WORD FOR WINDOWS ™
COMPANION

WORD FOR WINDOWS™
COMPANION

Mark W. Crane

with

Gena Cobb
Allan McGuffey
Jeff Yocom

Edited by

Linda Watkins

PUBLISHED BY
Microsoft Press
A Division of Microsoft Corporation
One Microsoft Way
Redmond, Washington 98052-6399

ISBN 0-936767-15-4

Printed and bound in the United States of America.

789   RRD-C   54321

Distributed to the book trade in Canada by Macmillan of Canada,
a division of Canada Publishing Corporation

Distributed to the book trade outside the United States
and Canada by Penguin Books Ltd.

Penguin Books Ltd., Harmondsworth, Middlesex, England
Penguin Books Australia Ltd., Ringwood, Victoria, Australia
Penguin Books N.Z. Ltd., 182-190 Wairau Road, Auckland 10, New Zealand

PostScript® is a registered trademark of Adobe Systems, Inc. Type Director™ is a trademark of Agfa
Corporation, AGFA Compugraphic Division. Paradox® is a registered trademark of Ansa Software, a
Borland Company. Apple,® LaserWriter,® LaserWriter II,® LaserWriter Plus,® and Macintosh® are
registered trademarks of Apple Computer, Inc. Quattro® is a registered trademark of Borland International, Inc. Compaq® is a registered trademark of Compaq Computer Corporation. Epson LQ-1000™
is a trademark and Epson® is a registered trademark of Epson America, Inc. Hercules® is a registered
trademark of Hercules Computer Technology. HP® and LaserJet® are registered trademarks of
Hewlett-Packard Company. Intel® is a registered trademark of Intel Corporation. AT,® IBM,® PC/XT,®
and PS/2® are registered trademarks of International Business Machines Corporation. Lotus,® 1-2-3,®
and Symphony® are registered trademarks of Lotus Development Corporation. Windows™ is a trademark and Microsoft® and MS-DOS® are registered trademarks of Microsoft Corporation. OverVUE™
is a trademark and ProVUE® is a registered trademark of ProVUE Development Corporation.
JetScript™ and PS Jet Plus™ are trademarks of QMS, Inc. WordPerfect® is a registered trademark of
WordPerfect Corporation.

Editing: Linda Watkins, Clyde Zellers, Jody Gilbert, Mary Welp
Production: Maureen Pawley, Beth Riggle
Design: Julie Baer Tirpak, Karl Feige

TABLE OF CONTENTS

Dedication

This book is dedicated to my father, Wendell Earl Crane:
Thanks, Dad, for being more than everything a father should be.
MWC

Acknowledgments

Douglas Cobb, for the opportunity and advice—without you, there wouldn't be a Cobb Group. Tom Cottingham, our big cheese, for managing a strange, stubborn, and colorful team of experts.

Linda Watkins and Clyde Zellers, for putting a few months of their lives on hold to finish this book. Jody Gilbert and Mary Welp, for their eyes and judgment. Linda Baughman and Lori Lorenz, for going above and beyond the call of duty.

Maureen Pawley and Beth Riggle, for putting it all together. Julie Tirpak and Karl Feige, for the slick cover design. Mike Tonegawa, for the picture on the back cover. Dave and Jo-Ann Parks at Printer's Type Service, for putting up with our ridiculous schedule.

Bud and Wanda, for the opportunities. Nita, for donating countless hours of your boyfriend's quality time to The Cobb Group—and not complaining about it.

Tim Landgrave, for encouragement, advice, and friendship—even when I don't make it four days a week. Brian Tirpak, for keeping B-ball on my itinerary. Michael Girard and Marshall Smith, for providing the very best technical support anywhere.

Finally, to the rest of The Cobb Group—Lou Armstrong, Becky Ballard, Gary Barnhart, Lisa Beebe, Doug Been, Julia Bennett, Tara Billinger, Toni Bowers, Jenny Camacho, Martha Clayton, Steve Cobb, Teresa Codey, Gordon Colby, Jeff Crane, Donald Fields, Luanne Flynn, Shalana Hampton, Laura Heuser, Godwin Ighodaro, Lori Junkins, Ginger Kepple, Kathleen Lane, Marco Mason, Elayne Noltemeyer, Mike O'Mara, Beth Ording, Joe Pierce, Jonathan Pyles, Blake Ragsdell, Ann Rockers, Raven Sexton, Brent Shean, Patricia Shields, Gina Sledge, Tracy Smith, Kim Spalding, Duane Spurlock, Jeff Warner, Jim Welp, Kellie Woods, and Peggy Zeillmann—thanks for being The Best in all that you do.

Preface

*T*here's no doubt about it—Microsoft Word for Windows is the most powerful word processor ever for the PC. From the first time we saw Word for Windows, in the summer of 1988, we knew it was going to be a hit. We also knew it was a product we wanted to write about.

Word for Windows offers all the editing features you would expect from a top-notch word processor, plus built-in Outline, Spelling, and Style Sheet facilities, a hyphenation dictionary, sophisticated multicolumn formatting capabilities, the ability to use borders and other graphic elements, the ability to create tables of contents and indexes, and much more. With Word for Windows' page view feature, you can review and edit a full-size representation of each document page on your screen, with columnar formatting, headers, footers, footnotes, and other elements in place. Another impressive feature of the program is the Position... command, which allows you to position an object on a page and flow text around it. And, with Word for Windows' customizing capabilities, you can quickly modify the menus and design your own keyboard shortcuts. These features combine to make Word for Windows the most powerful word processor available for any personal computer.

In short, Word for Windows has the depth and sophistication you need to create every kind of document imaginable, from simple memos and reports to newsletters and books. However, all this power is not without a price. If you've ever spent a couple of hours trying to develop a multicolumn layout or cursing because tabular data keeps jumping from place to place, you know that Word for Windows is a complex tool. Although the program's sophisticated word process-ing, formatting, editing, and design tools are intuitive and easy to use, you may find that it takes months to explore all the intricacies of this powerful program. Even with the user-friendly features of the Microsoft Windows operating environ-ment, learning Word for Windows is a big job.

ABOUT THIS BOOK

We wrote *Word for Windows Companion* to help make Word for Windows easier to learn and use. Regardless of your level of expertise, you'll find a great deal of useful information on the following pages. If you are new to word processing and desktop publishing, you can use this book as a tutorial to help you get started. If you are an experienced word processor, you can use this book as a reference guide to help you solve specific design and technical problems.

We had three goals in mind as we created this book. First, we wanted to help you learn to use Word for Windows efficiently—after all, a productivity tool is supposed to save time. Second, we wanted to provide an in-depth source of reference information that you will return to time and time again, whether you're a Word for Windows novice or an expert. Third, we wanted to introduce you to some of the basic concepts of word processing, typography, and design so that you'll be able to create professional-looking documents with confidence and ease. We think we've achieved all of these goals.

Organization

Word for Windows Companion has three sections. Section 1 will get you started by showing you how to install Word for Windows, taking you on a brief tour of the screen, and discussing file management. If you are new to Word for Windows, you will want to read this section carefully before you dive into the more complex aspects of the program. If you have been using Word for Windows for a while, we suggest that you skim this section to familiarize yourself with our terminology and approach before moving on to Sections 2 and 3. In Section 2, we cover Word for Windows basics—creating documents, editing, formatting, printing, and designing page layouts. Then, in Section 3, we explain the special features that make Word for Windows much more than a word processor. There, you will learn about such features as the Style Sheet, Outline, and Print Merge facilities.

Index

At The Cobb Group, we take pride in our comprehensive indexes. *Word for Windows Companion's* index contains almost two thousand entries covering all the concepts, topics, and applications we discuss. In addition, many entries are cross-referenced to facilitate your search for a particular subject. If you have a question about any command or feature in Word for Windows, the index will help you locate the answer in a matter of seconds.

ABOUT THE AUTHORS

Mark W. Crane is the co-author of several Cobb Group books, including *LaserJet Companion*, *HyperPAD Companion*, and *Quattro Companion*. He is the former editor-in-chief of three monthly Cobb Group journals: *The Expert*, *Excellence*, and *For Quattro*. Mark holds a B.S. in electrical engineering from Purdue University. Before joining The Cobb Group, he served as a PC specialist with IBM and with the Citizens Fidelity Corporation in Louisville, Kentucky.

Gena Cobb is the co-author of several books, including *Word 4 Companion, Word Companion, Doug Cobb's Tips for Microsoft Excel, Douglas Cobb's 1-2-3 Handbook, Mastering Symphony,* and *Write Companion.* She is the editor-in-chief of *Inside Word for Windows* and *Inside Word.* Gena received a B.S. from the University of Virginia and an M.B.A. from the Harvard Business School.

Allan McGuffey co-authored *Write Companion, Word 4 Companion,* and *Works 2 Companion* for the Cobb Group. He also co-authored *Excel in Business, 2nd edition* for Microsoft Press.

Jeff Yocom is editor-in-chief of *Inside WordPerfect* and the *Paradox User's Journal.* He co-authored *Douglas Cobb's Paradox 3 Handbook, Hands-On Paradox 3, LaserJet Companion,* and *HyperPAD Companion.* Jeff holds a B.A. in psychology from the University of Louisville and was a writer and software specialist at that university's Office of News and Public Information before joining The Cobb Group.

THERE'S MORE

In developing *Word for Windows Companion,* we spent months exploring every feature of Word for Windows—poking, prodding, and putting the program through its paces. We came up with more material than we could conceivably include in one book. Even as we go to press, we continue to discover new tips, traps, techniques, and shortcuts that we'd like to share.

If you're interested in learning more about Word for Windows, we urge you to subscribe to The Cobb Group's monthly journal for Word for Windows users: *Inside Word for Windows.* Each month, this journal provides tips and techniques that will help you become more proficient with this powerful word processor. It allows us to share all the new capabilities and techniques we uncover as we continue to use the program. To receive a free issue of *Inside Word for Windows,* simply fill out and return the card located in the back of this book.

SATISFACTION

The Best

GUARANTEED

The Preliminaries

Section 1
The Preliminaries

Section 1 lays the groundwork for using Microsoft Word for Windows. In this brief section, we'll introduce Word and show you how to get started with the program. You'll find it well worth the time to become familiar with the concepts presented here before you launch into a full-scale assault on Word, particularly if the program is new to you.

We'll assume throughout the course of this book that you are familiar with Microsoft Windows elements that are common to all programs—the mouse, menu commands and icons, dialog boxes, and so forth. If you are not comfortable with these basics, we suggest that you read Appendix 1 before you proceed. You'll find it much easier to come up to speed on Word if you have a feel for the general workings of Microsoft Windows first.

In this chapter

Before You Begin 1

*I*n this chapter, we'll show you how to get started with Microsoft Word for Windows. First, we'll describe the hardware necessary to run Word, and talk about some of the optional hardware accessories the program currently supports. Next, we'll show you how to install Word on your computer's hard disk and explain a few ways to load it.

Although the information in this chapter is sufficient to get you started in Word, you can call Microsoft for help if you have trouble installing and loading Word. The telephone number for Microsoft's Product Support Line is listed in the materials included with your Word for Windows packaging.

HARDWARE REQUIREMENTS

Word for Windows is designed to run on the IBM Personal System/2 (Model 50 or higher), an IBM PC AT, a Compaq Deskpro 286 or 386, or any 100% compatible computers that use Intel's 80286 or 80386 microprocessor. Your computer must have a minimum of 640 Kb of memory, one floppy disk drive, and a hard disk with at least 4 Mb of free space. It must operate under the MS-DOS or PC-DOS operating system, Version 3.0 or later.

Your computer must also have a graphics display adapter card. You can use IBM's VGA or EGA graphics card, the Hercules Graphics Card, or other graphics cards compatible with Microsoft Windows Version 2.03 or later. (We'll discuss Microsoft Windows in more detail in a moment.)

Optional components

You can add several optional components to your system that may help speed up your work with Word. The optional components we'll discuss range from the Microsoft Mouse to the Hewlett-Packard LaserJet printer. For advice on which items are best suited for your needs, consult your local hardware dealer.

Mouse

Although you can use Word without a mouse, we strongly recommend that you purchase one for your system. As you'll see when we tour the Word screen, Word's graphical user interface, which solicits input via pull-down menus and icons, is optimized for the mouse. Consequently, you can perform most operations much faster and easier with the mouse than with the keyboard.

When you purchase a mouse for your system, make sure it is either the Microsoft Mouse or one that is 100% compatible with the Microsoft Mouse. You can buy the Microsoft Mouse in either the serial or bus version. As you might guess, the serial version connects directly to one of your computer's serial ports. The bus version, on the other hand, connects to an adapter card that you must install in one of your computer's expansion slots. The version you choose will depend primarily on which output ports you use for your printer, communication devices, and so forth. For example, if your computer has an available serial port and no available expansion slots, you'll want to buy a serial mouse. If you don't have an available serial port, but have several unused expansion slots, you're better off purchasing a bus mouse.

The Microsoft Mouse has two buttons. If you're like most Word users, you'll usually use the left button. In some instances, however, Word (and several other Windows programs) take advantage of the right button. By default, the left mouse button is the primary button (the one you'll press when you want to highlight text, pull down a menu, and so forth), while the right mouse button is the secondary button (used only for a few specific tasks). If you prefer to use the right mouse button as your primary button, you can run the Windows Control Panel program to make the change. Refer to your *Microsoft Windows Reference Guide* for more information on Windows' Control Panel program.

Microsoft Windows

Microsoft Windows is an extension of the MS-DOS operating environment. As you probably know, Windows features a sophisticated graphical interface that lets you run two or more applications concurrently. Windows even lets you transfer data from one program to another via a facility called the Clipboard, and also lets you establish links between documents created in different Windows programs. In addition, Windows offers an MS-DOS Executive facility that gives you easy access to many common DOS functions, such as formatting diskettes, creating directories, and copying and deleting files.

Word for Windows must run under Microsoft Windows Version 2.03 or later. You can buy the latest copy of Windows at your local computer store or through many mail-order companies. If you don't want to purchase a new copy of Windows, however, you can run Word under the RunTime version of Windows that is bundled with your Word for Windows software. The RunTime version is much like the full-featured version—it provides Word with essential elements of the Windows operating environment. Unlike the full-featured version of Windows, however, RunTime Windows does not allow you to run programs concurrently or access the MS-DOS Executive facility.

Whether you should purchase the full-featured version of Windows or use the built-in RunTime version depends on your particular needs. If Word is the only Windows program you plan to use, the RunTime version will suffice. On the other hand, if you plan to use several Windows programs and want to quickly switch from one program to the next, or if you want to access the MS-DOS Executive facility, you'll need to purchase the full-featured version of Windows.

If your computer uses the Intel 80386 microprocessor, you'll want to run Word under Microsoft Windows/386, which allows Word to run much faster by taking advantage of the 80386's special features. If you're using a computer board on the Intel 80286 microprocessor, you'll need to run Word under Microsoft Windows/286. For more information on Microsoft Windows/286 and Microsoft Windows/386, consult your local computer vendor.

Printers and plotters

The main purpose of a powerful word processor like Word for Windows is to produce hard-copy output—letters, memos, reports, and so forth. For this reason, the printer you use to print your Word documents is undoubtedly the most important component in your system. Even if you already own a quality printer, you might want to talk to a few computer professionals to make sure you're using the printer that's best suited for your personal tastes and needs.

Dozens of printers are compatible with Word, ranging from state-of-the-art laser printers, such as the Hewlett-Packard LaserJet and the IBM PagePrinter, to the popular Epson FX 80 and IBM Proprinter. As you probably know, laser printers have many advantages over dot-matrix and daisy-wheel printers—they're faster and quieter, and allow tremendous font flexibility via font cartridges and soft fonts. Most importantly, they can produce great-looking text and/or graphics on a single page.

Local area networks

You can install Word for Windows on a computer connected to a local area network, which allows two or more users to share data stored on a common network drive. Word supports most major network software packages, including Microsoft LAN Manager and its licensees (IBM, 3COM, Ungermann Bass, etc.), and Novell Netware. For more information about how to install and run Word on a local area network, call Microsoft's Product Support Line.

Expanded and extended memory

As we mentioned earlier, you need a minimum of 640 Kb of memory to run Word. Depending on your speed requirements, the size of your documents, and your plans to run other Windows applications concurrently, you may need to install additional memory.

There are two kinds of additional memory you can add to your computer: expanded and extended. Both expanded and extended memory can significantly improve Word for Windows' performance. For information on how to take advantage of these memory options, refer to your Microsoft Windows documentation or consult your local computer vendor.

INSTALLING WORD FOR WINDOWS

Once you've assembled the hardware components of your system, you're ready to install Word on your hard disk. Although Word's program files occupy several diskettes, the installation process is relatively straightforward and simple.

Before you begin the installation procedure, you must prepare to answer several questions about your computer system. Specifically, you must know what type of PC, monitor, display adapter, mouse, and printer you're using.

To begin the installation, insert the Word for Windows Setup disk into drive A, type *A:SETUP* at the DOS prompt, and press [Enter]. The Setup program will take it from there, prompting you for information about your system, instructing you to change disks, and copying the appropriate files from the floppy disks to your hard disk.

LOADING WORD FOR WINDOWS

After you've installed Word on your computer, you're ready to load the program and begin working. Like most Windows programs, there are several ways to load Word. In this section, we'll explain each of these start-up techniques.

Starting from the DOS prompt

To start Word from the DOS prompt, first use the DOS command *CD* to move into the directory in which you've installed Word, then enter the command *WINWORD*. For example, if you've installed the program in the directory C:\WINWORD, first type *C:* and press [Enter] to make drive C your default drive, then type the command *CD \WINWORD* and press [Enter] to move into the \WINWORD directory. Next, type *WINWORD* and press [Enter] to tell your computer to load Word. When you do this, you'll see a box containing copyright information, followed by a screen like the one shown in Figure 1-1.

When this screen appears, enter your name and initials into the Name and Initials text boxes, then choose OK to bring up the screen in Figure 1-2. As you can see, Word creates a new, blank document named Document1, ready for your input. (Of course, you can save the document under any name you like. We'll show you how to do that in Chapter 3.)

Starting from Windows

If you've installed the RunTime version of Windows, you can start Word only from the DOS prompt. However, if you've installed the full-featured version of Windows on your hard disk along with Word, you'll sometimes want to start Word while you're in the Windows environment.

To enter the Windows environment, type *WIN* at the DOS prompt, then press [Enter]. Your computer will then load the Windows program and present an MS-DOS Executive window like the one shown in Figure 1-3 on page 8.

Figure 1-1

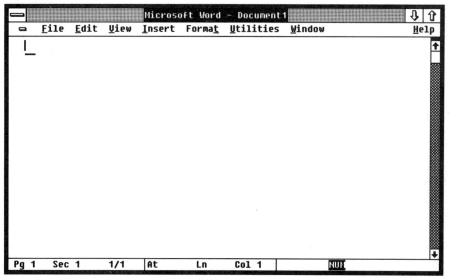

The first time you load Word, you'll need to enter your name and initials.

Figure 1-2

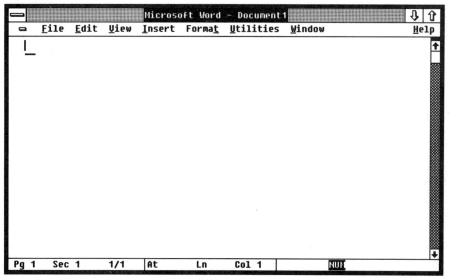

Word automatically opens a new document named Document1 each time you begin a new session.

Figure 1-3

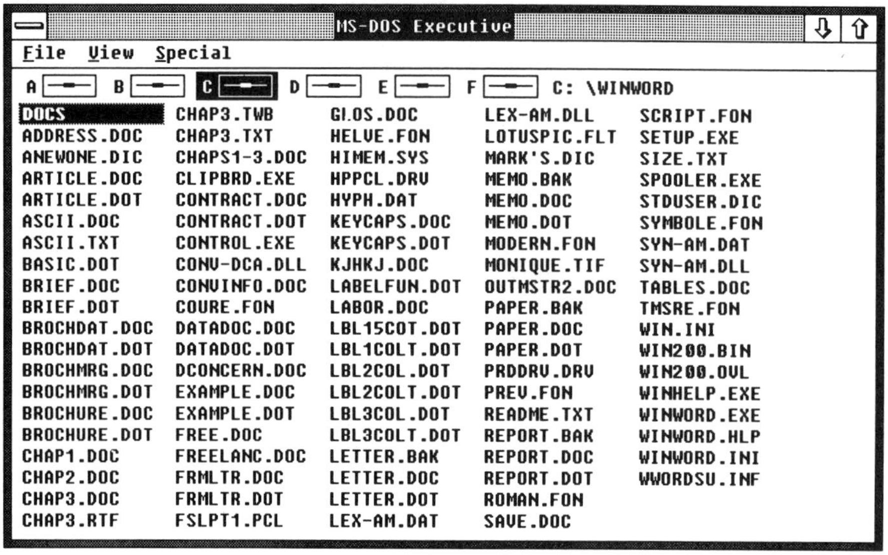

```
┌─────────────────────────────────────────────────────────────────────┐
│ ▭      ▓▓▓▓▓▓▓▓▓▓▓▓▓▓▓▓▓ MS-DOS Executive ▓▓▓▓▓▓▓▓▓▓▓▓▓▓▓      ⇩  ⇧  │
├─────────────────────────────────────────────────────────────────────┤
│  File   View   Special                                                │
├─────────────────────────────────────────────────────────────────────┤
│  A ▭—▭  B ▭—▭  C ▭—▭  D ▭—▭  E ▭—▭  F ▭—▭  C: \WINWORD               │
├─────────────────────────────────────────────────────────────────────┤
│ DOCS           CHAP3.TWB       GLOS.DOC        LEX-AM.DLL      SCRIPT.FON
│ ADDRESS.DOC    CHAP3.TXT       HELVE.FON       LOTUSPIC.FLT    SETUP.EXE
│ ANEWONE.DIC    CHAPS1-3.DOC    HIMEM.SYS       MARK'S.DIC      SIZE.TXT
│ ARTICLE.DOC    CLIPBRD.EXE     HPPCL.DRV       MEMO.BAK        SPOOLER.EXE
│ ARTICLE.DOT    CONTRACT.DOC    HYPH.DAT        MEMO.DOC        STDUSER.DIC
│ ASCII.DOC      CONTRACT.DOT    KEYCAPS.DOC     MEMO.DOT        SYMBOLE.FON
│ ASCII.TXT      CONTROL.EXE     KEYCAPS.DOT     MODERN.FON      SYN-AM.DAT
│ BASIC.DOT      CONV-DCA.DLL    KJHKJ.DOC       MONIQUE.TIF     SYN-AM.DLL
│ BRIEF.DOC      CONVINFO.DOC    LABELFUN.DOT    OUTMSTR2.DOC    TABLES.DOC
│ BRIEF.DOT      COURE.FON       LABOR.DOC       PAPER.BAK       TMSRE.FON
│ BROCHDAT.DOC   DATADOC.DOC     LBL15COT.DOT    PAPER.DOC       WIN.INI
│ BROCHDAT.DOT   DATADOC.DOT     LBL1COLT.DOT    PAPER.DOT       WIN200.BIN
│ BROCHMRG.DOC   DCONCERN.DOC    LBL2COL.DOT     PRDDRV.DRV      WIN200.OVL
│ BROCHMRG.DOT   EXAMPLE.DOC     LBL2COLT.DOT    PREV.FON        WINHELP.EXE
│ BROCHURE.DOC   EXAMPLE.DOT     LBL3COL.DOT     README.TXT      WINWORD.EXE
│ BROCHURE.DOT   FREE.DOC        LBL3COLT.DOT    REPORT.BAK      WINWORD.HLP
│ CHAP1.DOC      FREELANC.DOC    LETTER.BAK      REPORT.DOC      WINWORD.INI
│ CHAP2.DOC      FRMLTR.DOC      LETTER.DOC      REPORT.DOT      WWORDSU.INF
│ CHAP3.DOC      FRMLTR.DOT      LETTER.DOT      ROMAN.FON
│ CHAP3.RTF      FSLPT1.PCL      LEX-AM.DAT      SAVE.DOC
└─────────────────────────────────────────────────────────────────────┘
```

To bring up Windows' MS-DOS Executive, type WIN *at the DOS prompt.*

When the MS-DOS Executive window appears, use the Change Directory... command on the Special menu to move into the directory containing Word. Then, you can load the program by using the mouse to double-click on the file name WINWORD.EXE. If your computer is not equipped with a mouse, you can load Word by using the arrow keys to highlight the file name WINWORD.EXE, then pressing [Enter].

Starting Word and opening a document simultaneously

Although Word automatically opens a blank document named Document1 whenever you begin a new Word session, it is possible to start Word and open an existing document simultaneously.

To do this, simply follow the command WINWORD with the full path name of the file you want to open. For example, to start Word and open the document C:\BUDGET.DOC, enter the command *WINWORD C:\BUDGET.DOC*.

To start Word and open a document simultaneously from the Windows environment, double-click on the name of the document file you want to open. If you aren't using a mouse, highlight the name of the appropriate file and press [Enter].

In this chapter

A Brief Tour 2

*I*n this chapter, we'll take a tour of the Microsoft Word for Windows screen and introduce some key concepts and terms you'll need throughout the rest of the book. If you are new to Word, read this chapter carefully. It lays the groundwork for everything to follow. If you've been using Word for a while, we suggest that you skim this chapter just to be sure that you're familiar with our terminology.

If Word is the first program you've used that runs under Microsoft Windows, you need to read Appendix 1 before you read this chapter. In Appendix 1, you'll learn the concepts common to all Windows applications, including Word. However, if you've already worked with another Windows program, such as Microsoft Excel or Aldus PageMaker, you can dive right into this chapter and refer to Appendix 1 only when necessary.

We'll cover the topics in this chapter at a very general level. If you do not understand all the concepts presented here, don't worry about it. We'll discuss these topics in more detail throughout the course of the book.

THE WORD SCREEN

Whenever you begin a new Word session, you'll see a screen like the one shown in Figure 2-1 on the following page. If you've worked with other applications that run under Windows, some of the screen elements in Figure 2-1 should look familiar. Much of what you see, however, is unique to Word.

The large, empty area that occupies the bulk of the screen is the document window—your workspace. The document window is where all the creating will take place—your *tabula rasa*, so to speak. Through this window, you will create, edit, format, and view your documents.

At this point, your document window will be empty except for a blinking vertical bar called the insertion point marker. Since *insertion point marker* is a rather long phrase, we'll refer to it as the *cursor* throughout the remainder of this book. As you might have guessed, the cursor indicates your current position in the Word document. As you'll see when you begin working with text, the cursor moves one space to the right each time you type a character in your document. You'll also use the cursor to specify the point at which you want to edit text. If you have worked with other PC-based word processors, you'll find that Word's cursor is similar to theirs.

Figure 2-1

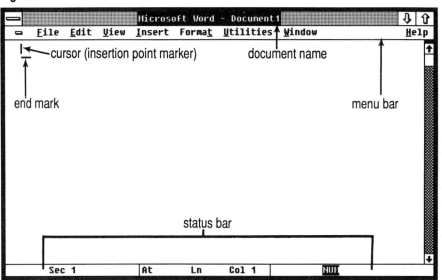

This screen will appear each time you begin a new Word session.

THE MENU BAR

Immediately above the document window is the menu bar, which you will use to send instructions to Word. As you can see, Word's menu bar initially offers nine menus to choose from: ▭ (the document Control menu), File, Edit, View, Insert, Format, Utilities, Window, and Help.

Each of these menus contains a different set of commands—a different group of tools to work with. As we explain in Appendix 1, the document Control menu lets you control the size and position of the document window. The File menu contains document-handling and printing commands. On the Edit menu, you'll find a series of commands that let you copy and move text, search for text, replace text, go to a specified page in your document, and define a header and/or footer. The View menu lets you control the way Word is displayed on the screen, and control the contents of the menus themselves. On the Insert menu, you'll find a group of commands that allow you to insert some special codes into your document—codes that create page breaks, footnotes, page numbers, and so forth. The Format menu lets you control the appearance of the text in your document.

From the Utilities menu, you can instruct Word to spell-check, repaginate, hyphenate, and sort the entries in your document. The Window menu lets you create new windows so you can view different parts of your document, and lets you move between document windows. Finally, you can access the Help menu when you need some assistance with Word. (When you activate the Full Menus mode, you'll see an additional menu—Macro—which you can use to record, run, and edit macros. We'll elaborate on this mode in a moment.)

To select a command from a menu, you can use the mouse to point to that menu and then press the mouse button. When the list of available commands appears below the menu name, point and click on the command you want. To select a command using the keyboard, press the [Alt] key to activate the menu bar, type the letter that is underlined in the menu you want to use, then type the letter that is underlined in the appropriate command name. (For a detailed discussion of selecting commands from menus, refer to Appendix 1.)

Issuing a command

As you glance through the Word menus, notice that several key names, such as Ctrl, Shift, F5, and so forth, appear to the right of many commands. These notations indicate that you can use keyboard shortcuts to issue the commands without accessing the menus. For example, since the key combination Shift+F12 appears next to the Save command on the File menu, you can press [Shift][F12] to save a document rather than select the Save command. Similarly, you can press [F5] instead of selecting Go To... from the Edit menu. You can also use the keyboard to perform many actions that are not listed on the Word menus. For example, you can use the [Ctrl][Shift]5 key combination to highlight all the text in the current document (you must press 5 on the numeric keypad). Appendix 3 provides a complete list of the keyboard shortcuts available in Word.

Keyboard shortcuts

When you first open Word, you will see only some of the commands that are actually available to you. This is because Word is initially loaded in the Short Menus mode. When Word is in this mode, it will display only the most common commands and options. If you want to see all the commands available in Word, you can switch to the Full Menus mode by selecting the Full Menus command from the View menu. Once you've placed Word in the Full Menus mode, a Macro menu will appear and the other menus will display an expanded list of commands.

Short vs. Full Menus

By the way, Full Menus is a toggle command, meaning that the command changes each time you issue it. After you select the Full Menus command from the View menu, Works will change that command to Short Menus. If you then issue the Short Menus command, Word will again display the condensed form of each menu and change the Short Menus command back to Full Menus. Since we'll be exploring all of Word's capabilities throughout the course of this book, you'll want to activate Full Menus. Figure 2-2 shows the list of commands available under both the Short and Full Menus.

Figure 2-2

Short menus

Full menus

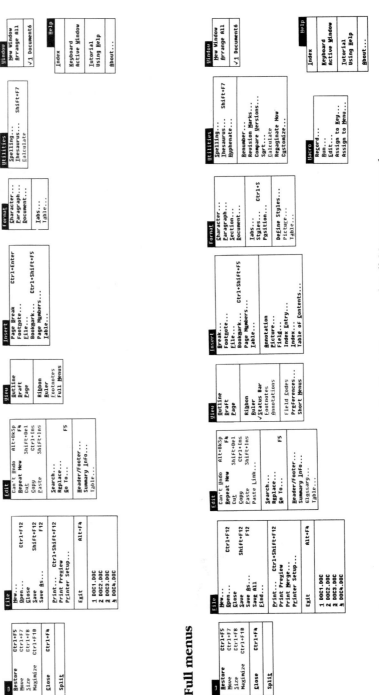

The contents of your menus vary when you toggle the Short Menus and Full Menus commands.

The simplest way to format characters in a document is with the ribbon. (An alternative way is with the Character... command.) You can use the ribbon to assign font types, point sizes, and other characteristics, such as boldface, italics, and underlining.

To access the ribbon, select the Ribbon command from the View menu. The ribbon will then appear above the document window, as shown in Figure 2-3.

THE RIBBON

Figure 2-3

		Microsoft Word - Document1		⇩ ⇧
▭	**File Edit View Insert Format Utilities Macro Window**			**Help**
Font:	Tms Rmn	↓ Pts: 10 ↓	B I κ U W D ‡	✖

| Pg 1 | Sec 1 | 1/1 | At 1" | Ln 1 | Col 1 | | NUI |

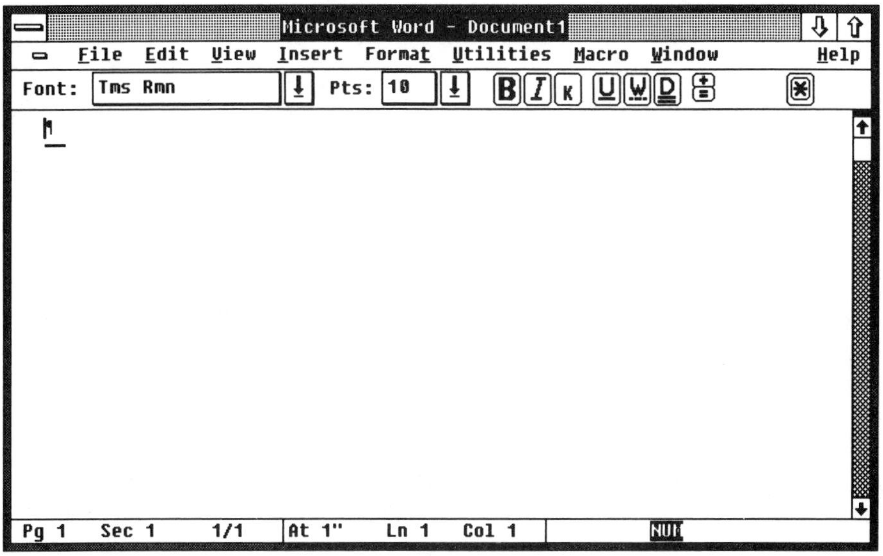

Selecting the Ribbon command from the View menu displays the ribbon above the document window.

As with most of the commands on the View menu, Word uses a check mark to indicate the ribbon's current display status. When you issue the Ribbon command, Word will place a check mark next to the command.

If you want to suppress the ribbon display, simply reselect the Ribbon command. Word will then remove both the ribbon from the screen and the check mark next to the Ribbon command. Of course, the formatting changes you've specified with the ribbon will remain in effect after you've suppressed its display. In Chapter 5, we'll show you how to use the ribbon to format characters.

You can specify formatting features, such as line lengths, paragraph indentions, paragraph justification, line spacing, and tab settings, by using the ruler. To access the ruler, select the Ruler command from the View menu. When you do, the ruler will appear above the document window, as shown in Figure 2-4. Also, Word will place a check mark next to this command on the View menu.

THE RULER

Figure 2-4

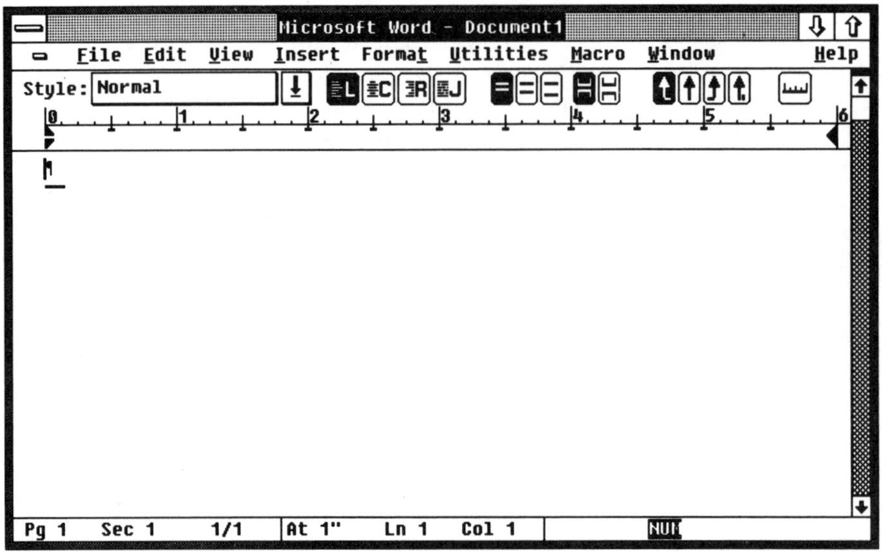

The ruler appears above the document window when you select the Ruler command from the View menu.

Once you've specified your ruler settings, you may prefer to suppress the ruler display to make more of your document visible on the screen. To do this, simply select the Ruler command a second time. Word will then remove both the ruler from the screen and the check mark next to the Ruler command on the View menu. You won't see the ruler on the screen, but the ruler specifications you've chosen will remain in effect.

Though you can see only about 6 inches of the ruler on your screen at a time, the ruler actually extends from -11 to 22 inches. You can see the remainder of the ruler by using the horizontal scroll bar, which we'll discuss in Chapter 4.

The ruler has three possible views: the paragraph view (the default), the margin view, and the column view. When you're using the paragraph view, the ruler shows the width of your document's text area. The margin view of the ruler shows your left and right margin settings relative to the width of the paper. The column view shows the boundaries of your text when you're working in a table. We'll discuss the ruler in more detail in Chapter 5.

THE STATUS BAR

Word uses the status bar, located at the bottom of the screen, to display messages, informational prompts, and status information. For instance, when you activate a menu, Word will display a short message in the status bar that explains the purpose of the highlighted menu name or command.

While you're creating or editing a document, Word uses the status bar to indicate your relative position in that document. Table 2-1 lists some sample codes that can appear in the status bar as you are working in a document.

Table 2-1

Status bar indicator	Meaning
Pg 1	Page 1 of the document is currently displayed
Sec 3	Section 3 of the document is currently displayed
13/56	The 13th page of a 56-page document is currently displayed
At 5"	The cursor is 5 inches from the top edge of the page
Ln 7	The cursor lies in the seventh line of the current page
Col 34	There are 34 characters between the cursor and the left margin
REC	The macro recorder is on
EXT	The [Extend Selection] key is on
COL	The [Column Selection] key is on
OVR	Word is in Overwrite mode
MRK	Word is in Mark Revisions mode
CAPS	The [Caps Lock] key is on
NUM	The [Num Lock] key is on

If you pull down the View menu while the status bar is displayed on your screen, you'll see a check mark next to the Status Bar command. To turn off the display of the status bar and remove the check mark, simply reselect the command. To redisplay the status bar, select the command again. As with the ribbon and ruler, we'll sometimes turn off the display of the status bar in our figures.

As you may have noticed, your mouse pointer takes on a number of different **THE POINTER** shapes as you move it around the screen. Table 2-2 on the following page shows the various mouse pointer icons you'll see as you work in Word.

You'll use the I-beam pointer to highlight text and move the cursor around your screen. The I-beam will probably be the most common pointer as you edit and format text.

Do not confuse the I-beam pointer with the cursor. You use the I-beam pointer to position the cursor, but the cursor does not move to the desired spot until you actually click the mouse button to position the cursor in your text. In fact, if you use the scroll bars to move through your document, your cursor might be in a part of the document that is completely different from the part you are viewing on your screen. Make sure the cursor is in the correct spot before you begin typing or editing text.

Table 2-2

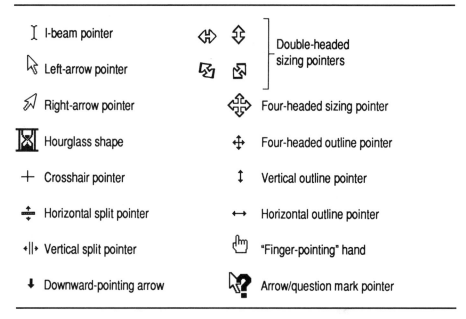

I-beam pointer	Double-headed sizing pointers
Left-arrow pointer	
Right-arrow pointer	Four-headed sizing pointer
Hourglass shape	Four-headed outline pointer
Crosshair pointer	Vertical outline pointer
Horizontal split pointer	Horizontal outline pointer
Vertical split pointer	"Finger-pointing" hand
Downward-pointing arrow	Arrow/question mark pointer

The arrow that points diagonally to the left appears whenever you point to the menu bar, title bar, scroll bars, or dialog box options. Of course, you'll use this arrow to select commands and options, and to move through a document with the scroll bars. This arrow also appears when you are dragging the size handles to resize or crop a graphic, and when you are recording a macro. (We'll discuss graphics and macros later in the book.)

The arrow that points diagonally to the right appears only when you point to the far-left side of a document window. There is an invisible selection bar in this area. When the pointer takes on this shape, you know that you are in the selection bar. You can then use this pointer to highlight lines, paragraphs, table rows, an entire table, or an entire document.

The hourglass shape indicates that Word is working to execute your last command. While this hourglass appears, you cannot use the mouse pointer to issue any other commands or to select text.

The crosshair pointer appears when you use the Print Preview command to see how your document will look when it's printed. You can use the crosshair pointer to reposition items on the page.

The horizontal split pointer appears when you either issue the Split command on the document Control menu, or when you position the mouse pointer on the split box in the vertical scroll bar.

You'll see the vertical split pointer when the mouse pointer is positioned on the style area split bar. (We'll discuss the style area in Chapter 8.)

The downward-pointing arrow appears when you move the pointer over the top of a table column. You can use this pointer to select an entire column of a table. (We'll discuss tables in Chapter 11.)

A double-headed sizing pointer appears when you position the mouse pointer on a window's border. When you see one of these pointers, you can use the mouse to manually resize that window. Similarly, the four-headed sizing pointer appears when you issue the Move command on a window's Control menu. For a detailed discussion on sizing and moving windows, refer to Appendix 1.

The four-headed outline pointer appears when you point to a heading or body-text icon. The vertical outline pointer appears when you drag the heading up or down. The horizontal outline pointer appears when you drag the heading left or right to promote or demote the heading. We'll cover Word's outlining features in Chapter 9.

You'll see the "finger-pointing" hand when you position the mouse pointer on a jump term or a glossary term in a Help window. Pressing the mouse button when this hand appears tells Word to bring up help information on that term. Finally, you'll see the arrow/question mark pointer when you press [Shift][F1] to access Word's Help facility. We'll take a look at the Help facility next.

GETTING HELP

If you forget how to use a command or some other feature of Word, you can use Word's Help facility to remind you how that particular feature works. There are two ways to bring up a Help window in Word. First, you can search through Word's extensive help information by using the commands on the Help menu. Alternatively, you can get context-sensitive help using the [F1] key or the [Shift][F1] key combination.

Using the Help menus

If you pull down the Help menu, you'll see the six commands shown in Figure 2-5 on the following page. Four of the commands on this menu—Index, Keyboard, Active Window, and Using Help—bring up a window containing help information. As you might guess, the Tutorial command runs the Microsoft Word Tutorial, while the About... command brings up a box containing the Word program version number, the amount of available memory, and the amount of available disk space.

Getting information on Help

The Using Help command tells you how to use Word's Help facility. When you select this command, Word will present the Help window shown in Figure 2-6 on the next page.

Figure 2-5

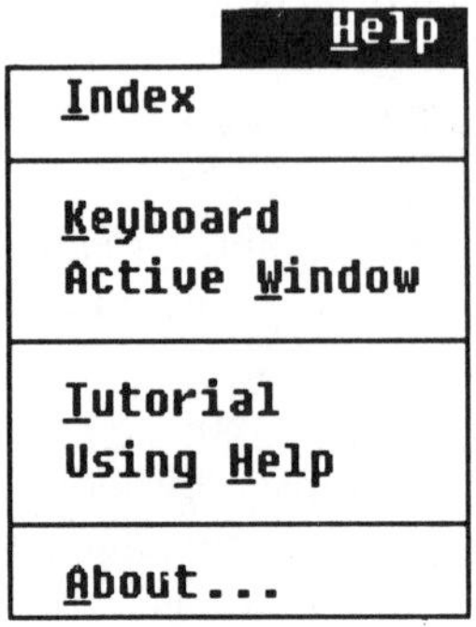

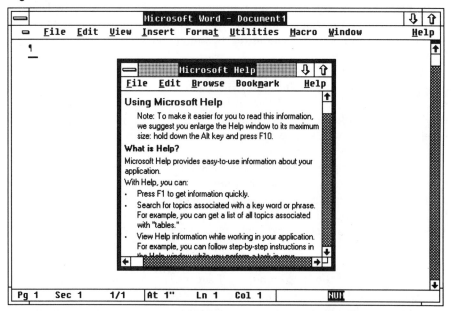

You can get help simply by selecting the commands on Word's Help menu.

Figure 2-6

If you select Using Help from the Help menu, you'll see this window.

Like all Help windows, this one contains a title bar, a Control menu, Maximize and Minimize boxes, a menu bar, and scroll bars. If you are not familiar with these essential window elements, read Appendix 1 before you attempt to navigate through the Help windows.

Navigating through the Help windows

You can scroll through the information in a Help window by using the mouse pointer and scroll bars. You also can scroll through information by using the keys listed in Table 2-3.

Table 2-3

Press...	to scroll...
[Page Down]	one window down
[Page Up]	one window up
[Ctrl][Home]	to the beginning of the topic
[Ctrl][End]	to the end of the topic

As you scroll through Word's Help windows, you'll see several words and phrases that appear with a solid underline. Word calls these jump terms. You might think of jump terms as cross-references you normally see in reference books.

When you position the mouse pointer on a jump term, the pointer will take on the shape of a finger-pointing hand. If you press the mouse button while the pointer is positioned on a jump term, Word will bring up a Help window on that topic. If you are using the keyboard to navigate through the Help windows, you can bring up a jump term's Help window by first using the arrow keys to move the highlight to the appropriate term, and then pressing [Enter].

After you read the information in the jump term's Help window, you can return to the original Help window either by selecting the Backtrack command from the Help window's Browse menu or by pressing the [Backspace] key. As you will see, this cross-referencing system works quickly and easily.

Many of the words and phrases in the Help windows will contain dotted underlines. Word calls these glossary terms. As with jump terms, positioning the mouse pointer on a glossary term turns the mouse pointer into a finger-pointing hand. Holding down the mouse button at this point will bring up a small window containing the definition of that term. Releasing the mouse button will remove the definition. To bring up a glossary term's definition using the keyboard, simply use the arrow keys to highlight the term, then hold down the [Enter] key. When you release the [Enter] key, Word will remove the glossary term's definition.

Jump terms and glossary terms

As you can see in Figure 2-5, the Help menu contains the Index, Keyboard, and Active Window commands in addition to the Using Help command. Issuing the Index command tells Word to bring up the window shown in Figure 2-7 on the following page, which lists a variety of general help topics. In this window, you can select one of the jump terms presented and continue "stepping down" until you find the appropriate Help window.

Other commands on the Help menu

The Keyboard command lets you bring up a list of keyboard topics. You'll want to use this command whenever you forget a keyboard shortcut required to execute some task within Word.

Finally, you can use the Active Window command to bring up help for the document's current view (normal editing, page, Print Preview, outline, or draft).

Figure 2-7

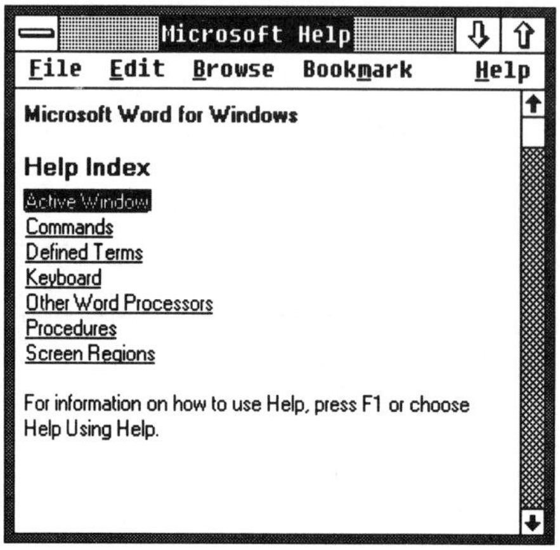

If you select Index from the Help menu, you'll see this list of general topics.

Getting context-sensitive help

Instead of navigating through Word's help menus to find out something about a particular command or option, you can quickly obtain information from Word's context-sensitive Help facility. As you might expect, you can request context-sensitive help with either the mouse or the keyboard.

Using the mouse

To access context-sensitive help with the mouse, first hold down the [Shift] key and press [F1]. When you do this, the mouse pointer will take on the shape of an arrow/question mark. At this point, you should point and click on the command or on the area of the screen for which you would like to obtain help. Instead of presenting a list of help topics from which you can choose, Word will go directly to the Help window that explains the feature you've selected.

For example, suppose you want to use the mouse to learn about the Section... command on the Format menu. To bring up Word's Help window for this command, first press [Shift][F1] to transform the pointer into an arrow/question mark. Next, use the pointer to select the Section... command. After a short pause, Word will present the Help window for the Section... command, as shown in Figure 2-8.

Using the keyboard

To bring up context-sensitive help using the keyboard, just highlight the appropriate command, bring up the appropriate dialog box, or generate the appropriate message, then press [F1]. Word will then bring up help information for the active command, dialog box, or message. If you do not activate a command, dialog box, or message before pressing [F1], Word will display the Help Index shown in Figure 2-7.

For example, suppose you want to use the keyboard to learn more about the Section... command. To do this, press [Alt] to activate the menus, press *T* to pull down the Format menu, then press the ↓ key twice to highlight the Section... command. Now, press [F1] to bring up the Help window shown in Figure 2-8. As you can see, Word takes you directly to the Help window for the Section... command instead of making you sift through the entire list of help topics.

Figure 2-8

To get context-sensitive help, just press [Shift][F1] and select a command or option.

More about Help

For more information on the Help facility, issue the Using Help command and choose the appropriate topic. In addition to the information we've presented in this section, Word's Help facility will tell you how to annotate Help windows, define bookmarks, and so forth.

In this chapter

File Handling 3

*I*n Section 2, we'll show you how to create, edit, and format documents. Before you invest your time and energy in building a document, however, you should learn the procedures for opening, closing, deleting, and saving files in Word. You'll also want to become familiar with Word's Summary Info dialog box, which simplifies the process of indexing and retrieving your Word documents.

In this chapter, we'll show you seven of the commands on Word's File menu: New…, Open…, Close, Save, Save As…, Save All, and Exit. In Chapter 17, we'll explore some additional document-retrieval features.

As we explained in Chapter 1, when you begin a new Word session by selecting WINWORD.EXE in the Windows operating environment, Word will automatically open a new blank file named Document1 (the name *Document1* will appear in the document's title bar). If you want to open an existing Word document and start Word at the same time, just double-click on the name of the file you want to open in the Windows operating environment.

CREATING AND OPENING DOCUMENTS

If you need to create a new document while you are working in Word, you can always select the New… command from the File menu. When you do, the dialog box shown in Figure 3-1 on the following page will appear on the screen.

As you can see, Word selects the Document option by default. To open a new Word document, just choose the OK button. If you have already created one new document, the next document you create will be called Document2. As you create documents during the current session, Word will number those documents sequentially—Document3, Document4, and so forth.

If you have already created a document file and you want to retrieve it from disk while working in Word, select the Open… command from the File menu. When you do, Word will display a dialog box like the one shown in Figure 3-2.

Opening existing documents

Figure 3-1

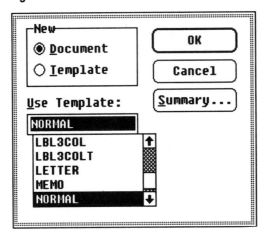

The New dialog box allows you to open a new document in Word.

Figure 3-2

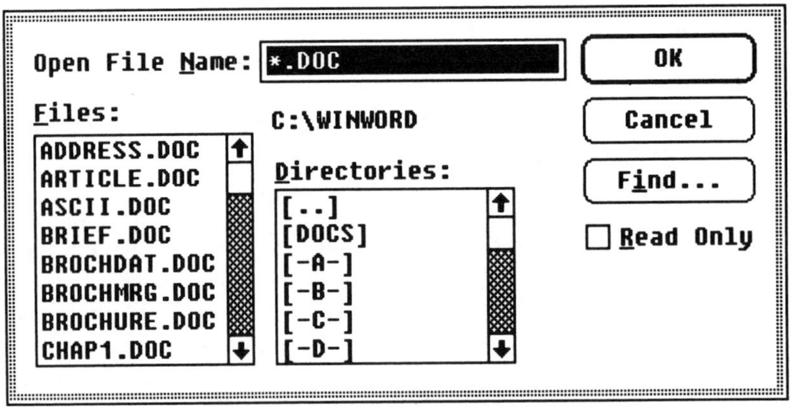

You'll use the Open dialog box to retrieve files.

The Open File Name text box at the top of the dialog box lets you specify the name of the document file you want to open. The default entry in this text box is *.DOC, which tells Word to list all the Word files (the files with a .DOC file-name extension) in the Files list box on the left side of the dialog box. If the name of the file you want to open appears in the Files list box, simply select that file name, then choose OK. If you're using a mouse, you can open a document simply by double-clicking on its file name.

If the document file you want to open does not appear in the Files list box, you'll need to change the current directory. Word lists the name of the current directory just below the Open File Name text box. (The current directory in the sample dialog box is C:\WINWORD.) To change the current directory, simply select the appropriate directory in the Directories list box and choose OK. (Mouse users can save time by double-clicking on the appropriate directory name.)

If your document file is stored in a directory that is located back a level or two on the current disk drive, select the [..] option in the Directories list box. Choosing this option moves back one level in the directory structure. Of course, if you need to specify a directory that is located on a different disk, first select the name of the appropriate disk in the Directories list box, then choose the appropriate directory. As you step through the directories on your disks, Word will keep the default entry *.DOC in the Open File Name text box so that you can view the Word files stored in each directory. If you want to view all the files in a directory, type *.* into the text box.

You can open a Word document by typing the full name of the document file into the Open File Name text box instead of selecting it in the Directories and Files list boxes. For example, if you've created a document named BUDGET.DOC, and you've stored it in your C:\WINWORD directory, you can open that document by typing the file name *C:\WINWORD\BUDGET.DOC* in the Open File Name text box, and choosing OK.

The Find... button on the right side of the dialog box performs the same task as the Find... command on the File menu. As we'll explain in Chapter 17, both the Find... button and the Find... command let you locate and open hard-to-find documents quickly and easily.

Finding a document

If you want to view the contents of a document file without saving any changes to disk, you can select the Read Only check box before you open it. When you do, Word will let you browse through the document and even make changes to it, but will not let you save that document under its original file name. To save the changes you've made to a document that was opened with the Read Only option, you must issue the Save As... command and save that document under a new file name. (We'll discuss the Save and Save As... commands in a moment.)

The Read Only check box

Fortunately, Word provides an easy way to reopen the documents you've used most recently. As you can see at the bottom of Figure 3-3 on the next page, when you pull down the File menu, you'll see the name of the last four document files you've opened. If you want to reopen any of these documents, just select the appropriate file name from the menu.

Opening recently used documents

The documents you create in Word reside in your computer's random access memory (RAM). Because RAM gets erased when you turn off your computer, you must save your documents as disk files to make them permanent. Once you save a document to disk, the document will remain there until you delete it.

SAVING YOUR WORK

Figure 3-3

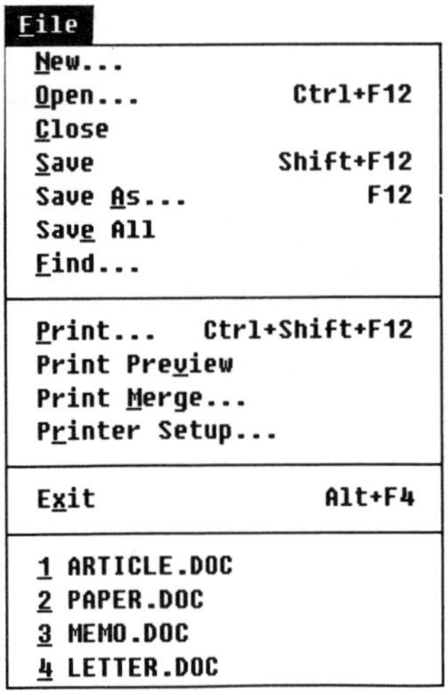

File
New...
Open... Ctrl+F12
Close
Save Shift+F12
Save As... F12
Save All
Find...
Print... Ctrl+Shift+F12
Print Preview
Print Merge...
Printer Setup...
Exit Alt+F4
1 ARTICLE.DOC
2 PAPER.DOC
3 MEMO.DOC
4 LETTER.DOC

The file names at the bottom of the File menu provide an easy way to reopen the documents you've used most recently.

The tools you'll normally use to save a document are the Save and Save As... commands on the File menu. The first time you issue either of these commands, Word will present the Save As dialog box shown in Figure 3-4. Once you've saved a document under a file name, however, you can bypass this dialog box by issuing the Save command instead of the Save As... command.

Figure 3-4

Save File Name:
OK
C:\WINWORD
Cancel
Directories:
Options >>
[..]
[DOCS]
[-A-]
[-B-]
[-C-]
[-D-]

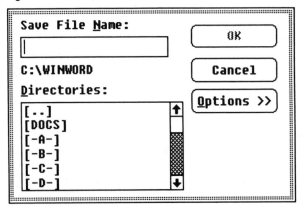

The Save As dialog box appears when you issue the Save or Save As... command to save a file for the first time.

When the Save As dialog box appears on your screen, you must specify a target directory and a file name. The current directory is shown just below the Save File Name text box (in this case, C:\WINWORD). If you want to store your document in a different directory, simply select another directory in the Directories list box.

Once you've specified the appropriate directory, type the name you want to assign to the file in the Save File Name text box, then choose OK to bring up the Summary Info dialog box shown in Figure 3-5. To complete the save, choose OK in this dialog box. (We'll discuss this box in more detail in a moment.)

Figure 3-5

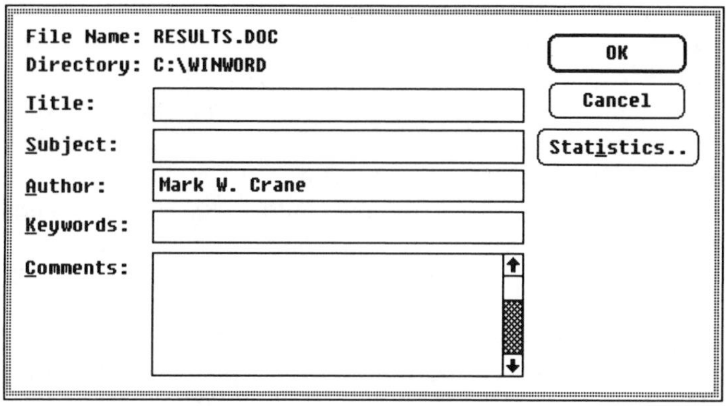

```
┌────────────────────────────────────────────────────────┐
│ File Name: RESULTS.DOC                                   │
│ Directory: C:\WINWORD            ┌──────────────┐        │
│                                  │      OK      │        │
│ Title:    ┌──────────────────┐   └──────────────┘        │
│           └──────────────────┘   ┌──────────────┐        │
│ Subject:  ┌──────────────────┐   │    Cancel    │        │
│           └──────────────────┘   └──────────────┘        │
│ Author:   ┌──────────────────┐   ┌──────────────┐        │
│           │ Mark W. Crane    │   │ Statistics.. │        │
│           └──────────────────┘   └──────────────┘        │
│ Keywords: ┌──────────────────┐                           │
│           └──────────────────┘                           │
│ Comments: ┌──────────────────┐                           │
│           │                  │                           │
│           │                  │                           │
│           └──────────────────┘                           │
└────────────────────────────────────────────────────────┘
```

The Summary Info dialog box appears when you choose OK in the Save As dialog box.

For example, suppose you wanted to save your current document on the diskette in drive A under the name BUDGET.DOC. To do this, select the Save As… command from the File menu, select the [-A-] option in the Directories list box, type the name *BUDGET* in the Save File Name text box, and choose OK. When the Summary Info dialog box in Figure 3-5 appears, choose OK to complete the command.

File-name rules

There are several important file-name rules you must follow when you save documents. First, the name you specify for a document can be no longer than eight characters. In addition to the name, you can specify a three-character file-name extension. If you do not supply an extension, Word will automatically supply the extension .DOC. For example, if you issue the Save As… command and supply the name AGENDA, Word will save the current document to disk under the file name AGENDA.DOC.

File names and extensions can include any letter of the alphabet. If you include any lowercase letters in a file name, however, Word will convert those letters to uppercase before it saves the file. In addition to letters, you can include the digits 0 through 9, the underline character, and most symbols. However, your file names cannot include blank spaces or any of the following symbols:

' * ? : ; , \ / &

If you accidentally include these symbols in your file name, Word will not save your document. Instead, depending on the symbol, it will either display a message box that notifies you of the problem or keep the Save As dialog box on the screen and not return you to the document.

File-name extensions

Word lets you save a file with any extension you want. All you have to do is type a period and the extension you want to use after the file name. For example, if you want to save a document under the file name MEMO.JAN, select the Save As... command, type *MEMO.JAN*, and press [Enter].

As we mentioned earlier, if you do not supply an extension when you save your documents, Word will supply the extension .DOC. We will refer to file-name extensions other than .DOC as non-standard extensions. If you want to save a document without including a file-name extension, simply type the file name, followed by a period.

Although Word lets you specify non-standard file-name extensions, it's difficult to use them efficiently. For instance, when you issue the File menu's Open... command to open a document you've stored on disk, Word will show you a list of only those files that have a .DOC extension. To view the files that have non-standard extensions, you must perform the additional (and bothersome) step of entering *.* into the Open File Name text box.

Table 3-1 lists some of the extensions you'll see in the file names in your Word directory. Although you'll typically create files with only .DOC extensions, this table might come in handy when you need to clean up the files stored on your disk. You'll seldom want to erase any of the files whose names include the extensions listed in this table.

Table 3-1

Extension	Meaning
.BAK	Backup file
.DAT	Data files for spell-checking, thesaurus, and hyphenation
.DIC	Dictionary file
.DOC	Document file
.DOT	Document template file
.DRV	Device driver file
.EXE	Program file
.FON	Font file
.INI	Initial settings file
.TMP	Temporary file used only during a Word session

In addition to specifying the file name and directory, you can specify several other file options when you save a document with the Save As… command. To access these options, choose the Options >> button in the Save As dialog box. When you do, the dialog box will expand, as shown in Figure 3-6.

Figure 3-6

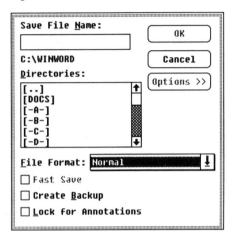

Choosing the Options >> button in the Save As dialog box lets you access more file-management options.

As you can see, the expanded area of the Save As dialog box contains a File Format pull-down list box, as well as three check boxes: Fast Save, Create Backup, and Lock for Annotations. You can use these dialog box options to select a different file format, adjust Word's fast-save feature, create backup document files, and protect the document from unwanted annotations.

Although Word usually saves your document in its Normal file format, it can save your document in several other file formats as well. You'll want to specify a different file format when you need to use a Word document with another application. As you might have guessed, you must use the File Format list box to change the file format of a Word document.

As you can see in Figure 3-6, the default setting in the File Format list box is Normal, which indicates that Word will save the current document in its own file format—regardless of the file name and extension you've specified. To save your document in a different file format, simply choose the appropriate format from the File Format list box, then choose OK. In Chapter 21, we'll talk about saving documents in other file formats.

The Fast Save check box

The first time you save a document with the Save or Save As... command, a dimmed option called Fast Save will appear in the expanded Save As dialog box. A little later in this chapter, we'll show you how to use this option to control Word's fast-save feature.

Creating backup document files

When you use the Save command to save a revised version of a document, Word will overwrite the copy you've saved to disk with the newly revised version. In most cases, this is what you'll want. Sometimes, however, you might want to make a backup copy of your original document before you overwrite it.

To make backup copies of your documents as you save them, you must use the Create Backup check box in the expanded Save As dialog box. When you save a file after activating this check box, Word will not overwrite the previously saved version of your document with the new version. Instead, it will change the previously saved version's file-name extension from .DOC to .BAK, then save the updated version into a new file under the original name.

For example, suppose you've saved a document to disk under the file name REPORT.DOC. Now, suppose you open REPORT.DOC, make a few changes, then save those changes with the Create Backup check box selected. When you do this, Word will change the name of the REPORT.DOC file to REPORT.BAK, and will save the new version of the document into a new file named REPORT.DOC. If you continue saving this document with the Create Backup option, Word will continue to change REPORT.DOC to REPORT.BAK and save the new document into a new file named REPORT.DOC. Of course, each time Word makes a backup copy of a document, it overwrites the existing copy of REPORT.BAK, if one exists.

Locking out annotations

The Lock for Annotations check box allows you to put a "lock" on a document, which prevents other people from altering it. When you save a document after activating this check box, only you (the original author) can make changes to the document and remove the lock. We'll discuss the Lock for Annotations check box in more detail in Chapter 17, and talk about annotations in Chapter 13.

Summary information

The first time you save a new document, Word will present a Summary Info dialog box like the one shown in Figure 3-5. If you enter the appropriate information into this dialog box, you can later use the Find... command on the File menu to look up that document by its title, subject, author, keywords, or comments. As you'll see in a moment, the Statistics... button in the Summary Info dialog box lets you view a variety of statistics on the document.

You will usually make entries into the Summary Info dialog box when you save a new document for the first time. If you want, however, you can fill out this dialog box before you begin creating a document by selecting the Summary... button in the New dialog box. You can also bring up a document's Summary Info dialog box at any time by selecting Summary Info... from the Edit menu.

You probably noticed that Word automatically includes the file name and directory information at the top of the dialog box. As you might expect, this information cannot be changed within this dialog box. To change the file name or directory, you'll need to use the Save As... command to resave the document.

Word lets you enter a descriptive title for your document in the Title text box. Unlike the file names in DOS, which are restricted to eight characters, the name you enter into the Title text box can be as long as 255 characters. In addition, the Title text box will accept any character or symbol (including spaces) that you can type on your keyboard. For example, if you're composing a newspaper article on Darrell Griffith of the NBA's Utah Jazz, you might save the document under the file name GRIFFITH.DOC, but enter the title *Jazzy Griffith Still Thrills Fans* in the Title text box, as we've done in Figure 3-7.

Entering summary information

Figure 3-7

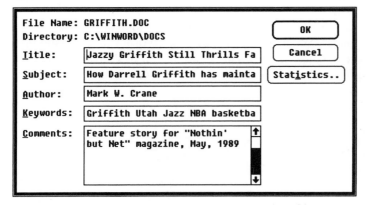

We've entered some sample information into this Summary Info dialog box.

In addition to specifying a title, you can explain the subject matter of the document in the Subject text box. Like the Title text box, the Subject text box will let you enter any combination of 255 characters. For our sample document, we've entered the text *How Darrell Griffith has maintained his "money player" status with the NBA's Utah Jazz.*

By default, Word enters into the Author text box the name you specified the first time you loaded Word. Of course, you can modify this name to include additional authors, or change the name altogether. If you want to change the default name that Word presents, choose the Customize... command on the Utilities menu and enter a new name into the Your Name text box. (We'll show you how to use the Customize... command in Chapter 20.)

You can create an index for your Word documents by entering a list of keywords into each document's Keywords text box. The keywords you specify should be words that indicate the document's contents. For example, for our sample document, we might enter the keywords *Griffith*, *Utah Jazz*, *NBA*, and *basketball*. (Notice that we've used a space to separate each keyword in the list.) Whenever you enter keywords into a document's Summary Info dialog box and then save that document, you can later locate and open the document by selecting the Find... command from the File menu and specifying any of the keywords you've entered in the Keywords text box. (We'll discuss the Find... command in more detail in Chapter 17.)

The last option in the Summary Info dialog box is the Comments text box. (Unlike the other text boxes you've seen so far, this text box features a scroll bar that lets you navigate through its contents.) As you might guess, you can type any remarks concerning your document into this text box. You also can use up to 255 characters and any symbols you want. For instance, in our sample document's Comments text box, you might want to enter the comments *Feature story for "Nothin' but Net" magazine, May, 1989.*

Statistical information

If you want to see a variety of statistics on your document, choose the Statistics... button in the Summary Info dialog box. Word will then bring up a Statistics dialog box like the one shown in Figure 3-8. As you can see, this dialog box tells you the document's date and time of creation, revision number, total editing time, and so forth.

Figure 3-8

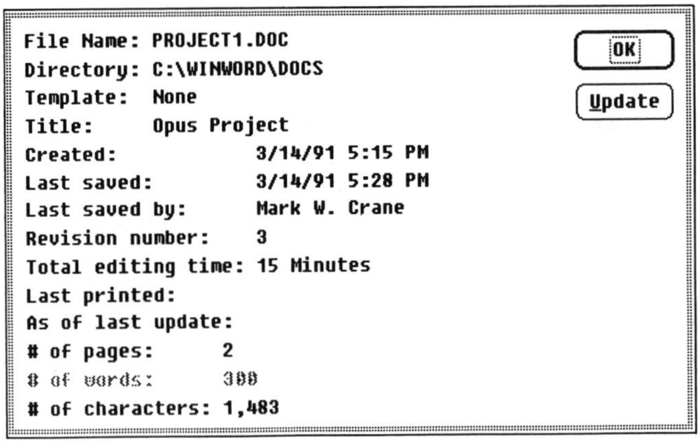

```
File Name: PROJECT1.DOC                      [ OK ]
Directory: C:\WINWORD\DOCS
Template:  None                              [ Update ]
Title:     Opus Project
Created:              3/14/91 5:15 PM
Last saved:           3/14/91 5:28 PM
Last saved by:        Mark W. Crane
Revision number:     3
Total editing time: 15 Minutes
Last printed:
As of last update:
# of pages:          2
8 of words:          300
# of characters: 1,483
```

The Statistics dialog box includes some information about your document.

You cannot edit the data in the Statistics dialog box. Each time you save your document to disk, Word automatically updates the Last Saved, Last Saved By, Revision Number, and Total Editing Time information. Similarly, each time you print your document, Word updates the Last Printed, # of Pages, # of Words, and # of Characters data. If you want to update the data in the Statistics dialog box without printing the document, you can choose the Update button in the upper-right corner of the dialog box. To exit from the Statistics dialog box and return to the Summary Info dialog box, choose OK.

Use the Cancel button in the Summary Info dialog box with care. As we have said, the Summary Info dialog box will appear the first time you use the Save or Save As... command to save a document. If you choose the Cancel button when the dialog box appears, Word will cancel the entire Save command and will not save your document. For this reason, you should choose OK—even if you don't enter anything into the Summary Info dialog box.

A word of caution

If there is not enough room on the active disk to save your document, you'll see a message box like the one shown in Figure 3-9. When you choose OK, Word will close this message box and return you to the document. At this point, you can either reissue the Save or Save As... command and save the document to a different disk, or use the Find... command to delete some of the documents on the disk (we'll show you how to do this at the end of this chapter).

Figure 3-9

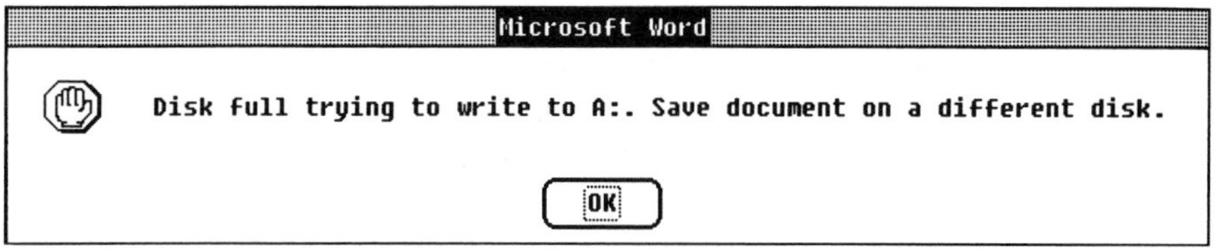

You'll see this message box if there is not enough room to save your document on the active disk.

If you enter into the Save File Name text box a name that already exists on the active disk, you'll see a message box like the one shown in Figure 3-10 on the following page. If you want to replace the existing file with the document that is currently open on your screen, choose Yes; otherwise, choose No. If you click No, Word will redisplay the Save As dialog box and allow you to enter a new document name into the Save File Name text box.

Once you've saved a document under a file name, it is not necessary to use the Save As... command again unless you want to either save that file under a new name or change one of the file options we've discussed. To save the changes to a file that has previously been saved, simply select Save from the File menu. Word will then overwrite the last version of the file with the current version and allow you to continue editing the document.

Saving a document again

Figure 3-10

Word will ask you to verify your file name when you assign the same name to two documents.

If you choose the Save As... command to save a file that has previously been saved, you'll see a Save As dialog box similar to the one shown in Figure 3-4. However, Word will automatically present the name under which you last saved the file in the Save File Name text box. If you want to save the document under a new name, type that name into the text box and choose OK. Word will then save the current document under the new file name and leave the previous version of the file intact under the old name.

If you use the Save As... command to save a document under its own name, Word will assume that you want to save the revised document under its existing name. In other words, Word will replace the version that is stored on disk with the revised version.

Adjusting Fast Save

By default, Word uses a technique called fast save to substantially shorten the amount of time required to save your documents. Here's how this technique works: When you use the Save command to perform a full-fledged save, Word completely rewrites your document to disk and accordingly updates all of the disk's pointer tables. When Word performs a fast save, however, it simply appends to the end of the document the changes you've made since the last save. Consequently, fast-saving your files will cause them to become longer with each successive save. To keep your document from becoming too long, Word will occasionally perform a full-fledged save to rewrite your changes, then update the disk's pointer tables. Of course, whenever you issue the Close or Exit commands, Word will perform a full-fledged save to record your changes.

To take advantage of Word's fast-save technique, simply leave the Fast Save check box selected in the expanded Save As dialog box. If you want Word to perform a full-fledged save each time you issue the Save command, simply deselect this check box.

Unfortunately, you cannot use the Create Backup and Fast Save options simultaneously. However, you can switch options at any time by issuing the Save As... command, then selecting the appropriate option in the expanded Save As dialog box. For example, suppose you have been using the Fast Save option to save your revisions, and you now want to keep the saved version of your file intact while you make some changes to it. To do this, select the Save As... command, choose the Options >> button to expand the Save As dialog box, select the Create Backup option, then choose OK. Now, reissue the Save As... command and reselect the Fast Save option in the expanded Save As dialog box to continue making quick saves as you work.

If you issue the Save command to save a file you opened with the Read Only check box, Word will display a message box like the one shown in Figure 3-11.

Saving a Read Only document

Figure 3-11

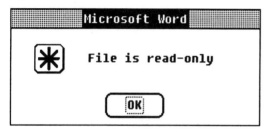

If you try to save a Read Only file, Word will display this message box.

After you select OK, Word will automatically present the Save As dialog box. If you attempt to assign to the altered file the same name that you used for the original, Word will once again present the message box.

To save your changes to the file, you must assign a new name to the document. Although the Read Only option is hardly a foolproof security device, you may find it a convenient way to protect your files from inadvertent changes.

In addition to saving individual files, you can save everything that is open on the Word desktop (including documents, templates, macros, and glossaries) by using the Save All command on the File menu. The Save All command comes in handy when the current document is very complex or is using macros.

Saving everything on the Word desktop

To save everything on the desktop, simply select the Save All command. When you do, Word will save all documents, templates, macros, and glossaries to disk.

As you may have learned the hard way, a momentary power outage can cost you a lot of hard work. If you issue the Save command to save your files regularly, however, you can prevent data loss while you are working in Word. Unfortunately, you may become so involved in your work that you forget to issue the Save command at regular intervals.

Reminding yourself to save

Word's autosave feature can help remedy this problem. This feature works like an alarm clock—it automatically prompts you to save your document at the interval you specify. You can set up reminder intervals of High (every 10 to 30 minutes), Medium (every 20 to 45 minutes), Low (every 30 to 60 minutes), or Never (which turns off the autosave feature).

To activate this feature, select the Customize... command from the Utilities menu to bring up the dialog box shown in Figure 3-12. In the Customize dialog box, choose the appropriate Autosave Frequency option. When you choose OK, the autosave feature will go into effect. When the interval you've specified passes, Word will display the dialog box shown in Figure 3-13.

Figure 3-12

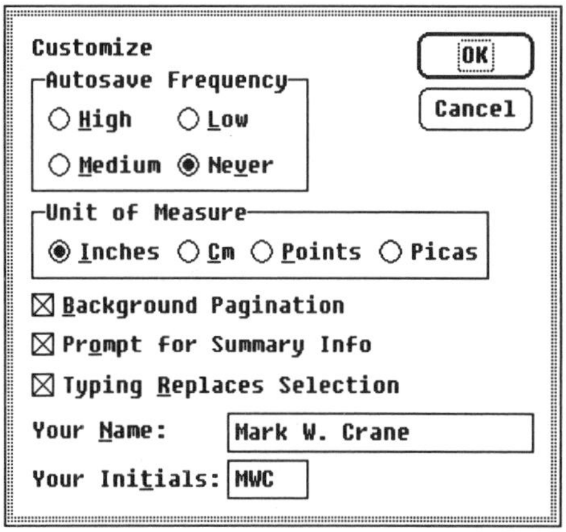

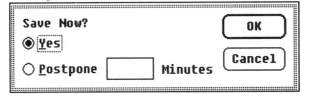

```
Customize                    [ OK ]
┌Autosave Frequency┐
  ○ High    ○ Low          [ Cancel ]
  ○ Medium  ⦿ Never
 ┌Unit of Measure─────────────────┐
  ⦿ Inches ○ Cm ○ Points ○ Picas

 ⊠ Background Pagination
 ⊠ Prompt for Summary Info
 ⊠ Typing Replaces Selection

 Your Name:    │ Mark W. Crane        │
 Your Initials:│ MWC │
```

You can control Word's autosave frequency with the Customize dialog box.

Figure 3-13

```
Save Now?                    ( OK )
 ⦿ Yes
                   ┌─────┐      ( Cancel )
 ○ Postpone        │     │ Minutes
                   └─────┘
```

The Autosave dialog box reminds you to save your documents on a regular basis.

When the Autosave dialog box appears, you can either save the document at that instant or postpone the save for a few minutes. If you tell Word to postpone saving for ten minutes, for example, Word will display the dialog box in Figure 3-13 ten minutes later. When the dialog box reappears, you can again choose to either save the document or postpone the save. If you choose the Cancel button in the Autosave dialog box, Word will restart the autosave clock.

Using the Close and Exit commands

If you issue the Close command on the File menu without saving the changes you've made to a document (or after entering text into a new document), Word will present a message box like the one shown in Figure 3-14.

Figure 3-14

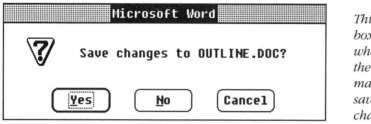

This message box appears when you issue the Close command without saving your changes.

If you choose Yes and the current document has previously been saved, Word will automatically save the document under its current name, then close the document. If the document has never been saved, Word will present the Save As dialog box shown in Figure 3-4. However, if you choose No in the message box, Word will close the current document without saving the changes you've made since the last save.

The Exit command on the File menu tells Word to close all documents on the desktop and return to the Windows operating environment. Therefore, if you issue the Exit command after you've made changes to any of the documents on the desktop, you'll see a message box like the one shown in Figure 3-14 for each document that has been changed since your last save (including dictionary, glossary, and macro files, which we'll discuss later in the book). As you'd expect, you can elect to save or discard your changes to each file.

To delete a file in Word, first select the Find... command from the File menu. When you do, Word will display a message box telling you that it is searching for files on your active disk. After Word has searched your entire disk, it will display a Find dialog box like the one shown in Figure 3-15.

DELETING A FILE

Figure 3-15

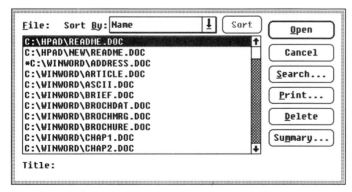

You can delete a file by using the Find dialog box.

In the File list box, select the document file you want to delete. If the file is stored on another disk or in another directory, choose the Search... button to find it (we'll discuss Word's search feature in Chapter 6). Once you select the file you want to delete, choose the Delete button. Word will then display a message box like the one shown in Figure 3-16. If you want to delete the file you've selected, choose Yes. If you select No, Word will return you to the document without deleting the file.

Figure 3-16

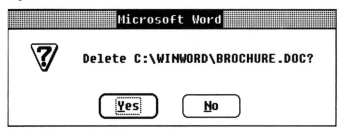

Word will ask if you want to delete the selected file.

If you want, you can delete more than one file at once. To do this, hold down the [Shift] key as you click on each file you want to delete. To deselect a file once you've selected it, keep holding down the [Shift] key and click on it again.

If your computer is not equipped with a mouse, you can use the following technique to select multiple files. First, position the highlight on the first file you want to select. Then, hold down the [Ctrl] key and use the ↑ or ↓ key to position the dotted-line highlight over the next file you want to select. When the highlight is in position, press the [Spacebar] to add the file to the selection. Now, continue holding down the [Ctrl] key and using the ↑, ↓, and [Spacebar] keys to select the desired files from the list. If you accidentally select a file, just press the [Spacebar] a second time to deselect it. When you're finished selecting the files from the list, release the [Ctrl] key and choose the Delete button to delete all the selected files.

SATISFACTION GUARANTEED

The Best

Working with Word

Section 2
Working with Word

Now that you've learned the basics, it's time to get some work done! Your first step, of course, will be to enter some text into a Word document. Then, you can use Word's formatting and editing tools to create a polished document. When you complete this section, you will have mastered the basic skills you need to use Word.

In this chapter

Word Basics 4

*A*fter you open a new Word document, you'll want to enter some text, then edit and format it to suit your needs. In this chapter, we'll show you how to enter text in Word and introduce some navigational and selection techniques you can use to view, edit, and format that text. We'll wrap up the chapter with some basic editing skills that will set the stage for our discussion of Word's formatting and editing commands in Chapters 5 and 6.

On the following pages, you'll find dozens of keyboard shortcuts and special techniques. We urge you to practice these techniques; they will help you work more efficiently in Word. For easy reference, see Appendix 3 for a summary of these keyboard shortcuts.

Entering text in Word is actually easier than typing text on a typewriter. A special facility called Wordwrap lets you type a constant stream of characters without pressing a carriage return at the end of each line. If you are new to word processing, you may be tempted to press the [Enter] key as you near the end of a line of text in order to move to the next line. Don't worry—if there's not enough room on the current line for the word you are typing, Word will wrap it to the beginning of the next line automatically.

In fact, the only time you need to press the [Enter] key as you enter text in Word is when you want to start a new paragraph. You can significantly hinder your editing and formatting capabilities by placing a carriage return at the end of each line. If you later decide to insert or delete text or change the widths of your margins, you'll have to edit each line manually in order to reset your line breaks. If you let Wordwrap handle this task for you, you can easily change the content, format, and layout of your document and have Word automatically reflow the text for you.

ENTERING TEXT

A sample document

To illustrate some basic entry, selection, and editing techniques in Word, we'll enter the text shown in Figure 4-1 into a new Word document. If you've just loaded Word, you can enter the sample text into the blank document entitled *Document1*. If you need to open a new blank document, however, select the New… command from the File menu. When the New dialog box appears, choose OK to bring up the new, blank document.

Figure 4-1

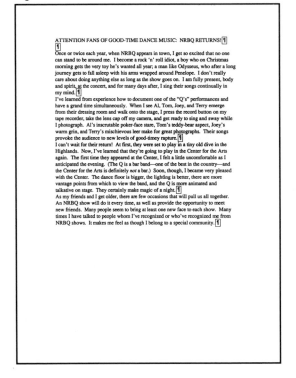

We'll use this sample document to illustrate some entry, selection, and editing techniques.

As we'll explain in Chapter 13, Word displays your document in one of five views: normal editing view, page view, Print Preview, outline view, or draft view. As you'll see in Chapter 7, you'll use the Print Preview command on the File menu to access Print Preview. You'll use the commands on the View menu, however, to access the other four views. To determine which of the four views you're currently in, pull down the View menu to see which view name has a check mark beside it. If there is no check mark next to any of the view names, Word is in normal editing view.

All the documents in this chapter will be shown in normal editing view. To make your documents look like the ones in our examples, you'll want to make sure none of the view names on the View menu is selected. If a check mark appears beside one of the view names, simply select that name to remove the check mark and return to the normal editing view.

The default font for a new document is 10-point Tms Rmn. However, if you told the Windows Setup program that you're using a PCL laser printer (such as the HP LaserJet Series II), the text you see on your screen will not appear in the Tms Rmn font unless you use the Printer Setup... command to tell Word that your printer is equipped with that font. For information on how to use the Printer Setup... command, refer to Chapter 7.

In order to make our figures more legible, we'll enter our documents' text in 12-point Tms Rmn instead of in the default 10-point Tms Rmn. To change the size of your document's text from 10 to 12 points, simply choose the Character... command from the Format menu, select 12 from the Points list box, and choose OK. Any new text you enter at the cursor will now appear in 12-point Tms Rmn. (We'll explain changing fonts in detail in Chapter 5.)

Once you've entered the normal editing view (and, if you wanted, chosen the 12-point Tms Rmn font), begin entering text by typing the first line shown in Figure 4-1. As you type, keep your eye on the blinking vertical cursor. This cursor will move one space to the right as you type each character, indicating your position in the document.

If you make an error as you are typing, just press the [Backspace] key to move the cursor back one space at a time and erase your mistakes. Then, you can resume typing as usual. If you don't notice an error until you are several words along, don't worry about it at this point. We'll show you how to correct those mistakes in a few pages.

When you reach the end of the first one-line paragraph shown in Figure 4-1 (this will become a headline when we begin formatting the text in Chapter 5), press the [Enter] key twice to begin two new paragraphs. Continue typing the sample text, pressing [Enter] only when you need to begin a new paragraph. Notice that we have included ¶ marks in our sample document to indicate where paragraph breaks are needed. You will not see these marks in your Word document at first. You must turn them on by selecting the Preferences... command from the View menu, selecting the Paragraph Marks check box, and choosing OK.

Don't worry if some of the text scrolls out of view as you type. As you'll see in a moment, you can use Word's scrolling features to bring that text back into view.

As we mentioned, we've used 12-point Tms Rmn to create the sample document in Figure 4-1. If you are using another point size or font (such as the default 10-point Tms Rmn), your line breaks may look a bit different from ours. We'll talk about changing fonts and formatting a document in Chapter 5.

**DISPLAYING
SPECIAL MARKS IN
YOUR DOCUMENT**

One of Word's best features is its graphical interface. Word lets you see on the screen almost exactly what your text will look like when it's printed. You don't have to litter the on-line version of your document with hard-to-read codes every time you want to begin a new paragraph, change margin widths, or assign a special format to some element of your text. This on-line display is whimsically referred to as the WYSIWYG (What You See Is What You Get) feature.

You might be surprised to learn, however, that you enter special coding information every time you create a new paragraph or make some formatting change to your document. Word does a lot of work behind the scenes as it implements your editing and formatting instructions. Some of this work is evident in a set of special marks that indicate where paragraph breaks, line breaks, blank spaces, optional hyphens, and so forth, occur in your document.

To see the special marks you've entered into your document, you'll need to turn on a few settings in the Preferences dialog box. To do this, simply choose the Preferences... command from the View menu. As you can see in Figure 4-2, the check-box options in the Preferences dialog box allow you to display on your screen special marks that indicate where you've entered tabs, spaces, paragraphs, optional hyphens, and hidden text. This dialog box also lets you turn on or off your horizontal and vertical scroll bars. For example, if you select the Spaces check box and the Paragraph Marks check box, you'll see a series of • and ¶ marks in your document window, as shown in Figure 4-3. These marks do not appear when you print your document; they appear on the screen only for your orientation.

Figure 4-2

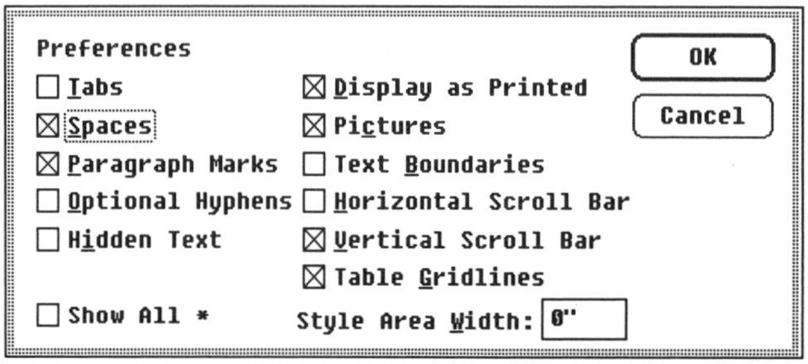

*The Preferences dialog box lets you display special for-
matting characters, like tabs, spaces, and paragraphs.*

The Preferences settings are an integral part of your document. When you change a default in the Preferences dialog box, then save your document, Word will save those changes as well.

We'll sometimes display the various marks in our figures to help you interpret the content and design of our sample documents. We think you will find these marks helpful as you follow along with our examples of selecting, editing, and formatting text.

Figure 4-3

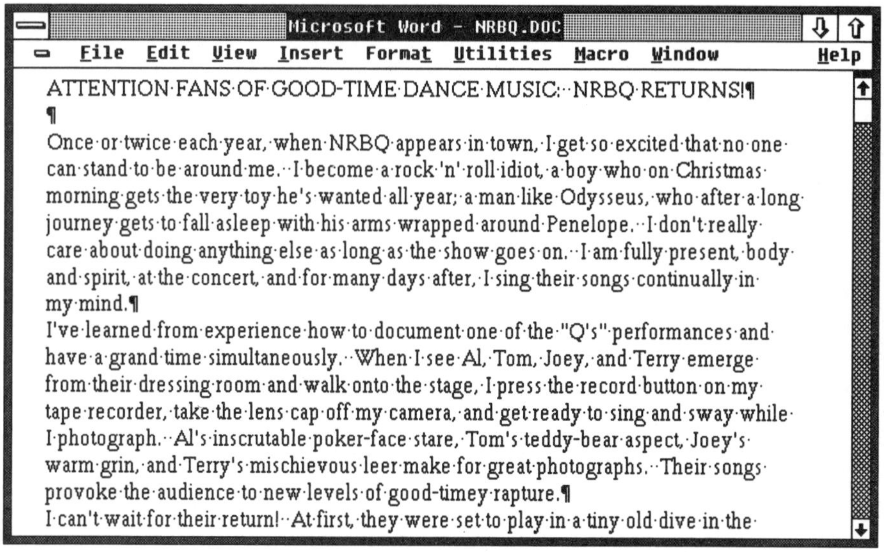

```
┌─────────────────────────────────────────────────────────────────┐
│ ▭        ▓▓▓▓▓Microsoft Word - NRBQ.DOC▓▓▓▓▓          ⇩ ⇧ │
│  ▭   File  Edit  View  Insert  Format  Utilities  Macro  Window     Help │
│ ┌───────────────────────────────────────────────────────────────┬─┐│
│ │ ATTENTION·FANS·OF·GOOD-TIME·DANCE·MUSIC:··NRBQ·RETURNS!¶        │↑││
│ │ ¶                                                               │ ││
│ │ Once·or·twice·each·year,·when·NRBQ·appears·in·town,·I·get·so·excited·that·no·one·│ ││
│ │ can·stand·to·be·around·me.··I·become·a·rock·'n'·roll·idiot,·a·boy·who·on·Christmas·│ ││
│ │ morning·gets·the·very·toy·he's·wanted·all·year;·a·man·like·Odysseus,·who·after·a·long·│ ││
│ │ journey·gets·to·fall·asleep·with·his·arms·wrapped·around·Penelope.··I·don't·really·│ ││
│ │ care·about·doing·anything·else·as·long·as·the·show·goes·on.··I·am·fully·present,·body·│ ││
│ │ and·spirit,·at·the·concert,·and·for·many·days·after,·I·sing·their·songs·continually·in·│ ││
│ │ my·mind.¶                                                       │ ││
│ │ I've·learned·from·experience·how·to·document·one·of·the·"Q's"·performances·and·│ ││
│ │ have·a·grand·time·simultaneously.··When·I·see·Al,·Tom,·Joey,·and·Terry·emerge·│ ││
│ │ from·their·dressing·room·and·walk·onto·the·stage,·I·press·the·record·button·on·my·│ ││
│ │ tape·recorder,·take·the·lens·cap·off·my·camera,·and·get·ready·to·sing·and·sway·while·│ ││
│ │ I·photograph.··Al's·inscrutable·poker-face·stare,·Tom's·teddy-bear·aspect,·Joey's·│ ││
│ │ warm·grin,·and·Terry's·mischievous·leer·make·for·great·photographs.··Their·songs·│ ││
│ │ provoke·the·audience·to·new·levels·of·good-timey·rapture.¶     │ ││
│ │ I·can't·wait·for·their·return!··At·first,·they·were·set·to·play·in·a·tiny·old·dive·in·the·│↓││
│ └───────────────────────────────────────────────────────────────┴─┘│
└─────────────────────────────────────────────────────────────────┘
```

We've turned on the display of space and paragraph marks in our sample document.

As you already know, the ¶ mark represents the end of a paragraph in your Word document. Among other things, it indicates where you want to begin a new line of text. As you'll learn when we begin formatting text in Chapter 5, the ¶ mark also "stores" the formatting characteristics that you have assigned to your text.

The dots (·) that appear between the words and sentences in Figure 4-3 represent blank spaces. It's a little difficult at first to distinguish the space marks from periods, but if you look closely, you'll see that the space marks sit slightly higher than the periods.

Word allows you to turn on the display of tabs, spaces, paragraph marks, optional hyphens, hidden text, text boundaries, and table gridlines by selecting the Show All check box in the Preferences dialog box. (If you display your ribbon as you work, you can quickly activate the Show All check box by using the mouse to select the Show-all icon (⊠) at the right edge of the ribbon.) If you are already in the habit of displaying a few of the special marks on your screen, activating the Show All check box will not deactivate the ones you have on. It will merely activate the rest of the special marks. As you'll see later in this book, activating this check box also displays field codes.

In addition to these special marks, the Show All check box affects the display of dates, times, page numbers, and footnote entries in your Word documents. We'll discuss each of these topics as they arise throughout this book. For now, let's explore some of the effects of the · and ¶ marks on your Word document.

**DEFINING THE
BASIC ELEMENTS
OF A DOCUMENT**

Now that we've entered some text and have seen how Word displays marks in a document, let's review some basic definitions. As you begin selecting, editing, and formatting text in your document, you'll need to understand how Word defines elements like characters, words, sentences, and paragraphs. While these concepts are not difficult to grasp, they can differ from the definitions you may have become accustomed to in writing or typing text. Many new users find themselves extremely frustrated as they begin editing and formatting documents because they've never been exposed to this terminology.

Characters

The most basic element of text in your Word document is a character. A character can be any element you enter onto the screen: a blank space, letter, number, punctuation mark, or any other special mark. Words, sentences, and paragraphs are nothing more than predefined combinations of characters.

Blocks

In Word, a block of text refers to any group of two or more adjacent characters. Usually, a block of text forms a sentence, a paragraph, or a cluster of paragraphs. However, even a part of a word or one or more complete words constitutes a block of text in Word.

Words

Word, of course, does not look at words in your document as nouns, verbs, adjectives, and so forth. To Word, a word is any group of alphabetic and/or numeric characters set apart by one or more blank spaces or by a period, comma, hyphen, colon, semicolon, question mark, exclamation point, or quotation mark. Other characters that can serve as word separators include parentheses, braces, brackets, greater than or less than signs, the pound sign, the @ symbol, the dollar sign, the ampersand, left and right slash marks, and the asterisk.

Oddly enough, characters like <, ?, >, !, @, -, +, and = mark the end of a word only when they are mixed with alphabetic or numeric characters—not when they are grouped. For example, the character string =-+ would be interpreted as one word, but the character string *abc+=-def* would be considered as three words: *abc, +=-,* and *def.*

In short, all the characters below serve as word delimiters, except when they are grouped:

~ ' ! @ # $ % ^ & * ( ) - = + [ ] { } ; : " , . < > \ | / ?

Keep in mind that a blank space always marks the end of a word, even when it is used in conjunction with the characters above. When an apostrophe falls between two letters, it doesn't end a word since that character is commonly used in contractions and in creating the possessive form of a noun.

With all of these definitions in mind, it still may surprise you how many words make up the sentence *ATTENTION FANS OF GOOD-TIME DANCE MUSIC:*

NRBQ RETURNS! at the beginning of the document shown in Figure 4-3. By Word's definition, there are actually 12 distinct words in this sentence, as shown by the vertical lines below:

ATTENTION• |FANS• |OF• |GOOD |– |TIME• |DANCE• |MUSIC |:•• |NRBQ• |RETURNS |!|¶

The ¶ mark at the end of the sentence also counts as a word, but Word does not consider the ¶ mark as part of the sentence.

As you know by now, Word always tries to keep words together in your document. That is, if a word is too long to fit at the end of a line, the Wordwrap feature will push it to the beginning of the next line. There are two exceptions to this. In keeping with our definitions above, if a word contains a hyphen, Word will treat it as two words. Thus, if a hyphenated word will not fit on one line, all the characters up to and including the hyphen will appear at the end of the first line, while the remaining characters will wrap to the beginning of the next line. You can control these breaks to some extent with Word's special hyphenation features, which we'll cover in Chapter 6.

The only other time that Wordwrap will not keep all the characters in a word together is when the word is simply too long to fit on a single line. This most likely will be a problem when you are working with very narrow columns. For example, in Figure 4-4, we typed the word *supercalifragilisticexpialidocious* into a blank Word document with a 1-inch column width (more on column widths in Chapters 5 and 12). As you can see, Word included as many characters in the first line as possible, allowing the remaining characters to flow to the next line.

Figure 4-4

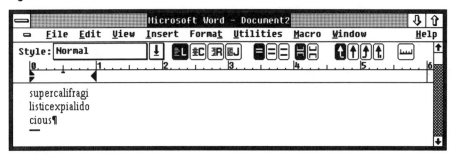

If all the characters in a word will not fit on one line, Word will allow the remaining characters to flow to the next line.

A sentence is a group of characters and words set apart by a period, exclamation point, or question mark. A forced line break (which is represented by the ↵ symbol and entered into a document by pressing the [Shift] and [Enter]

Sentences

keys) or a ¶ mark may also mark the end of a sentence. Of course, as you may have guessed from our discussion of words, any character that marks the end of a sentence also marks the end of the last word in that sentence.

For example, consider the sentence *Once or twice...I get so excited that no one can stand to be around me.* in the third paragraph of our sample document. The period at the end of this series of characters marks the end of the sentence, as well as the end of the word *me*.

Paragraphs

A paragraph can be any combination of characters, words, and symbols, set apart by a ¶ mark. Keep in mind that the ¶ mark at the end of a paragraph is considered part of that paragraph. In fact, the ¶ mark is treated as an individual word, which marks the end of the last word and the last sentence in a paragraph. And, as you might have guessed, the first sentence at the beginning of a paragraph is delimited by the ¶ mark at the end of the previous paragraph. Similarly, the first word in a paragraph is delimited by the ¶ mark from above.

For example, in the sample document shown in Figure 4-3, the ninth line ends with a ¶ mark, which signals the end of the sentence that begins *I am fully present*, as well as the third paragraph. It also marks the beginning of the first word and sentence in the next paragraph, *I've*.

These definitions may seem a bit esoteric at this point, but they will become important to you when you begin selecting text blocks and editing your document. As you will learn in Chapter 6, a thorough understanding of these definitions is also critical to using Word's Search... and Replace... commands effectively.

SELECTING TEXT

Now that you know how Word defines the basic elements of your document, it's time to learn how to edit and format those elements. Before you can edit or format any of the text you have created in Word, you must select that text.

When you select text in Word, that block of characters will appear in inverse video—that is, you'll see white type on a black background rather than the normal black on white. Throughout this book, we'll refer to this inverse video as highlighted or selected text.

If you've used other products that run under Microsoft Windows, you are probably aware that you can speed up most of your text selection and navigation if you use a mouse. If you don't have a mouse, we strongly recommend that you purchase and install one for your system. If you're forced to run Word for Windows on a mouseless system, however, Word provides several keyboard shortcuts to help you select text and move around your document. Let's begin by discussing the standard mouse selection techniques, then explore Word's keyboard selection techniques.

Click and drag

The most basic mouse selection technique is the click-and-drag method. To demonstrate this technique, suppose you want to select the words *poker-face stare* in line 14 of the sample document. To do this, begin by positioning the I-beam pointer just to the left of the letter *p* in the word *poker*. Next, press and hold the left mouse button. Now, without releasing the mouse button, drag to the right until the desired characters are highlighted, as shown in Figure 4-5. When you release the mouse button, the characters you dragged across will remain highlighted. You can use this click-and-drag method to select any size block of text, from a single character to an entire document.

Figure 4-5

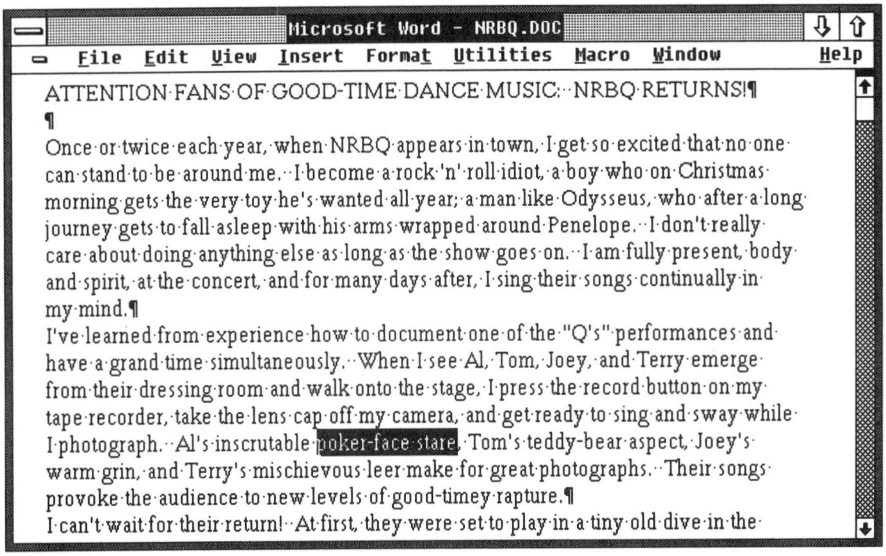

You can select a block of text by clicking at the beginning of the block and dragging to the end.

Double-clicking

To select an entire word, simply double-click (press the mouse button twice in quick succession) anywhere on that word. For example, to select the word *ATTENTION* in the first line of our sample document, just place the pointer over any portion of that word, and double-click. As you can see in Figure 4-6 on the following page, Word will highlight the entire word, as well as any blank spaces to the right of the word.

If you double-click on a word that is followed by a period, comma, or some other delimiting character, Word will not highlight the delimiting character or blank spaces after that word. For example, if you double-click on the word *year* in the third line of our sample document, Word will highlight only the characters *year*—not the comma or the blank space following that word. Instead, those trailing characters will be treated as a separate word. In fact, if you double-click just to the right of the word *year*, Word will highlight the comma and blank space that mark the end of that word.

Figure 4-6

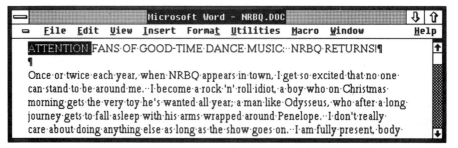

To select an entire word, double-click anywhere on that word.

You can use the double-click technique in combination with the click-and-drag method to highlight a group of words quickly and easily. After you double-click on a word, continue holding down the mouse button, and drag. As you do this, Word will not highlight individual letters, but instead will highlight entire words. This technique saves you time because it allows you to be less precise with your pointing and dragging.

The click/[Shift]-click method

Of course, if you need to select a large block of text, you might find it tiresome to drag through line after line of text. To save time when you need to select a large block of text, you can use the click/[Shift]-click method. To do this, first click at the beginning of the block, then hold down the [Shift] key and click at the end of the block. That's all there is to it!

For example, suppose you want to highlight all the text beginning with the words *I get so excited* and ending with *as long as the show goes on* in the third paragraph. Begin by clicking just to the left of the word *I*, then release the mouse button, press the [Shift] key, and click just to the right of the period that follows the word *on*. Figure 4-7 shows the results.

The [Ctrl]-click method

Word provides a technique specifically for selecting an entire sentence. Just press [Ctrl], then click the mouse button anywhere in the sentence you want to select. Word will highlight the entire sentence, as well as the period and any blank characters that appear after the sentence. If the sentence is the last in a paragraph, Word will not highlight the ¶ mark. Like the period and blank spaces in word selection, the ¶ mark is treated separately when you are selecting sentences.

The selection bar

To select an entire line or paragraph in Word, use the invisible selection bar on the left side of your document window. Although you cannot see the selection bar, you will know you are there when your I-beam pointer takes on the shape of a right arrow.

Figure 4-7

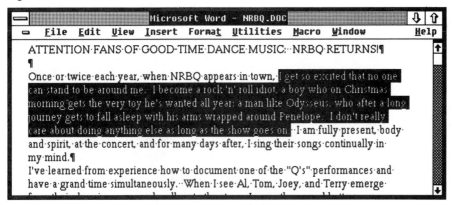

You can select any size block of text by clicking at the beginning of the block, then pressing the [Shift] key and clicking at the end of the block.

To select an entire line of text, just move the pointer to the left side of the screen until it takes on the right arrow shape, then point to the line of text you want to select, and click. For example, if you click in the selection bar to the left of the line that begins *I've learned from experience* in the fourth paragraph in the sample document, your screen will look like the one in Figure 4-8.

Figure 4-8

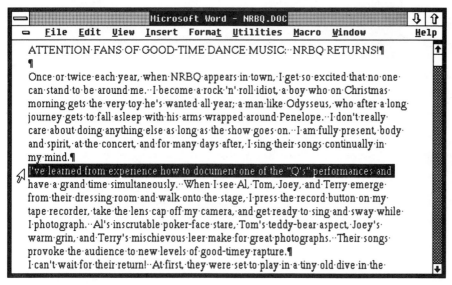

To select an entire line, click next to that line in the selection bar.

To select an entire paragraph, move your pointer to the selection bar and double-click the mouse button. Figure 4-9 shows the Word screen after we selected the entire fourth paragraph of the document. As you can see, the ¶ mark at the end of the paragraph is also highlighted. Notice the right-arrow pointer as it lies in the selection bar in Figures 4-8 and 4-9.

Finally, to select the entire Word document, move the pointer to the selection bar and press the [Ctrl] key as you click. All of your text will appear highlighted in inverse video to indicate your selection. As you will learn in Chapter 5, this technique is particularly helpful when you need to make a global change to your document—like changing the indentions for all your text.

Figure 4-9

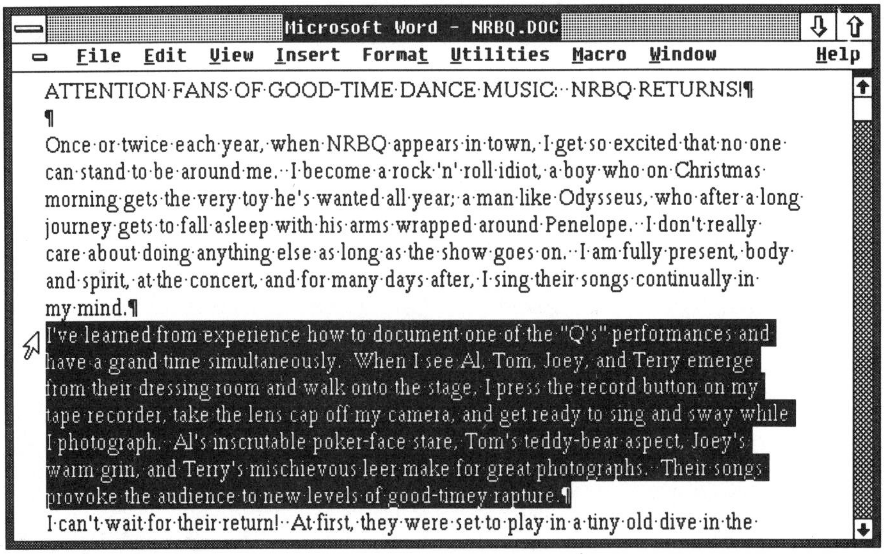

Double-click in the invisible selection bar to select a paragraph of text.

Making block selections

A selection technique that you'll find particularly convenient when you're working with tabular data is the block selection. To make a block selection, first position the pointer at one corner of the block you want to select. Next, press the right—not the left—mouse button, and drag to the opposite corner of the block.

Suppose you want to select the block of text shown in the sample document in Figure 4-10. To do this, position the I-beam pointer just to the left of the word *experience* in the first line of the fourth paragraph, press the right mouse button, and drag to the right of the word *new* in the seventh line of the paragraph.

As you can see, Word has highlighted a section of text from the middle of the document with no regard for word, sentence, or paragraph breaks. In fact, some of the characters in the selection are only partially highlighted. When you make block selections, Word considers any character that is more than half highlighted to be part of the selection. We'll discuss this technique in more detail in Chapter 11 when we talk about formatting and editing tables.

Figure 4-10

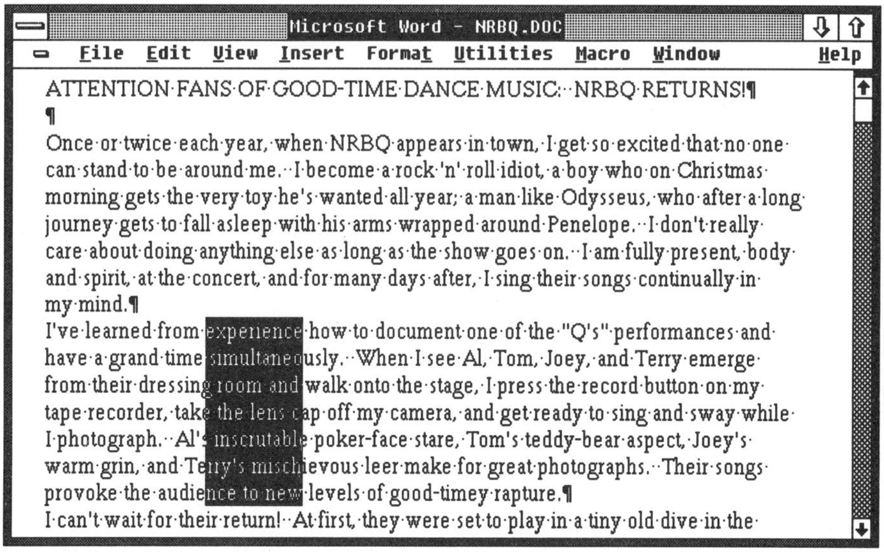

```
┌─────────────────────────────────────────────────────────────────────┐
│ ▭          Microsoft Word - NRBQ.DOC                          ⇩ ⇧ │
├─────────────────────────────────────────────────────────────────────┤
│ ▭    File  Edit  View  Insert  Format  Utilities  Macro  Window   Help│
├─────────────────────────────────────────────────────────────────────┤
│ ATTENTION·FANS·OF·GOOD-TIME·DANCE·MUSIC:··NRBQ·RETURNS!¶          ▲ │
│ ¶                                                                    │
│ Once·or·twice·each·year,·when·NRBQ·appears·in·town,·I·get·so·excited·that·no·one· │
│ can·stand·to·be·around·me.··I·become·a·rock·'n'·roll·idiot,·a·boy·who·on·Christmas· │
│ morning·gets·the·very·toy·he's·wanted·all·year;·a·man·like·Odysseus,·who·after·a·long· │
│ journey·gets·to·fall·asleep·with·his·arms·wrapped·around·Penelope.··I·don't·really· │
│ care·about·doing·anything·else·as·long·as·the·show·goes·on.··I·am·fully·present,·body· │
│ and·spirit,·at·the·concert,·and·for·many·days·after,·I·sing·their·songs·continually·in· │
│ my·mind.¶                                                            │
│ I've·learned·from·experience·how·to·document·one·of·the·"Q's"·performances·and· │
│ have·a·grand·time·simultaneously.··When·I·see·Al,·Tom,·Joey,·and·Terry·emerge· │
│ from·their·dressing·room·and·walk·onto·the·stage,·I·press·the·record·button·on·my· │
│ tape·recorder,·take·the·lens·cap·off·my·camera,·and·get·ready·to·sing·and·sway·while· │
│ I·photograph.··Al's·inscrutable·poker-face·stare,·Tom's·teddy-bear·aspect,·Joey's· │
│ warm·grin,·and·Terry's·mischievous·leer·make·for·great·photographs.··Their·songs· │
│ provoke·the·audience·to·new·levels·of·good-timey·rapture.¶          │
│ I·can't·wait·for·their·return!··At·first,·they·were·set·to·play·in·a·tiny·old·dive·in·the· ▼ │
└─────────────────────────────────────────────────────────────────────┘
```

To make a block selection, press the right mouse button, then drag through the desired text.

When you select text, your cursor serves as the pivot or anchor point for one end of the selection. Whether you drag or click above, below, to the left, or to the right of the cursor, it always represents one edge of your selection. For example, if you click to the left of the word *simultaneously* in line 11 of our sample document, then drag down and to the left of the comma after the word *stage*, your screen will look like the one in Figure 4-11 on the next page. However, if you now drag up and to the left of the word *from* in the previous line without releasing the mouse button, your screen will look like the one in Figure 4-12 on the next page. As you can see, the initial anchor point is now the endpoint of your selection. You can continue to change the size and shape of your selection by dragging around this anchor point, as long as you don't release the mouse button.

The easiest way to see the effect of the anchor point is to click in the middle of a line of text in your document and move your mouse in a broad circular motion. As you drag up, right, down, and left, the size and shape of your highlighted selection will change, but the cursor will always mark one end of your selection.

Anchoring your selection

Figure 4-11

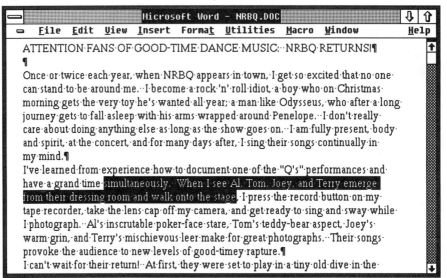

The cursor marks the start of a selection if you drag down or to the right.

Figure 4-12

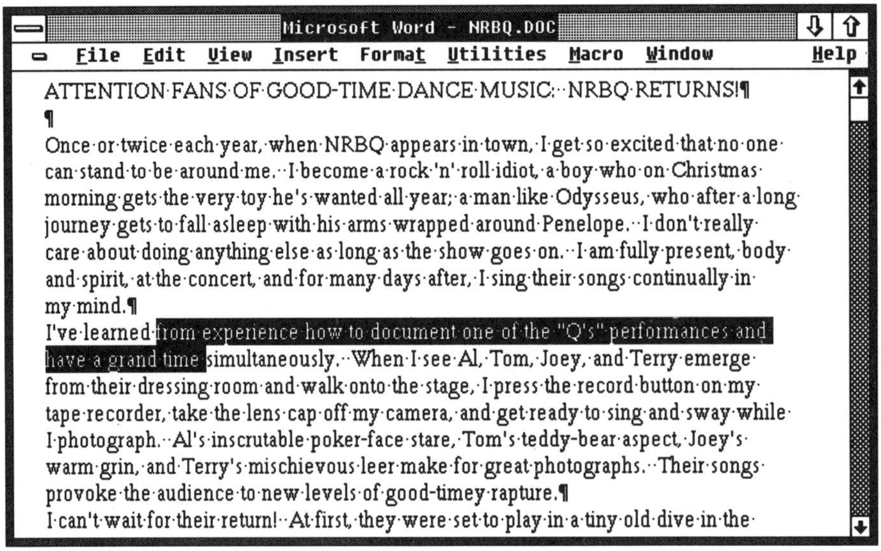

The cursor marks the end of a selection if you drag up or to the left.

Interestingly, when you use one of the mouse selection techniques described above, Word will "remember" that technique as you drag through additional text. For example, suppose you have double-clicked on a word to select it. In effect, you have entered the "word selection mode." If you drag to the right or left, Word will highlight the next word your pointer touches. Even if you drag up or down through several lines, Word will continue to highlight single words.

Selection modes

Similarly, if you press the [Ctrl] key and click on a sentence to select it, you can select adjacent sentences by dragging through them. The selection mode that you started with will remain in effect until you release the mouse button.

If your computer is not equipped with a mouse, you won't be able to use any of the convenient selection techniques we've discussed so far. Instead, you'll have to use the keyboard techniques Word provides to select text in a document.

Keyboard selection techniques

The most commonly used keyboard selection tool is the [Extend selection] key ([F8]). When you press this key, the letters *EXT* will appear in the status bar, indicating that the Extend Selection mode is active. While you are in this mode, you can highlight text by pressing the arrow keys. The initial position of the cursor serves as the anchor point for one end of the selection. As you highlight text with the arrow keys, the cursor's position always represents one end of the selection.

For example, if you move the cursor to the left of the word *simultaneously* in line 11 of our sample document, then press the [Extend selection] key and move the cursor to the left of the comma after the word *stage*, your screen will look like the one in Figure 4-11. However, if you now move the cursor to the left of the word *from* in the previous line, your screen will look like the one in Figure 4-12. The cursor's position now becomes the endpoint of the selection.

If you want to highlight entire words, sentences, paragraphs, or documents, you can take advantage of the [Extend selection] key's special features. After you've pressed this key once to enter the Extend Selection mode, you can press it a second time to highlight the word on which the cursor is positioned. The third time you press the [Extend selection] key, Word will highlight the sentence in which the highlighted word appears. With the fourth pressing of this key, Word will highlight the paragraph in which the highlighted word appears. Finally, the fifth time you press this key, Word will highlight your entire document. To cancel the Extend Selection mode, press the [Esc] key, then press one of the cursor-movement keys to remove the highlight.

In addition to the [Extend selection] key, you can use the [Shift] key in conjunction with the cursor-movement keys to select text. For instance, if you hold down the [Shift] key and repeatedly press the ➡ key, Word will highlight the characters to the right of the cursor. We'll mention the [Shift] key technique again after we explain Word's navigational techniques.

By the way, Word offers one keyboard selection technique that frequently comes in handy. To select an entire Word document, you can hold down the [Ctrl] key and press the number 5 on the numeric keypad.

NAVIGATION

As we said earlier, you often cannot view an entire document on your screen at one time. In fact, whenever you create a document that is more than 18 or 20 lines long, the beginning of your document will scroll off the top edge of your screen. The amount you can view at one time depends, of course, on the size of the window and the size of the type you are using.

To move around in a large document, you'll need to use Word's navigational tools. Some of these tools involve the mouse, while others require only the keyboard. After we explain how to navigate with the mouse, we'll show you some keyboard navigational devices.

Navigating with the mouse

A technique you'll often use to navigate through your document is called scrolling. As you learned in Chapter 2, the gray bars on the right side and at the bottom of your document window are called scroll bars. (Recall that the horizontal scroll bar at the bottom of each window shows up only when you've selected the Horizontal Scroll Bar check box in the Preferences dialog box.) The white boxes within the scroll bars are called scroll boxes, and the white arrows at either end of each scroll bar are called scroll arrows.

To move through your document a line at a time, simply click on the scroll arrows that appear above and below the vertical scroll bar. For example, in Figure 4-12, the first 17 lines of the document are in view. If you click on the scroll arrow at the bottom of the vertical scroll bar, you'll see lines 2 through 18. Line 1 will move out of view, as shown in Figure 4-13.

Figure 4-13

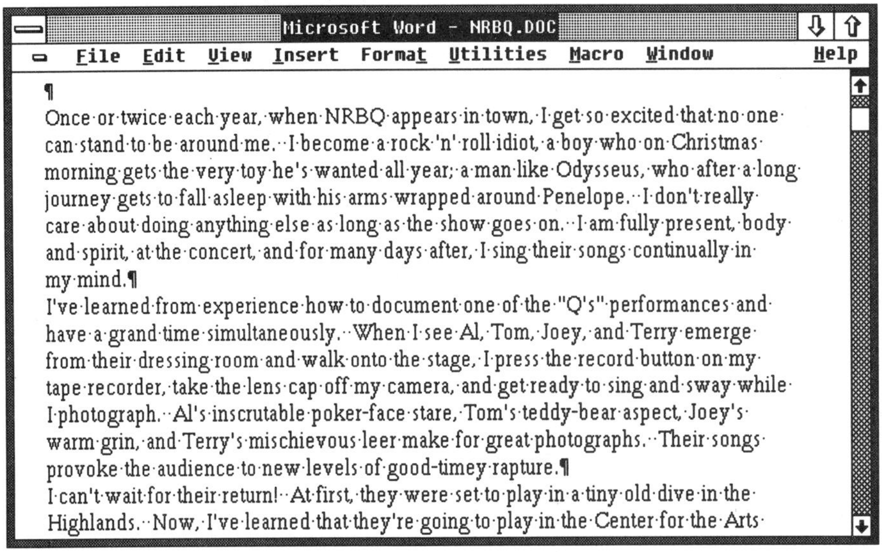

Use the scroll arrows at either end of the vertical scroll bar to move through your document one line at a time.

Moving through your text line by line is satisfactory for a short document, but you'll soon find this method tedious in a long document. To move through your document a full screen at a time, click in the gray area of the scroll bar above or below the scroll box. When you do this, the next screenful will scroll into view.

For example, if you click below the scroll box in the vertical scroll bar while lines 1 through 17 of the sample document are in view, your screen will look like the one in Figure 4-14. As you can see, lines 16 through 29 are now in view, along with four blank lines. Notice that Word carries two lines over to the top of the second screen to help you get your bearings.

Figure 4-14

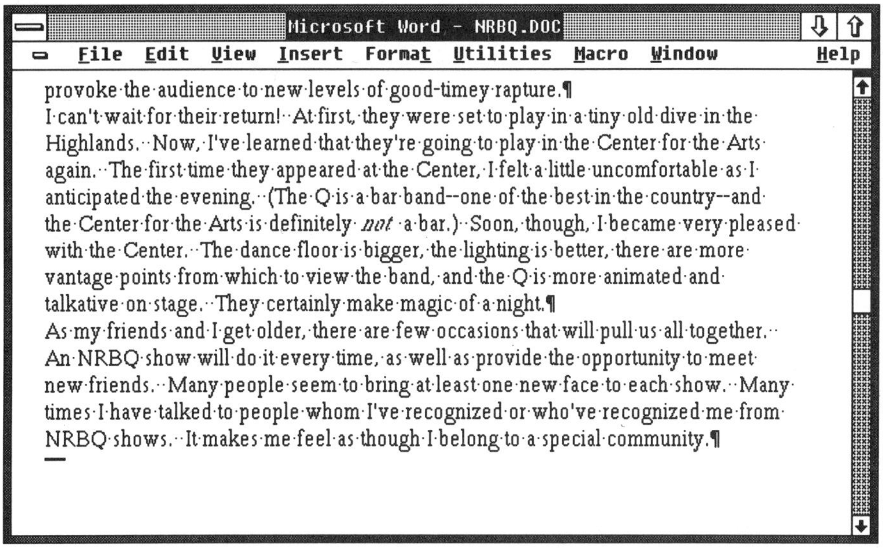

To view a new screenful of data, click in the gray area of the scroll bar.

Of course, the distance you scroll depends on the size of the document window. For example, if you reduce your document to the size shown in Figure 4-15 on the next page, only the first eight lines will be in view. If you click below the scroll box, Word will bring lines 7 through 14 into view. In Figure 4-16 on the next page, the last two lines from the bottom of the previous screen now appear at the top of the current screen.

You can also drag the scroll box to the desired position in the scroll bar to move long distances through your document. The distance you travel by dragging the scroll box depends on the length of your document.

The scroll bar reflects the length of your document. Therefore, in a very short document like the one containing the sample NRBQ.DOC text, dragging the scroll box to the middle of the scroll bar will advance you to the fourth paragraph of the document. However, if you drag to the middle of the vertical scroll bar in a 50-page document, you'd be scrolling through 25 pages of text. If you drag the scroll box to the top of the scroll bar, you'll see the first screen of your document; if you drag the scroll box to the bottom of the scroll bar, you'll see the last screenful of information.

Figure 4-15

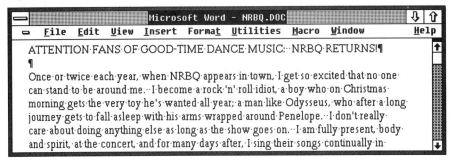

We have reduced our document window to eight lines to show how window size affects scrolling.

Figure 4-16

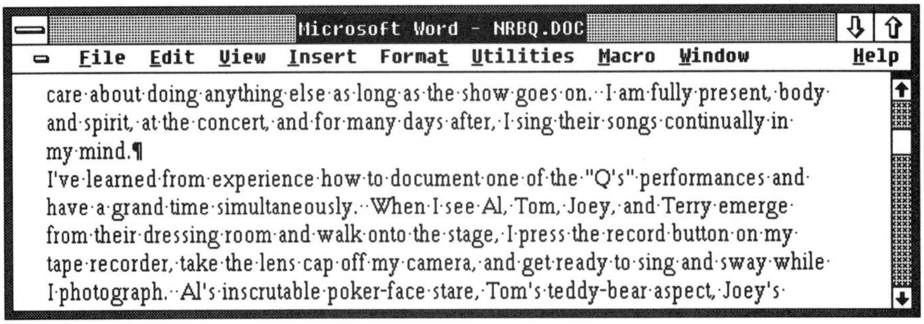

	Microsoft Word - NRBQ.DOC	⇩ ⇧
▭	**File Edit View Insert Forma̱t Utilities Macro Window**	**Help**

care·about·doing·anything·else·as·long·as·the·show·goes·on.··I·am·fully·present,·body·
and·spirit,·at·the·concert,·and·for·many·days·after,·I·sing·their·songs·continually·in·
my·mind.¶
I've·learned·from·experience·how·to·document·one·of·the·"Q's"·performances·and·
have·a·grand·time·simultaneously.··When·I·see·Al,·Tom,·Joey,·and·Terry·emerge·
from·their·dressing·room·and·walk·onto·the·stage,·I·press·the·record·button·on·my·
tape·recorder,·take·the·lens·cap·off·my·camera,·and·get·ready·to·sing·and·sway·while·
I·photograph.··Al's·inscrutable·poker-face·stare,·Tom's·teddy-bear·aspect,·Joey's·

Word will bring lines 7 through 14 into view when you click below the scroll box.

Using the horizontal scroll bar

If you are working with a document that is too wide to be displayed on one screen—for example, if you are using a wide page width or if you are viewing your text through a partial-screen window—you can use the scroll arrows at either end of the horizontal scroll bar to move right and left through your document. To access the horizontal scroll bar, select the Preferences... command from the View menu, then select the Horizontal Scroll Bar check box. Horizontal scrolling is much like vertical scrolling: Simply use the scroll arrows to move short distances through your document; click in the scroll bar to move a new screenful of information into view; and drag the scroll box to reposition the window manually.

Let's look at a few examples of moving through text with the horizontal scroll bar. First, narrow your sample document window so that only the first 4 inches of the document are visible, as shown in Figure 4-17. (Notice that we've activated the ruler with the Ruler command on the View menu, and that the menu bar has wrapped onto a second line.) To see the remaining text on the right side of the document, you can click on the right scroll arrow. As you can see in Figure 4-18, Word scrolls the document window $^3/_4$ inch to the right. If you click on the left scroll arrow, your screen will again look like Figure 4-17.

Figure 4-17

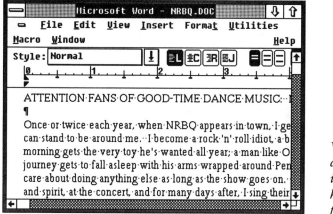

We've narrowed our document window to illustrate Word's horizontal scrolling features.

Figure 4-18

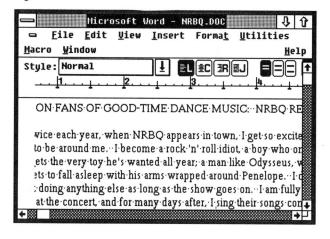

When you click on a scroll arrow, the next $^3/_4$ inch of the document will scroll into view.

When you click in the gray area of the scroll bar, to the left or right of the scroll box, Word will move the document window a full screen to the left or right. Again, the distance you travel depends on the size of the document window. Word will scroll the width that's shown on the screen. For example, when your screen looks like the one in Figure 4-17, if you click to the right of the scroll box, Word will bring about 4 more inches of the document into view, as shown in Figure 4-19. If you now click to the left of the scroll box, your screen will again look like the one in Figure 4-17.

Unlike the vertical scroll bar, the distance you travel when you drag the scroll box in the horizontal scroll bar is constant. Although only about 6 inches of your document is visible in a full-screen window, Word actually allows you to create columns as wide as 22 inches. Thus, if you drag the scroll box to the extreme right side of the horizontal scroll bar, you'll travel 22 inches; if you drag the scroll box to the middle of the horizontal scroll bar, you'll travel approximately 11 inches.

Figure 4-19

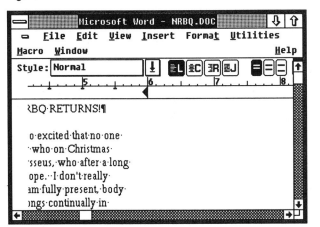

You can click in the gray area of the scroll bar to bring a new screenful of information into view.

Scrolling as you select text

Often, you'll want to select a block of text that is too large to display on one screen. In this event, you'll need to combine the selection technique described earlier in this chapter with the navigational techniques we've just discussed.

For example, suppose the first three paragraphs of the sample document are in view and you want to select the block of text that begins with *I am fully present* in the third paragraph and ends with *When I see Al* in the fourth paragraph. Although the last part of this text block is not visible on the screen when you begin your selection, clicking to the left of the word *I* in line 7 and dragging downward past the horizontal scroll bar brings the rest of your text into view, one line at a time. The text that was displayed at the top of the window will scroll out of view, as shown in Figure 4-20.

Figure 4-20

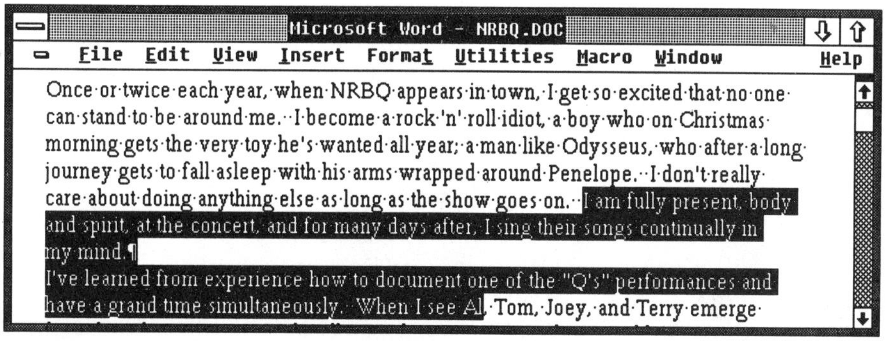

```
┌─────────────────────────────────────────────────────────────────┐
│ ═══            Microsoft Word - NRBQ.DOC                  ⇩ ⇧ │
│ ▭   File  Edit  View  Insert  Format  Utilities  Macro  Window      Help │
├─────────────────────────────────────────────────────────────────┤
│ Once·or·twice·each·year,··when·NRBQ·appears·in·town,·I·get·so·excited·that·no·one·  ▲ │
│ can·stand·to·be·around·me.··I·become·a·rock·'n'·roll·idiot,·a·boy·who·on·Christmas·  │
│ morning·gets·the·very·toy·he's·wanted·all·year;··a·man·like·Odysseus,·who·after·a·long·  │
│ journey·gets·to·fall·asleep·with·his·arms·wrapped·around·Penelope.··I·don't·really·  │
│ care·about·doing·anything·else·as·long·as·the·show·goes·on.··I·am·fully·present,·body·  │
│ and·spirit,·at·the·concert,·and·for·many·days·after,·I·sing·their·songs·continually·in·  │
│ my·mind.¶  │
│ I've·learned·from·experience·how·to·document·one·of·the·"Q's"·performances·and·  │
│ have·a·grand·time·simultaneously.··When·I·see·Al,·Tom,·Joey,·and·Terry·emerge·  ▼ │
└─────────────────────────────────────────────────────────────────┘
```

If you drag past the bottom of the document window, Word will scroll succeeding lines of text into view.

Similarly, if you drag toward the top of the screen, Word will scroll the document window upward as your mouse pointer comes in contact with the menu bar at the top of the document window. Word will automatically highlight the text as you drag.

If you have resized your window so that your text extends beyond the left or right edge of the window, you can select text by dragging horizontally beyond either edge. Word will scroll the document window so you can see your selection.

Fortunately, you can use the scroll bars in conjunction with the click/[Shift]-click technique described on page 54 to see all the text you are selecting. Simply click at the beginning of your selection, scroll to the end of the block you want to highlight, press the [Shift] key, and click at the end of the block.

Keyboard navigational techniques

If your computer is not equipped with a mouse, you can use the keyboard to move through your Word text. Keep in mind, however, that when you use most of the keyboard techniques described on the following pages, your cursor will travel with you as you navigate through your document window. (This is different from navigating with the mouse using the scroll bars. The mouse techniques we've described only scroll the document inside the document window—they do not move the cursor.) Table 4-1 on the following page summarizes all the techniques we'll discuss in this section. You might want to keep a copy of this table near your computer for handy reference.

Moving short distances

You'll find that the ↑, ↓, ←, and → arrow keys are tremendously convenient for moving short distances in your document. As you might expect, the ↑ and ↓ keys let you move the cursor up and down one line at a time. Generally, when you use the ↑ and ↓ keys, your cursor will move in a straight line. However, because line lengths vary and characters occupy different amounts of space, you may notice that your cursor jumps around a bit as you press the ↑ and ↓ keys. If you press the ↑ or ↓ key while the cursor is at the top or bottom of the document window, Word will scroll additional text into view automatically.

Table 4-1

These keys...	move the cursor...
← and →	left and right one character
↑ and ↓	up and down one line
[Ctrl]← and [Ctrl]→	left and right one word
[Ctrl]↑ and [Ctrl]↓	up and down one paragraph
[Page Up]	up one screen
[Page Down]	down one screen
[Ctrl][Page Up]	to the top of the screen
[Ctrl][Page Down]	to the bottom of the screen
[Home]	to the beginning of the current line
[End]	to the end of the current line
[Ctrl][Home]	to the top of the document
[Ctrl][End]	to the bottom of the document

When you press the ← or → key, the cursor will move one space to the left or right. When you press ← at the beginning of a line, the cursor will move to the end of the previous line. Similarly, when you press → at the end of a line, the cursor will move to the beginning of the next line.

It can be difficult to click in the exact location you need, particularly when you are working with very small point sizes or with text that is formatted in italics. The ← and → keys are very convenient for fine-tuning your selection once you've clicked in the general area in which you want to work.

Moving long distances

Using the arrow keys to move line by line is satisfactory in a short document, but you will want to cover ground more quickly in a long document. To move through your document a full screen at a time, you can use the [Page Up] or [Page Down] key. To move up one screen, press [Page Up]; to move down one screen, press [Page Down].

Of course, the distance that the [Page Up] and [Page Down] keys will scroll depends on the size of the document window. For example, if you reduce your document window to the size shown in Figure 4-15, only the first eight lines of the document will be in view. Pressing the [Page Down] key at this point will tell Word to bring lines 7 through 14 into view.

Using the [Page Up] and [Page Down] keys to scroll through a document moves the cursor through the document. As you scroll new portions of the document into view, the cursor will remain in the same relative position on the screen. For example, suppose the cursor rests between the third and fourth characters of a line, and you press the [Page Down] or [Page Up] key. When the new portion of the document appears in the window, the cursor will still be in the same relative position on the screen.

In addition to the techniques we've explained so far, you can use the [Home] and [End] keys to move to the beginning of the current line and to the end of the current line, respectively.

You can also use the [Ctrl] key in conjunction with the [Home] and [End] keys to move the cursor to the beginning or end of your document. Regardless of your current location, [Ctrl][Home] will place the cursor on the very first character space in your document, and [Ctrl][End] will place the cursor on the very last character space in your document.

Word offers several [Ctrl] key shortcuts that let you navigate through words, sentences, and paragraphs. To move from one word to the next, just hold down the [Ctrl] key as you press the ← or → key. The [Ctrl]← key combination lets you move one word to the left, while the [Ctrl]→ key combination lets you move one word to the right. In either case, the cursor will land just to the left of the next word, between the first character in that word and any preceding blank spaces or delimiting characters.

Navigating by words, sentences, and paragraphs

To move to the top or bottom of the current screen, just use the [Ctrl] key in conjunction with the [Page Up] or [Page Down] key. Pressing [Ctrl][Page Up] will take you to the top of the screen, while pressing [Ctrl][Page Down] will take you to the bottom of the screen.

Finally, to move through your document a paragraph at a time, just press the [Ctrl] key as you press the ↑ or ↓ key. If your cursor is currently in the middle of a paragraph, the [Ctrl]↑ combination lets you jump to the beginning of that paragraph. If your cursor is already at the beginning of a paragraph, [Ctrl]↑ will take you to the beginning of the previous paragraph. Similarly, pressing the [Ctrl]↓ combination will take you to the beginning of the following paragraph.

When you are editing a document, you'll often find yourself skipping from one spot to another to move text or to make minor changes. Word offers a navigational feature to help streamline this process: the [Go back] key ([Shift][F5]). You can quickly return to your last insertion point by pressing the [Go back] key. (The last insertion point is the place where you last made a change in your document—it is not necessarily the place where the cursor last appeared.)

Moving the cursor to its previous location

This technique is convenient for toggling between two remote areas of your document when you need to compare two sets of text. For example, suppose you have just finished editing a table that appears on the first page of your document, then you move to the end of your document to transfer some of the data from that table into your text. To move back to the table to pick up more information, just press the [Go back] key.

Word can remember as many as three insertion points in addition to your current location. For example, suppose you have made editing changes in the four locations marked in the sample screen in Figure 4-21. After making your change at point 4, if you press the [Go back] key, Word will move you back to point 3. Pressing the [Go back] key again will take you to point 2, and pressing it a third time, to point 1. If you press the [Go back] key a fourth time, Word will return to point 4 again. (Keep in mind that you must make editing changes of some sort for Word to remember your cursor was there. Merely moving the cursor onto a word doesn't cause Word to remember that location.)

Figure 4-21

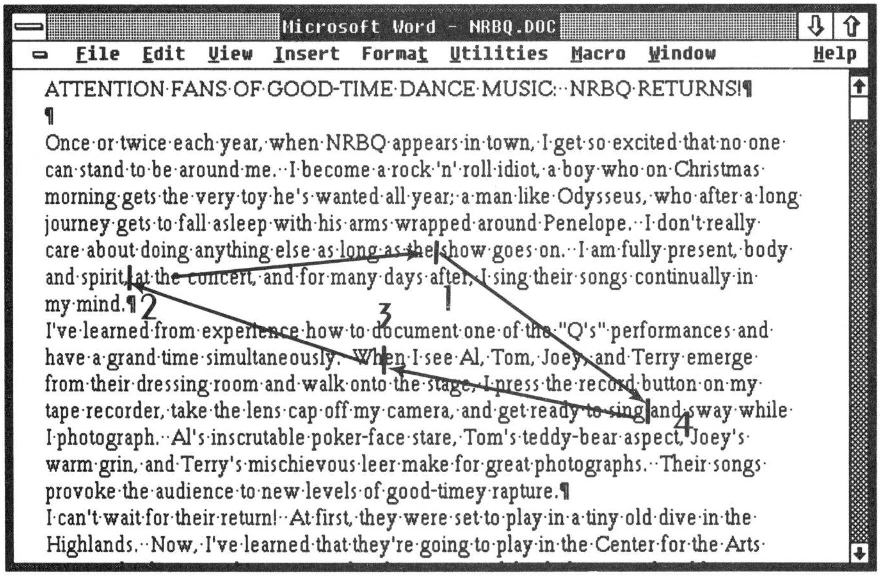

Word will remember the last three insertion points and the current location.

Selecting text with the [Shift] key

If you don't feel overwhelmed yet by all the selection and navigation techniques we've explored in this chapter, here's one more technique to try: Press the [Shift] key as you use the various navigational devices described above to select text as you move around in your Word document.

For example, you already know that you can press [Ctrl][Home] to move to the first character space in your document. If you press [Shift] along with [Ctrl][Home], Word will highlight everything from the current cursor position to the beginning of the document.

Similarly, you can press [Ctrl][Shift]➜ to select words as you scroll through your document or [Ctrl][Shift]⬇ to select entire paragraphs. In short, all the navigational techniques we have discussed in this section (except [Shift][F5]) double as selection techniques when you add the [Shift] key to the original key combination.

The Search... command on the Edit menu lets you search for specific text, formats, or a combination of text and formatting. The Search dialog box, shown in Figure 4-22, allows you to match whole words or any combination of upper-case and lowercase characters in any format you choose. You can also search for any sequential block of text, such as the end of one word through the beginning of another word.

**The Search...
command**

Figure 4-22

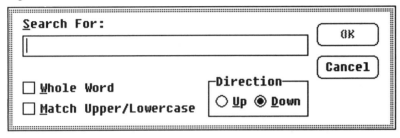

The Search dialog box lets you specify text, formats, or both.

The Search... command offers an alternative method to Word's Spelling facility. For instance, if you need to correct a misspelled word, you can locate it by using the Search... command instead of the Spelling... command.

You can begin a search from any point in your document. If you begin searching in the middle of your document, Word will ask whether you want to continue searching from the opposite end when it reaches the document's boundary. Refer to Chapter 6 for a detailed discussion of the Search... command.

In addition to the scroll bars and the Search... command, you can use the Go To... command on the Edit menu to move to the top of a specific page in your document. When you issue the Go To... command, Word will present the dialog box shown in Figure 4-23 on the next page. Fortunately, there is a keyboard shortcut you can use to access the Go To... command. To bring up the *Go to:* prompt in the status bar, simply press the [Go to] key ([F5]). To access the Go To dialog box, press the [Go to] key a second time.

When Word displays the Go To dialog box or prompt, simply type the number of the page you want to view and press [Enter]. Word will then display the first line of the specified page at the top of your document window and place the cursor at the beginning of that line. The page numbers, which appear at the left edge of the status bar, relate to the way the document will appear when it is printed. We'll tell you more about page numbering in Chapter 7.

In addition to finding a particular page, the Go To... command lets you find bookmarks you've inserted into your text. As we'll explain in Chapter 13, bookmarks are short, easy-to-remember codes that mark selected areas of text.

**The Go To...
command**

Figure 4-23

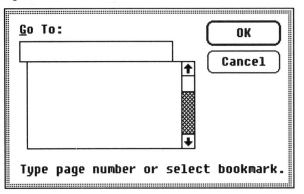

You can use the Go To dialog box to move quickly to a specified page in your document.

BASIC EDITING TECHNIQUES

The simplest way to edit text in your Word document is to insert new characters, delete existing characters, or overwrite the characters you want to change. These three techniques are among Word's most basic—and important—editing features. Although we'll talk much more about editing in Chapter 6, we'll introduce these three editing techniques here because they relate closely to the selection and navigation techniques we've explored over the last several pages.

As we mentioned earlier, the Wordwrap feature lets Word reflow your text whenever you make editing or formatting changes, which is why we cautioned you against entering carriage returns at the ends of lines of text. As we discuss the insertion, deletion, and overwriting techniques in the next few pages, notice the way Word reflows your text to adjust for your changes. As you'll see, Wordwrap is one of the features that make word processing so popular. This vital feature makes editing text virtually effortless.

Inserting new text

Inserting text into your Word document is as easy as typing. To insert a block of text into an existing document, move the cursor to the spot where you want to insert the text. To move the cursor with the mouse, position the I-beam pointer over the desired spot and click. To move the cursor using the keyboard, use the arrow keys or any of the navigational techniques we discussed earlier. When the cursor is in place, just begin typing.

For example, suppose you want to change the phrase *when NRBQ appears in town* in line 3 of our sample document to read *when the rock group NRBQ appears in town.* To do this, place the cursor just to the right of the space after the word *when,* and type the rest of the new phrase.

As you can see in Figure 4-24, when you type the new characters, Word will push the remaining characters on the line to the right to make room for your insertion. Thanks to Wordwrap, Word also will push the words at the end of the line to the beginning of the next line, reflowing your existing text all the way to the end of the document, if necessary, to make room for the new characters.

Figure 4-24

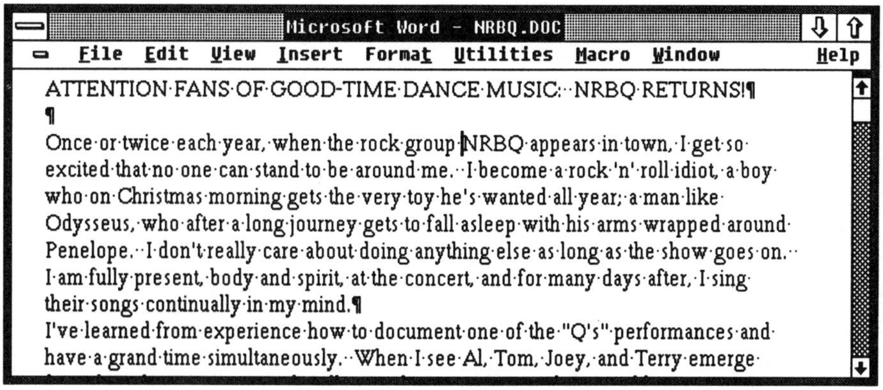

```
┌──────────────────────────────────────────────────────────────┐
│ ▭        Microsoft Word - NRBQ.DOC                      ⇩  ⇧  │
│ ▢   File  Edit  View  Insert  Format  Utilities  Macro  Window        Help │
├──────────────────────────────────────────────────────────────┤
│ ATTENTION·FANS·OF·GOOD-TIME·DANCE·MUSIC:··NRBQ·RETURNS!¶    ▲  │
│ ¶                                                             │
│ Once·or·twice·each·year,·when·the·rock·group│NRBQ·appears·in·town,·I·get·so· │
│ excited·that·no·one·can·stand·to·be·around·me.··I·become·a·rock·'n'·roll·idiot,·a·boy· │
│ who·on·Christmas·morning·gets·the·very·toy·he's·wanted·all·year;·a·man·like· │
│ Odysseus,·who·after·a·long·journey·gets·to·fall·asleep·with·his·arms·wrapped·around· │
│ Penelope.··I·don't·really·care·about·doing·anything·else·as·long·as·the·show·goes·on.·· │
│ I·am·fully·present,·body·and·spirit,·at·the·concert,·and·for·many·days·after,·I·sing· │
│ their·songs·continually·in·my·mind.¶                          │
│ I've·learned·from·experience·how·to·document·one·of·the·"Q's"·performances·and· │
│ have·a·grand·time·simultaneously.··When·I·see·Al,·Tom,·Joey,·and·Terry·emerge·  ▼  │
└──────────────────────────────────────────────────────────────┘
```

As you insert new text, Word will reflow your text to make room for your changes.

Deleting text

The easiest way to delete individual characters in your text is to click to the right of the character(s) you want to delete and press the [Backspace] key. Word will delete the characters immediately to the left of the cursor one at a time, pulling the characters to the right of the cursor one space to the left as you go.

To delete several characters at once, you can highlight the unwanted block, then press the [Delete] key to delete the entire selection. For example, suppose you want to delete the phrase *at the concert* in line 8 of the document shown in Figure 4-24. To do this, select the phrase *at the concert* along with the trailing comma and space, and press the [Delete] key to erase the highlighted block. As you can see in Figure 4-25 on the following page, Word will delete the selected characters and automatically fill in the gap by pulling the remaining characters in your document up and to the left.

If you press the [Backspace] key while your cursor is at the beginning of a line, Word will move the cursor to the end of the previous line and delete the last character in that line. Similarly, if you press [Backspace] while the cursor is at the beginning of a paragraph, Word will delete the ¶ mark at the end of the previous paragraph and reflow your text to combine the two paragraphs.

If you hear a beep when you try to press [Backspace] at the beginning of a paragraph, Word is probably trying to tell you that it cannot combine the two paragraphs because they carry different formatting characteristics. If you're determined to combine the two paragraphs anyway, you'll have to select the ¶ mark at the end of the first paragraph and press [Backspace] or [Delete]. The combined paragraph will take on the formatting characteristics of the second paragraph. We'll talk more about this topic in the next chapter.

Figure 4-25

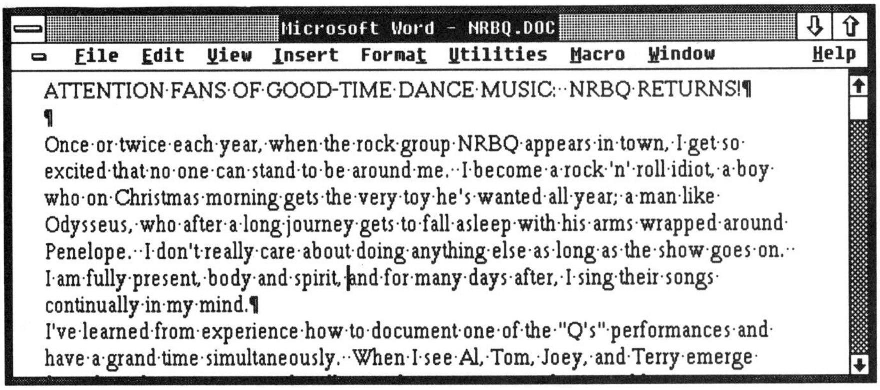

```
┌──────────────────────────────────────────────────────────────┐
│ ▭         Microsoft Word - NRBQ.DOC                     ⇩  ⇧  │
├──────────────────────────────────────────────────────────────┤
│  ▭   File  Edit  View  Insert  Format  Utilities  Macro  Window        Help │
├──────────────────────────────────────────────────────────────┤
│ ATTENTION·FANS·OF·GOOD-TIME·DANCE·MUSIC:··NRBQ·RETURNS!¶        ▲│
│ ¶                                                              │
│ Once·or·twice·each·year,·when·the·rock·group·NRBQ·appears·in·town,·I·get·so· │
│ excited·that·no·one·can·stand·to·be·around·me.··I·become·a·rock·'n'·roll·idiot,·a·boy· │
│ who·on·Christmas·morning·gets·the·very·toy·he's·wanted·all·year;·a·man·like· │
│ Odysseus,·who·after·a·long·journey·gets·to·fall·asleep·with·his·arms·wrapped·around· │
│ Penelope.··I·don't·really·care·about·doing·anything·else·as·long·as·the·show·goes·on.·· │
│ I·am·fully·present,·body·and·spirit,·and·for·many·days·after,·I·sing·their·songs· │
│ continually·in·my·mind.¶                                       │
│ I've·learned·from·experience·how·to·document·one·of·the·"Q's"·performances·and· │
│ have·a·grand·time·simultaneously.··When·I·see·Al,·Tom,·Joey,·and·Terry·emerge· ▼│
└──────────────────────────────────────────────────────────────┘
```

When you delete a block of text, Word will reflow your document to fill the gap.

Deletion shortcuts

In addition to the [Backspace] and [Delete] keys, Word offers some special keyboard shortcuts for deleting text. For example, instead of using the [Backspace] key to delete the characters to the left of the cursor one at a time, you can press [Ctrl][Backspace] to delete the entire word to the left of the cursor. If you want to delete the space to the right of the word as well, position the cursor to the right of that space before you press [Ctrl][Backspace].

If you position the cursor in the middle of a word and press [Ctrl][Backspace], Word will delete all the characters to the left of the cursor up to, but not including, the blank space that divides the current word from the previous word.

As you might expect, you can delete the word to the right of the cursor by pressing [Ctrl][Delete]. If you position the cursor just to the left of the first character of a word, pressing [Ctrl][Delete] will cause Word to delete all of that word, as well as the space following that word. On the other hand, if you position the cursor in the middle of a word, pressing [Ctrl][Delete] will delete only the characters between the cursor and the space following that word—it will not delete that word's trailing space mark.

Overwriting text

When you delete a block of text, you'll often need to insert new text to replace the text you deleted. If you have selected the Typing Replaces Selection check box in the Customize dialog box, you can overwrite existing characters by selecting them and typing your new text. Word will automatically delete the existing characters and replace them with the new characters you type. You can think of this overwriting technique as a combination deletion/insertion process. Also, once you've selected the Typing Replaces Selection check box, you will be able to delete highlighted text with the [Backspace] key.

To activate this option, simply select the Customize… command from the Utilities menu, select the Typing Replaces Selection check box, and choose OK.

As an example, suppose you want to replace the phrase *Once or twice each year, when* in line 3 with the new phrase *Each time.* Just drag through the characters *Once or twice each year, when* and type the replacement text. As you can see in Figure 4-26, Word replaces the old characters with the new ones and reflows the remaining text in your document.

Figure 4-26

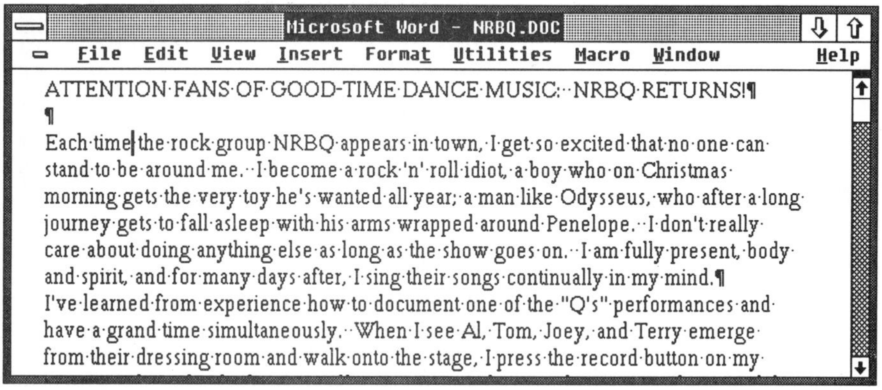

```
┌─────────────────────────────────────────────────────────────────────────┐
│ ═       │▓▓▓▓▓▓▓▓ Microsoft Word - NRBQ.DOC ▓▓▓▓▓▓▓▓│          ⇩  ⇧ │
├─────────────────────────────────────────────────────────────────────────┤
│  ▭   File   Edit   View   Insert   Format   Utilities   Macro   Window   Help │
├─────────────────────────────────────────────────────────────────────────┤
│ ATTENTION·FANS·OF·GOOD-TIME·DANCE·MUSIC:··NRBQ·RETURNS!¶              ↑ │
│ ¶                                                                        │
│ Each·time|the·rock·group·NRBQ·appears·in·town,·I·get·so·excited·that·no·one·can· │
│ stand·to·be·around·me.··I·become·a·rock·'n'·roll·idiot,·a·boy·who·on·Christmas· │
│ morning·gets·the·very·toy·he's·wanted·all·year;·a·man·like·Odysseus,·who·after·a·long· │
│ journey·gets·to·fall·asleep·with·his·arms·wrapped·around·Penelope.··I·don't·really· │
│ care·about·doing·anything·else·as·long·as·the·show·goes·on.··I·am·fully·present,·body· │
│ and·spirit,·and·for·many·days·after,·I·sing·their·songs·continually·in·my·mind.¶ │
│ I've·learned·from·experience·how·to·document·one·of·the·"Q's"·performances·and· │
│ have·a·grand·time·simultaneously.··When·I·see·Al,·Tom,·Joey,·and·Terry·emerge· │
│ from·their·dressing·room·and·walk·onto·the·stage,·I·press·the·record·button·on·my· ↓ │
└─────────────────────────────────────────────────────────────────────────┘
```

If you've selected the Typing Replaces Selection check box, you can overwrite text simply by selecting the characters you want to delete, then typing the replacement text.

You should note that Word will not allow you to overwrite a ¶ mark by selecting it and typing unless you select a block of text that falls both before and after the ¶ mark. Of course, if you replace the ¶ mark with new text, Word will combine the current paragraph with the paragraph below. As a result, Word will assign the paragraph formats associated with the second paragraph to the entire combined paragraph. We'll talk in detail about the ¶ mark in Chapter 5.

Cutting text

In addition to the techniques we've discussed so far, Word provides the Cut command on the Edit menu for deleting text. Unlike the other deletion techniques we've discussed, however, the Cut command stores the deleted text in a special place called the Clipboard. Although the Clipboard is actually a large chunk of memory, you might think of it as a temporary storage place for text. Once you've placed something on the Clipboard with the Cut or Copy command, you can paste its contents anywhere in your Word document with the Paste command. We'll talk more about the Cut, Copy, and Paste commands in Chapter 6.

Editing notes for mouse users

As you may know, when you double-click on a word to select it, Word automatically highlights any blank spaces that fall after that word. Naturally, if you press the [Delete] key to delete that word, those trailing blank spaces will be deleted as well. However, if you double-click on a word, then overwrite it by typing new characters, Word will leave any trailing blank spaces intact. Basically, the program assumes that you are replacing one or more words with another word and saves you a few keystrokes by leaving the blank spaces intact.

This technique works even if you have selected several words. As long as you entered the word selection mode by double-clicking on a word and dragging through additional words, Word will apply this treatment. The last set of blank spaces will be deleted if you press [Delete] but will be left intact if you overwrite the selected text.

If you double-click in the selection bar to highlight an entire paragraph, Word will use a similar technique to decide whether the ¶ mark at the end of the paragraph should stay or go. As you might have guessed, if you press [Delete] to delete the paragraph, the ¶ mark will disappear as well. However, if you overwrite the paragraph, the ¶ mark will remain in place.

As long as you entered the paragraph selection mode by double-clicking in the selection bar to select the paragraph, Word will apply this technique, no matter how many paragraphs you have selected. The ¶ mark that signals the end of the last paragraph in your selection will remain intact if you type new text and will be deleted if you press [Delete].

CANCELLING AND REPEATING ACTIONS

When you insert, delete, or overwrite text in your document, Word remembers the last set of keystrokes you pressed. Word does this so you can often undo an editing change or repeat a command or a series of keystrokes automatically. Let's explore the workings of the Undo command, then see how you can use the Repeat command to repeat a command or a series of keystrokes in Word.

Undoing an action

The Undo command is one of the most significant commands in Word because it gives you a second chance when you make a mistake. To issue the Undo command, simply choose Undo from the Edit menu. As you'll undoubtedly learn at some time in your work with Word, Undo can be a real lifesaver when you find that you have inadvertently altered a critical passage in your document.

Undo is a context-sensitive command. It changes to reflect your last action. If you've inserted new text or overwritten existing text, you'll see the Undo Typing command at the top of the Edit menu. If you have used the [Delete] key to delete some characters, you'll see the Undo Edit Clear command.

In fact, you can even undo an Undo command. When you issue the Undo command, Word will change that command to Undo Undo. Thus, if you delete a block of text, then select Undo Typing, you can select Undo Undo to delete the text again. You should keep in mind, however, that the Undo command remains in effect only until you issue another command or begin typing new text. As soon as you perform another action, Word will change the Undo command to reflect your new activity.

In addition to undoing the manual editing procedures we have discussed in this chapter, you can undo many of Word's other commands. Table 4-2 lists the commands that you can undo.

Table 4-2

Menu	Commands you can undo
Edit	All except Search… and Go To…; you can undo only the last change made by the Replace… command, and you can do this only if you selected the Confirm Changes check box.
Insert	All except Page Numbers…
Format	All except Define Styles…
Utilities	All except Repaginate Now and Customize…; you can undo all changes made with the Hyphenate… command.

We'll be talking more about these commands later. For now, just make a mental note of which actions in Word are easily remedied. Some commands—like Character…, which we'll discuss in Chapter 5—can easily be undone by reissuing the command and selecting the correct options. However, if you use the Find… command to erase a file, or you accidentally overwrite a file with the Save As… command, you won't be able to reverse that action. For this reason, you should be extremely careful when handling files.

Repeating an action

As we mentioned, Word remembers the last action you performed so that it can undo that action. Word also remembers your last action so that it can repeat a command or a series of keystrokes automatically. To repeat an action, all you need to do is choose the Repeat command from the Edit menu.

Like the Undo command, the Repeat command is context-sensitive and will change to reflect your last action. For example, if you use the Character… command on the Format menu to change the formatting of some text in your document, you'll see the command Repeat Character at the top of the Edit menu.

Similarly, if you insert a series of characters at one spot in your document, then decide that you need to insert the same series of characters in another location, you can click in the second location and choose the Repeat Typing command to "replay" your keystrokes.

In this chapter

Formatting 5

*O*ne of the main advantages of using a state-of-the-art word processor like Word for Windows is that it offers you a terrific amount of flexibility in formatting your documents. And, unlike most other word processing programs that run on the IBM PC, Word for Windows lets you see on your screen how your document will look when it's printed. Not only can you see the position of characters and paragraphs, you can also see special formatting effects, including fonts, borders, and such character styles as bold and italics.

Because Word offers so many options for controlling the appearance of your documents—and because these options often interact—formatting is a vast and complex topic. But don't be intimidated: Once you've learned a few basic techniques, you should be able to handle the majority of your formatting needs. In this chapter, we'll introduce you to those basic techniques: setting margins, applying paragraph formats, and formatting individual characters and words. We'll also talk about some related topics, including page breaks and special characters. In Chapter 8, we'll explain style sheets and, in Chapters 11 and 12, we'll address a variety of advanced formatting topics, including tables, multicolumn formatting, and headers and footers.

Formatting a document in Word occurs on four levels: the overall document level, the section level, the paragraph level, and the character level. Any changes you make at one level can affect the formatting characteristics of subsequent levels. For example, if you change your document's margins (a document-level formatting change), you'll affect every paragraph in the document. Because the different formatting levels are interrelated, it makes sense to design your documents from the top down.

TOP-DOWN DOCUMENT DESIGN

Top-down document design means moving from the general to the specific. Decide first on the most general aspects of your document layout (your paper size and margins, for example); then, fine-tune factors like paragraph and character formats. You'll find that this approach simplifies the document design process and eliminates a lot of backtracking. Figure 5-1 illustrates the general concept of top-down document design.

Figure 5-1

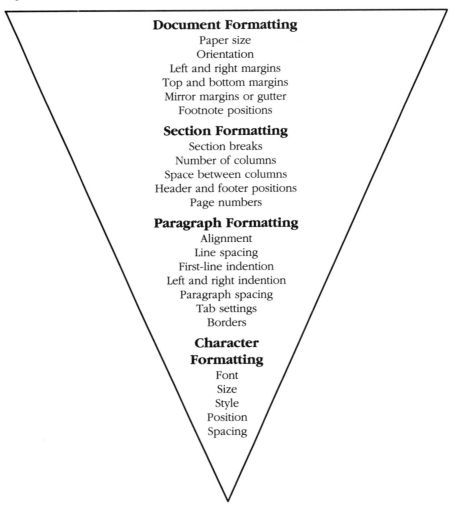

Document Formatting
Paper size
Orientation
Left and right margins
Top and bottom margins
Mirror margins or gutter
Footnote positions

Section Formatting
Section breaks
Number of columns
Space between columns
Header and footer positions
Page numbers

Paragraph Formatting
Alignment
Line spacing
First-line indention
Left and right indention
Paragraph spacing
Tab settings
Borders

Character Formatting
Font
Size
Style
Position
Spacing

You can simplify the document design process by moving from the general to the specific.

In this chapter, we'll look at three of Word's four formatting levels: document, paragraph, and character formatting. We'll save our discussion of section-level formatting for later in the book, since it applies only to documents with multiple sections. Generally, you'll use multiple sections when you need to change certain characteristics—such as the number of columns on a page or the header or footer text—from one part of a document to another.

In top-down document design, the first step in formatting a document is to establish your overall page layout. In a simple document, there are three factors that affect your page layout: paper size, margin settings, and print orientation. In a more complex document, you may also have to consider such factors as multiple columns, mirror margins (different margins on the right and left pages, as you often see in bound documents), headers, and footers. We'll cover these topics in detail in Chapter 12. For now, however, let's consider how paper size, margin settings, and orientation work together to determine your page layout.

BASIC PAGE LAYOUT

Figure 5-2 on the following page shows a sketch of Word's default page layout characteristics. Notice that the page size is assumed to be 8 $\frac{1}{2}$ inches wide by 11 inches tall. In addition, Word assumes that you're using Portrait orientation—that is, printing your document with the lines of text running across the short side of the paper. The default Left and Right margin settings are each 1.25 inches, and the Top and Bottom margin settings are each 1 inch. These margin settings indicate the amount of white space between the edge of the paper and the edge of the text area.

As Figure 5-2 illustrates, your paper size, margins, and orientation determine the width and height of your document's text area. Word determines the width of the text area by subtracting the left and right margins from the width of the paper, like this:

Determining the size of the text area

Width of text area = paper width - left margin - right margin

Similarly, Word determines the height of your text area by subtracting the top and bottom margins from the height of the paper:

Height of text area = paper height - top margin - bottom margin

When you're using Word's default settings, your text area on each page will be 6 inches wide (8 $\frac{1}{2}$ - $1\frac{1}{4}$ - $1\frac{1}{4}$) and 9 inches high (11 - 1 - 1).

In a multicolumn document or a table, the text area is divided into two or more text columns. In the documents we'll look at in this chapter, only one column of text will appear in the text area. Unless you change the indents on your paragraphs, the width of the text column will be the same as the width of the text area.

Figure 5-2

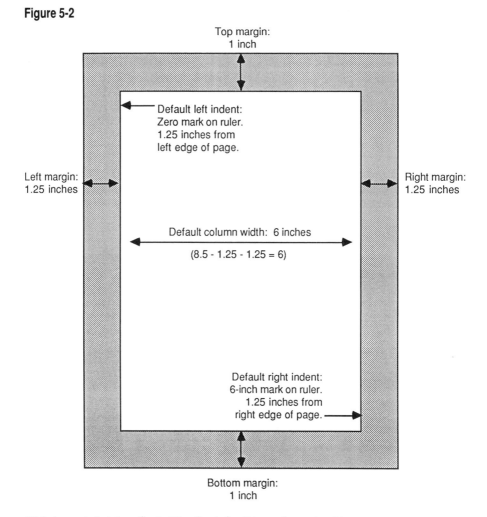

Top margin:
1 inch

Default left indent:
Zero mark on ruler.
1.25 inches from
left edge of page.

Left margin:
1.25 inches

Right margin:
1.25 inches

Default column width: 6 inches

(8.5 - 1.25 - 1.25 = 6)

Default right indent:
6-inch mark on ruler.
1.25 inches from
right edge of page.

Bottom margin:
1 inch

This layout sketch reflects Word's default page layout settings.

Since the size of your document's text area will affect the appearance of each paragraph within the document, you should establish your paper size, margin settings, and orientation before you do any other formatting. If you change the size of your text area after you've made other kinds of formatting changes, you may need to redo some of your section or paragraph formatting in the document. (We'll discuss section formatting in Chapter 12.)

The key to establishing your paper size and margin settings is the Document dialog box, which is shown in Figure 5-3. To open this dialog box, select the Document... command from the Format menu.

Figure 5-3

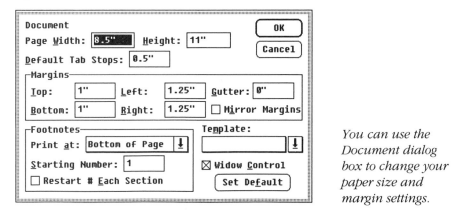

You can use the Document dialog box to change your paper size and margin settings.

As you can see, the Document dialog box contains text boxes for setting the Page Width and Height, as well as text boxes for the Top, Bottom, Left, and Right margin settings. In Figure 5-3, these text boxes all contain Word's default settings. We'll discuss the other elements in this dialog box later in this chapter and in other parts of this book.

If you're using a laser printer with Word, you can use the printer settings box to tell Word to print in either portrait or landscape orientation. To open this box, first choose Printer Setup… from the File menu. The ensuing dialog box will display the names of the printers you've installed. At this point, highlight the printer you plan to use, then choose the Setup… button. If you're using an HP LaserJet Series II printer, Word will present the printer settings box shown in Figure 5-4 on the next page. (We'll look at other printer settings boxes in Chapter 7.)

Although there are several options in this box, for now, we're interested only in the Orientation options: Portrait and Landscape. As you can see, Word's default orientation is Portrait. In a moment, we'll show you how changing the orientation to Landscape will affect your page layout. Before we change the orientation or the Document dialog box settings, however, let's take a look at how these settings affect the appearance of the ruler on your screen.

The ruler

As you might guess, the ruler that you can display at the top of a document window gives some helpful clues about the page layout of a document. When we introduced the ruler in Chapter 2, we explained that it can have three possible views: the paragraph view (the default), the margin view, and the column view. When you're using the paragraph view, the ruler shows you the width of your document's text column. The margin view of the ruler shows your left and right margin settings relative to the width of the paper, and the column view shows the boundaries of your text when you're working in a table. Since the column view of the ruler applies only to tabular text, we'll save our discussion of the column view for Chapter 11. For now, however, let's see how your paper size and margin settings affect the appearance of the ruler in the first two views.

Figure 5-4

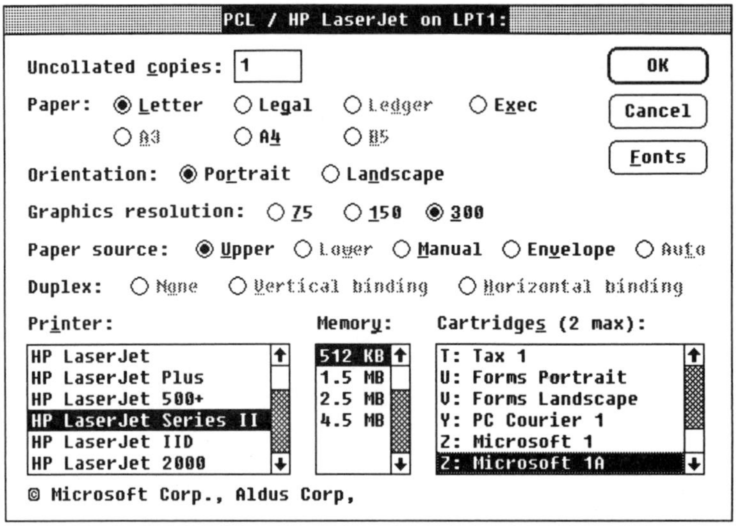

```
┌─────────────────────────────────────────────────────────────────┐
│░░░░░░░░░░░░░░░░░░░░░░PCL / HP LaserJet on LPT1:░░░░░░░░░░░░░░░░░░░│
│                                                                  │
│  Uncollated copies: │1          │         ┌──────────────┐       │
│                     └───────────┘         │     OK       │       │
│  Paper: ⦿ Letter  ○ Legal  ○ Ledger  ○ Exec └──────────────┘      │
│                                           ┌──────────────┐       │
│         ○ A3      ○ A4     ○ B5           │   Cancel     │       │
│                                           └──────────────┘       │
│  Orientation: ⦿ Portrait  ○ Landscape     ┌──────────────┐       │
│                                           │   Fonts      │       │
│  Graphics resolution: ○ 75  ○ 150  ⦿ 300  └──────────────┘       │
│                                                                  │
│  Paper source: ⦿ Upper  ○ Lower  ○ Manual  ○ Envelope  ○ Auto    │
│                                                                  │
│  Duplex:  ○ None  ○ Vertical binding  ○ Horizontal binding       │
│                                                                  │
│  Printer:              Memory:     Cartridges (2 max):           │
│  ┌─────────────────┬─┐ ┌────────┬─┐ ┌──────────────────────┬─┐   │
│  │HP LaserJet      │▲│ │512 KB  │▲│ │T: Tax 1              │▲│   │
│  │HP LaserJet Plus │ │ │1.5 MB  │ │ │U: Forms Portrait     │░│   │
│  │HP LaserJet 500+ │░│ │2.5 MB  │░│ │V: Forms Landscape    │░│   │
│  │HP LaserJet Series II│ │4.5 MB  │░│ │Y: PC Courier 1       │░│   │
│  │HP LaserJet IID  │░│ │        │ │ │Z: Microsoft 1        │░│   │
│  │HP LaserJet 2000 │▼│ │        │▼│ │Z: Microsoft 1A       │▼│   │
│  └─────────────────┴─┘ └────────┴─┘ └──────────────────────┴─┘   │
│  © Microsoft Corp., Aldus Corp,                                  │
└─────────────────────────────────────────────────────────────────┘
```

You can use the Printer Setup dialog box to change the orientation of your printed document.

When you're using Word's default settings, the paragraph view of the ruler will look like Figure 5-5. In the paragraph view, the zero point on the ruler always indicates the left edge of your text column—regardless of what you've specified as your Left margin setting or what paper size or orientation you're using. For example, with Word's default Left margin setting of 1.25, the zero point on the ruler represents a position that is $1\frac{1}{4}$ inches from the left edge of the paper. If you change your Left margin setting to 3, the zero point on the ruler will represent a position that is 3 inches from the left edge of the paper.

The right edge of your text—or the width of your text column—is marked by a vertical line that extends below the horizontal measuring line on the ruler. Unless you move the right indent marker (◀), you won't be able to see this line. As we've mentioned, when you're using Word's default paper size and margin settings, the width of your text column will be 6 inches. Thus, the vertical line appears at the 6-inch position on the ruler in Figure 5-5.

Figure 5-5

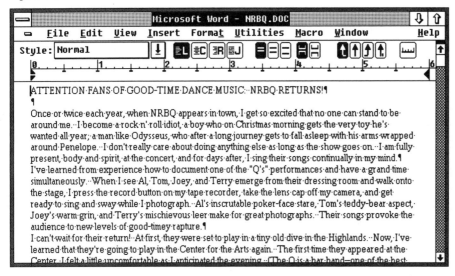

This is how the ruler's paragraph view will look when you're using Word's default paper size and margin settings.

Initially, Word will always align the right indent marker with the vertical line marking the right edge of your text. Similarly, Word will always align the first-line and left indent markers with the zero point on the ruler. You should not confuse these indent markers with your left and right margins. Although the indent markers will initially be aligned at the left and right edges of your text area, you can drag them along the ruler to change the left or right boundary of the text area in one or more paragraphs. (We'll talk more about this when we discuss paragraph formatting later in this chapter.) When you move an indent marker, however, you do *not* change your overall document margins—you merely change the position of text relative to those margins. To change your document margins, you must enter new settings in the Document dialog box or drag the margin markers in the margin view of the ruler. When you do this, Word will automatically adjust the width of your text column and move the vertical line that appears on the ruler in the paragraph view. Before we demonstrate changing margins, however, let's look at the ruler in the margin view.

To change from the paragraph view to the margin view, click the Ruler-view icon (⊟) in the far-right portion of the ruler. Word will then switch to the margin view of the ruler, as shown in Figure 5-6.

Figure 5-6

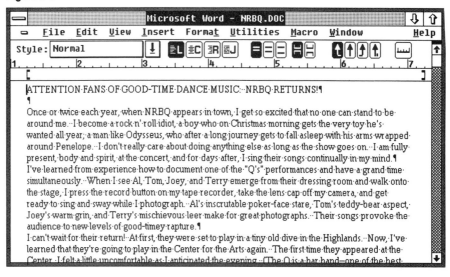

The ruler's margin view shows your left and right document margins relative to the width of the paper.

The main difference between the paragraph view and the margin view of the ruler is the orientation of the numbers on the ruler. As we mentioned, in the paragraph view, the zero point on the ruler represents the left edge of your text column. In the margin view, however, the ruler's zero point represents the left edge of the paper. The length of the ruler is determined by the Page Width setting in the Document dialog box. For example, if your Page Width setting is 8.5, the ruler in the margin view will be $8\frac{1}{2}$ inches long.

Instead of using indent markers and a vertical line to mark the boundaries of the text, the margin view shows two margin markers ([and]). The position of these markers corresponds to your Left and Right margin settings in the Document dialog box. When you're using Word's default settings, the left margin marker will appear at the $1\frac{1}{4}$-inch position on the ruler, and the right margin marker will appear at the $7\frac{1}{4}$-inch position. Let's look at how you can change your document's margins using either the ruler or the Document dialog box.

Changing margins

Probably the easiest way to change the left and right margins of a document is to switch to the margin view and drag the margin markers to the appropriate positions. Alternatively, you could open the Document dialog box and enter new margin settings in the Left and Right text boxes.

When you enter margin settings in the Document dialog box, you can specify your measurements in inches, centimeters, points, or picas by using the abbreviations *in, cm, pt,* or *pi.* If you're using the default unit (inches, unless you've specified a different default), you don't need to type a unit abbreviation.

For example, suppose you want to create a document on $8\frac{1}{2}$- by 11-inch paper on which your text lines are $4\frac{1}{2}$ inches wide and your left and right margins are of equal width. To determine how to change your margin settings to fit these specifications, subtract the desired text width from the paper width, then multiply by $\frac{1}{2}$, like this:

$$\text{Margin settings} = (\text{paper width - text area}) * \frac{1}{2}$$
$$= (8\frac{1}{2} - 4\frac{1}{2}) * \frac{1}{2}$$
$$= 2$$

As you can see, you should specify both a Left and Right margin setting of 2 inches to produce this document.

To change your margins on the ruler, you would first click on the Ruler-view icon to switch to the margin view (if you're not already in the margin view). Then, drag the left margin marker to the 2-inch position on the ruler and drag the right margin marker to the $6\frac{1}{2}$-inch position. To change your margins using the Document dialog box, choose Document… from the Format menu and enter *2″* in both the Left and Right text boxes.

Figure 5-7 on the next page shows the sample document from Figure 5-6 with new margin settings. Figure 5-8 on the following page shows this same document after we switched to the paragraph view on the ruler. As you can see, Word not only changed the appearance of the ruler, but also rewrapped the text of the document to reflect the new margin settings.

In the paragraph view of the ruler shown in Figure 5-8, Word has automatically moved both the right indent marker and the vertical line that marks the right edge of the text to the $4\frac{1}{2}$-inch position on the ruler.

Now, suppose you decide to change your left margin to $1\frac{1}{2}$ inches, but you want to leave your overall text width at $4\frac{1}{2}$ inches. To determine what your Right margin setting should be, subtract the left margin and the text width from the width of your paper, like this:

$$\text{New right margin} = \text{paper width - left margin - text area}$$
$$= 8\frac{1}{2} - 1\frac{1}{2} - 4\frac{1}{2}$$
$$= 2\frac{1}{2}$$

Therefore, changing the Left margin setting to $1\frac{1}{2}$ inches requires that you change the Right margin setting to $2\frac{1}{2}$ to maintain the same $4\frac{1}{2}$-inch text width.

Figure 5-7

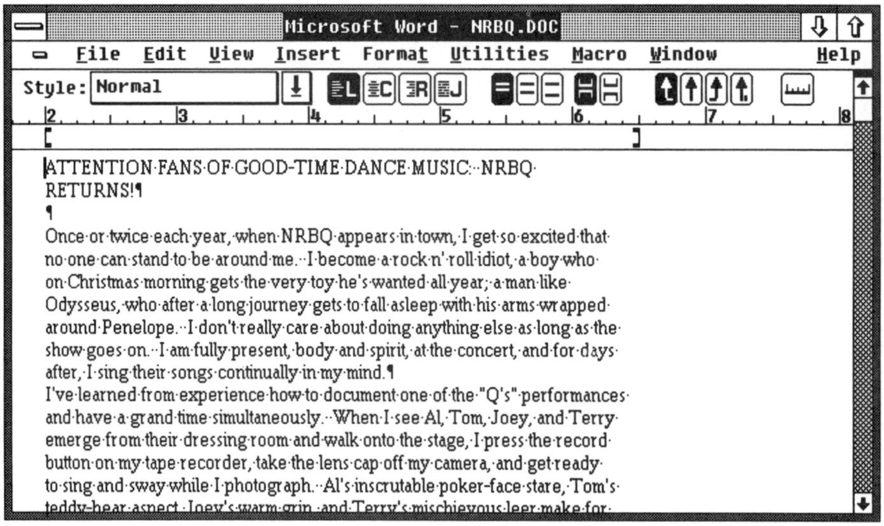

The margin markers on the ruler define the new margins in this document.

Figure 5-8

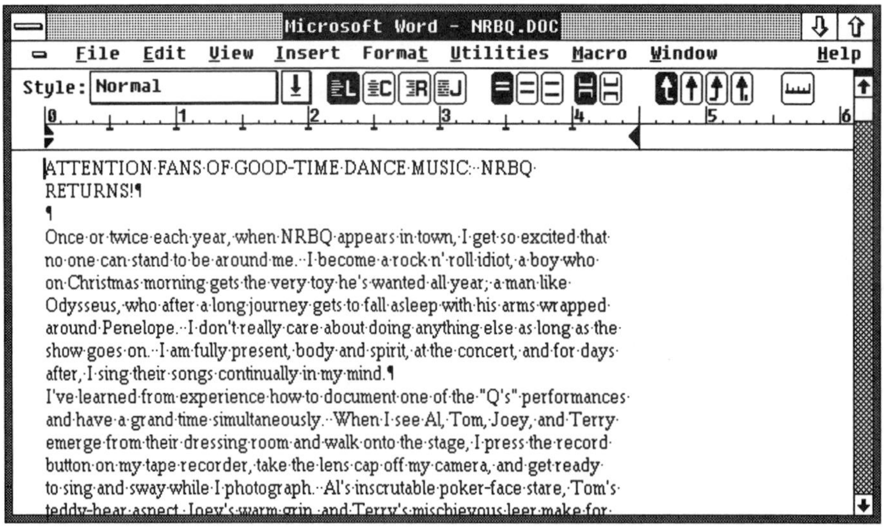

Using the paragraph view on the ruler, you can see that the new margin
settings reduce the width of the text area to 4 ¹/₂ inches.

After you specify these new margin settings in the Document dialog box or on the ruler, you won't see any change in the paragraph view of the ruler or in the text on your screen. The left edge of your text will still begin at the zero point, and the vertical line marking the right edge will still appear at the 4 $\frac{1}{2}$-inch position. However, if you switch to the margin view of the ruler, you'll see that the left margin is now narrower than the right margin, indicating that the text has been shifted left on the page. In other words, the width of your text area hasn't changed—only its position on the page.

In order to change the top or bottom margin in a document, you must use the Document dialog box—you cannot change these margins using the ruler. When you increase the size of the top and/or bottom margin, you decrease the size of your text area and, consequently, the number of lines that can fit on each page. On the other hand, when you decrease the top and/or bottom margin, you increase the size of your text area.

Changing the top and bottom margins

Suppose you want to increase the top margin of a document to 1 $\frac{1}{2}$ inches and increase the bottom margin to 2 inches. Simply open the Document dialog box, select the default *1"* in the Top text box, and replace it by typing *1.5"*. (Because Word's default unit of measure is inches, you can omit the inch sign, if you want.) Similarly, select the *1"* in the Bottom text box and replace it with *2"*. After changing your margins, the height of your text area will be reduced to 7 $\frac{1}{2}$ inches (11 - 2 - 1.5 = 7 $\frac{1}{2}$).

In our discussion of margins and ruler settings, we've assumed that your document will be printed on paper that is 8 $\frac{1}{2}$ inches wide and 11 inches long. If you change either the Page Width or Height setting in the Document dialog box, however, those changes will affect your margins. Moreover, if you change the Page Width setting, that change will be reflected on the ruler (and in any text you have entered).

Specifying paper size

For example, Figure 5-5 shows some text that we entered using Word's default Document settings. Now, let's see what happens when we change the Page Width setting in the Document dialog box from 8.5" to 7.5". When we choose OK to close the dialog box and lock in the new setting, our screen will look like Figure 5-9 on the next page.

Notice that the width of the text area has decreased from 6 inches to 5 inches. Word is still using the default Left and Right margin settings of 1.25 inches. However, these margins are now being subtracted from a narrower page width, which results in a narrower text area. If you switched to the margin view of the ruler, you would see that the right margin marker now appears at the 6 $\frac{1}{4}$-inch position on the ruler, as shown in Figure 5-10 on the following page.

Again, the Right margin setting has not changed from the default 1.25. However, since the right edge of the paper is assumed to be at the 7 $\frac{1}{2}$-inch position, Word has shifted the right margin marker accordingly.

Figure 5-9

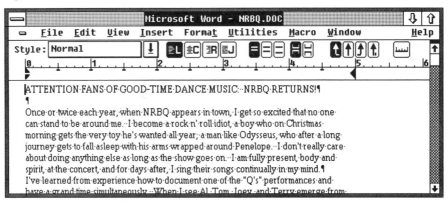

Word has adjusted our text to fit the new page width we indicated in the Document dialog box.

Figure 5-10

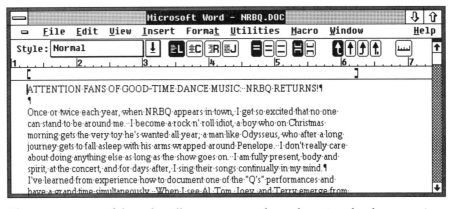

The margin view of the ruler allows you to see how changing the document's page width affects the right margin.

If you increase the Page Width setting, Word will widen the text area. For example, if you change the Page Width setting from 8.5 to 9, Word will shift the right edge of your text by $1/2$ inch. In the paragraph view of the ruler, the edge of your text will be at the $6\,1/2$-inch position, and in the margin view, the right margin marker will be at the $7\,3/4$-inch position on the ruler.

The Page Width and Height settings in the Document dialog box should match the size of the paper in your printer. If you're using anything other than letter-size paper, you'll need to use the Printer Setup... command on the File menu to choose a different paper size. Once you've selected a new paper size, Word will remind you to enter corresponding Page Width and Height settings into the Document dialog box. We'll discuss the Printer Setup… command in Chapter 7.

Changing the print orientation

As we mentioned earlier, laser printers can print documents in either portrait or landscape orientation. In most cases, when you use the Printer Setup… command to change the Orientation setting from Portrait to Landscape, the effect is similar to increasing your Page Width setting in the Document dialog box. When the Portrait orientation setting (Word's default) is in effect, Word assumes that you want to print your document across the width of the page. An $8\frac{1}{2}$- by 11-inch page, then, will be taller than it is wide.

Landscape orientation, on the other hand, will cause Word to print your document across the length of the page—as though the paper were rotated 90 degrees. A document printed on $8\frac{1}{2}$- by 11-inch paper will be wider than it is tall. Figure 5-11 shows a layout sketch of a page that uses Word's default page size and margin settings and landscape orientation. Notice that the top and bottom margins now appear on the long sides of the paper, while the left and right margins lie along the short sides of the paper.

Figure 5-11

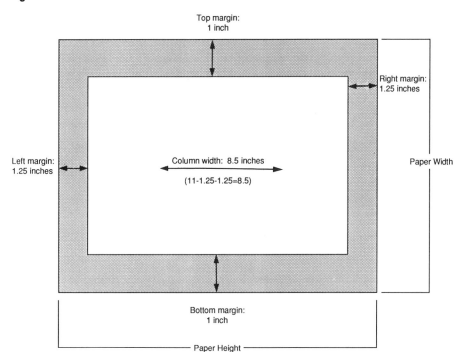

When you use landscape orientation, Word will rotate your page 90 degrees.

After you've used the Printer Setup... command to change the Orientation setting from Portrait to Landscape, Word will present a message box like the one shown in Figure 5-12. In this box, you should choose Yes, which tells Word to swap the Page Width and Height settings in the Document dialog box. If you choose No, you'll run into problems when you use the Print... command to print the document. We'll discuss the Print... command in Chapter 7.

Figure 5-12

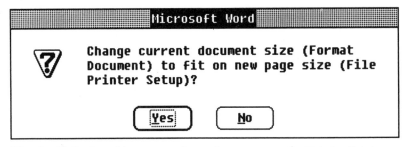

Word will display this message box when you use the Printer Setup... command to specify landscape orientation.

Figure 5-13 shows the document from Figure 5-6 after we changed the Orientation setting from Portrait to Landscape. (If you've selected the Display as Printed check box in the Preferences dialog box, your landscape document will look like Figure 5-13 only if you've installed the 12-point Tms Rmn landscape font on your printer.

Figure 5-13

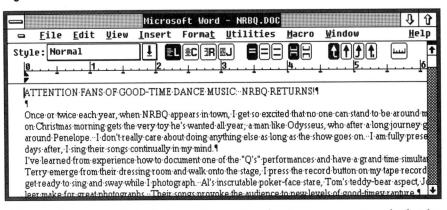

After we change our Orientation setting to Landscape, we cannot see both edges of the document without scrolling.

The document's text area is now so wide that you cannot see the end of each line without scrolling horizontally. In fact, if you're using the paragraph view of the ruler and you click on the horizontal scroll bar, you will see that the vertical line marking the right edge of your text area now appears at the $8\frac{1}{2}$-inch position. Word arrived at this new text width by subtracting the Left and Right margin settings from the width of the paper, like this:

$$\text{New text width} \quad = \text{paper width - left margin - right margin}$$
$$= 11 - 1\frac{1}{4} - 1\frac{1}{4}$$
$$= 8\frac{1}{2}$$

If you're changing only your margin settings, your paper size, or the orientation of text on the page, it's fairly easy to predict the result. When you need to change several of these settings, however, it's easy to get lost. If you're new to this process, we recommend that you make one change at a time and view your document after each change. You may even want to use the Print Preview window to get a better idea of how each change affects your document layout. (We'll discuss Print Preview in Chapter 7.)

CONTROLLING LINE AND PAGE BREAKS

As we've illustrated, the size of the text area determines how long individual lines of text can be and how many lines can fit on a page. Word offers a number of options that let you control where your line and page breaks occur.

Line breaks

Word automatically breaks lines of text at the right margin of your document. You can, however, create your own line breaks. One way to do this is by pressing the [Enter] key, which also starts a new paragraph. (If you're displaying paragraph marks on your screen, you'll see the ¶ mark at the point where you press [Enter].) If you want to start a new line without beginning a new paragraph, press [Shift][Enter]. Word will mark the line break on your screen with a ↵ symbol. The new line will be contained in the same paragraph as the line preceding it.

When we discuss paragraph formatting in the next section of this chapter, we'll show you how to narrow and widen paragraphs by moving the indent markers on the ruler.

Page breaks

As you're creating a document, Word automatically calculates where the page breaks will occur. If you want Word to calculate page breaks only when you tell it to, you can turn off the Background Pagination option. To do this, select the Customize... command from the Utilities menu, deselect the Background Pagination check box, and choose OK. Because it takes Word a while to repaginate a long document, you may want to automatically repaginate your short documents but manually repaginate your long ones.

To tell Word to repaginate your document, select the Repaginate Now command from the Utilities menu. Word will also repaginate your document when you preview it with the Print Preview command, when you print it, or when you issue the Page command on the View menu to enter the Page View mode.

As you work on a document in Page View mode, Word will repaginate from the beginning of the document through the current page. As you move the cursor forward in the document, Word will repaginate through that page.

As we pointed out in Chapter 2, Word displays the current page number (the number of the page containing the cursor) in the status bar. If you've selected the Background Pagination check box, the page number you see will always be accurate. If you've turned off Background Pagination, however, the status bar will accurately reflect the current page number only immediately after you issue the Repaginate Now command.

Manual page breaks

Sometimes, you'll need to force a page break at a particular location in your document. To do this, move the cursor to the spot where you want the new page to begin, select the Break… command from the Insert menu, leave the Page Break option selected in the Break dialog box, and choose OK. Alternatively, you can press [Ctrl][Enter] to insert a manual page break. When you use either technique, Word will insert a manual page-break marker after the cursor.

Like the automatic page breaks that appear when you repaginate your document, your manual page breaks will be represented by a single dotted line. However, manual page-break markers are slightly finer than automatic page-break markers. Figure 5-14 shows an example of an automatic and a manual page-break marker.

Figure 5-14

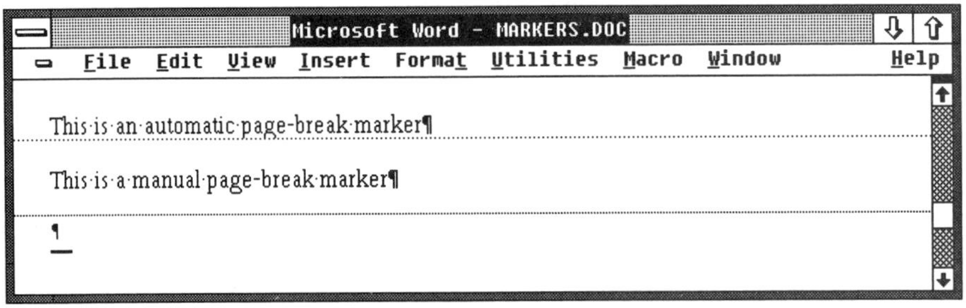

Word's manual page-break markers appear slightly finer than its automatic page-break markers.

Keep in mind that automatic page-break markers will change position each time you repaginate your document. Any manual page breaks you have inserted, however, will always occur at the location in which you inserted them. For this reason, we suggest you use manual page breaks sparingly. Otherwise, if you reformat or edit your document, these page breaks could cause unwanted gaps and awkward breaks in your printed document. To delete a manual page break, select it, or place the cursor in front of it, and press the [Delete] key.

If there is a paragraph that you want Word to always place at the top of a page, you may want to assign the Page Break Before option to that paragraph. We'll consider this option in more detail later in this chapter when we discuss the Paragraph dialog box.

Although the jargon is none too progressive, the term *widow* refers to those straggling single lines of text that appear at the top or bottom of a printed page. (Sometimes, *widow* refers only to the last line of a paragraph that appears at the top of a printed page, while *orphan* refers to the first line of a paragraph that appears at the bottom of a page. In Word, both of these situations are considered widows.) Generally, it is considered good style to keep at least two lines of a paragraph on a page. That is, the first or last line of a paragraph should never stand alone. If there isn't room for at least two lines of a paragraph at the bottom of a page, you should push the entire paragraph to the beginning of the next page. By the same token, if there is room at the bottom of a page for all but the last line of a paragraph, you should pull a line from the top of the second page to the bottom of the first page.

Widow control

The Widow Control check box in the Document dialog box ensures that no single line of text from a paragraph (unless, of course, it is a single-line paragraph) stands alone on a page. If you use this option, Word will automatically adjust your page breaks to ensure that at least two lines of a paragraph appear on a page. In some cases, this means that Word will not print the maximum number of lines on a page, making your bottom margin slightly larger.

When we discuss paragraph formatting later in this chapter, we'll look at the Keep Paragraph Together option, which goes a step further than Widow Control. When you apply this option to a paragraph, Word will print that paragraph in its entirety on a single page. If an entire paragraph cannot fit at the bottom of one page, Word will push it to the top of the next page.

So far, we've considered the basics of page layout in Word and looked at the primary factors that affect the positioning of page breaks in a document. In later chapters of this book, we'll look at other elements that can affect page breaks. In Chapter 7, we'll consider headers and footers—text that appears at the top or bottom of each printed page. As you'll see, Word may automatically adjust your top and/or bottom margin to make room for multiline headers and footers. In Chapter 12, we'll look at multisection documents. When you create a document with two or more sections, you can specify that each section should begin on a new page. Naturally, this will affect the location of page breaks that occur after

Other factors that affect page breaks

the start of a new section. Chapter 12 will also cover the Position... command which may affect a document's page breaks as well. Finally, in Chapter 14, we'll explain footnotes, which you can place at the bottom of a page, at the end of each section, or at the end of a document. Footnotes that are printed at the bottom of a page will likely change the location of page breaks.

PARAGRAPH FORMATTING

Once you've established the page layout of a document, you're ready to move on to formatting individual paragraphs. Word's paragraph formatting options cover a lot of territory, including indentions, alignment, line spacing, and before and after spacing. In many simple documents, your paragraphs may all conform to one or two formats, so you won't need to do much in the way of individual paragraph formatting. In some documents, however, you may need to create a variety of paragraph formats.

Word's paragraph formatting commands always apply to whole paragraphs. Therefore, to indicate which paragraph you want to format, place the cursor anywhere in that paragraph or select some or all of the text in the paragraph. If you want to format two or more paragraphs at once, first select any portion of the text in those paragraphs.

In this section, we'll show you how to apply Word's paragraph formatting features, using both the ruler and the Paragraph dialog box. In Chapter 8, we'll show you how to use a style sheet to name and save various combinations of paragraph formatting. As you'll see, using a style sheet can greatly speed up and simplify the process of formatting paragraphs. For now, however, let's begin by reviewing Word's default paragraph formats.

The defaults

Word's default settings for a paragraph are flush left, single-spaced, with no first-line, left, or right indents. The term *flush left* refers to how the text is aligned— with an even left and "ragged" right margin. As you'll see in a moment, you can also format paragraphs using centered, flush-right, or justified alignment.

Single-spacing refers to the amount of leading between lines of text. Word automatically adds 1 point of space (approximately $\frac{1}{72}$ of an inch) between lines of text to create buffers between the ascenders and descenders of characters on adjacent lines. You can increase or decrease this line spacing to suit your needs.

Word's default paragraph formatting calls for no indents, meaning that all the text is aligned within the text column established by your document's margins. By dragging the ruler's indent markers, you can increase or decrease the width of one or more paragraphs. For example, if you need to set a quotation off from the rest of your document, you might adjust the left and right indent markers to narrow that paragraph. You can also indent the first line of text in a paragraph.

(A note of warning: You may be tempted to change your overall margin settings by moving the indent markers on the ruler. We strongly urge you to resist this temptation. As we said earlier, if you later make any changes to your page size, margins, or print orientation, Word will automatically move the indent markers on the ruler to reflect the new settings—and will thoroughly scramble the "margins" you established with the indent markers.)

Earlier in this chapter, we explained how the ruler can show you the width of your text column and your page margins. The ruler also can be used to apply most paragraph formatting features and show you which of these features are in effect for any paragraph in a document. To display the ruler at the top of a document window, choose Ruler from the View menu. Immediately, Word will display the ruler shown in Figure 5-15. (The ruler display is associated with a specific document. If you have more than one document window open, you can choose to view the ruler in some document windows and not in others.)

Ruler icons

Figure 5-15

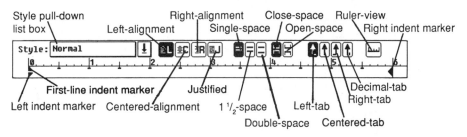

You can use the ruler icons to format your paragraphs.

As you can see from the tick marks along the ruler line, Word divides the ruler into $\frac{1}{8}$-inch increments. However, as we'll demonstrate in this chapter, you can position the indent markers and tabs along the ruler at more precise intervals.

In the paragraph view of the ruler, you'll see indent markers at either end of the ruler. In any of the ruler views, you'll also see icons above the ruler line that allow you to control paragraph alignment, line spacing, the space before a paragraph, and tabs. The ruler also contains a pull-down list box that you can use to apply styles. We'll show you how to use this list box in our discussion of style sheets in Chapter 8.

The ruler offers an excellent visual summary of most formatting features that have been applied to any paragraph in your document. If you place the cursor on a paragraph while the ruler is displayed, the ruler icons, indent markers, and tab marks will show you how that paragraph is formatted. Word will highlight the appropriate icons and move the tabs and indent markers to the correct positions. For example, the ruler in Figure 5-15 shows all of Word's default paragraph formats. The icons for left alignment, single spacing, and closed spacing are all highlighted; the first-line and left indent markers are at the zero position; and the right indent marker is at the 6-inch position.

If you select two or more paragraphs whose formatting differs, Word will dim all or part of the icons and indent markers. For example, suppose a document contains two adjacent paragraphs whose formatting is identical, except the first paragraph has left alignment and the second paragraph has centered alignment. If you select both paragraphs (or some text in both paragraphs), Word will dim the alignment icons on the ruler. All the other icons and the indent markers will be displayed normally.

Now that you've seen how the ruler can display a paragraph's format, we need to look at how you can use the ruler icons and indent markers to change a paragraph's format. After we discuss the ruler, we'll show you how to use the Paragraph dialog box to format paragraphs. Then, we'll demonstrate how to create tab stops in your text.

Indents

As we said earlier, your overall document margins are controlled by the margin settings in the Document dialog box or by the margin markers on the ruler in the margin view. Initially, Word will align the first-line and left indent markers with the left edge of your text and the right indent marker with the right edge of your text. You can move these markers when you need to change the width of the text in one or more paragraphs. In fact, you might think of the indent markers as tools for making a temporary margin change in a document. While the Left and Right margin settings control the margins throughout an entire document, the indent markers can control the margins or text width of a paragraph.

Changing indents using the mouse

To change the width of a paragraph with the mouse, first make sure that the ruler is in the paragraph view. Then, click anywhere on the paragraph and drag the left and right indent markers. For example, the second paragraph of text in the sample document in Figure 5-16 is a quotation from James Joyce's *Dubliners*. To set this quotation apart from the rest of the text, begin by clicking on or selecting a portion of the paragraph, then point to the left indent marker (the bottom of the two indent markers on the left side of the ruler), and drag it to the $\frac{1}{2}$-inch position. The first-line indent marker will move with the left indent marker. Next, to indent the right edge of the paragraph, point to the right indent marker and drag it to the $5\frac{1}{2}$-inch position. Figure 5-17 shows the results.

As you move the indent markers, remember that your paragraph indentions are relative to the margin settings you have specified in the Document dialog box or on the margin view of the ruler. In our sample document, the quotation will appear $1\frac{3}{4}$ inches from the left and right edges of the page.

Figure 5-16

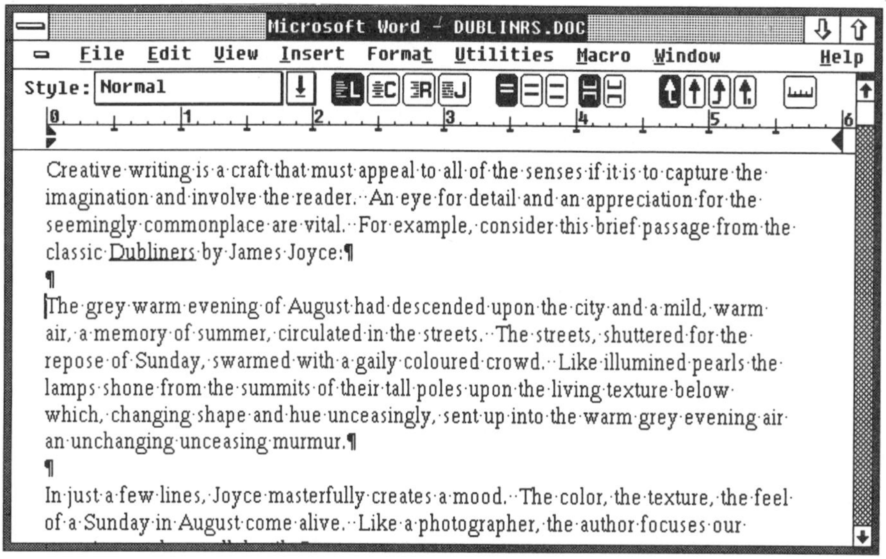

```
┌─────────────────────────────────────────────────────────────────┐
│ ═         Microsoft Word – DUBLINRS.DOC              ⇩ ⇧          │
│ ⊡  File  Edit  View  Insert  Format  Utilities  Macro  Window   Help │
│ Style:│Normal          │↓│ ▣L≣C≣R▣J  ≡≡≡ ≡≡  ⬆⬆⬆⬆  ⊡      ↑│
│ │0. . . │1 . . . │2 . . . │3 . . . │4 . . . │5 . . . │6│
│ ▼                                                            ◄    │
│ Creative·writing·is·a·craft·that·must·appeal·to·all·of·the·senses·if·it·is·to·capture·the· │
│ imagination·and·involve·the·reader.··An·eye·for·detail·and·an·appreciation·for·the· │
│ seemingly·commonplace·are·vital.··For·example,·consider·this·brief·passage·from·the· │
│ classic·Dubliners·by·James·Joyce:¶ │
│ ¶ │
│ The·grey·warm·evening·of·August·had·descended·upon·the·city·and·a·mild,·warm· │
│ air,·a·memory·of·summer,·circulated·in·the·streets.··The·streets,·shuttered·for·the· │
│ repose·of·Sunday,·swarmed·with·a·gaily·coloured·crowd.··Like·illumined·pearls·the· │
│ lamps·shone·from·the·summits·of·their·tall·poles·upon·the·living·texture·below· │
│ which,·changing·shape·and·hue·unceasingly,·sent·up·into·the·warm·grey·evening·air· │
│ an·unchanging·unceasing·murmur.¶ │
│ ¶ │
│ In·just·a·few·lines,·Joyce·masterfully·creates·a·mood.··The·color,·the·texture,·the·feel· │
│ of·a·Sunday·in·August·come·alive.··Like·a·photographer,·the·author·focuses·our· │
│                                                                           ▼ │
└─────────────────────────────────────────────────────────────────┘
```

The second paragraph in this sample document is a quotation.

Figure 5-17

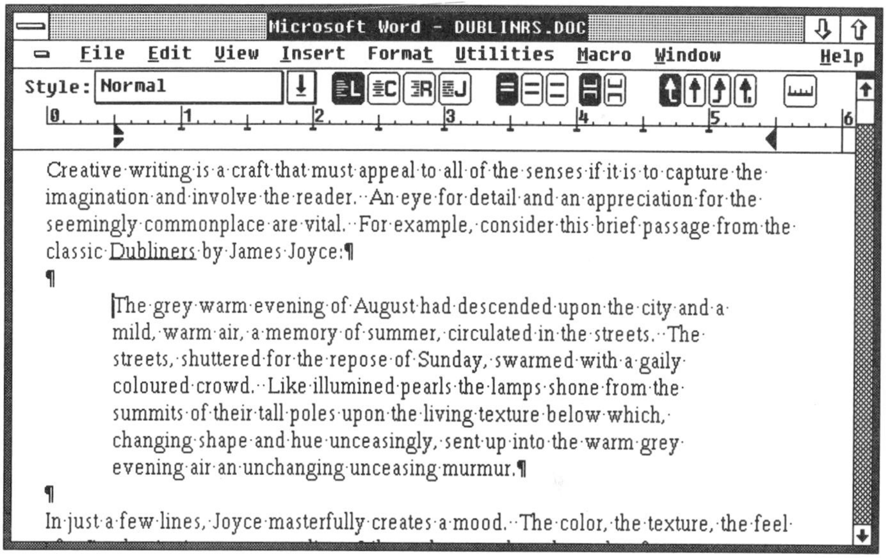

```
┌─────────────────────────────────────────────────────────────────┐
│ ═         Microsoft Word – DUBLINRS.DOC              ⇩ ⇧          │
│ ⊡  File  Edit  View  Insert  Format  Utilities  Macro  Window   Help │
│ Style:│Normal          │↓│ ▣L≣C≣R▣J  ≡≡≡ ≡≡  ⬆⬆⬆⬆  ⊡      ↑│
│ │0. . . │1 . . . │2 . . . │3 . . . │4 . . . │5 . . . │6│
│ ▼        ▲                                            ◄         │
│ Creative·writing·is·a·craft·that·must·appeal·to·all·of·the·senses·if·it·is·to·capture·the· │
│ imagination·and·involve·the·reader.··An·eye·for·detail·and·an·appreciation·for·the· │
│ seemingly·commonplace·are·vital.··For·example,·consider·this·brief·passage·from·the· │
│ classic·Dubliners·by·James·Joyce:¶ │
│ ¶ │
│        The·grey·warm·evening·of·August·had·descended·upon·the·city·and·a· │
│        mild,·warm·air,·a·memory·of·summer,·circulated·in·the·streets.··The· │
│        streets,·shuttered·for·the·repose·of·Sunday,·swarmed·with·a·gaily· │
│        coloured·crowd.··Like·illumined·pearls·the·lamps·shone·from·the· │
│        summits·of·their·tall·poles·upon·the·living·texture·below·which,· │
│        changing·shape·and·hue·unceasingly,·sent·up·into·the·warm·grey· │
│        evening·air·an·unchanging·unceasing·murmur.¶ │
│ ¶ │
│ In·just·a·few·lines,·Joyce·masterfully·creates·a·mood.··The·color,·the·texture,·the·feel· │
│                                                                           ▼ │
└─────────────────────────────────────────────────────────────────┘
```

To indent the left and right edges of a paragraph, move the indent markers on the ruler.

**Changing indents
using the keyboard**

You also can change your paragraph indents by using the keyboard instead of the mouse. After positioning the cursor on the paragraph you want to indent, press [Ctrl][Shift][F10] to activate the ruler. When the ruler appears, you'll see a square black cursor at its left edge, as shown in Figure 5-18. Using the arrow keys, you can position this cursor at various points along the ruler. Table 5-1 summarizes the ways you can move the cursor. (The increments stated in this table will change if you customize your ruler to show units of measure other than inches.)

Figure 5-18

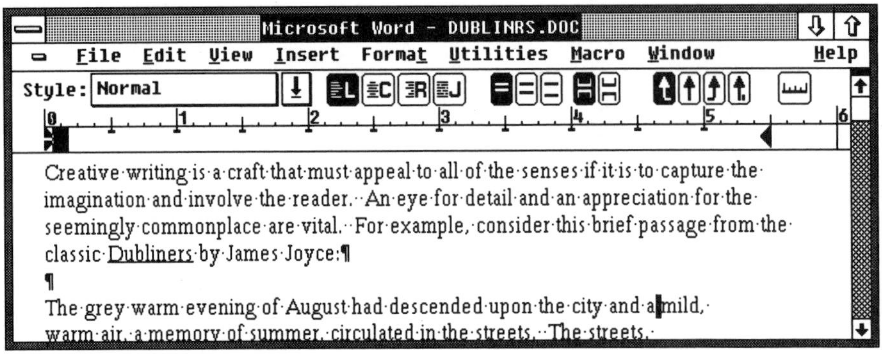

When you press [Ctrl][Shift][F10], Word will activate the ruler and display a ruler cursor at its left edge.

Table 5-1

This key...	moves the ruler cursor...
→	right in $1/_8$-inch increments
←	left in $1/_8$-inch increments
[Ctrl]→	right in 1-inch increments
[Ctrl]←	left in 1-inch increments
[End]	to the right edge of the text column
[Home]	to the zero position

After you've moved the cursor to the position you want to indent the paragraph, press *F* to move the first-line indent marker, *L* to move the left indent marker, or *R* to move the right indent marker.

For example, to move the left indent marker in our sample document, press [Ctrl][Shift][F10] to activate the ruler, then use the → key to position the cursor at the $1/_2$-inch position on the ruler. Next, press *L* to set the left indention. (The first-line indent marker will move to the same position.) After moving the left indent marker, you can use the arrow keys to position the cursor where you want the right indent marker to appear (the 5 $\frac{1}{2}$-inch position in our example), and press *R* to move the indent marker.

After placing the indent markers, you can press [Enter] to deactivate the ruler and return to your document. If you want to cancel the changes you've made on the ruler and return to your document, press [Esc].

Word offers a keyboard shortcut that lets you move the left indent of a paragraph by an amount equal to the width of a default tab stop. (Unless you change them, Word's default tab stops occur every $\frac{1}{2}$ inch along the ruler.) When you press [Ctrl]N, Word will "nest" the current paragraph(s). That is, Word will move its left indent to the right by $\frac{1}{2}$ inch. Each time you press [Ctrl]N, Word will nest the paragraph another $\frac{1}{2}$ inch (or the width of a default tab stop). To "unnest" a paragraph—that is, to move its left indent out by $\frac{1}{2}$ inch—press [Ctrl]M. You can use the [Ctrl]M technique independently of [Ctrl]N. Word will simply move the left indent marker for the current paragraph(s) so that the text hangs outside your left margin.

Paragraph nesting

Often, you'll want to indent only the first line of each paragraph in your documents to make it easier to distinguish paragraph breaks. That's why the indent marker on the left edge of the ruler is split. The top half of the marker (the first-line indent marker) lets you format the first line of a paragraph independently of the rest. To change your first-line indention using a mouse, drag the top marker.

Indenting the first line in a paragraph

For example, Figure 5-19 on the next page shows our sample document with a $\frac{1}{2}$-inch first-line indention added to each paragraph. As you can see on the ruler, the first-line indent marker for the first and third text paragraphs is at the $\frac{1}{2}$-inch position, while the left indent marker remains at zero. In the quotation paragraph, the first-line indent marker is at 1 inch and the left indent marker is at $\frac{1}{2}$ inch.

To move the first-line indent marker using the keyboard, first press [Ctrl][Shift][F10] to activate the ruler. Then, using the arrow keys, position the ruler cursor where you want the first-line indent marker to appear, and press *F*. Word will then move the first-line indent marker to the position you indicated.

Once you split the first-line indent and left indent markers, you can still move both markers simultaneously by moving the left indent marker. The distance between the two markers will remain unchanged. For example, suppose you want to shift the quotation in the sample document an additional $\frac{1}{2}$ inch to the right. You can point to the left indent marker and drag it to the 1-inch position on the ruler (or press [Ctrl][Shift][F10], move the ruler cursor to the 1-inch position, and press *L*). When you move the left indent marker, Word will move the first-line indent marker as well, so that it will be set at $1\frac{1}{2}$ inches.

If you want to move the left indent marker without changing the first-line indent, press the [Shift] key as you drag the marker with your mouse. Word will "release" the left indent marker, allowing you to move it independently. Unfortunately, if you don't have a mouse, there's no way to move the left indent marker without also moving the first-line indent marker. If you need to move the left indent marker, you may need to adjust the first-line indent as well.

Figure 5-19

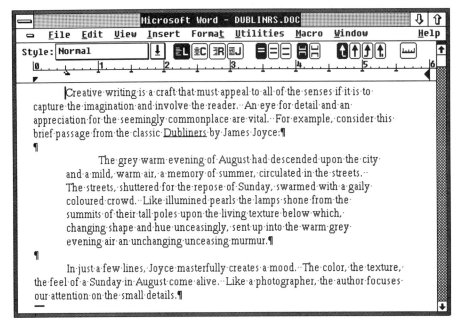

You can move the first-line indent marker to indent a paragraph.

Hanging indentions

Sometimes, you'll want to format a paragraph so that the first line starts to the left of the left indention. This is called a hanging indention, or outjustified text, since the first line "hangs" outside the left margin of the paragraph.

For example, to create the paragraph formatting shown in Figure 5-20, we moved the left indent marker to the $1/_2$-inch position and left the first-line indent at the zero position.

Hanging indentions are particularly useful when you want to create a numbered or bulleted list of items, placing your numbers or bullets outside the main list. We'll show you how to create this kind of list in Chapter 16.

Placing text in the margins

Generally, you'll use the first-line, left, and right indent markers to decrease the width of a selected paragraph, as illustrated in Figure 5-17. However, Word also lets you increase the width of a selected paragraph, placing text in the margin areas of your printed page. To do this, move the first-line and left indent markers to the left of the zero point on the ruler, and move the right indent marker to the right of the vertical line marking the edge of your text area. You can move the indent markers like this since the ruler (in the paragraph view) extends far beyond the 6 inches or so that are visible in a standard document window. (The ruler actually extends from -11 inches to 22 inches.) Figure 5-21 shows a printed document in which the title extends beyond the left and right margins of the main text area.

Figure 5-20

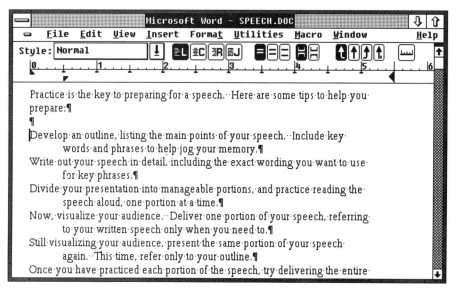

To create a hanging indention, drag the left indent marker to the right of the first-line indent marker.

Figure 5-21

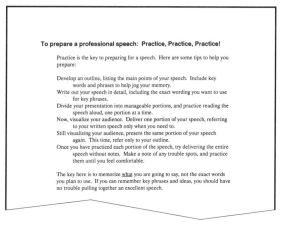

By moving the indent markers outside the text area, you can print text in the margins of your document.

To create this effect, first place the cursor on the title paragraph. Then, using either the mouse or the keyboard, move the right indent marker past the right margin (the 6-inch position, in this case), and move the first-line and left indent markers to the left of the zero point on the ruler. To move past the zero point, you need to press the [Shift] key as you drag the markers with a mouse. Alternatively, you can press the [Shift] key and click the left scroll arrow to bring the negative ruler values into view, then move the indent markers. To scroll negative values into view using the keyboard, press [Ctrl][Shift][F10] to activate the ruler, then hold down the [Shift] key as you press the ← key. Word will then shift the document window to the left, as shown in Figure 5-22.

Figure 5-22

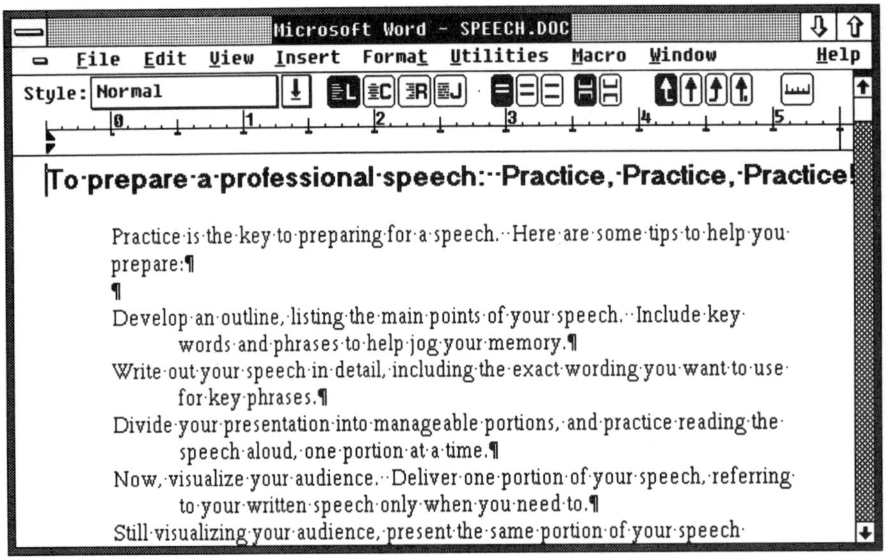

| Microsoft Word - SPEECH.DOC |
| File Edit View Insert Format Utilities Macro Window Help |

Style: Normal

|To·prepare·a·professional·speech:··Practice,·Practice,·Practice!

Practice·is·the·key·to·preparing·for·a·speech.··Here·are·some·tips·to·help·you·
prepare:¶
¶
Develop·an·outline,·listing·the·main·points·of·your·speech.··Include·key·
words·and·phrases·to·help·jog·your·memory.¶
Write·out·your·speech·in·detail,·including·the·exact·wording·you·want·to·use·
for·key·phrases.¶
Divide·your·presentation·into·manageable·portions,·and·practice·reading·the·
speech·aloud,·one·portion·at·a·time.¶
Now,·visualize·your·audience.··Deliver·one·portion·of·your·speech,·referring·
to·your·written·speech·only·when·you·need·to.¶
Still·visualizing·your·audience,·present·the·same·portion·of·your·speech·

To place text in the left margin, move the first-line and left indent markers to the left of the zero point on the ruler.

Another common use for negative indents is to place text or special symbols in the margin of a page to draw attention to certain paragraphs. For example, in Figure 5-23, we used a negative $1^1/_8$-inch first-line indent to display the words *Save 33%* to the left of the first paragraph. Notice that the left indent marker remains at the zero point so that the remainder of the paragraph is aligned with the rest of the text in the document.

When you enter text in the left margin like this, you may not be able to see that text after you scroll the document window to the right. (In addition, when you close a document and then reopen it, Word will automatically position the window so that the zero point appears at the left edge of the window, with the margin text out of view.) To scroll to the left of the zero point, press the [Shift] key as you click on the left scroll arrow. If you don't have a mouse, you can place the cursor on the line that contains the margin text, then use the arrow keys to move the cursor to the beginning of the line. As you move the cursor, Word will scroll the window to bring the margin area into view.

Figure 5-23

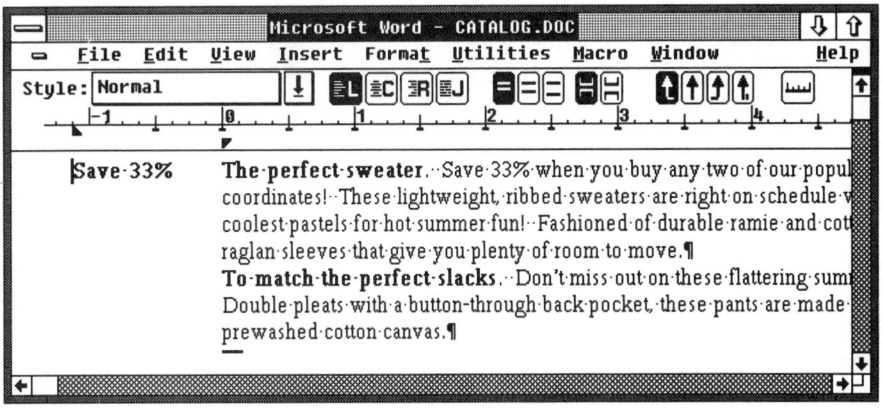

By moving the first-line indent marker, you can place text in the left margin to draw attention to certain paragraphs.

As you know, Word's default paragraph formatting aligns all the text in a document evenly with the left indent marker. The length of each line of text varies, creating a ragged right margin. To change this default alignment, place the cursor on the paragraph you want to format (or select some text in all the paragraphs you want to format) and click on one of the alignment icons on the ruler.

Alignment

If you're using the keyboard, place the cursor on the paragraph you want to format, then press one of the key combinations shown in Table 5-2 to select an alignment icon.

Table 5-2

This key combination...	selects this alignment...
[Ctrl]L	left
[Ctrl]C	centered
[Ctrl]R	right
[Ctrl]J	justified

The effects of the various alignment icons are fairly self-evident: The Centered-alignment icon instructs Word to center the selected text between the left and right indent markers; the Right-alignment icon aligns the text with the right indent marker, creating a ragged left margin; and the Justified icon aligns both edges of the text evenly with the left and right indent markers. When you choose justified alignment, Word may increase or decrease the width of the blank spaces in your text to keep the left and right edges of your text even.

By the way, Word always aligns text relative to the indent markers on the ruler, not to the page margins you've specified. This can have important implications for how your text is positioned on the page. For example, if you want to center your text, you must first be sure that your left and right margins are of equal width. Then, leave the indent markers at their default positions and select the Centered-alignment icon.

Let's use the title page in Figure 5-24 to illustrate Word's alignment features. Text that is all left-aligned does not make for a very interesting page. Now, notice the difference when we change the alignment of the various blocks of text, as shown in Figure 5-25.

Figure 5-24

All the text on this page is left-aligned.

Figure 5-25

> The Art of Flight:
> Fantasy and Inspiration
>
> We have always been fascinated by the romance and adventure of flight. Airplanes symbolize speed and liberation—a daring brush with the infinite. Beautiful in themselves, airplanes have also had their effect on the visual arts. In response to a universal dream, artists of the 20th century have drawn inspiration from the airplane.
>
> *Presented to the National*
> *Association of Visual Artists*
> *By Janet Morrison*
> *August 10, 1989*

You can dress up a page design by varying the alignment of paragraphs.

To format the first two lines of the sample page, we highlighted them and selected the Centered-alignment icon. Next, to place the summary paragraph in the center of the page, we selected it, placed the left and right indent markers at the 1-inch and 5-inch positions, respectively, then selected the Justified icon. To format the last four lines of text, we highlighted them and selected the Right-alignment icon.

By the way, when you use centered alignment, you'll generally want to keep the first-line and left indent markers at the same position on the ruler. A first-line indention may throw the first line of the paragraph out of balance with the remaining text.

As we mentioned earlier, Word automatically adds 1 point of leading, or spacing, between lines of text. This default spacing is called single spacing. For point sizes that are typically used in body text (10 or 12), single spacing tells Word to allow 1 point of space between the tallest ascender on one line and the lowest descender on the line immediately above. For example, if you're using 10-point Tms Rmn type, Word will allow 11 points from the bottom of one line to the bottom of the next line, creating 1 point of separator space between lines.

Line spacing

When you increase your point size, Word will increase the leading as well. For example, if you use 36-point Tms Rmn type, Word will allow 4 points of space between the characters on two adjacent lines. Figure 5-26 illustrates single spacing for several point sizes in the Tms Rmn font.

Figure 5-26

This is 10-point Tms Rmn text with default line spacing in effect.
This is 10-point Tms Rmn text with default line spacing in effect.

This is 12-point Tms Rmn text with default line spacing in
effect. This is 12-point Tms Rmn text with default line

This is 18-point Tms Rmn text with
default line spacing in effect. This is

This is 36-point
Tms Rmn Plain text

All the lines on this page are single-spaced.

The line-spacing icons on the ruler let you control the amount of space between lines of text in a paragraph. In addition to single-spaced lines, you can create $1^1/_2$-spaced and double-spaced lines of text. These two formats are convenient for creating manuscript pages because they give you extra room on the printed page for writing notes and corrections.

To apply the single-space, $1^1/_2$-space, and double-space line settings, place the cursor on (or select) the paragraph you want to format, then click on the appropriate ruler icon. If you're using the keyboard instead of a mouse, you can press the key combinations shown in Table 5-3 to choose the different line-spacing icons on the ruler.

When you use $1^1/_2$ line spacing, Word will increase the amount of space between lines to half of a line height. If you are using 10-point Tms Rmn type, this means that there will be 6 points of leading or white space between each line.

Table 5-3

This key combination...	selects...
[Ctrl]1	single spacing
[Ctrl]5	$1^1/_2$ spacing
[Ctrl]2	double spacing

When you use double spacing, Word will insert a full line of white space above each line of text. Again, if you are using 10-point Tms Rmn type, this means 12 points of leading. Figure 5-27 shows examples of single spacing, $1^1/_2$ spacing, and double spacing.

Figure 5-27

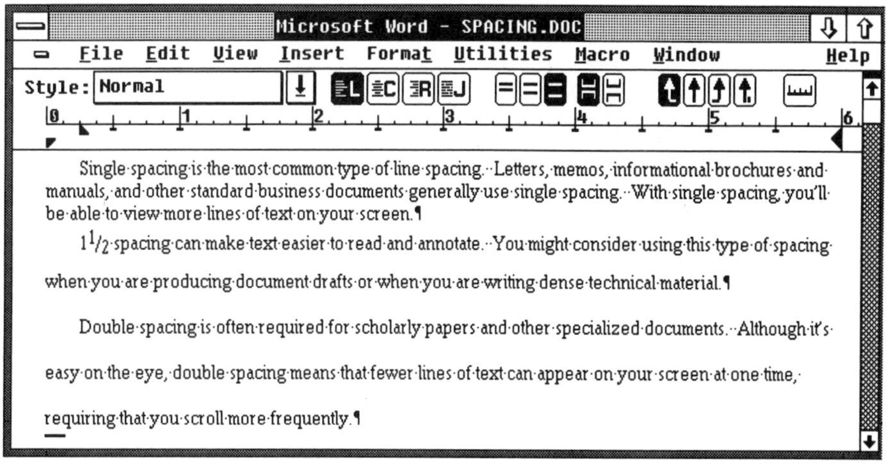

Using the ruler icons, you are able to create single spacing, $1^1/_2$ spacing, and double spacing.

You can use the Paragraph dialog box to create more precise line spacing than that allowed by the ruler icons. You also can create line spacing that's larger than double spacing or smaller than single spacing. We'll talk about the Line Spacing option in the Paragraph dialog box in a few pages.

Paragraph spacing is similar to line spacing except the spacing you choose applies only to the first line of the selected paragraph. Word offers two standard paragraph spacing options: open and closed. When you use closed paragraph spacing (the default), Word will not insert any extra spacing between paragraphs of text, other than the appropriate line spacing. When you use open paragraph

Paragraph spacing

spacing, Word will insert one line of white space before the first line of text in the selected paragraph(s). This space is in addition to any space created by the paragraph's line spacing setting.

To apply open and closed paragraph spacing, place the cursor on the paragraph you want to format (or select the paragraphs you want to format), then click on the appropriate ruler icon. If you're using the keyboard instead of a mouse, you can press [Ctrl]E to select the Close-space icon or [Ctrl]O to select the Open-space icon. Figure 5-28 shows a document in which the paragraphs have been assigned open spacing.

Figure 5-28

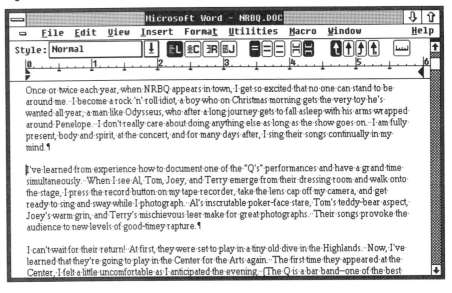

Use open spacing to create extra space between paragraphs.

You can also insert space before and after a paragraph by using the Before and After options in the Paragraph dialog box. These options have the advantage of allowing you to specify precisely how much space you want to insert rather than using Word's default spacing. We'll talk more about the Before and After spacing options later.

A paragraph
spacing tip

Many users create blank space between paragraphs manually by pressing the [Enter] key. When they reach the end of a paragraph, they simply press the [Enter] key twice to insert an extra blank paragraph and begin a new paragraph of text. This technique is inferior to using the Open-space icon in two important ways.

First, when you use the Open-space icon to add space between paragraphs, Word will omit that extra space if the new paragraph happens to fall at the beginning of a page. If you have manually inserted a blank paragraph, however, that extra space will appear regardless of the position of the text on the page. This means that if a paragraph falls at the top of a new page, it may not be properly aligned at the top margin, creating an unsightly gap in your document.

Using the Open-space icon is also advantageous if you decide to increase or decrease the amount of space between paragraphs. To make this kind of change, select all the paragraphs, then choose the Close-space icon or change the Before and/or After settings in the Paragraph dialog box. This will reformat all of the selected paragraphs. (You can also use style sheets to make this type of formatting change, as you'll learn in Chapter 8.)

The Paragraph dialog box

In many cases, the ruler offers the quickest and easiest way to format paragraphs, but it does not always let you create the various kinds of formatting you need. The Paragraph dialog box gives you some options that are not available on the ruler, and it allows you to specify some of the format settings—such as the position of indents and the amount of space between paragraphs—with more precision. If you do not have a mouse, you may find it easier to use the Paragraph dialog box to establish your formats than to activate the ruler and press various key combinations.

To open this dialog box, select the Paragraph... command from the Format menu. If you're using a mouse, you can open it quickly by double-clicking above the horizontal measuring line on the ruler. When Word displays the Paragraph dialog box, any settings that have been applied to the current paragraph will be selected. For example, if we place the cursor on the quotation in Figure 5-17 and choose the Paragraph... command, Word will display the dialog box shown in Figure 5-29 on the following page.

After you have changed some settings in the Paragraph dialog box, you can apply those settings and close the dialog box by choosing OK. If you want to close the dialog box without implementing any changes, choose Cancel.

Alignment, Indent, and Spacing options

If you've examined the various formatting options available on the ruler, most of the options in the Paragraph dialog box should look familiar. Choosing one of the Alignment options—Left, Center, Right, or Justified—has the same effect as clicking on the corresponding icon on the ruler. After you close the Paragraph dialog box, Word will automatically highlight the appropriate ruler icon to show which Alignment option you selected.

Indents can be specified in the three Indents text boxes: From Left, From Right, and First Line. Entering a value in these text boxes has the same effect as moving the indent markers on the ruler. However, when you move an indent marker on the ruler, you can place that marker with only $1/16$-inch precision (or

$^1/_8$-inch precision if you're using the keyboard). In the Indents text boxes, however, you specify the position of an indent with $^1/_{100}$-inch precision. If you don't want to use inches, you can specify your indent positions in centimeters, points, or picas by typing *cm, pt,* or *pi* after the number in the text box. If you don't specify a unit, Word will assume inches (or whatever unit you're using on the ruler).

Figure 5-29

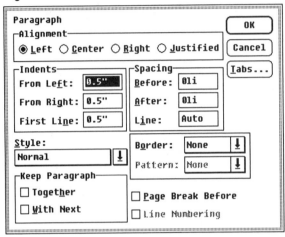

The Paragraph dialog box displays the formats of the current paragraph.

After you make an entry in one of the Indents text boxes and close the dialog box, Word will automatically move the appropriate indent marker to reflect the setting you specified. When you specify a first-line indent, Word assumes the measurement in the First Line text box is relative to the From Left indent setting. Thus, if you enter *0.5″* in the From Left text box and *0.5″* in the First Line text box, Word will position the first-line indent marker at the 1-inch position on the ruler—$^1/_2$ inch beyond the left indent.

The Spacing options in the Paragraph dialog box let you specify the amount of space you want to insert before and after a paragraph, as well as the line spacing within the paragraph. The Before setting is similar to the Open-space icon on the ruler. It allows you to specify the amount of space you want to insert before the first line of a paragraph. The After setting lets you insert space after the last line in a paragraph, and the Line setting lets you specify the total amount of space Word should allow for each line in the paragraph. (We'll talk more about line spacing in a moment.)

When you enter a Spacing setting, you can use inches, points, or lines as your unit of measure. Simply type a number followed by *in, ″, pt,* or *li.* Do not include a period after the unit's abbreviation—like *.25 in.* because Word will not be able to interpret your entry and will give you an error message. It's not necessary to include a space between the number you type and the unit of measure.

Often, Word will change the unit of measure you specify. For example, if you use lines as your unit of measure, Word will convert anything other than whole lines or half lines into inches. That is, if you enter *0.8 li* as your Line setting, then close the Paragraph dialog box and reopen it, you'll see *0.13"* in the Line text box.

If you do not specify a unit of measure, Word will assume that you intend to use lines. For example, if you type *0.8* in the Before text box, Word will assume that you want to insert $^3/_4$ line of space above the paragraph. Although Word assumes lines as the unit of measure, it still may convert your entry into inches. For instance, if you type *0.8* into the Before text box, you will see *0.13"* the next time you open the Paragraph dialog box.

When we explained the line-spacing icons earlier in this chapter, we mentioned that the Paragraph dialog box allows you to create more precise line spacing than the ruler icons do. The entry you make in the Line text box specifies the amount of space Word should allow from the bottom of one line to the bottom of the next. For example, if you enter *0.25"* into the Line text box, Word will allow $^1/_4$ inch of space from the bottom of one line to the bottom of the next. (With 10-point type, this is the same as $1^1/_2$ spacing.)

Normally, Word interprets the value you enter in the Line text box as a minimum line spacing value. If you have an unusually large character on a line, Word will increase the spacing between lines to accommodate that character. However, Word will never use less line spacing than you have specified. For example, Figure 5-30 shows some text in which we've entered a Line setting of 0.2". Notice that all the lines are spaced evenly except the fourth line, which contains some text formatted in a larger point size. Word increased the line spacing for this line to prevent the text from overlapping the line above.

More on line spacing

Figure 5-30

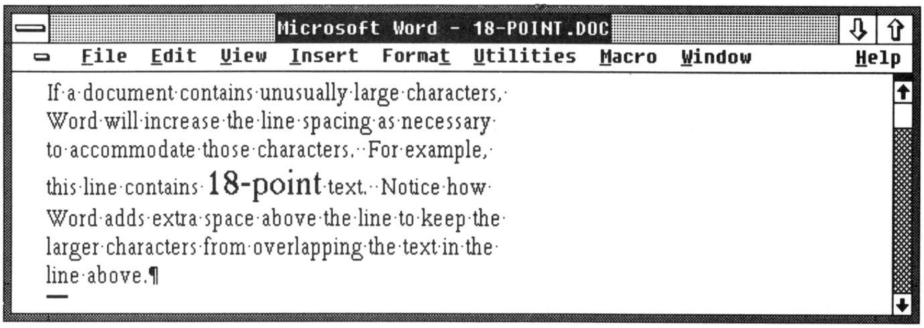

Word may increase line spacing on one line of text to accommodate larger characters.

If you want to override Word's automatic line spacing in order to overlap two or more lines of text, you can enter a negative number into the Line text box. The minus sign in front of the number does not indicate that you want to use negative spacing—if such spacing were possible. Instead, the minus sign indicates that you want the setting to be absolute. Thus, a -.2" Line setting tells Word that you want your line spacing to be $^2/_{10}$ of an inch, even if that means some characters will overlap. Figure 5-31 shows some overlapping printed text (24-point Tms Rmn) that we created by using a Line setting of -11 pt. When you use absolute line spacing, some of your characters may appear truncated on the screen. However, the characters will appear in their entirety when you print them.

Figure 5-31

You can create overlapping lines of text by entering a negative value in the Line text box.

Options that affect page breaks

The Paragraph dialog box includes three check-box options that allow you to control where page breaks occur relative to one or more paragraphs. These are the two Keep Paragraph check boxes—Together and With Next—that appear in the lower-left corner of the dialog box, and the Page Break Before check box.

You'll use the Keep Paragraph Together check box when you don't want Word to split a paragraph between pages. If you want to ensure that all of the lines in a paragraph appear on the same printed page, activate this check box. Then, if the paragraph happens to fall at the bottom of a page and Word does not have room to print the entire paragraph, Word will push all the lines of the paragraph to the beginning of the next page.

The Keep Paragraph With Next option tells Word to print a paragraph on the same page as the following paragraph. If there is not room for both paragraphs on the same page, Word will push them both to the top of the next page. You'll find that the Keep Paragraph With Next option comes in handy in many circumstances. For example, if your document contains subheadings, you might want to activate this option for each subheading to prevent Word from printing a subheading at the bottom of a page and the first text after the subheading at the top of the next page. When you create a list, you might assign the Keep Paragraph With Next option to related items. For example, if you're listing names and addresses, you could assign this option to each name to ensure that it appears on the same page as the address that follows it.

Keep in mind that the Keep Paragraph With Next option does not guarantee that all the lines in each paragraph will remain on the same page. If you have selected the Widow Control check box in the Document dialog box, Word will make certain that at least two lines from each paragraph appear together on a page. If you have deselected Widow Control, Word will ensure that at least one line from each paragraph appears on the same page as the adjacent paragraph. If you want Word to keep two paragraphs on the same page in their entirety, you must assign the Keep Paragraph Together option to both paragraphs and the Keep Paragraph With Next option to the first paragraph.

Finally, the Page Break Before check box, as its name implies, allows you to force a page break before a paragraph. This option is useful when you want a particular paragraph—such as a subheading—always to appear at the top of a page. Assigning the Page Break Before option to a paragraph is similar to pressing [Ctrl][Enter] to insert a manual page break before that paragraph. However, you won't see a line marking the page break on your screen until Word repaginates your document. (If Background Pagination is turned on, the line may appear a few seconds after you assign the Page Break Before option.) In addition, the manual page break will be permanently "attached" to the selected paragraph, just as any other paragraph format. If you use the Copy or Cut and Paste commands to copy or move the paragraph to another location in your document, the Page Break Before format will automatically move with the paragraph.

The Paragraph dialog box contains two list boxes that let you create a paragraph border and assign a pattern to it. You might want to use paragraph borders to call attention to an important paragraph in a document or to create a paragraph inset.

Adding borders

To add a border to the current paragraph, simply use the Border and Pattern pull-down list boxes to define the type of border you want. The Border list box offers five kinds of borders: None, Box, Bar, Above, and Below. Each of these border options is fairly self-explanatory. You'll use the Box option to create a border that "boxes in" the paragraphs you've selected. Choosing the Bar option tells Word to draw a vertical bar along the left side of the selected paragraphs. Finally, the Above and Below options let you draw a horizontal bar above or below the paragraphs you've selected.

The Pattern pull-down list box lets you tell Word what kind of line to use for the border: None, Single, Thick, Double, and Shadow. The Single option tells Word to draw a 1-point line, while the Thick option tells Word to draw a 2-point line. Choosing the Double option instructs Word to draw two 1-point parallel lines 2 points apart. You'll use the Shadow option in conjunction with the Box option in the Border list box to create a "shadow" effect around selected paragraphs. The Shadow option tells Word to place a 1-point line along the top and left edges of the paragraphs, and a 2-point line along the bottom and right edges.

As an example of using the Border and Pattern list boxes, suppose you want to draw a shadow box around the indented paragraph in Figure 5-32. To begin, move the cursor to that paragraph and choose the Paragraph... command. In the Paragraph dialog box, pull down the Border list box and choose the Box option.

Next, pull down the Pattern list box and choose the Shadow option. When you choose OK, Word will place a single line along the top and left edges of the paragraph and a thick line along the other edges, as shown in Figure 5-33.

Figure 5-32

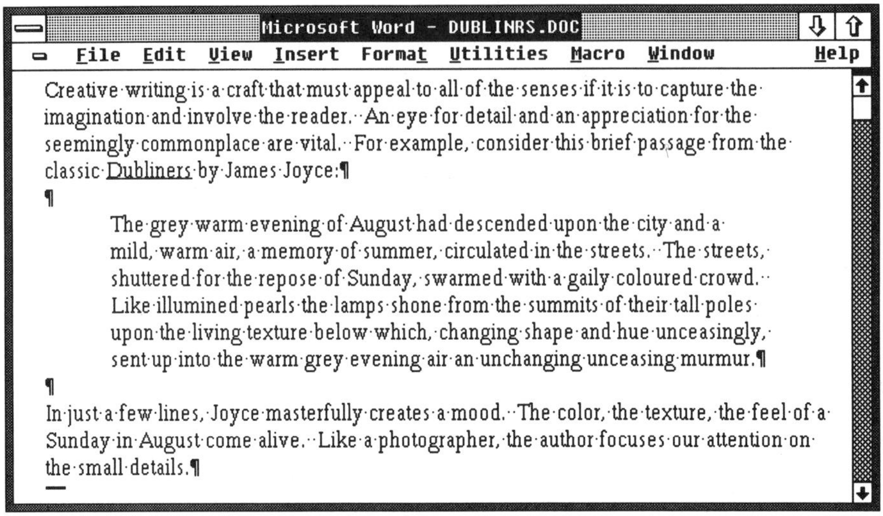

We'll use the Border and Pattern list boxes to add a border to this paragraph.

Figure 5-33

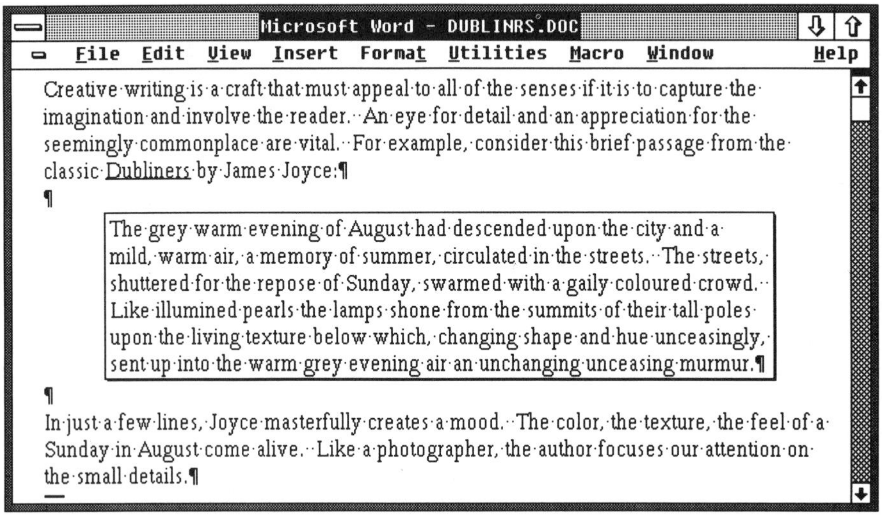

The Shadow option lets you create a shadow effect for a paragraph.

To delete a paragraph's border, select the paragraph, then open the Paragraph dialog box. Choose the None option from the Border list box, then choose OK.

There are two options in the Paragraph dialog box that we'll discuss in other parts of the book. The Style pull-down list box, which we'll discuss in Chapter 8, allows you to assign a named style to one or more paragraphs. We'll talk about the Line Numbering check box when we discuss line numbers in Chapter 16. Now, let's learn how to use the Tabs… button and the Tabs… command to control the tab stops in a paragraph.

Other Paragraph options

If you've used a typewriter or another word processor, you're probably familiar with tab stops, positions you set within the margins of a document for aligning text. Generally, tabs are used to create columnar text, such as tables and charts. On typewriters and in some word processors, you must also use tabs to create first-line or left indents. As you've already seen, however, Word handles indents with the indent markers on the ruler.

WORKING WITH TABS

In Word, you'll use tabs to create simple tables or to format documents that contain lists. When you need to create more complex tabular documents, you'll use Word's table feature, which allows you to do such things as wrap text within individual columns of a table. We'll look at this feature in detail in Chapter 11.

Working with tabs is a two-step process. First, specify your tab settings on the ruler, then use the [Tab] key to position text according to these settings. Each time you press the [Tab] key, Word will move the cursor to the next tab stop, creating a tab space. On your screen, a tab mark is designated by a right-pointing arrow (→).

If you press the [Tab] key without specifying any tab stops on the ruler, Word will use its default tab settings: left-aligned tab stops at every $1/2$ inch along the ruler. These default tab stops are indicated by inverted T marks (called tick marks) that hang below the ruler line (⊥). To change Word's default tab stops, choose the Document… command from the Format menu. In the Document dialog box, you'll see a text box labeled *Default Tab Stops*, with the setting *0.5″*. Enter a new tab interval that is less than the right edge of your text, and choose OK. For example, if you want default tab stops at every inch along the ruler, enter *1″* into the Default Tab Stops text box.

Default tab stops

When you need to use tabs, you probably won't want them to be spaced uniformly along the ruler line, as are Word's default tab stops. To set tabs at uneven intervals, you must create your own tab stops. Word allows you to create up to 50 tab stops for a single paragraph. When you create a tab stop, you can choose from four kinds of tab alignment: left, centered, right, and decimal. Table 5-4 shows the four tab-alignment icons that appear on the ruler. In a moment, we'll show you an example of each kind of tab alignment.

Creating, moving, and eliminating tab stops

Table 5-4

Icon	Alignment
↑	Left
↑	Centered
↑	Right
↑	Decimal

Word also lets you create tab leaders, which are a series of characters used to fill the tab space, such as a string of periods. As we'll show in a moment, you use the Tabs dialog box to specify a tab leader.

Manipulating tabs with the mouse

Before you create a tab stop, place the cursor on the paragraph you want to format. Next, use the mouse to click on the tab-alignment icon you want to use. When the appropriate icon is highlighted, click on the ruler at the position you want the tab to appear. For example, if you want to place a left-aligned tab at the 2-inch position on the ruler, first click on the Left-tab icon if it is not already selected, then click on the 2-inch position.

When you insert a tab on the ruler, Word will clear all default tab stops that appear to the left of the new tab. Continuing with our example, if you insert a tab at the 2-inch position, Word will delete the default tab stops at the $1/_2$-inch, 1-inch and $1^1/_2$-inch positions on the ruler. Word allows you to place tabs beyond the right indent marker and the dotted line that marks the right edge of the text on your page.

If you've already formatted the current paragraph by inserting tabs, Word will adjust the text in that paragraph according to the new tab stop(s) you create. Returning to our example, suppose that before you created the custom tab stop at the 2-inch position, you pressed the [Tab] key to move the text at the beginning of the current line to the first default tab stop at the $1/_2$-inch position. After you create the custom tab stop, Word will increase the tab space, moving the beginning of the line to the 2-inch position.

If you need to reposition a tab, use the mouse to point and click on the tab, and drag it to the new position. To clear a tab stop, drag the tab off the ruler.

Sometimes, when you're trying to insert a new tab stop very close to another one, Word will select the existing tab instead of inserting a new one. You can get around this problem by inserting the new tab in an empty area of the ruler and dragging it to the desired location.

Manipulating tabs with the keyboard

To create tabs using the keyboard, first press [Ctrl][Shift][F10] to activate the ruler. Then, using the arrow keys, position the ruler cursor where you want to create a tab stop. Next, press 1, 2, 3, or 4 to select the type of tab alignment you want to use: 1 for left-aligned, 2 for centered, 3 for right-aligned, and 4 for decimal. Word will highlight the appropriate icon on the ruler to show which type of alignment you've selected. Finally, press the [Insert] key to insert the tab on the ruler. The ruler will remain active so you can move the cursor to another position and create other tabs. When you press [Enter], Word will lock in your tab settings.

If you don't have a mouse, you can't move a tab by dragging it along the ruler. In order to move a tab, you must delete it and create a new one. To delete a tab, press [Ctrl][Shift][F10] to activate the ruler. Next, use the arrow keys to position the ruler cursor over the tab you want to delete, then press the [Delete] key. Pressing [Enter] will lock in the change.

Table 5-5 summarizes the keys you'll use to manipulate tab stops on the ruler. In a moment, we'll show you how to create, move, and eliminate tab stops using the Tabs dialog box. First, however, let's look at an example that illustrates how you might use tabs to create a simple table.

Table 5-5

This key...	has this effect...
1	selects the Left-tab icon or changes tab at ruler cursor position to have left alignment
2	selects the Centered-tab icon or changes tab at ruler cursor position to have centered alignment
3	selects the Right-tab icon or changes tab at ruler cursor position to have right alignment
4	selects the Decimal-tab icon or changes tab at ruler cursor position to have decimal alignment
[Insert]	inserts the selected tab type at the ruler cursor position
[Delete]	deletes tab at ruler cursor position
[Enter]	locks in new tab positions

Perhaps the easiest way to illustrate tabs is to work with a sample document like the one shown in Figure 5-34 on the next page. Although tables like this one require a little planning, they are not difficult to create. Let's walk through the process of building this table.

An example

Your first step is to decide how many columns you need and how much space you should allow for each column. The space required by each column depends on the size of the type you are using and the length of the entries in each column. To get your bearings, you may find it helpful to type the header line for the table and one or two sample lines. Don't worry about the proper ruler settings for now; just enter some sample text, pressing the [Tab] key at the end of each column to move to the next column. When you press the [Tab] key, Word will move your cursor to the next default tab stop.

Figure 5-34

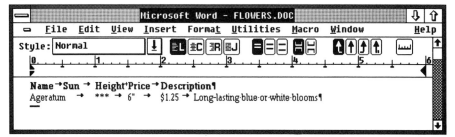

Name	Sun	Height	Price	Description
Ageratum	***	6"	$1.25	Long-lasting blue or white blooms
Alyssum	***	3"	.75	Great for rock gardens or borders
Aster	***	6" to 18"	$1.25	Blue, pink, or crimson blooms
Begonia	**	10" to 15"	$1.75	Easy to grow; blooms all summer
Caladium	*	8" to 20"	$1.99	Prefers humid climate and indirect sun
Calendula	**	12" to 15"	$1.99	Bright orange or yellow blooms
Candytuft	**	8"	.75	Hardy pink, white, or lavender blooms
Celosia	***	7" to 18"	$1.00	Feathery bright plumes
Cineraria	**	8" to 12"	$1.99	Blooms form colorful nosegays
Coleus	*	6" to 15"	$1.00	Beautiful multicolored leaves
Dahlia	**	12" to 20"	$2.25	Compact hardy growth; bright blooms
Fuchsia	*	12" to 20"	$2.75	Needs pampering, but well worth it!
Geranium	**	10" to 12"	$1.25	Long-time favorite for window boxes
Impatiens	**	12" to 20"	$1.00	Easy-care; blooms all summer
Marigold	***	18" to 20"	$1.25	Sturdy, bright blooms in lots of colors
Nasturtium	***	12" to 18"	$1.25	Cascades of sky-blue blooms
Pansy	**	7"	$1.75	Charming, delicate blooms; easy-care
Petunia	***	8" to 14"	$1.00	A window-box champion!
Phlox	**	7"	.75	Compact blooms; great ground cover
Portulaca	***	6"	$1.75	Roselike blooms; thrives in heat and sun
Snapdragon	***	12" to 20"	$1.75	Adds color and texture to any garden
Verbena	**	10"	$1.50	Brilliant colors; needs good drainage
Vinca	**	3" to 10"	.75	Fast-spreading hardy ground cover
Zinnia	***	10" to 18"	$1.75	A hardy sun-loving favorite

This table illustrates Word's four tab-alignment options.

Next, assign any character and paragraph formats to your text so you can get a feel for the amount of space required for each column. Figure 5-35 shows the first two lines of our table at this point. As you can see, our columns are not yet properly aligned because the entries in each line vary in length. As we pressed the [Tab] key, Word pushed each entry to the next $1/_2$-inch tab stop.

Figure 5-35

Microsoft Word - FLOWERS.DOC	⇩ ⇧
File Edit View Insert Format Utilities Macro Window	**Help**

Style: Normal

Name→Sun → Height'Price→Description¶
Ageratum → *** → 6" → $1.25 → Long-lasting·blue·or·white·blooms¶

Entering and formatting a few lines of sample text can help you determine the appropriate tab stops for a table.

After entering some sample text, you need to decide how you want to align and position the text in each column. Left-aligned tabs work best for text entries, like those in the first and fifth columns of our table. You can use a centered tab to align text or symbols, like those in the second column. To align a column of numbers, such as the third column of the table, use a right-aligned tab. When you're working with currency values, you may want to use decimal tabs to align the decimal points in each entry, as we've done in the fourth column.

In deciding where to position your tabs, try to allow enough room between each column to accommodate the longest entry in that column. For example, in the first column of our sample table, the word *Snapdragon* is our longest entry, extending almost to the 1-inch position. So, we decided to center our second column at the 1 $\frac{1}{8}$-inch position. Then, to position the third, fourth, and fifth columns, we used a right-aligned tab at the 2 $\frac{1}{4}$-inch position, a decimal tab at the 2 $\frac{7}{8}$-inch position, and a left-aligned tab at the 3 $\frac{1}{2}$-inch position. Figure 5-36 shows the results.

Figure 5-36

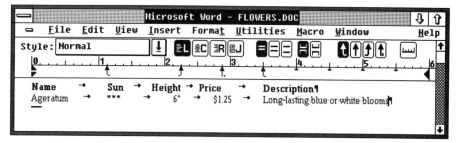

Position tab stops along the ruler according to the length and type of entries in each column.

If you use decimal tabs, you may have to make some adjustments to the header line of your table. As you can see in the Price column of Figure 5-36, our heading is not properly aligned with the subsequent currency values. When Word cannot locate a decimal point in a string of characters, it aligns the last character in that string flush right with the decimal tab stop.

To overcome this problem, we selected only the header line of the table and deleted the decimal tab at the 2 $\frac{7}{8}$-inch position. (Remember, to delete a tab with the mouse, point to the tab and drag it off the ruler. Using the keyboard, press [Ctrl][Shift][F10], move the ruler cursor to the tab, then press the [Delete] key.) Next, we added a right-aligned tab at the 3 $\frac{1}{16}$-inch position to reposition the fourth column of heading text. Figure 5-37 on the next page shows the result.

Once you have defined the width and alignment for each column in your table, you're ready to enter the remainder of your text. Notice that your ruler settings will carry over from one line to the next as you press the [Enter] key. So, once you have set up your tab stops, move the cursor just to the left of the ¶ mark at the end of the last line in your table, then press [Enter] to begin a new line.

If you need to adjust your tab stops later, highlight all the paragraphs in the table and move the tabs to new ruler positions. If you need to change a tab format, drag the old tab off the ruler, select the tab-alignment icon for the tab format you want to use, then click on the ruler again to specify the tab position. With the keyboard, you can press [Ctrl][Shift][F10] to activate the ruler, then move the ruler cursor to the tab whose alignment you want to change. Next, type the code for the alignment you want to use (1, 2, 3, or 4), and press [Enter] to lock in the change.

Figure 5-37

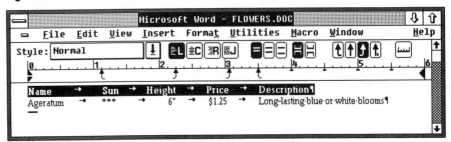

When you use a decimal tab, you may need to realign a line of text that does not have a decimal point, as we've done with the header line of this table.

The Tabs dialog box

So far, we've shown how you can use the ruler to create, move, and eliminate tab stops. The Tabs dialog box, shown in Figure 5-38, offers another way to manipulate tabs in your document. If you have a mouse, you'll probably find that it's more convenient to manipulate tabs by using the ruler. If you don't have a mouse, however, you may find that using the Tabs dialog box is easier. Regardless of whether you're using a mouse or the keyboard, the Tabs dialog box lets you do a couple of things that you cannot do with the ruler: position tabs more precisely and create tab leaders.

Figure 5-38

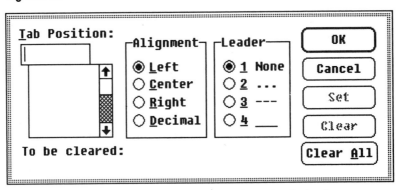

You can create, move, and delete tabs in the Tabs dialog box.

To open the Tabs dialog box, choose Tabs... from the Format menu. Alternatively, if you've already opened the Paragraph dialog box, you can select the Tabs... button to access this dialog box. Although you do not need to display the ruler on the screen in order to use the Tabs dialog box, you'll probably find it helpful to have the ruler in view as you work with tabs.

To create a tab stop using the Tabs dialog box, type the tab position in the Tab Position text box, then select the appropriate Alignment option, and choose the Set button. Like the Indents settings in the Paragraph dialog box, the tab position you enter can be expressed in inches (" or *in*), centimeters (*cm*), points (*pt*), or picas (*pi*). If you do not specify a unit of measure, Word will assume inches (or whatever unit of measure you're using on the ruler).

When you create a new tab stop, Word will add the tab position to the list box located just below the Tab Position text box. The Tabs dialog box will remain open, allowing you to create more tab stops or adjust existing ones. Since the position of the tab you create will appear in the Tab Position text box, you'll need to erase or edit the text box's contents before you can create a new tab. The tabs you create in the Tabs dialog box will not appear on the ruler until you choose OK to close the dialog box.

If you've already created some tab stops in the current paragraph, the positions of those tab stops will appear in the Tab Position list box when you open the Tabs dialog box. If you've selected text from two or more paragraphs that do not have identical tab settings, no tab stops will appear in the list box.

You can eliminate a tab stop by selecting it from the list (or typing its position in the text box) and choosing the Clear button. Word will then remove the tab stop from the list and display it next to the text that reads *To be cleared:*. If you decide that you don't want to delete a tab stop after all, you can choose the Cancel button. When you do this, however, Word will cancel all other actions you've taken while the Tabs dialog box has been open.

By the way, you can clear a tab stop and, while the Tabs dialog box is still open, recreate it. When you do this, the tab's position will still appear next to the *To be cleared:* notation, but Word will not remove the tab from the ruler when you close the dialog box.

You can remove all tab stops in the currently selected paragraph(s)—except the defaults—by choosing the Clear All button. When you do this, Word will remove all the custom tab positions from the list box and display the word *All* next to the *To be cleared:* notation. The tab stops won't actually be cleared until you choose OK. If you choose Cancel or press [Esc], however, Word will close the dialog box without eliminating the tab stops.

To change a tab's position, you must first clear the tab stop and then create a new one at the position you want. In the Tabs dialog box, you can specify a tab position with a great deal of precision—Word distinguishes tab positions to $1/_{100}$ of an inch.

Changing the alignment of a tab stop is even easier. Simply select from the list box the tab position you want to change. When you do this, Word will highlight the appropriate Alignment option for that tab. You can change the alignment by selecting a different option button and choosing Set. If you don't want to make further selections or changes in the Tabs dialog box, just choose OK.

Tab leader characters

As we've mentioned, the Tabs dialog box offers a way to create tab leaders quickly and easily. A tab leader is a character that's repeated on a line to fill in the space between columns of text. Tab leaders are often used to connect items in a table, guiding the reader from one column to the next. Word offers three kinds of tab leaders: periods, hyphens, and underline characters.

Figure 5-39 shows an example of a document that uses tab leaders. The periods help guide the reader's eye from the chapter names on the left to the page numbers on the right. We also used underline characters to help separate the different sections of the table.

Figure 5-39

CONTENTS

Section 1

Chapter 1	Worksheet Basics	3
Chapter 2	Formatting the Worksheet	25
Chapter 3	Editing the Worksheet	76
Chapter 4	Working with Windows	103

Section 2

Chapter 5	Built-in Functions	137
Chapter 6	Date and Time	165
Chapter 7	Other Worksheet Topics	200
Chapter 8	Printing the Worksheet	254

Section 3

Chapter 9	Basic Graphics Techniques	311
Chapter 10	Chart Formatting	349
Chapter 11	Advanced Charting Features	398

Section 4

Chapter 12	Database Management	444
Chapter 13	Working with a Database	490
Chapter 14	Sorting the Database	501

Section 5

Chapter 15	Macro Basics	555
Chapter 16	Command-Equivalent Functions	599
Chapter 17	User-Defined Functions	639

The periods help guide the reader from the chapter title column to the correct page number.

To add tab leaders, open the Tabs dialog box and select from the list box the tab-stop position where you want to create a leader. Then, choose one of the Leader options and choose Set. You can also specify a tab leader at the time you create a tab. After you type the tab position into the Tab Position text box and select an Alignment option, select the Leader option you want and choose Set.

If you're adding tab leaders to text you've already formatted with tabs, be sure to select the text before you open the Tabs dialog box. For example, suppose you have created a table of contents like the one shown in Figure 5-39, but you haven't yet inserted the tab leaders. Each of the lines on which a chapter name appears has a left-aligned tab at the $1^1/_2$-inch position and a right-aligned tab at the 6-inch position. To add the periods, select all the chapter names and page numbers in a section (for example, Chapters 1, 2, 3, and 4), then choose the Tabs... command. In the Tabs dialog box, select the 6" tab position from the list box, select the second leader option (...), and choose Set. When you choose OK, Word will insert the periods in your text, as shown in Figure 5-40. You follow a similar procedure to create the leaders for the rest of the table.

Figure 5-40

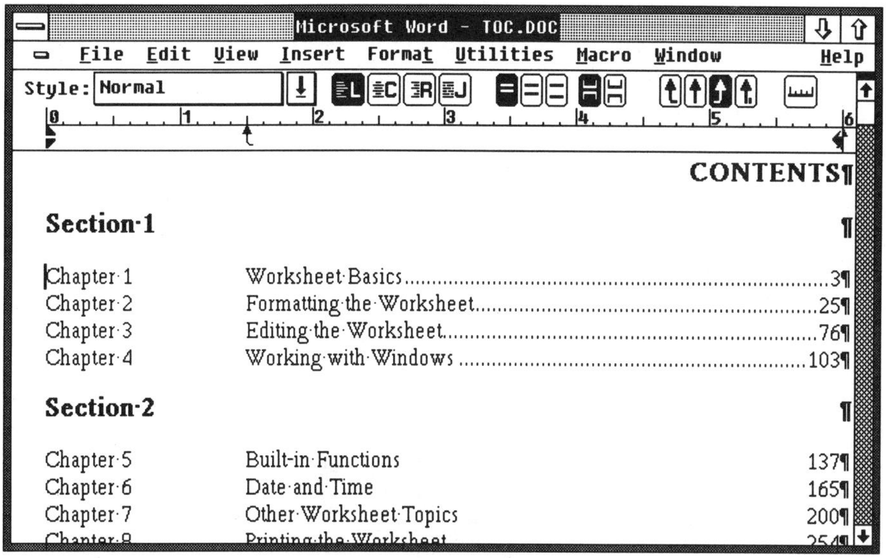

Microsoft Word - TOC.DOC

File   Edit   View   Insert   Format   Utilities   Macro   Window   Help

Style: Normal

CONTENTS¶

Section·1 ¶

Chapter·1	Worksheet·Basics	3¶
Chapter·2	Formatting·the·Worksheet	25¶
Chapter·3	Editing·the·Worksheet	76¶
Chapter·4	Working·with·Windows	103¶

Section·2 ¶

Chapter·5	Built-in·Functions	137¶
Chapter·6	Date·and·Time	165¶
Chapter·7	Other·Worksheet·Topics	200¶
Chapter·8	Printing·the·Worksheet	254¶

This is how the tab leaders will look on your screen.

As Figure 5-39 illustrates, you also can use a tab leader to create a horizontal line in your document. For example to create the line beside each section name, place the cursor on one of the section names and insert a left-aligned tab at the $1^1/_2$-inch position. Then, insert a right-aligned tab at the 6-inch position. The first

Using a tab leader to create a line

tab marks the start of the line where the leader characters will begin, and the second tab marks the end of the line. Now, while the cursor is still on the section-name paragraph, open the Tabs dialog box and select the 6" tab position from the list box. Then, choose the fourth Leader option (___) and choose Set.

After you close the Tabs dialog box, the horizontal line won't appear in your document until you press the [Tab] key. With the cursor positioned just after the section name, press the [Tab] key twice. The first time you press [Tab], Word will move the cursor to the first tab stop, which has no leader. When you press [Tab] again, Word will move the cursor to the second tab stop at the 6-inch position and will, at the same time, use the underline characters to fill in the space between the first and second tabs.

CHARACTER FORMATTING

We have now examined two formatting levels in Word: document-level formatting (which includes page layout) and paragraph-level formatting. Let's now look at the last formatting level in our top-down scheme of document design: character formatting.

When you format characters in your Word document, you need to make a number of decisions about how those characters will look: the font you want to use; the size of the characters; special emphasis, like bold, italics, and underlining; the position of those characters in relation to each other; and the amount of space between characters. In this section, we'll show you how to control these factors.

In most cases, you will select the text you want to work with before you apply character formats. All character formatting options—as the name implies—are applied on a character-by-character basis. Therefore, the text you format can be as small as a single character or as large as your entire document. Word will format only the text that is highlighted.

As you enter new text in a Word document, it will take on the formatting characteristics as the text immediately preceding it. For example, if you move the cursor to the middle of a line of text that is formatted in 18-point bold type, any new characters you type at that point will appear in 18-point bold as well. If you want to change formats in midstream, you can choose new formatting options without selecting any text. Word will apply those formats to the cursor. Then, as you begin typing, the text will appear with the formatting characteristics you have chosen. Those characteristics won't change unless you apply new formats or move the cursor to another part of your document.

Before we launch into the many character formatting options available in Word, let's consider a few typographical terms and concepts that will help you understand and apply character formats.

The language of type

As you've seen, Word's default character format is 10-point Tms Rmn. However, we've never really explained what this designation means. In this section, we'll briefly explore the concepts of fonts, point size, serifs, letter spacing, and line spacing.

In typographer's terms, a font is defined as a collection of type of one size and face. The term *face* refers to style elements like bold, italic, and so forth. Therefore, 18-point Tms Rmn type and 12-point Tms Rmn type are considered different fonts. Similarly, 18-point Tms Rmn bold type is considered a different font from 18-point Tms Rmn italic type. Though all of these faces are part of the same type family, each is defined as a distinct font.

In Word terminology, however, different point sizes and styles do not constitute different fonts. Instead, each family of type, with all its associated formatting options, is considered part of the same font. Therefore, 18-point Tms Rmn, 10-point Tms Rmn, 12-point Tms Rmn bold, and 12-point Tms Rmn italic are considered formatting variations of the same font—Tms Rmn. Choosing a font is, theoretically, a separate formatting decision from choosing a size and style. However, depending on the printer you have chosen, you probably will be limited to certain sizes for each font.

The issue of fonts can get pretty complicated, since it involves both hardware and software considerations. We'll talk more about fonts later in this chapter and in Chapter 7.

Fonts

You may also have wondered what the numeric point size specifications actually represent. It's not too hard to figure out that 18-point type is larger than 10-point, but what do these point sizes really mean?

In typography, a point is the unit used to measure the height of a character. A point is $\frac{1}{12}$ of a pica. If that doesn't help much, then you should also know that a pica is $\frac{1}{6}$ of an inch. Therefore, there are 72 points to an inch. (One point equals $\frac{1}{12} \times \frac{1}{6}$, or $\frac{1}{72}$ of an inch.) In other words, if you select a block of text and tell Word to display it in 72-point type, the characters you have selected will be 1 inch high. Similarly, if you specify 36 points, your type will be $\frac{1}{2}$ inch high; if you specify 18 points, your type will be $\frac{1}{4}$ of an inch high, and so forth.

Of course, not every letter in the alphabet is of the same height. The letter *b* is almost twice as high as the letter *e*. So how do point sizes relate to the height of any given letter in your text? Let's back up a step and introduce three new terms: ascender, descender, and x-height. As Figure 5-41 illustrates, the x-height represents the height of the "body" of the letter. Ascenders and descenders extend above and below the x-height of the letter.

Point sizes

Figure 5-41

48 points — abcdefgh — Ascender / X-Height / Descender

Point size is measured from the top of the letter's ascender to the bottom of its descender.

In typography, the height of a letter is determined by the distance from the bottom of the lowest descender to the top of the highest ascender. Therefore, the height of a letter in your document will depend on whether that letter has an ascender or descender. Even when you specify 36 points for your type, the typeface of any given letter might be only 30 points high. The remaining height is dedicated to the ascending and descending strokes, like the ascending vertical bars in the letters *h* and *k* and the descending strokes in the letters *g* and *q*.

The x-height of letters of the same point size and a different font may also vary significantly. (The x-height is equal to the distance between the mean line and the base line, the two gray lines that appear above and below the bodies of the letters in Figure 5-41.) For example, Table 5-6 shows the letters *h* and *g* in several typefaces. All the letters in this table appear in 18-point plain style. As you can see, however, even though the overall height of the letters is the same, the x-height of the letters varies significantly, depending on the emphasis given to ascenders and descenders.

Table 5-6

Tms Rmn	Helv	Palatino	Courier	Avant Garde
hg	hg	hg	hg	hg

Serifs

An important design decision in formatting a document is whether to use serif type. Serifs are the short crosslines that appear at the ends of the main strokes of a letter. Typefaces that use these crosslines are called serif fonts; those that do not are called sans serif fonts.

In Table 5-6, Tms Rmn, Palatino, and Courier are serif fonts; Helv and Avant Garde are sans serif fonts. Figure 5-42 shows a close-up of the letter *K* in Tms Rmn font with the serifs circled.

Generally, you'll find that either serif or sans serif type works fine for display type, such as headings. Studies have shown, however, that serif type is more readable in the body of a document because the serifs help the reader easily distinguish characters and words. They also add "horizontal stability," establishing a flow from left to right across a line of text.

Letter spacing

Word lets you manually control the amount of space between letters. You can adjust the letter spacing to open up crowded lines of text or to help balance two or more blocks of text. In typographer's terms, tightening the space between letters to achieve a more visually pleasing effect is called kerning. You sometimes may hear references to tighter kerning (less space between letters) or looser kerning (more space between letters).

Figure 5-42

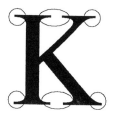

Serifs are the short crosslines at the ends of the main strokes of a letter.

Another factor that affects letter spacing is whether the font you choose is proportional or non-proportional—that is, whether the widths of the letters vary. In proportional fonts (also called variable-pitch fonts), the amount of horizontal space assigned to a letter varies according to the width of that letter. In non-proportional fonts (also called fixed-pitch fonts), every letter is assigned the same amount of space. Typewriters and daisy-wheel printers generally use non-proportional spacing. Therefore, even though the letters *i* and *l* are much narrower than the letters *m* and *w*, all four letters would occupy the same amount of space on the page when printed in a non-proportional font.

Table 5-7 on the following page shows some examples of proportional and non-proportional fonts. Generally, we think you'll find that a proportional font lends a more polished and professional appearance to a document. The two non-proportional fonts listed are included primarily for users whose printers cannot print proportionally spaced letters.

Line spacing, also referred to as leading, is similar to letter spacing except it applies to the vertical spacing between lines of type rather than the horizontal spacing between individual letters within a line.

Line spacing

Generally, Word considers line spacing to be a paragraph formatting feature. That is, the line spacing you select applies to an entire paragraph. You can, however, change the vertical position of one or more letters in a paragraph by applying the superscript and subscript formats. We'll look at superscripting and subscripting later in this section.

Now, let's apply these basic elements of typography to a Word document. The simplest way to format characters is to select a font, size, or style from the ribbon. To display the ribbon, choose Ribbon from the View menu. If you're displaying a ruler, Word will position the ribbon just above it.

The ribbon

Table 5-7

Proportional

Tms Rmn	Helv	Palatino	Helv Condensed
iwiw	iwiw	iwiw	iwiw
wiwi	wiwi	wiwi	wiwi

Non-proportional

Courier	Prestige Elite
iwiw	iwiw
wiwi	wiwi

As you can see in Figure 5-43, the ribbon contains a bar of icons and two pull-down list boxes. You can use these elements to select character formatting options and examine the formatting features that are in effect for the current text selection. As you'll see a little later in this chapter, you also can use the Character dialog box to select all the character formatting options on the ribbon, as well as additional formatting options.

Figure 5-43

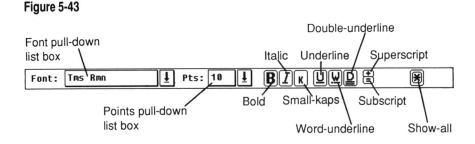

You can use the ribbon to apply character formatting features.

We'll use the document in Figure 5-44 to show you how to apply character formats from the ribbon. This document currently is formatted in 12-point Courier type. Suppose we decide to display the first line of this document (the title) in 12-point Helv bold type. We'll begin by selecting the title text, pulling down the Font list box on the ribbon, and choosing Helv. Next, we'll click on the Bold icon (🅱) or press [Ctrl]B to apply boldfacing. Figure 5-45 on the following page shows the results. (Depending on the printer you have installed and selected, you may not have 12-point Helv type available in Word.)

Figure 5-44

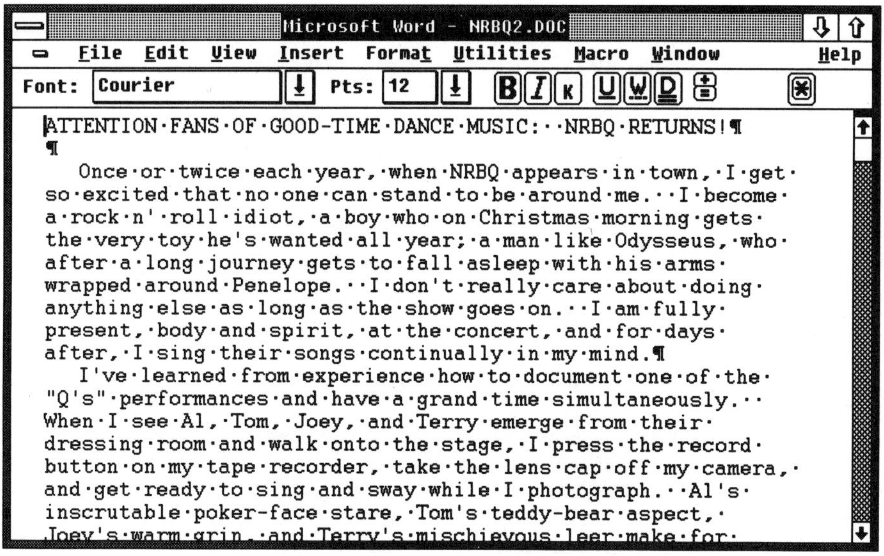

This sample document initially appears in 12-point Courier type.

Now, let's format the body of our document in 10-point Tms Rmn type. After selecting all the text below the title line, we'll pull down the Font list box and select Tms Rmn. Then, with the text still selected, we'll pull down the Points list box and choose 10. Figure 5-46 on the next page shows the results. (Again, depending on your hardware configuration, you may not have 10-point Tms Rmn available in your Points and Font list boxes.)

Notice that our line breaks have changed because we have selected a different font. Since our characters are now a different size, Word automatically reflowed the text within our document margins.

Figure 5-45

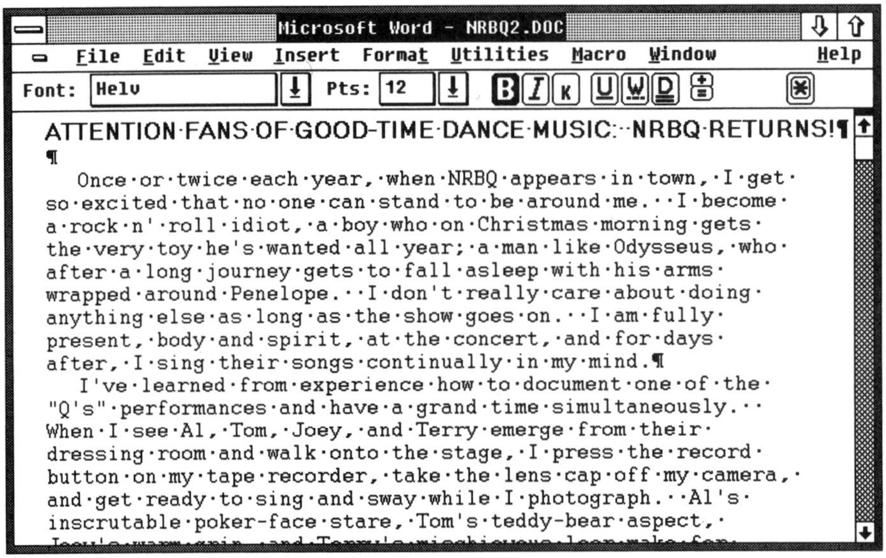

We've used the ribbon to assign 12-point Helv bold type to the first line of our document.

Figure 5-46

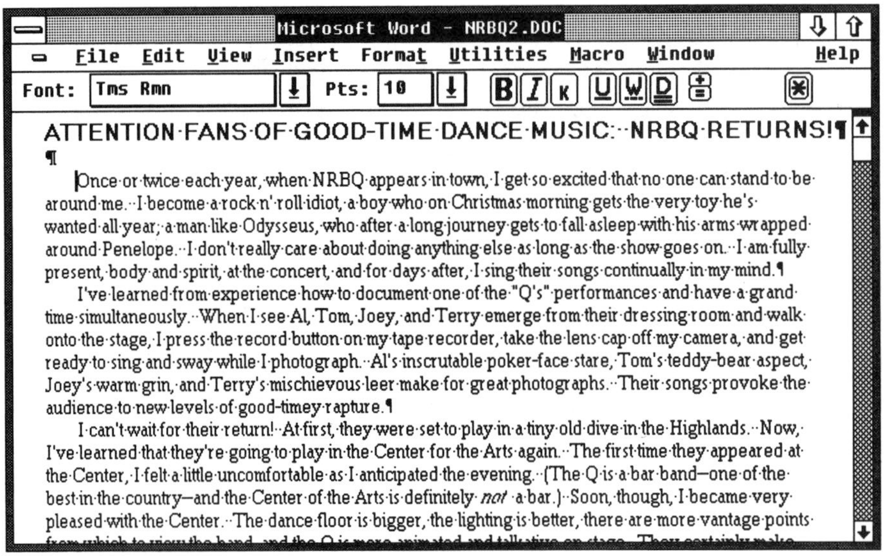

We've assigned 10-point Tms Rmn plain type to the body text in our document.

The example we just presented should give you a good idea of how the ribbon works. You just select the text you want to format and choose your formatting options from the ribbon. In addition to the Font list box, the Points list box, and the Bold icon, the ribbon includes icons for creating italic text, small capitals, underlined text, text with words underlined (not spaces), and text with double underlining. There are also icons for creating superscript and subscript text. Table 5-8 lists the formatting icons on the ribbon.

Table 5-8

This icon...	creates...
[B]	bold text
[I]	italic text
[K]	small kaps
[U]	underlining
[W]	word underlining
[D]	double underlining
[+]	superscript text
[=]	subscript text

If you're using a mouse, you can choose most of the formatting options on the ribbon by clicking on an icon. If you're using the keyboard, you can select these options by pressing the appropriate key combinations shown in Table 5-9 on page 140.

You can apply more than one formatting characteristic to the same text selection. For example, to create bold italic text, select both the Bold icon and the Italic icon. The three underlining options, on the other hand, are mutually exclusive. For example, if you apply double underlining, you cannot apply plain underlining or word underlining without "turning off" double underlining. Figure 5-47 on the next page shows some samples of printed text with various combinations of formatting. We printed this text on an HP Laserjet printer and used 12-point Tms Rmn font.

You also can use the ribbon to "turn off" a particular formatting characteristic. First, select the text whose format you want to change, then click on the icon for the format you want to remove. For instance, suppose you've formatted some text in both bold and italic. If you want to remove the boldfacing and retain the italic formatting, select the text and click on the Bold icon to deselect it.

Figure 5-47

This sentence appears in 12-point Tms Rmn Plain type.
You can use **boldface** to emphasize words.
Similarly, you can *italicize* words that require special attention.
If you want, you can apply SMALL KAPS formatting.

You can abbreviate the number 1,000,000 with the notation 10^6
Getting thirsty? Have a little H_2O.

You can combine various character format options to create all kinds of interesting effects.

The Character dialog box

Although the ribbon offers the easiest way to apply most character formats, there will be times when you need to access formatting options that are not available on the ribbon. That's when you'll use the Character… command on the Format menu to open the Character dialog box shown in Figure 5-48.

Figure 5-48

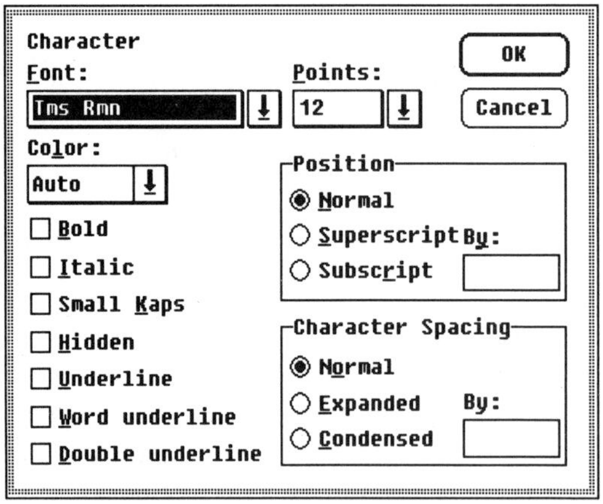

You can use the Character dialog box to apply character formatting.

The first two items in the Character dialog box should look familiar. The contents of the pull-down list boxes for fonts and point sizes are identical to the ones on the ribbon.

Just under the Font list box, you'll see a pull-down list box labeled *Color.* This feature allows you to assign color to your text—something you can't do from the ribbon. The Character dialog box also contains check-box options for seven other formatting features (your Word manual calls them "emphases"). All of these features, with the exception of Hidden, are represented as icons on the ribbon.

The Position options allow you to assign superscripting and subscripting. Unlike the ribbon, however, the Character dialog box lets you specify how many points you want to superscript or subscript text. The Character Spacing options in the lower-right corner of the dialog box let you adjust the spacing between characters, creating expanded and condensed text. This option also cannot be applied from the ribbon.

The options available in the Font and Points list boxes depend on the printer you have installed and selected. In general, Word will not include in these list boxes any font or point size that your printer is not capable of producing on paper. For example, if you have installed and selected an IBM Proprinter, your Font list box will include several variations of Courier, plus Helv, Modern, Preview, Roman, Script, Symbol, System, and Tms Rmn. On the other hand, if you have installed and selected an HP LaserJet printer (the original LaserJet with no cartridge capability), your Font list box will include only Courier, Modern, Roman, and Script. (In Chapter 7, we'll explain how to install and select different printers. If you are interested in knowing how to access more fonts and point sizes, you may want to skip ahead to that chapter.)

Fonts and point sizes

After you have selected a font, you can pull down the Points list box to see one or more sizes listed for that font. These are the standard sizes for the selected font. Although you can use a size other than one of the standard sizes (by typing a size in the Points box), the results will be unpredictable. In some cases, your printer will substitute a standard point size for the non-standard size you specified. If the font you have chosen is one of the Windows stroke fonts—Modern, Roman, or Script—your printer must enter a graphics mode in order to print the characters. While in graphics mode, your printer can create characters of non-standard size, but they probably will not be very attractive. In general, therefore, we recommend that you stick with the standard sizes offered in the Points list box.

If you're using a printer that is equipped with PostScript capabilities, you will have much more flexibility in specifying different sizes. PostScript printers are able to create different point sizes as they print.

Word may not be able to display your text in all the fonts available to your printer. Unless you purchase and install additional screen fonts, Word will be able to display only six fonts on your screen: Courier, Helv, Modern, Roman, Script, and Tms Rmn. (Some printers will also allow you to display text in the System and Terminal fonts. System is the font you see in your various screen items, such as menus and dialog boxes, and the Terminal font is used by the Windows Terminal application.) If you want to use optional screen fonts, you'll need to purchase and install those fonts separately from Word. For information on optional screen fonts, contact your local computer dealer.

Font substitution

If you select a printer font that does not correspond to one of Windows' screen fonts, Windows will substitute one of its screen fonts that most closely matches the font you have selected. For example, if you have installed and selected the HP LaserJet Series II printer, one of the fonts available in the Font list box will be LinePrinter. If you use this font to format some text, Word will substitute Courier in your screen display.

Even if the font you have chosen corresponds to one of the standard Windows screen fonts, there still may be some differences between the way your printer prints that font and the way that font looks on your screen. These differences can cause your printed document to have different line breaks and line spacing from the text that you see on your screen. For example, many printers offer a Times Roman font that is similar to (but not exactly like) the Windows Tms Rmn font. Since Word can display only Windows' Tms Rmn font, that's what you'll see on your screen. In most cases, this will present no problems at all. Sometimes, however, your printed document may not *exactly* match your screen display.

When Windows makes a font substitution, you no longer have true WYSIWYG (What You See Is What You Get) operation in Word. Word attempts to diminish this problem by offering a Display as Printed option. When you select Preferences... from the View menu, Word will open the Preferences dialog box, which includes a check box labeled *Display as Printed.* When you select this check box, Word will not necessarily allow you to see on screen every font your printer can produce. It will, however, let you see how your printer will handle line spacing and line breaks for any fonts that cannot be displayed on your screen. For example, in Figure 5-49, we've formatted our text in the LinePrinter font and deselected the Display as Printed check box. Since Word cannot display LinePrinter on the screen, this text appears in the Courier font.

Figure 5-49

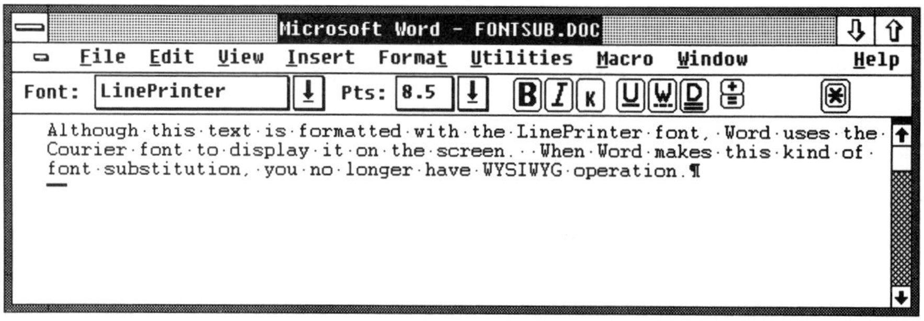

Although this text is formatted in the LinePrinter font, Word substitutes the Courier font in the screen display.

Figure 5-50 shows what happened after we selected the Display as Printed check box. Notice that Word has extended each line of text beyond the right margin. This does not mean that our margins or the width of our text area have changed in any way. It simply means that, when we print this document, we'll be able to fit more characters on each line, since LinePrinter is a more compact font than the Courier font Word has used as a substitute in the screen display. Figure 5-51 shows the printed text.

Figure 5-50

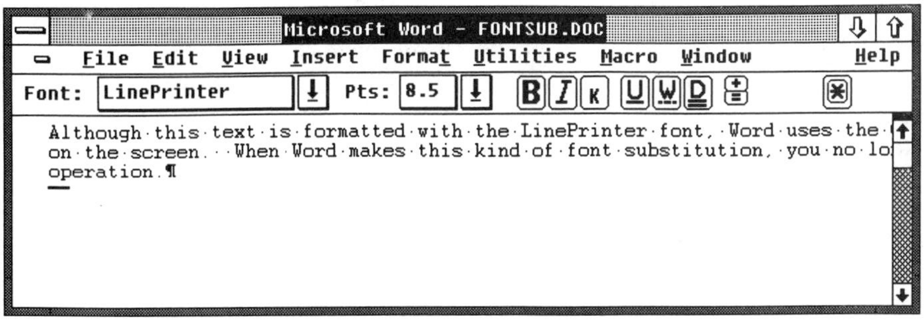

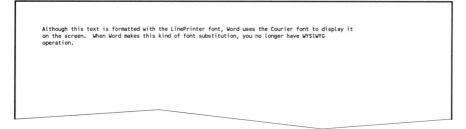

After we selected the Display as Printed check box, Word changed the line breaks in our document to show how they would occur when we printed.

Figure 5-51

Although this text is formatted with the LinePrinter font, Word uses the Courier font to display it
on the screen. When Word makes this kind of font substitution, you no longer have WYSIWYG
operation.

This is how the document in Figures 5-49 and 5-50 will appear when it is printed.

As you might guess, selecting the Display as Printed check box can make it more difficult to work with some documents. For instance, in Figure 5-50, you cannot see the right edge of each line of text without scrolling. Although this will not always be the case, we recommend that you try using the Display as Printed option to see how it affects your screen display. If Display as Printed makes it a nuisance to scroll parts of your document into view, you should turn it off until you're ready to print. Then, you may want to activate this option in order to check for awkward line and page breaks.

Matching screen fonts to printer fonts

You can use special utility programs to create Windows screen fonts that match any of the soft fonts available for the HP LaserJet printers. In addition, you can obtain Windows screen fonts to match any of the printer fonts that are resident in PostScript printers and PostScript adapter boards, such as QMS's JetScript adapter. For more information on Windows screen fonts, contact your local computer vendor.

Character styles

You've already seen how you can apply special formatting options, such as bold, italic, and underlining, from the ribbon. To apply these features from the Character dialog box, select the check box next to the appropriate item. Since check-box options are not mutually exclusive, you can apply almost any combination of formatting features you want. However, Word limits you to only one underline option at a time. You can activate the Underline, Word Underline, or Double Underline option along with any of the other style options, but you cannot activate more than one of the underline options.

Hidden text

Although the Hidden option is grouped with the other character styles, this feature is really in a category by itself. Hidden text is designed primarily for allowing you to conceal special items, such as index notations and confidential information. However, you also might use it to hide questions, notes, or other temporary text you've inserted into your document.

The Hidden option offers a way to vary the content of a document. For example, in our sample announcement in Figure 5-52, we added a new paragraph regarding complimentary tickets for the upcoming concert. We plan to send these complimentary tickets to selected persons on our mailing list. One way to vary the content of the document for other readers is to hide the optional paragraph when we don't need it. To do this, we would select the optional paragraph, open the Character dialog box, select the Hidden check box, then choose OK.

The Hidden Text check box in the Preferences dialog box controls the way Word displays hidden text in your document. If you select this check box, Word will place a dotted line below the document's hidden text, as shown in Figure 5-52. To suppress the display of hidden text, deselect the Hidden Text check box. (Make sure that the Show All check box is deselected as well.) When you suppress the display of hidden text, it will disappear from your screen, but will remain in your document "behind the scenes." Figure 5-53 shows the document from Figure 5-52 after we've hidden the optional paragraph. Notice that Word not only hid the text but also closed up the surrounding space so that there is no clue to where the hidden text was displayed.

You can redisplay hidden text by reissuing the Preferences… command and selecting the Hidden Text or Show All check box. You also can bring hidden text into view by selecting the Show-all icon (▣) at the right edge of the ribbon. Of course, this will also bring into view other special marks on your screen, such as paragraph, tab, and space marks.

Figure 5-52

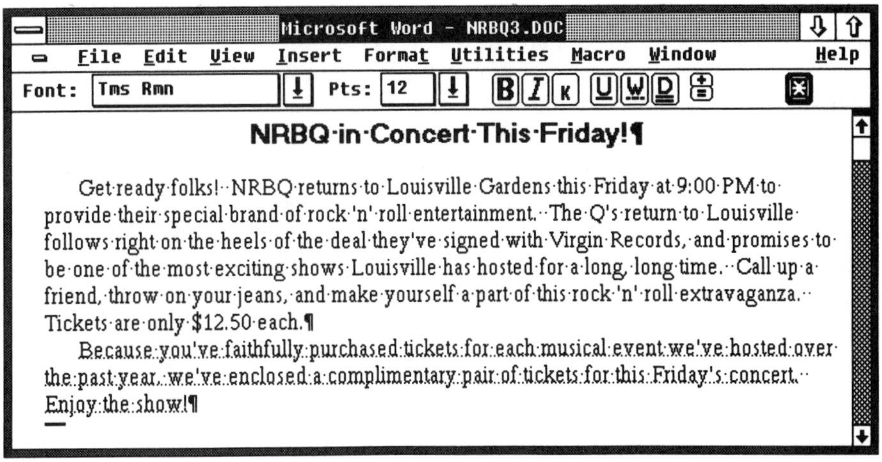

Since the last paragraph in this document is optional, we assigned it the hidden format.

Figure 5-53

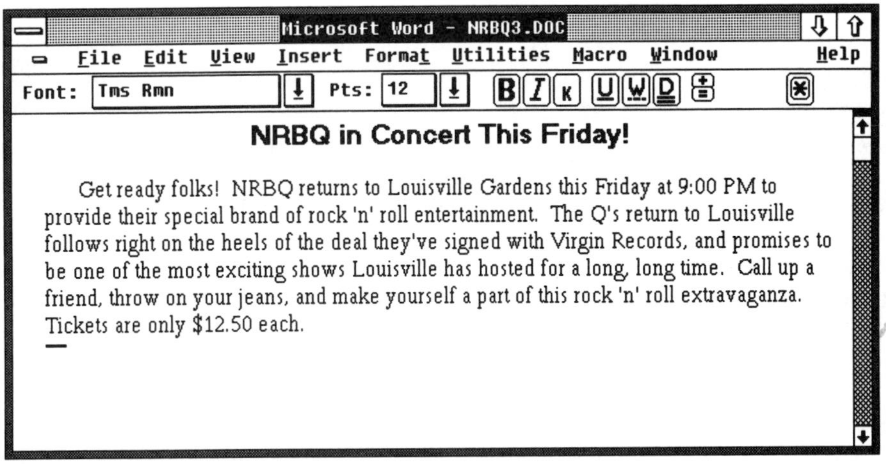

To suppress the display of hidden text, deselect the Hidden Text check box in the Preferences dialog box.

When we discuss printing in Chapter 7, we'll show you how to suppress hidden text in your printed documents. It's important to note that Word allows you to separately control the display of hidden text on your screen and in your printed documents.

Color

You can apply one of eight colors to a text selection. When Auto (the default Color choice) is in effect, Word will use the color you selected for your window text in the Windows Control Panel (probably black).

Using different colors throughout a document allows you to do such things as flagging text or emphasizing words or phrases. As we'll explain in the next chapter, Word lets you search for text of a particular color. Therefore, you might use the same color for certain items in a document—such as all proper names— and later use the Search… command to locate those items.

Of course, you must have a color monitor in order to see different colors of text on your screen. If you don't have a color monitor, you can still assign different colors in the Character dialog box. Those colors won't show up until you view your document on a color monitor or print it with a color printer.

To change the color of some text, select it, open the Character dialog box, pull down the Color list box, and choose the color you want to use: Black, Blue, Cyan, Green, Magenta, Red, Yellow, or White. When you choose OK, Word will change the color of the text you've selected. While the text is highlighted, however, it will not appear in the color you selected. Instead, it will appear in a contrasting color. For example, if you choose Green in the Character dialog box, Word will display the formatted text in magenta while it's highlighted.

Position

In Table 5-8, we've already shown how you can use the Superscript and Subscript icons on the ribbon to raise or lower a character's position. Superscripting and subscripting are used most commonly for mathematical notations like exponents and fractions. However, you may also be able to find more creative applications for these options.

When you use either the Superscript or Subscript icon on the ribbon, you cannot control the amount of space Word will superscript or subscript your text. Word will always superscript or subscript characters by 3 points. In the Character dialog box, however, Word lets you specify exactly how many points you want to superscript or subscript. Next to the Superscript and Subscript options, you'll see a text box labeled *By*. When you select either the Superscript or Subscript option, Word will display the default *3pt* in this text box. You can change this setting to anything from 0 to 63.5 points for superscripting and from 0 to 64 points for subscripting.

Word may have to adjust your line spacing to prevent the superscript and subscript characters from overlapping preceding or succeeding lines of text. Adding a 3-point superscript to a line of text will have the same effect as using a point size that is 3 points larger than the rest of the text on the line. If you find the change in line spacing unattractive, you may be able to reduce the size of the superscript or subscript characters. For example, Figure 5-54 shows some text that includes a mathematical expression. We reduced the point size of the superscripted and subscripted characters to keep our line spacing uniform and to give the formula a more polished appearance.

Figure 5-54

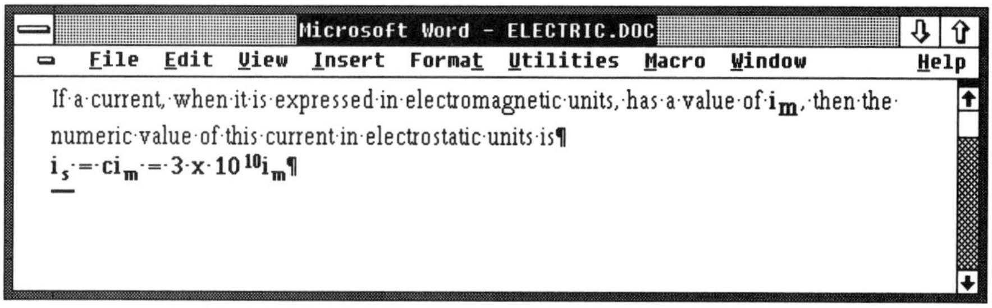

Microsoft Word - ELECTRIC.DOC
File Edit View Insert Format Utilities Macro Window Help
If a current, when it is expressed in electromagnetic units, has a value of i_m, then the numeric value of this current in electrostatic units is¶
$i_s = ci_m = 3 \times 10^{10} i_m$¶

You can reduce the size of superscripted and subscripted characters to help maintain uniform line spacing.

Character spacing

The Character Spacing options in the Character dialog box allow you to alter the kerning or amount of space between selected characters. To increase the amount of space between characters, select the characters you want to format, open the Character dialog box, then choose the Expanded option. Word will then activate the By text box, displaying *3pt*. This tells you that Word will add 3 points to the normal letter spacing. You can expand your letter spacing by a different amount by entering a value from 0 to 14 (points) in the By text box. If you use a decimal value, Word may round your By setting somewhat.

Similarly, if you want to decrease the amount of space between characters, select the characters you want to format, open the Character dialog box, and choose the Condensed option. Word will display its default value, *1.5pt* in the By text box. You can change this to anything from 0 to 1.75 points. Again, if you enter a decimal value, Word may round your By setting slightly.

Figure 5-55 shows the effects of Normal, Expanded, and Condensed spacing on 14-point Tms Rmn type.

Figure 5-55

Microsoft Word - LSPACING.DOC
File Edit View Insert Format Utilities Macro Window Help
This is Normal character spacing
This is Expanded character spacing
This is Condensed character spacing

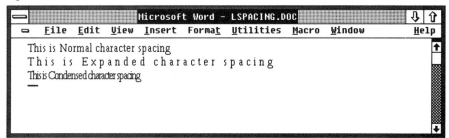

The Normal, Expanded, and Condensed options control the amount of space between characters.

Character formatting shortcuts

In addition to the ruler and Character dialog box, Word gives you a number of keyboard shortcuts for formatting characters. To use these shortcuts, press [Ctrl] as you press the appropriate key.

For example, to subscript a block of characters, you can press [Ctrl]=. To assign italics, press [Ctrl]I. To remove all character formatting, press [Ctrl][Spacebar]. Table 5-9 summarizes the common [Ctrl] key shortcuts you can use to format characters in Word.

In order to use three of the shortcuts in this table, you must take additional steps. If you press [Ctrl]F or [Ctrl]P, Word will highlight either the Font or Points text boxes on the ribbon. If the ribbon is not displayed, Word will present the prompt *Which font name?* in the status bar when you press [Ctrl]F, or the prompt *Which font size?* when you press [Ctrl]P. In response to these prompts, you can type a font name or size, or press ↑ or ↓ to cycle through Word's list of available options. To lock in your selection, press [Enter]. If you press [Ctrl]V, Word will display the prompt *Which color?* in the status bar. In response, you should type the name of the color you want to assign to the selected text, then press [Enter].

Table 5-9

Press...	to assign this format...
[Ctrl]B	bold
[Ctrl]I	italic
[Ctrl]K	small kaps
[Ctrl]U	underlining
[Ctrl]W	word underlining
[Ctrl]D	double underlining
[Ctrl]+	superscripting
[Ctrl]=	subscripting
[Ctrl]F	font
[Ctrl]H	hidden
[Ctrl][Spacebar]	plain
[Ctrl]P	point size
[Ctrl]V	color

USING SPECIAL CHARACTERS

In this chapter, we've shown how you can control the formatting of individual characters in a document. Word also offers several special characters that can be helpful as you're formatting a document, including non-breaking spaces, optional hyphens, non-breaking hyphens, and smart quotes.

Non-breaking spaces

A non-breaking space is a space Word treats like a character. If you place a non-breaking space (or several non-breaking spaces) between two words, Word will not split those words at the end of a line. As far as Word can tell, the two words and the non-breaking space are a single unit.

To create a non-breaking space, press [Ctrl][Shift][Spacebar]. If you are displaying space marks on your screen, each non-breaking space will look like a degree character (°) on your screen. Of course, these special characters will not appear in your printed document; instead, Word will print a blank space.

Non-breaking spaces can be useful when you want to keep two or more words together on the same line. For example, when you enter a date like *July 23, 1990*, in a document, it's a good idea to enter non-breaking spaces between *July* and *23* and before the year *1990*. You also might use non-breaking spaces between the different portions of a multipart number, such as a social security number, between a person's first name and middle initial, and between the words that comprise a single proper noun, such as New York.

One important characteristic of a non-breaking space is that it always has a specific width. You may have noticed that the width of a regular space may vary in a justified paragraph as Word increases or decreases the space between words to keep the left and right margins aligned. A non-breaking space, on the other hand, is always about the width of a lowercase *n*. (Word adjusts the width of non-breaking spaces according to the point size you have selected for your text and any character formatting you may have assigned. For instance, a non-breaking space that appears in the middle of a line of bold text will be slightly larger than one that falls in the middle of plain text.)

Hyphens

In addition to a regular hyphen, Word offers an optional hyphen and a non-breaking hyphen. For the most part, Word treats a regular hyphen, which you enter by pressing the - ([hyphen]) key, like any other character in your document. If the hyphenated word falls at the end of a line, however, Word will split that word between two lines. All the characters to the left of the hyphen and the hyphen itself will appear on the first line, and the characters to the right of the hyphen will wrap to the beginning of the next line.

Optional hyphens

As the name implies, an optional hyphen appears only when the hyphenated word is broken at the end of a line. When you use the Hyphenate… command on the Utilities menu to insert hyphens automatically, Word will insert only optional hyphens. (We'll discuss the Hyphenate… command in Chapter 6.) If you want to create an optional hyphen manually, press the [Ctrl] key as you type the hyphen. To display optional hyphens on your screen, choose Preferences… from the View menu and select either the Optional Hyphens or Show All check box. Alternatively, you can select the Show-all icon on the ribbon. Optional hyphens are displayed on the screen as ¬. When you choose not to display optional hyphens, Word will completely remove them from your screen unless one of the optional hyphens occurs at a line break. In that case, it will look exactly like a regular hyphen and will appear on the screen regardless of whether you've chosen to show optional hyphens.

We recommend that you use an optional hyphen whenever you hyphenate a word at the end of a line. That way, if you later revise your document so that the word does *not* fall at the end of a line, Word will not hyphenate the word in the middle of a line.

Non-breaking hyphens

A non-breaking hyphen is similar to a non-breaking space. If you hyphenate a word, such as *great-grandfather*, and it occurs at the end of a line, Word may break the word at the hyphen. If you don't want a word to break at the hyphen, you should use a non-breaking hyphen. For example, suppose you are writing about the software program Lotus 1-2-3. To prevent Word from breaking 1-2-3 at the end of a line, you should always use non-breaking hyphens between the *1* and *2* and between the *2* and *3*.

To create a non-breaking hyphen, press the [Ctrl] and [Shift] keys as you type a hyphen. Non-breaking hyphens are always visible on your screen, though they appear slightly longer than regular hyphens when you select the Show-all icon or the Optional Hyphens check box. To display non-breaking hyphens as regular hyphens, deselect the Show-all icon and turn off the Optional Hyphens check box in the Preferences dialog box. Of course, on your print-outs, non-breaking hyphens will look just like regular hyphens.

Smart quotes, em dashes, and en dashes

In addition to the character we've discussed, Word lets you create single smart quotes (' and '), double smart quotes (" and "), and em and en dashes (dashes the width of the letters *m* and *n*, respectively). We'll show you how to create these characters when we discuss symbols in Chapter 16.

Using ASCII and ANSI characters

ASCII, which stands for American Standard Code for Information Interchange, is the language that Word and other programs use to define the characters you enter into your document. Every letter, number, punctuation mark, and other symbol is defined by an ASCII code. Special instructions, like paragraph breaks, page breaks, and tabs, are also defined by an ASCII code.

ANSI, which stands for American National Standards Institute, is a superset of ASCII. In addition to the 128 ASCII characters, it contains foreign characters (like å and ç) for Western European countries. To see a complete listing of the characters in the ANSI character set, refer to Appendix 5.

Fortunately, Word lets you create characters by typing their ANSI codes. To do this, first turn on Num Lock, hold down the [Alt] key, and type the decimal number that represents the ANSI character you want to enter (you must use the numbers on the numeric keypad—not those across the top of your keyboard). After you type the code, release the [Alt] key. Word will then insert into your document the character represented by that code.

In this chapter

Editing 6

Word puts a number of tools at your disposal for editing text. In Chapter 4, we covered Word's most basic editing functions: inserting, deleting, and overwriting text. In this chapter, we'll introduce you to the "scissors and glue" functions—the Cut, Copy, and Paste commands.

In addition, we'll explore some of the more sophisticated editing features, like searching and replacing, spell-checking, and automatic hyphenation. We'll also show you how the Clipboard facility is designed to aid your editing tasks.

As we discussed in Chapter 4, your first task in editing a document is to select the text you want to work with. We suggest that you refer to the selection and navigation techniques presented in that chapter as you practice the editing concepts presented here. By learning to select text blocks quickly and accurately, you will reduce your editing time significantly.

COPYING AND MOVING TEXT

Word's Cut, Copy, and Paste commands are the scissors and glue that make editing your text a snap. With just a few keystrokes or mouse clicks, you can easily reorganize your document or duplicate a block of text—and simultaneously reflow the entire document to adjust for your changes. You can also copy items from one Word document to another. In this chapter, we'll cover copying and moving text within Word. In Chapter 21, we'll show you how to share information with other programs.

Copying and moving text involves selecting the text you want to duplicate or reposition, then choosing the location in which you want to paste that text. Word also offers a few keyboard shortcuts that let you copy character or paragraph formats only. Let's start with the more straightforward Cut, Copy, and Paste commands, then take a look at several keyboard techniques and shortcuts.

Copying text

Rather than typing the same block of text over and over, you can use the Copy and Paste commands to copy a selected block and paste it in one or more locations throughout your document. As you might expect, the Copy command can save time when you need to duplicate a word, a paragraph, or even an entire document in another location.

To copy a block of text, begin by highlighting the characters you want to copy, then select the Copy command from the Edit menu. Next, position the cursor where you want the copy block to appear. When you select Paste from the Edit menu, a copy of the text you selected will appear to the left of the cursor, and the cursor will move to the end of the pasted block. The original block of text will remain unchanged.

For example, suppose you want to insert the word *revitalization* to the left of the word *efforts* in the third body-text paragraph of the document shown in Figure 6-1. Instead of retyping the word *revitalization,* you could select it from the second body-text paragraph, issue the Copy command, position the cursor to the left of the word *efforts*, and issue the Paste command. As you can see in Figure 6-2, a duplicate of the copied word will appear to the left of the word *efforts*.

Figure 6-1

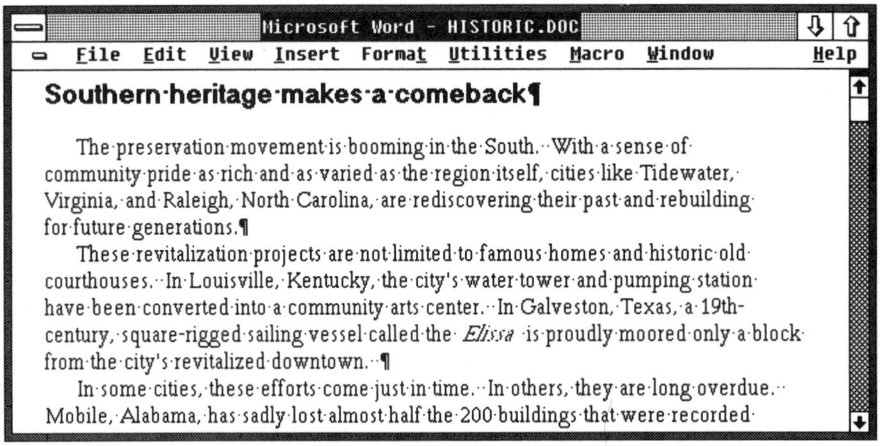

```
 ▭ ▐▓▓▓▓▓▓▓▓▓▓▓▓▓▓▓ Microsoft Word - HISTORIC.DOC ▓▓▓▓▓▓▓▓  ⇩ ⇧
 ▭    File  Edit  View  Insert  Forma_t  Utilities  Macro  Window      Help
┌──────────────────────────────────────────────────────────────────┐ ⬆
│ Southern·heritage·makes·a·comeback¶                                │
│                                                                    │
│    The·preservation·movement·is·booming·in·the·South.··With·a·sense·of·│
│ community·pride·as·rich·and·as·varied·as·the·region·itself,·cities·like·Tidewater,·│
│ Virginia,·and·Raleigh,·North·Carolina,·are·rediscovering·their·past·and·rebuilding·│
│ for·future·generations.¶                                            │
│    These·revitalization·projects·are·not·limited·to·famous·homes·and·historic·old·│
│ courthouses.··In·Louisville,·Kentucky,·the·city's·water·tower·and·pumping·station·│
│ have·been·converted·into·a·community·arts·center.··In·Galveston,·Texas,·a·19th-│
│ century,·square-rigged·sailing·vessel·called·the· *Elissa* ·is·proudly·moored·only·a·block·│
│ from·the·city's·revitalized·downtown.··¶                           │
│    In·some·cities,·these·efforts·come·just·in·time.··In·others,·they·are·long·overdue.··│
│ Mobile,·Alabama,·has·sadly·lost·almost·half·the·200·buildings·that·were·recorded·│ ⬇
└──────────────────────────────────────────────────────────────────┘
```

We need to insert the word revitalization *in the third body-text paragraph of this sample document.*

When you indicate your paste position with the cursor, Word will insert your copy block to the right of the cursor. When the paste is completed, your cursor will move to the end of the pasted text. If you are pasting a large block of text, Word will automatically scroll the end of the pasted block into view for you.

Figure 6-2

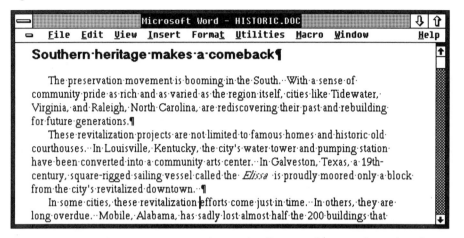

When you issue the Paste command, Word will insert the copied word to the
right of the cursor.

You can use the keyboard shortcut [Ctrl][Insert] to copy the selected block of text and, after you have selected a new insertion point, press [Shift][Insert] to paste it. Table 6-1 lists the keyboard shortcuts for the Cut, Copy, and Paste commands. If you can't remember these keyboard shortcuts, just pull down the Edit menu and look at the key combinations at the right of these commands.

Table 6-1

Command	Keyboard shortcut
Cut	[Shift][Delete]
Copy	[Ctrl][Insert]
Paste	[Shift][Insert]

If you want to paste your copy block over an existing block of text, you must first turn on the Typing Replaces Selection option in the Customize dialog box. Then, select the text you want to overwrite before issuing the Paste command. Returning to the sample document shown in Figure 6-2, suppose you want to change the word *revitalization* in the third body-text paragraph to read *preservation* instead. First, activate the Typing Replaces Selection option. Then, highlight the word *preservation* in the first paragraph of body text and choose the Copy command. Next, highlight the word *revitalization* and choose the Paste command. As you can see in Figure 6-3, Word will overwrite the highlighted text with the copied text.

Replacing
as you paste

Figure 6-3

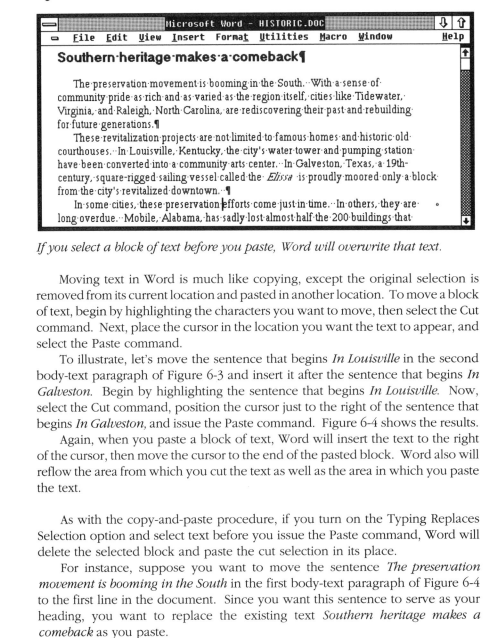

If you select a block of text before you paste, Word will overwrite that text.

Moving text

Moving text in Word is much like copying, except the original selection is removed from its current location and pasted in another location. To move a block of text, begin by highlighting the characters you want to move, then select the Cut command. Next, place the cursor in the location you want the text to appear, and select the Paste command.

To illustrate, let's move the sentence that begins *In Louisville* in the second body-text paragraph of Figure 6-3 and insert it after the sentence that begins *In Galveston.* Begin by highlighting the sentence that begins *In Louisville.* Now, select the Cut command, position the cursor just to the right of the sentence that begins *In Galveston,* and issue the Paste command. Figure 6-4 shows the results.

Again, when you paste a block of text, Word will insert the text to the right of the cursor, then move the cursor to the end of the pasted block. Word also will reflow the area from which you cut the text as well as the area in which you paste the text.

Replacing as you paste

As with the copy-and-paste procedure, if you turn on the Typing Replaces Selection option and select text before you issue the Paste command, Word will delete the selected block and paste the cut selection in its place.

For instance, suppose you want to move the sentence *The preservation movement is booming in the South* in the first body-text paragraph of Figure 6-4 to the first line in the document. Since you want this sentence to serve as your heading, you want to replace the existing text *Southern heritage makes a comeback* as you paste.

Begin by selecting the sentence and issuing the Cut command. Next, highlight the heading and issue the Paste command. Figure 6-5 shows the result.

Figure 6-4

You can use the Cut and Paste commands to transpose sentences.

Figure 6-5

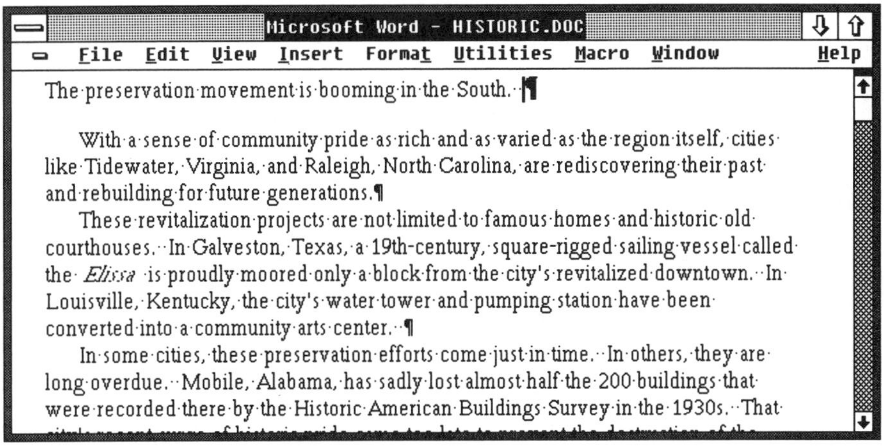

You can overwrite a block of text by using the Cut and Paste commands.

As you can see, Word replaced the heading with the selected sentence. However, since Word honors the character formatting of the pasted text, you need to apply the heading formatting to the pasted text. We'll discuss copying and moving formats in a moment.

Occasionally, you may want to use the same block of text in two or more Word documents. Rather than retyping this text, you can copy the original block to your

Pasting to other
Word documents

other documents. For example, consider the two document windows in Figure 6-6. Suppose you want to copy the paragraph that is displayed in the top document window (SALES1.DOC) and place it after the first paragraph in the second document (SALES2.DOC).

Figure 6-6

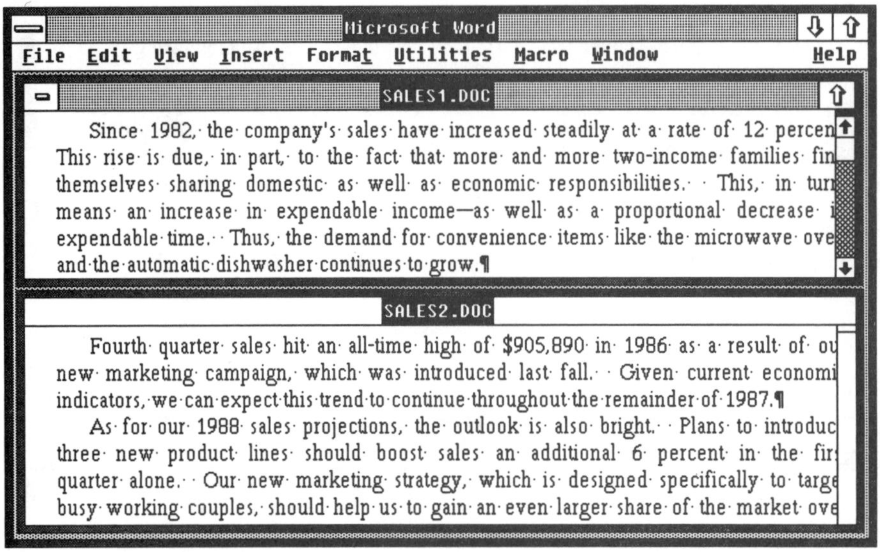

We want to copy the first paragraph from the top document window into the bottom document window.

First, activate the SALES1.DOC window, highlight the paragraph you want to copy, and issue the Copy command. Next, activate the SALES2.DOC window, click to the left of the word *As* in the second paragraph, then issue the Paste command. As you can see in Figure 6-7, a copy of the paragraph from the SALES1.DOC window now appears in the SALES2.DOC window.

By the way, you can use Word's File and Window menu commands to open new documents, retrieve existing files, or activate an open document window before you paste. Word will remember your copy block until you issue another Cut or Copy command or until you quit from the program.

The Clipboard

When you issue the Cut or Copy command, Word places the text you have selected in a special place called the Clipboard. The Clipboard is a temporary holding area where Word stores your cut and copy blocks until you need them. You can paste the contents of the Clipboard anywhere in a Word document by using the Paste command.

Figure 6-7

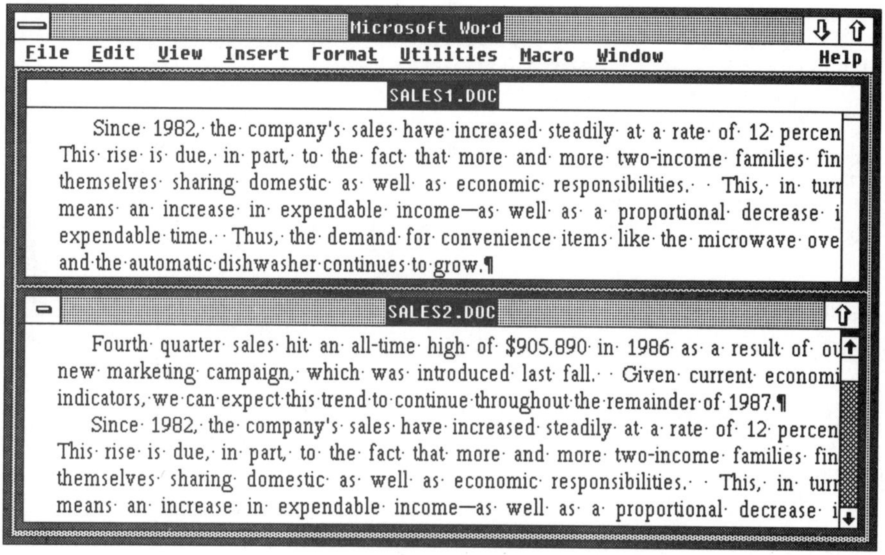

A copy of the paragraph now appears in the bottom document window as well.

Although the Clipboard can accommodate any size text block—from one character to an entire document (memory permitting)—it is important to understand that the Clipboard can hold only one selection at a time. If you issue the Cut or Copy command, then issue another Cut or Copy command before you paste the first selection into your document, Word will erase your first selection. Of course, if you are only copying the text, you have lost nothing but time. You must reselect the block and issue a new Copy command. If you issue the Cut command, however, and then cut or copy another block of text before pasting the first block, you'll lose the first block.

You can paste a cut or copied selection as many times as you like, as long as you don't overwrite the contents of the Clipboard by issuing another Cut or Copy command. Word will remember the current contents of your Clipboard even if you issue other commands or edit your document before you paste. You can even open and edit new documents without losing the contents of your Clipboard.

If you are doubtful about the last selection you have cut or copied, you can view the contents of the Clipboard by bringing up the Clipboard window. To do this, select the Run... command from Word's Control menu, choose the Clipboard option in the Run dialog box, and choose OK. Figure 6-8 shows the contents of the Clipboard after we copied the paragraph from the document in Figure 6-6.

Figure 6-8

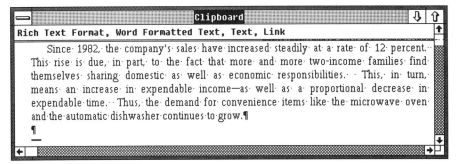

The Clipboard window indicates the last selection you cut or copied.

You can also save commonly used data in a glossary file or in the spike, as we'll explain in Chapter 13. However, you won't be able to transfer that data to other programs.

Keyboard shortcuts

In addition to the Cut, Copy, and Paste commands, Word provides two keyboard shortcuts that let you copy and move text from one location to another. These shortcuts also allow you to rearrange text without disturbing the contents of the Clipboard.

The [Copy] key

Rather than using the Copy and Paste commands to copy text, you can use Word's [Copy] key ([Shift][F2]). With the [Copy] key, you can duplicate text, insert it anywhere in your document, and leave the contents of your Clipboard intact. This is advantageous if you need to copy a block of text that is different from that stored on your Clipboard but want to retain the contents of the Clipboard.

To use this shortcut, first highlight the text you want to copy, then press the [Copy] key. Word will display the prompt *Copy to where?* at the bottom of the screen. Now, place the cursor where you want the copied text to appear, and press [Enter] to complete the copy. If you've activated the Typing Replaces Selection option in the Customize dialog box, you can overwrite existing text by highlighting it before pressing [Enter].

If you press the [Copy] key before highlighting any text, Word will display the message *Copy from where?* at the bottom of the screen. At this point, select the text you want to copy. (Instead of showing the selected text in inverse video, Word will place a dotted line under it.) Next, press [Enter] to complete the command. Word will then copy the text you've selected and insert it at the place marked by the cursor.

An alternative to the Cut and Paste commands is the [Move] key ([F2]). With the [Move] key, you can identify the text you want to move and choose its destination in one step. Like the [Copy] key, the [Move] key does not disturb the contents of the Clipboard.

The [Move] key

To use this shortcut, first highlight the text you want to move, then press the [Move] key. Word will then display the prompt *Move to where?* at the bottom of the screen. Next, place the cursor where you want to move the selected text, and press [Enter].

If you press the [Move] key without first highlighting any text, Word will assume that you want to move text to the current insertion point, and will present the prompt *Move from where?* at the bottom of the screen. At this point, select the text you want to move. (Word will place a dotted line under the selected text.) When you press [Enter], Word will move the selected text to the place marked by the cursor.

If you plan to move text using the keyboard rather than a mouse, you should get into the habit of using the [Move] key. It's much more expedient than the Cut and Paste commands.

When you copy or move a block of text, Word will generally retain the original character formats you assigned to that text as it pastes the characters in the new location. When you copy or move an entire paragraph, Word will also retain the paragraph formats of the copied selection when you paste. However, if you copy or move only a portion of the paragraph and the ¶ mark is not included in your selection, Word will use the paragraph formats assigned to the surrounding text in the paste area.

Copying and moving formats

You may need to revise the character and paragraph formats of the pasted text to match the formats of the surrounding text. Fortunately, you can use a couple of shortcuts to copy character or paragraph formats without copying any text. We'll discuss these shortcuts in a moment.

The effects of your Paste command may vary slightly if you are using Word's Style Sheet facility to format your document. In Chapter 8, we'll talk about the effects of editing text that is formatted with style sheets.

If you have a mouse, you can use a shortcut to copy character or paragraph formats without copying any text. First, highlight the text you want to format. Next, if you want to copy a character format, hold down [Ctrl][Shift] and click on the source character; to copy a paragraph format, hold down [Ctrl][Shift] and click in the invisible selection bar next to the source paragraph. Word will apply the formats of the source character or paragraph to the highlighted text.

Copying formats with the mouse

To demonstrate this shortcut, suppose you want the second body-text paragraph in Figure 6-9 to appear in the same format as the heading at the top of the document. Rather than reformatting the text manually, select the entire paragraph, hold down [Ctrl][Shift], and click on any letter in the heading. When you do, your document will look like the one in Figure 6-10. As you can see, Word has changed the character formats of the text in the paragraph.

Figure 6-9

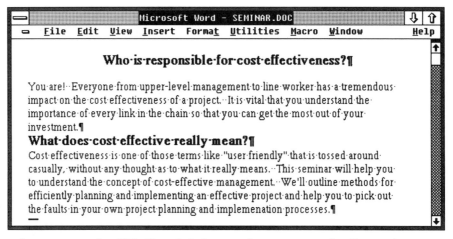

We want to copy the character formats from the heading to the second paragraph of body text.

Figure 6-10

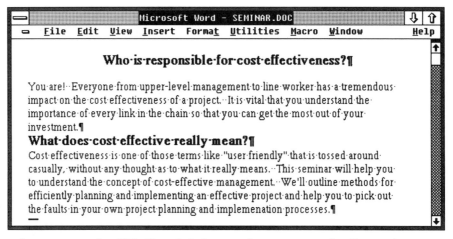

When you press [Ctrl][Shift] and click on a character, Word will copy that character's formats to the text you've highlighted.

Notice that Word has copied the character formats from the heading to the second paragraph of body text, but not the paragraph formats. The heading has centered alignment with spacing above and below the paragraph, while the body-text paragraph displays left alignment and no paragraph spacing. If you want to copy the paragraph formats, place the cursor anywhere in the body-text paragraph (or highlight some of its text), hold down [Ctrl][Shift], and click in the selection bar next to the heading. As you can see in Figure 6-11, Word will transfer the paragraph formats.

Figure 6-11

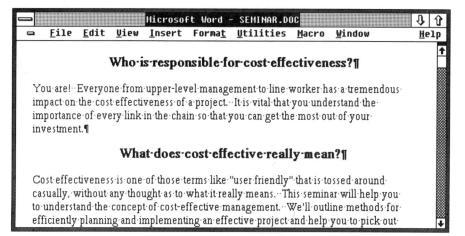

The destination paragraph now carries the same character and paragraph formats as the source paragraph.

If you don't have a mouse, you'll need to use Word's CopyFormat macro to copy character and paragraph formats. To copy a character format, first highlight the source character, then select the Run... command from the Macro menu. Next, type *copyformat* into the Run Macro Name text box, and choose OK. At this point, Word will display the prompt *Format to where?* at the bottom of the screen. Highlight the text you want to format and press [Enter]. Immediately, Word will transfer the character formats of the source character to the text you highlighted.

Copying formats with the keyboard

To copy a paragraph format with Word's CopyFormat macro, first highlight the entire source paragraph (including the ¶ mark). Next, select the Run... command, type *copyformat* into the Run Macro Name text box, and choose OK. At this point, Word will display the prompt *Format to where?* at the bottom of the screen. Place the cursor in the paragraph you want to format and press [Enter]. When you do, Word will transfer the paragraph formats of the source paragraph to the paragraph you highlighted.

Copying a ¶ mark

Another way to copy a paragraph format is to copy the ¶ mark from the end of one paragraph and paste it over the ¶ mark at the end of another paragraph. When you do this, Word will transfer the formats from the source paragraph to the destination paragraph. (Before you can use this technique, you'll need to display ¶ marks in your document by either selecting the Show-all icon on the ribbon or by activating the Paragraph Marks option in the Preferences dialog box.) If the source paragraph has been assigned a named style, Word will apply that style to the destination paragraph. We'll talk about styles in Chapter 8.

**THE SEARCH...
AND REPLACE...
COMMANDS**

Like most word processors, Word allows you to search through a document to find visible occurrences of a particular word or character sequence. Word also lets you locate a character sequence and replace it with a different character sequence. The term *character sequence* refers to any string of characters—from a single letter to several sentences. However, the sequence for which you are searching cannot exceed 256 characters. Typically, your character sequence will be only one or a few words.

Searching and replacing can be two of the most useful capabilities in any word processing program. Word takes these capabilities a step further than most word processors, letting you change formats as well as characters. In this section, we'll explain how to use the Search... and Replace... commands on the Edit menu. We'll also show you a few special ways to apply these features and warn you about certain problems that can arise when you use these commands.

Searching for text

To find a character sequence, just select the Search... command from the Edit menu to bring up the dialog box shown in Figure 6-12. When it first appears, you'll see a blinking cursor in the Search For text box. Type the characters you want to locate (this is called your search text), then choose OK to begin the search.

Figure 6-12

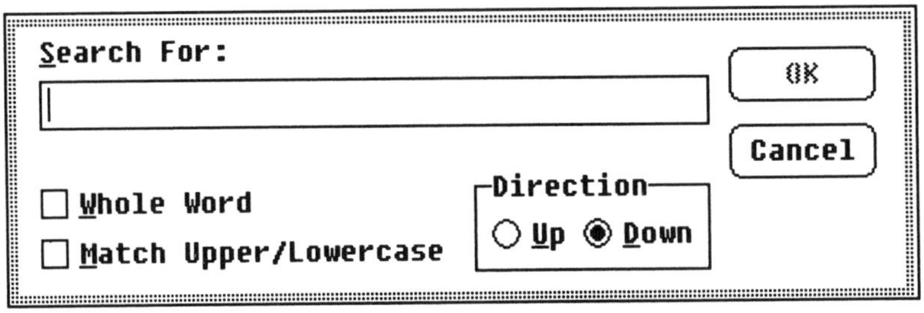

To find a specific character sequence, enter your search text into the Search dialog box.

Although there is room in the Search For text box to display only about 37 characters, your search text can be as long as 256 characters. The characters on the left side of the text box will scroll out of view as you type, but you can scroll the hidden portion of the search text into view by dragging to the left or right.

By default, Word begins at the current location of the cursor and scans forward to the end of the document. If you want Word to scan backward to the beginning of the document, choose the Up option button before you choose OK.

When Word finds the first occurrence of your search text, it will highlight that occurrence on your screen and halt the search procedure. At this point, you can edit that portion of your document or continue searching. To continue the search, you can either reissue the Search… command and choose OK in the Search dialog box, or you can press the [Repeat search] key ([Shift][F4]). As we'll discuss in a few pages, this shortcut is particularly helpful when you want to edit your document as you look for the search text.

If you press the [Repeat search] key, Word will not redisplay the Search dialog box; instead, it will continue scanning for the search text. The search text you specify in the Search For text box will not change until you replace or remove it, or until you quit from Word. You can even open another document file or activate another document window to search for the same character sequence in two or more documents. However, the next time you issue the Search… command, Word will highlight the contents of the Search For text box so you can overwrite its current contents.

As Word scans your document looking for the search text, it will scroll the document on your screen to bring the next occurrence of the search text into view. When Word has searched to the end of the document, you'll see the message box shown in Figure 6-13 on the following page. This does not necessarily mean that the search is complete; it just tells you that Word has reached the end of your document. If you want Word to cycle back to the beginning of the document and continue the search, choose Yes in this message box. (When Word reaches the end of the document for the second time, you'll see the message box again.) If you want to halt the search procedure, choose No.

If Word searches through the entire document without locating your search text, it will display the message box shown in Figure 6-14. If you're puzzled that no match was found, you might try retyping the search text. Keep in mind that Word looks for exact matches to your search text. (Capitalization does not matter unless you click the Match Upper/Lowercase option in the Search dialog box, which we'll talk about in a few pages.) Therefore, if you've entered extra blank spaces or typed a single character incorrectly in the Search For text box, Word won't be able to locate the search text in your document.

Figure 6-13

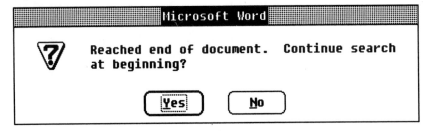

To search from the top of your document, choose Yes when this message box appears.

Figure 6-14

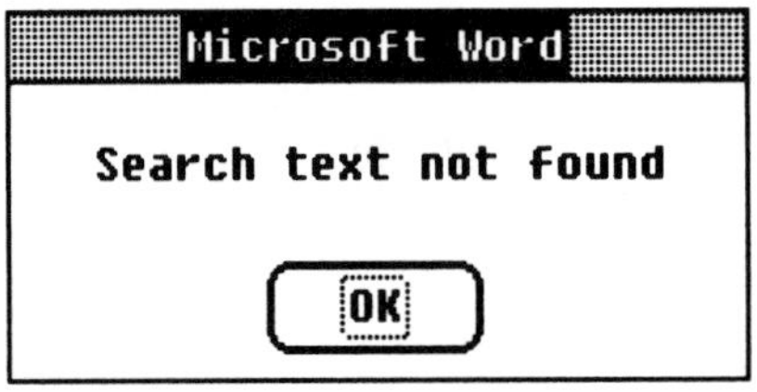

Word will display this message box if
it is unable to find the search text.

If you issue the Search... command while the cursor is positioned somewhere other than the top of your document, then choose Yes when Word asks if should continue searching from the beginning, Word will not tell you when it has completed one pass through the entire document. That is, when Word has scanned the document from the current cursor location to the end of the document, then scanned from the beginning of the document back to the cursor location, it will not automatically end the search procedure. You must watch the text on your screen, then cancel the procedure when you've searched the entire document, unless you want to search part or all of your document again. Therefore, if you want to search your entire document only once, you may find it easier to move to the beginning of the document before you issue the Search... command. That way, you'll know that you've searched through the entire document when you see the message box shown in Figure 6-13.

Navigating with the Search... command

The Search... command offers a quick way to jump from one part of your document to another as you make revisions. For example, suppose you want to edit a section of your document that appears under the heading named *Part II*. To move quickly to this section of your document without scrolling, you can issue the Search... command and enter *Part II* into the Search For text box. When you choose OK, Word will scroll your document on the screen to bring the *Part II* heading into view. You can then perform any necessary revisions.

The Search dialog box offers three options: the Whole Word and Match Upper/Lowercase check boxes and the Direction option. The Whole Word check box is used primarily when your search text is a short word, such as *the* or *for*. If you do not select this check box, Word will search for any character sequence that matches your search text, even if it occurs in the middle of another word. For example, if you type *for* in the Search For text box, Word will highlight occurrences in such words as *forecast* and *platform*. To avoid this, just select the Whole Word check box before you choose OK.

Search options

You can also use the Whole Word option when you want to find only the singular form or present tense of a word. For instance, suppose you enter the word *book* as your search text. By selecting the Whole Word check box before you begin searching, you will avoid finding the plural form of the word *books* or the past tense *booked*. Although you'll sometimes want to find different forms of a word, in general, we recommend that you select the Whole Word check box before you start your search. Of course, you can always activate this option in the middle of a search. To do this, just reissue the Search... command, choose the Whole Word check box, then choose OK. Once you've selected this option, it will remain in effect until you deselect it or exit Word.

The Match Upper/Lowercase check box works exactly as you might expect. If you do not activate this check box, Word will ignore case as it looks for occurrences of your search text. For example, if you enter *Microsoft* as your search text and do not select the Match Upper/Lowercase check box, Word will highlight such occurrences as *microsoft*, *MicroSoft*, and *MICROSOFT*. However, if you select this check box, Word will find only those occurrences whose capitalization exactly matches that of your search text.

The Match Upper/Lowercase option can be helpful when you need to search for a proper noun that has the same spelling as a common noun. Suppose you want to search a document for all references to the software program *Word*. However, you do not want to find other occurrences of the word *word*. Enter *Word* as your search text, then select the Match Upper/Lowercase check box before you start the search. (You may also want to activate the Whole Word check box.)

There's one possible disadvantage to using the Match Upper/Lowercase option. If you've accidentally used the improper case in some instances—say, if you've entered the name of the software program as *word* instead of *Word*—your search procedure will not highlight these occurrences. Sometimes, you may want to perform a search without activating the Match Upper/Lowercase check box so you can check for the correct case of a certain word throughout your document.

The Direction option lets you specify the direction in which you want Word to search through your document. The Down option tells Word to start at the position of the cursor or the rightmost character in the selected text and search to the end of the document. When Word reaches the end of the document, it will present a message box asking if you want to continue searching from the beginning of the document.

If you choose the Up option, Word will begin searching from the position of the cursor or from the leftmost character in the selected text, and will scan backward through the beginning of the document. When Word reaches the beginning of the document, it will present a message box asking if you want to continue searching from the end of the document.

Using the question mark as a wildcard

A helpful feature of the Search… command is its ability to use a question mark (?) as a wildcard. You can use a question mark in place of any single character in your search text. For example, if you enter *ba?e* as your search text, Word will highlight occurrences of *bale, base, bane, bake,* and other words that begin with *ba* followed by a single character and an *e.*

The ? wildcard comes in handy in various situations. For example, suppose you are working on a document in which you have not been consistent in spelling the name *Anderson.* In some cases, you have entered *Anderson;* in other cases, you've entered *Andersen.* You can find all occurrences of the name by using the Search… command and entering *Anders?n* as your search text. You will probably want to change some of the occurrences so that the spelling will be consistent throughout the document. We'll show you how to do that when we discuss the Replace… command.

If you want to search for a literal quotation mark in a document, you must precede the ? with a caret (^), like this: ^?. For instance, if you want to search for the character sequence *Why not?,* you must enter into the Search For text box the search text *Why not^?.* To search for the ^ character, simply use another caret, like this: ^^.

Finding hidden text

Word will not be able to locate occurrences of your search text if it is hidden from view. If you want Word to locate occurrences of your search text within a hidden text block, you must activate the Hidden Text option in the Preferences dialog box before you begin the search.

Finding formats

Word lets you search not only for a character sequence, but also for characters that exhibit particular character formats. When you perform this type of search, Word will find only the text that exhibits the formats you specify.

In addition to searching for specific character formats, Word lets you search for text that carries particular paragraph formatting. If you need to locate the next single-spaced paragraph, for example, Word will find it, regardless of that paragraph's character formatting.

If you want, you can use the Search… command to locate text that has a specific character *and* paragraph format. In this case, Word will find only specially formatted characters located in specially formatted paragraphs. One handy application for this feature is for moving quickly among headings in a large document. If you have formatted a document's first-level headings in 12-point

Helv bold type, you can search for one heading, then press the [Repeat search] key to move directly to the next heading that carries the same formats.

To define formatting characteristics along with the text in the Search For text box, you'll need to use the special key combinations listed in Table 6-2 on the next page. Unfortunately, when you've opened the Search dialog box, you won't be able to issue commands from another dialog box, the ruler, or the ribbon.

Let's demonstrate how you can use a key combination to find formatted text in your document. Suppose you want to locate all the occurrences of bold text in your document. To do this, first select the Search... command to open the Search dialog box. Next, press [Ctrl]B to specify bold text. Word will then display the word *Bold* just below the Search For text box, as shown in Figure 6-15. Now, to begin the search, just choose OK. Word will then locate the first occurrence of text that has been assigned the bold character format.

Figure 6-15

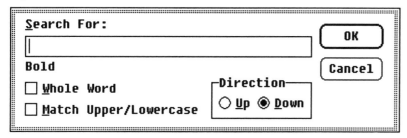

When you use the key combinations in Table 6-2, Word will indicate the formatting criteria just below the Search For text box.

To search for a particular character sequence that exhibits the bold character format, just enter that sequence in the Search For text box before you choose OK. To specify additional formatting criteria, just bring up the Search dialog box and press the appropriate key combinations listed in Table 6-2. To remove a formatting criterion from the Search For text box, press the appropriate key combination a second time. For example, to remove the Bold criterion from the Search dialog box, just press [Ctrl]B again. Like [Ctrl]B, all the key combinations in Table 6-2 are toggle commands.

Another useful feature of the Search... command is its ability to find special characters, such as paragraph marks, non-breaking spaces, and optional hyphens. To find a special character, you must insert a caret (^) in your search text. Table 6-3 on page 163 lists the characters you can search for and the corresponding character combination for each.

Finding special characters

Table 6-2

Type this...	to specify this character format...
[Ctrl]=	subscript, 3 points
[Ctrl]+	superscript, 3 points
[Ctrl]B	bold
[Ctrl]D	double underline
[Ctrl]F	font name: each press scrolls forward through the list of fonts one at a time
[Ctrl][Shift]F	font name: each press scrolls backward through the list of fonts one at a time
[Ctrl]H	hidden
[Ctrl]I	italic
[Ctrl]K	small kaps
[Ctrl]N	new text entered while Word was in the Mark Revisions mode
[Ctrl]P	point size: each press displays the next point size in half-point increments, from 4-127
[Ctrl][Shift]P	point size: each press displays the previous point size in half-point increments, from 127-4
[Ctrl][Spacebar]	remove all character formatting from the text you've specified in the dialog box
[Ctrl]U	underline
[Ctrl]V	each press displays the next available color
[Ctrl][Shift]V	each press displays the previous available color
[Ctrl]W	word underline
[Ctrl]Z	text deleted while Word was in the Mark Revisions mode

Type this...	to specify this paragraph format...
[Ctrl]1	single-spacing
[Ctrl]2	double-spacing
[Ctrl]5	$1^1/_2$-spacing
[Ctrl]C	centered alignment
[Ctrl]E	close space before
[Ctrl]J	justified alignment
[Ctrl]L	left alignment
[Ctrl]O	open space before
[Ctrl]R	right alignment
[Ctrl]X	remove all paragraph formatting from the text you've specified in the dialog box

Table 6-3

This code...	represents this character...
?	any single character
^	question mark
^^	caret
^p	paragraph mark (¶)
^t	tab mark (➡)
^n	newline mark (↵)
^s	non-breaking space (°)
^d	section-break marker (:::::::)
^w	white space
^—	non-breaking hyphen
^-	optional hyphen (¬)
^*0nnn*	ANSI character in *nnn* (decimal) form

Word can find special characters in your text even when they are not visible on the screen. For example, if you haven't activated the Paragraph Marks option in the Preferences dialog box, the ¶ marks at the end of every paragraph will not be visible on your screen. However, if you use the code ^*p* in your search text, Word will highlight the space following each paragraph. Similarly, Word can find tab marks, optional hyphens, and end-of-line marks, even when they are not displayed on the screen.

One item in the table, ^*w*, needs a little explaining. When you specify ^*w* as your search text, Word will find the blank space that appears between any two characters in your document. This will include the single spaces between words, as well as tab spaces.

As you might guess, your search text can include any combination of these special characters and other text. For example, to find every instance of a paragraph that begins with the word *For,* you can choose the Search... command and enter ^*pFor* into the Search For text box. When you choose OK, Word will highlight the ¶ mark at the end of the preceding paragraph as well as the word *For* at the beginning of the following paragraph.

In addition to using the special characters listed in Table 6-3, you can search for any character by entering a caret followed by a zero and the character's three-digit ANSI code. For example, if you enter ^*0097* as your search text, Word will find every occurrence of the letter *a.* Interestingly, even though 097 is the ANSI code for a lowercase *a* and 065 is the ANSI code for an uppercase *A,* Word will find every *a,* regardless of case, unless you activate Match Upper/Lowercase.

As we've mentioned, you can use the [Repeat search] key ([Shift][F4]) to repeat a search instead of reopening the Search dialog box. Whenever you close the

Shortcuts

Search dialog box, Word will remember the contents of the Search For text box. Consequently, when you press the [Repeat search] key, Word will be able to locate the next occurrence of the search text you entered.

Here's another shortcut you can use when editing text as you search. After you make a change to one occurrence of your search text, you can make the same editing change to the next occurrence simply by pressing the [Repeat] key ([F4]). For example, suppose you want to boldface your company name everywhere it appears in a document. Begin by opening the Search dialog box, entering the company name into the Search For text box, then choosing OK. When Word highlights the first occurrence of the company name, click on the Bold icon on the ribbon or press [Ctrl]B. After boldfacing the first occurrence, press the [Repeat search] key to go to the next occurrence of the company name. Then, either press the [Repeat] key or [Ctrl]B to boldface this occurrence as well. You can continue this procedure until you have boldfaced every occurrence of your company name in the document.

If you do not want to boldface every occurrence, you can skip some of them without losing the shortcut advantage. Just press the [Repeat search] key to skip from one occurrence to another, and press [Repeat] only when you reach an occurrence that you want to change. Because the [Repeat] key repeats only your most recent editing change, use it only when you haven't made an intermediate editing change to your document.

Replacing text

Like the Search… command, the Replace… command lets you find a character sequence in your document. However, the difference between the two commands is that you can use the Replace… command to replace the search text with new text throughout the entire document.

When you issue the Replace… command on the Edit menu, Word will display the dialog box shown in Figure 6-16. In this dialog box, type the search text into the Search For text box, then type the replacement text into the Replace With text box. Next, choose OK to begin the replace procedure. Once you've issued the Replace… command, Word will remember the entries you've made in the Search For and Replace With text boxes and will present those entries as the new defaults.

Although there is room in the Search For and Replace With text boxes to display only about 37 characters, each can hold up to 256 characters. Those on the left side of the text box will scroll out of view as you type, but you can scroll the hidden portion of the text into view by dragging to the left or right.

As you can see in Figure 6-16, the Confirm Changes check box, which we'll discuss in a moment, is activated by default. When you choose OK to begin the replace procedure, Word will start at the current location of the cursor and scan forward to the end of your document. When it finds the first occurrence of the search text, it will highlight that occurrence on the screen and present a second Replace dialog box. Figure 6-17 shows the dialog box that appears when Word finds an occurrence of the word *silver.*

Figure 6-16

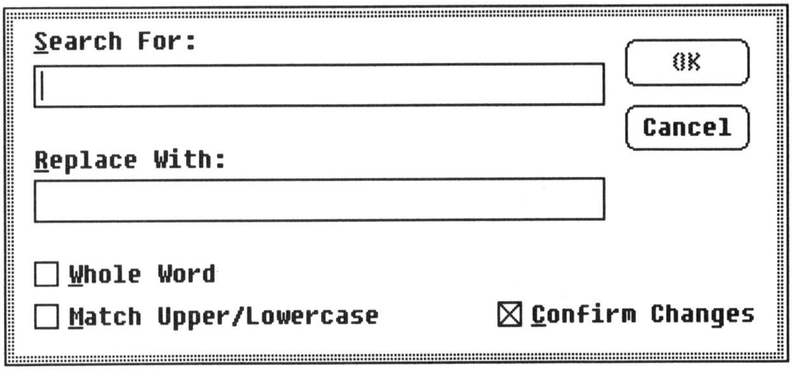

The Replace dialog box lets you locate and replace text in a single step.

Figure 6-17

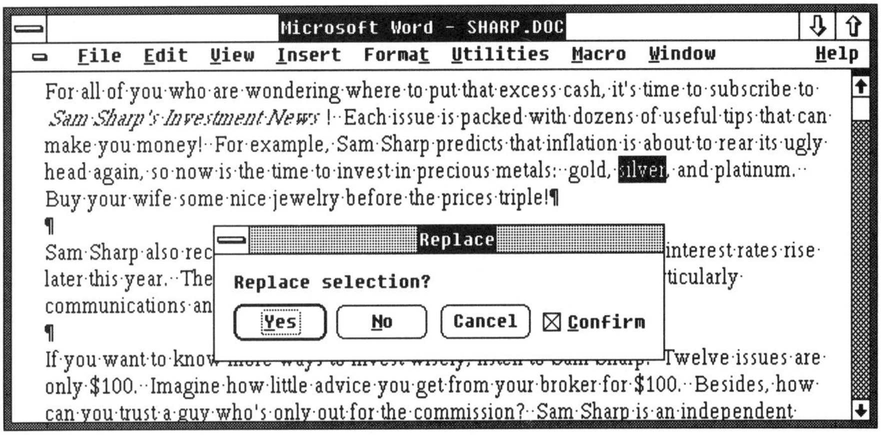

When Word finds an occurrence of the search text, it will present a dialog box like this one.

If you want to change every occurrence of the search text in your document, turn off the Confirm Changes check box shown in Figure 6-16 and choose OK. Word will then begin replacing every occurrence of your search text with the replacement text you specified. As the replacement text is pasted into your document, it will assume the same format as the search text it replaces. (If you leave the Replace With text box blank, Word will delete every occurrence of the search text when you choose Yes.)

For example, suppose you're working in the document shown in Figure 6-18 and you decide to change every occurrence of the word *year* to the word *period*.

To execute this, move the cursor to the beginning of the second body-text paragraph, then open the Replace dialog box. Enter *year* into the Search For text box and *period* into the Replace With text box. Then, turn off the Confirm Changes check box, and choose OK. Word will then start the replace procedure. When Word reaches the end of the document, it will present the message box shown in Figure 6-19.

Figure 6-18

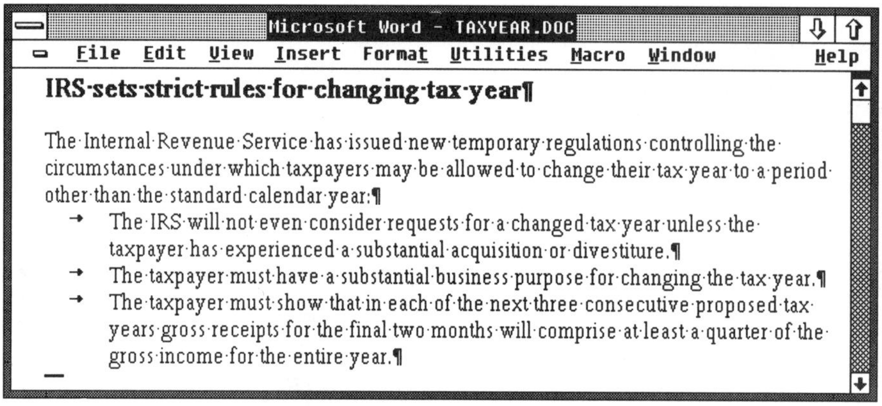

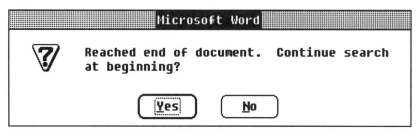

We'll use this sample document to demonstrate Word's Replace... command.

Figure 6-19

Word will present this message box when it reaches the end of the document during a replace procedure.

At this point, Word has replaced all the occurrences of the word *year* in the last three paragraphs with the word *period*. However, Word has not changed the text in the first two paragraphs. When you start a search-and-replace procedure from the middle of your document, Word will replace every occurrence of the search text from the cursor through the end of your document. To continue the replace procedure starting from the beginning of the document, choose Yes in the message box. To halt the replace procedure at this point, choose No. If you do, Word will display at the bottom of the screen the number of changes made, then close the Replace dialog box.

If you choose Yes to continue the replace procedure from the beginning of your document, Word will change all occurrences of the search text from the beginning of the document to the original cursor location. When Word has completed all the changes, you'll see a message at the bottom of the screen telling you how many changes were made. Figure 6-20 shows our sample document after replacing all occurrences of the word *year* with *period.*

Figure 6-20

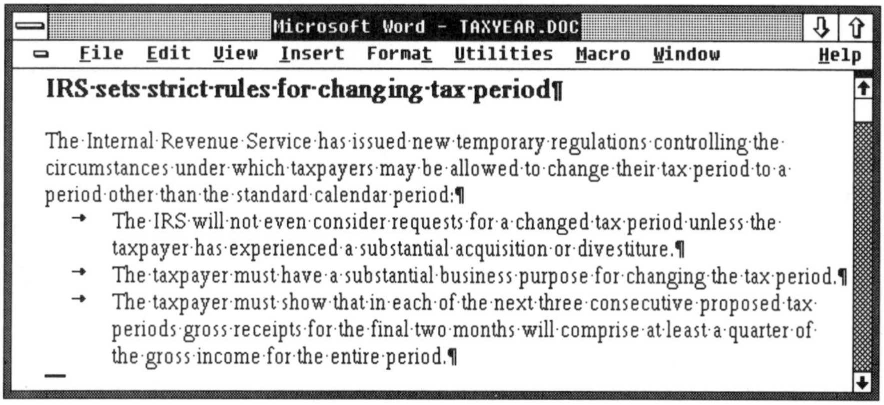

Word has replaced all occurrences of the word year *with the word* period.

Selective replacing

In many cases, you will not want to replace every occurrence of your search text. Fortunately, Word provides two ways to perform selective changes in a document. First, you can examine each occurrence of the search text before you decide whether you want to change it. Alternatively, you can change every occurrence of the search text within only a selected portion of your document.

Examining text before replacing it

If you want to examine each occurrence of your search text before you decide whether to change it, leave the Confirm Changes check box selected during the replace procedure. Beginning with the current cursor location, Word will highlight each occurrence of the search text on the screen and will present a second Replace dialog box asking if you want to replace the selection. If you want to change the selected occurrence, choose Yes. If you want to skip this occurrence and examine the next one, choose No.

In either case, Word will follow your instructions, then highlight the next occurrence of the search text on your screen. Again, it will present the second Relace dialog box, in which you can choose either Yes or No. As Word executes a replace procedure, it will scroll your document on the screen to bring new occurrences of the search text into view. Occasionally, you may need to move the second Replace dialog box out of the way so you can see the highlighted search text in your document.

As you examine each occurrence of the search text, you may want to make changes directly to the document. To do this, choose Cancel to reactivate your document, then type characters from the keyboard or access any of Word's menu commands. When you reissue the Replace… command, Word will begin where it left off.

This technique is useful when you want to use a different tense or form in the replacement text. For example, suppose you are changing the word *walk* to *run*. As you're going through the document, you find a past tense occurrence of the search text, *walked*. If Word were performing the replace procedure automatically, this occurrence would become *runed*. However, when you find an occurrence like this, you can choose the Cancel button to reactivate your document, replace the word *walk* with *run*, and reissue the Replace… command. (Another way to solve this type of problem is to select the Whole Word option, which we'll discuss in a minute.)

As you can see in Figure 6-19, when Word reaches the end of your document, it will ask whether you want to continue the search from the beginning of the document. You can stop the replace procedure at this point, or you can continue your selective replacing, starting at the beginning of the document. If you choose to return to the beginning of your document and resume the replace procedure, Word will continue to look for the search text until it reaches the point where the procedure began.

Replacing the search text in a selected area

If you select a portion of your document before you choose the Replace… command, you can change all occurrences of the search text within just that selection. Returning to the sample document in Figure 6-18, suppose you want to change the word *year* to *period* within only the first body-text paragraph. Begin by selecting that paragraph and choosing the Replace… command from the Edit menu. Next, enter *year* into the Search For text box and *period* into the Replace With text box. Finally, deselect the Confirm Changes check box and choose OK. Word will automatically change every occurrence of the search text within the paragraph you selected. Afterward, Word will display at the bottom of the screen the number of changes it has made.

Replace options

You've probably noticed that the Replace dialog box offers the same two options that appear in the Search dialog box: Whole Word and Match Upper/Lowercase. The Whole Word check box works exactly like the Whole Word check box in the Search dialog box. When you activate this check box, Word will change only whole-word matches to your search text. Again, this option is likely to be important when your search text is a single short word. For example, suppose you want to replace every occurrence of the word *top* with the word *bottom*. If you do not activate the Whole Word check box, Word will replace the characters *top* in such words as *topic* and *stop*. Your document may end up with such nonsensical words as *bottomic* and *sbottom*.

The Whole Word option also can come in handy when the word you are changing appears in more than one tense or form throughout your document. For example, suppose you want to change every occurrence of the word *boy* to *child*. If your document happens to contain the plural form, *boys*, and you do not select the Whole Word check box, Word will change *boys* to *childs*. To avoid this kind of problem, you can use the Whole Word check box to perform separate replace procedures for each form of the word.

The Match Upper/Lowercase option works a little differently in a replace procedure than it does in a search procedure. You may recall that when you activate this option in the Search dialog box, Word will look only for character sequences whose capitalization exactly matches that of the search text. This rule still applies when you issue the Replace… command. However, the Match Upper/ Lowercase option also affects your replacement text. If you do not activate this option during a replace procedure, and you enter your replacement text in lowercase letters, Word will use the existing capitalization of each occurrence of the search text to determine the capitalization of the replacement text.

For example, suppose you want to replace the word *May* with the word *April* throughout the sample document shown in Figure 6-21. If you enter your search and replacement text in all lowercase letters and do not activate the Match Upper/ Lowercase option, Word will find all occurrences of *may*, ignoring case, and replace them with the word *april*, as shown in Figure 6-22.

Figure 6-21

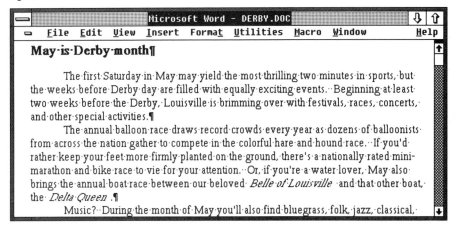

We want to change the word May *to* April *in this sample document.*

Figure 6-22

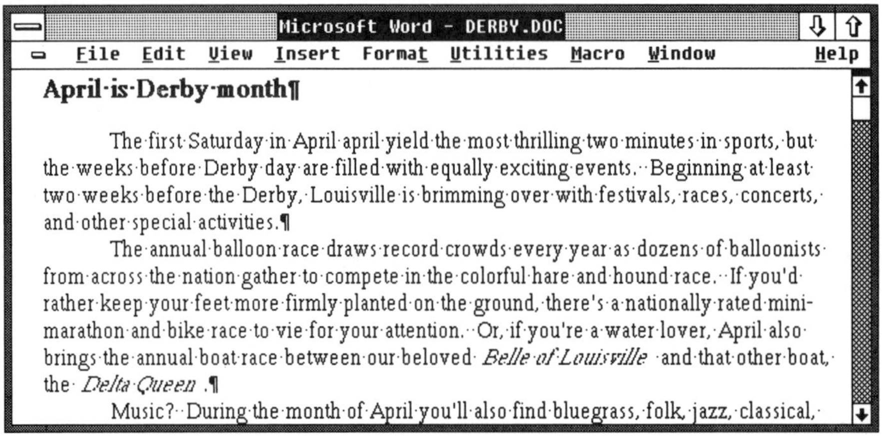

If you enter your search and replacement text in all lowercase letters and do not activate the Match Upper/Lowercase option, Word will retain the document's existing capitalization.

Notice that every instance in which the word *may* appeared capitalized, Word also capitalized the replacement text *april*. However, if you capitalize the word *april* in the Replace With text box, Word will capitalize all instances of the replacement text when it executes the Replace… command, as you can see in Figure 6-23.

Figure 6-23

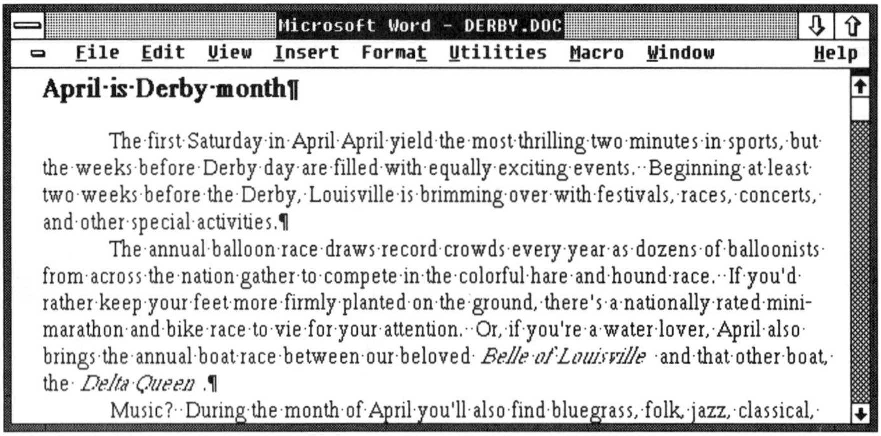

If you capitalize any of the letters in the Replace With text box, Word will use that case when it places that text in the document.

In the first body-text paragraph in Figure 6-22, notice that Word changed *may* to *april,* even though we intended to change only the month names with our search-and-replace procedure. We could get around this problem by using the Match Upper/Lowercase option.

If you activate the Match Upper/Lowercase check box, Word will find only those occurrences of the search text whose capitalization exactly matches that in the Search For text box. In addition, Word will always paste in your replacement text exactly as you have entered it in the Replace With text box, rather than adapting the replacement text to fit the style of each occurrence of the search text. Figure 6-24 shows the effect of the Replace... command on our sample document when we used the Match Upper/Lowercase option to change *May* to *April.* Notice that the second occurrence of the word *may* in the first body-text paragraph remains unchanged in this example.

Figure 6-24

When you use the Match Upper/Lowercase option, Word will change only those words that exactly match the capitalization of the search text.

You can use the ? wildcard only in the Search For text box. If you include a ? in the Replace With text box, Word will interpret it as a literal question mark. Sometimes, the ? wildcard can enable you to perform only one replace procedure where you otherwise might need two. For example, suppose you want to replace every occurrence of *software* and *hardware* with the words *computer supplies.* After you choose the Replace... command, enter *????ware* as your search text, then enter *computer supplies* as your replacement text. Word will look for all words that begin with any four characters followed by *ware,* then replace those words with *computer supplies.*

Using wildcards

Changing hidden text

The Replace... command will affect hidden text only if you have chosen to display it on your screen. If you use the Preferences... command to suppress the display of any text that carries the hidden format, Word will ignore that text when it performs the search-and-replace procedure. For this reason, if you want to change hidden text, you must activate the Hidden Text or Show All option in the Preferences dialog box, or select the Show-all icon on the ribbon before you begin a replace procedure.

Replacing text and formats

Earlier in this chapter, we showed you how to use the Search... command to search for text that has specific character and/or paragraph formats. If you want, you can use a similar procedure to tell Word how to format your replacement text. In addition, you can change the format of text without altering its content. Finally, you can use the Replace dialog box to strip the formatting from text.

To define formatting characteristics along with the text in the Replace With text box, you'll need to use the same formatting instructions you use in the Search For text box. Table 6-2 on page 162 lists the key combinations that specify character and paragraph formatting in the Search For and Replace With text boxes.

To paste some replacement text into your document in a special format, first type the replacement text into the Replace With text box. Then, press the appropriate key combination to format your text. As you might expect, Word will display a formatting criterion below the Replace With text box to indicate the format you've assigned to this text. If you want to assign more than one format, just issue the additional key combinations, and Word will display the corresponding criteria below the text box. Since the key combinations in Table 6-2 are toggle commands, you can remove a format you've assigned by pressing that format's key combination again. After you've assigned the appropriate formats to your replacement text, choose OK to tell Word to begin the replace procedure.

Replacing from the Clipboard

In some situations, you'll want to use the text on the Clipboard as your replacement text. First, because text you store on the Clipboard is not bound by the 256-character limitation that applies in the dialog box, you can use the Clipboard whenever your replacement text is particularly long. Second, when your replacement text is on the Clipboard, it will come into your document with its formatting intact. Consequently, you can use the Clipboard to include special style characteristics (different fonts, point sizes, character formats, and so forth) in your replacement text.

To use the Clipboard's contents as your replacement text, just enter the characters ^c in the Replace With text box. For instance, suppose you want to replace every occurrence of the words *The Expert* with the full title *The Expert: The Microsoft Excel User's Journal* in the sample document shown in Figure 6-25. You want this title to appear in bold italic type as well.

Figure 6-25

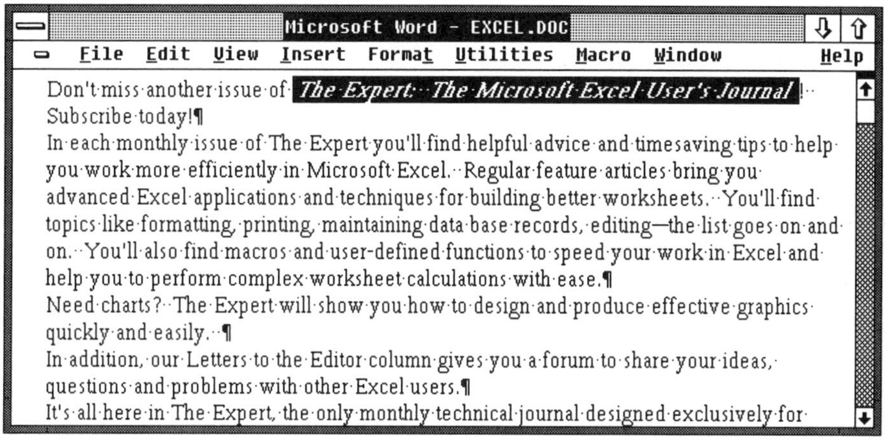

We want to change all occurrences of The Expert *to* The Expert: The Microsoft Excel User's Journal, *then format the replacement text in bold italic type.*

To do this, begin by highlighting the first occurrence of the full title *The Expert: The Microsoft Excel User's Journal* in line 1, as we've done in Figure 6-25. Then, select the Copy command from the Edit menu to place a copy of the formatted title on the Clipboard. Next, move the cursor to the beginning of the second paragraph, issue the Replace... command, and enter *The Expert* into the Search For text box. Now, enter ^c into the Replace With text box to tell Word to use the Clipboard's contents as the replacement text. At this point, the Replace dialog box will look like the one shown in Figure 6-26 on the next page. Next, make sure the Confirm Changes check box is deactivated, then choose OK. Word will begin replacing the search text with the text on the Clipboard. When Word reaches the end of the document and asks if you want to continue searching from the beginning, choose No. The resulting document will look like Figure 6-27 on the following page. (By the way, you will not want to type ^c in the Search For text box. If you do, Word will highlight every occurrence of the letter *c* in your document.)

Just as Word lets you use special formatting in your replacement text, you can use the Replace... command to search for one format and replace it with another. For instance, if you decide that you don't like the bold format you added to *The Expert: The Microsoft Excel User's Journal*, you can use the Replace... command to remove the format. To do this, first open the Replace dialog box. Then, erase the contents of the Search For text box and press [Ctrl]B and [Ctrl]I to assign the bold and italic formats to the search text. Next, erase the contents of the Replace With text box and press [Ctrl]I to assign only the italic format to the replacement text. Finally, deactivate the Confirm Changes check box, and choose OK to initiate the replace procedure.

Figure 6-26

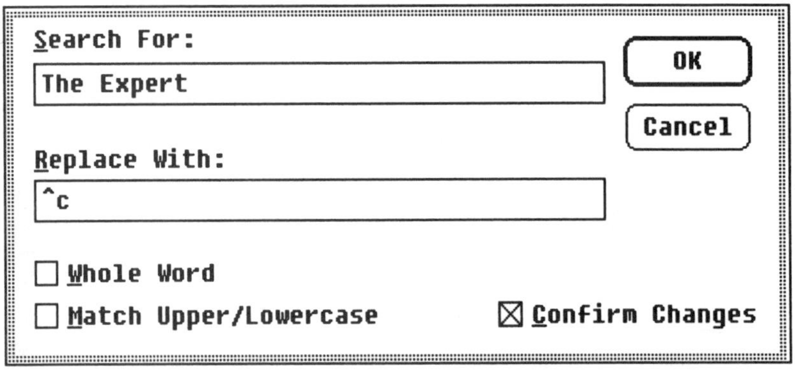

We've entered the code ^c into the Replace With text box to specify the text on the Clipboard as the replacement text.

Figure 6-27

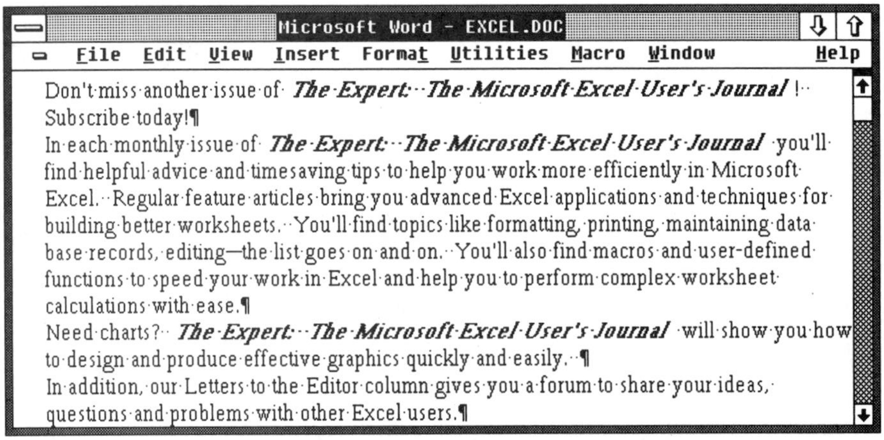

The replacement text exhibits the same formatting characteristics that appeared on the Clipboard.

Replacing styles

Word allows you to replace styles in your document. To specify a style in the Replace dialog box, type ^*y*, followed by the style name. You must not leave a space between ^*y* and the style name. Additionally, the style name must not be followed by text. For example, if you want to assign the style *heading 3* to all the paragraphs that are currently assigned the style *level C*, simply enter ^*ylevel C* into the Search For text box and enter ^*yheading 3* into the Replace With text box.

When you combine character and paragraph formatting in your instructions in the Replace dialog box, Word will find all the text in your document with the specified character formatting only if it is in paragraphs that match the specified paragraph formatting. Remember that Word applies paragraph formats to the entire paragraph, while it applies character formats only to the characters you have indicated.

Combining character and paragraph formatting

Earlier in this chapter, we explained how to use special codes in the Search For text box to search for special characters in a document. For example, if you want to search for every ¶ mark, you can enter ^p as your search text. Fortunately, you can use most of these same codes in the Replace With text box to specify your replacement text. Table 6-3 on page 163 summarizes the available codes.

Using special characters in the replacement text

For example, suppose you want to replace every regular hyphen in your document with an optional hyphen. (As we explained in Chapter 5, a regular hyphen always appears in your document, while an optional hyphen appears only when a word breaks at the end of a line.) First, choose the Replace... command and type a hyphen into the Search For text box. Then, enter ^- into the Replace With text box. As with any replace procedure, you can choose to deactivate the Confirm Changes check box and replace every occurrence at once.

Your replacement text also can consist of a ^ followed by a 0 and a character's three-digit decimal ANSI code. For instance, if you enter *^0065* as your replacement text, Word will paste an uppercase *A* in your document as the replacement for each occurrence of the search text. If you enter *^0097*, Word will paste a lowercase *a* in your document if the selected occurrence of the search text is lowercase, or an uppercase *A* if the selected occurrence is uppercase.

Word provides a main dictionary file of more than 130,000 words. Word uses this dictionary to identify misspelled words in a document. In addition to the main dictionary, you also can develop two custom dictionaries to locate and correct misspelled words. Typically, these two user-created dictionaries will contain proper nouns, technical terms, and other frequently used words that are not found in the main dictionary.

CHECKING SPELLING

To check the spelling in a document, begin by choosing the Spelling... command from the Utilities menu to open the Check Spelling dialog box shown in Figure 6-28 on the following page. We'll be exploring the various elements in this dialog box as we go along, but for now, let's briefly look at each item.

On the left side of the Check Spelling dialog box is the Word text box, where you can type the word whose spelling you want to check. Below the text box are two dimmed buttons: Check and Delete. Word will activate the Check button after you type text into the Word text box.

A quick tour of the Check Spelling dialog box

Figure 6-28

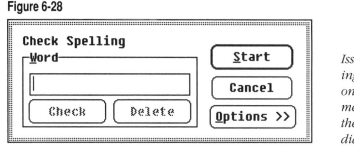

Issuing the Spelling... command on the Utilities menu displays the Check Spelling dialog box.

Along the right side of the dialog box are three buttons. The Start button is active when the dialog box first appears on the screen. Choosing this button will initiate the spell-check procedure. The Cancel button will halt the procedure and return you to your document. The Options >> button will expand the dialog box, as shown in Figure 6-29. As you can see, Word lets you select three dictionaries: the main dictionary, the user dictionary STDUSER.DIC, and the user dictionary you choose in the Supplemental pull-down list box. When Word finds a word that is not in any of these dictionaries, it will highlight that word in your document, then display a Spelling window containing that word. We will discuss the Spelling window shortly.

Figure 6-29

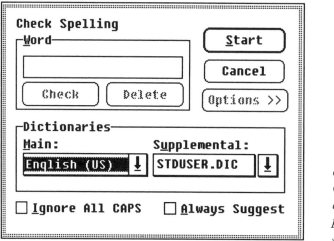

Choosing the Options >> button displays the expanded Check Spelling dialog box.

At the bottom of the expanded Check Spelling dialog box, you will see two check-box options: Ignore All CAPS and Always Suggest. If you select the first check box, Word will save time by passing over words that appear entirely in capital letters. (It's a good idea to turn this feature on if your document contains specific terms or acronyms that do not appear in the dictionaries.) If you select the Always Suggest check box, Word will suggest alternatives to every word that it can't find in its dictionaries.

After you've opened the Check Spelling dialog box, you can choose the Start button to begin scanning forward from the word on which the cursor is positioned. At first, it may appear as if nothing is happening. However, if you watch the status bar, you'll see the message *Checking... Press Esc to cancel.* When Word finds a word it does not recognize—that is, a word that is not in its dictionaries—it will highlight that word in your document, then display it in the text box of the Spelling window, as shown in Figure 6-30.

Finding and correcting misspelled words

Figure 6-30

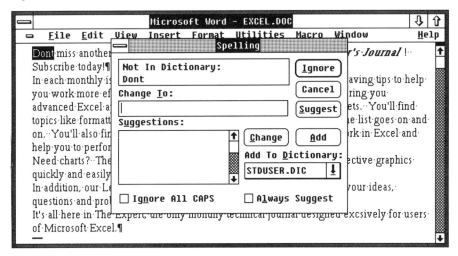

When Word finds a word that it does not recognize, it will highlight that word in your document and display it in the Spelling window.

At this point, you have several options. If you want to leave the word as it is, just choose the Ignore button. Word will then continue scanning the document until it finds another word it does not recognize. (By the way, after you've chosen Ignore once for an unrecognized word, Word will not display subsequent occurrences of that term in the Spelling window.)

If you want to change the unknown word, there are several approaches you can take. First, you can simply type a new word in the Change To text box, then

Making manual corrections

choose the Change button. Word will replace the misspelled word in your document with the word you type in the Change To text box and automatically continue checking for more unrecognized words.

Sometimes, the error in your document may be the result of an unintentional blank space or other error that cannot be corrected directly in the Change To text box. In that case, you need to select the Cancel button (or press [Esc]) to return to your document and change the text manually. Once you have made your change, you can use the Spelling… command to restart the spell-check procedure.

Using the
Suggest button

Another way to change a misspelled word is to choose the Suggest button. When you do, Word will display a list of alternatives in the Suggestions list box. For example, after Word finds the misspelled word *tihs*, choosing the Suggest button will cause Word to display the list of words shown in Figure 6-31.

Figure 6-31

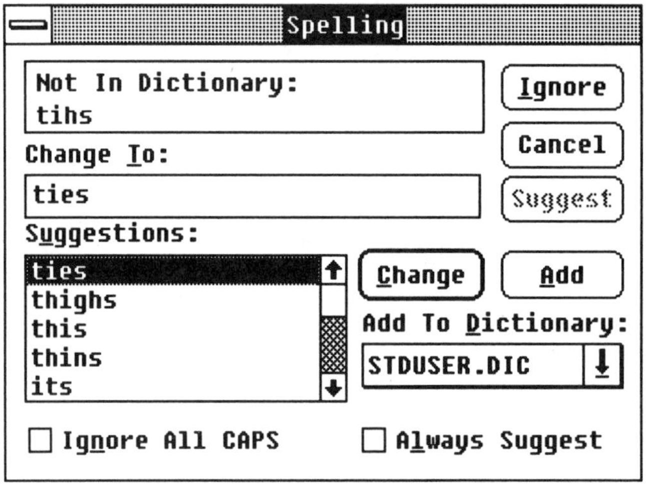

You can use the Suggest button to see a list of suggested alternatives for a misspelled word.

Notice that the first word in the list of suggested words also appears in the Change To text box. If you want to substitute this word for the misspelled word, just choose the Change button. Word will make the substitution and continue checking your document. If you want to use a different word in the list as your replacement, just select that word before you choose Change.

For example, suppose that when you see the window displayed in Figure 6-31, you realize that you want to use the word *this* instead of the suggestion in the text box, *ties*. You can simply select *this* in the Suggestions list box to display that word in the Change To text box, then choose the Change button. At this point, Word will substitute the word *this* in the Change To text box for the unrecognized word in your document, and continue scanning for other possible misspellings.

By the way, if the unknown word in your document begins with an upper-case letter, then the suggested list of alternatives in the Suggestions list box will also appear in this form. For example, suppose your document contains a reference to a book entitled *Business Statistics*, and you have misspelled the word *Business*. When Word flags this misspelling and you press the Suggest button, you'll see a list of alternatives that all begin with a capital *B*. In the same way, if a misspelled word appears in your document in all uppercase letters, the suggested alternatives will also appear in all uppercase letters. (If you've activated the Ignore All CAPS option, Word will skip over any misspelled words that appear in all uppercase letters.)

Occasionally, Word will be perplexed by the unknown word and will not be able to make an intelligent guess about alternatives. If that happens, you'll see the message *(No Suggestions)* in the Suggestions list box. At this point, you must type the correct word into the Change To text box. Another problem with the Suggest option is that it occasionally gives you a list of alternatives that are not even close to the correct answer. This is most likely to happen when the first letter of a word is incorrect. For example, when we misspelled the word *during* as *suring*, Word suggested alternatives that all began with the letter *s, c, or u,* such as *souring, sorting, currying, and using.*

As we mentioned above, you can use the Change To text box to enter an alternative for a misspelled word or to correct a misspelled word. By using the Change To text box creatively, you can make even more significant changes to a document without having to return to your document window and halt the spelling check. Returning to our example in Figure 6-31, suppose that you've misspelled the word *this* as *tihs* in your document. After Word catches the misspelling and suggests *this* as a possible alternative, you realize that, instead of the word *this*, you want to use the word *these*. All you have to do is change *this* in the Change To text box to *these*, then choose the Change button. Word will substitute *these* for the misspelled word in your document and continue scanning for more unrecognized words.

Using the Change To text box

When you're editing the contents of the Change To text box, you are not limited to typing a single word. Although the text box can display only about 30 characters at a time, you can type several more characters than this. You can even type a sentence or more, if you want.

If you have made the same spelling error more than once in your document, Word will remember the last editing change you made and make that correction each time it encounters the error in your document. Word will make these corrections without notifying you.

Repeated misspellings

For example, suppose you commonly transpose the letters *a* and *h* in the word *that*. The first time Word highlights the character sequence *taht*, type *that* into the Change To text box, then choose the Change button. The next time Word encounters the character sequence *taht*, it will automatically replace it with the word *that*.

Capitalization, prefixes, suffixes, and hidden text

In addition to misspelled words, the Spelling… command will find words that appear to have unusual patterns of uppercase and lowercase letters. For example, Word will flag such occurrences as BOok, boOk, and BooK, regardless of whether the Ignore All CAPS option is activated.

Word also can recognize most words that are created by adding common prefixes and suffixes. However, the program is not totally foolproof in this regard; it's possible that Word will not flag an illogical combination of a word and a prefix or suffix.

If you have assigned the hidden format to text in your document, Word will check the spelling of that text as long as it is displayed in the document window. However, if you use the Preferences… command to suppress the display of your hidden text, Word will not check the spelling of any hidden words.

Halting the spelling check

When Word has checked every word through the end of your document, it will close the Spelling window. Then, you'll briefly see the message *Spell check completed* in the status bar. If you started the spelling check in the middle of your document, Word will display a message box that asks *Continue checking at beginning of document?*. If you choose Yes, Word will go to the beginning of the document and continue checking for misspelled words until it reaches the point where the spelling check began. If you choose No, Word will halt the spelling check and remove the Spelling window from your screen.

You can cancel the spelling check at any time by pressing [Esc]. If Word is not scanning your document, you can cancel the spelling check by choosing the Cancel button. When you do, Word will close the Spelling window, then display *Spell check completed* in the status bar.

Spell-checking a selected portion of a document

Word makes it easy to check for spelling errors in only a selected portion of a document. All you have to do is highlight the portion of the document you want to check, then issue the Spelling… command and choose the Start button. Immediately, Word will proceed to scan only the text you have selected and flag any unrecognized words.   After scanning the entire selection, you'll see the message *Spell check completed* in the status bar.

If you want, you can use the [Spelling] key ([F7]) to tell Word to spell-check a selected portion of the document. Simply highlight the portion you want to check and press the [Spelling] key. Word will bypass the Check Spelling dialog box, display the message *Checking… Press Esc to cancel* in the status bar, and scan the words in the selection. The Spelling window will appear if Word finds any unrecognized words. After Word has scanned the entire selection, you'll see the message *Spell check completed* in the status bar.

To check the spelling of a single word, just select that word, issue the Spelling… command, and choose the Check button. Word will check to see if the word exists in any of its three open dictionaries. If the word is valid, Word will display a message indicating that the word was found in a dictionary. If Word does not recognize the word, it will display the Spelling window. You can then correct the word using the methods we described earlier, or you can choose the Ignore button to leave the word as it is. At this point, Word will close the Spelling window and terminate the spelling check.

Instead of using the Spelling… command to spell-check a word, you can use the [Spelling] key ([F7]). When you press this key, Word will display the message *Checking… Press Esc to cancel* in the status bar, and spell-check the selected word. Of course, the Spelling window will appear if Word cannot find the word in any of the open dictionaries. If the word is valid, however, you'll see the message *Spell check completed* in the status bar.

If you want, you can also use the Spelling… command or the [Spelling] key to check the spelling of text in your header, footer, and footnote panes. We'll talk about headers and footers in Chapter 7 and footnotes in Chapter 14.

In order to use Word's Spelling… command efficiently, you will almost certainly want to use a custom user dictionary in conjunction with the main dictionary. Chances are, your documents will contain one or more frequently used words (such as proper nouns, product names, and acronyms) that are not in the main dictionary file. It can be annoying and time-consuming for the program to flag these words as unknown when they are perfectly legitimate terms. You can get around this problem by adding these words either to the standard user dictionary file—STDUSER.DIC—or to another user dictionary you've created. Since Word automatically checks your document against three different dictionaries (main, STDUSER.DIC, and the user dictionary you specify), it will be able to recognize any specialized words you've stored in a user dictionary. Of course, if your document contains a specialized word that is misspelled, Word will flag it during a spelling check. You will then be able to consult your user dictionary to obtain the correct spelling for that word.

There are a couple of ways to add new words to a user dictionary. First, you can add them during a spelling check. Whenever Word finds a legitimate word that is not in its main dictionary, you can simply add it to a user dictionary. Second, you can add words by typing them directly into the Check Spelling dialog box. We will discuss both of these methods shortly.

In addition to adding words to a user dictionary, you can revise and delete current entries. You also can copy words from one user dictionary to another. Although Word offers a great deal of flexibility with user dictionaries, it does not allow you to make changes to the main dictionary. The main dictionary file is protected so you cannot add, delete, or revise its entries.

Spell-checking a word

User dictionaries

Adding new words to STDUSER.DIC

When you issue the Spelling... command for the first time during a Word session, Word automatically opens a dictionary called STDUSER.DIC (in addition to opening the main dictionary). Unless you've added words to this dictionary, the STDUSER.DIC dictionary will be empty. When you choose the Start button in the Check Spelling dialog box, and Word comes across a word that is not in the main dictionary, it will display that word in the Spelling window. To add the highlighted word to the STDUSER.DIC file, just choose the Add button. Once you have "legitimized" the word by adding it to the dictionary, Word will remove it from the Not In Dictionary area of the Spelling window and proceed with the spelling check.

Creating a new user dictionary

As we've mentioned, Word can use two user dictionaries in addition to the main dictionary to spell-check the words in your document. Actually, you can create as many user dictionaries as you want, but can activate only two at a time—STDUSER.DIC and another one of your choice.

To create a new user dictionary, simply rename STDUSER.DIC to the name of your choice. For instance, if you use a number of special words in the documents you send to your customers, you may want to store a list of these words in a dictionary file called CUSTOMER.DIC. To create this dictionary file, choose the Spelling... command to bring up the Check Spelling dialog box, and select the Options >> button to expand the dialog box. Next, use the [Tab] key to highlight the name STDUSER.DIC in the Supplemental list box, then type the name you want to use for the new dictionary—*CUSTOMER.DIC.* (Word uses the extension .DIC to identify dictionary files.) At this point, choose the Start button to begin the spelling check. Immediately, Word will present the message box shown in Figure 6-32. Since you want to create a new user dictionary, you should choose Yes. Word will then begin comparing every word in your document to the words in the main dictionary and STDUSER.DIC. When Word finds a word that is not in either dictionary, you'll see a Spelling window like the one shown in Figure 6-33.

Figure 6-32

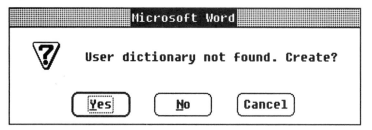

Word will present this message box when you specify a new user dictionary in the expanded Check Spelling dialog box.

Figure 6-33

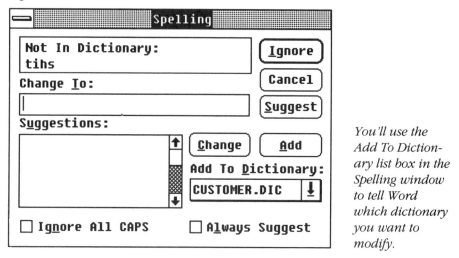

You'll use the Add To Dictionary list box in the Spelling window to tell Word which dictionary you want to modify.

Notice that Word places the name of your new dictionary, CUSTOMER.DIC, in the Add To Dictionary list box. To add the unknown word to this dictionary, simply select the Add button. If you want to add the word to another dictionary— either STDUSER.DIC or another user dictionary you've created—select the appropriate dictionary from the Add To Dictionary list box before you choose Add. When you choose Add, Word will add the unknown word to the selected dictionary and continue spell-checking the rest of the document.

The next time you use the Spelling... command to spell-check your document, Word will automatically use the custom user dictionary you last appended along with the main dictionary and the user dictionary STDUSER.DIC. To specify a different user dictionary before you begin the spelling check, open the expanded Check Spelling dialog box and choose the name of the desired dictionary from the Supplemental list box before selecting the Start button.

Capitalization

Before you add a new word to a user dictionary, you need to know how Word deals with capitalization during a spelling check. If the word you add to a dictionary is in all lowercase letters, Word will be able to recognize any occurrence of that word in a document, no matter what case is used. If you use one or more uppercase letters in the word you add to a dictionary, Word will be able to recognize only occurrences that have the same letters in uppercase. For example, suppose you add the name *McDonald* to a user dictionary. In performing a spelling check, Word will flag any occurrence of this name where either the *M* or the *D* is not capitalized. Therefore, *Mcdonald, mcdonald,* and *mcDonald* would all be unrecognized words.

Because of the way Word handles capitalization, you should be sure that you add any common terms in all lowercase letters. For example, the word *reboot* is not in the main dictionary. If you add this word to a user dictionary, be sure that you enter it in all lowercase letters. For instance, if you enter it with an uppercase *r*, Word will flag all occurrences in which the *r* is not capitalized.

Capitalization also affects the way Word displays dictionary terms in the Suggestions list box. If the unrecognized term is capitalized, Word's suggested alternatives will also appear capitalized.

Editing a user dictionary

Fortunately, Word's user dictionaries are very flexible. Not only can you add new terms to a dictionary, you also can revise existing terms, delete terms, and even copy terms from one user dictionary to another. If there's a dictionary that you use during most of your spelling checks, you will probably need to make frequent changes to that file in order to adapt it to different situations.

Deleting a dictionary term

To delete a term, type it into the Word text box of the Check Spelling dialog box, then choose Check. When Word displays the box with the message *Word was found in User dictionary*, choose OK, then choose the Delete button in the Check Spelling dialog box. This will remove the word from the dictionary. If you want, you can then select another dictionary in the expanded Check Spelling dialog box and add the term to that dictionary.

Revising a dictionary term

To revise a dictionary term, first delete it. Next, choose the Start button. When the term appears in the Not In Dictionary area of the Spelling window, make sure the correct dictionary name is displayed in the Add To Dictionary list box, then choose the Add button. Your replacement term will be stored in the user dictionary you selected.

Saving, opening, and closing a user dictionary

Fortunately, Word automatically saves the additions and deletions you make to your dictionaries. For this reason, you don't need to worry about issuing any Save commands.

After Word saves a user dictionary to disk, you can open it by issuing the Spelling... command, choosing the Options >> button to expand the Check Spelling dialog box, then choosing the appropriate user dictionary from the Supplemental list box. When you choose the Start button, Word will begin the spelling check using the dictionaries you've specified in the Main and Supplemental list boxes, along with the user dictionary STDUSER.DIC. To close a user dictionary, select the name of a different dictionary in the Supplemental list box.

A final note

We must remind you that Word's ability to find misspelled words does not necessarily mean it will discover every incorrect word in a document. The program has no way of recognizing incorrect tense or form or improper usage of a word. Always supplement your spelling checks with a thorough reading.

Word's Thesaurus is a treasury of terms. It provides a storehouse of synonyms you can use as alternatives. For instance, if you write quickly to get your ideas on paper, then revise your documents later to spruce up the phrasing, you'll find Word's Thesaurus offers invaluable assistance in avoiding repetition.

THE THESAURUS

To use the Thesaurus, pull down the Utilities menus and select the Thesaurus... command. When the Thesaurus dialog box shown in Figure 6-34 appears, Word will display the current selection in the Look Up text box. Word considers the current selection to be the word in which the cursor is positioned or, if the cursor is positioned between two words, the word to the left of the cursor.

Figure 6-34

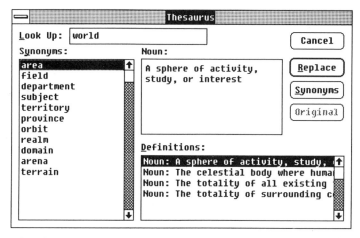

The Thesaurus dialog box displays the current selection in the Look Up text box.

If you want to check the synonyms for a particular word in your document, you should highlight the word or position the cursor in or next to the word, then issue the Thesaurus... command. Word will place the highlighted word in the Look Up text box and provide a list of synonyms for the word. If you highlight more than one word before issuing the Thesaurus... command, Word will narrow the selection to the leftmost word before it opens the dialog box

For example, to find a synonym for the word *world*, highlight that word in your document and select the Thesaurus... command. As you can see in Figure 6-34, the dialog box that appears will initially suggest 11 alternatives in the Synonyms list box.

The Synonyms list box presents only the synonyms for the definition you've selected in the Definitions list box. If you highlight a different definition in the Definitions list box, Word will place it in the area directly above the Definitions

Finding the right synonym

list box and change the list of words in the Synonyms list box. For instance, if you select the second definition shown in Figure 6-34, Word will place the text *The celestial body where humans live* in the area above the Definitions list box and display only one synonym in the Synonyms list box—*earth*. Notice that both the Definitions list box and the area containing the full definition indicate the word's part of speech in the context of the definition.

Occasionally, you may want to see some synonyms for a word that appears in the Synonyms list box. For instance, after you open the dialog box in Figure 6-34, you may want to see synonyms for the word *area.* To do this, highlight the word and select the Synonyms button. Word will then place the word you selected in the Look Up text box and will display the appropriate entries in the Synonyms and Definitions list boxes.

Making the switch

Once you've identified a suitable synonym for the word in your document, simply select that word in the Synonyms list box, then choose the Replace button. Word will then close the Thesaurus dialog box and replace the highlighted word in your document with the synonym you specified.

Recalling the original list

If you choose the Original button in the Thesaurus dialog box, Word will recall the list of synonyms it displayed when you first issued the Thesaurus... command. For instance, after perusing the definitions for *earth* and *area,* you could redisplay the synonyms and definitions for *world* by selecting the Original button.

Finding synonyms using the Look Up text box

The Thesaurus dialog box will show you synonyms for any valid word you enter into the Look Up text box. Once you've typed the word into this text box, choose the Synonyms button to bring up a list of synonyms for that word. This technique lets you review a list of words that you're considering using later in your document. When you're ready to close the Thesaurus dialog box after using this technique, however, make sure you do so by choosing the Cancel button. If you inadvertently close the Thesaurus dialog box by choosing the Replace button, Word will replace the currently selected word in your document with the highlighted entry in the Synonyms list box.

HYPHENATION

Like many other word processing programs, Word offers a hyphenation feature. Word will not automatically hyphenate words as you enter text. However, you can use the Hyphenate... command on the Utilities menu to hyphenate text you've already created. Of course, the benefit of using hyphenation is that it allows you to create more attractive documents. Hyphenation is particularly helpful when you are using justified paragraphs and/or narrow columns of text. By hyphenating selected words, you can avoid the unsightly extra spaces that Word occasionally inserts to achieve a justified right margin. If you are using left-aligned paragraphs instead of justified paragraphs, hyphenation can help you create more uniform lines of text.

Word's Hyphenate… command allows you to hyphenate an entire document or only a selected portion of a document. You also can check each possible hyphenation as you go or have Word perform all the hyphenation automatically. We'll talk about the different hyphenation options as we explain how to use the Hyphenate… command.

One major advantage of Word's hyphenation feature is that it inserts optional hyphens instead of "real" hyphens. An optional hyphen appears in your printed document only if the word you have hyphenated occurs at a line break. If you edit or reformat your text so that the hyphenated word gets shifted to the middle of a line, Word will not print the optional hyphen. (You can create an optional hyphen manually by pressing [Ctrl] as you type a hyphen.)

The optional hyphen is one of Word's two special hyphens. Word also offers a non-breaking hyphen, which you can create by pressing [Ctrl][Shift] as you type a hyphen. This will appear on your screen as a long hyphen if you have activated the Optional Hyphens option in the Preferences dialog box. (Activating Optional Hyphens also tells Word to display all optional hyphens.) If you haven't activated this option, the non-breaking hyphen will look like a regular hyphen, and optional hyphens will appear only if they exist at the end of a line.

To hyphenate your current document, choose Hyphenate… from the Utilities menu. When the Hyphenate dialog box appears, just choose OK to start the hyphenation procedure. Starting at the position of the cursor, Word will look through your document for the first possible word to hyphenate, then display that word in the Hyphenate At text box. Word also will highlight the suggested word break in your document. For example, Figure 6-35 shows how the Hyphenate dialog box will look when Word has found a word to hyphenate.

Using the Hyphenate… command

Figure 6-35

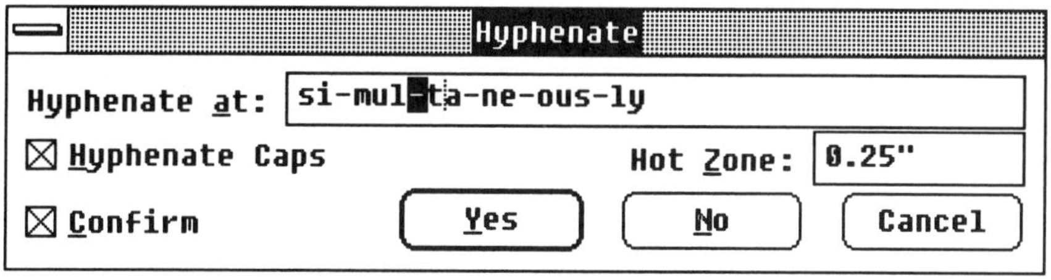

Word will suggest a word break when it locates a candidate for hyphenation.

If you want to change the hyphenation point that Word suggests, use the left or right arrow keys or the mouse to select a new hyphenation point in the Hyphenate At text box, then choose Yes to accept that hyphenation point. If you don't want to hyphenate the word, choose No to skip the word, or choose the Cancel button to cancel the procedure and close the dialog box. If you specify a hyphenation point that occurs after the line break, Word won't use your suggestion. Word will, however, remember it the next time that word needs to be hyphenated. If you edit your text later, and the word's position shifts, Word may be able to use your suggested hyphenation point.

By the way, you can hyphenate a word between any two letters—you do not have to break it between syllables. If you place the cursor somewhere other than at a syllable break in the text box, Word will display a vertical cursor at that place rather than highlighting the break. You will find this flexibility in controlling word breaks very helpful in those few situations in which Word's syllable breaks are unacceptable.

You might notice a dotted vertical line that appears on the word in the text box. This line indicates the approximate number of characters that will fit on the current line. In general, if you try to hyphenate the word to the right of the dotted line, there will not be enough room on the previous line of text to hold the first part of the hyphenated word. Word will still insert the optional hyphen in your document, however, without breaking the word. For instance, in the dialog box shown in Figure 6-35, if you placed the cursor between *simultaneous* and *ly*, Word probably would not be able to break the word. However, it still would place an optional hyphen in your document at that location.

After Word has scanned to the end of your document looking for possible word breaks, you'll see the message box shown in Figure 6-36. If you want to cycle back to the beginning of the document and look for more word breaks, choose Yes. If you want to stop the hyphenation procedure, choose No. Word will then close the Hyphenate dialog box and return to the document.

Figure 6-36

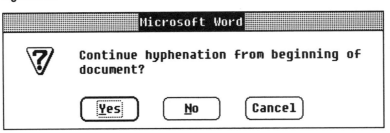

You'll see this message box when Word has hyphenated through the end of your document.

Automatic hyphenation

If you want Word to hyphenate your document automatically, just deselect the Confirm check box in the lower-left corner of the Hyphenate dialog box before you choose OK to begin hyphenation. As Word hyphenates the document, it will automatically decide which words to break between lines and how to break each word. This automatic hyphenation occurs very rapidly and affects all the text between the cursor and the end of the document. During hyphenation, the status bar will display the percentage of the document that has been hyphenated. When Word reaches the end of the document, you will see the message box shown in Figure 6-36.

Once again, you can continue hyphenating from the beginning of the document by choosing Yes; you can stop hyphenating and return to the document by choosing No or Cancel. If you want, you can undo hyphenation after the procedure is completed. We will explain a couple of methods for undoing hyphenation in a moment.

In general, we recommend that you avoid automatic hyphenation since it can lead to some problems. First, Word may hyphenate words at the end of two or more consecutive lines in your document. This is not good form since it makes the document more difficult to read. Second, Word may hyphenate words that already are hyphenated. For example, if your document contains the word *long-suffering*, Word may hyphenate the *suffering* portion at the end of a line. A final reason for avoiding automatic hyphenation is that Word's syllable breaks are not always correct. For example, in one of our documents, Word hyphenated the word *dictionary* between *dictio* and *nary*, rather than between *diction* and *ary*. If you use confirming hyphenation instead of automatic hyphenation, you can avoid these kinds of problems during the hyphenation procedure.

Problems with automatic hyphenation

The Hyphenate Caps check box in the Hyphenate dialog box lets you tell Word to either hyphenate or ignore capitalized words. As you can see in Figure 6-35, the Hyphenate Caps check box is selected when you first open the Hyphenate dialog box. If you do not want to hyphenate words that begin with an uppercase letter, deselect this check box.

The Hyphenate Caps option

You've probably noticed that Word presents a second text box in the Hyphenate dialog box: Hot Zone. This text box allows you to set the distance between the right indent and the end of the line. By adjusting the size of the hot zone, you can adjust the unevenness of the line along the right margin, as well as the number of hyphenated words that appear in the document.

Adjusting the Hot Zone setting

If the distance between the indention and the end of the line is greater than the value in the Hot Zone text box, Word will try to hyphenate the first word on the next line so part of the word will appear on the preceding line. When you first issue the Hyphenate... command, the default Hot Zone measurement is 0.25". If you want to decrease the "raggedness" of the words along the right margin, or you want to reduce the amount of space that appears between words in justified text, you'll want to enter a smaller Hot Zone setting. On the other hand, if you want to hyphenate as few words as possible, or you dislike seeing short single syllables at the beginning of lines, you'll want to enter a larger Hot Zone setting.

**Hyphenating a
selected part of
a document**

If you want to hyphenate only a portion of your document, just select that portion before you issue the Hyphenate... command. Your selection can be as small as a single word, although you probably will want to select at least a paragraph or more. Again, you will have the choice of using either automatic or confirming hyphenation. When Word has completed hyphenating the selection, it will close the Hyphenate dialog box.

**Editing after
you hyphenate**

If you make substantial changes to a document after you've used the Hyphenate... command, you will probably change the location of a number of hyphenated words. Instead of occurring at the end of lines, some hyphenated words will end up in the middle of lines. Additionally, you'll probably need to hyphenate a number of words that now appear at the end of a line. Of course, you can solve the second problem by issuing the Hyphenate... command again. Before you reissue the command, however, you may want to delete the hyphens that appear in the middle of lines of text. To do this quickly, you might want to use the search-and-replace procedure we explained earlier in this chapter to remove the unnecessary hyphens from your document. If you don't delete these hyphens, however, they will not affect the appearance of your printed document since Word does not print optional hyphens unless they appear at line breaks.

In general, we recommend that you delete any unnecessary optional hyphens before you rehyphenate your document. That way, you can activate the Optional Hyphens option in the Preferences dialog box to display long hyphens without cluttering up your screen. For example, the document shown in Figure 6-37 has been through several hyphenation procedures. Although none of the midline optional hyphens will appear in the printed document, they make it difficult to read and edit the document's text on the screen.

Figure 6-37

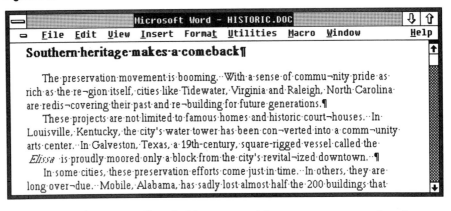

*To eliminate clutter, you'll probably want to delete unnecessary optional
hyphens from your document.*

After you have hyphenated a document or a selected portion of a document, you have the option of using the Undo Hyphenate command on the Edit menu to delete all of the hyphens that Word has just added. As with other Undo commands, you must select Undo Hyphenate immediately after you complete the hyphenation procedure. As soon as you do something else—type a character, change a format, etc.—the Undo Hyphenate command will no longer be available.

Fortunately, there's another way to undo hyphenation. By using the Replace... command, you can delete all the hyphens Word added during a hyphenation procedure. To do this, just choose Replace... from the Edit menu and enter a caret followed by a hyphen (^-) in the Search For text box. Leave the Replace With text box blank. Now, turn off the Confirm Changes option and choose OK. Immediately, Word will delete every optional hyphen in your document. If you want to delete only some of the hyphens, turn on Confirm Changes before you choose OK to begin the replace procedure. Word will then pause at each optional hyphen and give you the choice of deleting it.

Undoing hyphenation

In this chapter

Printing 7

*A*fter creating, formatting, and editing a document, you're ready to print it. Of course, if you're like most word processing users, you'll probably print at least one draft of your document before you complete all of your editing and formatting changes. Fortunately, the default settings in the Print and Document dialog boxes are generally adequate for printing quick drafts and simple documents. After you have installed and selected a printer, you simply choose the Print... command from the File menu and choose OK in the ensuing dialog box.

Of course, with a program as powerful as Word, it's no surprise that printing can also be a very complex issue. Word lets you specify a number of settings that apply directly to printing, such as the number of copies you want to create, which part of a document you want to print, and how you want to feed the paper into the printer. In addition, you can add certain elements to a document that enhance the printed pages, such as page numbers and headers and footers.

In this chapter, we'll explore the various settings that can affect printing and show you how to number your pages and create headers and footers. Then, we'll show you how to use the Print Preview window and the page view to see how the printed document will look—without actually printing. Let's begin, however, with a look at the procedures you follow to install and select a printer.

INSTALLING A PRINTER

When you ran the Windows Setup program, you probably specified at least one printer that you planned to use. Once you are in Word, you can install additional printers if you want and "uninstall" printers that you previously installed. Depending on the amount of memory in your computer, you may find that it's practical to have only one or two printers installed at any given time. More than this can lead to a warning message indicating that you're running low on memory.

To install an additional printer, choose Run… from Microsoft Word's Control menu, then choose Control Panel as the application you want to run. When the Control Panel appears on your screen, choose Add New Printer… from the Control Panel's Installation menu. You'll then see the Add Printer dialog box shown in Figure 7-1.

Figure 7-1

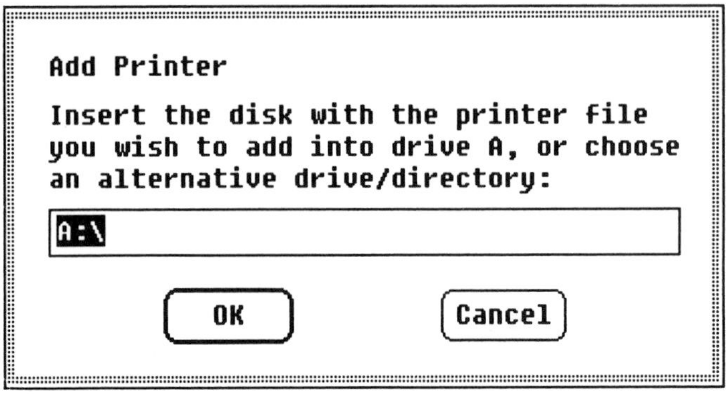

```
┌───────────────────────────────────────────────────────┐
│                                                       │
│   Add Printer                                         │
│                                                       │
│   Insert the disk with the printer file               │
│   you wish to add into drive A, or choose             │
│   an alternative drive/directory:                     │
│                                                       │
│   ┌─────────────────────────────────────────────┐     │
│   │ A:\                                         │     │
│   └─────────────────────────────────────────────┘     │
│                                                       │
│        ┌──────────┐        ┌──────────┐               │
│        │    OK    │        │  Cancel  │               │
│        └──────────┘        └──────────┘               │
│                                                       │
└───────────────────────────────────────────────────────┘
```

You'll use the Add Printer dialog box to specify which disk contains the driver for the printer you want to install.

If the driver for the printer you want to install is stored on a floppy disk (such as your Windows Utilities 1 disk), insert that disk into drive A and choose OK. If the driver for the printer is located on your hard disk, or if you want to use a drive other than A, type the full path name for the drive in which the printer driver is located, then choose OK.

You will then see a dialog box like the one in Figure 7-2, which lists all the printers whose drivers are stored on the drive you specified. Select the printer you want to install from this list and choose Add. You will then see a dialog box asking if you want to copy into your current directory the driver file for the printer you selected. At this point, you should choose Yes, which will tell Windows to install the printer driver and update your WIN.INI file.

By the way, if you're using an HP LaserJet printer equipped with a JetScript board, giving the printer PostScript capability, you must install the QMS-PS 800 Plus or the Apple LaserWriter Plus printer driver in order to take advantage of the printer's PostScript capability.

Specifying a printer port

After you install a new printer using the Control Panel, you need to specify to which port you've connected the printer. While the Control Panel is still open, choose Connections… from the Setup menu. This will bring up the Connections dialog box shown in Figure 7-3.

Figure 7-2

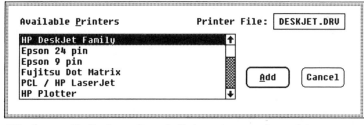

Windows will display a list of all the printers whose drivers are stored on the drive you specified.

Figure 7-3

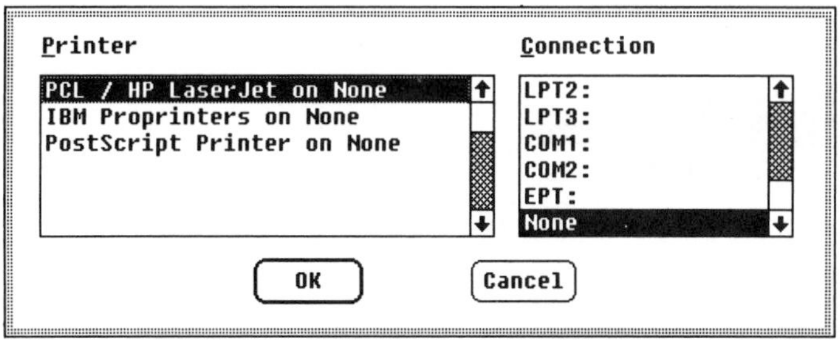

```
┌─────────────────────────────────────────────────────────┐
│  Printer                        Connection                │
│ ┌──────────────────────────┬─┐ ┌───────────────────────┬─┐│
│ │PCL / HP LaserJet on None │↑│ │LPT2:                  │↑││
│ │IBM Proprinters on None   │ │ │LPT3:                  │ ││
│ │PostScript Printer on None│ │ │COM1:                  │ ││
│ │                          │ │ │COM2:                  │ ││
│ │                          │ │ │EPT:                   │ ││
│ │                          │↓│ │None                   │↓││
│ └──────────────────────────┴─┘ └───────────────────────┴─┘│
│         ┌────────┐        ┌──────────┐                    │
│         │   OK   │        │  Cancel  │                    │
│         └────────┘        └──────────┘                    │
└─────────────────────────────────────────────────────────┘
```

Use the Connections dialog box to specify which port you plan to use for the printer you just installed.

The printer you just installed will appear last in the list of printers on the left. Highlight the appropriate printer name, select a printer port from the Connection list box, and choose OK. If you want, you also can use the Connections dialog box to change a printer port.

To uninstall a printer, you must again use the Control Panel. Choose Run... from Word's Control menu, then choose the Control Panel option. When the Control Panel appears on your screen, choose Delete Printer... from the Installation menu. You will then see the Delete Printer dialog box, which lists all the currently installed printers. Highlight the name of the printer you want to delete and choose the Delete button. You'll then see a dialog box asking if you want to delete the printer driver file from disk. Choose either Yes or No. If you have plenty of room on your hard disk and you think you may need to use the printer again, you probably should choose No. Then, the next time you want to install that printer, you won't need to insert another disk in your floppy drive. After deleting an installed printer, you can close the Control Panel and continue working in Word.

Deleting an installed printer

**SELECTING
A PRINTER**

If you have installed more than one printer, you will need to specify which one you want to use. If you do not select a printer, Windows will automatically use the first printer you installed.

There are two ways to select a printer: You can use the Printer... command on the Control Panel's Setup menu, or you can choose the Printer Setup... command from Word's File menu. Both of these commands will display a dialog box containing a list of installed printers. When you choose Printer Setup... from the File menu, you will see a Printer Setup dialog box like the one in Figure 7-4. If you choose Printer... from the Control Panel's Setup menu, however, you will see a Printer dialog box that contains two Printer Timeouts settings, as shown in Figure 7-5.

Figure 7-4

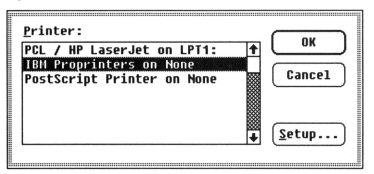

You'll see this dialog box when you choose Printer Setup... from Word's File menu.

Figure 7-5

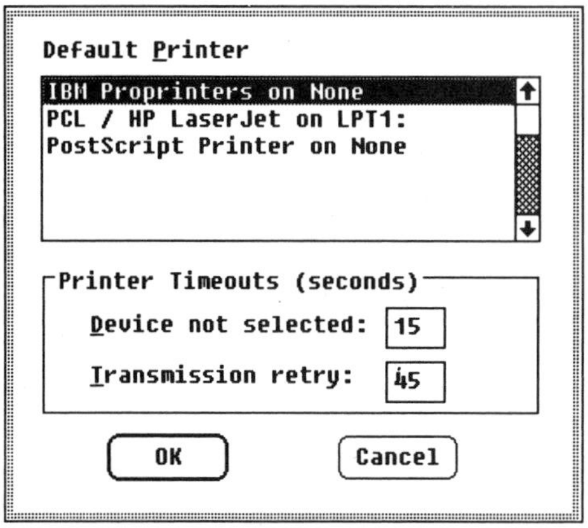

This is the dialog box you will see when you choose Printer... from the Control Panel's Setup menu.

The main difference between the dialog boxes in Figures 7-4 and 7-5 is the appearance of two Printer Timeouts settings. These settings determine how long (in seconds) your computer will wait before informing you of a problem during printing. The Device Not Selected text box specifies the number of seconds that must elapse before Windows alerts you that the printer is not responding to your initial print request. For example, suppose this setting is 15 and you try to print a document while your printer is not turned on or is not on-line. Your computer will continue its attempt to print until 15 seconds has elapsed. Following this, an error message will appear on your screen. If you want your computer to pause for a shorter or longer period, you can change the value in the Device Not Selected text box. **Printer Timeouts**

The Transmission Retry text box specifies the number of seconds that must elapse before Windows alerts you of a problem that occurs during printing. For example, suppose this setting is 45. If your printer runs out of paper or jams during the printing process, your computer will continue its attempt to print the document until 45 seconds has elapsed. Then, Windows will display an error message on your screen. If you want your computer to wait for a shorter or longer period before displaying an error message, you can change the value in the Transmission Retry text box.

The Printer Timeouts settings are not dependent on the printer you select. The settings you specify will apply regardless of the printer you decide to use.

To choose a printer in the Printer Setup dialog box, just highlight the name of the installed printer you want to use. If you're using Word's Printer Setup... command, you can then choose OK to lock in your new printer choice and close the dialog box. Alternatively, you can choose the Setup... button to bring up a dialog box of settings for the printer you have selected. Throughout this chapter, we'll refer to this dialog box as a printer settings box. We'll look at several printer settings boxes in more detail a little later in this chapter. **Choosing a printer**

If you're using the Control Panel, Windows will automatically display a printer settings box when you choose OK to lock in your printer selection. If you do not want to change any of the Setup options, just choose OK to close the dialog box. Windows will also close the dialog box shown in Figure 7-5 and return you to the Control Panel. Since the printer selection process is now complete, you can close the Control Panel window and return to Word.

A note of warning: If you're using the Control Panel, you must choose OK in both the dialog box shown in Figure 7-5 and in the ensuing printer settings box in order for Windows to accept your default printer selection. If you choose Cancel in either dialog box, Windows will not record your printer selection. In general, we recommend that you use Word's Printer Setup... command to select a printer. With this command, you can select a printer without having to open the printer settings box.

PRINTER SETTINGS

After selecting a printer, you will probably need to specify some additional settings in the printer settings box. As you've seen, you can access this dialog box by choosing the Setup... button in Word's Printer Setup dialog box or by choosing OK in the Control Panel's Printer dialog box. The size and contents of the printer settings box depend on the printer name you selected in the Printer Setup (or Printer) dialog box. In this section, we'll look at several of these printer settings boxes for various printers.

The HP LaserJet and other PCL printers

If the printer you have selected is one of the HP LaserJet printers or another Printer Command Language (PCL) printer, such as the Wang LDP8 or the NEC SilentWriter LC860, the printer settings box you see when you choose the Setup... button will look like the one in Figure 7-6.

Figure 7-6

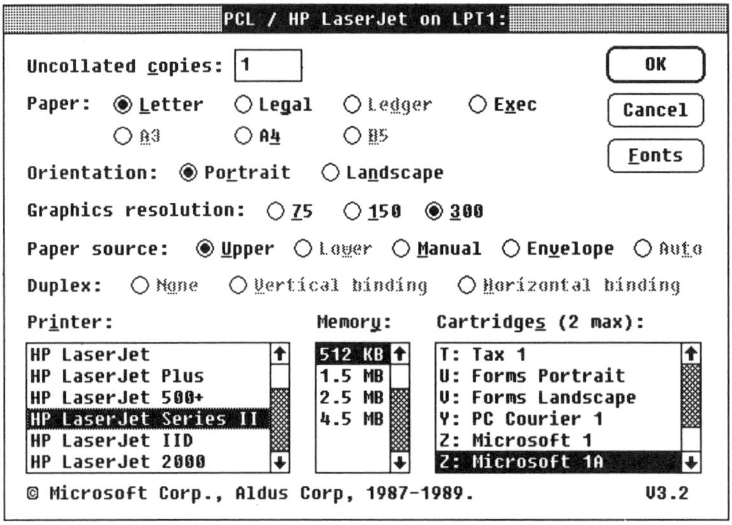

```
┌─────────────────────────────────────────────────────────────────┐
│                 PCL / HP LaserJet on LPT1:                        │
│                                                                   │
│  Uncollated copies: │1    │              ┌──────────┐            │
│                                           │    OK    │            │
│  Paper:  ◉ Letter   ○ Legal   ○ Ledger  ○ Exec      │            │
│                                           ┌──────────┐            │
│          ○ A3        ○ A4      ○ B5       │  Cancel  │            │
│                                           └──────────┘            │
│  Orientation: ◉ Portrait  ○ Landscape    ┌──────────┐            │
│                                           │  Fonts   │            │
│  Graphics resolution:  ○ 75   ○ 150  ◉ 300                       │
│                                                                   │
│  Paper source:  ◉ Upper  ○ Lower  ○ Manual  ○ Envelope  ○ Auto   │
│                                                                   │
│  Duplex:  ○ None  ○ Vertical binding  ○ Horizontal binding        │
│                                                                   │
│  Printer:                 Memory:      Cartridges (2 max):        │
│  ┌──────────────────┬─┐  ┌────────┬─┐  ┌──────────────────────┬─┐│
│  │HP LaserJet       │↑│  │512 KB  │↑│  │T: Tax 1              │↑││
│  │HP LaserJet Plus  │ │  │1.5 MB  │ │  │U: Forms Portrait     │ ││
│  │HP LaserJet 500+  │ │  │2.5 MB  │ │  │U: Forms Landscape    │ ││
│  │HP LaserJet Series II│ │4.5 MB │ │  │Y: PC Courier 1       │ ││
│  │HP LaserJet IID   │ │  │        │ │  │Z: Microsoft 1        │ ││
│  │HP LaserJet 2000  │↓│  │        │↓│  │Z: Microsoft 1A       │↓││
│  └──────────────────┴─┘  └────────┴─┘  └──────────────────────┴─┘│
│  © Microsoft Corp., Aldus Corp, 1987-1989.            V3.2        │
└─────────────────────────────────────────────────────────────────┘
```

This is the printer settings box for the HP LaserJet printer.

You will probably change some of the settings that appear in this box only once. For example, once you select a printer name and a memory setting, it is unlikely you will need to change these settings. On the other hand, you may need to change some settings quite frequently, such as the print orientation. Let's look at each of the settings you can specify for PCL printers.

Specifying a printer type

Probably the most important setting is the printer name you select from the Printer list box in the lower-left corner of the PCL/HP LaserJet printer settings box. This list box includes the names of all printers in the HP LaserJet family, as well as several LaserJet/PCL-compatible printers available from other manufacturers. From this list, you should choose the name of the particular printer you are using.

The printer you select will directly affect the availability of many of the other options in the printer settings box. For example, if you choose the HP LaserJet 2000 printer, you can access the Auto Paper Source option. This option will not be available if you choose the HP LaserJet Series II printer.

The printer you select will also affect the fonts that are available for formatting your Word documents. As we explained in Chapter 5, Word will allow you to format a document using only the fonts that your selected printer can produce. Different printers have different resident (built-in) fonts. For example, the HP LaserJet Series II printer has both Courier and LinePrinter as built-in fonts, while the HP LaserJet 2000 printer has these two fonts, as well as Helv, LineDraw, Prestige Elite, and Tms Rmn.

Most of the printers listed in the PCL/HP LaserJet printer settings box have at least two possible memory configurations. After you have selected a printer, you will see its various memory settings in the Memory list box. You should choose from this list (or single item, if your printer has only one memory configuration) the amount of memory that is installed in the printer you have selected.

Specifying the amount of printer memory

Most of the printers listed also can accept font cartridges. After you have selected a printer, a list of its available font cartridges (if any) will appear in the Cartridges list box. Just above the list box, you'll see the maximum number of cartridges you can select for the printer you are using. For example, if you have selected a HP LaserJet Plus printer, you will see *(1 max)* above the Cartridges list box. On the other hand, if you have selected an HP LaserJet Series II printer, you'll see *(2 max)*. If you don't have a font cartridge, you should select the None option that appears at the top of the Cartridges list. You can select font cartridges by clicking on their names with your mouse. To select more than one cartridge, press the [Shift] key as you click   To select a font cartridge using the keyboard, first press [Alt]S to activate the Cartridges list box. Then, press the [Ctrl] key as you use the ↑ and ↓ keys to move the dotted outline to a font cartridge name. Finally, press the [Spacebar] to select that name. To select a second or third font cartridge, just repeat this procedure.

Identifying font cartridges

The font cartridges you select, like the printer name you chose, will affect the list of available fonts in the Character dialog box and in the Font list box on the ribbon. Any fonts on the cartridges you select will also appear in these lists.

You use the Uncollated Copies text box to tell Word how many copies of your document you want to print. As the setting name implies, when you print multiple copies of a document, Word will not collate the document pages during printing. Instead, it will print the specified number of copies of the first page, followed by

Printing multiple copies

all the copies of the second page, and so forth. Because it does not collate multiple copies of a document, Word considerably speeds up the printing operation. This time-saver is especially significant when your document contains graphics or several fonts. Whenever you print a document, Word spends a certain amount of time converting each page to a data format that your printer can recognize. Windows spends additional time transmitting this data to the printer. By printing all copies of each page at once, Word has to convert the data for that page and send it to the printer only one time instead of several times.

Choosing paper

Each of the PCL printers listed in the Printer list box can use several types of paper stock. When you choose a printer, the Paper options that are available for that printer will appear in black, while options that are not available for that printer will be dimmed. You select one of the available options to tell Word what kind of paper you plan to use. Table 7-1 lists the most common paper options and their corresponding sizes.

Table 7-1

Paper option	Size
Letter	8.5 by 11 inches
Legal	8.5 by 14 inches
Exec	7.25 by 10.5 inches
A4	8.3 by 11.7 inches
B5	7.2 by 10 inches

It's important for you to match the Page Width and Height settings in the Document dialog box with the Paper option you select in the printer settings box. If you specify a paper size other than Letter, Word will present a message box like the one shown in Figure 7-7 when you choose OK in the Printer Setup dialog box. When you see this message box, you should choose OK and then select the Document... command from the Format menu. When the Document dialog box appears, change the Page Width and Height settings to match the new paper size you've specified in your printer settings box.

If you attempt to print a document whose Page Width and Height settings don't reflect the paper size you've selected in the printer settings box, Word will present the message box shown in Figure 7-8. If you see this message box, choose No to halt the Print... command, then use the Printer Setup... command to check the paper size you selected. After you've selected the appropriate paper size, you'll need to open the Document dialog box and adjust the Page Width and Height settings accordingly.

Figure 7-7

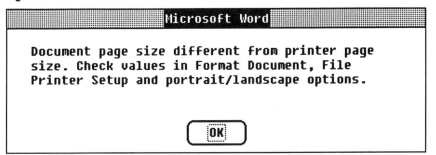

If you use a paper size other than Letter, make sure you adjust the Page Width and Height settings in the Document dialog box.

Figure 7-8

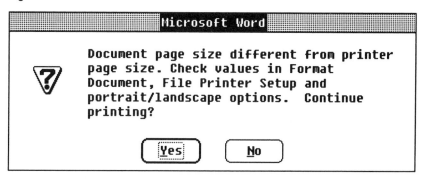

Word will present this message box if you attempt to print a document whose Page Width and Height settings don't match the paper size specified in the printer settings box.

We introduced the concept of print orientation in Chapter 5. As we explained there, if you choose portrait orientation, Word will print your text across the short side of the paper; if you choose landscape orientation, Word will print your text across the long side of the paper. In other words, with portrait orientation, Word prints lines of text across what you normally would consider the x-axis of a page. Similarly, with landscape orientation, Word prints the lines of text across what you normally would consider the y-axis of a page. Portrait is the default orientation for printing. You can change this setting by selecting the Landscape option.

If you change the Orientation setting in the printer settings box, Word will present a message box like the one shown in Figure 7-9 after you've closed both the printer settings box and the Printer Setup dialog box. When you see this message box, you should choose the Yes button, which will tell Word to swap the

Choosing print orientation

current Page Width and Height settings in the Document dialog box. If you don't choose Yes in this message box, Word will present the message box shown in Figure 7-8 when you issue the Print... command. Whenever you see this message, you should choose No to halt the Print... command, then adjust the Page Width and Height settings in the Document dialog box to match the paper size and orientation you've specified in the printer settings box.

Figure 7-9

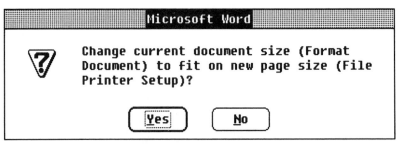

When you change the Orientation setting in the printer settings box,
Word will present this message box, allowing you to automatically
swap the Page Width and Height settings in the Document dialog box.

Specifying graphics resolution

The HP LaserJet and compatible printers are based on the Canon laser engines, which can print graphics at a maximum resolution of 300 dots per inch. These printers can also produce resolutions of 150 and 75 dots per inch. Specify the resolution you want to use by choosing the 75, 150, or 300 Graphics Resolution setting.

The number of dots per inch directly affects the quality of the graphic images (but not text) in your printed document. However, the greater the resolution setting, the slower the print speed. If quality is important, you should choose the highest resolution setting that your printer supports. On the other hand, if speed is your main concern, you'll want to choose one of the lower settings.

Choosing a paper source

Most of the PCL printers that Word supports offer at least two ways to feed paper into the printer: using the paper tray and manual feeding. Some printers have two paper trays, allowing you to use different paper stocks in each tray. You use the Paper Source options in the PCL/HP LaserJet printer settings box to tell Word which paper source you want to use. Just select the option you want—Upper, Lower, Manual, Envelope, or Auto.

Printing on both sides of the paper

The HP LaserJet IID and LaserJet 2000 printers have the ability to print documents on both sides of a page. If you have selected one of these printers from the Printer list box, the Duplex options will become available. If you have selected a different printer, the Duplex options will appear dimmed.

As you can see, there are three Duplex printing options: None, Vertical Binding, and Horizontal Binding. If you do not want to print text on both sides of a page, you should choose the None option. If you want to print text on both sides of the page so you can bind the pages along the long edge, you should choose the Vertical Binding option. Choose the Horizontal Binding option if you want to print text on both sides of a page so that you can bind the pages along the short edges.

Many of the PCL printers you can use with Word can accept soft fonts, which are fonts that you can download from the computer to the printer. If you've used a font management program (like Hewlett-Packard's Type Director) to generate and install soft fonts, you probably won't need to use Windows' Soft Font Installer—your font management program should take care of everything for you. However, if you've purchased a set of bitmapped soft fonts that you cannot resize, you'll need to run Windows' Soft Font Installer in order to use those fonts in your Word documents.

Using soft fonts

To run Windows' Soft Font Installer, simply choose the Fonts button in the PCL/HP LaserJet printer settings box. Immediately, the Soft Font Installer window, shown in Figure 7-10, will appear on your screen.

Figure 7-10

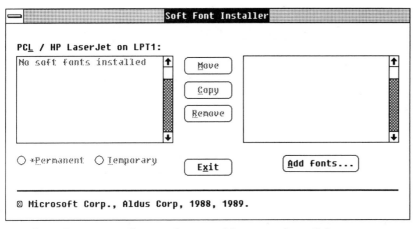

Use the Soft Font Installer window to add support for soft fonts.

In the Soft Font Installer window, choose the Add Fonts... button to bring up the Add Fonts dialog box shown in Figure 7-11. As you can see, this dialog box asks you to insert the disk containing your soft font files in drive A or to specify another drive/directory in which the font files are located. If you are installing soft fonts from a floppy disk, just insert that disk into drive A and choose OK. If you want to install soft fonts that are stored on your hard disk or on another floppy disk drive, enter the full path name for the directory in which those files are stored and choose OK.

Figure 7-11

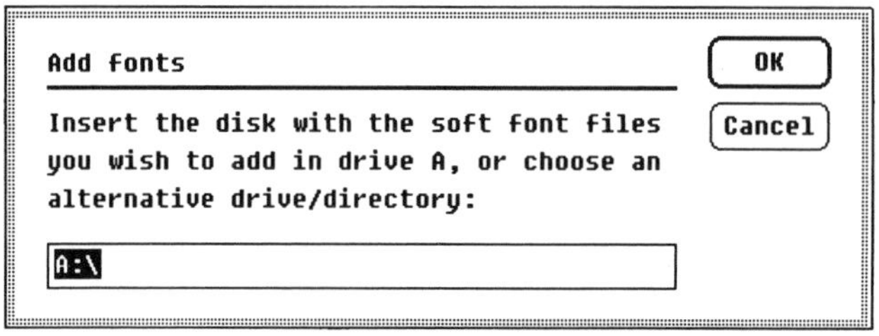

```
┌──────────────────────────────────────────────────────┐
│                                                        │
│  Add fonts                              ┌──────────┐   │
│                                         │    OK    │   │
│  Insert the disk with the soft font files ──────────   │
│  you wish to add in drive A, or choose an ┌──────────┐ │
│  alternative drive/directory:            │  Cancel  │ │
│                                          └──────────┘ │
│  ┌──────────────────────────────────────────────────┐ │
│  │A:\                                               │ │
│  └──────────────────────────────────────────────────┘ │
│                                                        │
└──────────────────────────────────────────────────────┘
```

In the Soft Font Installer window, enter the name of the drive and directory in which your soft font files are located.

Once the Soft Font Installer locates your soft font files, those files will appear in the list box on the right of the Soft Font Installer window. For example, in Figure 7-12, this list box contains the names of all the soft fonts that are stored on drive C in the directory \PCLFONTS. Notice that the list box is now labeled with the drive/directory name *Drive C:\PCLFONTS*. Notice also that the Add Fonts... button in the Soft Font Installer window is now labeled *Close drive*.

Figure 7-12

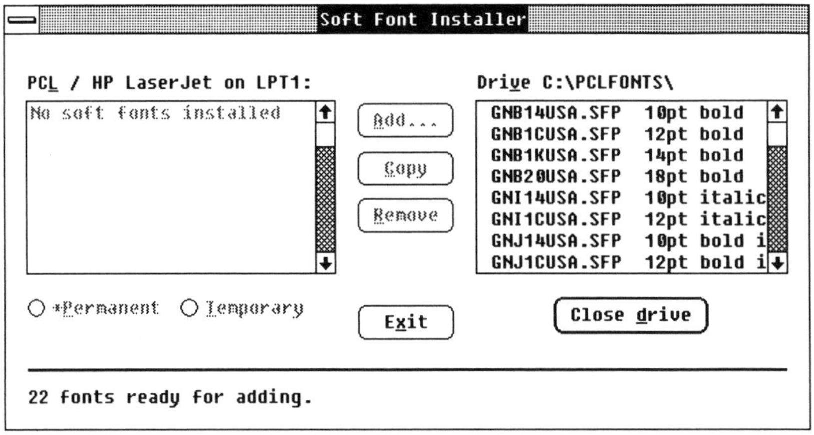

```
┌──────────────────────────────────────────────────────────────┐
│ ═   ░░░░░░░░░░░░░░░  Soft Font Installer  ░░░░░░░░░░░░░░░░░░░░  │
├──────────────────────────────────────────────────────────────┤
│                                                                │
│  PCL / HP LaserJet on LPT1:              Drive C:\PCLFONTS\     │
│  ┌──────────────────────────┐ ┌──────────┐ ┌──────────────────┐│
│  │No soft fonts installed ▲ │ │  Add...  │ │GNB14USA.SFP 10pt bold ▲││
│  │                        ▒ │ └──────────┘ │GNB1CUSA.SFP 12pt bold  ││
│  │                        ▒ │ ┌──────────┐ │GNB1KUSA.SFP 14pt bold  ││
│  │                        ▒ │ │  Copy    │ │GNB20USA.SFP 18pt bold  ││
│  │                        ▒ │ └──────────┘ │GNI14USA.SFP 10pt italic││
│  │                        ▒ │ ┌──────────┐ │GNI1CUSA.SFP 12pt italic││
│  │                        ▒ │ │  Remove  │ │GNJ14USA.SFP 10pt bold i││
│  │                        ▼ │ └──────────┘ │GNJ1CUSA.SFP 12pt bold i▼││
│  └──────────────────────────┘             └──────────────────┘│
│                                                                │
│  ○ *Permanent  ○ Temporary   ┌────────┐    ┌──────────────┐    │
│                              │  Exit  │    │  Close drive │    │
│                              └────────┘    └──────────────┘    │
│ ─────────────────────────────────────────────────────────────│
│  22 fonts ready for adding.                                    │
└──────────────────────────────────────────────────────────────┘
```

The Soft Font Installer window will list each of the soft font files stored in the directory you specify.

Your next step is to select the fonts you want to install from the list box on the right. If you're using a mouse, you can select two or more fonts by pressing the [Shift] key as you click on the font names. If you're using the keyboard, press

[Alt]V to activate the list of fonts, then use the ↑ and ↓ keys to move through the list to the first font you want to install. To select the first font, press the [Ctrl] key. If you want to select additional fonts, continue holding down the [Ctrl] key while you use the arrow keys to move the dotted outline up or down through the list. When you've highlighted another font you want to install, press the [Spacebar] to select it. Continue holding down the [Ctrl] key until you've selected every font you want to install.

After selecting the fonts, choose the Add… button. When you do this, the dialog box shown in Figure 7-13 will appear, asking you to specify the directory in which the font files should be copied. If you want to use the default directory, C:\PCLFONTS, just choose OK. To specify a different directory, type the full path name of that directory and choose OK. (If you choose the default directory, C:\PCLFONTS, and that directory does not yet exist, you will see a message box asking if this directory should be created.)

Figure 7-13

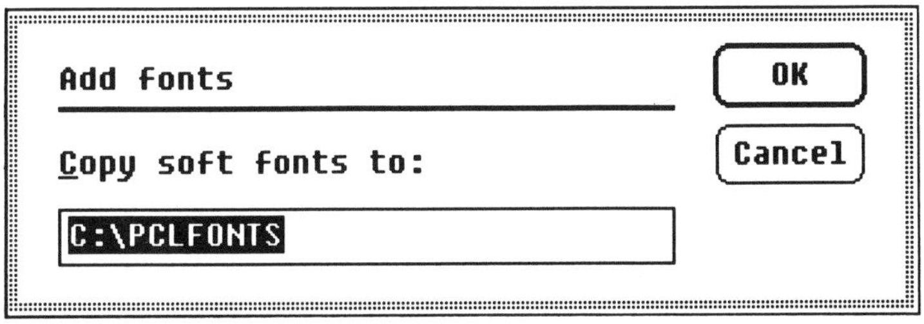

```
┌─────────────────────────────────────────────────┐
│  Add fonts                          ┌──────────┐ │
│  ─────────────────────────────      │    OK    │ │
│                                     └──────────┘ │
│  Copy soft fonts to:                ┌──────────┐ │
│                                     │  Cancel  │ │
│  ┌───────────────────────────┐      └──────────┘ │
│  │ C:\PCLFONTS               │                   │
│  └───────────────────────────┘                   │
└─────────────────────────────────────────────────┘
```

When you see this dialog box, you can choose OK to install the new fonts in the C:\PCLFONTS directory.

At this point, the Soft Font Installer will copy your selected font files into the directory you specified and will install those fonts in Windows. All the font names will appear in the list box on the left side of the Soft Font Installer window. When you return to Word, you will find that the soft fonts you just installed also appear in the pull-down Font list boxes on the ribbon and in the Character dialog box.

All of the soft fonts you install have a permanent or temporary download status. If a font's download status is temporary, the PCL driver will download that font from your computer to your printer every time you print a document using that font. Once the document containing the font has been printed, the PCL driver will delete all the temporary soft fonts from your printer's memory.

If a font's download status is permanent, the PCL driver will assume that the font already has been downloaded when you print a document using that font. Fonts with a permanent download status can be downloaded to your printer automatically when you start up your computer, or can be downloaded during a

Changing a font's download status

Windows session. In either case, they will remain in your printer's memory after you print a document. Any soft fonts that you plan to print several times during a Windows session should have a permanent download status.

Initially, all the soft fonts you install will have a temporary download status. To change a font's download status to permanent, highlight the name of that font and select the Permanent option. (You can change the download status of several fonts at once by selecting those font names before you choose the Permanent option. To select more than one font, use the techniques we described earlier for selecting multiple font names.)

The first time you change a font's download status from temporary to permanent, the Soft Font Installer will display a message box that explains the ramifications of the change. If you want more information, choose the Help button. Otherwise, once you have read the explanation that appears in this message box, choose OK to return to the Soft Font Installer window.

After changing a font's status from temporary to permanent, that font's name will be marked by an asterisk in the list box on the left side of the window. When you select the Exit button to return to the PCL/HP LaserJet printer settings box, you will see a Download Options dialog box like the one in Figure 7-14. As you can see, this dialog box allows you to specify when and if the Soft Font Installer should download the font whose status has been changed to permanent.

Figure 7-14

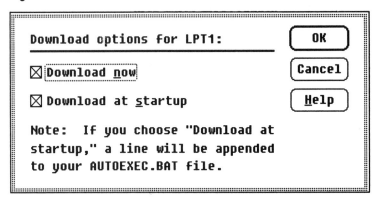

The Download Options dialog box lets you specify when and if the Soft Font Installer should download the font whose status has been changed to permanent.

If you want to download the font automatically when you turn on or reboot your computer, select the Download at Startup check box and choose OK. The Soft Font Installer will then add a line to your AUTOEXEC.BAT file so that each time you turn on or reboot your computer, a message will appear on your screen asking if you want to download PCL fonts to the specified printer port. You can choose Yes or No by typing *Y* or *N.* If you choose Yes, be sure that your printer is connected to the specified port.

If you want to use the font with a permanent download status during the current Windows session, choose the Download Now check box and then choose OK. When you do this, the Soft Font Installer will immediately download all the fonts with a permanent status. (Be sure your printer is connected to the specified port before you choose OK.)

In some cases, you may want to download one or more fonts for the current Windows session and tell your computer to download those fonts automatically each time you reboot your computer. To do this, select both the Download at Startup and the Download Now check boxes and choose OK. Finally, if you want to use a utility such as Hewlett-Packard's Type Director program to download your soft fonts, you should deselect both options in the Download Options dialog box and choose OK.

If you have access to more than one printer, you can use the Soft Font Installer to copy or move soft fonts from one printer port to another. To do this, pull down the Control menu in the Soft Font Installer window and choose the Copy between Ports... command. You will then see a Copy between Ports dialog box like the one in Figure 7-15. Select the port to which you want to copy or move the soft fonts, then choose OK. For example, suppose your first printer is connected to LPT1 and you want to use another printer on LPT2. Simply select LPT2 from the Copy between Ports dialog box and choose OK. The Soft Font Installer window will now look like Figure 7-16 on the next page.

Copying and moving soft font support

Figure 7-15

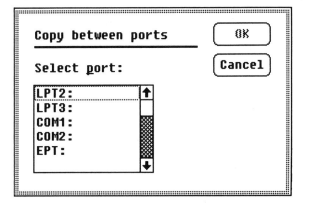

When you choose Copy between Ports... from the Control menu, this dialog box will ask you to identify the port to which you want to download soft fonts.

Figure 7-16

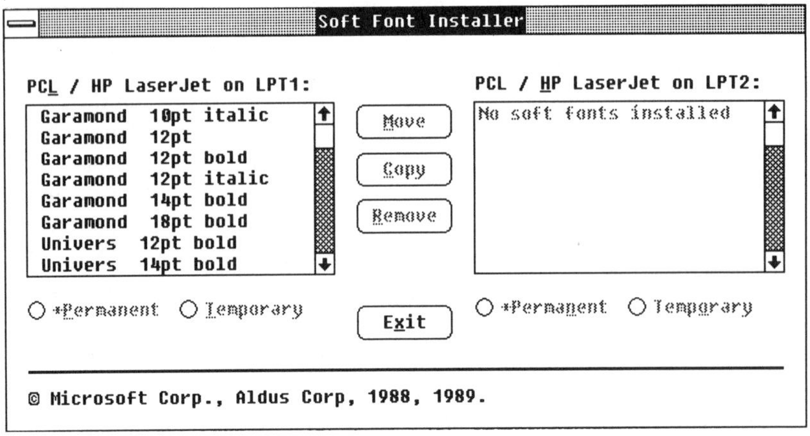

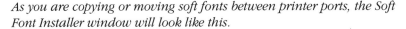

As you are copying or moving soft fonts between printer ports, the Soft Font Installer window will look like this.

The list box on the right side of the Soft Font Installer window will reflect the fonts supported by the printer that is connected to the port you selected. (As you can see, no fonts are currently installed.) In addition, the first button in the dialog box will be labeled *Move* instead of *Add....*

To copy support for a soft font from one printer port to another, highlight the name of the font and choose the Copy button. Similarly, to move a soft font from one printer port to another, highlight the font name and choose Move. After you copy or move a font to another port, the Permanent and Temporary option buttons will become active. You can use these option buttons to alter the status of any fonts on that port.

Once you have finished copying or moving support for soft fonts from one printer port to another, pull down the Control menu in the Soft Font Installer window and choose End between Ports.

Editing font metrics

Font metrics describes the information that identifies certain characteristics of a font. This information includes the font's name and point size, as well as the ID number you can use to select a font once you have downloaded it to a printer. When you install a soft font, the Soft Font Installer will create a data file to store font metrics information. You can change this information by enabling the Soft Font Installer's Edit button.

To enable the Edit button, pull down the Control menu and select the Enable Edit Button command. A button labeled *Edit* will then appear in the Soft Font Installer window, just below the Remove button, as shown in Figure 7-17.

Figure 7-17

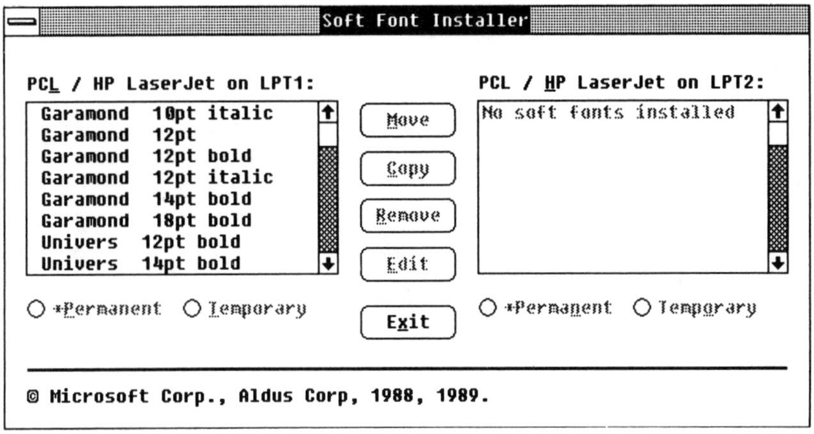

```
┌──────────────────────────────────────────────────────────┐
│ ═══           Soft Font Installer                          │
├──────────────────────────────────────────────────────────┤
│                                                            │
│ PCL / HP LaserJet on LPT1:        PCL / HP LaserJet on LPT2:│
│ ┌─────────────────────────┐┌─────┐ ┌───────────────────────┐│
│ │Garamond  10pt italic  ▲ ││Move │ │No soft fonts installed▲││
│ │Garamond  12pt           │└─────┘ │                       ││
│ │Garamond  12pt bold      │┌─────┐ │                       ││
│ │Garamond  12pt italic    ││Copy │ │                       ││
│ │Garamond  14pt bold      │└─────┘ │                       ││
│ │Garamond  18pt bold      │┌─────┐ │                       ││
│ │Univers   12pt bold      ││Remove│ │                       ││
│ │Univers   14pt bold    ▼ │└─────┘ │                      ▼││
│ └─────────────────────────┘┌─────┐ └───────────────────────┘│
│                            │Edit │                          │
│ ○ *Permanent  ○ Temporary  └─────┘ ○ *Permanent  ○ Temporary│
│                            ┌─────┐                          │
│                            │Exit │                          │
│                            └─────┘                          │
│ ─────────────────────────────────────────────────────────  │
│ © Microsoft Corp., Aldus Corp, 1988, 1989.                 │
└──────────────────────────────────────────────────────────┘
```

The Edit button allows you to make changes to font metrics.

When you select the name of the font you want to edit and choose the Edit button, you'll see a Font Metrics dialog box like the one in Figure 7-18. This dialog box contains information that identifies the font as well as the name of the file in which that font is stored.

Figure 7-18

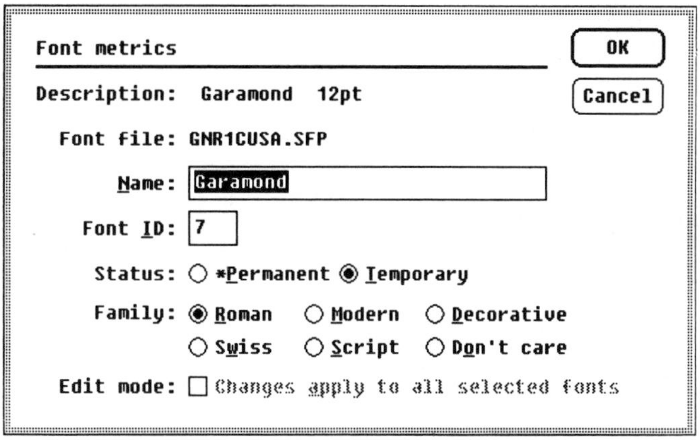

```
┌────────────────────────────────────────────────────┐
│                                                    │
│  Font metrics                         ┌──────────┐ │
│                                       │    OK    │ │
│  Description:  Garamond  12pt         └──────────┘ │
│                                       ┌──────────┐ │
│    Font file: GNR1CUSA.SFP            │  Cancel  │ │
│                                       └──────────┘ │
│        Name: ┌─────────────────────────┐           │
│              │Garamond                 │           │
│              └─────────────────────────┘           │
│     Font ID: ┌───┐                                 │
│              │ 7 │                                 │
│              └───┘                                 │
│      Status: ○ *Permanent  ◉ Temporary             │
│      Family: ◉ Roman   ○ Modern   ○ Decorative     │
│              ○ Swiss   ○ Script   ○ Don't care     │
│   Edit mode: □ Changes apply to all selected fonts │
│                                                    │
└────────────────────────────────────────────────────┘
```

The Font Metrics dialog box lets you make changes to the information that identifies a font.

If you want to change the name Word will use to identify the font, type a new name in the Name text box. Similarly, if you want to change the soft font ID number that Word will use to select a font once it has been downloaded to a printer, enter a number between 0 and 999 in the Font ID text box. You also can change the font's download status to permanent or temporary by choosing the appropriate option button. Finally, if you want, you can change the font's Family setting. After making your changes in the Font Metrics dialog box, choose OK to return to the Soft Font Installer window.

Removing support for a soft font

To remove support for a soft font you have installed, just highlight the font name in the list that appears in the Soft Font Installer window, then choose the Remove button. You can remove support for several fonts at once by highlighting all of their names before you select Remove. After you choose the Remove button, you will see a dialog box asking if you want to remove the font file(s) from disk as well. You can respond by choosing Yes, No, or Cancel. If you choose Yes, you will not only remove support for the font(s), but will also delete the file(s) containing the font information from the directory in which it was originally installed. If you choose No, you will remove support for the selected font(s) without deleting the file(s) from disk.

PostScript printers

If you've installed a PostScript printer, your printer settings box will look like the one in Figure 7-19. (If you are using an HP LaserJet printer, you can purchase a PostScript accessory that will give your printer PostScript capabilities.) Many of the options in this printer settings box are similar or identical to those in the printer settings boxes for the HP LaserJet and other PCL printers. Let's take a close look at each of these options.

Figure 7-19

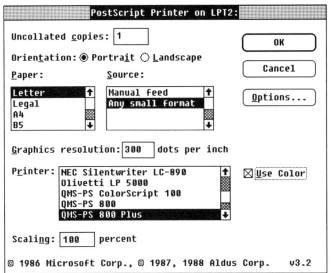

This is the printer settings box for Post-Script printers.

When you set up a PostScript printer, you should first select a printer from the Printer list box in the lower portion of the PostScript printer settings box. The printer you select will directly affect the availability of certain options in the printer settings box. It also will provide the PostScript driver with information about the fonts that are resident in your printer.

If you are using an HP LaserJet printer equipped with PostScript capabilities, you need to select the name of a compatible PostScript printer from this list. The manual included with your PostScript system may list the names of compatible printers. If not, you must obtain this information from the manufacturer or your dealer. For example, the manual included with the QMS JetScript system states that an HP LaserJet Series II printer equipped with the JetScript board is compatible with the Apple LaserWriter Plus and the QMS-PS 800 Plus. Therefore, you would choose one of these printers from the list box.

Specifying a printer type

If you want to print more than one copy of a document, just enter the number of copies into the Uncollated Copies text box. As the setting name implies, Word will not collate the copies as it prints. Instead, it will print all the specified copies of page 1, then all the copies of page 2, and so forth, until it has printed multiple copies of every page in the document. As we explained in our discussion of settings for PCL printers, printing multiple copies in this page-by-page fashion is much faster than printing multiple copies of a document one set at a time.

Printing multiple copies

The Orientation setting allows you to specify whether you want your lines of text to be printed across the short or long side of the paper. If you want to print your document in the conventional fashion, with lines running across the short side of the paper, choose the Portrait option. On the other hand, if you want your lines of print to be rotated 90 degrees and to run across the long side of the paper, choose Landscape.

Choosing print orientation

If you change the Orientation setting in the PostScript printer settings box, Word will present a message box like the one shown in Figure 7-9 on page 202 after you've closed both the printer settings box and the Printer Setup dialog box. When you see this message box, you should choose Yes, which will tell Word to swap the current Page Width and Height settings in the Document dialog box. If you don't choose Yes in this message box, Word will present the message box shown in Figure 7-8 on page 201 when you issue the Print... command. Whenever you see this message, you should choose No to halt the Print... command, and then adjust the Page Width and Height settings in the Document dialog box to match the paper size and orientation you've specified in the PostScript printer settings box.

The PostScript printer settings box offers more paper size options than any printer settings box in Windows. Although you can choose any of the paper sizes

Choosing paper

available in the dialog box, you'll probably choose either letter or legal size. The specific options that are available will depend on the type of printer you have chosen. Table 7-2 lists the most commonly used paper sizes.

Table 7-2

Paper option	Size
Letter	8.5 by 11 inches
Legal	8.5 by 14 inches
A4	8.3 by 11.7 inches
B5	7.2 by 10 inches

It's important for you to match the Page Width and Height settings in the Document dialog box with the Paper option you select in the PostScript printer settings box. If you specify a paper size other than Letter, Word will present a message box like the one shown in Figure 7-7 on page 201 when you choose OK in the Printer Setup dialog box. When you see this message box, you should choose OK, and then select the Document... command from the Format menu. When the Document dialog box appears, change the Page Width and Height settings to match the new paper size you've specified in your printer settings box.

If you attempt to print a document whose Page Width and Height settings don't reflect the paper size you've selected in the printer settings box, Word will present the message box shown in Figure 7-8 on page 201. In this message box, choose No to halt the Print... command, then use the Printer Setup... command to check the paper size you selected. After you've done this, open the Document dialog box and adjust the Page Width and Height settings.

Specifying graphics resolution

With a PostScript printer (or a PCL printer with PostScript capability), you can print graphics at a resolution of 75, 100, 150, and 300 dots per inch. (The Graphics Resolution setting does not affect text, which is always printed at a resolution of 300 dots per inch.) As you might guess, the higher the resolution, the better looking the graphic. However, higher resolution graphics take much longer to print than lower resolution graphics. Consequently, if you're more concerned about quality than about time, choose a high graphics resolution. If you need to print graphics quickly, however, you should choose a lower resolution and sacrifice print quality.

Specifying a paper source

Some PostScript printers offer an upper and lower tray for feeding paper to the printer. These printers allow you to preload two types of paper. Other printers offer both automatic paper feeding (from a paper tray or other source) and manual paper feeding. When a printer has two or more options for paper feed, you must select one of the Source options. Sometimes, this is a matter of selecting the Manual Feed or Any Small Format options, as shown in Figure 7-19. In other cases, you must choose from a few paper tray options. The type of printer you have selected will determine what Source options are available.

Dot-matrix printers

If you've installed a dot-matrix printer, the options available in your printer settings box will depend on your particular printer's capabilities. Although some of these printers offer unique printing options, most dot-matrix printers let you specify the paper size, orientation, and graphics resolution. Let's briefly discuss some important issues related to these three print settings.

Paper size

If you specify a paper size other than letter ($8\frac{1}{2}$ by 11 inches), Word will present the message box shown in Figure 7-7 on page 201 when you choose OK in the Printer Setup dialog box. If you see this message box, you should choose OK, then select the Document... command from the Format menu. When the Document dialog box appears, change the Page Width and Height settings to match the paper size you've selected in your printer settings box.

If you attempt to print a document whose Page Width and Height settings don't reflect the paper size you've selected in the printer settings box, Word will present the message box shown in Figure 7-8. If you see this message box, choose No to halt the Print... command, then use the Printer Setup... command to check the paper size you selected. After you've selected the appropriate paper size, open the Document dialog box and adjust the Page Width and Height settings.

Orientation

The Orientation setting in Figure 7-19 lets you specify whether your lines of text should be printed across the short or the long side of the paper. If you want to print your document with lines running across the short side of the paper, choose the Portrait option. If you want to print your document with lines running across the long side of the paper, choose Landscape.

If you change the Orientation setting in the printer settings box, Word will present a message box like the one shown in Figure 7-9 on page 202 after you've closed both the printer settings box and the Printer Setup dialog box When you see this message box, you should choose Yes, which will tell Word to swap the current Page Width and Height settings in the Document dialog box. If you don't choose Yes in this message box, Word will present the message box shown in Figure 7-8 on page 201 when you issue the Print... command. Whenever you see this message, you should choose No to halt the Print... command, then adjust the Page Width and Height settings in the Document dialog box to match the paper size and orientation you've specified in the printer settings box.

Graphics resolution

With most dot-matrix printers, you can print graphics at various resolutions. The higher the resolution, the better looking the graphic. However, higher resolution graphics take much longer to print than lower resolution graphics. Consequently, if you're more concerned about quality than about time, choose a high graphics resolution. If you need to print graphics quickly, you should choose a lower resolution.

Other printers

It is beyond the scope of this book to discuss the printing options available for all the printers you can connect to your computer. To control the print settings for a printer that is not discussed in this chapter, simply keep the same basic rules in mind that we've outlined for other printers, and make intelligent selections from the printer settings box. The owner's manual for your printer should explain the settings you'll see in the printer settings box. If you have trouble installing or setting up your printer, contact either your local hardware dealer or the printer manufacturer.

USING THE PRINT... COMMAND

Once you've installed and selected your printer, you can use Word's Print... command to send your document to the printer. When you issue the Print... command, Word will always print the currently active document. Word will not print any other documents that happen to be open unless you activate those document windows individually and issue a Print... command for each.

When you issue the Print... command, Word will present the Print dialog box shown in Figure 7-20. At the top of this dialog box, Word lists the current printer and port. If you want to change the printer or port, you'll need to follow the instructions we provided earlier in this chapter.

Figure 7-20

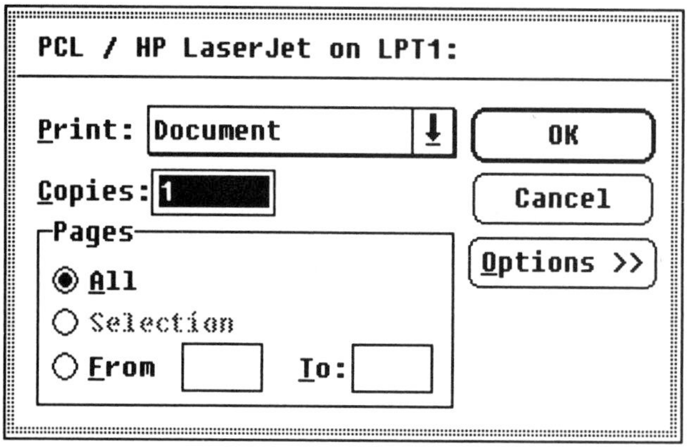

```
╔════════════════════════════════════════════════════╗
║ ┌────────────────────────────────────────────────┐ ║
║ │  PCL / HP LaserJet on LPT1:                      │ ║
║ │                                                  │ ║
║ │  Print: │Document            │ ↓│  ┌──────────┐  │ ║
║ │                                  │    OK    │  │ ║
║ │  Copies:│1       │               └──────────┘  │ ║
║ │  ┌Pages─────────────────────┐  ┌──────────┐    │ ║
║ │  │ ◉ All                    │  │  Cancel  │    │ ║
║ │  │ ○ Selection              │  └──────────┘    │ ║
║ │  │ ○ From │    │  To: │    │ │ ┌────────────┐   │ ║
║ │  └──────────────────────────┘  │ Options >> │   │ ║
║ │                                 └────────────┘   │ ║
║ └────────────────────────────────────────────────┘ ║
╚════════════════════════════════════════════════════╝
```

The Print... command is the tool you'll use to send documents to the printer.

In the Print dialog box, choose OK to send your entire document to the printer. Word will then display a message in the status bar that lets you know the status of the print job. For example, if you use the Print... command to send the document BUDGET.DOC to the printer, Word will display the message *Printing BUDGET.DOC. Press Esc to cancel.* When the entire document has been sent, Word will remove the message from the status bar and return you to the active document.

If, for any reason, Word cannot communicate with your printer successfully, it will present the Spooler message box shown in Figure 7-21. If this message box appears, make sure that the printer cable is firmly seated in both the printer and in your computer, and that the printer is on and on-line. Once you've corrected the problem, choose the Retry button in the Spooler message box to resend the document. Choosing the Cancel button cancels the Print... command and returns you to the document.

Figure 7-21

The Spooler message box will appear whenever Word cannot communicate with your printer successfully.

With luck, you will produce a printed document that looks just as you expected. Later in this chapter, we'll show you how to use the Print Preview command to reduce unexpected surprises at print time. For now, however, let's discuss the ways you can control printed documents with the options in the Print dialog box.

Printing part of a document

The Pages options in the Print dialog box are self-explanatory. To print the entire document, just leave the default All option button selected. If you want to print only part of the document, use the Selection or From and To options.

The Selection option tells Word to print only the part of your document that is highlighted on the screen. This option provides a quick way to print only a few lines or paragraphs of text. Just select the text you want to print, open the Print dialog box, choose the Selection option, and choose OK.

When you print a selection, Word will print the highlighted text, beginning at the upper-left corner of the page, even if the text you have selected would normally appear in the middle of a page. If you have added any page numbers, headers, or footers to your document, they will not appear when you use the Selection option.

For example, suppose you've printed the document shown in Figure 7-22, and you want to reprint the third body-text paragraph only. To do this, you would select that paragraph, open the Print dialog box, then choose the Selection option. As you can see in Figure 7-23, Word will reprint the selected paragraph, beginning at the upper-left corner of the page.

Figure 7-22

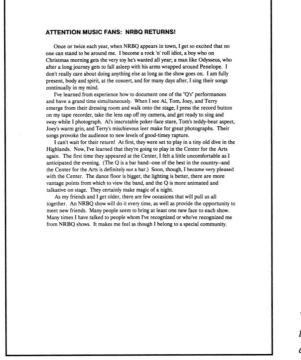

We want to reprint the third paragraph in this document.

Figure 7-23

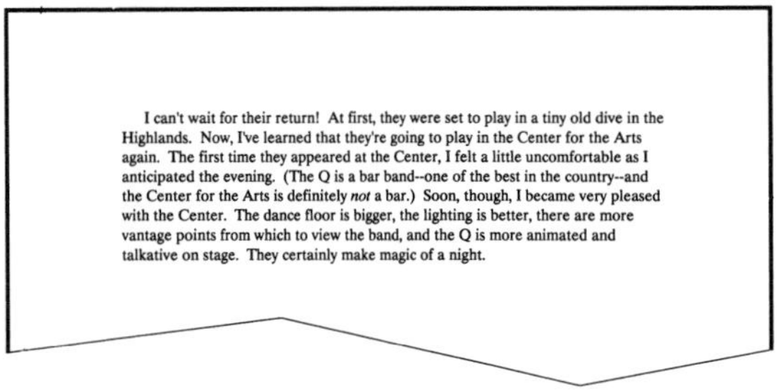

Notice that Word begins printing the selected text at the very top of the page.

If you need to print several consecutive pages of a document, you'll probably want to use the From and To settings rather than highlighting the text you want to print. If you select the option button that appears to the left of the From text box (or press [Alt]F), Word will prompt you for the From and To settings by displaying a cursor in the From text box. At this point, you should specify the appropriate range of pages. If you click in the From or To text box instead of first clicking the From/To option button, Word will automatically select the From/To option button for you.

Suppose you want to print pages 5 through 11 of a 25-page document. After you issue the Print... command, just click either on the From/To button or in the From text box (or press [Alt]F), then type the value *5*. Next, press the [Tab] key, or click in the To text box, and type the value *11*.

If you make an entry in the To text box but leave the From text box blank, Word will assume that you want to begin printing with the first page of the document and print to the end of the specified To page. Similarly, if you make an entry in the From text box but leave the To text box blank, Word will assume that you want to start printing at the beginning of the specified From page and print to the end of the document.

For example, to print pages 1 through 10 of your 25-page document, you can leave the From text box blank and simply enter the value *10* in the To text box. To print from page 10 to the end of the document, you can leave the To text box blank and type the value *10* in the From text box. To print only one page of a document, enter the same number in the From and To text boxes. For example, if you want to print only the third page of a document, enter *3* in both the From and To text boxes.

As you've seen, specifying a page range is generally as simple as typing the starting and ending page numbers in the Print dialog box. Things can get a little complicated, however, if you are using various numbering schemes for different sections of your document. We'll talk more about numbering schemes when we look at the Section... command in Chapter 12.

Printing multiple copies

If you want to print more than one copy of your document at a time, just type the number of copies you want in the Copies text box. If the document you are printing is longer than one page, Word will begin by printing a single copy of the entire document, then print another copy, and so forth, until it has printed the document the number of times specified in the Copies text box.

If you're printing to a laser printer, you can save time by using the Uncollated Copies setting in the printer settings box instead of the Copies setting in the Print dialog box. As we explained earlier, when you adjust the Uncollated Copies setting in the printer settings box, Word will print all the copies of the first page, followed by all the copies of the second page, and so forth. This method of printing multiple copies is faster than printing one complete document and then repeating the process for each new copy. However, if you use the Uncollated Copies setting to print multiple copies, you'll need to collate the pages after they come out of the printer.

Printing related document information

In addition to printing the current document, Word lets you print information relating to that document, like summary information, annotations, styles, glossary, and key assignments. To print related document information instead of the document itself, simply pull down the Print list box, as we've done in Figure 7-24, and choose the appropriate option from the list.

Figure 7-24

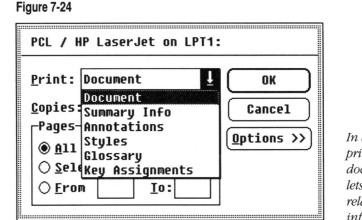

In addition to printing the current document, Word lets you print related document information.

As you've probably noticed by now, an Options >> button appears on the right side of the Print dialog box. When you choose this button, the Print dialog box will expand to reveal a few additional print options, as shown in Figure 7-25. We'll refer to some of the options in the expanded Print dialog box as we discuss printing related document information.

Printing summary information

To print all the document's summary information, which is the same information you can access with the Summary Info... command on the Edit menu, choose the Summary Info option in the Print list box. After you do this, choose OK to tell Word to send the summary information to the printer.

As you'll see in moment, you can use the Options >> button in the Print dialog box to tell Word to print both your document and its summary information at the same time. To do this, you'll need to leave the Document option selected in the Print list box, then select the Summary Info check box in the expanded Print dialog box. We'll talk more about the Options >> button in a moment. For a detailed discussion of a document's summary information, see Chapter 3.

Figure 7-25

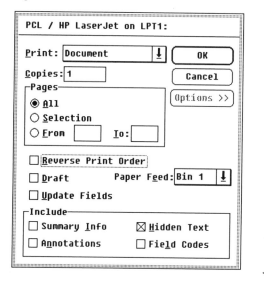

Selecting the Options >> button in the Print dialog box will reveal a few additional print options.

Choosing the Annotations option from the Print list box tells Word to print the annotations that have been made to a document. For example, suppose you use Word to write a letter to a prospective client, and then give your boss the disk containing the letter. If your boss uses Word's Annotations facility to add a couple of paragraphs, you can then use the Annotations option to print only the annotations that your boss has attached.

Printing annotations

By printing a list of annotations, you can review all the annotations at once instead of searching the entire document for them. In addition, you can use your entire screen area to view the document as you scroll, rather than having to relinquish part of the screen area for the annotation pane.

You can use the Options >> button in the Print dialog box to tell Word to print both your document and its annotations at the same time. To do this, you'll need to leave the Document option selected in the Print list box, then select the Annotations check box in the expanded Print dialog box. We'll talk more about the Options >> button in a moment. For more information on how to manipulate annotations in a Word document, see Chapter 13.

If you want to print a copy of the style sheet for the current document, choose the Styles option in the Print list box. When you choose OK, Word will print the entire style sheet in the printer's default font. Figure 7-26 shows a sample page from a styles listing.

Printing a style sheet

Figure 7-26

```
footer
        Normal + Tab stops: 3" Centered; 6" Right Flush

header
        Normal + Tab stops: 3" Centered; 6" Right Flush

heading 1

NextStyle:    Normal
        Normal + Font: Helv, Bold, Space Before 8pt

heading 2

NextStyle:    Normal
        Normal + Font: Helv, Indent: Left 0.25"

heading 3

NextStyle:    Normal Indent
        Normal + Font: Helv, Italic, Indent: Left 0.5"

heading 4

NextStyle:    Normal Indent
        Normal + Font: Helv, Indent: Left 0.75"

heading 5

NextStyle:    Normal Indent
        Normal + Font: Helv, Indent: Left 1"

mark's test
        Normal + Bold

New Chapter

NextStyle:    heading 1
        heading 1 + Font: 14 Point, Underline

Normal
        Font: Tms Rmn 12 Point, Flush left

Normal Indent

NextStyle:    Normal
        Normal + Indent: Left 0.5"
```

The Styles option in the Print list box lets you print a listing of all the styles in the current document.

Printing the glossary

As we'll explain in Chapter 13, Word lets you create a glossary of terms for each of your Word documents. To print a listing of the current document's glossary entries, choose the Glossary option from the Print list box. When you choose OK to complete the command, Word will print a listing of glossary entries in the printer's default font. Figure 7-27 shows a sample glossary listing.

Printing key assignments

In Chapter 19, we'll show you how to create macros and assign them to various key combinations. Once you've assigned a few macros to key combinations, you'll want to keep a reference sheet handy that shows the key assignments you've established. To print a listing of key assignments, choose the Key Assignments option from the Print list box, then choose OK.

Printing hidden text

You can use the Hidden Text check box in the expanded Print dialog box to instruct Word to send both the unhidden and hidden text in your document to the printer. Hidden text will appear in the printed report wherever you have entered it into your document, and it will have no distinguishing marks or formatting characteristics.

Figure 7-27

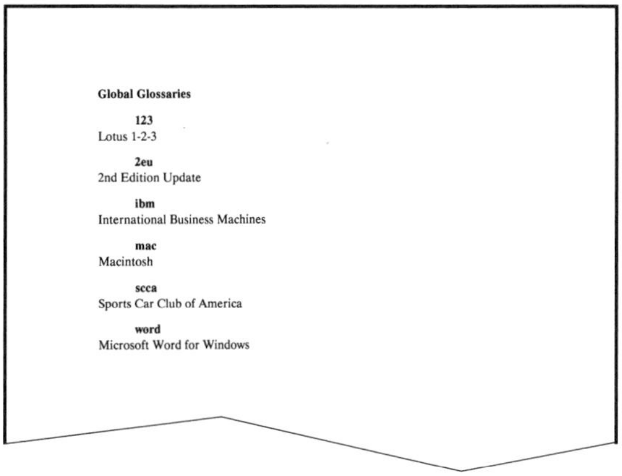

```
Global Glossaries

    123
Lotus 1-2-3

    2eu
2nd Edition Update

    ibm
International Business Machines

    mac
Macintosh

    scca
Sports Car Club of America

    word
Microsoft Word for Windows
```

The Glossary option in the Print list box tells Word to print the glossary terms associated with the current document.

Of course, if you print a document's hidden text, it will affect the document's page breaks. In addition, Word will update the # of Pages, # of Words, and # of Characters fields in the Statistics dialog box to reflect the addition of the document's hidden text in the print-out.

Printing field codes

In Chapter 10, you'll learn how to create and insert fields into your Word document. You might think of fields as formulas that return a result in your document. For example, the field {DATE} retrieves the current date and places it in your document. After you enter the field {DATE} into your document, however, you'll typically want to see that field's result instead of its field code ({DATE}).

If you want to print a document showing the field codes instead of the field results, select the Field Codes check box in the expanded Print dialog box. When Word prints the document, it will indicate the field code entries by placing a set of braces ({}) around them.

Printing a document's field codes will affect your document's page breaks. Since most field codes are much shorter than their results, printing a document with the Field Codes check box selected will typically result in a shorter document.

Specifying additional options

Although we've discussed a few of the options in the expanded Print dialog box, there are still some options we need to cover. These options let you reverse the order of printed pages, print the document without formatting, update the document fields, and select a method of paper feed. Let's consider each option in detail.

Reverse Print Order

The Reverse Print Order option tells Word to print the pages of your document in reverse order. Whether you use this option will depend on the way your printer stacks its printed pages. If your printer stacks pages with the printed side face up, then the pages of your document will be stacked in the reverse order from which they were printed. For example, if you print a ten-page document on a laser printer that stacks pages face up, Word will print the pages in order from 1 to 10. However, when you retrieve the printed pages from the paper tray, you'll have to reverse the order of the pages since page 10 will be on top of page 9, page 9 will be on top of page 8, and so forth.

To get around this problem, select the Reverse Print Order check box. Word will then print the pages in reverse order—from 10 to 1—so that they will be in the correct order when you retrieve the printed pages from the paper tray. The Reverse Print Order option is particularly convenient when you are printing long documents or when you are printing multiple copies of a document.

If you are using a printer that stacks pages face up instead of face down, you won't need to select the Reverse Print Order check box. When you retrieve your printed document, the pages will already appear in the order in which they were printed. Of course, if you want to retrieve the pages in reverse order, you can select Reverse Print Order.

Draft

The Draft option in the expanded Print dialog box is one of Word's biggest time-savers. The effect this option has on your printed documents depends on the kind of printer you're using. If you're using a dot-matrix printer, selecting the Draft check box will tell Word to print the entire document in the printer's default font and to underline the characters that have been assigned formatting characteristics. If the document contains an imported graphic, Word will print an empty box frame in place of that graphic.

If you're using a laser printer, selecting the Draft check box simply tells Word not to print the bitmapped graphics you've imported into the document. Your printed document will still retain all of its character formatting.

Update Fields

Although Word updates many of the fields in your document before it sends the document to the printer, it does not update some fields automatically. If you select the Update Fields check box in the expanded Print dialog box, however, Word will update the document's fields before it prints.

Paper Feed

Unlike the first generation of printers that were developed for personal computers, most of today's printers can accept paper from more than one source. For instance, many laser printers, like the HP LaserJet IID, have an upper and lower paper tray. Because many printers have multiple paper source options, Word includes a Paper Feed list box in the expanded Print dialog box.

The items you'll see in the Paper Feed list box depend on the type of printer you're using. If your printer can draw paper from only one source, the Paper Feed list box will appear dimmed and will not be selectable. Let's consider how each of the options that can appear in the Paper Feed list box affect the way your printer prints a Word document.

If your printer lets you feed sheets of paper manually, the Manual option will appear in the Paper Feed list box. If you select the Manual option and then choose OK, the printer will prompt you for a sheet of paper. For more information on manually feeding paper to your printer, see your printer manual.

The Auto option in the Paper Feed list box will cause your printer to use paper from its default paper source. For instance, if you're using a laser printer and you want the printer to draw paper from its paper tray, you'll want to select the Auto option.

If your printer can access multiple paper bins, you can use the Bin 1, Bin 2, and Bin 3 options to specify which bin you want the printer to use.

Finally, the Mixed option in the Paper Feed list box tells the printer to print page 1 of your document on the paper stored in bin 1, and to print the rest of the document on the paper stored in bin 2. If you load company letterhead into bin 1 and regular paper into bin 2, you can use the Mixed option in the Paper Feed list box to print business letters of more than a page long.

USING THE SPOOLER

The Spooler is a Windows program whose sole purpose is to print documents in the background as you continue to use your machine. In this section, we'll take a look at the Spooler and discuss what you should know about it in order to print documents successfully. We'll also show you how to turn the Spooler off in case you are running Windows on a floppy-based system or network.

Running the Spooler

Whenever you tell Word to print a document, one of three things will occur. First, if the Spooler is not running, it will start up automatically and send your document directly to its queue, where the document will wait to be printed. If you own a full-featured copy of Microsoft Windows, you can run the Spooler any time using the Windows MS-DOS Executive. To run the Spooler, double-click on the file name SPOOLER.EXE, or highlight the file name with the cursor, pull down MS-DOS Executive's File menu, and select Run.

If the Spooler is already running when you issue the Print… command, Word will send the document to the Spooler, which will handle the actual task of sending it to the printer. While the Spooler is sending the document to your printer, you can continue using Word (or any Windows application).

After the Spooler receives a document, you can allow it to print the document, or you can interfere by activating the Spooler window. To activate the Spooler window, click on the Spooler icon shown in Figure 7-28 or press [Alt][Tab].

Figure 7-28

 You can activate the Spooler by clicking on this icon or by pressing [Alt][Tab].

Fortunately, you can move and size the Spooler window just as you would any other window. Of course, the size and position of the Spooler window does not affect its operation.

Whenever the Spooler window is active, it displays a list of the printers currently installed on your system. Below the names of each of these printers, the Spooler window will display a list of any documents that are currently being printed or are waiting in the queue. Figure 7-29 shows a sample window.

Figure 7-29

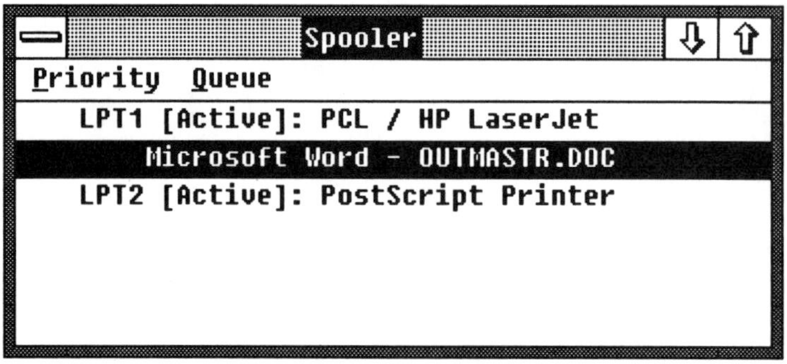

```
╺╺┈┈┈┈┈┈┈┈┈┈┈┈┈┈ Spooler ┈┈┈┈┈┈┈┈┈┈┈┈┈┈  ⇩ ⇧
 Priority  Queue
      LPT1 [Active]: PCL / HP LaserJet
          Microsoft Word - OUTMASTR.DOC
      LPT2 [Active]: PostScript Printer



```

When the Spooler window is active, it will display a list of the currently installed printers, as well as a summary of files that are printing or waiting in the queue.

Controlling the queue

As you can see in Figure 7-29, when the Spooler's window is active, the Spooler displays a list of all the documents that are printing or waiting to be printed. Fortunately, you can use the menu commands in the Spooler window to stop printing the current document or to remove a document from the Spooler's queue. To do this, activate the Spooler window and select the document you want to terminate. Next, pull down the Queue menu and select the Terminate command. The Spooler will then display the message box shown in Figure 7-30. This message box gives you the opportunity to cancel your decision to terminate the document. If you want to terminate the document, choose OK. If you don't, choose Cancel.

If a problem develops with your printer, you may want to pause the Spooler temporarily. For example, if you're using a laser printer, and its EP cartridge runs out of toner, you may want to stop the Spooler from sending additional pages until you've replaced the cartridge. To suspend printing, activate the Spooler window and select the name of the printer whose output you want to suspend. Next, pull down the Queue menu and select the Pause command. When you are ready to allow the Spooler to resume sending the document to the printer, select the printer's name again, and choose the Resume command from the Queue menu.

Figure 7-30

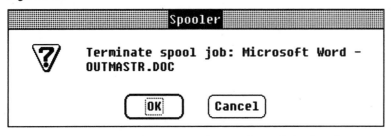

When you terminate a document, the Spooler will display this message box.

If you don't plan to work in Word while the Spooler is printing your document, you may want to increase the speed of the Spooler at the expense of decreasing the speed of Word. To devote more CPU (Central Processing Unit) time to the Spooler, pull down the Spooler's Priority menu, and select Hi. When you do this, the Spooler will print faster, while Word (and any other Windows applications) will run more slowly.

Setting priority

If an error occurs as the Spooler is printing a document, you will not immediately see an error message. Instead, the Spooler will flash the title bar of the currently active application to alert you that an error has occurred. When you see this flash, you should activate the Spooler window by double-clicking on its icon or by pressing [Alt][Tab]. When the Spooler window appears, it will display a message that identifies the error.

Receiving messages from the Spooler

While most people will always want to use the Spooler, some will not. For example, if you are running Windows on a computer not equipped with a hard disk, you may want to turn off the Spooler to conserve disk space and to speed operation. Likewise, if your computer is connected to a network that offers print spooling, it is advantageous to turn the Spooler off. Otherwise, you will end up spooling output twice. However, if you find that the Windows Spooler is faster than the network spooler, you may want to turn off the network spooler instead.

Turning off the Spooler

You can turn the Windows Spooler on and off by using Word to open the file WIN.INI, and changing the Spooler setting in the [windows] section of that file to spooler=no. After you save the change, end your current Windows session and restart Word for Windows.

Unless you specifically instruct it to do so, Word will not automatically add page numbers to each page of your printed document. There are two ways to add page numbers: using the Page Numbers… command on the Insert menu or using the Header/Footer… command on the Edit menu. If you want to print only the number of each page in your document, you'll find it easiest to use the Page

ADDING PAGE NUMBERS TO YOUR PRINTED DOCUMENT

Numbers... command. On the other hand, if you want to include additional information at the top or bottom of the page, such as the document name or the current date, or if you want to print the page number in a special format, you'll want to use Word's Header/Footer... command to add page numbers. We'll first explain how to add page numbers with the Page Numbers... command, then we'll look at headers and footers.

To add page numbers to your printed document, just choose the Page Numbers... command on the Insert menu to bring up the Page Numbers dialog box shown in Figure 7-31.

Figure 7-31

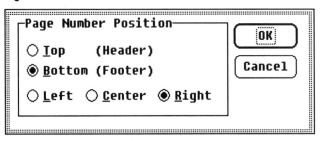

The Page Numbers dialog box lets you add page numbers to your document quickly and easily.

As you can see, the Page Numbers dialog box lets you print the page numbers at either the top or bottom of each page, and lets you position the page number along the left edge, center, or right edge of the page. After you choose the appropriate options from the Page Numbers dialog box, choose OK. Word will insert the field *{page}* into your header or footer and return you to the document. The next time you print your document, Word will place the current page number at the location you've specified on every page except page 1. (The Page Numbers dialog box will not insert a page number on the first page of your document.)

If, prior to issuing the Page Numbers... command, you've used either the Page Numbers... or Header/Footer... command to set up a header or footer in your document, Word will present the message box shown in Figure 7-32 when you choose OK in the Page Numbers dialog box. If you respond by choosing the Yes option, Word will replace your existing header or footer with a new one that contains only a page number. If you want to cancel the Page Numbers... command and retain your existing header or footer, choose No so that Word will return you to your document without creating a new header or footer.

CREATING HEADERS AND FOOTERS

You see headers and footers in just about every book, magazine, and other publication you read. Generally, headers and footers serve as guideposts for the reader, carrying such information as page numbers and the name of the publication. Longer publications sometimes have variable headers and footers that reflect the names of sections and chapters as well. On dated materials, like periodicals or technical materials that are subject to frequent updates, information such as the date of publication and volume and issue numbers commonly appear in the header or footer.

Figure 7-32

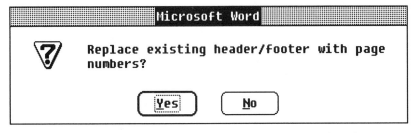

If you issue the Page Numbers... command after you've already set up a header or footer, Word will make sure you want to replace the existing header or footer with one that contains only a page number.

Word offers the most flexible system we've seen for creating, formatting, and editing headers and footers. In Word, headers and footers can carry any character and paragraph formats you choose and can be as short as a single character or as long as several paragraphs. You can also vary the appearance and content of headers and footers for odd and even pages and even control the appearance of headers and footers on the first page of a document or section.

In this section, we'll show you how to create, format, position, and edit headers and footers. In the next section of this chapter, you'll also see how you can use the Print Preview window to reposition headers and footers quickly.

As the names imply, headers generally appear at the top of each page in your document while footers appear at the bottom. However, Word allows you to control the positioning of headers and footers so that you can place them anywhere on the printed page.

While you're using the normal editing or draft view, the headers and footers you create will not appear in your document window. Instead, they will be tucked out of sight in separate panes that are stored along with your document when you save it to disk. To see how the header or footer will appear on each document page, you must switch to the page view or use the Print Preview window.

Let's get started by creating a sample header, then we'll look at some of the handy tools that Word offers for tailoring headers and footers to fit your publication needs. The steps you follow to create, format, and position headers are almost identical to those you follow to create, format, and position footers. If you know how to work with headers, you will be able to work with footers as well. Therefore, in this section, we will illustrate Word's header and footer techniques with examples that focus mainly on headers. Of course, we'll address any minor differences relating to footers as they arise.

A brief tour

To add a header or footer to your document, begin by selecting the Header/ Footer... command from the Edit menu. If you are in normal editing or draft view when you issue this command, the dialog box shown in Figure 7-33 will appear on your screen.

Figure 7-33

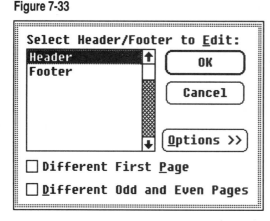

The Header/Footer dialog box is the tool you'll use to create headers and footers for your Word documents.

Since the Header option is selected in the Header/Footer dialog box by default, just choose OK to create a new header. When you do, Word will bring up the header pane at the bottom of your screen, as shown in Figure 7-34.

Notice that your cursor initially appears at the first character space in the empty header pane, much as it does in a new document window. The horizontal bar that currently appears just below the cursor serves as an end mark—just like the one you see in your document window.

In many ways, the header pane functions just like the standard document pane. You'll use the ruler and ribbon to control the appearance of the header, and you'll use the Preferences... command to control the appearance of tab marks, paragraph marks, scroll bars, and so forth. The status bar will also change to reflect the current status of the header pane.

The bar that appears across the top of the header pane displays the word *Header* to help you identify the contents of the pane. (In a footer pane, you'll see the word *Footer.*) As we'll demonstrate a little later, Word allows you to create a separate header and/or footer on the first page of a document. When you open the header or footer pane for this page, you'll see *First Header* or *First Footer* at the top of the pane.

Besides the word *Header*, you'll also see notations like *(S1)* and *(S2)* that tell you which section's header you're working with. If you're using different headers or footers on right and left pages, Word will display *Even Header*, *Odd Header*, *Even Footer*, or *Odd Footer* at the top of the pane to tell you what type of header or footer you are working with. (See Chapter 12 for a complete discussion of multisection documents and even/odd—or right/left—page layouts.)

Figure 7-34

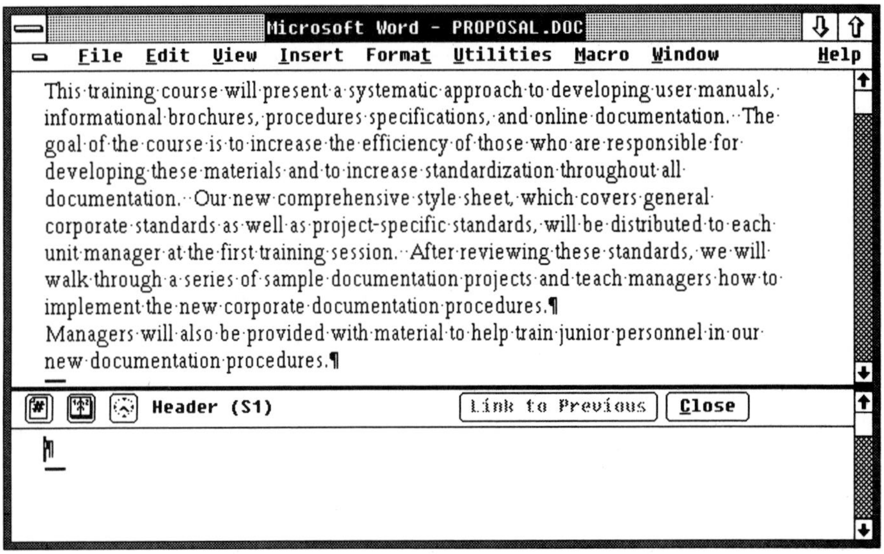

The header pane will appear at the bottom of your screen when you are in the normal editing view.

At the top of the header pane, you'll also find three new icons. As you'll see in a few moments, you can use these icons to add dynamic page numbers, dates, and times to your headers and footers.

Finally, two buttons appear at the top of the header pane: Link to Previous and Close. Choosing the Close button closes the header pane. We'll discuss the Link to Previous button, which is dimmed in Figure 7-34, in Chapter 12.

As we have said, a new footer pane looks exactly like a header pane, except the word *Footer* appears at the top of the pane. (As we will explain in Chapter 8, Word automatically creates the styles named *header* and *footer*, which you can use to format your header and footer text.)

Creating a header

Let's type some text into our empty header pane and see how we go about formatting that information. Suppose you are creating a project proposal called *Managing Computer Documentation Projects*, and you want the name of the report to appear at the top of each page. Begin by typing the phrase in the empty header pane, as shown in Figure 7-35 on the following page.

If you turn on the ruler while the cursor is in the header pane, you'll see that the header's text initially appears in Word's default font—10-point Tms Rmn. In addition, the header's paragraph formats are initially flush left, with a centered tab at 3 inches and a right-aligned tab at 6 inches. The header pane's right indent marker will fall at the 6-inch mark if you are using Word's default Document dialog box settings. Of course, the ruler settings in the header pane will vary according to the Document options you specify, just as they do in your document pane.

Figure 7-35

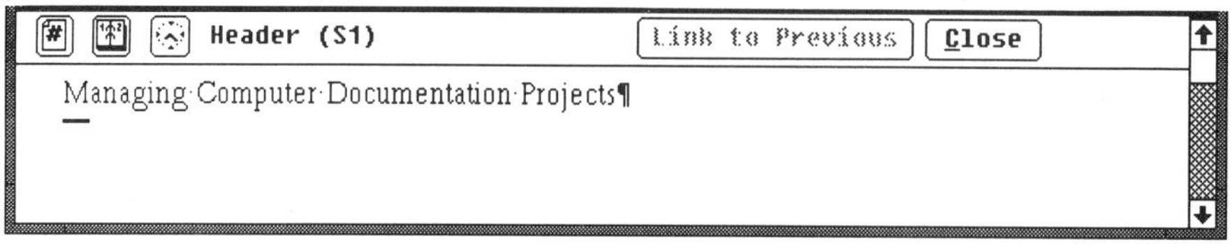

| # | 👤 | 🔍 | Header (S1) | Link to Previous | **Close** | ↑ |

Managing·Computer·Documentation·Projects¶

To create a header, just type the text you want to use in the header pane.

Although we'll want to do some more work on this sample header, let's pause for a moment to see how this header will look when we print the document. To save the new header you've created, choose the Close button at the top of the header pane. Word will then remove the header pane from the screen.

After you close the header pane, switch to the page view by choosing Page from the View menu. If you use the scroll bars to bring the very top of the page into view, you'll see the header at the top of the page. You'll often save yourself some bad print runs if you check your header in the page view before your issue the Print... command. When you send the sample document to the printer, the resulting page will look like the one shown in Figure 7-36.

Figure 7-36

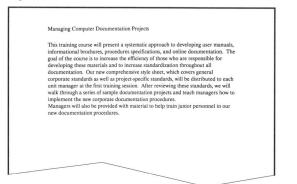

The sample document looks like this when printed on an HP LaserJet printer.

As you can see in Figure 7-36, when Word prints the sample document, the header appears $1/2$ inch from the top of the page. The body of the document begins $1/2$ inch below the top of the header line, 1 inch from the top of the page. Notice also that the header begins $1^1/_4$ inches from the left side of the page, in alignment with the body text.

Although you can format your headers in either the page view or the draft view, you'll probably want to use the page view so that you can monitor the effects of your formatting changes. For instance, suppose you want the header text in the sample document to appear in 14-point Helv bold type, centered on the page. To achieve this effect, first select all the text that appears in the header, then format it using either the ribbon or the Character… command, just as you would in a document pane. After you've assigned the 14-point Helv bold font to the text, select the Centered-alignment icon on the ruler. At this point, your document will look like the one shown in Figure 7-37.

Formatting and positioning the header text

Figure 7-37

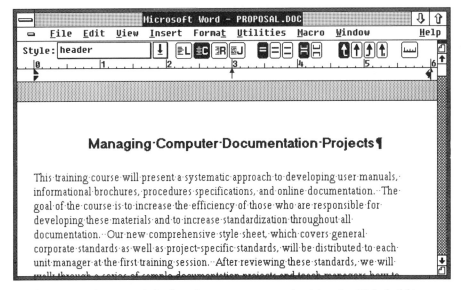

We have now formatted the header text to appear in 14-point Helv bold type with centered alignment.

If you format the header text in the draft view, Word will not show the header text in the new font you've defined. Instead, Word will underline the text in the header to indicate that you've assigned some special formatting to that text.

When you print the sample document with the newly formatted header, Word will center the formatted header text between the left and right margins, as shown in Figure 7-38 on the following page.

If you want to right-align your header text, just select the Right-alignment icon on the ruler. If you're creating a multiline header, you may want to use the Justified icon to align the left and right margins of your header text. You also might use borders to jazz up your headers and help separate them from your body text.

Figure 7-38

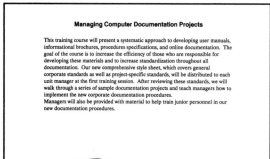

The formatted header text is centered between the left and right margins.

Placing headers in the left and right margins

Occasionally, you may want your header text to appear in your document margins rather than aligned with your main body text. For example, on the sample page shown in Figure 7-39, we've placed our header—consisting of the document title and current date—in the left margin of the page. (We'll show you how to add a date to a header in a few pages.) To create this header, we used a left indent of negative $1\frac{1}{4}$ inch, as shown in the header pane in Figure 7-40.

Figure 7-39

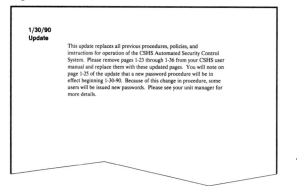

You can place headers and footers in the left and right margins.

To create the negative indent, you must first display the ruler. Then, hold down the [Shift] key while dragging the first-line and left indent markers to the left of the zero point on the ruler. If you're using the keyboard, follow the techniques we presented in Chapter 5 to adjust the indent markers.

If you want to place your header in the right margin of the printed page, just drag the right indent marker to the right, then move the first-line and left indent markers past the line that marks your right margin. (For more on changing a paragraph's left and right indents, see Chapter 5.)

Figure 7-40

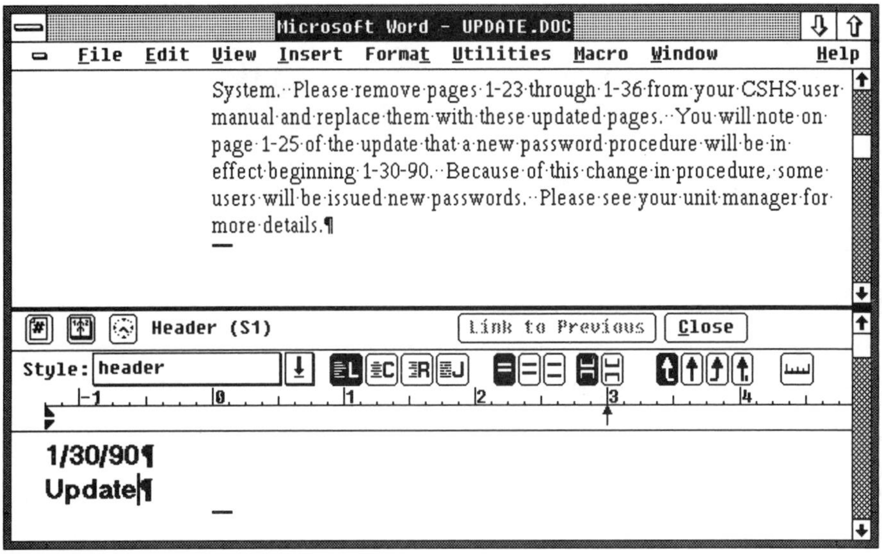

We used a negative left indent to format this header.

Notice that the sample header in Figure 7-40 is two lines long. As we mentioned earlier, your header (or footer) can contain as many lines of text as you like. For example, you might want to create your company's letterhead in the header pane, as shown in Figure 7-41 on the following page. The resulting printed header is shown in Figure 7-42.

Word will automatically expand the top margin of a document to make room for a multiline header. For example, in Figure 7-42, the first line of text in our document, which normally starts 1 inch from the top of the page, now appears about $1^3/_4$ inches from the top of the page. If we look at our Document dialog box, however, we'll see that Word has not changed our default Top margin setting of 1 inch. It simply overrode this margin setting to avoid overlapping the header text and the main body of the document.

You'll see a similar situation when you create a multiline footer. Word will automatically expand the bottom margin of your document to accommodate the footer text. However, your Bottom margin setting in the Document dialog box will not change.

Notice that Word does not add any extra space between the header and the first line of text. If you want to insert extra space between the header and the first line of text in your document, you'll need to change your Top margin setting in the Document dialog box or use the Spacing Before and After settings in the Paragraph dialog box. This brings us to the next topic: controlling the vertical positioning of headers and footers.

Multiline headers

Figure 7-41

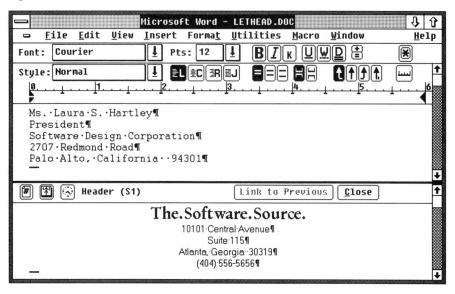

Your header can contain more than one line of text.

Figure 7-42

Word expands the top margin to make room for a multiline header.

Vertical positioning

As you have seen, you can alter the horizontal positioning of the header simply by moving the cursor into the header pane and then using the alignment icons or indent markers on the ruler. However, we haven't yet shown how you can move the header vertically on the page. As you know, the distance between the top of the page and the first line of regular text on the page is controlled by the Top margin setting in the Document dialog box. However, the distance between the top of the page and the first line of a header is controlled by a setting in the expanded Header/Footer dialog box. The distance between the bottom of the page and the last line of a footer is controlled by a similar setting in that dialog box.

To bring up the Header/Footer dialog box, just select the Header/Footer… command from the Edit menu. When the dialog box appears on your screen, choose the Options >> button to bring up the expanded dialog box shown in Figure 7-43. As you can see, the expanded Header/Footer dialog box contains two Distance From Edge settings: Header and Footer. Initially, these settings are 0.5".

Figure 7-43

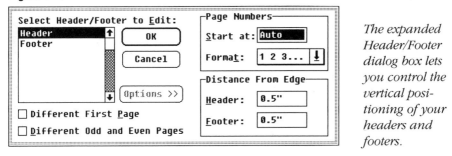

The expanded Header/Footer dialog box lets you control the vertical positioning of your headers and footers.

Because the default Top margin setting is 1 inch, the default Header Distance From Edge value leaves $1/_2$ inch between the header and the first line of text in your document. However, as you saw in Figure 7-42, if your header takes up more than $1/_2$ inch of space (because of the number of lines in the header and/or because of the font size you've chosen), Word will expand the top margin to make room for the header.

Suppose you decide to add extra space between the top of the page and the first line of your header in the sample page shown in Figure 7-42. To do this, simply select the Header/Footer… command, choose the Options >> button in the Header/Footer dialog box, and type a new value—1.5", for instance—in the Header Distance From Edge text box. If you choose OK to close the dialog box, then print the document, the result will look like Figure 7-44.

Figure 7-44

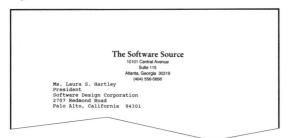

The Header Distance From Edge setting in the expanded Header/Footer dialog box lets you add extra space above a header.

As you can see, Word adds an extra inch between the top of the page and the first line of the header. Word also pushes the first line of text in our sample document down an inch to make room for our expanded header space.

Now, suppose you want to add extra space between the last line of the header and the first line of text on your sample page. To do this, simply select the Document... command from the Format menu, and enter a new value in the Top margin text box. Since the header occupies about $1\,^{3}/_{4}$ inches (including the space between the top line of the header and the top edge of the page), you might set your top margin to $2\,^{3}/_{4}$ inches by typing *2.75"* in the Top margin text box. This new setting would provide about an inch of space between the bottom of the header and the top of the text area.

Using the Before and After settings

In addition to changing the Distance From Edge settings in the Header/Footer dialog box, you can alter the distance between your header and footer text and the top and bottom of the page by using the Before and After settings in the Paragraph dialog box. For example, to open more space between your header and the top of the page, select the first paragraph of header text, then choose Paragraph... from the Format menu. In the Paragraph dialog box, enter a number—such as *12pt*—in the Before text box, then choose OK. Word will then automatically allow 12 points of space above your header text—in addition to the amount of space specified in the Header Distance From Edge text box of the expanded Header/Footer dialog box. As usual, Word will also expand the top margin to make room for the additional space that you've inserted in the header.

Similarly, you can add more space between a header or footer and the body text of a document by using the Before and After settings. For example, returning to Figure 7-42, suppose you want to insert another three lines of space between the header and the first line of document text. Begin by selecting the last paragraph of your header text, then open the Paragraph dialog box. Type *3 li* in the After text box, then choose OK. Word will add three lines of space ($^{1}/_{2}$ inch) below the header text and expand the top margin to accommodate the extra space. Figure 7-45 shows the resulting document. (For more on the Before and After settings in the Paragraph dialog box, see Chapter 5.)

Figure 7-45

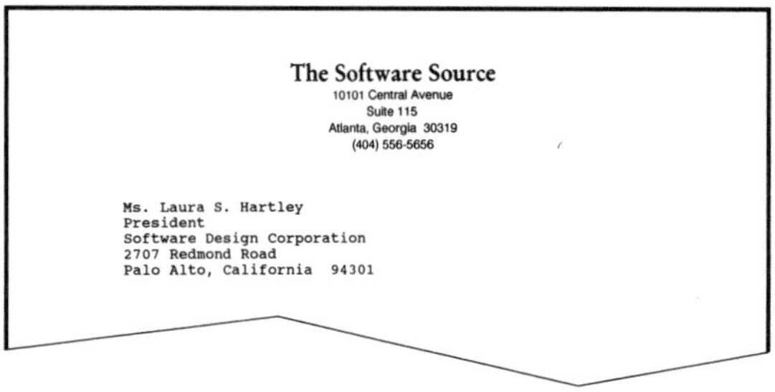
The Software Source
10101 Central Avenue
Suite 115
Atlanta, Georgia 30319
(404) 556-5656

Ms. Laura S. Hartley
President
Software Design Corporation
2707 Redmond Road
Palo Alto, California 94301

We've used the Paragraph dialog box to add $^{1}/_{2}$ inch of space between the header and the body text.

Although it is convenient that Word automatically adjusts your top margin to make room for long headers, you may occasionally want to override this automatic adjustment to enter your header below the top margin of the page. In other words, you may want to place your header in your text area. To override Word's automatic top margin adjustment, precede the margin setting in the Document dialog box with a minus sign. The minus sign doesn't tell Word to create a negative margin—it simply indicates that you want to make your 1-inch margin setting absolute. This absolute margin setting prevents Word from adjusting the top margin to accommodate the header.

Placing headers in the text area

Consider the sample header we created in Figure 7-39. We assigned a negative $1^1/_4$-inch left indent to this header so that we could print it in the left margin of the page. Now, suppose we want to print this header in the left margin and align it with the top line of the body text. We want both the header and the first line of text to begin 1 inch from the top of the page. As you learned in the previous examples, if you simply add extra space above the header, Word will move down your first line of text to accommodate the larger header area. To override Word's automatic top margin adjustment, however, you can precede the Top margin setting with a minus sign. Just choose the Document... command from the Format menu, type the value *-1"* in the Top margin text box, and choose OK.

Next, to place the header 1 inch from the top of the page, choose the Header/Footer... command from the Edit menu, choose the Options >> button to expand the dialog box, and type *1"* in the Header Distance From Edge text box. Finally, choose OK to complete the command.

If you print the sample document on an HP LaserJet printer, you'll see the page shown in Figure 7-46. Notice that the header and body text are now aligned 1 inch from the top of the page.

Figure 7-46

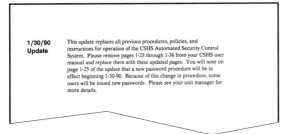

Both the header and the main body text now appear 1 inch from the top of the page.

Another way to place a header in the margin of a page is to use the Position... command. As we'll explain in Chapter 12, you can use this command to place selected text in a fixed position on the page and let Word flow the rest of the text around it.

Formatting headers and footers with the style sheet

It's easy to select and format text in a header pane; the process is no different from selecting and formatting text in your main document window. However, as you'll learn in Chapter 8, you also can format your header text by altering the definition of the style named *header* on your style sheet. (Word automatically adds this style to the style sheet whenever you create a header.) Similarly, you can format the text in a footer pane by using either manual formatting techniques or by altering the *footer* style on the style sheet. If you've used different headers and footers for different sections of a document, the *header* and *footer* styles will apply to all sections. Word does not create a separate style to format the header and footer of each new section. In some cases, you can use this to your advantage. When your document contains variable headers and/or footers, you can format all of them consistently by changing the *header* or *footer* style instructions. In situations where you want to use a different format for the headers and footers of each section, however, you can use manual formatting techniques.

Adding page numbers, dates, and times

The icons at the top of the header pane let you insert the current page number, date, and time into your header text. (These icons are also available in the footer pane.) Table 7-3 identifies these icons.

Table 7-3

This icon...	inserts a dynamic...
[#]	page number
[1↕8]	date
(clock)	time

Each of the icons in Table 7-3 enters a dynamic entry into your header or footer; that is, Word updates the page number, date, and time whenever you print your document so that they remain current. (By the way, to adjust the date and time settings, you'll need to use DOS's DATE and TIME commands to update your computer's system clock.) The page number that appears in the header pane reflects the number of the page that is currently displayed in your document window. Of course, when you print the document, the page number entry will change for each page in the document.

To insert a dynamic page number, date, or time entry into your header text, place the cursor at the spot where you want the entry to appear, then click on the appropriate icon at the top of the header pane. Figure 7-47 shows a sample header pane in which we've entered the time, date, and page number. When we print the document, Word will insert the entries at the positions we've specified.

Figure 7-47

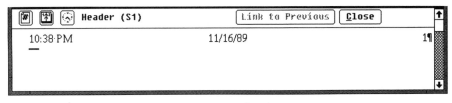

You can enter dynamic times, dates, and page numbers into your header.

As we'll explain in Chapter 10, Word uses a special kind of entry called a field to insert dynamic page numbers, dates, and times into your header. In fact, if you turn on the Field Codes setting on the View menu, you'll see the field codes *{PAGE}*, *{DATE}*, and *{TIME}* in the header pane instead of an actual page number, date, and time. Unless you turn on the Field Codes setting in the expanded Print dialog box, however, Word always displays the actual page number, date, or time in the printed document. Refer to Chapter 10 for a detailed discussion of fields.

You can assign any character formats you want to your page number, date, and time entries. In addition, you can change the form in which the entries are displayed. For example, you can number pages with Roman numerals; display the date 11/29/90 as *November 29, 1990*; and display 3:25 PM as *15:25*. We'll show you how to change the display form of your dates and times in Chapter 10. Now, however, let's investigate the techniques you'll use to change the format of your page numbers.

Working with page numbers

When you add a dynamic page number entry to your header text, Word will format the page numbers according to the numbering scheme you've selected in the expanded Header/Footer dialog box. When you bring up the expanded Header/Footer dialog box and pull down the Page Numbers Format list box, you'll see the five numbering schemes listed in Table 7-4.

Table 7-4

This option...	produces these page numbers...
1 2 3...	1 2 3 4 5 6 7 8 9 10...
a b c...	a b c d e f g h i j...
A B C...	A B C D E F G H I J...
i ii iii...	i ii iii iv v vi vii viii ix x...
I II III	I II III IV V VI VII VIII IX X...

To change the page number format in your document, simply choose the appropriate option from the Page Numbers Format list box, then choose OK. Suppose you want the page number in the sample header shown in Figure 7-47 to appear as a lowercase Roman numeral instead of in Word's default Arabic format. To make the change, bring up the expanded Header/Footer dialog box and choose the *i ii iii* option from the Page Numbers Format list box. When you choose OK to close the dialog box, the document's header will contain Roman numerals.

If your document contains more than one section, you can apply the same numbering scheme to all sections, or you can apply a different numbering scheme to each section. In Chapter 12, we'll explain how to control page numbering on a section-by-section basis.

Creating a different first-page header

Often, you'll want the first page of a document to display a different header or footer than the rest of the document. In fact, you may not want the first page of a document to display a header or footer at all. To change the header or footer on the first page, just select the Different First Page check box in the Header/Footer dialog box. When you do, you'll see two new options appear in the dialog box's list box: First Header and First Footer. If you choose one of these options and choose OK, Word will open a new header or footer pane with the words *First Header* or *First Footer* in the title bar. For example, Figure 7-48 shows a first-page header pane.

Figure 7-48

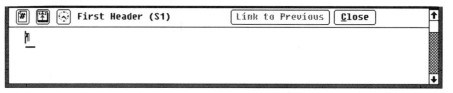

When you select the Different First Page check box in the Header/Footer dialog box, Word will create a new header or footer pane for the first page.

The first-page header and first-page footer panes will initially be blank. To eliminate the header or footer on the first page of a document, choose the Close button in the first-page header or first-page footer pane. To create a new header or footer for the first page, enter the text in the first-page header or first-page footer pane. If your document contains more than one section, you can create special first-page headers and footers for any or all of the sections. We'll show you how to do this in Chapter 12.

Editing headers and footers

In general, you edit headers and footers as you edit any other text in your document. All the techniques for selecting, inserting, deleting, and overwriting text that we discussed in Chapters 4 and 6 apply here as well. You can use the Cut, Copy, and Paste commands in the header and footer panes just as you do in a document pane. You also can copy and move text between your header, footer, and document panes. In fact, you can even use Word's Search..., Replace..., Spelling..., and Hyphenate... commands in your header and footer panes.

When you edit a header or footer pane for one section of your document, your changes may also affect any subsequent "linked" headers or footers. As we'll explain in Chapter 12, the effects of your editing changes depend on which header or footer pane you edit and whether you have broken the link between that header or footer and subsequent headers or footers.

When you are copying or moving text, you treat your header and footer panes just as you would treat any document pane. For example, suppose you have included the heading *Policies and Procedures* in your document, and you decide to use this title in your document header. Rather than retyping the text, just highlight the heading in your document, and issue the Copy command. Next, select the Header/Footer... command from the Document menu, and choose OK to bring up the header pane. Finally, position the cursor where you want to add the heading, and issue the Paste command. After you've finished editing and formatting your header, just choose the Close button at the top of the header pane to lock in your changes and close the pane.

Because the header or footer pane will remain open on your screen until you choose the Close button, you can easily copy several items between your document and header or footer. You may want to temporarily reposition the split bar that separates the document and the header or footer pane on your screen to make it easier to access the document and the header or footer pane.

Unfortunately, you can open only one header or footer pane at a time. For example, if you are using a first-page header and you want to copy an item from the first-page header pane to the regular header pane, you must first open the first-page header pane, select the text you want, and issue the Copy command. Then, you must use the Header/Footer... command to open the regular header pane, and issue the Paste command. As we'll discuss in Chapter 12, if you have created a multisection document and you want to copy a selection from one section header to another, you must issue separate Header/Footer... commands to access the header panes for each section.

When you use Word's Search... and Replace... commands to locate text or to replace one series of characters with another, Word finds and changes only the occurrences in the active pane. This means that Word won't typically locate occurrences of your search text in a header or footer pane, even if that pane is open on your screen when you issue the Search... or Replace... command.

If you want to perform a search or replace operation in a header or footer pane, however, just activate that pane before you issue the Search... or Replace... command. If the pane is already open on your screen, click on the pane to activate

Copying and moving text in header and footer panes

Advanced editing of headers and footers

it or press the [Next pane] key ([F6]). If the header or footer pane you want to work with is not currently open, use the Header/Footer dialog box to display it on your screen. Then, while the header or footer pane is active, start the search-and-replace procedure as you normally would in the document pane. If you are using different odd, even, or first-page headers and footers, you'll have to open each header or footer pane in turn and perform separate search-and-replace procedures. In a multisection document, you'll have to activate the appropriate section of your document, then open the header or footer pane for that section.

In a similar way, when you use the Spelling... or Hyphenate... commands in your document, Word will not automatically check your header and footer after it checks the main document. You must activate each of your header and footer panes before you can use the Spelling... and Hyphenate... commands in those panes. Once you activate the header or footer pane you want to check, you can proceed with your editing just as you would in a standard document pane. (See Chapter 6 for more on the Search..., Replace..., Spelling..., and Hyphenate... commands.)

Deleting headers and footers

To delete a header or footer, open the header or footer pane, select all the text, then press the [Delete] key. (You also can choose Cut from the Edit menu to delete the text.) After you've deleted the text, just close the header or footer pane.

PREVIEWING A PRINTED DOCUMENT

We've talked about a number of commands and settings that let you control the appearance of your printed document. However, it can sometimes be a bit confusing to figure out how all of these elements work together. Fortunately, Word offers two features, the page view and the Print Preview window, that let you preview your document before you print.

The Print Preview command, which is located on the File menu, gives you a bird's-eye view of your document, allowing you to see entire page layouts on the screen. The Page command on the View menu, which also can be accessed by selecting the Page View button in the Print Preview window, lets you see a full-size preview of your printed document with headers, footers, and other special elements in place. However, because Word displays the text in full size, you'll be able to see only a portion of the page on the screen. Both the Print Preview window and the page view can help you avoid time-consuming (and possibly costly) bad print runs. We'll look first at the Print Preview window, then we'll talk about using the page view.

The Print Preview window

When you choose the Print Preview command from the File menu, Word will display a window like the one shown in Figure 7-49. The buttons that appear just below the menu bar let you send the document to the printer, display boundary lines, change the margins, and switch to page view.

Figure 7-49

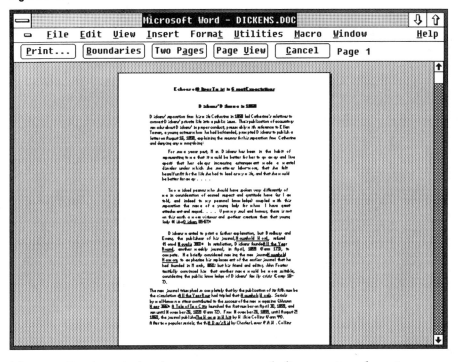

The Print Preview window lets you preview and alter your page layout.

The first time you use the Print Preview command, Word will display one document page on your screen. If you want to see two pages, you can select the Two Pages button at the top of the window. When you select this button, Word will display a two-page spread, as shown in Figure 7-50 on the following page. Notice that the Two Pages button now reads *One Page*. To bring the one-page display back, just select the One Page button.

To close the Print Preview window, just select the Page View or Cancel button. As you might guess, choosing the Page View button will display your document in the page view. Choosing the Cancel button will display your document in whatever view was active (normal editing, page, outline, or draft) at the time you issued the Print Preview command.

When you issue the Print Preview command, Word will automatically repaginate your document through the page that is currently visible on your screen and then display a preview of that page and the following page. The number of the page or pages that are currently being previewed will appear next to the Cancel button at the top of the preview screen.

Navigating in the Print Preview window

Figure 7-50

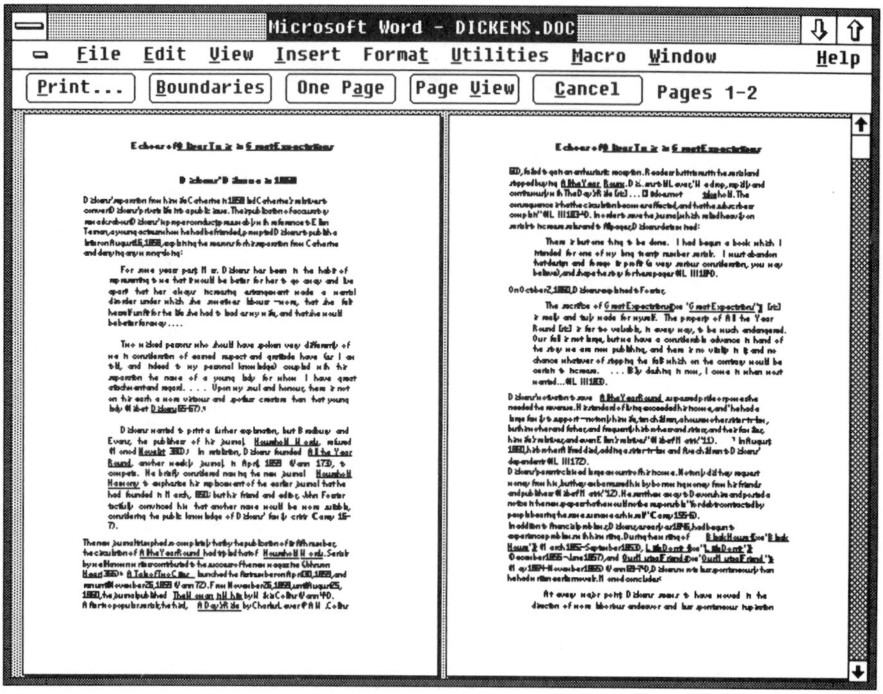

Selecting the Two Pages button at the top of the Print Preview window tells Word to display a two-page spread.

If you want to see a different page while the preview screen is open, you can use the vertical scroll bar on the right side of the preview screen or the arrow keys to bring other pages into view. Click on the scroll arrows or in the gray area of the scroll bar to move through the document a page at a time. Or, you can press the ↓ key to move forward one page, or press the ↑ key to move back one page. If you want to move through several pages on the preview screen, just drag the scroll box.

Generally, if you are using a two-page display, moving forward by one page will cause the page on the right side of your preview screen to move to the left, while a new page is brought into view on the right side. When you move back by one page, the effect is the opposite: the page on the left side shifts to the right side and a new page is brought into view on the left. For example, if you are viewing pages 4 and 5 on the preview screen and you click on the down scroll arrow, Word will display pages 5 and 6.

Navigating from page to page is a bit different if you have activated Mirror Margins or specified a Gutter setting in the Document dialog box, or if you've selected Different Odd and Even Pages in the Header/Footer dialog box. Word will always display an odd page on the right side of the preview screen and an even page on the left. When you're viewing the beginning of a document, page 1 will appear on the right side of your screen, and the page opposite page 1 will be blank. As you move forward or backward in a document, Word will shift both of the display pages in order to maintain this even-odd layout. For example, if you are viewing pages 4 and 5 on the screen and you click the up scroll arrow, Word will bring pages 2 and 3 into view.

Word will not let you edit your document or change its character and paragraph formatting while you are viewing it through the Print Preview window. However, if you notice an error or an item that you want to change while you are viewing a page in the Print Preview window, you can quickly go to that area of your document by choosing the Close button. When you close the Print Preview window, Word will display the text that is currently visible in that window. If, after making your editing or formatting change, you want to preview the results of your efforts, just issue the Print Preview command again. As long as the text you want to view is visible in your document window, Word will display the page on which that text is located when you choose the Print Preview command.

The sample preview screens you've seen so far have been standard letter-size pages in portrait orientation. If you use other page sizes or landscape orientation, however, Word will adjust the size and proportion of your preview pages to reflect your Document and Printer Setup dialog box specifications.

Page size

For example, the preview screen in Figure 7-51 on the next page shows a letter-size page that we've set up to print in landscape orientation, while the preview screen in Figure 7-52 on page 247 shows a page that we've set up to print on 3-by-5 index card stock. To create the 3-by-5 index card layout, we selected the Document... command on the Format menu, specified a custom paper size with a Page Width setting of 3 inches and a Height setting of 5 inches, and then specified Top and Bottom margin settings of .5 inch and Left and Right margins of .35 inch. Notice that Word rotated the page on the preview screen to match the orientation we selected, and that it adjusted the size of the preview page image to display as much detail as possible.

You can change many of your page layout specifications while the Print Preview window is open. For example, you can reposition page numbers, move your document margins, change your document's page breaks, and reposition your headers and footers. We suspect that many users will find it easier to format their documents "visually" in the Print Preview window, rather than using the Document dialog box. While you're viewing the Print Preview window, Word also lets you move items that have been positioned with the Position... command. We'll talk more about this in Chapter 12 when we explain the Position... command. For now, let's look at how you can use the Print Preview window to change margins, page breaks, and headers and footers.

Formatting in the Print Preview window

Figure 7-51

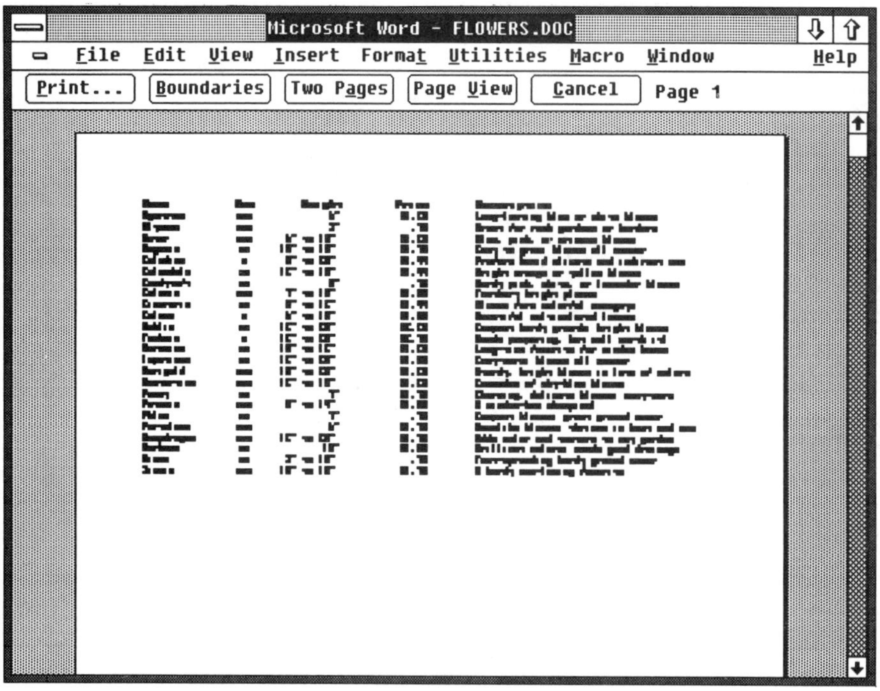

We've set up this sample document to print in landscape orientation.

Changing margins

In Chapter 5, we showed how you can set margins by entering Top, Bottom, Left, and Right margin settings in the Document dialog box. You also can set— or change—your margins in the Print Preview window. To do this, begin by choosing the Boundaries button. Then, if you are viewing two pages, click on the page you want to work with. At this point, Word will display dotted lines that represent your current margin positions, as well as your header and footer positions and page breaks, as shown in Figure 7-53 on page 248. If you have used the Position... command to place an object on the page you're previewing, the boundaries of that object will also be marked with a dotted line when you select the Boundaries button.

Notice the black squares or handles that appear at the edge of the top, bottom, left, and right margin lines on your screen. To change a margin setting, first use the mouse to position the mouse pointer above the appropriate margin handle. (At this point, the mouse pointer will assume the shape of a crosshair.) Next, press the mouse button and drag the margin line to the desired location on the page. As you drag the margin line across the page, notice that Word displays the value of the new margin setting in the upper-right portion of your screen. The value

that is displayed when you release the mouse button to lock in your change will
be transferred to the appropriate margin text box in the Document dialog box.

Figure 7-52

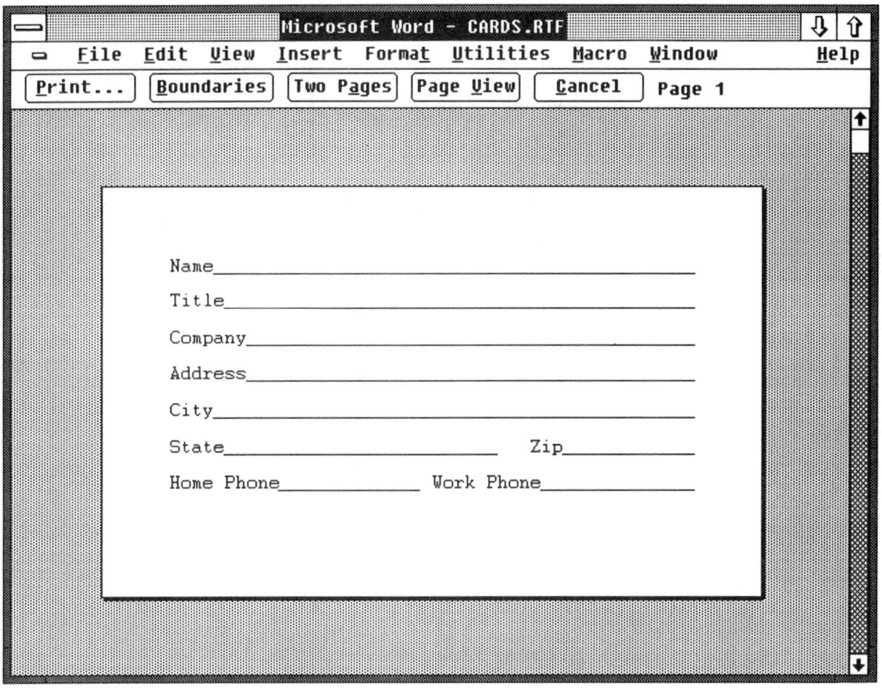

We've set up this sample document to print on 3-by-5 index cards.

For example, suppose you want to increase the Left and Right margin settings
for the sample document shown in Figure 7-53 to $1^3/_4$ inches each. Begin by
selecting the Boundaries button, then click on the handle at the bottom of the left
margin line and drag to the right. Release the mouse button when you see the
value *1.75"* at the top of the screen. To adjust the right margin, click on the handle
at the bottom of the right margin line and drag it to the left. Again, release the
mouse button when you see the value *1.75"*.

To change the margin settings in the Print Preview window with the keyboard,
first select the Boundaries button by pressing *B*, then press the [Tab] key until Word
activates the margin line you want to move. (The line will temporarily disappear
when Word activates it.) Once you've activated the appropriate margin line, use
the arrow keys to move the margin line to the desired location. Again, Word will
display the value of the margin setting in the upper-right portion of the window
as you move the margin line around on the page.

Figure 7-53

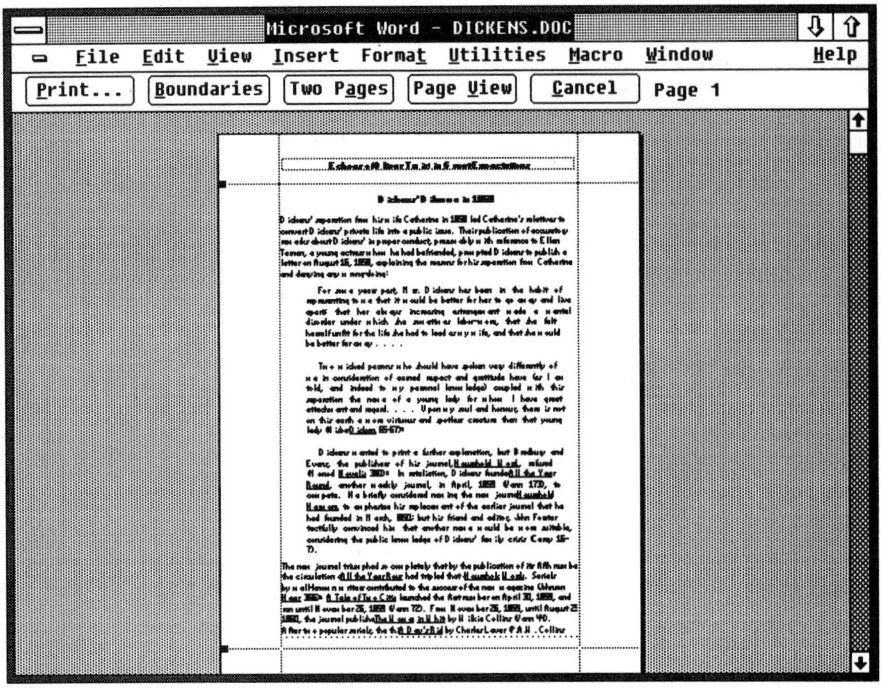

When you choose the Boundaries button, Word will display dotted lines that represent the current page layout settings.

Once you've positioned your margins, you can see the effects of your changes by either choosing the Boundaries button or clicking anywhere outside the page display portion of the screen. If you're using the keyboard, you can see the effects of your changes by first pressing [Enter] to lock in the new positions, and then pressing *B* to select the Boundaries button. Word will repaginate your document and redraw the pages on your screen to reflect the new margins. Keep in mind that your margin settings apply to your entire document, not just to the page or section you are previewing.

Changing page breaks

You can also insert manual page breaks into your document from the Print Preview window by dragging the page-break line that appears below the last line of text on the page. This line looks slightly different from the margin line and does not extend all the way to the edge of the page, as do your top and bottom margin lines. In addition, a page-break line does not have a handle—you simply point to any part of the line to drag it. When you release the mouse button, Word will immediately repaginate the document. If you move the page-break line up, any text that appears below that line will move to the top of the next page. If you drag the page-break line down, Word will pull text from the top of the next page down to the bottom of the current page. Of course, if the Widow Control option in the Document dialog box is selected, Word will not leave the first line of a paragraph "stranded" at the bottom of a page or move the last line of a paragraph to the top of the next page.

For example, suppose you want to move the last three lines at the bottom of page 1 in Figure 7-53 to the top of page 2. All you need to do is drag the page-break line up three lines, as shown in Figure 7-54. As you can see, Word will reflow the document and reposition the lines. When you return to your document window, you'll also see that Word has inserted a manual page-break marker at this position in your document.

Figure 7-54

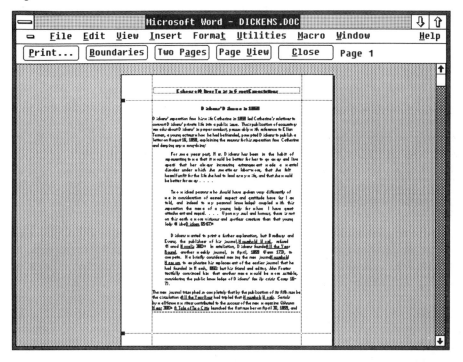

Word automatically inserts a manual page break and reflows your text when you drag the page-break line.

By the way, the page-break line will often appear just above the line marking the bottom margin. This can make it difficult for you to distinguish the page-break line from the margin line. However, you can move the page-break line without affecting your bottom margin line. In order to drag the page-break line, you must click between the left and right margins on the preview screen. Since the bottom margin line must be dragged by its handle—which appears on the left edge of the page—you'll be able to move the page-break line independently of the margin line. Word will not let you use the page-break line to flow text past the bottom margin line. However, if you have inserted a manual page break in your document and you decide to remove it, you can drag the page-break line past the bottom margin line on the preview screen. Word will reflow your document to fill the current page.

Repositioning headers and footers

When you select the Boundaries button in the Print Preview window, Word will display a dotted border around your headers and footers. To reposition a header or footer, just click anywhere within this border and drag the header or footer up or down to the desired position. This action is equivalent to changing the values in the Distance From Edge text boxes in the expanded Header/Footer dialog box. As you drag the header or footer, Word will display the distance from the edge of the page at the top of the screen.

To change the position of the header and footer in the Print Preview window with the keyboard, first select the Boundaries button by pressing *B*, then press the [Tab] key until Word activates the header or footer. (The header or footer will temporarily disappear when Word activates it.) Once you've activated the header or footer, use the arrow keys to move it to the desired location. Again, Word will display the distance from the edge of the page in the upper-right portion of the screen as you move the header or footer around on the page.

After you drag the header or footer, choose the Boundaries button or click in the gray area of the screen. If you're using the keyboard, press [Enter] before you choose the Boundaries button. Word will then redraw the screen to show the header or footer in its new position.

If your headers and footers require more space than is currently available in the top and bottom margin areas, you'll want to reposition your top and bottom margin lines before you move the headers and footers. Word will not allow you to drag a header or footer past your top or bottom margin line.

For example, suppose you want the header shown in Figure 7-54 to appear 1 inch from the top of the page. Because the current Top margin setting is 1 inch, you'll need to drag the top margin line down before you can move the header. To do this, simply click on the handle on the right side of the top margin line and drag it until you see *1.75"* at the top corner of the preview screen. Then, click on the header and drag it to the 1-inch position. You'll also want to remove the manual page break that was inserted earlier by dragging it off the page. Figure 7-55 shows the results.

To drag a header or footer past the current top or bottom margin so that it will print in the text area, just press the [Shift] key as you drag the header or footer.

This is equivalent to using a minus sign to type an absolute Top or Bottom margin setting in the Document dialog box. (See page 237 for more on placing headers and footers in the text area.)

Figure 7-55

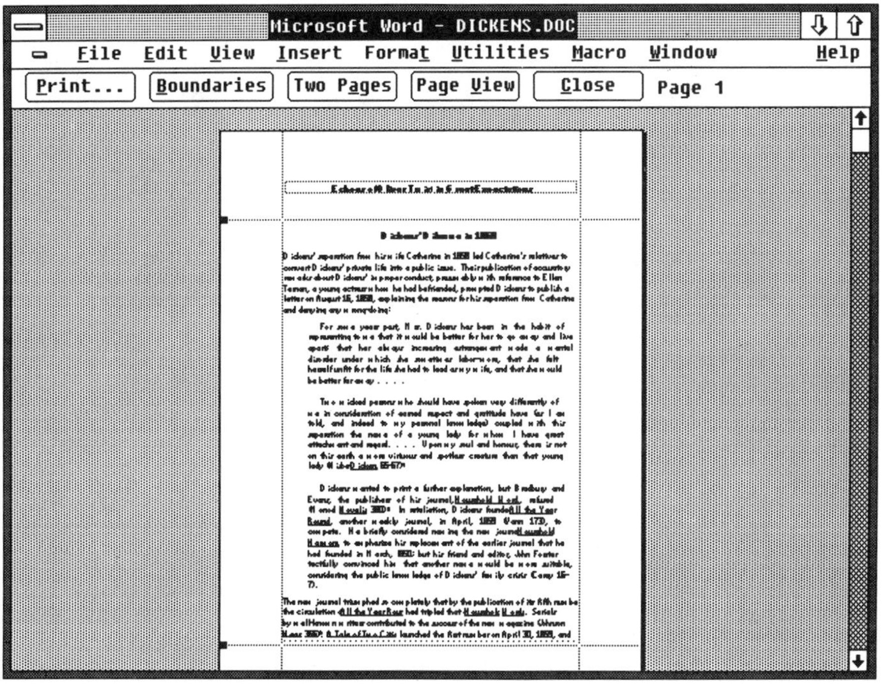

To reposition a header or footer, just drag it to the desired position on the page.

If you're working in a multisection document, your changes to the header and footer positions will apply to the current section only. If you want to change the header and footer positions in more than one section, you may find it easier to highlight some text in two or more sections in your document window and then use the Section… command to make your adjustments. (Chapter 12 explains this process in more detail.)

If you've used the Position… command on the Format menu to place an object into your Word document, Word will represent the object in the Print Preview window with an empty box frame. If you want to reposition the object, first select the Boundaries button to display the boundaries of the object. Next, if you're using a mouse, just place the mouse pointer inside the frame, where it will assume a

Repositioning absolute-positioned objects

crosshair shape, then click and drag the object to the desired position. If you're using the keyboard, use the [Tab] key to highlight the object, then use the arrow keys to change the object's position.

As you move the object around in the Print Preview window, Word will display its horizontal and vertical position coordinates at the top of the window. These coordinates represent the position of the left and top boundaries of the positioned object relative to the left and top edges of the page. For example, the coordinates *(1.5, 2.25)* tell you that the left boundary of the object is $1^1/_2$ inches from the left edge of the page, and the top boundary of the object is $2\,^1/_4$ inches from the top edge of the page. After you position the object to your liking, click in the gray area of the screen to move the boundary lines for the positioned object and redraw the screen showing the new flow of text.

Of course, if you want to see a closer view of a positioned object, select the Page View button at the top of the Print Preview window, or choose Page from the View menu.

Printing from the Print Preview window

You can send a Word document to the printer directly from the Print Preview window by choosing the Print... button. When you choose this button, Word will open the Print dialog box. At this point, you can adjust the print settings (if necessary), then choose OK to print the document. After Word sends your document to the printer, it will return you to the Print Preview window.

Specifying margin settings with the Document... command

Although the easiest way to position your margins, header, and footer is with the Boundaries button in the Print Preview window, you can still issue the Document... command from the Print Preview window and specify your margin settings in the Document dialog box. When you choose OK to close the dialog box, Word will adjust the display in the Print Preview window to reflect the settings you defined.

Using page view

Another useful Word for Windows feature is the page view. Like the preview screen that you see when you choose the Print Preview command, the page view shows you a preview of your printed document pages with headers, page numbers, footnotes, and other special elements in place. However, unlike the preview screen, the page view displays your page and text in their full size and lets you make changes as you're viewing those pages.

Although the page view is quite helpful for viewing the layout of your printed pages, you'll find that Word runs significantly more slowly when the page view is active. Therefore, you probably will not want to use it for the majority of your text creation, editing, and formatting. We recommend that you use the normal editing view most of the time and use the page view only to check the layout of your document in the final stages.

There are two ways to access the page view. First, you can simply select the Page command from the View menu. When you do this, Word will refresh your screen, changing from the view you were using (normal editing, Print Preview, draft, or outline) to the page view. The Page command is a toggle command—when you want to turn off the page view and switch to the normal editing view, just choose the command again. To change from the page view to the draft or outline view, choose Draft or Outline from the View menu. Word always indicates which view is currently active by placing a check mark next to the appropriate command on the View menu.

Another way to access the page view is to choose the Page View button at the top of the Print Preview window. This allows you to move from the bird's-eye view of the preview screen to the close-up view of the page view screen.

When you choose the Page command, Word will repaginate your document from the first page through the page on which the cursor is located. If the document is long, you may have to wait several seconds before the page view screen appears. While you're in page view, if you move forward to another page in the document, Word will repaginate through that point as well.

Let's use the page view to take another look at the sample document shown in Figure 7-53. When you issue the Page command, Word will display the screen shown in Figure 7-56.

Accessing page view

A brief tour

Figure 7-56

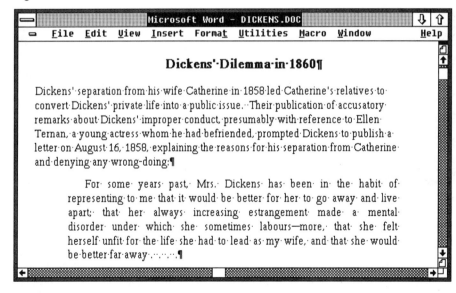

The page view will display the main text area of the current page at the top of the screen.

When you first switch to the page view, Word will display the main text area of the current page at the top of the screen. For example, if your document has a 1-inch top margin with a header, that margin and header will be just out of view, with the first line of your document's main body text appearing at the top of the window. To bring other parts of the page into view, just click on the vertical or horizontal scroll bar. To see a different page, you can drag the scroll boxes or click on the Page-back and Page-forward icons ( ) at the top and bottom of the vertical scroll bar. (We'll discuss these icons in a moment.)

When you scroll in page view, Word will show you the edges of a page instead of marking page breaks with a dotted horizontal line, as it does in the normal editing view. Figure 7-57 shows the page from Figure 7-56 after we scrolled the upper-left corner into view. Notice that Word uses a shaded background to help distinguish the page area. Notice also that you now can see the header at the top of the page. If this were not the first page in the document and we continued scrolling up, Word would display the bottom of the previous page.

Figure 7-57

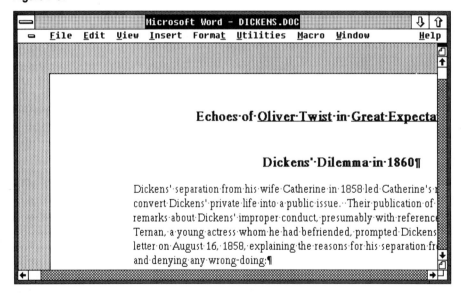

You can scroll the edges of a page into view on the page view screen.

Text areas

In page view, different elements of your page layout are considered separate text areas. In a simple page layout, you would have only one text area—the single column of text that's bounded by your left, right, top, and bottom margins. In a multicolumn layout, each column is a separate text area. Each header and footer is also considered a text area, as are fixed-positioned objects, tables, and individual cells of a table.

The concept of text areas becomes significant as you move around and select text in page view. As you'll see in a moment, Word offers a couple of keyboard shortcuts for moving from one text area to another. In addition, each text area in page view has its own selection bar. Before we talk about these topics, however, let's look at one way you can identify the separate text areas on a page.

To help you keep your bearings and distinguish individual text areas as you scroll around in the page view, Word can display boundaries, or dotted lines, around the different text areas in a document. These boundary lines are similar to the margin, header, and page-break lines you can see in the Print Preview window, although you cannot drag the boundary lines in page view.

Boundary lines

To toggle the display of the boundary lines while you are working in page view, simply click on the Show-all icon (▨) at the right edge of the ribbon, or select the Show All check box in the Preferences dialog box. Figure 7-58 shows the page from Figure 7-57 after we turned on the display of boundary lines.

Figure 7-58

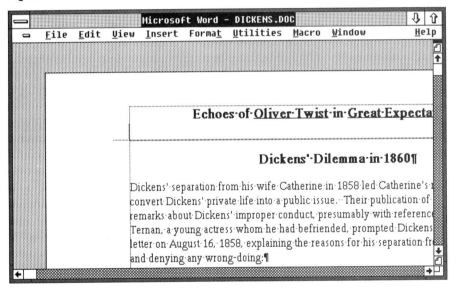

You can turn on the display of boundary lines by clicking on the Show-all icon at the right edge of the ribbon.

To turn on the display of boundary lines but suppress the display of tabs, spaces, paragraph marks, optional hyphens, and hidden text, select the Text Boundaries check box in the Preferences dialog box.

In Figure 7-58, you can see two types of boundary lines. The vertical and horizontal lines that intersect below the header in the upper-right corner of the page are the margin boundaries. If you scrolled to any corner of the page, you would see these intersecting lines. Above the line that marks the top margin, you'll see the header boundary. This line appears $1/2$ inch from the top edge of the page—the distance we've specified as the Header Distance From Edge setting in the expanded Header/Footer dialog box. If a page contains a footer, the bottom boundary of the footer will be marked by a similar line.

If your page is laid out in two or more snaking columns, each column will be surrounded by its own boundary line. Any object to which you have assigned a special position using the Position... command will also appear within its own boundary. Additionally, boundary lines will appear around tables you have created with the Table... command, and around each cell in the table.

Navigating in page view

In addition to using the vertical and horizontal scroll bars to navigate in page view, you can use the Page-back and Page-forward icons located at the top and bottom of the vertical scroll bar. When you click on the Page-back icon, Word will bring the top of the previous page into view. Clicking the Page-forward icon will bring the top of the next page into view. In both cases, Word will move the cursor to the beginning of the new page.

To move quickly through a large part of your document, drag the scroll boxes, or issue the Go To... command and specify the page number you want to see.

Word also offers a couple of keyboard shortcuts—[Alt]↓ and [Alt]↑—for moving around in page view. Pressing [Alt]↓ moves the cursor to the beginning of the next text area, while pressing [Alt]↑ moves it to the beginning of the previous text area. (We'll discuss the concept of text areas in Chapter 12.) If you use the ↑ and ↓ keys by themselves to move around in a multicolumn document in the page view, Word will move the cursor through one column before moving to the next column on the same page.

As you navigate in the page view, you'll notice that Word always aligns the zero point of the ruler with the left boundary of the current text area's first paragraph. For example, consider the two-column document shown in Figure 7-59. As you can see, when you place the cursor in the left column (as we've done in the top window of Figure 7-59), Word will align the zero point of the ruler with the left boundary of the first paragraph in that text area. When you move the cursor to the right column (as we've done in the bottom window), Word will move the ruler's zero point to the left boundary of the first paragraph in that text area.

Selecting text in page view

We mentioned earlier that each text area in the page view has its own selection bar. You can see evidence of this as you move the pointer around on the screen. Each time the pointer moves over the selection bar for a text area, it will change from the I-beam shape into a right-arrow pointer. Suppose you are working with a two-column layout in page view. Your document window will have a selection bar on the far left as it normally does, but this selection bar is for the left column only. There will be another selection bar just to the left of the right column. If you want to select a paragraph of text in the right column, move the pointer into the selection bar to the left of that paragraph and double-click.

Figure 7-59

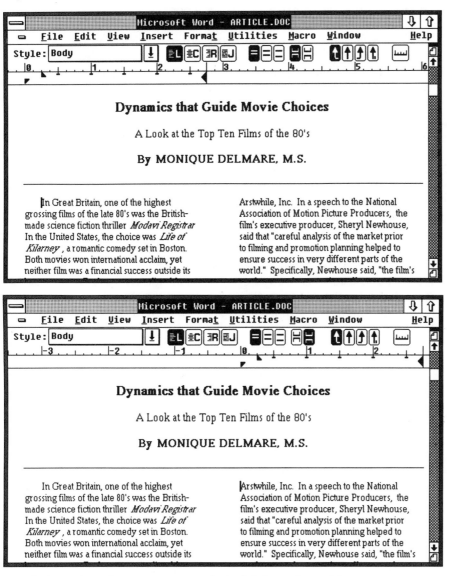

Word aligns the ruler's zero point with the left boundary of the current text area's first paragraph.

If you want to select all the text in a document, just move the pointer to any selection bar—except the selection bar for a header or footer—and press the [Ctrl] key as you click the mouse button. Other selection techniques that we describe in Chapter 4 work the same in the page view as in the normal editing view. You can even select text on two or more pages by dragging your selection beyond the top or bottom border of the window. However, you'll find that making a selection like this is much slower in page view than in normal editing view.

Editing and formatting in page view

Although you'll probably want to use the normal editing view for most of your editing and formatting, you'll often need to make minor changes in the page view as well. For example, if you spot a misspelled word in your header, you can simply click on the misspelling and correct it. There's no need to return to the normal editing view and open the header pane. As you're viewing your document, you also might discover that your margins aren't as wide as you would prefer. To correct this, just select the Document... command and enter new settings. You can open the Document dialog box quickly in page view by double-clicking in the corner of a page, between intersections of the lines that mark your side and top or bottom margins. Of course, you also can change your margins by issuing the Print Preview command, clicking on the Boundaries button, and dragging your margin lines.

In short, you can make any editing and formatting changes in the page view that you can make in the normal editing view. This includes altering your Document, Section, Paragraph, and Character dialog box settings; changing style definitions; and cutting, copying, pasting, finding, and changing text. You also can insert page breaks and section breaks and use any of Word's special features, including the Spelling..., Hyphenate..., and Sort... commands.

Working with headers, footers, and footnotes in page view

The page view shows you the position of each page's header and footer. If you want to alter a header or footer, just click on the text and make your change. Word will apply your change to all headers (or footers) in the current section. If your document has multiple sections, changing a header or footer on one page will affect any linked headers or footers in subsequent sections. (We'll explain sectional headers and footers in detail in Chapter 12.)

To add a header or footer in the page view, just choose the Header/Footer... command from the Edit menu. Word will then bring up the Header/Footer dialog box shown in Figure 7-60. When you select either the Header or Footer option and choose OK, Word will move the cursor to the first character in the header or footer area of the current page. You can then enter and format that text. If you have selected the Different Odd and Even Pages check box in the Header/Footer dialog box, Word will use the text that you enter only on like pages. For example, suppose you create a header on page 2. If you scroll to page 3, you won't see the header because that is an odd page. However, if you scroll to page 4, the header text from page 2 will appear. As long as you're in the page view, only the options *Header* and *Footer* will appear in the Header/Footer dialog box. However, when you switch to the normal editing view, you'll see a full range of options in the Header/Footer dialog box when you select the Different First Page and/or Different Odd and Even Pages check boxes.

Figure 7-60

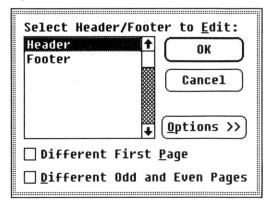

You can use the Header/ Footer dialog box while working in the page view to create or edit headers and footers.

Footnotes function very much like headers and footers in the page view. When you use the Footnote... command to insert a footnote while working in the page view, Word will insert the appropriate footnote reference mark into the document's text and move the cursor to the footnote area at the bottom of the page. At this point, you can type the footnote exactly as you want it to appear.

Although page view is a helpful feature, there are a number of instances when it cannot give you an accurate representation of your printed document. Additionally, as long as the Hidden Text check box is selected in the Preferences dialog box, any text assigned the hidden format will appear in page view—even if you've deselected the Hidden Text check box in the expanded Print dialog box. If you've chosen to use line numbers in a document, these will not appear in page view, though they will show up in the Print Preview window.

Finally, if you are printing to a laser printer, your printer must have access to the fonts you've used in the document. For instance, if you've assigned the 12-point Tms Rmn font to the text in your document, and your printer is not equipped with this font, the document you see in page view will look quite different from the one your printer will print.

Limitations of page view

Advanced Techniques

Section 3
Advanced Techniques

In Section 2, we showed you the fundamentals of working with Word. By now, you should have mastered such skills as creating, selecting, editing, formatting, and printing text. You should also have a handle on designing a page layout, creating and using document windows, and navigating in Word.

In this section, we'll go beyond these Word basics to look at a number of special features, such as style sheets, outlining, the glossary, indexes, multicolumn formatting, footnotes, form letters, and character formulas. You'll also learn how to customize your Word menus and control many default settings so that you can tailor the program to suit your needs. We'll show you how to share data with other programs—including Microsoft Excel—and describe how you can integrate graphics into your Word documents. We'll also introduce Word's powerful macro capability.

We encourage you to explore these powerful features and take advantage of them. These are the features that take Word beyond simple word processing into the realm of desktop publishing.

In this chapter

Style Sheets 8

*F*ew features in Word are as powerful and helpful as the Style Sheet facility. With style sheets, you can define the character and paragraph formats you want to use for various parts of your document and instruct Word to apply those formats automatically. Style sheets can save you a tremendous amount of time by ensuring that your document is formatted consistently. As you'll learn in this chapter, you can even copy style sheets from one document to another in order to maintain consistent formatting.

In the publishing industry, a style sheet is a listing of rules that specify how different portions of a printed document should look. In Word, each document includes its own style sheet, which contains a collection of named styles. A named style is simply a set of instructions for formatting a paragraph. These instructions control the appearance of a paragraph by specifying both the character formats, such as the font and point size, and the paragraph formats, such as indents and line spacing. (By the way, keep in mind that a paragraph in Word may be a block of text or a single line of text.)

WHAT IS A STYLE SHEET?

Typically, the instructions for a named style will control a combination of formatting features that you need to use in many paragraphs throughout a document. By recording these instructions on a style sheet, you won't need to repeat the formatting process for similar paragraphs. Instead, you can simply apply a named style from the style sheet.

For example, a style named *Figure Caption* might control all the formatting features you want to apply to each figure caption in a document. Every time you create a figure caption, you can format it by using a single command to select the *Figure Caption* style, instead of issuing two or three commands and clicking on various ruler icons.

While formatting a paragraph with one command instead of three is nice, the real beauty of style sheets is that they make it much easier and faster to modify a document's formatting. To illustrate the purpose of a style sheet, consider the process of painting a new house. Suppose you decide to paint the house blue and the trim around windows and doors white. After applying these colors to the entire house, you realize that the trim would look better if it were painted gray instead of white. To make this change, you would need to apply gray paint to all the trim. Imagine how nice it would be, however, if you could instantly change the color of everything painted white to gray or, if you decide you'd prefer a yellow house, change the color of everything painted blue to yellow.

Just as you paint different parts of the house certain colors, you assign different character and paragraph formats to certain parts of your document. When you want to assign a new format to certain paragraphs, you probably highlight each of those paragraphs and manually apply the new format. You can avoid the hassle of manually reformatting multiple paragraphs, however, if you use style sheets. After applying a style name to some paragraphs in your document, you can, in a single step, alter the format of all those paragraphs. In other words, although it's impossible to instantly change the color of your house's trim from white to gray, style sheets make it possible to change, for instance, every figure caption in your document from 10-point Helv type to 12-point Helv bold type.

To further illustrate the benefit of style sheets, consider the following situation. Suppose you've created a document that includes 18 excerpts from a novel. To set off these excerpts, which are scattered throughout the document, you use the ruler to indent them an inch from the left edge of the text column. After you've written the entire document, you decide that you'd like to reduce the excerpts' indent by $1/_2$ inch. If you manually formatted each excerpt rather than using a style sheet, you would need to search for each excerpt and adjust all 18 sets of margins separately. However, if you used the document's style sheet to format the excerpts, you could change all of them simply by modifying the appropriate style name. Using style sheets would allow you to get the same amount of work done with a fraction of the effort, and would guarantee that all excerpts were formatted the same.

Although style sheets are pretty complex, the time they can save you definitely makes them worth mastering. Once you begin to use style sheets, you'll find that they are one of the most valuable tools available in Word.

STYLE SHEET BASICS

Whenever you start a new document, Word automatically creates a style sheet for it. Initially, the default style sheet will contain only four styles: *Normal, heading 1, heading 2*, and *heading 3*. You can modify the default style sheet to include other styles, if you want. (We will explain how to do this in the section called "Changing Defaults" near the end of this chapter.)

Each document's style sheet is permanently linked to that document. You can change a document's style sheet by adding, modifying, deleting, and even borrowing styles from other documents. When you save a document, the style sheet—including any changes you've made—is saved automatically.

Every document uses a different style sheet. If you have more than one document open, each will have its own style sheet. Of course, several documents can use an identical collection of named styles. In fact, this is likely if you create several documents based on the same template or if you copy named styles from one document to another. (We'll explain how to do that later in this chapter.)

If you want to view the style sheet for a document, choose Styles... or Define Styles... from the Format menu. You can use the Styles... command to apply styles in your document and the Define Styles... command to edit your style sheet. For example, if you use the New... command to create a new document based on the Normal template, issuing the Styles... command will open the dialog box shown in Figure 8-1.

Figure 8-1

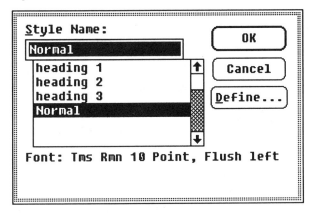

In a new document, Word's default style sheet will contain these four automatic styles.

As you can see, the default *Normal* style specifies 10-point Tms Rmn type with flush-left paragraph alignment. Text formatted with the *Normal* style will also have single spacing between lines and no indents. (As you may remember from Chapter 5, these are the default paragraph and character formats in Word.) If you want, you can change these default specifications for the *Normal* style.

Word uses the *Normal* style to format the main body text in a document. In fact, you can think of the *Normal* style as the default style for a document—any text that is not specifically assigned a different style will be formatted in this style. Figure 8-2 shows how text in the default *Normal* style will appear on your screen if you use a VGA display system. (The *Normal* style will look different if you use a different display system, such as EGA or CGA.)

Figure 8-2

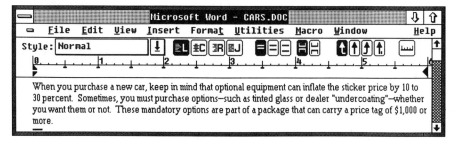

This screen shows how Word's default Normal *style will format text.*

Word gives you a couple of ways to apply styles other than *Normal*. On the left side of the ruler is the Style pull-down list box, which contains all the document's styles. You can use this list box to apply any style you want.

Although the Style list box is a convenient tool for selecting a named style, it does not let you see the formatting characteristics you've assigned to the style names. If you're not sure which style you want to assign, simply open the Styles dialog box and view the characteristics assigned to each style name.

In addition to the Styles... commands and the Style list box, the [Style] key ([Ctrl]S) is a useful tool for applying styles. If you press [Style] while the ruler is visible, Word will move the cursor to the Style list box, enabling you to select a named style. If you press [Style] while the ruler is not visible, Word will display the prompt *Which style?* in the status bar at the bottom of the screen. You can then apply any style by typing its name at this prompt and pressing [Enter]. If you are unsure of the style name you want to apply, you can press [Style] again to open the Styles dialog box. You can then select the appropriate style from the Style Name list box.

Named styles

A style sheet might contain as few as four or as many as 220 styles. Each named style consists of a set of formatting instructions that control the appearance of a paragraph. We've already seen how the definition for the default *Normal* style affects the appearance of text. That definition is fairly simple and straightforward. In many cases, however, a style's definition will be more complicated than the one you see in Figure 8-1. For example, Figure 8-3 displays the definition for the default style named *heading 1*.

You can use any named style on the style sheet to format a paragraph in a document, and you can apply a named style to as many paragraphs as you want. However, you cannot use a named style to format less than a full paragraph. For example, although you can use a named style to format the subheadings in a document, you cannot use a style to format only one word in a subheading. (There are exceptions to this "full paragraph" rule. Word uses a named style to format footnote and annotation reference marks in the body text of a document, and to format page and line numbers.)

Figure 8-3

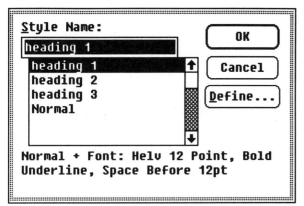

Normal + Font: Helv 12 Point, Bold
Underline, Space Before 12pt

Style definitions can become fairly lengthy and complex.

Whether you choose to format your document using named styles or format the text manually, every paragraph in a document will have a named style associated with it. Word always displays the style name for the current paragraph in the Style box on the ruler.

Unless you specifically choose another style, Word will assign the *Normal* style to each paragraph in a document. This does not necessarily mean that each paragraph will manifest all the formatting characteristics of the *Normal* style. The appearance of a paragraph can be controlled by both a named style and other formatting changes you implement using menu commands and ruler and ribbon icons. However, you probably will use named styles almost exclusively as you become familiar with style sheets. With a named style, you can control every aspect of a paragraph's appearance. Table 8-1 on the following page summarizes the characteristics that a named style can control.

In addition to the characteristics listed in Table 8-1, a named style can control which style should be used next in a document. For example, every style sheet includes the style named *heading 1*, which you can use to control the appearance of some of the headings in your document. The definition for this default style also specifies that the first paragraph after a *heading 1* paragraph should be assigned the *Normal* style. Thus, when you type a *heading 1* paragraph and press [Enter], Word will automatically start a new paragraph that is formatted in the *Normal* style. We will explain the Next Style option in the expanded Define Styles dialog box, and other style characteristics, later in this chapter.

Table 8-1

A named style can control:
First-line, left, and right indents
Tab placement
Tab alignment (left, centered, right, decimal)
Tab leaders
Paragraph alignment (left, centered, right, justified)
Line spacing within a paragraph
Spacing above and below a paragraph
Paragraph borders
Other paragraph formats (Keep Paragraph With Next, Page Break Before, etc.)
Font
Point size
Character formats (Bold, Italic, Underline, etc.)
Character spacing (Normal, Expanded, Condensed)
Character position (Normal, Superscript, Subscript)
Character color

Viewing the definition of a named style

If you want to view the definition for a particular named style, choose either Styles... or Define Styles... from the Format menu and select from the list box the name of the style whose definition you want to see. (If the style sheet contains more than a few styles, you may need to scroll more names into view in order to select the name of the style you want.) Word will then display the definition for the selected style. Figures 8-1 and 8-3 show how the Styles dialog box will display the definition for a named style. Figure 8-4 shows the Define Styles dialog box, in which we've highlighted the style name *Normal*.

Although the Define Styles dialog box looks similar to the Styles dialog box, you might notice that it includes several additional buttons. Specifically, it includes buttons that let you define character and paragraph formats and specify tabs and line positions. When you choose the Character..., Paragraph..., Tabs..., or Position... button, Word will display the dialog box summoned by the corresponding commands on the Format menu. The only difference is that when you use the Define Styles... command to open these dialog boxes, the formats you select affect every paragraph formatted with the style you are defining, rather than just highlighted text or paragraphs.

In addition to these four buttons, the Define Styles dialog box also includes an Options >> button that lets you define additional aspects of a style. For example, if you choose Options >> while defining the *heading 1* style, Word will expand the Define Styles dialog box, as shown in Figure 8-5. This expanded dialog box tells you that the *heading 1* style is based on the *Normal* style and that *Normal* is the next style after *heading 1*.

Figure 8-4

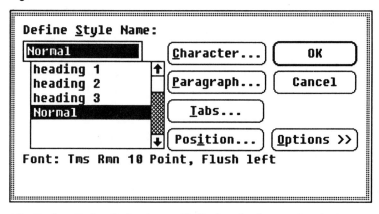

The Define Styles dialog box will display the formatting instructions for the style you select.

Figure 8-5

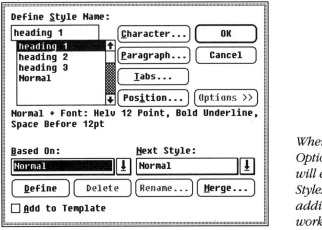

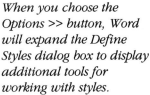

When you choose the Options >> button, Word will expand the Define Styles dialog box to display additional tools for working with styles.

The Define button below the Based On text box lets you lock in any changes you have made to a style without closing the Define Styles dialog box. You can use the Delete button to remove the selected style from the style sheet, and the Rename... button to change the name of the selected style. The Merge... button lets you copy styles between a document and a template, or merge styles from other documents or templates into the current document. We'll discuss deleting, renaming, and merging styles in more detail later in this chapter.

By the way, if you compare the definition for the *Normal* style in Figures 8-1 and 8-4 with the list of characteristics in Table 8-1, you'll see that the definition for the *Normal* style does not spell out every formatting characteristic. For example, the *Normal* style uses no indents, but this is not specifically stated in the definition. Except for the font, point size, and paragraph alignment, a style's definition will not include formatting characteristics that are set to Word's defaults.

Linked styles

Often, the definition for one named style will be based on the definition for another style. In this case, Word considers the two styles linked. The dependent style is the style whose definition is based on another style, and the Based On style is the style on which the dependent style is based.

Many styles can be linked to the same Based On style. For example, one style sheet might contain a dozen or more styles that are based on the *Normal* style. When you view the definition for a dependent style, you'll see that it begins with the name of the Based On style. The remainder of the style's definition will specify only those characteristics that are different from the definition for the Based On style. For example, Figure 8-5 shows the expanded Define Styles dialog box for the style named *heading 1*. The definition (*Normal + Font: Helv 12 Point, Bold Underline, Space Before 12pt)* is merely a shorthand way of saying, "Use the style definition of the style named *Normal*, but change the font to Helv 12-point bold underline and insert 12 points of space above the paragraph."

As you're setting up a style sheet, it's possible to link more than two styles. For example, you might have a style named *Style2*, which is based on a style named *Style1*. *Style1*, in turn, might be based on the style named *Normal*. In this case, *Style2* would be indirectly based on *Normal*. Consequently, if you changed the *Normal* style, *Style2* and *Style1* would probably change as well.

In this chapter, we will explain more about linked styles—how you can create a linked style, when you should link styles, and how to unlink two styles.

Automatic and custom styles

A final topic we need to cover in our discussion of style sheet basics is the difference between automatic and custom styles. Automatic styles are predefined styles that are designed to format certain common elements of a document, such as headings, footnotes, headers, and footers. In fact, Word comes with a built-in "library" of 34 automatic styles.

The styles *Normal, heading 1, heading 2,* and *heading 3,* which always appear on the default style sheet, are just a few of these automatic styles. Although the other automatic styles are among Word's defaults, they do not appear on the style sheet initially. However, Word will place them on a document's style sheet as you add different elements to the document. For example, if you add a header to a document, Word will automatically format the header, adding an automatic style named *header* to that document's style sheet.

All the automatic styles are based on the *Normal* style. Therefore, the formatting instructions for each automatic style begin with *Normal +*. As we'll explain in a few pages, Word allows you to modify the instructions for any of its automatic styles. However, you cannot delete or rename any of them.

In addition to automatic styles, a style sheet can contain custom styles that you create and name. There are a couple of ways to customize a style, as we will explain later in this chapter. Before we talk about automatic styles, custom styles, and other style sheet concepts, however, let's look at an example of creating, applying, and modifying styles.

Suppose you've just entered the title *Helping Your Kids Make a Career Choice* **An example** into a new document, as shown in Figure 8-6. As you can see, this title is formatted in Word's default *Normal* style, but you want it to appear in 14-point Modern bold type, with centered alignment and 12 points of space after the title.

Figure 8-6

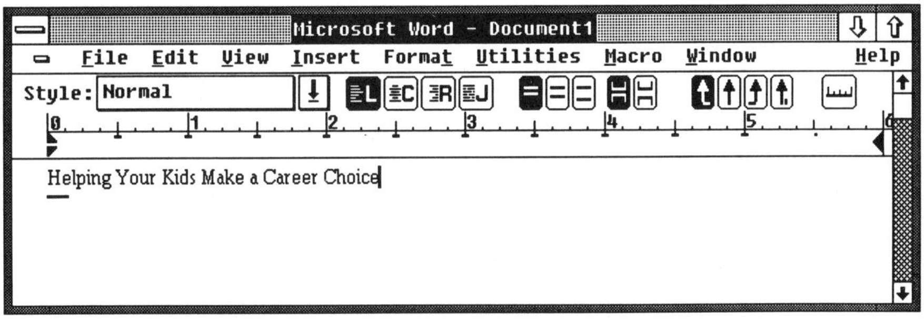

This screen shows the title for a new document.

To create this style, choose the Define Styles… command to open the Define Styles dialog box, and enter the name *Title* into the Define Style Name text box. Next, use the buttons in the dialog box to format the title of the document. First, select the Character… button to open the Character dialog box, choose Modern from the Font pull-down list box, choose 14 from the Points pull-down list box, and select the Bold check box. After you've defined the character formats, select OK to return to the Define Styles dialog box. Choose the Paragraph… button to open the Paragraph dialog box. Enter *12pt* in the Spacing After text box, choose the Center Alignment option, and choose OK to close the Paragraph dialog box.

When Word returns to the Define Styles dialog box, choose the Options >> button to expand the dialog box, then select *Normal* from the Next Style pull-down list box. When you've completed these steps, the dialog box should look like the one in Figure 8-7 on the next page.

To close the Define Styles dialog box, choose OK. Next, place the cursor anywhere in your title text, and select the new *Title* style from the Style list box on the ruler to apply that style to your document title. Word will then format the title according to the instructions you just specified in the dialog box.

After you've applied your new custom style, place the cursor at the end of the title and press [Enter]. Word will then start a new paragraph and format it using the *Normal* style. (Recall that we chose *Normal* in the Next Style text box of the Define Styles dialog box.) Figure 8-8 shows how your screen will look after you've formatted the title and entered some body text.

Figure 8-7

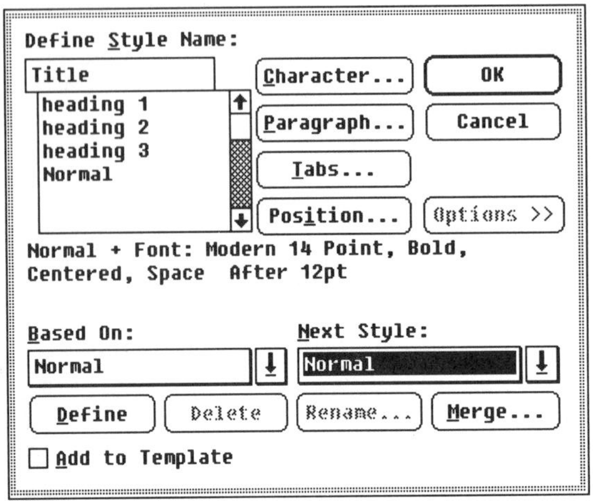

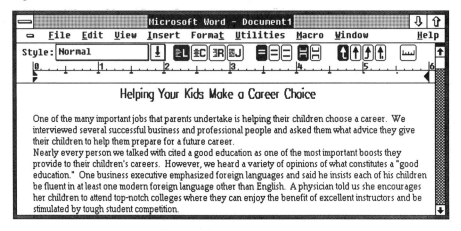

As you're defining a new style, Word will record your formatting instructions in the Define Styles dialog box.

Figure 8-8

This screen shows the formatted document title and several lines of text in the default Normal *style.*

Now, suppose you decide to change the main body text in this document from 10-point Tms Rmn to 12-point Tms Rmn, and you want to indent the first line of each paragraph by $1/4$ inch. By changing the definition of the *Normal* style, you can automatically reformat all text that uses this style. Begin by opening the Define Styles dialog box and selecting the style name *Normal.* Next, choose the Character... button to open the Character dialog box, select 12 from the Points list box, and choose OK. Choose Paragraph... to open the Paragraph dialog box, enter *.25"* into the First Line Indents text box, and select OK to close the Paragraph dialog box. To lock in the changes and close the Define Styles dialog box, choose OK. Figure 8-9 shows how your screen will appear at this point.

Figure 8-9

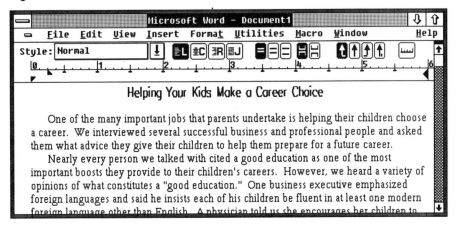

After you alter the definition for the Normal *style, Word will automatically reformat the body text of the document.*

Notice that you did not need to select any text before altering the *Normal* style. Word automatically applied the *Normal* style's formatting instructions to all the text carrying this named style. Of course, in this example, the *Normal* style was applied to only a few paragraphs. You could easily have selected these paragraphs and reformatted them manually. If you were working with a longer document, however, you might have *Normal* text scattered among text of different formats—such as figure captions, subtitles, and so forth. In such cases, changing the *Normal* style on the style sheet saves you the trouble of selecting and reformatting each paragraph of body text.

In the example we just discussed, you probably would not need to apply any styles on the style sheet since you've already formatted the title, and since Word would continue to use the *Normal* style to format the remainder of the document. However, in many of your documents, you'll need to switch from one style to another as you create and format different sections of the document. Later in this chapter, we'll elaborate on the techniques for applying styles. First, however, let's look at Word's automatic styles.

AUTOMATIC STYLES

As we explained earlier, Word predefines a number of automatic styles. We use the term *automatic* because, in most cases, Word will place a predefined style on the style sheet automatically as it's needed. As you'll see in a minute, you also can add these styles manually.

The *Normal* style

The *Normal* style is the predominant automatic style in Word. As we've mentioned, whenever you start a new document, the style sheet for that document will contain a style named *Normal*. Because the *Normal* style is linked to most of the other named styles in a document, it also helps to control the formatting of other elements in a document.

If you're like most users, you'll find the default *Normal* style unsuitable for many of your documents, and you probably will want to modify it each time you start a new document. Of course, it's not imperative that you change the definition for the *Normal* style on the style sheet. Instead, you can simply issue a few commands to alter the text on your screen in any way you want. However, there are certain advantages to modifying the *Normal* style instead of manually formatting the text in your document.

You can modify the *Normal* style before you enter text into a document. To do this, you follow the same steps you would to redefine the *Normal* style for existing text. That is, choose the Define Styles… command and use the buttons in the Define Styles dialog box to change the formats of the *Normal* style. After you redefine the *Normal* style in this manner, all the text you enter in paragraphs based on the *Normal* style will be formatted according to your new definition.

Redefining the *Normal* style will change this automatic style for your current document only. When you alter the *Normal* style definition, your document will be formatted with all the characteristics you chose after issuing the Define Styles… command. If you create a new document in Word, however, the *Normal* style in that document will once again have the default style definition (10-point Tms Rmn font with single spacing, flush-left alignment, and no indents). Later in this chapter, we'll explain how you can modify the default *Normal* style.

Although we recommend that you change the *Normal* style before you type any text into a new document, you can change the style at any time. As we demonstrated in our example earlier, if you have already typed some text using the default *Normal* style, Word will automatically reformat that text according to any changes you make to the style's definition.

Other automatic styles

Although a complete list of Word's 34 automatic styles doesn't initially appear on the default style sheet, you can see all of them by pressing [Ctrl]A while viewing the list of styles in the Styles or Define Styles dialog box. (Word will not be able to display all the automatic styles at one time, but you can scroll through the list in the pull-down list box.) Table 8-2 summarizes the name and purpose of each automatic style, and Table 8-3 on page 278 lists Word's default definitions for the automatic styles.

Table 8-2

Word uses this style...	to format...
annotation reference	text in the annotation reference mark that appears in a document
annotation text	text in an annotation pane
footer	text in a footer pane
footnote reference	the number or symbol that designates a footnote in the document
footnote text	text in a footnote pane
header	text in a header pane
heading 1, heading 2, ...heading 9	heading levels you create in the outline view
index 1, index 2,...index 7	levels of entries in an index
index heading	heading separators in a compiled index
line number	line numbers
Normal	all text that has not been assigned another style
Normal Indent	any text you want formatted in the *Normal* style, but with left indention
toc 1, toc 2,...toc 8	levels in the table of contents text

As we've said, Word will place automatic styles on a document's style sheet when you add certain elements to that document. For example, if you add one or more footnotes to a document, Word will automatically place two styles on the style sheet: *footnote reference*, used to format the number or symbol you place in the main body of your document to designate a footnote; and *footnote text*, used to format the footnote itself.

Word adds all the automatic styles to the style sheet in this way, except the *heading* styles. The first three *heading* styles appear on the default style sheet, while the rest of the *heading* styles, which are designed to format different levels of headings in a document, originate in the outline view.

Whenever you use Word's outline view to manipulate the headings in a document, Word will format those headings according to the automatic *heading* styles. Word also will add these named styles to the style sheet. If you do not begin your document in the outline view, Word will not automatically use the *heading* styles to format your headings. (Without an outline, Word has no way of distinguishing a heading from the rest of the document text.) In Chapter 9, we will talk about the link between Word's outline view and the *heading* styles.

Adding an automatic style to a style sheet

Table 8-3

Style names	Default definitions
annotation reference	Normal + Font: 8 Point
annotation text	Normal + (Next Style: *annotation text*)
footer	Normal + Tab stops: 3" Centered; 6" Right Flush (Next Style: *footer*)
footnote reference	Normal + Font: 8 Point, Superscript 3 Point
footnote text	Normal + (Next Style: *footnote text*)
header	Normal + Tab stops: 3" Centered; 6" Right Flush (Next Style: *header*)
heading 1	Normal + Font: Helv 12 Point, Bold Underline, Space Before 12pt
heading 2	Normal + Font: Helv 12 Point, Bold, Space Before 6pt
heading 3	Normal + Font: 12 Point, Bold, Indent: Left 0.25" (Next Style: *Normal Indent*)
heading 4	Normal + Font: 12 Point, Underline, Indent: Left 0.25" (Next Style: *Normal Indent*)
heading 5	Normal + Bold, Indent: Left 0.5" (Next Style: *Normal Indent*)
heading 6	Normal + Underline, Indent: Left 0.5" (Next Style: *Normal Indent*)
heading 7-heading 9	Normal + Italic, Indent: Left 0.5" (Next Style: *Normal Indent*)
index 1	Normal +
index 2-index 7	(Same as *index 1*, except each level is indented from left in increments of .25")
index heading	Normal + (Next Style: *index 1*)
line number	Normal + (Next Style: *Normal*)
Normal	Font: Tms Rmn 10 Point, Flush left
Normal Indent	Normal + Indent: Left 0.5" (Next Style: *Normal Indent*)
toc 1	Normal + Indent: Right 0.5", Tab stops: 5.75" …; 6" Right Flush
toc 2-toc 8	(Same as *toc 1*, except each level is indented from left in increments of .25")

If you want to use one of the automatic styles to format part of a document, you do not have to wait for Word to add that style name to the style sheet. Instead, you can add the style manually. To do this, choose the Define Styles… command and press [Ctrl]A. This will display all of Word's automatic styles in the list in the dialog box. Select the name of the style you want to add to the style sheet, then choose OK. Word will then close the dialog box and add the selected automatic style to your document's style sheet. The next time you view the list of named styles in the Styles or Define Styles dialog box, or in the Style list box on the ruler, the automatic style you defined will appear on the list.

If you want to add an automatic style to the style sheet, but you don't want to close the Define Styles dialog box, you should choose the Define button instead of the OK button. To make the Define button available (it doesn't appear in the initial Define Styles dialog box), you must choose the Options >> button after you open the dialog box. When the dialog box expands to include additional options, you will see the Define button in the lower-left corner. After you've selected and defined all the desired automatic styles, you can close the Define Styles dialog box by choosing OK.

All of Word's automatic styles are based on the *Normal* style. This has two important consequences. First, the format specified by each automatic style will be similar to the *Normal* style. For example, notice the definition for the *header* style in the Styles dialog box shown in Figure 8-10 on the following page. You can interpret this definition as "Use all the formatting characteristics of the *Normal* style and add two tab stops: one centered tab at the 3-inch ruler position and one right tab at the 6-inch ruler position." If the *Normal* style specifies 10-point Tms Rmn type (Word's default), the text in a document's header also will appear in 10-point Tms Rmn. Similarly, because the other automatic styles are based on *Normal*, other elements you add to a document, such as a footer, page numbers, headings, and so forth, will use 10-point Tms Rmn—or whatever font you've specified in the definition for the *Normal* style.

Another consequence of the link between automatic styles and the *Normal* style is that any change you make to the *Normal* style may affect the other automatic styles. For example, if you change the font for the *Normal* style from Tms Rmn to Helv, most of the other automatic styles will use the Helv font as well. Of course, the purpose of this link is to help you maintain consistency of appearance among the different parts of a document.

We've explained how you can modify the definition for the *Normal* style and, in fact, recommended that you do this each time you start a new document or create a new template. This recommendation is especially important because all the other automatic styles are based on the *Normal* style. By changing the *Normal* style first, you may be able to save yourself the trouble of changing each of the

The link between *Normal* and other automatic styles

other automatic styles. On the other hand, if you do not modify the *Normal* style, but manually format the main body text in your document, you probably will need to adjust the formats of other document elements as well.

Figure 8-10

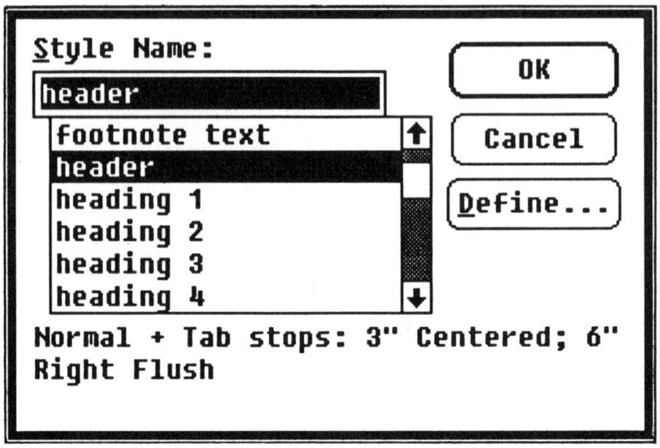

This dialog box shows the default definition for the automatic style named header.

For example, suppose you don't modify the definition for the *Normal* style. You then create a document and manually format the main body text to appear in 12-point Helv type. Suppose you then decide to add a header to the document. Figure 8-11 shows how Word will format the text in the header pane.

Notice that the text of the header does not match the main body text of the document. Instead, it appears in 10-point Tms Rmn since it is based on the *Normal* style. If you want the format of the header to be consistent with the rest of the document, you must either manually reformat the text in the header pane or open the Define Styles dialog box and modify the definition for the automatic style named *header.* The same thing will happen if you add a footer, page numbers, footnotes, or any other document element that is formatted according to one of Word's automatic styles. Each element will come into your document in a format that is related to the *Normal* style but inconsistent with the main body text, which you formatted manually.

To avoid the hassle of reformatting each document element or making extensive changes to the style sheet, simply modify the definition for the *Normal* style as soon as you create the document. Then, you won't need to worry about inconsistencies between the main body text and the various elements you add to the document.

Although modifying the *Normal* style offers an excellent starting point for changing Word's other automatic styles, you can, of course, change each of these styles directly. You also can break the link between any automatic style and the *Normal* style. We will talk about the various techniques for modifying styles in a few pages. However, since style modification techniques apply to both custom and automatic styles, we should first consider how you can add custom styles to a style sheet.

Figure 8-11

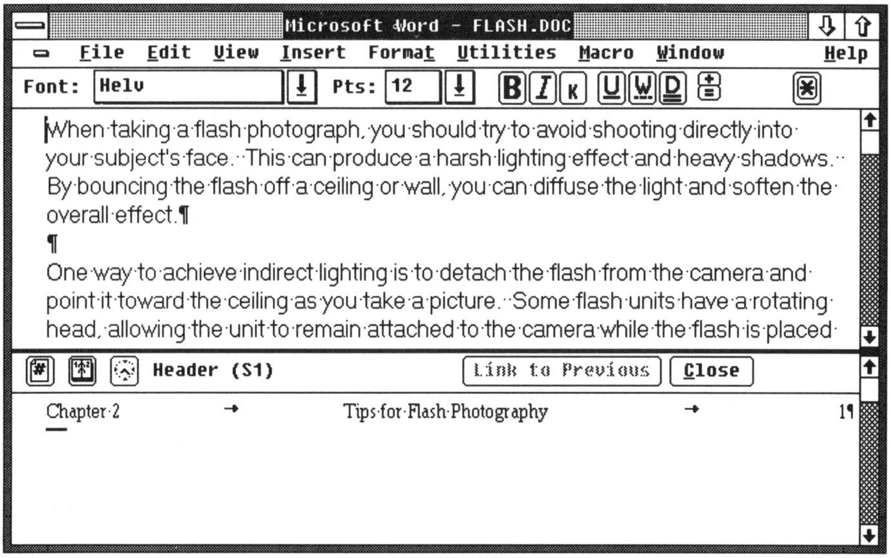

The appearance of text in a header pane will reflect the formatting instructions of the Normal *style.*

CUSTOM STYLES

There are two basic ways to create a custom style First, you can choose the Define Styles… command, enter the name of a new custom style in the Define Style Name text box, use the buttons in the Define Styles dialog box to specify the instructions for the new style, then choose OK or Define to save the new style. This process is very similar to the steps we explained earlier for changing the definition of a style, except you begin by entering the name of a new style rather than selecting an existing named style. For purposes of our discussion, we will refer to this method as defining "by selection" since it involves selecting formatting options through Word's dialog boxes.

Another method for defining a new style is "by example." In other words, you can format a paragraph in your document to have all the characteristics you want to include in a named style (using either the commands on the Format menu or the icons on the ruler and ribbon), then create a named style based on the example you have defined. Once you format your sample paragraph, you can create a style based on it by placing the cursor in that paragraph, choosing either the Styles or Define Styles… command, then entering the style's name in the Style Name or

Define Style Name text box. You can also define the new style by placing the cursor in your formatted paragraph, then entering the new style name in the Style box on the ruler.

The main difference between the "by selection" and "by example" methods is that when you're defining by example, you issue all of the formatting commands before you actually name the style. One major advantage of defining a style by example is that you can see the effects of your formatting specifications before you add them to your style sheet. This is especially helpful when you are designing a new style that may require quite a bit of fine-tuning to achieve exactly the appearance that you want.

In addition, formatting by example can come in handy when you've manually formatted a paragraph, then decide that you want to use that format in other locations in your document. Rather than manually reformatting the other text, you can use the first paragraph as your example to define a new style. Then, you can apply the style to all the paragraphs you want to format with the style's characteristics. Let's consider how you might use each of the methods for defining a new style.

Defining by selection

Suppose you want to create a new style named *Figure Caption*, which specifies 8-point Tms Rmn bold type with centered alignment. The style definition will also specify a 12-point line space both above and below the formatted text. To define this style by selection, first open the Define Styles dialog box, then choose the Options >> button. Word will then expand the dialog box, as shown in Figure 8-12.

Figure 8-12

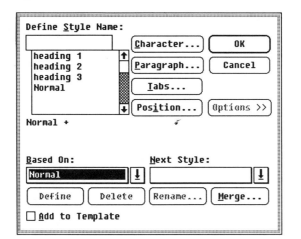

To create a new style by selection, begin by opening the expanded Define Styles dialog box.

There are two things you should notice about this dialog box. First, you can see that the Define Style Name text box is blank. Each time you open the Define Styles dialog box, Word assumes you want to add a new style to the style sheet.

Notice that Word has begun the definition for the new style with *Normal +* and that it has placed the style name *Normal* in the Based On text box in the lower-left corner of the dialog box. Whenever you define a new style, Word assumes that you want the style to be based on the style of the current paragraph (the paragraph in which the cursor is located when you issue the Define Styles... command). In our example, we positioned the cursor on a paragraph formatted in the *Normal* style before we selected Define Styles.... Therefore, Word assumed that we wanted to create a new style that would be based on the *Normal* style.

In most cases, you will want to base each new style on an existing style, just as we've done in our example. In a few pages, we will discuss the Based On style in more detail and explain how you can create a style that's *not* based on an existing style. For now, let's continue the process of defining the new style.

After you've opened the expanded Define Styles dialog box, enter a style name, then select the formatting features you want that style to use. It makes no difference which you do first. In our example, you can begin by entering the style name *Figure Caption* in the Define Style Name text box. Then, select the Character... button. When Word displays the Character dialog box, choose 8 in the Points pull-down list box, select the Bold check box, then choose OK. Next, select Paragraph... in the Define Styles dialog box, enter *12pt* into the Spacing Before and Spacing After text boxes, and choose the Center Alignment option. Finally, choose OK to close the Paragraph dialog box. At this point, the Define Styles dialog box will look like the one in Figure 8-13. Notice that Word has recorded all of the format selections in the style's definition.

Figure 8-13

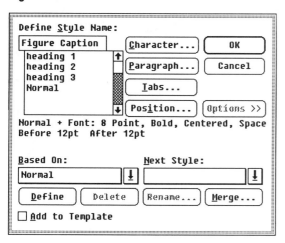

As you're creating a new style, Word will record your format selections in the definition for that style.

The last step in defining the new style is to add it to the style sheet by choosing OK or Define. If you choose OK, Word will add the new style name to the list of styles and close the Define Styles dialog box. Then, you can apply the new style to paragraphs in the document. If you choose Define, Word will place the style name *Figure Caption* in the list of styles and leave the dialog box open, allowing you to define additional styles.

Defining by example

Now, let's consider how you might define this same style by example instead of by selection. Suppose you have entered the text for a figure caption in a document, and you want to format that text. First, you would select the caption paragraph, then format it by using the commands on the Format menu, the icons on the ruler and ribbon, or a combination of both.

For example, to format the highlighted text shown in Figure 8-14, select the entire paragraph as we've done, choose 8 from the Points pull-down list box on the ribbon and select the ribbon's Bold icon. (Alternatively, you could choose Character... from the Format menu, enter 8 in the Points list box, and select the Bold check box.) Then, select Paragraph... from the Format menu, enter *12pt* in both the Spacing Before and Spacing After text boxes, select the Center Alignment option, and choose OK to close the Paragraph dialog box. (You could also center the text by choosing the Centered-alignment icon on the ruler, but you would still need to use the Paragraph dialog box to set the before and after spacing.) When you close the Paragraph dialog box, your figure caption will look like the one in Figure 8-15.

Figure 8-14

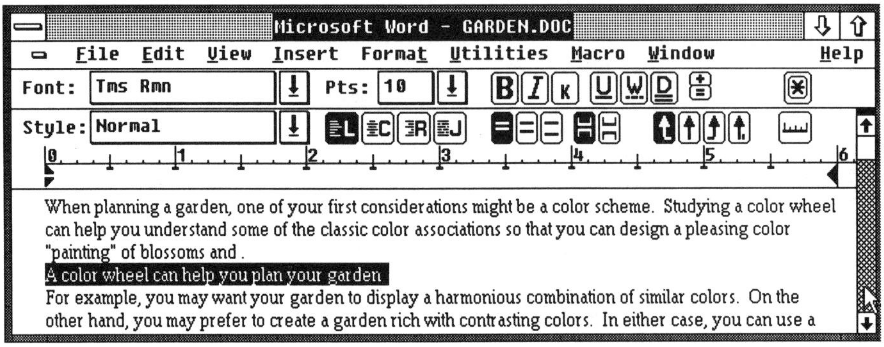

To define a new style by example, begin by entering and selecting the text you want to format.

Of course, in most cases, you won't be able to arrive at an acceptable format for a new style so quickly. Usually, the process of designing a format for a particular part of a document—such as a figure caption—is a matter of trial and error. That's why you might want to experiment with the format on your screen before you define it as a named style.

Figure 8-15

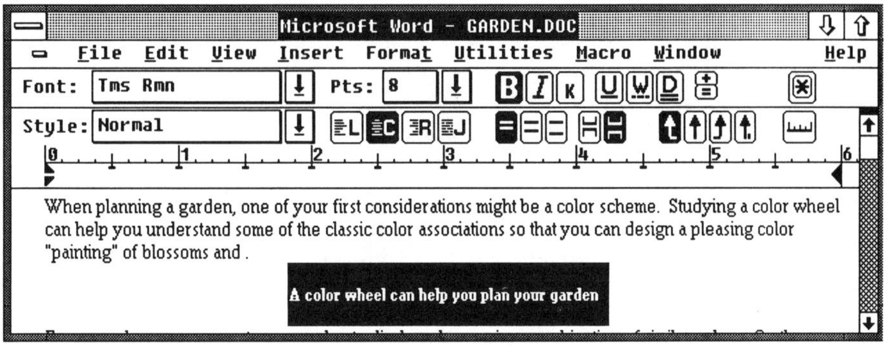

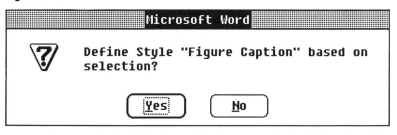

This screen shows the formatted text that will be the example for a new style.

The quickest way to save your sample format on the style sheet is to enter the new style name in the Style box on the ruler while the cursor is in your formatted paragraph. After you type in the new style name and press [Enter] (or click anywhere else on the screen), Word will display a message box like the one shown in Figure 8-16. If you select Yes, Word will create the new style based on the format of the current paragraph and assign the new style to the current paragraph. If you select No, Word will restore the style name that previously appeared in the Style box. This style name will reflect the example paragraph's original style.

Using the ruler to define by example

Figure 8-16

```
╔══════════════ Microsoft Word ══════════════╗
║                                             ║
║   ┏━━━┓                                      ║
║   ┃ ? ┃   Define Style "Figure Caption" based on ║
║   ┗━┳━┛   selection?                         ║
║     ▼                                        ║
║                                             ║
║        ┌───────┐      ┌───────┐             ║
║        │ Yes   │      │ No    │             ║
║        └───────┘      └───────┘             ║
╚═════════════════════════════════════════════╝
```

Word will ask you to verify that you want to create a new style based on the current paragraph.

As we mentioned, you can move the cursor directly to the Style box by pressing the [Style] key ([Ctrl]S) while the ruler is displayed on the screen. If you want to define a new style based on the current paragraph, but the ruler is not on the screen, you can press [Style] to summon the prompt *Which style?* in the status bar. After you type the new style name and press [Enter], Word will display a message box like the one shown in Figure 8-16 to verify that you want to create the new style.

Because the Style text box and the [Style] key offer the simplest and most intuitive techniques for creating a custom style by example, you'll probably want to use them most of the time.

Using the Format menu to define by example

You can also use the Styles... and Define Styles... commands to define a new custom style by example. Both of these techniques require that you first format your example paragraph, then place the cursor in that paragraph.

If you choose Styles... while the cursor is in your example paragraph, Word will display a standard Styles dialog box. The Style Name text box will list the name of the style that was originally applied to your example. To create a new style based on your example, simply type the new style name in the text box and choose OK. At this point, Word will display a message box similar to the one shown in Figure 8-16 (the only difference is the addition of a Cancel button). If you choose Yes, Word will add the new style name to the style sheet and assign the new style to your example paragraph. If you choose No, Word will close the dialog box and return you to the Styles dialog box. Choosing the Cancel button will make Word close both the message box and the Styles dialog box without adding the new style to the style sheet.

If you choose Define Styles... from the Format menu while the cursor is in your example paragraph, Word will display the Define Styles dialog box. After you type the name of the new style in the Define Style Name text box and choose OK, Word will add the new style to the style sheet and close the dialog box. However, Word will not assign the new style to the example paragraph as it does when you choose OK in the Styles dialog box.

If you use the Define Styles... command to define a new style, you can add the new style to the style sheet without closing the Define Styles dialog box. To define a new style without closing the dialog box, you must first choose the Options >> button to expand the dialog box, which will then include the Define button. If you enter a new style name into the Define Style Name text box and choose Define, Word will add the new style name to the list of styles but will leave the dialog box open. Using the Define button in this manner can be handy if you want to create several similar styles. You can define the first style by example, then use Define to add it to the style sheet. Then, you can use the options in the dialog box to make changes to the new style. Whenever you're ready to save the modified style, enter a new style name in the Define Style Name text box and choose Define again. When you are finished defining styles, you can choose OK to close the dialog box.

In our discussion of defining styles by example, we have assumed that your example consists of a single paragraph with uniformly formatted text. You can select an example paragraph by placing the cursor in it before defining a new style. However, Word actually allows you to use any amount of selected text as an example when creating a new style. This text can contain fonts of several typefaces, sizes, and formats and can include paragraphs of different formats.

Word used two rules to determine which formatting characteristics it will apply when the example includes several paragraph and character formats. If the selected example includes more than one paragraph, Word uses the paragraph formatting applied to the first paragraph in the example. The character formats of the new style depend on the formatting attributes shared by the majority of the characters in the example. For instance, if the majority of the characters in the example are bold, then the new style will make all characters bold. If more than half the characters are in the Courier font, then the new style will change all characters to Courier.

Understanding these rules can be helpful when you are defining styles based on existing text in a document. However, when you are creating a style by example, you often will create your example from scratch, using a new paragraph that contains uniformly formatted characters. As long as you select your example by placing the cursor in the paragraph (as opposed to highlighting it), you won't need to worry about unexpected results in your custom styles.

Multiple formats in an example

We have already explained how one style can be based on or linked to another style. The link between *Normal* and Word's other automatic styles causes each of the automatic styles to reflect, to some degree, the characteristics of the *Normal* style. Moreover, any change you make to the *Normal* style will affect the other automatic styles as well.

Whenever you define a custom style for a style sheet, Word assumes you want that new style to be based on an existing style. If you define a new style by example, Word will automatically use the style that was previously applied to your example paragraph as the Based On style. If you use the Define Styles… command to define a new style by selection, Word will use the style of the current paragraph as the Based On style.

When we defined a style by selection a moment ago, we created a new style that was based on *Normal* because the cursor was in a *Normal* paragraph when we issued the Define Styles… command. When we defined a style by example, our example paragraph had been formatted in the *Normal* style before we modified it to define the new style. When you create a new style, however, that style won't necessarily be based on *Normal*. It's a good idea, therefore, to think about which style you want to use as your Based On style before you begin to define a new style. That way, you may be able to save time in defining the new style's formatting instructions.

The Based On style

For example, suppose you want to create a new style named *Style1*, which has all the characteristics of the default *Normal* style except the first line of each paragraph is indented $^3/_4$ inch. Since this new style is so similar to *Normal*, it would make sense to use *Normal* as the Based On style. Therefore, before you begin defining *Style1*, you should be sure that the cursor is positioned on a *Normal* paragraph. Then, when you choose Define Styles…, Word will automatically enter *Normal* in the Based On text box and begin the definition for the new style with *Normal +*. (The style definition will be visible in the Define Styles dialog box, but you'll have to select the Options >> button to see the Based On text box.) To complete the definition of *Style1*, you need only select the Paragraph… button in the Define Styles dialog box, enter *.75"* in the First Line Indents text box, and choose OK to close the Paragraph dialog box. Then, choose OK in the Define Styles dialog box to close it and add *Style1* to the style sheet. Word will borrow the formatting instructions of the *Normal* Based On style and add the left indention to them when creating the *Style1* style.

If you were going to define *Style1* by example, you would first apply the *Normal* style to a paragraph, then use the Paragraph… command on the Format menu to add the $^3/_4$-inch indention. Next, you could use either the Define Styles… command or the Style box on the ruler to define the *Style1* style based on your example paragraph.

Now, suppose you want to create a new style named *Style2* that is identical to *Normal*, except the first line of each paragraph is indented $^3/_4$ inch and the characters appear in italic. Since you've already defined *Style1*, which includes the desired indention, you can save time by using this style as the Based On style for *Style2*. Then, you will only need to explicitly define the italic format when creating your new style. Word will automatically copy the left indention from the definition for *Style1*.

Specifying a different Based On style

When you're defining a new style, you don't have to use the Based On style that Word suggests. Instead, you can enter a different style name in the Based On text box of the expanded Define Styles dialog box. You can use the pull-down list attached to this text box to change the Based On style.

Creating a new style that is not based on an existing style

When you want to create a style that is completely independent of the other styles in your style sheet, you can simply delete the contents of the Based On text box as you are creating the new style.

For instance, suppose you're defining the *Figure Caption* style we described previously. When you open the expanded Define Styles dialog box, you'll see that the style's definition begins with *Normal +* and that the word *Normal* appears in the Based On text box. If you want to make the *Figure Caption* style independent of the *Normal* style, delete the word *Normal* from the Based On text box, then choose the Define button. If you select the *Figure Caption* style in the Define Style Name list box, the Define Styles dialog box will look like Figure 8-17.

Figure 8-17

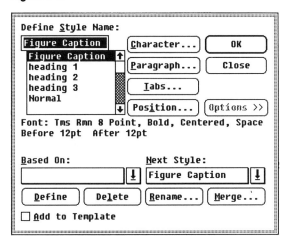

If you break the link to the Based On style, the definition for the dependent style will specify all the characteristics of the former Based On style.

As you can see, the definition is the same as the one shown in Figure 8-13, with two exceptions. First, the definition no longer begins with *Normal+*. Second, the definition now specifies the Tms Rmn font. When you eliminate the Based On style, the style that you're defining will retain all the formatting characteristics of the former Based On style. However, these characteristics will now be stated explicitly in the style's definition instead of being implicit in the name of the Based On style.

Although it's possible to create a style independent of any other style, you'll want to avoid this in most cases. For example, if you eliminate the link between the *Figure Caption* style and the *Normal* style, the left and right indents for *Figure Caption*—which determine the placement of each line—will no longer be tied to the indents for the *Normal* style. If you do not make any changes to the *Normal* style, this should be of no consequence. Suppose, however, you decide to modify the *Normal* style by adding a right indention of 1 inch. Word will change the right margin on the main body text in your document by 1 inch. However, since the *Figure Caption* style is no longer linked to *Normal*, any text that was formatted with that style will not have a right indention. In other words, all your figure captions will appear off-center from the main body text.

A word of warning

One style can be indirectly linked to several styles. However, a style can be directly based on only one style. For example, you might have a document in which *Style3* is based on *Style2*, which is based on *Style1*, which is based on *Normal*. In this case, *Style3* is indirectly linked to two styles, *Style1* and *Normal*, but it is directly based on only one style, *Style2*.

Notes on linked styles

Word will not allow you to create circular style references. For example, suppose *Style3* is based on *Style2*, which is based on *Style1*. If you then try to make *Style3* the Based On style for *Style1*, Word will beep and display the message *Style has circular Based On list.*

You will also see an alert message if you try to create more than nine levels of linked styles. For example, you can create a style sheet in which *Style8* is based on *Style7*, which is based on *Style6*, which is based on *Style5*, and so forth, through *Style1*, which is based on *Normal*. However, if you try to create a *Style9* that uses *Style8* as its Based On style, Word will not accept it and will display the message *Style has too many Based On ancestors.*

Of course, this does not mean you cannot have more than nine styles that are indirectly linked. For example, Figure 8-18 shows a diagram that illustrates how you might set up 14 styles in a style sheet that are all directly or indirectly linked to *Style1*, which is directly linked to *Normal*. Notice, however, that this style sheet contains only five levels of directly linked styles.

The Next Style

When you open the expanded Define Styles dialog box, you will see a Next Style text box beside the Based On text box. You use the Next Style text box to specify the style you want to apply immediately after a paragraph that's formatted with the style you're currently defining. To enter a style name in the Next Style text box, simply select a style name from the pull-down list attached to the text box or type the name of the style in the text box. Then, choose Define or OK to lock in your Next Style specification.

For example, suppose you are defining a style named *Figure Caption*, which you'll use to format the figure captions in your document. You'll probably want to follow each caption with a paragraph that is formatted according to the *Normal* style. Therefore, as you are defining the *Figure Caption* style, you should enter *Normal* into the Next Style text box.

The Next Style option comes into play only when you press [Enter] to end a paragraph. In our example, suppose you apply the style *Figure Caption* to a line of text in your document. When you press [Enter] at the end of that line, Word will begin a new paragraph that is formatted in the *Normal* style. On the other hand, if you placed the cursor in the middle of the figure caption text and pressed [Enter], Word would break that text into two separate paragraphs but would not apply the Next Style format to the second paragraph. Instead, Word would retain the *Figure Caption* style for the second paragraph.

As you're defining a new style, if you do not enter a style name into the Next Style text box, Word will use the style you are defining as the Next Style. For example, if you define the style named *Figure Caption*, but you don't specify a Next Style, Word will assume that the paragraph following the figure caption text should also be formatted according to the *Figure Caption* style.

Figure 8-18

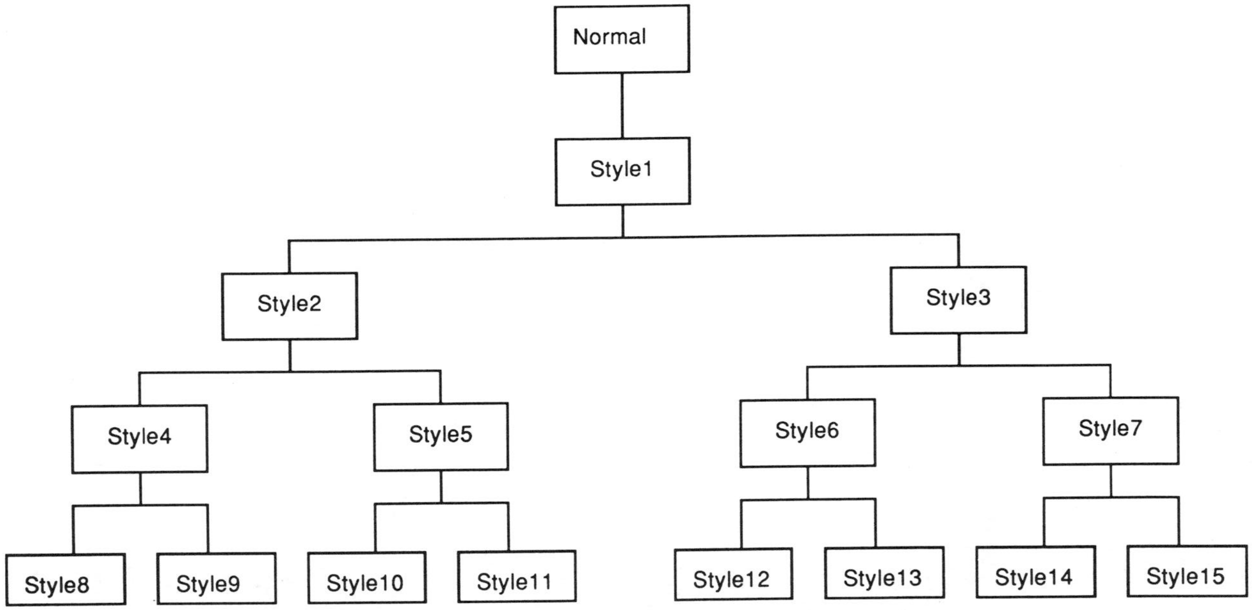

This diagram shows how you might set up links between Style1 and 14 other styles on the style sheet.

**Taking advantage
of the Next Style**

By carefully specifying the Next Style for each style on a style sheet, you can make one style automatically flow into another throughout a document. Each time you press [Enter] to begin a new paragraph, Word will use a different style to format that paragraph. This can be especially helpful when you're creating a document in which you must frequently switch from one style to another. For example, suppose you want to create a list of names and addresses, like the one shown in Figure 8-19.

Figure 8-19

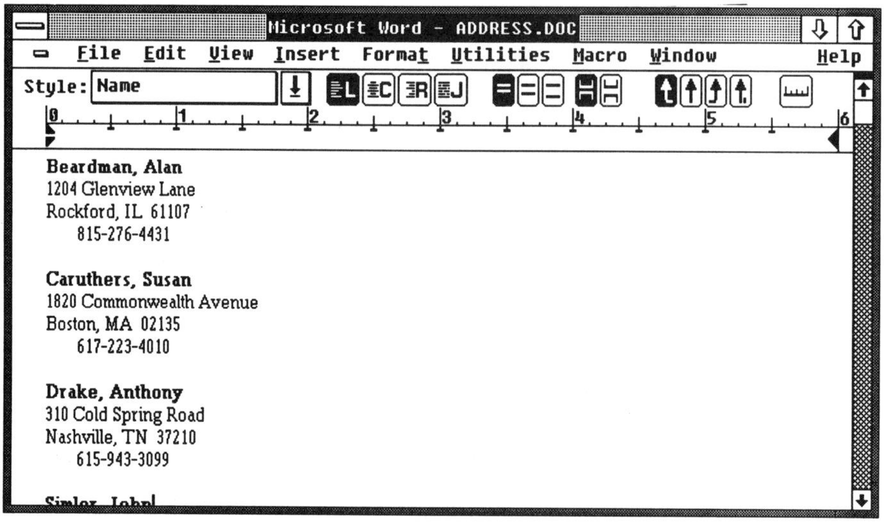

A list of names and addresses might be formatted with several styles.

One way you can greatly speed up the process of creating this list is to set up a style sheet with four styles: *Name*, *Address1*, *Address2*, and *Phone*. You can use the *Name* style to format each person's name; the *Address1* style to format the first line of each person's address; the *Address2* style to format the second line of each address; and the *Phone* style to format each phone number. To help speed up your text entry, you should ensure that the *Name* style uses *Address1* as its Next Style; the *Address1* style uses *Address2* as its Next Style; and the *Address2* style uses *Phone* as its Next Style. Finally, to complete the loop, the style named *Phone* should specify *Name* as its Next Style.

Once you have set up the style sheet, just use the *Name* style as you enter the first name in the list. Each time you press [Enter], Word will automatically cycle into *Address1*, *Address2*, *Phone*, and back to *Name*.

By the way, there's one minor constraint you need to keep in mind as you are specifying the Next Style. You must enter a valid style name in the Next Style text box. This can present a problem if you haven't yet created the style you want to use as the Next Style. For example, if you are defining the *Name* style but you haven't yet created the style named *Address1*, Word will not allow you to enter *Address1* in the Next Style text box. To get around this problem, you may need to modify a style after you've created it, specifying the correct Next Style. (Later in this chapter, we will explain how to modify an existing style.)

Another way to work around this constraint is to define your styles in reverse order. In other words, the first style you define should be the last style you plan to use in your sequence of styles. In our example, you might begin by defining the *Phone* style. Next, you would define *Address2*, *Address1*, and finally, *Name*. As you're defining *Address2*, *Address1*, and *Name*, the style you want to use as the Next Style would already exist so you wouldn't have any problem entering its name in the Next Style text box.

Style names

Although Word will accept a style name of up to 20 characters, you'll find that shorter names are easier to work with. One problem with extremely long names is that you may not be able to see the full style name in the text boxes and list boxes of the Styles or Define Styles dialog box. Most of these text and list boxes display fewer than 18 characters of a style's name.

Each style on a style sheet must have a unique name. If you enter the name of an existing style in the Define Style Name text box of the expanded Define Styles dialog box, then choose Define, Word will display the message box shown in Figure 8-20. If you choose Yes when you see this message, Word will replace the existing definition for the named style with the formatting instructions you have defined for the new style. If you select No, Word will not alter the existing style. If you choose Cancel in response to the message, Word will return you to the dialog box.

Figure 8-20

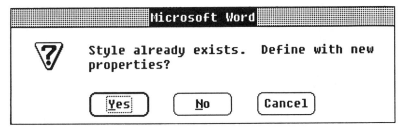

If you enter an existing style name when you're changing the name of a style, you will see this message box.

Word does not distinguish between uppercase and lowercase letters in a style name. As a result, a style sheet cannot include two style names that differ only in case, such as *Paragraph1* and *paragraph1*.

APPLYING STYLES

Now that we have covered all the details of creating named styles, let's look at how you can use a style sheet to format a document. In the next sections, we'll show you how to apply existing styles in a document, make global changes with a style sheet, and copy styles from one document to another.

Selecting named styles in a document

There are several techniques you can use to apply a named style to a document's text. Some of these techniques work best with a mouse, while others are designed for the keyboard. The method you use to apply a style will depend on whether you are using a mouse and on your personal preferences.

Choosing a style name from a list

Choosing a style from the Style box on the ruler is an efficient way to apply a style in a document. First, position your cursor anywhere on the paragraph you want to format, then turn on your ruler if it is not displayed on your screen. Select from the Style box the name of the style you want to apply to your paragraph. Immediately, Word will format that paragraph with the style you've selected.

You also can use the Styles dialog box to apply a style to a paragraph. Again, begin by positioning the cursor anywhere on the paragraph you want to format. Then, choose Styles… from the Format menu. In the Styles dialog box, select the name of the style you want to apply to the current paragraph, and choose OK. Word will apply the style and close the dialog box.

Notice that you do not have to select an entire paragraph to apply a style— it's sufficient to place the cursor anywhere on the paragraph before you make a selection from the Style box on the ruler or choose the Styles… command. However, if you want to apply a style to more than one paragraph in a single step, you must select some text in all of those paragraphs before you choose the style name you want to apply.

Typing in a style name

If you know the name of the style you want to use, you can also type the name of a style in the Style box on the ruler and press [Enter] to apply it. You can move the cursor directly to the Style box by clicking in the box or by pressing the [Style] key ([Ctrl]S). If you press [Style] while the ruler is not visible, the prompt *Which style?* will appear in the status bar. You can type the name of a style at this prompt and press [Enter] to apply that style to the currently selected paragraph(s).

Sometimes, you may have trouble remembering the exact name of the style you want to apply after you have placed the cursor in the Style box or summoned the *Which style?* prompt. In these cases, you can bring up the Styles dialog box by pressing the [Style] key again. As long as the cursor is in the Style box or at the *Which style?* prompt, pressing [Style] will bring up the Styles dialog box. Then, you can select a style from the dialog box's Style Name list box.

A note

In our explanations of how to apply styles, we assumed you had already entered some text you wanted to format. However, you can select a style before you type the text to which you want to apply the style. With the cursor positioned at the beginning of a new paragraph, select a style from the style sheet. Word will apply that style as you begin typing.

As you're formatting a document, you can combine manual format changes with style sheet formatting. In most cases, Word will simply add your manual changes to the formatting features specified by the named styles. For example, suppose your document's style sheet includes a style named *Style1* that specifies 12-point Courier bold type. Figure 8-21 shows some text with this style.

Manual formatting vs. style sheet formatting

Figure 8-21

```
━━        Microsoft Word - BATHROOM.DOC           ⇩ ⇧
 ▢   File  Edit  View  Insert  Format  Utilities  Macro  Window        Help
Style: Style1            ↓  ▣L▣C▣R▣J  ▣▣▣ ▣▣   ⬆⬆⬆⬆  ▭       ↑
   |0. . . ↓ . . |1. . . ↓ . . |2. . . ↓ . . |3. . . ↓ . . |4. . . ↓ . . |5. . . ↓ . . |6
 ▶                                                                         ◀

   One of the most popular home improvement projects is the
   addition of a bathroom.  A new bathroom is not only a nice
   convenience, but often can be a wise investment as well.  Most
   houses, especially older houses will appreciate in value with
   the addition of a bathroom.  This is especially true for houses
   that include a proportionally small number of bathrooms compared
   to the number of bedrooms.  As anyone with a large family can
   attest, the balance between the number of bathrooms and bedrooms
   can make a house much more comfortable to live in.              ⬇
```

This screen shows some text that has been formatted in Style1.

If you select a paragraph to which you've applied this style, then use the Character dialog box to select Italic, that paragraph will display italic formatting in addition to the boldfacing and other features specified by *Style1*. Furthermore, you can change the indents, margins, and other paragraph formatting features of the paragraph. Figure 8-22 on the following page shows a paragraph that we formatted in both *Style1* and italics. We've also changed the first-line indent of this paragraph from the zero position on the ruler to the $1/2$-inch position, and we've changed the alignment from left to justified.

When you change the paragraph formatting of some text—for example, the indents or alignment—Word will continue to display the original style name in the Style box on the ruler. Manual formatting changes, however, will usually take precedence over style sheet formatting. If you manually assign a format to some text, and that format conflicts with the definition of the style you've applied to the text, then your manual formatting will override the style definition. Returning to our example, suppose that after you've applied *Style1* to a paragraph, you select that paragraph and move the indent markers. Word will reformat the text in that paragraph according to the new margins instead of maintaining the margins specified by the style definition.

Figure 8-22

We formatted this text in Style1, *then manually added other features.*

After manually changing the format of a paragraph, you may decide that you want to remove the manual formatting, leaving only the format characteristics that are specified in the paragraph's style. To remove manual paragraph formatting, simply reapply the paragraph's original style.

In addition to the regular tools for applying styles, Word includes a shortcut for removing manual formatting and reapplying the original style of a paragraph. You can remove manual formatting from a paragraph by placing the cursor in the paragraph, then pressing [Ctrl]X. Word will then instantly reapply the paragraph's style, erasing the manual formatting that you added to the style's formatting.

You should be careful when removing manual formatting from large sections of a document. If you select several paragraphs and press [Ctrl]X, Word will apply the style associated with the first paragraph in the selection to every paragraph in the selection. Of course, this will result in incorrect formatting for paragraphs whose styles differed from those of the first paragraph. To remove manual formatting from several paragraphs based on different styles, you should select one paragraph at a time and press [Ctrl]X for each.

While reapplying a paragraph's style removes manual paragraph formatting, manual character formatting is another story. In the next section, we'll discuss the effects of applying and reapplying styles on manual character formatting.

Applying a named style after making manual format changes

So far, we've focused on what will happen when you make manual formatting changes after applying a style. If you format some text manually before you apply a named style to that text, the rules change a bit. If you manually change the paragraph formatting characteristics of some text (indents, line spacing, alignment, and so forth), then assign a style to that text, the style's formatting instructions will always take precedence over your manual paragraph formatting.

Manual changes to character formats work differently. Word will sometimes combine the formatting characteristics of the named style with the character formats you assign manually. Other times, however, Word will override your manual formatting. The following rules dictate whether Word preserves your manual format changes or overrides them: If your manual format changes affect a majority of the characters in a paragraph (more than half the characters), Word will override those changes when you apply a style. On the other hand, if your manual formatting is applied to fewer than half the characters in a paragraph, Word will not override that formatting when you apply a style.

For example, suppose you have created a paragraph, consisting of 200 characters, in Word's default *Normal* style. You then select a word in that paragraph and apply bold formatting. If you later click on the paragraph and reapply the *Normal* style, Word will not remove the bold formatting from that word. Suppose, however, that instead of applying bold formatting to a single word, you've applied it to the entire paragraph. If you then apply the *Normal* style, Word will remove all the bold formatting.

Because the paragraph consists of 200 characters, you can apply manual character formatting to 100 or fewer characters, and Word will not override that formatting if you later apply the *Normal* style. However, if you apply manual formatting to 101 or more characters in the paragraph, Word will override that formatting when you reapply the *Normal* style.

There is a sound reason for these formatting rules. If you manually format fewer than half the characters in a paragraph with a particular characteristic, then Word will assume that the formatted text is supposed to stand out from the rest of the text in the paragraph. In order to allow the text to continue to stand out, Word will leave the characteristic intact when applying the named style. However, if more than half the characters in a paragraph are formatted with a characteristic, Word will treat the characteristic as the norm for the paragraph and override it with the character formatting defined in the definition of the named style.

This same "majority" rule will affect how Word toggles formats on and off. In fact, you may get unexpected results when you combine manual character formatting that can be toggled on and off (such as italics or boldfacing) with style sheet formatting. If your manual formatting affects fewer than half the characters in a paragraph, and you later apply a style specifying the same format, Word will toggle off your manual formatting. However, if you've applied manual formatting to the majority of the characters in a paragraph, then apply a style whose formatting instructions specify that same format, Word will not toggle off your manual formatting, but will apply the style's formatting to the entire paragraph.

Returning to our example, suppose you've applied bold formatting to one word in a paragraph. Then, you apply to that paragraph a style specifying bold as part of its formatting instructions. Word will format the entire paragraph in bold except the word to which you manually applied bold formatting. Now, suppose you format an entire paragraph to appear in bold, then apply to that paragraph a style specifying bold. Word will not toggle off your manual formatting, but will continue to display the entire paragraph in bold.

When you reapply a style to remove manual character formatting, Word will use the same rules we've explained regarding manual paragraph formatting. In other words, reapplying a style may or may not remove manual character formatting from a paragraph. If you've manually formatted more than half the characters in the paragraph with a characteristic that contradicts the style's character formatting, Word will remove that formatting. However, if you have formatted fewer than half the characters in the paragraph with a characteristic, Word will leave the manual character formatting intact when you reapply the style.

MODIFYING STYLES

After you've started to work with named styles, you may need to make a minor change to one or more of them. Just as you can define a new style "by selection" or "by example," you use both of these methods to modify an existing style.

Modifying by selection

To modify a style by selection, just choose the Define Styles... command, then select the name of the style you want to change from the Define Style Name list box. With the style name selected, use the buttons in the dialog box to activate the various formatting dialog boxes. As you choose formatting options, Word will record your changes in the instructions for the selected style. After you press OK to close each formatting dialog box, Word will return you to the Define Styles dialog box. Then, you can lock in your changes by choosing OK (or Define in the expanded dialog box). When Word returns to the document, the text will reflect the changes you've made.

For example, suppose you've used the automatic style named *heading 1* to format some of the headings in a document, and you decide to change the appearance of those headings. The default definition for the *heading 1* style specifes *Normal* plus 12-point Helv type, with boldfacing, underlining, and a 12-point line space above the heading. Suppose you want your *heading 1* entries to appear in 14-point Helv bold type, with centered alignment and a 10-point line space above each heading. You also want to remove the underlining that Word adds automatically to each heading.

To make these changes, first issue the Define Styles... command. When Word displays the Define Styles dialog box, select the *heading 1* style to display the definition for that style, as shown in Figure 8-23.

To modify this style, choose the Character... button to open the Character dialog box and deselect the Underline option. Then, enter *14* into the Points text box and choose OK to close the Character dialog box. To change the line spacing above the heading, choose the Paragraph... button to open the Paragraph dialog box. Enter *10pt* in the Spacing Before text box, select the Center Alignment option, and choose OK to close the Paragraph dialog box. At this point, the Define Styles dialog box will display the altered definition for the *heading 1* style, as shown in Figure 8-24.

Figure 8-23

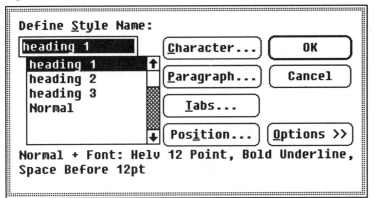

To modify a style, begin by opening the Define Styles dialog box and selecting the style's name.

Figure 8-24

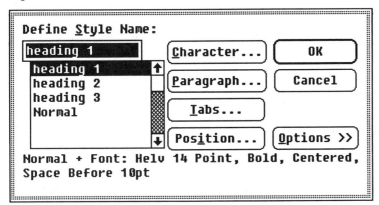

As you select new formats in the Define Styles dialog box, Word will alter the style definition to reflect your changes.

To complete the process of modifying this style, choose OK (or Define if you have expanded the Define Styles dialog box). If you choose OK, Word will redefine the *heading 1* style on the style sheet and close the dialog box. Word will also reformat any text in your document that has been formatted with the *heading 1* style. If you choose Define, Word will redefine the *heading 1* style and apply its new formatting instructions to text that has been assigned that style. Word will not close the dialog box until you choose OK.

However, before Word does anything in this particular case, it will display the message box shown in Figure 8-25 to confirm that you want to change one of the automatic styles. Word displays this dialog box whenever you choose OK or Define to change the default definition of an automatic style. Word will not display this message box if you change one of your custom styles or if you modify an automatic style that has already been changed. If you choose Yes, Word will save the *heading 1* style's new definition. Selecting No will make Word erase the changes you made to the *heading 1* style and return to the Define Styles dialog box, while choosing Cancel will return you to the Define Styles dialog box without altering the modified *heading 1* definition.

Figure 8-25

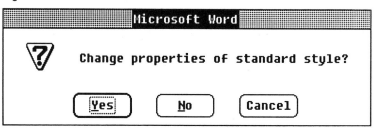

Word will display this message box when you attempt to change the default definition of an automatic style.

The Cancel and Close buttons

You can use the Cancel button in the Define Styles dialog box to remove new formatting instructions you have added to a style's definition. For example, suppose you open the Define Styles dialog box, change the size of the *Normal* style from 10 point to 14 point, then decide you don't want to change the point size after all. You could choose Cancel to close the Define Styles dialog box without saving the change to the style.

You lose the ability to erase changes to a style's definition the moment you choose the Define button to lock in the changes. When you choose Define in the expanded Define Styles dialog box, the name of the Cancel button will change to Close. If you then alter another style, you can use the Close button to close the Define Styles dialog box without saving the changes to this style. However, if you choose Define to lock in the changes to this style, those changes will become a permanent part of the style sheet.

The Define... button

The Styles dialog box includes one button not found in the Define Styles dialog box: the Define... button. You can use this button to move directly to the

Define Styles dialog box. The Define... button is useful if you open the Styles dialog box to apply a style, but upon seeing the style's definition, decide that you want to change it.

Word offers a number of keyboard shortcuts that can help you modify a style's Shortcuts definition. If you want to delete all the paragraph formatting instructions for a style, select the style name in the Define Styles dialog box and press [Ctrl]X. For example, suppose you want to delete the paragraph formatting instructions for the *heading 1* style that are displayed in Figure 8-24. Figure 8-26 shows how Word will alter the definition for this style if you press [Ctrl]X.

Figure 8-26

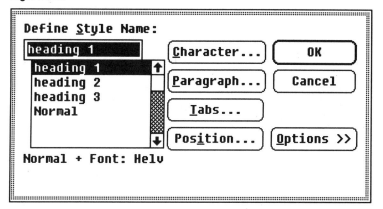

When you press [Ctrl]X, Word will delete all the paragraph formatting instructions for a style.

You can use a similar shortcut to delete only the character formatting instructions for a style. After you open the Define Styles dialog box and click on the name of the style you want to modify, press [Ctrl][Spacebar]. Word will then delete such characteristics as underlining, font type, and point size from the style's definition. For example, Figure 8-27 on the next page shows how the Define Styles dialog box from Figure 8-24 will look if you press [Ctrl][Spacebar].

You can also use the [Fonts] ([Ctrl]F) and [Points] ([Ctrl]P) keys to change a style's character formatting while you're in the Define Styles dialog box. Pressing the [Fonts] key changes a style's font type to the font immediately following the current font on the Font pull-down list box on the ribbon. For example, if you press [Fonts] while changing the *Normal* style, which uses the 10-point Tms Rmn font, Word will change the font for that style to the font immediately following Tms Rmn in the Font list box. Word will change the style's instructions without displaying the list of fonts. If you press [Ctrl][Shift]F, Word will select the font immediately preceding the Tms Rmn font on the list. The [Points] key works a little differently. If you press [Points], Word will increase the size for the font by $\frac{1}{2}$ point. If you press [Ctrl][Shift]P, Word will decrease the size by $\frac{1}{2}$ point.

Figure 8-27

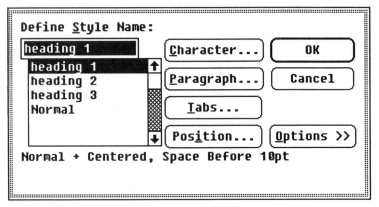

When you press [Ctrl][Spacebar], Word will delete all the character formatting instructions for a style.

You can also use the [Color] key ([Ctrl]V) while you're in the Define Styles dialog box to change the color of text defined in a style's definition. Pressing [Color] while defining a style scrolls forward through the list of colors displayed in the Character dialog box, while pressing [Ctrl][Shift]V scrolls backward through the list. Again, Word will make these changes to the style's definition without ever displaying the actual list of colors.

In addition to these shortcuts, you can use all the character and paragraph formatting shortcuts that we described in Chapter 5. (Appendix 3 includes a summary of these shortcuts.) For example, to specify centered alignment while defining a style, you can press [Ctrl]C, or to select boldfacing, you can press [Ctrl]B.

Modifying a
style by example

To modify a style by example, begin by placing the cursor in a paragraph formatted with the style you want to change. Next, manually reformat the paragraph, creating an example of how the modified style should look. You can use icons on the ruler and ribbon or commands on the Format menu to reformat the paragraph. Then, choose the name of the style from the Style box on the ruler or from the Styles dialog box, as if you were going to reapply the style to the example paragraph. When you attempt to apply the style, Word will present a message box like the one shown in Figure 8-28. If you choose Yes, Word will redefine the style based on the format of the example paragraph. Word will also use the style's new definition to reformat every paragraph to which the style is already applied. If you choose No, Word will reapply the style's original instructions to the example paragraph. (Earlier in this chapter, we explained that choosing No removes manual formatting.) If you choose Cancel, Word will remove the dialog box from the screen without altering the style's definition or reapplying the style to the example paragraph.

Figure 8-28

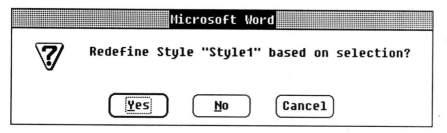

When you change the formatting of a paragraph and then reapply the style name to that paragraph, Word will display this message box.

Modifying a style by example imposes some limitations not inherent in modifying a style by selection. You cannot alter a style's name, its Based On style, or its Next Style without opening the Define Styles dialog box. However, if you want to make some simple formatting changes to a style, modifying by example is usually the simpler of the two methods.

Other modifications

In the example we presented earlier in this section, we showed you how you can modify the formatting instructions for one of Word's automatic styles. To modify the formatting instructions for a custom style, you would follow the same procedure.

In most cases, when you modify a style, you'll change that style's formatting instructions. However, there are other modifications you may want to make as well, such as changing a style's name or specifying a different Based On style or Next Style. Let's look at how you might implement these other style modifications.

Changing a style's name

To change the name of a style, open the Define Styles dialog box and choose Options >> to expand it. Select the name you want to change, then choose the Rename... button under the Next Style text box. Word will then display a dialog box like the one shown in Figure 8-29. Type the style's new name in the New Style Name text box and choose OK. When you do, the new style name will replace the original one in the list of styles.

Figure 8-29

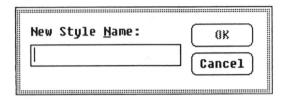

Word will display the Rename dialog box when you choose the Rename... button in the Define Styles dialog box.

Once you enter a new name for a style, Word will not let you cancel the action. In fact, when you choose OK to close the Rename dialog box, the name on the Cancel button in the expanded Define Styles dialog box will change to Close. However, you can always restore a style's original name by choosing Rename... again and entering the style name.

When you enter a new name in the New Style Name text box, be sure that you do not type a name that already exists. If you do this, Word will display the message shown in Figure 8-30. When you choose OK in this box, Word will return to the Rename dialog box.

Figure 8-30

Word will display this message box if you attempt to rename a style using an existing style name.

Although you can change the formatting instructions for Word's automatic styles, you cannot rename them. Whenever you select the name of an automatic style in the expanded Define Styles dialog box, the Rename... button will become dimmed, indicating that it is inactive.

Specifying a different Based On style

To change the Based On style, open the expanded Define Styles dialog box and select the name of the style whose Based On style you want to change. Then, type the name of the style you want to use in the Based On text box, or select the style name from the pull-down list attached to the text box. Finally, choose OK or Define to lock in the change.

Because specifying a new Based On style changes the foundation of a style, it can drastically change the attributes of the current style. For example, suppose you're working with a style sheet that contains styles named *Style1* and *Style2*. The *Normal* style specifies 10-point Tms Rmn type with flush-left alignment and no indents. *Style1* is based on *Normal,* and its definition reads *Normal + Bold Italic, Indent: Left 0.5" Right 0.5", Justified, Space Before 10pt. Style2* is identical to *Style1,* except it specifies 12-point type. Figure 8-31 shows the definition for *Style2.*

Figure 8-31

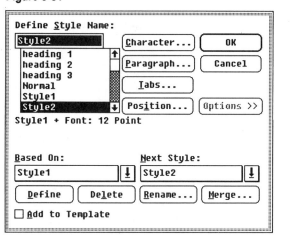

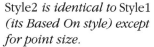

Style2 *is identical to* Style1
*(its Based On style) except
for point size.*

Suppose you want to change the Based On style for *Style2* to *Normal* instead of *Style1.* After opening the Define Styles dialog box and choosing Options >> to expand it, select the style name *Style2* in the Define Style Name list box. Next, select *Normal* as the name of your new Based On style and choose the Define button. Then, reselect *Style2* in the Define Style Name list box. Figure 8-32 shows the results.

Figure 8-32

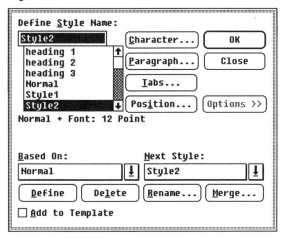

*After you change the
Based On style, Word will
change only the first
element in the instructions
for the dependent style.*

Notice that Figure 8-32 now shows that *Style2* is based on the *Normal* style. The formatting instructions for *Style2* build only on those in the *Normal* style and do not include the instructions added to *Style1*. As a result, text formatted with the *Style2* style will look similar to *Normal* text, except it will feature 12-point, rather than 10-point characters. Text formatted with *Style2* will no longer include the paragraph formatting of *Style1*.

There is a purpose in specifying a different Based On style. As we've mentioned, any changes you make to a Based On style are carried over into the instructions for the dependent style (or styles). Thus, you'll generally specify a new Based On style in order to link two or more styles that are used to format similar elements of a document. Linking styles in this manner helps to ensure that the formatting instructions of these styles are similar.

Breaking the link to the Based On style

Instead of changing the Based On style, you can delete it altogether. Just select the style name in the Based On text box, then press [Delete]. Choose the Define button to lock in the change. You might recall from our earlier discussion that, in general, it's not a good idea to have a style that is not based on another style. However, if you want to ensure that certain style formats remain unchanged no matter what style changes you make to other text in your document, you may want to eliminate the Based On style.

Specifying a different Next Style

Another modification you may want to make to a style is to specify a different Next Style. Just open and expand the Define Styles dialog box, select the style, then change the name in the Next Style text box and select OK or Define. When you specify a different Next Style, Word will not reformat your existing text. The new Next Style will affect only text you enter after the change has been made.

By default, Word uses each named style as its own Next Style. If you leave the Next Style text box blank, Word will automatically fill it with the name of the style you are defining. For example, suppose you delete the entry in the Next Style text box while redefining the *Style1* style, then choose the Define button. The next time you view the definition of the *Style1* style in the Define Styles dialog box, Word will list *Style1* as the Next Style.

The effects of modifying a style

Once you have made changes to a named style, those changes will affect any text in your document that has been formatted with that style. That text does not have to be selected at the time you modify the style in order to be reformatted. For example, suppose your style sheet includes the automatic style named *heading 1*, which you've used to format several headings throughout your document. If you change the style definition for *heading 1*—to specify a different font, for example—Word will automatically reformat all the *heading 1* paragraphs so that they are displayed in the new font. Of course, this automatic reformatting is one of the most important features of Word's style sheets. Since Word applies style sheet changes throughout the entire document, it saves you the time and trouble of reformatting individual sections of the document manually.

When you save a document after you've modified a style, the changes in the instructions will be saved along with the document text. This is true for both automatic and custom styles. Of course, if you modify one of Word's automatic styles, your modifications will *not* affect the default instructions for that style. If you create a new document that uses the automatic style, Word will return to its default instructions for that style. However, you can change the default instructions for an automatic style by changing the automatic styles in Word's default template, NORMAL.DOT. We'll show you how to do this later in this chapter.

If you make changes to a style that serves as the Based On style for other styles, your changes may affect those other styles. For example, earlier in this chapter, we explained how any changes you make to the instructions for the *Normal* style can affect the other styles that are based on *Normal*. Of course, it's possible to make some changes to a Based On style without affecting any dependent styles.

Modifying a Based On style

Once you've applied named styles throughout a document, you can make significant formatting changes to it merely by changing the instructions of one or more styles. When you change the style sheet, Word will reformat your document text according to those changes. You don't need to select any text before you modify a style's instructions—Word will automatically change any text to which that style has been applied. We've already seen examples of what can happen in a document when you modify the instructions for one style. Now let's consider an example that shows how you might make extensive formatting changes by modifying several styles.

Making global changes with a style sheet

Figure 8-33 on the following page shows part of a document in which three styles have been applied. The title has been formatted with a style named *Title* that specifies 14-point Tms Rmn bold type, flush-left alignment, and a 9-point space below the paragraph. The subheading has been formatted with a style named *Subheading*, which uses *Title* as its Based On style but specifies 12-point size and a 4-point line space before and a 2-point line space after the subheading. Finally, the body text in this document has been formatted with the default *Normal* style, which specifies 10-point Tms Rmn type and flush-left alignment.

Suppose you want to change the title and subheading in the document to appear in the Modern font with centered alignment. Since the Modern font is somewhat smaller than the Tms Rmn font, you want to change the size of the title to 18 points and the subheading to 14 points. You also want to change the main body text to 12-point Helv type with justified alignment. In just a few easy steps, you can apply all these formatting changes throughout the entire document.

Begin by opening the Define Styles dialog box, selecting the *Normal* style in the Define Style Name list box, and choosing Options >> to expand the dialog box.

Then, choose the Character... button to open the Character dialog box, and type *Helv* in the Font text box and *12pt* in the Points text box. Select OK to close the Character dialog box. Next, choose the Paragraph... button to open the Paragraph dialog box, choose the Justified Alignment option, and select OK to close the Paragraph dialog box. Then, choose Define to lock in these changes to the *Normal* style. Now, select *Title* in the Define Style Name list box and open the Character dialog box. Choose Modern from the list of fonts and 18 from the list of sizes, then select OK to close the Character dialog box. Open the Paragraph dialog box, choose the Center Alignment option, and select OK to close the Paragraph dialog box. Again, choose Define to lock in these changes. When you change the font and alignment for the *Title* style, Word will transfer those changes to the instructions for the *Subheading* style as well. Finally, select *Subheading* from the Define Style Name list box. Since the *Subheading* style is based on the *Title* style, you only need to change the point size for this style. To do this, open the Character dialog box, choose 14 from the list of sizes, select OK to close the dialog box, then choose Define to save the change.

Figure 8-33

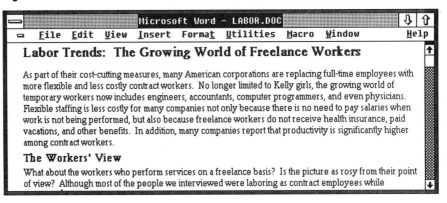

This document has three styles: Title, Subheading, *and* Normal.

After altering all the style definitions, choose OK or Close to close the Define Styles dialog box. Figure 8-34 shows how your document will appear at this point.

As we've mentioned, one of the nicest advantages of style sheets is that you don't need to select any text before making your formatting changes. When you alter a style's formatting instructions, Word will automatically change any text to which that style has been applied.

Merging styles from another document

Word allows you to copy or "merge" styles from other documents and templates and import them into your current document. You can borrow styles one at a time or import all the styles on another document's style sheet into your current document. Either way, the ability to copy style definitions from document to document can save you the time of redefining styles for each new document and can provide an efficient way to reformat text.

Figure 8-34

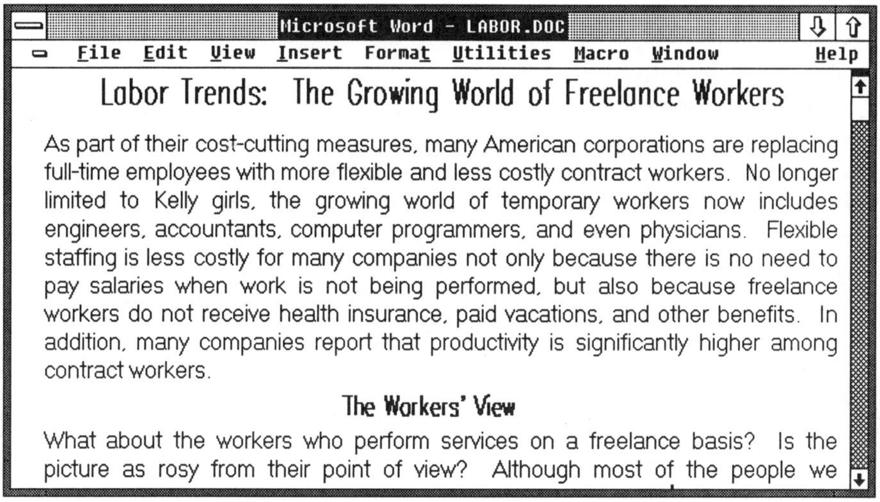

A few simple changes to the style sheet can significantly alter the appearance of a document.

If you want to copy a style from one document to another, simply copy some text that has been formatted with that style. When you paste the formatted text into a document, Word will also add the style name and style definition to that document's style sheet. For example, suppose you're working on a document named INTRO in which you've created a style named *First ¶*. You want to use this style in a document named SUMMARY. In the document named INTRO, select some text that has been formatted with the *First ¶* style. Then, choose Copy from the Edit menu. Next, open the SUMMARY document and choose Paste from the Edit menu. Word will copy the text you selected in INTRO—with all its formatting—into the SUMMARY document. If you then choose Styles... or Define Styles... from the Format menu, or pull down the Style list box on the ruler, you will see that the style named *First ¶* is now part of SUMMARY's style sheet.

Copying one style

When you use this technique, there are rules you must follow. First, the text you select and copy must include an entire paragraph. If you copy only part of one (not including the ¶ mark), Word will not transfer any of the text formatting or the style name to the other document. When you paste the text in the second document, it will be formatted according to that document's *Normal* style.

Second, you need to be aware of how Word handles duplicate style names. Returning to our example, suppose the style sheet for the SUMMARY document already contained a style named *First ¶*. When you paste the *First ¶* text from INTRO into SUMMARY, Word will use the existing formatting instructions for *First ¶* to format that text rather than importing the new instructions from the INTRO file. In cases of identical style names, the instructions for the style in the destination document will always take precedence over the instructions for the duplicate style name in the source document.

Third, if the style definition for the paragraph you are copying includes a Based On style, Word may need to alter the instructions when you paste the text into the destination document. If the paragraph you copy is based on a style that is not defined in your destination document, Word will use *Normal* as the Based On style for the style you are copying. However, Word will retain all the character and paragraph formats you assigned to that paragraph in the source document by creating a more specific set of instructions for that style.

For example, suppose you are working in a document that contains styles named *Sub1* and *Sub2*. The formatting instructions for *Sub1* specify 14-point Helv type. *Sub2*, which is based on *Sub1*, specifies 12-point Helv type. Thus, the formatting instructions for *Sub2* read *Sub1 + Font: 12 Point*. Now, suppose you decide to copy a *Sub2* paragraph into a new document window. The only styles on the style sheet in this new document are Word's default *Normal, heading 1, heading 2*, and *heading 3* styles. After pasting the *Sub2* text into this document, Word will add the *Sub2* style to the style sheet. However, since *Sub2*'s Based On style (*Sub1*) does not appear in this new document, the formatting instructions for *Sub2* will read *Normal + Font: Helv 12 Point*.

If the Based On style of the paragraph you are copying appears in your destination document's style sheet, Word will continue to use that Based On style. Again, Word will not change the formatting characteristics of the copied style in any way. In the example above, suppose you decide to copy some *Sub2* text into a document that already contains a style named *Sub1* (the name of the Based On style for *Sub2* in the source document). However, in the destination document, the formatting instructions for *Sub1* specify 14-point Tms Rmn italic type. When you copy the *Sub2* text into this document, Word will add the style name *Sub2* to the style sheet. However, its formatting instructions will now read *Sub1 + Font: Helv 12 Point, Not Italic*. In other words, *Sub1* is still the Based On style for *Sub2* in the new document. However, in this new document, Word has changed the formatting instructions for *Sub2* so that they spell out all the differences between *Sub2* and *Sub1*.

The best way to avoid uncertainty about the effect of copying some formatted text from one document to another is to make sure you don't have duplicate style names. Of course, you can't avoid having a *Normal* style in each of your documents. So, one of your first steps in setting up a new document should be to alter the *Normal* style to suit that particular document. Then, as you copy styles based on *Normal* from one document to another, you'll need to watch carefully for any unwanted format changes and handle these as they occur.

Copying one style at a time can be useful in many instances, but you often will find that it's more efficient to import an entire style sheet rather than copy individual styles.

To import a style sheet from a file on disk, issue the Define Styles… command and choose Options >> to expand the dialog box. Next, choose the Merge… button in the lower-right corner of the dialog box. Word will present a dialog box like the one shown in Figure 8-35. You use this dialog box to select the Word file whose styles you want to merge into your document. You can merge styles from either another document file or a template file. Notice that when the Merge dialog box first appears, the Files list box lists the names of templates in the current directory. The names of templates appear because the file description in the Merge File Name text box is *.DOT, which is the extension Word assigns to template files. Word assigns the extension .DOC to the names of regular document files. If you want to see a list of document names, type *.DOC* in the Merge File Name text box and choose OK. After you do this, the Files list box will list all files in the current directory whose names end with the extension .DOC. If you know the name of the file from which you want to merge styles, you can simply type this file name in the Merge File Name text box.

Importing a complete
style sheet

Figure 8-35

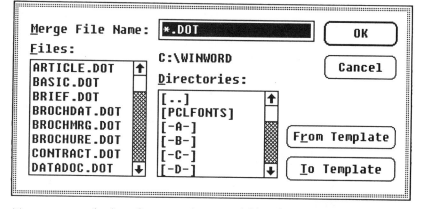

To merge a style sheet from another Word file, choose Merge… in the expanded Define Styles dialog box to open the Merge dialog box.

If the file containing the style sheet you want to use is not in the current directory or on the current disk drive, you can use the Directories list box to access other directories and disk drives. Once you see the name of the file that contains the style sheet you want to import, select that name, then choose OK (or simply double-click the file name). Word will then display the message shown in Figure 8-36. You should choose Yes to complete the style merger or select No to return to the dialog box.

Figure 8-36

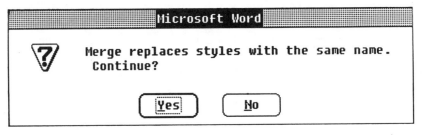

Word displays this message box to remind you of the consequences of merging styles.

If you choose Yes, Word will add the styles from the selected document to your current style sheet. (Your style sheet will contain both its original styles and all the styles from the style sheet of the disk file.) If the disk file contains one or more styles with the same name as one of the styles in your current document, the style from the disk file will overwrite the existing style. Any text in your document that has been formatted with that style will be reformatted according to the instructions of the new style from the disk file.

For example, every document's style sheet contains the *Normal* style, but the formatting instructions for *Normal* will vary from document to document. Suppose you're working in a document in which the *Normal* style specifies 10-point Tms Rmn type (Word's default), and you import a style sheet whose *Normal* style specifies 12-point Courier type. Word will replace the instructions for the *Normal* style on your style sheet with the new instructions from the disk file. In addition, the main body text in your current document will be reformatted to display 12-point Courier type.

Of course, if the names of all or most of the styles on your current style sheet are identical to the style names you import, your document may be radically reformatted. In some cases, this may be exactly what you want. Borrowing another document's style sheet offers an excellent way to reformat an entire document rapidly.

Saving a style sheet in a template

If you plan to use similar formats in several documents, you may want to store those formats in the style sheet of a template. As we'll explain in Chapter 18, a template is a special type of Word document that serves as a pattern for other documents.   Templates can contain a number of named styles, as well as text, fields, macros, and keyboard and menu assignments. You can open and change templates just like regular Word documents. When you create a new document, Word will use all the features of a template as the starting point for the new document. Each new document begins its life with the styles, text, fields, macros, and keyboard and menu assignments it inherits from its parent template.

By default, Word uses the template stored under the file name NORMAL.DOT (which we'll refer to as the Normal template) when you create a new document. All the examples we've used in this chapter assumed that you were using a document based on this template. When you create a document using the New… command, the New dialog box will allow you to choose a different template upon which to base the new document. If you anticipate creating several documents with similar formats, you'll probably want to create a template with the styles you'll be using. Then, you can select this template as you create each of the documents and avoid having to format each document from scratch.

In Chapter 18, we'll show you how to create and modify templates and how to merge style sheets between a document and its template.

DELETING STYLES

To delete a named style from a style sheet, just open the Define Styles dialog box, choose Options >> to expand the dialog box, then select the name of the style you want to delete. With that name selected, choose the Delete button. Word will then display a message box asking if you want to delete the selected style. If you choose Yes, Word will pause a few seconds, then eliminate that style from the style sheet.

Once you delete a named style, any text that was formatted with that style will lose its special formatting. However, Word will automatically assign the *Normal* style to all the paragraphs that previously were associated with the deleted style.

As we've said, Word will not allow you to delete or rename any of its automatic styles. Whenever you select an automatic style in the Define Style Name list box, the Delete button will become dimmed, indicating that it is inactive.

If you delete a Based On style, the dependent style will retain all the formatting characteristics of the deleted style. Of course, any formatting characteristics that were derived from the Based On style will now be stated explicitly in the style definition. In addition, Word will automatically make *Normal* the Based On style in place of the style that was deleted.

If you delete a style that appears in another style's Next Style text box, Word will automatically use *Normal* in place of the style you deleted. Word also will reformat any existing text that was formatted with the deleted style according to the instructions of the *Normal* style.

CHANGING DEFAULTS

If you use certain styles in almost every document you create, you may want to change the default style sheet stored in the Normal template so that those styles are automatically available each time you start a new document in Word. In addition, you might want to change the default formatting instructions of some of Word's automatic styles, particularly the *Normal* style. Because Word uses the Normal template's style sheet as the default style sheet for new documents, you can change Word's default style sheet by modifying the style sheet of the Normal template. As a result, changing default styles is no more complicated than changing styles for any regular document.

Modifying the Normal template's style sheet

Initially, the only styles on the default style sheet are the *Normal, heading 1, heading 2,* and *heading 3* styles. To add styles (custom or automatic) to this default style sheet, all you need to do is open the Normal template and use the techniques we've explained in this chapter to define the new styles. To open the Normal template, choose the Open… command on the File menu. When Word presents the Open dialog box, enter *NORMAL.DOT* in the Open File Name text box and choose OK. Word will then display the Normal template in a new window.

Once the Normal template is open, you can modify the automatic styles already on the default sheet or add automatic or custom styles. After you save your changes to the Normal template's style sheet, all new documents will include the modified default style sheet. The only exceptions to this rule will be those documents that are based on templates other than Normal. The modified default styles will not affect any existing document based on the Normal template unless you merge the new style sheet into the existing document. We'll discuss changing the Normal template in more detail in Chapter 18.

Returning to the original defaults

If, after making changes to the default style sheet, you want to restore it and return the automatic styles to their original forms, you can erase the Normal template from your hard disk. The next time you start Word for Windows, the program will automatically create a new Normal template using the original default settings.

To erase the Normal template from your hard disk, first return to DOS and move into the directory containing your Word for Windows program files. For instance, if you've installed Word for Windows in the directory C:\WINWORD, enter the command *CD \WINWORD* at the DOS prompt. Once you've moved into the appropriate directory, issue the command *ERASE NORMAL.DOT.*

Of course, if you erase your Normal template, you'll change more than the default styles. You also will erase any text, fields, macros, or menu changes you made to the Normal template. We'll further discuss this topic in Chapter 20.

DISPLAYING THE STYLE AREA

While the Style box on the ruler always displays the name of the current paragraph's style, it is possible to display the style names for all the paragraphs. You can see all the styles used in a document by opening the style area, which is a window that runs along the left edge of the document window. The name of the style applied to each paragraph appears in the style area next to the paragraph itself.

To display the style area, first make sure you are not in the page view, then select the Preferences… command on the View menu to display the Preferences dialog box shown in Figure 8-37. Notice the Style Area Width text box in the lower-right corner of this dialog box. This text box contains the entry 0" because, by default, Word does not display the style area. If you enter a value greater than 0 in this text box, Word will display the style area with the specified width along the left edge of the screen. After changing the entry in the text box, choose OK to lock in the new width and close the Preferences dialog box.

Figure 8-37

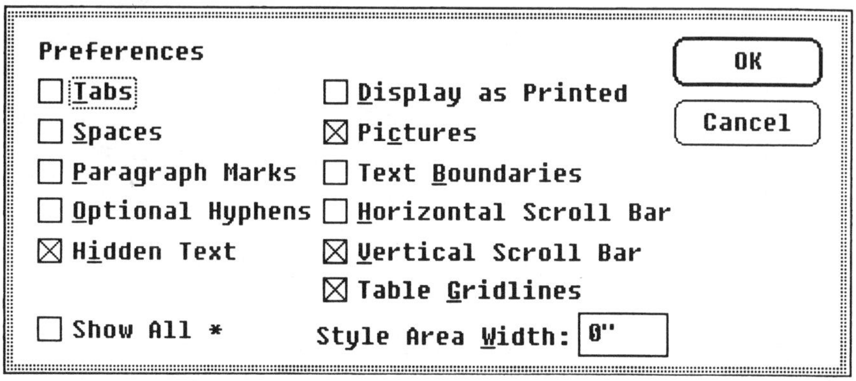

```
┌──────────────────────────────────────────────────────────┐
│                                                            │
│  Preferences                          ┌──────────────┐     │
│                                       │      OK       │    │
│  ☐ Tabs          ☐ Display as Printed └──────────────┘     │
│  ☐ Spaces        ☒ Pictures           ┌──────────────┐     │
│  ☐ Paragraph Marks ☐ Text Boundaries  │   Cancel      │    │
│  ☐ Optional Hyphens ☐ Horizontal Scroll Bar └─────────┘    │
│  ☒ Hidden Text   ☒ Vertical Scroll Bar                     │
│                  ☒ Table Gridlines                         │
│  ☐ Show All *    Style Area Width: ┌────┐                  │
│                                    │ 0" │                  │
│                                    └────┘                  │
└──────────────────────────────────────────────────────────┘
```

You can display the style area by changing the Style Area Width setting in the Preferences dialog box.

For example, if you open the Preferences dialog box while editing the document shown in Figure 8-34, enter 1" in the Style Area Width text box, and choose OK, Word will display a 1-inch-wide style area, as shown in Figure 8-38 on the next page.

When sizing the style area, you should make it just large enough to display the longest style name on your document's style sheet. If you make the style area too large, your document's text may run off the right side of your screen.

If you want to resize the style area after displaying it, just issue the Preferences… command again, enter a new width in the Style Area Width text box, and choose OK. You can also use your mouse to resize the style area. If you move the mouse pointer over the style area split bar (the vertical line along the right edge of the style area), the pointer will change as shown in the upper-left portion of Figure 8-39. When the pointer changes shape, click the mouse button, drag the style area split bar to its new location, then release the mouse button.

Figure 8-38

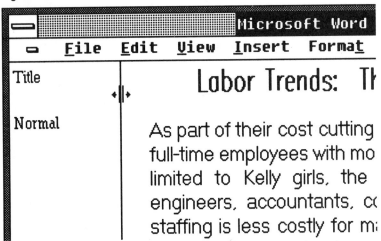

	Microsoft Word - LABOR.DOC ⇩ ⇧
▭	**File** **Edit** **View** **Insert** **Forma<u>t</u>** **Utilities** **Macro** **Window** **Help**
Title	Labor Trends: The Growing World of Freelance Wc
Normal	As part of their cost-cutting measures, many American corporations
	full-time employees with more flexible and less costly contract worker
	limited to Kelly girls, the growing world of temporary workers n
	engineers, accountants, computer programmers, and even physicia
	staffing is less costly for many companies not only because there i
	pay salaries when work is not being performed, but also becau
	workers do not receive health insurance, paid vacations, and other
	addition, many companies report that productivity is significantly hi
	contract workers.
Subheading	The Workers' View
Normal	What about the workers who perform services on a freelance ba
	picture as rosy from their point of view? Although most of the

The style area displays the style names for all the paragraphs in a document.

Figure 8-39

▭		Microsoft Word
▭	**File** **Edit** **View** **Insert** **Forma<u>t</u>**	
Title	◀‖▶	Labor Trends: Tf
Normal		As part of their cost cutting
		full-time employees with mo
		limited to Kelly girls, the
		engineers, accountants, cc
		staffing is less costly for m;

The pointer will change shape when you move it over the style area split bar.

To close the style area, open the Preferences dialog box, enter *0"* in the Style Area Width text box, and choose OK. You can close the style area with your mouse by dragging the style area split bar to the left edge of the document window. After you open the style area in a document, Word will display it for every new document you create or open until you close the style area.

To print a list of all the styles on a style sheet, choose Print… from the File menu, then select Styles from the Print pull-down list box. When you choose OK, Word will print a list like the one shown in Figure 8-40. As you can see, this list includes the style names in bold and the definition for each style.

PRINTING A STYLE SHEET

Figure 8-40

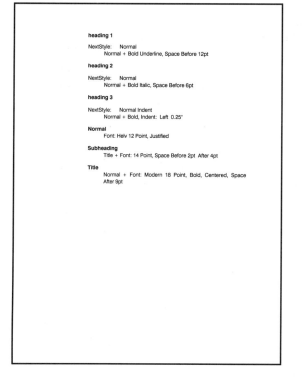

Word can print a list of the styles and definitions on the current style sheet.

In this chapter

Outlining 9

$\mathcal{S}$ometimes when you create a document, you know exactly what you want to say and how you want to say it. At other times, however, you just can't seem to get started, or you have so much information that structuring it seems overwhelming. Fortunately, Word comes to your rescue with the outline view, which helps you organize your thoughts and build a document from the ground up.

Although Word's outline view is easy to use, it is highly sophisticated. As you'll see, the outline view works in conjunction with many of Word's other special features to help you create, edit, and organize your text. The combined power of the outline view and style sheets lets you format your documents quickly and easily. In addition, you can use the outline view to create a table of contents (more on this topic in Chapter 14), to navigate through long documents, and to rearrange blocks of text with only a few keystrokes.

To activate the outline view, select the Outline command from the View menu. When you do, you'll see an icon selection bar just below the menu bar, as shown in Figure 9-1. Because the Outline command is a toggle command, you can reselect it to return to the normal editing view.

Figure 9-1

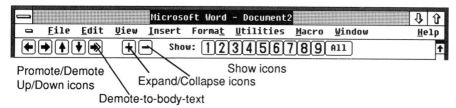

When you issue the Outline command, you'll see this set of icons at the top of your screen.

As you assemble your outline, you'll use the icons to organize and assign priorities to the information in your document, and to expand and collapse your view of the document. We'll look at each of these features as we examine the process of creating and editing text using the outline view.

HEADINGS AND BODY TEXT

Word's outline view divides your document text into two categories: headings and body text. Generally, you'll enter the headings in the outline view, then return to the normal editing view to enter the body text. Each heading is assigned a level labeled *heading 1* through *heading 9*. The remainder of the text is body text.

Heading 1 entries represent the broadest or most important categories of ideas, while *heading 2* through *heading 9* entries represent subordinate levels of ideas under the main headings. You can use all of these entries as headings in your finished document, or you can opt to hide them from view once you have completed the document.

Word helps you visualize the relationships between outline topics by indenting the different levels of text that appear in the outline view. Main topics— those labeled *heading 1*—start at the left margin, while subordinate headings are indented. *Heading 2* entries are indented $^1/_2$ inch, *heading 3* entries are indented 1 inch, and so forth—with each new level indented an additional $^1/_2$ inch. Any body text you enter while in the outline view will be indented $^1/_4$ inch from where the preceding heading begins. (Actually, the amount of indention Word uses for the different levels in the outline view corresponds to the Default Tab Stops setting in the Document dialog box. If you change this setting, Word will change the amount of indention for each level of text in the outline.)

BUILDING AN OUTLINE

The easiest way to become familiar with the outline view is to create a sample document. To illustrate, we'll create an article about free-lancing. We'll use the outline view to organize our ideas, then we'll build on the outline to create a finished document. If you'd like to follow along with our example, open a new document, select the Ruler command from the View menu, then select the Outline command. Word will place a check mark next to these commands to indicate that they've been selected.

Figure 9-2 shows a portion of our sample article's outline. To create this outline, start by typing the first heading, *Cutting loose*, then press [Enter] to start a new paragraph. Whenever you begin a new outline, Word assumes that your first paragraph will be a *heading 1* entry. It also assumes that all subsequent paragraphs will be entered at the same level as the previous entry unless you indicate otherwise.

To create the subordinate heading on the second line of the sample outline, begin by clicking the ➡ (Demote) icon at the top of the screen or pressing the [Alt][Shift]➡ keys. Then, type the phrase *Is freelancing for you?* You will notice that Word has "demoted" your second paragraph to the *heading 2* level, and has indented the paragraph $^1/_2$ inch from the left margin to indicate that this heading is subordinate to the first heading. Press [Enter] again to begin the third paragraph, then demote this entry to the *heading 3* level by clicking the ➡ icon or by pressing the [Alt][Shift]➡ keys.

Figure 9-2

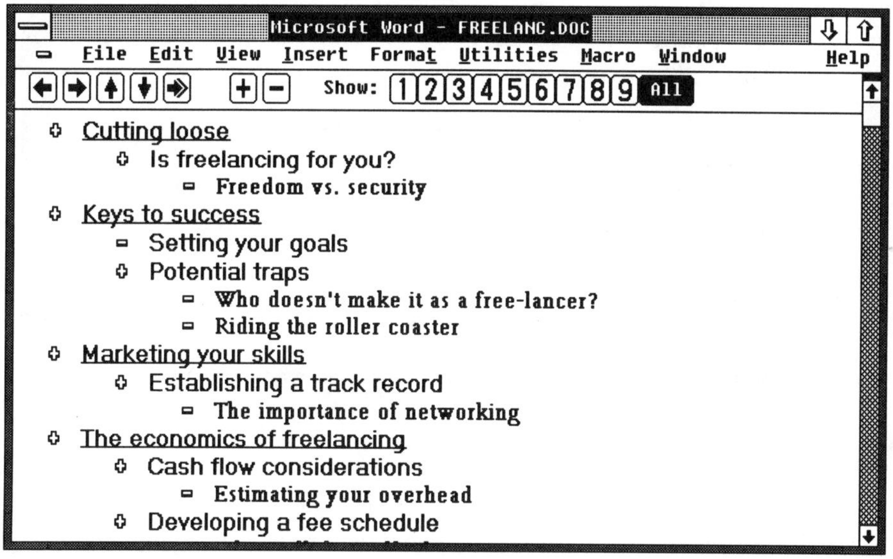

We'll start by entering our headings in the outline view and assigning priority levels to each.

In addition to the various levels of indention, notice that Word has assigned different character formats to the heading levels in the outline. As we'll explain later in this chapter, your document's style sheet controls the formats for these headings. If you prefer not to show these various heading formats, you can select the Draft command from the View menu, which allows you to hide formatting in the outline view. When you do this, Word will display all the document's text in the Microsoft Windows System font, as shown in Figure 9-3 on the following page. You may find that this simplified, unformatted display makes it easier to interpret the structure of your document. To redisplay character formatting, just reselect the Draft command.

After you type the text for the third heading, you're ready to move on to your next major topic: *Keys to success.* Notice that this paragraph is of the same level as the first heading in Figure 9-2. When you press [Enter] at the end of the third paragraph to enter this heading, however, Word will assume that you want this new paragraph to become a *heading 3* entry as well. To "promote" the fourth paragraph to a *heading 1* entry, click the ◀ (Promote) icon twice or press [Alt][Shift]◀ twice.

Figure 9-3

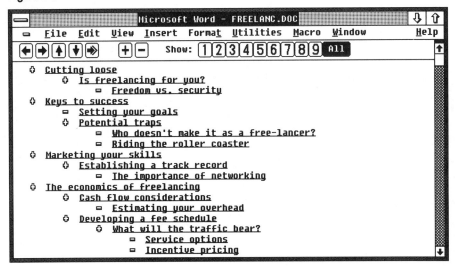

You can select the Draft command from the View menu to suppress character formatting in the outline view.

To complete the outline, continue typing the sample text shown in Figure 9-2, clicking the ← and → icons to promote and demote each heading as needed. (Of course, you can also use the [Alt][Shift]← and [Alt][Shift]→ key combinations to promote and demote your headings.)

Although our sample outline uses only four heading levels, Word allows you to create as many as nine. Generally, the more detailed your outline, the greater the number of heading levels you will use.

Before continuing, you should familiarize yourself with the heading and body-text icons you will encounter as you enter, promote, and demote text. You'll see these icons to the left of the heading paragraphs in the outline view. The icon's shape indicates whether a paragraph is a heading or body text. The ▫ icon signals a paragraph of body text. The ✪ and ▬ icons signal heading text: ✪ indicates a heading with subordinate text, while ▬ indicates a heading without subordinate text. (By subordinate text, we mean all the headings and body text between the current heading and the next heading of an equal or higher level.)

Viewing an outline in the normal editing view

As you enter the outline text, keep in mind that the outline view is just another type of document view, as far as Word is concerned. Any actions you take in the outline view will also affect what you see in each of the other views. For example, when you use the Outline command to return to the normal editing view after typing the sample outline shown in Figure 9-2, your screen will look like the one in Figure 9-4. As you can see, Word makes it easy to identify the relationship among the headings.

Figure 9-4

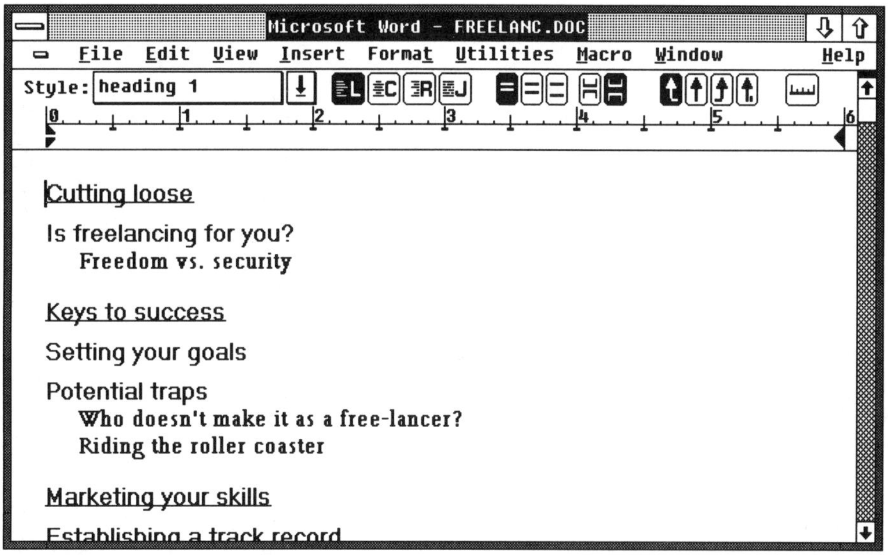

When you toggle back to the normal editing view, the document's text will look like this.

When you return to the normal editing view, you'll see that each heading level carries different character and paragraph formats. If you keep your eye on the Style box on the ruler as you move the cursor to the various headings, you'll see that Word has remembered the heading level you assigned to each paragraph.

While you create an outline, Word is busy behind the scenes creating a style sheet for your document. For each heading level you enter into the document in the outline view, Word creates a corresponding set of style definitions. We'll show you later in this chapter how to use these automatic styles to format your document. First, let's add some body text to our outline and explore techniques for editing our document in the outline view.

After you've established the headings in an outline, you can fill in your document by adding body text. To do this, first activate the normal editing view. Next, place the cursor just before the ¶ mark at the end of the first paragraph, then press [Enter] to begin a new paragraph. As you type the body of the document, part of which is shown in Figure 9-5, Word will automatically format the text in the default *Normal* style—10-point Tms Rmn.

ADDING BODY TEXT

Figure 9-5

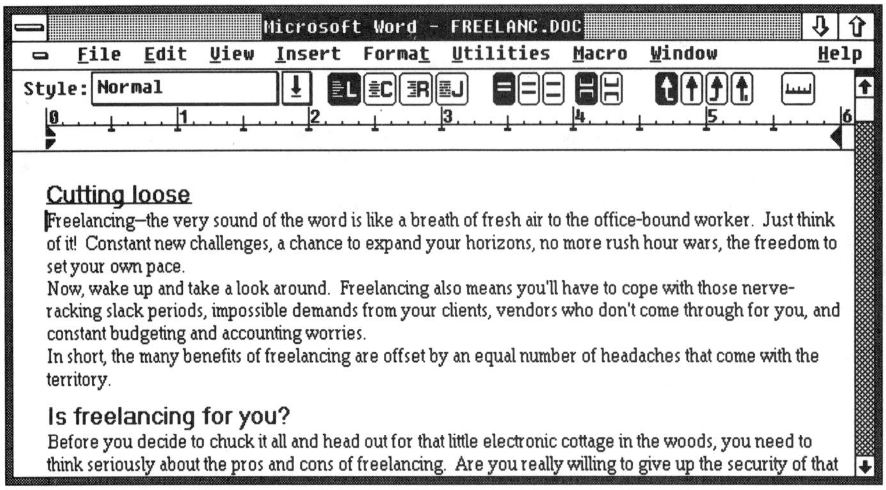

When you position the cursor after a heading paragraph and press [Enter], Word will automatically assign the Normal *style to the body-text paragraph.*

After entering some body text, toggle back to the outline view and notice what has happened to the outline. As you can see in Figure 9-6, Word redisplays your indentions to give you a clear view of the relationship between each heading in the document. Also, notice that each body-text paragraph is indented $1/4$ inch to the right of the heading under which it falls. This half-level indention gives you another visual clue to the organizational structure of your document.

Simplifying the outline view

To help you reduce clutter in the outline view and better see the structure of your document, Word offers a way to toggle the display of body text. When you press [Alt][Shift]F, Word will condense each paragraph of body text to only one line—just enough text to remind you of the topic of each paragraph. As you can see in Figure 9-7, when you condense the body text in the outline view, Word will place ellipses at the end of each line of body text to indicate that additional text follows. If you want to view the full text of your document again, press [Alt][Shift]F a second time.

SELECTION TECHNIQUES

Once you have entered your headings and drafted the body text, you'll probably need to make some changes and reorganize the information in your document. Word offers several shortcuts for editing a document in the outline view. As in the normal editing view, however, you must select the text before you can edit it. Let's look at a couple of special selection techniques that Word makes available in the outline view.

Figure 9-6

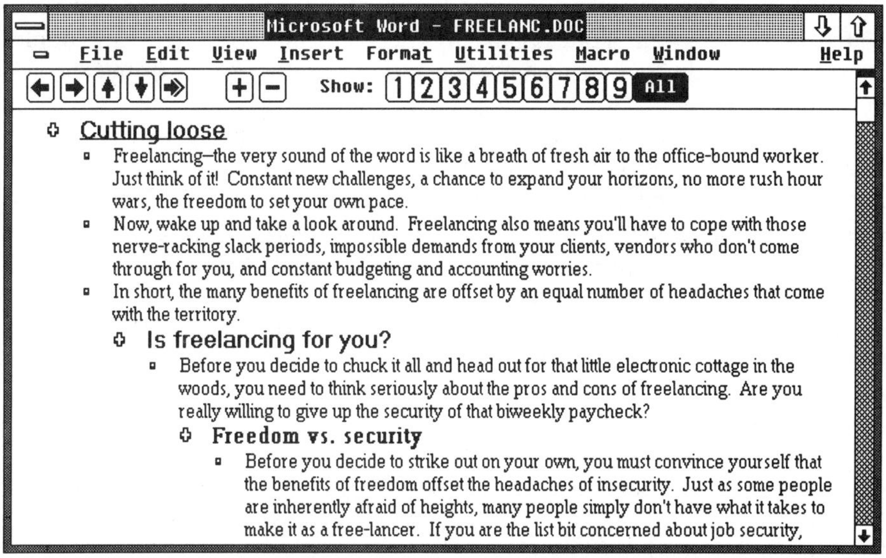

```
┌─────────────────────────────────────────────────────────────────────┐
│ ▭         Microsoft Word - FREELANC.DOC                      ⇩ │ ⇧ │
│ ▭   File   Edit   View   Insert   Format   Utilities   Macro   Window        Help │
│ ◀ ▶ ▲ ▼ ➡   ＋ －   Show: [1][2][3][4][5][6][7][8][9] [All]            ↑ │
│ ✛  Cutting loose                                                        │
│    ▫  Freelancing—the very sound of the word is like a breath of fresh air to the office-bound worker. │
│       Just think of it!  Constant new challenges, a chance to expand your horizons, no more rush hour │
│       wars, the freedom to set your own pace.                           │
│    ▫  Now, wake up and take a look around.  Freelancing also means you'll have to cope with those │
│       nerve-racking slack periods, impossible demands from your clients, vendors who don't come │
│       through for you, and constant budgeting and accounting worries.   │
│    ▫  In short, the many benefits of freelancing are offset by an equal number of headaches that come │
│       with the territory.                                               │
│       ✛  Is freelancing for you?                                        │
│          ▫  Before you decide to chuck it all and head out for that little electronic cottage in the │
│             woods, you need to think seriously about the pros and cons of freelancing.  Are you │
│             really willing to give up the security of that biweekly paycheck? │
│          ✛  Freedom vs. security                                        │
│             ▫  Before you decide to strike out on your own, you must convince yourself that │
│                the benefits of freedom offset the headaches of insecurity.  Just as some people │
│                are inherently afraid of heights, many people simply don't have what it takes to │
│                make it as a free-lancer.  If you are the list bit concerned about job security,  ↓ │
└─────────────────────────────────────────────────────────────────────┘
```

When you return to the outline view, you'll see that each body-text paragraph is indented $\frac{1}{4}$ inch to the right of the heading under which it falls.

Figure 9-7

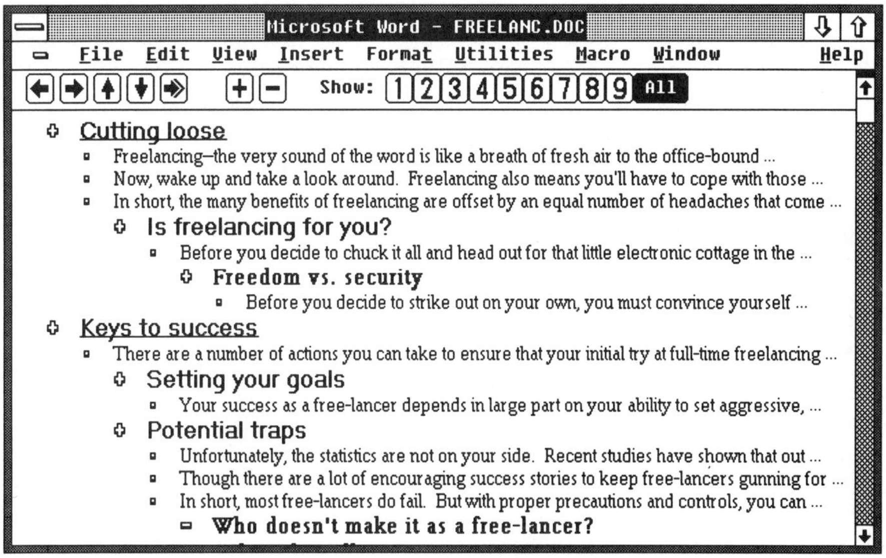

```
┌─────────────────────────────────────────────────────────────────────┐
│ ▭         Microsoft Word - FREELANC.DOC                      ⇩ │ ⇧ │
│ ▭   File   Edit   View   Insert   Format   Utilities   Macro   Window        Help │
│ ◀ ▶ ▲ ▼ ➡   ＋ －   Show: [1][2][3][4][5][6][7][8][9] [All]            ↑ │
│ ✛  Cutting loose                                                        │
│    ▫  Freelancing—the very sound of the word is like a breath of fresh air to the office-bound ... │
│    ▫  Now, wake up and take a look around.  Freelancing also means you'll have to cope with those ... │
│    ▫  In short, the many benefits of freelancing are offset by an equal number of headaches that come ... │
│       ✛  Is freelancing for you?                                        │
│          ▫  Before you decide to chuck it all and head out for that little electronic cottage in the ... │
│          ✛  Freedom vs. security                                        │
│             ▫  Before you decide to strike out on your own, you must convince yourself ... │
│ ✛  Keys to success                                                      │
│    ▫  There are a number of actions you can take to ensure that your initial try at full-time freelancing ... │
│       ✛  Setting your goals                                             │
│          ▫  Your success as a free-lancer depends in large part on your ability to set aggressive, ... │
│       ✛  Potential traps                                                │
│          ▫  Unfortunately, the statistics are not on your side.  Recent studies have shown that out ... │
│          ▫  Though there are a lot of encouraging success stories to keep free-lancers gunning for ... │
│          ▫  In short, most free-lancers do fail.  But with proper precautions and controls, you can ... │
│             ▭  Who doesn't make it as a free-lancer?                  ↓ │
└─────────────────────────────────────────────────────────────────────┘
```

To simplify your view of the document, press [Alt][Shift]F to condense each body-text paragraph to one line.

When you are working within a single paragraph of an outline, you can use Word's standard selection techniques (described in Chapter 4) to select the text you want to work with. For example, to select an entire word, you can double-click on that word. To select an entire sentence, press the [Ctrl] key and click on that sentence.

In the normal editing view, you can select an entire paragraph by double-clicking in the selection bar next to that paragraph. In the outline view, however, things work a little differently. You need only click once in the selection bar to select an entire heading. (Each heading comprises one paragraph.) You also can select a heading by first placing the cursor anywhere on the heading, then pressing the [Shift] key and clicking on the heading's icon.

If you double-click in the selection bar, Word will highlight not only the heading next to the pointer, but all the subordinate text below that heading. Another way to make this type of selection is to click once on the appropriate heading icon.

For example, if you click once in the selection bar next to the *heading 1* entry *Cutting loose* at the top of the outline view in Figure 9-7, Word will highlight that entire paragraph. If you double-click in the selection bar next to this heading, however, your screen will look like the one in Figure 9-8. As you can see, Word highlights the paragraph containing the text *Cutting loose* as well as the subordinate text up to the next *heading 1* paragraph. (You can also make this selection by clicking once on the heading icon to the left of the *heading 1* entry *Cutting loose.*)

COLLAPSING AND EXPANDING THE OUTLINE

Even if you have instructed Word to display the first line of each paragraph of body text in the outline view, your outline can get pretty lengthy once you've created several levels of headings and inserted body text under each. If you lose a sense of the document's organization, you can eliminate some of the clutter by collapsing the outline to hide selected headings and body text from view.

For example, suppose you want to see only the *heading 1* entries in your outline. To collapse the outline, click on the *1* icon at the top of the screen (this is called the Show-1 icon). As you can see in Figure 9-9, Word will hide all the body text and subheadings under your *heading 1* entries. In addition, Word will underline those headings whose subordinate text is hidden from view.

To expand the outline again, select another Show icon. For example, if you select the Show-3 icon, Word will expand the outline to display all of the *heading 1*, *heading 2*, and *heading 3* entries. Your body text will remain hidden from view. To bring all your headings and the first lines of body text back into view, simply select the Show-All icon, press the [Alt][Shift]A keys, or press the * key on the numeric keypad.

While the Show icons affect the display of your entire outline, the Expand and Collapse icons—represented by the + and - symbols at the top of the screen—

affect only selected portions of your outline display. You can also use the gray + and - keys on your numeric keypad or the [Alt][Shift]+ and [Alt][Shift]- keys on your keyboard to expand and collapse portions of your outline.

Figure 9-8

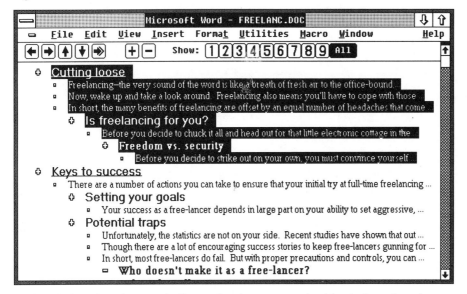

To highlight a heading and all its subordinate text, double-click in the selection bar next to the heading or click once on the heading icon.

Figure 9-9

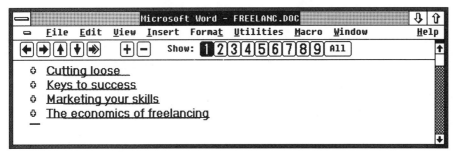

When you select the Show-1 icon, Word will collapse your outline to show only heading 1 *entries.*

Suppose you want to collapse the headings and body text that appear below the second *heading 1* entry in the document shown in Figure 9-8. To do this, click on the heading, then click on the - icon or press the - key on your numeric keypad. As you can see in Figure 9-10, Word will collapse all the body text that originally appeared under that heading. If you click on the - icon or press the - key again, Word will collapse all the *heading 3* entries below that heading; repeating the procedure will collapse all the *heading 2* entries. To reverse this process, simply click on the heading again, then click on the + icon or press the + key on your numeric keypad.

Figure 9-10

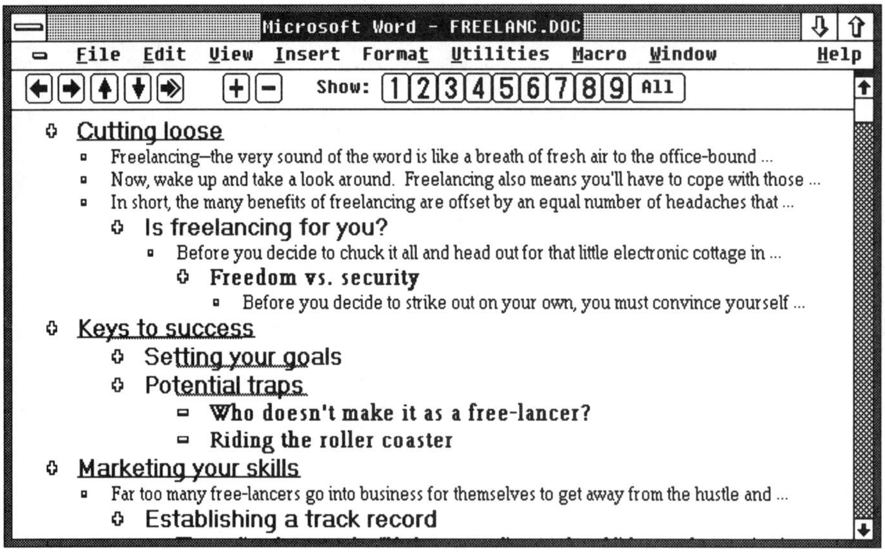

You can use the - icon or the - key on your numeric keypad to collapse selected portions of the outline.

When you use these expand and collapse techniques, Word will not act upon the other text in your outline; instead, it will act only upon the text that falls between the current heading and the next heading of an equal or higher level. In our example, Word collapsed only the text between the second and third *heading 1* entries. You could also click on the *heading 2* entry *Setting your goals* to collapse all the text between that heading and the next heading of equal or higher value, *Potential traps*.

To expand or collapse all the subordinate text below a heading in one step, double-click the appropriate heading icon. You also can click in the selection bar to highlight the entire heading paragraph, then click the - icon. Alternatively, you can select the heading and its subordinate text, then press - on the numeric keypad. This method presents an interesting problem if you try to reverse the command by clicking the + icon or by pressing the + key on the numeric keypad. You'll need to press the + key (or click the + icon) repeatedly to regain all the levels of text you collapsed.

For example, to collapse all the subheadings and body text under the heading *Keys to success* in our sample outline, double-click the heading icon next to this heading. Word will hide the subheadings and body text between that heading and the next *heading 1* entry, *Marketing your skills*. Figure 9-11 shows the results.

Figure 9-11

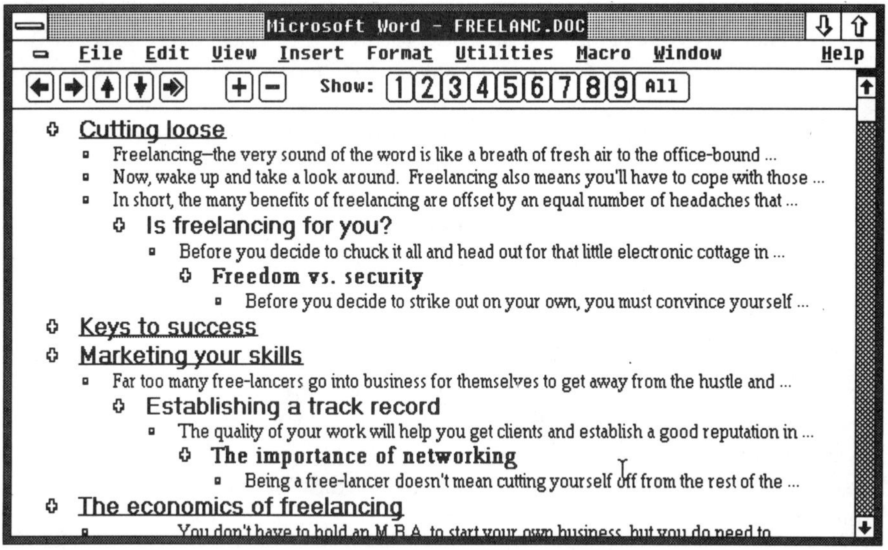

To collapse all the subordinate text under a heading, double-click on its heading icon.

To expand the heading, you can double-click the heading icon once again. You also can select the entire paragraph containing the heading *Keys to success*, and click the + icon or press the + key on the numeric keypad to redisplay all the text between that heading and the next *heading 1* entry. In addition, you can expand a heading by moving the cursor to it and pressing the + key on the numeric keypad.

A navigation tip

When you are working with a long document and want to move to a particular area of it, you can use the outline view to navigate quickly through the document. Just toggle to the outline view, then collapse the outline to the *heading 1* entries by using any of the techniques we discussed earlier. If the *heading 1* entries are too general for you to find your place, keep expanding the outline until you locate the spot you want. Next, highlight the heading or body text that represents the section you want to work with. Finally, scroll the highlighted text to the top of your screen. When you select the Outline command to toggle back to the normal editing view, Word will display the desired section on the screen.

EDITING IN THE OUTLINE VIEW

You can use any of the editing techniques described in Chapters 4 and 6 to edit text in the outline view. However, when you use the Search... and Replace... commands in the outline view, Word will not operate on any text that is collapsed under a heading.

For example, when you issue the Search... command, Word will not find any occurrences of your search text that are located in a collapsed portion of the outline. If you want to search through all the text in your document, you'll probably find it easier to perform the search operation in the normal editing view. However, if you want to find or change occurrences of a text string that appears only in your document's headings, you may be able to streamline your search-and-replace procedure by working in the outline view.

In addition to these standard editing techniques, Word offers a number of special editing features to help you work with text in the outline view. Let's look at some of these features.

Changing a heading level

You can easily change the level of a heading in your outline at any time. To do this, begin by clicking on the heading or by selecting the paragraph containing the heading, then click on the ← or → (Promote or Demote) icon. To change the level of a heading using the keyboard, move the cursor to that heading and press either the [Alt][Shift]← or [Alt][Shift]→ keys. In addition to changing the level number of the selected heading, Word will change the indention of that paragraph to reflect its new level. Word will also adjust the indention of any body text that appears immediately below the selected heading to indicate that it still "belongs to" that heading.

Unless you specifically instruct it to do so, however, Word will not change the levels of other subordinate text in the outline. If you want to promote or demote a heading and all its subordinate text, you must click once on the heading icon or double-click in the selection bar to select the heading and its subordinate text. Then, click on the ← or → icon. Alternatively, you can click on the heading icon and drag it to the left or right. As you drag, your pointer will take on the shape of a double-headed arrow, and a dotted vertical line will indicate where the heading will appear when you release the mouse button. From the keyboard, you can use [F8] and the arrow keys to highlight a block of text, and use [Alt][Shift]← or [Alt][Shift]→ to promote or demote that block.

For example, suppose you want to demote the *heading 1* entry *Keys to success* in Figure 9-7 to a *heading 2* entry. If you click on that heading and click the → icon, the outline will look like Figure 9-12. From the keyboard, you can demote this text by placing the cursor on the paragraph *Keys to success* and pressing [Alt][Shift]➡. As you can see, Word did not demote any of the headings below *Keys to success*.

Figure 9-12

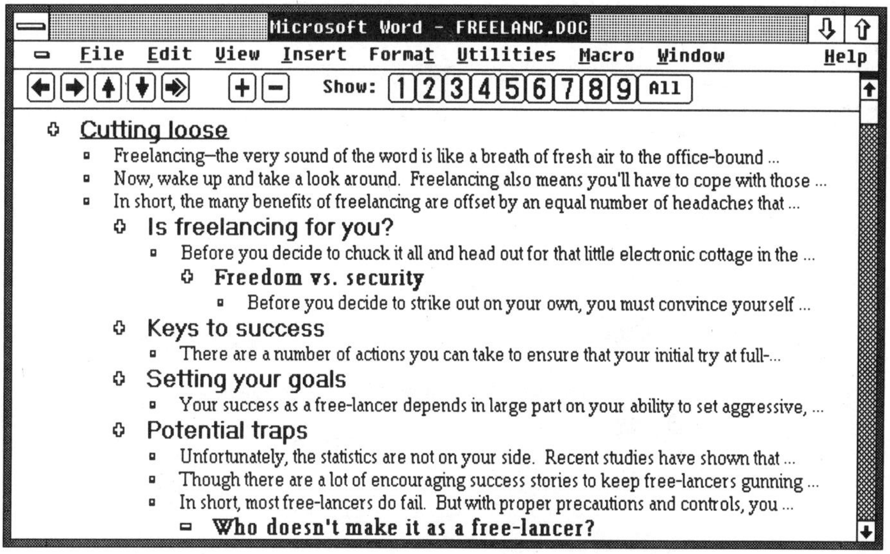

If you click on a heading, then click the ⬅ *or the* ➡ *icon, Word will promote or demote the heading and its body text.*

In addition, any heading can be promoted or demoted by using the [Style] key ([Ctrl]S). For example, to demote *Keys to success* to a *heading 5* entry, place the cursor on that paragraph and press the [Style] key. The status bar will display the message *Which style?* When you type *heading 5* and press [Enter], Word will demote *Keys to success* to a *heading 5* entry. Also, Word will demote any body text associated with that heading.

If you click on the heading icon next to *Keys to success* in Figure 9-7 (or double-click in the selection bar to select the heading and its subordinate text), then click the ➡ icon, your outline will look like the one in Figure 9-13 on the next page. It will also look like Figure 9-13 if you click on the heading icon and drag it one level to the right.

If you're using the keyboard, place the cursor before the word *Keys* in the *heading 1* entry and use the [F8] and the ⬇ key to select all the subordinate headings and body text up to the next *heading 1* entry. To demote the highlighted text, press [Alt][Shift]➡. Figure 9-13 illustrates how Word will demote all the subordinate headings and body text between the *Keys to success* heading and the next *heading 1* entry. In effect, the *Keys to success* heading and its subordinate text now fall under the first *heading 1* entry *Cutting loose*.

Figure 9-13

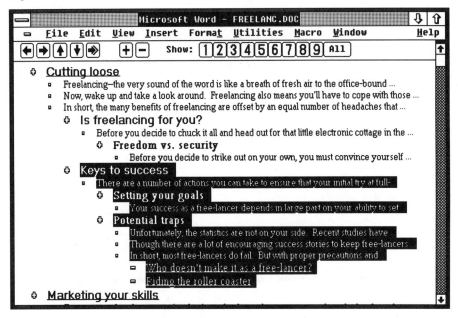

To promote or demote a heading and its subordinate text, double-click in the selection bar before you click the ← *or* → *icon.*

Converting body text to a heading

If you click on a body-text paragraph in the outline view, then click the ← icon or press [Alt][Shift]←, Word will convert that body text to the same level as its immediate superior heading. For example, if you click on the body-text paragraph that begins *Freelancing—the very sound* in the second line of our sample outline, then click the ← icon, Word will promote that entire paragraph to a *heading 1* entry. As you can see in Figure 9-14, when you convert the paragraph to a heading, Word will display the entire contents of that heading rather than only the first line. You might use this technique to view or edit the contents of a body-text paragraph in the outline view, then convert that paragraph back to a body-text paragraph when you're through.

Converting a heading to body text

To convert a heading to body text, click on the heading and click the ⇒ (Demote-to-body-text) icon. Alternatively, you can hold down [Alt] and [Shift], then press 5 on the numeric keypad.

Figure 9-14

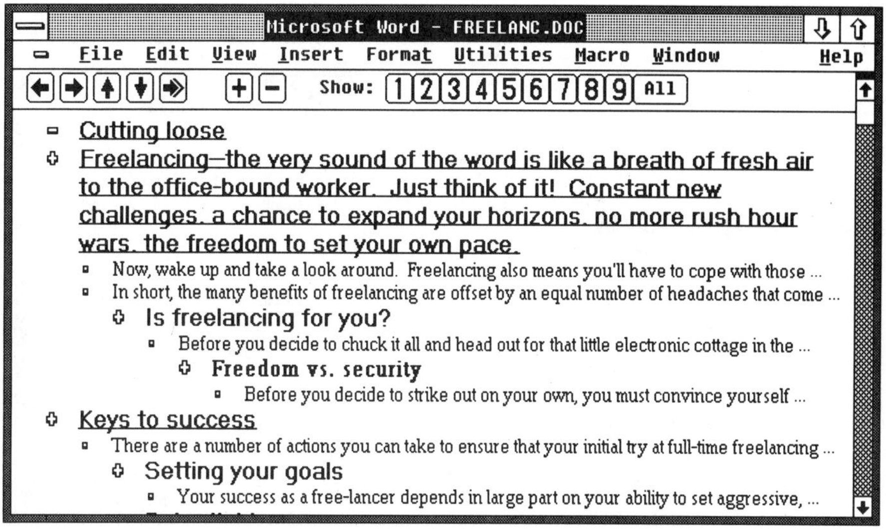

We've converted the first paragraph of body text to a heading 1 *entry.*

When you convert a heading to body text, Word will change the indention of that heading—and any subordinate body text immediately below the heading—to appear $^1/_4$ inch to the right of the heading immediately preceding it. In short, the heading and its body text become part of the subordinate body text for the preceding heading.

For example, if you select the *heading 2* entry *Is freelancing for you?* and click the ➡ icon, your screen will look like the one in Figure 9-15 on the following page. Notice that the body text that was formerly attached to this *heading 2* entry now carries the same indention as the rest of the body text for the *heading 1* entry *Cutting loose*. As you can see, however, Word did not change the *heading 3* entry *Freedom vs. security* that appears below the converted *heading 2* entry.

Dragging text

Just as you can drag a heading icon left and right to promote and demote headings, you can drag a body-text icon to promote and demote body text. If you drag left, you'll promote the body text; if you drag right, you'll demote it.

Inserting a new heading

The easiest way to insert a new heading into an outline is to click in front of the paragraph that is immediately below the spot where you want to place the new heading, then press [Enter]. Word will then insert a new ¶ mark and a heading icon on the line above.

Initially, the new heading will appear at the same level as the heading you clicked on before pressing [Enter]. Of course, you can use the ← and → icons to change the heading level of the paragraph.

Figure 9-15

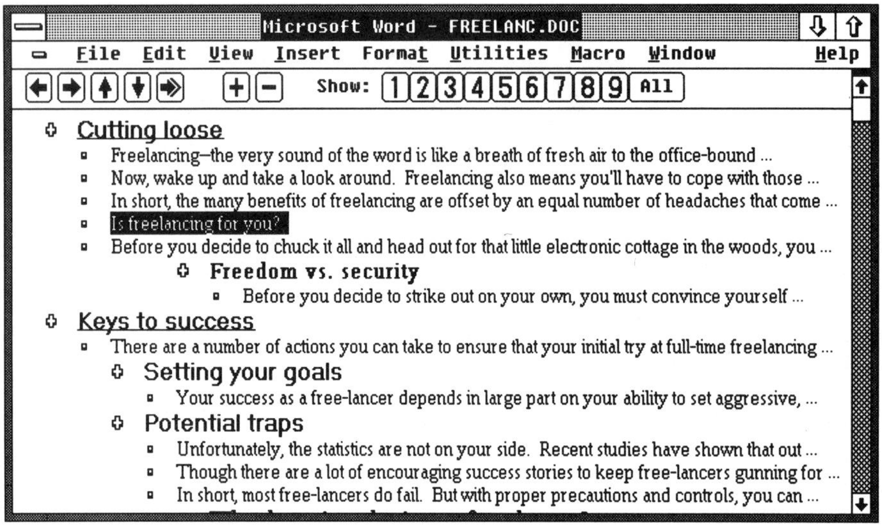

You can use the ➡ *icon to convert any heading in your outline to standard body text.*

Continuing with our sample outline, imagine you want to add a new *heading 2* entry—*Success stories*—between the *heading 3* entry *Freedom vs. security* and the *heading 1* entry *Keys to success.* If you click at the end of the *heading 3* entry and press [Enter], your new heading will appear between the *Freedom vs. security* heading and the text paragraph that begins *Before you decide.*

To get around this problem, place the cursor in front of the *heading 1* entry *Keys to success,* and press [Enter]. As you can see in Figure 9-16, Word will push the heading down a line and insert a new paragraph for you. Now, all you need to do is click the ➡ icon or press [Alt][Shift]➡ to demote this paragraph, then type your new text. Figure 9-17 shows the results.

Deleting a heading

To delete a heading from your outline, be sure to expand the outline before you begin. Otherwise, you may inadvertently delete all the subordinate text for that heading as well. When you select a heading in a collapsed outline, you also select all the subordinate text for that heading.

For example, if you select the *heading 1* entry *Cutting loose* in Figure 9-9, then click the Show-All icon, Word will highlight all the subordinate text between the first and second *heading 1* entries in the outline view. In short, any changes you make to a heading while the outline is collapsed will affect all the subordinate text below that heading.

Figure 9-16

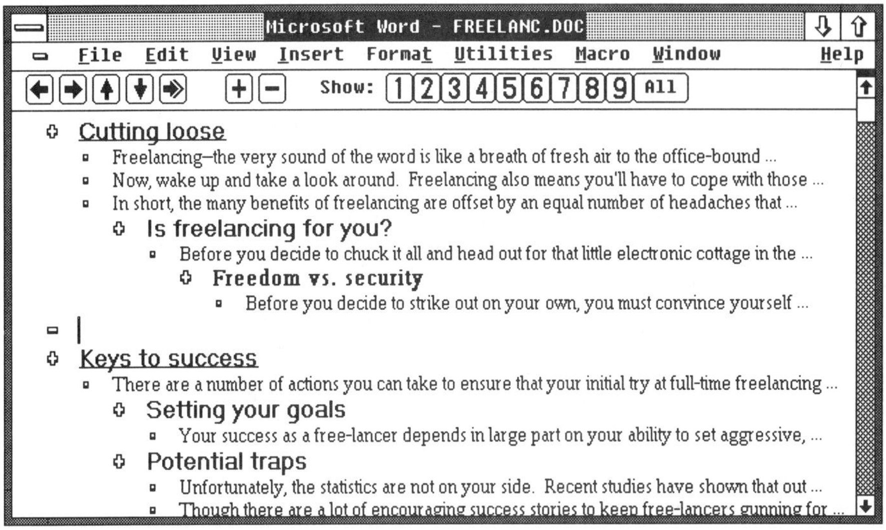

To insert a new heading, click in front of the paragraph immediately below the spot where you want your new heading to appear, and press [Enter].

Figure 9-17

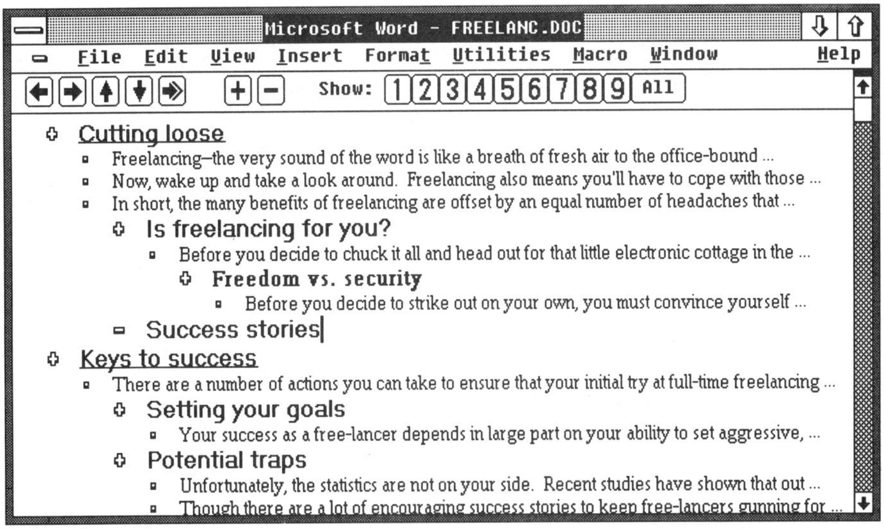

After you create your new blank paragraph, assign the appropriate level and type the new heading text.

Once you have expanded the outline and selected the heading or body-text paragraph you want to delete, press the [Delete] key or issue the Cut command on the Edit menu to remove that heading.

Moving a heading

There are three ways to move blocks of text in the outline view. The first is the standard cut-and-paste procedure—just select the heading and any subordinate text you want to move, issue the Cut command, select the spot where you want to place the text, and issue the Paste command. You also can use the ↑ (Move-up) and ↓ (Move-down) icons or the [Alt][Shift]↑ and [Alt][Shift]↓ keys to move text, or you can click on a heading icon and drag text.

When you use the Cut command to delete or move text in the outline view, your changes may affect more than the text that is visible on your screen. As we've mentioned, selecting a heading with collapsed subordinate text automatically selects that text as well. If you do not want Word to move the subordinate text along with the selected heading, you'll need to expand your outline before you select the heading and issue the Cut command. However, if you want Word to include the subordinate text in your selection, you may find it easier to collapse the outline before you begin the cut-and-paste procedure.

Similarly, when you select your paste area, you may want to expand any collapsed text in that area to ensure that you are not inserting text between a heading and its subordinate text.

In addition to the Cut and Paste commands, you can use the ↑ and ↓ icons in the outline view to rearrange blocks of text. For example, suppose you decide to move the *heading 2* entry *Setting your goals* and its subordinate text. You want to place this text just below the body-text paragraph that begins *Before you decide*. If the portion of the outline you want to move is collapsed, click on the heading icon or in the selection bar next to the heading to select that heading and all of its subordinate text. If your outline is not collapsed, you'll need to double-click in the selection bar or click once on the heading icon to make your selection.

Now, click the ↑ icon or [Alt][Shift]↑ to move the selected text block toward the beginning of the document. When you do this, Word will move the selected block up through the outline one heading at a time. Just keep clicking the ↑ icon or pressing [Alt][Shift]↑ until the text block is in the position you want. (If you need to move the text block a long distance, you can save time by collapsing some or all of the outline text before you begin.) Figure 9-18 shows the results.

Just as you can drag text left and right in the outline view, you can click on a heading icon and drag a heading and its subordinate text up or down to reposition it in your document. By the way, you'll notice that when you move a block of text vertically in the outline view, you change the order of the document's paragraphs, but you do not change the heading levels or the relationship between the headings and body text.

Figure 9-18

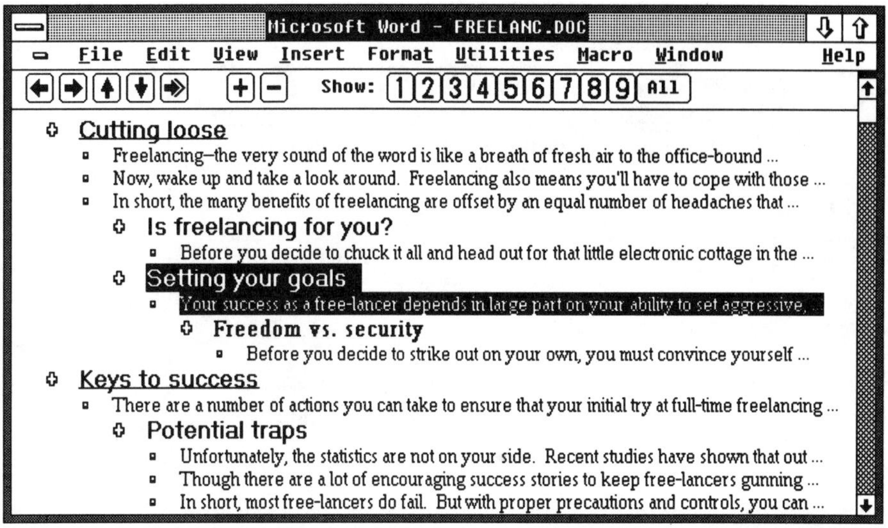

To reposition a selection in the outline view, you can click the ↑ *and* ↓ *icons or press the [Alt][Shift]*↑ *and [Alt][Shift]*↓ *keys.*

As we mentioned at the beginning of this chapter, Word's outline view is designed to work in conjunction with the Style Sheet facility. When you edit a document in the outline view, Word assumes that you will want to use each topic in the outline as a heading in your document. When you switch from the outline view to the normal editing view, Word will automatically set up a style sheet, assigning a different style name to each level of the outline.

To illustrate, let's continue with our sample article. If you switch to the normal editing view, you'll see a style name displayed in the Style box on the ruler. This name reflects the style applied to the paragraph on which the cursor is positioned.

Each level you use in the outline view has a corresponding style name on the document's style sheet. If you choose the Styles… or Define Styles… command from the Format menu, you'll see that the style sheet in our sample document includes the style names *heading 1, heading 2, heading 3,* and *heading 4.* Like other document style sheets, this one will also include the style named *Normal,* as shown in Figure 9-19 on the next page.

Although Word gives you a head start by setting up styles named *heading 1, heading 2,* and so forth, it does not provide much distinction in the formatting of these styles. Table 9-1 shows the default definitions for each style.

THE OUTLINE VIEW AND STYLE SHEETS

Figure 9-19

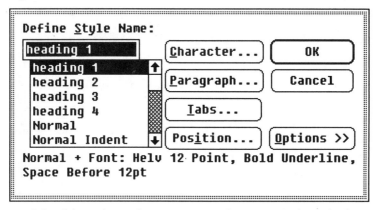

Each level from the outline is now a style name on the style sheet.

Table 9-1

Style name	Default definitions
heading 1	Normal + Font: Helv 12 Point, Bold Underline, Space Before 12pt
heading 2	Normal + Font: Helv 12 Point, Bold, Space Before 6pt
heading 3	Normal + Font: 12 Point, Bold, Indent: Left 0.25"
heading 4	Normal + Font: 12 Point, Underline, Indent: Left 0.25"
heading 5	Normal + Bold, Indent: Left 0.5"
heading 6	Normal + Underline, Indent: Left 0.5"
heading 7	Normal + Italic, Indent: Left 0.5"
heading 8	Normal + Italic, Indent: Left 0.5"
heading 9	Normal + Italic, Indent: Left 0.5"

Let's suppose you want the main body text in your document to appear in 12-point Helv type with a $^1/_4$-inch indent on the first line of each paragraph. To alter the *Normal* style to meet these specifications, choose Define Styles… from the Format menu and select *Normal* as the style name. Then, open the Character dialog box, choose Helv from the Font list box, choose 12 from the Points list box, and choose OK. Next, open the Paragraph dialog box, enter *0.25"* for the first-line indent, and choose OK. Finally, close the Define Styles dialog box by selecting OK. Figure 9-20 shows how the screen from Figure 9-5 will look after you've modified the *Normal* style. Notice that all the text from the outline now appears in 12-point Helv with a $^1/_4$-inch indent.

Once you've modified the *Normal* style, you can make additional changes to the definitions for each of the *heading* styles. Continuing with our example, imagine you want the *heading 1* entries to appear in 14-point bold, the *heading 2* entries to appear in 14-point plain, and the *heading 3* entries to appear in 14-point italic. You also want each heading to be aligned with the left margin instead of being indented like the *Normal* text, and you want to retain the existing paragraph spacing settings for the *heading 1* and *heading 2* entries.

Figure 9-20

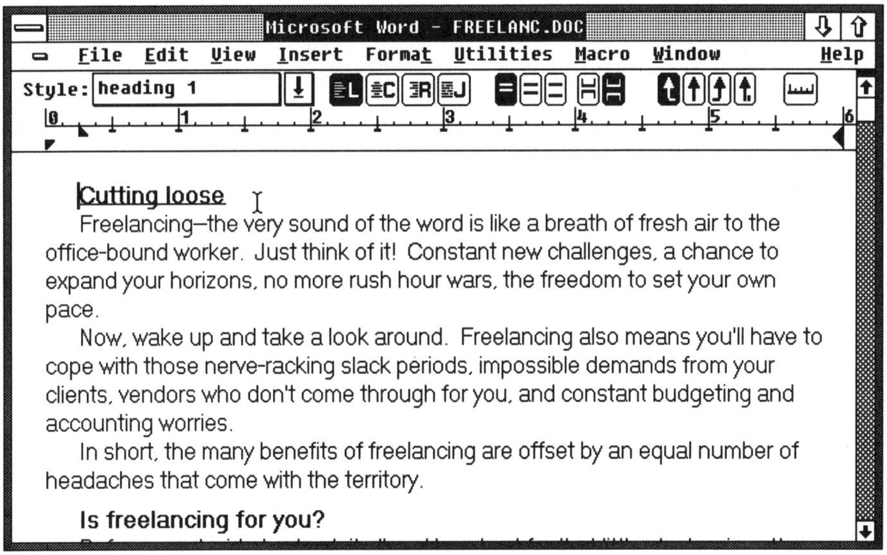

When you modify the Normal *style, Word will also change the formatting of each* heading *style based on* Normal.

To modify each style, simply follow the standard procedure that we described in Chapter 8. Open the Define Styles dialog box, select the name of the style you want to modify, then select the character and paragraph formats for this heading level. When you choose OK in the Define Styles dialog box, Word will apply the specified formats to the headings in your document. Figure 9-21 on the following page shows the first few headings in our sample document after we modified the *heading* styles.

If you decide you don't want all of your headings to appear in your finished document, simply change the style definition for that heading level to include the hidden format. When you deselect the Hidden Text check box in the Preferences dialog box, Word will hide the selected headings in both the normal editing and outline views.

As you're changing the definitions for each *heading* style, you may want to change the Based On style in the expanded Define Styles dialog box as well. Instead of using *Normal* as the Based On style for each of the *heading* styles, you may want to base each *heading* style on the next highest *heading* style. Specifically, the *heading 3* style could be based on *heading 2*, which could be based on *heading 1*, which could be based on *Normal.* That way, when you make format changes to the *heading 1* style—new indention settings, for example— those changes will affect all headings.

Figure 9-21

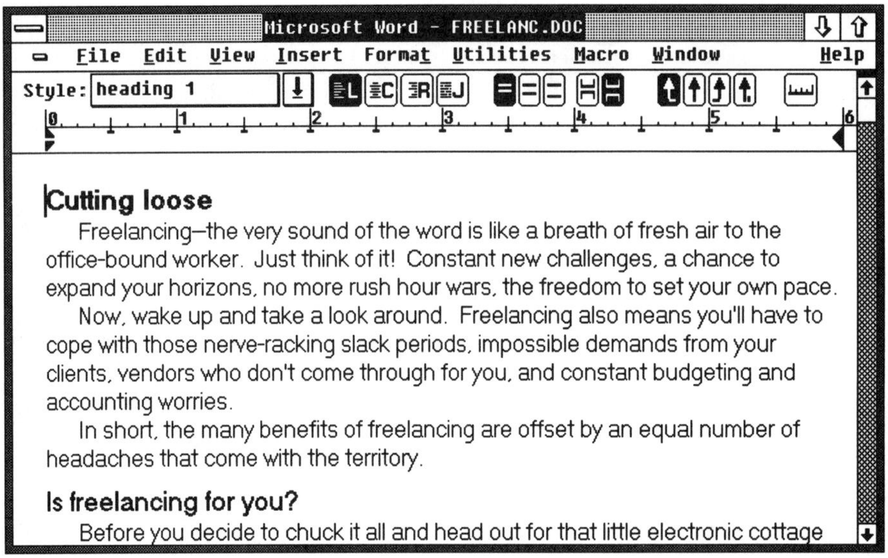

When you modify the definitions for each heading level, Word will apply those new formatting instructions to your document.

In the expanded Define Styles dialog box, you'll also notice that Word uses the Next Style specification *Normal* for all of the *heading* styles. As you saw earlier, when you click at the end of a heading in the normal editing view and press [Enter] to begin a new paragraph, Word assumes you want that text to appear in the *Normal* style. If you want to use a different format for the body text, you can change the Next Style setting.

As you already know, while you're viewing the document in the outline view, you can change the level of any heading by placing the cursor on it and clicking the ← or → icon or using the [Alt][Shift]← or [Alt][Shift]→ keys. Word will, of course, change the indention and heading number of the text in the outline view. In addition, when you switch to the normal editing view, you'll see that Word has reformatted that text by applying a different style.

If you want, you can change the level of any heading in the normal editing view with the Define Styles... or Styles... command. When you return to the outline view, your heading will be promoted or demoted to the appropriate level.

To print your document outline, just activate the outline view and issue the Print... command. You can control which headings are included in the printed outline by expanding or collapsing the outline on the screen. If the first lines of any body-text paragraphs are visible in the outline view, Word will print those paragraphs in their entirety.

In the outline view, Word ignores any paragraph formats you may have assigned to the text in the normal editing view, but recognizes your character formats as well as the settings in the Document and Section dialog boxes, when it prints the outline. Any headers, footers, section breaks, or manual page breaks you may have created will also be included in your printed outline. Figure 9-22 shows the printed version of the outline, collapsed to show only heading levels 1, 2, and 3.

PRINTING THE OUTLINE

Figure 9-22

Cutting loose
　　Is freelancing for you?
　　　　Freedom vs. security
Keys to success
　　Setting your goals
　　Potential traps
　　　　Who doesn't make it as a free-lancer?
　　　　Riding the roller coaster
Marketing your skills
　　Establishing a track record
　　　　The importance of networking
The economics of freelancing
　　Cash flow considerations
　　　　Estimating your overhead
　　Developing a fee schedule
　　　　What will the traffic bear?

You can use the Print... command on the File menu to generate a printed copy of your outline.

Once you have created an outline, you can use Word's Renumber... command on the Utilities menu to number some or all of the outline's headings and body text. As you modify the outline, Word will automatically update the numbers next to the headings and body text. Additionally, you can choose between three numbering styles: legal, outline, or sequence. We will show you how to add numbers to an outline in Chapter 16.

NUMBERING THE OUTLINE

In this chapter

Fields **10**

*I*n this chapter, we'll introduce you to one of Word's most exciting capabilities—fields. We'll start by telling you what fields are and showing you how to enter them into your document. Then, we'll show you how to display and recalculate a field's result, how to edit a field, and how to change the format of a field's result. Finally, we'll examine Word's DATE and TIME fields, summary info fields, and statistical fields. We will discuss the rest of Word's fields in the appropriate places later in the book.

WHAT ARE FIELDS?

The ability to insert fields into a document is a feature that distinguishes Word for Windows from other word processing programs. Fields provide you with tremendous flexibility and power and, in fact, redefine the whole function of word processing. A field is a special code you can enter into a document. All of Word's fields fall into one of three categories: result, marker, or action. We'll explain each of these field categories before we show you the forms of fields.

Result fields

A result field retrieves a particular piece of information and places it into the document. An example of a result field is the DATE field, which retrieves the current date from your computer's system clock. Similarly, the AUTHOR field retrieves the name of the document's author from the Summary Info dialog box and places it into the document.

Most of the fields you'll enter into your documents will be result fields. We'll look at several examples of these fields in this chapter and in other chapters throughout the book.

Marker fields

A marker field merely supplies information about the document to Word—it does not return a result. For example, the Index Entry field (XE) marks the words that should appear as an entry in the document's index. The Index Entry field does not return a result of its own—it merely provides information that Word uses when it compiles the index.

Action fields

Unlike result and marker fields, actions fields tell Word to perform an action. For example, the FILLIN field tells Word to prompt the user for some information and to store that information in the document. Some action fields tell Word to perform the action only when you update the fields in the document. Others instruct Word to perform the action automatically.

THE FORMS OF FIELDS

While fields can perform many different tasks, all fields have similar forms. For instance, all fields have names. A field's name is a short, descriptive word that identifies what the field does. In addition, many fields have one or more arguments or switches. A field's arguments might tell the field what to act upon, or they might control the way the field's result is displayed in the document. For example, in the field

{DATE \@ "MMM-yy"}

the field name is DATE and the arguments are \@ and *MMM-yy*. This field tells Word to retrieve the current date from your computer's system clock and to display it in the MMM-yy format.

Field names

As we mentioned, a field's name is a short description of the field's purpose. For example, the DATE field returns the current date. Similarly, the NUMWORDS field returns the number of words in the current document. (Throughout this book, we will display all field names in uppercase.)

Field names are always enclosed in the field characters { and }. These characters tell Word that the enclosed text is a field and not just regular text. Although the field characters look like regular braces, you cannot generate these characters by typing them from your keyboard. Instead, you'll need to enter these characters with the [Insert field] key ([Ctrl][F9]). We'll show you how to do this in a moment.

Arguments

Many fields require one or more arguments. A field's argument either tells Word what to operate on or how to display the field's result. For example, the single argument of the field *{INCLUDE "BUDGET.DOC"}* is the document name BUDGET.DOC. This field tells Word to place the contents of the document BUDGET.DOC into the current document. Notice that the argument appears within quotation marks. Although Word requires you to place quotation marks only around multiple-word arguments, we recommend that you enclose all arguments within quotation marks to establish consistency and to avoid errors. You must use double quotation marks (" ") to enclose arguments; single quotation marks will not work.

When a field requires more than one argument, you must use a space to separate the arguments. For example, the field *{SET "Chapter4" "Word Basics"}* has two arguments: the bookmark name *Chapter4* and the text *Word Basics*. This field assigns the name *Chapter4* to the text *Word Basics*. You will notice that the two arguments in this field are enclosed in quotation marks and are separated by a single space. If you need to use a literal quotation mark within an argument, you must precede it with a backslash (\). If you need to include a backslash as part of an argument, you must type two backslashes (\\).

Several fields require no argument at all. For example, the field {AUTHOR}, which returns the name of the document's author, accepts no arguments, nor does the field {NUMWORDS}, which returns the number of words in the document.

The arguments of fields can be literal text, literal values, expressions, bookmarks, identifiers, switches, or other fields. Let's look briefly at some examples of each type of argument.

Some fields accept literal text as an argument. For example, if you want to use the INCLUDE field to place the contents of the document BUDGET.DOC into the current document, you can use the field

Literal text

{INCLUDE "BUDGET.DOC"}

Notice that, in this case, you type the name of the appropriate document as the field's argument. In Chapters 12 and 21, we'll show you other ways to use the INCLUDE field.

You'll sometimes need to supply a mathematical expression as the argument for a field. The = field (often called the Expression field in Word's documentation) calculates the mathematical expression you supply and returns the result. For example, the field

Expressions

{= 2+2}

returns *4*. You'll notice that the = field is the only field that does not accept quotation marks around its argument. In Chapter 16, we'll show you examples of using the = field.

As you'll learn in Chapter 13, a bookmark is a name you assign to some selected text in the document. For instance, you might assign the name *conclusion* to the last paragraph in your document. Once you've created a bookmark, you

Bookmarks

can supply its name as an argument to several fields. For example, if you've created the bookmark *conclusion*, the field

{PAGEREF "conclusion"}

will return the number of the page that contains the conclusion. We'll discuss the PAGEREF field in detail in Chapter 13.

Identifiers

Some fields require an identifier argument. The best way to illustrate the purpose of an identifier argument is to show you an example of a field that uses identifiers. As we'll explain in Chapter 13, you can use the SEQ field to label a series of items, such as figures, tables, or illustrations. Because you'll sometimes need to label two separate series of items in a single document, you'll need to supply an identifier argument to the SEQ field so that it numbers the items in each series separately. For example, to create sequential numbers for a series of figures, you would use the field

{SEQ "figure"}

To create the numbers for a series of tables in the same document, you would use the field

{SEQ "table"}

The identifier arguments *figure* and *table* allow the SEQ field to correctly number both the document's figures and tables.

Switches

In addition to the types of arguments we've mentioned, fields can contain switches. A switch, which consists of a backslash (\) followed by a single character, changes the way a field works or the way it formats its result. Some switches are followed by an additional argument that further defines the effect.

For example, the field {TIME} returns the current time in h:m AM/PM format. If you want it to return the current time in 24-hour format, you can use the field

{TIME \@ "HH:mm"}

The \@ switch tells the field {TIME} to display its result in a special format—the one specified by the argument *HH:mm*. We'll discuss switches and the TIME field later in this chapter.

ENTERING FIELDS

Now that we've given you an overview of fields, we'll discuss the techniques you'll use to enter them into a document. Fortunately, Word provides multiple techniques for entering fields, using both the command menus and the keyboard.

Because Word offers dozens of fields, and because many fields accept several arguments, it will take you a little while to learn the forms of the fields you'll want to use. Fortunately, the Field... command on the Insert menu makes it easy to enter a field even if you haven't memorized its form.

Entering fields with the Field... command

To enter a field into your document, begin by moving the cursor to the position in which you want to place the field. Next, select the Field... command to bring up the Field dialog box shown in Figure 10-1.

Figure 10-1

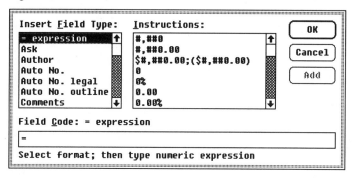

The Field dialog box makes it easy to enter fields.

The Insert Field Type list box in the upper-left corner of the Field dialog box allows you to select the type of field you want to insert. (This list box shows a long version of each field name instead of the standard field names.) The Instructions list box lets you specify special instructions, such as how you want Word to format the field's result. The Field Code text box at the bottom of the dialog box lets you customize the field code.

Once the Field dialog box appears, you should choose the type of field you want to insert from the Insert Field Type list box. You'll notice that as you select different field types in the list box, Word will automatically place the selected field's code in the Field Code text box at the bottom of the dialog box. Word also will display the proper syntax for that field just above the Field Code text box and present an instructional prompt just below it. After you choose a field type, move to the Instructions list box and specify any necessary, additional information. Finally, choose OK to enter the field into the document.

Suppose you want to use a DATE field to insert the current date at the top of the document shown in Figure 10-2. To do this, move the cursor to the top of the document, then select the Field... command to display the Field dialog box shown in Figure 10-1. At this point, select the Date option from the Insert Field Type list

An example

box, and choose OK. Figure 10-3 shows the result. As you can see, Word displays the field code *{date }* instead of the field's result. We'll show you how to display a field's result in a moment.

By the way, as you can see in Figure 10-3, the Field... command enters the field name in lowercase. However, to help you distinguish field names from the rest of the text in this book, we'll display field names in uppercase.

Figure 10-2

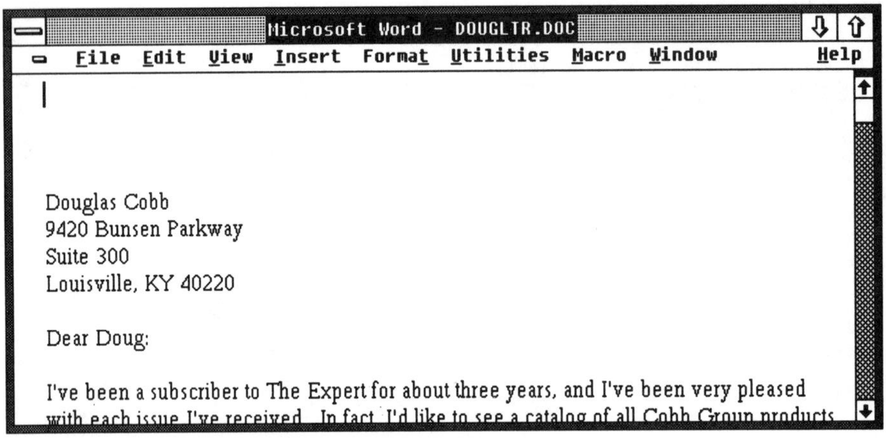

We'll insert a DATE field at the top of this document.

Figure 10-3

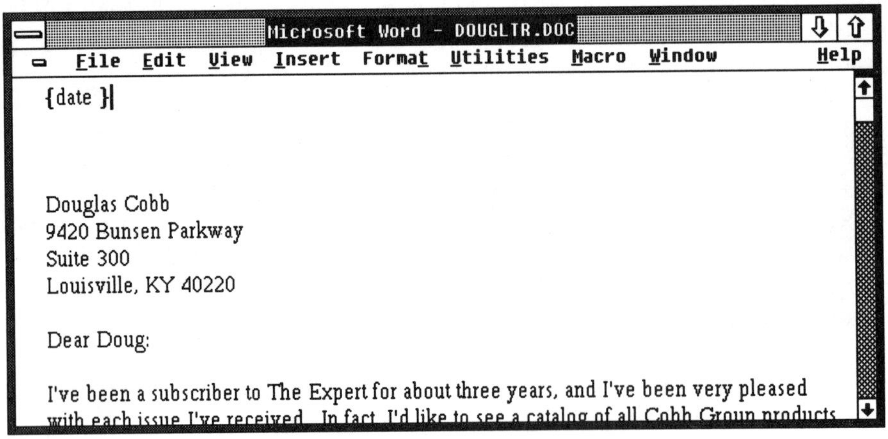

Word initially displays a field's code instead of its result.

As an alternative to the Field... command, Word provides a keyboard technique for inserting fields into the document. First, move the cursor to the appropriate place in the document, then press the [Insert field] key ([Ctrl][F9]). Word will then enter a pair of field characters ({}) into the document and place the cursor between them. At this point, type the appropriate field name and any necessary arguments.

For example, suppose you want to enter the field {AUTHOR} at the current position of the cursor. To do this, begin by pressing the [Insert field] key. When you do, Word will insert a pair of field characters and place the cursor between them. Finally, complete the field entry by typing *AUTHOR*.

The [Insert field] key

Once you've entered a field into a document, you'll want to make sure the field returns the correct result. Consequently, you need to know how to tell Word to display field results instead of field codes, and how to update a field's result. Let's consider each of these topics in detail.

DISPLAYING FIELD RESULTS

As you noticed in the example above, Word displays a field's code the first time you enter a field into a document. To display the field's result instead of its code, you'll need to switch from the Show Codes mode to the Show Results mode. To make the switch, you'll need to toggle the Field Codes setting on the View menu shown in Figure 10-4. The check mark next to the Field Codes setting indicates that Word is currently in the Show Codes mode. If you select Field Codes, Word will remove the check mark and toggle to the Show Results mode.

Toggling the Field Codes setting

Figure 10-4

```
┌─────────┐
│ View    │
├─────────┴──────────┐
│  Outline           │
│  Draft             │
│  Page              │
├────────────────────┤
│  Ribbon            │
│  Ruler             │
│  Status Bar        │
│  Footnotes         │
│  Annotations       │
├────────────────────┤
│ √Field Codes       │
│  Preferences...    │
│  Short Menus       │
└────────────────────┘
```

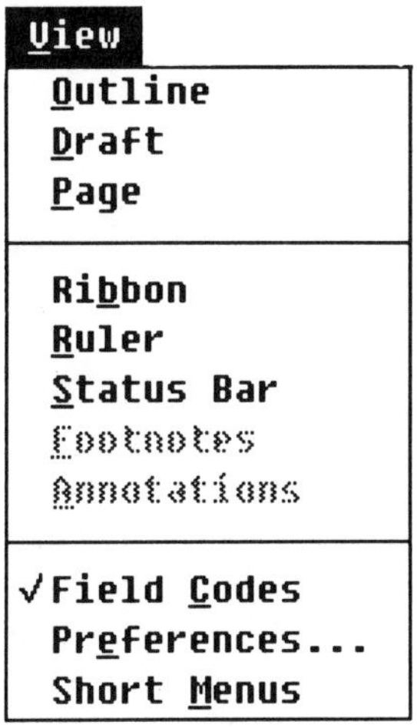

Selecting the Field Codes setting on the View menu toggles Word between the Show Codes and Show Results modes.

For example, suppose you've inserted the field {DATE} into your document, as we've done in Figure 10-3. To display this field's result instead of its code, pull down the View menu and select the Field Codes setting. Word will then display the field's result in place of its code, as shown in Figure 10-5.

Figure 10-5

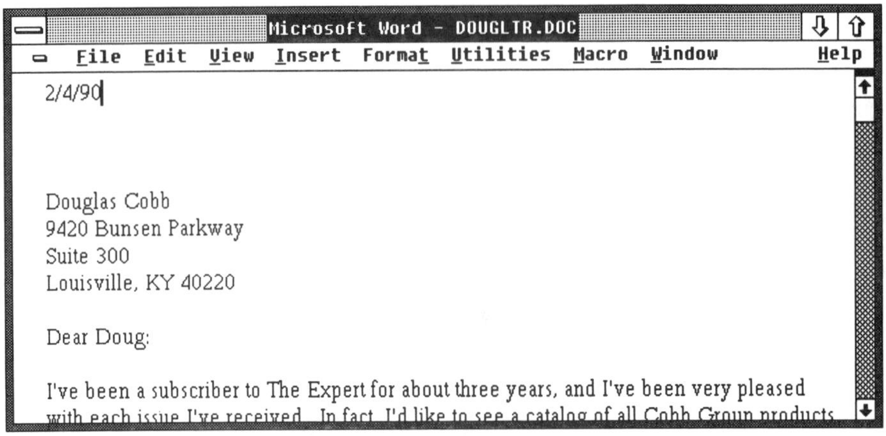

Deselecting the Field Codes setting allows you to see the results of all the fields in the document.

If you want, you can toggle a field between the Show Results and Show Codes modes. To do this, highlight the field or place the cursor somewhere within the field's code or result, and press the [Toggle field codes view] key ([Shift][F9]). Word will then toggle the display of the selected field. If you toggle the view mode of a field that appears in multiple panes or windows, Word will toggle that field's setting only in the current pane or window.

Updating a field's result

Word automatically recalculates most result fields whenever you issue the Print Merge... or Print... command on the File menu. However, you can use the [Update field] key ([F9]) to update a field's result anytime you want. Fortunately, Word allows you to update a field's result in either the Show Codes or Show Results mode.

To update a field, first highlight its field code or field result. If you want, you can just place the cursor anywhere within the field characters, { and }, or within the field's result text instead of highlighting the entire field. Then, press the [Update field] key. If you're in the Show Results mode, you'll immediately see Word replace the old result with the new one. If you're in the Show Codes mode, you won't notice a change until you activate the Show Results mode.

As you might expect, updating a field automatically updates all of its nested fields. (We will discuss nested fields later in this chapter.) In addition, the [Update field] key will not update marker and action fields or locked fields. If you accidentally update a field, you can use the Undo command to restore the field's previous result.

Displaying a field's code and result simultaneously

Fortunately, Word provides you with a way to view both a field's code and its result simultaneously. To do this, use the split box at the top of the vertical scroll bar to split the document window into two different views. (Appendix 1 shows you how to do this.) Next, place the cursor in the portion of the document below the split bar, then toggle the Field Codes setting on the View menu to change the view mode of that portion. Finally, adjust the size and position of the document on either side of the split bar so you can see both the field code and its result on the screen at the same time. At this point, you can view field codes on one side of the split bar and the results of those fields on the other side.

For example, consider the screen shown in Figure 10-6. The top portion of this screen shows the document's field codes, while the bottom portion shows the document's field results. By setting up our screen in this fashion, we can modify the field codes in the top portion and view the results of our changes in the bottom portion.

Figure 10-6

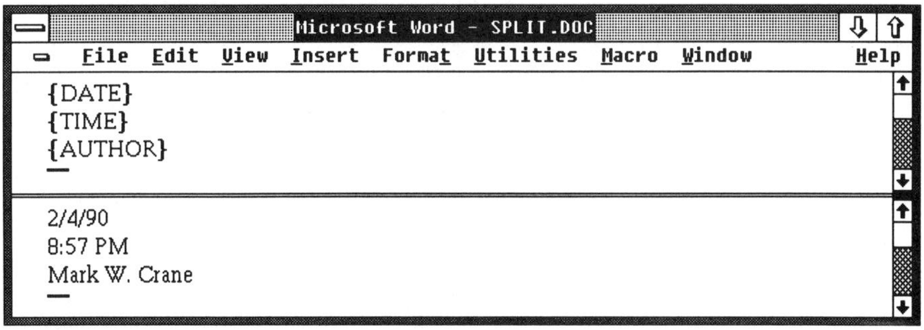

Splitting the document window into two panes lets you see field codes and their results at the same time.

Locking a field

If you want to prevent Word from updating a field's result, you can "lock" that field. To do this, either highlight the field or place the cursor within the field code or result, and press the [Lock field] key ([Ctrl][F11]). Unfortunately, locked fields don't look any different from unlocked fields. In fact, the only way to tell if a field is locked is to select it and press the [Update field] key. When you do this, your computer will beep and not update the selected field.

To unlock a field, highlight the field or position the cursor within it, and press the [Unlock field] key ([Ctrl][Shift][F11]). Again, you won't realize the effects of unlocking a field until you use the [Update field] key to recalculate the field's result.

Unlinking a field

Although you can always use the [Lock field] key to prevent Word from changing a field's results, you'll sometimes want to use Word's [Unlink field] key to accomplish this task. When you select a field and press the [Unlink field] key ([Ctrl][Shift][F9]), Word will replace the selected field with its most recent result. If the selected field has no result, pressing the [Unlink field] key will delete the field. Of course, if you accidentally press the [Unlink field] key, you can use the Undo command to restore the field.

Moving to the next or previous field

Word provides a couple of handy keyboard techniques for moving to the next or previous field in a document. To move the highlight to the next field, press the [Next field] key ([F11]); to move the highlight to the previous field, press the [Previous field] key ([Shift][F11]).

If you've entered some hidden fields into your document, there are a couple of rules you'll want to keep in mind. If you press the [Next field] key to move to the next field in your document and that field is hidden from view, Word will move the cursor to the place where the field exists in the document even though you can't see the field on the screen. In order to see the field, you'll need to select the Hidden Text check box in the Preferences dialog box.

Interestingly, the [Next field] and [Previous field] keys will skip over Word's marker fields (such as XE and TC), which are automatically assigned the hidden format. To move to a marker field, you'll need to select the Hidden Text check box and use the Search... command to search for the field's name.

EDITING FIELDS

Once you've entered a field into a document, you can edit the text in that field much like you edit other text. Of course, the effect of your editing changes depends on whether you're viewing field codes or field results.

Editing field codes

If you're viewing field codes instead of field results, you can edit any of a field's characters except { and }. For instance, if you accidentally enter the field {SAVEDATE}, and you want to change it to the field {CREATEDATE}, you can highlight the word *SAVE* inside the field characters, and then type the word *CREATE*. Similarly, if you enter the field

{DATE \@ "d-MMM-yy"}

and you want to change the field's argument from *d-MMM-yy* to *MMMM, yy*, you can just use standard editing techniques.

If you're viewing field results instead of field codes, you can edit only the text returned by result fields. In fact, you can add to, delete, or copy the text returned by a result field. However, if you make some changes to a field's result text, and then update that field, Word will replace the changes you've made with the field's new result. For this reason, we advise against modifying a field's result. Instead, if you want to display something other than a field's true result, first hide or delete the field, then type in the text you want to display.

Editing field results

To delete a field, highlight the entire field and press [Delete]. If you are viewing field codes, you can highlight the entire field by highlighting either the { or } field character. If you are viewing field results, you can highlight an entire result field by double-clicking on the first or last word in the field's result.

Deleting and copying a field

If you want to remove a field from a document but retain a copy of it on the Clipboard, highlight the field and issue the Cut command on the Edit menu. After you've placed the field onto the Clipboard, you can use the Paste command to paste it back into that document or into another document.

To make a copy of a field, first highlight the entire field, then issue the Copy command to place a copy of the field onto the Clipboard. At this point, simply move the cursor to the place where you want to insert the copy, and issue the Paste command.

You cannot edit a field that is hidden unless you activate the Hidden Text option in the Preferences dialog box. Once you've activated this option to display all the hidden fields in the current document, you can edit the hidden fields just as you would a normal field.

Working with hidden fields

Remember that you can use the [Next field] ([F11]) and [Previous field] ([Shift][F11]) keys to help you locate hidden fields in the current document. If the next or previous field is hidden, pressing the [Next field] or [Previous field] key will move the cursor just in front of the first character in the field. However, these keys will not move to Word's marker fields.

Fortunately, Word provides several ways to control how it displays a field's result. In this section, we'll explore all of Word's field formatting techniques.

FORMATTING FIELDS

Word makes it easy to assign character formats to a field's result. To do this, first activate the Field Codes setting on the View menu, then apply the desired character format to the first character in the field's name. As you know, you can use either the Character... command on the Format menu or the ribbon to apply character formats. Once you've applied the new formatting, update the field to show the result in the new format.

Character formatting

For example, suppose you want the result of the field {DATE} to appear in bold. To do this, simply assign the bold format to the letter *D* in the field name, like this:

{**DATE**}

Then, while the cursor is still within the field, press the [Update field] key to update that field. You can use this technique to apply any of Word's character formats to a field's result. To remove character formatting after you've applied it, reformat the first character in the field's name.

If you apply character formats to more than just the first character in the field name, Word will ignore those formats. The only character that controls the format of the field's result is the first character in the field's name.

You might be wondering what will happen if you display the result of a field and then apply character formatting to some text in that result. If you do this, Word will recognize the formatting you apply until it updates the field. Each time Word updates the field, it will lose the formatting you applied.

The only fields upon which this "first character" formatting technique will not work are fields that import data from other programs. To apply character formats to the results of these fields, you'll need to add a couple of arguments to your field code. We'll explain how to do this in a moment.

Format switch

The format switch, *, lets you apply some special formatting to a field's result. Specifically, you can use the format switch to control case, to change the numeric format, or to apply character formatting. The form of the format switch is

* *formatName*

where *formatName* is the argument that defines the special formatting you want to apply.

Controlling case

Word offers four arguments that control the case used to display the field's result: *upper, lower, firstcap, and caps.* As you would expect, including the argument *upper* after the format switch tells Word to display every character in the field's result in uppercase. The argument *lower* tells Word to display all the characters in the field's result in lowercase. The argument *firstcap* converts the first character in the result to uppercase, and the remaining characters to lowercase. Finally, the argument *caps* instructs Word to uppercase the first character of each word and to lowercase the remaining characters.

To illustrate how these four arguments control a field's result, let's suppose you've entered the text *A Passion for Excellence* into the Title text box in the Summary Info dialog box. Table 10-1 shows how each of the four case arguments will affect the result of the TITLE field.

Table 10-1

Field code	Result
{TITLE}	A Passion for Excellence
{TITLE * "upper"}	A PASSION FOR EXCELLENCE
{TITLE * "lower"}	a passion for excellence
{TITLE * "firstcap"}	A passion for excellence
{TITLE * "caps"}	A Passion For Excellence

Word's format switch not only allows you to convert the case of a field's result, it also allows you to convert a field's result to several numeric formats. Table 10-2 lists these formats along with their corresponding arguments.

Controlling numeric formats

Table 10-2

Format	Argument
Arabic number	arabic
Ordinal number	ordinal
Roman numeral	roman
Alphabetic characters	alphabetic
Cardinal text	cardtext
Ordinal text	ordtext
Hexidecimal number	hex
Cardinal text with a fraction	dollartext

To display a field's result in one of these formats, you simply supply to the field the format switch and the appropriate argument. Table 10-3 on the following page uses the NUMPAGES field to illustrate how you can convert a result to each of the available formats.

You may have noticed that the first letter in the *roman* and *alphabetic* arguments controls the case of the result. If the argument's first letter is lowercase, the result will appear in lowercase as well. If you uppercase the first letter in the *roman* and *alphabetic* arguments, Word will display the result in all uppercase. The case of the other arguments in Table 10-2 has no effect on the result.

The last two arguments you can use along with the format switch are the *charformat* and *mergeformat* arguments. You'll need to use these arguments only in fields that import information from other programs. The *charformat* argument tells Word to display the field's result in the format you've applied to the field code's first letter. The *mergeformat* argument, on the other hand, tells Word to merge the format of the field code's first letter with the format applied to the imported information.

Formatting fields that import data

Table 10-3

Field code	Result
{NUMPAGES}	11
{NUMPAGES* "arabic"}	11
{NUMPAGES* "ordinal"}	11th
{NUMPAGES* "roman"}	xi
{NUMPAGES* "Roman"}	XI
{NUMPAGES* "alphabetic"}	k
{NUMPAGES* "Alphabetic"}	K
{NUMPAGES* "cardtext"}	Eleven
{NUMPAGES* "ordtext"}	Eleventh
{NUMPAGES* "hex"}	B
{NUMPAGES* "dollartext"}	Eleven and NO/100

For example, suppose you're using the field

{INCLUDE "C:\\FORECAST.XLS"}

to import a Microsoft Excel worksheet named FORECAST.XLS. In this case, let's assume that all the data in the source worksheet is assigned the italic format.

Now, to import the data and display it in bold (not italic), you would enter the field

{INCLUDE "C:\\FORECAST.XLS" * "charformat"}

Notice that you must apply bold formatting to the first letter in the field name and include the arguments * *charformat* in order to display the worksheet data in bold.

If you want to import the italicized data and display it in both italic and bold, you can use the argument *mergeformat* instead of *charformat*, like this:

{INCLUDE "C:\\FORECAST.XLS" * "mergeformat"}

We'll discuss importing data from other programs in detail in Chapter 21.

Numeric picture switch

As you will learn, many fields return a numeric result. For instance, the field {NUMCHARS} returns the number of characters in the current document, and the field {EDITTIME} returns the total number of minutes the current document has been open. Later in this book, you'll learn how to use the = (Expression) field to compute the result of a mathematical expression.

Unless you specify otherwise, Word will always display numeric results in a general numeric format. Specifically, Word does not add special characters, like commas or percent signs, to the result, and it displays only two digits after the decimal point. If you want, however, you can use the numeric picture switch, \#, to change the way Word formats a field's numeric result. For instance, if a field returns the value *1234.1*, you might want to use the numeric picture switch to tell Word to display that result as *1,234.10* or *$1234*.

If you include the numeric picture switch in a field that does not return a value, the switch will not affect the field's result. We'll examine the numeric picture switch later in the book.

Date-time picture switch

Word offers five fields that return dates or times: DATE, TIME, CREATEDATE, PRINTDATE, and SAVEDATE. By default, the results of these fields will appear in the format you've specified in the Microsoft Windows Control Panel.

Fortunately, Word lets you use the date-time picture switch, \@, to change the format it uses to display the results of these fields. For example, if a field returns the date *3/31/92*, you can use the date-time picture switch to display the resulting date in the form *March 31, 1992*, *Mar-31, 1992*, or any form you want.

If you include the date-time picture switch in a field that does not return a date or time, the switch will not affect the field's result. We'll examine the date-time picture switch when we discuss the DATE and TIME fields.

NESTING FIELDS

Occasionally, you'll want to use a field as an argument to another field. For example, you might use a couple of FILLIN fields as arguments to an INFO field, like this:

{INFO {FILLIN "Which item?"} {FILLIN "New entry"}}

The FILLIN fields in this example collect input from the user and return that input as arguments to the INFO field. As in this example, Word always evaluates the innermost field first and the outermost field last. You'll see several examples of nested fields throughout the rest of this book.

DATE AND TIME FIELDS

Now that we've given you an overview of fields, let's consider two of Word's most important fields—the DATE and TIME fields. After we show you how to insert a DATE and TIME field in one of Word's standard formats, we'll show you how to insert the date and time in your own custom format.

The DATE field

The DATE field returns the current date, which is stored in your computer's system clock. The form of this field is simply {DATE}. By default, Word displays the date in the format you've defined in the Microsoft Windows Control Panel. If you want, however, you can display the date in a format that is not the default.

One of the most common places to display the current date, of course, is in a document's header or footer. For this reason, Word provides a Date icon in the header and footer panes. As we explained in Chapter 7, you can click on this icon in a header or footer pane to place the field {DATE} in the header or footer. Of course, if you want to display the date in a format other than the default, you'll need to use either the Field... command on the Insert menu or the [Insert field] key ([Ctrl][F9]).

To insert the current date using the Field dialog box, first place the cursor where you want the date to appear. Next, select the Field... command to bring up the Field dialog box shown in Figure 10-1. Then, choose the Date option from the Insert Field Type list box. At this point, Word will present a list of date formats in the Instructions list box. You should now choose the format you want from this list box.

As you can see, Word uses a series of abbreviations to identify the available date formats. Table 10-4 lists these formats, along with the time formats, and shows examples of how the date October 15, 1992, and the time 1:30 PM would look in each format.

Table 10-4

Format	Example
d MMMM, yy	15 October, 92
d-MMM-yy	15-Oct-92
M/d/yy	10/15/92
M/d/yy h:mm AM/PM	10/15/92 1:30 PM
MMM-yy	Oct-92
MMMM d, yyyy	October 15, 1992
MMMM, yy	October, 92
H:mm	13:30
h:mm AM/PM	1:30 PM

After you've chosen the date format you want, choose OK to insert the DATE field into your document. To use a date format that is not listed in the Instructions list box, you can create your own custom format. We'll show you how to do that in a moment.

An example

Suppose you want to insert the current date at the top of the letter shown in Figure 10-7. You want the month name first, followed by the day and the year, like this: February 4, 1990. To do this, move the cursor to the top of the letter and select the Field... command. In the Field dialog box, choose the Date option from the Insert Field Type list box. Next, choose from the Instructions list box the date format in which you want the date to appear—MMMM d, yyyy (the sixth option in the list box). At this point, the dialog box should look like the one shown in Figure 10-8. To complete the process, choose OK. If you deactivate the Field Codes setting on the View menu, the resulting letter will look like the one shown in Figure 10-9 on the next page.

Figure 10-7

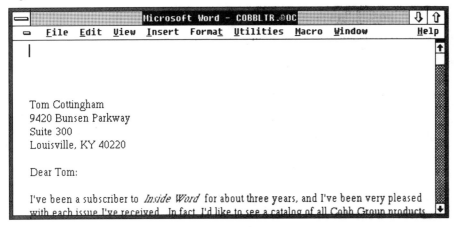

We'll insert a DATE field above the address in this letter.

Figure 10-8

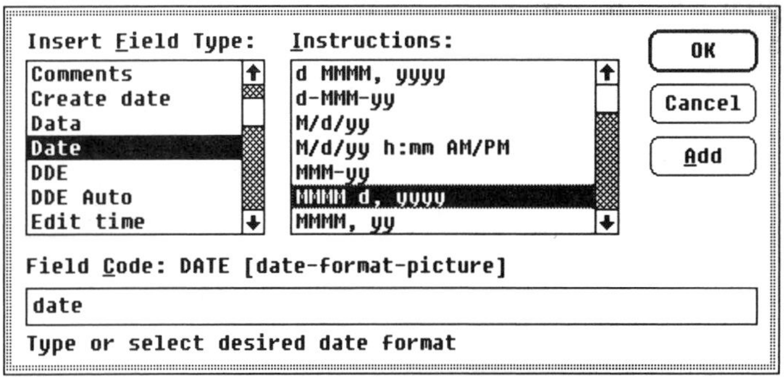

This dialog box shows the settings for inserting the date in our sample letter.

The TIME field

Now that you've seen how the DATE field works, let's take a look at the TIME field, which returns the current time. Inserting a TIME field into a document is essentially the same as inserting a DATE field, except you choose the Time option from the Insert Field Type list box, then select one of the time formats from the Instructions list box.

Figure 10-9

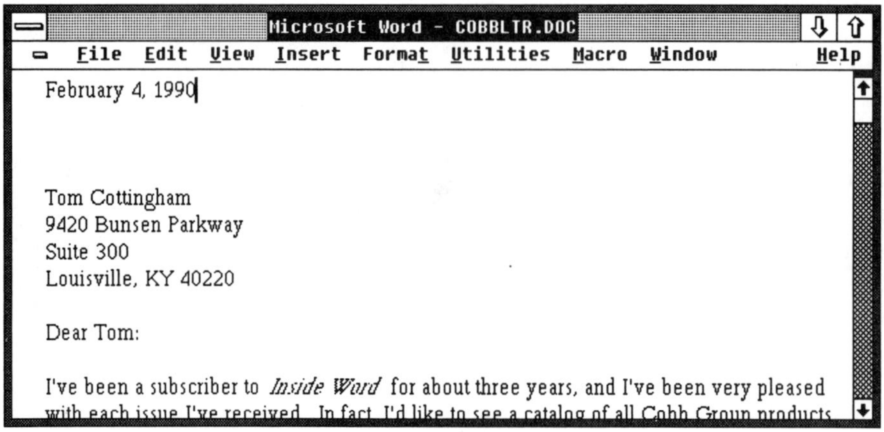

When the Field Codes setting on the View menu is turned off, Word will display the result of the DATE field.

For example, suppose you want to insert the current time into a letter you're writing. First, position the cursor where you want the time to appear. Next, open the Field dialog box and choose the Time option from the Insert Field Type list box. Then, choose one of the time formats from the Instructions list box and choose OK to insert the field into your letter.

Like the DATE field, the TIME field usually appears in a document's header or footer. For this reason, Word provides a Time icon in the header and footer panes. As we explained in Chapter 7, you can click on this icon to place the field {TIME} in the header or footer. Of course, if you want to display the time in a format other than the default, you'll need to use the Field... command or manually enter a TIME field with the date-time picture switch.

Formatting DATE and TIME fields

As we mentioned, you can change Word's default date and time format with the Microsoft Windows Control Panel. To do this, pull down Word's Control menu either by clicking on it or by pressing [Alt][Shift][Spacebar], then select the Run... command. When the Run dialog box appears, choose the Control Panel option and then choose OK. At this point, you can select the date and time formats you want to use as your defaults.

Of course, you can use the Field... command to display a date or time in any of the formats listed in the Instructions list box. In addition to the built-in formats Word supplies, however, you can assign a custom date or time format to the dates and times in your document. With custom formats, you can create DATE and TIME fields that return the day of the week in addition to the date, month, and year. You can also create combinations of dates and times in the same field.

To create custom formats, you need to use the date-time picture switch (\@). This switch is an optional argument you can supply to a DATE or TIME field to tell Word exactly how to format the date or time. The form of this switch is

\@ *dateTimePicture*

where *dateTimePicture* is a string of special abbreviations and literal text that defines the date or time format. Table 10-5 lists all the available date and time abbreviations that Word will recognize. Of course, you've seen some of these abbreviations in the built-in formats that appear in the Instructions list box in the Field dialog box. Some of the abbreviations, however, are available only in custom formats. If you add any literal text in the date-time picture, including commas and spaces, Word will enter that text in the field's result.

Table 10-5

Abbreviation	Description	Example
M	Number of month	1 through 12
MM	Number of month with leading zeros	01 through 12
MMM	Three-letter month abbreviation	Oct
MMMM	Full month name	October
yy	Year as two digits	92
yyyy	Year as four digits	1992
d	Date as one or two digits	1 through 31
dd	Two-digit date with leading zeros	01 through 31
ddd	Three-letter day of the week	Wed
dddd	Full day name	Wednesday
h	Hours on a 12-hour clock	1 through 12
hh	Hours on a 12-hour clock with leading zeros	01 through 12
H	Hours on a 24-hour clock	1 through 24
HH	Hours on a 24-hour clock with leading zeros	01 through 24
m	Minutes	1 through 59
mm	Minutes with leading zeros	01 through 59
AM/PM	Uppercase AM or PM	9 AM, 5 PM
am/pm	Lowercase am or pm	9 am, 5 pm
A/P	Uppercase AM or PM	9A, 5P
a/p	Lowercase am or pm	9a, 9p

When you include a date-time picture switch in a DATE or TIME field, the entire field code will take one of the following forms:

{date \@ *dateTimePicture*}
{time \@ *dateTimePicture*}

To insert a custom date or time format, start as if you were going to insert a DATE or TIME field using a built-in format. Just position the cursor, open the Field dialog box, and select either the Date or Time option from the Insert Field Type list box.

Next, instead of selecting a format from the Instructions list box, move the cursor to the Field Code text box, which, at this point, will contain only the field name *date* or *time*. To specify a custom format, type the characters \@ after the field name, then a space, and finally the desired date-time picture, enclosed in quotation marks. For example, if you want to assign the format MMM-d to a date field, the text box should contain the entry

date \@ "MMM-d"

After you've typed the appropriate entry into the Field Code text box, choose OK to insert the field into your document.

By the way, whenever you use a date-time picture to define a custom format, it makes no difference whether you use a DATE or a TIME field—both will return the same result. In addition, if you include the date-time picture switch in a field that does not return a date, that switch will not affect the field's result.

An example

Let's suppose you want to insert a DATE field into your document that includes the day of the week, as well as the month, day, and year, such as Wednesday, October 15, 1992.

To create this format, open the Field dialog box and choose the Date option from the Insert Field Type list box. Next, move to the Field Code text box and append the text \@ *"dddd, MMMM d, yyyy"*. (You'll want to always include the appropriate spaces and commas in your date-time picture.) Figure 10-10 shows the Field dialog box at this point.

After you've entered the appropriate text into the Field Code text box, choose OK to insert the new field into your document.

Modifying a built-in format

If you want to define a custom date-time picture that is very similar to one of Word's built-in formats, you can save time by editing an existing format. To do this, bring up the Field dialog box and choose the Date or Time option from the Insert Field Type list box. Next, select the format you want to modify from the Instructions list box. When you do this, you'll notice that the Add button on the right side of the dialog box will become active. If you choose the Add button at this point, Word will place the switch \@ and the appropriate date-time picture in the Field Code text box. You can then edit the built-in date-time picture and choose OK to insert the new field.

Figure 10-10

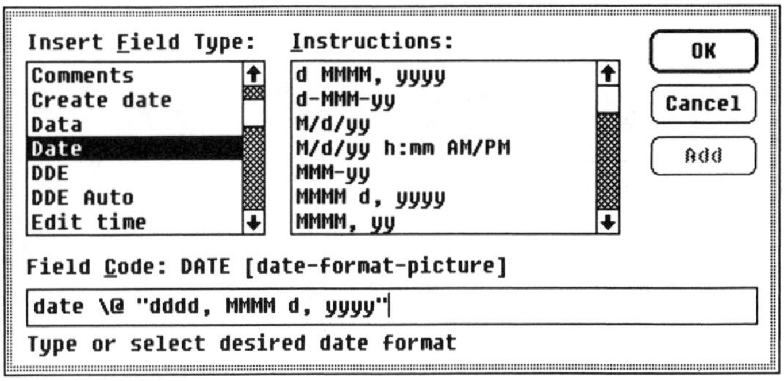

```
╔════════════════════════════════════════════════════════════╗
║ Insert Field Type:   Instructions:              ┌────────┐  ║
║ ┌──────────────┬─┐   ┌────────────────────────┬─┐│   OK   │  ║
║ │Comments      │▲│   │d MMMM, yyyy            │▲│└────────┘  ║
║ │Create date   │▒│   │d-MMM-yy                │▒│┌────────┐  ║
║ │Data          │▒│   │M/d/yy                  │▒││ Cancel │  ║
║ │Date          │▒│   │M/d/yy h:mm AM/PM       │▒│└────────┘  ║
║ │DDE           │▒│   │MMM-yy                  │▒│┌────────┐  ║
║ │DDE Auto      │▒│   │MMMM d, yyyy            │▒││  Add   │  ║
║ │Edit time     │▼│   │MMMM, yy                │▼│└────────┘  ║
║ └──────────────┴─┘   └────────────────────────┴─┘           ║
║ Field Code: DATE [date-format-picture]                      ║
║ ┌────────────────────────────────────────────────────────┐ ║
║ │date \@ "dddd, MMMM d, yyyy"│                            │ ║
║ └────────────────────────────────────────────────────────┘ ║
║ Type or select desired date format                          ║
╚════════════════════════════════════════════════════════════╝
```

You can define a custom date or time format by typing a date-time picture in the Field Code text box.

As we said, the DATE and TIME fields will return the same result when you include a date-time picture. Consequently, you can use any combination of the abbreviations in Table 10-5 to create a field that displays both the date and time. For example, if you want to insert a field that returns the date and time in the following format

> Oct-15, 1992 at 5:30 PM

you can enter either of the following fields:

> {date \@ "MMM-d, yyyy at h:mm AM/PM"}
> {time \@ "MMM-d, yyyy at h:mm AM/PM"}

Combining dates and times

Up to this point, we've been using the Field dialog box in our examples to insert DATE and TIME fields into a document. After a while, you'll probably find it easier to insert these fields manually with the [Insert field] key rather than with the Field dialog box.

To manually enter a DATE or TIME field, press the [Insert field] key ([Ctrl][F9]). Next, type the field name (*DATE* or *TIME*), followed by the date-time picture switch, \@, and the appropriate date-time picture. For example, to manually insert the field we entered in Figure 10-10, press the [Insert field] key to insert the special field characters { and }, and type *DATE \@ "dddd, MMMM d, yyyy"*.

Manually entering DATE and TIME fields

**SUMMARY
INFO FIELDS**

Word offers six fields that return information stored in the Summary Info dialog box: TITLE, SUBJECT, AUTHOR, KEYWORDS, COMMENTS, and INFO. Figure 10-11 uses a split screen to show how Word's summary info fields appear in a document. The top portion of this screen shows the field codes, while the bottom portion shows the field results. Let's look at each summary info field.

Figure 10-11

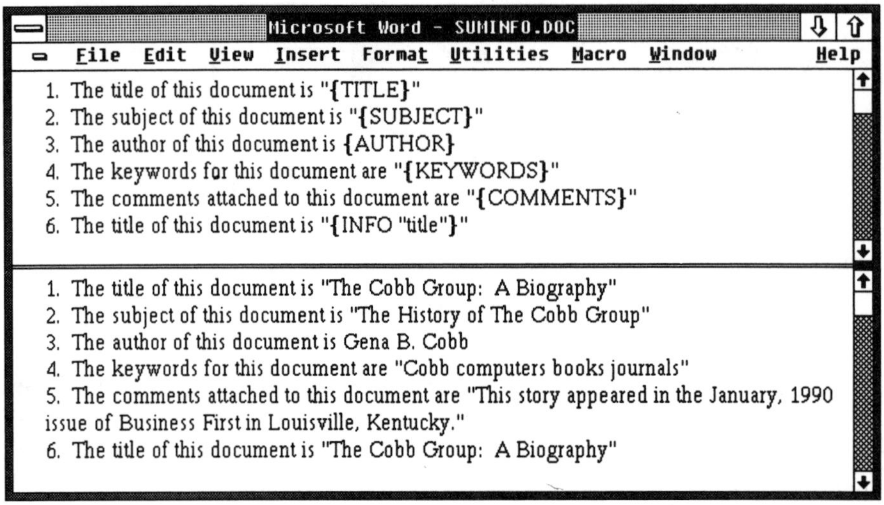

```
┌──────────────────────────────────────────────────────────────────────┐
│ ▭               Microsoft Word - SUMINFO.DOC              ⇩ ⇧          │
│ ▭   File  Edit  View  Insert  Format  Utilities  Macro  Window   Help │
├──────────────────────────────────────────────────────────────────────┤
│  1. The title of this document is "{TITLE}"                         ↑ │
│  2. The subject of this document is "{SUBJECT}"                       │
│  3. The author of this document is {AUTHOR}                           │
│  4. The keywords for this document are "{KEYWORDS}"                   │
│  5. The comments attached to this document are "{COMMENTS}"           │
│  6. The title of this document is "{INFO "title"}"                  ↓ │
├──────────────────────────────────────────────────────────────────────┤
│  1. The title of this document is "The Cobb Group: A Biography"     ↑ │
│  2. The subject of this document is "The History of The Cobb Group"  │
│  3. The author of this document is Gena B. Cobb                      │
│  4. The keywords for this document are "Cobb computers books journals"│
│  5. The comments attached to this document are "This story appeared in the January, 1990 │
│  issue of Business First in Louisville, Kentucky."                   │
│  6. The title of this document is "The Cobb Group: A Biography"     ↓ │
└──────────────────────────────────────────────────────────────────────┘
```

Summary info fields retrieve information from the Summary Info dialog box.

The TITLE field

The TITLE field returns the title stored in the current document's Summary Info dialog box. The forms of this field are

{TITLE}
{TITLE *newTitle*}

You'll typically use the first form of this field, which returns the entry stored in the Title text box in the Summary Info dialog box. For example, line 1 of the document shown in Figure 10-11 contains the text

The title of this document is "{TITLE}"

If the title of the current document is *The Cobb Group: A Biography*, Word will substitute this title in place of the TITLE field when it updates the field, as shown in the bottom portion of Figure 10-11.

If you want, you can use the second form of the TITLE field to change the Title entry in the Summary Info dialog box. Simply include a *newTitle* argument, enclosed in quotation marks, after the field name. For example, if you enter and update the field

{TITLE "The Plight of Douglas Cobb"}

Word will change the Title entry in the Summary Info dialog box to *The Plight of Douglas Cobb* and will return that entry as the field's result.

Word will update the TITLE field when you select it and then press the [Update field] key ([F9]) or when you issue the Print Merge… command on the File menu. If you enter a TITLE field into a header or footer, Word will automatically update the field the first time you issue the Print… command.

The SUBJECT field returns the entry stored in the Subject text box in the Summary Info dialog box. The forms of this field are

The SUBJECT field

{SUBJECT}
{SUBJECT *newSubject*}

As you'd expect, the first form of this field simply retrieves the Subject entry in the Summary Info dialog box. The second line of Figure 10-11 shows how you might use this form of the SUBJECT field in a document.

You can use the second form of the SUBJECT field to change the Subject entry in the Summary Info dialog box. Just include a *newSubject* argument, enclosed in quotation marks, after the field name. For example, if you enter and update the field

{SUBJECT "How Doug Cobb Achieved Fame"}

Word will change the Subject entry in the Summary Info dialog box to *How Doug Cobb Achieved Fame* and will return that entry as the field's result.

Like the TITLE field, Word will update the SUBJECT field when you select it and press the [Update field] key or when you issue the Print Merge… command. If you enter a SUBJECT field into a header or footer, Word will automatically update the field the first time you issue the Print… command.

The AUTHOR field returns the name of the person who created the document. The forms of this field are

The AUTHOR field

{AUTHOR}
{AUTHOR *newName*}

As you'd expect, the first form of this field simply retrieves the Author entry in the Summary Info dialog box. The third line of Figure 10-11 shows how you might use this form of the AUTHOR field in a document.

You can use the second form of the AUTHOR field to change the Author entry in the dialog box. Simply include a *newName* argument, enclosed in quotation marks, after the field name. For example, if you enter and update the field

{AUTHOR "Steve Cobb"}

Word will change the Author entry in the Summary Info dialog box to *Steve Cobb*, and will return that entry as the field's result.

Word will update the AUTHOR field when you select it and then press the [Update field] key or when you issue the Print Merge... command. If you enter an AUTHOR field into a header or footer, Word will automatically update it the first time you issue the Print... command.

The KEYWORDS field

The KEYWORDS field returns the entry stored in the Keywords text box in the Summary Info dialog box. The forms of this field are

{KEYWORDS }
{KEYWORDS *newKeywords*}

As you'd expect, the first form of this field retrieves the Keywords entry in the Summary Info dialog box. The fourth line of Figure 10-11 shows how you might use this form of the KEYWORDS field in a document.

Like the other summary info fields we've covered, the KEYWORDS field has a second form that lets you change the Keywords entry in the dialog box. Just include a *newKeywords* argument, enclosed in quotation marks, after the field name. For example, if you enter and update the field

{KEYWORDS "Cobb 1-2-3 Louisville"}

Word will change the Keywords entry in the Summary Info dialog box to *Cobb 1-2-3 Louisville* and will return that entry as the field's result.

Word will update the KEYWORDS field when you select it and press the [Update field] key or when you issue the Print Merge... command. If you enter a KEYWORDS field into a header or footer, Word will automatically update it the first time you issue the Print. command.

The COMMENTS field

The COMMENTS field returns the comments stored in the Comments text box in the Summary Info dialog box.. The forms of this field are

{COMMENTS }
{COMMENTS *newComments*}

The first form of this field retrieves the Comments entry in the Summary Info dialog box. The fifth line of Figure 10-11 shows how you might use this form of the COMMENTS field in a document.

You can use the second form of the COMMENTS field to change the Comments entry in the Summary Info dialog box. Simply include a *newComments* argument, enclosed in quotation marks, after the field name. For example, if you enter and update the field

{COMMENTS "This story is not yet complete"}

Word will place the text *This story is not yet complete* in the Comments text box in the Summary Info dialog box, and will return that entry as the field's result.

Like all summary info fields, Word will update the COMMENTS field when you select it and press the [Update field] key or when you choose Print Merge.... If you enter a COMMENTS field into a header or footer, Word will automatically update it the first time you issue the Print... command.

The INFO field

The INFO field allows you to retrieve or change any of the entries in the Summary Info dialog box. The forms of this field are

{INFO *infoType*}
{INFO *infoType newEntry*}

If you use the first form of this field, you must supply an *infoType* argument, which specifies the entry you want to retrieve from the dialog box (Title, Subject, Author, Keywords, or Comments). For example, if you enter the field

{INFO "title"}

as we've done in the sixth line of Figure 10-11, Word will return the Title entry in the dialog box.

The second form of the INFO field lets you change an entry in the Summary Info dialog box. Simply include a *newEntry* argument, enclosed in quotation marks, after the *infoType* argument. For example, if you want to change the title of the document to *The Plight of Douglas Cobb,* use the field

{INFO "title" "The Plight of Douglas Cobb"}

As with all the fields we've discussed in this section, Word will update the INFO field when you select it and press the [Update field] key or when you choose Print Merge.... If you enter an INFO field into a header or footer, Word will automatically update it the first time you issue the Print... command.

As you may have noticed, you can use the INFO field as an alternative to the other five summary info fields we have discussed in this section. For instance, the fields *{INFO "title"}* and *{TITLE}* return the same result, as do the fields *{INFO "author" "Steve Cobb"}* and *{AUTHOR "Steve Cobb"}*.

The INFO field really comes in handy if you want to let a user specify summary information. To do this, you can embed some FILLIN fields within an INFO field, like this:

{INFO {FILLIN "Change which info item?"} {FILLIN "Change
    to what?"}}

STATISTICAL FIELDS

Word offers 11 fields that return statistical information about the current document: CREATEDATE, EDITTIME, FILENAME, LASTSAVEDBY, NUMCHARS, NUMPAGES, NUMWORDS, PRINTDATE, REVNUM, SAVEDATE, and TEMPLATE. All of these fields return the results that you see when you choose the Statistics... button in the Summary Info dialog box. Word will update each of these fields when you select them and press the [Update field] key or when you issue the Print Merge... command. If you enter any of these fields into a header or footer (with the exception of the NUMCHARS, NUMPAGES, and NUMWORDS fields), Word will automatically update them the first time you issue the Print... command.

Figure 10-12 uses a split screen to show you how Word's statistical fields appear in a document. The top portion of this screen shows the field codes, while the bottom portion shows the field results. Let's consider each field in detail.

The CREATEDATE field

The CREATEDATE field returns the date on which the document was created. The form of this field is simply {CREATEDATE}. The first line of Figure 10-12 shows how the CREATEDATE field appears in a document.

The EDITTIME field

The EDITTIME field returns the total number of minutes the document has been open since it was created. The form of this field is {EDITTIME}—it does not accept an argument. The second line of Figure 10-12 shows how the EDITTIME field appears in a document.

The FILENAME field

The FILENAME field returns the file name of the current document. The form of this field is {FILENAME}. Like many other result fields, this field does not accept an argument. The third line of the figure shows how you might use the FILENAME field in a document.

The LASTSAVEDBY field

The LASTSAVEDBY field returns the name of the person who last saved the document. The form of this field is {LASTSAVEDBY}—the field accepts no arguments. The fourth line of the figure shows how you might use the LASTSAVEDBY field in a document.

Figure 10-12

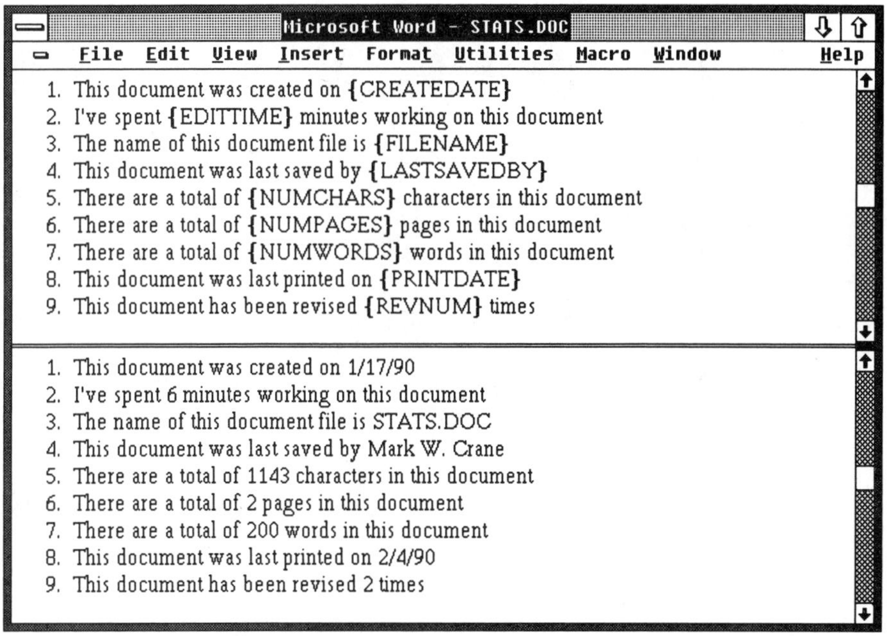

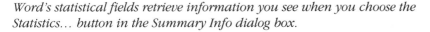

```
┌─────────────────────────────────────────────────────────────────────┐
│ ▭       █████████████ Microsoft Word - STATS.DOC ████████████    ⇩ ⇧ │
│ ▭   File  Edit  View  Insert  Format  Utilities  Macro  Window  Help │ ↑
│  1. This document was created on {CREATEDATE}                         │
│  2. I've spent {EDITTIME} minutes working on this document           │
│  3. The name of this document file is {FILENAME}                     │
│  4. This document was last saved by {LASTSAVEDBY}                    │
│  5. There are a total of {NUMCHARS} characters in this document      │
│  6. There are a total of {NUMPAGES} pages in this document           │
│  7. There are a total of {NUMWORDS} words in this document           │
│  8. This document was last printed on {PRINTDATE}                    │
│  9. This document has been revised {REVNUM} times                    │ ↓
├─────────────────────────────────────────────────────────────────────┤
│  1. This document was created on 1/17/90                             │ ↑
│  2. I've spent 6 minutes working on this document                    │
│  3. The name of this document file is STATS.DOC                      │
│  4. This document was last saved by Mark W. Crane                    │
│  5. There are a total of 1143 characters in this document           │
│  6. There are a total of 2 pages in this document                   │
│  7. There are a total of 200 words in this document                 │
│  8. This document was last printed on 2/4/90                         │
│  9. This document has been revised 2 times                          │ ↓
└─────────────────────────────────────────────────────────────────────┘
```

Word's statistical fields retrieve information you see when you choose the Statistics… button in the Summary Info dialog box.

The NUMCHARS field

The NUMCHARS field returns the number of characters in the document. This number is stored in the Statistics dialog box and is computed each time you print the document or choose the Update button in the Statistics dialog box.

The form of this field is {NUMCHARS}—the field accepts no arguments. The figure's fifth line shows how you might use the NUMCHARS field in a document.

The NUMPAGES field

The NUMPAGES field returns the total number of pages in the document. If you've divided the document into sections, Word obtains the total number of pages by adding the number of pages in each section. This number is stored in the Statistics dialog box and is computed each time you print the document or choose the Update button in the dialog box.

The form of this field is simply {NUMPAGES}—the field accepts no arguments. The sixth line of the figure shows how you might use the NUMPAGES field in a document.

The NUMWORDS field

The NUMWORDS field returns the number of words in the document. This field considers a word to be any group of alphabetic characters surrounded by white space, a tab, or a punctuation mark. This number is stored in the Statistics dialog box and is computed each time you print the document or choose the Update button in the dialog box.

The form of this field is {NUMWORDS}—the field accepts no arguments. The figure's seventh line shows how to use the NUMWORDS field in a document.

The PRINTDATE field

The PRINTDATE field returns the date on which the document was last printed. The form of this field is simply {PRINTDATE}. By default, Word will display the date in the format you've defined in the Control Panel. If you want, however, you can use a date-time picture switch to change the format in which the date is displayed. The eighth line of the figure shows how you might use the PRINTDATE field in a document.

The REVNUM field

The REVNUM field returns the revision number of the current document. The form of this field is {REVNUM}—the field accepts no arguments.

When you create a new document, its revision number will be 1. Each time you save the document, Word will increment its revision number by one. The ninth line of the figure shows how you might use the REVNUM field in a document.

The SAVEDATE field

The SAVEDATE field returns the date that the document was last saved. The form of this field is simply {SAVEDATE}. By default, Word will display the date in the format you've defined in the Control Panel. If you want, you can use a date-time picture switch to change the format in which the date is displayed. The first line of Figure 10-13 shows how you can use the SAVEDATE field in a document.

Figure 10-13

```
┌──────────────────────────────────────────────────────────────────┐
│ ▭           Microsoft Word - STATS2.DOC                    ⇩  ⇧   │
├──────────────────────────────────────────────────────────────────┤
│ ▭   File   Edit   View   Insert   Format   Utilities   Macro   Window        Help │
├──────────────────────────────────────────────────────────────────┤
│  1. This document was last saved on {SAVEDATE}.                    ↑ │
│  2. The name of this document's template is {TEMPLATE}.            ▓ │
│                                                                    ↓ │
├──────────────────────────────────────────────────────────────────┤
│  1. This document was last saved on 2/4/90.                        ↑ │
│  2. The name of this document's template is STATEMNT.DOT.          ▓ │
│                                                                    ↓ │
└──────────────────────────────────────────────────────────────────┘
```

The SAVEDATE and TEMPLATE fields are two more statistical fields you can use in a document.

The TEMPLATE field

The TEMPLATE field returns the name of the document's template. The form of this field is {TEMPLATE}—the field accepts no arguments. (If the current document uses the default template NORMAL.DOT, the field {TEMPLATE} will not return a result.) The second line of Figure 10-13 shows how you might use the TEMPLATE field in a document.

In this chapter

Building Tables **11**

One of Word's most useful features is its table capabilities. You can use tables to create simple tabular layouts, such as a two-column list, or more complex page designs, such as elaborate forms or side-by-side text and graphics. In this chapter, we'll show you how to create a simple table. Then, we'll demonstrate the various editing and formatting techniques you can use to alter a table to suit your needs.

There are two ways to create a table in Word. First, you can use the Table... command on the Insert menu to create a blank table. Second, you can convert existing text into a table. We'll begin our discussion by showing you how to create an empty table and fill in the text. Later in this chapter, we'll show you how to convert existing text into table format.

CREATING A TABLE

Let's begin by creating the two-column table shown in Figure 11-1 on the following page. Although this is a fairly simple document, notice that the text in the second column wraps from one line to the next. Although you could create this effect using tabs, a table makes this type of formatting much easier.

First, place the cursor where you want the table to appear, then choose the Table... command from the Insert menu. Word will present the Insert Table dialog box shown in Figure 11-2 on the next page. As you can see, Word initially suggests two columns and one row for the table. Since our sample table has two columns, we won't need to change the Number of Columns setting. However, since our table has three rows, we'll need to change the Number of Rows setting to 3.

The Insert Table dialog box also lets you specify a column width. As you can see, the default setting is Auto, which tells Word to automatically determine the appropriate column width for your table. To arrive at a column width, Word divides the total width of the text area by the number of columns in the table. As you may recall from Chapter 5, when you use Word's default Document dialog box settings, the width of your total text area will be 6 inches. In a single-column layout, the text column is the same width as the text area—6 inches. Thus, Word will set the width of each column in a two-column table at 3 inches (6 inches ÷ 2 columns). We'll leave the Initial Col Width setting on Auto for now. Later, we'll show you how to change the widths of your table's columns.

Figure 11-1

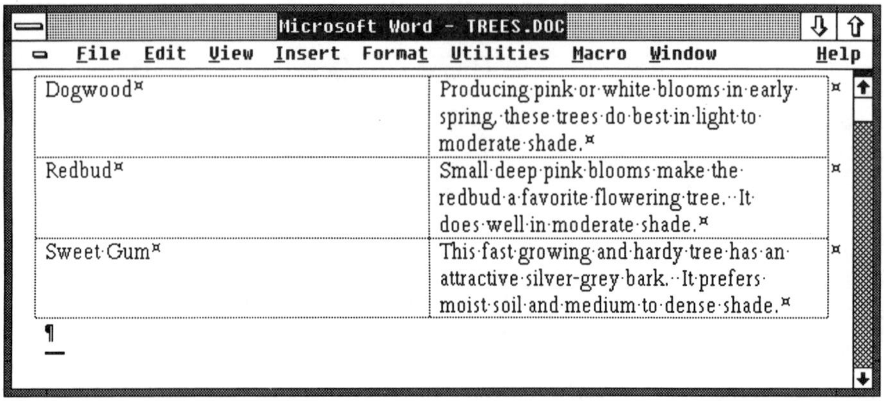

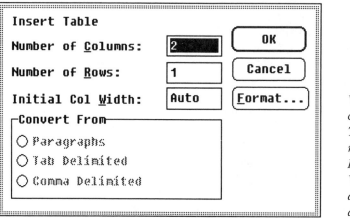

The Table... command on the Insert menu makes it easy to create tables like this one.

Figure 11-2

When you choose the Table... command on the Insert menu, Word will display this dialog box.

After specifying the number of columns and rows for your table as well as an initial column width, choose OK in the Insert Table dialog box. Word will then insert a blank table in your document, as shown in Figure 11-3.

Figure 11-3

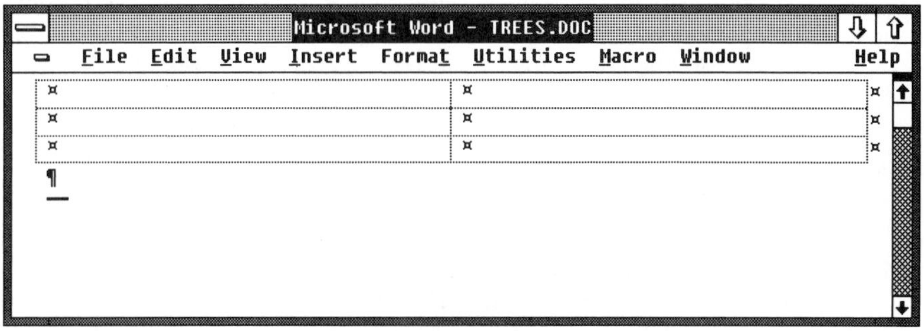

We used the Table... command to create this blank table in our document.

When you insert a table into a document that has a multicolumn format, Word will determine the automatic column width by dividing the width of the current text area by the number of columns in the table. For example, suppose you are working in a two-column document in which each text column is 2 inches wide. If you use the Table... command to insert a two-column table, the Auto setting in the Initial Col Width text box will cause Word to insert a table with two 1-inch-wide columns.

As you can see in Figure 11-3, our blank table contains gridlines that define the rows and columns of the table. The intersection of each row and column is called a cell. Each cell contains an end-of-cell mark (¤), which shows how far the text in that cell extends. (Since there is no text in the table yet, the end-of-cell mark appears at the left edge of each cell.) Another ¤ character, called the end-of-row mark, appears just to the right of each row. This marker comes into play when you want to append a new column onto the right edge of a table.

Getting your bearings

If you do not see the gridlines and ¤ characters after you create a new table, don't panic. There are a couple of ways to turn on the display of these elements. First, you can choose the Show-all icon on the ribbon. When you do, Word will display table gridlines and end-of-cell and end-of-row marks. Alternatively, if you select the Table Gridlines and Paragraph Marks check boxes in the Preferences dialog box, Word will display gridlines and end-of-cell and end-of-row marks, even when you haven't selected the Show-all icon. In fact, the only way to suppress the gridlines and marks is to deselect the Table Gridlines and Paragraph Marks check boxes in the Preferences dialog box, then deselect the Show-all icon on the ribbon.

You almost undoubtedly will want to display gridlines while you're working with a table. Without gridlines, it can be virtually impossible to discern many important characteristics of a table, such as the width of columns, the alignment of rows, and the depth of rows.

By the way, if a cell in a table contains no text or only a single paragraph of text, Word will not display a ¶ mark in that cell. Nevertheless, Word considers the text in separate cells to be in separate paragraphs. Consequently, the end-of-cell mark defines both the end of the cell and the end of the last paragraph of text in a cell.

Of course, Word will not include the gridlines and end-of-cell and end-of-row marks in a printed document. You can, however, print gridlines in a table by adding borders. We'll show you how to use borders in a table later in this chapter.

Using the ruler with a table

As you work with tables, you'll need to be familiar with the ways in which Word displays the ruler. As we explained in Chapters 2 and 5, Word can show a ruler in three views: the paragraph view, the column view, and the margin view. Let's begin with the paragraph view. Figure 11-4 shows our blank table from Figure 11-3 after we've turned on the ruler display.

Figure 11-4

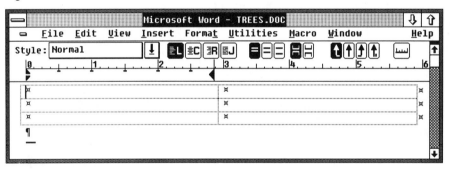

In the paragraph view, the ruler shows the width of the text area for the current cell in our blank table.

You might recall from Chapter 5 that the ruler in the paragraph view shows the width of your document's text area. The left edge of the text area begins at the zero point on the ruler, while the right edge of the text area is marked by a vertical line. When you're working in a table, the paragraph view on the ruler is somewhat different. Instead of showing the width of your total text area, the ruler shows you the width of the current cell's text area. Again, the left edge of the text area begins at the zero point on the ruler and the right edge of the text area is marked by a vertical line.

For example, in Figure 11-4, the cursor is in the first cell of the table. The text area of this cell begins at the zero point on the ruler and extends to the $2\frac{7}{8}$-inch position. You may wonder why the line marking the right edge of this cell's text area does not appear at the 3-inch position on the ruler, since each of our columns is 3 inches wide (according to the Initial Col Width setting in the Insert Table dialog box). The reason is that Word allows some space between the columns of a table so that the text in adjacent cells won't overlap. We'll talk more about this space in a moment. First, however, let's see what happens when we move the cursor to a cell in the second column of the table.

Figure 11-5 shows our table with the cursor in the second column. Notice that the ruler display has shifted so that the zero point is aligned with the left edge of the second column's text area. Similarly, the vertical line at the $2\,^{7}/_{8}$-inch position now marks the right edge of this cell's text area.

Figure 11-5

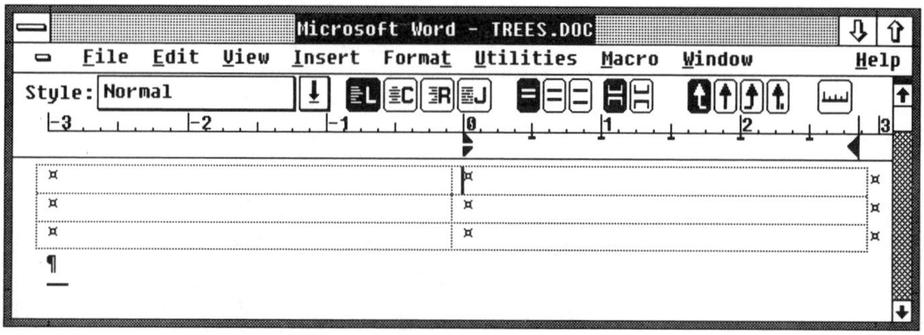

When we move the cursor to the right column, Word will shift the ruler display.

Now, let's select the Ruler-view icon at the far right side of the ruler to switch to the column view. Figure 11-6 shows our document after making this change As you can see, when you activate the column view, the zero point on the ruler will represent the edge of your document's left text column—more on this later.

Figure 11-6

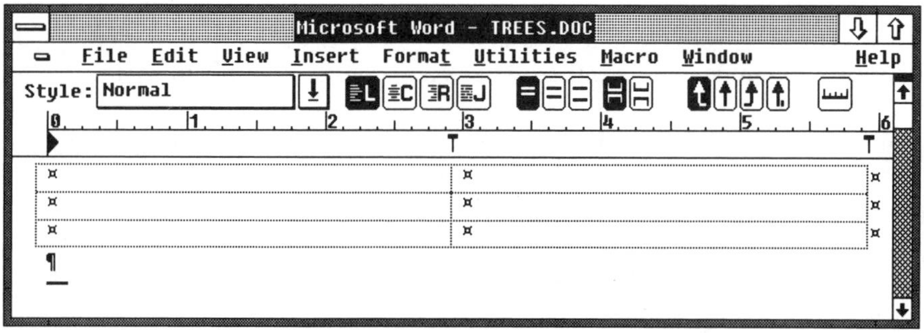

When we switch to the column view on the ruler, Word will mark the position of our column boundaries.

The position of the left edge of the table is denoted by a row indent marker (▶). Unlike the first-line and left indent markers that appear on the ruler in the paragraph view, the row indent marker is a solid arrowhead. In Figure 11-6, the row indent marker is aligned with the zero point on the ruler. As we'll show you later, this won't always be the case.

The ruler's column view also displays a ⊤ marker just below the ruler line to denote the right edge of each cell in the current row. Notice in Figure 11-6 that each ⊤ marker corresponds to a cell boundary, without taking into account the space between cells. You can drag these ⊤ markers to change your column widths. We'll show you how to do this in a moment.

Now, let's click on the Ruler-view icon once more to see the ruler in the margin view. As you can see in Figure 11-7, positioning the cursor in a table does not affect the appearance of the ruler in the margin view. As we explained in Chapters 2 and 5, this view shows the width of your page, with brackets marking the left and right margin positions.

Figure 11-7

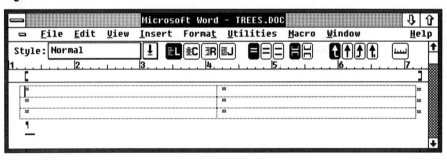

The ruler in the margin view shows the position of our left and right document margins relative to the edges of the page.

Entering text into a table

Now that we have created a blank table, let's enter some text. Entering text in a table is the same as entering text in a document. You simply move the cursor to the place where you want the text to appear, and begin typing. The text will appear in the *Normal* style for the current document, unless you assign different character and paragraph formats. (In our sample trees table, the *Normal* style definition calls for 12-point Tms Rmn text.)

To create the sample table shown in Figure 11-1, we moved the cursor into the first cell of the table and typed the word *Dogwood*. Then, we clicked on the first cell in the second column and entered the descriptive text that begins *Producing pink or white blooms*. (We also could have pressed the [Tab] key to move the cursor from the first cell to the second cell. We'll talk about this and other navigational techniques shortly.)

If the text you enter is longer than the width of the current cell, Word will wrap the text within the cell. For example, Figure 11-8 shows our sample table after we entered the descriptive text in the first cell of the second column. Notice that Word increased the depth of the adjacent cell in the first column, even though it contains only one line of text.

Figure 11-8

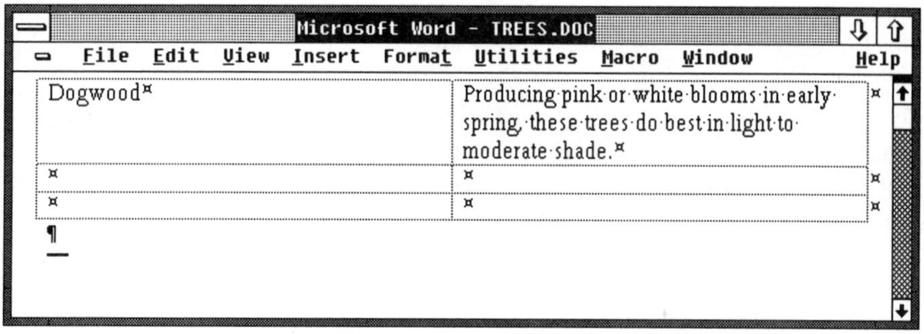

Word can wrap text within each cell of a table.

To complete the table, we clicked on each cell (or pressed the [Tab] key to move from cell to cell) and then typed the text for that cell. Figure 11-1 shows our sample table after we filled in all the text.

Now that we've shown how to create a table and enter text, let's consider some techniques for moving around in a table and selecting text.

Perhaps the easiest way to move around in a table is simply to use the mouse to click in the location you want to work, but you also can press the [Tab] key to move from cell to cell in a table. Each time you press [Tab], Word will move the cursor one cell to the right and position it in front of the first character space in that cell. If you press [Tab] while the cursor is on the last cell of a row, the cursor will jump to the first cell of the next row. (If you're in the last cell of the last row of the table, pressing [Tab] will append a new row to the end of the table.)

Similarly, pressing [Shift][Tab] will move you to the cell immediately to the left of the current cell. If you press [Shift][Tab] while the cursor is on the first cell of a row, Word will move it to the last cell of the row immediately above. (However, if the cursor is on the first cell of the first row of the table, pressing [Shift][Tab] will have no effect.)

You can also use the cursor-movement keys to navigate in a table. Pressing ↑ will move the cursor to the cell immediately above. Pressing ↓ will move the cursor to the cell immediately below. Pressing ← will move the cursor one cell to the left. Finally, pressing → will move the cursor one cell to the right.

Navigating within a table

Table 11-1 summarizes the keyboard shortcuts that are available while you're working in a table.

Table 11-1

This key combination...	does this...
[Tab]	moves right one cell
[Shift][Tab]	moves left one cell
[Alt][Home]	moves to the first cell in the current row
[Alt][End]	moves to the last cell in the current row
[Alt][Page Up]	moves to the first cell in the current column
[Alt][Page Down]	moves to the last cell in the current column
[Alt]5 (on numeric keypad)	selects the entire table
[Ctrl][Shift][Enter]	splits the table into two tables, inserting a ¶ mark above the row in which the cursor is positioned

SELECTING TEXT IN A TABLE

In many respects, selecting text in a table is the same as selecting text in any other part of a document. For instance, you can use your mouse to drag through text to select it, and you can double-click on a word to select it. You also can use the technique described in Chapter 4 of clicking at the beginning of the text you want to select, moving the cursor to the end of the area you want to select, and pressing [Shift] as you click once more.

If you are using your keyboard to select text in a table, you can press the [Extend selection] key ([F8]) in combination with the arrow keys. You can also select text by holding down the [Shift] key as you press the arrow keys.

Whenever you select text in two or more cells, Word will highlight those cells in their entirety. In other words, Word will not let you select only part of the text in two or more cells. For example, suppose you click to the left of the last word in a cell and then drag down. As soon as you cross the cell boundary, Word will select all the text in the original cell and all the text in the cell immediately below.

In addition to the click-and-drag method, Word also offers several special techniques that mouse users can employ to select text in a table. To use these techniques, you need to be aware that each cell and each column in a table has its own invisible selection bar. If you move the pointer to the left edge of a cell, you'll see that it assumes the shape of a right-pointing arrow, telling you that the pointer is in the cell's invisible selection bar. Similarly, if you move the pointer over the top of a column, you'll notice that it assumes the shape of a downward-pointing arrow, as shown in Figure 11-9. This tells you the pointer is in the column's invisible selection bar.

Figure 11-9

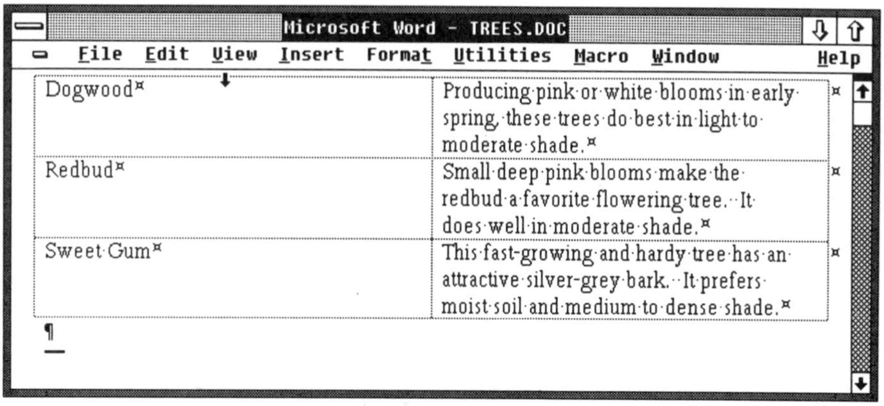

The downward-pointing arrow indicates that the pointer is in the selection bar for a column.

You can select the contents of a cell by clicking once anywhere in that cell's selection bar. To select an entire row, place the pointer in the selection bar for any cell in that row and double-click. For example, suppose you want to select the second row in the sample table. First, move the pointer to the left edge of either the first or the second column on the second row of the table. When the pointer assumes the shape of a right-pointing arrow, just double-click. At this point, Word will select the entire row, as shown in Figure 11-10.

Figure 11-10

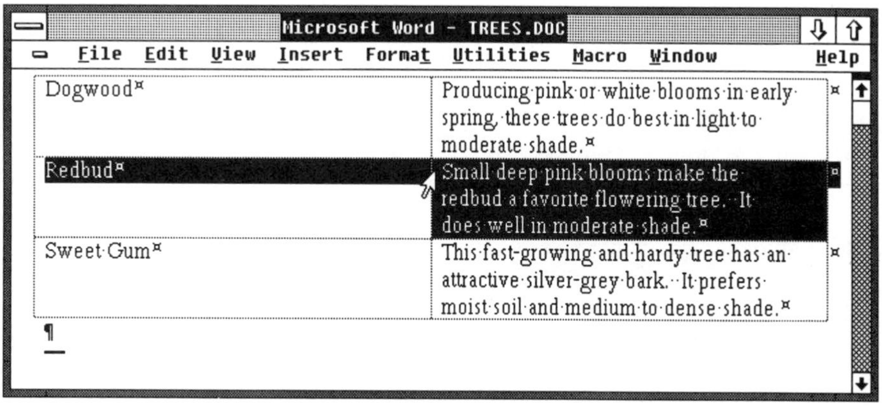

You can select a row in a table by double-clicking in the selection bar for any cell in that row.

To select an entire column of text, click in the column's selection bar or position the pointer anywhere in the column and press the right mouse button. To select an entire column using the keyboard, press the [Column selection] key ([Ctrl][Shift][F8]), then use the arrow keys to highlight the column.

To select an entire table, click the right mouse button anywhere in the first column, then drag to the rightmost column in the table. (You also can just drag through the entire table.) To select the entire table using the keyboard, hold down the [Alt] key and press 5 on the numeric keypad.

CHANGING THE LAYOUT OF A TABLE

After you create a table, you may want to change its appearance by altering the width of one or more columns, changing the spacing between columns, or adding and deleting rows and columns. In fact, you may want to use a different number of columns in certain parts of the table. You also may want to change the alignment of some of the table's rows. In this section, we'll explain how to make these kinds of changes using two commands: the Table... command on the Format menu and the Table... command on the Edit menu.

Adjusting cell and column widths

One way to change a table is to alter the width of individual cells or the width of entire columns. Changing the width of a column in a table is simply a matter of changing the width of all the cells in that column. Let's look first at how you would change the width of an individual cell, then we'll consider how to adjust entire and partial columns.

Changing the cell width with the mouse

To change the width of a cell with the mouse, first click on the Ruler-view icon until you've placed the ruler in the column view. Next, click on the row containing the cell, and drag the appropriate ⊤ marker that appears on the ruler. If you want to change the width of two or more cells in a column, select those cells before you drag the ⊤ marker. If you simply click on one cell and drag a ⊤ marker, Word will adjust the width of that cell only without changing any other cells in the column. (Of course, you can use this to your advantage when you need to create a table with different cell widths on different rows.)

When you drag a ⊤ marker on the ruler, Word will simultaneously move all ⊤ markers that appear to the right of that marker. This allows you to change the width of one cell without affecting the width of other cells on the same row.

Changing the cell width with the keyboard

You also can use the keyboard to adjust the width of a cell or a column. First, move the cursor into the cell whose width you want to change (or highlight all the cells whose widths you want to adjust). Then, choose the Table... command from the Format menu. Word will then display the dialog box shown in Figure 11-11. (You also can access this dialog box by clicking the Format... button in the Insert Table dialog box.)

Figure 11-11

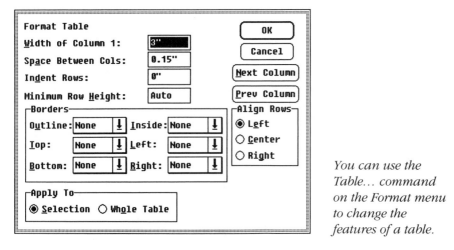

You can use the Table... command on the Format menu to change the features of a table.

Notice that the first text box in the dialog box is labeled *Width of Column 1*. The column number in this label will change depending on where the cursor is positioned or what part of the table is selected. If you've selected cells in two columns, the label will read *Width of Columns 1-2*.

Normally, the Width of Column text box will display the width of the current cell(s). However, if you've selected two or more cells of different widths, the text box will be blank.

To change the width of the cell(s) you have selected, just enter a measurement in the Width of Column text box and choose OK. You can enter your width measurement in inches, centimeters, points, or picas. If you don't specify a unit of measure (such as *in* or *"*, *cm*, *pt*, or *pi*), Word will assume inches (or whatever unit you've chosen for your default in the Customize dialog box).

Just below the OK and Cancel buttons in the Format Table dialog box, you'll see two buttons labeled *Next Column* and *Prev Column*. When you choose the Next Column button, Word will select the cell to the right of the current cell and display its width in the Width of Column text box. Similarly, when you choose the Prev Column button, Word will select the cell to the left of the current cell and display its width in the Width of Column text box. If you click Next Column when the last cell on a row is selected, Word will select the first cell in the row. By the same token, if you click the Prev Column button when the first cell in a row is selected, Word will highlight the last cell in that row.

If you have selected two or more cells in a row and you choose the Next Column button, Word will select the first cell to the right of the highlighted cells. If you have highlighted two or more cells in a row and you choose the Prev Column

Using the Next Column and Prev Column buttons

button, Word will select the cell to the left of the first cell in your selection. For example, suppose you have selected the second and third cells in a four-cell row. If you choose the Prev Column button, Word will select the first cell in that row.

The Next Column and Prev Column buttons can be particularly useful when you want to assign different widths to different cells on the same row. You can select one cell in the row, open the Format Table dialog box, and specify a Width of Column setting. Then, instead of choosing the OK button, which will close the dialog box, choose the Next Column or Prev Column button to move to a different cell on the row. You can specify a width for this cell, then move to another cell by choosing Next Column or Prev Column. After you've adjusted all the cells in the row, choose OK to assign all the widths you've defined.

Changing the column width with the mouse

As we mentioned, changing the width of a column in a table is really just a matter of changing the widths of all the cells in that column. Fortunately, however, you don't have to change each cell individually.

If you want to use the ruler to change the width of a column, first select that entire column. Then, place the ruler in the column view and drag the ⊤ marker for the boundary of the column. If there are cells of different widths in the column, Word will dim the ⊤ markers on the ruler and display the width of the top cell only. However, the new width you create by dragging the dimmed marker will apply to all the cells in the selected column.

Again, Word will automatically move any ⊤ markers to the right of the one that you drag. Because you've selected the entire column, however, Word will shift the cells in all the columns that appear to the right of the current column.

For example, let's reduce the width of the first column in our sample table. First, we'll highlight that column by positioning the pointer over the column's invisible selection bar (at which point the pointer will take on the shape of a downward-pointing arrow), and click. Figure 11-12 shows the column after we highlighted it.

After highlighting the column, we'll click on the ⊤ marker that appears near the 3-inch position on the ruler and drag it to the $1\frac{1}{2}$-inch position. When we release the mouse button, the ⊤ marker near the 6-inch position will move to the $4\frac{1}{2}$-inch position. Figure 11-13 shows the results.

Changing the column width with the keyboard

You also can use the Format Table dialog box to change the width of an entire column. To do this, simply select the entire column whose width you want to change, then choose Table... from the Format menu. In the Format Table dialog box, enter the column width you want to use in the Width of Column text box, then choose OK.

To change the width of two or more columns, just highlight those columns before you open the Format Table dialog box. Then, specify a Width of Column setting and choose OK.

Figure 11-12

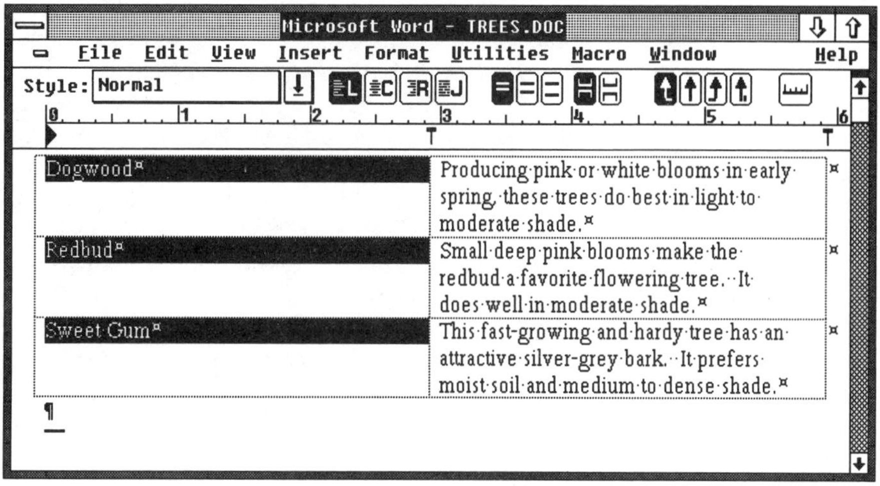

To change a column width using the ruler, first highlight the entire column.

Figure 11-13

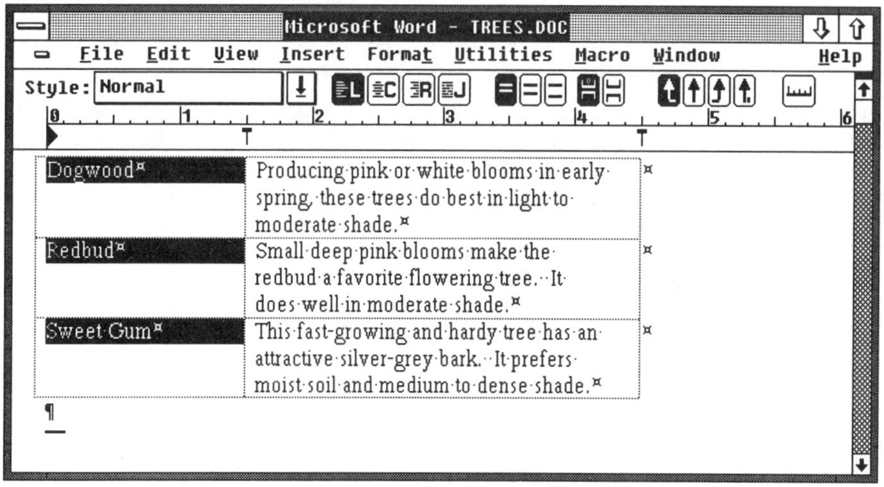

We dragged a ⊤ marker on the ruler to decrease the width of the left column.

As you're adjusting column widths in the Format Table dialog box, you can use the Next Column and Prev Column buttons we described earlier to move from one column to another. For example, after specifying a new Width of Column setting for one column, you can choose Next Column or Prev Column to select a different column and adjust its width as well. When you choose OK to close the dialog box, Word will assign all of the column widths you've defined.

Before we move on, let's take a look at the two Apply To options in the Format Table dialog box: Selection and Whole Table. If you choose Selection after specifying a new column width, Word will change the width of only the cell on which the cursor is positioned (or only the cells you selected before opening the Format Table dialog box) when you choose OK. If you choose Whole Table, however, Word will change the width of every cell in the entire table.

Partial columns

So far, we've considered how you might change the widths of individual cells or entire columns. As you might guess, you also can change the width of any block of cells in a column. After highlighting the cells whose widths you want to change, drag the **T** markers on the ruler or specify a Width of Column setting in the Format Table dialog box. If you choose the Next Column or Prev Column button in the Format Table dialog box, Word will select the corresponding cells in an adjacent column. For example, suppose you've selected the last two cells in the first column of a table. If you open the Format Table dialog box and choose Next Column, Word will select the last two cells in the second column of the table.

Adjusting the space between columns

When you create a table, Word automatically will allow some space between the text in each column. This space is not marked on your screen by any gridlines or other indicators. However, as you enter text in a cell, you'll notice that Word allows some space between the left edge of that cell and the first text character. Similarly, Word will not let the text flow all the way to the right edge of a cell; instead, it will wrap the text to a new line, leaving some space between the last character on each line and the right cell boundary.

Word's default spacing between columns is .15". When you create a new table and open the Format Table dialog box, you'll see the value *0.15"* displayed in the Space Between Cols text box. This Space Between Cols setting can be pretty confusing for several reasons. First, this setting actually determines the maximum space between the *text areas* of adjacent columns; it does not change the boundaries of the columns themselves. For example, if you increase the Space Between Cols setting, you won't see any change in the width of your table cells. (However, you will notice that Word shifts your cells to the left and rewraps the text in each cell.)

Another confusing characteristic of the Space Between Cols setting is that you cannot specify a different spacing setting for different cells on the same row. Unlike the Width of Column setting, the Space Between Cols setting that you specify affects all the cells on the current row(s).

Finally, the way Word creates the spacing between columns is a little odd. Word divides the value in the Space Between Cols text box between both ends of each cell on a row. For example, suppose you have specified .5" as your Space Between Cols setting. Word will allow $\frac{1}{4}$ inch of space at both the left and right edge of each cell. You won't be able to enter text in these areas unless you change the indents for that text (more on this later). By combining the $\frac{1}{4}$ inch of space at the left edge of one cell with the $\frac{1}{4}$ inch of space at the right edge of an adjacent cell, Word achieves the $\frac{1}{2}$-inch column spacing you've specified. However—and this is the strange part—Word also inserts the $\frac{1}{4}$-inch space at the left edge of the first cell on the row and at the right edge of the last cell on the row. Obviously, this space will not fall "between columns" as the setting name declares.

To get a better handle on the Space Between Cols setting, let's look at the ruler. Figure 11-14 shows a four-column table in which each column is 1 inch wide. Currently, the table is formatted with Word's default Space Between Cols setting of .15".

Figure 11-14

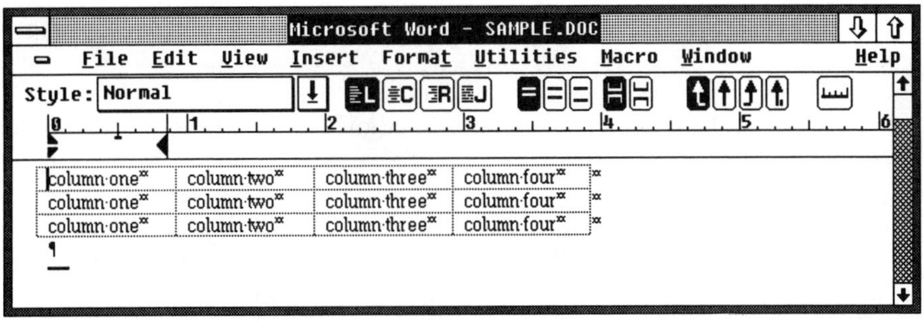

This table displays Word's default Space Between Cols setting of .15".

With the ruler in the paragraph view, you can see that the width of the text area in the current cell is slightly less than 1 inch, extending from the zero point on the ruler to the vertical line. This width reflects the width of the cell (1 inch) less the default space between columns (.15").

If you look carefully at Figure 11-14, you'll see that the line marking the left boundary of the table falls just to the left of the zero point on the ruler. However, the cursor (and the text in the first column of the table) is aligned with the zero point. The space between the table's left boundary line and the left edge of the text in each cell is the "space between columns" that Word has allotted to this end of the cell.

Now, let's see what happens when we increase the Space Between Cols setting to .5". After selecting all the cells in one column, we'll open the Format Table dialog box and enter .5" in the Space Between Cols text box. Figure 11-15 shows our table after making this change.

Figure 11-15

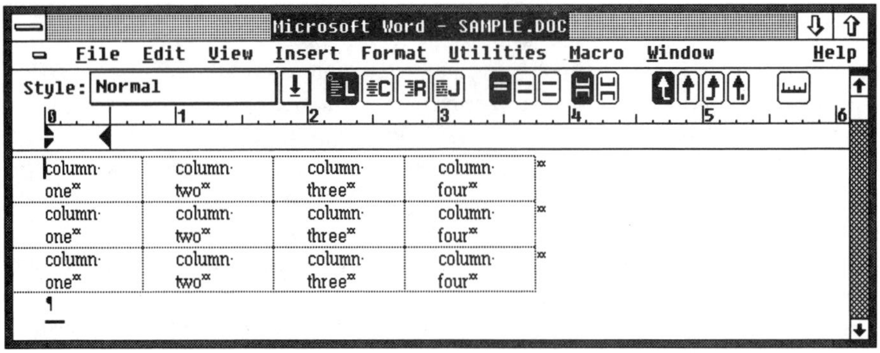

We've now increased the Space Between Cols setting to .5".

As you can see, the left boundary of the table is no longer visible on the screen. With the increased Space Between Cols setting, Word now allots $1/4$ inch of space to each end of each cell. To create this space, Word has simply shifted the left edge of all the column boundaries to the left.

In increasing the space between columns, however, Word does not change the relative alignment of the text in the table. To illustrate, notice that the cursor in the first cell is still aligned with the zero point on the ruler. Similarly, the left edge of the text in all the columns has retained its original alignment.

Notice also that the text area on the ruler is now only $1/2$ inch wide. After subtracting the $1/2$-inch space between columns from the 1-inch cell width, only $1/2$ inch is left for text in each cell. Thus, Word has had to wrap the text in each row to a new line.

Let's see how changing the Space Between Cols setting affects the ruler in the column view. Figure 11-16 shows our original table from Figure 11-14 with the default .15" Space Between Cols setting. Figure 11-17 shows the table after we increased the Space Between Cols setting to .5".

As you can see, when we change the Space Between Cols setting, Word will shift the **T** markers on the ruler to reflect the change in the column boundaries. Interestingly, Word does not shift the row indent marker at the zero point on the ruler. This marker shows the left edge of the text in the first column, not the left boundary of that column.

Unfortunately, this makes it difficult to figure out how wide each cell is just by looking at the ruler. The positions of the **T** markers do not correspond to absolute cell widths. For example, in Figure 11-17, the first **T** marker appears at the $3/4$-inch position on the ruler. However, each cell in the first column of the table is actually 1 inch wide. One-fourth inch of each cell's width falls to the left of the zero point on the ruler.

Figure 11-16

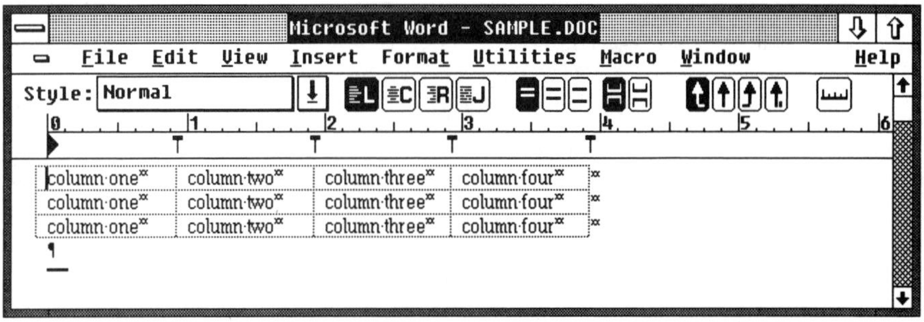

When we switch the ruler to the column view, τ markers will show the location of column boundaries.

Figure 11-17

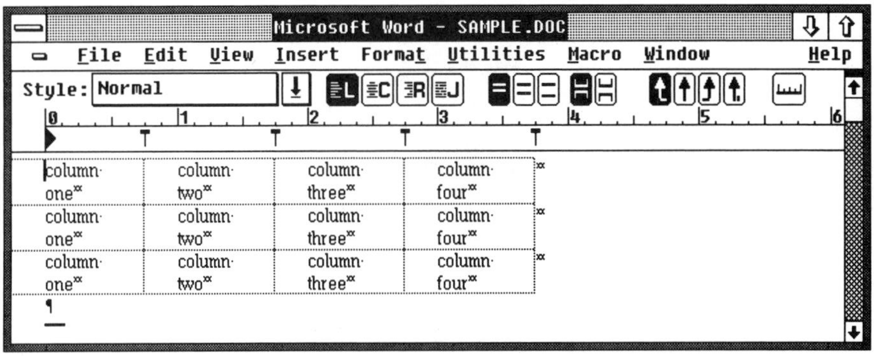

After we increased the Space Between Cols setting, Word shifted the τ markers to reflect the new column boundaries.

If you're finding the whole topic of column spacing thoroughly confusing, you're probably not alone. However, if you keep just a few key points in mind, you should be able to adjust the space between columns to suit your needs. First, remember that Word subtracts your Space Between Cols setting from the cell width, thus decreasing the width of the area available for text in a cell. Second, Word creates space between columns by allotting a blank area at either end of each cell in a row. This blank area appears at the beginning of the first cell on a row as well as at the end of the last cell on a row. Finally, changing the Space Between Cols setting does not affect the horizontal alignment of text on a row. It may, however, change the way Word wraps text and breaks lines within each cell.

Key points

As we'll see later in this chapter, you can use paragraph formatting techniques to change the alignment of text within cells (and of individual paragraphs in the same cell). By moving the indent markers on the ruler, you can actually "pull" text into the blank area that Word allots at either end of a cell. We'll also show you how to shift the entire table to the right or left.

Adjusting row height

As you enter text in a table, Word will automatically adjust the height of individual rows to accommodate the text. Both the size of the characters and the number of text lines will affect the height of a row. For example, in the sample table in Figure 11-13, notice how Word has adjusted the height of all the cells in each row to accommodate the wrapping text lines in the second column. If we selected the text in our table and applied a larger font size, Word would increase the row height even more.

Word lets you increase the height of rows to allow more white space between the text on each row. For example, going back to the table in Figure 11-13, let's see what happens when we increase the height of the rows in this table. To begin, position the cursor anywhere in the table, and then open the Format Table dialog box. In the Minimum Row Height text box, let's replace the word *Auto* with .75". Then, choose the Apply To Whole Table option and choose OK. Figure 11-18 shows the result.

Figure 11-18

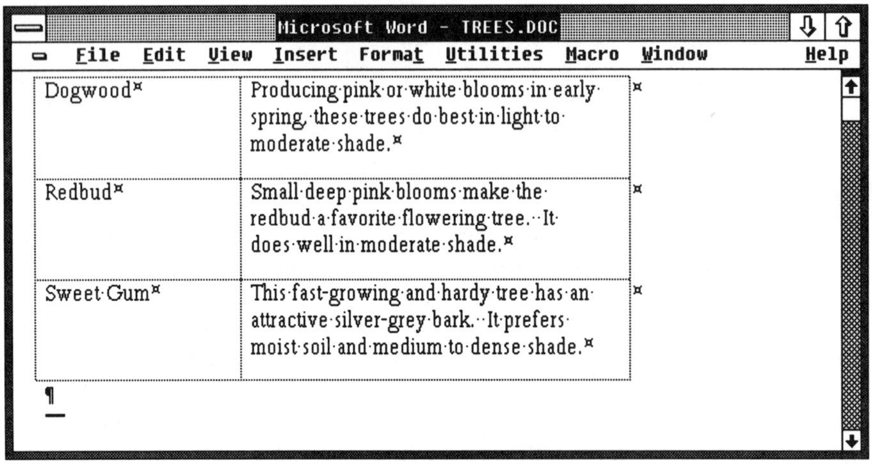

This is how our trees table will look after we increase the row height slightly.

Notice that when Word increases the height of a row, it inserts the additional space below the text. If we want to insert space above the text, we'll need to use the Open-space icon on the ruler or the Before setting in the Paragraph dialog box. (We'll discuss spacing later in this chapter.)

Notice also that the Minimum Row Height setting affects all the cells on a row. Word will not allow you to have cells of different heights on the same row. Moreover, the label for the text box—*Minimum Row Height*—should give you a clue as to how Word interprets your setting. Word will not allow the rows you've formatted to appear smaller than the specified height. However, Word will increase the height of those rows as necessary to accommodate additional text or different formatting.

If you enter a setting that is smaller than the amount of space Word needs to separate the text in adjacent rows, Word will ignore your setting and use automatic spacing so that the rows of your table don't overlap. You can override Word's "overlap protection" by entering a negative value as the Minimum Row Height setting. Word will then use the absolute value of that number and overlap the rows of text. (This is similar to how Word handles a negative Line Spacing setting in the Paragraph dialog box, which is explained in Chapter 5.)

To return a row to the default height, just open the Format Table dialog box and enter *0* or *Auto* in the Minimum Row Height text box.

Adding rows

To add a row to the end of a table, just place the cursor anywhere in the rightmost cell of the last row and press the [Tab] key. A new blank row will appear at the bottom of the table. This new row will have the same format settings (alignment, indent, and row height) as the last row of the table. For example, to add another tree description to our sample table, we can just move the cursor to the last cell of the table (where the description of the Sweet Gum tree appears), and press [Tab] once. Figure 11-19 on the next page shows the result. Using this new row, we can add a new tree description, as shown in Figure 11-20 also on the next page.

To add a row to any other part of a table, you must use the Table... command on the Edit menu. This command allows you to insert a row above the current row. For example, suppose we want to add a row to the top of the sample table. We'll begin by clicking on any cell in the top row of the table. Then, we'll choose the Table... command from the Edit menu. At this point, Word will display the dialog box shown in Figure 11-21 on page 393.

Figure 11-19

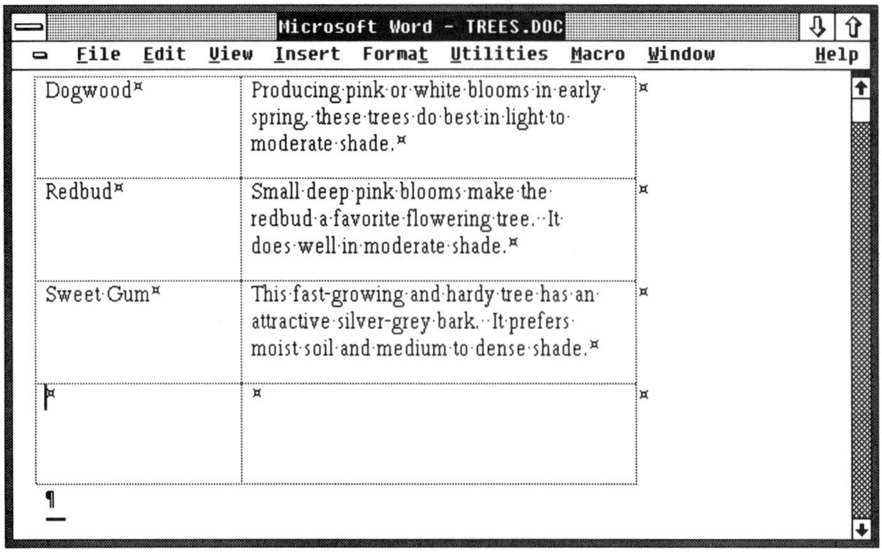

To append a new row onto the end of a table, just click on the last cell of the table and press the [Tab] key.

Figure 11-20

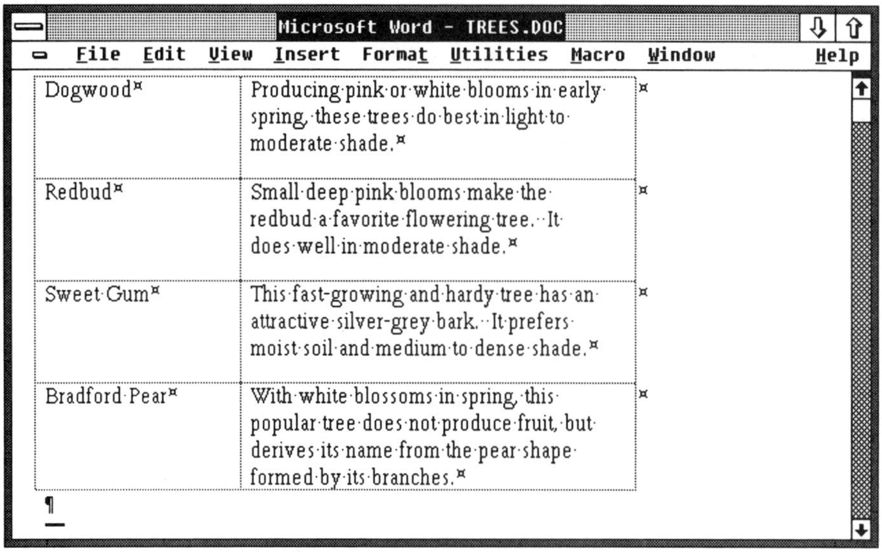

We used the new row to add another tree description to the table.

Figure 11-21

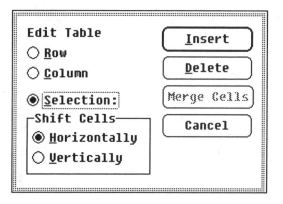

The Edit Table dialog box allows you to insert and delete rows and columns.

In the Edit Table dialog box, Word will suggest the type of insertion we need to make: Row, Column, or Selection. Since we selected less than a full row or column, Word automatically activated the Selection option. Because we want to add an entire row to the table, we'll choose the Row option, then choose the Insert button. Word will then insert a new row, as shown in Figure 11-22, which will have the same formats as the row immediately below. In Figure 11-23 on the next page, we decreased the row height after entering the title text in each column.

Figure 11-22

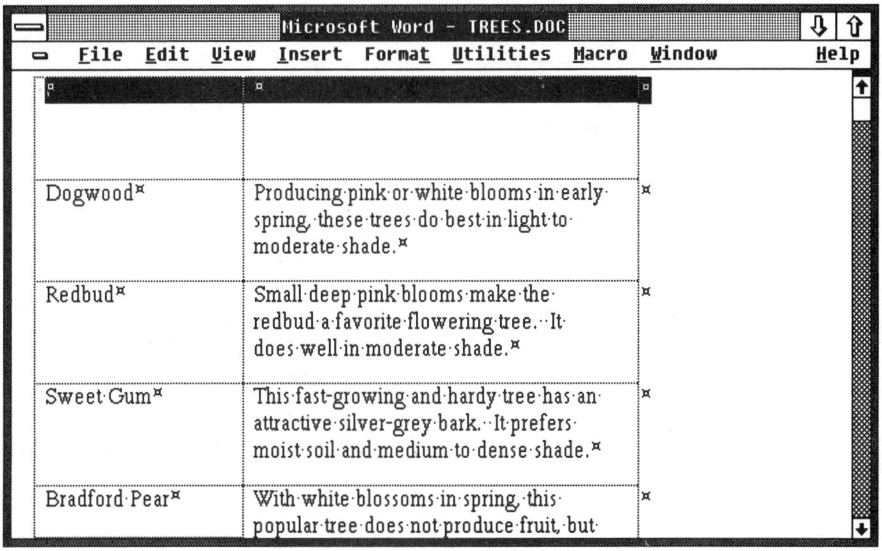

Microsoft Word - TREES.DOC	⇩ ⇧
▭ **File** **Edit** **View** **Insert** **Format** **Utilities** **Macro** **Window**	**Help**

Dogwood ⌐	Producing·pink·or·white·blooms·in·early· spring, these·trees·do·best·in·light·to· moderate·shade. ⌐
Redbud ⌐	Small·deep·pink·blooms·make·the· redbud·a·favorite·flowering·tree.·· It· does·well·in·moderate·shade. ⌐
Sweet·Gum ⌐	This·fast-growing·and·hardy·tree·has·an· attractive·silver-grey·bark.·· It·prefers· moist·soil·and·medium·to·dense·shade. ⌐
Bradford·Pear ⌐	With·white·blossoms·in·spring,·this· popular·tree·does·not·produce·fruit,·but·

Using the Row option in the Edit Table dialog box, we inserted a new row at the top of our sample table.

Figure 11-23

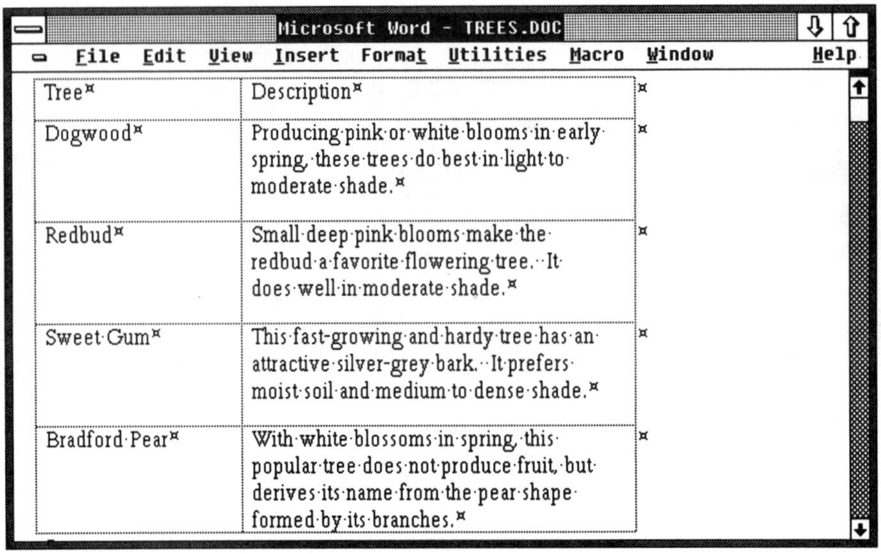

Tree✕	Description✕	✕
Dogwood✕	Producing·pink·or·white·blooms·in·early· spring,·these·trees·do·best·in·light·to· moderate·shade.✕	✕
Redbud✕	Small·deep·pink·blooms·make·the· redbud·a·favorite·flowering·tree.··It· does·well·in·moderate·shade.✕	✕
Sweet·Gum✕	This·fast-growing·and·hardy·tree·has·an· attractive·silver-grey·bark.··It·prefers· moist·soil·and·medium·to·dense·shade.✕	✕
Bradford·Pear✕	With·white·blossoms·in·spring,·this· popular·tree·does·not·produce·fruit,·but· derives·its·name·from·the·pear·shape· formed·by·its·branches.✕	✕

We used the new row in our table to display a title for each column.

Adding multiple rows

You can add two or more rows to a table in one step. First, select one or more cells in the number of rows you want to insert. For example, if you want to insert three rows in a table, you should select one or more cells in three rows. (Of course, you can just select three rows in their entirety.) Keep in mind that the rows you insert will appear above the first row in your selection.

After making your selection, choose the Table... command from the Edit menu. In the Edit Table dialog box, choose the Row option and click Insert. Word will then add the new rows just above the rows you selected. The new rows will have the same format (alignment, indent, and row height) as the top row in your selection.

Deleting rows

To delete one or more rows in a table, you must use the Edit Table dialog box. First, select one or more cells in the row(s) you want to delete. (If you want to delete only one row, click anywhere in that row.) Then, open the Edit Table dialog box, choose the Row option, then choose the Delete button. Word will remove the selected rows and move up any rows below so no gap appears in the table.

If you mistakenly delete rows that you need to keep in your table, you can use the Undo command to recover those rows. Because Word does not place deleted rows on the Clipboard, however, you cannot recover deleted rows by pasting them back into your document.

By the way, if you attempt to use normal editing techniques—like the Cut command or the [Delete] key—to delete a row, Word will merely delete the text in the selected row. You must use the Edit Table dialog box to remove a row from a table.

Inserting columns in a table is similar to inserting rows. Normally, the new column(s) will appear to the left of the current column. You also can insert new columns to the right of the table. We'll show you how to do this in a moment.

Adding columns

Suppose we want to insert a new column in our sample table to display the mature height of each tree. First, we'll place the cursor anywhere in the second column of the table, then choose the Table... command from the Edit menu. In the Edit Table dialog box, we'll choose the Column option, then choose the Insert button. Word will then insert a new column, as shown in Figure 11-24.

Figure 11-24

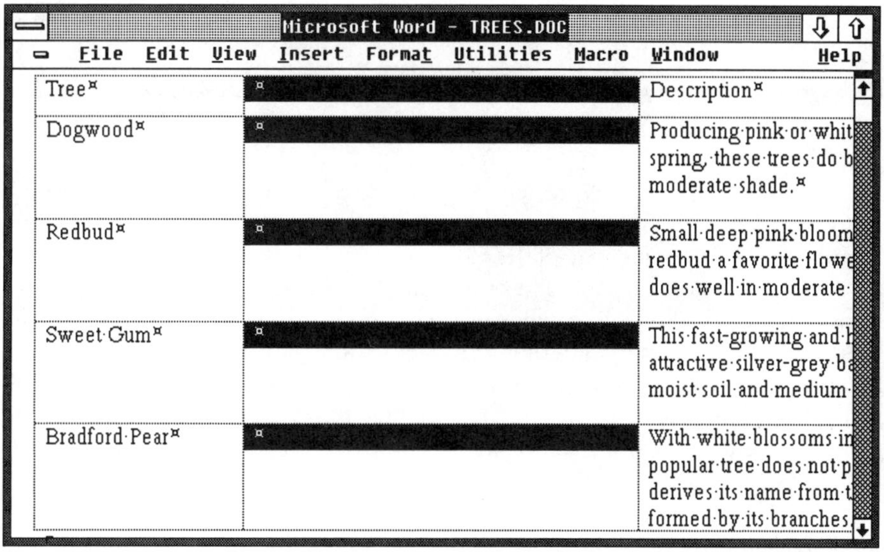

With the Table... command on the Edit menu, you can insert a new column in a table.

The cells in the new column have the same width as the first cell in the column immediately to the right (the column that contained the cursor before we inserted the new column). Of course, you can change the width of the cells in a new column using the techniques we have described. For instance, after inserting the new column in our sample table, we reduced its width to $1\frac{1}{4}$ inches, then added text. Figure 11-25 shows the result.

Figure 11-25

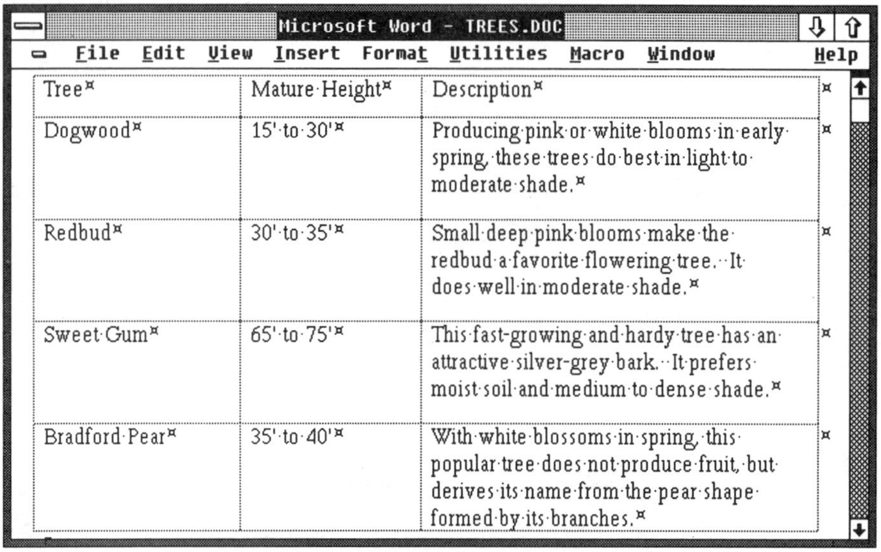

Tree^x	Mature·Height^x	Description^x	
Dogwood^x	15'·to·30'^x	Producing·pink·or·white·blooms·in·early· spring,·these·trees·do·best·in·light·to· moderate·shade.^x	^x
Redbud^x	30'·to·35'^x	Small·deep·pink·blooms·make·the· redbud·a·favorite·flowering·tree.···It· does·well·in·moderate·shade.^x	^x
Sweet·Gum^x	65'·to·75'^x	This·fast-growing·and·hardy·tree·has·an· attractive·silver-grey·bark.···It·prefers· moist·soil·and·medium·to·dense·shade.^x	^x
Bradford·Pear^x	35'·to·40'^x	With·white·blossoms·in·spring,·this· popular·tree·does·not·produce·fruit,·but· derives·its·name·from·the·pear·shape· formed·by·its·branches.^x	^x

A new column in this table displays the mature height of each tree.

Adding a column to the right of a table

As we've mentioned, Word lets you append a column to the right side of a table. To add a new column to our sample table, begin by placing the cursor in the area outside the right edge of the table. Word will position the cursor between the edge of the table and the end-of-row mark just outside the table.

Next, open the Edit Table dialog box, choose the Column option, and choose Insert. Word will insert a new column, as shown in Figure 11-26. As you can see, the new column displays the same width as the column immediately to the left. In fact, in Figure 11-26, we scrolled to the right in our document window in order to display the new column. (Since we won't be needing this extra column, we'll delete it before creating any more examples.)

Adding multiple columns

Word lets you add multiple adjacent columns with one Table… command. To add columns to a table, first select one or more cells in the number of columns you want to add. For example, if you want to insert two columns in a table, you should select one or more cells in two columns. (Of course, you can select two columns in their entirety.) The columns you insert will appear just to the left of the first column in your selection.

After making your selection, open the Edit Table dialog box, choose the Column option, and choose Insert. The new columns Word inserts will have the same width as the top cell in the first column of your selection.

Figure 11-26

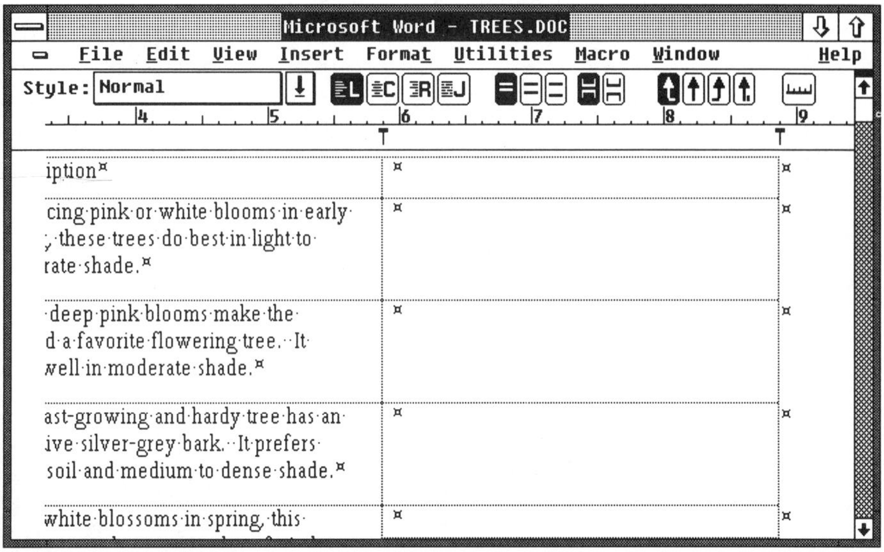

With the Edit Table dialog box, you can add a new column to the right side of a table.

To append two columns to the right edge of a table, you use the same technique, except you must highlight the last column in the table and the end-of-row marks. When you open the Edit Table dialog box, choose the Column option and choose Insert. Word will then append two columns to the end of your table. You can extend this technique to append several columns to the end of your table.

The technique you use to delete a column is similar to the one you use to delete a row. Begin by selecting one or more cells in the column(s) you want to delete. (If you want to delete only one column, just move the cursor anywhere in that column.) Then, open the Edit Table dialog box, choose the Column option, and choose Delete. Word will remove the selected column(s) and shift the remaining columns so that no gap appears in the table. When it shifts the remaining columns, Word will maintain your row alignment (left, centered, or right).

Deleting columns

If you mistakenly delete columns that you need to keep in your table, you can use the Undo command to recover them. Because Word does not place the deleted columns on the Clipboard, you cannot recover deleted columns by pasting them back into your document.

Again, if you try to use normal editing techniques—the Cut command or the [Delete] key—to delete a column, Word will merely delete the text in the selected column. It will not remove the column from the table.

**Adding and
deleting cells**

You've probably noticed that the Edit Table dialog box includes two Shift Cells options: Horizontally and Vertically. You use these options when you want to insert or delete less than a full column or full row of cells. These options tell Word which way to shift the cells of the table in order to perform the insertion or deletion. Now, we'll consider an example of how you might insert or delete partial rows and columns.

Figure 11-27 shows a simple four-column by six-row table. Notice that we have selected two cells in the second row. To delete these two cells, we'll open the Edit Table dialog box. At this point, Word already will have selected the Shift Cells Horizontally option. If we click on the Delete button while this option is selected, the remaining rows will shift to the left and the result will look like Figure 11-28. If we decide that we don't want to delete the cells after all, we can use the Undo command to recover them.

Figure 11-27

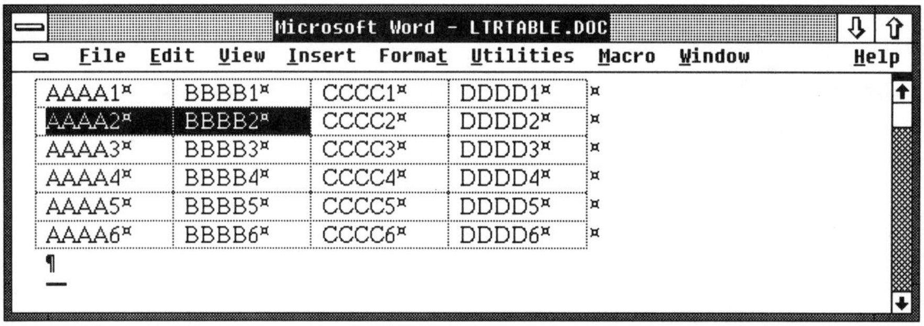

We'll use this simple table to illustrate inserting and deleting cells.

Figure 11-28

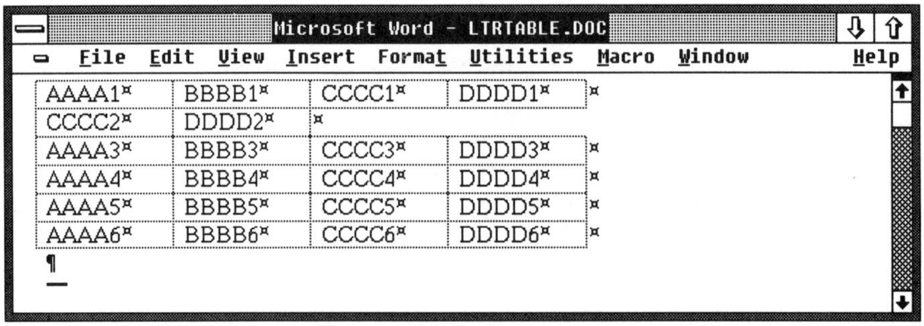

This is the effect of deleting the selected cells and shifting the remaining cells horizontally.

Figure 11-29 shows what happens when we use the Shift Cells Vertically option to delete the selected cells in the second row. As you can see, Word has moved up by one row all the cells in the first and second columns and the third through sixth rows. Notice that two blank cells now appear in the sixth row of the table.

Figure 11-29

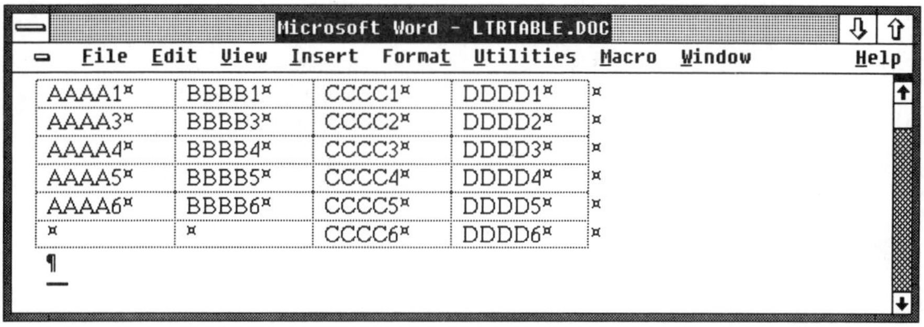

When you choose the Shift Cells Vertically option and delete cells, Word will move up the cells in the rows below.

Combining and splitting cells

Word allows you to merge two or more cells on the same row. (You cannot merge cells in the same column.) To merge cells, just select the cells you want to combine, open the Edit Table dialog box, and choose the Merge Cells button. Word will remove the boundaries between the selected cells and create one cell whose width is equal to the combined widths of the merged cells.

One excellent use for cell merging is creating a title that stretches across two or more columns in a table. For example, let's add a title row to the table shown in Figure 11-25. The first step is to add a new row to the top of the table. After clicking on one of the cells in the top row, we'll open the Edit Table dialog box, select the Row option, and click the Insert button. Word will then add a new row, as shown in Figure 11-30 on the following page.

The next step is to merge the cells in this new row into one cell. Since the row is already highlighted, we'll open the Edit Table dialog box and click the Merge Cells button. Figure 11-31 on the next page shows the result. Notice the two paragraph marks that appear in the merged cell along with the end-of-cell mark. We'll delete these before entering our text.

After entering the title text *Popular American Trees* in the new cell, we'll center that text by using the Centered-alignment icon on the ruler. Figure 11-32 on page 401 shows the table with the title in place.

Figure 11-30

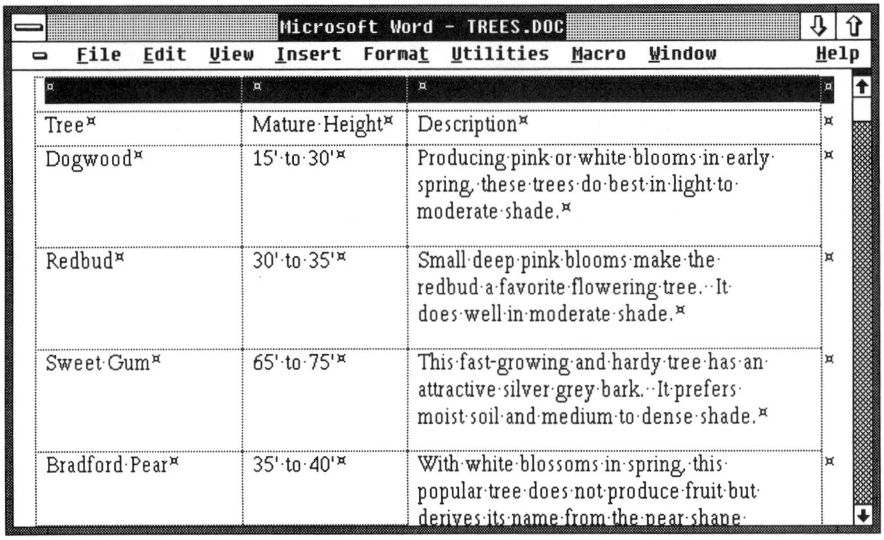

Tree¤	Mature·Height¤	Description¤	¤
Dogwood¤	15'·to·30'¤	Producing·pink·or·white·blooms·in·early·spring,·these·trees·do·best·in·light·to·moderate·shade.¤	¤
Redbud¤	30'·to·35'¤	Small·deep·pink·blooms·make·the·redbud·a·favorite·flowering·tree.··It·does·well·in·moderate·shade.¤	¤
Sweet·Gum¤	65'·to·75'¤	This·fast-growing·and·hardy·tree·has·an·attractive·silver·grey·bark.··It·prefers·moist·soil·and·medium·to·dense·shade.¤	¤
Bradford·Pear¤	35'·to·40'¤	With·white·blossoms·in·spring,·this·popular·tree·does·not·produce·fruit·but·derives·its·name·from·the·pear·shape	¤

To create a title for our sample table, we'll begin by adding a new row to the top of the table.

Figure 11-31

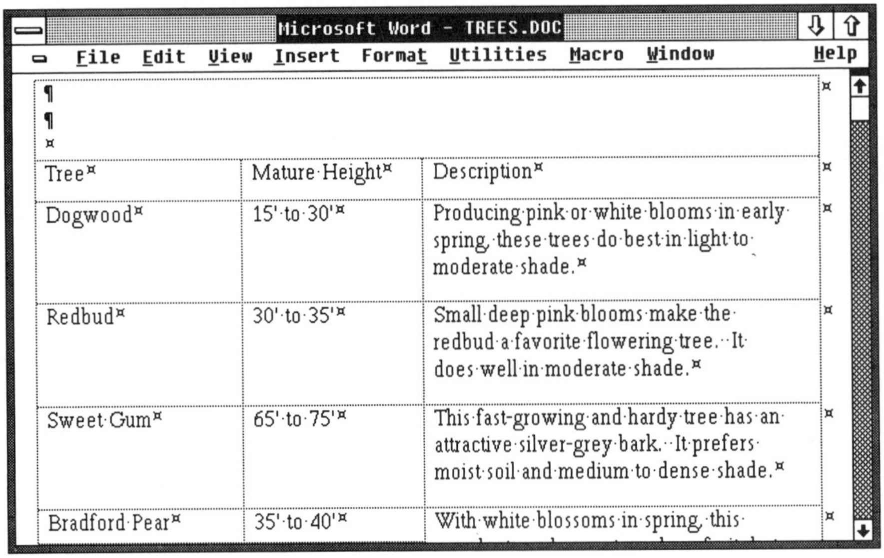

Tree¤	Mature·Height¤	Description¤	¤
Dogwood¤	15'·to·30'¤	Producing·pink·or·white·blooms·in·early·spring,·these·trees·do·best·in·light·to·moderate·shade.¤	¤
Redbud¤	30'·to·35'¤	Small·deep·pink·blooms·make·the·redbud·a·favorite·flowering·tree.··It·does·well·in·moderate·shade.¤	¤
Sweet·Gum¤	65'·to·75'¤	This·fast-growing·and·hardy·tree·has·an·attractive·silver-grey·bark.··It·prefers·moist·soil·and·medium·to·dense·shade.¤	¤
Bradford·Pear¤	35'·to·40'¤	With·white·blossoms·in·spring,·this·	¤

Word has merged the cells in the new row into a single cell.

Figure 11-32

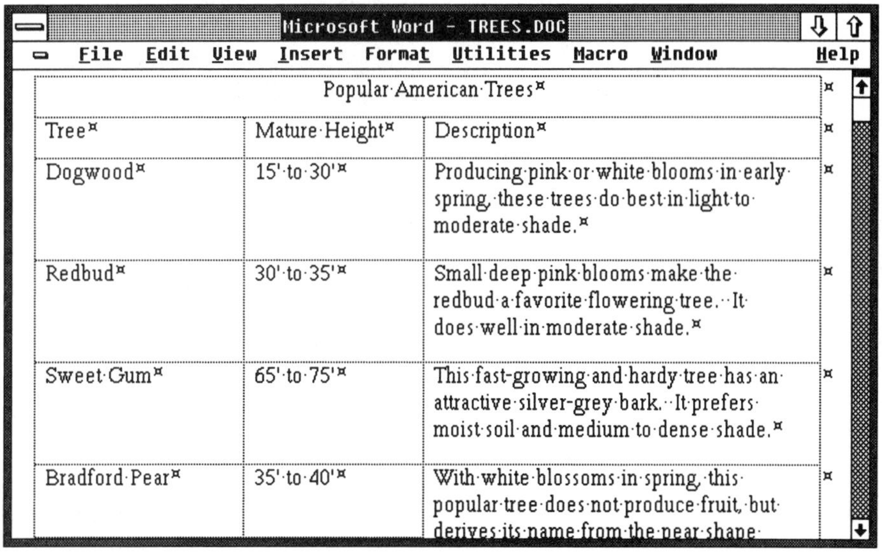

Microsoft Word - TREES.DOC	⇩ ⇧
□ **File** **Edit** **View** **Insert** **Forma t** **Utilities** **Macro** **Window**	**Help**

Popular·American·Trees×	×	↑
Tree×	Mature·Height×	Description×	×	
Dogwood×	15'·to·30'×	Producing·pink·or·white·blooms·in·early· spring,·these·trees·do·best·in·light·to· moderate·shade.×	×	
Redbud×	30'·to·35'×	Small·deep·pink·blooms·make·the· redbud·a·favorite·flowering·tree.··It· does·well·in·moderate·shade.×	×	
Sweet·Gum×	65'·to·75'×	This·fast-growing·and·hardy·tree·has·an· attractive·silver-grey·bark.··It·prefers· moist·soil·and·medium·to·dense·shade.×	×	
Bradford·Pear×	35'·to·40'×	With·white·blossoms·in·spring,·this· popular·tree·does·not·produce·fruit,·but· derives·its·name·from·the·pear·shape	×	↓

We entered our title text into the top row of the table and formatted it with centered alignment.

After merging two or more cells, you can use the Undo command to cancel the merge—provided that you choose Undo before you perform any other action. You also can use the Edit Table dialog box to "unmerge" a cell. If you move the cursor into a cell that you created by merging some cells, then open the Edit Table dialog box, you'll see that the Merge Cells button has been replaced by a Split Cells button. This button appears only after you have used the Merge Cells button to combine cells. In other words, you cannot split any cells other than the ones that were created by merging. When you click the Split Cells button, Word will break the merged cell into its original cell components.

By the way, you cannot combine a merged cell with another cell. For example, suppose you have merged the first two cells in a four-cell row. You then decide that you really wanted to merge all the cells in that row. You select the new merged cell and the other cells on that row and open the Edit Table dialog box. When you do this, you'll see that the Merge Cells button is dimmed, indicating that it is not available.

As we've illustrated, when you first create a table, Word aligns the left edge of the text area in the first column with the left edge of your document's text column. Assuming you're working in a single-column layout and you haven't moved the first-line or left indent markers on the ruler, the position of the left edge

CHANGING TABLE AND ROW ALIGNMENT

of the table text will correspond to the zero point on the ruler. However, the left boundary of the table itself (marked by a dotted line on your screen) will appear just to the left of the zero point.

Using the Format Table dialog box (shown in Figure 11-11), you can change the alignment of individual rows in a table or the alignment of an entire table. In other words, you can shift the boundaries of the table horizontally. Changing the alignment of a table is evident only when the total width of a table is less than the total width of the current text column.

The three Align Rows options in the Format Table dialog box allow you to change the alignment of a table relative to the current text column. The Left option (the default) will align the left boundary of the table with the left edge of the text column (actually, slightly to the left of the edge of the text column due to the Space Between Cols setting). So far, all the tables we have shown in this chapter display left alignment.

With the Center option, you can center the boundaries of a table within your document's text column. With the Right option, you can align the right edge of a table with the right edge of your document's text column. With right alignment, Word actually aligns the right table boundary with the right edge of the text column. It doesn't attempt to compensate for the Space Between Cols setting.

When you choose one of the Align Rows options, you can apply that alignment to some of the rows in a table or to the entire table. If you select one or more cells in every row of the table, Word will automatically apply the Align Rows option you select to the entire table. If you do not select a cell in every row of the table or if you simply move the cursor into a single cell, you can use the Apply To options—Selection or Whole Table—to specify how you want to apply the Align Rows option.

If you choose Apply To Selection, Word will apply the alignment you choose only to the row in which the cursor is located (or to all the rows in the current selection if you've selected cells in more than one row). If you choose Apply To Whole Table, Word will apply the alignment option to the entire table.

For example, let's center the table shown in Figure 11-27. After moving the cursor into a cell, we'll issue the Table… command on the Format menu, select the Center option, then choose the Apply To Whole Table option. When we choose OK, the table will look like Figure 11-33.

Although in most simple table applications, you'll want all of your rows to display the same alignment, there may be times when you need to use a different alignment on different rows to create a special effect. For example, if you use a table to design a complex form, you may want to change the alignment of selected rows in the table. In these situations, you can select some cells on just those rows whose alignment you want to change, then choose an alignment option and click the Apply To Selection option. For example, Figure 11-34 shows the sample table from Figure 11-27 after we applied centered alignment to only two rows.

Figure 11-33

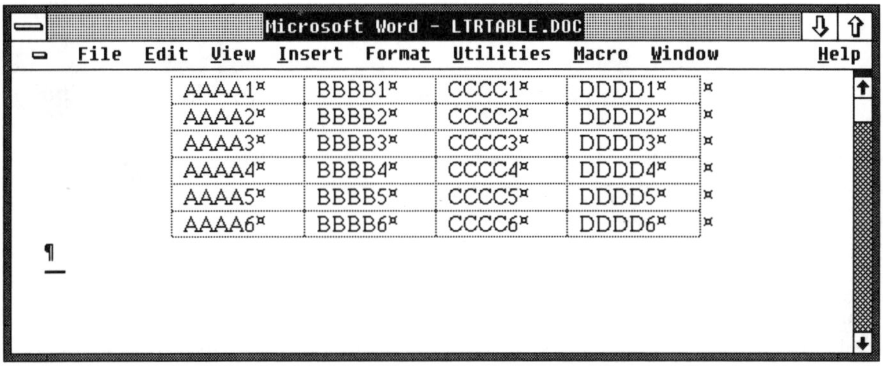

This is how the sample table from Figure 11-27 will look if we choose the Center and Apply To Whole Table options.

Figure 11-34

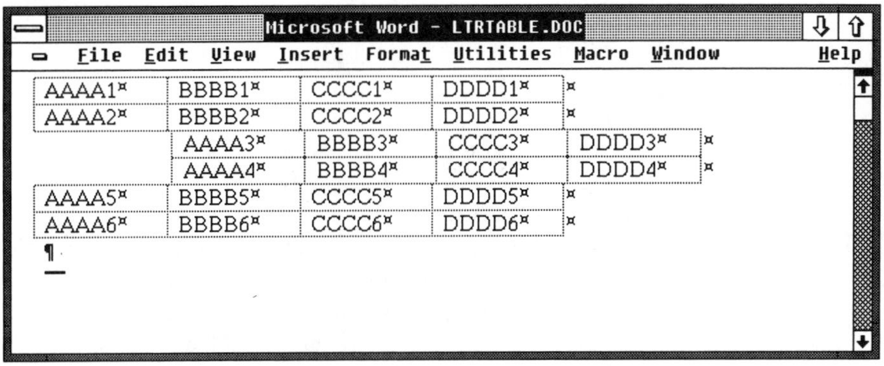

Word allows you to change the alignment of selected rows in a table.

You should note that the alignment of a table (or a row) has nothing to do with the alignment of the text within individual cells of that table. As we'll demonstrate a little later, Word allows you to change the alignment of text in a table without affecting the alignment of the table boundaries. Therefore, you do not need to change the alignment of entire rows in order to achieve different text alignment within a table.

Indenting rows

Besides alignment options, the Format Table dialog box also includes an Indent Rows setting that you can use to shift one or more rows—or the entire table—to the left or right. For example, suppose you're using the default left alignment and you want to shift the entire table $^1/_2$ inch to the right. After opening the Format Table dialog box, enter *.5″* in the Indent Rows text box and choose the Apply To Whole Table option. When you choose OK, Word will shift all the rows of the table $\frac{1}{2}$ inch to the right.

Since Word allows you to place a row in the margin area of your page, you can cause part of your table to "hang" outside the margin by adjusting the indent on one or more rows. For example, suppose you are working on a table that is left-aligned. You click on one row, open the Format Table dialog box, and enter an Indent Rows setting of -.5″. If you use the Apply To Selection option, Word will shift the current row $\frac{1}{2}$ inch to the left.

When you use an Indent Rows setting other than the default of 0, that setting will affect the table's alignment. For example, suppose you specify an Indent Rows setting of .5″, then you select Center as your Align Rows option and choose the Apply To Whole Table option. Instead of centering the table between the left and right edges of the current text column, Word will center the table between the $\frac{1}{2}$-inch indent that you've specified and the right edge of the text column.

If you have a mouse, you can use the ruler in the column view to indent one or more rows in a table. As we've pointed out, in the column view, the ruler displays a row indent marker (▶) at the zero point. By dragging this marker, you can change the indention of selected rows or an entire table. For example, to indent an entire table by $\frac{1}{2}$ inch, select any column in the table. Then, just drag the row indent marker $\frac{1}{2}$ inch to the right.

SPLITTING A TABLE

To split a table horizontally, you must insert a ¶ mark between two rows in that table. To do this, begin by placing the cursor on the row that appears below the place you want the split to occur. Then, press the [Column break] key ([Ctrl][Shift][Enter]). For example, suppose you want to split the six-row table shown in Figure 11-33 into two three-row tables. First, click anywhere on the fourth row of the table, then press the [Column break] key. Word will insert a ¶ mark between the third and fourth rows, as shown in Figure 11-35. You can enter any text or other data in the blank area between the two smaller tables.

Another way to split a table horizontally is to select one or more entire rows in the table and then choose the Table to Text… command on the Insert menu. (This command replaces the Table… command on the menu when you select at least one entire row in a table.) In the Table to Text dialog box, select one of the three Convert Table To options (Paragraphs, Tab Delimited, or Comma Delimited), and choose OK. Word will convert your selected rows to normal text. This text will split the original table into two separate tables. If the rows you selected were blank, Word will create a blank paragraph for each row to divide the table. We'll talk more about the Table to Text… command later in this chapter.

Word does not offer a method for splitting a table vertically between columns. In other words, you cannot create two tables that appear side by side in a document. However, you can achieve the same effect simply by inserting one or more new columns in the middle of a table. Just use the Insert button in the Edit Table dialog box as we've described to insert a new column where you want the vertical "split" to occur.

Figure 11-35

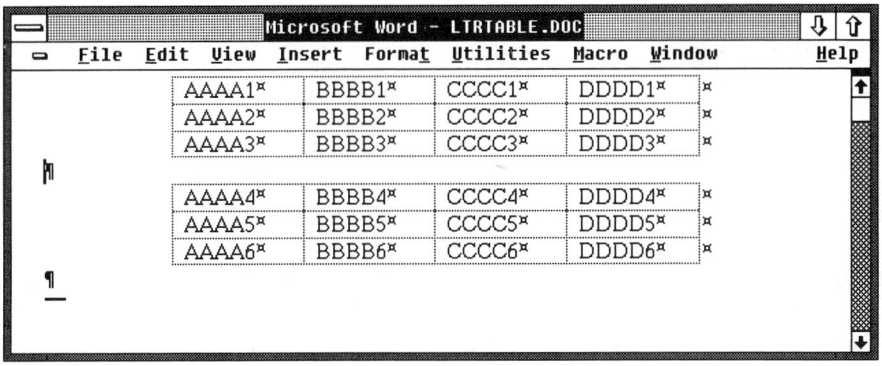

You can split a table by pressing the [Column break] key.

Inserting text above a table

Suppose you've inserted a table at the top of a new document, and you decide to enter some document text above that table. To do this, you must insert a blank paragraph above the table by clicking anywhere on the first row of the table, then pressing the [Column break] key. Word will shift the table down slightly and place a ¶ mark above the table.

WORKING WITH TEXT IN A TABLE

Word lets you edit and format the text in a table much as you would edit and format any other document text. There are a few differences, however, which we'll point out. We've already shown you how to select text in a table. Now, we'll show you how to edit your table text, then teach you how to format it.

Editing text in a table

To edit text in a table, you can use many of the same procedures and commands that you use to edit normal document text. For example, you can use all the basic editing techniques we described in Chapter 4 for inserting new text and overwriting or deleting existing text. When you press the [Enter] key, Word will begin a new paragraph in the same cell of the table—it won't move the cursor to the next row of the table.

When you use Word's Cut, Copy, and Paste commands, there are a few rules that you need to observe. First, when you copy and paste or cut and paste, the results of your paste will vary, depending on whether you copied or cut an end-of-cell mark. If the selection you copy or cut includes an end-of-cell mark, when you paste that text to another cell in the table, Word will replace the contents of that cell. (By the way, after you've cut or copied an end-of-cell mark, the Paste command on the Edit menu will change to Paste Cells.)

For example, suppose you want to replace the contents of the last cell in the fourth column of the table in Figure 11-33 with the contents of the second cell in the first column. To do this, first select the entire upper-left cell, including the end-of-cell mark. Figure 11-36 shows the table at this point.

Figure 11-36

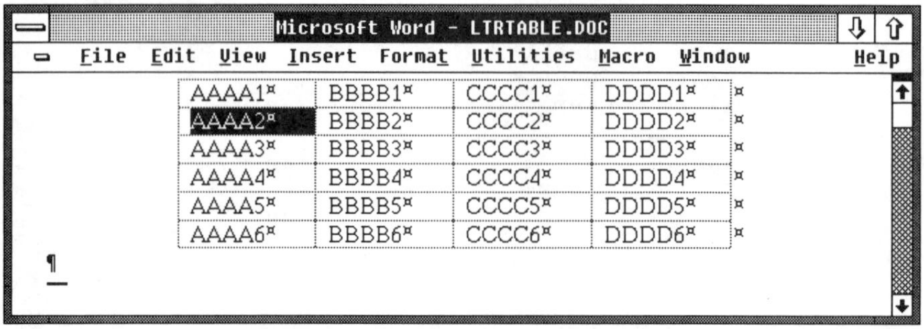

AAAA1ᵡ	BBBB1ᵡ	CCCC1ᵡ	DDDD1ᵡ	ᵡ
AAAA2ᵡ	BBBB2ᵡ	CCCC2ᵡ	DDDD2ᵡ	ᵡ
AAAA3ᵡ	BBBB3ᵡ	CCCC3ᵡ	DDDD3ᵡ	ᵡ
AAAA4ᵡ	BBBB4ᵡ	CCCC4ᵡ	DDDD4ᵡ	ᵡ
AAAA5ᵡ	BBBB5ᵡ	CCCC5ᵡ	DDDD5ᵡ	ᵡ
AAAA6ᵡ	BBBB6ᵡ	CCCC6ᵡ	DDDD6ᵡ	ᵡ

Microsoft Word – LTRTABLE.DOC
File Edit View Insert Format Utilities Macro Window Help

We've selected both the text and the end-of-cell mark in a cell.

Now, suppose you choose the Copy command, move the cursor into the last cell in the fourth column of the table, and choose the Paste Cells command. Figure 11-37 shows the result. As you can see, the copied text *AAAA2*, has replaced the text *DDDD6* that formerly appeared in the last cell of the table.

Figure 11-37

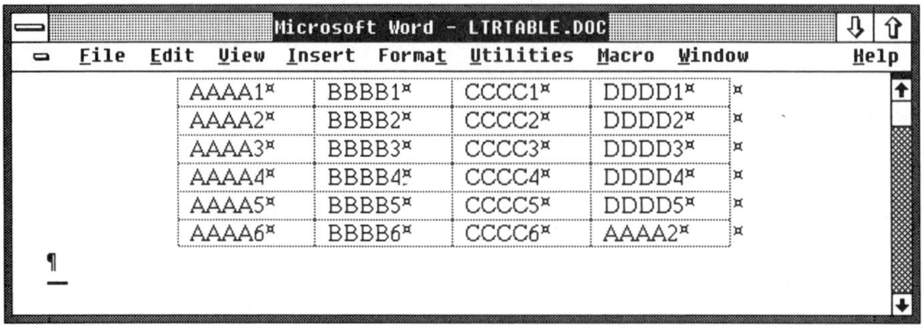

Microsoft Word – LTRTABLE.DOC
File Edit View Insert Format Utilities Macro Window Help

AAAA1ᵡ	BBBB1ᵡ	CCCC1ᵡ	DDDD1ᵡ	ᵡ
AAAA2ᵡ	BBBB2ᵡ	CCCC2ᵡ	DDDD2ᵡ	ᵡ
AAAA3ᵡ	BBBB3ᵡ	CCCC3ᵡ	DDDD3ᵡ	ᵡ
AAAA4ᵡ	BBBB4ᵡ	CCCC4ᵡ	DDDD4ᵡ	ᵡ
AAAA5ᵡ	BBBB5ᵡ	CCCC5ᵡ	DDDD5ᵡ	ᵡ
AAAA6ᵡ	BBBB6ᵡ	CCCC6ᵡ	AAAA2ᵡ	ᵡ

Because we copied the end-of-cell mark, Word replaced the contents of the last cell on the last row of the table.

If the selection you copy or cut does not include an end-of-cell mark, Word will simply add that text to the cell in which you paste it. For example, suppose the selection in the table shown in Figure 11-36 included only the text *AAAA2* and not the end-of-cell mark. Figure 11-38 shows the result of copying and pasting this text into the last cell of the table. (We also inserted a space between the original and copied text.)

Figure 11-38

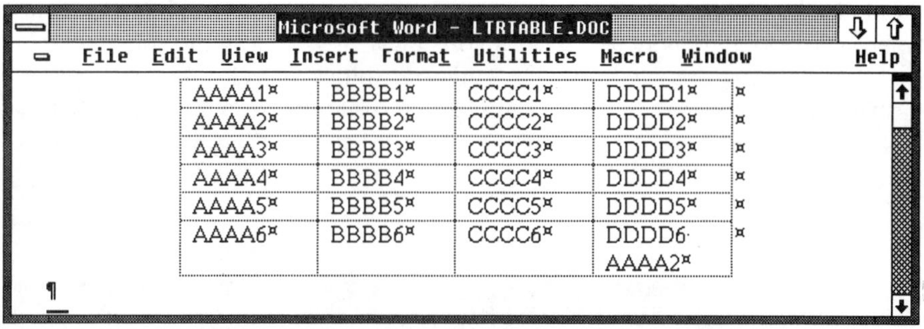

When the text selection does not include an end-of-cell mark, Word will add the selection to the text in the cell in which you paste.

As we pointed out earlier, there's no way to select text from two or more cells without also selecting the end-of-cell marks. If you want to copy and paste text from two or more cells into another cell—without deleting the contents of that cell—you must perform separate copy procedures for each cell whose text you want to duplicate. Similarly, if you want to cut text from two or more cells and paste it into another cell without losing the original contents of that cell, you must issue a separate Cut command for each cell whose contents you want to move.

Selecting a paste area within a table

When you move or copy cells within a table, you'll want to select a paste area that corresponds in both size and shape to the area that you cut or copied. For example, suppose you want to copy the first two rows of the table shown in Figure 11-36 and paste them into the last two rows of that table. To begin, select the first two rows and issue the Copy command. Next, select the last two rows in their entirety and then choose the Paste Cells command. If you select a paste area that does not match the copy area—for example, if you select only the first cells in the last two rows—Word will not execute the paste and will display the message *Copy and Paste areas are different shapes.* To correct the problem, choose OK in the message box and select a new paste area.

There is one exception to the rule we've stated for pasting cells: Word lets you specify the paste area by moving the cursor into a single cell. When you move the cursor into a single cell and issue the Paste Cells command, Word will extend the paste area to match the size and shape of the cut or copy area. The cell containing the cursor becomes the upper-left corner of the paste area. (By the way, if you're familiar with copying, cutting, and pasting in a spreadsheet, such as Microsoft Excel, you can see that copying and pasting in a Word table is similar.)

Pasting text outside a table

The results of moving and copying text within a table will vary depending on whether the text you select to cut or copy includes an end-of-cell mark. The end-of-cell mark also affects what happens when you paste text outside a table. If the text you select in a table includes an end-of-cell mark and you paste that text outside a table, Word will create a new table. This new table will have the same dimensions and alignment as the cells you cut or copied from the original table. For example, suppose we copied the selected block of cells shown in Figure 11-39 to an area outside the table. Figure 11-40 shows the results. Notice that the cells are the same size as the original cells and that Word has applied centered alignment to this new table.

Figure 11-39

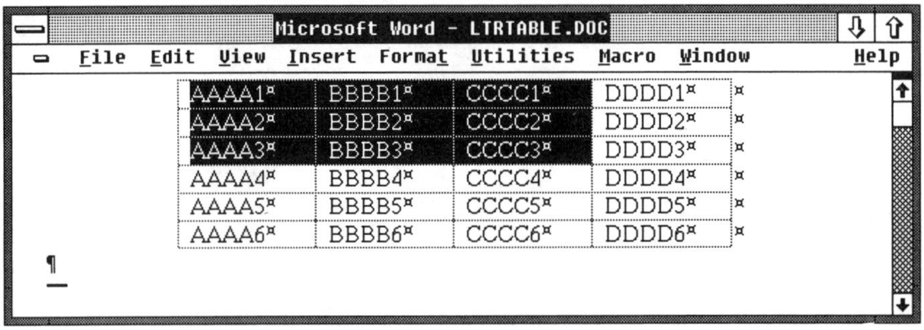

We'll copy this block of cells outside the table.

Figure 11-40

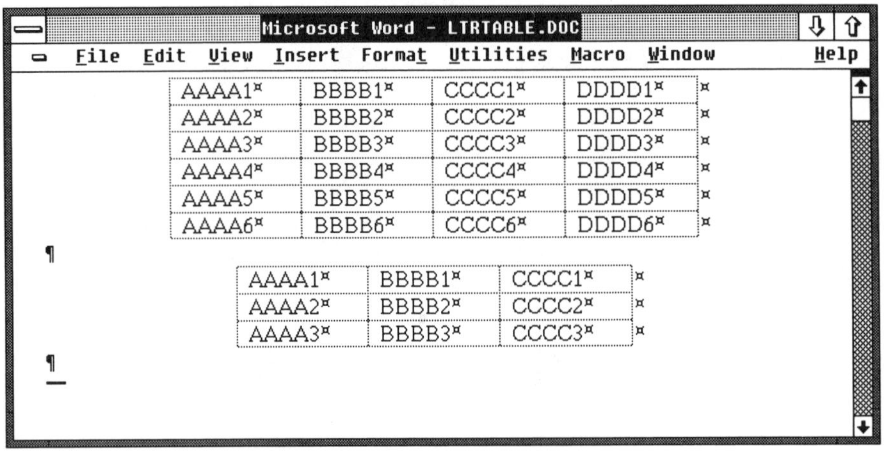

When we paste the selected block of cells outside the table, Word will create a new table.

When we performed the copy procedure shown in Figures 11-39 and 11-40, we left a blank paragraph between the original table and the copied cells. If we had not done this, Word would have appended the cells onto our original table, as shown in Figure 11-41.

Figure 11-41

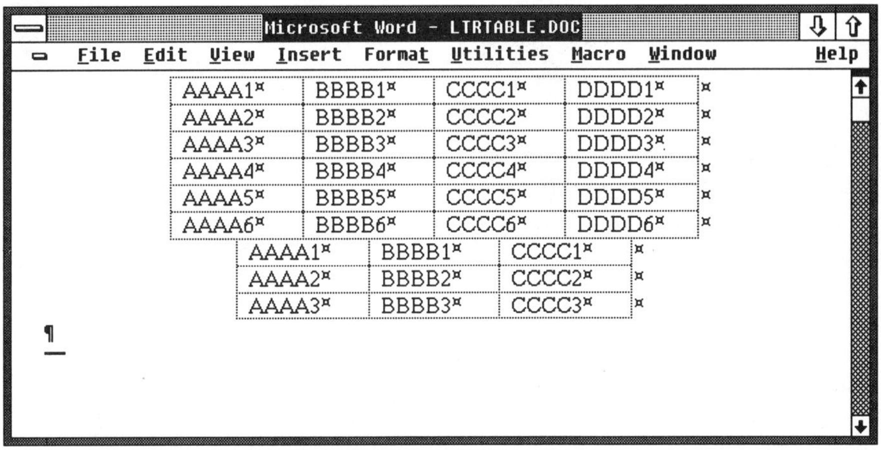

If you don't allow a blank paragraph between the original table and the copied cells, Word will append those cells onto the original table.

If you select some text in a table and your selection does not include an end-of-cell mark, you can copy or move that text outside the table without creating a new table. For example, suppose we select only the text in the first cell of the table shown in Figure 11-39, issue the Copy command, click outside the table, then choose Paste. Figure 11-42 on the next page shows the result. Notice that we did not need to leave a blank paragraph between the table and the copied text.

Formatting text in a table

One of the nicest features of tables is the tremendous amount of flexibility you're allowed in formatting the table text. You can apply any combination of character and paragraph formatting to the text of a table. To make formatting faster and easier, you can define and apply styles to your table text.

Each of the paragraphs in a table can be formatted independently of other paragraphs. Thus, text that appears in the same row or the same column—or even the same cell—of a table can display different indents, alignment, line spacing, tabs, and so forth. There are only a few restrictions that Word imposes on formatting the text in a table. First, you cannot force table text to flow across a cell boundary. You also cannot create a table within a table.

Figure 11-42

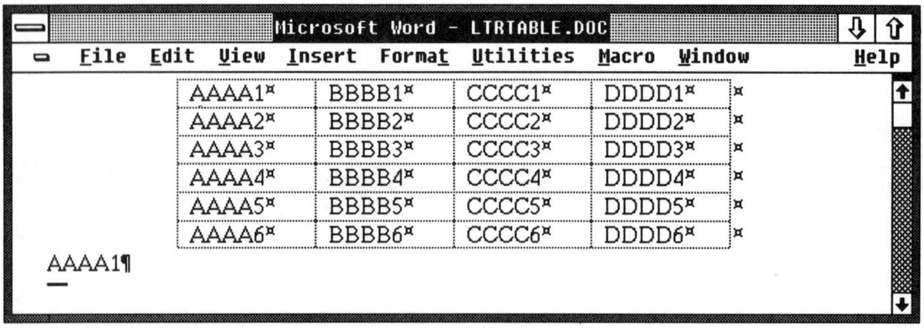

```
┌─────────────────────────────────────────────────────────────────────────┐
│ ═  │░░░░░░░░░░░░░░░░░░Microsoft Word - LTRTABLE.DOC░░░░░░░░░░░░░░│ ⇩ │ ⇧ │
├───────────────────────────────────────────────────────────────────────────┤
│ ═   File  Edit  View  Insert  Format  Utilities  Macro  Window        Help │
│            ┌────────┬────────┬────────┬────────┐                       ▲   │
│            │ AAAA1ˣ │ BBBB1ˣ │ CCCC1ˣ │ DDDD1ˣ │ ˣ                     █   │
│            │ AAAA2ˣ │ BBBB2ˣ │ CCCC2ˣ │ DDDD2ˣ │ ˣ                     █   │
│            │ AAAA3ˣ │ BBBB3ˣ │ CCCC3ˣ │ DDDD3ˣ │ ˣ                     █   │
│            │ AAAA4ˣ │ BBBB4ˣ │ CCCC4ˣ │ DDDD4ˣ │ ˣ                         │
│            │ AAAA5ˣ │ BBBB5ˣ │ CCCC5ˣ │ DDDD5ˣ │ ˣ                         │
│            │ AAAA6ˣ │ BBBB6ˣ │ CCCC6ˣ │ DDDD6ˣ │ ˣ                         │
│    AAAA1¶  └────────┴────────┴────────┴────────┘                           │
│    ─                                                                       │
│                                                                            ▼ │
└─────────────────────────────────────────────────────────────────────────┘
```

If the text you select does not include an end-of-cell mark, you can paste that text outside the table without creating a new table.

To show how to format text in a table, we'll apply some character and paragraph formatting to our sample trees table shown in Figure 11-32. We'll begin by formatting the title of the table to appear in 14-point bold type. To do this, we'll select the title text (*Popular American Trees*), choose 14 from the ribbon's Points pull-down list box, and select the ribbon's Bold icon. We'll also add 8 points of space before and after the title by opening the Paragraph dialog box, entering *8pt* into the Spacing Before and After text boxes, and choosing OK.

Next, we'll add bold formatting, centered alignment, and spacing before and after each of the column headings (*Tree, Mature Height,* and *Description*) by first selecting the row on which these titles appear, then choosing the Bold icon on the ribbon. Next, we'll open the Paragraph dialog box and enter *2pt* in both the Spacing Before and After text boxes. Finally, we'll select the Centered-alignment icon on the ruler. Figure 11-43 shows the result of our formatting changes.

Using named styles in a table

When you first create a table, Word will assign to every cell in that table the style of the paragraph on which the cursor was positioned at the time you issued the Table... command on the Insert menu. If you create a table in a new blank document, every cell will automatically carry the *Normal* style. You can, of course, apply other named styles to format the text in a table. For example, let's format the tree names in the first column of the table by defining a style named *trees* and applying it. To determine what characteristics we want the *trees* style to have, let's format the first tree name, *Dogwood,* then use it as the "example" for our new style. After moving the cursor into the cell that contains the name *Dogwood,* we'll select the Centered-alignment icon on the ruler. Then, we'll select the Open-space icon.

Now, to define these characteristics as a new style, we'll highlight the current style name that appears in the Style text box on the ruler. Next, we'll type our new style name, *trees,* and press [Enter]. When Word displays the message *Define Style "trees" based on selection?,* we'll choose the Yes button.

Figure 11-43

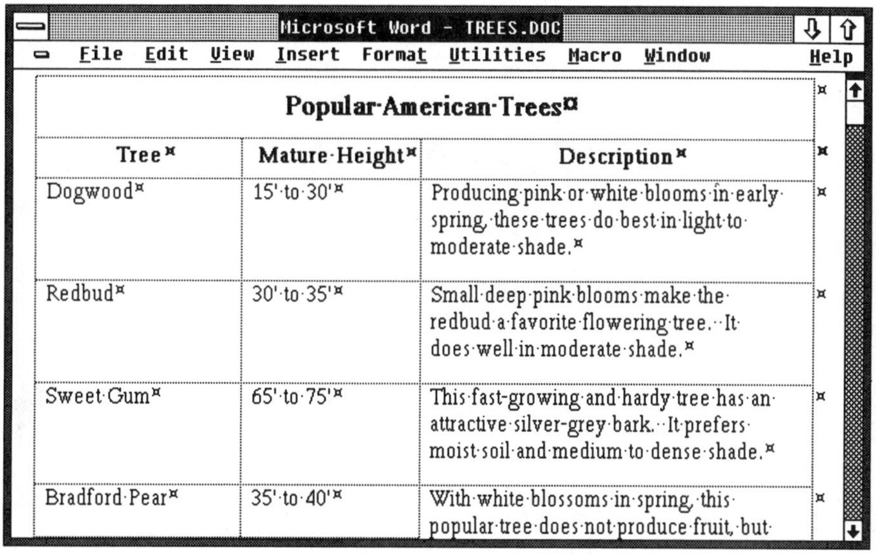

We've added some formatting to the title and column headings in our table.

To apply this new style to the other tree names, we'll simply select those cells and choose the style name *trees* from the Style list box on the ruler.

We could follow a similar procedure to define the styles *height* and *description* to format the second and third columns of the table. The *height* style, like the *trees* style, would call for centered alignment and open spacing. The *description* style would call for 6 points of space above each paragraph. Figure 11-44 on the following page shows the table after applying our named styles.

When you use styles in a table, those styles will not "carry over" from one cell to the next as you are entering text. For example, suppose you have applied a style named *cells* to the first cell in a table. After typing some text in this cell, you press the [Tab] key to move to the adjacent cell. When you begin typing there, Word will use the *Normal* style to format your text (or whatever style has been applied to that cell). If you want to use the *cells* style again, you must apply it to the cell.

Of course, if you press [Enter] to start a new paragraph in the same cell, Word will continue to use whatever style you applied to the previous paragraph—unless that style specifies a different Next Style.

With styles, you also can preformat individual cells of a table. After you have created a new, blank table, just apply the appropriate style names to the different cells in the table. Then, as you move from cell to cell and enter text, Word will automatically apply the style that's defined for each cell. Of course, instead of preformatting the cells of a table as we've described, you can enter all the text in a table and then apply various styles to individual cells and blocks of cells to format the text.

Figure 11-44

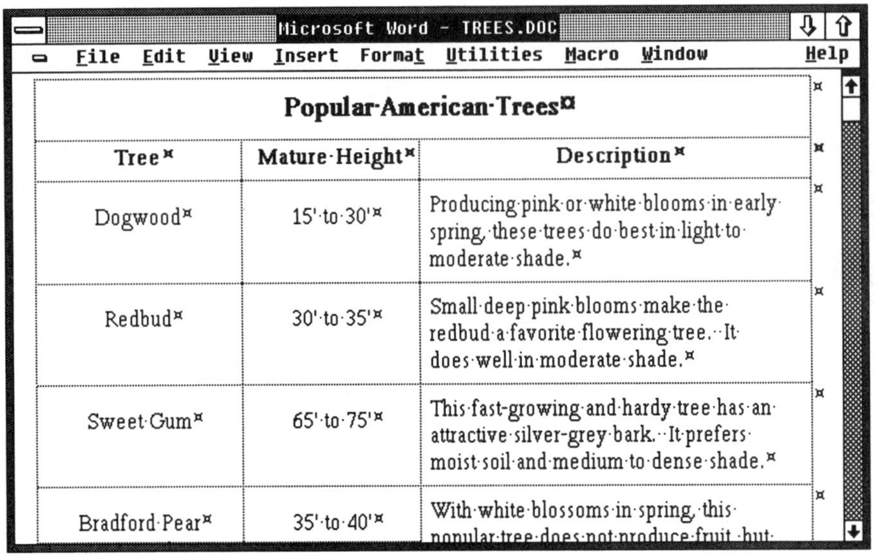

Popular American Trees		
Tree	Mature Height	Description
Dogwood	15' to 30'	Producing pink or white blooms in early spring, these trees do best in light to moderate shade.
Redbud	30' to 35'	Small deep pink blooms make the redbud a favorite flowering tree. It does well in moderate shade.
Sweet Gum	65' to 75'	This fast-growing and hardy tree has an attractive silver-grey bark. It prefers moist soil and medium to dense shade.
Bradford Pear	35' to 40'	With white blossoms in spring, this popular tree does not produce fruit but

We used named styles to format the columns of our table.

Indenting table text

If you have a mouse, you can change the alignment of text in a table by moving the indent markers on the ruler. To change the indents, first make sure the ruler is displayed in the paragraph view. Then, highlight the text you want to indent and drag the indent markers on the ruler. If a cell contains two or more paragraphs, you can change the indents for only one of those paragraphs by clicking on it and moving the indent markers on the ruler. The other paragraphs in the cell will not be affected.

You can simultaneously change the indents for two or more adjacent cells in a column. Just select those cells and drag the indent markers on the ruler. (If the cells in your selection have different indent settings, Word will dim the ruler and display the indent markers for the top cell in the selection.)

You can also use the ruler to simultaneously change the indent settings for two or more cells in a row. If you select two or more adjacent cells in a row, the ruler will display a dimmed set of indent markers that reflects the indents for only the first (leftmost) cell in the selection. If you change the position of the dimmed indent markers, all the selected cells will maintain the same amount of space between the indent markers and the cell's left and right cell boundaries. For example, if you highlight two adjacent cells in the same row and move both the left and right indent markers inward $^1/_2$ inch from the cell boundary, Word will move both the left and right indent markers of the two selected cells inward $^1/_2$ inch from their respective cell boundaries.

If you don't have a mouse, you can use the Paragraph dialog box to change the indents of the text in your tables. To do this, simply select the Paragraph... command from the Format menu, enter a new setting into two of the Indents text boxes—From Left and From Right—then choose OK.

Changing indents can have an effect similar to changing the Space Between Cols setting in the Format Table dialog box—it will move your text closer to or farther from the left and right boundaries of the cell. However, you can change indents on a selective basis, whereas the Space Between Cols setting always applies to every cell in a row.

In fact, by moving the indent markers on the ruler, you can override the Space Between Cols setting. As we explained earlier, Word divides the Space Between Cols setting between the left and right ends of each cell. Therefore, if you specify a Space Between Cols setting of .5" for one row of a table, Word will insert $^1/_4$ inch of space at either end of each cell on that row. This can create unwanted space between the left and right boundaries of the table and the table text. To push your table text closer to the cell boundaries, just select the cells you want to format and move the indent markers on the ruler.

For example, Figure 11-45 on the next page shows a table that has two 2-inch-wide columns and a Space Between Cols setting of .5". We've also applied centered alignment to this table. Suppose we want the text in the first column to appear closer to the left table boundary and we want the text in the second column to appear closer to the right table boundary. We'll begin by selecting the first column and, with the ruler in the paragraph view, we'll drag the first-line and left indent markers $^1/_4$ inch to the left. Next, we'll select the second column and drag the right indent marker $^1/_4$ inch to the right. Figure 11-46 on the following page shows the result.

The Spacing Before and After settings in the Paragraph dialog box (and the Open-space icon on the ruler) offer a way to create space between the text in a table and the top and bottom boundaries of each cell. When you add space before and/or after the text in a cell, Word will adjust the height of that cell (and other cells on the same row) as necessary to accommodate the additional space. In this respect, adding space before and after the table text is similar to changing the Minimum Row Height setting in the Format Table dialog box. However, there's one important difference. When you adjust the height of a row in the Format Table dialog box, Word does not increase the spacing between the text in that row and the top boundary of that row. With the Before and After settings, however, you can increase the height of a row and control the position of the text in that row relative to the top and bottom cell boundaries.

Adding space before and after the table text

Figure 11-45

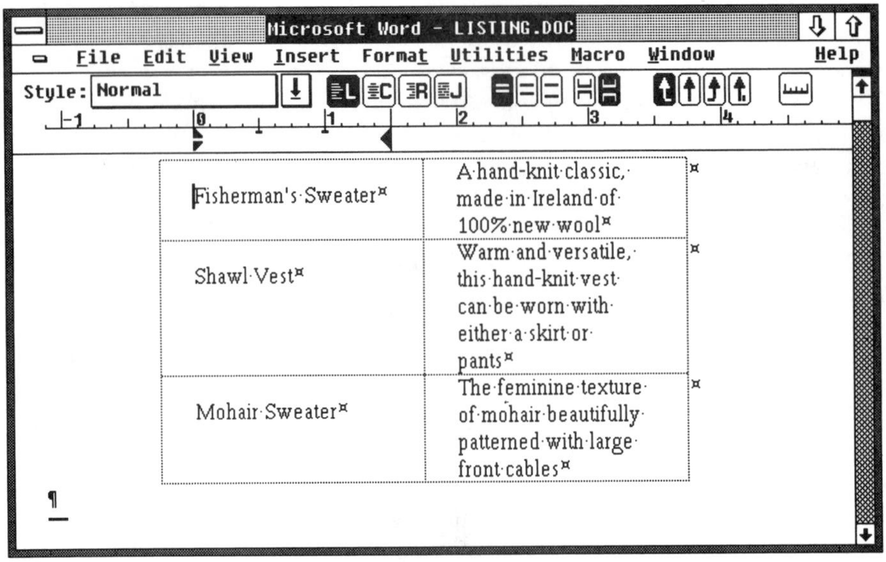

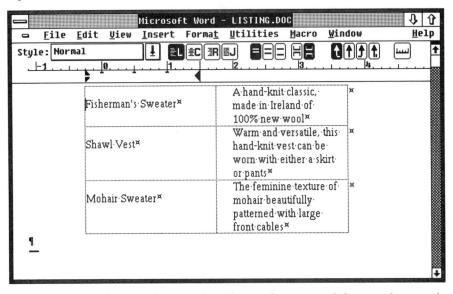

This table has a Space Between Cols setting of .5", which creates extra space between the table boundaries and the table text.

Figure 11-46

By moving the indent markers on the ruler, we have moved the text closer to the table boundaries.

For example, we used the Before setting to format some of the paragraphs in our trees table shown in Figure 11-44. This moved the text away from the top boundary of each cell, making the table more attractive and easier to read.

Word allows you to use tabs to align the text in one or more cells of a table. With tabs, you can split the contents of a cell into two or more "columns" without having to insert a new cell. This can be convenient when only one cell (or a few cells) on a row needs columnar formatting.

Tabs also allow you to create decimal alignment for a column of numbers in a table. In fact, if you format a cell with a decimal tab, Word will automatically align the contents of that cell with the decimal tab. (For more on creating and using tabs, see Chapter 5.)

There's one important difference between tabs that appear in a table and tabs that appear in other parts of a document. To move the cursor to the next tab stop in a table, you must press [Ctrl][Tab]. As we explained earlier, when you press only the [Tab] key, Word will move the cursor to the next cell on the same row.

Figure 11-47 shows an example of a table that includes tabs. As you can see on the ruler, we used a decimal tab to align the numbers in the second column of the table. We also used a right-aligned tab to align the words *(through Dec. 10)* in the last cell of the first column. Instead of using a tab in this last cell, we could have used the Table… command on the Edit menu to insert an extra cell in the fourth row of the table, then adjusted the widths of the cells to align the text properly. However, inserting a single tab is a more efficient way to accomplish the same goal.

Using tabs in a table

Figure 11-47

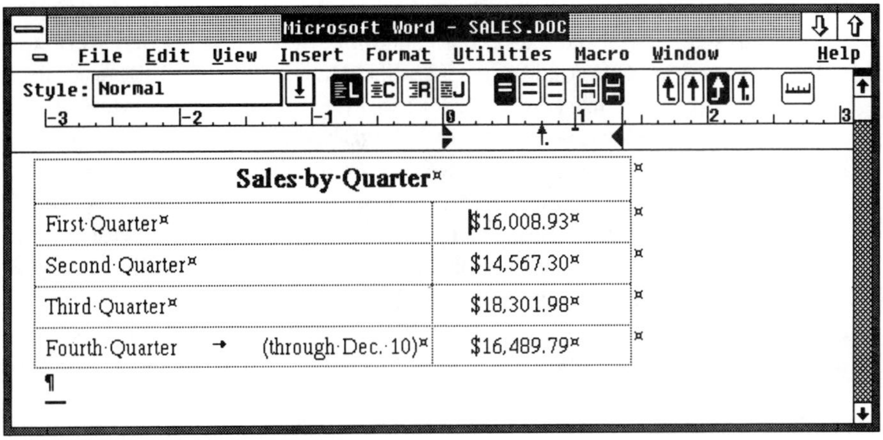

You can use tabs in a table to align text and numbers.

ADDING BORDERS TO A TABLE

As we've mentioned, the gridlines that define the row and column boundaries of a table on your screen do not appear when you print the table. If you want the printed table to include gridlines, you can format the table with borders. When you use borders in a table, you do not need to display lines between every row and every column. You can apply borders selectively to certain rows and columns or even to individual cells. You also can surround an entire table with a border.

To add a border to a table, first select the portion of the table where you want the border to appear. Then, choose the Table... command from the Format menu to bring up the Format Table dialog box shown in Figure 11-48.

Figure 11-48

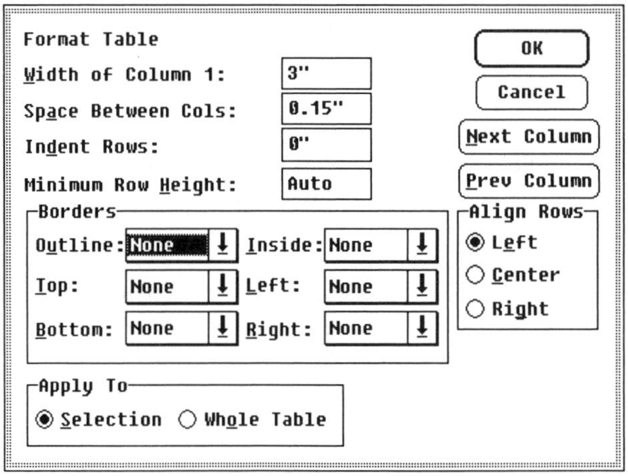

```
┌─────────────────────────────────────────────────────────────┐
│  Format Table                          ┌──────────────┐      │
│  Width of Column 1:      │3"      │     │     OK       │      │
│                                        └──────────────┘      │
│  Space Between Cols:     │0.15"   │    ┌──────────────┐       │
│                                        │   Cancel     │       │
│  Indent Rows:            │0"      │    └──────────────┘       │
│                                       ┌──────────────┐        │
│  Minimum Row Height:     │Auto    │   │ Next Column  │        │
│  ┌Borders──────────────────────────┐ └──────────────┘        │
│                                       ┌──────────────┐        │
│   Outline:│None   ↓│ Inside:│None ↓│ │ Prev Column  │        │
│                                       └──────────────┘        │
│   Top:    │None ↓│ Left:  │None ↓│   ┌Align Rows─┐            │
│                                       │ ◉ Left    │            │
│   Bottom: │None ↓│ Right: │None ↓│   │ ○ Center  │            │
│                                       │ ○ Right   │            │
│                                                               │
│  ┌Apply To────────────────────────┐                          │
│  │ ◉ Selection  ○ Whole Table      │                          │
│  └─────────────────────────────────┘                          │
└─────────────────────────────────────────────────────────────┘
```

Use the Format Table dialog box to create borders in a table.

As you can see, the Format Table dialog box includes six pull-down list boxes in the Borders section of the dialog box: Outline, Inside, Top, Left, Bottom, and Right. You use the Top list box to draw a border along the top edge of the highlighted cells. Similarly, you use the Left, Bottom, and Right list boxes to draw borders along the left, bottom, and right edge of the highlighted cells. The Outline list box lets you draw a line around the outside of the highlighted cells. (As you'll see in a moment, the Outline list box simply enters the appropriate settings into the Top, Left, Bottom, and Right list boxes.) Finally, the Inside list box lets you draw lines between the cells that lie inside the highlighted range.

As an example, suppose you want to draw a plain, box border around the table in Figure 11-44. To begin, highlight the entire table and choose the Table... command from the Format menu. When the Format Table dialog box appears, pull down the Outline list box and choose the Single option. Word will then automatically select the Single option in each of the Top, Left, Bottom, and Right list boxes. When you choose OK to complete the command, Word will surround the table with a single line, as shown in the print-out in Figure 11-49.

Figure 11-49

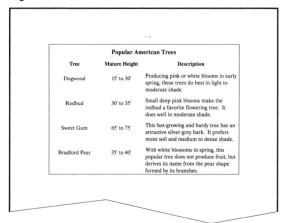

The Outline option lets you add an outline to your tables.

Suppose you now want to add borders to the inside of your table in addition to the outline border. To do this, simply highlight the entire table, bring up the Format Table dialog box, pull down the Inside list box, and choose the Single option. When you choose OK, Word will add borders around the cells of the table, as shown in the print-out in Figure 11-50.

Figure 11-50

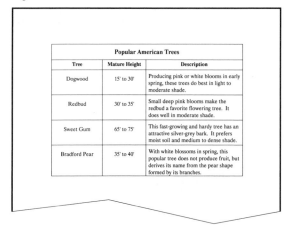

The Inside list box lets you draw lines along the borders of all the cells in the table.

Each of the Borders pull-down list boxes contains four options: None, Single, Thick, and Double. The Single option tells Word to draw a 1-point line, while the Thick option tells Word to draw a 2-point line. The Double option instructs Word to draw two 1-point parallel lines 2 points apart.

The Outline list box also contains a Shadow option, which creates a shadow effect by placing a single line along the top and left edges of the selected area, and a thick line along the bottom and right edges. You can often enhance the appearance of your borders by using these alternative line types.

Deleting borders

To delete the borders in a table, begin by selecting the cells whose borders you want to remove and opening the Format Table dialog box. In the dialog box, Word will present the current line types in each of the six Borders list boxes. To remove all borders, just change the settings in each of these list boxes to None, and then choose OK. To remove only selected parts of the border, just change the appropriate list box settings to None. For example, if you wanted to delete only the top border on the selected cells, you would change the Top list box setting to None—you wouldn't alter the settings in the other five list boxes.

In some cases, the portion of the table you highlight will not have the same border type along one of its edges. When this happens, Word will present the word *None* in the appropriate list box in the Borders section. To remove the borders along that side, first pull down the appropriate list box. When you do this, you will notice that Word will remove the word *None* from the text box at the top of the list. At this point, choose None from the list to return the word *None* to the text box, then choose OK. Word will then remove all borders along that edge of the table.

SORTING IN A TABLE

In Chapter 16, we'll explain the Sort... command on Word's Utilities menu. You can use this command to sort all or part of a table. When you sort a table, Word will follow most of the same rules for sorting that we will explain in Chapter 16.

Word always sorts a table by rows. In other words, you cannot use the Sort... command to rearrange the cells in a row. Furthermore, in determining how to sort a table, Word looks at the first character (or first few characters) in each cell. If a cell contains more than one paragraph, the Sort... command will not affect the order of those paragraphs within the cell.

Suppose you want to sort the information in the sample trees table so that it appears in alphabetical order by tree name. To do this, begin by selecting just the tree names in the first column. (It's important that you do not select the column heading.) You can select entire rows of the table instead of selecting just the tree names. After making your selection, choose the Sort... command from the Utilities menu. At this point, Word will display the dialog box shown in Figure 11-51. To sort the tree names alphabetically, just choose OK to complete the command. Figure 11-52 shows the result.

As you can see, Word sorts the text in *all* the columns of the table—not just the column(s) you select. The column you select (or the leftmost column in a selection) serves as the "key" to the sort procedure. To sort the sample trees table by height, begin by selecting the second column of the table. (You also could select the second and third columns.) Then, open the Sort dialog box and choose OK. Figure 11-53 on the next page shows the result.

Figure 11-51

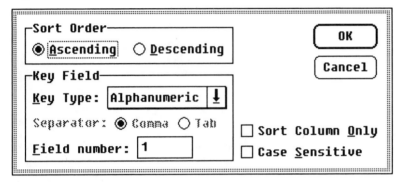

The Sort dialog box lets you rearrange the rows in your table.

Figure 11-52

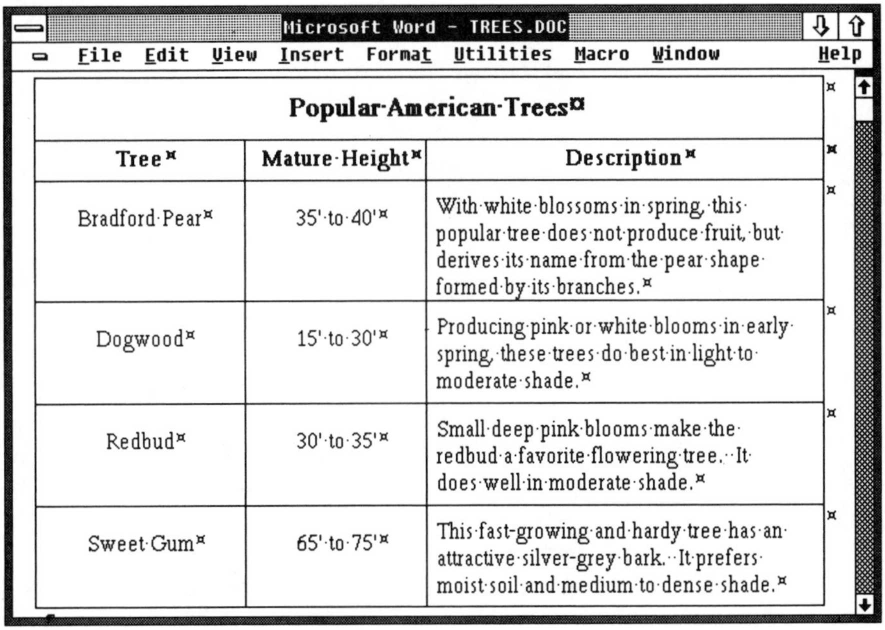

Popular American Trees		
Tree	**Mature Height**	**Description**
Bradford Pear	35' to 40'	With white blossoms in spring, this popular tree does not produce fruit, but derives its name from the pear shape formed by its branches.
Dogwood	15' to 30'	Producing pink or white blooms in early spring, these trees do best in light to moderate shade.
Redbud	30' to 35'	Small deep pink blooms make the redbud a favorite flowering tree. It does well in moderate shade.
Sweet Gum	65' to 75'	This fast-growing and hardy tree has an attractive silver-grey bark. It prefers moist soil and medium to dense shade.

Word arranged the table in alphabetical order by tree name.

Figure 11-53

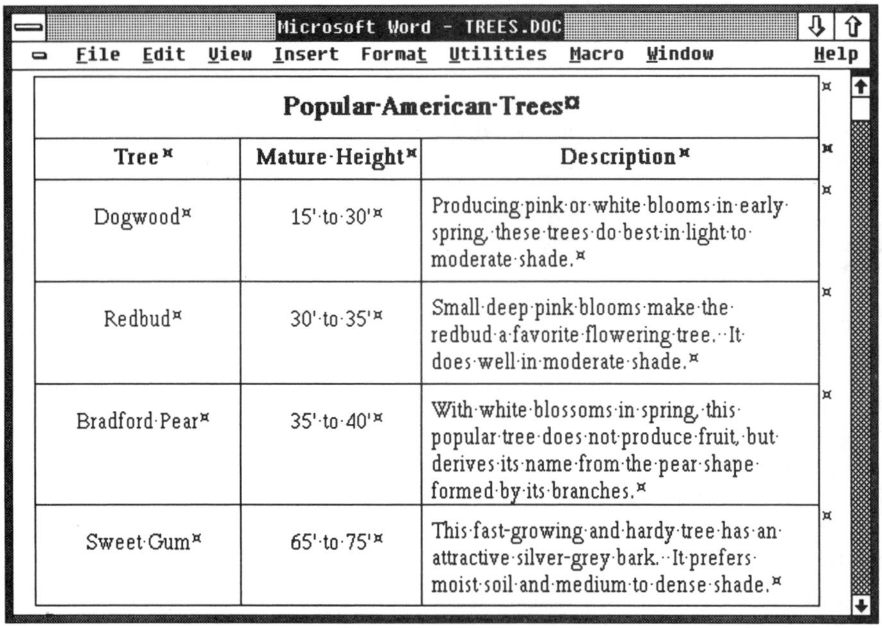

Popular·American·Trees¤		
Treeˣ	**Mature·Height**ˣ	**Description**ˣ
Dogwoodˣ	15'·to·30'ˣ	Producing·pink·or·white·blooms·in·early· spring,·these·trees·do·best·in·light·to· moderate·shade.ˣ
Redbudˣ	30'·to·35'ˣ	Small·deep·pink·blooms·make·the· redbud·a·favorite·flowering·tree.··It· does·well·in·moderate·shade.ˣ
Bradford·Pearˣ	35'·to·40'ˣ	With·white·blossoms·in·spring,·this· popular·tree·does·not·produce·fruit,·but· derives·its·name·from·the·pear·shape· formed·by·its·branches.ˣ
Sweet·Gumˣ	65'·to·75'ˣ	This·fast-growing·and·hardy·tree·has·an· attractive·silver-grey·bark.··It·prefers· moist·soil·and·medium·to·dense·shade.ˣ

Our table is now arranged in ascending order by height.

As we'll explain in Chapter 16, you can use the Sort Column Only option in the Sort dialog box to sort only the entries that appear in the column you've highlighted. For example, if you highlight the second column of the table in Figure 11-53, open the Sort dialog box, select the Sort Column Only check box, and then choose OK, Word will sort the entries in the second column, but will not change the order of the entries in the first or third columns.

SETTING UP A SPREADSHEET WITH A TABLE

If you've ever worked with a spreadsheet application like Microsoft Excel, you've probably noticed a few similarities between spreadsheets and the tables you can create in a Word document. Although Word cannot perform most of the complex tasks that are normally associated with spreadsheet programs, you can use Word's table capabilities along with fields to set up a simple spreadsheet in your document.

We've already shown you how to make text and numeric entries in a Word table—two types of entries that are essential to spreadsheets. What we haven't shown you yet is how to enter formulas that refer to other cells in a table. Let's discuss how to refer to cells in a table.

All cell references take the form [*rncn*], where *r* stands for row and *c* stands for column. The *n's* stand for the row or column offset from the upper-left corner of the table. For example, [r1c1] refers to the cell that lies in row 1, column 1, while [r3c2] refers to the cell that lies in row 3, column 2. Although we'll always use lowercase *r's* and *c's* in our range references, Word allows you to use either uppercase or lowercase letters in your range references.

If you want to refer to a group of adjacent cells (called a *range* of cells), type a colon between the upper-left and lower-right cells of the range. For example, the range reference [r1c1:r2c2] refers to four cells: r1c1, r1c2, r2c1, and r2c2. If you want to refer to an entire row or to an entire column, type the appropriate row or column reference. For example, the reference [r3] refers to all the cells in row 3, while the reference [c2] refers to all the cells in column 2.

Referencing cells

Consider the table shown in Figure 11-54. As you can see, this table breaks down a company's sales figures by month and by region. If you want to calculate the total sales for January, move the cursor into the last row of the January column, then press the [Insert field] key ([Ctrl][F9]) to insert the field characters {}. Now, enter the Expression field

An example

{=SUM([r2c2:r5c2])}

as we've done in Figure 11-54. As you can see, this field uses a SUM function to add the values in the range r2c2:r5c2. When you update this field and display its result, Word will display the sum of the values in cells r2c2, r3c2, r4c2, and r5c2—19232—in the cell containing this field, as shown in Figure 11-55 on the next page.

Figure 11-54

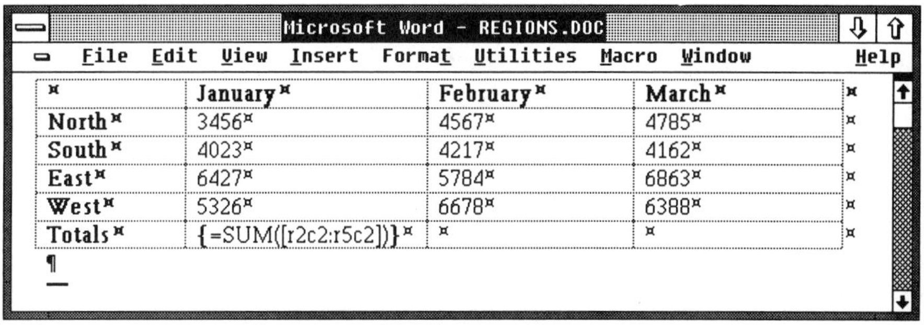

	January *	February *	March *	
North *	3456 *	4567 *	4785 *	*
South *	4023 *	4217 *	4162 *	*
East *	6427 *	5784 *	6863 *	*
West *	5326 *	6678 *	6388 *	*
Totals *	{=SUM([r2c2:r5c2])} *	*	*	*

Microsoft Word — REGIONS.DOC
File   Edit   View   Insert   Format   Utilities   Macro   Window   Help

We've entered a field into this table to calculate the January sales totals.

The SUM function we used in the previous example is only one of the 16 functions you can use in a Word table. Table 11-2 lists all 16 of these functions, which we'll explain in Chapter 16.

Field functions

Figure 11-55

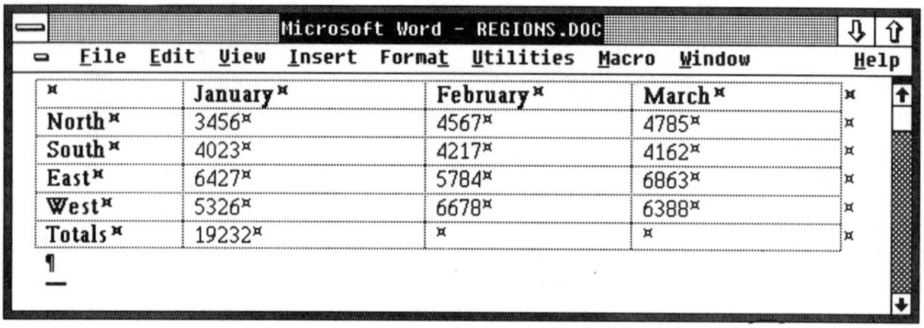

When you update the field in Figure 11-54 and display its result, the field will return the January total—19232.

Table 11-2

ABS	MIN
AND	MOD
AVERAGE	NOT
COUNT	OR
DEFINED	PRODUCT
IF	ROUND
INT	SIGN
MAX	SUM

Of course, Word doesn't offer nearly as many functions as most spreadsheet programs. If you find that Word's spreadsheeting capabilities are too limited for your needs, you might want to use Microsoft Excel to create a spreadsheet, then paste that spreadsheet into a Word document. In Chapter 21, we'll show you how to exchange data between Word for Windows and Microsoft Excel.

DELETING A TABLE

There are several techniques you can use to delete an entire table from your document. First, you can select the table, then choose Table… from the Edit menu and choose the Delete button in the Edit Table dialog box. You also can select all the cells in one column of the table, open the Edit Table dialog box, select the Row option and then click the Delete button. This tells Word to delete all the rows in which you've selected a cell—or the entire table. Finally, you can select an entire row of the table, open the Edit Table dialog box, click the Column option, then click the Delete button.

If you delete a table by mistake, you can use the Undo command to recover it. Remember that Word does not place the deleted table on your Clipboard. As a result, you cannot recover a table by pasting it back into your document.

As we mentioned earlier, Word allows you to convert existing text into a table. More often, you'll convert side-by-side paragraphs or tab-delimited text into a table. You also can convert comma-delimited text, such as a database that you've imported from another program. Finally, you can create a table by converting plain paragraphs with no tabs, commas, or special formatting.

CONVERTING EXISTING TEXT INTO A TABLE

To convert existing text into a table format, first select that text. Then, select the Table... command from the Insert menu. When the Insert Table dialog box appears, you'll see that the Convert From options at the bottom of the dialog box are active, as shown in Figure 11-56. (Normally, these options are dimmed.)

Figure 11-56

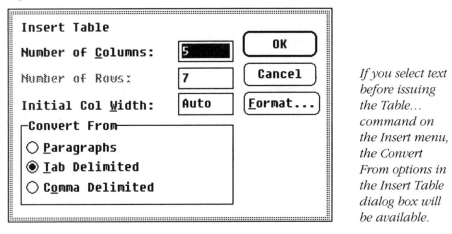

If you select text before issuing the Table... command on the Insert menu, the Convert From options in the Insert Table dialog box will be available.

Word will usually select the Convert From option that best describes the type of text you are converting. If your selected text contains a mixture of types—for example, some tab-delimited lines and some comma-delimited lines—Word will be able to convert only one type correctly. For instance, suppose you select one line of text that is delimited by tabs and another line that is delimited by commas. Then, you open the Insert Table dialog box. Word will automatically select the Tab Delimited option. When you choose OK to create the table, Word will place all the text in the comma-delimited line in a single cell. On the other hand, if you select the Comma Delimited option, Word will place all the text in the tab-delimited line in a single cell of the new table.

When you convert existing text into a table, Word will suggest a Number of Columns and an Initial Col Width setting based on your text selection. If you select the Tab Delimited option, Word will use the paragraph containing the greatest number of tabs to determine its suggested Number of Columns setting. Similarly, if you select the Comma Delimited option, Word will use the paragraph containing the greatest number of commas to determine its suggested Number of Columns setting. Word will then determine the Initial Col Width setting by dividing the width of the current text column by the number of columns.

As you can see in Figure 11-56, the Number of Rows setting in the Insert Table dialog box is dimmed. Word automatically sets the number of rows in the new table to the number of paragraphs you are converting to table format.

Let's consider an example of how you might convert existing text to table format. Figure 11-57 shows a document that lists name and address information. You might use a document like this as the data document in a merge procedure (which we'll discuss in Chapter 15). As you can see, the fields in this document (LastName, FirstName, Address, and so forth) are separated by tabs. To convert this text to a table, select all the rows of information, then choose the Table... command from the Insert menu. In the Insert Table dialog box, Word will automatically suggest the correct settings for the table, so you can simply choose OK to complete the procedure. Figure 11-58 shows the result.

Figure 11-57

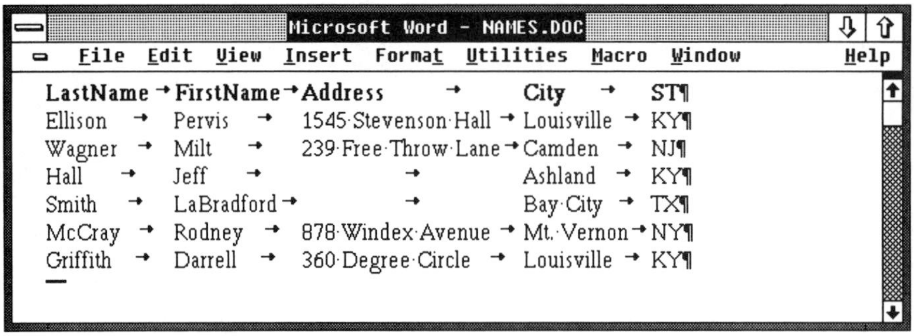

You can convert tab-delimited text like this to table format.

In the third column of Figure 11-58, notice that Word has wrapped some of the address information onto two lines in order to fit it within the cell boundaries. Of course, you can always widen this column if you want each address to appear on a single line. If the text wraps, however, Word will have no trouble interpreting the information in a merge procedure.

CONVERTING ALL OR PART OF A TABLE INTO TEXT

Word makes it easy to convert selected rows of a table—or an entire table—to text. To do this, select the row(s) you want to convert. It's important that you select whole rows; otherwise, Word won't be able to convert the table to text. After making your selection, choose the Table to Text... command on the Insert menu.

(This command replaces the Table… command when you select an entire row in a table.) Word will then display the dialog box shown in Figure 11-59. Next, choose one of the Convert Table To options and choose OK.

Figure 11-58

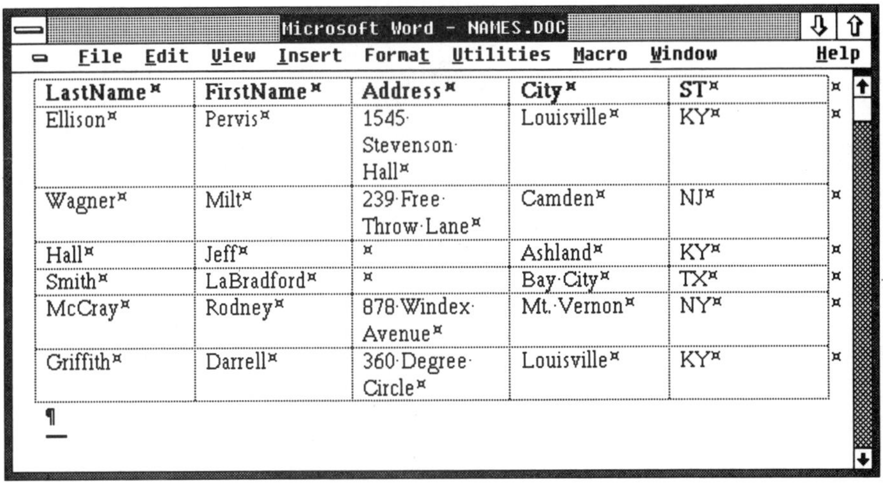

LastName✕	FirstName✕	Address✕	City✕	ST✕	✕
Ellison✕	Pervis✕	1545 Stevenson Hall✕	Louisville✕	KY✕	✕
Wagner✕	Milt✕	239 Free Throw Lane✕	Camden✕	NJ✕	✕
Hall✕	Jeff✕	✕	Ashland✕	KY✕	✕
Smith✕	LaBradford✕	✕	Bay City✕	TX✕	✕
McCray✕	Rodney✕	878 Windex Avenue✕	Mt. Vernon✕	NY✕	✕
Griffith✕	Darrell✕	360 Degree Circle✕	Louisville✕	KY✕	✕

This is the table that Word created from the document shown in Figure 11-57.

Figure 11-59

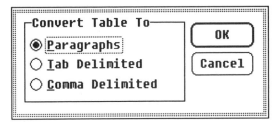

Word will display this dialog box when you choose the Table to Text… command.

If you select the Convert Table To Paragraphs option, Word will place the text in each table cell in a separate paragraph. However, if a cell contains two or more paragraphs, those paragraphs will remain separate after the conversion. In addition, any paragraph formatting you have applied to the table text, such as indents or line spacing, will be preserved.

If you select the Convert Table To Tab Delimited or Convert Table To Comma Delimited option, Word will use tabs or commas to separate the text of each cell on a row. Word will convert each row of the table into a single paragraph unless one of the cells on a row contains two or more paragraphs. In that case, Word will recognize the additional paragraphs as it converts the text.

In this chapter

Advanced Document Design 12

*I*n Chapter 5, we explained the basics of formatting your documents in Word. We showed you how to determine the layout of your document pages, format individual paragraphs, and apply character formatting, such as fonts and point sizes. In this chapter, we'll cover Word's more complex formatting features.

We'll begin by looking at multisection documents and show you how to use the various options in the Section dialog box. Then, we'll show you how to set up different right and left page layouts, or "mirror margins." After we look at multicolumn layouts and explain how to create snaking columns, we'll cover the Position… command, which lets you flow text around a positioned object. We'll wrap up the chapter with a discussion of Word's ability to create long documents by linking two or more shorter documents.

When you create a long or complex document, you may need to break it into two or more sections. Dividing a document into sections allows you to control certain elements of the document that Word would normally handle automatically. For example, in a multisection document, you can create a separate header and footer for each section instead of using the same header or footer throughout the document. You also can number the pages of each section independently, and use a different numbering scheme for each chapter or section of a long document.

MULTISECTION DOCUMENTS

Although multiple sections are useful in longer documents, there are times when you'll need to break a shorter document into sections as well. For example, if you want to vary the number of columns from one part of a document to another—or use a varying number of columns on a single page—you'll need to divide the document into different sections. We'll show you how to handle multicolumn formatting a little later in this chapter. For now, however, let's consider how you can create multiple sections in a document.

Dividing a document into sections

Every new Word document initially consists of only one section. If you want to create a new section, place the cursor where you want that section to begin, and choose the Break... command from the Insert menu to bring up the Break dialog box shown in Figure 12-1. As you can see, this dialog box allows you to insert a page break, a column break, and four types of section breaks. Let's look at each section break option.

Figure 12-1

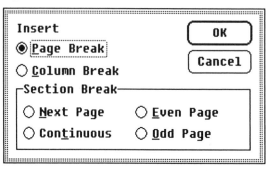

The Break dialog box lets you insert four kinds of section breaks into your document.

If you use the Next Page option in the Break dialog box to insert a section break, Word will print the first paragraph in the new section at the top of a new page. As a result, part of the previous page may be left blank.

If you choose the Continuous option, Word will print the new section immediately below the previous section. As you will see a little later in this chapter, the Continuous option lets you create different columnar layouts on the same page.

Finally, if you choose the Even Page or Odd Page option in the Break dialog box, the new section will begin at the top of the next even-numbered (left) or odd-numbered (right) page. These options sometimes force a blank page to appear in the document. For example, in books, it's common practice to begin each chapter on an odd page. If you are creating a technical publication that contains charts and descriptions, you may want to ensure that all the charts appear on even pages while their corresponding descriptions appear on odd pages.

Although you do not have to use mirror margins or a Gutter setting in order to select the Even Page or Odd Page option, you will often find these options useful when the document has different right and left page layouts. (We'll discuss right and left page layouts later in this chapter.)

After you select a section break in the Break dialog box, choose OK to complete the command. Word will then mark the section break on your screen with a double dotted line, as shown in Figure 12-2. Like page-break markers, section-break markers will not appear in a printed document.

Figure 12-2

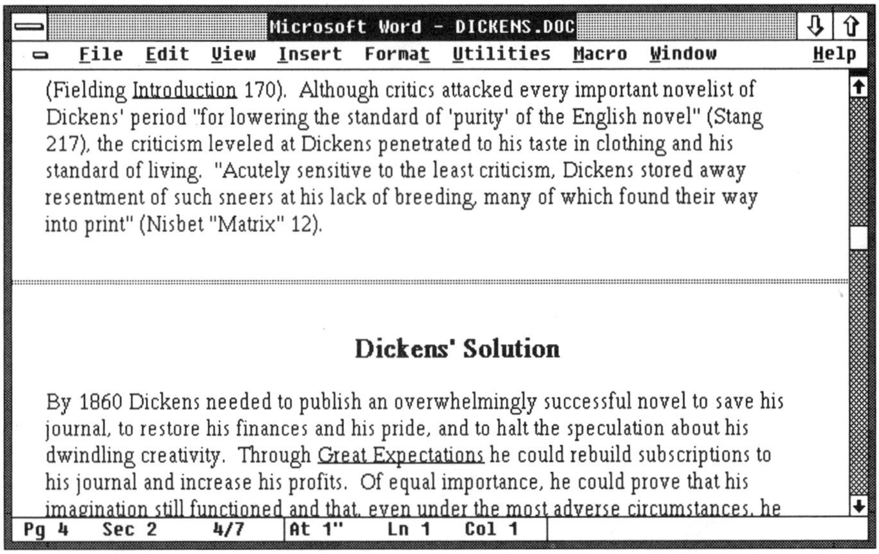

```
┌─────────────────────────────────────────────────────────────────────┐
│ ▭        ▓▓▓Microsoft Word - DICKENS.DOC▓▓▓           ⇩ ⇧ │
│ ▫   File  Edit  View  Insert  Format  Utilities  Macro  Window   Help │
├─────────────────────────────────────────────────────────────────────┤
│ (Fielding Introduction 170). Although critics attacked every important novelist of │ ▲
│ Dickens' period "for lowering the standard of 'purity' of the English novel" (Stang │
│ 217), the criticism leveled at Dickens penetrated to his taste in clothing and his │
│ standard of living. "Acutely sensitive to the least criticism, Dickens stored away │
│ resentment of such sneers at his lack of breeding, many of which found their way │
│ into print" (Nisbet "Matrix" 12).                                      │
│ ═════════════════════════════════════════════════════════════════════ │
│                                                                        │
│                          Dickens' Solution                             │
│                                                                        │
│ By 1860 Dickens needed to publish an overwhelmingly successful novel to save his │
│ journal, to restore his finances and his pride, and to halt the speculation about his │
│ dwindling creativity. Through Great Expectations he could rebuild subscriptions to │
│ his journal and increase his profits. Of equal importance, he could prove that his │
│ imagination still functioned and that, even under the most adverse circumstances, he │ ▼
├─────────────────────────────────────────────────────────────────────┤
│ Pg 4    Sec 2    4/7  │At 1"    Ln 1    Col 1 │                        │
└─────────────────────────────────────────────────────────────────────┘
```

Section breaks are marked on your screen by a double dotted line.

Once you've divided a document into two or more sections, Word will use the *Sec* indicator in the status bar to indicate the section in which the cursor is located. For instance, notice that the status bar in Figure 12-2 now displays *Pg 4 Sec 2*. This tells you that the cursor lies on the fourth page and in the second section of this document.

The Section dialog box

As we mentioned in Chapter 5, you can format a Word document on four levels: the overall document level, the section level, the paragraph level, and the character level. The various options for section-level formatting are found in the Section dialog box, which is shown in Figure 12-3 on the following page. To open this dialog box, just choose the Section… command from the Format menu.

Like the Paragraph and Character dialog boxes, the Section dialog box displays the settings for the current section. (The dialog box in Figure 12-3 displays Word's default Section settings.) If you select text in two or more sections before you open the Section dialog box, all the text boxes will appear blank and the check-box options will be dimmed.

When you enter settings and choose options in the Section dialog box, your selections will apply to the section in which the cursor is currently located (or to all the sections in which you've selected text). If you select a section-break marker before opening the Section dialog box, the settings you select in the dialog box will apply to all the text preceding the section-break marker, up to the next section-break marker or to the beginning of the document if there is no preceding section. If you have not inserted any section breaks in your document, Word will treat the entire document as one section and will apply your Section dialog box settings to the entire document.

Figure 12-3

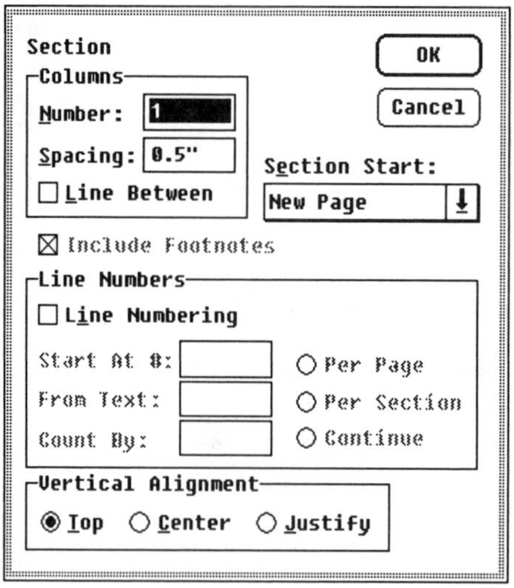

The Section dialog box lets you vary certain characteristics of your document from one section to another.

The Section Start options

When you pull down the list of Section Start options in the Section dialog box, you'll see the items shown in Figure 12-4. These options specify where the section will begin—that is, whether the first paragraph in the section will appear at the top of the next column or page, or whether it will start on an even or odd page.

Figure 12-4

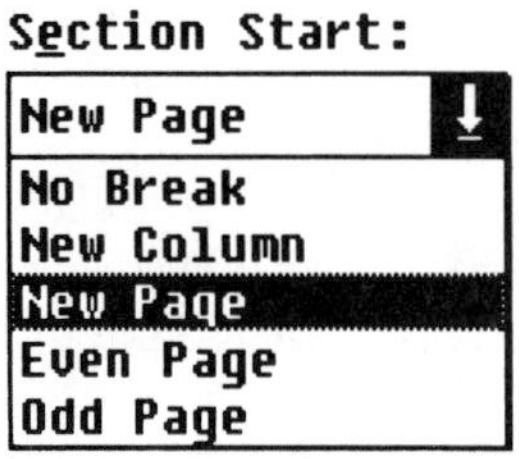

Word offers five Section Start options in the Section dialog box.

As you may have figured out, Word automatically chooses the appropriate Section Start option for a new section when you insert a section break with the Break... command on the Insert menu. Table 12-1 shows the Section Start options that correspond to options in the Break dialog box in Figure 12-1.

Table 12-1

Choosing this option in the Break dialog box...	selects this Section Start option in the Section dialog box...
Next Page	New Page
Continuous	No Break
Even Page	Even Page
Odd Page	Odd Page

Although the Break... command automatically selects the appropriate Section Start option, you can open the Section dialog box and change the Section Start option manually anytime you want.

By the way, it's important to remember that the Column Break option in the Break dialog box does not create a new section. It simply inserts a manual column break, which is very similar to a manual page break. We'll discuss column breaks when we discuss multicolumn formatting later in this chapter.

The Vertical Alignment options at the bottom of the Section dialog box allow you to tell Word how to position text between the page's top and bottom margins. Figure 12-5 shows how each of the Vertical Alignment options affects a sample printed page.

Vertical alignment

Figure 12-5

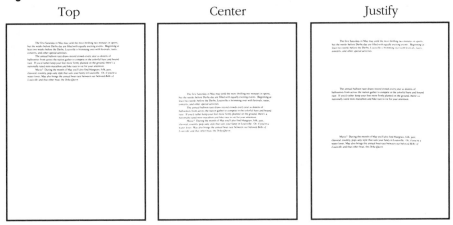

The Vertical Alignment options in the Section dialog box let you control the vertical position of a page's text.

By default, Word selects the Vertical Alignment Top option, which places the first line on each page at the position indicated by the Top margin setting in the Document dialog box. If there are not enough lines of text to fill the text area between the page's top and bottom margins, Word will leave white space at the bottom of the page, as shown in Figure 12-5.

If you want to center text between a page's top and bottom margins, choose the Vertical Alignment Center option. As you'll see in a moment, this option comes in handy when you want to create a title page.

The Vertical Alignment Justify option tells Word to insert an equal amount of space between the paragraphs on each page that contains a manual page break. Selecting this option will not affect the spacing between the lines within an individual paragraph.

Let's use the Vertical Alignment Center option to create a title page for the document shown in Figure 12-6. At the top of the document, enter and format the text you want to appear on the title page. Next, move the cursor to the end of the last paragraph on the title page, select the Break... command from the Insert menu, choose the Next Page option, then choose OK. Figure 12-7 shows how our sample document appears at this point.

Next, open the Section dialog box, choose the Vertical Alignment Center option, and choose OK. Figure 12-8 on page 434 shows how the resulting title page will appear when you print the document.

Figure 12-6

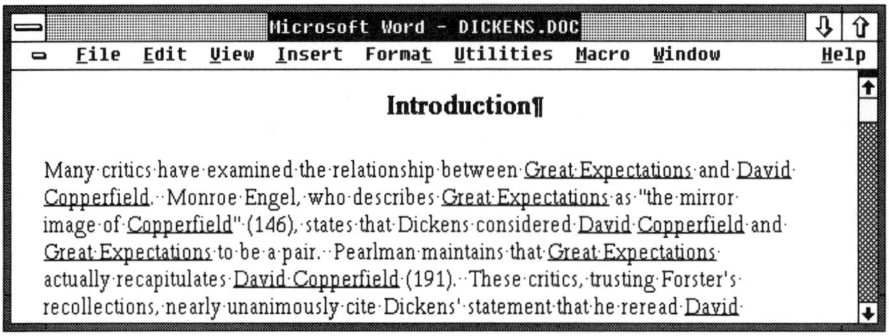

We'll create a title page for this sample document.

Changing page numbers from one section to another

In Chapter 7, we explained how to number the pages of a document either by inserting a page number in a header or footer or by using the Page Numbers... command on the Insert menu. We also introduced the five numbering schemes available in Word and explained how to position page numbers in the header.

Fortunately, you can control your page numbering on a section-by-section basis. In other words, you can do such things as number the pages in each section separately or use a different numbering scheme in different sections.

Figure 12-7

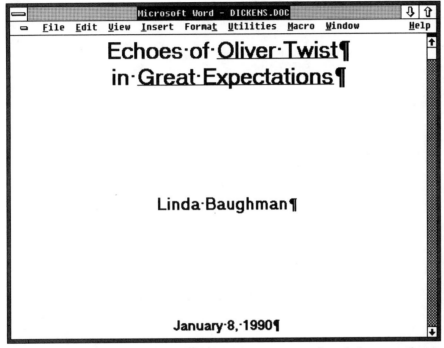

We'll use the Vertical Alignment Center option to center the title between the top and bottom margins.

Since page numbers are stored in the document's header and footer, you must use the expanded Header/Footer dialog box to control your section page numbering. To bring up this dialog box, select the Header/Footer... command from the Edit menu, then choose the Options >> button. When you do this, you'll see the dialog box shown in Figure 12-9 on the next page.

To change the vertical position of page numbers from one section to another, you must change the position of the header or footer that contains the page number. To do this, just move the cursor into each section, bring up the expanded Header/Footer dialog box, and specify the Distance From Edge settings you want to use for that section.

Changing the position of section page numbers

Figure 12-8

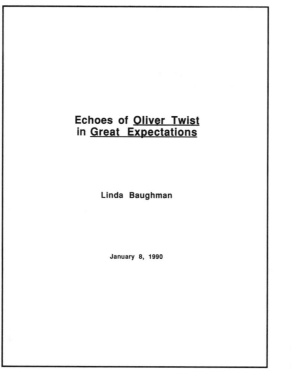

This is the title page we created for our sample document.

Figure 12-9

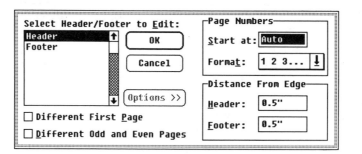

Word's expanded Header/Footer dialog box lets you control your page numbering on a section-by-section basis.

Numbering sections separately

If you want the pages of each section to be numbered separately, move the cursor into each section, bring up the expanded Header/Footer dialog box, and enter *1* in the Page Numbers Start At text box. (If you want, you can number the first page of each section with a number other than 1.) If you have chosen a numbering scheme other than the default Arabic numerals, Word will begin numbering the pages of each section with *a, A, i,* or *I.*

If you start each section with page 1, Word will change the page numbers in the status bar to reflect this. For example, suppose you are working with a ten-page document that you have divided into two sections. The first section occupies pages 1 through 4, and the second section occupies pages 5 through 10. If you move the cursor into the second section, bring up the expanded Header/Footer dialog box, and enter *1* in the Page Numbers Start At text box, Word will use the numbers 1 through 6 to number the pages in the second section As you scroll through this part of the document, the status bar will display *Pg 1 Sec 2, Pg 2 Sec 2,* and so forth.

Like the position of your page numbers, the numbering scheme you use can change from one section to another. For instance, it's common to use lowercase Roman numerals to number the front matter pages (preface, table of contents, and so forth) of a publication, and Arabic numerals to number the pages of the main body of the document. To change schemes, move the cursor into each section, bring up the expanded Header/Footer dialog box, and select the type of numbering you want to use from the Page Numbers Format pull-down list box.

Changing the numbering scheme

When you change numbering schemes in a document section, you'll almost certainly want to restart the page numbering for that section by entering *1* in the Page Numbers Start At text box. For example, suppose you have used the lowercase Roman option (i, ii, iii) to number the front matter of the document. This section occupies ten pages, which are numbered *i* to *x.* When you reach the first chapter of the document, you start a new section and specify the Arabic scheme *(1, 2, 3).* If you don't specify a Page Numbers Start At setting of 1 for this new section, your page numbers will start at 11.

In Chapter 7, we introduced the Print dialog box and explained how you can use the Pages From and To settings to print a specified range of pages. As we mentioned, specifying a range of pages in a multisection document can become pretty complicated. For example, suppose you have created a document that uses a numbering scheme like the one shown in Table 12-2 on the following page, and you want to print page B from the fifth section of the document (the appendix). How can you specify a page number without adding all your pages to determine the actual value for page B in the appendix? Chances are, you won't know the correct number for the page you want to print.

Specifying a range for printing

After Word repaginates a multisection document, the status bar will indicate which page contains the cursor, displaying both the section number and page number. For example, the first page in the Introduction would be labeled *Pg 1 Sec 1.* The first page in Chapter 1 would be labeled *Pg 1 Sec 2.* Since you did not restart the numbering with page 1 in Chapters 2 and 3, the first pages of these chapters would be labeled *Pg 11 Sec 3* and *Pg 17 Sec 4*, respectively. Finally, the first page in the appendix would be labeled *Pg 1 Sec 5*. As you can see, Word always uses Arabic numerals to indicate the current page in the status bar instead of using the numbering scheme assigned to that section.

Table 12-2

Section	Name	Numbered	Actual page
1	Introduction	i to iv	1 to 4
2	Chapter 1	1 to 10	5 to 14
3	Chapter 2	11 to 16	15 to 20
4	Chapter 3	17 to 23	21 to 27
5	Appendix	A to H	28 to 35

When you specify a page range in the Print dialog box, you can enter values like *P15 S2* and *P2 S5* in the From and To text boxes. (You can drop the *P* if you like and just enter *15 S2* or *2 S5*, and you don't have to type the space between the page number and the section number.) Just as Word uses Arabic numerals to label pages in the status bar, you must use Arabic numerals when specifying a page range in the Print dialog box. For instance, to print page C from section 5 of your document, you'll have to enter *P3 S5* in the From and To text boxes. If you try to enter *PC S5* or *C S5*, Word will display the message *Not a valid print range*. Table 12-3 shows several combinations of From and To settings you can use to print the sample document pages in Table 12-2.

Table 12-3

To print this range...	enter these settings...	
introduction only	From P1 S1	To P4 S1
chapters only	From P1 S2	To P23 S4
appendix only	From P1 S5	To P8 S5
introduction and first five pages of Chapter 1	From P1 S1	To P5 S2
Chapter 2 and first two pages of Chapter 3	From P11 S3	To P18 S4
last three pages of Chapter 3 and Appendix	From P21 S4	To P8 S5

If the pages of a multisection document are numbered sequentially, you can print any part of the document simply by specifying the correct From and To page numbers; there's no need to specify a section component as well. For example, suppose you have a 20-page document that's divided into two sections, as shown in Table 12-4. You've numbered these pages sequentially, with pages 1 through 12 in the first section and pages 13 through 20 in the second section.

Table 12-4

Section number	Page numbers
1	1 to 12
2	13 to 20

If you want to print pages 8 through 15 of this document, enter *8* as your From setting and *15* as your To setting. If you want, you can also enter *P8 S1* as the From setting and *P15 S2* as the To setting, but this isn't necessary.

By the way, if you specify incompatible page and section combinations in the From and To text boxes, Word may not be able to execute the Print... command. For example, suppose you're printing the document pages in Table 12-4, and you enter *P15 S1* and *P18 S1* as your From and To settings, respectively. Because pages 15 through 18 are in the second section of the document, and you've included the *S1* component along with these page numbers, Word will not print anything.

When you want to go to a specific page in a multisection document, you can select the Go To... command from the Edit menu and enter a value like *P2 S5* in the Go To text box (the case of the *P* and *S* is not important). This will move the cursor to the second page of the fifth document section. If the pages of your multisection document are numbered consecutively, you do not need to specify a section number. For example, suppose you are working in a three-section document in which the pages of the first section are numbered 1 through 12, the pages of the second section are numbered 13 through 20, and the pages of the third section are numbered 21 through 34. If you want to go to page 25, you would simply choose the Go To... command, enter *25* in the Go To text box, and choose OK. There's no need to specify a section number.

The Go To... command

When you use the *Pn Sn* format to specify a page number in the Go To dialog box, you must use Arabic numerals, even if you've arranged the pages of one or more sections in your document using letters or Roman numerals. Word will not accept a value like *Pi S1* or *PA S5* in the Go To text box.

Word does not automatically repaginate your document when you issue the Go To... command. If you want to be sure you are going to the correct page, issue the Repaginate Now command before you issue the Go To... command.

Sectional headers and footers

In Chapter 7, we introduced headers and footers, showing you how to create, position, and format them, and how to create a special header or footer for the first page of a document. As we mentioned, when a document is divided into sections, you can vary the headers and footers from one section to another. In most cases, your section breaks will correspond to major document divisions, such as chapters. However, you can change headers and footers at any location in a document by adding a section break.

When you divide a document into sections, each will initially carry identical headers, footers, and Header/Footer dialog box settings. In addition, each header or footer will be linked to the headers and footers in subsequent sections of the document. Any changes you make to the header or footer in one section of a document will apply to all the headers or footers in subsequent sections.

To vary the text or format of a particular section's header or footer, first place the cursor within that section. Next, make sure you're in either the normal editing or draft view, and select the Header/Footer... command from the Edit menu. When the Header/Footer dialog box appears, choose the Header option from the list box and choose OK. At this point, Word will display the section number at the top of the header or footer pane to indicate to which section your changes will apply. For example, the header pane in Figure 12-10 carries the notation *(S1)*, indicating that it is the header for the first section of a document. After opening the header pane, you can edit or format the text to suit your purposes.

Figure 12-10

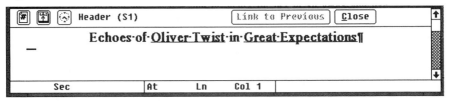

The top of the header pane displays the section number of that header.

As we've mentioned, when you reformat or edit the contents of a header or footer pane, Word will apply your changes to all successive headers or footers in the document. Any headers or footers that appear before the current section, however, will not be affected. In addition, once you edit a header or footer, you break the link between it and any previous headers or footers.

For example, suppose you have divided a document into four sections. You enter the text *Chapter 1* in the header pane for the first section. If you then open the header panes for the second, third, and fourth sections of this document, you'll see that they also contain the text *Chapter 1*. Now, suppose you click in the third section of the document, open the header pane, and change the header text to read *Chapter 3.* The headers for both the third and fourth sections will now read *Chapter 3.* However, the headers for the first and second sections will still read *Chapter 1.* If you move back to the first section at this point and edit the header text for that section, your change will apply to the first and second sections only. The third and fourth sections will be unaffected by your changes since they are no longer linked to the previous sections' headers.

You can change any of the Section dialog box settings for two or more sections of a document by highlighting all or part of the sections you want to work with before issuing the Section... command. Unfortunately, this technique does not work for changes you make to the text or formats of your headers and footers. If you select two or more sections of your document and issue the Header/Footer... command, the header or footer pane will display the header or footer for the first section only. Any changes you make in this pane will apply to only the first section in your selection, unless the sections you've selected are still linked. In that case, Word will carry your changes through to the other sections in your selection as well. However, if you have created different headers or footers for different sections of a document, you cannot use this technique to make a global change to all the headers and footers. You can, however, make global formatting changes to headers and footers by altering the definition of the *header* and *footer* styles. (See Chapter 8 for more on style sheets.)

Fortunately, if you want to change the Distance From Edge settings for the headers and footers in two or more sections, you can do so by selecting text in those sections, opening the expanded Header/Footer dialog box, and making new entries in the Distance From Edge text boxes. Interestingly, if you change a Distance From Edge setting in the Header/Footer dialog box without selecting any text, your changes will apply only to the headers and footers in the current section, even if the headers and footers in successive sections are linked to the current section. If you want your header and footer positions to be consistent from one section to the next, you must select your entire document before you change the Distance From Edge settings.

If you want a header or footer to contain the same text and formats as the header or footer in the previous section of a document, you can choose the Link to Previous button that appears at the top of a header or footer pane. Word will copy into the current pane the header or footer text and formats from the previous section. In addition, Word will re-establish the link between the current header or footer and the previous section's header or footer. Once the link is re-established, you can change the contents of the first header or footer pane, and Word will automatically update the second header or footer pane to reflect the changes you've entered.

The Link to Previous button

If the contents of the header or footer pane are already identical to the previous section's header or footer, the Link to Previous button will be dimmed. However, if the current header or footer text differs from the header or footer for the previous section, this button will be available for selection.

The Different First Page option

In Chapter 7, we explained how you can use the Different First Page option in the Header/Footer dialog box to create a unique header and/or footer on the first page of a document or to eliminate the header or footer from the first page altogether. This option also allows you to create a unique header and/or footer for the first page of each section in your document.

Selecting the Different First Page check box brings up the First Header and First Footer options in the Header/Footer dialog box. If you select the First Header option and then choose OK, Word will print that header on only the first page of the current section. To place the same header on the first page in other sections of your document, you'll need to move the cursor into each section, and then use the Header/Footer dialog box to select the Different First Page check box.

If you want the first-page header of one section to look different from the first-page header of another section, just bring up the Header/Footer dialog box and choose the First Header option from the list box. You can then edit and format your header text.

As with regular headers and footers, if you change the text or formatting in one of the first-page header or first-page footer panes, you will break the link between that header or footer and the first-page header or first-page footer for previous sections in the document. However, you can re-establish the link by choosing the Link to Previous button.

Merging two document sections

If you want to merge two adjacent document sections, just delete the section-break marker between them. To delete a section-break marker, move the cursor to the line containing the marker, then press the [Delete] key. If the two sections have different Section dialog box settings, the new, merged section will display the settings of the original second section. (This is similar to what happens when you merge two paragraphs by deleting the ¶ mark at the end of the first one. The merged paragraph will display the paragraph format settings of the second paragraph, whose ¶ mark was not deleted.)

RIGHT AND LEFT PAGES

If you plan to print a document using both sides of each sheet of paper, then bind that document, you probably will want to take advantage of Word's ability to create different odd and even (or right and left) page layouts. This type of page layout is sometimes referred to as "facing pages" or "mirror margins," since the left and right margins of facing pages will mirror each other.

There are a couple of ways you can create a document with different formats on right and left pages. First, you can set up "inside" and "outside" margins. In other words, instead of specifying a left and right margin measurement, you specify an inside margin—or the margin that will appear on the binding edge of your paper—and an outside margin, which is the margin that appears opposite the binding edge. On odd-numbered pages, the left side of the page is considered the binding edge, where your inside margin will appear. On even-numbered pages, the right side of the page is considered the inside margin and the binding edge. Generally, you will make your inside margin larger than your outside margin to allow room for binding.

Another approach to creating right and left page layouts is to use standard right and left margin settings, but add a page gutter to allow room for binding. This gutter will always be added to the binding edge of a page. Again, on odd-numbered pages, the gutter will appear on the left edge, and on even-numbered pages, it will appear on the right edge.

Finally, Word allows you to specify both inside/outside margins and a page gutter. In this situation, the space on the binding edge of each page consists of the inside margin measurement plus the page gutter.

The tools you'll use to set up different right and left page layouts are the Document... and Header/Footer... commands. When you bring up the Document dialog box, you'll see two special margin settings: the Mirror Margins check box and the Gutter text box. To set up headers and footers for odd and even pages, you'll use the Different Odd and Even Pages check box in the Header/Footer dialog box.

Now that you have a general idea of the tools and capabilities Word offers to set up odd and even pages, let's look at them in detail.

The Mirror Margins check box in the Document dialog box lets you establish inside and outside margins on your document pages. When you select this check box, Word will change the labels on the Left and Right margin text boxes to read *Inside* and *Outside*.

Setting up mirror margins

For example, suppose you want to create a document with margins that are $1^1/_4$ inches wide, and you want to allow an additional $^1/_2$ inch for binding. To begin, select the Document... command from the Format menu and select the Mirror Margins check box. Next, specify an Inside setting of *1.75"* and an Outside setting of *1.25"*. At this point, your Document dialog box will look like Figure 12-11 on the following page.

When you print your document, page 1 will have a left margin that is $1^3/_4$ inches wide and a right margin that is $1^1/_4$ inches wide. On page 2, these margins will be reversed: The left margin will be $1^1/_4$ inches wide, while the right margin will be $1^3/_4$ inches wide.

Figure 12-11

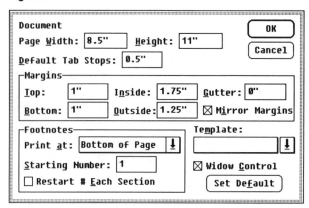

When you activate the Mirror Margins option, the Left and Right margin text boxes will be labeled Inside *and* Outside.

Using gutters

Another way to set up the same page layout is to specify a page gutter in the Gutter text box of the Document dialog box. You do not need to activate Mirror Margins in order to specify a gutter. You could use Word's default Left and Right margin settings of 1.25", then enter .5"in the Gutter text box. When you print this document, Word will add the $\frac{1}{2}$ inch of gutter space to the left edge of all odd-numbered pages and to the right edge of all even-numbered pages.

Combining mirror margins and gutters

As we've mentioned, you can combine inside and outside margins with a page gutter. In this situation, the binding edge of each page will have white space that is equal to the Inside margin setting plus the Gutter setting. For example, suppose you have activated the Mirror Margins check box in the Document dialog box, and you've specified an Inside margin setting of 1.25", an Outside margin setting of 1.5", and a Gutter setting of .75". When you print this document, Word will allow a total of 2 inches of white space (the Inside margin setting plus the Gutter setting) on the binding edge of each page.

Using the ruler with right and left pages

When you use inside and outside margins or a page gutter, Word will adjust the appearance of the ruler on your screen. As we explained in Chapter 5, when you display the ruler in the paragraph view, it shows the width of your current text column. In a single-column layout, the width of the text column is the same as the width of the text area on the page. The left edge of your text area always begins at the zero point on the ruler, while the right edge of the text area is marked by a vertical line. In order to compute the width of the text area, Word subtracts the Left and Right margin settings from the width of your paper.

When you use inside and outside margins, Word again computes the width of your text area by subtracting these margin settings from the width of your paper, like this:

Width of text area = width of paper - inside margin - outside margin

If you've specified a page gutter, Word will subtract the Gutter setting as well as your margins settings in order to obtain the width of the text area, like this:

Width of text area = width of paper - left margin - right margin - gutter

or, like this:

Width of text area = width of paper - inside margin - outside margin - gutter

For example, suppose you are using Word's default Left and Right margin settings of 1.25. As you know, this will create a text area that is 6 inches wide (assuming that you're using paper that is $8\frac{1}{2}$ inches wide). Now, let's suppose you decide to specify a Gutter setting of .5 inches. This will reduce the width of your text area by $\frac{1}{2}$ inch, so the vertical line marking the right edge of your text will move to the $5\frac{1}{2}$-inch position on the ruler.

When you enter the page view and place the ruler in the margin view, Word will account for your Inside and Outside margin settings as well as your Gutter setting in determining the placement of the ruler's margin markers. As you scroll from an odd page to an even page, Word will shift the margin markers accordingly. For example, suppose you've specified an Inside margin setting of 1.75" and an Outside margin setting of .75". When you are viewing an odd page on the screen with the ruler displaying the margin view, the margin marker on the left side of the ruler will appear at the $1\frac{3}{4}$-inch position. The margin marker on the right side of the ruler will appear at the $7\frac{1}{4}$-inch position. When you scroll to an even page, Word will display the margin marker on the left side of the ruler at the $\frac{3}{4}$-inch position. The margin marker on the right side of the ruler will move to the $6\frac{3}{4}$-inch position.

Right and left headers and footers

As you've seen, the Header/Footer dialog box contains a check box labeled *Different Odd and Even Pages*. This setting allows you to vary the content and format of your headers and footers between right and left pages. You've probably noticed that many books use this type of feature by placing the book's title at the top of even pages and the chapter title at the top of odd pages. Even when the text of a header or footer is the same on both right and left pages, it's common to vary the position of certain elements. For example, in a magazine, you might see page numbers on the outside edge, the name of the publication in the center, and the date on the inside edge of each page.

The Different Odd and Even Pages option in the Header/Footer dialog box acts independently of the Mirror Margins and Gutter settings in the Document dialog box. This means that you can vary your headers and footers between the right and left pages of your document even if you are not using inside and outside margins or a page gutter.

When you select the Different Odd and Even Pages check box, Word will display four new options in the list box that appears in the Header/Footer dialog box: Even Header, Even Footer, Odd Header, and Odd Footer. You use these four options to set up the headers and footers on your left and right pages.

For example, Figures 12-12 and 12-13 show a pair of even and odd header panes that we used to create the headers for a book called *Fear and Loathing on the Remodeling Trail.* In the even header pane, we placed our page number on the left and used a right-aligned tab at the 6-inch position to align our book title with the right margin. In the odd header pane, we placed the chapter title *Dream Kitchen or Nightmare?* on the left and used a right-aligned tab at the 6-inch position to align our page numbers with the right margin. Figure 12-14 shows how these headers will appear when the document is printed.

Figure 12-12

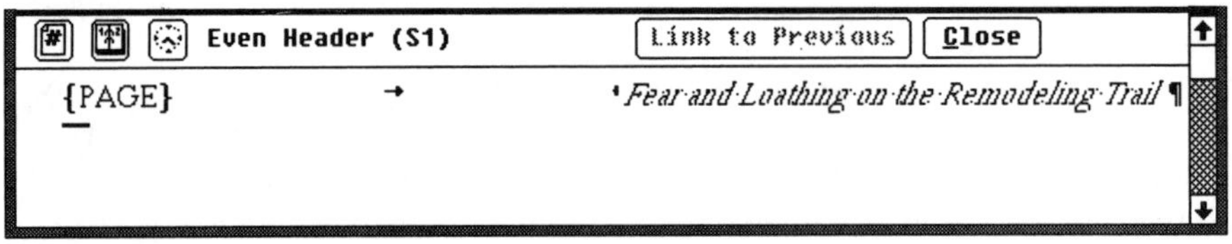

This header is designed for the even pages of a book.

Figure 12-13

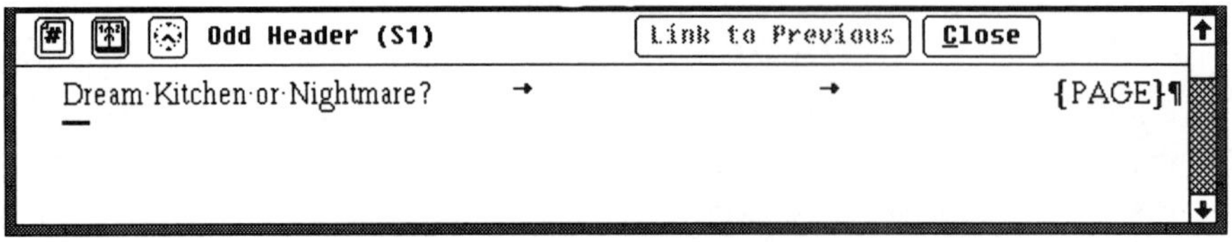

This header is designed for odd pages.

Figure 12-14

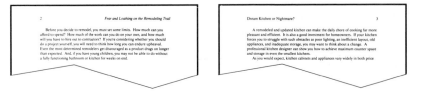

When we print the document, our page numbers will be aligned with the outside edge of each page, while our book and chapter titles will be aligned with the inside margins.

In our discussion of multisection documents, we described how the headers and footers for each section are linked to the headers and footers of subsequent sections. When you are using even and odd headers with a multisection document, the situation becomes a bit more complicated. Basically, the headers and footers for the first section "set the tone" for the corresponding headers and footers in subsequent sections.

For example, assume you are working with a single-section document with no Different Odd and Even Pages or Different First Page options activated. You issue the Header/Footer… command, choose OK in the Header/Footer dialog box to add a header, then enter the text *Title* in the header pane. Now, suppose you open the Header/Footer dialog box and activate the Different Odd and Even Pages check box. When you do this, Word will present the options Even Header, Even Footer, Odd Header, and Odd Footer. When you open each of these header and footer panes, you'll see that Word presents the default text *Title* only in the odd header pane. The even header pane will be blank until you enter some text in it. Similarly, if you choose the Different First Page option, the first-page header pane will initially be blank.

Now, suppose you decide to split your document into three sections. Initially, both the even header and odd header panes in the second and third sections will have "inherited" the same text that appears in the even header and odd header panes for the first section. To create a special first-page header in the second and third sections, you'll need to highlight each section and choose the Different First Page option in the Header/Footer dialog box. Once you've done this, Word will use the same first-page header for the other sections that it uses for the first section.

If you change the even header pane in the second section of your document to read *Chapter 2*, you will break the link between that header and the even header of the first section. In addition, the even header of the third section will automatically change to match the new header in the second section. In fact, any changes you make to the text of the even header for the second section will carry over to the even header for the third and following sections.

Linking right and left headers and footers

To re-establish the link between the even header for the second section and the even header for the first section, choose the Link to Previous button in the even header pane for the second section.

The same basic rules apply when you modify first-page headers and footers. When you change a first-page header in a document section, that header will no longer be linked to the previous section's first-page header. In addition, Word will automatically change the first-page headers in any subsequent sections so that they are identical to the header you changed.

Returning to our example, suppose you are working in a three-section document. You created the text *First Page* in the first-page header pane of the first section, and the first-page header panes of the second and third sections inherited this text. Now, suppose you open the first-page header pane in the second section and change the text to read *Another First Page*. If you then move the cursor to the third section of the document and open the first-page header pane, you'll see that it also reads *Another First Page*. This header pane is still linked to the first-page header pane for the second section of the document. Therefore, it displays identical text.

If, at any time, you deselect the Different Odd and Even Pages option, Word will use the text in the odd header pane in each section of your document as the header text for both the odd and even pages in that section. Similarly, if you deselect the Different First Page option, Word will treat the first page of a section just like any other odd or even page. However, if you reselect the Different First Page or Different Odd and Even Pages options, Word will remember the original text and formats for those headers.

Page numbers

Unfortunately, you cannot use the Page Numbers... command on the Insert menu to insert page numbers into odd and even headers or footers. As soon as you choose OK in the Page Numbers dialog box, Word will present a message box asking *Replace existing header/footer with page numbers?*. If you choose Yes in this message box, Word will automatically deselect the Different Odd and Even Pages option in the Header/Footer dialog box and replace the existing text in the header or footer pane with a single PAGE field. For this reason, if you want to add page numbers to your odd and even headers or footers, you'll need to open each header or footer pane and insert a PAGE field using either the Page-number icon, the [Insert field] key ([Ctrl][F9]), or the Field... command on the Insert menu. For more information on entering page numbers into your headers and footers, refer to Chapter 7.

Bar borders

As you may recall from Chapter 5, one of the paragraph border options in the Paragraph dialog box is Bar. As we pointed out, when you select the Bar option, Word will print a bar along the left edge of the paragraph. However, when you activate either the Mirror Margins or Different Odd and Even Pages option, or enter a Gutter setting, Word will always print the bar along the outside edge of the paragraph—that is, on the side opposite the binding edge of the page. On right (odd-numbered) pages, the bar border will appear on the right side of the paragraph, and on left (even-numbered) pages, Word will print the bar border on the left side of the paragraph. Figure 12-15 shows a couple of printed pages in which we've used the Mirror Margins option and a bar border.

Figure 12-15

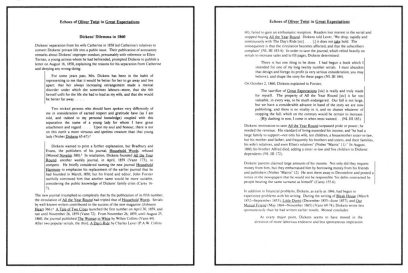

When you use a right and left page layout, Word will print your paragraph bar borders on the side opposite the binding edge of the page.

Unfortunately, Word will display the bar borders in their correct positions only in the Print Preview window. In the normal editing view, page view, and draft view, the bar borders will always appear on the left side of the paragraph.

MULTICOLUMN FORMATTING

So far, most of the page designs we've shown and discussed have consisted of a single column of text that extends from the left margin to the right margin of the printed page. Of course, there are a lot of publications—such as newspapers and journals—that contain two or more columns of text on each page.

Word offers two kinds of multicolumn formats: snaking columns and tabular (or side-by-side) columns. The text in snaking columns, as shown in Figure 12-16, automatically wraps or "snakes" from the bottom of one column to the top of the next. Tabular formatting, on the other hand, can be used to place individual paragraphs next to each other on the page. For example, in Figure 12-17, we've used a table to place headings beside our body text.

Figure 12-16

The text in snaking columns wraps or "snakes" from the bottom of one column to the top of the next.

Figure 12-17

By building a table, you can align individual paragraphs in two or more columns.

In Chapter 11, we showed you how to set up tabular paragraphs. Now, let's learn how to set up snaking columns.

Creating snaking columns is easy. Begin by choosing the Section... command from the Format menu. In the Number text box of the Section dialog box, type the number of columns you want. In the Spacing text box, indicate the amount of gutter space that you want to appear between columns. Word's default Spacing setting is .5".

Snaking columns

(The word *gutter* refers to the space between columns of text as well as to the extra binding space you use when printing facing pages. Throughout the remainder of this chapter, we'll use the term *column gutter* to refer to the space between columns and the term *page gutter* to refer to the extra left and right margin space that appears on facing pages.)

When you choose OK to close the Section dialog box and return to your document, your text will appear in one narrow column on the screen. You will not be able to see both columns in your document window as they will appear on the printed page unless you switch to the page view or issue the Print Preview command.

For example, to create the sample page shown in Figure 12-16, we started with Word's default Document and Section dialog box settings. Then, we issued the Section... command, specified a Number setting of 2, and used Word's default Spacing setting of .5". Figure 12-18 on the next page shows how this document appears on the screen in the normal editing view. As you can see, we also applied justified alignment to the text.

Notice that the default right edge for our columnar text (indicated by the vertical line on the ruler) now appears at the $2\,^{3}/_{4}$-inch position on the ruler instead of at the 6-inch position. However, if you check the Document dialog box, you'll see that Word has not changed the default Right margin setting of 1.25". When you use the snaking column format, the width of your columns depends on a number of factors, including the width of your document's text area, the number of columns to be placed on a page, and the column gutter. Let's back up a moment and consider how Word calculates column width.

To determine the width of each column in a multicolumn layout, begin by calculating the width of your total text area. This tells you how much space you have to work with on the printed page. This space must then be divided among the text columns and the column gutter.

Calculating column width

As you may remember from previous discussions, to determine the width of a document's text area, you need to take into account the page size and orientation, as well as your Left and Right margin settings (or your Inside and

Outside margin settings). If you are using a page gutter, you also need to consider the width of your Gutter setting. Therefore, to calculate the width of a document's text area, use this formula:

Width of text area = page width - left margin - right margin

Figure 12-18

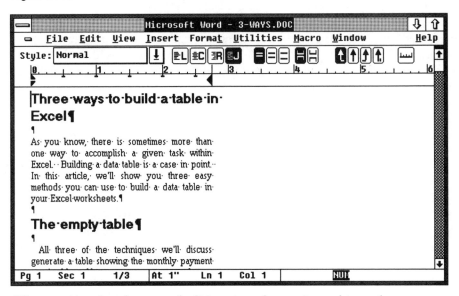

When you're using the normal editing view, the text in snaking columns appears on your screen as one long column.

A document's text area, of course, must accommodate the columns of text as well as the column gutter. For example, in the sample document shown in Figure 12-16, Word divided the 6-inch text area into two columns, allowing 3 inches for each column. Then, to create the $\frac{1}{2}$-inch column gutter, Word subtracted an equal amount, $\frac{1}{4}$ inch, from each column. This resulted in a width of $2\frac{3}{4}$ inches for the text in each column.

To determine the width of your columns in any document, you can use the standard formula

Column = width of text area - (column gutter * (number of columns - 1))
width   number of columns

Although this formula looks a little complicated, you'll find that it's quite simple if you take it a step at a time. Let's look first at the formula's numerator. You already know how to compute the *width of text area* component. The *(column gutter * (number of columns - 1))* portion of the numerator computes the total amount of space that will be allotted to column gutters. You must subtract this space from the width of your text area before you can determine the amount of space available for the columns of text.

You need to subtract 1 from the number of columns in order to determine the amount of gutter space. Because column gutters appear *between* columns—not to the left or right of each column—you will always have one fewer gutter than text columns. For instance, in a two-column page layout, you'll have one column gutter; in a three-column layout, you'll have two column gutters; and so forth.

After computing the amount of space available for the columns of text, you must divide that result by the number of columns. The formula's denominator is simply the Number setting you specify in the Section dialog box.

Let's use this formula to compute the column widths for the sample page shown in Figure 12-16.

$$\text{Column width} = \frac{6 - (.5 * (2-1))}{2} = \frac{6 - .5}{2} = 2.75$$

As you can see, the formula results in the column width shown in Figure 12-18, $2\,^3/_4$ inches. If you are creating a three-column layout, you would determine the total column width using a formula like this:

$$\text{Column width} = \frac{6 - (.5 * (3-1))}{3} = \frac{6 - 1}{3} = 1.66$$

This formula allows room for two $^1/_2$-inch column gutters, rather than one. Thus, you must subtract a total of 1 inch from your text area before you can determine the width of each column.

To test this three-column formula, let's go back to the sample document window shown in Figure 12-18 and issue a new Section... command. If we specify a Number setting of 3 and leave the Spacing setting at .5", our document window (in the normal editing view) will look like the one in Figure 12-19. Notice that Word has now narrowed our columns to a little more than $1^1/_2$ inches. Figure 12-20 shows the resulting printed page.

Figure 12-19

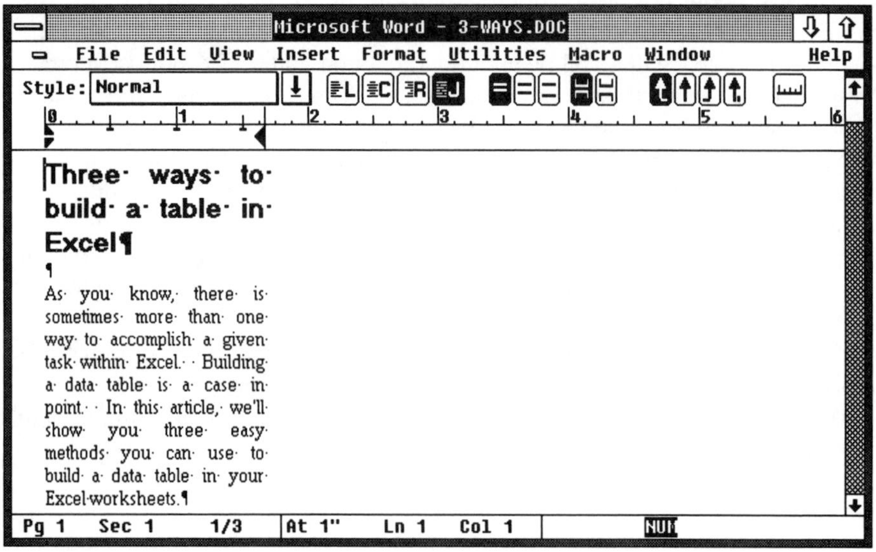

When we use a Number setting of 3 and a Spacing setting of .5", Word will narrow each column to 1.66 inches.

If you find these formulas hard to grasp, you may find it easier to visualize the effects of your column settings by creating a layout sketch of your multicolumn page. For example, Figure 12-21 on page 454 shows a layout sketch of the three-column page we created in Figure 12-20.

Controlling column breaks

In Chapter 5, we presented several techniques for controlling page breaks in documents. Most of the same techniques can be applied in multicolumn documents to control column breaks. For example, you can use the Widow Control option in the Document dialog box to ensure that no single line from a paragraph will appear alone at the top or bottom of a column. You can also use the Keep Paragraph Together option in the Paragraph dialog box to prevent Word from splitting a paragraph between two columns. Similarly, the Keep Paragraph With Next option in the Paragraph dialog box will ensure that a paragraph appears in the same column as the succeeding paragraph. (When you use these features, Word may need to repaginate your document in order to display the correct column breaks.)

Figure 12-20

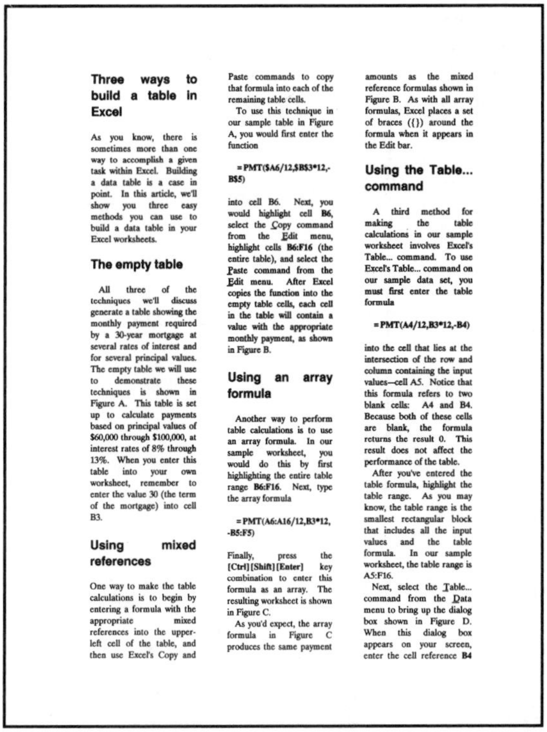

Three ways to build a table in Excel

As you know, there is sometimes more than one way to accomplish a given task within Excel. Building a data table is a case in point. In this article, we'll show you three easy methods you can use to build a data table in your Excel worksheets.

The empty table

All three of the techniques we'll discuss generate a table showing the monthly payment required by a 30-year mortgage at several rates of interest and for several principal values. The empty table we will use to demonstrate these techniques is shown in Figure A. This table is set up to calculate payments based on principal values of $60,000 through $100,000, at interest rates of 8% through 13%. When you enter this table into your own worksheet, remember to enter the value 30 (the term of the mortgage) into cell B3.

Using mixed references

One way to make the table calculations is to begin by entering a formula with the appropriate mixed references into the upper-left cell of the table, and then use Excel's Copy and Paste commands to copy that formula into each of the remaining table cells.

To use this technique in our sample table in Figure A, you would first enter the function

=PMT($A6/12,$B$3*12,-B$5)

into cell B6. Next, you would highlight cell B6, select the Copy command from the Edit menu, highlight cells B6:F16 (the entire table), and select the Paste command from the Edit menu. After Excel copies the function into the empty table cells, each cell in the table will contain a value with the appropriate monthly payment, as shown in Figure B.

Using an array formula

Another way to perform table calculations is to use an array formula. In our sample worksheet, you would do this by first highlighting the entire table range B6:F16. Next, type the array formula

=PMT(A6:A16/12,B3*12,-B5:F5)

Finally, press the [Ctrl][Shift][Enter] key combination to enter this formula as an array. The resulting worksheet is shown in Figure C.

As you'd expect, the array formula in Figure C produces the same payment amounts as the mixed reference formulas shown in Figure B. As with all array formulas, Excel places a set of braces ({}) around the formula when it appears in the Edit bar.

Using the Table... command

A third method for making the table calculations in our sample worksheet involves Excel's Table... command. To use Excel's Table... command on our sample data set, you must first enter the table formula

=PMT(A4/12,B3*12,-B4)

into the cell that lies at the intersection of the row and column containing the input values—cell A5. Notice that this formula refers to two blank cells: A4 and B4. Because both of these cells are blank, the formula returns the result 0. This result does not affect the performance of the table.

After you've entered the table formula, highlight the table range. As you may know, the table range is the smallest rectangular block that includes all the input values and the table formula. In our sample worksheet, the table range is A5:F16.

Next, select the Table... command from the Data menu to bring up the dialog box shown in Figure D. When this dialog box appears on your screen, enter the cell reference B4

This printed page shows the results of our three-column page layout.

When you are working with snaking columns, the only way to tell where the column breaks will occur in your document is to switch to the page view on your screen. When you repaginate a document that contains two or more columns, Word will display only your page breaks—not your column breaks—in the normal editing view. The page view, on the other hand, shows snaking columns side by side on the screen. If you've selected the Show-all icon on the ribbon or the Show All check box in the Preferences dialog box, Word will also display dotted lines around the column boundaries. For example, Figure 12-22 on page 455 shows the document from Figure 12-20 in the page view. Notice that Word adjusts the location of the zero point on the ruler (in the paragraph view) to show the width of the current column. In Figure 12-22, for example, the cursor is in the middle column, shifting the zero point on the ruler toward the right.

Figure 12-21

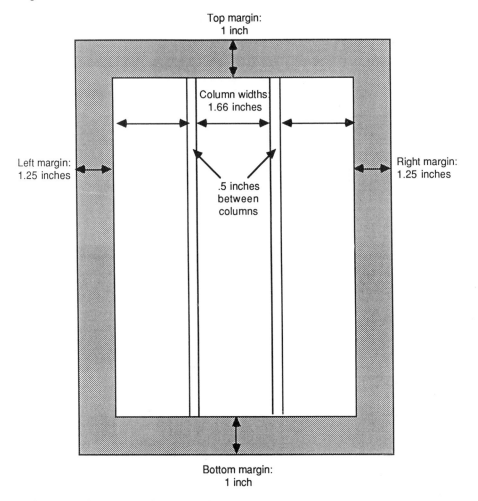

When you design a multicolumn layout, a sketch like this one may help you determine your column widths.

The column boundaries you see in the page view show how much space remains at the bottom of a column that does not quite fill a page. They also show you where Word has created one or more extra blank lines in a column in order to control a widow, keep two paragraphs together, or keep all the lines of one paragraph in a single column.

Figure 12-22

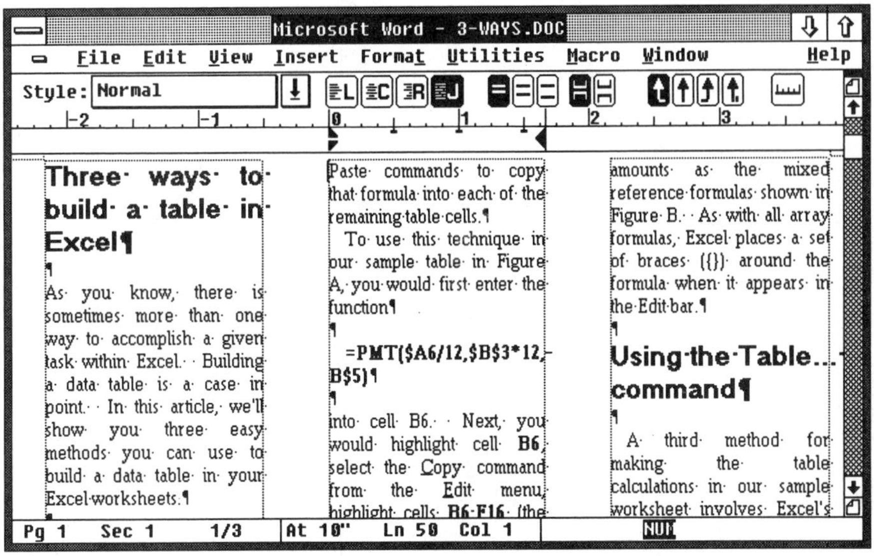

When you switch to the page view, you can see columns of text on the screen as well as dotted lines marking the column boundaries.

Fortunately, Word makes it easy for you to insert a column break in a document. Simply place the cursor where you want the column break to occur, and select the Break... command from the Insert menu to bring up the dialog box shown in Figure 12-1. At this point, select the Column Break option and choose OK. Word will then insert a column-break marker, which looks identical to a page-break marker. If you're in the page view, Word will also move the text immediately following the column-break marker to the top of the next column. If you want, you can bypass the Break dialog box by pressing the [Column break] key ([Ctrl][Shift][Enter]) to insert a column break.

For example, in the printed document shown in Figure 12-20, suppose you want the heading *Using an array formula,* which appears near the middle of the second column, to appear at the top of the third column. To insert the column break, first move the cursor to the left of the paragraph that contains this heading. Then, open the Break... dialog box, select the Column Break option, and choose OK. At this point, Word will insert a column-break marker just above the heading. When you print the document, you'll see the page shown in Figure 12-23.

Figure 12-23

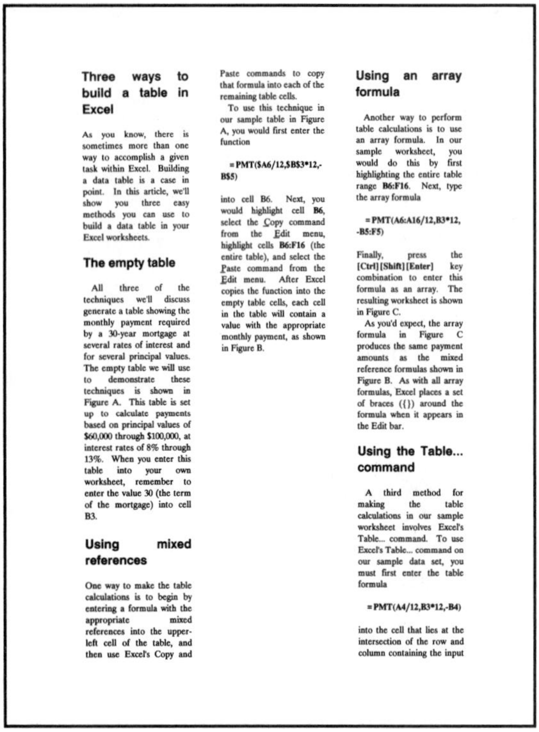

To force a column break in a document, use the Column Break option in the Break dialog box.

Combining single and multiple columns

Because snaking columns are controlled by the Section… command, you can change the number of columns in a document on a section-by-section basis. Thus, to use two or more column formats in the same document, just start a new section and indicate the desired number of columns in the Section dialog box. You can use two or more column formats on a single page. For example, you might display part of a page in a one-column format and part of it in a two-column format. Each time you want to change column formats, first move the cursor where you want the break to occur, then use the Break… command on the Insert menu to insert a continuous section break. Once you've done that, click in the new section, open the Section dialog box, and specify the number of columns you want. When you choose OK, Word will split the page into the two column formats you've specified.

For example, consider the sample page shown in Figure 12-24. To create this page layout, we first placed the cursor between the introductory paragraph and the list of names. Next, we split our document into two sections by opening the Break dialog box, selecting the Continuous option, and choosing OK. At this point, our document looked like the one shown in Figure 12-25 on page 458.

Then, we moved the cursor to the second section (where the list of names appears), opened the Section dialog box, and entered Number and Spacing settings of 2 and .5", respectively. Finally, we chose OK to complete the process.

Figure 12-24

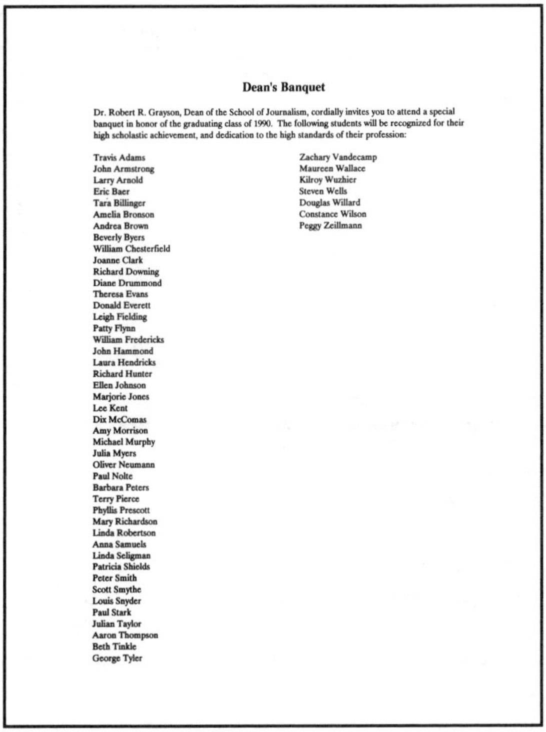

Word allows you to combine single and multicolumn layouts on the same page.

In Figure 12-24, notice that the text in the second section begins just below the section break and extends to the bottom margin, thus creating the first column. Word wraps the text in the second section back to the top of the section—not to the top of the page—creating the second column.

You also can use section breaks to create columns of equal length. Whenever a page contains one or more sections with multicolumn formatting, Word will break the columns at the section boundaries and wrap the columnar text. In other words, inserting a continuous section break does not cause the text from one section to flow into the text of the next section. Instead, it causes Word to place the text from separate sections on the same page, wrapping the columnar text within each section separately from the text in other sections. Thus, the location of your section breaks determines the depth of the columns within each section.

Creating columns of equal length

Figure 12-25

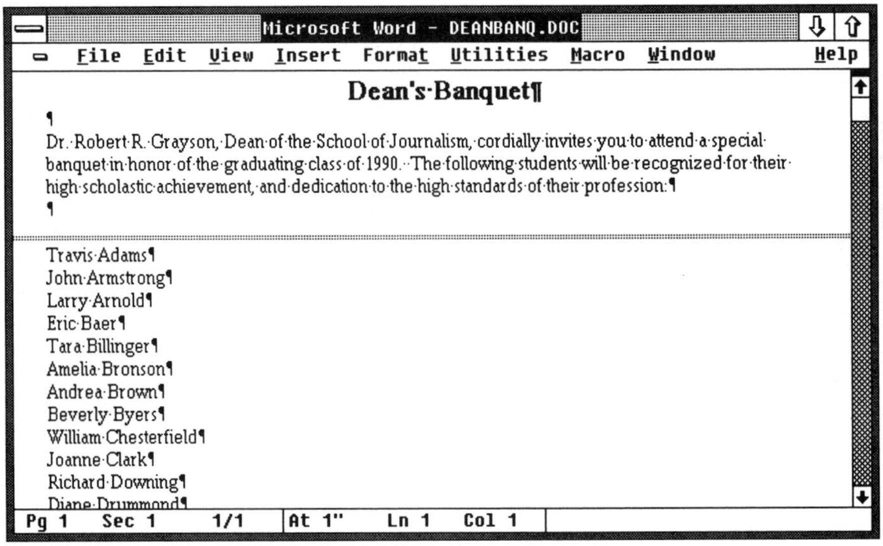

```
⊟                    Microsoft Word - DEANBANQ.DOC              ⇩ ⇧
  ▭    File   Edit   View   Insert   Format   Utilities   Macro   Window              Help
                          Dean's·Banquet¶                                    ↑
      ¶
      Dr.·Robert·R.·Grayson,·Dean·of·the·School·of·Journalism,·cordially·invites·you·to·attend·a·special·
      banquet·in·honor·of·the·graduating·class·of·1990.··The·following·students·will·be·recognized·for·their·
      high·scholastic·achievement,·and·dedication·to·the·high·standards·of·their·profession:¶
      ¶
      ·············································································
      Travis·Adams¶
      John·Armstrong¶
      Larry·Arnold¶
      Eric·Baer¶
      Tara·Billinger¶
      Amelia·Bronson¶
      Andrea·Brown¶
      Beverly·Byers¶
      William·Chesterfield¶
      Joanne·Clark¶
      Richard·Downing¶
      Diane·Drummond¶                                                        ↓
   Pg 1    Sec 1    1/1   │ At 1"    Ln 1    Col 1
```

To change columnar layouts, open the Section dialog box for the new section, and enter a new Number setting.

For example, in the document shown in Figure 12-24, the two columns are not of the same length. To solve this problem, we might insert another continuous section break just below the last line of text in the two-column section. Word will then wrap the two-column text between the section breaks, as shown in the print-out in Figure 12-26. (As you can see, we have created a third section and formatted it to have only one column. However, if our only goal in adding this third section were to align the columns in the two-column section, we could simply have entered a section break without typing any text.)

Creating long headings

In a newspaper-style layout, you may want to create headings that stretch across two or more columns. To accomplish this, you might be tempted to click on your heading text and drag the right indent marker to the right so that the heading extends across the width of the page. If you use this method, however, the text in your second column will overlap your heading text.

For example, as we pointed out earlier, Word marks the right edge of the text column in the sample document in Figure 12-18 with a vertical line at the $2\,{}^{3}/_{4}$-inch position on the ruler. Suppose we decide to alter the heading of this document to read *Three ways to build a table in an Excel worksheet*, and to adjust the heading's format so that it stretches across both columns. To do this, we'll place the cursor in the heading and then drag the right indent marker to the 6-inch position, as shown in Figure 12-27.

Figure 12-26

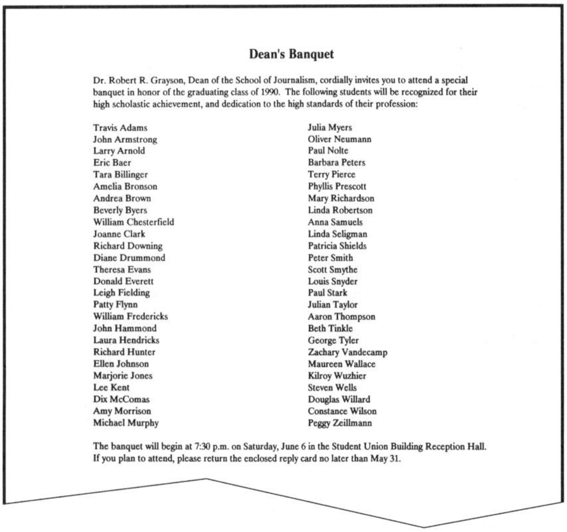

*We divided our document
into three sections to create
this page layout.*

Figure 12-27

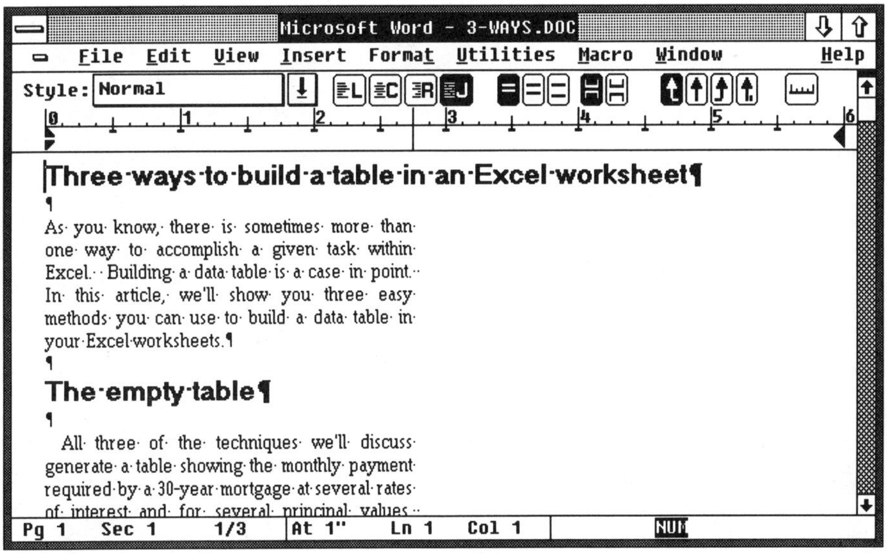

*To format the heading for this document, we dragged the right indent marker
to the 6-inch position on the ruler.*

Figure 12-28 shows what happens when we print this document. Although
our heading extends across both columns, the text in the second column wraps
to the top of the page and overlaps the heading text.

Figure 12-28

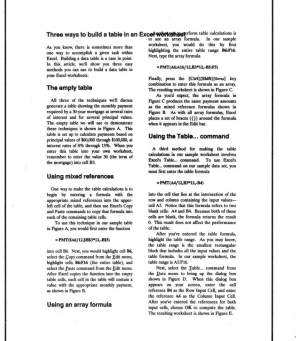

When we print the document, the text in the second column will overlap our heading.

To get around this problem, we placed our heading in a separate section. We began by moving the cursor to the beginning of the first line after the heading and using the Break… command to insert a continuous section break. Then, we placed the cursor within the first section (which contains the heading text), opened the Section dialog box, and changed the Number setting to 1. As you can see in Figure 12-29, when we print this document, the text in the second column starts on the same line as the text in the first column, rather than wrapping to the top of the page.

SPECIAL POSITIONING

Another useful Word feature is the Position… command, which allows you to place a paragraph, picture (or graphic), or table anywhere on a page, with text flowing around that item. This command lets you create sidebars, which you commonly see in newspapers, or side headings, which often appear in books. You also can use the Position… command to place one or more rows from a table anywhere on a page. This new capability is an important tool for anyone who uses Word for desktop publishing applications.

Figure 12-29

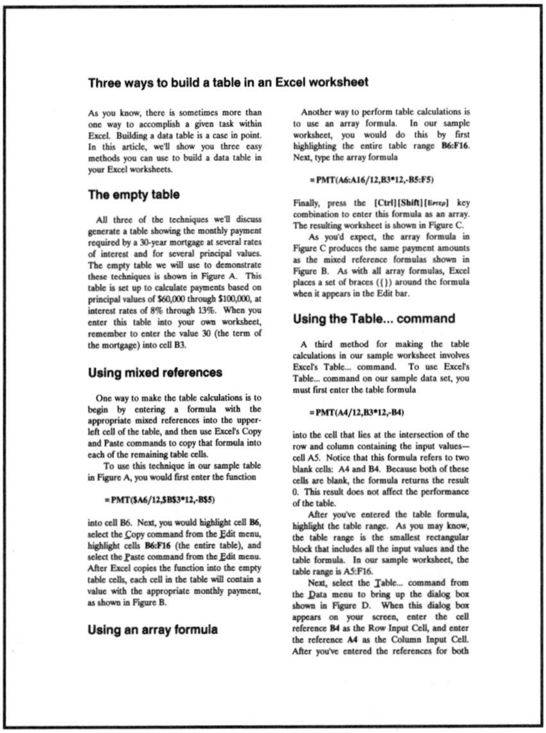

To avoid the overlapping shown in Figure 12-28, we placed our long heading in a separate, one-column section.

When you place an item with the Position... command, that item is called a positioned object. For example, Figure 12-30 on the next page shows a page of text with a table positioned in the center.

As you can see in Figure 12-30, Word automatically flows the text around a positioned object on a page. You won't be able to see the flowed text, however, unless you're in the page view or you issue the Print Preview command. As long as you're in the normal editing or draft view, the text will appear in a single column—as it normally would—displaying any formats you have assigned.

To position a paragraph, picture, or table row, first highlight it. To position a full table, you must highlight the entire table; to position two or more rows in a table, you must highlight the first cell in each row. Once you've highlighted the appropriate object, select the Position... command from the Format menu. Word will then display the dialog box shown in Figure 12-31.

Positioning an object

Figure 12-30

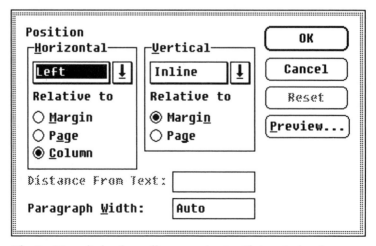

You can use the Position… command to place a paragraph, picture, or table anywhere on a page.

Figure 12-31

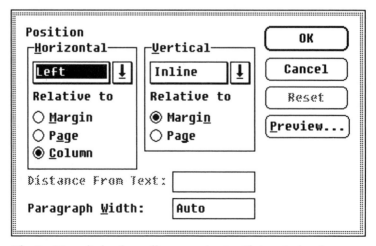

The Position dialog box allows you to specify precisely where you want to place an object on a page.

The settings in this dialog box let you specify the position of the selected object on a page. Notice that there are two pull-down list boxes labeled *Horizontal* and *Vertical.* Below each pull-down list, you'll see the Relative To options. As these items suggest, positioning an object is simply a matter of specifying its horizontal and vertical position relative to a specific part of the page. The horizontal position can be relative to the left and right document margins, the left and right edges of your page, or the boundaries of a text column. (If your document contains only one column of text, the Margin and Column options have the same effect.) The vertical position can be relative to either the top and bottom margins, or to the top and bottom edges of the page.

Figure 12-32 shows the options available on the Horizontal and Vertical pull-down lists. Instead of choosing one of these standard options, you can type a value in the text box at the top of the list. We'll show you how to use values for your Horizontal and Vertical settings a little later in this chapter.

Figure 12-32

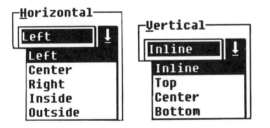

Word offers several standard options for specifying the horizontal and vertical positions of an object.

The first step in specifying an object's position is to choose one of the Relative To options. In other words, you need to decide what part of the page you want to use as your point of reference in positioning the object. Then, you can specify how you want to align the object either by selecting an alignment option from the Horizontal and Vertical list boxes or by typing a numerical measurement in the text box at the top of the list.

After you've specified a position, choose OK to apply it and return to your document. Alternatively, you can choose the Preview... button in the Position dialog box to go directly to the Print Preview window and see how Word will place the object on the printed page.

For example, Figure 12-33 shows a picture we've positioned 2 inches from the top margin, aligned with the left edge of the text column. We specified the horizontal position of this object by choosing Left from the Horizontal list box and selecting the Relative To Column option below this list box. Then, to specify the vertical position, we typed *2in* in the Vertical text box and chose the Relative To Margin option.

Figure 12-33

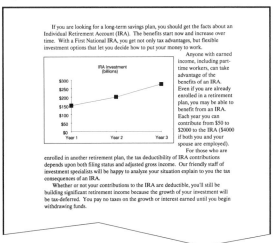

We positioned this picture 2 inches from the top margin, aligned with the left edge of the text column.

Alignment options

When you first open the Position dialog box, you'll notice that Word's default horizontal alignment is Left Relative To Column. The default vertical alignment is Inline. With these settings, the object will appear with no special positioning. Let's look at how you can use the other alignment options to change an object's position in relation to page margins and text.

Horizontal options

As you can see in Figure 12-32, the alignment options in the Horizontal list box are Left, Center, Right, Inside, and Outside. Left will align the left edge of the selected object with the left margin, the left edge of the page, or the current column (depending on the Relative To option you select: Margin, Page, or Column). Similarly, the Right option will align the right edge of the selected object with the right margin, the right edge of the page, or the current column. When you choose Center, Word will center the object between the margins, the edges of the page, or the current text column. Figures 12-34 and 12-35 illustrate uses of the Left, Center, and Right Horizontal options.

The Inside and Outside options allow you to specify a position that changes depending on whether the positioned object falls on a right or left (odd or even) page. You will typically use these options only when you've activated the Mirror Margins option or specified a Gutter setting in the Document dialog box. However, these options are available even if you have not set up different right and left page layouts.

Figure 12-34

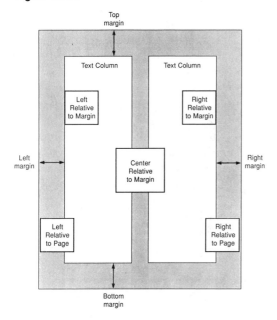

This layout sketch illustrates horizontal alignment relative to the left and right margins and the left and right edges of the page.

Figure 12-35

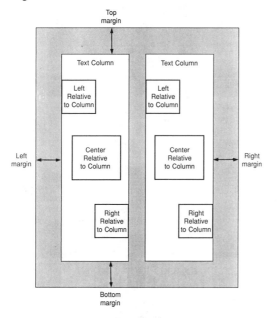

This layout sketch illustrates horizontal alignment relative to column boundaries.

The Inside option will align the edge of an object with the inside margin, the inside edge of a page, or the inside edge of a column. On odd-numbered (right) pages, the left edge of the object will be aligned with the left margin, the left edge of the page, or the left edge of the text column. On even-numbered (left) pages, the right edge of the object will be aligned with the right margin, the right edge of the page, or the right edge of the text column.

Similarly, the Outside option will align the edge of an object with the outside margin, the outside edge of a page, or the outside edge of a column. On odd-numbered pages, the right edge of the object will be aligned with the right margin, the right edge of the page, or the right column boundary. On even-numbered pages, the left edge of the object will be aligned with the left margin, the left edge of the page, or the left column boundary. Figures 12-36 and 12-37 on the following pages illustrate how the Inside and Outside options will align an object.

Vertical options

The Vertical list box in the Position dialog box offers the Inline, Top, Center, and Bottom options. The Top, Center, and Bottom options are fairly self-explanatory. Top will align the top edge of the selected object with the top of the page or with the top margin (depending on whether you've selected Margin or Page as your Relative To option). The Bottom option will align the bottom edge of the selected object with the bottom of the page or with the bottom margin. If you select Center, Word will center the positioned object either between the top and bottom margins or between the top and bottom edges of the page.

The Inline option works a little differently. It does not change the normal vertical alignment of an object on a page. When you choose Inline, Word will position the object relative to its surrounding document text. If you insert or delete text above the positioned object, Word will adjust the vertical position of that object accordingly. The Relative To options for vertical positioning have no effect when you choose the Inline option.

Since the Inline option does not change the vertical position of an object, you may be wondering what purpose it serves. By using this option along with one of the Horizontal options (or a measurement in the Horizontal text box), you can change an object's horizontal position without changing its alignment relative to preceding and subsequent text. This is similar to adjusting the left indent on a paragraph, with one important difference: When you specify a horizontal position and use the Inline Vertical option, Word will flow text around the positioned object. In fact, if you specify a Horizontal setting of Left Relative To Margin and a Vertical setting of Inline, Word will position the object just as it normally would, but will flow text around that object (assuming that there's room for the text).

For example, Figure 12-38 on page 469 shows some text that we've positioned using Inline as our Vertical setting and Left Relative To Margin as our Horizontal setting. Notice how the main body text of our document flows around the positioned paragraph. (To create this effect, we specified a Paragraph Width setting of 3.25". We'll talk more about this Position dialog box setting in a moment. As you can see, we also created a border around the positioned paragraph.)

Figure 12-36

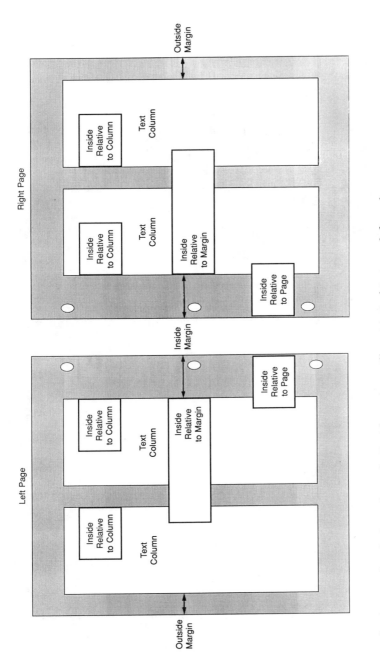

This layout sketch shows how the Inside option will position objects on left and right pages.

Figure 12-37

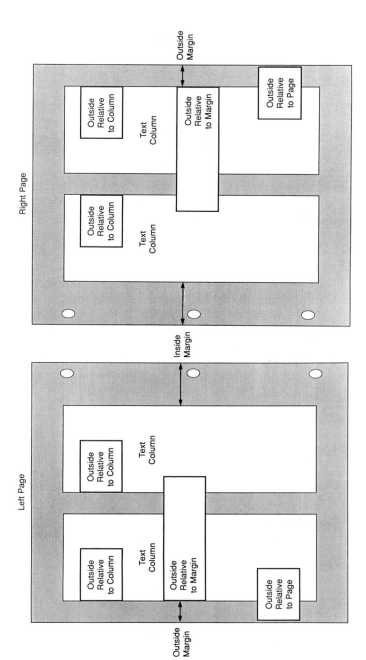

This layout shows how the Outside option will position objects.

Figure 12-38

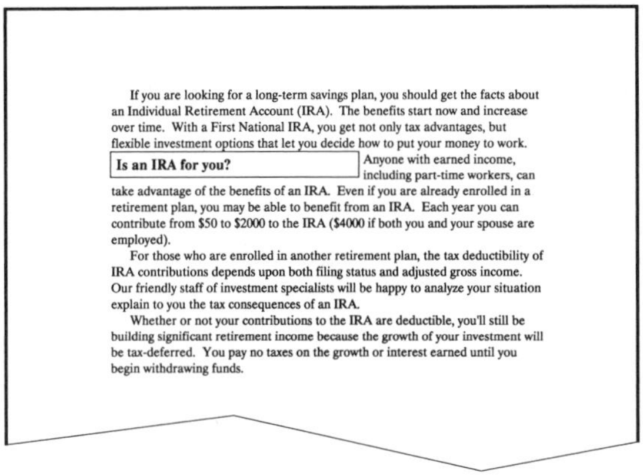

If you are looking for a long-term savings plan, you should get the facts about an Individual Retirement Account (IRA). The benefits start now and increase over time. With a First National IRA, you get not only tax advantages, but flexible investment options that let you decide how to put your money to work.

Is an IRA for you? Anyone with earned income, including part-time workers, can take advantage of the benefits of an IRA. Even if you are already enrolled in a retirement plan, you may be able to benefit from an IRA. Each year you can contribute from $50 to $2000 to the IRA ($4000 if both you and your spouse are employed).

For those who are enrolled in another retirement plan, the tax deductibility of IRA contributions depends upon both filing status and adjusted gross income. Our friendly staff of investment specialists will be happy to analyze your situation explain to you the tax consequences of an IRA.

Whether or not your contributions to the IRA are deductible, you'll still be building significant retirement income because the growth of your investment will be tax-deferred. You pay no taxes on the growth or interest earned until you begin withdrawing funds.

When you use the Inline Vertical option, Word will not change the vertical position of an object but will flow text around it.

Instead of selecting an option from the Horizontal or Vertical list box, you can type a measurement in the Horizontal or Vertical text box. The measurement you type must be a positive number, expressed in inches, centimeters, points, or picas. If you do not include a unit (*in* or ", *cm*, *pt*, or *pi*) in your entry, Word will assume inches (or whatever unit you have chosen as your default in the Preferences dialog box). In addition, Word will convert any entries you make in centimeters, points, or picas to inches (or the default unit of measure).

When you use a measurement to specify an object's horizontal position, Word will align the left edge of that object relative to the left margin, the left edge of the page, or the left column boundary, depending on the Relative To option you select. For example, suppose you enter *.5"* in the Horizontal text box and click the Relative To Page option. Word will position the selected object $^1/_2$ inch from the left edge of your page.

Similarly, when you use a measurement to specify an object's vertical position, Word will position the object relative to the top edge of your paper or to the top margin. For example, suppose you enter *3"* in the Vertical text box and choose the Margin option. Word will position the selected object 3 inches from the top margin on the page.

As you've seen, when you position text or a picture, Word will flow the remainder of the text on the page around the positioned object. Normally, Word allows .13 inches (about $^1/_8$ inch) of space between the positioned object and the text that flows around it. This space is determined by the Distance From Text setting in the Position dialog box. As you might guess, you can change the amount of space between a positioned object and its surrounding text by changing the default setting (.13") in the Distance From Text text box.

Specifying an alignment measurement

Specifying the Distance From Text setting

Your Distance From Text setting can be as small as 0 or as large as 22 inches. Word will add the number you enter to its minimum spacing. Thus, if you specify 0 as your Distance From Text setting, Word will still allow about $^1/_8$ inch of space between the positioned object and its surrounding text. A relatively large setting—a few inches or more—may cause the positioned object to appear on a page by itself. When this happens, Word will not "carry over" any of the space you've specified in the Distance From Text setting to the previous or subsequent pages. In other words, Word will place the positioned object on one page, and place the text on the pages before and after the object in the normal text area.

Although Word succeeds in controlling the horizontal distance between a positioned object and its surrounding text, you may find that the space between your text and the top or bottom edge of a positioned object does not exactly match the Distance From Text setting. The reason for this inaccuracy is that Word must consider the leading of the text that flows around the positioned object as well as the Distance From Text setting. Word won't adjust the line leading to create the correct amount of space between a positioned object and surrounding text.

For example, Figure 12-39 shows a printed document in which one paragraph has been assigned special positioning. The text flowing around the paragraph is 12-point type. We've specified a Distance From Text setting of .2" for this paragraph. Notice, however, that the distances between the top and bottom edges of the paragraph and the surrounding text are considerably greater than the distances between the left and right paragraph edges and the surrounding text.

Figure 12-39

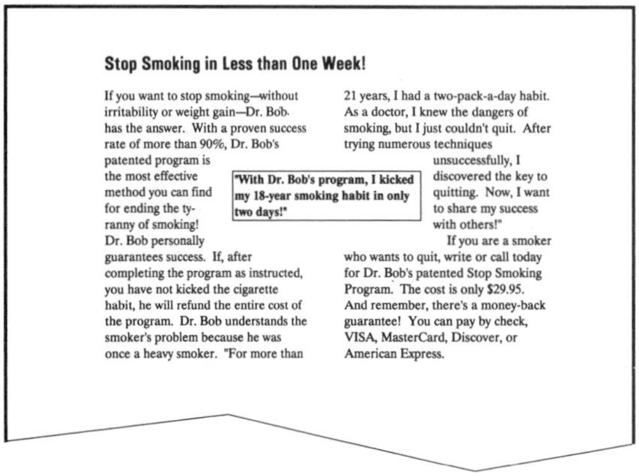

Stop Smoking in Less than One Week!

If you want to stop smoking—without irritability or weight gain—Dr. Bob has the answer. With a proven success rate of more than 90%, Dr. Bob's patented program is the most effective method you can find for ending the tyranny of smoking! Dr. Bob personally guarantees success. If, after completing the program as instructed, you have not kicked the cigarette habit, he will refund the entire cost of the program. Dr. Bob understands the smoker's problem because he was once a heavy smoker. "For more than 21 years, I had a two-pack-a-day habit. As a doctor, I knew the dangers of smoking, but I just couldn't quit. After trying numerous techniques unsuccessfully, I discovered the key to quitting. Now, I want to share my success with others!"

"With Dr. Bob's program, I kicked my 18-year smoking habit in only two days!"

If you are a smoker who wants to quit, write or call today for Dr. Bob's patented Stop Smoking Program. The cost is only $29.95. And remember, there's a money-back guarantee! You can pay by check, VISA, MasterCard, Discover, or American Express.

To maintain proper line leading, Word may not be able to create the correct amount of space between the top and bottom edges of a positioned object and surrounding text.

As you specify a Distance From Text setting, you should be aware that this setting will affect how Word flows text around the positioned object. To flow text beside an object, Word must have at least 1 inch of space between a positioned object and the boundary of a text column. In determining whether there is 1 inch of available space, Word considers not only an object's horizontal position but also the Distance From Text setting. If Word cannot maintain the specified distance between an object and its surrounding text and still have at least 1 inch of space available for text, it will not flow the text.

For example, suppose you have positioned a picture 1 inch from the left margin, and you have specified .1" as your Distance From Text setting. Word will not be able to flow text on the left side of that picture because only $9/_{10}$ inch remains after allowing for the .1" Distance From Text setting. To flow text on the left side of the picture, you must make sure that the picture is at least $1^1/_{10}$ inches from the left margin. In other words, you must specify a Horizontal setting of at least 1.1 inches and choose Relative To Margin.

If you position an object at the edge of a page, the Distance From Text setting will determine how much space appears between that object and the text column. For example, suppose you have positioned a picture by choosing Right from the Horizontal list and choosing the Relative To Page option. You've also specified 0 as the Distance From Text setting. Word will not align the right edge of the picture with the right edge of the page. Instead, it will align the left edge of the picture with the right edge of the text column. If you then change the positioned picture's Distance From Text setting to .25", Word will allow $1/_4$ inch of space between the left edge of the picture and the right edge of the text column. Of course, when you position an object near the edge of a page, keep in mind that a laser printer, such as the Hewlett-Packard LaserJet, cannot print anything that falls less than about $3/_8$ inch from the edge of the paper.

We've just seen how the Distance From Text setting can affect the way Word flows text around a positioned object. Another factor that affects the flow of text is the width of the object. The default width of a positioned picture is simply the width of the frame that appears above the picture. Similarly, the default width of a positioned table is no different from the width of the table without any special positioning. Therefore, when you apply special positioning to a picture or table, Word will automatically flow text around that object if there is sufficient room.

Specifying a width

Positioned paragraphs work a little differently. Initially, the width of a positioned paragraph is determined by the width of the text column. For example, if you're using Word's default Document dialog box settings, and you have only one column of text, each paragraph—regardless of whether you assign a special position—will be 6 inches wide. If you are using snaking columns, the width of each paragraph will be equal to the width of a column.

Because Word considers positioned paragraphs to be the same width as the text column, it may not be able to flow text on the right or left side of the paragraph. Even if you move the indent markers on the ruler to make a positioned paragraph narrower or wider, Word will consider that paragraph to be the same width as your text column for positioning purposes.

You can see the width of a positioned paragraph by switching to the page view and selecting either the Show-all icon on the ribbon or the Show All or Text Boundaries check box in the Preferences dialog box. When you do this, Word will mark the paragraph's boundaries on your screen with dotted lines. For example, let's go back to the printed document shown in Figure 12-38. Before we changed the Paragraph Width setting on the positioned paragraph, Word considered that paragraph to have the same width as the document's text area. Figure 12-40 shows this document in the page view before we changed the Paragraph Width setting. As you can see, a dotted line marks the boundaries of the positioned paragraph. Although the text of this paragraph is quite short, Word extends its boundaries to the full width of the text area and is unable to flow text to the right of the paragraph.

Figure 12-40

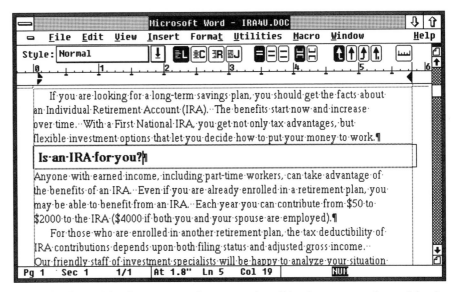

Initially, the width of a positioned paragraph will be the same as the width of a document's text column.

Changing the width of a positioned paragraph

To make the text flow around the positioned paragraph shown in Figure 12-40, you must specify a Paragraph Width setting in the Position dialog box. When you specify a Paragraph Width that is less than the width of the text area, Word will rewrap the paragraph text, if necessary, to comply with that setting. In addition, Word will flow text around the paragraph. For example, Figure 12-41 shows our sample paragraph from Figure 12-40 after we changed its Paragraph Width setting to 3.25 inches.

Figure 12-41

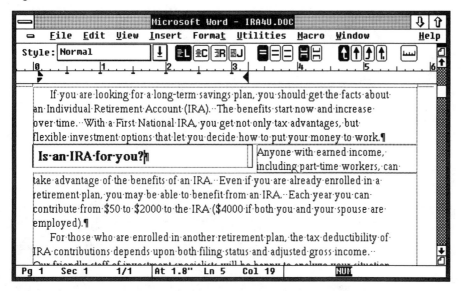

After changing the Paragraph Width setting, Word is able to flow text around the positioned paragraph.

You also can specify a Paragraph Width setting that is greater than the width of your text column. When you do this, Word will rewrap the text in the paragraph to align it within the specified width.

Although you can use the Paragraph Width setting with a positioned table or picture, you probably will want to leave this setting on Auto. If you specify a setting that is greater than the initial width of the table or picture, Word will not enlarge the table or picture; it will simply add some additional white space to the right of the object. However, if you specify a Paragraph Width setting that is less than the initial width of a table or picture, Word will truncate the positioned object by cropping part of its right edge.

Changing the
width of a positioned
table or picture

You can use the ruler and the Paragraph dialog box to change the alignment and other paragraph formatting characteristics of a positioned paragraph. When you move the cursor to a positioned paragraph, the ruler (in the paragraph view) will display the width of that paragraph, with the zero point on the ruler representing the left edge of the paragraph and the vertical line representing the paragraph's right boundary (as determined by the Paragraph Width setting). For example, notice in Figure 12-41 that the vertical line on the ruler appears at the

Formatting a
positioned paragraph

$3\frac{1}{4}$-inch position on the ruler. Initially the first-line and left indent markers for the paragraph will be aligned with the zero point on the ruler, and the right indent marker will be aligned with the vertical line.

Changing alignment and indention

If you change the alignment or indention of a positioned paragraph, those changes will be made relative to the paragraph's boundaries. For example, suppose we apply right alignment to the positioned paragraph shown in Figure 12-41. As you can see in Figure 12-42, Word will align the paragraph with its right boundary. (If we were to move the right indent marker on this paragraph, Word would align the paragraph with the indent marker rather than with the right boundary.)

Figure 12-42

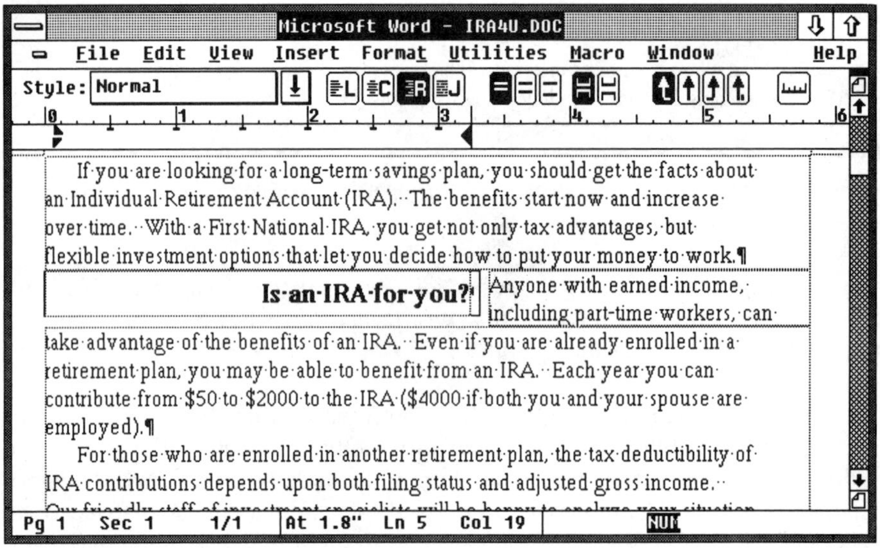

We have applied right alignment to the paragraph shown in Figure 12-41.

Because Word aligns the indent markers relative to a paragraph's boundaries, you should not move these markers until you have specified a Paragraph Width setting. If you move the markers before you change this setting, you may get unexpected results. For example, Figure 12-43 shows a document whose text area is 6 inches wide (Word's default). As you can see, we have moved the right indent marker for the positioned paragraph to the 4-inch position on the ruler. We've also assigned a special position to this paragraph: The Horizontal setting is Center Relative To Column and the Vertical setting is Inline. We used Word's default Distance From Text setting of .13".

Figure 12-43

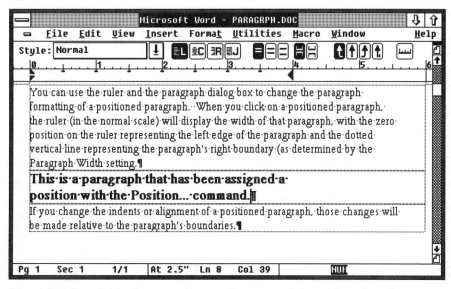

The right edge of this document's second paragraph has a 2-inch indention.

To flow text around the positioned paragraph, we will need to make sure that there is at least 1.13 inches of space on either side of the paragraph (1 inch for the text and .13 inch for the Distance From Text setting). To create this space, we need to change the Paragraph Width setting. If we simply move the indent markers on the ruler, Word will wrap the paragraph text in a narrower area, but the paragraph boundaries will remain aligned with the left and right edges of the text column.

Suppose we open the Position dialog box and specify a Paragraph Width setting of 3". This will create $1^1/_2$ inches of space on either side of the positioned paragraph. (The text column is 6 inches wide. Subtracting 3 from this gives us 3 inches in which to flow text. Word will put half of this space on either side of the positioned paragraph, creating $1^1/_2$ inches of space.)

Figure 12-44 on the next page shows the positioned paragraph after we changed its Paragraph Width setting. Notice that Word has maintained the 2-inch right indent so that the text is now wrapped within a 1-inch-wide column.

Fortunately, you can correct the problem shown in Figure 12-44 by moving the right indent marker on the ruler to the vertical line that marks the right boundary of the paragraph. Figure 12-45 shows the corrected document.

Figure 12-44

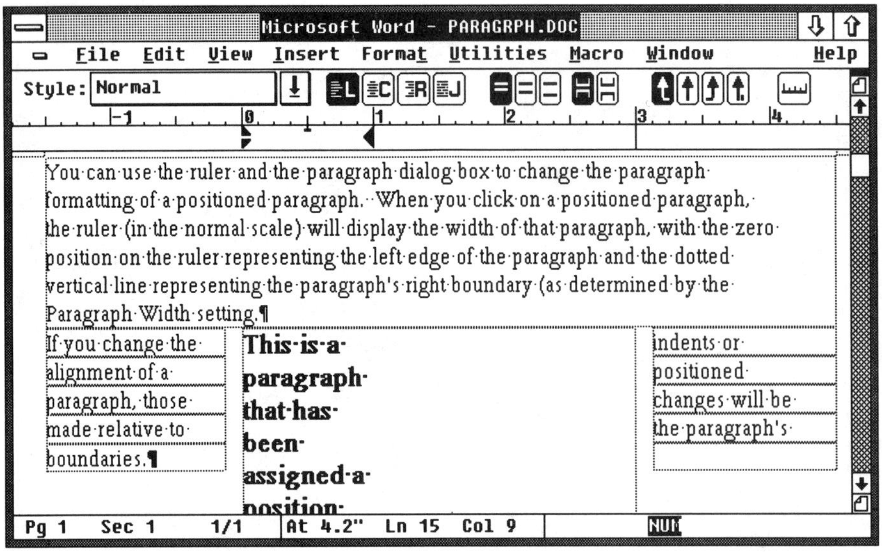

When we change the Paragraph Width setting to 3", Word will maintain the 2-inch right indention, wrapping the text in a 1-inch-wide area.

Figure 12-45

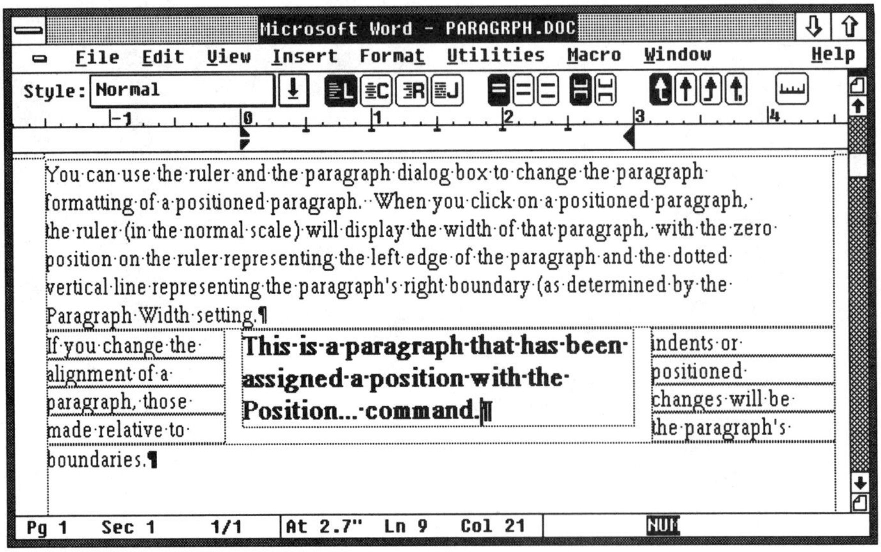

We moved the right indent marker to the 3-inch position on the ruler in order to wrap the positioned paragraph within its 3-inch boundary.

To avoid the type of problem shown in Figure 12-44, we recommend that you use the Paragraph Width setting—not the indent markers on the ruler—to adjust the width of a positioned paragraph. After setting the Paragraph Width, you may want to move the indent markers on the ruler to fine-tune the appearance of the positioned paragraph.

By the way, Word allows you to move the indent markers beyond the left and right boundaries of the positioned paragraph. That is, you can move the first-line and left indent markers to the left of the zero point on the ruler, and you can move the right indent marker to the right of the vertical line. Generally, you'll want to avoid doing this. When you use the indent markers to move the positioned object into the surrounding text, Word will truncate part of that object.

Another way you can format a positioned paragraph is to change its line spacing. For example, a document may contain a positioned paragraph with double spacing, while the text that flows around that paragraph may have single spacing. You also can create tab stops in a positioned paragraph or add a border.

Other paragraph formatting

With the Spacing Before and After settings in the Paragraph dialog box, or the Open-space icon on the ruler, you can change the amount of space between the top and/or bottom edges of a positioned paragraph and its surrounding text. In other words, when you insert space before or after a positioned paragraph, Word will place that space within the paragraph's boundary.

As we have mentioned, to see special positioning on your screen, you must turn on the page view or use the Print Preview window. When you use the Print Preview window, you can change the position of an object by dragging it. To do this, you must first select the Boundaries button to display the boundaries of the object. For example, Figure 12-46 on the following page shows the printed document from Figure 12-30 in the Print Preview window.

Viewing the positioned object

After selecting the Boundaries button, you can move the pointer over the positioned object, where it will assume a crosshair shape. When you click on the object, Word will display its horizontal and vertical position coordinates at the top of the Print Preview window. These coordinates represent the position of the left and top boundaries of the positioned object relative to the left and top edges of the page. For example, the coordinates *(1.5, 2.25)*"tell you that the left boundary of the object is $1^1/_2$ inches from the left edge of the page, and the top boundary of the object is $2^1/_4$ inches from the top edge of the page. Word will display new coordinates as you drag the object to a new position. After you've repositioned the object and clicked in the gray area of the window, Word will remove the boundary lines for the positioned object and redraw the screen to show the new flow of text.

If you want to reposition objects in the Print Preview window with the keyboard, first select the Boundaries button to display the boundary lines, then press the [Tab] key until Word highlights the object you want to reposition. At this point, use the arrow keys to move the object around on the page. When you've placed the object in the desired position, press [Enter] twice to remove the boundary lines and redraw the screen to show the new flow of text.

Figure 12-46

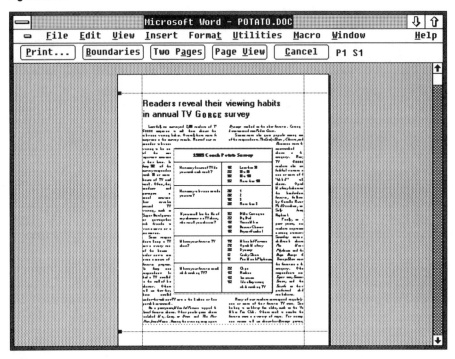

When you select the Boundaries button in the Print Preview window, Word will display boundary lines around a positioned object.

If you want a closer view of a positioned object, select the Page View button at the top of the Print Preview window or choose Page View from the Document menu. Figure 12-47 shows the document from Figure 12-46 in the page view.

Returning to normal positioning

If you decide that you do not want a paragraph, picture, or table to have special positioning in your document, you can choose the Reset button in the Position dialog box. This will return the object to a normal position. The Horizontal setting will become Left Relative To Column, the Vertical setting will become Inline, and the Paragraph Width setting will return to Auto.

Figure 12-47

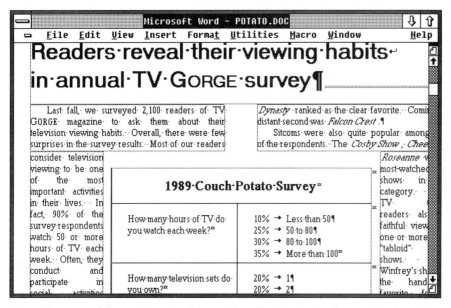

For a close-up of the positioned object, select the Page View button in the Print Preview window.

Specifying positioning in a style definition

In many respects, applying special positioning to a paragraph is no different from applying other, more conventional paragraph formatting. In fact, as you may know, you can use the settings in the Position dialog box as part of a style definition. For example, suppose you want to place the illustrations throughout a document in one of four standard positions on a page. The easiest way to do this would be to define four named styles whose definitions include your position settings. To do this, just choose Define Styles... from the Format menu and, in the Define Style Name text box, type a name for the style—such as *position1*. Next, choose the Position... button, specify your Position settings, and choose OK. Finally, choose the OK button in the Define Styles dialog box to complete the style definition. Now, when you want to position one of your illustrations, just click on the illustration to select its frame, then apply the *position1* style.

Tips on positioning

Whenever you want to use the Position... command to place an object in a particular location on a page, we strongly recommend that you first create and format your entire document without any positioned objects. Then, repaginate the document and add the positioned objects, beginning at the top of the document and working your way to the end. After positioning each object, you should repaginate again. We recommend this approach because it's possible for Word to move a positioned object from one page to another as you add and delete text. Keep in mind that the Position... command does not specify on which printed page a positioned object should appear. It merely specifies the location of an object on the current page. Therefore, if you edit a document, changing the location of its page breaks, it's likely that an object with fixed positioning will be moved to a different page.

You probably will want to avoid placing a positioned object in the middle of a wide text column—for example, in the middle of the page that contains only one column of text. When you do this, Word will split lines of text at the edge of the positioned object, making it difficult to read the document. In fact, in the sample documents we've shown in this section, whenever we've centered an object on a page, we've used a two-column text layout. In this way, each text column flows around one side of the positioned object, and the lines of text are not split by the object.

We mentioned at the beginning of this section that you can use the Position... command to position one or more rows of a table, rather than an entire table. To do this, apply a position to the first cell(s) of the row(s) you want to position. In order to position the row(s), Word may split the table between different parts of the page.

If you're positioning a picture and some text below it, Word will automatically set the width of the text to be the same as the width of the picture. This feature is particularly handy when you need to use the Position... command to place an illustration and its caption in a certain area of the page.

Although the Position... command is a powerful feature, we have found that it often requires some trial and error to create an attractive page layout. We recommend that you have a good working knowledge of Word's Document, Paragraph, and Character formatting features before you attempt to use the Position... command.

WORKING WITH LONG DOCUMENTS

Although your Word for Windows documentation states that the length of your documents is limited only by memory and disk space, you'll probably find that documents any longer than about 80 pages become slow to work with and difficult to handle. Of course, the practical size limit of a document also depends somewhat on the document's complexity.

If you have created a very long document that is divided into several sections, you may want to consider splitting it into a few smaller documents. When you've finished editing the smaller documents, you can use a master document to link them and print them consecutively. You can also use the master document to generate a table of contents and an index for the linked documents.

The INCLUDE field is the tool you will use to compile several smaller docu- **The INCLUDE field**
ments into a single master document. This field takes the form

{INCLUDE *filename*}

where *filename* is the full path name of the document file you want to include.
(You must double the backslash character in the file's path name). The result of
an INCLUDE field is all the text stored in *filename*.

For instance, imagine you have created a 250-page document that consists of
three chapters. Because you want to vary the headers and footers within each
chapter and use multicolumn formatting on some pages, you've divided each
chapter into several sections. As you might imagine, procedures such as searching
and replacing, hyphenating, spell-checking, repaginating, and saving will slow
down considerably when you're working with a document of this length.

To solve this problem, use the Cut and Paste commands to divide this
document into three smaller documents named CHAP1.DOC, CHAP2.DOC, and
CHAP3.DOC. Once you've created these three smaller documents, you can work
with them individually, thereby reducing the amount of time required to perform
hyphenation, repagination, and so forth.

After you've divided your long document into three smaller documents, you'll
want to create a master document like the one shown in Figure 12-48. As you can
see, this document contains only the fields

{INCLUDE "C:\\CHAP1.DOC"}
{INCLUDE "C:\\CHAP2.DOC"}
{INCLUDE "C:\\CHAP3.DOC"}

When you are ready to print the three chapters, activate the master document,
choose the Print… command from the File menu, select the Update Fields check
box in the expanded Print dialog box, and choose OK. Word will then print the
text in the three documents consecutively.

Figure 12-48

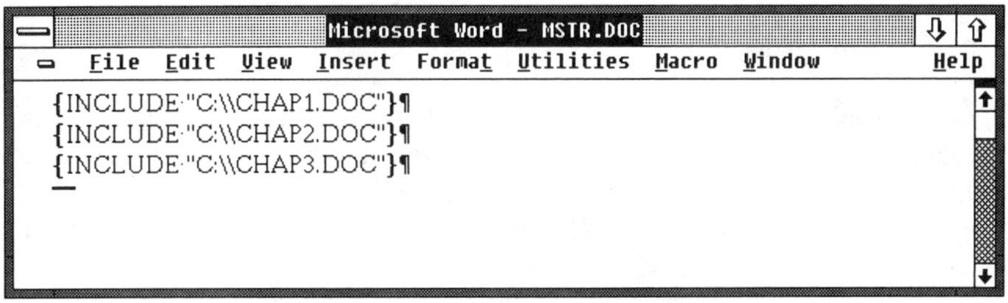

*The INCLUDE field allows you to consolidate several documents into a single
master document.*

It's important that you update the INCLUDE fields in your master document before you send it to the printer. As we've demonstrated, the easiest way to do this is to select the Update Fields check box in the expanded Print dialog box.

In Chapter 14, we'll show you how to use a master document to generate a table of contents and an index for a series of documents.

More about the
INCLUDE field

If you want your master document to include only a portion of the text stored in another document file, you can first define a bookmark that names the text you want to include. Then, you can enter into the master document an INCLUDE field in the form

{INCLUDE *filename bookmark*}

where *filename* is the name of the source file and *bookmark* is the name of the text you want to insert.

Once you've entered some INCLUDE fields into your master document, you can display the text from the source documents by activating the master document and turning off the Field Codes setting on the View menu. If you want, you can make changes to the text returned by the INCLUDE fields, and then use Word's UpdateSource macro to copy your changes back to the source document. To run this macro, place the cursor anywhere within the modified text and press [Ctrl][Shift][F7]. Word will then copy your changes to the source document stored on disk.

The RD field

In addition to the INCLUDE field, Word offers an RD field for consolidating multiple documents into a single master document. (RD stands for Referenced Document.) The form of the RD field is similar to that of the INCLUDE field:

{RD *filename*}

The difference between the INCLUDE field and the RD field is that the INCLUDE field returns the text from the source document as its result, while the RD field returns no result of its own. The RD field is designed exclusively for allowing you to create a master table of contents or index. We'll show you some examples of this field in Chapter 14.

Margins, headers,
and footers

When you use a master document to link multiple documents, Word will use the margin settings in the master document's Document dialog box to format all the linked documents. In addition, when you send the master document to the printer, Word will ignore the headers and footers in the linked documents and print the master document's header and footer on each page. If you want each of your linked documents to carry a unique header or footer, you'll need to insert section breaks between the INCLUDE fields in the master document, then use the techniques we explained earlier in this chapter to set up a different header or footer for each section.

Fortunately, your master document automatically assigns consecutive page, line, and footnote numbers to your printed documents. If you want Word to number all the pages, lines, and footnotes consecutively, beginning with the first document and continuing through the last document, you don't need to adjust the starting numbers for these items in your linked documents.

Page, line, and footnote numbers

If you don't want to assign consecutive page, line, or footnote numbers to all the pages in your linked documents, however, you'll first need to insert section breaks between the appropriate INCLUDE fields in the master document. Then, if you want to assign a new starting page number to a section, use the techniques we've discussed earlier in this chapter to change the section's starting page number. In Chapter 14, we'll show you how to restart the footnote numbers in a section of your document, and in Chapter 16, we'll discuss line numbering.

When you link a series of documents, you can use the Pages From and To options in the Print dialog box to print any series of pages. Because Word numbers the pages in your master document sequentially, you can just type the From and To values you want into the Print dialog box. For example, suppose you want to print a portion of the master document in Figure 12-48. Also, assume that Chapter 1 in your series is 85 pages long and Chapter 2 is 97 pages long. If you issue the Print... command and enter a From setting of *80* and a To setting of *110*, Word will print the last six pages of Chapter 1 and the first 25 pages of Chapter 2. Of course, Word will number the pages 80 through 110.

Printing selected pages

In this chapter

Advanced Editing Techniques 13

*A*fter you've mastered Word's basic editing techniques, you'll want to explore its advanced editing features. In this chapter, we'll discuss many of the advanced features you can use to create long, complex documents. We'll begin by giving you an overview of the five ways to view your document, then we'll cover the glossary and the spike—two features that you'll find in few other PC word processors. We'll also discuss bookmarks, references, and advanced navigational techniques, and show you how to annotate and revise a Word document stored on disk.

As you edit and format documents with Word, you'll want to take advantage of the five ways you can view a document. Of course, each of the views Word offers has its advantages and disadvantages. In this section, we'll summarize each view's features and point out some situations that call for a particular view.

VIEWING YOUR DOCUMENT

By default, Word places you in the normal editing view when you create a new document. This view is a WYSIWYG (What You See Is What You Get) view because what you see on the screen is what you'll get when you print the document. For instance, the normal editing view allows you to see the document's character and paragraph formatting, line and page breaks, and tab-stop alignment. Figure 13-1 on the next page shows a sample document in the normal editing view.

Unfortunately, the normal editing view does not offer true WYSIWYG capability, since it doesn't show you how headers, footers, footnotes, and side-by-side snaking columns will appear on the printed page. Additionally, the normal editing view will not show you how text wraps around fixed-position paragraphs, tables, and pictures.

Normal editing view

Figure 13-1

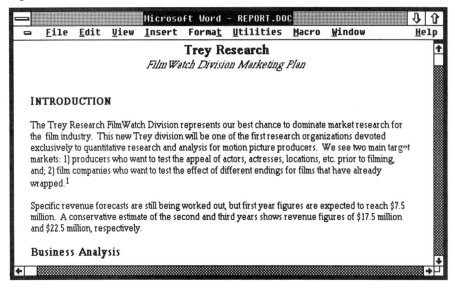

The normal editing view offers a good combination of WYSIWYG features and system speed.

You'll want to use the normal editing view most of the time, since it offers a good array of WYSIWYG features and allows Word to perform at a reasonably good rate of speed.

Page view

Generally speaking, Word's page view provides an on-screen representation of your printed document, giving you true WYSIWYG capability. In addition to the features offered by the normal editing view, the page view allows you to see how headers, footers, and footnotes will appear in the printed document. It also displays side-by-side snaking columns and shows how text wraps around fixed-position objects.

Although the page view is quite helpful for seeing how your printed pages will actually appear, Word runs significantly slower in the page view than in the normal editing view. For this reason, you probably will not want to use the page view for the majority of your text creation, editing, and formatting. We recommend that you stay with the normal editing view and use the page view only to check the layout of your document in its final stages.

There are two ways to access the page view. First, you can select the Page command from the View menu. If you do this, Word will indicate that the page view is active by placing a check mark next to the Page command. Another way to access the page view is to choose the Page View button at the top of the Print

Preview window. This allows you to move from the bird's-eye view of the preview screen to the close-up view of the page view screen.

When you first switch to the page view, Word will display the main text area of the current page at the top of the screen. For example, if your document has a 1-inch top margin with a header, that margin and header will be just out of view, with the first line of your document's main body text appearing at the top of the window. To bring other parts of the page into view, just use the vertical or horizontal scroll bar. To see a different page, you can drag the scroll boxes or click on the Page-back and Page-forward icons (⛶) at the top and bottom of the vertical scroll bar. (We'll discuss these icons in a moment.)

When you scroll in page view, Word will show you the edges of a page instead of marking page breaks with a dotted horizontal line, as it does in the normal editing view. For example, Figure 13-2 shows the page from Figure 13-1 after we issued the Page command and scrolled the upper-left corner into view. Notice that Word uses a shaded background to help distinguish the page area. Notice also that you now can see the header at the top of the page. If this were not the first page in the document and we continued scrolling up, Word would display the bottom of the previous page.

Figure 13-2

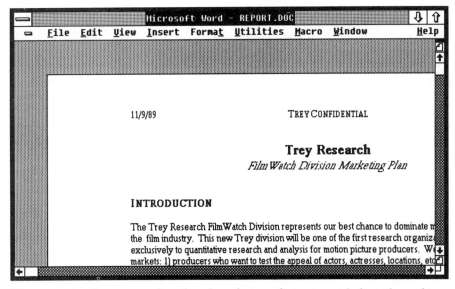

The page view lets you see how headers, footers, footnotes, side-by-side snaking columns, and fixed-position objects will appear in the printed document.

Like the Print Preview window, the page view really comes in handy when you want to preview the effect of a formatting change before you send the document to the printer. Keep in mind, however, that the page view cannot always give you an accurate representation of your printed document. For instance, if you've added line numbers to your document, those numbers will not appear in the page view. In addition, if you've used a font that is not installed in your printer, the document you see in page view will look quite different from the one you'll print. For a detailed discussion of the page view, refer to Chapter 7.

Print Preview

The Print Preview window gives you a bird's-eye view of your document, allowing you to see entire page layouts on the screen. To activate the Print Preview window, simply choose the Print Preview command from the File menu. Figure 13-3 shows the document from Figure 13-1 in the Print Preview window.

Figure 13-3

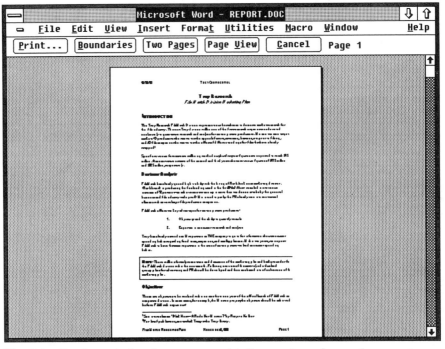

The Print Preview window lets you see a bird's-eye view of your document.

As you might expect, the Print Preview window can help you avoid time-consuming (and possibly costly) bad print runs. For a detailed discussion of the Print Preview window, refer to Chapter 7.

Word's outline view allows you to plan and analyze a document's structure. The combined power of the outline view and style sheets lets you format your document with ease. In addition, you can use the outline view to create a table of contents for your document, navigate through long documents quickly, and rearrange blocks of text with just a few keystrokes.

Outline view

To activate the outline view, simply choose the Outline command on the View menu. Figure 13-4 shows our sample document in the outline view. For details on Word's outline view, refer to Chapter 9.

Figure 13-4

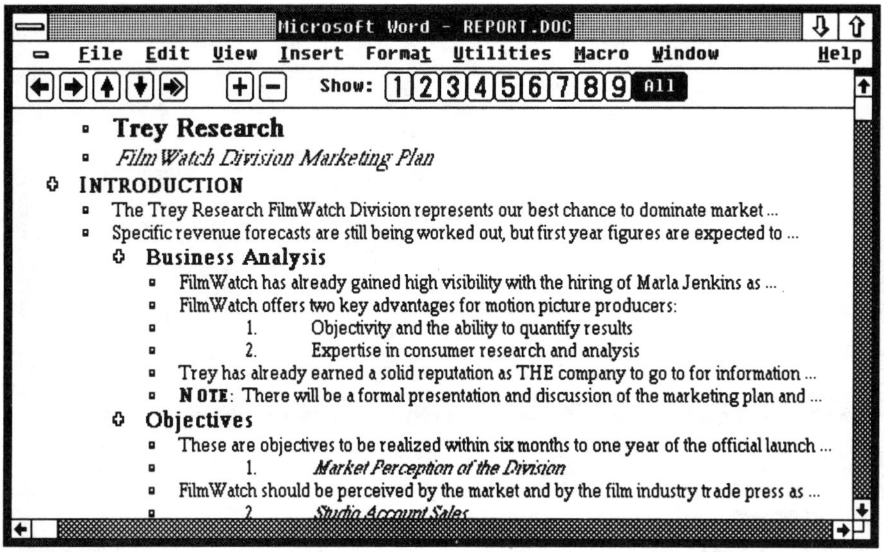

The outline view lets you plan and analyze your document's structure.

As your documents become longer and more complex, it will take Word longer to display and print them. If you become frustrated with the amount of time required to format or scroll through your document, you might want to take advantage of Word's draft view.

Draft view

In a nutshell, the draft view allows Word to operate much faster by removing most of the document's formatting from the display. When you choose the Draft command on the View menu to enter the draft view, Word will display all of the document's text in the Microsoft Windows System font (the font used in the menu bar and dialog boxes), and will display any pictures you've imported as empty boxes. If you've applied character formatting to some of the document's text, Word will underline that text.

For example, Figure 13-5 shows our sample document in the draft view. Although this document looks much better in normal editing view, you can format or scroll through the document in the draft view much quicker than you can in the normal editing view (or any of the other views).

Figure 13-5

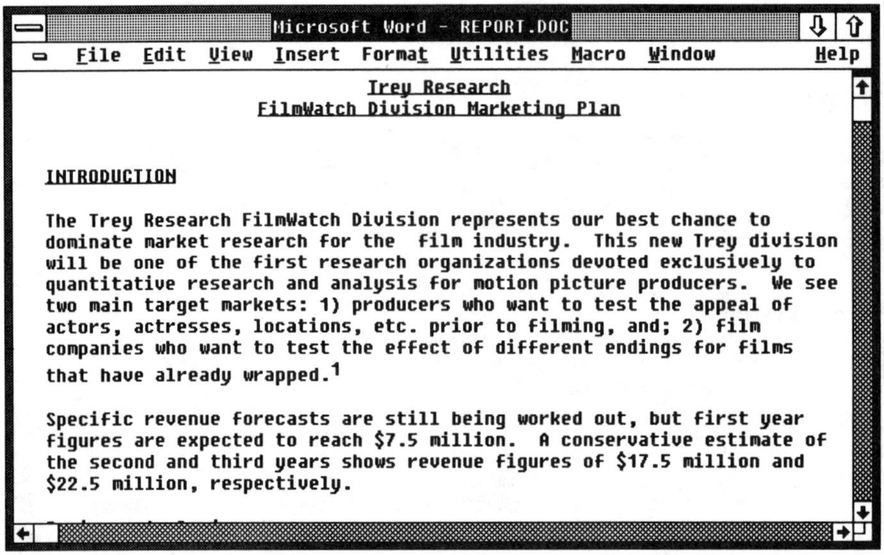

The draft view sacrifices WYSIWYG capabilities for speed.

By the way, one instance where the draft view comes in handy is when you're editing a document whose text appears in a very small point size. By working with such a document in the draft view instead of in one of the other views, you might find it easier to read and select its text.

Keep in mind that the Draft command controls only the way Word displays the document on your screen—it does not affect the way the document looks when you print it. If you want to print a document in the Draft View mode, you must select the Print... command, choose the Options >> button in the Print dialog box to bring up the expanded Print dialog box, select the Draft check box, then choose OK. When you do this, Word will print the document in your printer's default font and will underline text that has been assigned character formats.

Although you'll seldom want to, you can work in both the Draft View and Outline View modes at the same time. When you activate both modes on the View menu, Word will display unformatted text in the outline view.

You've probably seen many books that include a glossary, or listing of special terms and their definitions. In Word, the glossary serves a slightly different purpose from what you might expect. Instead of containing definitions for special terms, the Word glossary stores frequently used terms and their abbreviations. The entries you store in the glossary might include words that require special formatting or long words or phrases that are difficult to spell. Glossary text can be as short as a single character or as long as several pages. Word even allows you to store pictures in a glossary.

In this section, we'll begin with an example that demonstrates the usefulness of the glossary. Then, we'll explain how to add, revise, and delete a glossary entry, and how to insert glossary text into a document. Finally, we'll show you how to store fields and pictures in the glossary, then show you how to save and print it.

Suppose you are creating a document into which you must frequently type the name of your company, International Consolidated Systems, Inc. Since this is a long name that you need to use repeatedly, it makes sense to add it to the glossary. To do this, first type the full company name anywhere in your document. Then, highlight that text, and choose Glossary… from the Edit menu to open the Glossary dialog box shown in Figure 13-6. When this dialog box appears, type an appropriate abbreviation in the Glossary Name text box. For example, you might type the abbreviation *ics*. Finally, choose the Define button. Word will then close the dialog box and return to the document.

Figure 13-6

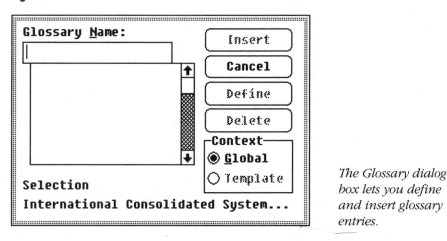

The Glossary dialog box lets you define and insert glossary entries.

The next time you need to use the company name in your document, you can insert it by using the [Expand glossary name] key ([F3]). To do this, simply position the cursor where you want the name to appear (except in the middle of an existing word), type *ics,* and press the [Expand glossary name] key. Immediately, Word will replace the glossary term *ics* with the glossary text *International Consolidated Systems, Inc.* Alternatively, you can use the Glossary... command to insert the company name into the document. To do this, place the cursor in the appropriate spot, select the Glossary... command, click on the term *ics* in the Glossary Name list box, then choose the Insert button. Word will then close the Glossary dialog box and insert the full text for the glossary entry—*International Consolidated Systems, Inc.*—into the document at the position of the cursor.

The example we just presented describes the most basic glossary-related task. However, using the glossary can become more complicated in other situations. In the remainder of this section, we'll go into much more detail about the specifics of working with the glossary.

Glossary basics

In addition to adding new entries to the glossary, Word lets you revise and delete the glossary's existing entries. The list box in the Glossary dialog box lists existing entries in alphabetical order. If there are more entries in the list box than Word can display at one time, you can use the scroll bar to bring the additional entries into view.

Earlier, we mentioned that you can use Word's glossary to store frequently used terms and their abbreviations. The list box that you see in the Glossary dialog box shows only the abbreviations. In this chapter, we will use the word *glossary term* when we refer to one of the items in this list. The term *glossary text* will refer to the longer text that a glossary abbreviation represents. Finally, we'll use the term *glossary entry* to denote a complete glossary item—both the glossary term and the text it represents.

If you want to see what a particular glossary term stands for, you can open the Glossary dialog box and select that term in the list box. In the lower-left corner of the dialog box, Word will display the glossary text that the selected term represents. For example, suppose you've defined the term *scca* and you've forgotten what this term represents. To find out what *scca* stands for, simply click on this term in the list box, as shown in Figure 13-7.

Notice that when you select a glossary term, Word automatically enters it into the Glossary Name text box. Notice also that the text *Sports Car Club of America* appears in the lower-left corner of the dialog box. This tells you that the glossary term *scca* represents this glossary text.

Sometimes, the text for a glossary term will be too long for Word to display in the dialog box. In that case, Word will display only as much of the text as will fit in the dialog box, followed by an ellipsis (...). If you want to see all the text, you must click the Insert button to paste it into your document. Then, you can use either the Undo Expand Glossary or the Cut command to remove the text from your document.

Figure 13-7

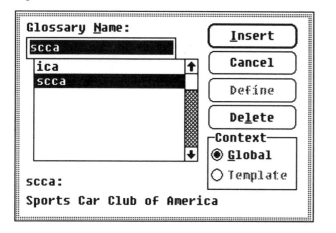

When you click on a term in the list box, Word will display the text for that term in the lower-left corner of the dialog box.

As we demonstrated in our example, the first step in adding a new glossary entry is to type the glossary text anywhere in your document. Next, highlight that text and choose the Glossary... command to open the Glossary dialog box. In the dialog box, type the appropriate glossary term (abbreviation) in the Glossary Name text box, then choose the Define button to complete the process and close the dialog box.

Adding a new glossary entry

When you type a glossary term into the Glossary Name text box, there are a few rules to keep in mind. First of all, Word will not allow you to enter an existing glossary term when you are creating a new glossary entry. If you type into the Glossary Name text box a term that has already been defined, Word will display a message box containing the question *Redefine glossary?*, as shown in Figure 13-8. Choosing the Yes button tells Word to replace the old entry with the new text you've selected. Choosing No returns you to the Glossary dialog box without modifying the existing entry.

Rules for glossary terms

Figure 13-8

If you try to assign an existing term to a new glossary entry, Word will present this message box.

In determining which terms have already been used, Word does not consider case. For example, a lowercase *g* is considered to be the same as an uppercase *G*. As you'll see, the fact that Word does not distinguish case in glossary terms can make the glossary easier to use.

You can use any characters you want in a glossary term, including punctuation marks and other characters you can generate with the keyboard. A glossary term can consist of two or more words, but cannot exceed 31 characters. However, you'll want to keep each glossary term as short as possible so you can type it quickly and remember it easily.

Formatted glossary text

When you select text for a new glossary entry, Word stores the formatting for that text in the glossary. Returning to our previous example, suppose you add bold formatting to the name *International Consolidated Systems, Inc.* before you create the glossary entry. Each time you use the glossary term *ics*, Word will insert the full name—including bold formatting—into your document.

In addition to bold formatting, Word will store fonts, point sizes, superscripting, italics, and any other character formatting you may have assigned to your glossary text. If your glossary text is a complete paragraph (or several paragraphs), Word will store the paragraph formatting as well—including margins, line spacing, indention, and so forth.

Although Word maintains the formatting for your glossary text, it will not display that formatting when you view the glossary text in the dialog box. As with any other dialog box, Word displays all the text in the Glossary dialog box in the Microsoft Windows System font.

Revising an existing glossary entry

After you have added entries to the glossary, you may need to change the text to which a glossary term refers. Changing the text for a glossary term is similar to creating a new glossary entry. Word will not allow you simply to edit the existing glossary text; instead, you must replace it with new text. To do this, first type into your document the word or phrase that you want to use as your replacement text (if those words do not already exist in your document). Then, select that text and choose the Glossary... command. In the Glossary dialog box, click on the term whose text you want to replace. Word will display that term in the Glossary Name text box and display all or part of the glossary text for that term in the lower-left corner of the dialog box. To complete the replacement, choose the Define button. At this point, Word will present the message box shown in Figure 13-8. If you choose Yes, Word will redefine the entry you've selected and close the message box.

For example, suppose your glossary includes the term *2EU*, which stands for *2nd Edition Update*. You would like to change the text for this glossary entry to *Current Edition Update*. To do this, first type the words *Current Edition Update* anywhere in your document. Then, select that text and issue the Glossary...

command.. In the Glossary dialog box, select the term *2EU*, as we've done in Figure 13-9, then choose the Define button to bring up the dialog box shown in Figure 13-8. When you choose Yes, Word will replace the existing text for that term, *2nd Edition Update*, with the text you've selected in your document, *Current Edition Update*, and close the dialog box.

Figure 13-9

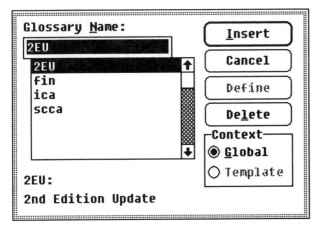

You can redefine glossary text by replacing it with new text.

    Unfortunately, you can't use the Glossary dialog box to redefine an existing glossary term (the abbreviation). If you want to change the term that refers to some glossary text, you'll need to reselect that text in the document, then use the Glossary dialog box to create a new glossary term. Once you've done this, you can use the procedure described in the next section to delete the old entry.

    To delete a glossary entry, just open the Glossary dialog box, select the glossary term assigned to the entry, and choose the Delete button. Immediately, Word will remove the selected entry from the glossary. The Glossary dialog box will remain open on your screen so you can insert or delete more entries.
    Word will allow you to delete only one glossary entry at a time. If you need to eliminate several entries in the glossary, you must choose Delete for each entry.

Deleting a glossary entry

    As we mentioned, there are a couple of ways to insert glossary text into your document. The first step with either is to position the cursor at the location where you want to insert the text. Then, you can issue the Glossary... command and select the glossary term whose text you want to insert. Finally, choose the Insert button to close the dialog box and place the glossary text in your document.
    Unless you need to view the text for a glossary entry or you cannot remember a glossary term, opening the Glossary dialog box and clicking the Insert button is not the most efficient way to insert glossary text into a document. Word offers

Inserting glossary text into your document

a much easier way. First, position the cursor at the location where you want to insert the text. Then, type the glossary term (the abbreviation) for the text you want to insert in your document, and press the [Expand glossary name] key ([F3]). Word will then replace the abbreviation with the glossary text. Of course, in order to use this technique, you must remember the correct glossary term so that you can type it into the document. Capitalization does not matter when you enter a glossary term.

The GLOSSARY field

Another way to insert glossary text into your document is to use the GLOSSARY field. The form of this field is {GLOSSARY *glossaryTerm*}, where *glossaryTerm* is the abbreviation for the glossary text you want to insert. If you redefine the glossary text associated with a glossary term, Word will not change the result of the GLOSSARY field until you place the cursor in that field and press the [Update field] key ([F9]).

Storing fields in the glossary

If you include a field in your glossary text, Word will store that glossary item a little differently than regular text. For example, suppose you've entered the field

{DATE \@ "MMM-d"}

into your document, and you want to assign this field to the glossary term *date*. For the sake of this example, let's also assume that the field currently returns *Oct-26* as its result. To add this field to the glossary, simply highlight it in the document, then bring up the Glossary dialog box shown in Figure 13-10.

Figure 13-10

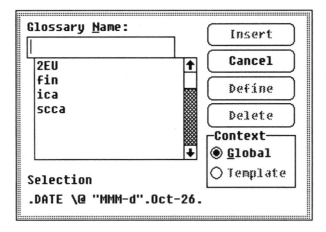

When you include a field in your glossary text, Word will store both the field's code and its most recent result.

Notice that the selection Word displays at the bottom of the Glossary dialog box includes both the field's code and its most recent result. Whenever Word displays a field at the bottom of the Glossary dialog box, it displays it in the form

.fieldCode.result.

where *fieldCode* is the text that appears between the two special field characters, { and }, and *result* is the result the field returned when it was last updated.

As you might expect, when you insert glossary text that contains a field, Word will insert the appropriate field code. In addition, the field you've inserted will return the same result as the field that was used to define the glossary text. For example, if you use the Glossary dialog box to insert the sample DATE field into a document, Word will insert the field code *{DATE \@ "MMM-d"}*, and that field will initially return the result *Oct-26*. Of course, the next time you update this field, Word will return the current date.

Storing pictures in the glossary

Although you'll probably use the glossary mainly to store text, you can also use it to store pictures. Most pictures consist of a graphic or chart created in another Microsoft Windows program, then inserted into a Word document. Word considers each picture a single character that you can cut, copy, or paste, just as you would regular characters.

To add a picture to the glossary, you must first paste that picture into a Word document. (We'll explain how to do this in Chapter 21.) Then, the procedure you use to add the picture to the glossary is the same you follow to add any other glossary entry. First, select it with the mouse by clicking anywhere on the picture. (You'll be able to tell that the picture is selected by the small black boxes or "handles" that appear around its frame.) To select a picture with the keyboard, place the cursor along the left edge of the picture, then press the [Shift]→ key combination. With the picture selected, open the Glossary dialog box, type a name for the glossary entry in the Glossary Name text box, and choose the Define button. (By the way, if you change the size of the picture before you add it to the glossary, Word will store the picture in its new size.)

Once a picture is stored in the glossary, you can use any of the techniques we have described to paste that picture into your document. You can open the Glossary dialog box, select the glossary term for the picture, then choose the Insert button. Alternatively, you can enter the glossary term into the document and press the [Expand glossary name] key.

Saving the glossary

You might be surprised to learn that Word stores glossary entries in a document template file rather than in a separate glossary file. By default, your glossary entries are stored in the standard document template NORMAL.DOT. All the glossary entries stored in NORMAL.DOT are global entries, which means that you can access them while working in *any* Word document—not just documents based on the template NORMAL.DOT.

If you're working with a document that is based on a template other than NORMAL.DOT, you can tell Word to save a glossary entry in that document's template instead of in NORMAL.DOT. When you save a glossary entry in a template other than NORMAL.DOT, however, you can access that entry only when you activate a document that is based on the template containing the entry. For instance, suppose you are working with a document based on the template MEMO.DOT. If you save a glossary entry in MEMO.DOT, then open an existing document based on the template NORMAL.DOT, you will not be able to access that glossary entry.

To tell Word you want to store a glossary entry in the active document's template instead of in NORMAL.DOT, first highlight the glossary text in your document, and bring up the Glossary dialog box. Next, type the name of the glossary term in the Glossary Name text box, then change the Context setting in the lower-right corner of the dialog box from Global to Template. (If the active document is based on the template NORMAL.DOT, the Template option will be dimmed and unavailable for selection.) Finally, choose the Define button to define the new entry and close the dialog box.

Word won't actually save your glossary changes as soon as you define them. Instead, it will keep the glossary items in memory and save them to disk in either of two ways, depending on which template's glossary you've changed. If you make any changes to the global glossary (the one stored in NORMAL.DOT), Word won't save the changes to disk until you exit from Word. When you issue the Exit command on the File menu, however, Word will display the message box shown in Figure 13-11. To save the glossary changes you've made, choose Yes. If you don't want to save your glossary changes, choose No. Choose Cancel if you don't want to exit from Word.

Figure 13-11

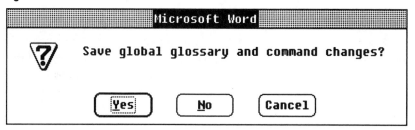

Word will save your global glossary changes to NORMAL.DOT when you exit from the program.

If you've modified the glossary for a template other than NORMAL.DOT, Word will save those glossary changes when you close the document based on that template. When you close the document, Word will bring up a message box like the one shown in Figure 13-12. To update the changes you've made to the template's glossary, choose Yes. If you don't want to save the glossary changes you've made, choose No. Choose Cancel if you want to cancel the close procedure and return to the document.

Figure 13-12

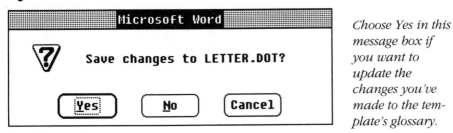

Choose Yes in this message box if you want to update the changes you've made to the template's glossary.

If you want to get a print-out of the glossary's contents, choose the Print... command from the File menu to bring up the Print dialog box, select the Glossary option from the Print pull-down list box, and choose OK. Word will then print a listing of each glossary term and the text for that term. Figure 13-13 shows a sample glossary listing.

Printing the glossary

Figure 13-13

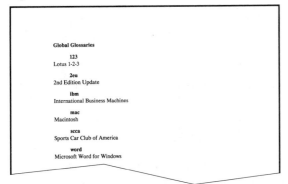

You can print the contents of the glossary.

Word features a special kind of glossary entry called the spike. The spike gets its name from the physical spike that many small businesses use to hold bills, receipts, or other pieces of paper.

USING THE SPIKE

Before we explain how to use Word's spike, let's think about how you might use a physical spike to store information. Imagine you are the owner and operator of a hardware store. Next to your cash register, you've placed a spike to hold copies of the store's sales receipts. Each time a customer buys something in the store, you hand a copy of the sales receipt to the customer and place the store's copy on the spike. At the end of the day, you take all the receipts off the spike, and log the total of each sale into a journal. When business begins the next day, the spike will be empty and ready to store that day's receipts.

Like a physical spike, Word's spike is useful for collecting and storing multiple pieces of related information, and then depositing that information into a single location. Of course, the information you store on Word's spike isn't a group of receipts or bills—it's text or pictures you've entered into your document. After you've stored something on the spike, you can empty the spike's contents into a single location in the document.

What is the spike?

The spike is actually a special glossary entry named *Spike*. The main difference between the glossary term *Spike* and other glossary terms is that when you store text or a picture under the glossary term *Spike*, Word doesn't replace its contents with the new text or picture—instead, it adds that text or picture to what's already stored there. In all other respects, *Spike* is like any other glossary term.

Placing text on the spike

To place some text from your document on the spike, first highlight that text, then press the [Spike] key ([Ctrl][F3]). Word will then remove the text from the document and add it to the contents of the spike. Each time you press the [Spike] key, Word will continue adding the text you've highlighted to the spike.

For example, suppose you've entered *Total Sales: $1,000* into a document, and you want to place this text on the spike. To do this, simply highlight that text and press the [Spike] key. Immediately, Word will remove the highlighted text from the document and place it on the spike.

Now, suppose you've also entered *Total Costs: $700* into the document, and you want to add this text to the spike. To do this, highlight that text and press the [Spike] key again. At this point, the spike will contain both pieces of text—*Total Sales: $1,000* and *Total Costs: $700*. Word will not remove this text from the spike until you tell it to do so with the [Unspike] key ([Ctrl][Shift][F3]).

Inserting the spike's contents

When you are ready to insert the contents of the spike back into a document, you can use either of two techniques. First, you can use the [Unspike] key, which empties the spike after inserting all of its contents into the document. Alternatively, you can use the Glossary... command or the [Expand glossary name] key ([F3]) to insert a copy of the spike in the document without removing its contents. (You cannot insert a portion of the spike into a document.) Let's consider each of these techniques in detail.

To empty the contents of the spike into a document, simply place the cursor in the appropriate spot and press the [Unspike] key. Immediately, Word will transfer the spike's contents into the document and empty the spike.

To insert a copy of the spike's contents into a document without emptying the spike, simply position the cursor in the appropriate spot, open the Glossary dialog box, and choose the term *Spike* from the list box. (This term will not appear until you place something on the spike.) At this point, Word will display the text stored in the spike at the bottom of the Glossary dialog box. Choosing the Insert button at this point will place a copy of the spike's contents into the document and close the dialog box.

An even easier way to insert a copy of the spike's contents into a document is by typing the word *spike* into the document at the appropriate location, then pressing the [Expand glossary name] key. Doing this has the same effect as choosing the Insert button in the Glossary dialog box to insert the glossary text represented by the glossary term *Spike*.

Let's briefly demonstrate both of the techniques we've discussed for inserting the spike's contents. Suppose the spike currently contains the text *stuff on the spike*, and you want to insert this text at the top of a new document. To insert the spike's contents without emptying the spike, simply position the cursor, type the word *spike*, and press the [Expand glossary name] key. To insert the spike's contents into the document and empty the spike, simply position the cursor and press the [Unspike] key.

USING BOOKMARKS

Like the spike, bookmarks are so named because they are similar to the regular bookmarks you use to mark a place in a book. Like regular bookmarks, Word's bookmarks let you mark a particular place in a document. Once you've defined a bookmark, you can use the Go To… command to immediately move to that spot from anywhere in the document.

Marking places in a document is only one of the many tasks for which you'll find bookmarks useful. You can also use bookmarks to name blocks of text, then use the bookmark name to refer to that text. For instance, you can use a bookmark name in the argument of a field or in an editing or formatting instruction in a macro.

Bookmarks have a few other uses as well, which we'll discuss later in the appropriate places of this book. For now, let's learn how to define bookmarks in a document, how to modify and delete an existing bookmark, and how to go to a bookmark with the Go To… command.

Defining a bookmark

Defining a bookmark in your document is much like creating a new glossary item. First, identify the place or the text to which you want to assign a bookmark name. Next, choose the Bookmark… command from the Insert menu to bring up

---

Emptying the spike

Copying from the spike

An example

the Bookmark dialog box shown in Figure 13-14. At this point, type the bookmark name you want to use into the Bookmark Name text box, then choose OK to define the bookmark and close the dialog box.

Figure 13-14

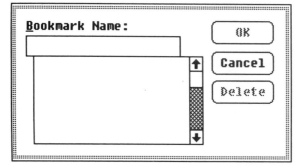

The Bookmark dialog box allows you to define bookmarks for your document.

An example

Suppose you've created the document shown in Figure 13-15, and you want to assign the bookmark name *intro* to the heading *INTRODUCTION* near the top of the screen. To define this bookmark, first highlight the text *INTRODUCTION*, then choose the Bookmark… command from the Insert menu. Next, enter the name *intro* into the Bookmark Name text box and choose OK.

Figure 13-15

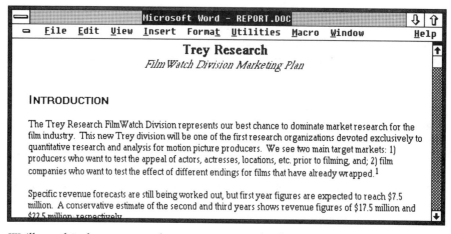

We'll use this document to demonstrate some bookmark basics.

Bookmark names

Bookmark names cannot exceed 20 characters, and each must begin with a letter of the alphabet. Additionally, the name can contain only letters, numbers, and the underline character—you cannot use spaces, punctuation marks, or any other symbols. If you enter an invalid bookmark name into the Bookmark Name text box, Word will present the message box shown in Figure 13-16 when you choose OK. In this message box, simply choose OK to return to the Bookmark dialog box, and enter a valid bookmark name.

Figure 13-16

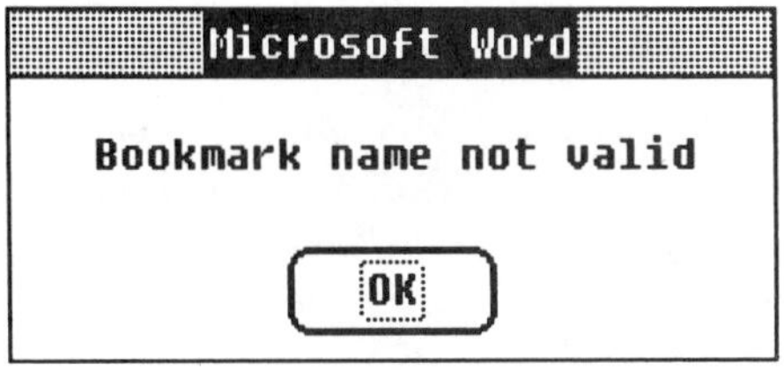

Word will present this message box if you attempt to define an invalid bookmark name.

If you want, you can redefine a bookmark name to refer to a different place or block of text. To do this, first select the place or block of text to which you want the existing bookmark name to refer. Next, select the Bookmark… command to open the Bookmark dialog box, and choose from the list box the bookmark name you want to redefine. When you choose OK, Word will close the Bookmark dialog box and redefine the bookmark name you selected.

Redefining a bookmark

To delete an existing bookmark, open the Bookmark dialog box and choose from the list box the bookmark name you want to delete. When you choose Delete, Word will delete the bookmark and remove its name from the list box.

Deleting a bookmark

One of the advantages of defining bookmarks is that they make it easy to go to a specific place in a document. After you've defined some bookmarks in your document, you can use either the Go To… command or the [Go to] key ([F5]) to move the cursor or the highlight to those bookmarks.

Going to a bookmark

To go to a bookmark, you can select the Go To… command on the Edit menu. When you do, Word will present a dialog box like the one shown in Figure 13-17 on the next page. At this point, simply choose the bookmark name from the list box and choose OK. If the bookmark you've specified marks a place in the document, Word will immediately move the cursor to that place. If the bookmark defines a block of text, however, Word will highlight that text.

Using the Go To… command

For example, suppose you want to go to the bookmark named *intro*, which we defined in our example. To do this, select the Go To… command from the Edit menu, choose *intro* from the list box, and choose OK. Word will then scroll into view the portion of the document shown in Figure 13-15 and highlight the word *INTRODUCTION.*

Figure 13-17

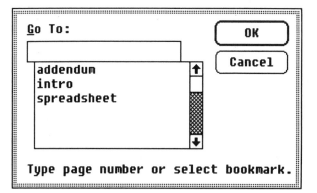

You can use either the Go To... command or the [Go to] key to go to a bookmark.

Using the [Go to] key

Another way you can go to a bookmark is to press the [Go to] key ([F5]). When you press the [Go to] key, Word will present the prompt *Go to:* at the bottom of the screen. At this point, you can type the name of the bookmark to which you want to go, and press [Enter]. Alternatively, you can press the [Go to] key a second time to bring up the Go To dialog box, select a bookmark name from the list box, and choose OK. When you use either of these techniques, Word will go to the specified bookmark.

For example, to go to the bookmark *intro* using the [Go to] key, press [Go to], type *intro* in response to the *Go to:* prompt, and press [Enter]. Word will immediately scroll into view the portion of the document shown in Figure 13-15.

CREATING REFERENCES

Often, you'll want to refer to something that appears several pages away in a long document. For example, you might instruct the reader to look at a table on an earlier page, or refer to a later section in the document for a detailed discussion of a particular topic. In this section, we'll show you how to create these kinds of references with Word. First, we'll show you how to create page-number references. Then, we'll explain how to use Word's referencing capabilities to create a sequentially numbered list of items. Finally, we'll discuss textual references and show you how to include them in a document.

Referring to a page number

Occasionally, you'll want to insert a page number into your document that directs the reader to a particular piece of information. To insert a page-number reference, you must use the PAGEREF field. The form of this field is

{PAGEREF *bookmark*}

where *bookmark* specifies the bookmark whose page number you want to insert. (You must use the Bookmark... command to define the bookmark before you can use the PAGEREF field to insert its page number.) This field returns the number of the page on which *bookmark* is located. If *bookmark* is a block of text that appears on more than one page, PAGEREF will return the number of the page on which *bookmark* begins. As you might expect, Word updates the PAGEREF field only when you issue the Print… command or when you update it manually with the [Update field] key ([F9]).

For example, suppose you've defined a bookmark named *table2* that marks the place where Table 2 begins. If you need to refer to Table 2 on a distant page, you could insert its page number with the field *{PAGEREF "table2"}*, like this:

These commands are listed in Table 2 on page {PAGEREF "table2"}.

When Word updates the field, which it will do only when you print the document or update the field manually, the PAGEREF field will return the page number on which the bookmark *table2* appears.

If you want the PAGEREF field to return a number in a non-standard format, use the format switch—*. As we explained in Chapter 10, you can use this switch to convert an ordinary page number into seven other formats, including Roman numeral and cardinal text. Refer to Chapter 10 for more information on the format switch.

You probably number the figures or tables in your documents sequentially, labeling the first figure *Figure 1*, the second one *Figure 2*, and so forth. Although you can type figure labels into a document as literal text, trouble sets in when you need to move or delete a figure that appears early in the document. For instance, if you've labeled the figures in a document *Figure 1* through *Figure 30*, and you need to delete Figure 2, you must manually change all the labels for Figures 3 through 30. Additionally, you'll need to change the references to those figures in the body text of your document—a time-consuming process that can drive you up the wall.

Fortunately, Word provides a tool that lets you avoid many of the hassles of relabeling figures or other sequentially numbered items in a document—the SEQ field. If you use the SEQ field to insert sequential numbers, Word will automatically adjust those numbers as you move or delete items in the sequence. This means that if you use the SEQ field to label your figures, you can delete any figure in the document and have Word adjust all the figure labels that follow.

An example

Choosing different number formats

Creating sequence references

The SEQ field

As we've said, you'll use the SEQ field to create sequential references in a document. The forms of this field are

{SEQ *identifier*}
{SEQ *identifier bookmark*}

where *identifier* identifies the sequence you're labeling, and *bookmark* is a bookmark you've previously defined. You can use three special switches with the SEQ field—\c, \r, and \h. Before we discuss these switches, however, let's look at an example that demonstrates the benefit of the SEQ field in its basic form.

An example

Suppose you're creating a document that will contain three tables, labeled *Table 1* through *Table 3*. Although you could label each table with the literal text *Table 1, Table 2,* and *Table 3,* you're better off labeling the table with the SEQ field.

Figure 13-18 shows how you would use the SEQ field to label the tables in a sample document. As you can see, each of the three tables is labeled

Table {SEQ "table"}

If you update the fields in Figure 13-18 and display the document's field results, the document will look like Figure 13-19.

Figure 13-18

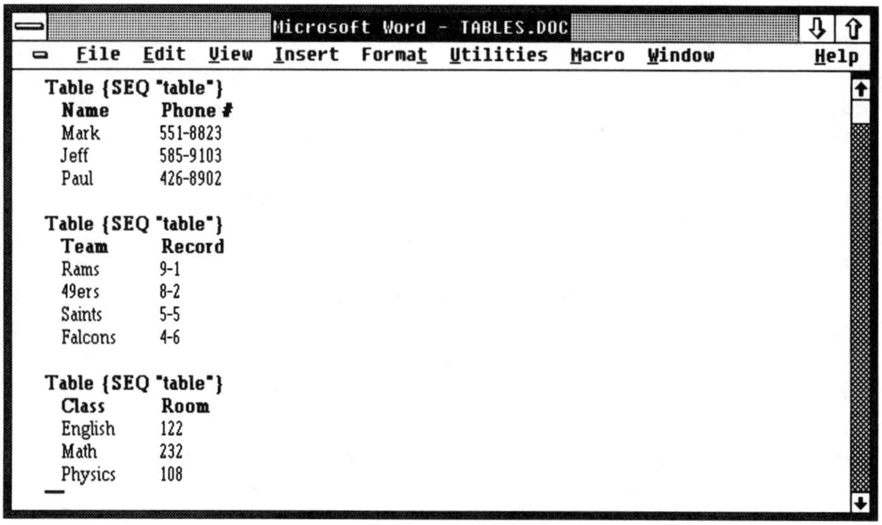

We've used the SEQ field to label the tables in this sample document.

Figure 13-19

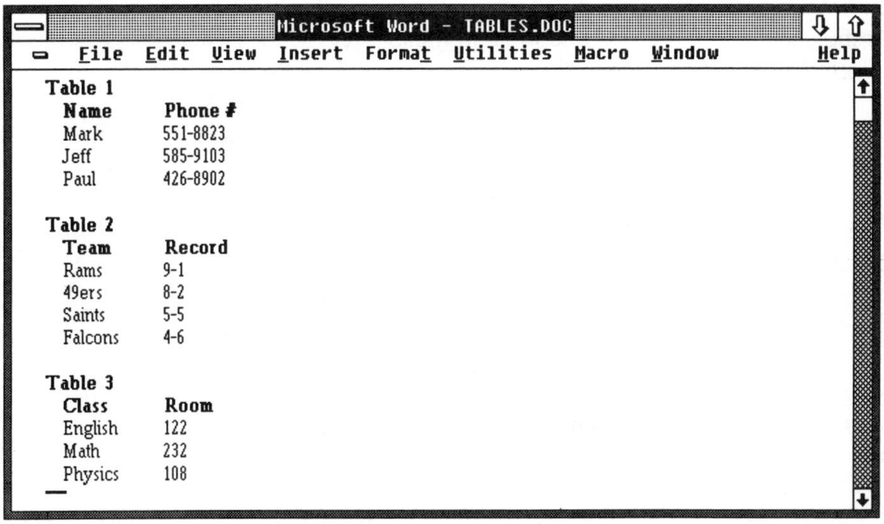

```
┌──────────────────────────────────────────────────────────────────────────┐
│ ⊟                   Microsoft Word - TABLES.DOC                      ⇩  ⇧  │
│  ⊟   File  Edit  View  Insert  Format  Utilities  Macro  Window    Help    │
├──────────────────────────────────────────────────────────────────────────┤
│   Table 1                                                             ▲    │
│     Name        Phone #                                              ░░░   │
│     Mark        551-8823                                             ░░░   │
│     Jeff        585-9103                                             ░░░   │
│     Paul        426-8902                                             ░░░   │
│                                                                      ░░░   │
│   Table 2                                                            ░░░   │
│     Team        Record                                              ░░░   │
│     Rams        9-1                                                        │
│     49ers       8-2                                                        │
│     Saints      5-5                                                        │
│     Falcons     4-6                                                        │
│                                                                            │
│   Table 3                                                                  │
│     Class       Room                                                       │
│     English     122                                                        │
│     Math        232                                                        │
│     Physics     108                                                   ▼    │
└──────────────────────────────────────────────────────────────────────────┘
```

When you update the SEQ fields, they'll return a list of sequential numbers.

Notice that we used the name *table* as our *identifier* argument. If we need to number another sequence of items in the same document, we could do so by using a different identifier as the argument to the SEQ field. For instance, to label a sequence of figures in this document, we could use the field {SEQ "figure"}.

Repeating the previous sequence number

If you want an SEQ field to return the same number as the previous SEQ field, you can achieve this effect by using the \c switch. For instance, if you've used the field {SEQ "table"} to generate a table number, and you need to generate the same table number again, you can use the field {SEQ "table" \c}.

Resetting the sequence number

To reset the sequence number to a particular value, use the \r switch. The form of this switch is

    \r *newValue*

where *newValue* is the value you want the field to return. Of course, an SEQ field that uses the \r switch will affect all the subsequent SEQ fields with the same identifier. For instance, if you want to use an SEQ field to return *Table 12*, use the field {SEQ "table" \r "12"}.

Creating a placeholder SEQ field

The SEQ field allows one additional switch—\h—that tells Word to update the sequence number according to the other switches in the field, but to not insert the field's result in the document. You must enter the \h switch after the other switches in the field code.

Using bookmarks in an SEQ field

If you need to refer to a particular figure, table, illustration, or some other item you've previously numbered with an SEQ field, you can first insert a bookmark just before that field, then enter an SEQ field that includes the bookmark name as its second argument. For instance, suppose you've labeled all the tables in your document like this:

Table {SEQ "table"}

Near the end of your document, you want to refer to a particular table containing information about your company's vacation policy. To refer to this table by number, first move back through the document and locate the SEQ field that creates the table's number. Next, insert a bookmark named *vacation* just in front of the SEQ field. Finally, create a reference to the table by entering another SEQ field that includes the bookmark name *vacation*, like this:

Your vacation benefits appear in Table {SEQ "table" "vacation"}

When you calculate the result of this new SEQ field, it will return the same result as the SEQ field next to the bookmark *vacation*. For instance, if the bookmark *vacation* resides in the same paragraph as an SEQ field that returns the number 7, the field *{SEQ "table" "vacation"}* will return the number 7 as well.

Creating textual references

Word offers a couple of fields that let you create textual references in a document—REF and STYLEREF. Let's look at each of these fields in detail and use some examples to illustrate when they'll come in handy.

The REF field

The REF field lets you insert into your document the text stored in any bookmark. The form of this field is

{REF *bookmark*}

where *bookmark* is the name of the bookmark whose text you want to insert. Word updates this field only when you issue the Print Merge… command or when you update the field manually with the [Update field] key ([F9]). If you insert the REF field in a header or footer, Word will also update the field the first time you issue the Print… command.

For example, suppose you've defined a bookmark named *chap9* that refers to the text *Managing Growth*. If you want to insert that text somewhere else in your document, you might do so like this:

We'll talk more about growth in Chapter 9, "{REF "chap9"}."

When you update this REF field, the sentence will look like this:

We'll talk more about growth in Chapter 9, "Managing Growth."

The STYLEREF field returns the text of the nearest paragraph that matches the style you specify. This field is used primarily in headers and footers to create dictionary-style headings in your document. The forms of this field are

The STYLEREF field

{STYLEREF *styleName*}
{STYLEREF *styleName* \l}

where *styleName* is the name of the style assigned to the paragraph you want to return. To search for one of Word's built-in *heading* styles (such as *heading 1, heading 2,* and so forth), you can use the appropriate number to abbreviate the heading names. For instance, you can use the number 1 to refer to the style *heading 1*. Word updates the STYLEREF field only when you issue the Print Merge… command or when you update it manually with the [Update field] key.

The method that Word uses to determine which paragraph is the "nearest" one depends on where the STYLEREF field appears in your document, and whether you've included the \l switch. Table 13-1 on the following page summarizes all of the possibilities. The \l switch lets you retrieve the style of the last paragraph on the page; you can only use this switch in STYLEREF fields that exist in a header or footer.

Since the STYLEREF field is most commonly used in headers and footers, let's look at a couple of sample documents that effectively use a STYLEREF field in their headers. First, consider the document shown in Figure 13-20 on page 511. Notice that we've assigned the style *heading 1* to the headings in this document, and that we've entered the header

{TITLE} — {STYLEREF "heading 1"}

When we update the fields in Figure 13-20 and display the field results, Word will insert into the header the document's title along with the nearest title in the style *heading 1*, as shown in Figure 13-21 on page 511.

Table 13-1

If STYLEREF appears...	Word will search...
In body text	from the field code to the beginning of the document. If Word doesn't find the specified style, it will search from the field code to the end of the document.
In headers and footers	from the beginning of the current page to the end of that page. If Word doesn't find the specified style, it will search from the end of the previous page to the beginning of the document. If Word still doesn't find the style, it will search from the beginning of the following page to the end of the document.
In headers and footers with the \l switch	from the end of the current page to the beginning of that page. If Word doesn't find the specified style, it will search from the end of the previous page to the beginning of the document. If Word still doesn't find the style, it will search from the beginning of the following page to the end of the document.
In footnotes and annotations	from the footnote reference mark or the annotation reference mark to the beginning of the document. If Word doesn't find the specified style, it will search from the footnote reference mark or the annotation reference mark to the end of the document.

Now, consider the document shown in Figure 13-22 on page 512. As you can see, this document contains a series of glossary terms, each assigned the style *heading 2*. To provide a set of keywords at the top of each page of this glossary, we've created the header text

{STYLEREF "heading 2"} — {STYLEREF "heading 2" \l}

The first field in this header retrieves the glossary term that appears nearest the top of the page, while the second field, which contains an \l switch, retrieves the glossary term nearest the bottom of the page. Figure 13-23 on page 512 shows how the document appears when we update and display the field results.

Figure 13-20

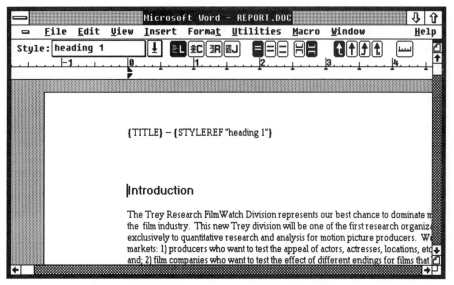

We've used the STYLEREF field in the header of this document to retrieve the nearest subtitle.

Figure 13-21

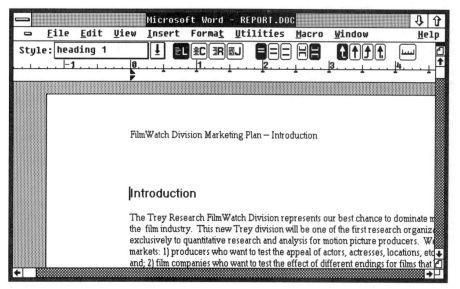

This is how the document shown in Figure 13-20 appears when we update the fields and show their results.

Figure 13-22

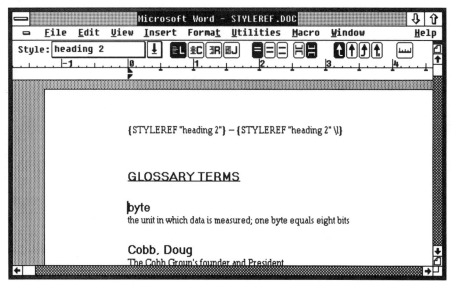

We've used a couple of STYLEREF fields in the header of this document to create dictionary-style headings.

Figure 13-23

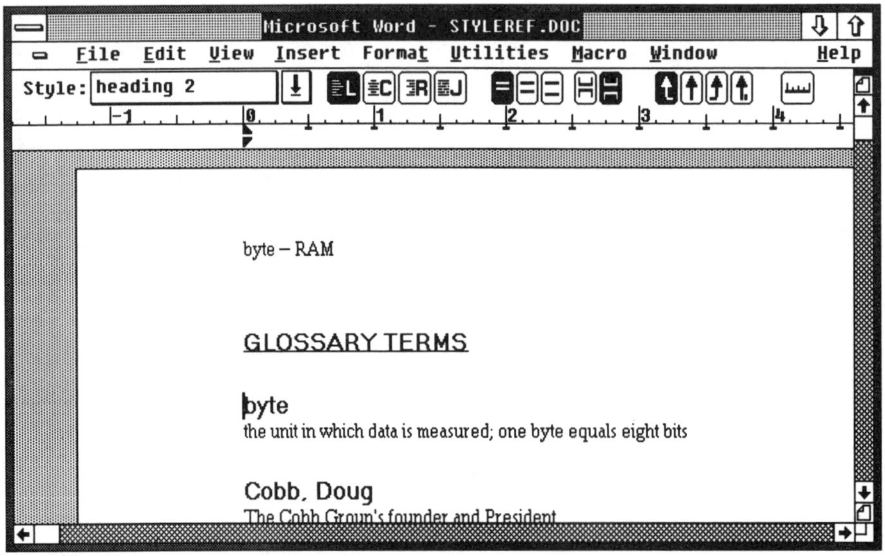

This is how the page shown in Figure 13-22 appears when we update the fields and show their results.

Earlier in this chapter, we showed you how to use the Go To... command to go to a bookmark in your document. In addition to moving to a bookmark, the Go To... command lets you move to a page, section, line, footnote, annotation, or percentage point.

ADVANCED GO TO TECHNIQUES

When you select the Go To... command, Word will present a Go To dialog box like the one shown in Figure 13-24. This dialog box contains a Go To text box and a list box containing the names of all the bookmarks you've defined in the document. At this point, you should tell Word where to go by typing an appropriate entry into the Go To text box. After you type your entry, choose OK.

Figure 13-24

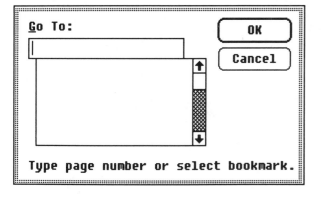

You can navigate through long documents by using the Go To dialog box.

If you want, you can use the [Go to] key ([F5]) instead of the Go To... command. When you press the [Go to] key, Word will present the prompt *Go to:* at the bottom of the screen. Then, you can type the appropriate entry and press [Enter]. Alternatively, you can press the [Go to] key a second time to bring up the Go To dialog box, type an entry into the Go To text box, and choose OK. When you use either of these techniques, Word will go to the destination you specify.

To go to a particular page in the document, simply type the desired page number into the Go To text box, or type the letter *p* followed by the page number. To go to page 5, for example, type either *5* or *p5*.

Going to a page

If you want to go to the next page in the document, you can just type *p*. If you want to go to a page that is a particular number of pages before or after the current page, type a minus sign (-) or a plus sign (+), respectively, followed by the appropriate number. For example, to go to the previous page, type *-1*. To go to the page after the next page, type *+2*.

The page numbers you enter into the Go To text box specify the number of pages from the beginning of the document—not the number that is assigned to that page. For this reason, if you're working with a two-section document that has two pages in section 1 and four pages in section 2, and you enter *4* into the Go To text box, choosing OK will tell Word to go to the second page in section 2.

Remember to repaginate your document before issuing the Go To... command. As you know, Word repaginates the document whenever you issue the Repaginate Now command, enter the Page View mode or the Print Preview window, or activate the Background Pagination setting in the Customize dialog box.

Going to a section

To move to a specific section in your document, type the letter *s* into the Go To text box, followed by the section number. To go to section 3, for instance, simply type *s3*.

If you want to go to the next section in the document, you can just type *s*. To go to a section that is a particular number of sections before or after the current section, type the letter *s* and a minus sign (-) or a plus sign (+), respectively, followed by the appropriate number. For example to go to the preceding section, type *s-1*. To go to the section after next, type *s+2*.

Going to a line

To move to a specific line in your document, type the letter *l* into the Go To text box, followed by the line number. To go to line 45, for instance, type *l45*.

If you want to go to the next line in the document, you can just type *l*. To go to a line that is a particular number of lines before or after the current line, type the letter *l* and a minus sign (-) or a plus sign (+), respectively, followed by the appropriate number. For example, to go to the preceding line, type *l-1*. To go to the line after next, type *l+2*.

Going to a footnote

To go to a footnote in your document, type the letter *f* into the Go To text box, followed by the footnote number. To go to the second footnote in the document, for instance, type *f2*. To go to a previous or following footnote, you can use the same minus sign and plus sign technique we discussed earlier for pages, sections, and lines.

Going to annotations

If you want to move to an annotation in your document, type the letter *a* into the Go To text box, followed by the desired annotation number, counted from the beginning of the document. To go to the second annotation in the document, for instance, type *a2*. To go to a previous or following annotation, you can use the same minus sign and plus sign technique we've discussed.

Specifying a combined destination

You can specify a combined destination with the Go To... command. For instance, you might want to tell Word to go to a line on a page in a particular section. To do this, simply combine the destination codes we've shown you so far in the Go To text box, and choose OK. The string you enter into the Go To text box may include codes for a section, page, and codes for either a line, footnote, or annotation.

As we've said, when a destination code for any item appears by itself in the Go To text box, Word counts the items from the beginning of the document. If you specify multiple destination codes, however, Word will count from the beginning of the most significant item to the least significant item, in this order: section; page; and line, footnote, or annotation. For example, the destination code *s2p4* takes you to the fourth page in the second section. Similarly, the code *s3p5l8* takes you to the eighth line on the fifth page in the third section.

You can use a plus and minus sign only with the most significant item in a combined destination. For example, you can enter the codes *s-2p4* or *p-2l8*, but not the codes *s2p-4* or *p2l-8*. Remember that the line, footnote, and annotation codes are mutually exclusive—you can specify only one of the three in a single destination string.

As you'll recall from Chapter 4, you can use the scroll bar to move to a particular percentage point in the document. To move to the document's halfway point, for instance, click on the scroll box and drag it to the center of the scroll bar. If your computer is not equipped with a mouse, however, you cannot use the scroll bar to move to a certain percentage of the document. Instead, you'll have to use the Go To dialog box.

Moving a percentage

In the Go To dialog box, simply type into the Go To text box the percent symbol (%), followed by the desired percentage value. For example, to go to the point that is exactly halfway between the beginning and end of the document, type *%50*. When you choose OK, Word will immediately move the cursor to that point in the document.

If you move the cursor to a different location in the document (either with the Go To... command or some other cursor-movement technique), you can return the cursor to its previous location by pressing the [Go back] key ([Shift][F5]). Pressing it repeatedly will cycle the cursor through its last three locations.

Returning to the previous location

The GOTOBUTTON field lets you set up a "button" in your document that goes to a specified destination in your document. This field takes the form

The GOTOBUTTON field

{GOTOBUTTON *destination buttonText*}

where *destination* is any destination you enter into the Go To dialog box, and *buttonText* is either the text or picture you want to serve as the button in the document. (We'll show you how to insert a picture into a document in Chapter 21.) If you use text as the *buttonText* argument, you don't need to enclose that text within quotation marks.

When you display the result of a GOTOBUTTON field, you'll see either the text or picture you've specified in the *buttonText* argument. If you want, you can apply some character formatting to the *buttonText* argument to help distinguish the field's result from the surrounding text. Unlike it handles most of the fields we'll discuss in this book, Word updates the result of the GOTOBUTTON field whenever you edit the field's code.

If you have a mouse, you can double-click on the text or picture returned by the GOTOBUTTON field to go to the destination specified in the field's *destination* argument. If you don't have a mouse, you will need to use the keyboard to highlight the text or picture returned by the GOTOBUTTON field, then press the [Do field click] key ([Alt][Shift][F9]) to go to the destination. Alternatively, you can highlight the text returned by the field and run Word's built-in DoFieldClick macro (we'll show you how to run a macro in Chapter 19).

As an example, suppose you've created the document shown in Figure 13-25, which discusses technology in the automotive industry. Elsewhere in the document, you've included some text that defines many of the document's special terms, including the term *Multi-valve Engine*, which we've highlighted in Figure 13-25. If you want to provide a way to move to the portion of the document that defines this term, you can replace the term with a GOTOBUTTON field. That way, the reader can double-click on that term to bring up its definition.

Figure 13-25

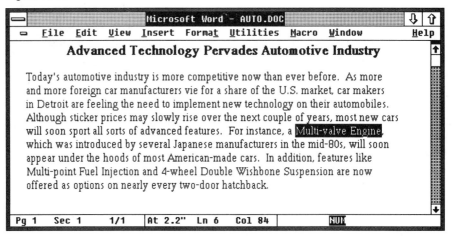

We'll use a GOTOBUTTON field in place of the term Multi-valve Engine *to access that term's definition.*

To set up this kind of button, first define a bookmark named *multivalve* at the place where you've defined *Multi-valve Engine* in the document. Next, return to the portion of the document shown in Figure 13-25, and replace the term *Multi-valve Engine* with the field

{GOTOBUTTON "multivalve" **Multi-valve Engine**}

as we've done in Figure 13-26. When you view the result of this field, you'll see the text *Multi-valve Engine,* as shown in Figure 13-27. Notice that we've displayed this text in bold to distinguish it from the surrounding text. Now, to bring up the definition of this term, just double-click on the term. Word will immediately move the cursor to the place in your document containing the bookmark *multivalve.*

Figure 13-26

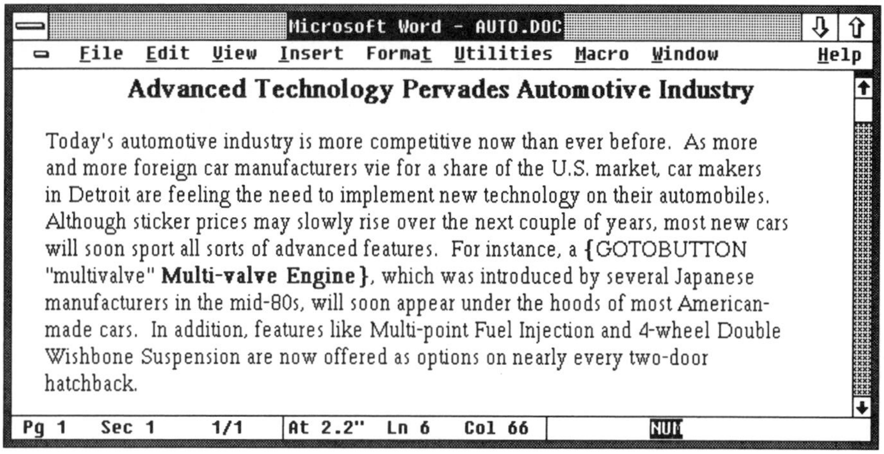

Word will exhibit the formatting you've applied to the buttonText *argument when it displays the field's result.*

Figure 13-27

You can now find the definition of the term Multi-valve Engine *by double-clicking on that term.*

**CREATING
ANNOTATIONS**

If you want to review and annotate a document written by someone else, you'll want to take advantage of Word's annotations feature. This feature lets you insert an initialed annotation reference mark into the document, then enter the annotation text into a special area of the screen called the annotation pane, leaving the original document intact. When the document's author reviews the annotations later, he or she can delete or include each annotation. In addition, if several people have inserted annotations, the initialed annotation reference marks in the document will allow the author to identify the person who made each annotation.

If you want, you can lock a document for annotations, which means that you can allow others to insert annotations into the document, but prevent them from making any changes to the document itself. You can also use the Print... command to print a document's annotations.

**Inserting an
annotation**

To insert an annotation into a document, simply move the cursor to the appropriate location and choose the Annotation command from the Insert menu. Word will then insert an annotation reference mark into the document and open the annotation pane at the bottom of the document window. At this point, you can type the annotation text into the annotation pane.

For example, suppose you're reading the document shown in Figure 13-28, and you want to insert the annotation

Additionally, total expenditures for the month were well over budget.

at the location of the cursor. To do this, just select the Annotation command from the Insert menu. Word will immediately insert an annotation reference mark at the cursor's location, then open the annotation pane at the bottom of the window, as shown in Figure 13-29.

Figure 13-28

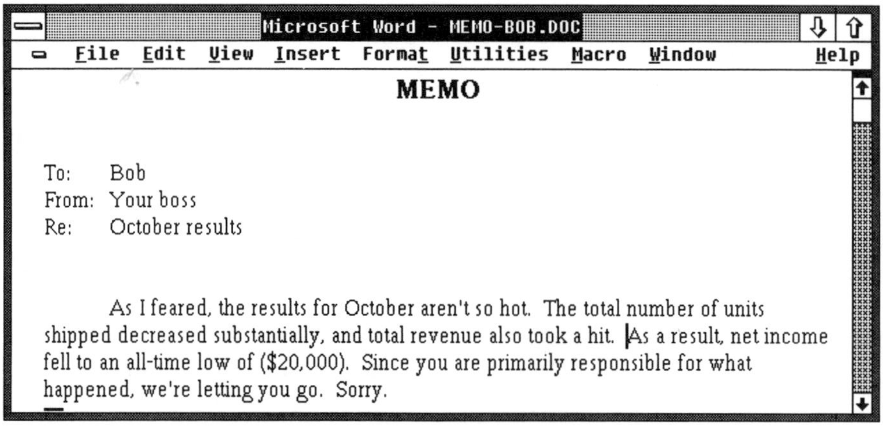

We'll use this document to demonstrate Word's annotations feature.

As you can see, the annotation reference mark consists of a pair of brackets ([]) that enclose the author's initials (in this case, MWC) and a number that reflects the annotation's order in the document. Now, finish inserting the annotation by typing the text next to the annotation reference mark.

The annotation reference mark that appears in your document is assigned the hidden text format. If you want to suppress the display of your documents annotation marks, you must select the Annotations command on the View menu. When you do this, Word will remove the check mark next to the Annotations command to indicate that it is inactive, and will not display any of the document's annotation reference marks or the annotation pane at the bottom of the screen. Because the annotation reference marks are hidden text, however, Word will continue displaying them if you select the Hidden Text check box in the Preferences dialog box.

Figure 13-29

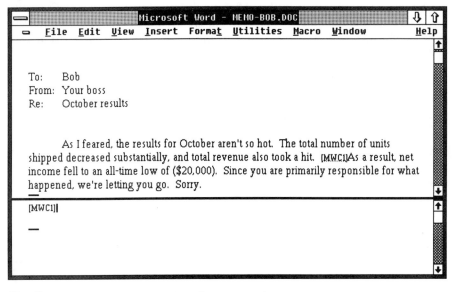

You'll type your annotations into the annotation pane.

If you want to redisplay the document's annotation reference marks and annotation pane, simply reselect the Annotations command from the View menu to turn the Annotations setting on. As long as the Annotations setting is turned on, Word will display the annotation reference marks in the document, even if you deselect the Hidden Text check box.

As you add annotations to a document, Word will continue numbering annotation reference marks sequentially. If you insert an annotation above existing ones, Word will renumber the existing annotations. For instance, if you insert an annotation at the top of the document shown in Figure 13-29, Word will insert the mark [MWC1] at the top of the document, and will change the existing mark from [MWC1] to [MWC2]. If other annotation reference marks appear in the document, Word will adjust the numbers in those marks as well.

Sizing the annotation pane

As you probably noticed, Word separates the document pane from the annotation pane with a split bar. If you want, you can adjust the size of the annotation pane by adjusting the position of the split bar. For a discussion of manipulating the split bar, refer to Appendix 1.

Moving between panes

Word offers a couple of techniques for moving the cursor between the annotation pane and the document pane. First, if you have a mouse, you can position the cursor by clicking at the desired spot in the appropriate pane. Alternatively, you can press the [Next pane] key ([F6]) to move between the two panes.

Editing an annotation

Editing annotation text in the annotation pane is no different from editing regular text in the document. Simply highlight the annotation text or place the cursor in the appropriate location, then use the appropriate editing and formatting tools to modify that text.

Deleting an annotation

As we mentioned earlier, when an author reviews the annotations made to his document, he or she will either delete or include each annotation. To delete an annotation from a document, simply highlight the annotation reference mark in the document pane, and either press [Delete] or issue the Cut command. Word will then remove both the mark and its associated annotation text from the annotation pane. In addition, Word will adjust the numbers of the document's remaining annotations to maintain a sequentially ordered list.

Including an annotation

If you want to include an annotation in your document, simply perform a standard cut-and-paste procedure. First, highlight the text you want to include in the annotation pane, then issue the Cut command. Next, return to the document pane, place the cursor in the appropriate location, and issue the Paste command Finally, delete the annotation reference mark by highlighting it and pressing [Delete].

To quickly replace the annotation reference mark in the document with the annotation text, highlight the mark before you issue the Paste command. This technique lets you avoid the final step of deleting the mark from the document.

For example, consider the document show in Figure 13-30. Let's suppose you want to include the annotation [MWC1] in the document. To do this, highlight the annotation text *Additionally, total expenditures for the month were well over budget.* in the annotation pane, and issue the Cut command. Next, move to the document pane and highlight the annotation reference mark [MWC1]. Finally, issue the Paste command. Figure 13-31 shows the resulting document. Notice that Word renumbered the marks [MWC2] and [MWC3] in both the document and annotation panes when we replaced annotation [MWC1].

Figure 13-30

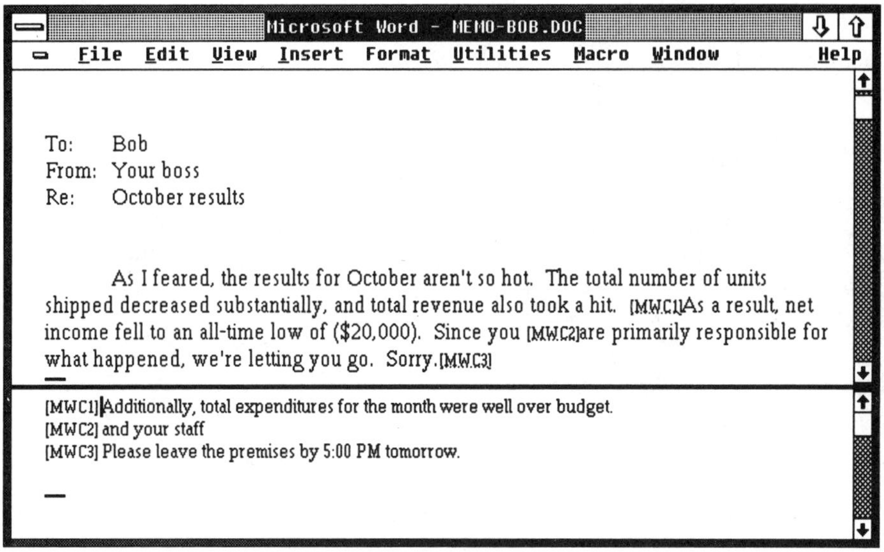

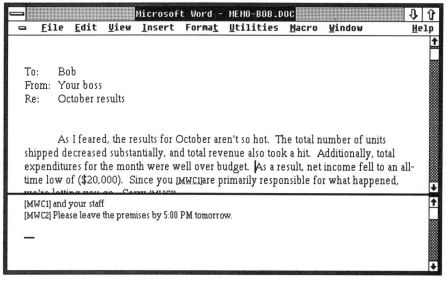

```
┌─────────────────────────────────────────────────────────────────┐
│ ▭    ▓▓▓▓▓      Microsoft Word - MEMO-BOB.DOC    ▓▓▓▓▓    ⇩  ⇧   │
│ ⊟   File   Edit   View   Insert   Format   Utilities   Macro   Window        Help │
├─────────────────────────────────────────────────────────────────┤
│                                                                      ↑ │
│                                                                        │
│     To:    Bob                                                         │
│     From:  Your boss                                                   │
│     Re:    October results                                            │
│                                                                        │
│                                                                        │
│          As I feared, the results for October aren't so hot. The total number of units │
│     shipped decreased substantially, and total revenue also took a hit. [MWC1]As a result, net │
│     income fell to an all-time low of ($20,000). Since you [MWC2]are primarily responsible for │
│     what happened, we're letting you go. Sorry.[MWC3]                   │
│     ▬                                                                ↓ │
├─────────────────────────────────────────────────────────────────┤
│   [MWC1]Additionally, total expenditures for the month were well over budget.    ↑ │
│   [MWC2] and your staff                                                │
│   [MWC3] Please leave the premises by 5:00 PM tomorrow.                 │
│                                                                        │
│     ▬                                                                ↓ │
└─────────────────────────────────────────────────────────────────┘
```

Including an annotation in a document requires a simple cut-and-paste procedure.

Figure 13-31

```
┌─────────────────────────────────────────────────────────────────┐
│ ▭    ▓▓▓▓▓      Microsoft Word - MEMO-BOB.DOC    ▓▓▓▓▓    ⇩  ⇧   │
│ ⊟   File   Edit   View   Insert   Format   Utilities   Macro   Window        Help │
├─────────────────────────────────────────────────────────────────┤
│                                                                      ↑ │
│                                                                        │
│     To:    Bob                                                         │
│     From:  Your boss                                                   │
│     Re:    October results                                            │
│                                                                        │
│                                                                        │
│          As I feared, the results for October aren't so hot. The total number of units │
│     shipped decreased substantially, and total revenue also took a hit. Additionally, total │
│     expenditures for the month were well over budget. As a result, net income fell to an all- │
│     time low of ($20,000). Since you [MWC1]are primarily responsible for what happened, │
│     we're letting you go. Sorry.[MWC2]                                  │
├─────────────────────────────────────────────────────────────────┤
│   [MWC1] and your staff                                                ↑ │
│   [MWC2] Please leave the premises by 5:00 PM tomorrow.                 │
│                                                                        │
│     ▬                                                                ↓ │
└─────────────────────────────────────────────────────────────────┘
```

We've included the annotation [MWC1] in this document.

Locking a document for annotations

If you want to prevent others from making changes to your document, but want to allow them to insert annotations, you can "lock" the document for annotations. Once you've locked a document, only you, the document's author, can modify that document and unlock it again. If someone else opens the document, Word will not allow that person to make any changes to the document's text, and will activate only the menu commands that don't affect the document's contents. The only exception to this rule is the Annotation command, which inserts hidden annotation reference marks into the document.

To lock a document for annotations, choose the Save As... command from the File menu, and choose the Options >> button to bring up the expanded Save As dialog box shown in Figure 13-32. Now, select the Lock for Annotations check box, as we've done in the figure, and choose OK.

Figure 13-32

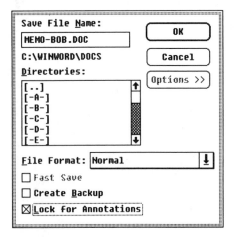

Selecting the Lock for Annotations check box prevents others from altering the contents of your document.

If you open a document that someone else has locked for annotations, you can turn on the ruler and ribbon to see how the document is formatted, but you cannot use them to reformat any of the document's text. In addition, most of the menu commands and a few dialog box options will be dimmed and unavailable. Table 13-2 lists the commands you cannot select as you work in the document pane and in the annotation pane of a locked document.

Unlocking a document

To unlock a document, reopen the expanded Save As dialog box, deselect the Lock for Annotations check box, and choose OK. If someone other than the document's author opens the expanded Save As dialog box, the Lock for Annotations option will be dimmed and inactive, preventing the user from removing the lock.

Table 13-2

Document pane

Menu	Unselectable commands
File	Lock for Annotations check box in Save As dialog box
Edit	Undo, Repeat, Cut, Paste, Paste Link..., Replace..., Header/Footer..., Summary Info..., Glossary..., Table...
Insert	All commands except Annotation
Format	All commands
Utilities	All commands except Customize...
Macro	Context Template options in Assign to Key and Assign to Menu dialog boxes

Annotation pane

Menu	Unselectable commands
File	Lock for Annotations check box in Save As dialog box
Edit	Header/Footer..., Summary Info..., Glossary..., Table...
View	Outline, Footnotes
Format	Section..., Document..., Styles..., Position..., Define Styles..., Picture..., and Table...
Utilities	Revision Marks..., Compare Versions..., Sort..., Repaginate Now
Macro	Context Template options in Assign to Key and Assign to Menu dialog boxes

---

In case you're wondering, the Lock for Annotations check box isn't a great security feature—anyone can "break the lock." To make changes to a document that has been locked for annotations, you can open the document, then use the Customize... command to change the entry in the Your Name text box to match the name of the person who locked the document. Once you've "tricked" Word into thinking that you are the document's original author, you can alter the document and deselect the Lock for Annotations check box.

To print a document's annotations, select the Print... command from the File menu to bring up the Print dialog box, and choose the Annotations option from the Print pull-down list box. When you choose OK, Word will print a listing of each annotation reference mark and its associated text, along with the page on which the mark appears. Figure 13-33 shows a sample annotations listing.

Printing annotations

Figure 13-33

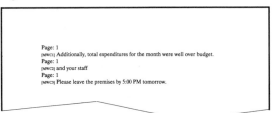

This figure shows a sample annotations listing.

If you want to print both a document and its annotations, you can use the following technique. First, open the Print dialog box and leave the default Document option selected in the Print pull-down list box. Next, choose the Options >> button to bring up the expanded Print dialog, then select the Annotations check box, as we've done in Figure 13-34. (Word will automatically select the Hidden Text check box when you select the Annotations check box.) Finally, choose OK to send the document and the annotations to the printer.

Figure 13-34

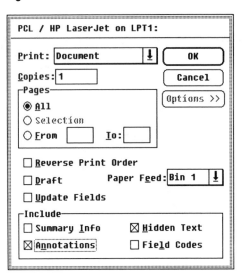

The expanded Print dialog box lets you print both a document and its annotations.

REVISION MARKS   Like annotations, Word's revision marks feature is designed for people who review documents written by someone else. Unlike annotations, however, which are entered into the annotation pane, revision marks are entered directly into the document. As the reviewer makes changes to the document, Word records those changes in a way that lets you see exactly what has changed. For instance, if you delete a block of text, Word strikes through that text instead of removing it from the document. If you add new text, it appears in the underline format. In addition, Word places vertical bars called revision bars alongside the revised lines in the document.

When the document's author reviews the revised document, he or she can either undo or accept the revisions. The author can do this in either a case-by-case fashion, reviewing each revision mark individually, or globally accept or undo all of the document's revisions in one fell swoop.

Besides adding revision marks to a document as you review it, you can compare a revised version of a document with the original version, and use revision marks to identify the portions of the document that have changed. Let's explore all of these features.

To make revision marks in the active document, first select the Revision Marks... command on the Utilities menu to bring up the Mark Revisions dialog box shown in Figure 13-35. When this dialog box appears, select the Mark Revisions check box in the upper-left corner, and choose OK. Word will then display the *MRK* indicator in the status bar to indicate that the Mark Revisions setting is on. Now, as you delete text in the active document with either the Cut command or the [Delete] key, Word will strike through that text. Additionally, Word will place an underline under any new text you insert into the document.

Marking up a document

Figure 13-35

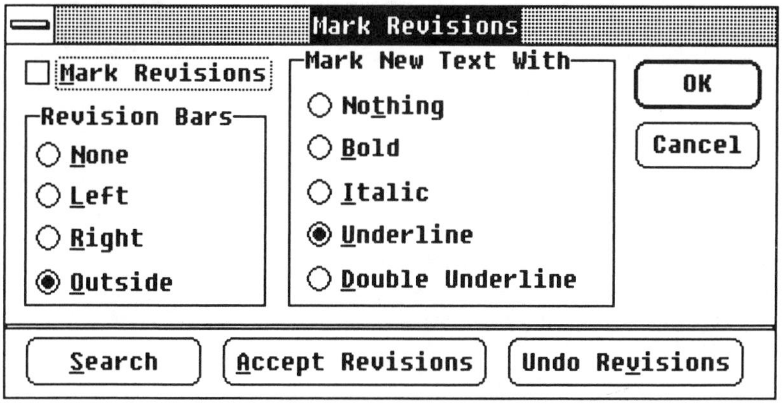

The Mark Revisions dialog box allows you to make revision marks in a document.

For example, let's suppose that someone has created the document shown in Figure 13-36, and that you want to make a few revisions to this document using Word's revision marks feature. To do this, simply activate the Mark Revisions check box, and then make the changes to the document in the usual way. Figure 13-37 shows how the sample document appears after we made a few revisions.

Figure 13-36

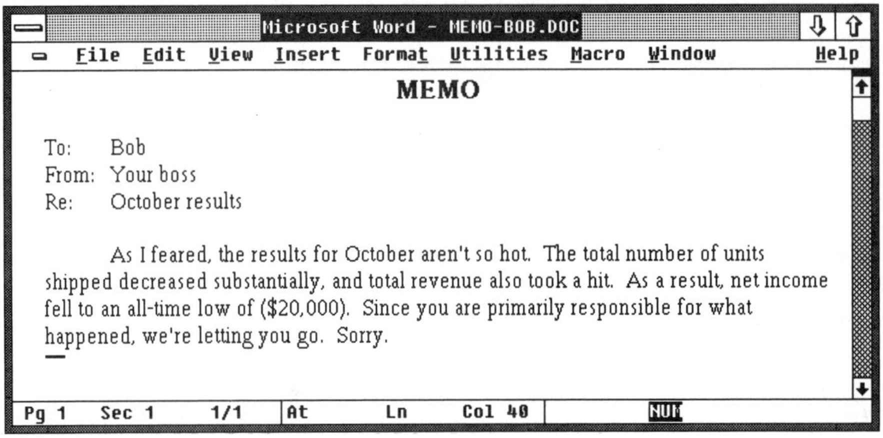

We'll use this sample document to illustrate Word's revision marks feature.

Figure 13-37

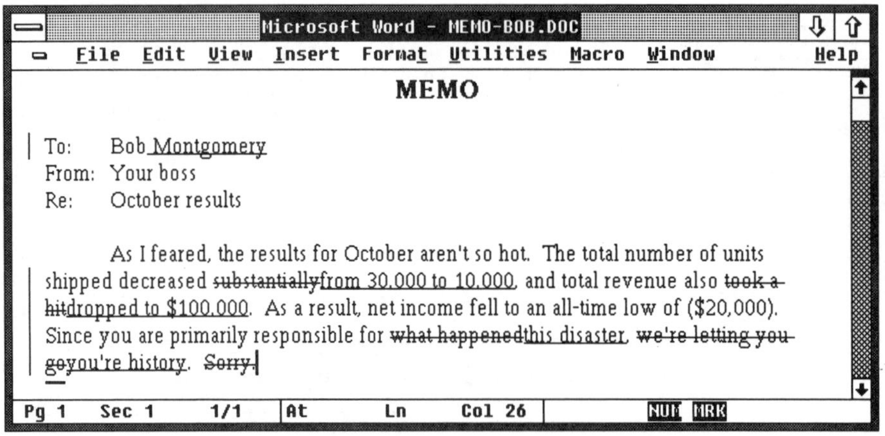

Word's revision marks make it easy to identify the changes you've made.

Occasionally, you'll accidentally mark some text for deletion, or insert some text that doesn't belong. In either of these cases, you can undo your revision by highlighting that text, bringing up the Mark Revisions dialog box, and choosing the Undo Revisions button. When you do, Word will restore the highlighted portion of the document to its original form.

For example, suppose you want to unmark the word *Sorry* at the end of the document in Figure 13-37, which you previously marked for deletion. To do this, highlight that word, select the Revision Marks… command from the Utilities menu, choose the Undo Revisions button in the dialog box, and choose either the Close button (formerly the Cancel button) or the OK button to return to the document.

As we mentioned, Word always uses the strikethrough format to identify text you've marked for deletion. If you want, however, you can change the format Word uses to display newly inserted text from underlining to any of the Mark New Text With formats in the Mark Revisions dialog box. When you choose a new Mark New Text With option and choose OK, Word will use that format to mark all the new text in the document.

Changing the format of inserted text

For example, suppose you've added the revision marks shown in Figure 13-37, and you want Word to draw a double underline under the new text you've added. To do this, open the Mark Revisions dialog box, choose the Double Underline option, and choose OK. Figure 13-38 shows the resulting document.

Figure 13-38

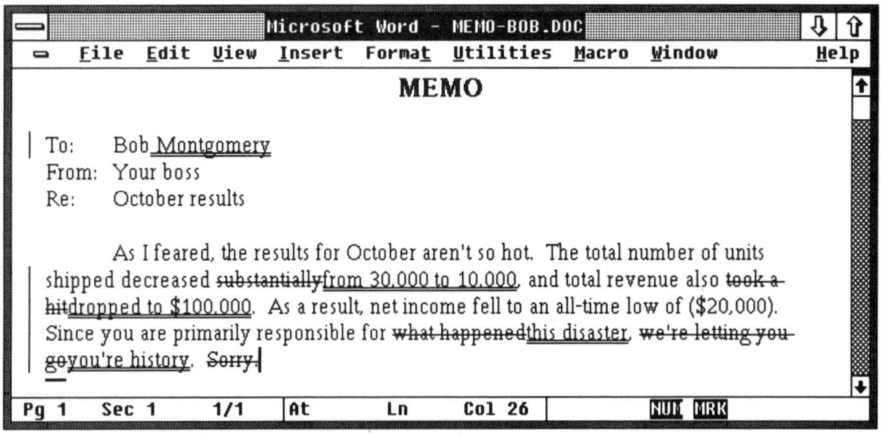

You can change the way Word displays new text by choosing a new Mark New Text With option in the Mark Revisions dialog box.

As we said earlier, Word places revision bars alongside the lines of text containing revision marks. Although these bars will always appear on the left of the screen, you can adjust their position in the printed document.

Moving the revision bars

By default, Word places revision bars along the outside edge of the page, which means the right edge on right-hand (odd-numbered) pages, and the left edge on left-hand (even-numbered) pages. If you want, you can tell Word to always print the revision bars along the left edge of the page, the right edge of the page, or not at all. To do this, simply choose the desired Revision Bars option in the Mark Revisions dialog box, and choose OK.

Reviewing the revisions

Fortunately, Word offers a set of sophisticated tools for working with a document that contains revision marks. As you'll see, Word lets you do either of two things with a revision: accept it or undo it. If you accept the revision, Word will remove the selected text if it's marked for deletion, or remove the special formatting from the text if it's new. If you undo the revision, however, Word will remove the revision from the document, restoring the document to its original form.

Word allows you to update all of a document's revisions in a single step, or to update each revision individually. Let's take a look at each of these cases.

Updating all revisions at one time

To accept or undo all of a document's revisions at once, first make sure you haven't highlighted any text in the document, then select the Revision Marks... command from the Utilities menu to bring up the Mark Revisions dialog box shown in Figure 13-35. As you can see, three command buttons appear along the bottom of this dialog box, two of which are labeled Accept Revisions and Undo Revisions. To accept all the revisions in the document, choose Accept Revisions. When you do, Word will present the message box shown in Figure 13-39.

Figure 13-39

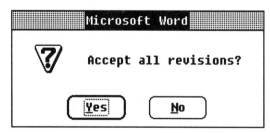

Word will ask you to confirm your decision to accept all the revisions in the document.

At this point, choose Yes to accept all of the document's revisions. Immediately, Word will highlight all the text in the document, delete all the text marked for deletion, and remove the special formatting for newly inserted text. If you choose the Accept Revisions button by mistake, of course, you should choose the No button to return to the Mark Revisions dialog box without altering the document's revision marks.

As you might expect, the Undo Revisions button in the Mark Revisions dialog box works much like the Accept Revisions button. To undo all of the document's revisions at once, make sure you haven't highlighted any text in the document, open the Mark Revisions dialog box, and choose the Undo Revisions button. When Word presents the message box asking *Undo all revisions?*, choose Yes to remove all of the document's revision marks. Of course, you can choose No if you've chosen the Undo Revisions button by mistake.

Although Word lets you update all revisions in a single step, you'll typically want to review and update each revision individually. Fortunately, Word provides a couple of quick-and-easy ways to do this.

Updating revisions individually

To accept or undo any particular revision in the document, simply highlight the revised text, bring up the Mark Revisions dialog box, and choose either the Accept Revisions or the Undo Revisions button. When you accept or undo a revision, Word will change the Cancel button in the dialog box to read *Close*. To return to the document, choose either the OK or Close button.

If you need to update more than just a few revisions, you'll want to take advantage of Word's searching capabilities. To do this, position the cursor anywhere in the document and open the Mark Revisions dialog box. Next, choose the Search button in the lower-left corner of the dialog box. Word will then highlight the next group of revised text in the document, but will keep the Mark Revisions dialog box on the screen. At this point, you can review the revision, then choose either the Accept Revisions or Undo Revisions button to update it. (You can move the Mark Revisions dialog box if it obstructs a portion of the document you need to see.)

After you accept or undo the selected revision, you can choose the Search button again to highlight the next revision in the document. If you want, you can pass over a revision and search for the next one by choosing the Search button again instead of choosing the Accept Revisions or Undo Revisions button. You can continue using this search-and-update technique until you reach the end of the document, at which point Word will present the message box shown in Figure 13-40 on the next page. If you choose Yes, Word will continue searching for revisions from the beginning of the document. If Word has made a pass through the entire document without finding any new revisions, it will present the message box shown in Figure 13-41 on the following page.

As an example, let's suppose you've just opened the document shown in Figure 13-38, and you want to use the search-and-update technique we've discussed. To do this, first bring up the Mark Revisions dialog box and choose the Search button. Figure 13-42 on the next page shows how the screen will appear at this point.

If you now choose the Accept Revisions button to accept the revision, Word will include the revision in the document. You can then choose the Search button again to continue updating the remaining revisions in the document.

Figure 13-40

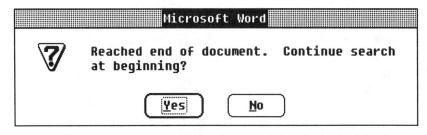

Word will present this message box when it reaches the end of the document while searching for revisions.

Figure 13-41

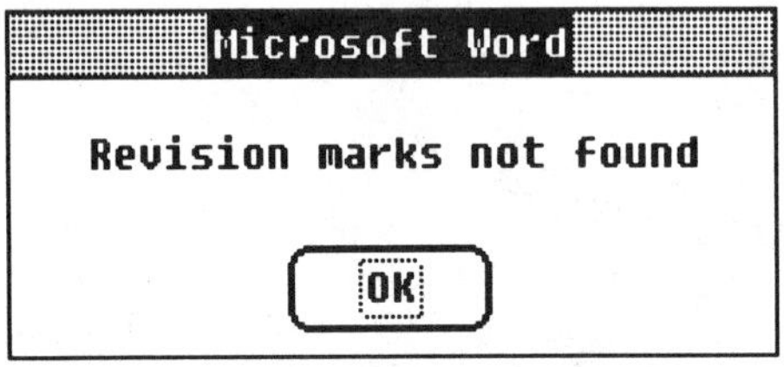

This message box will appear after Word has passed through the entire document without finding new revisions.

Figure 13-42

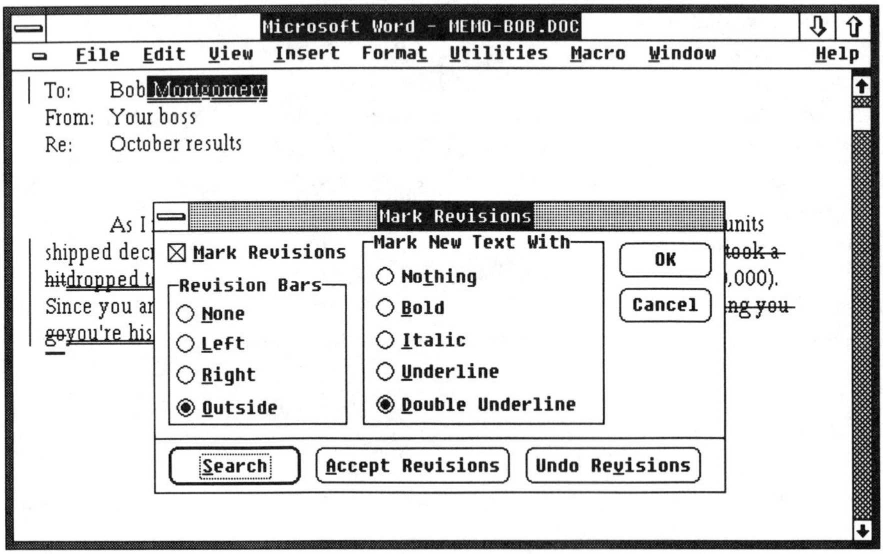

When Word highlights a revision, simply choose either the Accept Revisions or Undo Revisions button.

In addition to the revision-marking capabilities we've discussed so far, Word is able to compare two versions of a document and use revision marks to indicate which paragraphs of the document are different. This feature comes in handy in a couple of situations. First, if someone revises a document without activating the Mark Revisions check box, the author can compare the revised version of the document with the original version to identify which portions have changed.

Additionally, if a document passes between an author and a reviewer several times before it is completed, the author and the reviewer will, in the later review phases, want to pay more attention to the portions of the document that are still changing. By comparing the latest version of the document with the previous version, the author or reviewer can identify those key areas very quickly and therefore apply their efforts more efficiently.

To compare two versions of a document, first open the version you want to check (this is usually the most recently saved version). Next, select the Compare Versions… command from the Utilities menu to bring up the dialog box shown in Figure 13-43. Next, use the Files and Directories list boxes or the Compare File Name text box to select the document file you want to compare with the active document. Once you've selected the appropriate file, choose OK to perform the comparison. Word will use revision marks to identify the paragraphs of the active document that are different from the document you selected.

Comparing two versions of a document

Figure 13-43

```
Compare File Name: MEMO1.DOC              OK

Files:                C:\WINWORD\DOCS
18-POINT.DOC  ↑                           Cancel
ARTFLY.DOC            Directories:
ARTICLE.DOC          [..]            ↑
ASOPRESS.DOC         [-A-]
BIGROWS.DOC          [-B-]
BRIEF.DOC            [-C-]
BROCHDAT.DOC         [-D-]
BROCHMRG.DOC  ↓      [-E-]           ↓
```

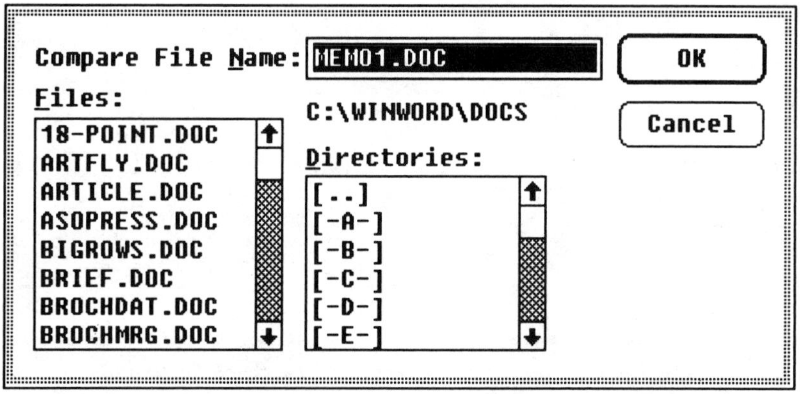

The Compare Versions dialog box lets you identify the portions of a document that are different.

For example, suppose you've opened the document shown in Figure 13-44 on the next page (MEMO1.DOC), and you want to compare it to the document shown in Figure 13-36, which is stored on disk under the file name MEMO-BOB.DOC. To do this, activate MEMO1.DOC, select the Compare Revisions… command from the Utilities menu, select the document file MEMO-BOB.DOC, then choose OK. Figure 13-45 shows how the screen will appear at this point.

Figure 13-44

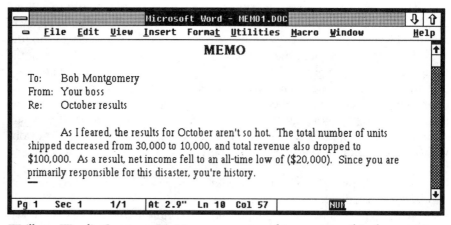

*We'll use Word's Compare Revisions... command to compare this document
with the one shown in Figure 13-36.*

Figure 13-45

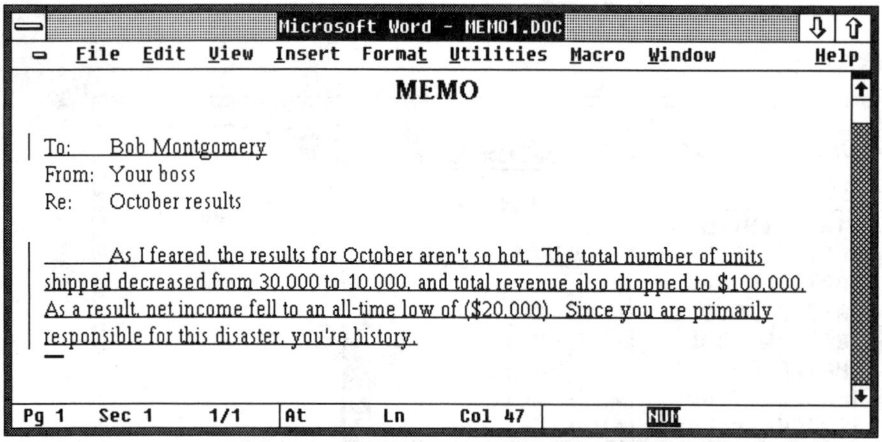

*Word's Compare Revisions... command marks the paragraphs in the active
document that are different from the document you specified.*

Word has underlined the paragraphs of the document that have changed, and
has placed revision bars along the sides of those paragraphs. At this point, you
can remove the revision marks from the document by highlighting the marked text,
opening the Mark Revisions dialog box, and choosing the Accept Revisions button.
Be careful not to highlight any marked text and choose the Undo Revisions button,
since this will tell Word to delete that text.

In this chapter

Adding a Table of Contents, 14
an Index, and Footnotes

One of the most time-consuming and monotonous tasks in creating a document is developing reference aids, such as tables of contents, indexes, and footnotes. Fortunately, Word takes much of the tedium out of these tasks by providing special Table of Contents, Index, and Footnote facilities.

The steps you follow to create indexes and tables of contents are quite similar. You simply enter fields into the body of your document to flag the entries you want to include. Then, you can use the Index… or Table of Contents… command to compile these entries.

Footnotes, on the other hand, are entered in a separate pane that is saved to disk with your document (much like a header or footer pane). Word will print your footnotes automatically when you print your document.

Because Word's Table of Contents and Index facilities are based on several fields, you should become familiar with the concepts we presented in Chapter 10 before reading this chapter. Since the table of contents is the simplest of the three features we'll discuss in this chapter, we'll look at it first; then, we'll discuss Word's indexing and footnoting capabilities.

CREATING A TABLE OF CONTENTS

Word gives you two ways to build entries for a table of contents. First, if you have used the Outline facility (described in Chapter 9) to create your document, you can instruct Word to compile a table of contents directly from the headings you have entered into the outline. Alternatively, you can enter TC fields into your document to flag the entries you want to include in your table of contents. We'll show you how to use both of these techniques in this section. If you're using Word to write chapters for a book, you'll want to pay close attention to the last section of this chapter, which covers a few table of contents and index features that are provided specifically for documents that contain a chapter of a book.

**Building a TOC
from the outline**

The easiest way to create a table of contents is by using Word's outline *heading* styles. As you'll recall from Chapter 9, the Outline facility allows you to assign a special set of style names to your document's headings. Major headings are assigned the style *heading 1*; subheadings are assigned the style *heading 2*, *heading 3*, and so forth. (Your document can contain as many as nine levels of headings.) If you're creating a table of contents for an existing document whose headings are not assigned the *heading* styles, you can modify your *heading* styles either with the Style pull-down list box on the ruler (which we covered in Chapter 8), or with the Outline facility.

**Compiling a
table using heading
paragraphs**

Once you've created a document that uses Word's outline *heading* styles, you can compile the table of contents with the Table of Contents... command on the Insert menu. When you issue this command, Word will display the dialog box shown in Figure 14-1.

Figure 14-1

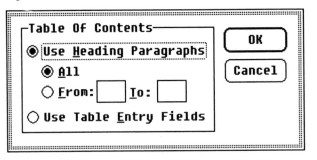

The Table of Contents dialog box makes it easy to compile a table of contents.

The option you select in the Table of Contents dialog box tells Word where to look for the table of contents entries. Since you want to use the paragraphs that appear in one of Word's outline *heading* styles, you'll want to leave the default setting—Use Heading Paragraphs—selected.

By default, Word includes in the table of contents all the paragraphs that carry the style names *heading 1, heading 2,* and so forth. These headings will become the text for your table of contents. As you might guess, your *heading 1* styles will become first-level table of contents entries, your *heading 2* styles will become second-level table of contents entries, and so forth. If you want to restrict the table's entries to a range of *heading* styles (like *heading 1* through *heading 3*), you can do so by entering the level numbers into the From and To text boxes in the Table of Contents dialog box. (When you type an entry into either of these boxes, Word will automatically deselect the All option button and select the From option button.) After you've specified the appropriate range, choose OK to begin compiling the table. If you need to halt the compilation for any reason, you can press [Esc] to cancel the procedure.

When you choose OK in the Table of Contents dialog box, Word will repaginate the entire document, search for the table of contents entries, compile the table of contents, and insert the text at the position of the cursor. During this process, Word will overlook any hidden text in your document. (By the way, in order to see the table's text, you must turn off the Show All option in the Preferences dialog box and turn off the Field Codes setting on the View menu.) If you've already compiled a table of contents from your outline headings, Word will highlight that table and ask if you want to replace it. Choosing Yes will tell Word to replace the existing table with the new one. Choosing No will cancel the Table of Contents... command and leave the existing table intact.

Since you'll typically want your table of contents to appear at the beginning of the document, you'll probably want to create a new section there and place the cursor in that section before issuing the Table of Contents... command.

Figure 14-2 shows a sample table of contents we compiled in Word. As you can see, each entry contains the table of contents text, followed by a tab mark, dot leaders, the page number, and a paragraph mark to end the entry. For each table of contents entry level you create, Word will add a style name to the document's style sheet. If you pull down the Style list box on the ruler or issue the Styles... command on the Format menu, you'll see that your document's style sheet includes the style names *toc 1, toc 2, toc 3*, and so forth. Later in this chapter, we'll show you how to change the table's format by modifying these styles.

Figure 14-2

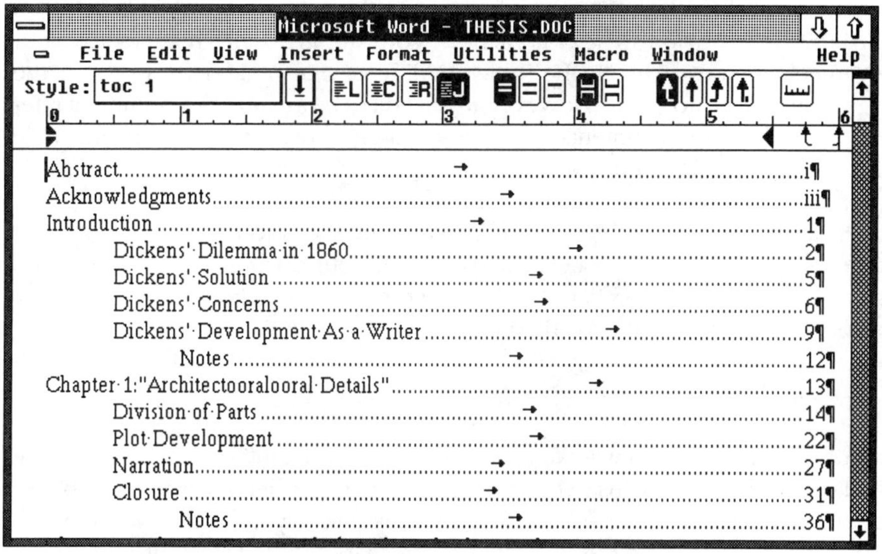

Your compiled table of contents will look like this.

The TOC field

The table of contents you see in your document is actually the result of a TOC field. To see the TOC field code instead of the TOC field result, either select the Show-all icon on the ribbon or activate the Field Codes setting on the View menu. When you do, you'll see that the field

{toc \o}

generates the table. The field argument \o tells Word to compile the table of contents from the document's outline headings. If you specified a range of headings in the From and To text boxes in the Table of Contents dialog box, the TOC field will take the form

{toc \o *startLevel-endLevel*}

where *startLevel* and *endLevel* are the heading levels you specified. We'll discuss the other forms of the TOC field in a moment.

Updating the table of contents

To update a document's table of contents, place the cursor anywhere within the table and press the [Update field] key ([F9]). Word will then repaginate the entire document, search for table of contents entries, and update all the entries in that table. Fortunately, you don't need to worry about suppressing the display of the document's hidden text before updating the table—Word automatically ignores hidden text as it compiles the table.

By the way, the best time to compile the table of contents is right before you print the final version of a document. Word automatically repaginates your document when you execute the Table of Contents… command to ensure that the page numbers are accurate. However, if you edit or reorganize the document after compiling the table of contents, the page numbers may change, causing the table of contents entries to be incorrect.

Building a table of contents from fields

In addition to using Word's outline *heading* styles to collect your table of contents entries, you can use TC fields (which your documentation sometimes calls TOC Entry fields) to flag the entries you want to include in your table of contents. The form of the TC field is

{TC *text*}

where *text* is the text you want to appear in the table of contents listing. Although you'll generally want to use your document's existing headings as the table of contents entries, you must specify the entry text literally in the *text* argument to a TC field. The TC field's sole purpose is to mark table of contents entries—it shows no result of its own. Later in this chapter, we'll show you how to use TC fields to create other kinds of tables, such as a table of figures or illustrations.

To enter a TC field in your document, you can use either the Field… command on the Insert menu or the [Insert field] key ([Ctrl][F9]). Unlike many of the fields you've worked with, Word automatically assigns the hidden format to TC fields. Consequently, to display TC fields in your document, you'll need to select either the Show-all icon on the ribbon or the Show All or Hidden Text check boxes in the Preferences dialog box.

We've used TC fields to create three table of contents entries in the document shown in Figure 14-3. The first field is *{TC "Division of Parts"}*. Notice that this field appears with a dotted underline, indicating that Word has assigned the hidden format to that field. To insert this field into a document, we simply activated the Hidden Text check box in the Preferences dialog box, pressed the [Insert field] key ([Ctrl][F9]), and typed *TC "Division of Parts"*. If we had wanted, we could have placed this field into the document by choosing the Field… command on the Insert menu, selecting the TC option from the Insert Field Type list box, editing the entry in the Field Code text box to read *tc "Division of Parts"*, and choosing OK.

The second table of contents entry in Figure 14-3, *{TC "Delineation of roles"}*, appears just after the first paragraph of body text. As you can see, this entry occupies an entire paragraph but is not part of our document text. Again, we entered this field into the document by pressing the [Insert field] key and typing *TC "Delineation of roles"*.

Figure 14-3

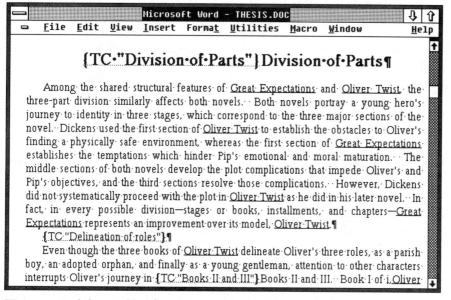

We've created three table of contents entries in this sample document.

The third table entry, *{TC "Books II and III"}*, which appears in the last line shown on the screen, is within the paragraph text.

Multilevel table of contents entries

Earlier in this chapter, we explained that Word can create a multilevel table of contents from the headings you've created in the outline view. Fortunately, Word can also create a multilevel table of contents from the TC fields you've entered into your document. The only extra step you need to perform is to include an \l (backslash and the letter *l*) switch in each TC field that defines the level of that particular entry. The form of this switch is

\l *level*

where *level* is a number from 1 to 9 that specifies the level at which you want that entry to appear. When Word compiles the table of contents from the TC fields you've entered, it will assign the style *toc 1* to the first-level entries, *toc 2* to the second-level entries, and so forth. If you do not include an \l switch in a TC field, Word will assume that the field defines a first-level entry.

For example, consider the document in Figure 14-4. As you can see, we've included the \l switch in the TC fields in this document to create a multilevel table of contents. The first field at the top of the page, *{TC "Division of Parts" \l 1}*, tells Word to include the entry *Division of Parts* and to assign it the style *toc 1*. The next field, *{TC "Delineation of roles" \l 2}*, tells Word to include the entry *Delineation of roles* and to assign it the style *toc 2*. Finally, the entry in the last line, *{TC "Books II and III" \l 3}*, defines a third-level entry, which will take on the style *toc 3*.

Compiling a table using TC fields

Compiling the table of contents from TC fields is similar to compiling it from outline headings. Once you've marked all of your table of contents entries by entering TC fields into the document, you can issue the Table of Contents... command to bring up the dialog box shown in Figure 14-1, and choose the Use Table Entry Fields option. When you choose OK to complete the command, Word will repaginate the entire document, search for TC fields, compile the table of contents, and insert at the position of the cursor a TOC field that generates the table text. As we mentioned earlier, you'll typically want to create a new section at the beginning of the document and place the cursor in that section before issuing the Table of Contents... command.

To see the TOC field code that returns the table of contents, either select the Show-all icon on the ribbon or activate the Field Codes setting on the View menu. When you do this, you will see the field

{toc \f}

Figure 14-4

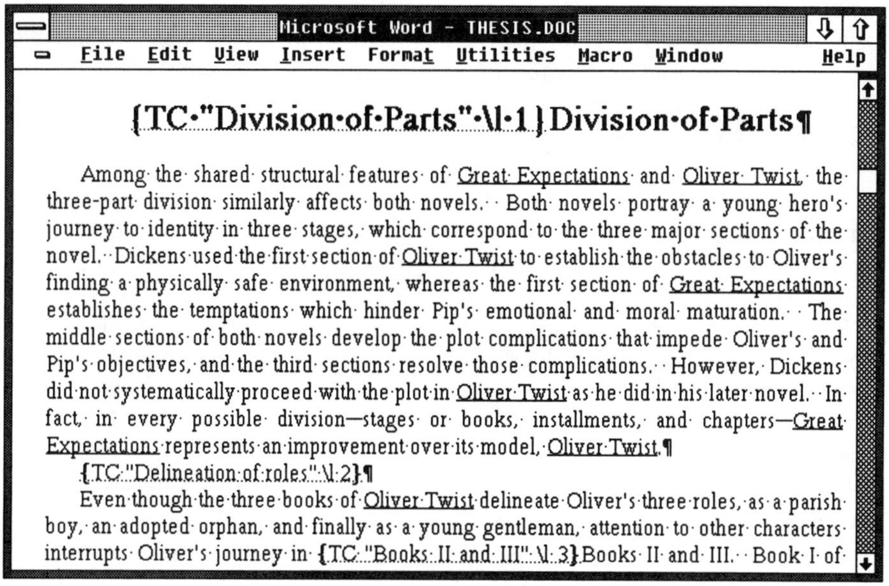

```
┌──────────────────────────────────────────────────────────────┐
│  ▭         Microsoft Word - THESIS.DOC              ⇩ ⇧        │
│  ▭   File  Edit  View  Insert  Format  Utilities  Macro  Window      Help │
│                                                              ⬆ │
│     {TC·"Division·of·Parts"·\l·1} Division·of·Parts ¶          │
│                                                              ▪ │
│        Among· the· shared· structural· features· of· Great· Expectations· and· Oliver· Twist,· the· │
│     three-part· division· similarly· affects· both· novels.·· Both· novels· portray· a· young· hero's· │
│     journey· to· identity· in· three· stages,· which· correspond· to· the· three· major· sections· of· the· │
│     novel.··Dickens·used·the·first·section·of·Oliver·Twist·to·establish·the·obstacles·to·Oliver's· │
│     finding· a· physically· safe· environment,· whereas· the· first· section· of· Great· Expectations· │
│     establishes· the· temptations· which· hinder· Pip's· emotional· and· moral· maturation.·· The· │
│     middle· sections· of· both· novels· develop· the· plot· complications· that· impede· Oliver's· and· │
│     Pip's·objectives,·and·the·third·sections·resolve·those·complications.··However,·Dickens· │
│     did·not·systematically·proceed·with·the·plot·in·Oliver·Twist·as·he·did·in·his·later·novel.··In· │
│     fact,· in· every· possible· division—stages· or· books,· installments,· and· chapters—Great· │
│     Expectations·represents·an·improvement·over·its·model,·Oliver·Twist.¶ │
│        {TC·"Delineation·of·roles"·\l·2}¶ │
│        Even·though·the·three·books·of·Oliver·Twist·delineate·Oliver's·three·roles,·as·a·parish· │
│     boy,·an·adopted·orphan,·and·finally·as·a·young·gentleman,·attention·to·other·characters· │
│     interrupts·Oliver's·journey·in·{TC·"Books·II·and·III"·\l·3}Books·II·and·III.··Book·I·of· ▼ │
└──────────────────────────────────────────────────────────────┘
```

We've created three levels of table of contents entries in this document.

Notice that the field argument \f appears in this field where the argument \o appeared earlier. The letter *f* tells Word to compile from TC fields, while the letter *o* instructs Word to compile from the outline headings.

If you want, you can bypass the Table of Contents… command and insert a TOC field into your document manually. To do this, press the [Insert field] key ([Ctrl][F9]), and type *toc* \f. When you place the cursor between the field characters ({}) and press the [Update field] key ([F9]) to update the field's result, you'll see the same table of contents generated by the Table of Contents… command.

You can tell Word to compile a table of contents for only a portion of a document. To do this, first define a bookmark that refers to the area of the document for which you want to compile the table. Once you've defined the bookmark, include the arguments

> Restricting the table of contents to an area of the document

\b *bookmark*

in the TOC field, where *bookmark* is the name of the bookmark you've defined. Finally, update the field's result to generate the desired table.

For example, suppose you want to create a table of contents for the first two pages in a document, using outline headings. To begin, highlight all the text on the first two pages, then select the Bookmark… command from the Insert menu.

When the Bookmark dialog box appears, type *pages1-2* into the Bookmark Name text box, and choose OK. Once you've defined the appropriate bookmark, position the cursor where you want the table of contents to appear (presumably in a preceding section), and enter the field

{TOC \o \b "pages1-2"}

Finally, press the [Update field] key while the cursor lies between the field characters. Immediately, Word will repaginate your document, compile the table of contents for the first two pages, and display the table as the field's result.

A summary of TOC field switches

Table 14-1 shows you a summary of the TOC field switches we've discussed. Although we've already explained each switch, this table will make a handy reference guide.

Table 14-1

Use this switch...	to...
\o *startLevel-endLevel*	compile a table of contents from outline headings that fall in the range *startLevel-endLevel*
\f	compile a table of contents from TC fields
\b *bookmark*	compile a table of contents for the area of the document defined by *bookmark*

Formatting the table of contents

When you create a table of contents using any of the methods we've discussed, the character formatting of the table will initially match the *Normal* style for your document. For example, if you're using Word's default *Normal* style, your table of contents text will appear in 10-point Tms Rmn plain type. (See Chapter 8 for more on style sheets and defining the *Normal* style.) Although Word does not assign any special character formats to a table of contents, it does assign certain paragraph formats to each entry in the table. This paragraph formatting determines the amount of indention for each entry level, as well as the tabs and dot leaders used to position the page numbers in the table.

Of course, once you've created a table of contents, you can change its character and paragraph formats. You also can use the Cut and Paste commands to move the table to another part of your document. The easiest way to reformat your table of contents text is to redefine the style definitions that Word has applied to the table. With that in mind, let's look at the relationship between the table of contents and Word's Style Sheet facility.

Like the Outline facility we discussed in Chapter 9, Word's Table of Contents facility is designed to work in conjunction with the Style Sheet facility. For each table of contents level you create, Word adds a style name to the document's style sheet. If you select the Styles... or Define Styles... command from the Format menu (or pull down the Style list box on the ruler) after creating a three-level table of contents, you'll see that your document's style sheet includes the style names *toc 1*, *toc 2*, and *toc 3*, as shown in Figure 14-5. Like every other document style sheet, this style sheet will also include the style named *Normal*. If you have used the Outline facility to build your document, you'll also see the style names *heading 1*, *heading 2*, and so forth.

Using the style sheet

Figure 14-5

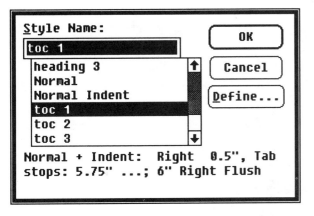

Each level in the table of contents is now a style name on the style sheet.

All the *toc* styles are based on the *Normal* style—that's why your table of contents will display the same character formats as the main body text in your document. All *toc* styles carry a $\frac{1}{2}$-inch right indention. That is, in a standard document that is 6 inches wide, the right indent marker will appear at the $5\frac{1}{2}$-inch position. All *toc* style definitions also contain two tab stops: a left-aligned tab with a dot leader at the $5\frac{3}{4}$-inch position and a right-aligned tab at the 6-inch position. (In Figure 14-2, you can see the right indent and tabs on the ruler.) In fact, the only difference between the various *toc* styles is that Word assigns different amounts of left indention to each level. In the default style, *toc 1* entries are not indented; they are aligned with the default left margin of your body text. However, each of the remaining *toc* styles is indented in $\frac{1}{2}$-inch increments. For example, *toc 2* entries are indented $\frac{1}{2}$ inch, *toc 3* entries are indented 1 inch, and so forth.

To modify one of your *toc* styles, choose Define Styles... from the Format menu. In the Define Styles dialog box, select the name of the style you want to modify, then select the character and paragraph formats you want to use for this level. Choose OK in the Define Styles dialog box, and Word will apply the new formatting to all the document's table of contents entries that carry that style name.

For example, in the sample document we used to create the table of contents shown in Figure 14-2, our *Normal* style specifies 12-point Tms Rmn plain type. As a result, our table of contents also appears in that type. Suppose we want the first-level headings in this table of contents to appear in 12-point Tms Rmn bold type. We can change the format of all the first-level entries by modifying the *toc 1* style on the style sheet. To do this, we first select the Define Styles... command from the Format menu, then select the name *toc 1* in the list that appears in the dialog box. Next, we select the Character... button, select the Bold check box in the Character dialog box, and choose OK to return to the Define Styles dialog box. When we choose OK to lock in this style change and return to the document, our table of contents will look like Figure 14-6.

Figure 14-6

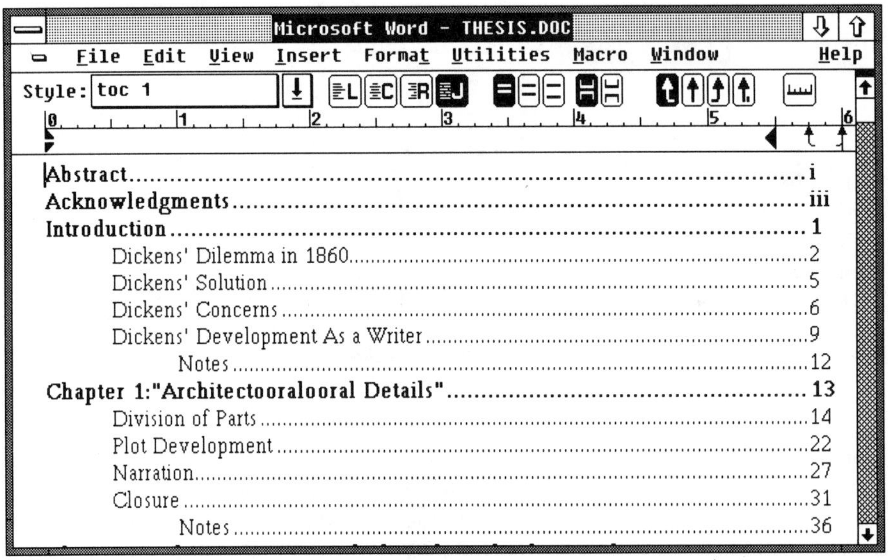

We used the Define Styles... command to apply bold formatting to the first-level table of contents entries in this document.

As you're changing the formatting instructions for each *toc* style, you may want to change the Based On style as well. Instead of using *Normal* as the Based On style for each *toc* style, you might want to base each *toc* style on the next highest *toc* style. This can help you maintain formatting consistency among the various levels in a table of contents. Specifically, *toc 4* could be based on *toc 3*, which could be based on *toc 2*, which could be based on *toc 1*, which could be based on *Normal.* As a result, when you make a formatting change to the *toc 1* style, your change will affect the other *toc* styles as well.

Numbering the table of contents pages

As we suggested earlier, you'll probably want to place the table of contents in its own section at the beginning of the document. Since the table of contents is generally considered part of the document's front matter, you might want to create a special numbering scheme for your table of contents pages (and any other front matter items, such as the title page, acknowledgments page, and so forth). Lowercase Roman numerals (i, ii, iii) are useful for this part of a document.

To number your table of contents pages, place the cursor anywhere in the section containing the table of contents, then select the Header/Footer... command from the Edit menu to open the Header/Footer dialog box. In this dialog box, choose the Options >> button to open the expanded Header/Footer dialog box shown in Figure 14-7, and choose the numbering scheme you want to use from the Page Numbers Format pull-down list box. Once you've done this, choose either the Header or Footer option from the list box on the left side of the dialog box, and choose OK to open that pane. Finally, use the Page-number icon at the top of the header or footer pane to insert a page number into the header or footer.

Figure 14-7

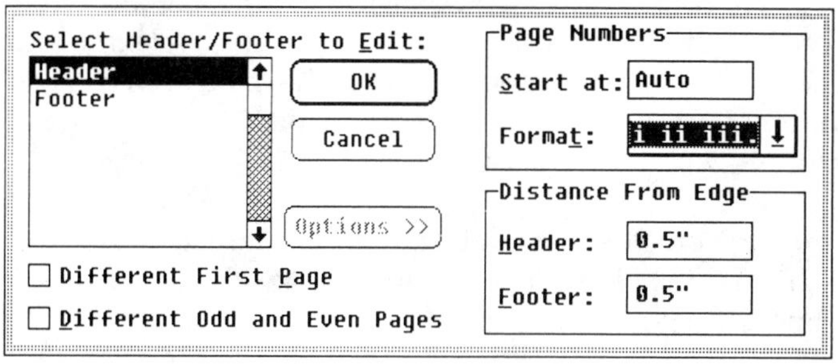

You can change the format of your page numbers with the expanded Header/Footer dialog box.

To use a different page numbering scheme for the body of your document, move the cursor to the first section of the main document and reopen the expanded Header/Footer dialog box. Now, select the appropriate numbering scheme from the Page Numbers Format list box, and change the Page Numbers Start At setting to 1. When you choose OK to close the dialog box (and open the header or footer pane), Word will reset the page number count to 1 and will display the document's page numbers in the format you selected.

Make sure you update the table of contents after you've adjusted all the page numbers in your document. Simply place the cursor anywhere within the table, and press the [Update field] key ([F9]).

Creating other table listings

You can use the Table of Contents... command to compile other types of tables, such as a list of illustrations or figures. In fact, Word lets you do this by using outline headings or fields.

Creating a table with outline headings

To define the table of contents entries with outline headings, assign one of the unused lower-level outline *heading* styles (like *heading 8* or *heading 9*) to each area of text you want to include in the table. When you're ready to compile the table, issue the Table of Contents... command, enter the same value into both the From and To text boxes, and choose OK. Word will then insert a table into your document that lists all the headings carrying the styles you specified.

For example, suppose you want to insert a table of illustrations at the top of your document. To begin, apply the style *heading 8* to each paragraph that labels an illustration. After you've applied this style to the appropriate paragraphs in the document, you'll probably want to use the Define Styles... command to redefine the style's character and paragraph formats to your liking. When you're ready to compile the table, move the cursor to the desired location and select the Table of Contents... command. When the Table of Contents dialog box appears, enter *8* into both the From and To text boxes, and choose OK. Word will then compile the table of illustrations and insert it into your document.

If you want to create a multilevel table listing using outline headings, just use enough *heading* styles to do the job, applying those styles to the paragraphs you want to include in the table. For instance, if you want to create a three-level table of illustrations, you can use the styles *heading 6, heading 7*, and *heading 8* to define the first-, second-, and third-level entries, respectively. When you compile the table with the Table of Contents... command, enter *6* in the From text box and *8* in the To text box.

Creating a table with fields

If you don't want to use Word's outline headings to define the entries in a table listing, you can use TC fields instead. To define a table entry with a TC field, you must append a switch to the field in the form

\f *identifier*

where *identifier* is a single letter from *a* to *z*—excluding *c*—that identifies the table with which it is associated (case isn't important). For instance, if you enter the field

{TC "Illustration 3" \f i}

Word will place the entry *Illustration 3* into the table identified by the letter *i*. (We chose the letter *i* simply because it is the first letter in the word *Illustration*.) Remember not to use the letter *c* as a table identifier. This letter is reserved for fields that define entries for the table of contents. In fact, entering the field *{TC "Introduction"}* is the same as entering the field *{TC "Introduction" \f c}*.

To compile your table, enter into the document a TOC field that includes the same \f switch and identifier you specified in your TC fields. For instance, if you've defined your table of illustrations entries with the arguments \f *i*, use the field

{TOC \f i}

to compile the table. As you'll recall, you can use either the Field... command on the Insert menu or the [Insert field] key ([Ctrl][F9]) to enter a TOC field into your document. Also recall that you will need to update the TOC field with the [Update field] key ([F9]) after you've entered it into the document.

We've entered a few TC fields into the document shown in Figure 14-8. As you can see, we've used the identifier *i* to denote entries for the table of illustrations, and the identifier *f* to denote entries for the table of figures. To compile the table of illustrations for this document, we would use the field *{TOC \f i}*. To compile the table of figures, we would use the field *{TOC \f f}*.

Figure 14-8

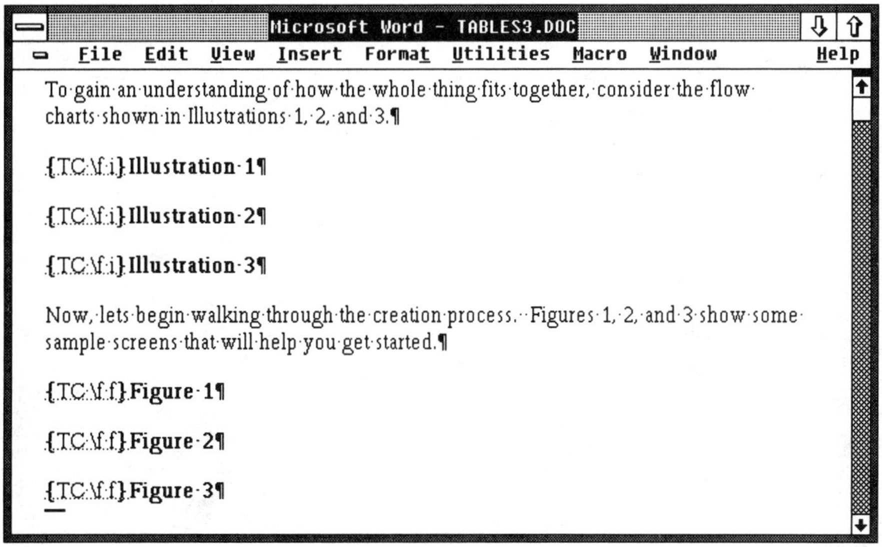

```
┌──────────────────── Microsoft Word - TABLES3.DOC ──────────────── ⬇ ⬆
│  ▭   File  Edit  View  Insert  Format  Utilities  Macro  Window        Help
├───────────────────────────────────────────────────────────────────────┤
│ To·gain·an·understanding·of·how·the·whole·thing·fits·together,·consider·the·flow·   ▲
│ charts·shown·in·Illustrations·1,·2,·and·3.¶
│
│ {TC\f:i}·Illustration·1¶
│
│ {TC\f:i}·Illustration·2¶
│
│ {TC\f:i}·Illustration·3¶
│
│ Now,·lets·begin·walking·through·the·creation·process.··Figures·1,·2,·and·3·show·some·
│ sample·screens·that·will·help·you·get·started.¶
│
│ {TC\f:f}·Figure·1¶
│
│ {TC\f:f}·Figure·2¶
│
│ {TC\f:f}·Figure·3¶
│                                                                              ▼
└───────────────────────────────────────────────────────────────────────┘
```

You can create several table listings for a single document by using different identifiers in the TC and TOC fields.

CREATING AN INDEX

Although the process is slightly different, creating an index is much like creating a table of contents. Index entries are defined by XE (Index Entry) fields, and the index is compiled by an INDEX field. You can enter these fields directly into your document with either the Field... command or the [Insert field] key, or you can enter them by using the Index Entry... and Index... commands on the Insert menu.

Word allows you to exercise a considerable amount of control over the way it formats an index. For example, you can display page number references in bold and/or italic, and you can change the character used to separate page numbers. We'll explore all of Word's indexing capabilities in this section.

A quick example

Let's suppose you've created the document shown in Figure 14-9, and you want to define the heading *Division of Parts* as an index entry. To define this entry, highlight the heading and select the Index Entry... command from the Insert menu to bring up the dialog box shown in Figure 14-10. (In this example, we'll assume that the Show All option in the Preferences dialog box is turned off, and that the Field Codes setting on the View menu is turned off as well.) As you can see, Word automatically places the text you've highlighted into the Index Entry text box. If you want the entry to read differently from the way it does in the text box, edit the entry, then choose OK. Word will then insert an XE field after the text you highlighted, as shown in Figure 14-11. (Since the field is assigned the hidden format, you'll need to activate the Hidden Text check box in the Preferences dialog box to display it on the screen.)

Figure 14-9

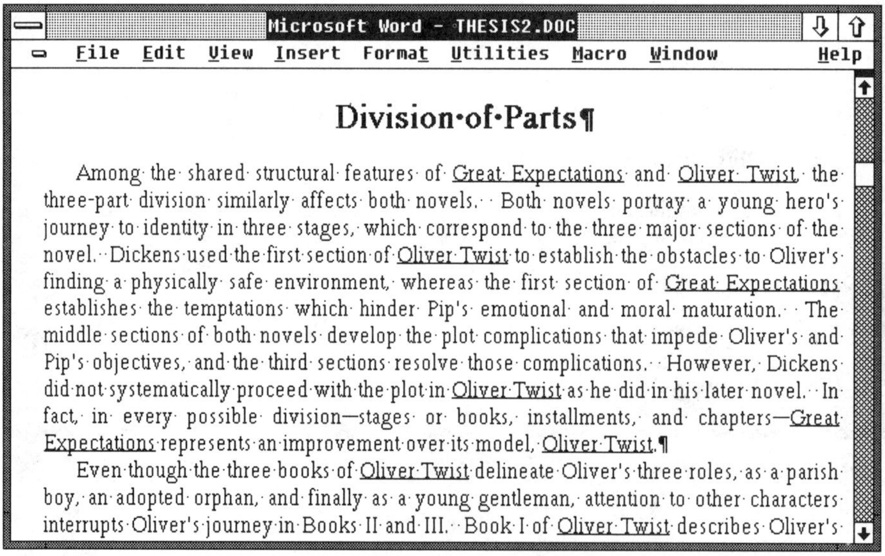

```
┌─┐                    Microsoft Word - THESIS2.DOC                      ⇩ ⇧
├─┤   File   Edit   View   Insert   Format   Utilities   Macro   Window        Help
│ □                                                                          ↑
│
│                          Division·of·Parts¶
│
│         Among· the· shared· structural· features· of· Great· Expectations· and· Oliver· Twist,· the·
│    three-part· division· similarly· affects· both· novels.· · Both· novels· portray· a· young· hero's·
│    journey· to· identity· in· three· stages,· which· correspond· to· the· three· major· sections· of· the·
│    novel.· Dickens· used· the· first· section· of· Oliver· Twist· to· establish· the· obstacles· to· Oliver's·
│    finding· a· physically· safe· environment,· whereas· the· first· section· of· Great· Expectations·
│    establishes· the· temptations· which· hinder· Pip's· emotional· and· moral· maturation.· · The·
│    middle· sections· of· both· novels· develop· the· plot· complications· that· impede· Oliver's· and·
│    Pip's· objectives,· and· the· third· sections· resolve· those· complications.· · However,· Dickens·
│    did· not· systematically· proceed· with· the· plot· in· Oliver· Twist· as· he· did· in· his· later· novel.· · In·
│    fact,· in· every· possible· division—stages· or· books,· installments,· and· chapters—Great·
│    Expectations· represents· an· improvement· over· its· model,· Oliver· Twist.¶
│         Even· though· the· three· books· of· Oliver· Twist· delineate· Oliver's· three· roles,· as· a· parish·
│    boy,· an· adopted· orphan,· and· finally· as· a· young· gentleman,· attention· to· other· characters·
│    interrupts· Oliver's· journey· in· Books· II· and· III.· · Book· I· of· Oliver· Twist· describes· Oliver's· ↓
```

We'll use this document to demonstrate Word's indexing capabilities.

As you can see, the field that defines our index entry is *{XE "Division of Parts"}*. Notice that this field appears with a dotted underline, indicating that Word has assigned it the hidden format.

You can continue using the Index Entry... command to define all the index entries for your document. When you are ready to compile the index, move the cursor to the appropriate spot (typically, the end of the document), and select the Index... command from the Insert menu to bring up the dialog box shown in Figure 14-12 on page 550.

Figure 14-10

Index Entry:
Division of Parts
OK
Cancel
Page Number
Range:
Bold
Italic

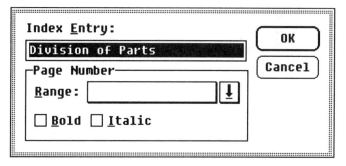

One way to define index entries in your document is by using the Index Entry dialog box.

Figure 14-11

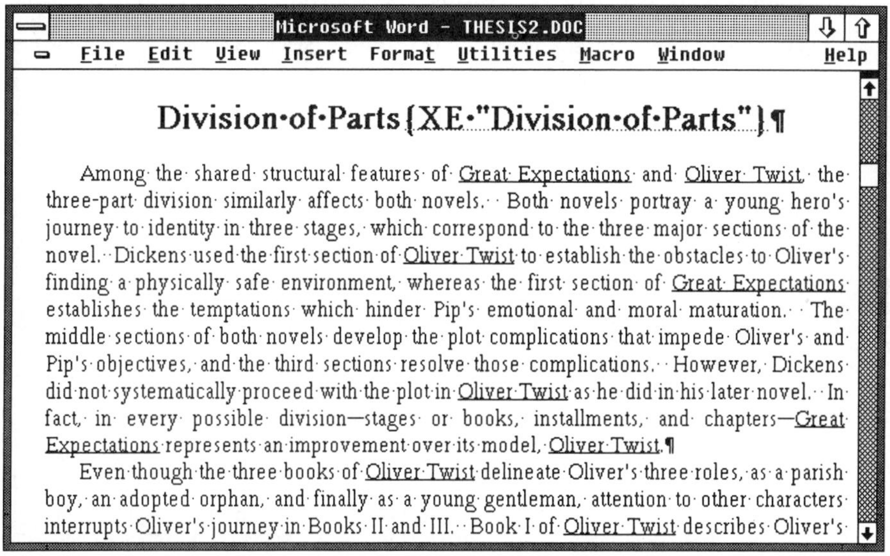

Microsoft Word - THESIS2.DOC
File Edit View Insert Format Utilities Macro Window Help
Division·of·Parts{XE·"Division·of·Parts"}¶
Among·the·shared·structural·features·of·Great·Expectations·and·Oliver·Twist,·the·three-part·division·similarly·affects·both·novels.··Both·novels·portray·a·young·hero's·journey·to·identity·in·three·stages,·which·correspond·to·the·three·major·sections·of·the·novel.··Dickens·used·the·first·section·of·Oliver·Twist·to·establish·the·obstacles·to·Oliver's·finding·a·physically·safe·environment,·whereas·the·first·section·of·Great·Expectations·establishes·the·temptations·which·hinder·Pip's·emotional·and·moral·maturation.··The·middle·sections·of·both·novels·develop·the·plot·complications·that·impede·Oliver's·and·Pip's·objectives,·and·the·third·sections·resolve·those·complications.··However,·Dickens·did·not·systematically·proceed·with·the·plot·in·Oliver·Twist·as·he·did·in·his·later·novel.··In·fact,·in·every·possible·division—stages·or·books,·installments,·and·chapters—Great·Expectations·represents·an·improvement·over·its·model,·Oliver·Twist.¶
Even·though·the·three·books·of·Oliver·Twist·delineate·Oliver's·three·roles,·as·a·parish·boy,·an·adopted·orphan,·and·finally·as·a·young·gentleman,·attention·to·other·characters·interrupts·Oliver's·journey·in·Books·II·and·III.··Book·I·of·Oliver·Twist·describes·Oliver's·

The Index Entry... command inserts an XE field immediately after the text you highlighted.

Since you want to create a normal index with no heading separators, leave the default options selected and choose OK to complete the command. Word will then repaginate your document, search for index entries, and insert an index like the one shown in Figure 14-13 on the following page.

Of course, this example illustrates only the basics of creating an index. For the remainder of this section, we'll explain all of Word's indexing features.

Figure 14-12

Insert
Normal Index
Run-in Index
OK
Cancel
Heading Separator
None
Blank Line
Letter

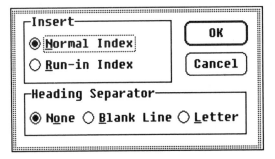

You can use the Index dialog box to compile all the index entries in your document.

Figure 14-13

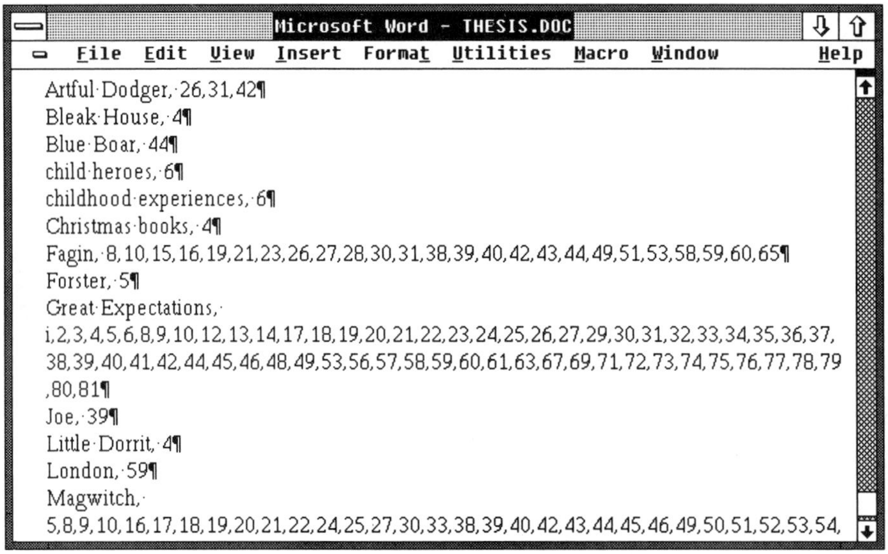

Microsoft Word - THESIS.DOC
File Edit View Insert Format Utilities Macro Window Help
Artful·Dodger,·26,31,42¶
Bleak·House,·4¶
Blue·Boar,·44¶
child·heroes,·6¶
childhood·experiences,·6¶
Christmas·books,·4¶
Fagin,·8,10,15,16,19,21,23,26,27,28,30,31,38,39,40,42,43,44,49,51,53,58,59,60,65¶
Forster,·5¶
Great·Expectations,·
i,2,3,4,5,6,8,9,10,12,13,14,17,18,19,20,21,22,23,24,25,26,27,29,30,31,32,33,34,35,36,37,
38,39,40,41,42,44,45,46,48,49,53,56,57,58,59,60,61,63,67,69,71,72,73,74,75,76,77,78,79
,80,81¶
Joe,·39¶
Little·Dorrit,·4¶
London,·59¶
Magwitch,·
5,8,9,10,16,17,18,19,20,21,22,24,25,27,30,33,38,39,40,42,43,44,45,46,49,50,51,52,53,54,

We've created this sample index with Word's default settings.

Defining index entries

Before you define an index entry in your document, you need to determine whether you want to create a term entry or a topic entry. A term entry always refers to a single page, like 49 or 156, while a topic entry may refer to a range of pages, like 49-51 or 156-162. Once you've decided which type of entry you want to create, you can take the appropriate steps to define that entry.

Word allows you to define both term and topic entries by issuing the Index Entry... command or entering XE (Index Entry) fields. After we show you how to define term and topic entries by using the Index Entry... command, we'll show you how to modify an XE field with a few optional arguments.

To create an index entry for a particular word or phrase in your document, start by highlighting that word or phrase. Then, select the Index Entry... command to bring up the dialog box shown in Figure 14-10. Word will place the text you highlighted in the Index Entry text box. (Word will accept no more than 64 characters in the text box.)

Defining term entries

If a colon appears in the text you highlighted, Word will automatically insert a backslash character (\) to the left of that colon in the Index Entry text box. (Word does this because the colon character is used to create multiple-level headings, which we'll explain in a moment.) To modify the entry's text, edit the text in the Index Entry text box. If you need to insert a colon into the Index Entry text box, precede it with a backslash, or you won't get the results you expect.

If you want the entry's page number reference to appear in bold and/or italic type, select the appropriate check boxes in the Index Entry dialog box. Finally, choose OK to define the index entry and return to the document. Unless you've told Word to suppress the display of hidden text, an XE field that defines your index entry will appear just after the text you highlighted in the document.

If you want, you can create an index entry for a term by manually entering an XE field into your document. Before you enter an XE field, however, turn on the display of hidden text by activating either the Show-all icon on the ribbon or the Hidden Text option in the Preferences dialog box. If you forget to turn on the display of hidden text, your XE field will disappear while you're entering the field in the document.

Manually entering an XE field

Once you've turned on the display of hidden text, position the cursor immediately after the appropriate term. Next, press the [Insert field] key ([Ctrl][F9]), and enter the field in the form

{XE *term*}

where *term* is the name of the term, enclosed in quotation marks, that you want to appear in the index. For example, if the term *HP LaserJet* appears in your document, and you want to define an index entry for that term, place the cursor immediately after the letter *t* in *LaserJet*, press the [Insert field] key, and type *XE "HP LaserJet"*.

If you want the page number reference in your index entry to appear in bold and/or italic type, append the switch \b and/or \i to the XE field. For example, to tell Word to display the page number reference for *HP LaserJet* in bold type, enter the field

{XE "HP LaserJet" \b}

Defining topic entries

The procedure for creating an index entry for a topic is slightly different from creating an entry for a term. Before you can create a topic entry with the Index Entry... command, you must use the Bookmark... command to assign a bookmark name to the block of text to which the entry will refer. For instance, if you want to create an index entry named *getting started*, which refers to the first five paragraphs in your document, you must first highlight those paragraphs, select the Bookmark... command from the Insert menu, type a name into the Bookmark Name text box (like *gettingStarted*), and choose OK.

After you've assigned a bookmark name to the appropriate block of text in the document, select the Index Entry... command. Then, replace the text in the Index Entry text box with the entry you want to appear in the index (for our example, we'll type *getting started*). At this point, pull down the Range list box and select the bookmark name you just defined—*gettingStarted*. Finally, choose OK to close the dialog box and return to the document. For our sample entry, Word will insert into the document the field

{XE "getting started" \r "gettingStarted"}

If you want to manually enter XE fields that define topic entries, make sure your fields follow the form

{XE *topic* \r *bookmark*}

where *topic* is the name of the topic you want to appear in the index, and *bookmark* is the name of the bookmark that defines the location of that topic within the document. Although it doesn't matter where you enter the field that defines a topic entry, we suggest you enter it immediately after the last paragraph in the bookmark so you'll know where to find it later.

Referring to other entries

Sometimes, you'll want to create an index entry that refers to another entry instead of to a page number. For instance, you might want to create the entry

Excel, see Microsoft Excel

To create entries like this, simply include the switch

\t *referenceText*

within the XE field, where *referenceText* is the text you want to use in place of the entry's page number. For instance, to create our entry, you would use the field

{XE "Excel" \t "see Microsoft Excel"}

Like fields that define topic entries, fields that refer to other entries can appear anywhere in the document. However, we recommend that you enter these fields at the end of the document, just above the INDEX field that compiles your entries, so you can easily modify or delete them later.

Word allows you to create multilevel entries, which are useful when you need to break down a large topic into several subtopics. For instance, you might want to create a group of entries like this:

printing
    envelopes, 326-29
    graphics, 325
    legal-size paper, 329-330
    margins, 322

Defining multilevel entries

To create multilevel entries in your index, you simply type an entry name in the form

1st level:2nd level:3rd level:...nth level

For example, to create the sample group of entries shown above, you would enter the following four fields into the appropriate place in your document:

{XE "printing:envelopes"}
{XE "printing:graphics"}
{XE "printing:legal-size paper"}
{XE "printing:margins"}

Table 14-2 shows a summary of all the switches you can include in an XE field. Although we've already explained each switch in detail, this table makes a handy reference guide.

A summary of XE field switches

Table 14-2

Use this switch...	to...
\r *bookmark*	create a topic entry; resulting index will refer to the pages defined by *bookmark*
\t *referenceText*	create an entry that refers to another entry
\b	display page number in bold type
\i	display page number in italic type

Compiling the index

Once you've defined the index entries in your document, you're ready to compile the index. To do this, issue the Index... command on the Insert menu or manually enter an INDEX field into your document. When you use either technique, Word will gather and alphabetize your entries, search for any duplicate entries and merge them, and eliminate any duplicate page number references for an entry. It will also compile the index, insert the correct page numbers, and insert the index at the location of the cursor.

Using the Index... command

To insert an index into your document with the Index... command, first move the cursor to the location in which you want the index to appear (this will typically be at the end of your document). Next, select the Index... command to bring up the dialog box shown in Figure 14-14.

Figure 14-14

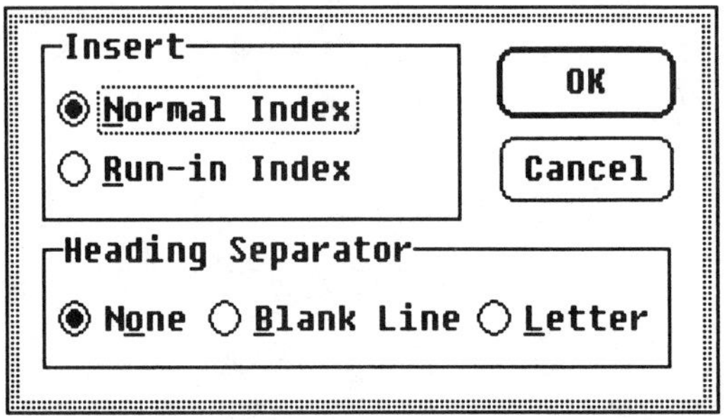

The Index dialog box lets you compile an index based on the index entries you've defined.

When the Index dialog box appears, you should choose the appropriate index type in the upper-left corner of the dialog box. If you choose the Normal Index option (the default), Word will indent each subentry on a new line under the main entry, as shown in Figure 14-15. If you choose the Run-in Index option, however, Word will include each subentry in the same paragraph as its main entry. Each subentry will be separated from the main entry by a colon and from other subentries by a semicolon, as shown in Figure 14-16.

After you've selected the appropriate index type, choose a heading separator. If you choose None (the default), Word will list all the index entries together with no separators. If you choose the Blank Line option, Word will insert a blank line between groups of entries that start with a new letter. Finally, choosing the Letter option will tell Word to precede each group of entries with a letter that identifies that group.

Once you've selected an index type and heading separator, choose OK to insert the index into your document. If you have already compiled an index for the document, Word will ask whether you want to replace the existing index. If you choose No, Word will cancel the Index... command and return to the document. If you choose Yes, Word will replace the old index with the new one.

Figure 14-15

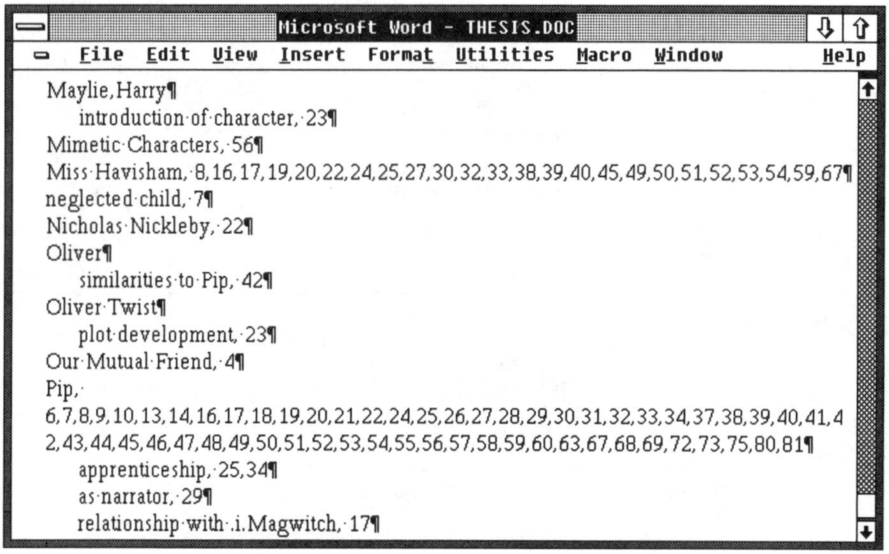

```
┌─────────────────────────────────────────────────────────────────┐
│ ▭      ▌▌▌▌▌▌  Microsoft Word - THESIS.DOC ▌▌▌▌▌▌        ⇩ ⇧      │
│  ▭    File   Edit   View   Insert   Format   Utilities   Macro   Window        Help │
├─────────────────────────────────────────────────────────────────┤
│ Maylie,Harry¶                                                   ↑ │
│     introduction·of·character,·23¶                                │
│ Mimetic·Characters,·56¶                                          │
│ Miss·Havisham,·8,16,17,19,20,22,24,25,27,30,32,33,38,39,40,45,49,50,51,52,53,54,59,67¶│
│ neglected·child,·7¶                                              │
│ Nicholas·Nickleby,·22¶                                          │
│ Oliver¶                                                          │
│     similarities·to·Pip,·42¶                                     │
│ Oliver·Twist¶                                                    │
│     plot·development,·23¶                                         │
│ Our·Mutual·Friend,·4¶                                           │
│ Pip,·                                                            │
│ 6,7,8,9,10,13,14,16,17,18,19,20,21,22,24,25,26,27,28,29,30,31,32,33,34,37,38,39,40,41,4│
│ 2,43,44,45,46,47,48,49,50,51,52,53,54,55,56,57,58,59,60,63,67,68,69,72,73,75,80,81¶│
│     apprenticeship,·25,34¶                                       │
│     as·narrator,·29¶                                            │
│     relationship·with··i.Magwitch,·17¶                          ↓ │
└─────────────────────────────────────────────────────────────────┘
```

When you choose the Normal Index option, Word will indent each subentry on a new line under the main entry.

Figure 14-16

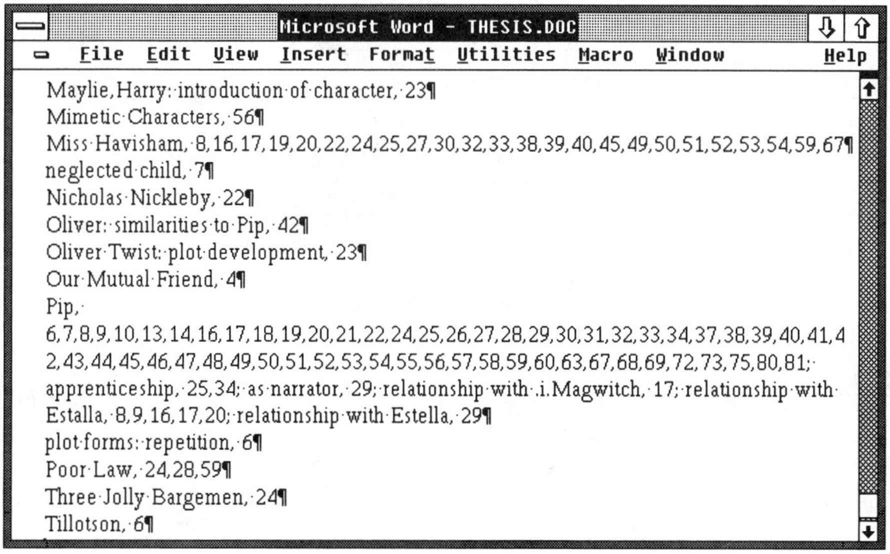

```
┌─────────────────────────────────────────────────────────────────┐
│ ▭      ▌▌▌▌▌▌  Microsoft Word - THESIS.DOC ▌▌▌▌▌▌        ⇩ ⇧      │
│  ▭    File   Edit   View   Insert   Format   Utilities   Macro   Window        Help │
├─────────────────────────────────────────────────────────────────┤
│ Maylie,Harry:·introduction·of·character,·23¶                    ↑ │
│ Mimetic·Characters,·56¶                                          │
│ Miss·Havisham,·8,16,17,19,20,22,24,25,27,30,32,33,38,39,40,45,49,50,51,52,53,54,59,67¶│
│ neglected·child,·7¶                                              │
│ Nicholas·Nickleby,·22¶                                          │
│ Oliver:·similarities·to·Pip,·42¶                                 │
│ Oliver·Twist:·plot·development,·23¶                             │
│ Our·Mutual·Friend,·4¶                                           │
│ Pip,·                                                            │
│ 6,7,8,9,10,13,14,16,17,18,19,20,21,22,24,25,26,27,28,29,30,31,32,33,34,37,38,39,40,41,4│
│ 2,43,44,45,46,47,48,49,50,51,52,53,54,55,56,57,58,59,60,63,67,68,69,72,73,75,80,81;·│
│ apprenticeship,·25,34;·as·narrator,·29;·relationship·with··i.Magwitch,·17;·relationship·with·│
│ Estalla,·8,9,16,17,20;·relationship·with·Estella,·29¶           │
│ plot·forms:·repetition,·6¶                                      │
│ Poor·Law,·24,28,59¶                                             │
│ Three·Jolly·Bargemen,·24¶                                       │
│ Tillotson,·6¶                                                   ↓ │
└─────────────────────────────────────────────────────────────────┘
```

When you choose the Run-in Index option, Word will include your subentries in the same paragraph as the main entry.

INDEX field options

If you select the Show-all icon on the ribbon or select the Field Codes setting on the View menu, you'll see that your document's index is actually the result of an INDEX field. For instance, if you use the Index... command to insert a normal index with no heading separator, Word will insert into your document the field *{index}*. If you want, you can use the [Insert field] key ([Ctrl][F9]) or the Field... command to manually enter an INDEX field into your document.

Like most fields, the INDEX field can accept several switches. Table 14-3 lists the switches you can include in an INDEX field. Let's examine each of these.

Table 14-3

Use this switch...	to...
\r	create a run-in index
\h *heading*	insert *heading* between groups of entries
\e *chars*	insert *chars* between index entries and their page numbers
\g *chars*	insert *chars* between the page numbers in a range reference
\l *chars*	insert *chars* between page number references
\b *bookmark*	compile an index for the portion of the document defined by *bookmark*
\p *range*	limit the index to entries that begin with the letters in *range*
\s *identifier*	insert a sequence name in front of each entry's page number
\d *chars*	insert *chars* between *identifier* in the \s switch and the page number

Creating a run-in index

If you want to create a run-in index by manually entering an INDEX field, add the switch \r. As we said earlier, a run-in index includes each subentry in the same paragraph as its main entry.

Creating custom separator characters

You'll use the \h switch to insert custom headings between groups of index entries. To create a custom heading, include in the INDEX field the switch

    \h *heading*

where *heading* is the text that defines your custom heading. If you include a letter in the *heading* argument, Word will substitute the appropriate letter for each group in the index.

For example, suppose you want to use a blank line as your heading separator. To specify this type of heading, you would use the field:

{INDEX \h " "}

To insert a single letter that identifies each group of entries, use the field:

{INDEX \h "A"}

Finally, you can include other characters in the *heading* argument, like this:

{INDEX \h "-A-"}

By default, Word uses a single blank space to separate every index entry from its page number. If you want to use a different character or group of characters to separate entries from their page numbers, include the \e switch along with your custom character(s). For instance, to insert an ellipsis between each entry and its page number, enter the field

{INDEX \e "..."}

Word uses a hyphen to separate a range of pages in an index. If you want to use a different character as the range reference separator, include the \g switch and your custom character(s). For instance, to create an index that refers to pages 1 through 4 as 1..4, enter the field

{INDEX \g ".."}

Finally, you can use the \l switch to change the character Word uses to separate page number references. By default, Word uses a comma. To define a different page number reference separator, just include the \l switch and the character(s) you want to use. For instance, to separate page number references with a semicolon, enter the field

{INDEX \l ";"}

If you want to compile an index only for a portion of your document, you can include the arguments

\b *bookmark*

Compiling an index for a portion of a document

in the INDEX field, where *bookmark* is the name of the bookmark that defines the area of the document you want to index. For example, if you've created a 50-page document, and you want to compile an index for pages 1 through 25, first use the Bookmark… command to assign a name to those pages. (For the sake of this example, let's suppose you use the bookmark name *part1*.) To compile an index for these pages, you would enter the field

{INDEX \b "part1"}

Other switches

The \p, \s, and \d switches are useful in creating indexes for relatively long documents. We'll cover these three switches when we talk about long documents in the last section of this chapter.

Updating the index

To update a document's index, simply place the cursor anywhere within the index and press the [Update field] key ([F9]). When you do, Word will repaginate the entire document, search for index entries, and recompile the index. Fortunately, you don't need to worry about suppressing the display of the document's hidden text before updating the index—Word automatically ignores hidden text as it compiles.

As with a table of contents, the best time to compile an index is right before you print the final version of a document. Word automatically repaginates your document when you issue the Index… command to ensure that the page numbers are accurate. However, if you edit or reorganize the document after compiling the index, the page numbers may change, causing the index entries to be incorrect.

Formatting the index

Initially, the character and paragraph formats of your first-level index entries will match the *Normal* style for your document. Subentries are identical to first-level entries, except Word indents each subentry $1/4$ inch.

Once you've inserted an INDEX field into your document, you can assign it any character and paragraph formats you like. You can also use the Cut and Paste commands to move the INDEX field to another part of your document. The easiest way to reformat your index text is to redefine the style definitions that Word applies to the index. Let's look at the relationship between the index and Word's Style Sheet facility.

Using the style sheet

Like the Outline and Table of Contents facilities, Word's Index facility is designed to work in conjunction with style sheets. If you create a normal index (as opposed to a run-in index), Word will create a style name for each index level in your document. These *index* styles, which are named *index 1, index 2,* and so forth, correspond to the various entry levels you have created for your index. In addition, Word creates an *index heading* style, which it assigns to the heading separators between groups of entries. Each style is based on the *Normal* style. If you choose the Styles… command from the Format menu after creating an index, you'll see a dialog box like the one in Figure 14-17.

Figure 14-17

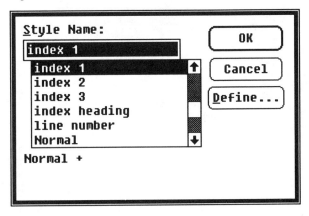

Each level of a normal index has a style name on the style sheet.

If you use the Run-in Index option to include all your index subentries in the same paragraph as your main entry (as shown in Figure 14-16), Word will create only one *index* style—*index 1*. Since each main entry appears in the same paragraph as all of its subentries, there is no need to create special formatting instructions for different index levels.

You can modify *index* styles by changing the style instructions on the style sheet. Just move the cursor to one of the index entries that belong to the level you want to format, then choose Define Styles... from the Format menu. In the Define Styles dialog box, select the name of the style you want to modify, then select the character and paragraph formats for that index level. When you choose OK in the Define Styles dialog box, Word will apply the specified formats to all the index entries in your document that carry that style name. (For a detailed discussion of modifying styles, see Chapter 8.)

For example, in the sample document we used to create the index shown in Figure 14-15, our *Normal* style, which formats the main body text of the document, specifies 12-point Tms Rmn plain type. As a result, our index also appears in that type. If you want the first-level headings in the index to appear in bold type, move the cursor to one of the first-level index entries in the document and issue the Define Styles... command. In the Define Styles dialog box, select the style name *index 1*, then choose the Character... button to open the Character dialog box. Next, select the Bold check box and choose OK to return to the Define Styles dialog box. When you choose OK to lock in this change and return to the document, your index will look like the one in Figure 14-18. Notice that any formatting change you make to an *index* style affects the entire index entry—both the text portion and the page number reference.

Figure 14-18

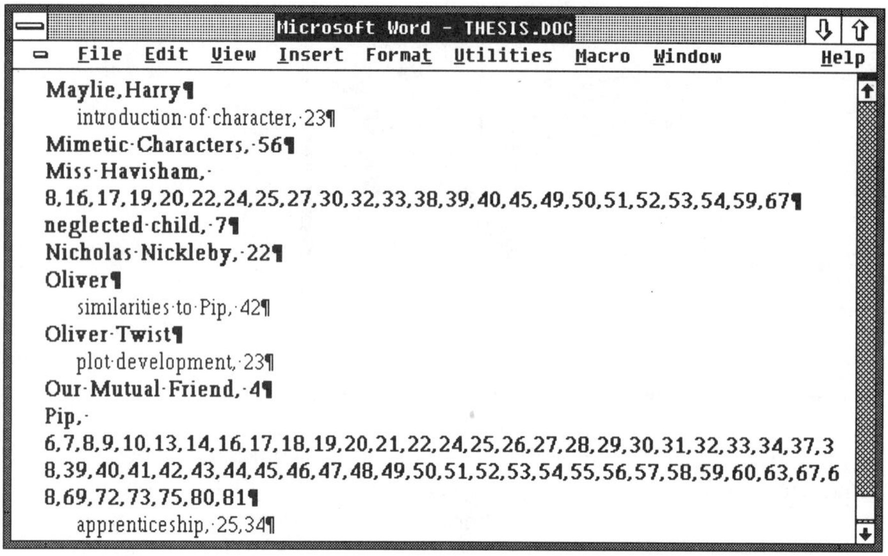

```
┌────────────────────────────────────────────────────────────┐
│ ▭        Microsoft Word - THESIS.DOC          ⬇ ⬆ │
│ ▭   File  Edit  View  Insert  Format  Utilities  Macro  Window      Help │
│ Maylie,Harry¶                                               ▲│
│     introduction·of·character,·23¶                          │
│ Mimetic·Characters,·56¶                                     │
│ Miss·Havisham,·                                             │
│ 8,16,17,19,20,22,24,25,27,30,32,33,38,39,40,45,49,50,51,52,53,54,59,67¶ │
│ neglected·child,·7¶                                         │
│ Nicholas·Nickleby,·22¶                                      │
│ Oliver¶                                                     │
│     similarities·to·Pip,·42¶                                │
│ Oliver·Twist¶                                               │
│     plot·development,·23¶                                   │
│ Our·Mutual·Friend,·4¶                                       │
│ Pip,·                                                       │
│ 6,7,8,9,10,13,14,16,17,18,19,20,21,22,24,25,26,27,28,29,30,31,32,33,34,37,3 │
│ 8,39,40,41,42,43,44,45,46,47,48,49,50,51,52,53,54,55,56,57,58,59,60,63,67,6 │
│ 8,69,72,73,75,80,81¶                                        │
│     apprenticeship,·25,34¶                                 ▼│
└────────────────────────────────────────────────────────────┘
```

We used the Define Styles… command to apply boldfacing to the first-level index entries in this document.

As you're changing the formatting instructions for an *index* style, you may want to change the Based On style as well. Instead of using *Normal* as the Based On style for each *index* style, you might want to base each *index* style on the next highest index style. Specifically, *index 4* could be based on *index 3*, which could be based on *index 2*, which could be based on *index 1*, which could be based on *Normal*. That way, when you make a formatting change to the *index 1* style, that change will affect not only the first-level index entries, but also the subsequent levels of index entries.

Word's page-numbering conventions

Word adheres to the page-number abbreviation conventions established in *The Chicago Manual of Style*, University of Chicago Press. Table 14-4 summarizes these conventions.

CREATING FOOTNOTES

The mere mention of footnotes strikes fear in the heart of anyone who has ever struggled through a term paper. But with Word, footnotes don't have to be frightening. Word's Footnote facility allows you to enter footnote text as you create your document (while the information is still fresh in your mind and at your fingertips). Word will automatically number and track the sequence of your footnotes—even if you modify the document by adding and deleting them. Then, when you are ready to print your document, you can tell Word where to place the footnotes and choose how they will be separated from the rest of the text on a page.

Table 14-4

If start number is...	stop number should...	Examples
less than 100	use all digits	7-13; 56-57
100 or multiple of 100	use all digits	100-104;
		1200-1213
101 through 109 (in multiples of 100)	use only the part that changes, omitting unnecessary zeros	103-4; 408-12; 1105-7
110 through 199 (in multiples of 100)	use two digits or more as needed	252-58; 578-601; 1283-87; 12561-612
	However, if page numbers are four digits long and three digits change, use all digits	1298-1314; 7856-7902

Let's start by showing how you would create a footnote in the sample document shown in Figure 14-19 on the next page. The first step is to place your cursor at the location you want your footnote reference mark to appear. In this example, we want to add our sample footnote reference mark at the end of the first paragraph of body text.

Once the cursor is in place, choose Footnote... from the Insert menu to bring up the dialog box shown in Figure 14-20 on the following page. We'll take a look at the Separator..., Cont. Separator..., and Cont. Notice... buttons in a few moments. First, let's examine the Footnote Reference Mark text box.

If you want Word to number your footnotes automatically, select the Auto-numbered Reference check box in the Footnote dialog box. If you'd rather use your own footnote reference mark, such as an asterisk, just type the appropriate character into the Footnote Reference Mark text box. You can enter as many as ten characters. Word will automatically deselect the Auto-numbered Reference check box when you type an entry into the Footnote Reference Mark text box.

When you choose OK, Word will insert the correct footnote number or other reference mark just to the right of the cursor in your document. If you're in the normal editing view, Word also will split your document window into two panes, as shown in Figure 14-21 on page 563, and display a corresponding footnote reference mark in the bottom pane.

Figure 14-19

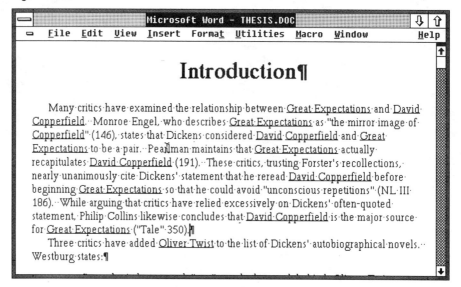

We'll insert a sample footnote reference mark into this document.

Figure 14-20

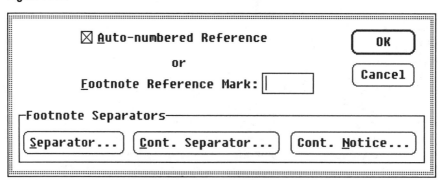

You'll use the Footnote dialog box to insert footnotes into a document.

At this point, all you need to do is type your footnote text after the footnote reference mark in the bottom pane. Figure 14-22 shows the text for our sample footnote. There is no limit to the length of the text or number of paragraphs you can include in a footnote. If your footnote text is too long to view in the bottom pane, you can use the vertical scroll bar in that pane to bring additional text into view, or you can move the split bar up to make the bottom pane larger. (See Appendix 1 for an explanation of how to move the split bar.)

Figure 14-21

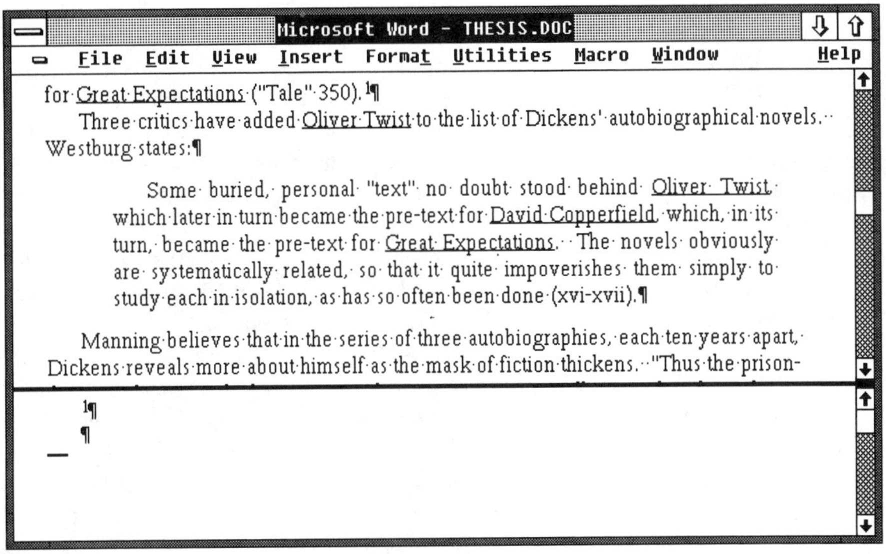

```
┌─────────────────────────────────────────────────────────────┐
│ ═     Microsoft Word - THESIS.DOC                       ⇩ ⇧  │
│  ▭  File  Edit  View  Insert  Format  Utilities  Macro  Window    Help │
├─────────────────────────────────────────────────────────────┤
│ for·Great·Expectations·("Tale"·350).¹¶                          │
│     Three·critics·have·added·Oliver·Twist·to·the·list·of·Dickens'·autobiographical·novels.· │
│ Westburg·states:¶                                              │
│                                                               │
│         Some· buried,· personal· "text"· no· doubt· stood· behind· Oliver· Twist, │
│     which·later·in·turn·became·the·pre-text·for·David·Copperfield,·which,·in·its· │
│     turn,· became· the· pre-text· for· Great· Expectations.··· The· novels· obviously· │
│     are· systematically· related,· so· that· it· quite· impoverishes· them· simply· to· │
│     study·each·in·isolation,·as·has·so·often·been·done·(xvi-xvii).¶ │
│                                                               │
│     Manning·believes·that·in·the·series·of·three·autobiographies,·each·ten·years·apart,· │
│ Dickens·reveals·more·about·himself·as·the·mask·of·fiction·thickens.···"Thus·the·prison- │
├─────────────────────────────────────────────────────────────┤
│     ¹¶                                                         │
│     ¶                                                         │
│ ─                                                             │
└─────────────────────────────────────────────────────────────┘
```

When you choose OK in the Footnote dialog box, Word will add a footnote reference mark and split your document window into two panes.

Figure 14-22

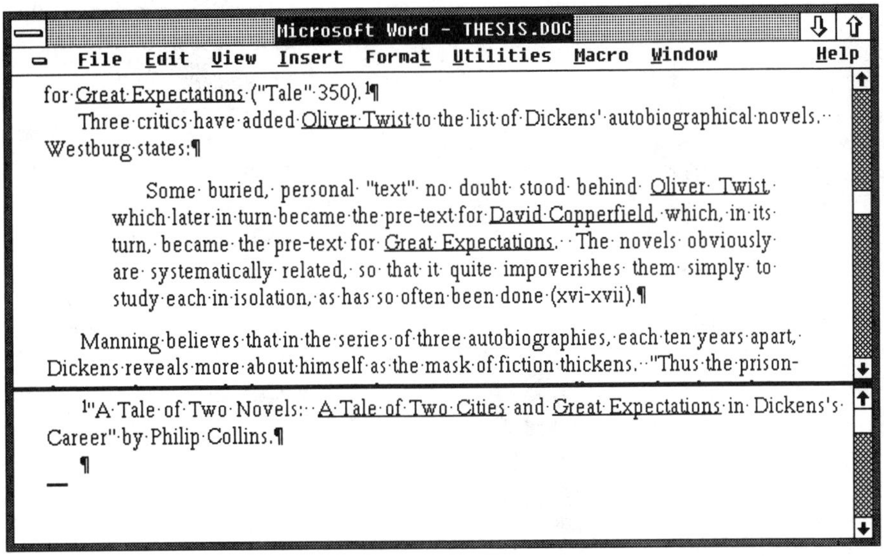

```
┌─────────────────────────────────────────────────────────────┐
│ ═     Microsoft Word - THESIS.DOC                       ⇩ ⇧  │
│  ▭  File  Edit  View  Insert  Format  Utilities  Macro  Window    Help │
├─────────────────────────────────────────────────────────────┤
│ for·Great·Expectations·("Tale"·350).¹¶                          │
│     Three·critics·have·added·Oliver·Twist·to·the·list·of·Dickens'·autobiographical·novels.·· │
│ Westburg·states:¶                                              │
│                                                               │
│         Some· buried,· personal· "text"· no· doubt· stood· behind· Oliver· Twist, │
│     which·later·in·turn·became·the·pre-text·for·David·Copperfield,·which,·in·its· │
│     turn,· became· the· pre-text· for· Great· Expectations.··· The· novels· obviously· │
│     are· systematically· related,· so· that· it· quite· impoverishes· them· simply· to· │
│     study·each·in·isolation,·as·has·so·often·been·done·(xvi-xvii).¶ │
│                                                               │
│     Manning·believes·that·in·the·series·of·three·autobiographies,·each·ten·years·apart,· │
│ Dickens·reveals·more·about·himself·as·the·mask·of·fiction·thickens.···"Thus·the·prison- │
├─────────────────────────────────────────────────────────────┤
│     ¹"A·Tale·of·Two·Novels:···A·Tale·of·Two·Cities·and·Great·Expectations·in·Dickens's· │
│ Career"·by·Philip·Collins.¶                                    │
│     ¶                                                         │
│ ─                                                             │
└─────────────────────────────────────────────────────────────┘
```

We have entered our footnote text in the bottom pane.

After you've finished inserting or editing footnote text in the footnote pane, you can return to your previous place in the document pane either by pressing the [Jump panes] key ([F6]) or by clicking anywhere in the document pane. Word will continue to display the footnote pane at the bottom of the screen.

The document and footnote panes you see in Figure 14-22 resemble the panes you create by dragging the split bar in your document window. However, the footnote pane is actually a separate entity. Although footnotes are saved to disk along with your document, Word does not consider footnotes to be a part of the body of the document.

As with headers and footers, Microsoft chose to use a split-window format for footnotes rather than create a new window. That way, it could create vertical scroll bars that allow you to move through your document and footnote text with ease. As you scroll through the document pane, Word will automatically scroll the contents of the footnote pane in order to display the footnote text that corresponds to the footnote reference mark on your screen. By the same token, when you scroll through your footnote entries in the bottom pane, Word will scroll the corresponding parts of your document text into view in the top pane.

To expand your view of the document pane, you can drag the split bar toward the bottom of the screen. To remove the footnote pane, you can either drag the split bar past the top or bottom of the document pane, or you can double-click on a footnote reference mark in the footnote pane.

You can bring your footnote text back into view using a variety of techniques. First, you can choose Footnotes from the View menu. Alternatively, you can hold down the [Shift] key as you click on the split box and drag the split bar. (When your document window is not split into panes, the split box will appear at the top of the vertical scroll bar.) Finally, you can double-click on a footnote reference mark in the document.

Inserting and deleting footnotes

As you might expect, your footnote reference marks are dynamic—that is, Word will adjust all of your footnote reference marks whenever you insert or delete an automatically numbered footnote. (By the way, a dotted border will appear around your footnote reference marks after you select either the Show-all icon on the ribbon or the Show All check box in the Preferences dialog box.)

To delete a footnote, just delete the footnote reference mark in your document pane. Word will automatically delete the corresponding footnote text as well. Even better, Word will renumber all subsequent footnotes automatically.

To insert a new footnote between existing footnotes, click at the location in the document pane where you want the footnote reference mark to appear, select the Footnote... command, then choose OK. Word will insert the correct footnote reference mark in the document, move the cursor to the correct location in the footnote pane, and create a new paragraph so you can enter the footnote text. Again, Word will renumber all subsequent footnotes automatically, both in your document and footnote panes.

If you have entered your own footnote reference mark (such as an asterisk), and you decide to use a different footnote reference mark, you'll need to change the mark in your document. In changing the footnote reference mark in your document, you should not attempt to edit it directly. If you do, Word will delete your footnote reference and text. Instead, select the footnote reference mark in your document, issue the Footnote... command and type a new reference mark in the Footnote Reference Mark text box. Word will change the entry in your document pane as well as in your footnote pane.

Editing footnotes

Once you have created a footnote, you can use Word's standard editing techniques to edit the footnote text. For example, you can insert, delete, cut, copy, and paste text just as you would in the document pane. You can also use the Search..., Replace..., Spelling..., Thesaurus..., and Hyphenate... commands to edit your footnote text. Unfortunately, Word will not check your footnote text when you issue one of these commands while the cursor is in the document pane.

Here's a handy shortcut for repeating a footnote entry in one or more locations in your document. If you select a footnote reference mark in your document, issue the Copy command, then paste that reference mark in another part of the document, Word will automatically copy the corresponding text for that footnote as well. The copied footnote text will appear in the appropriate location in the footnote pane. When you paste—if you copied an automatically numbered reference mark—Word will also change that number to reflect its new position in the document. Word will then renumber any subsequent reference marks.

Copying footnotes

When you insert a footnote into your document, Word will add two new style names to your style sheet: *footnote reference* and *footnote text*. As you can see in the Styles dialog box in Figure 14-23, the *footnote reference* style will format your footnote reference marks in 8-point type, superscripted 3 points. The *footnote text* style will format your footnote text in 10-point plain type. Both styles specify a *Normal* Based On style.

Formatting footnotes

The easiest way to change the format of your footnote text or footnote reference marks is to change the style definition of *footnote reference* or *footnote text* in the Define Styles dialog box. When you change the style definition for *footnote text*, Word will apply the new formatting instructions to all the footnote text in your document. Changing the style definition for *footnote reference*, however, will affect the format of only future footnote reference marks—not existing ones. To change the format of your existing footnote reference marks, you'll need to manually format each mark in both the document and the footnote pane. (For a discussion of modifying named styles, see Chapter 8.)

When you print a document, Word will automatically print its footnotes as well. As you can see in Figure 14-24, Word uses a short horizontal line between

Changing footnote separators

your document text and footnote text to separate the two elements on the printed page. When a footnote is too long to fit on one page or when all the footnotes for a page cannot appear at the bottom of that page, Word will automatically place the remaining text on the following page. To indicate that the footnote text on the next page is a continuation, Word uses a horizontal rule that extends from margin to margin.

Figure 14-23

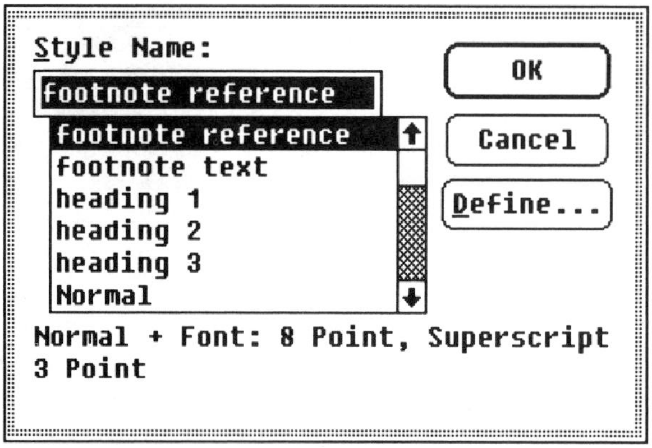

When you create a footnote, Word will add the footnote reference *and* footnote text *styles to the style sheet.*

Figure 14-24

Echoes of Oliver Twist in Great Expectations

Fagin's undoing results from his lesson to Noah Claypole, imparting so well the philosophy of "looking after Number One . . . that, feeble blockhead though he is, he yet becomes the instrument that betrays Fagin himself to the law" (Wilson Introduction 21). Oliver's half-brother's punishment reflects society's views of genteel crime and Dickens' sense of justice: Monks does not suffer punishment for his attempts to hide Oliver's heritage and transform the innocent child into a criminal. However, Monks' evil eventually consumes him, and he dies in prison in the New World. The evil Monks, though a gentleman, deports himself; and the evil Sikes, a vicious criminal, first imprisons and then hangs himself. Fagin's small, dark death cell, the epitome of the imagery associated with the bad characters, contrasts with the pastoral setting of Oliver's idyllic country home, where he lives surrounded by friends and his Aunt Rose.

In Oliver Twist Dickens intermittently, instead of steadily, developed his theme of society's inhumanity to the oppressed. He prepared readers for the theme of enlightened self-interest as practiced by both the respectable and criminal worlds and then interrupted the theme to explore the human potential for evil. Fagin explains to Noah the code which governs both criminal and upper classes:

> In a little community like ours . . ., we have a general number one, that is, you can't consider yourself as number one, without considering me too as the same, and all the other young people . . . . The more you value your number one, the more careful you must be of mine; so we come at last to what I told you at first - that a regard for number one holds us all together, and must do so, unless we would all go to pieces in company (387-8).

Dickens showed by Fagin's "little community" the effects of the code. He implied by extension that the same rules governed the workhouse system, the legal system, and even Mr. Brownlow's respectable system. However, Dickens interrupted his theme of the reliance of all segments of society on the same rules to pursue an additional theme of the duality of human nature.

[1] "Prisoners and Children: Forms of Growth in Dickens' novels" by William T. Lankford.
[2] Dickens and Ellen Ternan by Ada Nisbit.
[3] Dickens the Novelist Sylvere Monod.
[4] In 1861, J. Holsworth published Great Expectations, "a drama in three stages by Charles Dickens" (Morley, 79), indicating Dickens' continued preference for three-part division.

62

[5] "'Keystone' Structure in Dickens' Serial Novels" by William Axton.
[6] "Structural Patterns in Dickens's Great Expectations" by John H. Hagan, Jr.
[7] Dickens specified time of day, season, or an amount of elapsed time at the beginning of Chapters 2, 3, 9, 18, 20, 23, 33, 38, 47, 48, 49, 51, and 53.
[8] For examples of chapters which begin with vague references to time, see Chapters 10 and 32.
[9] Charles Dickens As Serial Novelist by Archibald C. Coolidge, Jr.
[10] According to Calder, the hulks were not used after 1852 (499); Edminson sets the date much earlier at 1837.
[11] Introduction to Great Expectations by Angus Wilson.
[12] "'The Parish Boy's Progress': The Evolving Form of Oliver Twist" by William Lankford.
[13] "The Popularity of Dickens" by Philip Collins.
[14] The Moral Art of Dickens by Barbara Hardy.
[15] The Heart of Charles Dickens by Edgar Johnson.
[16] "The Autobiographical Matrix of Great Expectations" by Ada Nisbet.
[17] Charles Dickens, A Critical Introduction by K. J. Fielding.
[18] "Great Expectations, The Culmination Of A Developing Art." by Archibald C. Coolidge, Jr.

63

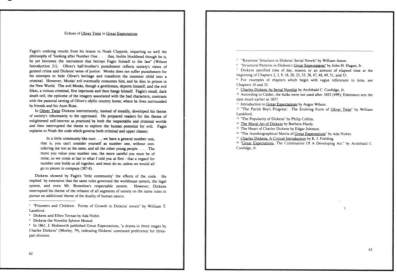

Word uses a short horizontal line to separate your footnotes from your body text and a margin-to-margin line to indicate that the footnotes continue from one page to the next.

If you like, you can create your own separators by using the Separator… and Cont. Separator… options in the Footnote dialog box. To access these options, first choose the Footnote… command. Then, rather than choosing OK to start a new footnote entry, select the Separator… button. When you do, Word will close the Footnote dialog box and open a Footnote Separator pane at the bottom of the document window, as shown in Figure 14-25.

Figure 14-25

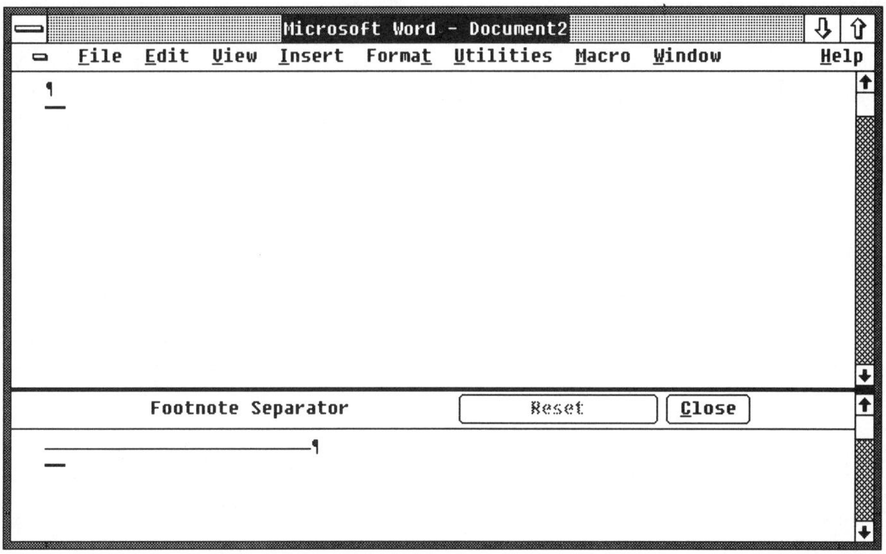

Use the Footnote Separator pane to customize the separator that divides your footnotes from your body text.

Notice that Word displays a horizontal line about 2 inches long in this pane. Although you cannot change the size or format of this line, you can add characters to this line, or you can delete the line altogether and insert your own separator characters. (We'll demonstrate this in a moment.) You also can insert any field into the Footnote Separator pane to add a dynamic page number, date and/or time to your separator.

When you choose the Cont. Separator… button in the Footnote dialog box, Word will open the Footnote Cont. Separator pane shown in Figure 14-26. As you can see, this pane contains the margin-to-margin line that Word uses as the default separator between document and footnote text when footnotes continue from one page to another. (This pane is identical to the Footnote Separator pane except for the length of the separator line.) Again, you can insert additional characters or overwrite the separator line.

Figure 14-26

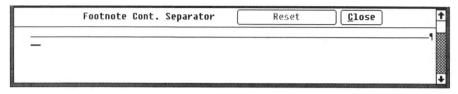

You can enter your own separator characters in the Footnote Cont. Separator pane to distinguish footnotes from text.

In addition to customizing your separators, Word allows you to place a notice at the end of your footnotes on one page to let the reader know that the footnote text continues on the next page. To do this, choose the Cont. Notice... button in the Footnote dialog box. You will then see a blank Footnote Cont. Notice pane like the one in Figure 14-27. In this pane, you can enter a phrase like *(continued on next page)*. Word will print the contents of the Footnote Cont. Notice pane only when footnote text flows from one page to the next.

Figure 14-27

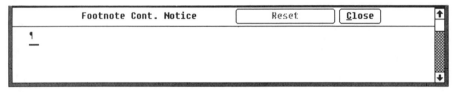

You can use this pane to notify the reader that the footnote text will continue on the next page.

To illustrate how you might use the Footnote Separator, Footnote Cont. Separator, and Footnote Cont. Notice panes, let's customize the footnote separators and create a continuation notice for the sample pages in Figure 14-24. First, select the Footnote... command from the Insert menu to open the Footnote dialog box. Next, choose the Separator... button to access the pane shown in Figure 14-25. Now, suppose you want to replace the default separator with the word *Footnotes*. You want this word to appear in 12-point Helv bold underlined type, centered between your document margins.

To do this, highlight the existing separator by double-clicking on it or by using the [Shift] and arrow keys, press [Delete], then type the word *Footnotes*. (Word will overwrite the line when you begin typing.) Next, highlight the word you just typed, then use the ribbon to choose the 12-point Helv bold underline format. Finally, choose the Centered-alignment icon on the ruler. (You also may want to click on the Open-space icon to create some extra white space between the last line of body text and your footnote separator.) Figure 14-28 shows the Footnote Separator pane at this point.

Figure 14-28

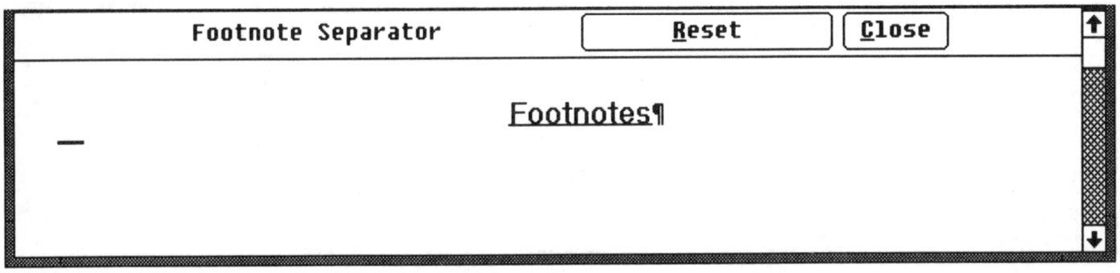

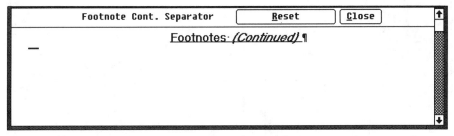

The word Footnotes *replaces Word's default separator.*

Now, to format the continuation separator, first choose the Close button in the Footnote Separator pane, then follow the same steps described above, except type the text *Footnotes (Continued)* in the Footnote Cont. Separator pane and format the word *(Continued)* in italics. Figure 14-29 shows the pane at this point.

Figure 14-29

Footnote Cont. Separator	**R**eset	**C**lose	↑
—	Footnotes· *(Continued)* ¶		

The continuation separator now displays the words Footnotes (Continued).

Finally, to create a continuation notice, close the window in Figure 14-29, open the Footnote Cont. Notice pane and enter a message like *(continued on next page)*. Format your continuation notice to appear in 12-point Helv plain type, as shown in Figure 14-30 on the next page.

Now, when you print your document, Word will use your new separators and print the continuation notice where necessary, as shown in Figure 14-31 on the following page.

Oddly enough, Word will not allow you to create different separators and continuation notices for different pages in your document. In fact, you cannot even change the separators or continuation notice from one section to another.

The Reset button

Any changes you make in these panes will affect your entire document. That being the case, you may wonder what purpose, if any, the Reset button serves in these three panes.

Figure 14-30

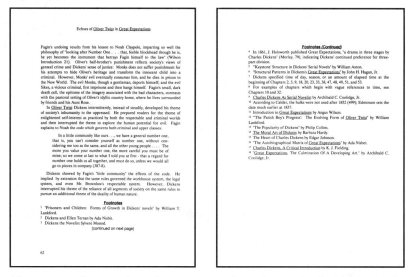

You can add a continuation notice to the Footnote Cont. Notice pane.

Figure 14-31

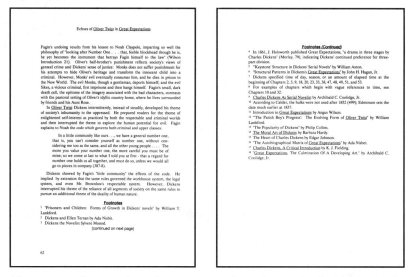

These printed pages show the customized separators and continuation notice.

The Reset button that appears in the Footnote Separator, Footnote Cont. Separator, and Footnote Cont. Notice panes is used to return the contents of the current pane to the default. For example, if you were to click this button in the pane shown in Figure 14-28, Word would remove the word *Footnotes* and replace it with the default separator.

Word gives you a number of choices for positioning your footnotes in a document: You can print each footnote on the same page as its footnote reference mark; you can group your footnotes at the end of a document section; or you can print all your footnotes at the end of your document. If you want each footnote to appear on the same page as its reference mark, you can tell Word to place the footnotes either at the bottom of the page or directly below the last paragraph on the page. (In some cases, the last paragraph on a page may occur somewhere other than at the bottom of the page.) You also can control whether your footnotes will be numbered consecutively throughout a document or separately on each page or in each section.

You can control the positioning of your footnotes by using the Document dialog box, which offers four options for positioning footnotes in the Print At pull-down list box: End of Section, Bottom of Page, Beneath Text, and End of Document. This dialog box, shown in Figure 14-32, also includes the Restart # Each Section check box, which determines whether your footnotes will be numbered consecutively throughout a document or numbered separately in each section. Finally, the Document dialog box includes a Starting Number text box, which allows you to begin your footnote numbers at something other than Word's default of 1.

Positioning and numbering footnotes

Figure 14-32

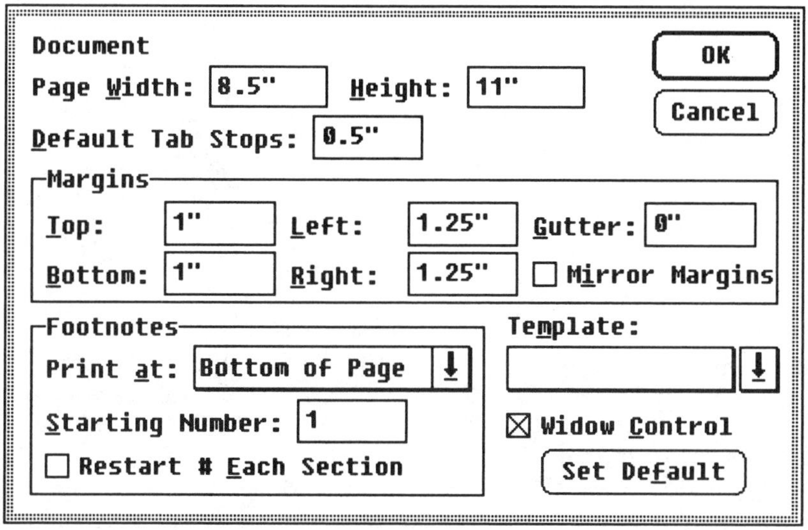

You can position footnotes with the settings in the Document dialog box.

If you select the Bottom of Page option from the Print At list box in the Document dialog box, each footnote will appear at the bottom of the page on which its reference mark appears, as shown in Figure 14-33. If you choose Beneath Text, your footnotes will appear on the same page as their reference marks, but Word will print them directly below the last paragraph on the page, as shown in Figure 14-34.

Figure 14-33

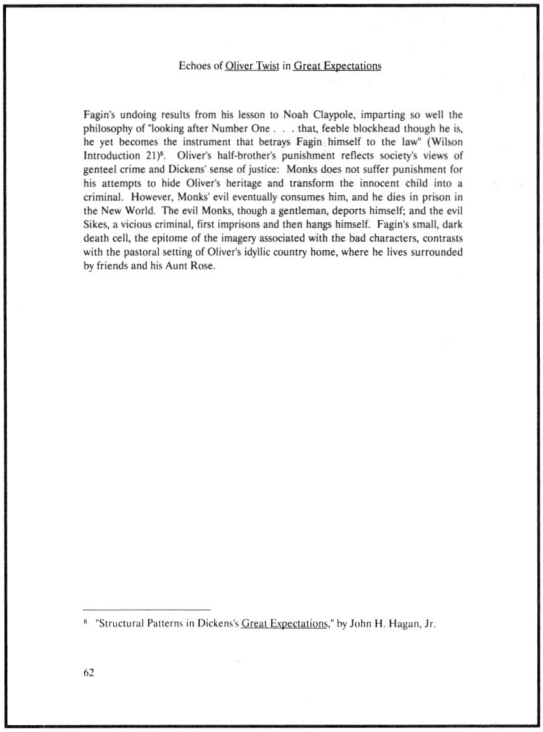

Echoes of Oliver Twist in Great Expectations

Fagin's undoing results from his lesson to Noah Claypole, imparting so well the philosophy of "looking after Number One . . . that, feeble blockhead though he is, he yet becomes the instrument that betrays Fagin himself to the law" (Wilson Introduction 21)[8]. Oliver's half-brother's punishment reflects society's views of genteel crime and Dickens' sense of justice: Monks does not suffer punishment for his attempts to hide Oliver's heritage and transform the innocent child into a criminal. However, Monks' evil eventually consumes him, and he dies in prison in the New World. The evil Monks, though a gentleman, deports himself; and the evil Sikes, a vicious criminal, first imprisons and then hangs himself. Fagin's small, dark death cell, the epitome of the imagery associated with the bad characters, contrasts with the pastoral setting of Oliver's idyllic country home, where he lives surrounded by friends and his Aunt Rose.

[8] "Structural Patterns in Dickens's Great Expectations," by John H. Hagan, Jr.

62

If you use the Bottom of Page option, the footnote text will appear at the bottom of the page on which its reference mark appears.

When you choose the Bottom of Page, Beneath Text, or End of Section option, you can number your footnotes separately in each section, or you can number them sequentially throughout the document. To restart the footnote numbers in each section, select the Restart # Each Section check box in the Document dialog box. If you deselect this check box, Word will number your footnotes continuously from section to section.

To group your footnotes at the end of a section in a document, select the End of Section option. Of course, if your document contains only one section, this option will place your footnotes at the end of the document (just as if you had chosen the End of Document option). If your document contains more than one section, and you choose the End of Section option, Word will automatically turn on the Include Footnotes option in the Section dialog box. This tells Word to include the footnotes for that section at the end of the section. If you turn off the Include Footnotes option for one or more sections, Word will place the footnotes for those sections at the end of the next section for which the Include Footnotes option is active (or at the end of your document if you have turned off the Include Footnotes option in all the remaining sections). This can be helpful when you have created separate sections for formatting purposes only.

Figure 14-34

If you use the Beneath Text option, the footnote text will appear directly below the last paragraph on the page.

When you group your footnotes at the end of each section, you can number your footnotes sequentially throughout the entire document, or you can number the footnotes separately in each section. The Restart # Each Section option in the Document dialog box determines whether you will have continuous footnote numbering. If you select this check box, Word will number the footnotes in each section separately. When this check box is not selected, Word will number all the footnotes in the document sequentially. By the way, when you choose the End of Section option, Word will always print your footnotes immediately after the last paragraph in a section. Word will not place the footnotes at the bottom of the last page or on a separate page.

If you want to place all your footnotes at the end of a document, just select the End of Document option. Word will then print the footnotes just below the last paragraph in the document. When your footnotes appear at the end of a document, Word will always number them sequentially from the beginning to the end of the document.

WORKING WITH LONG DOCUMENTS

As we explained in Chapter 12, you'll sometimes want to split a very long document into separate document files, then link the documents using either the INCLUDE or RD fields. If you use this technique to consolidate several short documents into one long document, Word can consolidate your table of contents, index, and footnote entries.

For example, suppose you've created three documents entitled CHAP1, CHAP2, and CHAP3, and you've linked them using the document shown in Figure 14-35. Let's use this sample document to illustrate how you'll consolidate your table of contents, index, and footnotes.

Figure 14-35

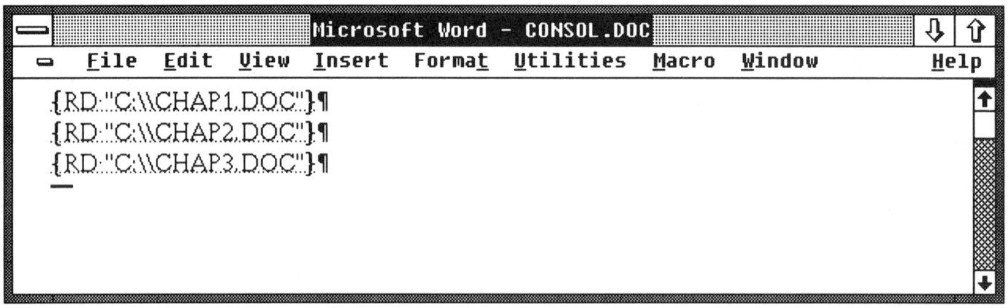

```
┌──┬─────────────────────Microsoft Word - CONSOL.DOC──────────────────⬇ ⬆┐
│ ▭  File  Edit  View  Insert  Format  Utilities  Macro  Window     Help│
├──────────────────────────────────────────────────────────────────────┤
│  {RD:"C:\\CHAP1.DOC"}¶                                               ⬆│
│  {RD:"C:\\CHAP2.DOC"}¶                                               ▓│
│  {RD:"C:\\CHAP3.DOC"}¶                                               ▓│
│  ▬                                                                   ▓│
│                                                                      ▓│
│                                                                      ⬇│
└──────────────────────────────────────────────────────────────────────┘
```

We'll use this sample document to illustrate Word's consolidation techniques.

Consolidating the table of contents and index

To create a master table of contents or index for a consolidated document like the one shown in Figure 14-35, follow a few simple steps. First, make sure you've entered the correct file names into each RD (or INCLUDE) field in the master document. Also, be sure that you've entered the correct page number in the Page Numbers Start At text box of the expanded Header/Footer dialog box for each document. (If you don't number the pages of your linked documents sequentially, the page number references in your index and table of contents will be incorrect.) Now, just move the cursor to either the beginning or end of the document and issue either the Table of Contents... or Index... command on the Insert menu. Word will then repaginate each of the linked documents on disk. If you're creating a table of contents, Word will insert into the document a TOC field at the location of the cursor. If you're compiling an index, Word will insert an INDEX field at the cursor's location. When you view the result of the field in the master document, you'll see the resulting table of contents or index. (If you've used INCLUDE fields instead of RD fields in the master document, you'll need to manually update the TOC and INDEX fields immediately after you enter them.)

If you later make a change to any of the documents you've included in the master document, make sure you remember to update the fields in your master document. Don't forget to update the INCLUDE fields along with the TOC and INDEX fields.

If you create an index that contains a few thousand entries, your computer may run out of memory (or run very slowly) when it compiles the index. Fortunately, Word provides a way to divide an index into multiple parts, then compile those parts independently.

Breaking up the index

To compile only a portion of an index, include the arguments

\p *startLetter-endLetter*

in the INDEX field, where *startLetter* and *endLetter* define the range of entries you want to compile. For example, if you want to divide an index into two parts, you might use the INDEX fields

```
{INDEX \p "a-m"}
{INDEX \p "n-z"}
```

When you're ready to recompile the index, update each INDEX field individually. If you want to break the index into even more parts, just add more INDEX fields and specify a smaller range in each field.

If you've created a master document with INCLUDE fields, and you want Word to group all your footnotes at the end of the last document rather than place them at the bottom of each page or at the end of each section, you'll need to select the End of Document option in the Document dialog box for each document. That's all there is to it. You don't need to give each document a new starting footnote number—Word automatically adjusts the footnote numbers when you update the fields in the master document. When you print the master document, your footnotes will be numbered sequentially, and Word will print all the footnotes at the end of the last document in the master list.

Numbering footnotes in multiple documents

If you use Word to create chapters for a book or manual, you might want to create a numbering scheme that reflects both the chapter number and the page number. For instance, you might want to refer to page 1 of Chapter 8 as *page 8-1*. Of course, if you create these kinds of page numbers, you'll want them to appear in the table of contents and in the index.

Creating chapter-page style numbers

The key to creating chapter-page style numbers is the SEQ field, which we discussed in Chapter 13. As you'll recall, Word provides the SEQ field to let you create sequential references in a document. The forms of this field are

{SEQ *identifier*}
{SEQ *identifier bookmark*}

where *identifier* identifies the sequence you're labeling, and *bookmark* is a bookmark you've previously defined.

Let's illustrate how you can take advantage of the SEQ field to set up a document that contains a chapter. Imagine that your document contains the text for Chapter 8 in your book, and the chapter is entitled *Advanced Techniques*.

You'll want to begin the document with

Chapter {SEQ "chapter" \r 8}, {SET "chapName" "Advanced
    Techniques"}{chapName}

which will return the result

Chapter 8, Advanced Techniques

The field *{SEQ "chapter" \r 8}* assigns the number 8 to the identifier *chapter* and returns the number 8 as its result. If you later want to change the chapter number, you can make the change throughout the entire document by replacing the number 8 in this SEQ field with the revised chapter number. The field *{SET "chapName" "Advanced Techniques"}* assigns the text *Advanced Techniques* to the bookmark *chapName*. This allows you to insert the chapter's title into the document by entering the field *{chapName}*, as we've done immediately after the SET field.

If you want to display the chapter number and title in the document's header, you can do so by entering into the header the text

Chapter {SEQ "chapter" \c}, {"chapName"}

which will return the result

Chapter 8, Advanced Techniques

To display the page numbers in the header or footer, just enter into the header or footer the text

Page {SEQ "chapter" \c}-{PAGE}

The first page of the document will show the result *Page 8-1*, the second page will show *Page 8-2*, and so forth.

To tell Word to use chapter-page style numbers in the table of contents and index, just include in the TOC or INDEX field the arguments

\s *identifier*

where *identifier* is the identifier you've used in the SEQ fields that return the chapter number. For example, to create a table of contents and index for our sample document, you would use the fields

{TOC \o \s "chapter"}
{INDEX \s "chapter"}

Finally, if you want to separate the chapter number from the page number with something other than a hyphen, you can include the arguments

\d *chars*

where *chars* represents the characters you want to use as the new separators.

In this chapter

Merging Documents **15**

*I*f you're like most people, a great deal of the business writing you perform each day is dull and repetitive—sending out billing notices to your clients or churning out dozens of personal invitations to the grand opening of your company's new production facility. If you find yourself stuck with these jobs very often, you'll be glad to know that Word's Print Merge facility can take the time and tedium out of these repetitive tasks.

The Print Merge facility is a powerful feature that lets you combine data from two or more documents to create any number of customized documents. You provide the standardized text in one document and the variable information in another document. When you issue the Print Merge… command, Word will print multiple versions of the main document, automatically customizing each with a name, address, account balance—or other data—from a second document.

For example, in your grand opening invitations, you might enter the text of your letter in one document and the names and addresses of each guest in another. When you merge the two files, Word will create a personal letter of invitation for each guest. Similarly, when you send out billing notices, you might store the text of the notice in one document and the names, addresses, and amounts due for each client in another document. Then, you can merge the information in these two files to create all of your billing statements.

You commonly hear Word's Print Merge facility referred to as a form-letter facility since it is often used to customize business letters. However, there are dozens of equally useful applications for this facility, such as mailing labels and management reports. For that reason, we'll use the term *Print Merge facility* rather than *form-letter facility*.

**USING THE PRINT
MERGE FACILITY**

As we mentioned, you'll need to create at least two files in order to generate a series of merge documents: a main document and a data document. The main document contains your standard text, which will remain constant for each merge document. The data document contains the text that will vary from one merge document to the next. Word combines the information from the data document and the main document to create a series of customized merge documents.

Why bother?

If you've ever dealt with a cantankerous word processor that makes your form letters look like glued-together bomb threats from an illiterate terrorist, you may feel doubtful about using the Print Merge facility. Perhaps you've even received computer-generated form letters in which half of your name is truncated on the mailing label, or you've found your name floating in the middle of a gappy line of text because it didn't fill the allotted space. For example, a name like Catherine Hammerschmidt can be rechristened Catherine Hammers (or, even worse, Catheri Hammersc), and Ann Lee can get lost in the middle of a sentence like

```
    Just for you, Ann Lee          , we've reserved a…
```

Well, you can now set your doubts to rest. Word has gone a step beyond most other programs to let you develop truly professional merge documents. Because the Print Merge facility includes a number of sophisticated capabilities for extracting and formatting variable information, your form letters don't have to look like conventional form letters. Word automatically adjusts the text in every merge document to accommodate entries of variable lengths. You can even choose to exclude blocks of text from selected merge documents without leaving gaping holes in your printed document.

There are a number of other advantages to using Word's Print Merge facility to create varied merge documents. The most obvious advantage is that you can compile and print all your merge documents with a single command—no more typing different names and addresses for each version of a form letter. This not only saves time, but also helps you avoid typographical errors and inconsistencies. You will save even more time—and disk space—by letting Word fill in the blanks for you as it prints, rather than creating and saving each version of your document to disk.

Although your main document and data document may take a little time and planning to develop, once you set them up, you can use those documents again and again. In addition, Word lets you combine information any way you like. That is, you can use the same data document to "feed" any number of main documents, and you can draw information from any number of data documents into a main document by directing Word to the document files you want to use.

Before we can put the Print Merge facility through its paces, we need to create a pair of main and data documents. We'll begin by setting up our data document, then we'll set up the main document and show you how to merge the information from the data document into the text of the main document.

SETTING UP THE DATA DOCUMENT

If you've ever worked with a database program, you should have no trouble mastering data documents in Word. A data document is nothing more than a specially structured collection of entries that are stored in a standard document. This document can contain any kind of information—from inventory numbers and prices to names, addresses, and telephone numbers.

Every data document consists of three elements: records, fields, and field headers. Each paragraph in a data document is a record and each column is a field. When you merge the data and main documents, each record provides the variable data needed to create one new merge document. The field header paragraph, which appears at the top of the data document, identifies the information that is stored in each field. As you'll see in a moment, these field headers are the key link between your data and main documents.

Figure 15-1 shows the sample data document we'll use to create our merge documents throughout this chapter. The first line in this document contains our field headers: LastName, FirstName, Address1, Address2, City, ST, ZIP, and Sign. Each row of text after this first one is a separate record, ending with a ¶ mark and containing information on each person.

Figure 15-1

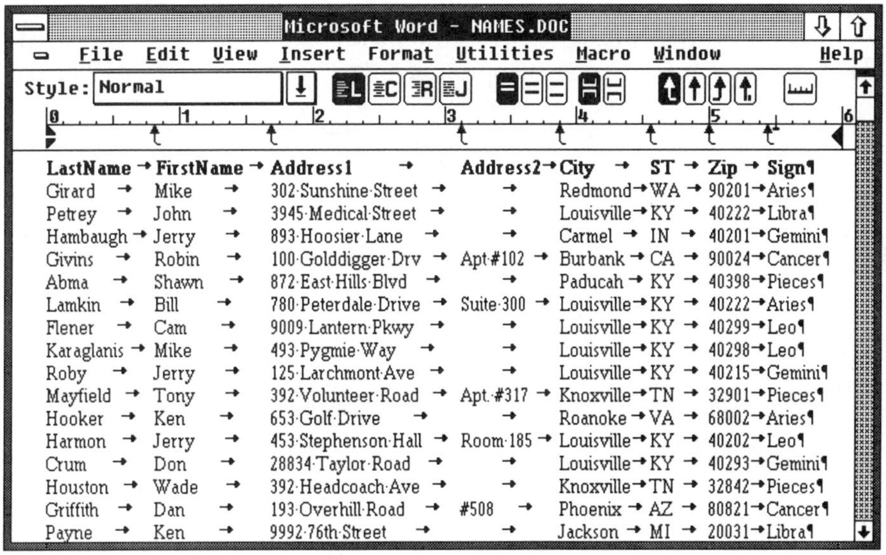

LastName	FirstName	Address1	Address2	City	ST	Zip	Sign¶
Girard	Mike	302·Sunshine·Street		Redmond	WA	90201	Aries¶
Petrey	John	3945·Medical·Street		Louisville	KY	40222	Libra¶
Hambaugh	Jerry	893·Hoosier·Lane		Carmel	IN	40201	Gemini¶
Givins	Robin	100·Golddigger·Drv	Apt·#102	Burbank	CA	90024	Cancer¶
Abma	Shawn	872·East·Hills·Blvd		Paducah	KY	40398	Pieces¶
Lamkin	Bill	780·Peterdale·Drive	Suite·300	Louisville	KY	40222	Aries¶
Flener	Cam	9009·Lantern·Pkwy		Louisville	KY	40299	Leo¶
Karaglanis	Mike	493·Pygmie·Way		Louisville	KY	40298	Leo¶
Roby	Jerry	125·Larchmont·Ave		Louisville	KY	40215	Gemini¶
Mayfield	Tony	392·Volunteer·Road	Apt.·#317	Knoxville	TN	32901	Pieces¶
Hooker	Ken	653·Golf·Drive		Roanoke	VA	68002	Aries¶
Harmon	Jerry	453·Stephenson·Hall	Room·185	Louisville	KY	40202	Leo¶
Crum	Don	28834·Taylor·Road		Louisville	KY	40293	Gemini¶
Houston	Wade	392·Headcoach·Ave		Knoxville	TN	32842	Pieces¶
Griffith	Dan	193·Overhill·Road	#508	Phoenix	AZ	80821	Cancer¶
Payne	Ken	9992·76th·Street		Jackson	MI	20031	Libra¶

We'll use this data document to create some sample merge documents.

Rules of the game   Although creating a data document is quite easy, there are a number of rules you must follow as you set up this document. First, your field headers, which the Word documentation calls *bookmark names,* must occupy the very first paragraph of the data document. Otherwise, Word will not be able to locate the correct field entries when you merge the main and data documents. In addition, each field header can be as long as 20 characters. For readability and ease of use, we suggest that you use short, easy-to-remember field headers.

Since field headers are the same as bookmark names, they are bound by the same rules as bookmark names. As you'll recall from Chapter 13, bookmark names can be no longer than 20 characters and must begin with a letter of the alphabet. The name can contain only letters, numbers, and the underline character—you cannot use spaces, punctuation marks, or other symbols.

Word uses a ¶ mark to signal the end of each record. If your data document contains several fields or if some field entries are very long, your records may wrap onto two or more lines. This is fine since Word will be able to interpret the data in each record as a unit as long as that information appears in a single paragraph and in the same order as the information in the field header paragraph.

Each row in your data document must contain the same number of entries as the header paragraph. If you want to omit an entry, simply press the [Tab] key to enter a placeholder and move to the next field. If you include a record in your data document that does not contain the same number of field entries as the header paragraph, Word will present a message box notifying you of the problem. For instance, if the third record of your data document does not contain as many field entries as the header paragraph, Word will present a message box like the one shown in Figure 15-2 when it attempts to merge the main and data documents. If you choose Yes in this box, Word will ignore the data in record 3 when it performs the print merge. Consequently, make sure you enter information (or a tab placeholder) into all the fields in each record of your data document, as we've done in Figure 15-1.

Figure 15-2

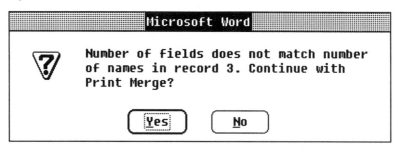

Make sure that each row in your data document contains the same number of entries (or entry placeholders) as the header paragraph.

You must also be sure your field entries are typed exactly as you want them to appear in your merge documents. For example, any extra blank spaces that you include in a field entry will also appear in the merge documents and may cause your text to be misaligned. You should be sure to use the correct case for your field entries—for example, you'll want to capitalize the first letter of each last name, first name, city, street, and sign entry. If you're using standard two-digit state abbreviations, you'll also want to type your state field entries in uppercase letters— KY, LA, and MO, for example.

Notice that we've used tab marks to separate the field headers and entries in our sample data document. If you want, you can use commas instead of tabs as your delimiters. Regardless of whether you use tabs or commas, you should try to use the same delimiters in your field header paragraph as you do in each record.

Field delimiters

We strongly recommend that you use tabs instead of commas to delimit the fields in your data document. Tab-delimited documents are much easier to read and, consequently, much easier to edit. Also, with tab marks, you often can tell at a glance if a particular record is missing a field entry or contains an extra field entry. And, because tabs create clearly defined columns, you will be able to select any field in your data document and sort the document on the contents of that field.

If you have imported your data document from another program, its records may be delimited automatically, with commas between the field entries. If this is the case, you can easily use the Replace... command, discussed in Chapter 6, to replace the commas with tab marks. Just enter a single comma (,) in the Search For text box, and type ^t in the Replace With text box. Then, deselect the Confirm Changes check box and choose OK to make the switch.

Since Word interprets tab marks and commas as field delimiters, you may be wondering how you can enter literal commas and tabs into your records. If you want to include a comma or tab within a field entry, you must enclose that entire entry in quotation marks. For example, you would enter the company name MegaCorp, Inc. as *"MegaCorp, Inc."* The quotation marks around this entry indicate that you want Word to interpret the contents as literal characters.

Special characters

You can also use quotation marks to include a ¶ mark in a data document. For example, if you specify the field entry

```
"line1¶
line2"
```

Word will interpret that entry as a single field entry containing two lines of text.

You may now be wondering how you can include quotation marks within one of your data documents. To do this, you must precede the quotation marks with a backslash character (\). For example, suppose you have a client who insists on calling himself Jim "Pop" Stallone. You would enter his name into the data document like this:

Jim \"Pop\" Stallone

The backslash characters tell Word to interpret the quotation marks as literal text within the field entry.

To include a backslash character in a data document, you must precede the backslash with another backslash. For example, to specify the directory name C:\BUDGETS in your data document, you would enter the directory name:

C:\\BUDGETS

If you include any result fields in your data document, such as {AUTHOR} or {CREATEDATE}, Word will interpret the field as a single entry. To place two or more result fields in a single entry, simply enclose the fields in quotation marks. For example, if you enter the result fields

{AUTHOR}{CREATEDATE}

into a data document, Word will consider these to be two separate field entries. To include both result fields in a single entry, you must enclose them in quotation marks, like this: *"{AUTHOR}{CREATEDATE}"*.

Table 15-1 shows how Word will interpret a few sample entries when it performs a print merge.

Table 15-1

To specify the entry...	type this...
Manager, Word Processing	"Manager, Word Processing"
"Jelly Bean" Woods	\"Jelly Bean\" Woods
C:\WINDOWS	C:\\WINDOWS

If you do not delimit the entries in your data document as we've described, Word will not be able to complete the merge procedure and will display an alert message when you issue the Print Merge... command.

Formatting and organizing your data document

As we've said, you should type your field entries exactly as you want them to appear in your merge documents, using the correct capitalization, spelling, spacing, and so forth. However, the character and paragraph formats you assign to the entries in your data document have absolutely no effect on the way that information will appear when you create your merge documents. You'll assign the formatting specifications for the merge documents when you create your main document. (This means that the same field entries can take on different formats in different merge documents. You can even format the same field entry in several ways within the same merge document.) Nevertheless, as you are creating a data document, you may want to use certain character and paragraph formats to make the records easy to read and edit.

For example, in Figure 15-1, we entered a series of manual tab stops on our ruler. These ensure that the entries in each column are aligned properly, allowing us to make certain that no information is missing. The tabs will also help us edit our field entries and make it easier to extract information from the data document later. However, formatting our fields with tabs is not required. It makes no difference to Word whether your data document is aesthetically pleasing, as long as all the information is in place and in order.

Organizational tips

Your data document will be much more useful if you organize your information carefully. As you set up your fields entries, think about how you will use the information when you create your merge documents. Then, try to design the fields so that you can easily access any piece of information. For example, you may be tempted to type your clients' names in a single field. Instead, consider using three separate fields to hold each person's first name, middle initial, and last name. You may also want to create additional fields for titles like Dr., Mr., and Ms. and for professional designations like C.P.A. and Vice President.

Although it may seem like a lot of trouble to create a separate field for every piece of information in your data document, the importance of this organizational issue will become clearer as you begin sorting data and extracting information from the data document. For instance, in the data document shown in Figure 15-1, we split our address information into five fields: Address1, Address2, City, ST, and Zip. This will allow us to extract exactly the address information we need in our main document.

Header documents

If you have imported the text for your data document from another program, your data document may not automatically include a field header paragraph like the one shown in Figure 15-1. In this case, you can either manually edit the imported file to create your field headers, or you can store your header paragraph in a separate header document.

To create a header document, just type your field entries into a new Word document. Separate the field headers with tabs or commas—just as if you were entering your headers into a standard data document. A little later, we'll show how you can use the information from a header document in your merge documents.

**Using tables in
the data document**

If you want, you can use a table to set up your records in the data document. Each row of the table functions as a paragraph and contains a single record, while each cell of the table holds a field entry. For information on setting up a table in a Word document, refer to Chapter 11.

**SETTING UP THE
MAIN DOCUMENT**

Once you have created your data document, you're ready to build your main document. You create, edit, and format this document exactly as you would any Word document, except you add merge instructions where you want Word to fill in variable information later. Figure 15-3 shows a sample main document that we have created to extract information from the FirstName, LastName, and Sign fields of our sample data document.

Figure 15-3

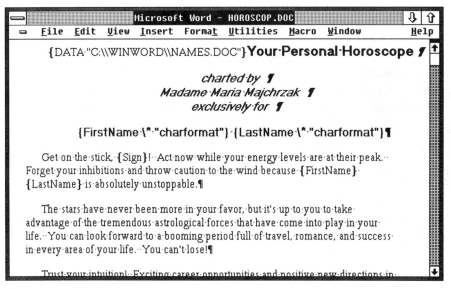

*The main document contains merge instructions that let you extract
information from the data document.*

Notice the instruction *{DATA "C:\\WINWORD\\NAMES.DOC"}*, which appears at the very beginning of this document. This instruction tells Word the name and location of the data document that contains the information needed to create the merge documents. This DATA instruction will not appear when you print your merge documents, nor will it affect the documents' line or character spacing. If you insert the DATA instruction in a paragraph by itself, however, Word will print a blank line at that location. (Because the term *field* is used in the Word documentation to describe both a merge instruction like DATA and a single category in a data document, we'll use the term *merge instruction* or simply *instruction* throughout the rest of this chapter to refer to instructions like DATA, which affect document merging.)

The fifth line of the main document contains two merge instructions, *{FirstName}* and *{LastName}*, which tell Word to extract the entries from the FirstName and LastName fields of the data document and place them into the main document. Therefore, when Word prints the first merge document, it will insert *Mike* and *Girard* in the appropriate places. In printing the second merge document, Word will plug in the FirstName entry *John* and the LastName entry *Petrey*. Unless we specify otherwise, Word will create a new merge document for each record in the data document, plugging in the appropriate entries for each new version of the merge document.

The main document includes three more merge instructions. In the first line of body text, we use the merge instruction *{Sign}* to extract the individual's astrological sign from the data document. Then, in the second and third lines of body text, we use the merge instructions *{FirstName}* and *{LastName}* again. When we create our merge documents, Word will again extract the appropriate information from each record and place it in its proper location in the document.

Before we see how our finished merge documents appear, let's look at some of the rules for entering merge instructions into the main document and for formatting the variable text.

Merge instruction basics

The sample document in Figure 15-3 uses the two most common merge instructions—the DATA and bookmark instructions. Later in this chapter, we'll show you some additional merge instructions you can use to vary the contents of your merge documents. Regardless of the type of instruction you are entering, however, the basic rules remain the same.

To enter a merge instruction into the text of your main document, you can use the Field... command on the Insert menu, or you can press the [Insert field] key ([Ctrl][F9]) and type the instruction manually. Since nearly all the merge instructions you'll enter will be either DATA or bookmark instructions, you'll probably find it easier to enter them manually with the [Insert field] key.

For example, suppose that you want to enter the merge instruction *{DATA "C:\\WINWORD\\NAMES.DOC"}* at the top of your document. To do this, first position the cursor at the beginning of the document, press the [Insert field] key, type *DATA "C:\\WINWORD\\NAMES.DOC"*, and then move the cursor outside the field characters ({}).

Now that you know how to enter a merge instruction into your main document, let's look at the two most commonly used instructions: the DATA and bookmark instructions.

The DATA instruction

The first merge instruction in your main document must be the DATA instruction, which takes the form

{DATA *dataDocument*}

where *dataDocument* is the full path name of the document file containing your records. This instruction tells Word where to find the variable information it will use to "fill in the blanks" in your merge documents. For example, the DATA instruction *{DATA "C:\\WINWORD\\NAMES.DOC"}* tells Word to look for the variable information in the file NAMES.DOC in the directory C:\WINWORD. Notice that you must double the backslash character in the document's full path name to avoid confusing this argument with a switch argument.

You might be wondering why you must specify the full path name of the data document in the DATA instruction instead of simply supplying the document name. When you don't supply the data document's full path name, Word looks only in the current directory for that document. Consequently, if the current directory doesn't contain the document, Word will generate an error message when you issue the Print Merge… command. To avoid this problem, always specify the full path name of the data document in your DATA instruction.

Word does not distinguish between uppercase and lowercase letters in your DATA instructions. For example, you can enter the first word of your DATA instruction as *data*, *DATA*, or *Data*, and the second word as *c:\\winword\\names.doc* or *C:\\WINWORD\\NAMES.DOC*. However, we'll generally use capital letters when we refer to the names of merge instructions and document files to distinguish them from the rest of the text.

Referring to a header document

Earlier, we mentioned how you can store your field headers in a separate document. When you have created and saved a header document, you'll need to add an additional argument to your DATA instruction to direct Word to the header document, like this:

{DATA *dataDocument headerDocument*}

For example, suppose you have stored the headers for a data document called CLIENTS.DOC in a document file named HEADERS1.DOC, and both document files are stored in the directory C:\WINWORD. To let Word know where your header text is stored, you would enter this DATA instruction:

{DATA "C:\\WINWORD\\CLIENTS.DOC"
"C:\\WINWORD\\HEADERS1.DOC"}

Keep in mind that the same header document can apply to any number of data documents. For this reason, you may find it convenient to store a set of headers in a separate document file when the information in your data documents must be updated frequently or when you have created several data documents that use the same headers. That way, you can be sure that all your data documents contain correct header information.

As we said earlier, the field headers at the top of your data document provide the link between your main document and the information stored in your data document. To plug in text from a specific field in your data document, simply press the [Insert field] key ([Ctrl][F9]) and type the appropriate field header. (Your Word documentation refers to field headers as *bookmark names*.) No other arguments are required for these instructions.

Bookmark instructions

You can refer to the same field as many times as you like in your main document, and you can enter your bookmark instructions in any order. As long as the bookmark names in your main document exactly match the field headers in the data document, Word will be able to extract the needed information from the appropriate field in each record.

As in the DATA instruction, Word does not consider case in your bookmark instructions. For example, we used the field header *FirstName* to identify our first name fields in the data document shown in Figure 15-1. If we use a bookmark instruction like *{firstname}* or *{Firstname}* in our main document, Word will locate the appropriate data when we merge the documents, even though the case in the bookmark instruction doesn't match the case in the field header.

Because you can't use spaces in your field headers, you might want to adopt the following convention. When you want to create a multiple-word field header, type the first letter of each word in uppercase, and the rest of the letters in lowercase. For example, in our data document, we used the field headers FirstName and LastName. We think you'll agree that this convention lets you create valid field headers and bookmark instructions that are easy to read.

By default, any merge text that Word pulls from the data document will appear in the character format defined by the document's *Normal* style. If you want to assign a special character format to the merge text, you must perform two simple steps. First, assign the desired format to the first letter—the letter that appears after the first { character—in the merge instruction. (If you want, you can assign this format to the entire instruction instead of just to its first letter.) Second, append to the instruction the arguments

Formatting your merge text

* charformat

These arguments tell Word to display the instruction's result in the same character format you've assigned to the first letter of the instruction. If you don't include these arguments in a formatted merge instruction, Word will display the instruction's result in the character format defined by the document's *Normal* style.

You may have noticed that we used this formatting technique in the merge instructions {FirstName *"charformat"} and {LastName *"charformat"} in the fifth line of Figure 15-3. As you can see, all the body text appears in the character format of this document's *Normal* style—12-point Tms Rmn. However, we've formatted our merge instructions to appear in 14-point Helv bold. Since we included the arguments *"charformat" in our formatted merge instructions, Word will format their results when it creates the merge documents.

In addition to character formatting, Word will format your merge documents using all the Document, Section, and Paragraph dialog box settings that you assign in your main document.

MERGING THE DOCUMENTS

Once you have created your data and main documents, you're ready to use the Print Merge... command to merge the two documents. Before you issue this command, however, you need to make sure that two conditions exist: you've activated the main document and you've set the current directory to the one containing the data document.

To change Word's current directory, select the Open... command from the File menu. When the Open dialog box appears, you'll see the name of the current directory near the center of the dialog box—just above the Directories list box. At this point, you should use the Directories list box to select the directory that contains your data document. Once you've done this, choose the Cancel button to return to the document. Although choosing Cancel isn't the standard technique to end a task such as this, it's the only way to complete this procedure without actually opening an existing document.

Once you've activated the main document and selected the directory containing the data document, you're ready to begin merging the documents. To begin the merge, select the Print Merge... command from the File menu. Word will then display a dialog box like the one in Figure 15-4.

Figure 15-4

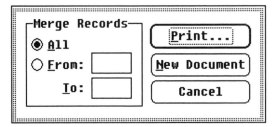

You'll see a dialog box like this one when you issue the Print Merge... command.

If you want to send your merge documents to the printer, just choose the Print... button. The From and To options in the Print Merge dialog box let you control which records you want to use in your merge documents. If you want to create merge documents for every record in your data document, leave the default All option selected. If you want to print only some of the records, enter the start and end ranges in the From and To text boxes. For example, if you want to merge the data from the fourth, fifth, and sixth records, type *4* in the From text box and *6* in the To text box.

When you select the Print... button, Word will present a Print dialog box exactly like the one you see when you issue the Print... command from the File menu. (See Chapter 7 for a complete description of the Print dialog box.)

Although a few of the options in the Print dialog box will not be active, the rest of the options will work just as they do when you print a standard Word document. Remember that the Pages options in the Print dialog box refer to the number of document pages you want to print, not the number of records; that setting is controlled in the Print Merge dialog box. If you specify a From and To value in the Print dialog box, Word will print the specified range of pages once for each record in your data document. In other words, if you have a four-page document, and you use From and To values of 2 and 3, Word will print pages 2 and 3 of the merge document for every record in your data document. (Of course, if you've instructed Word to merge only a subset of your records, then the page range will be printed once for each record you've selected.)

Similarly, the Copies option in the Print dialog box refers to the number of copies of each merge document you want to print, not the total number of documents you want to print. For example, if you use a Copies setting of 3, Word will print three copies of your merge document for each record in the data document. (Again, if you've chosen to merge only a subset of records from the data document, Word will print the specified number of copies for each record.)

Figures 15-5 and 15-6 on the next page show the first two merge documents that Word will create when you merge the NAMES.DOC data document with the HOROSCOP.DOC main document shown in Figures 15-1 and 15-3. As you can see, Word has printed the text of the main document, substituting the text from the FirstName, LastName, and Sign fields of the first and second records in the data document for each of the bookmark instructions in the main document.

After you choose OK in the Print dialog box, Word will create your merge documents and send them to the printer. If Word encounters any problem during the merge procedure, it will display a message box. Otherwise, your printer will create a merge document for each record you've entered in your data document.

Rather than routing your merge text directly to a printer, you can use the New Document button in the Print Merge dialog box to "print" your merge text to another Word document. When you do, Word will open a new Word document called Form Letters1. Like the documents that Word creates when you issue the New... command, each Form Letters document you create during a Word session will be numbered sequentially—Form Letters2, Form Letters3, and so forth.

Creating a merge document

Figure 15-5

To create this merge document, Word extracted information from the first record in our data document.

Figure 15-6

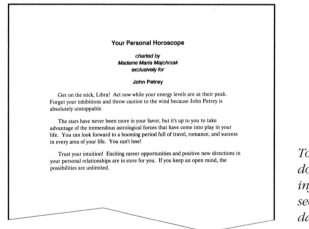

To create this merge document, Word used information from the second record in our data document.

Instead of creating a new file for each record in your data document, Word places all the merge text into a single Form Letters document. A section break will appear between the text for each record. For instance, if we were to select the New Document button as we merged the files in our example, Word would display the screen shown in Figure 15-7. As it creates this document, Word compiles the merge text for Mike Girard, then inserts a section-break marker and compiles the merge text for John Petrey. (By the way, you will not see the Print dialog box when you use the New Document option.)

Figure 15-7

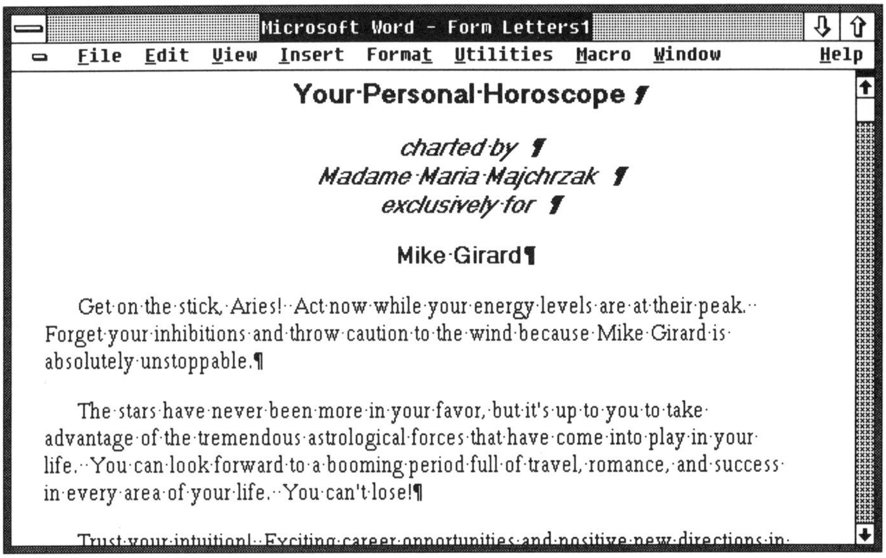

You can save your merge text in a document rather than print it.

You can save these Form Letters documents or use them as temporary documents to see the results of your merge instructions before you print. In order to get a better idea of how the printed merge documents will appear, you may want to use the Print Preview command, which we discussed in Chapter 7. If your data document contains several records, you may want to use the From and To options in the Print Merge dialog box to create a merge document for only a few records, then preview your merge documents. This spot-checking technique can save you a lot of time, frustration, and paper before you begin printing a series of merge documents.

If you decide to save your Form Letters document, you should remember that the file is static. That is, a Form Letters document is not linked in any way to your main document or data document. If you change the information in either document, you'll have to use another Print Merge... command to create a new, updated merge document.

Troubleshooting

Unfortunately, your merge documents won't always turn out perfectly the first time you print them. If you run into any problems during the merge procedure, Word will either display a message box on the screen, or it will display an error message in your merge documents. To minimize unexpected problems at merge time, try to avoid the following common pitfalls.

Failing to choose the appropriate directory

If Word displays the message box shown in Figure 15-8 during the merge procedure, you've probably failed to specify the appropriate directory in your DATA instruction. As we've said, Word will look only in the current directory for a data document if you don't provide a full path name. For this reason, you should follow the instructions we gave earlier for specifying the data document's name in your DATA instruction.

Figure 15-8

If Word presents this message box during a merge procedure, you probably failed to supply the full path name of your data document.

Misspelling instructions or bookmarks

When we showed you how to manually enter merge instructions into your main document earlier in this chapter, we mentioned that you must spell the names of your merge instructions correctly. If you misspell a merge instruction, Word will insert the message *Error! Bookmark not defined* in your merge documents. Whenever you see this message, you'll need to correct the spelling of the merge instruction that appears at the error message's location.

Forgetting to use the [Insert field] key

Another frequent mistake is the failure to use the [Insert field] key ([Ctrl][F9]) when entering your merge instructions. As you'll recall, you must press this key to enter a set of field characters ({}) into your document. Unfortunately, you'll often forget to use the [Insert field] key to enter the field characters and will type them manually instead. If you make this mistake, Word will not pull data from the data document and print it in place of the instruction. Instead, Word will print the merge instruction you've typed directly into each of the merge documents.

To solve this problem, return to the main document, delete the instruction and the field characters you typed in manually, and re-enter the instruction with either the [Insert field] key or the Field... command on the Insert menu.

SPECIAL INSTRUCTIONS

In addition to the DATA and bookmark instructions, Word offers special instructions that let you vary the contents of your merge documents. You can use these to insert text from other Word documents into your merge documents, to update selected information manually each time you issue the Print Merge... command, to create logical criteria, and to combine data from two or more records in the same merge document. Let's consider each of these instructions.

The INCLUDE instruction lets you extract text from another Word document file and insert it into your merge documents. This instruction takes a form similar to the DATA instruction that we discussed earlier:

{INCLUDE *filename*}

Filename is the full path name of the document file containing the text you want to insert. As we mentioned earlier, you must double the backslash character in the file's path name to distinguish it from a switch argument.

To use this instruction, simply type the INCLUDE instruction at the location you want the included text to appear. If any main document text appears after the INCLUDE instruction, Word will print that text immediately after the included text. If you want a page or section break to occur before the included text, just insert a manual page-break marker or section-break marker directly above the INCLUDE instruction. Similarly, if you want a page or section break to occur below the included text, you can insert one after the INCLUDE instruction.

As with the data document, any document files you want to include in your merge documents should be located on the same disk and in the same directory as your main document. Otherwise, Word will return as the result of the INCLUDE instruction the message *Error! Cannot open file.*

Suppose you want to include a "sun sign profile" after the text in our sample horoscope document. This additional text is located in a document file called PROFILE.DOC, shown in Figure 15-9 on the following page. To include the text from this document in the merge documents, type the instruction

{INCLUDE "C:\\WINWORD\\PROFILE.DOC"}

at the end of your main document text, as shown in Figure 15-10 on the next page. When you merge the main, data, and include documents, Word will create a series of merge documents like the one shown in Figure 15-11 on page 597.

Notice in Figure 15-9 that our PROFILE.DOC document also contains bookmark instructions to fill in the client's sign. Your INCLUDE instruction can contain any of the special instructions you use in your main document, except the DATA instruction. Word allows you to use only one DATA instruction in your main document, and it must be the first instruction in that document.

Once you've used the INCLUDE instruction to insert some text into your document, you can edit that text in any way you choose. Then, after you've made the change, you can use Word's UpdateSource macro to copy that change back to the include document. To run the UpdateSource macro, simply move the cursor anywhere within the modified result of the INCLUDE instruction, and press [Ctrl][Shift][F7]. Immediately, Word will copy your changes to the include document stored on disk.

Figure 15-9

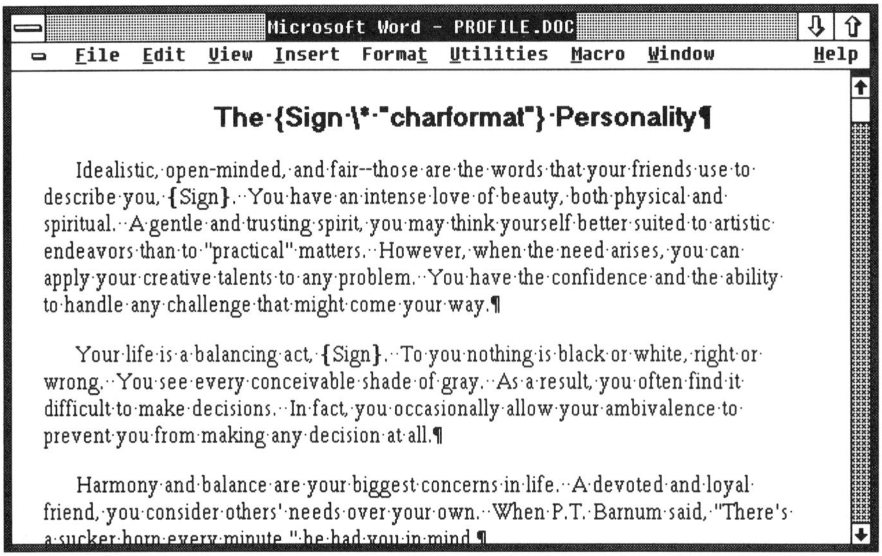

```
┌──────────────────────────────────────────────────────────────────┐
│ ▭          Microsoft Word - PROFILE.DOC                    ⇩  ⇧   │
│ ▭   File  Edit  View  Insert  Format  Utilities  Macro  Window  Help │
├──────────────────────────────────────────────────────────────────┤
│                                                                 ↑  │
│          The·{Sign·\*·"charformat"}·Personality¶                   │
│                                                                    │
│     Idealistic,·open-minded,·and·fair--those·are·the·words·that·your·friends·use·to· │
│  describe·you,·{Sign}.··You·have·an·intense·love·of·beauty,·both·physical·and· │
│  spiritual.··A·gentle·and·trusting·spirit,·you·may·think·yourself·better·suited·to·artistic· │
│  endeavors·than·to·"practical"·matters.··However,·when·the·need·arises,·you·can· │
│  apply·your·creative·talents·to·any·problem.··You·have·the·confidence·and·the·ability· │
│  to·handle·any·challenge·that·might·come·your·way.¶                 │
│                                                                    │
│     Your·life·is·a·balancing·act,·{Sign}.··To·you·nothing·is·black·or·white,·right·or· │
│  wrong.··You·see·every·conceivable·shade·of·gray.··As·a·result,·you·often·find·it· │
│  difficult·to·make·decisions.··In·fact,·you·occasionally·allow·your·ambivalence·to· │
│  prevent·you·from·making·any·decision·at·all.¶                      │
│                                                                    │
│     Harmony·and·balance·are·your·biggest·concerns·in·life.··A·devoted·and·loyal· │
│  friend,·you·consider·others'·needs·over·your·own.··When·P.T.·Barnum·said,·"There's· │
│  a·sucker·born·every·minute,"·he·had·you·in·mind.¶              ↓   │
└──────────────────────────────────────────────────────────────────┘
```

This document contains the sun sign profile text.

Figure 15-10

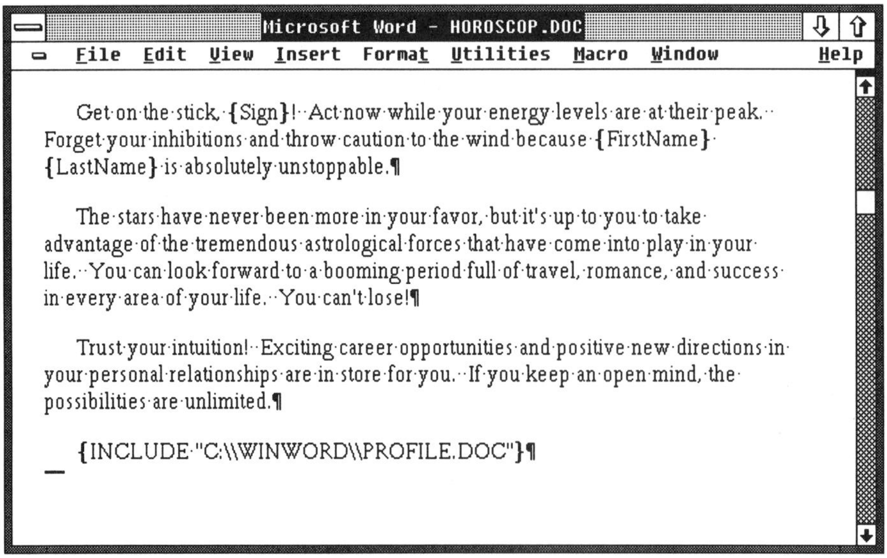

```
┌──────────────────────────────────────────────────────────────────┐
│ ▭          Microsoft Word - HOROSCOP.DOC                   ⇩  ⇧   │
│ ▭   File  Edit  View  Insert  Format  Utilities  Macro  Window  Help │
├──────────────────────────────────────────────────────────────────┤
│                                                                 ↑  │
│     Get·on·the·stick,·{Sign}!··Act·now·while·your·energy·levels·are·at·their·peak.·· │
│  Forget·your·inhibitions·and·throw·caution·to·the·wind·because·{FirstName}· │
│  {LastName}·is·absolutely·unstoppable.¶                            │
│                                                                    │
│     The·stars·have·never·been·more·in·your·favor,·but·it's·up·to·you·to·take· │
│  advantage·of·the·tremendous·astrological·forces·that·have·come·into·play·in·your· │
│  life.··You·can·look·forward·to·a·booming·period·full·of·travel,·romance,·and·success· │
│  in·every·area·of·your·life.··You·can't·lose!¶                      │
│                                                                    │
│     Trust·your·intuition!··Exciting·career·opportunities·and·positive·new·directions·in· │
│  your·personal·relationships·are·in·store·for·you.··If·you·keep·an·open·mind,·the· │
│  possibilities·are·unlimited.¶                                     │
│                                                                    │
│ —   {INCLUDE·"C:\\WINWORD\\PROFILE.DOC"}¶                          │
│                                                                 ↓  │
└──────────────────────────────────────────────────────────────────┘
```

Type the INCLUDE instruction where you want the additional text to appear.

Figure 15-11

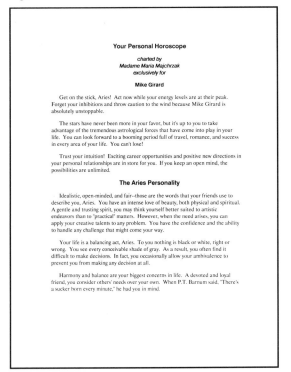

When you issue the Print Merge... command, Word will combine the text from all three documents.

There are a couple of reasons you would want to use the INCLUDE instruction to place additional text into your merge documents rather than simply entering that text into the main document. First, you can refer to the same include document file in any number of main documents, thus saving yourself the time, effort, and disk space required to enter the included text in several files.

In addition, as you'll see in a few pages, you can set up criteria that instruct Word to extract data from different include document files, depending on the results of certain conditional tests.

If you need to vary only a few words from one document to the next, you'll probably find it more efficient to use the SET instruction rather than the INCLUDE instruction to extract your variable text from a separate file. The SET instruction lets you manually change the contents of selected bookmarks in your merge documents each time you create a new set of merge documents.

The SET instruction takes the form:

{SET *bookmarkName text*}

The SET instruction

You use the *bookmarkName* argument to define the name of the bookmark you want to vary each time you create a new set of merge documents. Then, enter that name into the desired locations in your main document text in order to flag the areas you want Word to insert your text. You must use the [Insert field] key to enter the merge instructions. If you simply type the field characters instead of using the [Insert field] key, Word will not recognize the instruction.

The *bookmarkName* argument for your SET instruction should be different from the field headers that appear in your data document's field header paragraph. Like the field headers in your data document, your SET instruction bookmark names must be entered into your main document at each place you want to vary some text. However, instead of extracting text from the data document, when Word encounters a bookmark name in a SET instruction, it will use text you have provided in the instruction's *text* argument. If you use a bookmark name in your SET instruction that matches one of the field headers in your data document, Word will use the text you've assigned to the bookmark name with the SET instruction instead of pulling the appropriate field entry from the data document.

An example

Let's look at an example of how you can put the SET instruction to work. At the beginning of this chapter, we mentioned that you might want to use the Print Merge facility to create a series of personalized invitations to your company's grand opening. Suppose your grand opening party is going to be so extravagant that you must spread it over three days in order to accommodate all your guests.

In order to create three sets of form letters that carry different invitation dates, insert into your main document a SET instruction with a *bookmarkName* argument called *OpenDate*, like this:

{SET "OpenDate" "July 18"}

Then, to vary the definition of the OpenDate field, edit this SET instruction each time you issue the Print Merge... command so that it specifies a different date.

For example, Figure 15-12 shows an invitation letter in which this SET instruction appears immediately after the DATA instruction. After entering the SET instruction to define the OpenDate field, we typed the instruction *{OpenDate}* in the first and fourth lines of the letter's body text.

To divide our invitations into three groups (with a different invitation date for each), we issued three separate Print Merge... commands. Using the From and To options in the Print Merge dialog box, we specified a different subset of records for each merge procedure. For example, suppose our data document contains 300 records. We can use From and To arguments of 1 and 100 to print the first batch of invitations, 101 and 200 to print the second batch, and 201 and 300 to print the last batch.

To vary the invitation date from one group of letters to the next, we could simply change the text in the SET instruction before issuing the Print Merge...

command. In the second batch, for example, our SET instruction would read *{SET "OpenDate" "July 19"}*, while the SET instruction in the third batch would read *{SET "OpenDate" "July 20"}*.

Figure 15-12

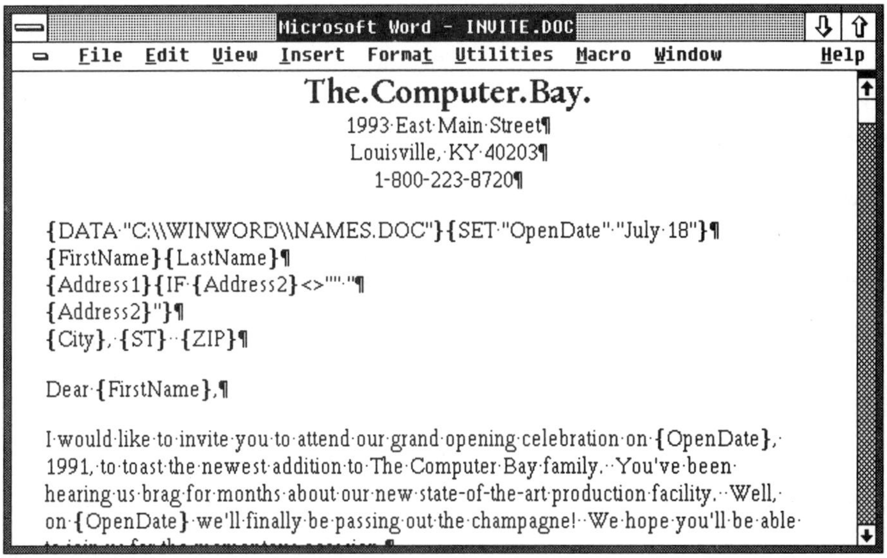

We used the SET instruction to vary our invitation dates in this form letter.

The ASK instruction

The ASK instruction is similar to the SET instruction except it tells Word to prompt you for the text you want to assign to a particular bookmark name. You can use ASK instructions only within the body of your document—not in headers, footers, footnotes, annotations, or macros.

The basic form of the ASK instruction is:

{ASK bookmarkName prompt}

As with the SET instruction, the *bookmarkName* argument defines a bookmark or placeholder that will appear in the main document. Again, this bookmark name cannot be the same as one of the headers in the field header paragraph of the data document.

The *prompt* argument in the last part of the ASK instruction tells Word to present an ASK dialog box that asks you to define the entry you want to assign to the specified bookmark name. This dialog box will appear before Word prints each merge document.

For example, suppose you decide to create a personalized greeting for each guest you plan to invite to your grand opening. To do this, you might set up a form letter like the one shown in Figure 15-13. The ASK instruction in the letter's salutation

{ASK "Greeting" "Enter a greeting"}

will cause Word to prompt you for a greeting before it prints each letter. When you type a greeting in the dialog box's text box and choose OK, Word will assign to the name *Greeting* the text you enter.

Figure 15-13

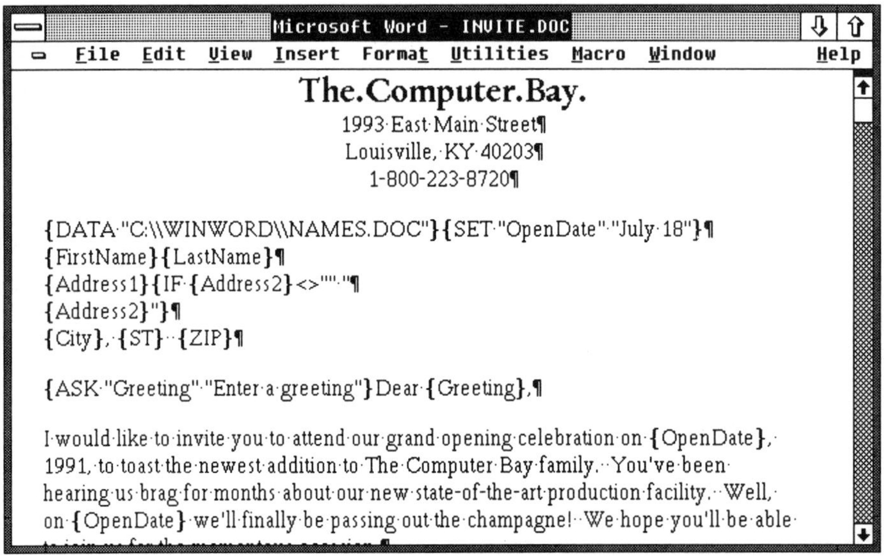

```
 ═                      Microsoft Word - INVITE.DOC                        ⇩ ⇧
 ▫    File   Edit   View   Insert   Format   Utilities   Macro   Window      Help
                        The.Computer.Bay.                                    ▲
                          1993·East·Main·Street¶
                          Louisville,·KY·40203¶
                            1-800-223-8720¶

 {DATA·"C:\\WINWORD\\NAMES.DOC"}{SET·"OpenDate"·"July·18"}¶
 {FirstName}{LastName}¶
 {Address1}{IF·{Address2}<>""·"¶
 {Address2}"}¶
 {City},·{ST}···{ZIP}¶

 {ASK·"Greeting"·"Enter·a·greeting"}·Dear·{Greeting},¶

 I·would·like·to·invite·you·to·attend·our·grand·opening·celebration·on·{OpenDate},·
 1991,·to·toast·the·newest·addition·to·The·Computer·Bay·family.··You've·been·
 hearing·us·brag·for·months·about·our·new·state-of-the-art·production·facility.··Well,·
 on·{OpenDate}·we'll·finally·be·passing·out·the·champagne!··We·hope·you'll·be·able·      ▼
```

You can use the ASK instruction to vary a field entry for each merge document.

Of course, once you've assigned some text to the bookmark name *Greeting*, you can use the instruction {Greeting} to place that text in the document. You'll notice that we've entered *Dear {Greeting}* in the letter's salutation to take advantage of the information we've gathered.

Nesting bookmark instructions

Unfortunately, as you respond to each ASK prompt, you may not be able to tell which record is being processed. Here's an easy way to get around that problem: Nest one or more bookmark instructions in your ASK instruction to identify which record is currently being processed. For example, rather than using the instruction

{ASK "Greeting" "Enter a greeting"}

you could use an instruction like

{ASK "Greeting" "How do you want to greet {FirstName} {LastName}?"}

When you issue the Print Merge… command, Word will present a dialog box like the one in Figure 15-14 as it creates the merge text for each record in your data document.

Figure 15-14

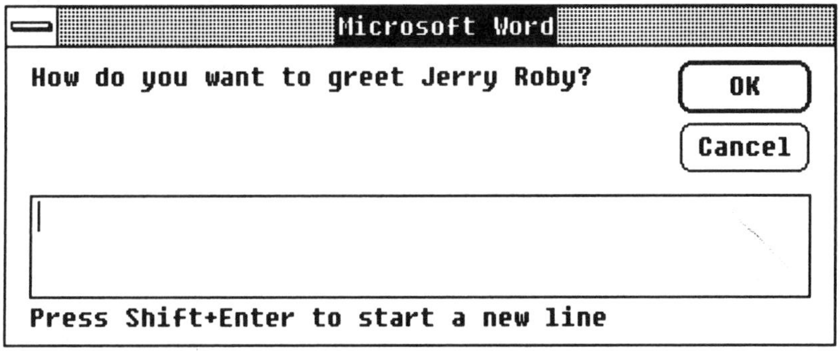

You can embed bookmark instructions in your ASK instructions to keep track of which record is being processed.

Whenever you use the ASK instruction to bring up an ASK dialog box, the entry that you last typed into an ASK dialog box will appear as the default. If you want to specify a different default, use a \d switch in the ASK instruction. An ASK instruction with a \d switch takes the form:

{ASK *bookmarkName prompt* \d *defaultText*}

For example, if you want the ASK instruction to prompt you for a greeting for your main document, and you want *Friend* to appear as the default entry each time the ASK instruction prompts you for the greeting, you can use the instruction

{ASK "Greeting" "Enter a greeting" \d "Friend"}

Specifying the ASK default

Although you need to surround the *defaultText* argument with quotation marks only when it's more than one word, we suggest that you get into the habit of using quotation marks all the time.

Asking only before printing the first merge document

As you know, the ASK instruction prompts for information before Word prints each merge document. However, you can tell the ASK instruction to prompt for information only once—just before Word prints the first document. To do this, simply append the \o switch to the ASK instruction, like this:

{ASK *bookmarkName prompt* \o}

If you want to use the \o and \d switches in a single ASK instruction, it doesn't matter which switch you specify first.

The IF instruction

In many instances, you'll want to create variations in your merge documents that can't be handled with a simple ASK or SET instruction. For example, you may need to insert into your merge documents special text that is dependent upon the information in one of the entries in your data document. Word's IF instruction lets you handle these situations by setting up conditional tests in your main document.

The form of the IF instruction is:

{IF *conditionalTest trueResult falseResult*}

The first argument of the IF instruction, *conditionalTest*, is an expression that is either true or false. If *conditionalTest* is true, then the instruction will return *trueResult*. If *conditionalTest* is false, the instruction will return *falseResult*.

The *conditionalTest* argument always uses one of the six conditional operators listed in Table 15-2. You can use all of these operators with both text and numeric entries. When an entry contains text, Word will use the ANSI value of that text to perform the conditional test. For example, all of the following expressions are conditional tests:

> {MStatus}="Single"
> {NumItems}>100
> {Spouse}<>""

Any expression that uses one of the conditional operators to make a comparison is either true or false. For example, consider the conditional test *{NumItems}>100*. If the NumItems field of the current record contains a value that is less than 100, this test will be false. If the NumItems field contains the value 100, this test also will be false. If the NumItems field contains a value greater than 100, however, this test will be true.

Table 15-2

Operator	Definition
>	Greater than
<	Less than
=	Equal to
>=	Greater than or equal to
<=	Less than or equal to
<>	Not equal to

The text you enter in the *trueResult* and *falseResult* arguments of your IF instructions can be any length and can contain page-break markers and section-break markers. You can even include special instructions, such as the SET, ASK, and INCLUDE instructions, within the *trueResult* and *falseResult* arguments. If either the *trueResult* or *falseResult* argument consists of only a single word or a single merge instruction, you don't need to surround the argument with quotation marks. In most cases, however, you'll want to use multiple-word arguments, so we recommend that you get into the habit of always surrounding these arguments with quotation marks.

Fortunately, you can use the IF instruction anywhere in your document, including the header, footer, and footnotes. To update all the IF instructions, move the cursor to one of them and press the [Update field] key ([F9]) or use the Print Merge... command to perform a merge procedure.

Now that we've covered the basics of the IF instruction, let's look at a few of its most common uses.

You'll often want to use the *conditionalTest* argument to determine whether a particular field in the current record contains an entry. For example, suppose your data document stores names in three separate fields: FirstName, MI, and LastName. If you want to include a person's full name in your main document, you might use the merge instructions:

{FirstName} {IF {MI}<>"" "{MI} "}{LastName}

Testing for
field entries

Notice that the conditional test *{MI}<>""* tests for the presence of an entry in the MI field of the data document. If there is an entry in the MI field, then the conditional test is true, and the IF instruction will print the text that appears in the *trueResult* argument *{MI}*. If the MI field is empty (that is, if you have inserted an extra comma or tab to skip that field in the data document), then the test is false, and the IF instruction will print the text that appears in the *falseResult* argument. (Since we did not specify a *falseResult*, Word will not print a middle initial in the merge document.)

Printing optional sentences and paragraphs

Let's look at another way to employ the IF instruction in the sample invitation letter shown in Figure 15-13. Suppose you want to include a note extending the invitation to your clients' spouses. In your data document, you have included a field that contains the name of each client's spouse—if he or she is married. For those who are single, this field is blank.

To test for the presence of an entry in the Spouse field of your data document and then print the appropriate text, you can use the IF instruction

{IF {Spouse}<>"" "Of course, we'd also be thrilled if {Spouse} would like to accompany you to our celebration as well! The more, the merrier!"}

as we've done in in Figure 15-15. If the Spouse field contains an entry, Word will print the text *Of course, we'd also be thrilled if {Spouse} would like to accompany you to our celebration as well! The more, the merrier!* (In printing this text, Word will substitute the name from the Spouse field for the {Spouse} instruction.) If the Spouse field is empty, however, Word will omit this paragraph.

Figure 15-15

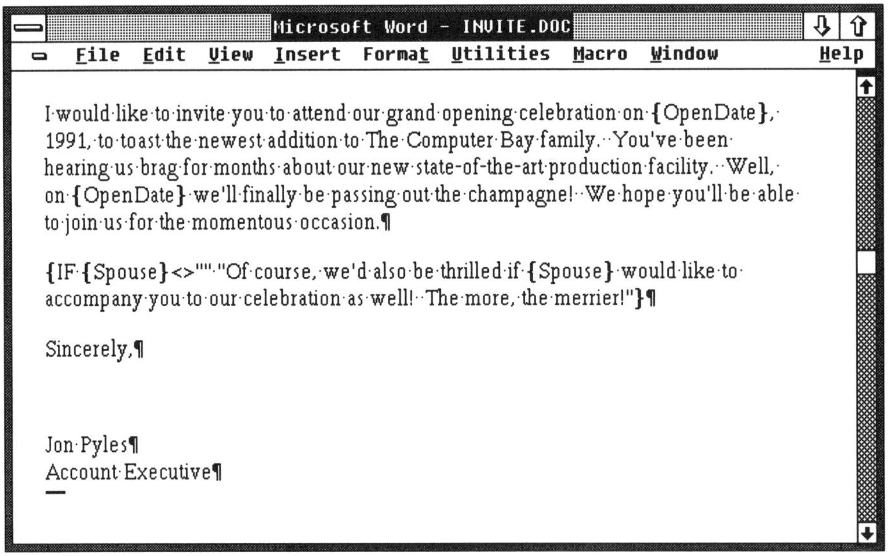

```
┌─────────────────────────────────────────────────────────────────────┐
│ ▭         Microsoft Word - INVITE.DOC                        ⇩ ⇧     │
│ ▭   File  Edit  View  Insert  Format  Utilities  Macro  Window  Help │
├─────────────────────────────────────────────────────────────────────┤
│ I·would·like·to·invite·you·to·attend·our·grand·opening·celebration·on·{OpenDate},· │
│ 1991,·to·toast·the·newest·addition·to·The·Computer·Bay·family.··You've·been· │
│ hearing·us·brag·for·months·about·our·new·state-of-the-art·production·facility.··Well,· │
│ on·{OpenDate}·we'll·finally·be·passing·out·the·champagne!··We·hope·you'll·be·able· │
│ to·join·us·for·the·momentous·occasion.¶ │
│                                                                       │
│ {IF·{Spouse}<>""··"Of·course,·we'd·also·be·thrilled·if·{Spouse}·would·like·to· │
│ accompany·you·to·our·celebration·as·well!··The·more,·the·merrier!"}¶ │
│                                                                       │
│ Sincerely,¶ │
│                                                                       │
│                                                                       │
│ Jon·Pyles¶ │
│ Account·Executive¶ │
│ ── │
└─────────────────────────────────────────────────────────────────────┘
```

This conditional text will appear only if there is an entry in the Spouse field.

Comparing text and numbers

Rather than simply testing for the presence of an entry in a field, you can use the IF instruction to compare the contents of a field to a string or value that you specify. Word lets you compare text entries as well as numeric values with this form of the IF instruction:

{IF {*bookmarkName*}=*comparisonText trueResult falseResult*}

Remember to enclose the last three arguments in the IF instruction—
comparisonText, trueResult, and *falseResult*—in quotation marks, or you won't get
the results you expect.

Returning to our sample horoscope document, suppose you want to include
a birthday greeting to those persons on the mailing list whose birthdays are
approaching. Let's assume that you will be mailing these letters in mid-September,
so the Libras are the next group of clients with birthdays on their astral horizons.
You could include a birthday greeting for clients with the Sign field entry *Libra*
by entering the IF instruction

{IF {Sign}="Libra" "Happy Birthday!"}

As you can see, Word checks to see if the entry in the Sign field of the data
document is *Libra.* If so, Word will insert the text *Happy Birthday!;* if not, Word
will not insert this special greeting.

Let's consider an example that demonstrates how Word handles numeric
expressions in the IF instruction's *comparisonText* argument. Suppose you've
compiled a listing of your clients in a data document named CLIENTS.DOC, and
you want to send a series of billing notices. Let's assume that the CLIENTS.DOC
data document includes an OD field listing the number of days that each payment
is past due.

If you want to issue a particularly strong message to those people whose
payments are more than 15 days late, you could use the IF instruction

{IF {OD}>"15" "Your bill is seriously past due!"}

This instruction checks to see whether the value in the OD field is greater than
15. If the logical test *{OD}>"15"* is true, Word will include the sentence *Your bill
is seriously past due!* in the billing notice for that client. If the payment is 15 days
overdue or less, this sentence will not appear in the merge document.

Word also allows you to create IF instructions that compare the contents of
one field to another within a single record. The form of this instruction is

{IF {*bookmarkName1*}={*bookmarkName2*} *trueResult falseResult*}

So far, all of our conditional tests have instructed Word to enter a text block
into our merge document when a given condition is true. As we've said, however,
there may be times when you want to print alternative text in your merge
document when a condition is false. Word's *falseResult* argument provides you
with the ability to accomplish this task.

Returning to the sample invitation letter shown in Figure 15-15, suppose you
want to add an alternative line of text for your unmarried clients (those with no

**Taking advantage
of *falseResult***

entry in the Spouse field), inviting them to bring a guest. You could accomplish this by changing your IF instruction to

> {IF {Spouse}<>"" "Of course, we'd also be thrilled if {Spouse} would like to accompany you to our celebration as well! The more, the merrier!" "Please feel free to invite a guest to help us celebrate this momentous occasion!"}

as we've done in Figure 15-16.

Figure 15-16

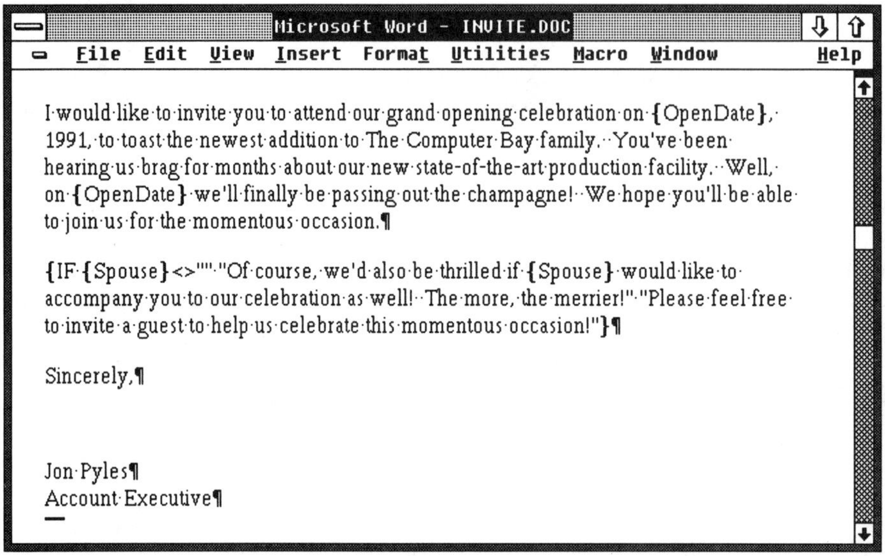

We used the falseResult *argument to add alternative text for single clients.*

As you can see, to create the alternative text, you simply add the argument *Please feel free to invite a guest to help us celebrate this momentous occasion!* to your IF instruction.

Using IF to control blank lines

In the sample letter in Figure 15-13, you may have noticed that we used the conditional instruction

> {IF {Address2}<>"" "¶
> {Address2}"}

to create the second line of our address block. In the sample data document shown in Figure 15-1, only some of the records contain entries in the Address2 field. The others simply contain extra tab marks as placeholders for this field.

To avoid printing a blank line in the address block whenever the Address2 field is empty, we used the {Address2} instruction in our conditional test. As you can see, we chose to place the ¶ mark inside the *trueResult* argument to ensure that no extra blank line occurs at this point when the Address2 field is empty. To enter the ¶ mark, just press the [Enter] key. (You won't see the ¶ mark unless you've selected the Paragraph Marks check box in the Preferences dialog box.)

Of course, when you press the [Enter] key to enter the ¶ mark into the *trueResult* argument, Word will move the cursor to the next line, just as it always does when you press [Enter]. Don't let this visual problem trouble you—continue typing the merge instruction on the next line just as you would if you were entering the entire instruction on a single line.

Nesting IF instructions

You've already seen several examples of nested instructions as we've created our sample merge documents throughout this chapter. For instance, we showed how you could nest a bookmark instruction within an ASK instruction and within an IF instruction. As you might have guessed, you can also nest two or more IF instructions in your main document to test for a number of possible conditions. In fact, by stringing together a group of IF instructions, you can create a fairly sophisticated series of conditional tests.

Depending on the form you use in combining your IF instructions, you can direct Word to print your conditional text only if all the IF instructions are true or if any one of the IF instructions is true. In other words, like many spreadsheet and database programs, Word allows you to create "logical AND" combinations and "logical OR" combinations. When all the IF instructions must be true in order for Word to print the conditional text, you might think of your IF instructions as being tied together with logical ANDs. On the other hand, if only one of the IF instructions must be true before Word prints the conditional text, you might think of the IF instructions as being combined with logical ORs.

Logical AND combinations

To combine IF instructions with a logical AND, you can string the instructions together like this:

{IF {*bookmarkName1*}=*comparisonText* {IF
    {*bookmarkName2*}=*comparisonText conditionalText*}}

For example, if you want to print the text *Congratulations, you've passed!* only when the TestAvg field is greater than 70 and when the Absences field is less than 10, you could use the following instruction:

{IF {TestAvg}>"70" {IF {Absences}<"10" "Congratulations, you've passed!"}}

Notice that Word will print the congratulatory note only when both the TestAvg and Absences fields meet their stated criteria.

Logical OR combinations

As we've mentioned, in a logical OR combination, only one IF instruction must be true in order for Word to print the conditional text. When you set up a logical OR combination, you must type the conditional text once for each IF instruction:

{IF {*bookmarkName1*}=*comparisonText   conditionalText* {IF
     {*bookmarkName2*}=*comparisonText conditionalText*}}

You can use either the same field name or different field names in each IF instruction. Unlike a logical AND combination, however, you can vary the conditional text for each IF instruction. For example, in the sample document shown in Figure 15-10, we showed how you could create an INCLUDE instruction to extract text from a file named PROFILE.DOC. Suppose you decide to create 12 separate profile documents—one for each astrological sign. We have named these documents Aries, Taurus, Gemini, and so forth. To select the appropriate profile for each client, you could string together a series of 12 IF instructions, like this:

{IF {Sign}="Aries" {INCLUDE Aries} {IF {Sign}="Taurus" {INCLUDE Taurus}
    {IF {Sign}="Gemini" {INCLUDE Gemini} {IF {Sign}="Cancer" {INCLUDE
    Cancer} {IF {Sign}="Leo" {INCLUDE Leo} {IF {Sign}="Virgo" {INCLUDE
    Virgo} {IF {Sign}="Libra" {INCLUDE Libra} {IF {Sign}="Scorpio" {IN-
    CLUDE Scorpio} {IF {Sign}="Sagittarius" {INCLUDE Sagittarius} {IF
    {Sign}="Capricorn" {INCLUDE Capricorn} {IF {Sign}="Aquarius" {IN-
    CLUDE Aquarius} {IF {Sign}="Pisces" {INCLUDE Pisces}}}}}}}}}}}}

Notice that the conditional text for each IF instruction is an INCLUDE instruction that directs Word to the appropriate profile document.

The NEXT instruction

As we have already explained, when you use the Print Merge… command to create a new Form Letters document, Word will insert a section-break marker between the end of the merge text for one record and the beginning of the merge text for the next record. Similarly, when you print your merge documents, Word again will insert a section break between the merge text for different records. Consequently, if the default Section Start setting in the Section dialog box is New Page, Word will automatically start on a new page each time it begins printing the text for a new record.

If you want to omit these page and section breaks, you can insert a series of NEXT instructions in your main document. The NEXT instruction tells Word to use the next record of the data document to fill the remaining bookmark instructions in the main document—without starting a new document or inserting a section break.

The NEXT instruction accepts no arguments and returns no result of its own. You insert it in front of other merge instructions to tell Word to extract information from the next record in your data document.

For example, suppose you want to create a list of your clients' names, with ten names printed on a page. If you created a main document with the simple instructions

{FirstName} {LastName}

Word would print only one client name on each page. In order to print ten names on a page, you must set up your main document so that it repeats these instructions ten times. After the first *{FirstName} {LastName}* sequence, you should include a NEXT instruction in front of the following *{FirstName} {LastName}* sequences, like this:

{NEXT}{FirstName} {LastName}

Each time Word encounters a NEXT instruction, it will extract the first and last name information from another record in the data document and merge it into the main document where the next *{FirstName} {LastName}* sequence appears.

The NEXTIF instruction is a combination of Word's NEXT and IF instructions. Instead of using both a NEXT and an IF instruction together like this:

The NEXTIF instruction

{IF *conditionalTest* "{NEXT}"}

you can use a NEXTIF instruction like this:

{NEXTIF *conditionalTest*}

The NEXTIF instruction does either of two things based on the result of the conditional test. If *conditionalTest* is false, the NEXTIF instruction will have no effect on the document whatsoever. If *conditionalTest* is true, however, the NEXTIF instruction will issue a NEXT instruction. As we explained earlier, the NEXT instruction tells Word to use the next record of the data document to fill the remaining bookmark instructions in the main document.

Like the NEXTIF instruction, SKIPIF is a variation of the basic IF instruction. The form of this instruction is:

The SKIPIF instruction

{SKIPIF *conditionalTest*}

The result of the SKIPIF instruction depends on the result of the conditional test. If *conditionalTest* is false, then the SKIPIF instruction has absolutely no effect on the merge document. If *conditionalTest* is true, however, SKIPIF tells Word to do two things: cancel the current page of the merge document and start a new page of the merge document that fills bookmark instructions with data from the next record of the data document.

Here's a situation in which you might want to use the SKIPIF instruction. Imagine you're running a little low on cash, and you decide it's time to send a persuasive letter to everyone who owes you money. In your data document, you've set up a field called Balance that shows the amount of money each person in your data document owes. Of course, the people to whom you owe money will show a negative balance in their Balance fields.

Figure 15-17 shows the kind of document you want to create. As you can see, the instruction

{SKIPIF {Balance}<="0"}

appears just after the DATA instruction. The SKIPIF instruction tells Word to check the value of the Balance entry in the current record. If the current Balance entry is less than or equal to zero, the conditional test will be true. SKIPIF will tell Word not to print a letter for the current record, and to restart the merging process with the next record in the data document. On the other hand, if the current Balance entry is greater than zero, the conditional test will be false, and Word will continue merging the data from the current record into the main document. When Word completes the merge procedure, it will have printed a letter for everyone in the data document with an outstanding positive balance.

Figure 15-17

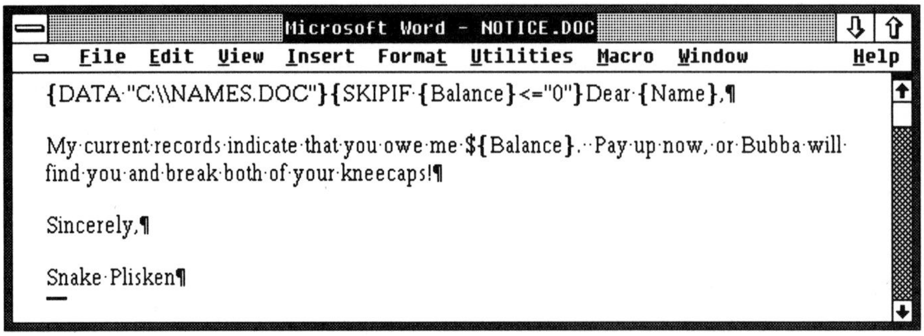

```
═══════════════ Microsoft Word - NOTICE.DOC ═══════════════  ⬇ ⬆
 ▭   File  Edit  View  Insert  Format  Utilities  Macro  Window      Help
   {DATA·"C:\\NAMES.DOC"}{SKIPIF·{Balance}<="0"}Dear·{Name},¶       ⬆

   My·current·records·indicate·that·you·owe·me·${Balance}.··Pay·up·now,·or·Bubba·will·
   find·you·and·break·both·of·your·kneecaps!¶

   Sincerely,¶

   Snake·Plisken¶
   —                                                                 ⬇
```

This document uses the SKIPIF instruction to print letters only for people who owe money.

The MERGEREC instruction allows you to enter the number of the current print merge record. The form of this instruction is simply *{MERGEREC}*—the instruction accepts no arguments.

When Word encounters the MERGEREC instruction during a merge procedure, it will draw the number of the current record from the data document and place it in the merge document. Word will assign the number *1* to the first record in the data document (not the header paragraph), the number *2* to the second record, and so forth.

As you know by now, the current record in the data document changes whenever Word encounters the NEXT instruction. The NEXTIF and SKIPIF instructions will also increase the current record number when their *conditionalTest* arguments are true.

You'll seldom want to use the MERGEREC instruction for typical merging tasks. In fact, since MERGEREC tells Word to print the current record number in the text of your document, you'll probably use it mostly as a debugging tool when you are creating your main documents.

Our discussion of merging would be incomplete without covering the topic of mailing labels (which are sometimes called *address labels* in Word's documentation). You might use Word's print merge capabilities to create mailing labels as often as you use them to do any other kind of merging. In this section, we'll cover the basics of creating mailing labels in Word.

The most difficult part of creating mailing labels with any word processor is formatting the text to fit within the label boundaries. Fortunately, Word takes this troubling step out of your way by providing a group of document templates that are formatted to print to the most commonly used sheets of labels. To print mailing labels with Word, you simply need to create a data document containing the names and addresses, open a new main document using the appropriate document template, and then issue the Print Merge… command. Let's examine each of these steps.

In order to use Word's preformatted label templates, you need to create a data document that conforms to the following rules. First of all, the first paragraph in the data document must contain the field headers

    name ➜ street ➜ city ➜ state ➜ zip

where ➜ represents a tab mark. Once you've entered the field headers, enter the names and addresses into the appropriate fields of the data document. Figure 15-18 shows the sample data document we'll use to create some mailing labels.

Figure 15-18

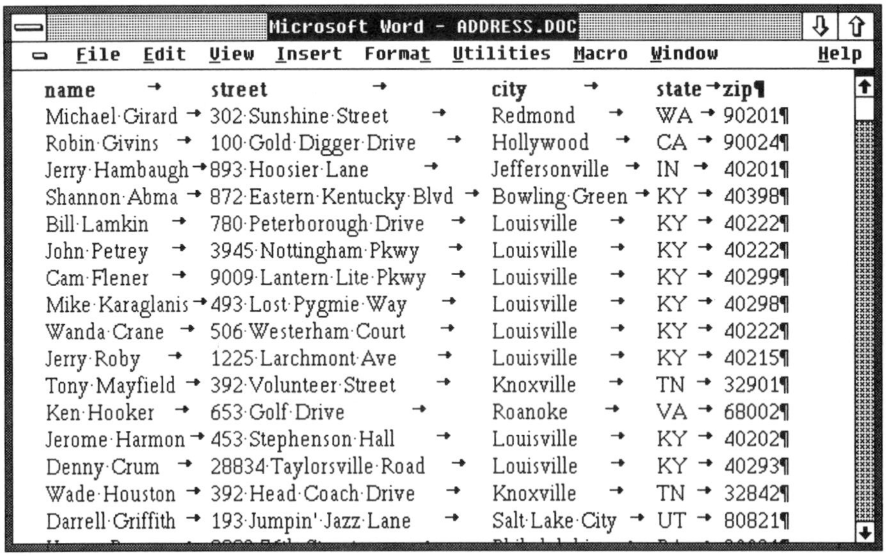

The field entries in your data document must appear in the order shown here if you want to use Word's built-in label templates.

If any of the field entries in your data document contain commas, remember to enclose those entries in quotation marks. For example, if you need to enter the street address *940 Bunsen Pkwy, Suite 300*, you must enclose that entire entry in quotation marks.

Once you've set up your data document, save it under the name ADDRESS.DOC. To do this, select the Save As… command from the File menu, type *ADDRESS* into the Save File Name text box, and choose OK.

Opening the main document

Once you've created your data document, you need to open a new main document that uses one of Word's built-in label templates. As we'll explain in Chapter 18, a template is essentially a pattern for a new document. Whenever you create a new document that is based on one of Word's built-in label templates, the new document will not be empty when it first appears. Instead, it will contain a collection of formatted merge instructions designed to print mailing labels.

To create a new main document for printing mailing labels, select the New… command from the File menu to bring up the dialog box shown in Figure 15-19. At this point, choose from the Use Template list box the name of the template that matches the kind of label sheets you're using. Table 15-3 lists the five available label templates and provides a brief description of each.

Figure 15-19

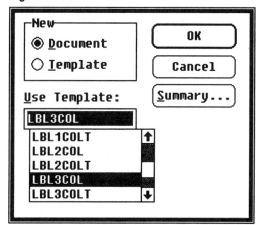

When the New dialog box appears, select the name of the appropriate label template from the Use Template list box.

Table 15-3

Template	Type of feed	Layout
LBL2COL	Sheet	2 columns of 1-inch-tall labels
LBL3COL	Sheet	3 columns of 1-inch-tall labels
LBL1COLT	Continuous	1 column of 1-inch-tall labels
LBL2COLT	Continuous	2 columns of 1-inch-tall labels
LBL3COLT	Continuous	3 columns of 1-inch-tall labels

After you select the appropriate template from the Use Template list box, choose OK to create a new document based on that template. Figure 15-20 on the next page shows a new document based on the template LBL3COL.

All documents based on one of Word's label templates contain a single table that fills the entire page. The table has as many rows as there are labels down each page, and contains as many columns as there are labels across each page. Additionally, each row of the table is an inch tall to match the size of the labels. (In other words, the table's Minimum Row Height setting in the Format Table dialog box is 1".)

Word's label template also sets up the document's margins to match those of the sheet containing the labels. As a result, you shouldn't have to bother trying to make the printed text line up properly with the labels. As long as you specify the correct template when you create the main document, the printed text should appear in the correct position.

Figure 15-20

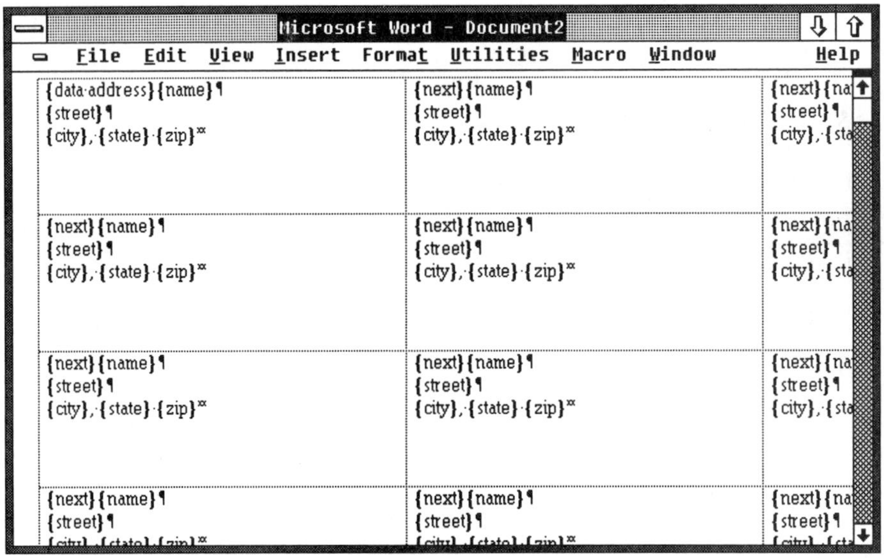

This main document is based on the template LBL3COL.

If you're using a dot-matrix printer, you'll need to make an additional adjustment before you can print your labels. Simply use the Printer Setup... command to access your printer settings box, then activate the No Page Break option (if one exists).

Printing the labels

After you've created both your data document containing the names and addresses, and a main document based on one of Word's label templates, you're ready to print the labels. To do this, activate your main document and select the Print Merge... command from the File menu. When the Print Merge dialog box appears, follow the steps we've explained to complete the merge procedure. Figure 15-21 shows a sample page of labels we printed using the data document in Figure 15-18 and the main document in Figure 15-20.

By the way, if a name or address is too long to fit on a single line of a label, Word will wrap the text to the next line of that same label. This will not only decrease the readability of that label, it will also disrupt the line spacing for all the labels that follow. Consequently, you should make sure that you keep your names and addresses short enough (or make sure the point size in which they appear is small enough) to prevent them from wrapping.

Customizing the main document

If you are like most Word users, you'll seldom have trouble using Word's label templates. In some cases, however, you may create a main document based on one of Word's label templates that doesn't quite get the job done. For instance, you might need to include an additional piece of data on each label. Or, if you're printing to an odd-size sheet of labels, your names and addresses may fall outside the label boundaries. In these situations, you'll need to customize your main document. Let's briefly take a look at the techniques you can use.

Figure 15-21

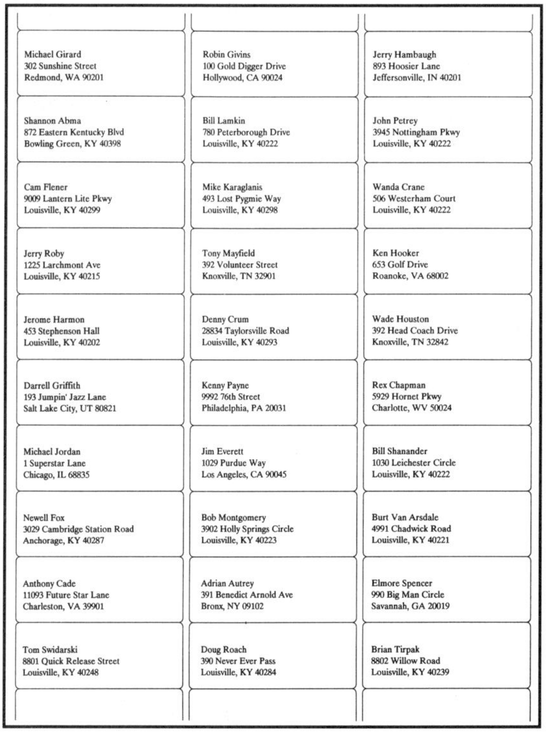

Michael Girard 302 Sunshine Street Redmond, WA 90201	Robin Givins 100 Gold Digger Drive Hollywood, CA 90024	Jerry Hambaugh 893 Hoosier Lane Jeffersonville, IN 40201
Shannon Abma 872 Eastern Kentucky Blvd Bowling Green, KY 40398	Bill Lamkin 780 Peterborough Drive Louisville, KY 40222	John Petrey 3945 Nottingham Pkwy Louisville, KY 40222
Cam Flener 9009 Lantern Lite Pkwy Louisville, KY 40299	Mike Karaglanis 493 Lost Pygmie Way Louisville, KY 40298	Wanda Crane 506 Westerham Court Louisville, KY 40222
Jerry Roby 1225 Larchmont Ave Louisville, KY 40215	Tony Mayfield 392 Volunteer Street Knoxville, TN 32901	Ken Hooker 653 Golf Drive Roanoke, VA 68002
Jerome Harmon 453 Stephenson Hall Louisville, KY 40202	Denny Crum 28834 Taylorsville Road Louisville, KY 40293	Wade Houston 392 Head Coach Drive Knoxville, TN 32842
Darrell Griffith 193 Jumpin' Jazz Lane Salt Lake City, UT 80821	Kenny Payne 9992 76th Street Philadelphia, PA 20031	Rex Chapman 5929 Hornet Pkwy Charlotte, WV 50024
Michael Jordan 1 Superstar Lane Chicago, IL 68835	Jim Everett 1029 Purdue Way Los Angeles, CA 90045	Bill Shanander 1030 Leichester Circle Louisville, KY 40222
Newell Fox 3029 Cambridge Station Road Anchorage, KY 40287	Bob Montgomery 3902 Holly Springs Circle Louisville, KY 40223	Burt Van Arsdale 4991 Chadwick Road Louisville, KY 40221
Anthony Cade 11093 Future Star Lane Charleston, VA 39901	Adrian Autrey 391 Benedict Arnold Ave Bronx, NY 09102	Elmore Spencer 990 Big Man Circle Savannah, GA 20019
Tom Swidarski 8801 Quick Release Street Louisville, KY 40248	Doug Roach 390 Never Ever Pass Louisville, KY 40284	Brian Tirpak 8802 Willow Road Louisville, KY 40239

We generated this page of labels using the data document in Figure 15-18 and the main document in Figure 15-20.

All five of Word's label templates insert the merge instruction *{data address}* at the very top of the document, which tells Word to use the names and addresses you've entered into the document named ADDRESS.DOC. For this reason, we instructed you to store your names and addresses in a document file named ADDRESS.DOC. In practice, however, you'll probably want to keep a permanent record of multiple collections of names and addresses. For example, you might want to store the names and addresses of your most important clients in a document file named VIPS.DOC, and the names of your prospective clients in a file named PROSPCTS.DOC. To tell Word to use the names and addresses in a file that is not named ADDRESS.DOC, change the DATA instruction's argument from *address* to the full path name of the appropriate document file.

Specifying
the data file

Modifying the information on each label

As you can see in Figure 15-20, each cell of the main document's table (except the first) contains the merge instructions:

{next}{name}¶
{street}¶
{city}, {state} {zip}

If you want to modify the instructions in any way, enter the appropriate merge instructions into each cell in the main document. For instance, if you set up FirstName and LastName fields in your data document instead of setting up a single name field, you'll need to replace the {name} instruction in each cell in your main document with the instructions {FirstName} and {LastName}, like this:

{next}{FirstName} {LastName}¶
{street}¶
{city}, {state} {zip}

As another example, if you've set up Address1 and Address2 fields to store the street address, as we did in the data document in Figure 15-1, you'll need to modify the cells in the main document to look like this:

{next}{FirstName} {LastName}¶
{Address1}{IF {Address2}<>"" "¶
{Address2}"}¶
{city}, {state} {zip}

Notice that you must use the IF instruction technique we demonstrated earlier to account for blank Address2 entries.

Adjusting the size and position of the label text

If you're using sheets of labels that do not conform to one of Word's built-in label templates, you should first create a new document based on the template that is most similar to the label sheets you're using, and then modify that document. Because documents based on Word's label templates use a table to format its text, you'll use Word's table commands along with the Document... command to modify the size and position of the label text. Because we covered document formatting in Chapter 5 and table commands in Chapter 11, we'll briefly explain how the settings in Word's Document and Format Table dialog boxes affect the size and position of the printed labels.

Adjusting the Document settings

The Page Width and Height settings in the Document dialog box shown in Figure 15-22 should match the width and height of the page containing your labels. If you change either of these settings, you should also use the Printer Setup...

command to specify the new paper size in your printer settings box. If your printer settings box doesn't offer a paper size that matches the size of your label sheets, you'll see a message box notifying you of the discrepancy when you issue the Print Merge... command. When this message box appears, choose Yes to continue printing the labels.

Figure 15-22

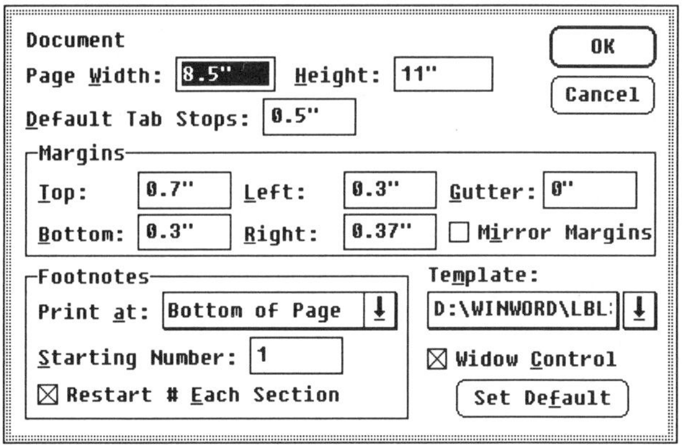

```
┌──────────────────────────────────────────────┐
│ Document                         ┌──────────┐ │
│ Page Width: 8.5"    Height: 11"  │    OK    │ │
│                                  └──────────┘ │
│ Default Tab Stops: 0.5"          ┌──────────┐ │
│ ┌Margins─────────────────────────│  Cancel  │ │
│ │ Top:    0.7"   Left:  0.3"   Gutter: 0"    │ │
│ │ Bottom: 0.3"   Right: 0.37"  ☐ Mirror Margins│
│ ┌Footnotes──────────┐  Template:               │
│ │ Print at: Bottom of Page ↓  D:\WINWORD\LBL: ↓│
│ │ Starting Number: 1        ☒ Widow Control    │
│ │ ☒ Restart # Each Section   ┌ Set Default ┐   │
└──────────────────────────────────────────────┘
```

The Page Width, Height, and margin settings in the Document dialog box affect the position of your printed labels.

The Top margin setting should equal the amount of space between the top edge of the page and the topmost label. Similarly, the Bottom margin setting should reflect the amount of space from the bottom edge of the paper and the bottom label.

Like the Top and Bottom margin settings, the Left and Right margin settings should reflect the amount of space between the edges of the page and the labels. However, if you're using a laser printer, the minimum Left and Right margin setting you can specify is .29". If less than .29 inches of space exists in the left and right margins of your page, you'll need to use the Table... command on the Format menu to display the Format Table dialog box, then slightly decrease the width of the first (and, if necessary, the third) column in the table.

Adjusting the Format Table settings

Now that we've discussed the Document settings that apply to merging, let's consider the significance of the settings in the Format Table dialog box, which is shown in Figure 15-23 on the next page. As we briefly mentioned earlier, the Minimum Row Height setting should match the height of the labels on your sheet. By default, this setting is initially 1". If you're using labels that are not an inch tall, change this setting to match your label height.

The Width of Column setting determines where the text for the adjacent column of labels will begin, as well as where line breaks will occur on each label in the current column. By default, the Width of Column setting for each column in the table should be approximately equal to the width of the labels. If the text for the second and/or third column is running off the left edge of the labels, however, you should increase the Width of Column setting for each column. If the names and addresses are running off the right edge of the labels, you'll want to decrease this setting.

Figure 15-23

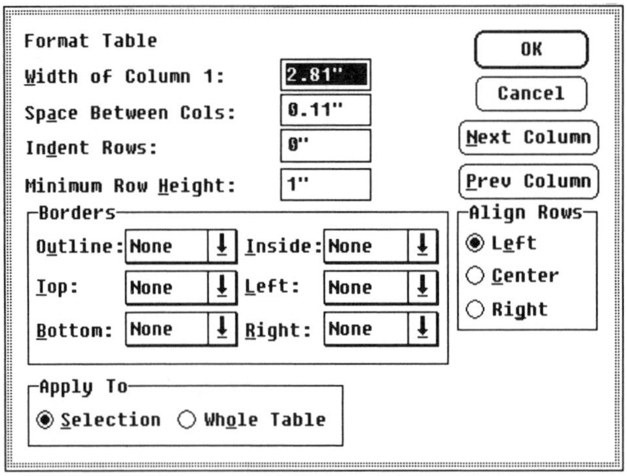

You'll use the Format Table dialog box to adjust the size and position of your label text.

If you're using a multiple-column label template, the Space Between Cols setting should match the amount of space between the columns of labels. Finally, the Indent Rows setting should remain at 0" for all label types.

If you change any of the settings in the Format Table dialog box, don't forget to choose the Apply To Whole Table option at the bottom of the dialog box before choosing OK. Refer to Chapter 11 for a more detailed discussion of each of the table settings we've mentioned here.

Saving the new main document

After you've made changes to your main document, you'll want to save those changes. Of course, you can save your changes either in the Normal file format or as a document template. To save your changes in the Normal file format, simply use the Save command as usual. To create a new document template, however, open the expanded Save As... dialog box, choose Document Template from the File Format list box, type a file name into the Save File Name text box, and choose OK. The next time you issue the New... command, you'll see the name of your custom template in the Use Template list box. We'll talk about document templates in detail in Chapter 18.

In this chapter

Special Features 16

*W*ord offers a number of special features and capabilities that are designed to make you work more efficiently. In previous chapters, we've looked at some important special features, including style sheets and outlining. In this chapter, we'll show you how to take advantage of Word's other capabilities. We'll begin by looking at line and paragraph numbering, then we'll move into sorting paragraphs and performing calculations in Word. After we examine Word's mathematical and scientific formulas, we'll look at some techniques for speeding up Word and optimizing the screen area.

LINE NUMBERING

To create line numbers in your documents, issue the Section… command on the Format menu to bring up a dialog box like the one shown in Figure 16-1 on the following page. In this dialog box, simply select the Line Numbering check box in the Line Numbers section, as we've done in the figure. When you do, all the options in the Line Numbers section will become available for selection. When you choose OK, Word will number all the lines in your document according to the default options in the dialog box.

Line numbers do not appear on your screen unless you print your document or open the Print Preview window. However, Word will include the line numbers in your printed document for all lines except those formatted as footnote, table, header, or footer text. Figure 16-2 on the next page shows part of a printed document with line numbers.

If your document contains a blank line you created by pressing [Enter], Word will number that line. However, if you've formatted a paragraph to have double line spacing or $1 \frac{1}{2}$ line spacing, Word will not number the blank lines between the lines of text in that paragraph. Similarly, if a paragraph's format specifies a certain amount of space before and/or after the text, Word will not assign a line number to those spaces.

Figure 16-1

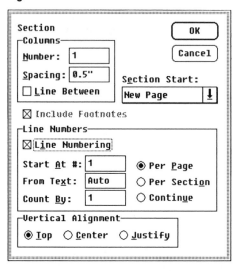

To number the lines in your document, select the Line Numbering check box in the Section dialog box.

Figure 16-2

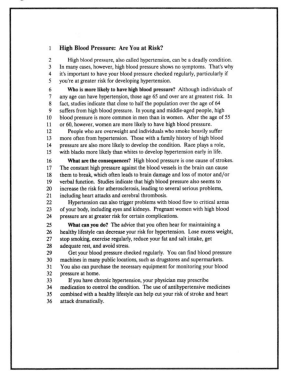

Line numbers appear in your printed document, but are not displayed on your screen unless you use the Print Preview command.

When you select the Line Numbering check box, you can control certain features about your line numbers. First, you can specify how often Word should restart its line numbers. You can restart the line numbers at the top of each new page, at the beginning of each new section, or you can number all the lines in a document continuously. Word's default is to restart line numbering on each page.

Numbering options

You can also control how frequently Word prints a line number. For example, you can print a number next to every line (this is the default), or you can display line numbers only on every fifth or tenth line. Whatever interval you choose, Word will still include each line in its line count; however, it will print only those line numbers that fall at the interval you specify.

Finally, Word lets you control the placement of line numbers relative to your document text. The default placement is $1/_4$ inch from the left edge of each line of text. Let's look at each of the options in the Line Numbers section of the Section dialog box.

In the Section dialog box, there are three line numbering options on the right side of the Line Numbers section: Per Page, Per Section, and Continue. The Per Page option tells Word to number the lines on each page separately, beginning with 1.

Restarting the line numbers

If you prefer to number all the lines in each section continuously without restarting the numbers on each new page, choose the Per Section option. Actually, this option allows you to restart your line numbers anywhere you want. Simply use the Break… command on the Insert menu to enter a section break whenever you want to restart your line numbering at 1. If your document contains only one section, the Per Section option will tell Word to continuously number all the lines in the document.

You can use the third option, Continue, to achieve continuous line numbering in documents with more than one section. When you choose this option, Word will number every line in the section without restarting the line count from the last section or page. In order for this option to work properly, you must be sure that you've activated line numbering in every section in your document and that you've clicked the Continue option for each section.

When you select the Per Page, Per Section, or Continue option, your selection will apply only to the current section (the section in which the cursor is positioned when you open the Section dialog box). This allows you more flexibility in numbering lines. For example, suppose your document contains three sections. You want to number the lines in the first section independently, then number the lines in the last two sections continuously. To achieve this, choose the Per Section option for both the first and second sections. Then, in the third section, choose the Continue option. This tells Word that you want the line numbers in the third section to be continued from the line numbers in the second section, rather than restarting at 1.

In some cases, you may want to begin numbering a section with a number other than 1. You can change the first line number in your document from 1 (Word's default) to another value by entering a beginning line number in the Start At # text box of the Section dialog box. For example, suppose you want the first line number in a document to be 463. Place the cursor in the first (and possibly only) section in the document, choose Section... from the Format menu, choose the Continue option, and enter *463* in the Start At # text box, as shown in Figure 16-3.

Figure 16-3

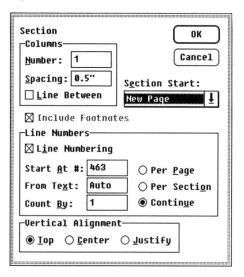

To specify a starting line number other than 1, enter the value in the Start At # text box.

By the way, if you choose the Per Page option, Word will begin numbering the lines on each page with the line number you've entered in the Start At # text box. However, if a section break occurs in the middle of a page, Word will not restart the numbering at the beginning of the new section. Instead, it will restart the line numbers at the beginning of the next page (the first complete page in the new section).

Any section for which you choose the Per Section option will begin with the specified Start At # value. A section with the Continue option will always continue the line count from the previous section, unless the section is the first in a document. In this case, Word will number the first line in the section (and document) with the Start At # value.

Line number frequency

As we mentioned, you can control the interval at which line numbers are printed in your document. The entry in the Count By text box in the Section dialog box determines the frequency of your printed line numbers. Word's default Count

By setting is 1; if you do not change this, Word will print a line number next to every line in your document, as shown in Figure 16-2. If you want to print line numbers at wider intervals, you should replace the 1 in the Count By text box with a greater value.

For example, suppose you want your line numbers to appear only on every fifth line. In that case, you should enter 5 in the Count By text box. Figure 16-4 shows the document from Figure 16-2 after we changed the Count By value to 5. Notice that the first line number that appears in this document is 5.

Figure 16-4

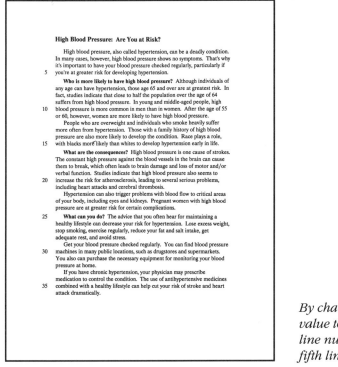

By changing the Count By value to 5, you can print line numbers only on every fifth line.

When you enter a Count By value other than 1 for one section in a multisection document, the results can sometimes be confusing because you can't see where one set of line numbers ends and another begins. For example, suppose your document contains several sections and you've activated the Per Section option in each section. If a new section starts in the middle of a page, Word will restart the line numbers at the section break. However, because your printed document does not show every line number, you won't be able to tell where the new section and the new set of line numbers begin. For instance, in the document shown in

Figure 16-5, a new section begins at the heading in the middle of the page (*Philosophy and Learning*). Notice that, because we've chosen to display line numbers on only every tenth line, there is an apparent gap in the flow of numbered lines around the section break. To make matters more difficult, there are two lines numbered 10—one in the first section and one in the second section.

Figure 16-5

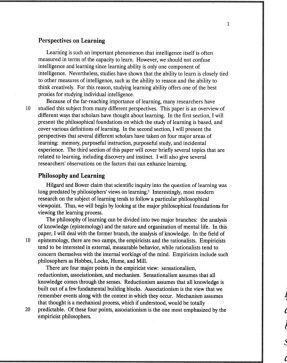

If you choose not to show all line numbers, you won't be able to see when a new set of line numbers begins at a section break.

Line number position

Word's default position for line numbers is $1/4$ inch from the left edge of each line of text. If you want to change this, enter a number in the From Text text box in the Line Numbers section of the Section dialog box. For example, to position your line numbers $1/2$ inch from the left edge of your text, enter *.5″* in the From Text text box.

In positioning line numbers, Word assumes that the left edge of your text is determined by your Left margin setting in the Document dialog box. If you've indented your text by moving the indent markers on the ruler, Word won't take this into account in positioning line numbers. For example, suppose your Left margin setting is 1.25″ (Word's default). Suppose also that you've formatted every paragraph in your document by moving the first-line and left indent markers to the 1-inch position on the ruler. This will create a total margin space of $2\frac{1}{4}$ inches in your printed document. If you activate line numbering in this document and enter .5" in the From Text text box, your line numbers will actually be printed $1\frac{1}{2}$ inches from the left edge of your text.

The From Text setting must be less than the width of the Left margin setting in the Document dialog box. Otherwise, Word will not be able to accommodate your line numbers on the printed page. Word doesn't allow you to enter negative numbers in the From Text text box.

If you're using a multicolumn page design, and you have selected the Line Numbering check box, Word will number the lines in each column. For example, Figure 16-6 shows a two-column document with numbered lines. Notice that the line numbering is continuous from the bottom of the first column to the top of the second column.

Multicolumn documents

Figure 16-6

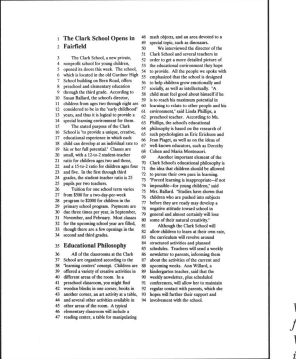

When you use columnar formatting in a document, Word will number the lines in every column.

When you number the lines in a multicolumn document, be sure that you allow enough space between columns to display the line numbers. The From Text setting for your line numbers must be less than the Spacing setting for your columns. Otherwise, your line numbers will not fit in the space between columns.

Selective line numbering

In some cases, you may want to assign line numbers only to certain parts of your document. There are a couple of ways you can number lines selectively. First, if you want to number the lines in only a small part of your document—say, a few paragraphs—you should place a section break both before and after that part of your document. To insert a section break, position the cursor where you want the break to appear, select the Break... command from the Insert menu, select the type of section break you want to insert (Next Page, Continuous, Even Page, or Odd Page), and choose OK. Word will display a double dotted line on your screen to mark the boundary of the new section. Figure 16-7 shows a document in which we've inserted Continuous section breaks both before and after a paragraph.

Figure 16-7

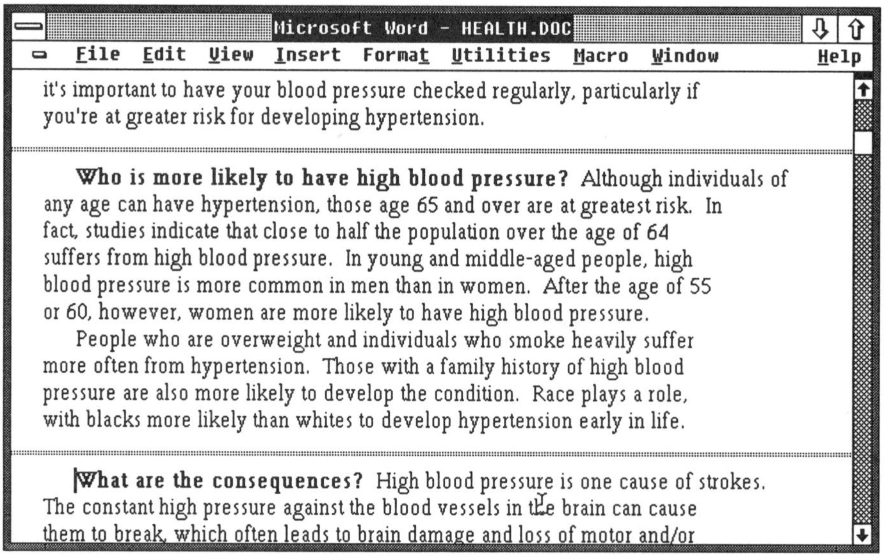

To number the lines in only a small portion of your document, place a section break both before and after that text.

After you've "sectioned off" a part of your document, position your cursor anywhere within the section you want to number, open the Section dialog box and select the Per Section option.

Another way you can control line numbering in a document is by turning off the line numbers on selected paragraphs. To do this, first select the paragraph(s) whose lines you do not want to number, then choose the Paragraph... command from the Format menu to open the Paragraph dialog box. As you can see in Figure 16-8, when you first open this dialog box, the Line Numbering check box will be selected. (When you select the Line Numbering check box in the Section dialog box, Word will activate the Line Numbering check box in the Paragraph dialog box as well.) Simply deactivate the Line Numbering check box in the Paragraph dialog box to turn off line numbering for the selected paragraph(s), then choose OK to close the dialog box.

Figure 16-8

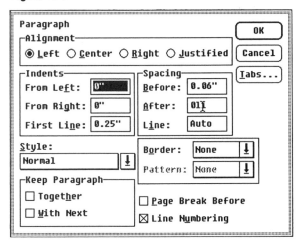

If you have activated line numbering in a section, Word will activate the Line Numbering check box in the Paragraph dialog box as well.

Although you can deactivate the Line Numbering check box in the Paragraph dialog box for certain paragraphs, you can't select this check box for a paragraph until you have activated that option in the Section dialog box. If you do not select the Line Numbering check box in the Section dialog box, the Line Numbering option in the Paragraph dialog box will be dimmed.

When you turn off the line numbers for a selected paragraph, Word will not print line numbers next to that text, nor will it include those lines in its line count. For example, Figure 16-9 on the next page shows a printed page from a document in which we've numbered all the lines except those in the second paragraph of body text. Notice that the last line before the unnumbered paragraph is 7, while the first line after the unnumbered paragraph picks up the count again with 8.

Word's Renumber... command on the Utilities menu lets you number paragraphs automatically throughout all or part of a document. If you don't select any text before issuing the Renumber... command, choosing OK in the Renumber dialog box will tell Word to assign a number to every paragraph in the current

NUMBERING PARAGRAPHS

document. If you select one or more paragraphs before you choose Renumber..., Word will assign numbers only to the selected paragraphs. (By the way, if you select less than a full paragraph of text—say, a word or two—before you choose Renumber..., Word will assume that you want to assign a number only to the paragraph that contains your selection.) In numbering paragraphs, Word doesn't recognize section breaks. The paragraphs before and after a section break will be numbered continuously.

Figure 16-9

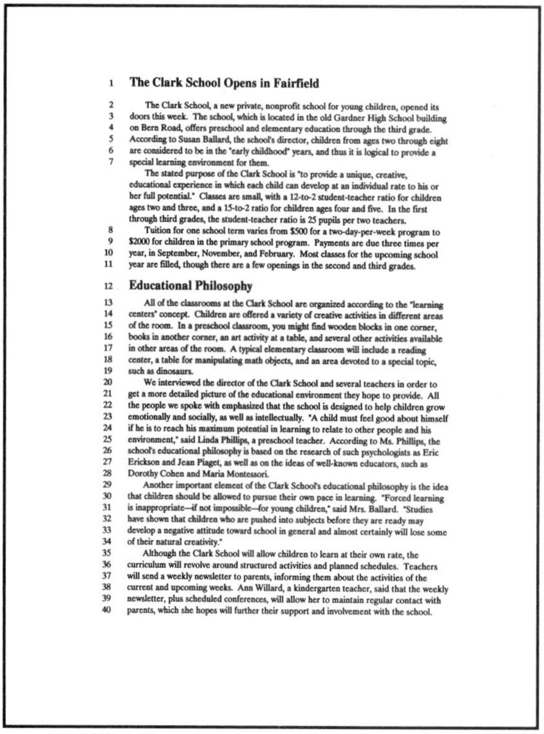

The Clark School Opens in Fairfield

The Clark School, a new private, nonprofit school for young children, opened its doors this week. The school, which is located in the old Gardner High School building on Bern Road, offers preschool and elementary education through the third grade. According to Susan Ballard, the school's director, children from ages two through eight are considered to be in the "early childhood" years, and thus it is logical to provide a special learning environment for them.

The stated purpose of the Clark School is "to provide a unique, creative, educational experience in which each child can develop at an individual rate to his or her full potential." Classes are small, with a 12-to-2 student-teacher ratio for children ages two and three, and a 15-to-2 ratio for children ages four and five. In the first through third grades, the student-teacher ratio is 25 pupils per two teachers.

Tuition for one school term varies from $500 for a two-day-per-week program to $2000 for children in the primary school program. Payments are due three times per year, in September, November, and February. Most classes for the upcoming school year are filled, though there are a few openings in the second and third grades.

Educational Philosophy

All of the classrooms at the Clark School are organized according to the "learning centers" concept. Children are offered a variety of creative activities in different areas of the room. In a preschool classroom, you might find wooden blocks in one corner, books in another corner, an art activity at a table, and several other activities available in other areas of the room. A typical elementary classroom will include a reading center, a table for manipulating math objects, and an area devoted to a special topic, such as dinosaurs.

We interviewed the director of the Clark School and several teachers in order to get a more detailed picture of the educational environment they hope to provide. All the people we spoke with emphasized that the school is designed to help children grow emotionally and socially, as well as intellectually. "A child must feel good about himself if he is to reach his maximum potential in learning to relate to other people and his environment," said Linda Phillips, a preschool teacher. According to Ms. Phillips, the school's educational philosophy is based on the research of such psychologists as Eric Erickson and Jean Piaget, as well as on the ideas of well-known educators, such as Dorothy Cohen and Maria Montessori.

Another important element of the Clark School's educational philosophy is the idea that children should be allowed to pursue their own pace in learning. "Forced learning is inappropriate—if not impossible—for young children," said Mrs. Ballard. "Studies have shown that children who are pushed into subjects before they are ready may develop a negative attitude toward school in general and almost certainly will lose some of their natural creativity."

Although the Clark School will allow children to learn at their own rate, the curriculum will revolve around structured activities and planned schedules. Teachers will send a weekly newsletter to parents, informing them about the activities of the current and upcoming weeks. Ann Willard, a kindergarten teacher, said that the weekly newsletter, plus scheduled conferences, will allow her to maintain regular contact with parents, which she hopes will further their support and involvement with the school.

When you eliminate line numbers from a selected paragraph, Word will not include that paragraph in its line count.

You can control several features of your paragraph numbers, including their alignment in relation to your text, the type of numbering scheme used, and the starting number for a sequence of paragraphs. If you decide to add, delete, or rearrange paragraphs, Word's Renumber... command will make it easy to put your paragraph numbers back in order.

When you number paragraphs, you can insert either literal numbers into your document or fields that automatically display a paragraph's number based on its position in the document. The literal numbers are known as manual numbers because you can change or delete them just like manually entered text. The results of the numbering fields are called automatic numbers because the numbers they return change automatically when you move or delete paragraphs in a document.

Paragraph numbering is particularly useful in documents with multiple levels of paragraphs—such as legal documents or outlines. In these cases, Word lets you control the numbering scheme of each level. For example, your first-level paragraphs may be numbered *1.*, *2.*, *3.*, and so forth, while your second-level paragraphs are numbered *1-A.*, *1-B.*, and so forth. Before we talk about numbering multiple levels of paragraphs, however, let's examine some of the basics of paragraph numbering. These basic concepts will apply whether your document contains only one level or several levels of paragraphs.

When you use automatic numbering, Word will insert a special field at the beginning of each paragraph. The names of these fields depend on the numbering scheme you apply. To insert automatic paragraph numbers in a document, just choose the Renumber... command from the Utilities menu. Word will then display the dialog box shown in Figure 16-10.

Automatic numbering

Figure 16-10

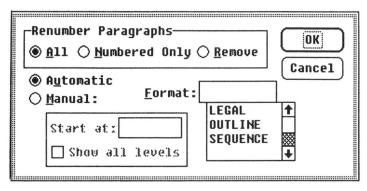

You'll see this dialog box when you choose Renumber... from the Utilities menu.

Notice that Word selects the Automatic and Renumber Paragraphs All options by default. When you see this dialog box, all you have to do is enter *SEQUENCE* into the Format text box (either by typing it or selecting it from the Format list box). The SEQUENCE format numbers paragraphs with Arabic numerals. When you choose OK, Word will close the dialog box and place an Arabic numeral followed by a period (*1.*, *2.*, *3.*, and so forth) at the beginning of each paragraph. Figure 16-11 shows an example of a document with automatic paragraph numbering.

Figure 16-11

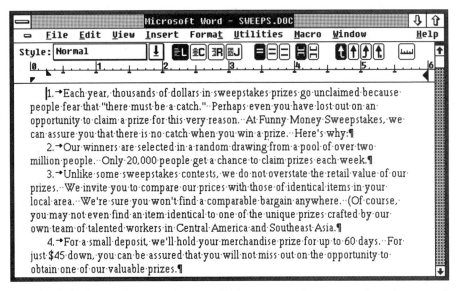

Word's default numbering scheme will place an Arabic numeral and a period at the beginning of each paragraph.

Notice that Word aligns each paragraph number with the first-line indent marker on the ruler. In this example, the first-line indent marker for each paragraph is positioned at the $1/_4$-inch position on the ruler. Therefore, each paragraph number is indented $1/_4$ inch. Notice also that Word inserts a tab space between the paragraph number and the paragraph text. This causes the first character of text to be positioned at the first tab after the initial indention. Since we have not changed Word's default tab stops, the first character of each paragraph is aligned with the default tab stop at the $1/_2$-inch position on the ruler. As we'll explain, you can change the alignment of paragraph numbers and text by manipulating your indent markers and tabs.

The numbers that appear next to each paragraph are actually fields. Figure 16-12 displays the same document shown in Figure 16-11 after we activated the Field Codes setting on the View menu. These AUTONUM fields automatically display the number of each paragraph based on its position in the document. As a result, if you remove a numbered paragraph from a document, Word will automatically renumber any displaced paragraphs based on their new positions.

Word counts all the previous automatically numbered paragraphs in a document when determining the number to be displayed by an AUTONUM field, even if there are unnumbered paragraphs among the numbered ones. For example, if the first and third paragraphs in your document are automatically numbered, but the second is not, Word will label the third paragraph as paragraph number 2. Word will ignore the second paragraph in the count because it is not marked with an AUTONUM field.

Figure 16-12

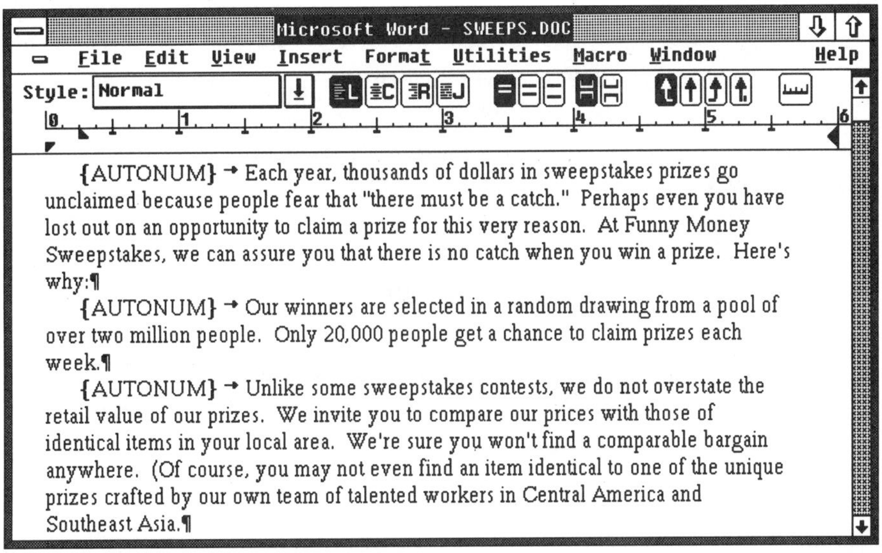

The AUTONUM field lets you use automatic page numbering.

Manual numbering

Rather than telling Word to insert automatic paragraph numbers, you can use the Renumber... command to insert manual paragraph numbers in your document. Manual paragraph numbering is useful when you want to include several groups of numbered paragraphs in a single document. All you have to do is select the first group of paragraphs, open the Renumber dialog box, choose the Manual option, and choose OK. When you are finished numbering the first group, simply repeat the process for each group of paragraphs you want to number. As you select and number different groups of paragraphs, Word will begin a new numbering sequence each time.

Manual paragraph numbering also offers some options not available with automatic numbering. When you use manual paragraph numbering, you can select both a start number and a numbering scheme.

Specifying
a start number

When you first issue the Renumber... command, the Start At text box will appear dimmed because you cannot specify a starting number for automatic paragraph numbering. Word always begins automatic numbering with the number 1. However, when you choose the Manual option, the Start At text box will become active, allowing you to specify a starting number. For example, if you want the first paragraph in the document or selection to be numbered 14, you should enter *14* in the Start At text box, as shown in Figure 16-13. Word will then number the second paragraph 15, the third paragraph 16, and so forth.

Figure 16-13

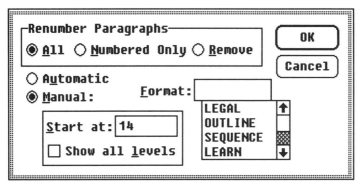

The entry in the Start At text box indicates the first paragraph number in your document or selection.

You can also use the Start At text box to change the starting number of a series of paragraphs to which you've already applied manual numbering. Just select the paragraphs (or, to renumber the entire document, don't select any text), then open the Renumber dialog box and enter the new starting number in the Start At text box. When you choose OK, Word will renumber the paragraphs, labeling the first with the new Start At value.

Choosing a numbering scheme

As we demonstrated in Figure 16-11, Word's default numbering scheme for paragraphs uses a simple sequence of Arabic numerals. If you prefer to use Roman numerals or letters, you can manually assign the desired numbering scheme to the first paragraph in the group before you open the Renumber dialog box.

The first time you open the Renumber dialog box, the Format text box will be blank, as it was in Figure 16-10. In fact, this text box will always be blank unless the first paragraph in your document (or the first paragraph in your selection) has been numbered. After you've numbered the first paragraph in your example format, however, the Format text box will display the entry *LEARN*, as shown in Figure 16-14. With the LEARN option, Word will manually number all the paragraphs in your document using the format you've assigned to the example paragraph (the first paragraph in your document or selection).

The appearance of the LEARN option in the Format text box is not the only difference you will see in the Renumber dialog box if you've already numbered the first paragraph. In addition, Word will select the Manual option instead of Automatic, and the Renumber Paragraphs Numbered Only option will replace the Renumber Paragraphs All option. To number all the paragraphs in your document according to the example format, just select the Renumber Paragraphs All option and choose OK.

Figure 16-14

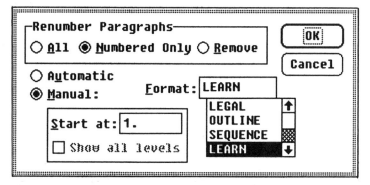

The Renumber dialog box will be slightly altered if you number the first paragraph before choosing the Renumber... command.

For example, suppose you want to use Roman numerals, rather than Arabic numerals, to number all the paragraphs in a document. First, type the Roman numeral *I* and a period at the beginning of the first paragraph, and press [Tab] to move the text in the paragraph to the first tab stop. Now issue the Renumber... command to access the dialog box shown in Figure 16-14, and select the Renumber Paragraphs All option. When you choose OK, all your paragraphs will be numbered with Roman numerals followed by a period.

As you're specifying a numbering scheme, you don't have to use the first letter of the alphabet, the Roman numeral *I*, or *1*. You can type any Arabic numeral to specify an Arabic numbering scheme, and you can enter any letter (except I, V, or X) to indicate that you want to use an alphabetic numbering scheme. Similarly, you can enter an I, V, or X to specify a Roman numeral numbering scheme. If you use a number greater than 1 or a letter after A to dictate a numbering scheme, Word will begin numbering paragraphs with the number or letter you specify. When you open the Renumber dialog box, the value in your example paragraph will appear in the Start At text box. However, if you replace the entry in the Start At text box, Word will begin the sequence with the number in the text box rather than with the value of your example. In such a case, Word will still use the numbering scheme demonstrated by your example.

Interestingly, the Start At entry does not have to be stated in the same format as your chosen numbering scheme. For example, suppose you want to use an alphabetic numbering scheme, and you want to begin labeling your paragraphs with the letter *d*. You can use any lowercase letter as your example and, when you open the Renumber dialog box, enter either *d.* or *4.* in the Start At text box (since *d* is the fourth letter of the alphabet). You can also use a different format when changing the starting number for paragraphs already numbered, as we described in the last section.

If, when entering your example number, you type a high Roman numeral that's only a single character—such as L, C, or M—Word will interpret your entry as an alphabetic character. However, if you enter a high Roman numeral that is composed of two or more characters—such as LIX or CM—Word will correctly interpret your entry as a Roman numeral.

If you choose an alphabetic or Roman numeral numbering scheme, Word will allow you to use either uppercase or lowercase for your paragraph numbers. The case you use for the example number will determine the case of the remaining numbers in your document. For instance, if you want to use a lowercase alphabetic numbering scheme, type a lowercase letter—such as *a*—as the number for the first paragraph. Similarly, if you want to use a lowercase Roman numeral numbering scheme (i, ii, iii, and so forth), you should enter a lowercase Roman numeral in the first paragraph, as we've done in Figure 16-15.

As you'll see in a few pages, specifying a starting number in a document with multiple levels of paragraphs is a little more complicated.

If you use manual numbering to create several series of numbered paragraphs, you can specify a different numbering scheme for each series. For example, you can use uppercase Roman numerals for one series of paragraphs and lowercase Roman numerals for another.

Choosing the separator characters

Word's default separator characters (the characters that separate a paragraph's number from its text) are a period and a tab space. If you want to use different separator characters, you must include them with the number or letter in your example number.

For instance, suppose you want to use a closing parenthesis as your separator character for a numbering scheme with lowercase Roman numerals. In that case, insert the characters *i)* at the beginning of the first paragraph you want to number. Figure 16-16 shows this example number in a document. After you open the Renumber dialog box, choose the Renumber Paragraphs All option, and choose OK, Word will use the specified separator characters while numbering all the paragraphs in the document.

You can use any of the standard non-alphanumeric characters as separator characters. For example, all the characters produced by pressing [Shift] and the numeric keys at the top of your keyboard are valid separator characters, including #, *, and -.

Figure 16-15

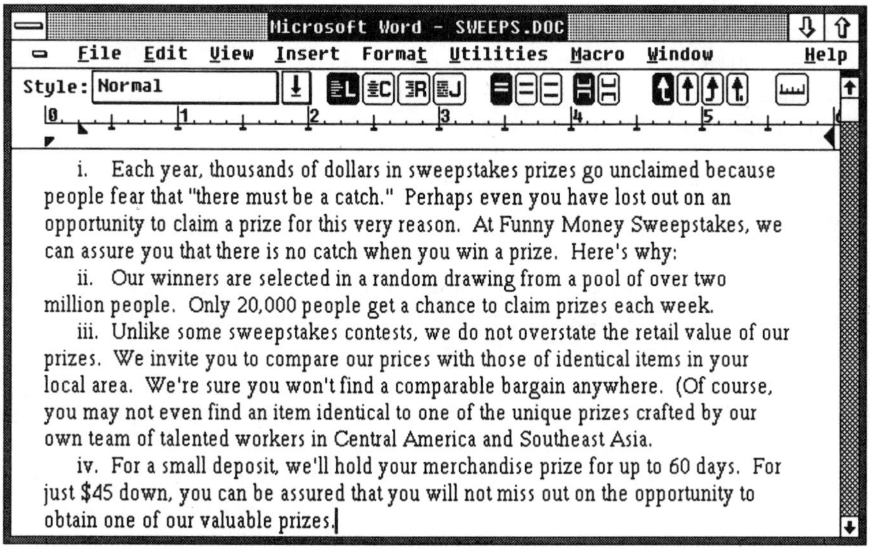

The example number in the first paragraph tells Word what kind of numbering scheme you want to use for your paragraphs.

Figure 16-16

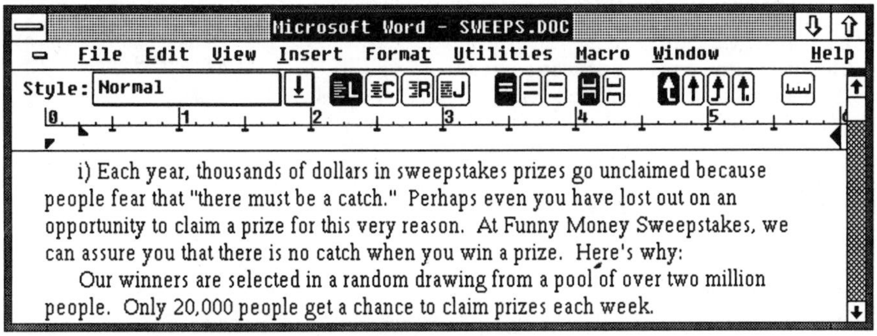

Your example number can also specify a separator character.

If you want to place a separator character to the left of the numbers in your paragraphs, you can't use the LEARN option—instead, you'll need to manually enter the desired numbering scheme into the Renumber dialog box's Format text box. For instance, to use a numbering scheme like *-1-* or *<i>*, you must type this entry into the Format text box. If you enter this type of numbering scheme into an example paragraph and leave the LEARN option displayed in the Format text box, Word will delete the leading separator character.

Word also will not allow any "extra" separator characters. If you place two or more separator characters after a number, such as *1***, Word will simply ignore all separator characters after the first one.

When you're numbering multiple levels of paragraphs, Word will let you use a different separator character between each level number. For example, third-level paragraphs might be numbered 1.1-a). We will discuss the format of multiple-level paragraph numbers later in this chapter.

Formatting your paragraph numbers

Whether you use automatic or manual paragraph numbering, Word will use the formatting features of the first character in each paragraph to determine the format of that paragraph's number. In other words, Word will match the character formatting of each paragraph's number—font, point size, and so forth—to the format of the first character in the paragraph. This automatic formatting can be especially helpful in documents in which you've used character formatting to distinguish different kinds of topics. For example, Figure 16-17 shows a document with various character formatting. Figure 16-18 shows this same document after we've numbered its paragraphs with the Renumber... command. Notice that some of the numbers appear in Tms Rmn bold type, while others appear in Helv italic.

Figure 16-17

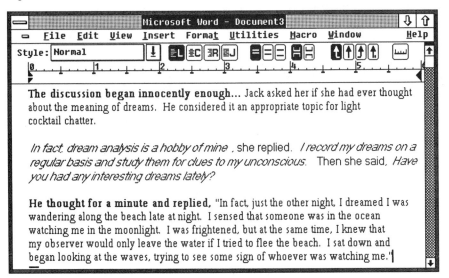

This document contains paragraphs with various character formatting.

After you have numbered your paragraphs, you can change the format of your paragraph numbers (whether they are manual or automatic). If you reformat the numbers, then change the numbering scheme, Word will not alter your manual format changes. (By the way, if your paragraph numbers are arranged in a column, keep in mind that you can use the [Column selection] key ([Crtl][Shift][F8]) or the right mouse button to make a columnar block selection and reformat all the numbers at once. In Chapter 4, we describe this block selection technique in greater detail.)

Figure 16-18

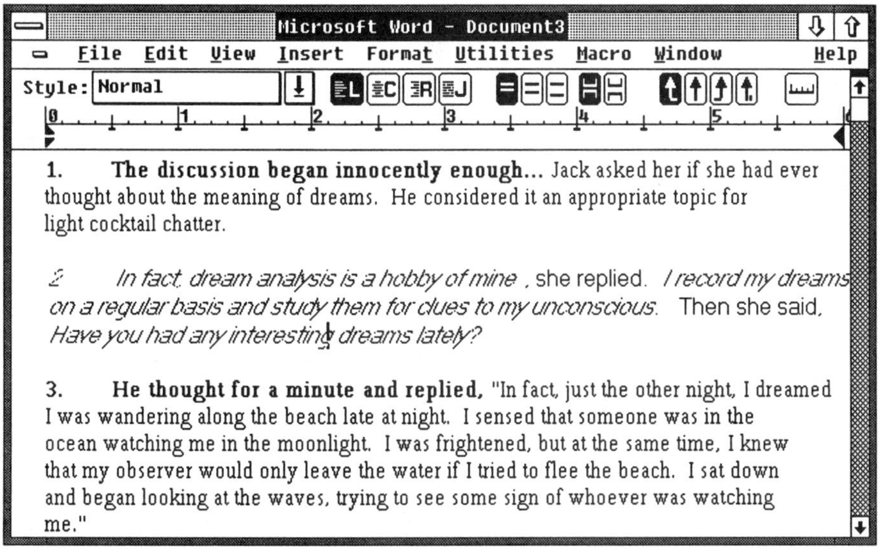

Word uses the formatting characteristics of the first character in each paragraph to determine the format of each paragraph number.

Word aligns each paragraph number with the first-line indent marker on the ruler. Word also inserts a tab space after each paragraph number so that the first character of paragraph text is aligned with the first tab after the indent. (Of course, the position of the first-line indent marker and the first tab can change from paragraph to paragraph in your document.)

To change the amount of space between a paragraph number and the first character of paragraph text, simply place a tab at the appropriate place on the ruler. For example, Figure 16-19 on the following page shows some numbered paragraphs in which each number is aligned at the left edge of the screen (since the first-line indent marker is at the zero point on the ruler), while the first character of text in each paragraph is aligned with the $1/2$-inch position on the ruler.

Let's say that you want to indent the first character of text by an additional $1/4$ inch. First, select these paragraphs, then insert a left tab stop at the $3/4$-inch position on the ruler. The result will look like Figure 16-20.

Aligning numbers and text

Figure 16-19

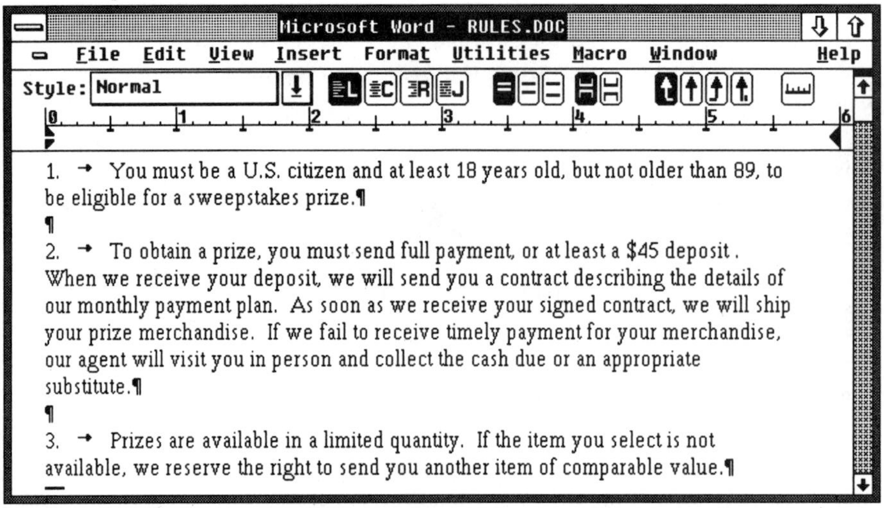

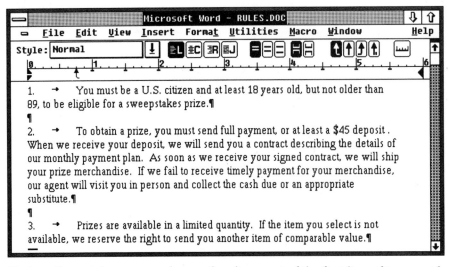

In these paragraphs, the numbers are aligned at the zero point on the ruler, while the first character of text in each paragraph is aligned at the ¹/₂-inch position.

Figure 16-20

By inserting a tab, you can change the alignment of the first line of paragraph text.

If you use Roman numerals or a large font for the paragraph numbers in your document, some of the larger numbers may actually reach beyond the first tab stop. As a result, the tab inserted after the paragraph number will force the text in some paragraphs to the second tab stop, ruining the alignment of your paragraphs. To accommodate the largest of the numbers, you can realign the text in the paragraphs by using the technique we just discussed to set a new first tab stop for all the paragraphs.

By moving the left indent marker, you can change the alignment of the paragraph text (after the first line) in relation to the paragraph number. For example, you can "hang" paragraph numbers outside the paragraph text. Figure 16-21 shows the paragraphs from Figure 16-20 after we moved the left indent marker to the $^1/_2$-inch position on the ruler. To change the alignment of all the paragraphs in the document, first select the paragraphs and then use either your mouse to drag the indent marker to the new position or the Paragraph... command on the Format menu to change the From Left setting in the Indents section to .5".

Notice in Figure 16-21 that the first line in each paragraph is no longer aligned with the tab stop at the $^3/_4$-inch position. Instead, it is aligned with the left indent marker at the $^1/_2$-inch position. In deciding where to align the first line of text, Word looks for the first "stopping place" on the ruler after the first-line indent. In many cases, the first stop will occur at a tab—either one of Word's default tabs or a tab you've insert manually. However, if you move the left indent marker to the right of the first-line indent marker, you may create a "stopping place" before a tab, as we've done in Figure 16-21. In that case, Word will align the first character of text with the left indent marker.

Figure 16-21

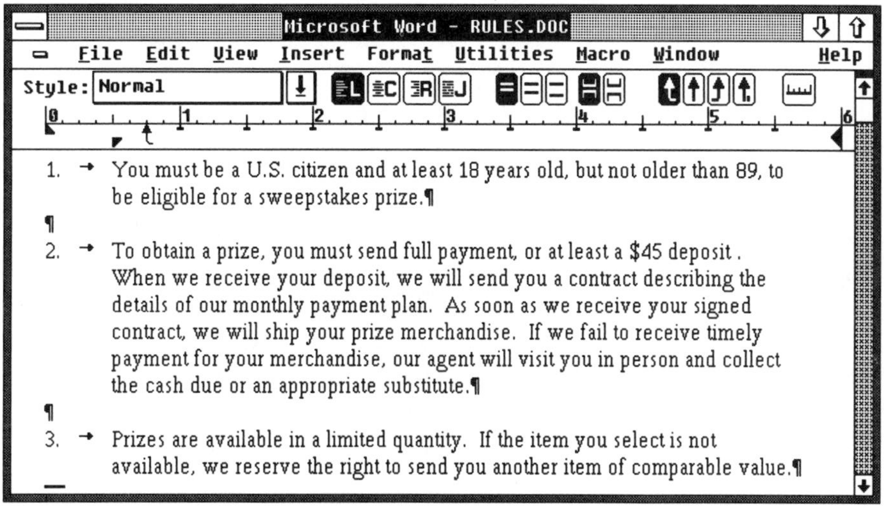

You can create "hanging" paragraph numbers with the left indent marker.

If you move the left indent marker to the right of the tab, your paragraphs will look like those in Figure 16-22. Notice that the first line of text in each paragraph is aligned at the tab that we've inserted at the $^3/_4$-inch position, while subsequent lines are aligned at the left indent marker, which occurs at the 1-inch position. As a result, both the paragraph numbers and the initial text in each paragraph hang outside the left margin.

Figure 16-22

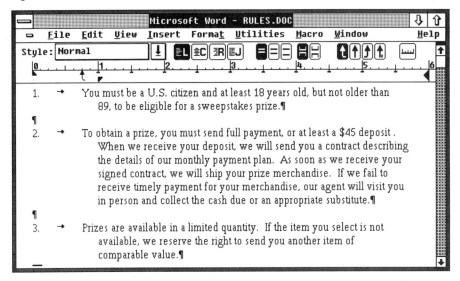

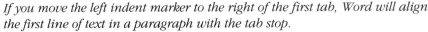

If you move the left indent marker to the right of the first tab, Word will align the first line of text in a paragraph with the tab stop.

Finally, by moving the left indent marker to the left of the first-line indent marker, you can cause the paragraph numbers to appear indented. For example, in Figure 16-23, we've moved the first-line indent marker to the $^1/_4$-inch position and the left indent marker to the zero point.

To change the alignment of only a few numbered paragraphs, you must select those paragraphs before you move the indent markers or insert tab stops. To change the alignment of all the paragraphs in a document, you must select the entire document before you make your ruler changes. A more efficient way to change the alignment of all the paragraphs in your document—or even a few paragraphs—is to alter the style definition(s) for those paragraphs on the style sheet. For information on how to use named styles to format paragraphs, see Chapter 8.

Figure 16-23

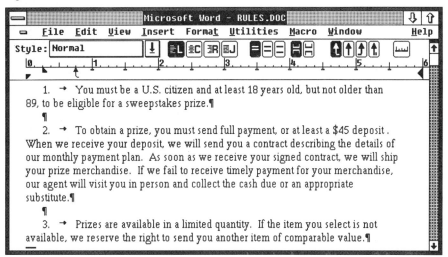

By moving the left indent marker to the left of the first-line indent marker, you can indent your paragraph numbers.

When you number the paragraphs in a document, you probably will want to exclude certain paragraphs, such as the title, subheadings, figure captions, and so forth. There are a few techniques you can use to selectively number paragraphs.

Selective numbering

If you want to use automatic paragraph numbering, Word makes it easy to selectively number paragraphs. Just number your document a few paragraphs at a time, selecting groups of paragraphs you want to number. For example, you can begin by selecting all the paragraphs after the main title and before the first subheading, then open the Renumber dialog box and select the Automatic option. After you number these paragraphs, you can select another group of paragraphs between the first and second subheadings, then reopen the Renumber dialog box. When you number this second group of paragraphs (and all subsequent paragraphs), be sure to select the Automatic option. If you accidentally choose the Manual option, Word will insert literal numbers rather than numbering fields. These literal numbers won't appear in sequence with the automatic paragraph numbers in the document.

If you want to use manual paragraph numbering, you can use a similar technique. Go through the entire document as we explained above, numbering groups of paragraphs, but select the Manual option each time you issue the Renumber... command. When you are finished, each group of paragraphs you selected will have its own sequence of numbers, beginning with 1. Now, without selecting any paragraphs, issue the Renumber... command again. When the Renumber dialog box appears, Word will automatically select the Manual option and the Renumber Paragraphs Numbered Only option. All you'll need to do is enter *1* in the Start At text box. (Word will automatically enter the number of the current paragraph in this text box, so you'll need to change the Start At setting if the cursor was not in the first numbered paragraph when you issued the Renumber... command.) When you choose OK to close the Renumber dialog box, Word will renumber all the paragraphs you had previously numbered, using one continuous sequence of numbers.

Another technique you can use to achieve selective manual numbering is to number all the paragraphs in your document, making sure to select the Manual option, then manually remove each unwanted number. After removing the numbers, you can issue the Renumber... command once more and choose the Renumber Paragraphs Numbered Only option. Word will then renumber your document, ignoring the paragraphs that don't already have numbers. In other words, the second time you issue the Renumber... command, Word will place all the remaining paragraph numbers in the correct order.

Using this technique with automatic numbering works a bit differently. First, you number all the paragraphs in your document, but then you must use the Renumber... command to remove the automatic numbering from selected paragraphs. To remove an automatic number from a paragraph, select that paragraph, then issue the Renumber... command and select the Renumber Paragraphs Remove option. When you choose OK, Word will remove the numbering field from the paragraph and adjust the remaining automatic numbers throughout the document.

Numbering blank paragraphs

Whenever you number the paragraphs in a document, Word will skip blank paragraphs—that is, paragraphs that consist of a ¶ mark with no associated text. However, there may be times when you want to number these blank paragraphs, perhaps so you can add text to these locations later. The method that you use to number blank paragraphs will depend on whether you are using automatic or manual paragraph numbers.

If you are using automatic numbers, you will need to insert some dummy text in the blank paragraphs before you number them, then delete the text. This dummy text can be a single character or several characters—including numbers, letters, or non-alphanumeric characters, such as # or $. After you number the lines and delete the dummy text, Word will leave the numbering field in place and adjust its displayed value whenever you add, delete, or move a paragraph.

To number blank paragraphs with manual numbers, you must first enter a number for each of these blank paragraphs. These numbers, which are simply placeholders, do not have to be in proper sequence, nor do they have to use the same numbering scheme as the rest of your paragraph numbers.

After you type a number in front of each blank paragraph, you can use the Renumber... command to make Word replace these placeholder numbers with correct numbers. The Renumber… command will number the blank paragraphs in sequence, using the same numbering scheme (Arabic, Roman, or alphabetic) as the rest of your paragraph numbers.

For example, suppose you want to number the blank paragraphs (along with the rest of the document) shown in Figure 16-24. Before you issue the Renumber… command, type *1* followed by a period at the beginning of the document's blank paragraphs. (The period is not necessary in this case. However, if you use a letter for your placeholder instead of a number, you must be sure to type a separator character so that Word can distinguish your entry from the paragraph text.)

Figure 16-24

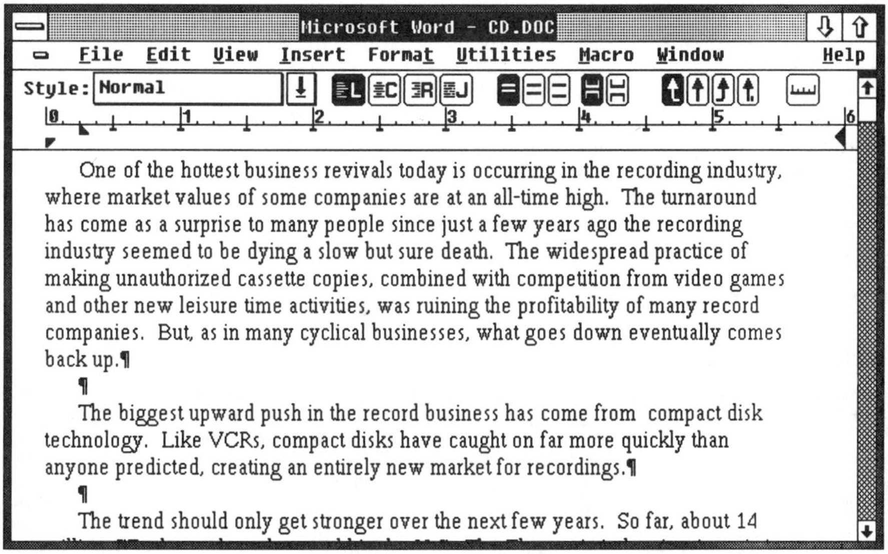

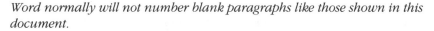

Word normally will not number blank paragraphs like those shown in this document.

In this example, let's assume you want to specify an uppercase alphabetic numbering scheme. To define the numbering scheme, insert the character *A* followed by a period and a tab at the beginning of the first paragraph in the document. Figure 16-25 shows the document with the placeholder numbers and the example number. Next, open the Renumber dialog box and choose the Renumber Paragraphs All option. (Word will automatically select the LEARN option in the Format list box and the Manual option.) After you choose OK, your document will look like Figure 16-26. Notice that Word has replaced each placeholder number with the correct letter for that paragraph.

Figure 16-25

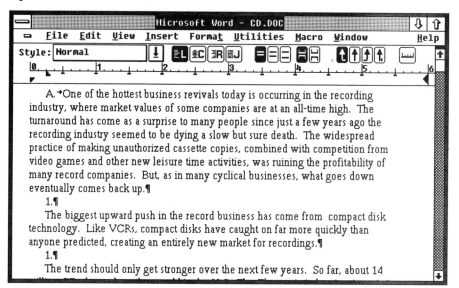

To manually number blank paragraphs, begin by entering placeholder numbers and an example number.

Figure 16-26

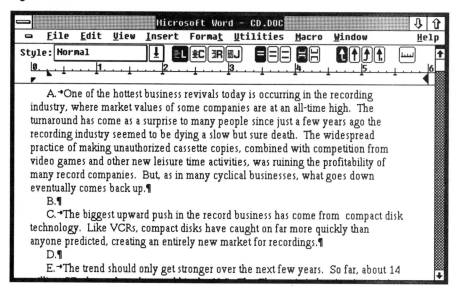

When you choose Renumber..., Word will replace each placeholder number with a properly formatted number or letter in the correct sequence.

By the way, you can use both the techniques discussed in this section to number blank paragraphs in documents that have multiple levels of paragraphs. When you execute the Renumber... command, Word will assign the correct number to each blank paragraph, regardless of its level.

As we've said, paragraph numbering is perhaps most useful in documents that contain multiple levels of paragraphs, such as legal documents or teaching materials. When you issue the Renumber... command, Word will recognize different levels of paragraphs based on their styles and assign a different set of numbers to each level. Word determines numbering levels based on the automatic styles that distinguish levels in an outline (*heading 1*, *heading 2*, etc.), applying a different numbering scheme to paragraphs at each outline level. As we explained in Chapters 8 and 9, you can apply these outline styles directly or let Word apply them as you create an outline.

Numbering multiple levels of paragraphs

For example, Figure 16-27 shows a document with four levels of paragraphs after we've numbered them with the SEQUENCE option. These levels are distinguished by the styles *Title*, *heading 1*, *heading 2*, and *Normal.* Notice that Word uses a different sequence of numbers for each level, restarting the count for each set of subordinate paragraphs.

Figure 16-27

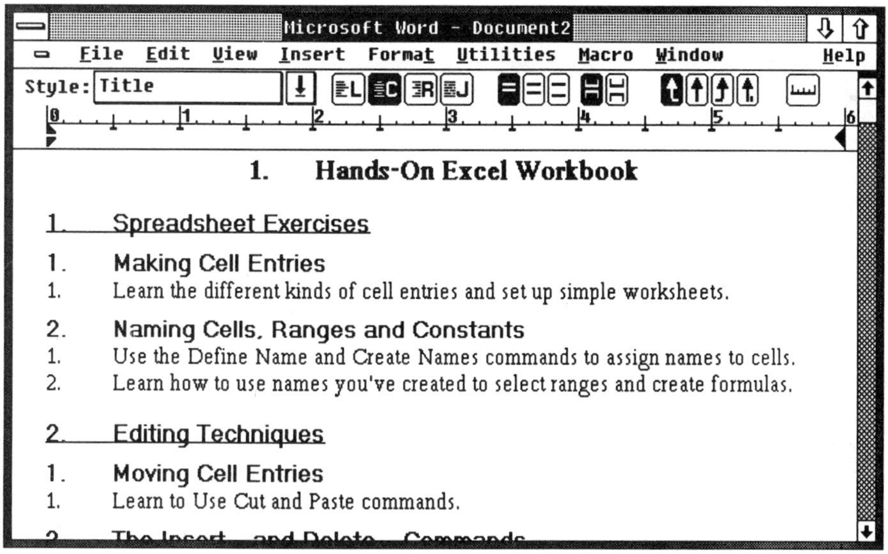

Word is able to assign a different set of numbers to each paragraph level in a document.

Not only is Word able to number each level separately, it can also use a different numbering scheme for each level. Word offers preset numbering schemes you can use to number multilevel documents as outlines or legal documents. To use one of these formats, select the appropriate option (OUTLINE or LEGAL) in the Format text box of the Renumber dialog box. You can use these preset formats to add automatic or manual numbering to paragraphs in a selection or document. As an alternative to Word's preset formats, you can also use the LEARN format we discussed earlier to define a different numbering scheme for every paragraph level. As we already explained, the LEARN option is available only when you are adding manual numbering to paragraphs. We'll look at Word's preset formats first, then show you an example of how you might define your own numbering schemes for a document with multiple levels of paragraphs.

Numbering an outline

When you number the paragraphs in a selection or document as an outline, Word will distinguish each paragraph level with a different numbering scheme, following the standards defined in the *Chicago Manual of Style*. For example, Word numbers first-level paragraphs formatted in the *heading 1* style with uppercase Roman numerals and numbers *heading 2* paragraphs with uppercase letters. Table 16-1 shows the numbering scheme Word uses for each heading level when you choose the OUTLINE option in the Format text box.

Table 16-1

Paragraph style	Numbering scheme & separator character	Example
heading 1	Uppercase Roman numerals, period	I.
heading 2	Uppercase letters, period	A.
heading 3	Arabic numerals, period	1.
heading 4	Lowercase letters, closing parenthesis	a.)
heading 5	Arabic numerals, parentheses	(1)
heading 6	Lowercase letters, parentheses	(a)
heading 7	Lowercase Roman numerals, parentheses	(i)
heading 8	Lowercase letters, parentheses	(a)
heading 9	Lowercase Roman numerals, parentheses	(i)
Other styles	Arabic numerals, period	1.

As you can see in Table 16-1, Word uses Arabic numerals and a period separator for any paragraphs not formatted with one of the *heading* styles. However, when you number a document as an outline, you'll probably want to exclude its title and any non-heading text from the numbering. (Titles and text will probably be formatted in the *Normal* style or another named style you've defined.) You can exclude these paragraphs by switching to the outline view and collapsing the outline to exclude non-heading paragraphs before you issue the Renumber... command. When you issue the Renumber... command in the outline view, Word will number only those paragraphs visible on the screen. As a result, when you leave the outline view, only the *heading* paragraphs will have numbers.

For example, suppose you want to number the paragraphs in the document shown in Figure 16-27 using the OUTLINE option. First, issue the Renumber... command, select the Renumber Paragraphs Remove option, and choose OK to remove the sequential numbering already in place. To exclude the title and text paragraphs from the new numbering scheme, issue the Outline command on the View menu, then choose one of the numbered Show icons (between 2 and 9, in this case) to reduce the scope of the outline. (You can also reduce the outline's scope by pressing [Alt][Shift] and the number of the lowest level heading you want to see.) Figure 16-28 shows the document in the outline view with the outline reduced to first- and second-level headings. Next, issue the Renumber... command, choose the OUTLINE option from the Format list box, and choose OK. Since Word applies automatic numbering by default, some numbering fields will appear at the beginning of each paragraph. If you turn on the Field Codes setting on the View menu, you'll see that these fields are labeled *AUTONUMOUT*. If you select the Manual option in the Renumber dialog box, Word will insert literal numbers instead of the AUTONUMOUT fields.

Figure 16-28

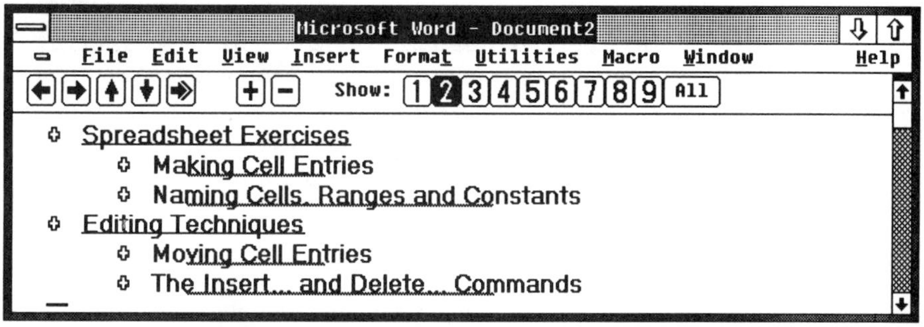

Collapsing an outline to show only heading paragraphs removes other paragraphs from the screen.

After numbering the heading paragraphs, you can issue the Outline command again to leave the outline view. Then, the document will look like Figure 16-29.

Figure 16-29

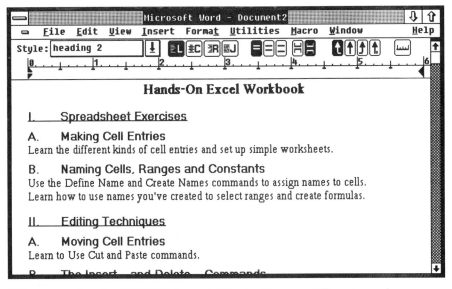

When you select the OUTLINE format, Word will use a different numbering scheme for each paragraph level.

Numbering text paragraphs

While you'll probably never want to number an outlined document's title, you may want to number the paragraphs of text. Whether you are applying automatic or manual numbers, do not switch to the outline view before you number your paragraphs. Simply use the Renumber... command and select the OUTLINE option to number all the paragraphs in the document. Word will use Arabic numerals to number the title, text, and any other paragraph not formatted with a *heading* style. Next, select the title paragraph and use the Renumber... command to remove its automatic numbering. You can also use this technique to selectively remove the automatic or manual numbers from other paragraphs as well.

The Show All Levels option

When you use the OUTLINE option to insert manual paragraph numbers, Word will allow you to create detailed outline numbers. For example, if you were to use this option, the paragraph number *I.B.3.* would identify a paragraph as the third-level paragraph (*3.*) subordinate to the second second-level paragraph (*B.*), which is in turn subordinate to the first first-level paragraph (*I.*) in the document.

To activate this option, simply select the Show All Levels check box in the Renumber dialog box. The Show All Levels option is available only when you have selected the Manual option and chosen the OUTLINE option in the Format list box. To give you a better idea of how the Show All Levels option affects a document's appearance, Figure 16-30 shows the document from Figure 16-29 after we selected the Show All Levels check box.

Figure 16-30

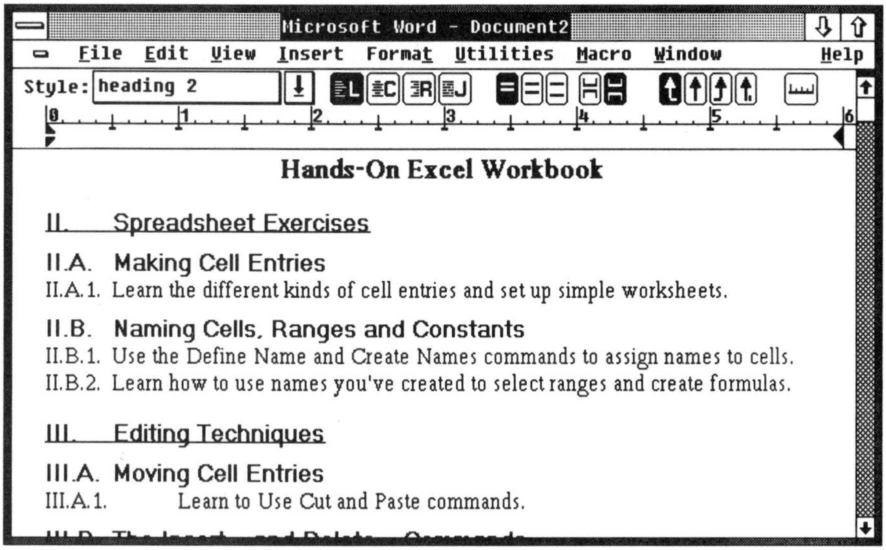

The Show All Levels option adds the numbers of a paragraph's superior paragraphs to a document's manual numbering.

Sometimes, you'll want the numbers for only some of your paragraphs to display their superior levels. Using the LEARN option in the Format list box, you can control the display of superior level numbers on a level-by-level basis throughout your document.

For instance, in the document shown in Figure 16-30, suppose you want to display the numbers of superior levels only on the text formatted in the *Normal* style. On the *heading 1* and *heading 2* paragraphs, you want to display only the number of the current level. Begin by displaying the numbers of superior levels on all your paragraphs as we've done in Figure 16-30. Then, for each level on which you do not want to display the numbers of superior levels, edit the number on the first paragraph in that level so that it no longer displays the superior levels. In our example, you must edit the number for the first second-level paragraph (*Making Cell Entries*), changing its number from *II.A* to simply *A..*

After editing the paragraph number, open the Renumber dialog box, choose the Renumber Paragraphs Numbered Only option, along with the Manual and LEARN options. When you choose OK, Word will change the paragraph numbers so that the format of each number at a given level matches the format of the first paragraph number in that level. Figure 16-31 shows our sample document with the numbers of superior levels displayed only on the third-level paragraphs.

Figure 16-31

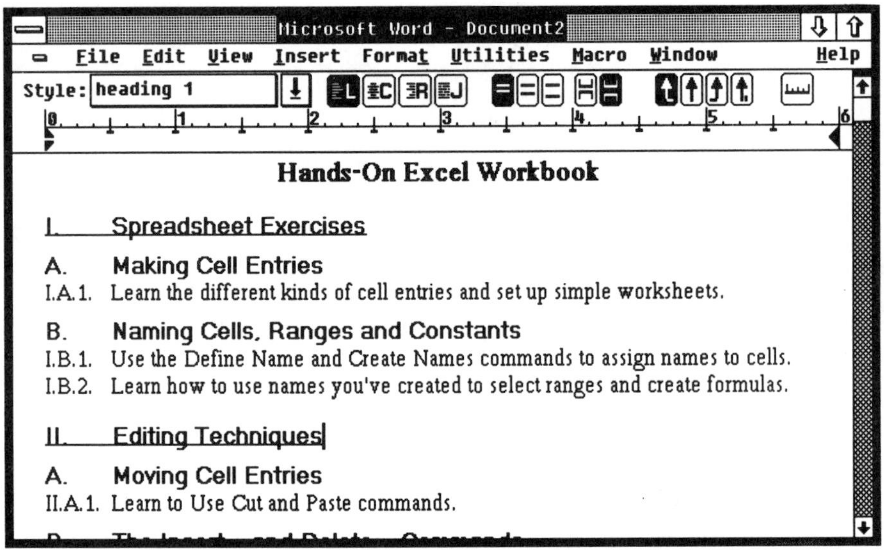

In this document, only the Normal *paragraph numbers display the numbers of superior levels.*

Numbering a legal document

The LEGAL option in the Format list box tells Word to number paragraphs as they would appear in a legal document. When you select the LEGAL option, Word will number each paragraph with a series of Arabic numerals, separated from the text by periods, that identify the number of each paragraph's superior paragraphs. For example, the paragraph number 2.1.2 would identify the second-level paragraph subordinate to the first second-level paragraph under the second first-level paragraph. Figure 16-32 shows the document from Figure 16-31 after we numbered the paragraphs with the LEGAL format.

If you select the LEGAL option while applying automatic paragraph numbering, Word will insert numbering fields named AUTONUMLGL. Like AUTONUM and AUTONUMOUT fields, an AUTONUMLGL field will automatically change its result whenever you add or delete numbered entries in your document.

Defining your own numbering schemes

Earlier in this chapter, we showed you how to use the LEARN option in the Format text box to define a single numbering scheme for manually numbered paragraphs. As you may recall, you had to insert an example of your numbering scheme in the first paragraph you wanted to number before issuing the Renumber... command. You can also use the LEARN option to define different manual numbering schemes for the various levels in a document that contains multiple levels of paragraphs. To define multiple numbering schemes, enter an example number in the first paragraph at each level.

Figure 16-32

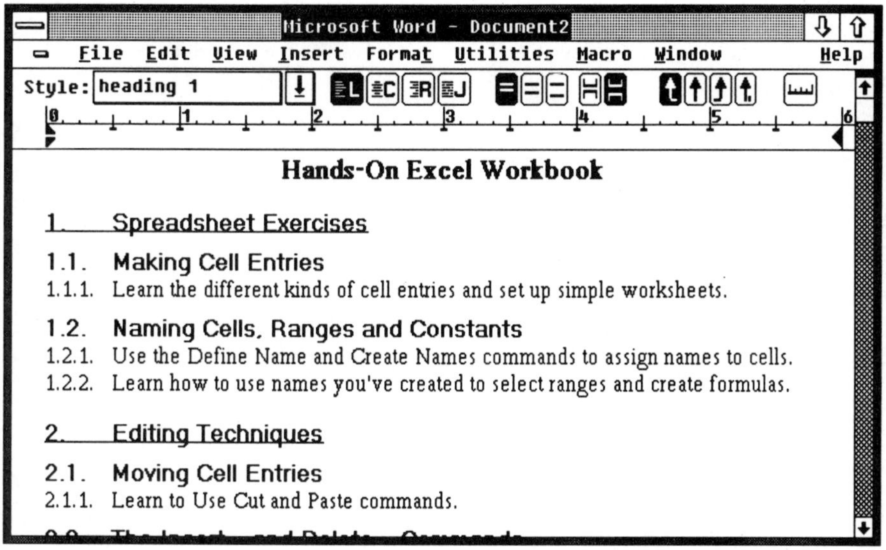

```
┌─────────────────────────────────────────────────────────────────────┐
│ ▭        Microsoft Word - Document2              ⇩ ⇧ │
├─────────────────────────────────────────────────────────────────────┤
│  ▭  File  Edit  View  Insert  Format  Utilities  Macro  Window    Help │
├─────────────────────────────────────────────────────────────────────┤
│ Style:│heading 1    │ ⬇ │ ☰L ☰C ☰R ☰J  ☰☰☰ ☰☰  ⬆⬆⬆⬆  ⎵ │ ⬆ │
│ 0. . . . 1. . . . 2. . . . 3. . . . 4. . . . 5. . . . 6  │
│                                                                        │
│            Hands-On Excel Workbook                                    │
│                                                                        │
│   1.     Spreadsheet Exercises                                        │
│                                                                        │
│   1.1.   Making Cell Entries                                          │
│   1.1.1. Learn the different kinds of cell entries and set up simple worksheets. │
│                                                                        │
│   1.2.   Naming Cells, Ranges and Constants                           │
│   1.2.1. Use the Define Name and Create Names commands to assign names to cells. │
│   1.2.2. Learn how to use names you've created to select ranges and create formulas. │
│                                                                        │
│   2.     Editing Techniques                                           │
│                                                                        │
│   2.1.   Moving Cell Entries                                          │
│   2.1.1. Learn to Use Cut and Paste commands.                         │
│                                                                      ⬇ │
└─────────────────────────────────────────────────────────────────────┘
```

*You can use the LEGAL option to number paragraphs as they should appear in
a legal document.*

For instance, suppose you want to renumber the paragraphs in the document
in Figure 16-29, using Arabic numerals followed by a closing parenthesis and tab
for first-level paragraphs and, for second-level paragraphs, use lowercase letters
followed by a closing parenthesis and tab. To begin, insert example numbers in
the first first-level and second-level paragraphs, as shown in Figure 16-33 on the
next page. Next, issue the Renumber... command. Assuming the cursor is still
in one of the paragraphs you've already numbered, Word will automatically select
the Manual option in the Renumber dialog box and the LEARN option in the
Format text box. (If you've moved the cursor, you'll need to select these options
yourself.) However, if the cursor is in a numbered paragraph, Word will also select
the Renumber Paragraphs Numbered Only option. (If you want to define a
numbering scheme for a previously unnumbered document, you'll need to select
the Renumber Paragraphs All option.) After you select OK, the renumbered
document will look like Figure 16-34 on the following page.

Notice that Word has numbered the title and text paragraphs with Arabic
numerals followed by a period, maintaining the Show All Levels setting from our
previous example. If you do not specify a numbering scheme for a paragraph level
when applying the LEARN format, Word will use this Arabic numbering scheme
for paragraphs at that level. If you select the LEARN option without inserting
example numbers for any level of paragraphs, Word will number every level with
Arabic numerals, as if you had chosen the SEQUENCE option.

Figure 16-33

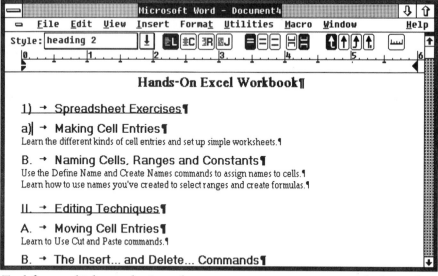

To define multiple numbering schemes, you must enter an example for each paragraph level.

Figure 16-34

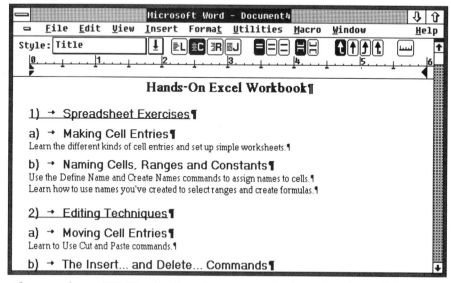

After you choose OK, Word will apply your numbering schemes to all the paragraphs in your document.

When numbering paragraphs with the LEARN option, you can include the numbers of all superior levels of paragraphs, as we did in this example. To display superior levels, you can either add the multiple levels to selected example paragraphs, as we demonstrated, or choose the Show All Levels check box in the Renumber dialog box.

When you're working with a selection in a document that contains multiple levels of paragraphs, specifying a Start At number for manual numbering can be a bit tricky. The number you enter in the Start At text box must include the number of all superior paragraph levels, but it must not include the numbers of subordinate levels below the level at which you want to begin renumbering. For example, Figure 16-35 shows a document with three levels of paragraphs that are numbered with a standard outline numbering scheme. As you can see, a new second-level topic has been inserted between paragraph A (*Software Issues*) and paragraph B (*Hardware Issues*). In addition, we've added a couple of third-level topics under the new second-level paragraph.

Specifying a Start At number

Figure 16-35

```
┌────────────────────────────────────────────────────────────┐
│ ▭          Microsoft Word - CONFER.DOC              ⇩ ⇧     │
│  ▭  File  Edit  View  Insert  Format  Utilities  Macro  Window  Help │
│ Style: heading 1    ↓  [≣L][≣C][≣R][≣J] [▬▬][▬▬][▬▬][▇▇] [↕][↑][↕][↑] [⌴]  ↑│
│ 0 ┊    ┊  1  ┊    ┊  2  ┊    ┊  3  ┊    ┊  4  ┊    ┊  5  ┊    ┊  6 │
│                                                            │
│              Technology Marketing Conference               │
│                                                            │
│  I.     Breakfast                                          │
│                                                            │
│  II.    Welcome                                            │
│                                                            │
│  III.   Morning Conference                                 │
│                                                            │
│  A.     Software Issues                                    │
│  1.     Marketing software for emerging standards. - Tom Wagner, ICS Corp. │
│  2.     Who should sell your product? - Barbara Kaplan, Medical Software Systems. │
│                                                            │
│  Artificial Intelligence Issues                            │
│  Long-term thinking in a fast-changing industry. - Phil Hopkins, Martin & Hopkins. │
│  The role of A.I in marketing new products. - Stuart Gatti, America Digital Systems, Inc. │
│                                                            │
│  B.     Hardware Issues                                    │
│  1.     New systems for printing and plotting. - Karen Emerson, Output Systems, Inc. │
│  2.     Keeping up with expanded memory configurations - John Grossman, IBM │
└────────────────────────────────────────────────────────────┘
```

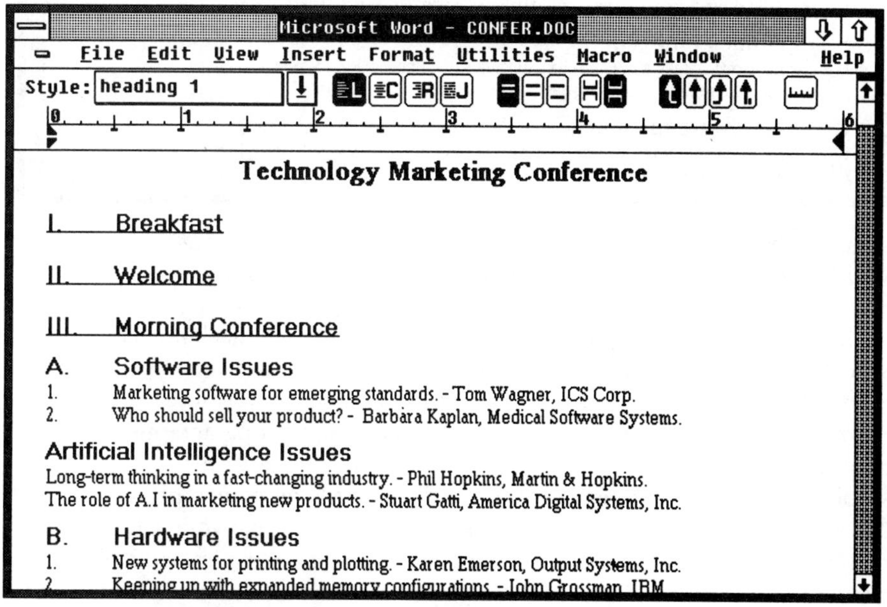

We inserted some new paragraphs in this three-level document.

To renumber this document, begin by selecting all the text beginning with the new second-level paragraph. (Select *Artificial Intelligence Issues* and the following text.) Then, open the Renumber dialog box and select the Manual and OUTLINE options. Enter *III.B* or *3.2* in the Start At text box and choose OK. Figure 16-36 shows the result.

Figure 16-36

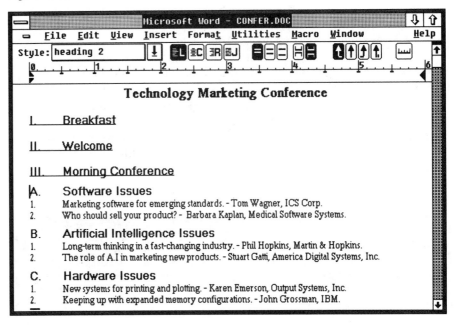

In renumbering paragraphs in a multiple-level document, the Start At number should include the number of any superior paragraph levels.

Remember, the examples in your document tell Word what kind of numbering scheme you want to use at the different paragraph levels (Roman numerals, Arabic numerals, or letters). The entry in the Start At text box simply indicates where in this numbering scheme you want to start numbering your paragraphs. A Start At number of *3.2*, like *III.B*, indicates that you want to start numbering with the second second-level paragraph after the third first-level paragraph.

Notice that, even though you want the first paragraph in your selection to be numbered with *B.*, the Start At number includes the *III* of the immediate superior paragraph. Had you entered *B* as your Start At number, Word would have misinterpreted your intentions. Word considers a *B* in the Start At text box to be the same as a *2*; both indicate that you want to begin numbering with the second number in the particular numbering scheme you've chosen. In the example, the entry *B* in the Start At text box would have caused the first paragraph in the selection to be numbered with II since our entry in the Format text box specifies a standard outline numbering scheme, in which the second first-level paragraph is always numbered II.

As we've demonstrated, Word's ability to update paragraph numbers is very flexible. Of course, Word adjusts the paragraph numbers displayed by AUTONUM, AUTONUMOUT, and AUTONUMLGL fields whenever you move or delete paragraphs. However, you can also easily update manual numbers to reflect any changes you make, such as adding, deleting, or moving text. If you want to maintain the format of manual numbers as you update them, be sure that the first paragraph number at each level is formatted properly.

Revising your paragraph numbers

If you add new paragraphs to your document, delete some paragraphs, or rearrange your existing paragraphs, you can easily update manual paragraph numbers by executing the Renumber… command. Just be sure that no text is selected when you choose Renumber… so that Word will be able to change all the numbers in your document and not just the numbers of selected paragraphs. Of course, there may be times when the changes you make affect only a limited area of your document. In those cases, you'll probably find it quicker to select just the affected area before you issue the Renumber… command.

Adding, deleting, and rearranging paragraphs

When you add or rearrange selected paragraphs, you may need to enter a new Start At number in the Renumber dialog box. If you do this, just be aware of how Word interprets the entry in the Start At text box.

After you issue the Renumber… command and choose OK, you can undo your numbering by selecting Undo Renumber from the Edit menu. If you select Undo Renumber after renumbering your document for the first time, Word will delete all the paragraph numbers. If you selected Renumber… to reformat or update your paragraph numbers, Undo Renumber will cancel the latest change.

Removing paragraph numbers

You can remove paragraph numbers at any time by selecting the Remove option in the Renumber dialog box. If you don't select any text before you do this, Word will remove all the paragraph numbers in your document. If you want to remove the numbers on only some of the paragraphs in your document, simply highlight those paragraphs before you choose the Renumber… command and select the Remove option.

Word's Sort… command lets you rearrange lists, paragraphs, and tables in either ascending or descending order. When you select the Sort… command from the Utilities menu, Word will display the Sort dialog box shown in Figure 16-37. You can change the settings in this box to make Word sort according to alphanumeric, numeric, or date values, and control other sorting options.

SORTING

Figure 16-37

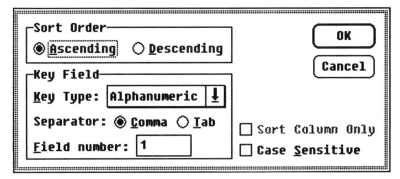

Word displays this dialog box when you issue the Sort... command.

If you don't select any text before you issue the Sort... command, Word will sort all the paragraphs in your document based on the first character in each paragraph. If two or more paragraphs begin with the same character, Word will compare the second characters, then the third, and so on, until it finds a variation on which it can sort or reaches the end of the identical paragraphs. In sorting the paragraphs, Word will ignore section boundaries. If you want to sort only a portion of a document, you can select the text you want to sort before you issue the Sort... command.

One of the most powerful features of the Sort... command is its ability to sort a table of information based on a single key column. We'll demonstrate this technique in a few pages. First, however, let's consider a few basic facts about sorting with Word.

Word's default sort order is ascending. However, you can sort in descending order by selecting the Descending option in the Sort dialog box. Once you've issued the Sort... command, you can undo your sort by choosing Undo Sort from the Edit menu. (Like other Undo commands, this one must be issued immediately after you sort, before you do anything else.)

Let's look at a simple example of sorting. Suppose you want to sort the used cars listed in the document shown in Figure 16-38 in ascending order based on the model name of each car. Since you want to sort only the paragraphs listing cars, begin by selecting those lines, as shown in Figure 16-39. Next, issue the Sort... command and choose OK in the Sort dialog box. Word will then sort the selected paragraphs as shown in Figure 16-40 on page 660.

Word can perform sorts based on several types of data. Based on the option you choose in the Sort dialog box, Word will sort the text in selected paragraphs as alphanumeric, numeric, or date values.

Figure 16-38

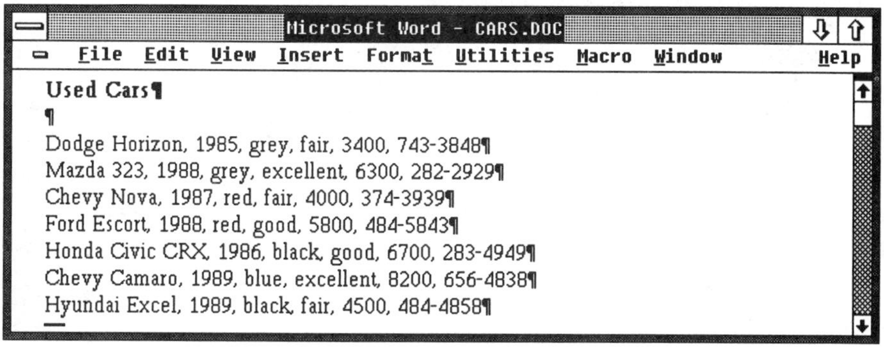

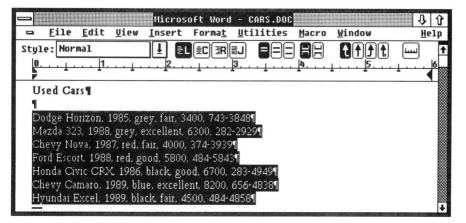

We'll sort the cars in this list according to their model names.

Figure 16-39

If you don't want to sort all the paragraphs in a document, you can make a block selection before issuing the Sort... command.

By default, Word sorts paragraphs as alphanumeric data, which can include letters of the alphabet, numbers, and any other printable character. As a result, the Alphanumeric option will appear in the Key Type text box the first time you issue the Sort... command during a Word session.

Word sorts alphanumeric data according to its own internal sort order table. When Word sorts alphanumeric data into ascending order, punctuation marks and other non-alphanumeric characters will precede numbers, and numbers will precede letters.

Alphanumeric sorts

Figure 16-40

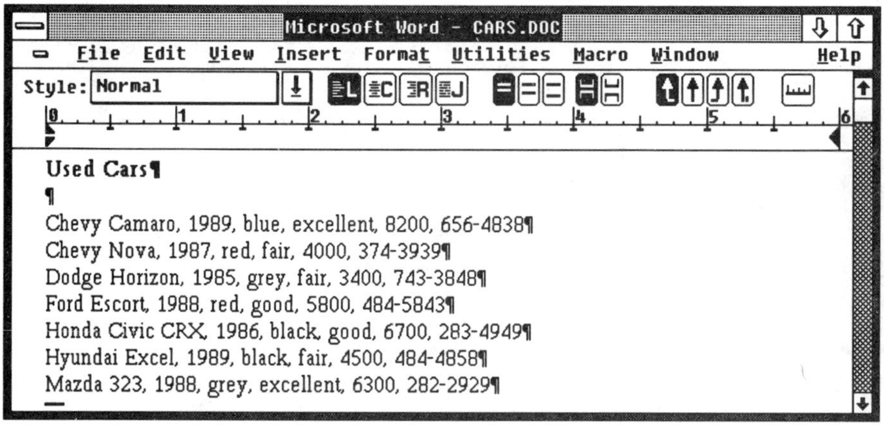

```
┌─────────────────────────────────────────────────────────────────────┐
│ ═══    ▓▓▓▓▓▓▓▓▓▓▓Microsoft Word - CARS.DOC▓▓▓▓▓▓▓▓▓    ⇩ │ ⇧ │
│  ▭   File  Edit  View  Insert  Format  Utilities  Macro  Window    Help│
│ Style: Normal        ⬇ ⬛L⬛C⬛R⬛J  ⬛⬛⬛ ⬛⬛  ⬛⬆⬆⬆  └─┘        ⬆│
│ 0......↓.....1......↓.....2......↓.....3......↓.....4......↓.....5......↓.....6│
│ ▶                                                                    ◀│
│ ───────────────────────────────────────────────────────────────────── │
│ Used Cars¶                                                            │
│ ¶                                                                     │
│ Chevy Camaro, 1989, blue, excellent, 8200, 656-4838¶                 │
│ Chevy Nova, 1987, red, fair, 4000, 374-3939¶                         │
│ Dodge Horizon, 1985, grey, fair, 3400, 743-3848¶                     │
│ Ford Escort, 1988, red, good, 5800, 484-5843¶                        │
│ Honda Civic CRX, 1986, black, good, 6700, 283-4949¶                  │
│ Hyundai Excel, 1989, black, fair, 4500, 484-4858¶                    │
│ Mazda 323, 1988, grey, excellent, 6300, 282-2929¶                    │
│ ═══                                                                 ⬇│
└─────────────────────────────────────────────────────────────────────┘
```

This screen shows the sorted list of cars.

If a paragraph begins with an indent, tab, or blank space, Word will ignore the space and sort the paragraph according to the first character after the indent, tab, or space. Similarly, if a paragraph begins with a quotation mark, Word will sort that paragraph according to the first character after the quotation mark. This rule does not apply to the single quotation mark ('). Blank paragraphs—that is, paragraphs that consist of a ¶ mark with no text—precede non-blank paragraphs in an ascending sort.

By default, Word ignores case when sorting letters. For example, a paragraph that begins with the word *able* will precede another paragraph that begins with *Apple* because *b* precedes *p* in the alphabet. However, you can enable case-sensitive sorting by selecting the Case Sensitive check box in the Sort dialog box. If you activate this check box, a paragraph that begins with *Apple* will precede one that begins with *able* simply because it begins with an uppercase A. The Case Sensitive option is available only when you've selected the Alphanumeric Key Type option.

Numeric sorts

You can sort paragraphs as numeric data by entering the Numeric option in the Key Type text box. (You can type selections in this text box or choose an option from the attached pull-down list box.) When Word sorts numbers, it considers each string to be digits in a numeric value; it does not simply look at the first digit in the series. For example, in sorting numbers, Word knows that the number 6 comes before the number 10, even though the first digit in 10—1—is less than 6.

Word's ability to sort by number offers an easy way to rearrange several paragraphs in a document. For instance, suppose you need to rearrange a group of paragraphs in a document. You could cut and paste each paragraph until they're all in the correct order. A faster method, however, is to type a number at the beginning of each paragraph, indicating the order in which you want to place that paragraph. For example, Figure 16-41 shows a document in which we've typed numbers at the beginning of some paragraphs. You must include at least one blank space between the number and the paragraph text. As you'll see in a moment, this will speed up the process of removing the numbers after you've rearranged the paragraphs.

Using numbered paragraphs to rearrange a document

Figure 16-41

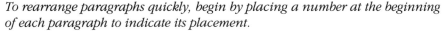

```
┌──────────────────────────────────────────────────────────────┐
│ ▭  ▭        Microsoft Word - SCHOOL.DOC              ⇩ ⇧ │
│ ⊖   File  Edit  View  Insert  Format  Utilities  Macro  Window        Help │
├──────────────────────────────────────────────────────────────┤ ▲
│  Educational Philosophy                                         │
│        3 All of the classrooms at the Clark School are organized according to │
│    the "learning centers" concept. Children are offered a variety of creative │
│    activities in different areas of the room. In a preschool classroom, you might │
│    find wooden blocks in one corner, books in another corner, an art activity at │
│    a table, and several other activities available in other areas of the room. │
│        1 We interviewed the director of the Clark School and several teachers │
│    in order to get a more detailed picture of the educational environment they │
│    hope to provide. All the people we spoke with emphasized that the school │
│    is designed to help children grow emotionally and socially, as well as │
│    intellectually.. │
│        2 Another important element of the Clark School's educational │
│    philosophy is the idea that children should be allowed to pursue their own │
│    pace in learning. "Forced learning is inappropriate—if not impossible—for │
│    young children," said Mrs. Ballard. "Studies have shown that children who │
│    are pushed into subjects before they are ready may develop a negative │ ▼
└──────────────────────────────────────────────────────────────┘
```

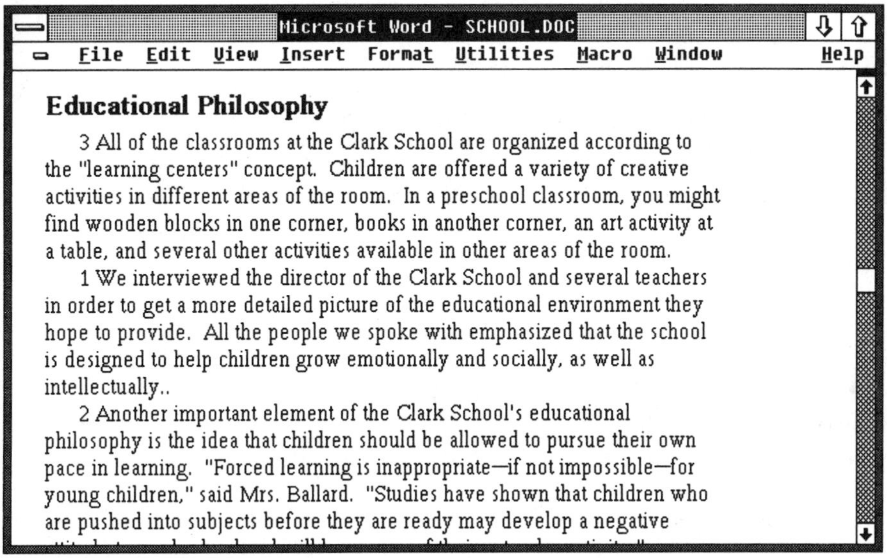

To rearrange paragraphs quickly, begin by placing a number at the beginning of each paragraph to indicate its placement.

Once you've numbered the paragraphs, select them, and choose Sort... from the Utilities menu, select the Numeric option in the Key Type list box, and choose OK. Word will then rearrange the paragraphs according to their numbers, as shown in Figure 16-42 on the following page.

You can now remove the numbers, either with manual editing techniques or by using Word's Renumber... command. To remove the numbers with the Renumber... command, open the Renumber dialog box, select the Remove option, then choose OK. This technique will work only if you've included at least one blank space between each number and the first character of paragraph text.

Figure 16-42

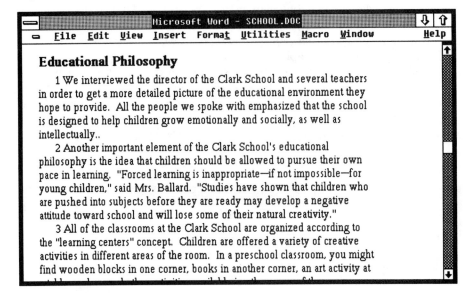

When you issue the Sort... command, Word will sort the paragraphs according to their numbers.

Unfortunately, you cannot use Roman numerals to sort paragraphs. However, you can sort Roman numerals up to VIII as alphanumeric values because the first eight Roman numerals fall into the correct order based on the letters they include (I before II, II before III, III before IV, and so on). In general, we recommend that you use Arabic numerals when numbering paragraphs that you intend to sort.

Date sorts

In addition to alphanumeric and numeric sorts, Word can sort properly formatted data as date values. In order for Word to recognize a string of text as a date value, the text must be organized in one of the formats in Table 16-2.

Table 16-2

Date formats	Example
MMM-yy	Jan-90
M/d/yy	1/23/90
M-d-yy	1-23-90
d-MMM-yy	23-Jan-90
MMMM d, yyyy	January 23, 1990
M/d/yy h:mm AM/PM	1/23/90 3:30 PM

Word will use all the information included in your date values when it performs the sort. For example, if you sort three paragraphs that begin with the dates Dec-89, Nov-89 and Jan-90, Word will arrange the paragraphs in the order Nov-89, Dec-89, and Jan-90. If you sort the dates 1/1/89 2:30 PM and 1/1/89 2:30 AM, Word will place the date with the time 2:30 AM before the same date with the time 2:30 PM.

The ability to base a sort on dates is a powerful tool when you are organizing a table or sorting lists. We'll demonstrate these useful features later in this chapter.

The Sort... command is available in the outline view, and Word distinguishes between the levels of an outline when you sort (just as it distinguishes between levels of numbered paragraphs). For example, Figure 16-43 shows what happened when we sorted the outline from Figure 16-28. (We issued the Sort... command before numbering the outline.) Notice that Word has moved the subordinate outline sections along with their superior headings. Whenever you sort in the outline view, Word sorts only the highest-level paragraphs selected, moving subordinate paragraphs with their superior paragraphs. You can sort the paragraphs that appear under the same superior paragraph by selecting them and then issuing the Sort... command.

Sorting in the outline view

Figure 16-43

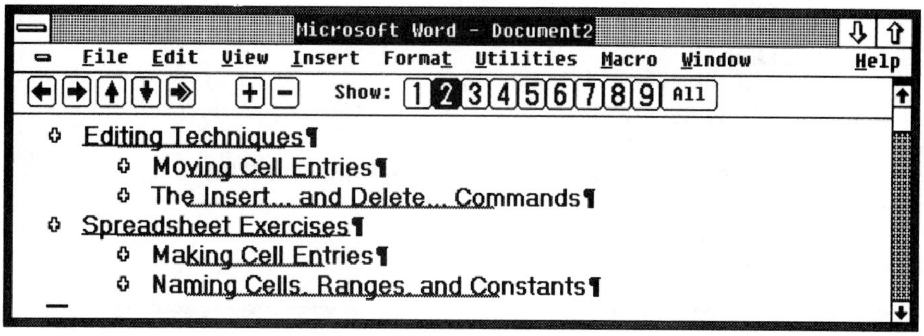

Word will keep subordinate paragraphs under their headings when you sort in the outline view.

If you want to rearrange sections in an outline, you can specify a new order by numbering the headings at different levels with letters or Arabic or Roman numerals, then sorting the collapsed outline. We already explained that the Sort... command cannot sort Roman numerals as numbers, and there are some other points you need to keep in mind when sorting an outline.

First, if you use letters to designate heading levels in your document, you need to select the Alphanumeric Key Type option when you sort the outline. However, if you select the Alphanumeric Key Type option, you can use numbers only at paragraph levels that include fewer than ten headings. Remember that Word will place a paragraph with the number 10 before another with the number 9 when performing an alphanumeric sort. As we've already explained, you can use Roman numerals only at levels that include no more than eight headings. If you want to use Arabic numerals to label a section that includes more than nine headings, you'll need to select the Numeric Key Type option and use Arabic numerals at every level throughout your outline.

For example, suppose you created an outline in the outline view, then you switched to the normal editing view and filled in the document text. Next, you returned to the outline view and selected the Show-2 icon, causing Word to display only the first two levels of headings, as shown in Figure 16-44.

Figure 16-44

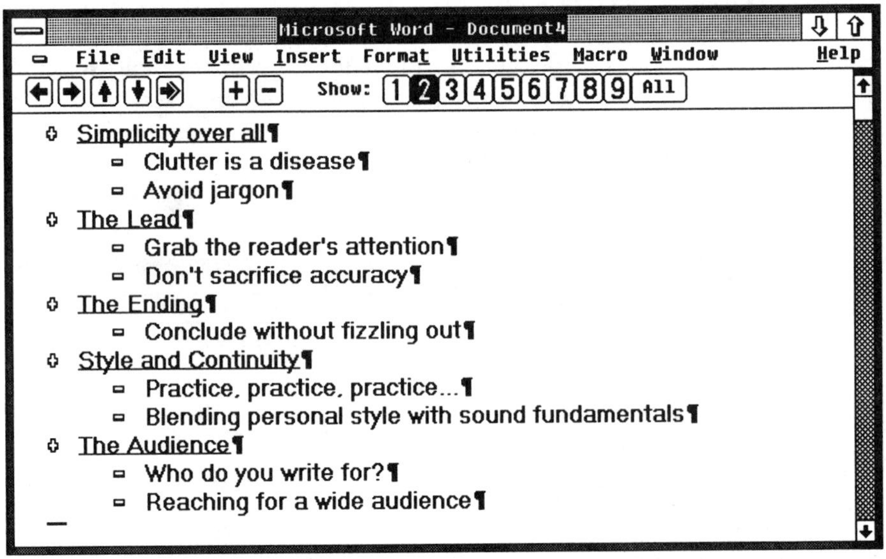

When you switch from the normal editing view to the outline view, you can use the Show icons to collapse the document to headings only.

This bird's-eye view can be very helpful in checking the organization and flow of your document. Then, if you decide to rearrange your document, you can do so easily in the outline view. For example, in the outline view, you can move one subheading and, in so doing, move all the subheadings and body text under that subheading as well. The Sort... command can be a handy tool for rearranging various parts of a document in the outline view. If you want to use the Sort... command, however, you must be sure to collapse out of view any portions of your document you do not want to sort.

For example, suppose you want to move the fourth first-level section (*Style and Continuity*) to the beginning of your document, and reverse the order of the two subsections within this section. To do this, number the first-level headings according to the desired order and similarly number the two second-level headings in the *Style and Continuity* section, as shown in Figure 16-45.

Figure 16-45

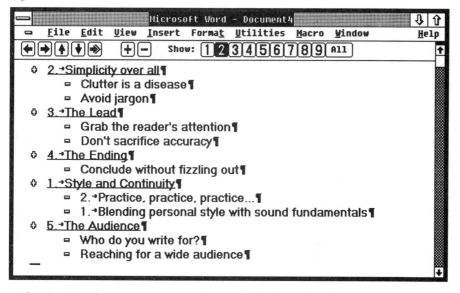

Before issuing the Sort... command, you should number the sections you want to sort.

After numbering the sections you want to rearrange, issue the Sort... command and select the Numeric Key Type option. When you choose OK, Word will sort the sections in the outline, as shown in Figure 16-46 on the next page. Next, select the two second-level paragraphs under *Style and Continuity* and issue the Sort... command again. When you choose OK this time, Word will sort the two second-level paragraphs, as shown in Figure 16-47 on page 667. Now, you can issue the Renumber... command and select the Renumber Paragraphs Remove option to remove the numbers from the document.

Word's ability to sort tables and lists of information is similar to that of many simple database programs. In most tables, information is listed in columns aligned at tab stops, with each paragraph constituting one row in the table. Each column represents one "field" in the table's structure. In a list of information, fields of data are separated by tabs or commas, and a paragraph can include as many lines as

Sorting based on a key field

are needed to hold all its fields. Although Word, by default, sorts on the information in the first column (field) of each paragraph, you can use the Sort dialog box to specify any column as the key field. We will begin by showing you how to sort based on a column in a table, then we will look at sorting lists on a specified column.

Figure 16-46

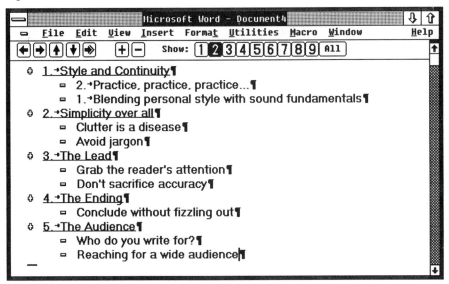

Word will sort the numbered sections when you select the Numeric Key Type option in the Sort dialog box.

Sorting a table by key column

Word can sort all the entries in one column of a table and rearrange the rest of the table according to that sorted column. It can also sort one column without disturbing other columns in the table. Let's consider a simple example that demonstrates Word's table-sorting capability.

Suppose your document contains the table of data shown in Figure 16-48. You want to sort this information into descending order by Start Date so that the most recently hired employees will appear at the top of the table. Since you want to exclude the column headings from the sort, begin by selecting only those lines that contain data, as shown in Figure 16-49 on page 668.

Next, open the Sort dialog box, choose the Descending option, and select the Date option in the Key Type text box. Since you are sorting a column, select the Tab Separator option. Finally, enter *2* in the Field Number text box to sort on the Start Date column, which is the second column (field) in the table. After you choose OK, Word will sort the table as shown in Figure 16-50 on page 668.

Figure 16-47

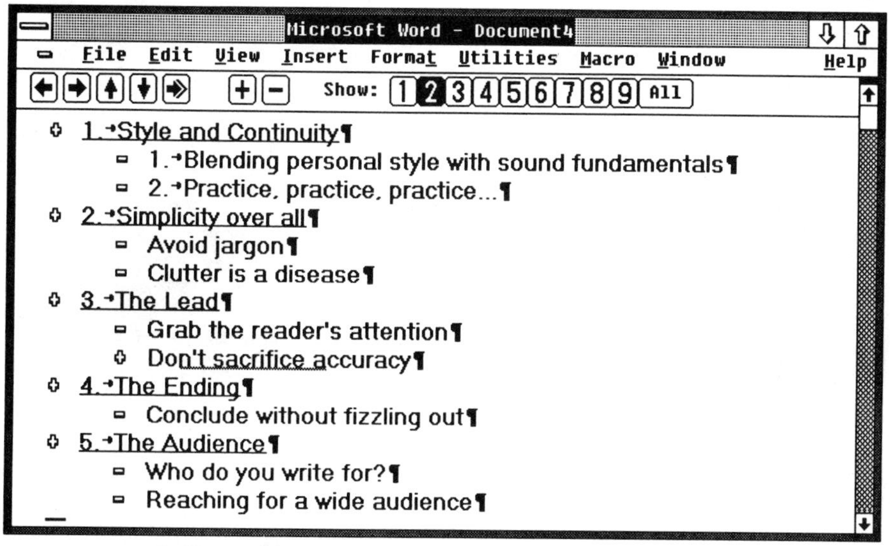

```
┌──────────────────────────────────────────────────────────────────┐
│ ⊟         Microsoft Word - Document4                        ⇩ ⇧   │
│ ⊟   File  Edit  View  Insert  Format  Utilities  Macro  Window  Help│
│ ◄ ► ▲ ▼ ➡   ⊞ ⊟   Show: 1 2 3 4 5 6 7 8 9 All                 ↑  │
│  ◊  1.→Style and Continuity¶                                       │
│       □  1.→Blending personal style with sound fundamentals¶       │
│       □  2.→Practice, practice, practice...¶                       │
│  ◊  2.→Simplicity over all¶                                        │
│       □  Avoid jargon¶                                             │
│       □  Clutter is a disease¶                                     │
│  ◊  3.→The Lead¶                                                   │
│       □  Grab the reader's attention¶                              │
│       ◊  Don't sacrifice accuracy¶                                 │
│  ◊  4.→The Ending¶                                                 │
│       □  Conclude without fizzling out¶                            │
│  ◊  5.→The Audience¶                                               │
│       □  Who do you write for?¶                                    │
│       □  Reaching for a wide audience¶                             │
│  ─                                                            ↓    │
└──────────────────────────────────────────────────────────────────┘
```

To sort subordinate paragraphs grouped under the same superior heading, select the subordinate paragraphs before you issue the Sort... command.

Figure 16-48

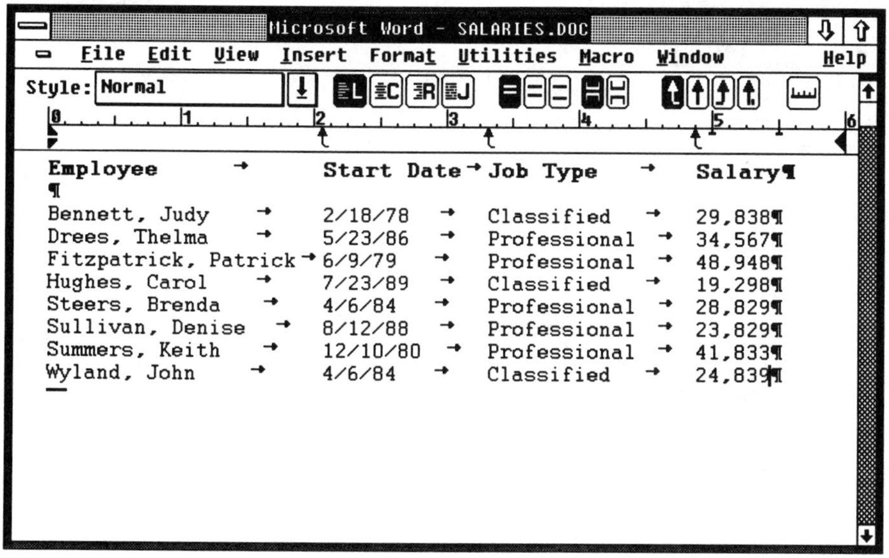

```
┌──────────────────────────────────────────────────────────────────┐
│ ⊟         Microsoft Word - SALARIES.DOC                     ⇩ ⇧   │
│ ⊟   File  Edit  View  Insert  Format  Utilities  Macro  Window  Help│
│ Style: Normal      ↓  L C R J  ▬ ▬ ▬ ▬  ↑ ↑ ↑ ↑  ▭         ↑  │
│ 0. . . . . 1. . . . . 2. . . . . 3. . . . . 4. . . . . 5. . . . . 6│
│                                                                    │
│ Employee          →    Start Date→Job Type      →   Salary¶        │
│ ¶                                                                  │
│ Bennett, Judy     →    2/18/78  →  Classified   →   29,838¶        │
│ Drees, Thelma     →    5/23/86  →  Professional →   34,567¶        │
│ Fitzpatrick, Patrick→6/9/79    →  Professional →   48,948¶        │
│ Hughes, Carol     →    7/23/89  →  Classified   →   19,298¶        │
│ Steers, Brenda    →    4/6/84   →  Professional →   28,829¶        │
│ Sullivan, Denise  →    8/12/88  →  Professional →   23,829¶        │
│ Summers, Keith    →    12/10/80 →  Professional →   41,833¶        │
│ Wyland, John      →    4/6/84   →  Classified   →   24,839¶        │
│ ─                                                            ↓    │
└──────────────────────────────────────────────────────────────────┘
```

You can use Word's Sort... command to sort a table like this one.

Figure 16-49

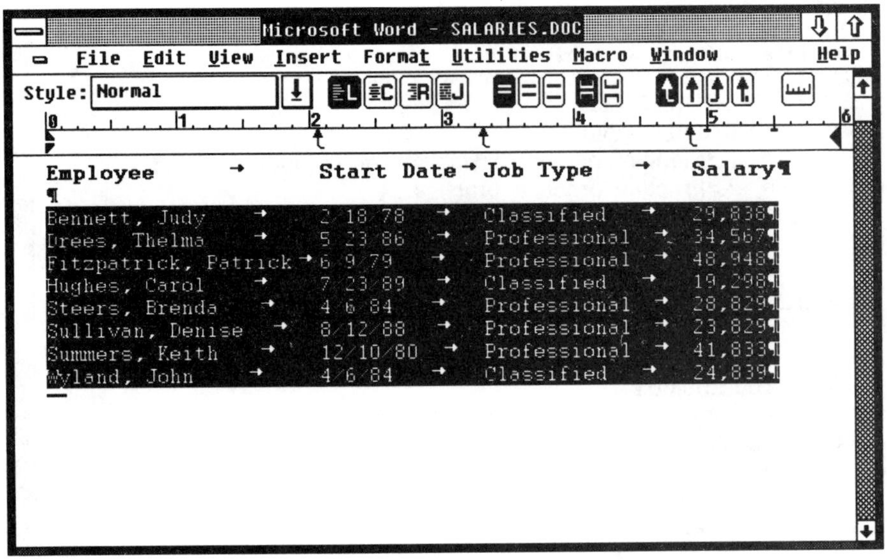

The first step in sorting the table is to select the lines of data you want to sort.

Figure 16-50

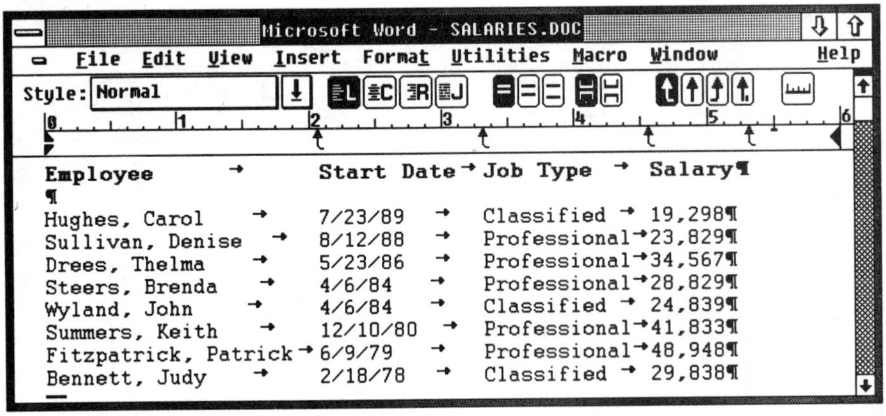

When you choose OK from the Sort dialog box, Word will sort the table according to the column you selected.

If you want to use multiple sort keys, you must sort on the primary sort key first, then go back and select each group of rows with the same value in their key columns, and sort them based on your secondary sort key. For example, suppose you want to sort the table shown in Figure 16-50 in ascending order based on the Job Type and Salary columns. In other words, you want to group those employees with the same job type, then sort according to the salary within each group.

The first step is to sort the table based on the Job Type column. To do this, select all the rows in the table, excluding the column headings and blank lines, and open the Sort dialog box. Next, choose the Ascending Sort Order, Alphanumeric Key Type, and Tab Separator options, and enter *3* in the Field Number text box. Choosing OK tells Word to sort the table as shown in Figure 16-51.

Figure 16-51

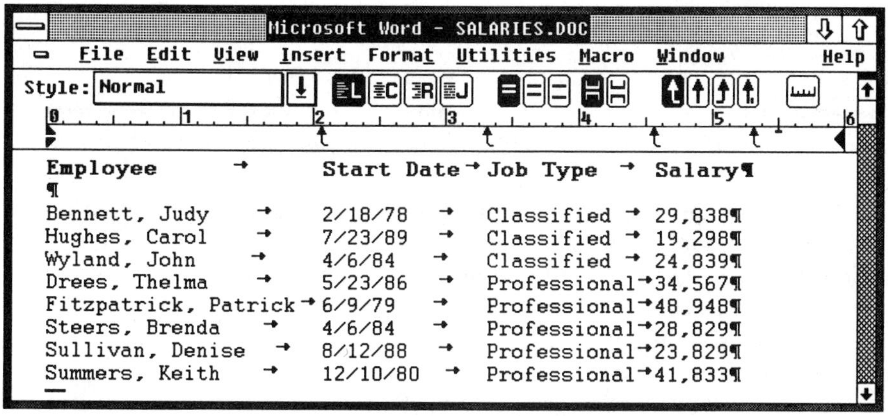
Microsoft Word - SALARIES.DOC
File Edit View Insert Format Utilities Macro Window Help
Style: Normal
Employee → Start Date → Job Type → Salary¶
¶
Bennett, Judy → 2/18/78 → Classified → 29,838¶
Hughes, Carol → 7/23/89 → Classified → 19,298¶
Wyland, John → 4/6/84 → Classified → 24,839¶
Drees, Thelma → 5/23/86 → Professional→34,567¶
Fitzpatrick, Patrick→6/9/79 → Professional→48,948¶
Steers, Brenda → 4/6/84 → Professional→28,829¶
Sullivan, Denise → 8/12/88 → Professional→23,829¶
Summers, Keith → 12/10/80 → Professional→41,833¶

This screen shows the result of sorting on the Job Type column.

Next, select only those rows with *Classified* in the Job Type column and open the Sort dialog box, choose the Numeric Key Type option, enter *4* (the number of the Salary column) in the Field Number text box, and choose OK. After you repeat these steps for the rows with *Professional* in the Job Type column, the table will look like Figure 16-52 on the following page.

Notice that we instructed you to change the Key Type option from Alphanumeric to Numeric before sorting based on the secondary key. This technique for multiple key sorting allows you to specify a different key type for each column on which you sort a table. Unfortunately, this technique becomes quite cumbersome if the column you use as your primary sort key contains several values.

Sorting data in a single column

In addition to sorting paragraphs or rows based on the entries in a column, Word can also sort the entries in a single column without moving other material in your document. This type of sort is useful when you are organizing a document that includes several unrelated columns.

Figure 16-52

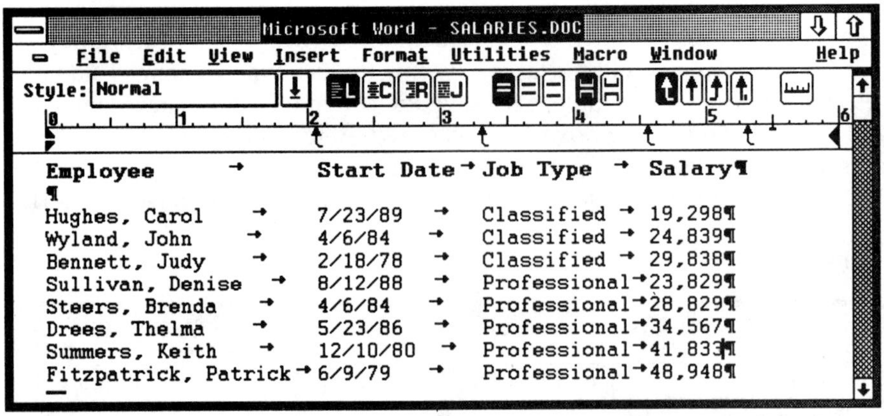

After you sort on the Job Type and Salary columns, the table will look like this.

To sort a single column, begin by pressing the right mouse button or the [Column selection] key ([Ctrl][Shift][F8]) to select a column, then open the Sort dialog box and select the Sort Column Only check box, which is available only when you select a column before issuing the Sort… command. When you choose OK, Word will sort the entries in the selected column but leave the other columns in your table intact.

Suppose that after creating the document shown in Figure 16-53, you want to sort both columns in the document in ascending order. To sort the column listing individual contributors, select the column, as shown in Figure 16-54. Next, open the Sort dialog box, select the Ascending, Alphanumeric Key Type, Tab Separator, and Sort Column Only options. When you choose OK, Word will sort the entries in the selected column. Next, select the column of corporation names, open the Sort dialog box, and choose OK. (The Alphanumeric Key Type and Sort Column Only options will still be selected from your last sort.) Figure 16-55 on page 672 shows the result: two independently sorted columns.

When you are selecting columns for independent sorting, you must select the entire width of each row in the column and select only those lines in the column that actually contain data. If you fail to select all the text on a line in the column, Word will not move the unselected text when it sorts the column, leaving some disjointed lines in the column. If you select lines that are blank in the column, Word will move the blank lines to the top of the column, rather than leaving them at the bottom where you most likely want them.

If you select a column in a table or document, then use the Sort… command without choosing the Sort Column Only option, Word will sort the entire document as if you had entered the selected column's number in the Field Number text box. So, Word actually provides two methods of specifying the column on which the rows in a table should be sorted.

Figure 16-53

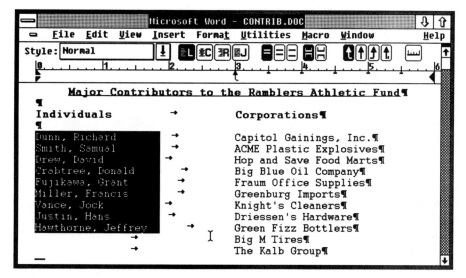

We'll sort both the columns in this document separately.

Figure 16-54

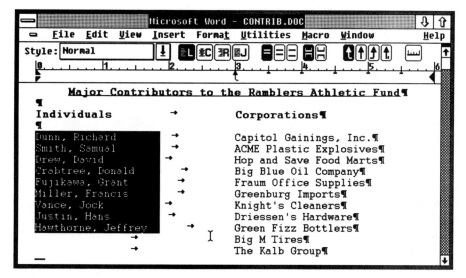

Before you can sort a column by itself, you must select the column.

Figure 16-55

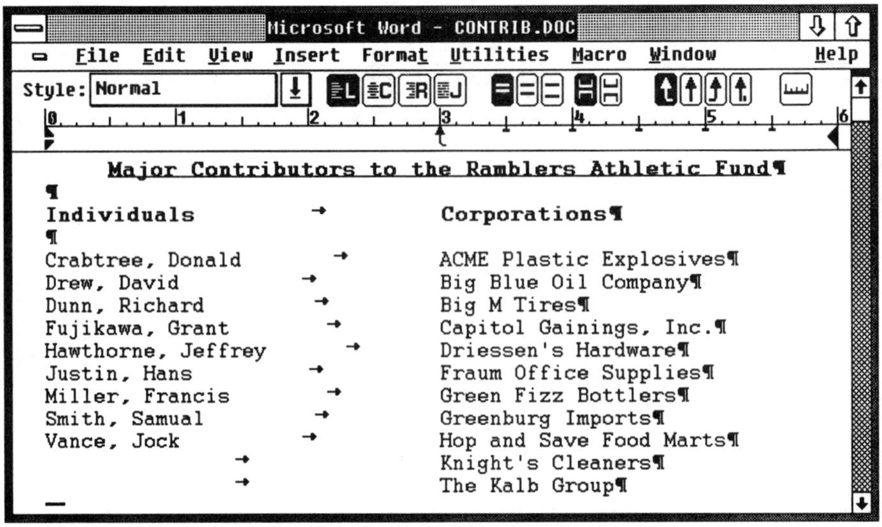

```
┌─────────────────────────────────────────────────────────────────────────┐
│ ▭▭▭▭▭▭▭▭▭▭▭▭▭▭▭▭  Microsoft Word - CONTRIB.DOC ▭▭▭▭▭▭▭▭▭▭▭▭   ⇩  ⇧       │
│  ▭  File  Edit  View  Insert  Forma̱t  Utilities  Macro  Window      Help │
│ Style: Normal        ⬇  ▣L ≡C ≡R ≡J  ≡≡ ≡≡ ⬒⬒  ⬆⬆⬆⬆  ⌂           ↑       │
│ ▐0. . . . . |1. . . . |2. . . . |3. . . . |4. . . |5. . . . |6         │
│ ▶                                  ┴                                      │
│ ┌─────────────────────────────────────────────────────────────────────┐ │
│ │      Major Contributors to the Ramblers Athletic Fund¶               │ │
│ │ ¶                                                                     │ │
│ │ Individuals          →            Corporations¶                      │ │
│ │ ¶                                                                     │ │
│ │ Crabtree, Donald      →           ACME Plastic Explosives¶           │ │
│ │ Drew, David          →            Big Blue Oil Company¶              │ │
│ │ Dunn, Richard         →           Big M Tires¶                       │ │
│ │ Fujikawa, Grant       →           Capitol Gainings, Inc.¶            │ │
│ │ Hawthorne, Jeffrey     →          Driessen's Hardware¶               │ │
│ │ Justin, Hans         →            Fraum Office Supplies¶             │ │
│ │ Miller, Francis       →           Green Fizz Bottlers¶               │ │
│ │ Smith, Samual         →           Greenburg Imports¶                 │ │
│ │ Vance, Jock           →           Hop and Save Food Marts¶           │ │
│ │                 →                 Knight's Cleaners¶                 │ │
│ │                 →                 The Kalb Group¶                    │ │
│ │ ▬                                                                  ▼  │ │
│ └─────────────────────────────────────────────────────────────────────┘ │
└─────────────────────────────────────────────────────────────────────────┘
```

This screen shows the document after you have sorted both columns separately.

Sorting lists

In addition to sorting rows and columns in tables, Word can also sort paragraphs that contain lists of entries separated by commas. The procedure for sorting lists is very similar to the one for sorting a table. You can sort lists in either ascending or descending order based on alphanumeric, numeric, or date sort keys. Because entries are separated by commas, rather than tabs, you must specify the Comma Separator option in the Sort dialog box when sorting lists.

For example, Figure 16-56 shows a document in which each paragraph lists a series of attributes describing cars for sale. Notice that each paragraph contains the same number of listed items arranged in the same order. Each paragraph lists the model name of the car first, then the year, color, condition, price, and phone number.

Earlier in this section, we sorted this document based on the model name of each car, which appears in the first entry (field) in each paragraph. Suppose you want to sort the paragraphs in this document in ascending order based on the year of each car, which is listed in the second entry (field). First, select the paragraphs listing car information, excluding the title and blank line at the top of the document. Then, issue the Sort... command and choose the Ascending Sort Order, Numeric Key Type, and Comma Separator options. To sort based on year, the second field in each list, enter *2* in the Field Number text box and choose OK. Word will then sort the document as shown in Figure 16-57.

Figure 16-56

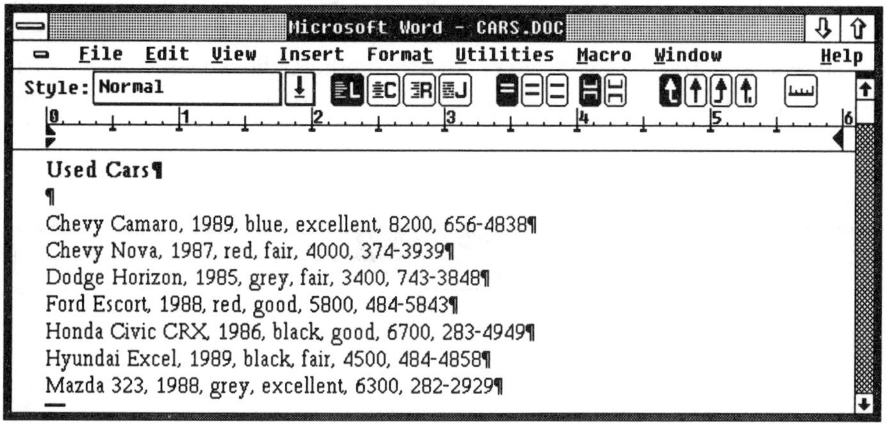

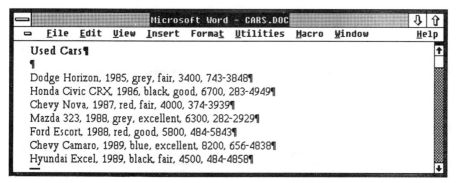

```
┌─────────────────────────────────────────────────────────────┐
│ ═     Microsoft Word - CARS.DOC            ⇩ ⇧               │
│  ▭  File  Edit  View  Insert  Format  Utilities  Macro  Window    Help │
│ Style: Normal      ↓  ▣L ▣C ▣R ▣J  ▤▤ ▤ ▤▤  ⬆⬆⬆⬆  ⌐⌐  ↑ │
│   0. . . .  1. . . .  2. . . .  3. . . .  4. . . .  5. . . .  6 │
│ ◄                                                              │
├─────────────────────────────────────────────────────────────┤
│ Used Cars¶                                                    │
│ ¶                                                             │
│ Chevy Camaro, 1989, blue, excellent, 8200, 656-4838¶          │
│ Chevy Nova, 1987, red, fair, 4000, 374-3939¶                  │
│ Dodge Horizon, 1985, grey, fair, 3400, 743-3848¶              │
│ Ford Escort, 1988, red, good, 5800, 484-5843¶                 │
│ Honda Civic CRX, 1986, black, good, 6700, 283-4949¶           │
│ Hyundai Excel, 1989, black, fair, 4500, 484-4858¶             │
│ Mazda 323, 1988, grey, excellent, 6300, 282-2929¶             │
│ ▬                                                         ↓   │
└─────────────────────────────────────────────────────────────┘
```

Each paragraph in this document contains a similar list of entries.

Figure 16-57

```
┌─────────────────────────────────────────────────────────────┐
│ ═     Microsoft Word - CARS.DOC            ⇩ ⇧               │
│  ▭  File  Edit  View  Insert  Format  Utilities  Macro  Window    Help │
│ Used Cars¶                                                 ↑  │
│ ¶                                                             │
│ Dodge Horizon, 1985, grey, fair, 3400, 743-3848¶             │
│ Honda Civic CRX, 1986, black, good, 6700, 283-4949¶          │
│ Chevy Nova, 1987, red, fair, 4000, 374-3939¶                 │
│ Mazda 323, 1988, grey, excellent, 6300, 282-2929¶            │
│ Ford Escort, 1988, red, good, 5800, 484-5843¶                │
│ Chevy Camaro, 1989, blue, excellent, 8200, 656-4838¶         │
│ Hyundai Excel, 1989, black, fair, 4500, 484-4858¶            │
│ ▬                                                         ↓   │
└─────────────────────────────────────────────────────────────┘
```

When you enter 2 into the Field Number text box, Word will sort the listed cars based on year.

In this example we selected the Numeric Key Type option even though we were interested in a date value expressed as a year. Because Word does not recognize a four-digit number, such as 1989, as a date value, you should always use the Numeric Key Type option when sorting simple year values.

Another special feature of Word is its ability to perform basic mathematical calculations. With this capability, you can perform calculations quickly, then plug their results into your document. Word can add, subtract, divide, and multiply values, and calculate roots and percentages.

PERFORMING MATHEMATICAL CALCULATIONS

For example, suppose you have created a table of cash receipts like the one in Figure 16-58. You want to compute your total receipts for the week and insert that value into the table. Begin by highlighting the cells in the second column of the table, then issue the Calculate command on the Utilities menu. As you can see in Figure 16-59, Word displays the total value *6025.09* at the bottom of the document window.

Figure 16-58

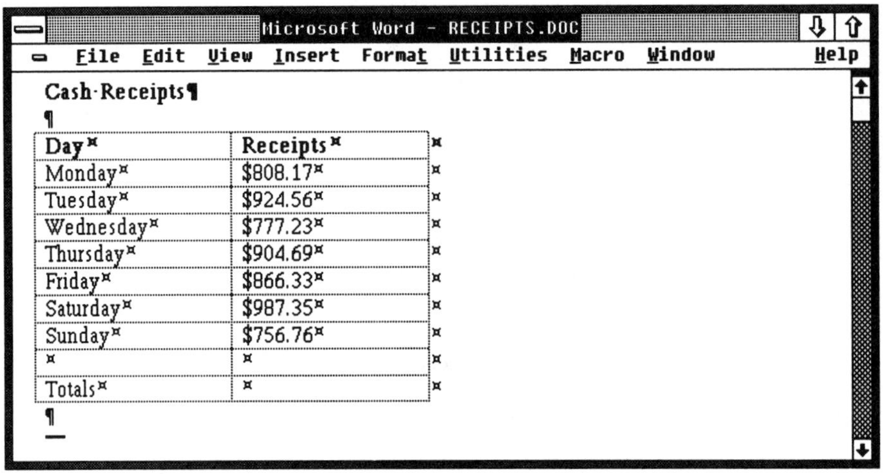

Word can add a column of numbers like the cash receipts shown in this table.

Figure 16-59

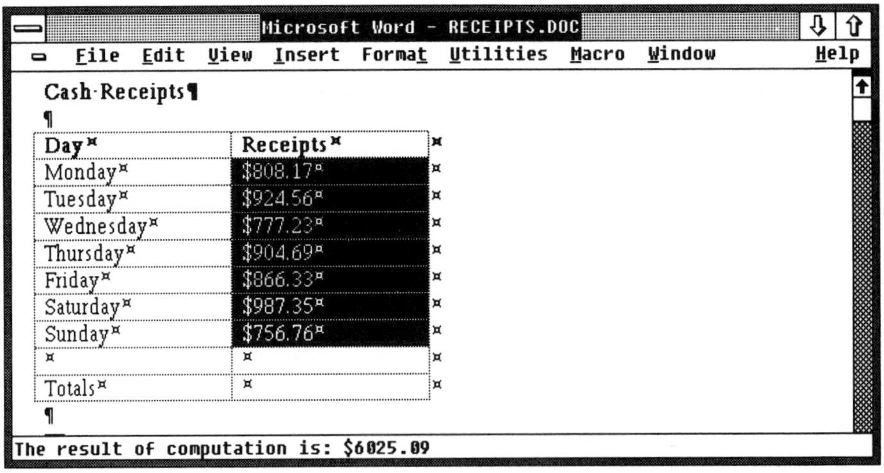

Word displays the result at the bottom of the document window.

Word also places a copy of this total value on your Clipboard so that you can issue the Paste command to enter the results of your calculation into your document. For example, if you move the cursor to the second column in the Totals row, then select Paste from the Edit menu, Word will paste the value *$6025.09* to the right of the insertion point, as shown in Figure 16-60.

Figure 16-60

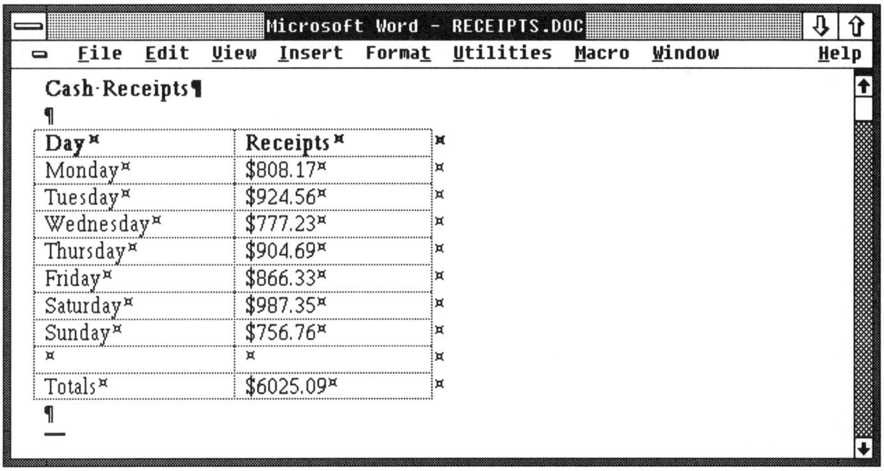

```
┌────────────────────────────────────────────────────────────────────┐
│ ▭          Microsoft Word - RECEIPTS.DOC                    ⇩ ⇧ │
│ ▢    File   Edit   View   Insert   Format   Utilities   Macro   Window        Help │
│  Cash·Receipts¶                                                      ↑│
│  ¶                                                                    │
│  ┌──────────────┬──────────────┐                                     │
│  │ Day ×        │ Receipts ×   │ ×                                   │
│  │ Monday ×     │ $808.17 ×    │ ×                                   │
│  │ Tuesday ×    │ $924.56 ×    │ ×                                   │
│  │ Wednesday ×  │ $777.23 ×    │ ×                                   │
│  │ Thursday ×   │ $904.69 ×    │ ×                                   │
│  │ Friday ×     │ $866.33 ×    │ ×                                   │
│  │ Saturday ×   │ $987.35 ×    │ ×                                   │
│  │ Sunday ×     │ $756.76 ×    │ ×                                   │
│  │ ×            │ ×            │ ×                                   │
│  │ Totals ×     │ $6025.09 ×   │ ×                                   │
│  └──────────────┴──────────────┘                                     │
│  ¶                                                                   ↓│
└────────────────────────────────────────────────────────────────────┘
```

You can paste the results of your calculations into the worksheet.

When you add a series of values, as we did in the previous example, Word will not require that you use any mathematical operators. Unless the text you select includes a mathematical operator, Word assumes you want to add the values in that selection.

Also, notice that you can highlight entire rows of text and numbers, rather than select only the individual values you want to total. (As you'll see in a moment, if you want to select individual columns from a table of values, you can use the right mouse button to narrow your selection.) When you use the Calculate command, Word will include in the addition all numbers that are preceded by a blank space. For example, Word will consider the entry *10a* as the number 10, but will ignore the entry *a10* in the calculation.

Word also ignores blank spaces and most punctuation and special markup characters like ?, #, @, ¶, and ↵. There are a few exceptions to this rule, such as commas, periods, and the +, -, *, /, %, and ^ characters. If a value is enclosed in parentheses—(100), for instance—Word treats that value as a negative number.

If you include commas between numbers—as in 100,100—Word will consider those numbers a single value. That's because Word treats commas as separators, dividing hundreds from thousands, thousands from millions, and so on. If a space appears before or after a comma, however, Word will treat the numbers as two separate values.

Similarly, if you include a period between two numbers—as in 100.25—Word will interpret the numbers as a single value since it recognizes the period as a decimal point. Again, if you enter a space before or after the decimal point, Word will ignore the period character and treat the numbers as two separate values. By the way, if any of the values you are using in your calculations contain commas, decimal points, and/or dollar signs, Word will display those characters in the result as well.

Other calculations

To perform calculations other than addition, you must enter mathematical operators into your document. The +, -, *, /, %, and ^ characters serve as mathematical operators when you are performing calculations in Word. The + sign, which is optional, tells Word to add a series of values, while the - sign tells Word to subtract. The * and / signs indicate multiplication and division, respectively. The % operator tells Word to calculate a percentage, and the ^ operator tells Word to calculate the power or root of a number. Table 16-3 summarizes these six operators.

Table 16-3

Character	**Operation**
+ (optional)	Addition
-	Subtraction
*	Multiplication
/	Division
%	Percentage (divide the number by 100 and then multiply the result)
^	Power (if the number is greater than or equal to 1) or root (if the number is between 0 and 1)

For example, to multiply 10 x 2, you would type

10*2

in your document, highlight those characters, and select the Calculate command from the Utilities menu. Word will display the result, *20*, at the bottom of the document window. Word also will place the result on the Clipboard so you can paste it anywhere in your document by moving the cursor to that spot and selecting Paste from the Edit menu.

You enter the +, -, *, and / operators to the left of the number you want to add, subtract, multiply, or divide by. However, you enter the % sign directly after the number to which you want it to apply. Therefore, you would use the expression

18%*70

to determine that 18 percent of 70 equals 12.6. When you place a % sign after a value, Word will convert that value to a decimal by dividing by 100. Thus, the expression above is equivalent to

.18*70

Similarly, the expression

20%+5

is equal to

.2+5

When more than one operator appears in the same expression, Word will rely on a rule known as operator precedence to determine the order in which it will evaluate the expression. For instance, when Word evaluates the expression *5+10*4*, operator precedence dictates that it will multiply 10 by 4, then add the result to 5. Table 16-4 shows the order in which Word evaluates operators.

Operator precedence

Table 16-4

Operator	Precedence
^, %	1
*, /	2
+, -	3

If you want, you can use parentheses to control operator precedence. For instance, consider the expression *20*4+5*. Normally, Word would evaluate the * operator first, meaning that it would multiply 20 by 4 to produce the value 80, which it would add to 5 to produce the value 85.

If you place the *4+5* portion of the expression within parentheses, as in *20*(4+5)*, Word will evaluate that portion before it evaluates the multiplication. In short, it will add 4 to 5 to produce the value 9, then multiply 9 by 20 to produce the value 180.

Using the =
(Expression) field

In addition to the Calculate command, Word offers the = (Expression) field for performing mathematical calculations. The form of this field is

{= *expression*}

where *expression* is the mathematical expression you want to evaluate. You can include in an = field any of the operators we've discussed (+, -, *, /, %, or ^), as well as the operators =, <, >, <=, or >=. Of course, the result of the = field is the calculated result of *expression*. Word will update the field's result only when you place the cursor within the field and press the [Update field] key ([F9]), or when you issue the Print Merge… command on the File menu.

For example, if you enter the field

{= 10*4}

into a document, Word will calculate the expression *10*4* and return the result— *40*—as the field's result.

Using bookmarks

You can use bookmarks to define numbers, then use bookmark names in the = field as your operands. For example, suppose you've assigned the bookmark name *SALES* to the number 1000, and the bookmark name *COGS* to the number 700. To calculate the value of *SALES-COGS*, you can enter the field

{= SALES - COGS}

into the document, which will return the value *300*. Notice that you must insert a space between the bookmark names and the operators.

Functions

In addition to using operators and bookmark names in an = field, you can use a set of built-in functions to build mathematical expressions. Table 16-5 lists all the available functions.

The ABS function

The ABS function returns the absolute (positive) value of a number or expression. The form of this function is

ABS(*expression*)

where *expression* is the number or expression whose absolute value you want to determine. For example, both of the fields

{= ABS(-5)}
{= ABS(5)}

return the value *5.*

Table 16-5

This function...	returns...
ABS	the absolute value of a number
AND	1 if both arguments are true; 0 if either argument is false
AVERAGE	average of a list of values
COUNT	the number of arguments in a list
DEFINED	1 or 0, depending on whether an expression can be calculated without error
IF	one of two values, depending on the outcome of a conditional test
INT	the greatest integer in a value
MAX	the highest value in a list
MIN	the lowest value in a list
MOD	the remainder of a division
NOT	the inverse of a logical value
OR	1 if either argument is true; 0 if both arguments are false
PRODUCT	the product of a list of values
ROUND	the rounded value of a number
SIGN	the sign of a value (-1, 1, or 0)
SUM	the sum of a list of values

You can use the AND function to join two logical expressions into a single complex expression. The form of this function is

The AND function

    AND(*logical1,logical2*)

where *logical1* and *logical2* are the two logical expressions you want to test. If both *logical1* and *logical2* are true, this function will return the value *1* (TRUE); if either *logical1* or *logical2* is false, the AND function will return the value *0* (FALSE). For example, the field

    {= AND(1<2,3<4)}

returns the value *1*, while the field

    {= AND(1<2,3>4)}

returns the value *0*.

The AVERAGE function

The AVERAGE function returns the average (arithmetic mean) of a list of values. The form of this function is

AVERAGE(*value1,value2,...valueN*)

where *value1, value2,* and so forth, are the values you want to average. For example, the field

{= AVERAGE(2,4,6)}

returns the average of 2, 4, and 6, which is 4.

The COUNT function

The COUNT function counts the number of arguments in a list. The form of this function is

COUNT(*value1,value2,...valueN*)

where *value1, value2,* and so forth, are the numbers you want to count. For example, the field

{= COUNT(3,49,10.8)}

returns the value *3*. If you want, you can specify a range of line numbers in the argument of a COUNT function, like this:

{= COUNT(line1:line60)}

This function will count the numbers that appear in lines 1 through 60.

The DEFINED function

The DEFINED function tells you whether an expression can be calculated without error. The form of this function is

DEFINED(*expression*)

where *expression* is the expression you want to check. If *expression* can be calculated without error, the function will return the value *1* (TRUE). If an error prevents *expression* from being calculated, the function will return the value *0* (FALSE). For instance, the field

{= DEFINED(5/0)}

returns the value *0*, while the field

{= DEFINED(5/1)}

returns the value *1*.

The IF function returns either of two values based on the result of a conditional test. The form of this function is

IF(*conditionalTest,trueResult,falseResult*)

The first argument is a conditional test that Word will evaluate as either true or false. If *conditionalTest* is true, the function will return *trueResult*. If *conditionalTest* is false, the function will return *falseResult*. For example, the field

{= IF(2<3,1,0)}

evaluates the conditional test *2<3*. Since *2<3* is true, the function returns the value in the *trueResult* argument, which is 1.

Like most programs, Word uses the number 1 to represent the value TRUE and the number 0 to represent the value FALSE. If you want, however, you can type *TRUE* and *FALSE* instead of 1 and 0 in the *conditionalTest* argument of the IF function. For instance, to test whether the expression *2<3* is false, you can use either *2<3=0* or *2<3=FALSE* as your *conditionalTest* argument.

The INT function returns the largest integer that is less than a specified value. The form of this function is

INT(*value*)

where *value* is the value whose integer portion you want to truncate. For example, the field

{= INT(45.8)}

returns the value *45*, while the field

{= INT(-45.8)}

returns the value *-46*.

The MAX and MIN functions let you find the highest or lowest values in a list. The forms of these functions are

MAX(*value1,value2,...valueN*)
MIN(*value1,value2,...valueN*)

The IF function

The INT function

The MAX and MIN functions

For example, if you want to find the highest value in the list 32, 19, 7, 78, and 34, you can use the field

{= MAX(32,19,7,78,34)}

which returns the value *78*. To find the lowest value in the list, you can use the field

{= MIN(32,19,7,78,34)}

which returns the value *7*.

The MOD function

The MOD function computes the modulus (or remainder) that results from dividing one value by another. The form of this function is

MOD(*dividend,divisor*)

The result of this function is the remainder that results from dividing *dividend* by *divisor*. For example, the field

{= MOD(5,2)}

returns the value *1*, since 5 divided by 2 equals 2 with a remainder of 1.

The NOT function

The NOT function inverts a logical value. The form of this function is

NOT(*logical*)

where *logical* is the logical value or expression you want to invert. For example, the field

{= NOT(2+2=5)}

returns the value *1* (TRUE), while the field

{= NOT(2+2=4)}

returns the value *0* (FALSE).

The OR function

You can use the OR function to join two logical expressions into a single complex expression. The form of this function is

OR(*logical1,logical2*)

where *logical1* and *logical2* are the two logical expressions you want to test. If either *logical1* or *logical2* is true, this function will return the value *1* (TRUE); if both *logical1* and *logical2* are false, the OR function will return the value *0* (FALSE). For example, the field

{= OR(1<2,3>4)}

returns the value *1*, while the field

{= OR(1>2,3>4)}

returns the value *0*.

The PRODUCT function multiplies all of its arguments and returns their product. The form of this function is

The PRODUCT function

PRODUCT(*value1,value2,...valueN*)

For example, if you want to multiply the numbers 3, 4, 5, 6, and 7, you can use the field

{= PRODUCT(3,4,5,6,7)}

which returns the value *2520*.

The ROUND function rounds the value specified by its first argument to the number of decimal places specified by its second argument. The form of this function is

The ROUND function

ROUND(*value,numPlaces*)

where *numPlaces* specifies the number of decimal places to which *value* should be rounded. For example, the field

{= ROUND(3.14159,3)}

returns the value that results from rounding the value 3.14159 to three decimal places—*3.142*.

The SIGN function returns the sign of a specified value. The form of this function is

The SIGN function

SIGN(*value*)

If *value* is positive, the function will return *1*; if *value* is negative, the function will return *-1*; if *value* is 0, the function will return *0*. For example, the field

{= SIGN(-32)}

returns the value *-1*, since its argument is negative.

The SUM function

The SUM function adds a list of values. The form of the SUM function is

SUM(*value1,value2,...valueN*)

For example, to add the numbers 3,4,5,6, and 7, you can use the field

{= SUM(3,4,5,6,7)}

which returns the value *25*.

CHARACTER FORMULAS

Another unique feature of Word is its ability to create special characters using the EQ (Formula) field. By using the EQ field, you can create complex scientific and mathematical formulas in your documents, such as

$$\int \frac{dx}{x^2\sqrt{27x^2 + 6 - 1}}$$

Character formulas can be useful to nearly any writer, not just those with a technical or scientific bent. With a little imagination, you can use character formulas to create a variety of special symbols and to present ordinary text in an unusual way.

You can create character formulas in your documents only if you've installed a PCL printer (such as the Hewlett-Packard LaserJet) or a PostScript printer (such as the Apple LaserWriter). In addition, you must install the Symbol font using the Windows Setup program. For information on installing the Symbol font, see your Word for Windows documentation.

The EQ field

The EQ field's most basic form is

{EQ *formulaDescription*}

where *formulaDescription* is a string of characters that defines the formula you want to create. This string is made up of both literal text and formula codes, which are similar to the switch arguments used in other fields. Each formula code you include in the *formulaDescription* argument begins with a backslash character (\)

and a letter, and is usually followed by some arguments enclosed in parentheses. The code tells the EQ field what action you want to perform, and the code's arguments indicate the character(s) to be acted upon.

For example, the box code is represented by \x. This code draws a border around the character(s) you specify in the code's argument. For instance, if you supply the *formulaDescription* argument \x*(Answer)* to an EQ field, like this:

{EQ \x(Answer)}

the field will return the word *Answer*, surrounded by a box, as shown at the bottom of Figure 16-61.

Unlike the fields we've discussed so far, Word updates the result of an EQ field as you modify its field code. You'll want to split your document window into two panes, as we've done in Figure 16-61, so you can edit an EQ field code in one pane as you view its result in the other. In Chapter 10, we discuss this efficient split-screen format.

Figure 16-61

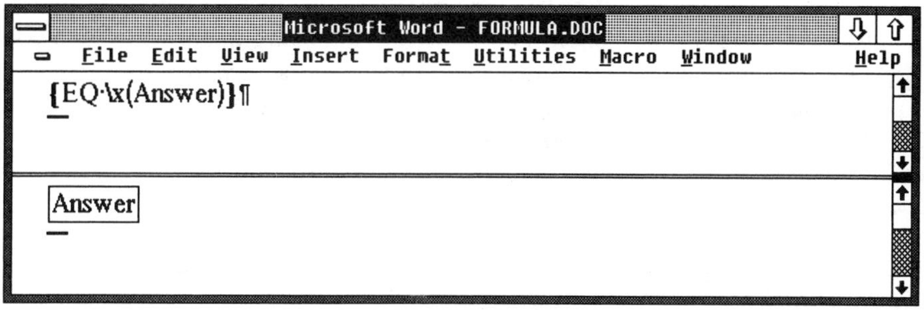

You'll want to split your document window into two panes so you can edit an EQ field code and view its result simultaneously.

With some formula codes, you can include options that affect the resulting formula. When you use an option with a code, you must enter that option between the code name and the code's argument. In addition, you must precede the option with the backslash character (\). If you use more than one option, each option must be preceded with a \.

For example, when you use the box code, you can include options that tell Word to draw only the top, bottom, right, or left edge of the box. You also can combine these options so that Word draws just the parts of the box you specify, such as the top edge and right edge. In a few cases, an option will require its own "argument"—a character that precisely defines how that option should affect the formula. We will describe these "option arguments" where appropriate as we explain each of Word's formula codes.

To summarize, the basic form of a *formulaDescription* argument is

\code\option(*a1,a2,...a*N)

where \code is the formula code; \option is the option; and *a1*, *a2*, and so forth, are the code's arguments.

Character formula rules

You can use either uppercase or lowercase letters for the formula codes and options. When you enter your code's arguments, however, be sure that you use the capitalization and formatting you want to exhibit in the final result. For example, if you want the EQ field's result to display a particular character in boldface, you must apply the bold format to the appropriate character as you're entering the field's *formulaDescription* argument.

By the way, if you enter an invalid *formulaDescription* argument, Word will not be able to evaluate the EQ field and will display the result *Error!*. When you see this result, carefully recheck your *formulaDescription* argument. The error will typically result from a misplaced parenthesis or comma.

Formula codes

Word offers ten formula codes, listed in Table 16-6, that you can use to build character formulas in the EQ field's *formulaDescription* argument. Although you often will use only a single formula code to achieve a certain result, you can combine different codes in a single argument. In our examples, we'll show you how to use each formula code and show how some codes are specifically designed to be used with another code.

Table 16-6

This formula code...	lets you...
\a (array)	create an array
\b (bracket)	enclose text within a specified set of brackets
\d (displace)	create a fixed amount of space in a line
\f (fraction)	create a fraction
\i (integral)	create an integral character
\l (list)	specify a list of arguments
\o (overstrike)	place two or more characters in the same space
\r (radical)	create a radical symbol
\s (superscript/subscript)	superscript or subscript characters
\x (box)	draw a border around characters

The \a (array) code creates a two-dimensional array using the arguments you specify. The simplest form of the \a code is:

\a(*a1,a2...a*N)

The arguments, *a1, a2*, and so forth, are the elements of the array you want to create. The simple form of the \a code creates a one-column array with the elements centered on top of one another. Figure 16-62 shows an example of the \a code. Notice that Word stacks the elements, with the first argument, *10*, at the top of the stack.

Figure 16-62

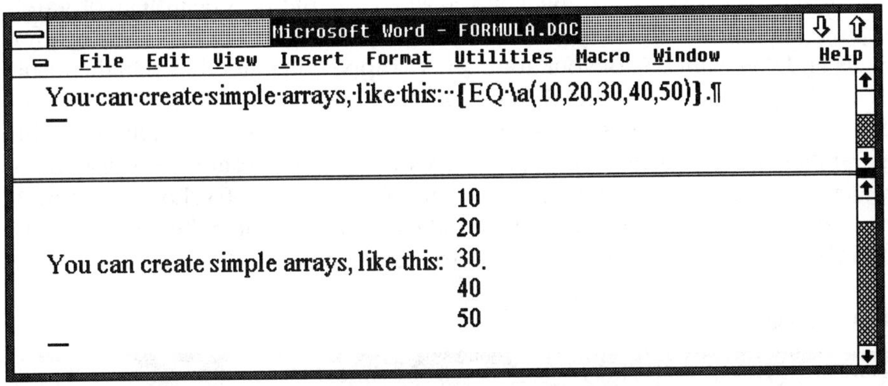

```
╔══════════════════════════════════════════════════════════╗
║         Microsoft Word — FORMULA.DOC            ⇩  ⇧      ║
║   File  Edit  View  Insert  Format  Utilities  Macro  Window    Help  ║
║ You·can·create·simple·arrays,·like·this:···{EQ·\a(10,20,30,40,50)}·.¶   ║
║                                                                        ║
║ ──────────────────────────────────────────────────────────────────── ║
║                              10                                        ║
║                              20                                        ║
║   You can create simple arrays, like this: 30.                         ║
║                              40                                        ║
║                              50                                        ║
║   ─                                                                    ║
╚══════════════════════════════════════════════════════════╝
```

In its simplest form, the \a code will create a one-column array.

There are several options you can type between the \a code and its arguments to control the number of columns in an array and to control the spacing and alignment of array elements. If you want to create a multicolumn array, you must use the \co*n* option, where *n* is a number that indicates how many columns you want to include in the array.

There also are options you can use with the \a code to control both the horizontal and vertical spacing of the array elements. Normally, Word does not place any space between the columns of an array. In addition, the amount of space between the rows in an array is equal to Word's default line leading. The \hs*n* option controls horizontal spacing and the \vs*n* option controls vertical spacing. In both cases, *n* is a whole number that indicates the amount of space, in points, that you want to add between the rows or columns of the array. For example, if you use the \hs1 option, Word will add 1 point of space between the columns of the array. This 1 point is in addition to the normal space that appears between characters. Similarly, if you use the \vs1 option, Word will add 1 point of space between the rows of the array.

Three more options you can use with the \a code to control the alignment of characters are \al, \ar, and \ac, which stand for align left, align right, and align center, respectively. If you do not use an alignment option, Word will create an array with centered alignment.

The \b (bracket) code

The \b (bracket) code encloses its argument within any character you specify. The simplest form of the \b code is:

\b(*a1*)

This code places parentheses around the argument *a1*. For example, the field *{EQ \b(ABC)}* will return the string *ABC* enclosed in parentheses, like this: *(ABC)*.

You're probably wondering why you would use the \b code instead of simply typing parentheses. Using the \b code is essential when you are building a formula and you want one of your arguments to appear in parentheses in the result. If you simply type the parentheses, you could invalidate another code in the formula. For example, suppose you want to enclose the fraction $^3/_4$ within parentheses. If you type the parentheses as part of the argument for the \f (fraction) code, you'll create an invalid formula. Figure 16-63 shows the correct way to place the fraction $^3/_4$ within parentheses. Notice that in the formula result, Word altered the size of the parentheses to accommodate the height of the fraction.

Figure 16-63

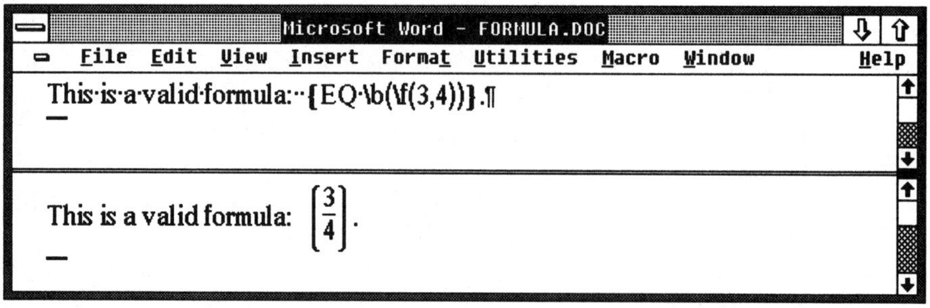

The \b code allows you to display parentheses in a formula result.

The \bc option lets you use characters other than parentheses as bracketing characters. The \bc option is always followed by \ and the character you want to use for bracketing. When you use this option, you need to specify only the opening (or left bracket) character—such as { or [—and Word will supply the closing bracket character.

The \lc and \rc options allow you to place a bracketing character on only the left or right of the argument. The \lc option places the character you specify on the left side of the argument. Similarly, the \rc option places the character you specify on the right side of the argument. As with the \bc option, each of these options must be followed by a \ and the character you want to use.

The \d (displace) code lets you move characters forward or backward by a specified number of points. The \d code is different from other codes in two important ways. First, it does not accept any arguments. Instead of acting upon an argument, this code always displaces the characters that immediately follow the code. Nevertheless, you must place a pair of parentheses after the \d code.

The \d (displace) code

Another important feature of the \d code is that it requires one of three options, \fo*n*, \ba*n*, or \li, which you can type between the \d code and its parentheses: The \fo*n* option moves characters forward on the line by *n* points. Similarly, the \ba*n* option moves characters backward by *n* points. The \li option draws a line from the end of the displaced character to the beginning of the next character. The \li option must always be used with either the \fo*n* or \ba*n* option.

The main purpose of the \d code is to give you precise control over the placement of characters on a line. For example, suppose you want to create exactly $\frac{1}{4}$ inch (or 18 points) of space between two words on a line. Figure 16-64 shows a formula that does this. Notice that we used the *fo18* option with this formula to create the 18 points of space.

Figure 16-64

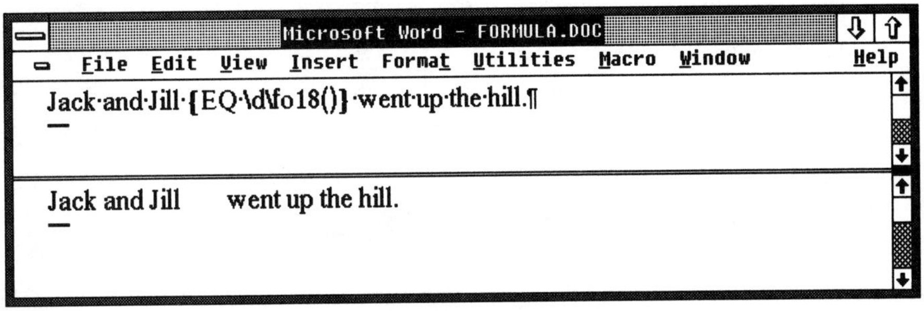

Use the \d code with the \fon option to insert a precise amount of horizontal space on a line.

The \fo*n* option moves *all* characters following the \d code on the current line forward by *n* points. If the *n* value is large enough, some characters on the current line will wrap to the next line. This may cause characters on the succeeding line to wrap to another line as well.

The \ba*n* option moves all characters that follow the \d code in the current paragraph backward by *n* points. Because the \d code does not affect the characters that precede the code, the displaced characters will probably overlap other characters on the same line. If the *n* value you specify is large enough, Word will displace characters beyond the beginning of the line. However, the displaced characters will not wrap to the previous line. Instead, Word will place them in the blank area of your screen beyond the left margin. If you want to view the displaced characters, you must use the horizontal scroll bar to bring this part of your screen into view.

The \li option draws a line in the space you create with the \d code. When you use the \li option with the \fo*n* option, Word will underline the space created by the \fo*n* option. If you use the \li option with the \ba*n* option, Word will draw the line under the characters that have been displaced by the \ba*n* option.

The \f (fraction) code

The \f (fraction) code does exactly what you would expect: It creates a fraction using the arguments you specify as the numerator and denominator. The form of the \f code is

\f(*a1,a2*)

where *a1* is the numerator and *a2* is the denominator. Figure 16-65 shows an example of this code.

Figure 16-65

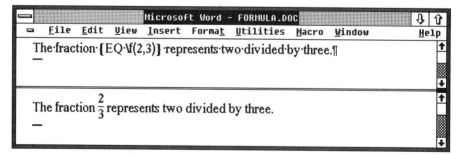

The \f code creates a fraction using the arguments you specify for the numerator and denominator.

The numerator and denominator arguments do not have to be simple whole numbers, like those used in Figure 16-65. You can use complex formulas, such as *4x+12y-23*, or even text, as either the numerator or denominator.

You can use the \i (integral) code to create integrals, summations, products, or any other formulas that take a similar form. The simplest form of this code is

\i(*a1*,*a2*,*a3*)

where *a1* is the lower limit, *a2* is the upper limit, and *a3* is the integral character. Figure 16-66 shows a simple example of the \i code. To enhance the appearance of the resulting integral formula (in the lower screen), we assigned a smaller point size to the first two arguments of the code.

Figure 16-66

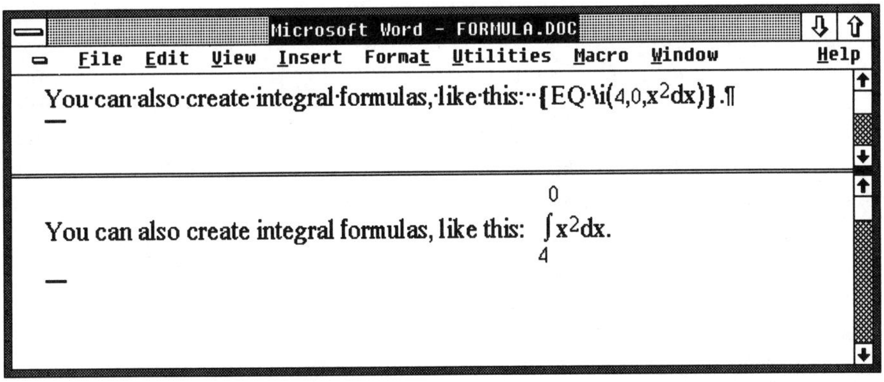

These screens show the \i code in its simplest form.

There are a couple of options you can type between the \i code and its arguments that allow you to display a summation symbol (Σ) or a product symbol (π) instead of the integral symbol ($\int$). To create a summation formula, type *su* immediately after the \i code in your integral formula. To create a product formula, type *pr* after the \i code.

You are not limited to the Σ, π, and $\int$ symbols when you use the \i code. By adding the \fc or \vc option to your formula, you can use any character on the keyboard in place of the default $\int$ symbol. The \fc option indicates a character of fixed height: Whatever character you type in the formula is the character Word will use in the resulting formula display. The \vc option, on the other hand, indicates a character of variable height. Word will change the size of the character you type to correspond to the size of the third argument in the formula. This option is particularly useful when the third argument of the \i code is a fraction. When you use either the \fc or \vc option, you must type that option immediately after the \i code, then type another \ before the character you want to substitute for the $\int$ symbol.

Another option you can use with the \i code, \in, changes the placement of the first two arguments in the formula result. Instead of the first two arguments appearing above and below the integral symbol (or whatever other symbol you use in the formula), the \in option causes them to appear to the right of the integral symbol in the "in-line" format.

The \l (list) code

Like the \b (bracket) code, the \l (list) code is designed to be used with other codes. This code simply creates a list, separated by commas, of the arguments you specify. The simplest form of the \l code is

\l(*a1,a2,...a*N)

and its result is simply a list of items separated by commas. Since Word normally interprets a comma as an argument separator, the \l code comes in handy whenever you want to use a list of items as a single argument. For example, suppose you want to create a list of numbers and draw a box around the list. Since the \x (box) code can accept only one argument, the field *{EQ \x(10,20,30,40,50)}* is invalid. As you can see, Figure 16-67 shows how the \l code can be used to overcome this limitation.

Figure 16-67

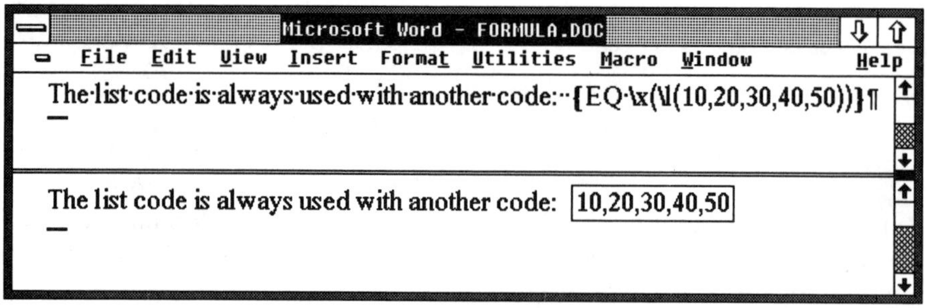

You can use the \l code when your formula result must display items separated by commas.

The \o (overstrike) code

The \o (overstrike) code (backslash and the letter *o*), places two or more characters in the same space. The form of this code is

\o(*a1,a2,...a*N*)*

where *a1, a2,* and so forth, represent the characters you want to place "on top of" one another. Each argument can be as short as a single character or as long as several words.

As an example of the \o code, suppose you want to print the character Ø, which is a combination of a zero and a slash. Figure 16-68 shows how you can use Word's \o code to produce this character.

Figure 16-68

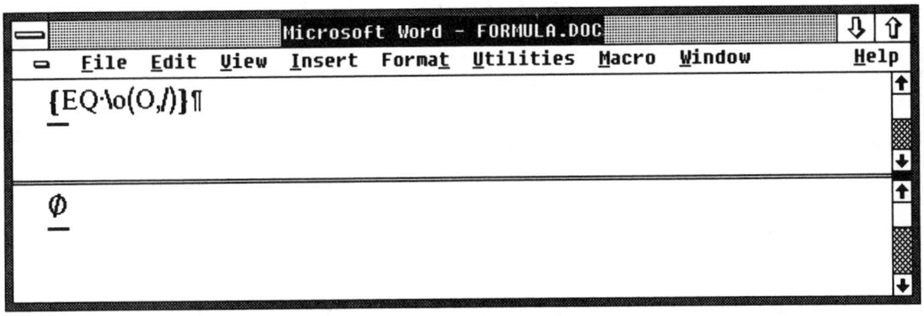

Use the \o code to position two or more characters in the same space.

There are three options you can type between the \o code and its arguments: \ar, \al, and \ac. These options, which stand for align right, align left, and align center, determine the placement of the character represented by the second argument in relation to the character represented by the first argument. If you do not choose one of these options, Word will assume you want centered alignment.

The \r (radical) code draws a radical or "square root" symbol. The form of the code is

The \r (radical) code

$\r(a1,a2)$

The second argument is optional. If you use only one argument, Word will place it inside the radical to create a square root. If you use two arguments, Word will place the second argument ($a2$) inside the radical and place the first argument ($a1$) above the radical to indicate the root being computed. For example, Figure 16-69 on the next page shows a formula that displays the square root of 100 and another formula that displays the cube root of 100.

When you use the second argument with the \r code, you may want to change the point size of the first argument so that the exponent outside the radical symbol is smaller than the number inside the radical.

The simplest form of the \s (superscript/subscript) code is:

The \s (superscript/ subscript) code

$\s(a1)$

Figure 16-69

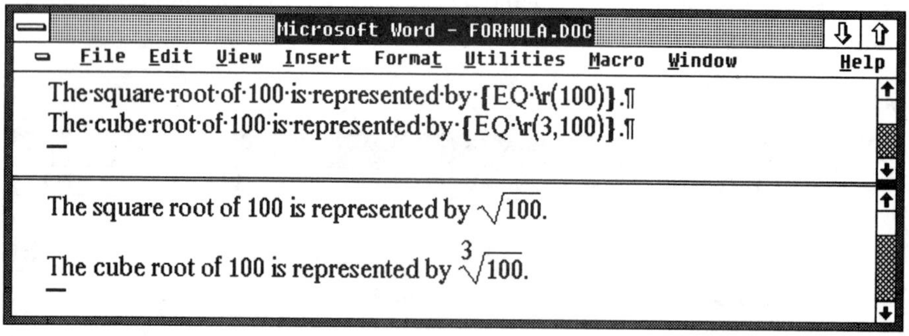

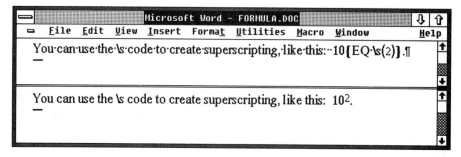

Use the \r code to display the radical symbol in a mathematical formula.

This code positions the single argument you specify as a superscript. For example, Figure 16-70 shows a formula in which we've created a superscripted 2. In this example, the 10 at the beginning of the formula is not really part of the formula; it merely serves as the "base" for the superscripted 2. (By the way, we reduced the point size of the argument, *2*, in order to enhance the appearance of the formula result.)

Figure 16-70

You can use the \s code to create superscripting.

When you use the \s code with no options, Word will superscript the argument you specify by 3 points. If you want to superscript the argument by a different number of points, you can insert an \up*n* option between the \s code and its argument, where *n* is a number of points by which you want to superscript the argument.

The \do*n* option allows you to create a subscript instead of a superscript. Again, *n* is the number of points by which you want to subscript the argument.

Whenever you use either the \up*n* or the \do*n* option, you must specify an *n* value. Otherwise, Word will assume an *n* value of 0 and will not superscript or subscript your argument.

You're probably wondering why anyone would use the \s code instead of simply choosing Character... from the Format menu and choosing the Superscript or Subscript option. There's really only one advantage. When you use two or more arguments with the \s code, Word will superscript the first argument and then "stack" the additional arguments in a column under the first argument. When you use multiple arguments with the \s code, the code will not recognize any \up*n* or \do*n* options. Therefore, there's no point in using the \up*n* and \do*n* options when your \s code has more than one argument.

The \x (box) code draws a border around the argument you specify. Unlike the Border options in the Paragraph dialog box, you can apply the \x code to single characters. The \x code takes the form

The \x (box) code

$$\text{\textbackslash}x(a1)$$

where *a1* is the character(s) you want to draw the box around.

For example, suppose you want the name of your company, *National Systems Corporation*, to appear in 14-point Helv type with a border around it. Figure 16-71 shows a formula that achieves this result.

Figure 16-71

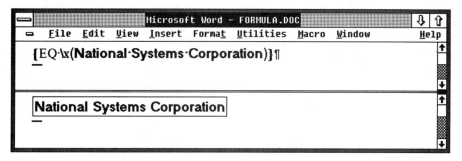

You can use the \x code to draw a border around several words.

The \x code can accept only one argument. If you want the argument to include a comma, you must precede it with the \ character. Otherwise, Word will think you are trying to enter more than one argument and will not be able to evaluate the field. If your argument must contain a lot of commas, it would be best to embed the \l (list) code within your argument for the \x code, rather than typing a separate \ character for each comma.

There are three options you can type between the \x code and its arguments: \to, \bo, \le, and \ri. These stand for top border, bottom border, left border, and right border, respectively. You can use one or more of these options when you want to draw only a partial border around your argument. You can combine these options in any way.

OPTIMIZING YOUR SYSTEM FOR SPEED

As the documents you create in Word become larger and more complex, you'll notice a decrease in overall system performance. However, by following the tips in this section, you will enable Word to run as fast as possible.

First, as we mentioned in Chapter 13, you can significantly speed up many aspects of Word by turning on the draft view. Although working in the draft view prevents you from taking advantage of Word's WYSIWYG capabilities, the draft view can enhance your system's performance as much as any other technique.

If you're running Word under a full-featured version of Microsoft Windows, make sure you minimize the size of the MS-DOS Executive window. You'll know that this window is minimized when you see a small disk icon in the lower-left corner on your screen. You can increase performance by opening only one document at a time and by maximizing the size of both the Microsoft Word window and the document window. If you don't know how to minimize and maximize windows, refer to Appendix 1.

Several Word features decrease system performance when they're activated, including all the options in the Preferences dialog box and the Background Pagination option in the Customize dialog box. In addition, the ruler, ribbon, and status bar slightly inhibit system performance when they're activated. For this reason, remember to turn off the options you don't need as you create and modify your documents.

If your computer is connected to a local area network, you might be able to enhance system performance by modifying the way Word is installed on your network. For instance, if Word is installed on a network drive, and you have plenty of available space on a local hard disk drive, you may want to reinstall Word on your local drive. Consult your network administrator for assistance on maximizing Word's performance on your network.

Finally, you can enhance Word's performance by configuring your computer with either a disk cache or a RAM disk. Consult your local PC vendor or expert for information on how to set up either of these facilities on your machine.

CREATING SPECIAL CHARACTERS

Nearly all the text we've shown in our sample documents so far consists of standard keyboard characters that you enter into your document by typing a letter or number, or by pressing the [Shift] key and typing a character. As we mentioned in Chapter 5, Word lets you create a number of special characters, including smart quotes, bullets, en and em dashes, math symbols, ® and ™ symbols, and Greek letters. In this section, we'll show you how to enter these special characters into your document.

As we explained in Chapter 5, the language that Word and other programs use to define the characters you type is ASCII (American Standard Code for Information Interchange). Every letter, number, punctuation mark, and other symbol you can type on a standard American keyboard is defined by an ASCII code that ranges from 0 to 127. Even special instructions, like carriage returns, paragraph breaks, page breaks, and tabs, are defined in an ASCII code table.

ASCII, ANSI, and OEM character sets

ANSI (American National Standards Institute) is a superset of ASCII. In addition to the 128 ASCII characters, it contains foreign characters, such as å and ç, for Western European countries. These 128 special characters are called *extended characters* and do not appear on a standard American keyboard. We'll show you how to enter these characters in a moment.

In addition to accessing characters in the ANSI character set, you can access characters that belong to the OEM (Original Equipment Manufacturer) character set, which is built into your computer. The first 128 characters of the OEM character set are identical to those in the ASCII and ANSI character sets. However, as you'll see in a moment, the extended OEM characters (128-255) differ from extended ANSI characters.

Table A5-1 in Appendix 5 lists the entire set of ANSI and OEM characters and their associated codes. Tables 16-7 and 16-8 on the following page show a few of the extended ANSI and OEM characters. Although these characters don't appear on your keyboard, it's easy to enter any of them into your document.

Entering ANSI and OEM characters

To enter an extended ANSI character, first turn on Num Lock, then hold down the [Alt] key. While holding down the [Alt] key, type 0 on the numeric keypad, then type the decimal code from Table A5-1 that represents the ANSI character you want to enter. (You must use the numbers on the numeric keypad.) After you type the last number in the code, release the [Alt] key. Word will then insert at the cursor position the character represented by that code. For example, to enter the ® character, hold down the [Alt] key, type *0174* on the numeric keypad, and release the [Alt] key.

To enter an extended OEM character into your document, hold down the [Alt] key, then type the decimal code that represents the OEM character you want to enter. (Notice that you do not precede the three-digit code with a 0 to produce an OEM character.) When you release the [Alt] key, Word will insert the appropriate OEM character into your document. For example, to enter the British pounds sterling (£), hold down the [Alt] key, type *156* on the numeric keypad, and release the [Alt] key.

If you've installed either a PCL laser printer (such as the Hewlett-Packard LaserJet) or a PostScript printer (such as the Apple LaserWriter), you can use the Windows Symbol font to create additional special characters. For instance, you can create all the letters in the Greek alphabet (both uppercase and lowercase), several math symbols, solid bullet characters, and so forth.

Using the Symbol font

Table 16-7

This code...	represents this ANSI character...
145	'
146	'
147	"
148	"
149	o
150	—
151	–
169	©
174	®

Table 16-8

This code...	represents this OEM character...
146	Æ
155	¢
156	£
164	ñ
225	ß

To create a character with the Symbol font, use the ribbon or the Character dialog box to apply the Symbol font to an ANSI or OEM character you've entered into your document. (The Symbol font will appear in the Font pull-down list box only if you've installed a PCL laser printer or a PostScript printer.) Table A5-2 in Appendix 5 shows the symbols that correspond to each ANSI and OEM character. Table 16-9 lists a few of the most popular characters you can create with this font.

Table 16-9

Assigning the Symbol font to this character...	creates this symbol...
OEM 83	Σ
OEM 132	™
OEM 156	$\leq$
OEM 157	∞
ANSI 188	...
ANSI 183	•

For example, to create a solid bullet character, first enter ANSI character 183 into your document by holding down [Alt], typing *0183* on the numeric keypad, and releasing the [Alt] key. At this point, a small dot will appear in the document. Now, highlight the character and use the ribbon or the Character dialog box to apply the Symbol font. When you do, the selected character will appear as a bullet (•). If you want, you can use the Points list box on the ribbon to change the size of the bullet to 8, 10, 12, 14, 18, or 24 points.

Although the ANSI and OEM character sets give you access to several characters, they are more difficult to enter than standard characters. For one thing, you'll need to refer to a table like the one in Appendix 5 whenever you want to use a special character.

Using the glossary to store symbols

To save yourself time and trouble, use Word's glossary feature to store the symbols you plan to use often. Once you've entered a character into your document, follow the procedures we outlined in Chapter 13 to place that character into the glossary. That way, you can later enter the character without having to refer to an ANSI or OEM character table. You'll find that the glossary is especially nice for storing commonly used characters, such as smart quotes, en and em dashes, and bullets.

TWO SPECIAL FIELDS

Although we've discussed nearly all the fields Word offers in previous sections of this book, two of its fields serve a somewhat unusual purpose—QUOTE and PRINT. Let's briefly discuss these fields.

The QUOTE field

The QUOTE field simply inserts literal text into your document. This field takes the form

{QUOTE *literalText*}

where *literalText* is the text (enclosed in quotation marks) you want to insert into the document. Word will update the QUOTE field as soon as you modify its field code. If you want, you can specify an ANSI character in the *literalText* argument by typing the appropriate ANSI code outside the argument's quotation marks. Appendix 5 offers a complete list of ANSI characters and their associated codes.

For example, if you enter the field

{QUOTE "Word for Windows Companion, c 1990"}

into a document, you'll see the text *Word for Windows Companion, c 1990* when you display the field's result. If you enter the field

{QUOTE "Word for Windows Companion, "169" 1990"}

it will return the text *Word for Windows Companion, © 1990.* Because the number *169* in the field's argument appears outside the quotation marks, Word substitutes ANSI character 169 (the © symbol) in the field's result.

The PRINT field

You can use the PRINT field to send printer control codes and PostScript programs to your printer. The PRINT field takes the form

{PRINT *printInstructions*}

where *printInstructions* are the codes or instructions, enclosed in quotation marks, you want to send to the printer. Because the PRINT field is an action field, it doesn't return a result. Instead, when you use the Print... command to print a document, the PRINT field sends the printer control codes you specify.

Every printer has its own set of printer control codes and instructions. For this reason, you'll need to consult your printer manual to determine which codes and instructions you can use. Unfortunately, Word cannot determine whether the *printInstructions* argument you specify is valid for your printer. If you specify an invalid set of printer control codes in the *printInstructions* argument, your printer will probably print those codes as literal text.

If you're using a PostScript printer, and you want to use a PostScript program as your *printInstructions* argument, you need to precede the argument with the \p switch. Consult your *Word for Windows Technical Reference Manual* for more information on sending PostScript programs with the PRINT field.

In this chapter

Advanced File Handling 17

*I*n Chapter 3, we introduced you to many commands on Word's File menu and showed you how to open, save, and close documents. In this chapter, we'll show you a few more file-handling procedures that should help make it easier to manage your Word documents. First, we'll show you how to take advantage of Word's sophisticated document retrieval facilities, including searching and sorting. Then, we'll show you how to protect your documents against unwanted modifications.

After you've worked with Word for a while, your hard disk will contain dozens (or even hundreds) of document files, such as old memos, letters, reports, price lists, and so forth. Of course, the more document files you store on your hard disk, the more difficult it is to find a particular document later. Fortunately, Word provides some document retrieval tools that help you locate and open hard-to-find documents.

RETRIEVING DOCUMENTS

In order to take full advantage of these tools, you need to complete the information in the Summary Info dialog box for each document you save to disk. As we explained in Chapter 3, the Summary Info dialog box contains important document information, such as who wrote the document, what it's about, and comments about the document. If you take an extra moment to fill out the Summary Info dialog box before you save your documents, you can later use Word's document retrieval tools to locate documents by using several criteria, including title, subject, author, creation date, and revision date.

The tool you'll use to locate and identify document files on your hard disk is the Find... command. To issue the Find... command, you can either select Find... from the File menu, or you can select the Open... command from the File menu and choose the Find... button in the Open dialog box. When you use either of these techniques, Word will present a message box like the one shown in Figure 17-1 while it looks for document files on the active disk drive. After Word has examined the entire disk, it will present a Find dialog box like the one shown in Figure 17-2.

Figure 17-1

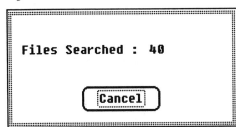

Word presents this message box while it looks for Word document files on your active disk.

Figure 17-2

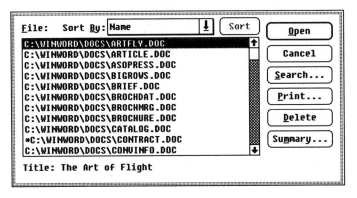

The Find dialog box allows you to perform a variety of document retrieval functions.

In addition to simply finding and opening a Word document, the Find dialog box lets you perform several other operations. Specifically, you can use this dialog box to send documents to the printer, delete documents, and display and edit a document's summary information. We'll show you how to perform each of these tasks in a moment.

Opening documents

You'll sometimes forget where you've stored an important document—especially if your disk is organized into several directories. If you find yourself using the Open... command to aimlessly search through your disk's directories for a document, you should take advantage of the Find... command's ability to search, sort, and open Word documents.

As you can see in Figure 17-2, the File list box in the Find dialog box shows you the full path name of every Word document file (files with a .DOC extension) on your active disk. To open a document file, select its file name and choose the Open button. If you're using a mouse, you can simply double-click on the file name of the document.

By the way, you probably noticed that one of the file names in Figure 17-2 (C:\WINWORD\DOCS\CONTRACT.DOC) appears with an asterisk. This indicates that the file has been saved in the Fast Save format. We'll come back to the subject of asterisks later in this chapter when we discuss searching for files.

If you want, you can open several document files at once. To do this with the mouse, press the [Shift] key as you click on the name of each file you want to open. After you've selected all the files, choose the Open button. If you're using the keyboard, first use the arrow keys to highlight the name of the first file you want to open. Next, hold down the [Ctrl] key while you use the arrow keys to move the dotted-line highlight to the name of the next file you want to open. When you've positioned the highlight over the appropriate file name, press the [Spacebar] to select that file. Continue using the [Ctrl] key, arrow keys, and the [Spacebar] in this fashion until you've selected all the files you want to open. Finally, to open them, choose the Open button.

Searching for files

As you've seen, it's quite simple to open a document with the Find... command when you know the name of the document file—even if you initially don't remember in which directory that file is stored. In many cases, however, you'll want to open a document whose file name you can't recall. Or, you might issue the Find... command and see several similar file names in the File list box— any of which might be the name of the document file you're trying to locate. Whenever you can't recall the document's exact file name or location, you'll want to take advantage of Word's searching capabilities.

To search for a particular document file, choose the Search... button in the Find dialog box. When you do, Word will present a Search dialog box like the one shown in Figure 17-3 on the following page. As you can see, this dialog box lets you specify both the list of directories to search and the search criteria. As we mentioned earlier, you can specify a variety of search criteria, including the document's title, subject, and author.

Specifying a search list

The Search List text box lets you specify the directories in which Word should look for your document files. Simply type into this text box the full path name of the directories, separating each path name with a semicolon. For example, if you want Word to look for files with .DOC extensions in the \WINWORD and \DATA directories, type *WINWORD;\DATA* into the Search List text box.

Figure 17-3

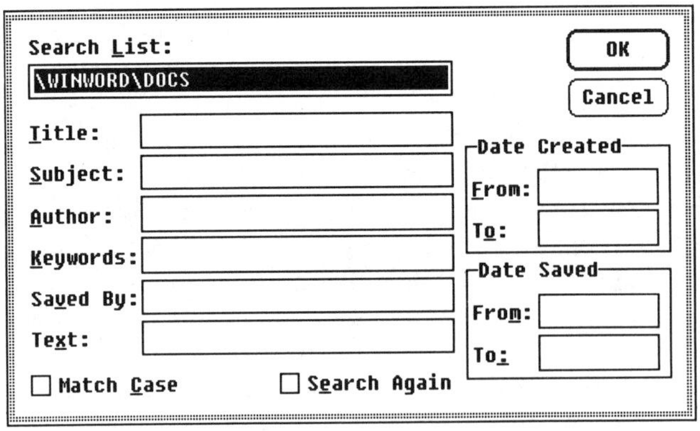

The Search dialog box makes it easy to find a particular document file.

Word will examine only standard Word documents (files with a .DOC file-name extension) when it searches the directories in the Search List text box. If you want to examine documents with non-standard extensions, you must indicate this by appending a file-name descriptor to the path names in the Search List text box. You can use the standard DOS wildcard characters (* and ?) to specify the types of files you want to locate. For example, if you want Word to examine all the files in the two directories that we specified earlier, you must enter *\WINWORD*.*;\DATA*.** into the Search List text box.

When you are ready to begin searching through the new directories you've specified, select the Search Again check box, then choose OK. After Word has searched through the specified directories, it will redisplay the Find dialog box with an updated list of files.

Specifying search criteria

Once you've used the Search List text box to specify the directories and types of files you want Word to look for, you will want to use the rest of the options in the Search dialog box to specify the appropriate search criteria. As we've said, you can specify all types of search criteria in the Search dialog box. Now, we'll consider each type.

Summary Info criteria

You can often find an elusive document file if you know something about the document's Summary Info dialog box. To identify all the document files whose summary information matches some known information, enter that information into the appropriate text box in Figure 17-3 (Title, Subject, Author, Keywords, or Saved By), and choose OK. As you may know, Word stores the name you entered when you first started Word in the Your Name text box in the Customize dialog box. When you save a document, Word saves that name along with the document. Consequently, if you are the original author of the document you're searching for, and the name *Fred* appears in the Your Name text box in the Customize dialog box, you can search for all the files you've written by typing *Fred* into the Author text box in Figure 17-3, and choosing OK.

Text criteria

The Text text box comes in handy when you can recall some of the text in the document you're trying to locate. To use this criteria, simply type some text that appears in the document you're searching for, and choose OK. As you might expect, it takes Word longer to find documents using text criteria than it does to find documents using other criteria. For this reason, we suggest that you specify text criteria only as a last resort, and use the other criteria whenever possible.

As we mentioned earlier, if a file has been saved in the Fast Save format, an asterisk will appear next to its file name in the Find dialog box. Unfortunately, Word cannot read all of a document's text if it is stored in the Fast Save format. To remedy this problem, you must open each document whose name appears with an asterisk, issue the Save As... command, deselect the Fast Save check box in the expanded Save As dialog box, and choose OK. If you plan to use text criteria to search for documents on a regular basis, you should refrain from activating the Fast Save check box when saving your documents.

Word provides a few special characters you might want to use in the search criteria text boxes we've discussed. Table 17-1 lists these special characters and their meanings.

Using special characters

Table 17-1

This character...	tells Word to...
? (question mark)	match any single character
* (asterisk)	match a group of characters
∧ (caret)	treat the following special character as a regular character
, (comma)	select a document if its summary information matches any or all items in the text box (analogous to a logical OR operation)
& (ampersand)	select a document if its summary information matches all of the items in the text box (analogous to a logical AND operation)
~ (tilde)	select a document if its summary information does not match the item in the text box (analogous to a logical NOT operation)

The ? and * are wildcard characters, just as they are in DOS. You can use the ? character whenever you need a single-character wildcard in your search criteria; you can use the * character whenever you need a multiple-character wildcard. For example, to search for all the documents written by Mark and Mary, you could enter the criterion *Mar?* in the Author text box in Figure 17-3, then choose OK. Similarly, to search for all the documents written by people whose name begins with the letter *M*, you could enter the criterion *M** in the Author text box.

The caret (^) lets you use any of the six special characters as a literal character in your search criteria text boxes. To use one of the six special characters as a literal character, precede the special character with a ^. For example, if you want to search for the document entitled *Bonnie & Clyde*, you could use the criterion *Bonnie^&Clyde* in the Title text box. Similarly, to search for the document entitled *What's Up Doc?*, you could use the criterion *What's Up Doc^?*.

The comma (,) tells Word to search for documents whose summary information contains any or all of the items you've listed in a search criteria text box. For instance, suppose you want to search for documents that were written by Mark or Allan. To do this, you could enter *Mark,Allan* in the Author text box. Similarly, to search for documents written by Doug, Steve, or Gena, you could enter *Doug,Steve,Gena*.

The ampersand (&) tells Word to search for documents whose summary information matches all the items in your search criteria text box. For example, to search for documents whose body text contains both the words *terminate* and *insubordination*, you would need to enter *terminate&insubordination* in the Text text box.

Finally, the tilde (~) tells Word to search for documents whose summary information does not match the stated criterion. For example, if you want to search for all the documents that were not originally written by Peggy, you could use the criterion *~Peggy* in the Author text box.

If you want, you can enter the tilde character in conjunction with the comma to specify a complex criterion. For example, if you want to search for all the documents that were written by anyone other than Joe or Jeff, you could enter *~(Joe,Jeff)* in the Author text box. Notice that we've used parentheses to surround *Joe, Jeff* in order to make the criterion valid.

Be careful when you specify your search criteria. Remember that if a document's summary information contains a superset of the criterion you specify, Word will select that document. Consequently, if you specify the criterion *Doug* in the Author text box, Word will select the documents written by Doug Cobb, Doug Been, Doug Roach, and so forth. Try to make your search criteria as specific as possible without excluding any of the documents you want to select. For instance, if you want to search for all the documents written by Mark and Mary, don't use the criterion *M** in the Author text box—instead use *Mar?*.

You've probably noticed that two check boxes appear near the bottom of the Search dialog box—Match Case and Search Again. As you'd expect, selecting the Match Case check box tells Word that case is important in the criterion you've specified. For example, if you enter the search criterion *Fred* into the Author text box and do not select the Match Case check box, choosing OK will tell Word to search for all the documents whose Author text box contains the word *Fred* in any case combination, including *Fred, FRED, fReD, fred,* and so forth. If you select the Match Case check box, however, Word will search only for documents whose Author text box contains the word *Fred*.

Matching case

In addition to searching for documents whose summary information matches some known criteria, you can search for documents that were created during a specific time period. To do this, simply enter the appropriate dates into the Date Created text boxes. For instance, if you want to search for all the documents created between January 1, 1990, and January 31, 1990, enter the date *1/1/90* into the Date Created From text box, then enter the date *1/31/90* into the Date Created To text box, then choose OK. If you want to search for documents created on a single day, enter the same date into both text boxes. If you leave the Date Created From text box empty, Word will search for all documents created before the Date Created To date. If you leave the Date Created To text box empty, Word will search for all documents created after the Date Created From date.

Date criteria

As you might guess, the Date Saved From and Date Saved To text boxes let you search for documents that were last saved during a specific time period. As with the Date Created text boxes, you can specify a single date criterion by entering the same date into both text boxes. If you leave the Date Saved From text box empty, Word will search for all the documents saved before the Date Saved To date. Similarly, if you leave the Date Saved To text box empty, Word will search for all the documents saved after the Date Saved From date.

In case you're wondering, you cannot use any of the special characters listed in Table 17-1 in the date criterion. These special characters work only in the six text boxes that appear immediately below the Search List text box.

After you've specified all of your search criteria in the Search dialog box, you need to make sure that the Search Again check box is set properly. If you don't select the Search Again check box before you choose OK, Word will search for only the files that are currently listed in the Find dialog box. If you select the Search Again check box before you choose OK, however, Word will search the files stored in all the directories listed in the Search List text box. Of course, if you haven't changed the list of directories in the Search List text box, the Search Again option will not affect the search.

Repeating the search

Sorting file names

Once you've used Word's searching capabilities to bring up a list of files in the Find dialog box's File list box, you may want to sort the list. By default, Word sorts the file names in alphabetical order. If you want, however, you can tell Word to sort the file names by author, by the date the document was created or last saved, by the name of the person who last saved the document, or by size. Table 17-2 lists the six keys upon which you can sort.

Table 17-2

This criterion...	sorts files...
Name	alphabetically
Author	alphabetically
Creation Date	chronologically, with most recently created listed first
Last Saved Date	chronologically, with most recently saved listed last
Last Saved By	alphabetically
Size	by size, with smallest document listed first

To sort the file names by any of these sort keys, first choose the appropriate option from the Sort By pull-down list box in the Find dialog box. When you choose a new sort key, the option you selected will appear in the Sort By text box. In addition, Word will activate the Sort button so that you can select it. To sort the file names by the sort key you've selected, simply choose the Sort button. Word will then rearrange the file names in the File list box according to that sort key.

In addition to rearranging the file names, Word will change the information displayed at the bottom of the Find dialog box to match the sort key. As you can see in Figure 17-2, Word displays the title of the file you've highlighted at the bottom of the dialog box when the files are sorted by name. However, when Word sorts the file names by author, it will display the author of the file you've highlighted, as shown in Figure 17-4. Similarly, when Word sorts the file names by any of the other sort keys, it will display the correct data at the bottom of the dialog box.

By the way, when Word sorts file names by author, it uses the leftmost characters of the author name you've entered to determine the sort order. For this reason, if you specify the author name in the Summary Info dialog box in the usual first-name last-name format, Word will sort files according to the author's first name. To sort files by the author's last name, you must enter an author name in each document's Summary Info dialog box in the last-name first-name format. For details on entering and editing summary information, refer to Chapter 3.

Figure 17-4

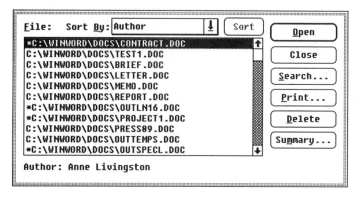

*When you sort Word files by author, Word will display the
author of the highlighted file at the bottom of the dialog box.*

Although you'll typically use the Print... command on the File menu to print
your Word documents, you can also print by using the Print... button in the Find
dialog box. Although the command and the button work in essentially the same
way, the Print... button lets you send multiple documents to the printer with a
single command.

To print a document from the Find dialog box, highlight the document you
want to print and select the Print... button. Word will then display the Print dialog
box shown in Figure 17-5. To complete the printing procedure, choose OK.

Printing documents

Figure 17-5

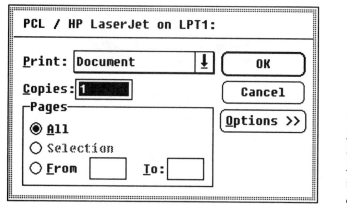

*You can open the
Print dialog box
by using the
Print... button
in the Find
dialog box.*

Printing multiple documents

If you want to send multiple documents to the printer with a single command, just highlight the name of each document you want to send in the File list box before you choose the Print... button. To highlight multiple documents with the mouse, hold down the [Shift] key as you click on the name of each document. If you're using the keyboard, first use the arrow keys to highlight the name of the first document you want to print. Next, hold down the [Ctrl] key while you use the arrow keys to move the dotted-line highlight to the name of the next document. When you've positioned the highlight over the appropriate document name, press the [Spacebar] to select that file. Continue using the [Ctrl] key, arrow keys, and the [Spacebar] in this fashion until you've selected all the files you want to print.

Notes

As we said, choosing the Print... button will instruct Word to present the Print dialog box shown in Figure 17-5. If you use the Print... button to print multiple documents, the settings you specify in the Print dialog box will apply to every document you print. For example, if you tell Word to print pages 1 through 3 in the Print dialog box, Word will print only pages 1 through 3 of each document you selected in the Find dialog box.

Deleting documents

As you create more and more Word documents, your disk will become cluttered with document files. To eliminate some of your old files and clean up your disk, you can use the Delete button in the Find dialog box.

To delete a file that appears in the File list box, select the file and choose the Delete button. Word will then present a message box like the one shown in Figure 17-6. If you've accidentally chosen the Delete button or have selected the wrong file, choose No to cancel the command and to return to the Find dialog box. If you've chosen the correct file, however, choose Yes to delete it and to return to the dialog box.

Figure 17-6

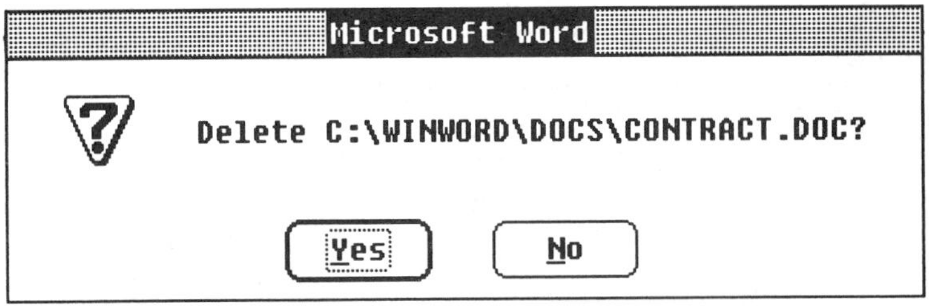

Word will ask you to confirm your decision to delete a file.

Like most of the buttons in the Find dialog box, the Delete button lets you operate on multiple files with a single command. To delete multiple files, select the names of all the files you want to delete in the File list box before you choose the Delete button. When Word presents the message box asking you to confirm the deletion, it will present the names of all the files you selected. To complete the command and delete all of the selected files, choose Yes.

Once you've opened the Find dialog box, you can display and edit the summary information for any file you see in the File list box. To display a file's summary information, simply highlight the appropriate file and choose the Summary... button. Word will then bring up the selected file's Summary Info dialog box. In fact, selecting a file and choosing the Summary... button is no different from choosing the Summary Info... command on the Edit menu while that document is active. For a detailed discussion of the Summary Info dialog box, refer to Chapter 3.

Reviewing summary information

Sometimes, the Summary... button in the Find dialog box will be inactive. Word dims the Summary... button whenever the File list box is empty or when nine documents are open at the same time. If you run into this situation, simply use the Search... button to bring some file names into the File list box, or close the Find dialog box and close some of the documents that are currently open.

Word provides two forms of security for your documents: the Read Only option in the Open dialog box and the Lock for Annotations option in the expanded Save As dialog box. Let's consider how you can use each option to prevent unwanted changes to your Word documents.

DOCUMENT SECURITY

If you open a document while the Read Only option is selected, Word will allow you to edit and format that document, but will not allow you to save the altered document under its original name. To save the changes you've made to a document that was opened with the Read Only option, you'll have to use the Save As... command to save that document under a new name.

The Read Only option

To open a Word document under Read Only status, first select the Open... command from the File menu to bring up the Open dialog box shown in Figure 17-7 on the next page. In this dialog box, select the Read Only check box in the lower-right corner. Once you've selected the check box, select the file you want to open in the Files list box, then choose OK.

In addition to the Read Only option, which you can select when you open a Word document, Word provides the Lock for Annotations option, which you can select when you save a document. This option allows you to put a "lock" on a document, which prevents other users from making changes to it. Once you've activated this option and saved a document, you can make changes to the document and turn off the Lock for Annotations option only if the name you've entered in the Your Name text box in the Customize dialog box matches the name of the document's original author.

The Lock for Annotations option

Figure 17-7

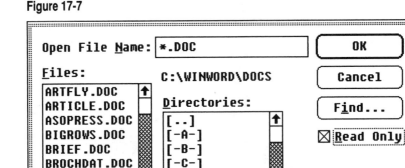

The Read Only check box in the Open dialog box protects your Word files against unwanted changes.

To save a document using the Lock for Annotations option, issue the Save As... command to bring up the Save As dialog box, then choose the Options >> button to bring up the expanded Save As dialog box shown in Figure 17-8. In this dialog box, select the Lock for Annotations check box, then choose OK.

Figure 17-8

When you save a document, you can use the Lock for Annotations option to prevent others from making changes to the document.

Although activating the Lock for Annotations option protects a document's contents, other users can still open, browse, and insert annotations into the document. For a detailed discussion on inserting and editing document annotations, see Chapter 13.

If you've locked a document with the Lock for Annotations option, you can unlock it again by reissuing the Save As... command, choosing the Options >> button, deselecting the Lock for Annotations check box, and choosing OK.

Although the Lock for Annotations option sounds like a great security feature, anyone can "break the lock" if they know the name of the document's author. To make changes to a document that has been saved with this option, first open the document, then issue the Customize... command on the Utilities menu. In the Customize dialog box, change the entry in the Your Name text box to match the name of the document's author. Once you've "tricked" Word into thinking that you are the document's original author, you can alter the document and the Lock for Annotations setting.

A warning

Although everyone can take advantage of Word's Read Only and Lock for Annotations features, your computer system might allow other forms of document security. Most disk operating systems and local area networks provide various ways to protect important files. To find out which forms of security are available, check with your information center specialist or with your local PC expert.

Other forms of security

During any typical Word session, Word will use several of the files stored on your hard disk. Table 17-3 on the following page lists the important Word for Windows files you'll see if you look at a listing of the files in your Word for Windows directory. Let's discuss a few of these files.

IMPORTANT FILES

WINWORD.EXE is Word's main program file. You must use this file to begin a new Word session. The WINWORD.INI file is Word's initialization file, which stores Word's default settings when you end a Word session. Each time you begin a new Word session, Word will use the WINWORD.INI file to restore your previous defaults. You cannot edit the contents of this file directly; instead, you must change the appropriate defaults during a Word session, then end that session.

WIN.INI is Windows' initialization file. If you've installed the RunTime version of Microsoft Windows, this file will appear in your Word for Windows directory. If you've installed a full-featured version of Microsoft Windows, WIN.INI will appear in your Windows directory. The WIN.INI file stores all your Windows defaults, as well as a few Word defaults. Each time you begin a new Word for Windows (or Windows) session, the settings in this file will restore the previous Windows defaults.

The NORMAL.DOT file is Word's default document template. If you use the New... command to create a new document and do not specify an existing document template, Word will use the NORMAL.DOT template to create the new document. As we'll explain in Chapter 18, you can modify this default template to suit your needs.

Table 17-3

File	Function
WINWORD.EXE	Word's main program file
WINWORD.INI	Word's initialization file
WINWORD.HLP	Word's Help file
WIN.INI	Windows' initialization file
WINWORD.CBT	Word's tutorial program file
NORMAL.DOT	Word's default document template
*.BAK	Backup files for documents and templates
*.DIC	Spelling dictionary files
*.DOC	Word document files
*.DOT	Word document template files
*.DRV	Driver files for the screen, mouse, and printer
*.FON	Screen font files
*.TMP	Temporary files used during a Word session
HYPH.DAT	Word's hyphenation data file
LEX-??.EXE	Spelling program files
LEX-??.DAT	Main spelling dictionary
SYN-??.EXE	Thesaurus program file
SYN-??.DAT	Thesaurus data file
CONV-??.EXE	Converter program file

The LEX-??.EXE files are Word's spelling program files. The two question marks in the file name are placeholders for a two-letter abbreviation for that file's language. For example, the file LEX-AM.EXE is the spelling program file for the U.S. dictionary, while the file LEX-BR.EXE is the spelling program file for the United Kingdom dictionary. The CONV-??.EXE files are Word's converted files. These files convert documents created in other applications into Word's Normal file format.

In this chapter

Document Templates **18**

*I*n several places throughout this book, we've mentioned document templates, which are involved in nearly everything from creating a new document to customizing Word's menus. In this chapter, we'll explain document templates in detail and show you how to open a new document based on a document template. We'll also show you how to create and edit your own document templates and how to use them to create custom forms.

A document template is a special type of Word document that serves as a pattern for other documents. Just as a shoemaker uses shoe templates to make shoes of different sizes, you can use document templates to create several types of documents.

WHAT IS A DOCUMENT TEMPLATE?

To illustrate the benefit of using document templates, suppose you print many of your Word documents on company letterhead. Each time you prepare to print such a document, you change its Left margin setting from 1.25" to 1", and its Top margin setting from 1" to 3". In addition, you always insert the current date at the top of the letter.

Instead of going through the process of changing the document's margins and entering the current date each time you begin a new letter, you can create a document template that automatically takes care of these tasks for you. All you have to do is select the New… command from the File menu, choose the name of the appropriate template in the Use Template list box, and choose OK. Word will then create a new document that already has the correct margin settings and the current date. You can then begin typing the new letter.

Although the process of setting up the document's margins and entering the current date doesn't require a great deal of time and effort, you might want to create templates that are much more complex. For instance, you might create a template for interoffice memos, another one for monthly status reports, and so forth. Of course, the time you invest in setting up a complex document template is well spent if you're likely to use the template to create several new documents.

Word stores every document template as a file with a .DOT file-name extension in the Word program directory. As you may have noticed, Word installs a few sample document templates for you when you run the Word for Windows Setup program. As you create and save your own document templates, Word will store those new template files in the Word program directory as well.

A document template can contain all the elements listed in Table 18-1. When you create a new document based on a template, the document will automatically contain all the elements stored in its template.

Table 18-1

This template element...	allows you to...
boilerplate text	include the same text in every document
Document and Section settings	automatically apply consistent document and section formatting
styles	use a style sheet to apply consistent paragraph and character formatting
glossary items	use standard glossary entries
macros	run macros you've created that perform editing and formatting tasks
menu and key assignments	invoke macros using the same key combinations and menu commands

Now that we've given you a general idea of what document templates are and how you can use them to work more efficiently, let's discuss the techniques you'll need to know in order to work with templates efficiently. Specifically, we'll explain how to create a new document based on a template, and how to create and edit custom templates.

CREATING A NEW DOCUMENT BASED ON A TEMPLATE

To create a new document based on a template, simply select the New... command from the File menu to open the dialog box shown in Figure 18-1. As you can see, Word chooses the New Document option by default, and presents a list of the available templates in the Use Template list box. This list includes all of Word's built-in templates as well as the templates you've created. (We'll show you how to create a template in a moment.)

Figure 18-1

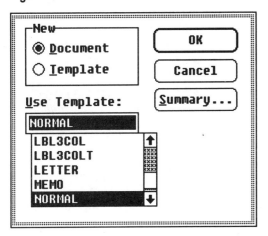

Word bases the new documents you create on the template selected in the Use Template list box.

By default, Word selects the NORMAL option in the Use Template list box. The Normal template initially contains all of Word's standard default Document and Section dialog box settings, as well as Word's standard menu and key assignments. It doesn't contain any text, glossary entries, or macros. If you're like most users, you probably base nearly all of your new documents on the Normal template, then modify your new document when it appears in the document window.

If you want to base a new document on a template other than Normal, simply select that template in the Use Template list box before choosing OK. When you choose OK, a new, untitled document will appear on the screen containing all the elements that are stored in the template you selected. You can then edit, format, save, and print the new document as usual.

Remember that when you open a document based on any document template other than Normal, Word will check to make sure that the document's template is present in the Word program directory. If Word cannot find the template, it will display the message box shown in Figure 18-2 on the next page. When you choose OK to close this message box, you can begin working with the document, but you will not be able to access any of the glossary terms, macros, custom key assignments, or custom menu commands stored in the document's template.

CREATING A NEW DOCUMENT TEMPLATE

Word offers several ways to create a new template. First, you can use the New... command to create a new template from scratch. You can also use the New... command to base a new template on an existing document or on an existing template. If you want to save one of your existing documents in the form of a document template, you can do so by using the Save As... command. Let's take a closer look at each of these techniques.

Figure 18-2

You'll see this message box if you open a document whose template cannot be located.

Creating a new template from scratch

To create a new template from scratch, select the New... command from the File menu, choose the New Template option, and choose OK. When you do this, Word will open a new document window entitled *Template1*. As you create new templates during the current session, Word will number those templates sequentially—Template2, Template3, and so forth.

Once you've created the new template, you can begin modifying it just as you modify a document. You can add, edit, and format text, define styles and glossary entries, and change the Document and Section dialog box settings. In Chapter 19, we'll explain how to store a macro you've created in a document template, and in Chapter 20, we'll explain how to store custom menu and key assignments.

When you're ready to save the template, choose the Save or Save As... command from the File menu to bring up the dialog box shown in Figure 18-3. At this point, type the name you want to assign to the new template in the Save File Name text box, and choose OK to bring up a Summary Info dialog box for the new template. After you type in the template's summary information, choose OK to complete the save. Word will then save the new template under the name you specify in your Word program directory, and will automatically append a .DOT file-name extension to its name. The next time you issue the New... command on the File menu, Word will include the name of the new template in the Use Template list box.

If you attempt to save a template under the same name as an existing template, Word will present a message box like the one shown in Figure 18-4. If you want to replace the existing template with the one you've created, choose Yes. Choosing No will tell Word to cancel the save and return to the dialog box in Figure 18-3, where you can type a new template name. If you want to cancel the save altogether and return to the template, choose Cancel.

Creating a new template from an existing document

If you have created a document you'd like to use as a template for new documents, you can use the Save As... command to save that document as a template. To do this, activate the document and select the Save As... command from the File menu to open the Save As dialog box. Next, choose the Options >> button to expand the Save As dialog box, and choose the Document Template option from the File Format pull-down list box, as we've done in Figure 18-5 on the following page. Word will then make sure the current directory name, which appears above the Directories list box, is the directory containing your Word program files. In addition, Word will deactivate the Directories list box to prevent you from saving the new template in another directory. Next, type the name you want to assign to the new template, then choose OK. When the Summary Info dialog box appears, enter the summary information and choose OK.

Figure 18-3

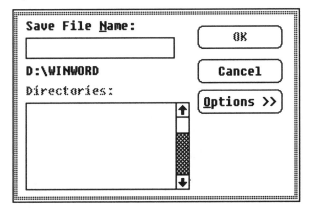

Word saves new templates in the Word program directory, and appends a .DOT file-name extension.

Figure 18-4

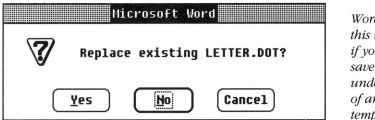

Word will present this message box if you attempt to save a template under the name of an existing template.

When you choose OK in the Summary Info dialog box, Word will save the new template under the name you specify in your Word program directory, and will automatically append a .DOT file-name extension to its name. The next time you issue the New... command on the File menu, Word will include the name of the new template in the Use Template list box.

If you attempt to save a template under the same name as an existing template, Word will present a message box like the one shown in Figure 18-4. If you want to replace the existing template with the one you've created, choose Yes.

Choosing No will tell Word to cancel the save and return to the dialog box in Figure 18-5, where you can type a new template name. If you want to cancel the save altogether and return to the template, choose Cancel.

Figure 18-5

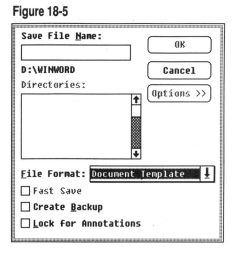

The expanded Save As dialog box lets you save the active document in the form of a template.

Basing a new template on an existing template

As with new documents, you can base new templates on existing templates. The procedure you'll use to base a new template on an existing template is similar to the one we described above. First, select the New... command to open the New dialog box. Next, choose the New Template option and select from the Use Template list box the template upon which you want to base the new template. When you choose OK, Word will create a new, untitled template window that carries the same elements as the template upon which it is based.

Instead of using the New... command to base a new template on an existing template, you can open the existing template, modify it, then use the Save As... command to save the modified template in a separate template file. If you use this technique, remember to choose the Document Template option from the File Format list box in the expanded Save As dialog box before you choose OK.

EDITING A DOCUMENT TEMPLATE

After you've created a document template, you can open and modify it just like a regular Word document. To open a document template, begin by selecting the Open... command from the File menu to bring up the Open dialog box shown in Figure 18-6. If the current directory is not set to your Word program directory, use the Directories list box to activate that directory.

As we explained in Chapter 3, the default entry in the Open File Name text box is *.DOC, which tells Word to list all the Word documents (the files with a .DOC file-name extension) in the Files list box on the left side of the Open dialog box. As we mentioned earlier, document template files have a .DOT file-name extension and therefore do not appear in the Files list box automatically. To display the names of your document template files in the Files list box, change the entry in the Open File Name text box to *.DOT and choose OK. Word will then display in the Files list box all of your document template files, as shown in Figure 18-7.

Figure 18-6

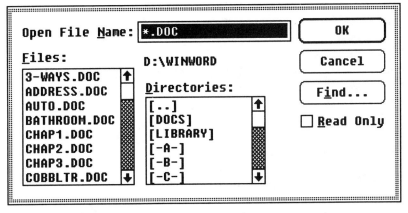

You'll use the Open... command to open document templates.

Figure 18-7

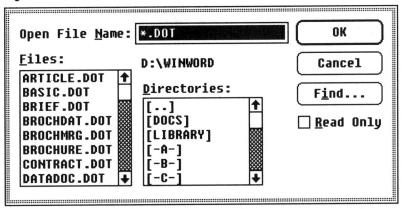

*Changing the entry in the Open File Name text box to *.DOT tells Word to display in the Files list box all of your document template files.*

After you've instructed Word to display the document template files in the Files list box, choose the name of the template you want to edit, and choose OK. Immediately, Word will open the template you selected. At this point, you can begin adding text, defining styles and glossary entries, and so forth. When you are ready to save your changes, use the Save or Close command to save the template just as you would after modifying a normal document.

After you alter a document template, any new documents you base on that template will carry all of the template's new elements, including text, Document and Section dialog box settings, styles, glossary items, macros, and menu and key assignments. However, when you open a document that was based on the unmodified version of that template, that document will not reflect the changes you've made to the template's text, Document and Section dialog box settings, or styles. On the other hand, any changes you've made to the template's glossary, macros, and menu and key assignments will be evident when you open the document and issue the Glossary… command or any of the commands on the Macro menu (except Record…).

Editing the Normal template

You might be surprised to learn that Word's Setup program does not place a copy of the Normal template in your Word program directory until you perform an action that modifies Word's default settings in some way. For this reason, if you haven't modified any of Word's default settings, you won't be able to open and modify the Normal template directly.

If you want to open and edit the Normal template, and the file name *NORMAL.DOT* doesn't appear in the Files list box in the Open dialog box, you can tell Word to create a NORMAL.DOT file by following this simple procedure: First, use the New… command to create a new document, then select the Document… command from the Format menu to open the dialog box shown in Figure 18-8. Next, change any of the settings in the Document dialog box, such as the Widow Control check box, and choose the Set Default button. Next, change the setting back to its original default, and choose the Set Default button again. Finally, choose the OK button to close the Document dialog box. (We'll discuss the Set Default button in detail in Chapter 20.)

After you close the Document dialog box, choose the Exit command from the File menu. When Word presents the message box shown in Figure 18-9, choose Yes to save the new NORMAL.DOT file and to exit from Word. Now, when you restart Word, issue the Open… command, and enter **.DOT* in the Open File Name text box, you'll see the file *NORMAL.DOT* in the Files list box. You can then select that file and choose OK to open the Normal template. After you make the desired modifications, choose the Close command from the File menu to save your changes and close the template.

Deleting document templates

As we mentioned earlier, Word stores all document templates as files with a .DOT file-name extension in the Word program directory. If you want to delete a document template (either one you've created or one of Word's built-in templates), delete the appropriate template file from the Word program directory. To learn how to delete a file, refer to Chapter 17.

Figure 18-8

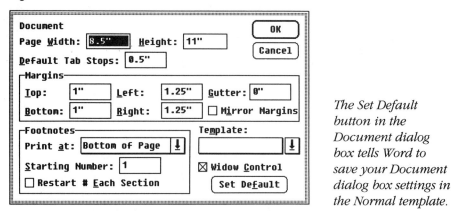

The Set Default button in the Document dialog box tells Word to save your Document dialog box settings in the Normal template.

Figure 18-9

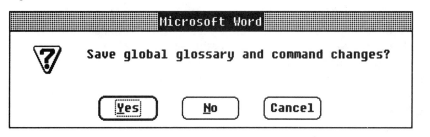

When you choose Yes in this message box, Word will save a new NORMAL.DOT file and exit from Word.

CREATING FORMS

One of the most popular uses for document templates is for creating forms. Forms are "fill-in-the-blank" documents that prompt you for specific pieces of information. Word allows you to create all kinds of forms, ranging from simple phone memos to complex tax forms. For instance, Figure 18-10 on the following page shows a phone memo form you can create in Word.

The basic building block of a Word form is a table. Some cells of the table will store the text that labels the form's blanks, while other cells will store the entries you supply. Chapter 11 explains how to insert a table into a document and customize it.

After you've created your form, save it to disk as a document template. Then, whenever you want to open a new copy of the form and fill in its blanks, just select the New... command from the File menu, select the name of the form in the Use Template list box, then choose OK. Word will then open a new, untitled document based on the form you selected. At this point, you can fill in the form's blanks, save the form to disk, print it, and so forth.

Figure 18-10

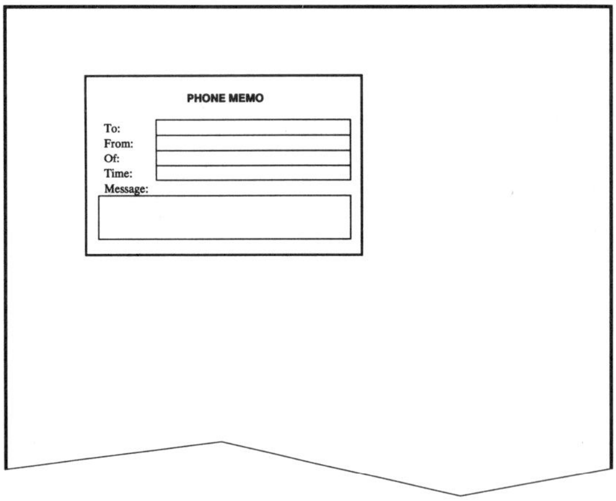

You can use document templates to create all kinds of forms.

A sample form

To demonstrate the process of creating a form, let's create the sample phone memo shown in Figure 18-10. To begin, select the New... command from the File menu, choose the New Template option in the New dialog box, and choose OK to open a new, untitled template. Next, use the Table... command on the Insert menu to insert a table with four columns and eight rows. Once you've done this, enter the memo's label text into the appropriate cells of the table, as shown in Figure 18-11.

Your next step is to use the techniques we discussed in Chapter 11 to format the table. For our sample phone memo, you'll want to adjust the widths of the columns, merge some cells, add single borders to a few cells, and add a thick border around the entire table. Figure 18-12 shows the table after we've performed these formatting tasks.

After you've finished customizing the table, you're ready to save the form to disk. To do this, select the Save or Save As... command from the File menu, type the name you want to assign to the new form (like *PHONE*), and choose OK.

After you've created the phone memo form, you're ready to open a new copy of that form and fill it out. To do this, select the New... command from the File menu, select PHONE from the Use Template list box, and choose OK. Word will then create a new, untitled document based on the phone memo form, as shown in Figure 18-13 on page 730.

When Word displays the new copy of the form, you can fill it out by moving the cursor to the appropriate cells and typing the missing information. When you've completed the form, you can save it to disk or print it.

Figure 18-11

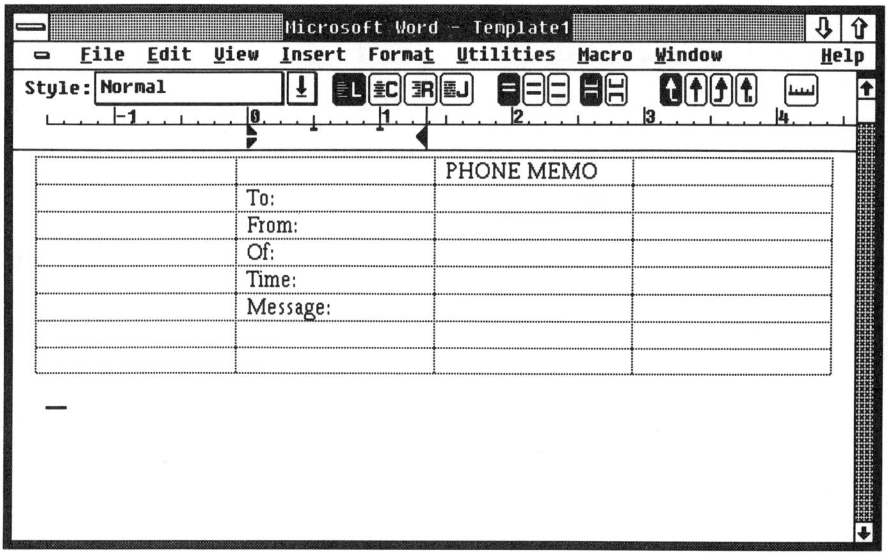

The first step in creating a form is to insert a table into your document and type the text that labels the form's entries.

Figure 18-12

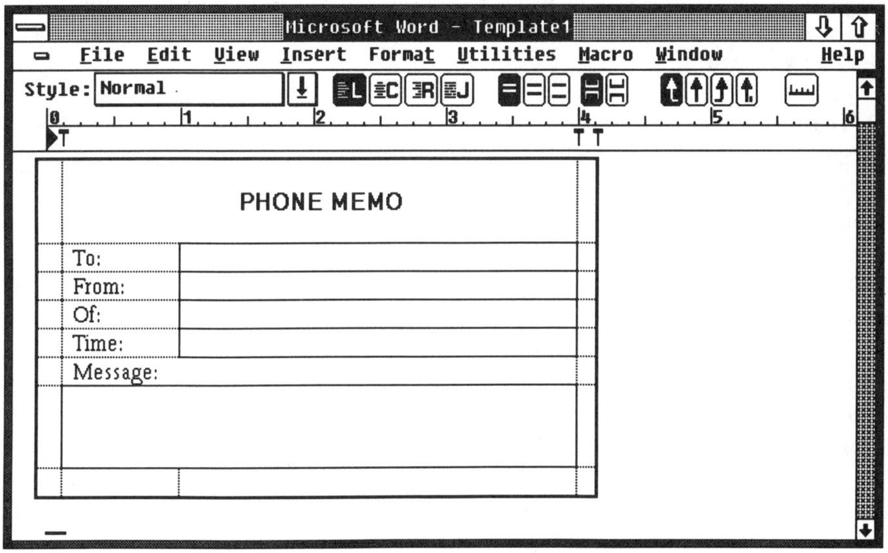

You can format the table by adjusting column widths, merging cells, and adding borders.

Figure 18-13

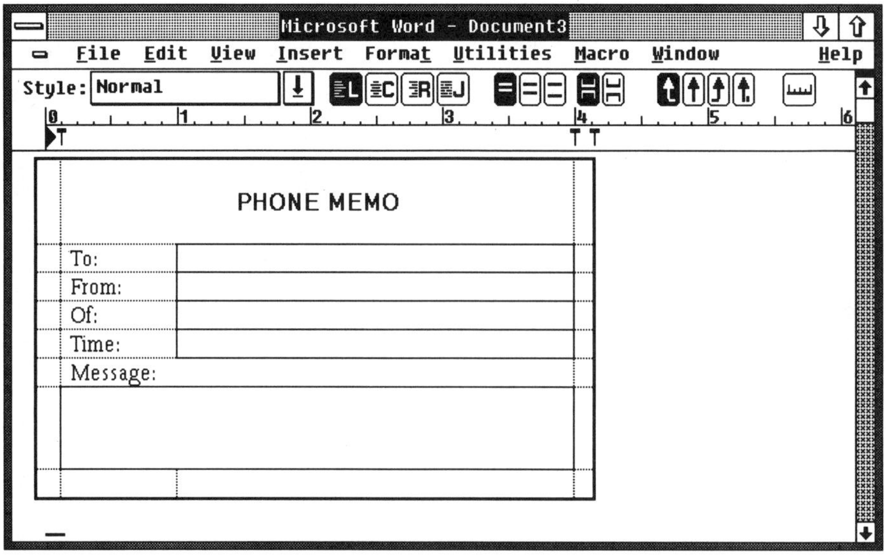

When you create a new document based on a custom template, that untitled document will initially look exactly like the template.

Prompting for the form's information

Instead of moving the cursor to the appropriate cells in a form and typing the missing information, you can instruct Word to prompt you for the information and enter your responses into the appropriate cells. To do this, you'll need to use either the FILLIN or ASK field.

The FILLIN field

The FILLIN field tells Word to prompt you for the text you want to insert into the current document. The form of this field is:

{FILLIN *prompt*}

When Word updates the FILLIN field, it will present a dialog box containing the text specified in the *prompt* argument. After you respond to the prompt and choose OK, Word will insert the text you've entered at the FILLIN field's location.

As with most fields, Word updates the FILLIN field whenever you highlight it and press the [Update field] key ([F9]). For this reason, you'll want to tell Word to update all of the form's FILLIN fields as soon as you create a new form. To do this, highlight the entire document and press the [Update field] key. After Word has prompted you for each piece of information, you'll see the information you supplied in the appropriate cells of the form. (You'll need to turn off the Field Codes setting on the View menu in order to see the results of the FILLIN fields.)

Let's illustrate the benefit of FILLIN fields by using them to prompt for the information in the phone memo form. First, use the Open... command on the File menu to open the template PHONE.DOT. Next, move the cursor to the cell that stores the To entry, press the [Insert field] key ([Ctrl][F9]), and enter the field:

{FILLIN "Who is the message for?"}

Now, in the cells that store the From, Of, Time, and Message entries, enter the following four fields, respectively:

{FILLIN "What is the caller's name?"}
{FILLIN "Which firm does the caller work for? (Leave blank if none)"}
{FILLIN "What time did the call come in?"}
{FILLIN "What is the message?"}

Figure 18-14 shows these fields in our sample form.

Figure 18-14

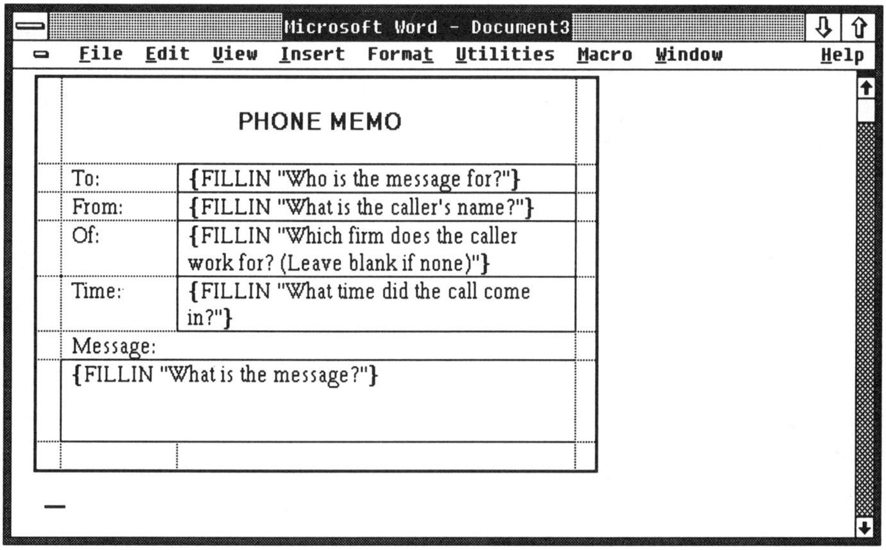

You can use FILLIN fields to prompt for a form's information.

After you've entered all the FILLIN fields into your form, select the Close command from the File menu and choose Yes in the ensuing message box to save your changes to disk.

Now, to use the modified form, select the New... command from the File menu, select PHONE from the Use Template list box, and choose OK to create a new copy of the phone memo form. Next, highlight the entire document and press the [Update field] key ([F9]). At this point, Word will update the first field in the document and present the dialog box shown in Figure 18-15. You can then type the name of the message's recipient and choose OK to insert that text into the document. Word will then present a similar dialog box for each FILLIN field you've entered in the form's template. After you've responded to all the prompts, you'll see the information you've supplied in the appropriate cells of the form. Figure 18-16 shows the sample form Word created after we responded to each of the FILLIN prompts. (Don't forget to turn off the Field Codes setting on the View menu in order to view the FILLIN fields' results instead of their field codes.)

Figure 18-15

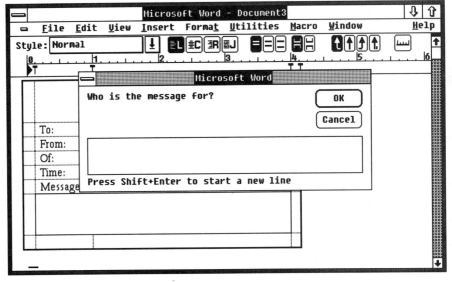

Word presents a dialog box like this when it updates a FILLIN field.

Although highlighting the entire document and pressing the [Update field] key is not a time-consuming process, you can use a macro that will automatically update all the fields in your document when you choose OK in the New dialog box. We'll show you how to do that in the next chapter.

If you want Word to provide a default entry in the dialog box generated by a FILLIN field, you can do so by using a \d switch. The form of the FILLIN field with a \d switch is

{FILLIN *prompt* \d *defaultText*}

where *defaultText* is the text you want to appear as the default entry. For example, if you want the entry *Please call back* to be the default for the Message entry in the sample phone memo, you would use the field:

{FILLIN "What is the message?" \d "Please call back"}

Figure 18-16

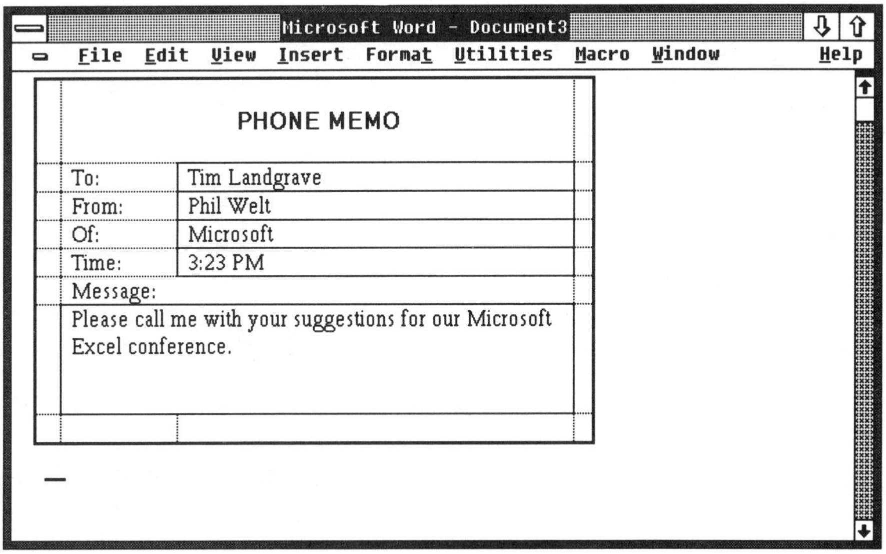

Word automatically inserts into the appropriate cells of the form your responses to the FILLIN prompts.

If a piece of information appears more than once in your form, you'll probably want to use an ASK field instead of a FILLIN field to prompt for information. The basic form of the ASK field is:

The ASK field

{ASK *bookmarkName prompt*}

As with a FILLIN field, when Word updates an ASK field, it will present a dialog box containing the text you specified in the *prompt* argument. Instead of storing your response directly in the document, however, Word will store it in the bookmark specified in the *bookmarkName* argument. That way, you can enter a REF field into the form wherever you want the typed response to appear.

For instance, instead of using a FILLIN field to collect the caller's name in the phone memo form, you could use the field

{ASK "recipient" "Who is the message for?"}

to present the dialog box shown in Figure 18-15. When you type a name and choose OK, Word will store your response in the bookmark *recipient.* You can then use the field

{REF "recipient"}

to insert the response anywhere in the form.

All the rules concerning updating FILLIN fields apply to ASK fields as well. In addition, the ASK field lets you use a \d switch to specify a default entry.

In this chapter

Macros **19**

As you use Word, you'll probably find yourself repeating certain tasks. For example, you'll frequently transpose letters, delete sentences, enter the current date, and so forth. Instead of performing these tasks manually, you can program them into macros. That way, you can accomplish these tasks simply by pressing a key or selecting a menu command.

Word's Macro menu contains all the commands you'll need for working with macros. In this chapter, we'll cover the commands you can use to record, run, edit, and debug macros. In Chapter 20, we'll cover the Assign to Key... and Assign to Menu... commands, which let you assign a key combination or menu command to the macros you create.

There are two ways to create a Word macro—by recording it or writing it. Of the two, recording is by far the easiest. When Word records a macro, it stores representations of the keys you press and the commands you issue in a portion of your computer's memory. While Word records these keystrokes and commands, it carries out whatever those actions normally tell it to do.

RECORDING A MACRO

To record a macro, select the Record... command from the Macro menu to bring up the Macro Record dialog box shown in Figure 19-1 on the following page. When this dialog box appears, you can type the name you want to assign to the macro in the Record Macro Name text box, or you can accept Word's default macro name—Macro1. (The next time you record a macro, Word will suggest the name Macro2, and so forth.) If you want, you can accept Word's default name for now, then rename the macro later with the Edit... command on the Macro menu. We'll show you how to do that in a moment.

The macro name you specify must begin with a letter of the alphabet. Additionally, the name may contain only letters and numbers; you cannot use spaces, the underline character, punctuation marks, or any other symbols as part of the macro name. If you enter an invalid macro name in the Record Macro Name text box, Word will dim the OK button in the dialog box to indicate that your macro name is invalid.

Figure 19-1

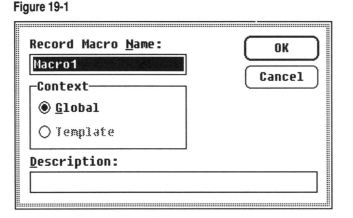

The Macro Record dialog box lets you specify a name and description of the macro you're about to record.

After you've specified a valid macro name, you can type a brief description of the macro in the Description text box. Although the macro description can be as long as you like, you should try to limit your description to 70 characters. You'll see why we've imposed this limitation later when we show you how to run a macro. If you don't want to provide a description of the macro, simply leave the Description text box blank.

Context options

The Context options in the Macro Record dialog box, Global and Template, determine where Word will save the macro. By default, Word will store the macro in the standard document template NORMAL.DOT, which allows you to run the macro while working in any Word document—not just documents based on the template NORMAL.DOT.

If you're working with a document that is based on a template other than NORMAL.DOT, however, you can use the Context Template option in the Macro Record dialog box to tell Word to save your macro in that document's template. (If the current document is based on the template NORMAL.DOT, the Template option will be dim and inactive.) When you save a macro in a template other than NORMAL.DOT, you will be able to access that macro only when you activate a document based on that template. For instance, if you use the Template option to save a macro in the template MEMO.DOT, then open a new document based on the template NORMAL.DOT, you will not be able to run or edit that macro.

Word won't actually save your macros as soon as you record them. Instead, it will keep the menu instructions in memory, then save them to disk in either of two ways, depending on which template you've chosen. If you save the macro in the template NORMAL.DOT, Word won't save the macro to disk until you exit from Word. When you issue the Exit command on the File menu, however, Word will display the message box shown in Figure 19-2. To save the macros you've recorded during the current Word session, choose the Yes button. If you don't want to save your macros, choose No. Choose Cancel if you don't want to exit from Word.

Saving macros

Figure 19-2

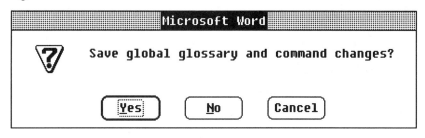

Word will save your global macros to NORMAL.DOT only when you exit from Word.

If you've used the Template option to save a macro in a template other than NORMAL.DOT, Word will perform the save when you use the Close command to close the document based on that template. When you close the document, Word will display a message box like the one shown in Figure 19-3 (in this case, we've made changes to the template EXAMPLES.DOT). To save the macro in that template, choose Yes. If you don't want to save the macro you've recorded, choose No. Choose Cancel if you want to cancel the Close command and return to the document.

Figure 19-3

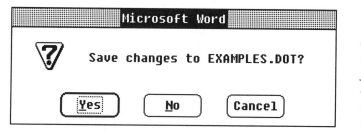

Word will update a template's macros when you close the document that is based on that template.

The recording process

Once you've specified a name, description, and context for the macro you want to record, choose OK. Word will then remove the Macro Record dialog box from the screen and begin recording your keystrokes and commands.

While you are recording a macro, you can do most things in Word as you normally would. However, Word will not let you use the mouse to move the cursor or to select text in the document. Instead, you'll need to use the keyboard techniques we discussed in Chapter 4 for moving the cursor and selecting text. Fortunately, you can use the mouse for everything else, such as issuing commands, selecting dialog box options, selecting ruler and ribbon options, and scrolling through the document.

Whenever you move the cursor or highlight within a document, Word will record the relative movement of the cursor. For example, suppose you're recording a macro, and the first thing you do is press the ➡ key three times to move the cursor three characters to the right. When you run the macro later, Word will initially move the cursor three characters to the right of its current position. Similarly, if you're recording a macro and you press the [Extend selection] key ([F8]) twice to highlight the current word, running that macro later will tell Word to highlight whatever word contains the cursor at the instant you invoke the macro.

Correcting mistakes

While you are recording a macro, you may make a mistake, such as typing a character you didn't intend to type, or issuing a command other than the one you wanted. If you type the wrong character, you can use the [Backspace] key to back up and correct the typing mistake. Instead of recording both the mistake and the correction, Word will record only the final group of characters you insert before issuing a command or moving the cursor.

If you accidentally use a command, the ruler, or the ribbon to make a change to your document, you have two choices: You can stop the recording and record your actions again, or you can correct the mistake by reissuing the command or reusing the ruler or ribbon. For example, if you use the ribbon to change the size of some 12-point text to 18 points, then realize that you wanted to change it to 14 points instead, you could use the ribbon again to change it to 14 points. When you do this, of course, Word will record the correction. If you want, you can edit the macro to correct the mistake after you've finished the recording. We'll show you how to do that later in this chapter.

Ending the recording of a macro

When you have completed the tasks you want to record, you should stop the recording. To do this, first pull down the Macro menu. At this point, you'll notice that the command *Stop Recorder* has replaced the Record... command. When you choose the Stop Recorder command, Word will close the Macro menu and stop recording your actions.

To demonstrate the process of recording a macro, let's record one that transposes two characters. This macro will simply swap the positions of the characters on either side of the cursor.

To begin recording this macro, position the cursor between any two characters you want to transpose. Next, choose the Record... command from the Macro menu to bring up the Macro Record dialog box shown in Figure 19-1. Now, enter *Transpose* into the Record Macro Name text box, and enter *Transposes two characters* into the Description text box. Finally, choose OK to begin recording.

To transpose the characters that are situated to the left and right of the cursor, begin by pressing the ➡ key while holding down the [Shift] key. This highlights the character to the right of the cursor—the one you want to move. Then, pull down the Edit menu and select the Cut command. When you do this, Word will cut the misplaced character and place it on the Clipboard. Next, press ⬅ to move the cursor one character to the left. Finally, pull down the Edit menu and select the Paste command. Word will then paste the misplaced character into its proper place—immediately to the left of the other character.

Once you have performed these actions, end the recording of the macro by choosing Stop Recorder from the Macro menu. Word will then stop recording your actions and return you to the document. At that point, you can transpose any two letters simply by moving the cursor between them and running the Transpose macro. We'll discuss running macros in a moment.

When you type text and issue commands during the recording of a macro, Word will record your actions as a series of WordBASIC instructions. WordBASIC, an implementation of the programming language BASIC, was designed specifically for use with Microsoft Word for Windows. Later in this chapter, we'll show you how to view and edit the WordBASIC instructions that comprise the macros you record.

Once you've recorded a macro, you can run it by using one of three methods. First, you can use the Run... command on the Macro menu. Alternatively, you can link a macro to a key combination, then press that key combination. Finally, you can add the macro name to one of Word's menus, then select the macro's name from the menu just as you select Word's built-in menu commands. In this section, we'll show you how to run a macro using the Run... command on the Macro menu. In Chapter 20, we'll show you how to use the Assign to Key... and Assign to Menu... commands to assign a macro to a key combination or menu.

To run a macro, choose the Run... command from the Macro menu. When you do this, Word will bring up a Macro Run dialog box like the one shown in Figure 19-4. The list box in this dialog box will contain all the macros you've created and saved in the current document's template. In the Run Macro Name text box, type the name of the macro you want to run, or select the appropriate macro name from the attached list box. If you entered a description for your macro when you first recorded it, Word will display that description in the Description box at the bottom of the dialog box. (This box can display only about 70 characters at a time.) Once you have selected the appropriate macro, choose the OK button to begin executing the macro's instructions.

Figure 19-4

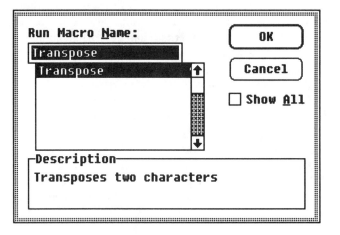

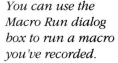

You can use the Macro Run dialog box to run a macro you've recorded.

By the way, selecting the Show All check box in the Macro Run dialog box tells Word to display in the list box the names of all of Word's built-in commands and macros along with the ones you've created. After you select the Show All check box, you can highlight the name of a built-in command or macro and see its description in the Description box at the bottom of the dialog box.

To demonstrate the process of running a macro, let's use the Transpose macro we recorded earlier to transpose the letters *d* and *n* in the word *Widnows,* which is shown in the document in Figure 19-5. First, place the cursor between the letters *d* and *n*. Next, select the Run... command from the Macro menu to bring up the Macro Run dialog box shown in Figure 19-4, and select Transpose from the list box. (Notice that Word displays the description we typed in the Description box at the bottom of the dialog box.) Finally, choose OK to begin running the macro. When you do this, Word will transpose the letters *d* and *n* to create the word *Windows,* as shown in Figure 19-6.

By using the techniques we'll demonstrate in Chapter 20, you can assign the Transpose macro to a key combination such as [Ctrl][Shift]T. That way, you can transpose two characters simply by positioning the cursor between them and pressing [Ctrl][Shift]T.

Figure 19-5

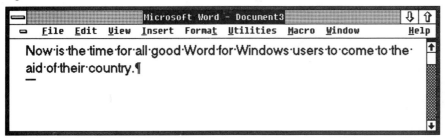

We'll use the Transpose macro we recorded earlier to transpose the letters d *and* n *in the word* Widnows.

Figure 19-6

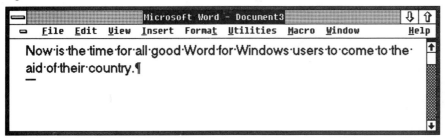

This is the document that results from running the Transpose macro in the document in Figure 19-5.

When Word runs a macro, it will repeat the actions you performed when you recorded that macro. Although Word won't actually pull down menus when it issues commands, it will carry out the effects of those commands in the active document. Of course, Word will speedily execute the recorded actions in the sequence you recorded them.

What happens when Word runs a macro

If a macro instructs Word to run another macro (which is called a submacro), Word will stop running the main macro and begin playing the submacro. As soon as Word reaches the end of the submacro, it will resume playing the main macro, starting with the instruction that immediately follows the command that invoked the submacro.

A macro that doesn't do what you intended can have disastrous effects. For example, it can erase a portion of a document you didn't intend to erase. For this reason, we strongly recommend that you save your active document before you run any macro that has the potential to do harm—especially macros you're testing for the first time.

A word of caution

**MODIFYING
A MACRO**

Once you've recorded a macro, you can modify it in several ways. For instance, you can rename it, delete it, and edit its instructions. To modify a macro, you'll need to select the Edit... command from the Macro menu to bring up a Macro Edit dialog box like the one shown in Figure 19-7. Let's learn how to use this dialog box to modify an existing macro.

Figure 19-7

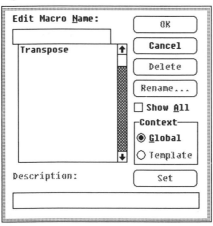

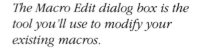

The Macro Edit dialog box is the tool you'll use to modify your existing macros.

Renaming a macro

To change the name of a macro after you've recorded it, first select its name in the Edit Macro Name list box. When you do this, the Rename... button, which formerly was dimmed and inactive, will become available for selection. If you choose the Rename... button, Word will display the Rename dialog box shown in Figure 19-8. At this point, you should replace the macro's existing name in the New Macro Name text box with the new name you want to assign. When you choose OK, Word will close the Rename dialog box and display the macro's new name in the Macro Edit dialog box.

Figure 19-8

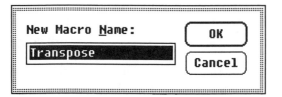

The Rename dialog box lets you change the name of an existing macro.

**Changing a
macro's description**

To change the description of an existing macro, first highlight its name in the Edit Macro Name list box. Next, type the new description for that macro in the Description text box at the bottom of the dialog box. (As we mentioned, you should limit this description to 70 characters.) Finally, choose the Set button, which tells Word to lock in the new macro description and keep the Macro Edit dialog box open.

To delete an existing macro, simply highlight its name in the Edit Macro Name list box, then choose the Delete button. Immediately, Word will delete the selected macro and remove its name from the list box. Unfortunately, you cannot use the Undo command to recover a macro you've deleted by accident. For this reason, make sure you want to delete the selected macro before you choose Delete.

Deleting a macro

As we mentioned, when you record a macro, Word will record your actions as a series of WordBASIC instructions. If you want, you can use Word's macro editing window to view and edit the instructions in any macro you've created.

To edit the instructions in a macro, simply select the name of the appropriate macro in the Macro Edit dialog box, and choose OK. Word will then open a macro editing window like the one shown in Figure 19-9.

Editing a macro

Figure 19-9

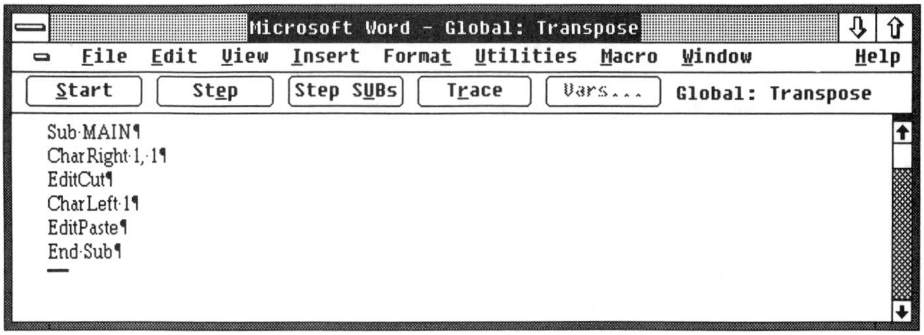

Word's macro editing window lets you review and edit the instructions that make up a macro.

As you can see, the macro editing window is similar to a standard document window. The name of this window is Global: Transpose because the macro we selected is named Transpose and is stored in the standard document template NORMAL.DOT. Notice that the Macro Edit icon bar, which contains five buttons, appears immediately below the menu bar. We will discuss each of these buttons in a moment.

Word will dim most of the commands on the menus while a macro editing window is open. You can access only those commands that are essential for editing the macro, such as Search..., Replace..., Glossary..., Preferences..., and so forth.

The text that appears in the window below the Macro Edit icon bar in Figure 19-9 are the WordBASIC instructions that Word will execute when running the Transpose macro recorded earlier. If you want to modify a macro's instructions, you can do so by using standard editing techniques. In fact, you can use the Cut, Copy, and Paste commands to move and copy text within the current macro or between two macros.

Before you attempt to modify a macro, you'll need to be familiar with the syntax of WordBASIC's various instructions. Unfortunately, a thorough explanation of WordBASIC and its program syntax is well beyond the scope of this book. For information on WordBASIC, refer to your *Word for Windows Technical Reference Manual.*

Every macro editing window functions much like a standard document window. For instance, after you open a macro editing window, you can activate another window on the desktop by choosing its name from the Window menu. In addition, you'll use the Close command on the File menu to close a macro editing window once you've opened it. As long as a macro editing window is open on the desktop, Word will continue to display the Macro Edit icon bar on the screen. You'll see why Word continues to display this icon bar in a moment, when we discuss debugging macros.

WRITING MACROS FROM SCRATCH

You can use a macro editing window to write a macro from scratch. Simply begin by choosing the Edit... command from the Macro menu. Next, type the name you want to assign to the new macro in the Edit Macro Name text box, then choose OK. At this point, Word will open a macro editing window like the one shown in Figure 19-10. As you can see, this macro editing window is empty except for the statements *Sub MAIN* and *End Sub*, which Word provides for you. You can begin writing your macro by inserting WordBASIC instructions between the two existing statements.

Figure 19-10

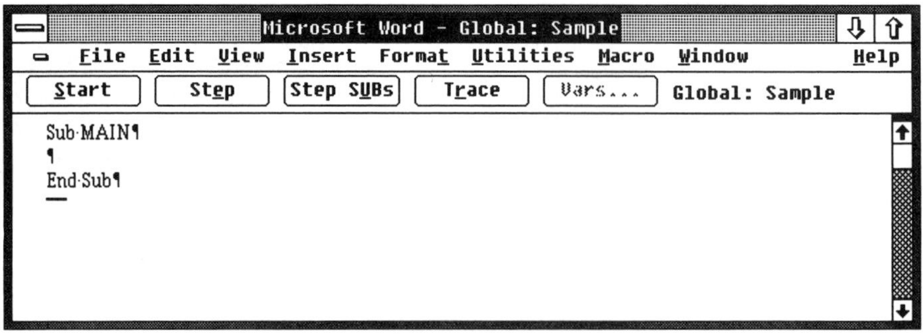

If you've learned WordBASIC, you can write macros from scratch.

When you are finished writing your macro, choose the Close command from the File menu. When Word asks if you want to save your changes to the macro, choose Yes. Word will then save your new macro and close the macro editing window. Word will not check for syntax errors in your macro until you run it.

DEBUGGING MACROS

If you get into the habit of using the macro editing window to modify a macro's instructions, or if you begin writing macros from scratch, you'll occasionally run a macro that doesn't perform as you expected. Fortunately, Word provides five buttons in the Macro Edit icon bar that help you debug the errors in a macro: Start, Step, Step SUBs, Trace, and Vars....

To take advantage of the five buttons in the Macro Edit icon bar, first adjust the size of your macro editing window and document window so you can see both on the screen simultaneously. Figure 19-11 shows a screen we've set up in this fashion. You'll notice that Word continues to display the Macro Edit icon bar at the top of the screen regardless of whether you activate the macro editing window or the document window.

Figure 19-11

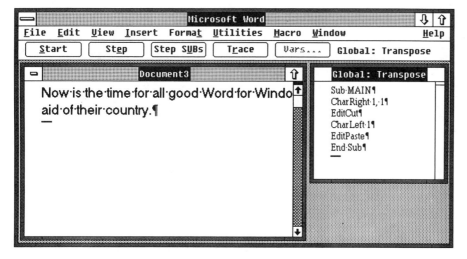

To take advantage of the buttons in the Macro Edit icon bar, you'll need to adjust the size of your macro editing and document windows so you can see both on the screen simultaneously.

You need to perform two additional tasks before you can begin the debugging process. First, you must make sure that the name of the macro you're debugging appears on the right side of the Macro Edit icon bar. If you've opened only one macro editing window on the desktop, the name of that macro will appear in the icon bar automatically. If you opened more than one macro editing window on the desktop, however, Word will display the name of the active macro in this icon bar. To activate a different macro, simply activate that macro's window.

Once you've done these things, you can activate the document window and move the cursor to the desired location. If you attempt to debug a macro without first activating the document window, the macro will attempt to act upon the text in its own window instead of acting upon the text in the document window.

The Start button

The Start button in the Macro Edit icon bar tells Word to run the active macro. Essentially, choosing this button is no different from selecting the active macro's name in the Macro Run dialog box and choosing OK. When you choose the Start button, the mouse pointer will take on the shape of the hourglass, and you will be able to see the macro's effect on the document as the macro runs. As you'll see in a moment, the Start button changes into a Continue button when you use the Step or Step SUBs button to debug a macro.

The Step button

The Step button tells Word to execute a single instruction in the active macro, and then stop. The first time you choose the Step button, Word will simply highlight, but not execute, the first instruction in the active macro. If you've set up your screen so you can view both the macro editing and document windows simultaneously, you can repeatedly choose the Step button to execute macro instructions one at a time, then view the effect of each in the document window.

After you've selected the Step button, you'll notice that the Start button in the icon bar will change to read *Continue*. When you choose the Continue button, Word will continue to execute the rest of the instructions in the macro without pausing. When Word reaches the end of the macro, the Continue button will change to read *Start* again.

The Step SUBs button

Like the Step button, the Step SUBs button tells Word to execute the instructions in the active macro one at a time. The difference between the Step button and the Step SUBs button comes into play only when the active macro contains an instruction that tells Word to run a submacro. If you're using the Step button to step through such a macro, Word will branch to the submacro and run through its instructions one at a time as you choose the Step button. After Word has executed all of the submacro's instructions, choosing Step again will cause Word to return to the main macro and continue executing instructions where it left off. However, if you're using the Step SUBs button to step through a macro, Word will not pause after each instruction in the submacro, but will execute all of the submacro's instructions in a single step.

The Trace button

The Trace button is similar to the Start button—it tells Word to execute all the instructions in the active macro until it reaches the end of the macro. However, unlike the Start button, the Trace button tells Word to highlight each instruction in the macro before executing it. This allows you to monitor the instruction that

Word is executing. Although Word will execute the macro's instructions in rapid succession, you will be able to follow the movement of the highlight.

The Vars… button in the icon bar is usually inactive. You can choose this button only when the active macro contains one or more variables in its instructions. If you've created a macro that uses one or more variables, choosing the Vars… button will tell Word to display the variables that the macro employs.

The Vars... button

To print the instructions in a macro, first use the Edit… command on the Macro menu to open the appropriate macro editing window. Then, simply use the File menu's Print… command in the usual fashion to send the macro to the printer.

PRINTING A MACRO

You can assign one of three special names to a macro—AutoNew, AutoOpen, or AutoExec—that will cause it to run automatically when a particular event occurs. Let's briefly discuss how Word will handle a macro that is assigned one of these names.

AUTO MACROS

If you assign the name AutoNew to a macro, Word will run that macro automatically each time you create a new document based on the template in which the macro is saved. For example, suppose you record a global macro named AutoNew that turns on the display of the ruler and ribbon. Each time you use the New… command to create a document based on the template NORMAL.DOT, Word will turn on the display of the ruler and ribbon (if they are not already turned on).

AutoNew

One way to take advantage of an AutoNew macro is to use it to update all of the ASK and FILLIN fields you've entered in a document template. For instance, if you create a memo template that uses FILLIN fields to prompt you for the recipient and subject of the memo, you'll want Word to update these fields as soon as you use the New… command to create a new document based on that template. To do this, simply enter the instructions

```
EditSelectAll
UpdateFields
```

between the statements *Sub MAIN* and *End Sub* in your AutoNew macro. The instruction *EditSelectAll* tells Word to select the entire document, while the instruction *UpdateFields* tells Word to update all the fields in the selection. Now, each time you use the New… command to create a new document based on your memo template, Word will automatically prompt you for the memo's recipient and subject.

When you assign the name AutoOpen to a macro, Word will run that macro whenever you open a document that is based on the template in which the macro

AutoOpen

is saved. For example, let's suppose you've created a global macro named AutoOpen that turns on the display of the ruler and ribbon. Each time you open a document based on the template NORMAL.DOT (using either the Open... or Find... commands on the File menu, or the file names at the bottom of the File menu), Word will turn on the display of the ruler and ribbon (if they're not already turned on).

AutoExec

The last of Word's three special names is AutoExec. If you save a macro named AutoExec in the template NORMAL.DOT, Word will run that macro automatically each time you start a new Word session. For example, you might want to record a global macro named AutoExec that opens the Preferences dialog box and turns on only the options you typically want to display on the screen.

If you want, you can start Word from the DOS prompt without running the AutoExec macro you've saved in NORMAL.DOT. Simply enter the command

WINWORD/M

at the DOS prompt.

One task you might want to perform in an AutoExec macro is to reopen the document that was open just before you ended your last Word session. To do this, simply enter the instruction

file1

in your AutoExec macro. The next time you start Word by typing *WINWORD* at the DOS prompt, you will not see an empty document named Document1, but instead will see the document you last opened during your previous Word session.

If you include the instruction *file1* in your AutoExec macro, and you use the technique we explained in Chapter 1 to start Word *and* open a specified document, Word will automatically open both the document you specify and your most recently opened document. For example, if you start Word by entering the command *WINWORD C:\LETTER.DOC* at the DOS prompt, Word will automatically open both the document C:\LETTER.DOC and the document you last opened during your previous Word session.

THE MACROBUTTON FIELD

The MACROBUTTON field lets you set up a "button" in your document that you can double-click to invoke a macro. This field takes the form

{MACROBUTTON *macroName buttonText*}

where *macroName* is the name of the macro you want the button to invoke, and *buttonText* is the text or graphic you want to serve as the button in the document. If you use text, don't enclose it within quotation marks in the field code.

When you display the result of the MACROBUTTON field, you'll see either the text or graphic you've specified as the *buttonText* argument. Word will update the field's result whenever you edit the *buttonText* argument.

If you have a mouse, you can double-click on the text or graphic returned by the MACROBUTTON field to run the macro specified in the field's *macroName* argument. If you don't have a mouse, you will need to use the keyboard to highlight the text or graphic returned by the MACROBUTTON field, and then press the [Do field click] key ([Alt][Shift][F9]) to run the specified macro. Alternatively, you can highlight the text or graphic returned by the field and run Word's built-in DoFieldClick macro.

As an example, suppose you've recorded a macro named PrintDocument that prints every page in the active document. Now, suppose you enter the field

{MACROBUTTON PrintDocument *PRINT*}

at the top of a document, as we've done in Figure 19-12. When you view the result of this field, you'll see the text *PRINT*, as shown in Figure 19-13. Now, to send the document to the printer, simply double-click anywhere on this text. Word will then send every page of the active document to the printer.

Figure 19-12

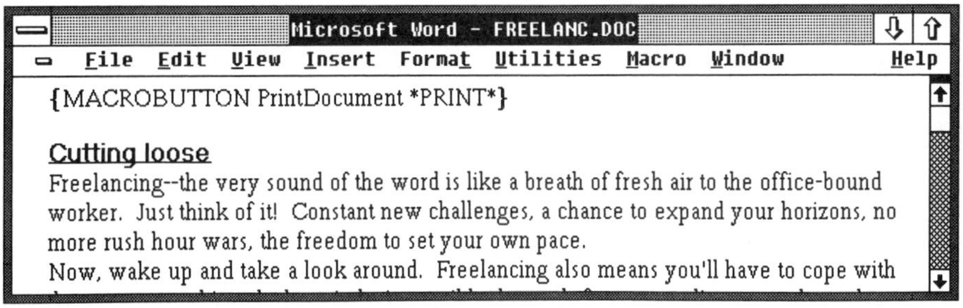

We've entered a MACROBUTTON field at the top of this document.

Figure 19-13

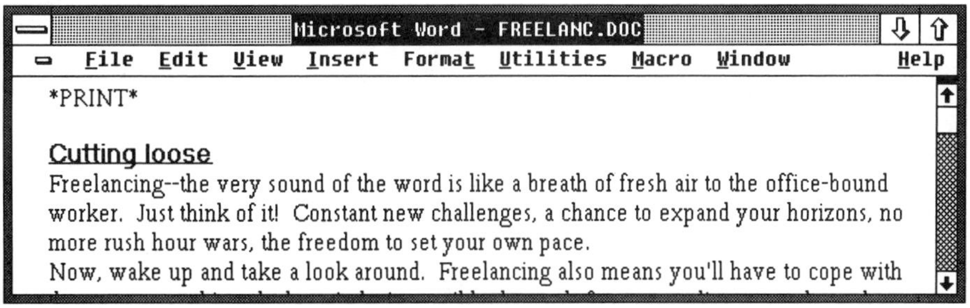

To print this document, you can simply double-click on the word *PRINT*.

In this chapter

Customizing Word **20**

*T*hroughout this book, we've shown you how to utilize many of Word's customizing features, including how to edit templates, design style sheets, create macros, and add dictionary and glossary terms. In this chapter, we'll explain how to further customize your copy of Word for Windows to match your personal tastes and needs. First, we'll show you how to use the Assign to Menu… command to change the commands that appear on Word's menus. Next, we'll show you how to use the Assign to Key… command to assign a specified key combination to a Word command or macro. Finally, we'll discuss Word's original default settings and explain how to change and restore those settings.

As you probably know by now, the Short Menus and Full Menus commands on the View menu let you run Word under two menu structures. If you're just getting started with Word, you'll probably want to use Short Menus, which contain only the commands necessary for creating simple documents, such as letters and memos. Once you've become familiar with Word, however, you'll want to use Full Menus, which contain all of Word's available commands.

CUSTOMIZING THE MENUS

Although Word's menu structures are intuitive and well-organized, you can modify the menus to accommodate your needs. For instance, if you prefer not to display the ruler, but frequently need to adjust your document's paragraph alignment, you can add four commands entitled *Left Para*, *Center Para*, *Right Para*, and *Justify Para* to the Format menu, then use those commands to control your document's paragraph alignment.

In addition to adding Word's built-in commands to its menus, you can add to a menu the name of a macro you've created, then invoke that macro simply by selecting its name from the menu. For instance, if you usually add a standard header to every document you create, you can use the techniques discussed in

Chapter 19 to create a macro named CreateHeader that builds your custom header automatically, then add the macro's name to Word's Edit menu. Once you've done this, you can create your custom header for all new documents in a single step by choosing CreateHeader from the Edit menu.

The command you'll use to customize your Word menus is the Assign to Menu... command on the Macro menu. When you issue this command, Word will present the dialog box shown in Figure 20-1. In this section, we'll show you how to use this dialog box to add and delete menu commands. After you customize your menus, they will not look like the menus shown in other chapters of this book. As you'll see in a moment, though, you can later restore Word's default menus after you've customized them.

Figure 20-1

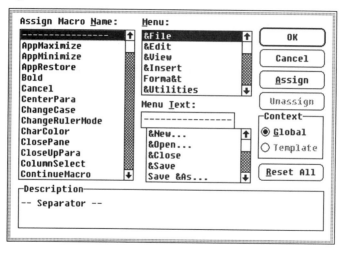

You'll use the Assign to Menu dialog box to customize Word's menus.

Adding menu commands

All the commands and macros you can place on Word's menus appear in the Assign Macro Name list box in the Assign to Menu dialog box. To add one of these commands or macros to a menu, first highlight the appropriate option in the Assign Macro Name list box. Word will describe the function of the highlighted option in the Description box at the bottom of the dialog box. For example, when you highlight the CenterPara command, Word will display the message *Centers paragraph between indents* in the Description box.

Notice that the first option in the Assign Macro Name list box is a broken horizontal line. You should select this option when you want to add a line across the bottom of a menu to separate groups of commands.

After you've highlighted the appropriate option in the Assign Macro Name list box, use the Menu list box to select the menu to which you want to add the new command. (As you might expect, you cannot add commands to a document's Control menu.)

Next, check the Menu Text text box to see if you are satisfied with the text Word will use to represent the command on the menu. You'll notice that Word will include an ampersand (&) to the left of the underlined character in the command name. As you probably know by now, the underlined character is the one you can press to select that command. If you want to change Word's default text, just edit the entry in the Menu Text text box. (Remember to include an ampersand to the left of the character you want underlined, and be sure to choose a character that is unique among the other command names on the same menu.

At this point, you should check the information you've specified in the dialog box to see if everything looks correct. When all is in order, choose the Assign button. Word will then add the new command to the specified menu, but will leave the dialog box open in case you want to add more commands. You'll also notice that choosing the Assign button causes the Cancel button to change to a Close button. To close the dialog box after you've chosen the Assign button, just choose Close.

If, after you've made your selections in the Assign to Menu dialog box, you choose the OK button instead of the Assign button, Word will both add the command you've specified and close the dialog box. Of course, choosing the Cancel button tells Word to cancel the Assign to Menu... command without taking any action.

An example

Let's suppose you want to add the Grow Font command to the bottom of Word's Format menu. To do this, first select the Assign to Menu... command from the Macro menu. When the Assign to Menu dialog box appears, leave the horizontal separator (----) selected in the Assign Macro Name list box, choose the Forma&t option from the Menu list box, and choose Assign to add the separator to the Format menu.

Next, highlight the GrowFont option in the Assign Macro Name list box. When you do this, Word will place the text *&Grow Font* in the Menu Text text box, and will display the text *Increases the point size of the selection* in the Description box in the dialog box. Now, leave the Forma&t option selected in the Menu list box, and choose Assign to add the Grow Font command to the Format menu. If you now choose the Close button to close the dialog box, then pull down the Format menu as we've done in Figure 20-2 on the next page, you'll see that Word has added a separator line and the Grow Font command to the bottom of the menu. Notice that Word automatically displays the keyboard shortcut for the Grow Font command (Ctrl+F2) at the right of the command.

Context options

The Context options in the Assign to Menu dialog box, Global and Template, determine where Word will save the changes you make to the menu structure. By default, your changes are stored in the standard document template NORMAL.DOT, which allows you to use your custom menus while working in any Word document—not just documents based on the template NORMAL.DOT.

Figure 20-2

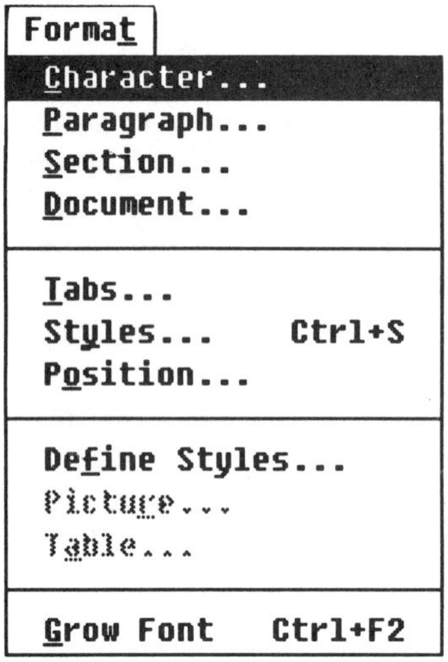

```
┌─────────────────────┐
│ Format │            │
├─────────────────────┤
│ Character...        │
│ Paragraph...        │
│ Section...          │
│ Document...         │
├─────────────────────┤
│ Tabs...             │
│ Styles...    Ctrl+S │
│ Position...         │
├─────────────────────┤
│ Define Styles...    │
│ Picture...          │
│ Table...            │
├─────────────────────┤
│ Grow Font    Ctrl+F2│
└─────────────────────┘
```

We've used the Assign to Menu... command to add the Grow Font command to Word's Format menu.

If you're working with a document that is based on a template other than NORMAL.DOT, you can use the Context Template option to tell Word to save your menu changes in that document's template. (If the current document is based on the template NORMAL.DOT, the Template option will be dimmed and inactive.)

When you save your changes in a template other than NORMAL.DOT, you will see your menu changes only when you activate a document that is based on that template. For instance, suppose you are working with a document based on the template MEMO.DOT. You open the Assign to Menu dialog box, choose the Context Template option, then use the Assign button to add a command to a menu. Now, if you open a new document based on the template NORMAL.DOT, you will not see the new command you added.

Word won't actually save your menu changes as soon as you make them. Instead, it will keep the menu changes in memory and save them to disk in either of two ways, depending on which template you've chosen. If you make any changes to the standard document template NORMAL.DOT, Word won't save the changes to disk until you exit from Word. When you issue the Exit command on the File menu, Word will display the message box shown in Figure 20-3. To save the menu changes you've made, choose Yes. If you don't want to save your menu changes, choose No. Choose Cancel if you don't want to exit from Word.

If you've modified the menus for a template other than NORMAL.DOT, Word will save those changes when you close the document based on that template. When you issue the Close command on the File menu, Word will bring up a message box like the one shown in Figure 20-4 (in this case, we've made changes to the template EXAMPLES.DOT). To update the changes you've made to the template's menus, choose Yes. If you don't want to save the menu changes you've made, choose No. Choose Cancel if you want to cancel the Close command and return to the document.

Figure 20-3

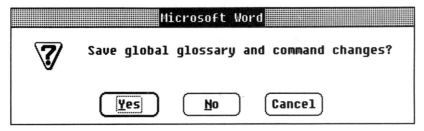

Word will save your global menu changes to NORMAL.DOT when you exit from the program.

Figure 20-4

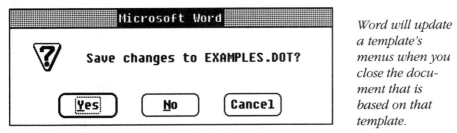

Word will update a template's menus when you close the document that is based on that template.

You can tell Word to revert to its default menus anytime you want. We'll show you how to do that later in this chapter.

Removing a command

The process you use to remove commands from Word's menus is similar to the one you use to add commands. To begin, open the Assign to Menu dialog box, then use the Menu list box to select the menu containing the command you want to remove. Word will then display the menu's commands in the Menu Text list box. At this point, you should select from the Menu Text list box the command you want to remove, then choose the Unassign button to remove the command from the menu. Word will then remove the command, but will not close the dialog box in case you want to modify other menus. You'll also notice that choosing the Unassign button causes the Cancel button to change to a Close button. To close the dialog box after you've used the Unassign button, just choose Close.

An example

Let's suppose you want to remove from the Format menu the Grow Font command we added in the previous example. (Of course, you can remove any menu command you want—not just the custom commands you've already added.) To do this, open the Assign to Menu dialog box and highlight the Forma&t option in the Menu list box. When you do this, Word will present all the commands on the Format menu in the Menu Text list box. At this point, highlight the &Grow Font option in the Menu Text list box, and choose the Unassign button to remove the Grow Font command from the menu. If you now choose the Close button to close the dialog box, then pull down the Format menu, you'll see that Word has removed the Grow Font command.

Resetting the menus

The Reset All button in the Assign to Menu dialog box lets you return all of Word's menus to their original forms. If you ever accidentally remove a command from a menu, or if you want to completely remove all the custom commands you've added, just choose the Reset All button to quickly reset the Word menus to their original defaults.

CUSTOMIZING THE KEYBOARD

If you're like most people, you'll use the mouse to highlight text, select commands, and choose options in dialog boxes. However, if you're strictly a keyboard user, or if you don't own a mouse, you'll want to memorize many of the keyboard shortcuts Word provides. To see a complete listing of Word's default key assignments, refer to Appendix 3.

Although you'll find that Word's default keyboard shortcuts are sufficient for most of your work, you may need to modify some shortcuts to suit your needs. You can assign a key combination to any Word command, then press that key combination instead of using the menu bar to issue that command. Similarly, if you've used the techniques discussed in Chapter 19 to create a macro, you can assign the macro to a key combination, then press that key combination whenever you want to invoke the macro.

The command you'll use to make custom key assignments is the Assign to Key... command on the Macro menu. When you issue this command, Word will present the dialog box shown in Figure 20-5. In this section, we'll show you how to use this dialog box to assign a particular key combination to a command or a macro, and to remove a key assignment. After you customize your key assignments, they will not match the ones listed in our book or in your Word documentation. As you'll see in a moment, however, you can easily return Word's key assignments to their defaults after you've customized them.

Making key assignments

All the commands and macros you can link to a key combination appear in the Assign Macro Name list box. To link one of these commands or macros to a key combination, first highlight the appropriate option in the list box. Word will describe the function of the highlighted option in the Description box at the bottom of the dialog box, and will display the key combination(s) currently assigned to that option in the Current Keys list box. For example, when you highlight the ChangeCase command, Word will display the message *Changes the case of letters in the selection* in the Description box, and will display *Shift+F3* in the Current Keys list box.

Figure 20-5

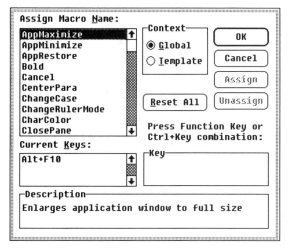

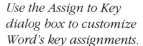

Use the Assign to Key dialog box to customize Word's key assignments.

If the option you've highlighted in the Assign Macro Name list box is already assigned to a key combination, Word will display that key combination in the Current Keys list box.

After you've highlighted the appropriate command in the Assign Macro Name list box, press the key combination to which you'd like to assign the new command. Available key combinations include a function key, a [Shift]-function key combination, a [Ctrl]-[Shift]-function key combination, a [Ctrl]-[Shift]-letter combination, or a [Ctrl]-letter combination.

When you press a valid key combination, Word will display the combination you've typed in the Key box of the dialog box. In addition, Word will show the command or macro that is currently assigned to the key combination you've typed. If no command or macro is currently assigned to that key combination, Word will display the message *[currently unassigned]* along with the key combination.

Once you've selected the appropriate option from the Assign Macro Name list box and entered a key combination in the Key box, choose the Assign button. Word will then assign the keys in the Key box to the selected command or macro, but will not close the dialog box in case you want to make more key assignments. You'll also notice that choosing the Assign button changes the Cancel button to a Close button. To close the dialog box after you've chosen the Assign button, just choose Close.

If, after you've selected a command and a key combination, you choose the OK button instead of the Assign button, Word will assign the selected command to the key combination shown in the Key box and close the dialog box. Of course, choosing the Cancel button tells Word to cancel the Assign to Key... command without taking any action.

An example

Suppose you want to assign the [Ctrl][Shift]X key combination to the Exit command on the File menu. To do this, open the Assign to Key dialog box, select the FileExit command in the Assign Macro Name list box, and press [Ctrl][Shift]X. At this point, Word will highlight the FileExit command in the Assign Macro Name list box, and will display *Ctrl+Shift+X [currently unassigned]* in the Key box, as shown in Figure 20-6. Now, to make the assignment, choose the Assign button. Word will then display *Ctrl+Shift+X* in the Current Keys list box, along with Word's built-in key combination for the FileExit command (Alt+F4). Now that you've assigned the [Ctrl][Shift]X key combination to this command as well, use the Close button to close the dialog box. You can then use either the [Ctrl][Shift]X or [Alt][F4] key combination to issue the Exit command.

Figure 20-6

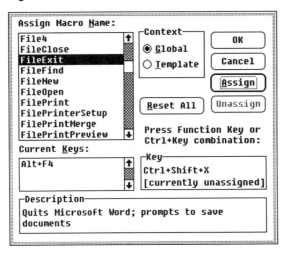

We'll use the Assign to Key dialog box to assign the key combination [Ctrl][Shift]X to the FileExit command.

Context options

The Context options in the Assign to Key dialog box, Global and Template, determine where Word will save your key assignments. By default, key assignments are stored in the standard document template NORMAL.DOT, which allows you to use a custom key combination while working in any Word document—not just documents based on the template NORMAL.DOT.

If you're working with a document that is based on a template other than NORMAL.DOT, however, you can use the Context Template option in the Assign to Key dialog box to tell Word to save your key assignments in that document's template. (If the current document is based on the template NORMAL.DOT, the Template option will be dimmed and inactive.)

When you save your key assignments in a template other than NORMAL.DOT, you can use your custom key combinations only when you activate a document that is based on that template. For instance, suppose you are working with a document based on the template MEMO.DOT. You open the Assign to Key dialog box, choose the Context Template option, then define a custom key combination. Now, if you open a new document based on the template NORMAL.DOT, you will not be able to use the key combination you defined.

Word won't actually save your key assignments as soon as you define them. Instead, it will keep the key assignments in memory and save them to disk in either of two ways, depending on which template you've chosen. If you make any changes to the template NORMAL.DOT, Word won't save the changes to disk until you exit from Word. When you issue the Exit command on the File menu, Word will display the message box shown in Figure 20-3. To save the key assignments you've made, choose the Yes button. If you don't want to save your key assignments, choose No. Choose Cancel if you don't want to exit from Word.

If you have made custom key assignments for a template other than NORMAL.DOT, Word will save your key assignments when you close the document based on that template. When you choose the Close command from the File menu, Word will present a message box like the one shown in Figure 20-4. To save the key assignments you defined, choose Yes. If you don't want to save your key assignments, choose No. Choose Cancel if you want to cancel the Close command and return to the document.

You can tell Word to revert to its default key assignments at any time. We'll show you how to do this in a moment.

Removing key assignments

Removing key assignments is similar to creating key assignments. First, issue the Assign to Key... command to bring up the dialog box shown in Figure 20-5. Then, press the key combination you want to remove. When you do this, Word will display that key combination in the Key box, along with the name of the command or macro currently assigned to that key combination. (If a command or macro is not assigned to that key combination, Word will display the message *[currently unassigned]*.) To remove the key combination from its command or macro, just choose the Unassign button. Word will then remove the key combination and erase the contents of the Key box.

When removing key assignments, you can choose the command or macro name in the Assign Macro Name list box rather than pressing the appropriate key combination. To use this technique, first select the appropriate command or macro name in the Assign Macro Name list box. At this point, Word will display the key combination(s) currently assigned to that command or macro in the

Current Keys list box. You should now select from this list box the key combination you want to remove. Word will then display that key combination in the Key box, along with the name of the selected command or macro. Finally, to remove the key combination from its command or macro, just choose the Unassign button. At this point, Word will remove the key combination and erase the contents of the Key box.

If you remove a key combination that originally had a built-in command assignment, Word will let you restore that key combination to its original command. To restore a built-in key assignment, press the key combination to place it in the Key box. At this point, the message *[currently unassigned]* will appear below the key combination in the Key box, and the Unassign button will change to a Reset button. Choosing the Reset button tells Word to restore the built-in command assignment that it had when you first installed Word.

After you're finished with the Assign to Key dialog box, just choose the Close button (which was formerly the Cancel button) to close the dialog box.

An example

To demonstrate the process of removing key assignments, let's suppose you want to remove the [Ctrl][Shift]X key combination from the Exit command, an assignment we made in the previous example. To do this, open the Assign to Key dialog box and press the [Ctrl][Shift]X key combination. When you do this, Word will display *Ctrl+Shift+X FileExit* in the Key box, as shown in Figure 20-7. At this point, choose the Unassign button. Word will then remove the [Ctrl][Shift]X key combination from the FileExit command and erase the contents of the Key box. If you press [Ctrl][Shift]X at this point, Word will display *Ctrl+Shift+X* in the Key box again, along with the message *[currently unassigned]*. Because Word does not assign the [Ctrl][Shift]X key combination to one of its built-in commands, the Unassign button will be dimmed at this point. However, if you had used the [Ctrl][Shift]X key combination for a command shortcut before you reassigned it, the Unassign button would have changed to a Reset button. Choosing Reset would have restored the built-in command assignment that the key combination had when you first installed Word.

Restoring all key assignments

The Reset All button in the Assign to Key dialog box lets you restore Word's command assignments to their original key combinations. If you accidentally reassign a built-in key combination, or if you want to completely remove all the custom assignments you've made, just choose the Reset All button to quickly restore all the key combinations to their original defaults.

Figure 20-7

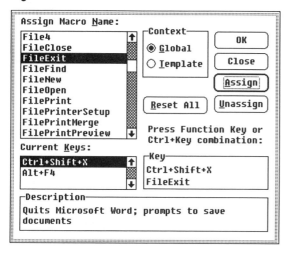

The Unassign button in the Assign to Key dialog box lets you remove key assignments.

Printing key assignments

After you've defined some custom key assignments, you'll probably want to keep a reference sheet handy that shows the key assignments you've established. To print a listing of your custom key assignments, select the Print... command from the File menu and choose the Key Assignments option from the Print pull-down list box, as we've done in Figure 20-8. When you choose OK to complete the Print... command, Word will print a key assignments listing like the one shown in Figure 20-9.

Figure 20-8

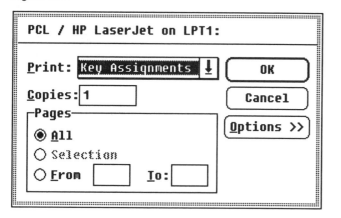

The Key Assignments option in the Print pull-down list box lets you print a listing of your custom key assignments.

Figure 20-9

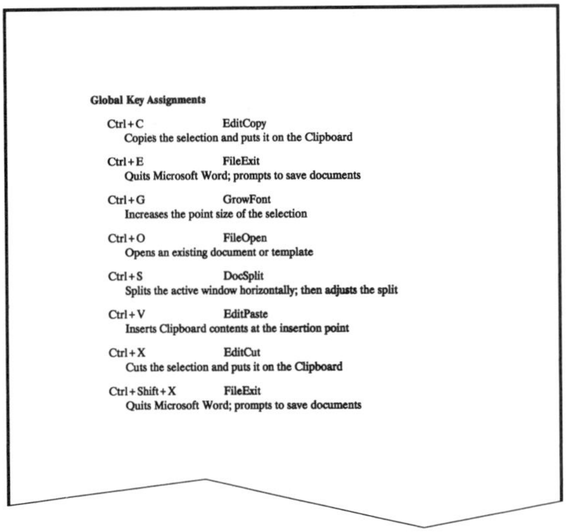

```
Global Key Assignments

Ctrl + C              EditCopy
        Copies the selection and puts it on the Clipboard

Ctrl + E              FileExit
        Quits Microsoft Word; prompts to save documents

Ctrl + G              GrowFont
        Increases the point size of the selection

Ctrl + O              FileOpen
        Opens an existing document or template

Ctrl + S              DocSplit
        Splits the active window horizontally; then adjusts the split

Ctrl + V              EditPaste
        Inserts Clipboard contents at the insertion point

Ctrl + X              EditCut
        Cuts the selection and puts it on the Clipboard

Ctrl + Shift + X      FileExit
        Quits Microsoft Word; prompts to save documents
```

You can print a sample key assignments listing.

WORD DEFAULTS

Like all software programs, Word comes with certain preset defaults. These default settings control such items as the appearance of the screen, character and paragraph formatting, page layout, and print settings. While working in a document, you are not restricted to using Word's default settings. If a particular setting is unsuitable for the document in which you're working, you can change it.

Word's default settings are stored in either the WINWORD.INI or the NORMAL.DOT file. Most of your general default settings, like those on the View menu and in the Preferences dialog box, are stored in the file WINWORD.INI. On the other hand, your document default settings, like Page Width and Height, Margins, and so forth, are stored in the file NORMAL.DOT. If you find that you're changing one or more default settings each time you start a new document, you should consider making a permanent change to that setting. For example, if you always change the Left and Right margin settings in the Document dialog box from 1.25" to 1", you probably should change Word's default settings for the left and right margins. Later in this chapter, we'll explain how to do this by using the Document dialog box's Set Default option.

To restore all of Word's original default settings, delete both the WINWORD.INI and the NORMAL.DOT files from your Word for Windows program directory. When you restart Word after deleting these files, Word will create new ones that contain the original default settings.

View menu defaults

Word has a number of default settings that affect various elements of your screen display. Nearly all of these settings are controlled by the View menu, including the display of the ruler, the ribbon, the status bar, and several special characters like tabs, spaces, and paragraph marks. Word stores all the settings controlled by the View menu in the file WINWORD.INI. If you delete this file, Word will automatically restore all of its original default settings the next time you start Word. Let's look at a few of these settings in detail.

As we explained in Chapter 2, Word's initial default menu configuration is Short Menus. You can change this by selecting Full Menus from the View menu. Once you change from Short Menus to Full Menus (or vice versa) and quit from Word, your change becomes the new default. Figure 2-2 on page 14 shows the different menu selections that are available in Short and Full Menus.

Using Short and Full menus

When you start Word for the first time, you won't see the ruler or ribbon at the top of the window. You must select the Ruler or Ribbon command from the View menu to bring these elements into view. Once you've activated the ruler or ribbon, it will remain on your screen until you reselect Ruler or Ribbon from the View menu to turn it off again.

Unlike the ruler and ribbon display, the display of the status bar is turned on by default. If you want to turn off the display of the status bar, select the Status Bar command from the View menu. Once you've turned off the display of the status bar, it will remain off until you reselect the Status Bar command.

Displaying the ruler, ribbon, and status bar

Throughout this book, we've referred to settings in the Preferences dialog box, which you can access by issuing the Preferences… command on the View menu. Figure 20-10 shows this dialog box with its default settings.

Displaying elements in the Preferences dialog box

Figure 20-10

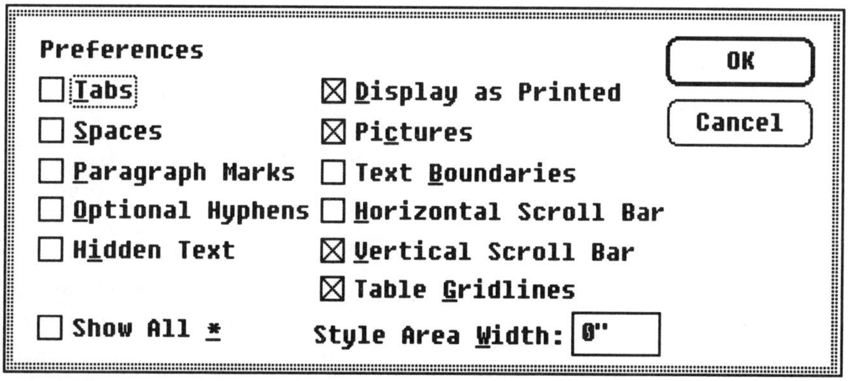

The Preferences dialog box lets you control the display of several screen elements.

The Show All check box overrides the settings in the other check boxes on the left side of the Preferences dialog box. In other words, selecting the Show All check box tells Word to display tabs, spaces, paragraph marks, optional hyphens, and hidden text—regardless of whether you've selected those options. As you probably know, Word allows you to toggle the Show All option by clicking on the Show-all icon (☒) on the ribbon.

Customize dialog box defaults

The Customize... command on the Utilities menu lets you modify some of Word's most important features. When you select the Customize... command, Word will present a dialog box like the one shown in Figure 20-11.

Figure 20-11

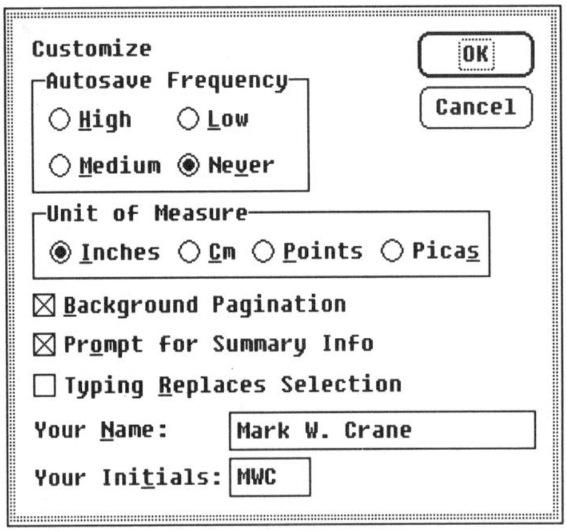

You'll use the Customize dialog box to specify several important features.

As you can see, the Customize dialog box lets you specify an autosave frequency, choose the default unit of measure, control background pagination, change the prompt for summary information, tell Word to use the characters you type to replace the document's selected characters, and specify your name and initials. Let's take a closer look at the default settings in the Customize dialog box and consider how you can use each setting to customize your Word program.

Autosave Frequency

As you may have learned the hard way, you should protect your work against tragedies like power outages or system crashes by issuing the Save command every few minutes. Unfortunately, you'll often get so involved in your work, you'll forget to issue the Save command at regular intervals.

As we explained in Chapter 3, Word's autosave feature can help remedy this problem. This feature works like an alarm clock—it automatically prompts you to save your document at the interval you specify. You can set up reminder intervals of High (every 10 to 30 minutes), Medium (every 20 to 45 minutes), Low (every 30 to 60 minutes), or Never (which turns off the autosave feature). Word sets the Autosave Frequency to Never by default. Refer to Chapter 3 for more information on this feature.

The default unit of measure on Word's ruler and in its dialog boxes is inches. If you want, however, you can change the unit to centimeters, points, or picas. To make the change, simply choose the Unit of Measure setting you want to use, then choose OK. (As you may know, 1 inch is the same as 2.54 centimeters, 72 points, or 6 picas.) Once you've selected a different unit of measure, Word will change the ruler's appearance to reflect the change. Figure 20-12 shows the same screen with the four types of rulers.

Unit of Measure

Figure 20-12

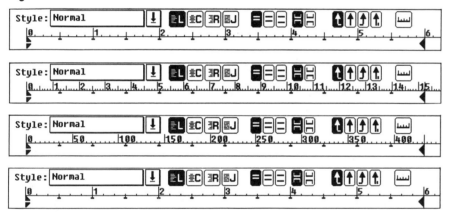

Word allows you to specify one of four units of measure on the ruler: inches, centimeters, points, or picas.

Word will not change the alignment of text on the screen when you change the unit of measure. All the indents and tabs will occur at the same positions. In other words, when you change the Unit of Measure setting in the Customize dialog box, Word will not only change the markings on the ruler; it also will convert the position of each indent and tab to the new unit of measure.

In addition to changing the appearance of the ruler, the Unit of Measure setting will determine the unit of measure in some of the text boxes in your dialog boxes. For example, if you change the Unit of Measure setting to centimeters, Word will display the margin settings in the Document dialog box in centimeters. Other dialog boxes that will be affected by a change in the unit of measure include the Paragraph, Section, Table, and Position dialog boxes.

Besides dialog boxes, the Unit of Measure option can affect your style definitions. Any named style that specifies one or more indents or tabs will use the new unit of measure in its style definition.

Finally, when you change the unit of measure, you'll notice a difference in the Print Preview window. If you select the Boundaries button at the top of the Print Preview window, then click on one of the margin "handles," Word will display the margin measurement in the upper-right corner of your window in the same units you've specified for the ruler. Word will also display the position of your page numbers, headers, footers, and page-break markers in these units.

Background Pagination

The Background Pagination option in the Customize dialog box lets you tell Word when to repaginate your document. Word activates this option by default. If you leave this option turned on, Word will automatically repaginate your document as you edit it in the page view. When you enter the page view while the Background Pagination option is selected, Word will repaginate your document from the first page through the page on which the cursor is located. If your document is quite long, you may have to wait several seconds or longer before Word redisplays the document in the page view. While you're in the page view, if you move forward to another page in the document, Word will repaginate through that point as well.

If you turn off the Background Pagination option, Word will repaginate your document only when you issue the Repaginate Now command on the Utilities menu, or when you use the Print Preview command to preview your document.

The only exception to the pagination rules we've stated is as follows: If you're working in page view and you've turned off the Background Pagination option, Word will repaginate your document when you make an editing or formatting change that causes text to flow from one page to the next. For example, if you insert a paragraph on a page, causing several lines to be pushed to the next page, Word will automatically repaginate in order to ensure that the page you're viewing reflects your current document layout. Similarly, changing your document margins will also tell Word to repaginate.

Prompt for Summary Info

Word keeps track of each document's title, subject, author, keywords, and comments in the Summary Info dialog box. By default, Word presets the Summary Info dialog box each time you save a new Word document. If you would rather not see the Summary Info dialog box each time you save a new document, however, just turn off the Prompt for Summary Info option in the Customize dialog box.

After you turn off this option, remember that you can still access the Summary Info dialog box by using two methods. First, you can bring up this dialog box before you open a new document by selecting the New... command from the File menu, choosing the Summary... button in the New dialog box, then choosing OK. In addition, you can bring up a document's Summary Info dialog box at any time by selecting the Summary Info... command from the Edit menu.

As we explained in Chapter 4, the Typing Replaces Selection option in the Customize dialog box controls the way Word responds when you highlight text and type a character. If you leave this option turned off, Word will insert new characters you type in the document, placing them to the left of the highlighted block of text. In other words, to change a block of text in a document, you must highlight the text you want to replace, press the [Delete] key to remove the text, then type the replacement text.

Typing Replaces Selection

If you select the Typing Replaces Selection check box, you can overwrite existing characters by selecting the characters you want to replace, then typing your new text. Word will automatically delete the existing characters and replace them with the new characters you type. You can think of this overwriting technique as a combination deletion/insertion process. Also, once you've selected the Typing Replaces Selection check box, you will be able to delete highlighted text with the [Backspace] key.

The text boxes at the bottom of the Customize dialog box let you specify your name and initials. If you are the only person using Word on your computer, then the Your Name and Your Initials text boxes will always contain the name and initials you specified the first time you started Word. You'll probably never need to change these entries. If others use Word on your computer, however, you'll want to update the Your Name and Your Initials text boxes as soon as you begin a new Word session.

Your Name and Your Initials

There are several reasons you'll want to keep these text box entries up to date while you're working in Word. First of all, when Word compiles summary information for a new document, it will insert into the Author text box of the Summary Info dialog box the name you've entered in the Your Name text box. By ensuring that the documents you create have *your* name in the Summary Info dialog boxes, you can easily use the search techniques we described in Chapter 6 to locate the appropriate documents.

Another reason you'll want to keep the Your Name entry up to date is for security purposes. As we explained in Chapter 13, you can prevent other people from modifying your document by locking it with the Lock for Annotations option in the expanded Save As dialog box. Once you've saved a document with the Lock for Annotations option selected, only you (the original author) can make changes to the document, and only you can turn off the Lock for Annotations option. Of course, if someone else's name appears in the Customize dialog box when you lock a document, you'll run into problems if you attempt to modify the document under your own name. For more information on the Lock for Annotations option, see Chapter 13.

In addition to the Your Name entry, you'll want to make sure your initials are entered correctly in the Customize dialog box. If you use the techniques described in Chapter 13 to make annotations to a document, Word will place the initials in the Customize dialog box next to the annotations you've made. Of course, if the initials in the Customize dialog box are not your own, and you annotate a document, the original author will think someone else made your annotations.

Page layout defaults   There are a number of settings that control the default layout of any document you create in Word. These settings appear in the Document and Section dialog boxes, which are shown in Figures 20-13 and 20-14.

Figure 20-13

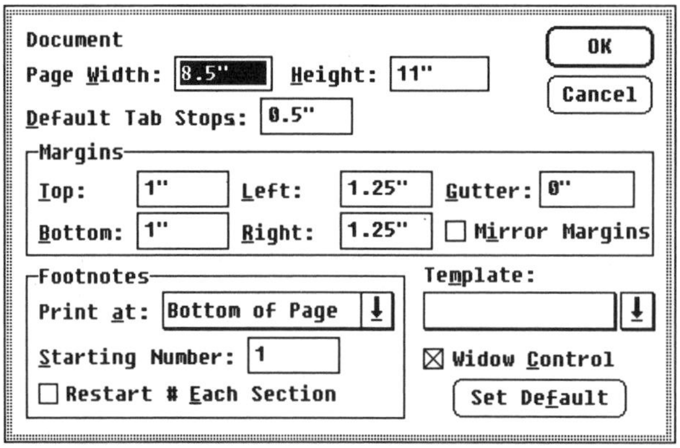

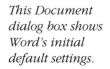

This Document dialog box shows Word's initial default settings.

Figure 20-14

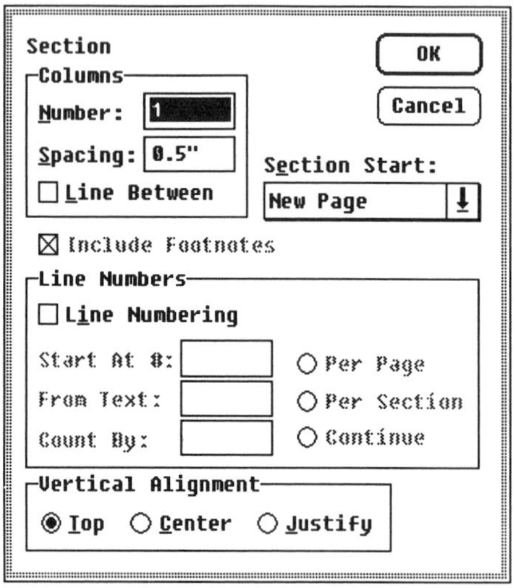

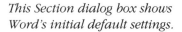

This Section dialog box shows Word's initial default settings.

You can change the default for any of the settings in the Document dialog box by entering a new value for that setting or selecting a new option, then choosing the Set Default button. When you choose this button, Word will save all the Document dialog box's current settings in the file NORMAL.DOT, which is the default template Word uses to create new documents.

If you change Word's default Document settings, those changes will not affect any documents previously saved to disk, and will not alter any open, unsaved documents. In this regard, the default Document settings are unlike the default screen display settings, which typically affect all documents, including those previously saved to disk.

You can change any of the Document settings for a particular document without affecting the default settings. Simply change the appropriate settings in the Document dialog box and choose OK. As long as you don't choose Set Default, the default values for those settings will not change.

As you can see in Figure 20-14, the Section dialog box doesn't offer a Set Default button. If you want to change any of the default settings in this dialog box, you'll need to modify the file NORMAL.DOT using the procedure we discussed in Chapter 18.

Margins

As we explained in Chapter 5, your document margins are controlled in the Document dialog box. Initially, Word's default margin settings are 1" for the top and bottom margins and 1.25" for the left and right margins. If you want to change Word's default margin settings, just enter new measurements in the Top, Bottom, Left, and/or Right text boxes of the Document dialog box, then choose the Set Default button.

Text area

While the margin settings determine the amount of space surrounding the text area on a page, the actual dimensions of the text area depend on your margin settings as well as on your Page Width and Height settings. Word's default Page Width and Height settings are 8.5" and 11", respectively. (For more on determining the size of the text area, see Chapter 5.)

If you want to change the default page size, just type the new setting in the Document dialog box, then choose Set Default. As we explained in Chapter 7, it's important that your Page Width and Height settings match the paper size you've specified in your printer settings box. Refer to Chapter 7 for more information on choosing paper size and print orientation.

Footnotes

Footnotes, like headers and footers, are controlled by settings in your Document and Section dialog boxes, as well as by style definitions. The Footnotes settings in the Document dialog box determine whether footnotes will appear at the bottom of each page, at the end of each section, beneath the last line of text on each page, or at the end of an entire document. These settings also determine whether your footnotes will be numbered separately on each new page, in each new section, or continuously throughout a document. (Chapter 14 explains footnotes in detail.)

The default Footnotes settings in the Document dialog box tell Word to place footnotes at the bottom of each page and to use a new set of footnote numbers on each page. Word's default starting number for the footnotes on each page is 1. If you want, you can change the default Footnotes settings, then choose the Set Default button. As usual, Word will record your new default settings in the file NORMAL.DOT.

There's only one footnote-related setting in the Section dialog box—Include Footnotes. Word initially dims this setting, making it inactive. Include Footnotes comes into play only when your document contains more than one section and you've selected the End of Section option in the Footnotes section of the Document dialog box. When this is the case, the Include Footnotes section in the Section dialog box instructs Word to print the footnotes for the current section at the end of that section, instead of printing them at the end of the entire document. If you want Word to print all of your footnotes at the end of the document, you should deactivate the Include Footnotes option. To make the deactivated Include Footnotes option Word's new default, you'll need to follow the procedures in Chapter 18 for modifying the file NORMAL.DOT.

Default Tab Stops

The Default Tab Stops setting in the Document dialog box controls the interval between Word's default tab stops. To change this setting, open the Document dialog box, enter a new measurement in the Default Tab Stops text box, and choose Set Default.

Widow Control

The Widow Control option in the Document dialog box prevents Word from placing one line of a paragraph on a page by itself. Normally, this check box is selected. If you want to change Word's default so that the Widow Control check box is deactivated, just open the Document dialog box, deselect this check box, then choose Set Default. Again, your changes to Word's default Document settings will be stored in the file NORMAL.DOT.

Formatting defaults

In Chapters 5 and 8, we described Word's default paragraph and character formats. You may recall that the default format for a paragraph specifies left-alignment, single spacing, no indents, no tabs other than the defaults, no before or after spacing (other than normal line spacing), no borders, and no special features (such as Keep Paragraph Together or Keep Paragraph With Next). Word's default character formatting calls for 10-point Tms Rmn type.

As we explained in Chapter 8, Word's default character and paragraph formats are controlled by the definition of the default *Normal* style. If you want to change Word's default character and/or paragraph formats, you can do so by first opening the file NORMAL.DOT, using the technique we explained in Chapter 18. Next, use the Define Styles… command on the Format menu to redefine the *Normal* style to your liking. Finally, close the file NORMAL.DOT and save your changes to disk.

For example, suppose you want to specify a default character format of 12-point Tms Rmn type instead of 10-point Tms Rmn. To do this, first use the Open… command to open the file NORMAL.DOT. Next, select the Define Styles… command from the Format menu and use the Define Styles dialog box to change the character formatting for the *Normal* style to 12-point Tms Rmn type. After you choose OK to close the dialog box, select the Close command from the File menu, and choose Yes in the ensuing message box to save your changes to the file. At this point, Word's new default character format will be 12-point Tms Rmn.

Other defaults

Word runs under Microsoft Windows, which has many default settings that come into play when you're running Word. For instance, you can use the Windows Control Panel to change the format in which dates and times appear on your screen. For information on changing Windows' default settings, refer to your Microsoft Windows documentation.

In this chapter

Sharing Data with *21*
Other Programs

*O*ne of Word for Windows' most helpful features is its ability to save and retrieve documents in various file formats. If you've written documents with another PC word processor, you'll probably be able to use Word for Windows to open, edit, and format those documents. Similarly, if you create a document in Word for Windows that you later want to edit in another word processor, you can tell Word for Windows to save that document in the appropriate format.

In this chapter, you'll learn how to open documents created with other applications and how to save documents into file formats that can be loaded into another program. We'll also show you how to insert into an existing document text and pictures created in another program. Finally, we'll talk about sharing data with IBM DisplayWrite, Microsoft Word for the Macintosh, and Microsoft Excel.

It's quite simple to open and save a document that is not saved in a standard Word for Windows file format. The first step, however, is to use the Word for Windows Setup program to install the appropriate converter files into your Word for Windows program directory. After you've done this, the technique you use to open and save non-standard documents is similar to the one used to open and save Word for Windows documents. Let's briefly discuss opening and saving documents in non-standard formats.

OPENING AND SAVING DOCUMENTS IN OTHER FORMATS

To open a non-standard document file into Word for Windows, begin by choosing the Open... command from the File menu to bring up the dialog box shown in Figure 21-1. As you can see, the entry in the Open File Name text box tells Word to display only those documents with a .DOC file-name extension in the Files list box.

Opening non-standard files in Word for Windows

Figure 21-1

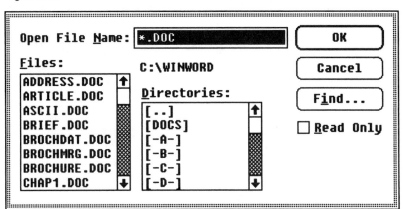

The Open dialog box initially displays only those files with a .DOC file-name extension.

Once the Open dialog box appears on your screen, you'll want to tell Word to display files with extensions other than .DOC in the Files list box. As we explained in Chapter 3, you can do this by changing the default entry in the Open File Name text box from *.DOC to *.*.

Once you've instructed Word to display all the files in the directory, use the Files and Directories list boxes to select the name of the file you want to open, then choose OK. Word will present a dialog box like the one shown in Figure 21-2, which asks you to confirm the file format Word has detected. If Word suggests the correct format, simply choose OK to begin converting the file into a Word for Windows document. You can monitor the progress of the conversion by watching the lower-left corner of the screen. When Word has finished reading and converting the entire file, the contents of that file will appear in a new document window on your screen under its original file name.

If you have not installed the necessary converter files into your Word for Windows program directory, you may see a message box telling you that Word cannot convert the non-standard document into a Word for Windows document. If such a message appears, rerun the Setup program on the Word for Windows Setup disk, and install the appropriate converter files.

By the way, if you deselect the Confirm File Format Conversion check box in the dialog box shown in Figure 21-2, Word will no longer present this dialog box when you open non-standard documents. Instead, Word will determine the file's format and immediately convert the file into a normal Word for Windows document. If Word cannot recognize the file's format, it will assume it is a Text Only file.

Figure 21-2

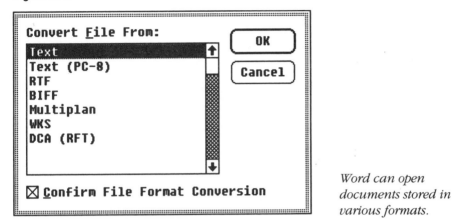

Convert File From:
- Text
- Text (PC-8)
- RTF
- BIFF
- Multiplan
- WKS
- DCA (RFT)

OK
Cancel

☒ Confirm File Format Conversion

Word can open documents stored in various formats.

In case you're wondering, the only way to tell Word to redisplay the dialog box in Figure 21-2 is to make a change to the WIN.INI file in your Windows directory. When you deselect the Confirm File Format Conversion check box, Word will add the line

CONVERSIONS=NO

to WIN.INI. If you change this line to read

CONVERSIONS=YES

Word will once again display the dialog box shown in Figure 21-2 each time you open a non-standard file.

Saving a Word document in non-standard formats

To save a Word for Windows document in a non-standard format, first select the Save As... command from the File menu, then choose the Options >> button to expand the Save As dialog box, as shown in Figure 21-3 on the following page. Next, pull down the File Format list box and choose the appropriate file format. At this point, the name of the format you've selected will replace the Normal file format in the File Format text box. When you choose OK to complete the command, Word will save the document in the format you've specified.

If you have not installed the necessary converter files into your Word for Windows program directory, you may see a message box stating that you cannot convert your Word for Windows document into the format you've chosen. If such a message appears, rerun the Setup program on the Word for Windows Setup disk, and install the appropriate converter files.

Figure 21-3

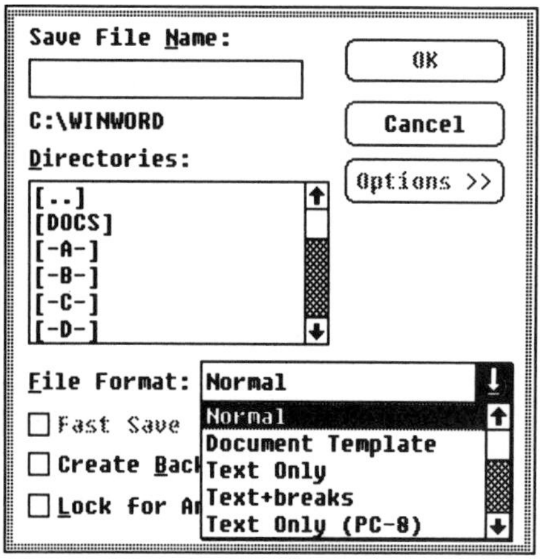

Save File **N**ame:

[   ]   [OK   ]

C:\WINWORD   [Cancel   ]

Directories:
[   ]   [**O**ptions >>]

[..]
[DOCS]
[-A-]
[-B-]
[-C-]
[-D-]

File Format: | Normal

☐ Fast Save | Normal
☐ Create **B**ac | Document Template
☐ **L**ock for A | Text Only
              | Text+breaks
              | Text Only (PC-8)

The expanded Save As dialog box lets you save Word for Windows documents in several formats.

As an example, suppose you've created a Word for Windows document named STATUS.DOC, and you want to give a copy of that document (on disk) to a friend who uses WordPerfect 5.0. To save a copy of STATUS.DOC in WordPerfect 5.0 format to the disk in drive A, first open the document, select the Save As... command from the File menu, select the [-A-] option from the Directories list box, and choose the Options >> button to expand the Save As dialog box. Next, select the WordPerfect 5.0 option from the File Format pull-down list box, and choose OK to complete the command. Your friend should now be able to use WordPerfect 5.0 to retrieve and edit the document you've saved to the disk in drive A. Remember, however, that some of the document's formatting may be lost in the conversion process.

**Using the
ASCII file format**

Most word processing programs, including Word for Windows, can save documents to disk in the ASCII file format. In addition, nearly every word processing program and many spreadsheet and database programs can read ASCII files. The ASCII system uses a three-digit code to represent each number, letter, and symbol. For example, your computer knows the letter *e* as ASCII code 101.

You might think of the ASCII file format as the "lowest common denominator" format. When you save a Word for Windows document in this format, you create a pure text file without any special character or paragraph formats. Similarly, when you load an ASCII file into Word, you will see plain text on your screen with no special character or paragraph formatting. It's the "plain jane" nature of ASCII files that makes them useful for moving documents from one program to another.

If you want to save a Word for Windows document into an ASCII file, open the expanded Save As dialog box, pull down the File Format list box, and choose either the Text Only, Text+breaks, Text Only (PC-8), or Text+breaks (PC-8) option. (The PC-8 options simply convert the document's upper-level ASCII characters from the Roman-8 character set to the PC-8 character set.) Next, enter a new file name with a different extension (like .TXT) into the Save File Name text box. Finally, choose OK to close the expanded dialog box and save the document.

When you execute the Save As... command, Word will save a copy of the current document to disk in the ASCII file format. To see the ASCII document you just saved, open it with the Open... command just as you would any normal Word for Windows document. As you'll see, none of the text in an ASCII document carries character, paragraph, or section formatting. However, the document's paragraph breaks will remain intact. If you selected the Text+breaks or Text+breaks (PC-8) option, you'll see additional paragraph breaks at the end of every line.

If the purpose in saving your document in the ASCII file format is to read it into another word processing program, you'll probably want to use the Text Only or Text Only (PC-8) option, not the Text+breaks or Text+breaks (PC-8) option. This second group of options is designed primarily for transferring information from Word to spreadsheet and database programs.

IMPORTING DATA FROM OTHER PROGRAMS

Word provides a couple of ways to insert data from other programs into an existing document. In this section, we'll show you how to insert data using the Clipboard or the File... command on the Insert menu.

Using the Clipboard

In many cases, the simplest way to exchange information between Word for Windows and other programs is to copy and paste (or cut and paste) that information via the Clipboard. (We discussed the Clipboard in Chapter 6.) Of course, it's easier to use the Clipboard if you load both Word for Windows and the other application simultaneously. However, even if you can't load more than one Windows application at a time, you can still use the Clipboard to transfer data between the two products.

To transfer information via the Clipboard, first open the file containing the graphic, worksheet data, or other information you want to copy into Word. Select the information you want to transfer, and choose the Copy command. Your selection will be copied to the Clipboard, where it will remain as long as you do not issue another Copy or Cut command or end the Windows session. Now, activate Word for Windows, open the document into which you want to paste the information you just copied or cut, and place the cursor in the location you want to insert the information.

At this point, you can use either the Paste or Paste Link... command on the Edit menu to insert the information into your document. If you issue the Paste command, the data you import will come in as either literal text or as a graphic image. If you issue the Paste Link... command, however, Word will present a Paste Link dialog box like the one shown in Figure 21-4. This dialog box lets you create two types of links between a Word for Windows document and the source application: regular links or auto update links.

Figure 21-4

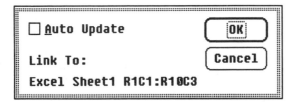

Word's Paste Link dialog box lets you create regular links and auto update links with the source application.

If you leave the Auto Update check box deselected and choose OK, Word will create a regular link between the document and the source application by inserting a DDE field into the document. You can update the result of a DDE field by selecting that field and pressing the [Update field] key ([F9]). On the other hand, if you select the Auto Update check box and choose OK, Word will create an auto update link between the document and the source application by inserting a DDEAUTO field into the document. Unlike DDE fields, DDEAUTO fields are updated automatically as soon as new data is available in the source application.

If you want, you can bypass the Paste Link... command and enter DDE and DDEAUTO fields directly into your document. The forms of these fields are

{DDE *appName filename [place/reference]*}
{DDEAUTO *appName filename [place/reference]*}

where *appName* is the full path name of the source application, and *filename* is the name of the source document, worksheet, or chart you want to insert. The optional argument *[place/reference]* lets you define a specific quantity of data, such as a range in a worksheet.

If you use the Field... command on the Insert menu to enter one of these fields, Word will update the field for you automatically as soon as it enters the field into your document. On the other hand, if you use the [Insert field] key ([Ctrl][F9]) to enter one of these fields, you'll need to update the field manually after you enter it by pressing the [Update field] key.

When we discuss exchanging data with Microsoft Excel later in this chapter, we'll show you how to use the DDE and DDEAUTO fields to insert data from an Excel worksheet into a Word for Windows document.

**Using the
File... command**

If the data you want to insert into your document is not likely to change, you might want to use the File... command on the Insert menu to insert that data into your document. When you issue this command, Word will bring up the dialog box shown in Figure 21-5.

When the Insert File dialog box appears, you'll want to change the entry in the Insert File Name text box from *.DOC to *.* so you can view all the files saved on your disk. Next, use the Files and Directories list boxes to select the data file you want to include in the document.

Figure 21-5

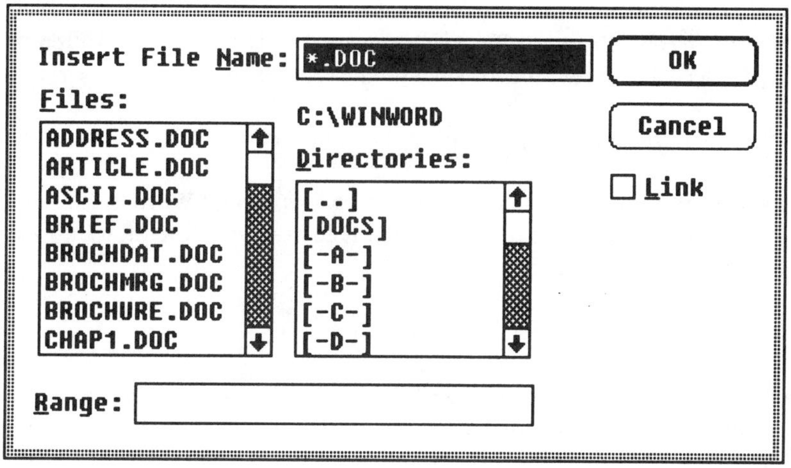

The Insert File dialog box lets you insert data stored in a file on disk.

If you don't want to link the imported data to the source data file, you should leave the Link check box deselected and choose OK to complete the command. When you do this, the data you specified will appear at the location of the cursor as literal text.

On the other hand, if you want to link the imported data to the source data file so that you can update the data later with the [Update field] key, select the Link check box before choosing OK. Immediately, Word will insert into the document an INCLUDE field that takes the form

{INCLUDE *filename [place/reference]*}

where *filename* is the full path name of the source data file, and *[place/reference]* is an optional argument that defines a specific quantity of data, such as a range in a worksheet. The INCLUDE field's result is the literal text in the source data file.

Word allows you to bypass the File... command on the Insert menu and enter an INCLUDE field directly into your document. If you do this, make sure you double the backslash character in the worksheet's full path name to avoid confusing this argument with a switch argument.

Updating the data

If the data stored in the source data file changes after you use an INCLUDE field to import it into Word, you can update the field's result by moving the cursor into the field code (or field result), and pressing the [Update field] key ([F9]). When we discuss exchanging data with Microsoft Excel later in this chapter, we'll show you how to use the INCLUDE field to insert data from an Excel worksheet into a Word for Windows document.

Specifying
a file format

Word will automatically determine the format of the data file you specify, and convert the file into Word's Normal file format as it opens it. If you want, however, you can use the \c switch to tell Word to convert the data file into a different format. The INCLUDE field with a \c switch takes the form

{INCLUDE *filename [place/reference]* \c *converterName*}

where *converterName* is the name of the converter file you want Word to use. For example, if you want to open the document LETTER.DOC and convert it into the Text Only format, use the field:

{INCLUDE "C:\\LETTER.DOC" \c "Text Only"}

PICTURES

Fortunately, Word provides several tools for manipulating pictures (graphics) in a document. After importing a picture into your document, you can size, crop, and position the picture to fit your layout needs. You can also place a border around a picture or insert an empty picture frame into a document to serve as a placeholder for photographs or illustrations that you'll manually paste in later.

Importing a picture

You can import into Word a picture from a graphics program, such as Microsoft Paint or PC Paintbrush, by using the Clipboard, as we described earlier in this chapter. If you're running a full-featured version of Windows and your computer has enough memory to run both Word for Windows and a graphics program, the fastest way to insert a picture into a Word for Windows document is to copy the picture to the Clipboard, then switch to Word and paste the picture into the desired location in your document.

For example, Figure 21-6 shows a Microsoft Paint screen in which we've created some artwork. Let's suppose that we now want to insert this artwork as a picture in a Word for Windows document. To do this, we select the artwork, issue the Copy command, switch to our Word for Windows document, move the cursor to the location in which we want to place the picture, and issue the Paste command. Word will then copy the picture from the Clipboard into the document window, as shown in Figure 21-7.

Inserting a TIFF file

Many graphics programs can save a picture to disk in a special format called TIFF, an acronym for Tagged Image File Format. Most scanners save their scanned images to disk in this form. If you want to insert a picture in the form of a TIFF file, move the cursor to the place where you want to insert the picture, and select the Picture... command from the Insert menu. Figure 21-8 on page 784 shows the dialog box that appears at this point.

Figure 21-6

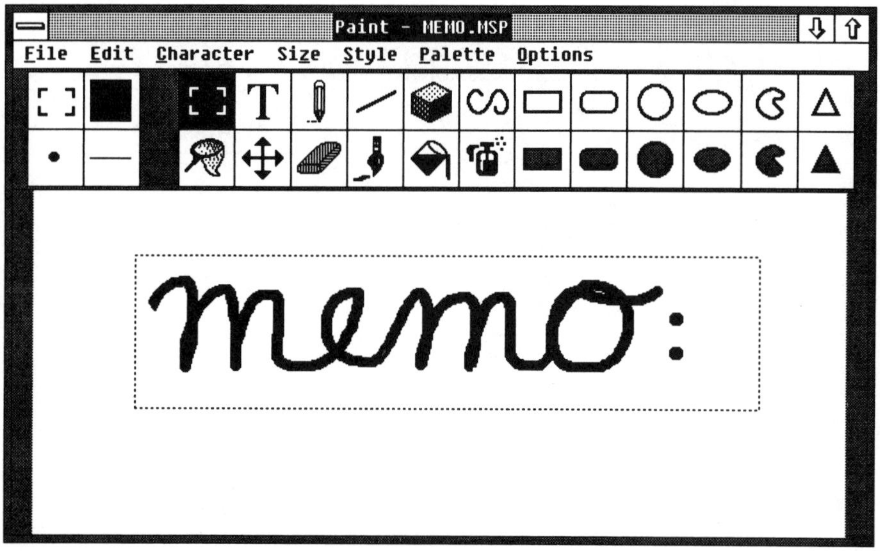

We created this picture in Microsoft Paint.

Figure 21-7

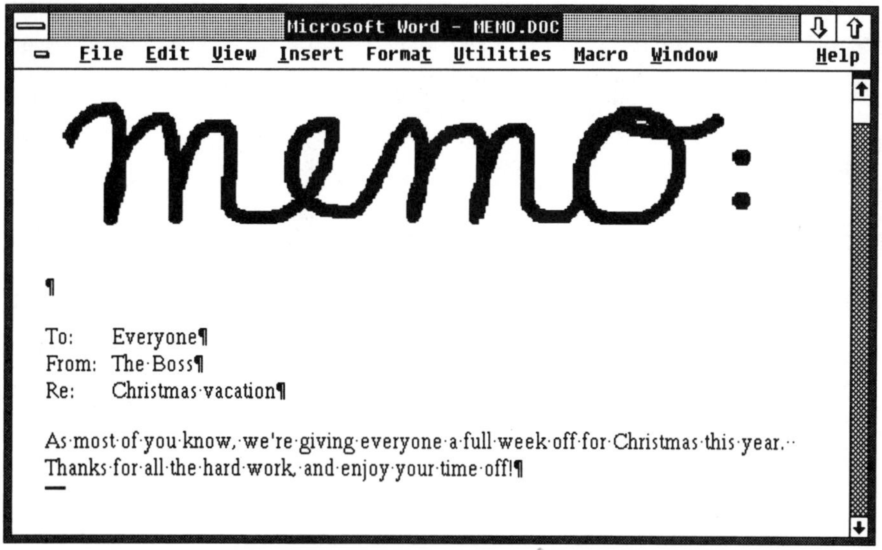

We pasted the picture into our Word for Windows document.

Figure 21-8

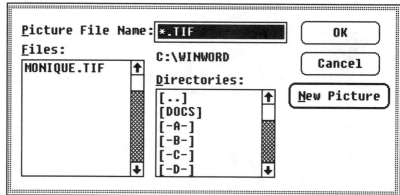

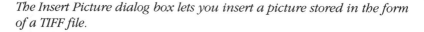

The Insert Picture dialog box lets you insert a picture stored in the form of a TIFF file.

In the Insert Picture dialog box, use the Directories and Files list boxes to select the appropriate TIFF file, and choose OK. Word will then insert an IMPORT field into your document that takes the form

{IMPORT *filename*}

where *filename* is the full path name of the file you specified in the Insert Picture dialog box. For example, if you select the file C:\MONIQUE.TIF in the dialog box in Figure 21-8, Word will insert the field:

{IMPORT C:\\MONIQUE.TIF}

The result of the field will be the picture saved in the file MONIQUE.TIF.

If you want, you can bypass the Picture... command on the Insert menu and manually enter an IMPORT field into your document. If you use an IMPORT field, however, don't forget to double the backslash in the file's path name.

Inserting an empty picture frame

If you want to manually paste artwork into your printed Word for Windows document, you might want to insert a picture frame into the document as a placeholder. To insert a picture frame, move the cursor to the place you want to insert the frame, then select the Picture... command from the Insert menu to open the dialog box shown in Figure 21-8. Now, if you choose the New Picture button, Word will insert a solid-line picture frame that measures a square inch. You can resize or reposition this frame any way you want.

By the way, to place a border around a picture you've inserted into a document, don't use the Picture... command on the Insert menu. Instead, use the Picture... command on the Format menu. We'll show you how to use this command in a moment.

To size a picture with the mouse, first click on the picture. When you do, Word will display a solid-line frame with eight small black squares or "handles" around the picture. For example, Figure 21-9 shows the picture from Figure 21-7 after we clicked on it to display its frame. As you can see, a handle appears at every corner and along every side of the frame. As long as the frame is larger than the picture, Word will center the picture within the frame.

Sizing a picture

Figure 21-9

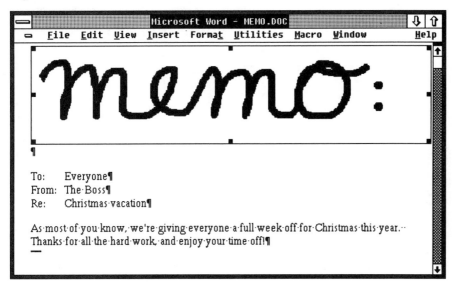

When you click on a picture, Word will display a frame with eight handles.

You can use the frame around a picture to change its size. Word lets you size a picture by cropping or scaling it. Let's take a look at each of these techniques.

To crop a picture—that is—to resize the frame without changing the scale of the picture—just drag one of its handles. You can use the handles at the top and bottom of the frame's edges to change only the height of the picture, and you can use the handles at the left and right to adjust the width. Dragging a corner handle will alter both the height and width, resizing the picture's frame without altering its original proportions.

Cropping a picture

When you crop a picture, Word will not change the actual size of the picture you have pasted into the document. Instead, it will change the amount of space allotted to the picture. If you increase the size of the picture frame, Word will insert more white space between the picture and its surrounding text. If you decrease the picture frame's height or width (or both), Word will display only as much of the picture as it can accommodate in the frame. As you drag a handle, Word will display information at the bottom of the screen telling you how much of the original picture you're cropping.

For example, if we click on the picture shown in Figure 21-9 and drag the lower-right corner handle up and to the left, Word will display only part of the original image, as shown in Figure 21-10.

Figure 21-10

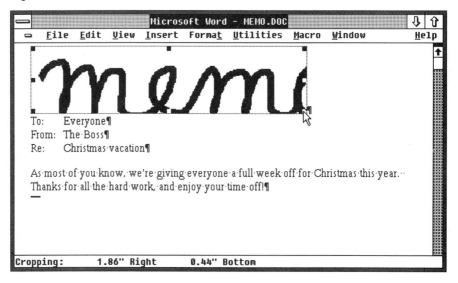

When you crop a picture frame, Word will display only as much of the picture as it can accommodate in the frame.

If you want to crop a picture using the keyboard, first select the picture by placing the cursor to the left of the picture and pressing [Shift]➡. Next, select the Picture… command from the Format menu to bring up the Format Picture dialog box shown in Figure 21-11. At this point, type the desired values into the Crop From text boxes. For instance, if you want to crop an inch from the right edge of the picture, enter *1"* into the Crop From Right text box. When you choose OK to return to the document, the picture will reflect the cropping measurements you specified.

Figure 21-11

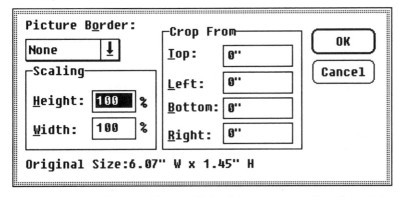

You can use the Format Picture dialog box to crop and scale a picture.

To scale a picture—that is, to change the actual size of the image rather than just the frame, you can press the [Shift] key as you drag a frame handle. As you drag a handle, Word will flash percentages—like *58% High 58% Wide*—at the bottom of the screen. This indicates the new size of the picture relative to the original size. For example, suppose you are viewing the sample picture shown in Figure 21-9. You press the [Shift] key and drag the picture's lower-right corner handle until you see the message *58% High 58% Wide* at the bottom of the screen. When you release the [Shift] key, Word will reduce the size of the entire picture, as shown in Figure 21-12 on the following page.

If you want to scale a picture using the keyboard, first select the picture and choose the Picture… command from the Format menu to open the Format Picture dialog box shown in Figure 21-11. At this point, simply enter the desired values into the Scaling Height and Width text boxes. When you choose OK to close the dialog box, Word will display the picture according to the new scaling measurements you've specified.

Scaling a picture

The frame that appears around a picture when you click on it will not appear in your printed document. If you want to place a border around a picture, select the picture, then choose the Picture… command from the Format menu to open the dialog box in Figure 21-11. At this point, choose the type of border you want to use from the Picture Border pull-down list box, then choose OK. Immediately, Word will place the border you selected around the picture. Figure 21-13 on the next page shows the picture from Figure 21-12 after we added a thick border.

Placing a border around a picture

If you press [Enter] to place a ¶ mark after a picture so that it occupies its own paragraph, you can assign paragraph formats to that picture to control how it is positioned in your text. For example, you can use the ruler alignment icons

Positioning a picture

to left-align, right-align, or center a picture in your document, and use the Paragraph… command to add space above and below the picture.

Figure 21-12

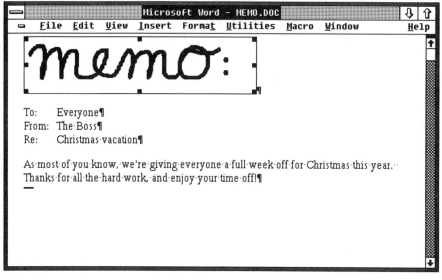

When you scale a picture, Word will change the size of the picture.

Figure 21-13

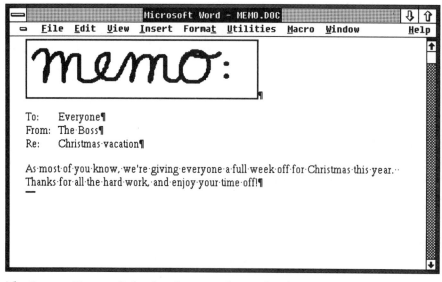

The Format Picture dialog box lets you place a border around a picture.

You also can use the Position... command to place a picture at any absolute position on the page. For a complete discussion of the Position... command, refer to Chapter 12.

Before you can open a DisplayWrite document in Word for Windows, you must first use DisplayWrite to save the document in the DCA/RFT file format. You can then use Word for Windows' Open... command to open the document. Of course, some of the document's formatting may not transfer into Word correctly.

To save a Word for Windows document in a form that you can open in DisplayWrite, access the expanded Save As dialog box, choose the DCA/RFT option in the File Format pull-down list box, and choose OK to complete the command. DisplayWrite will lose much of the formatting you've assigned to a Word for Windows document.

DISPLAYWRITE

Importing documents from Microsoft Word for the Macintosh (Mac Word) is a bit trickier than importing files from PC applications. If you've created a document with Mac Word, and you want to open that document in Word for Windows, you must first use Mac Word to save the document in the Interchange format (RTF). Once you've created the document file, you'll need to transfer that file from a disk formatted on the Macintosh to a disk formatted with MS-DOS. Several third-party manufacturers sell disk drives that are designed for exchanging data between a Macintosh and a PC. Consult your local computer vendor or consultant for help with this kind of conversion process.

Once you've transferred a Mac Word document in RTF format to an MS-DOS disk, you can use Word for Windows' Open... command to open that document. As usual, some of the document's formatting may not transfer into Word for Windows correctly.

To save a Word for Windows document into a file that Mac Word can read, access the expanded Save As dialog box, choose RTF from the File Format pull-down list box, and then choose OK. Next, you'll need to transfer the file from an MS-DOS disk to a Macintosh disk. Finally, use the Open... command in Mac Word to open the document.

MICROSOFT WORD FOR THE MACINTOSH

If you use Microsoft Excel, you'll sometimes want to import data from an Excel worksheet into a Word for Windows document. As you might expect, you can use the Open... command on the File menu to open an Excel worksheet as a Word for Windows document. If Word asks you to confirm the file format, just accept Word's suggested format (BIFF). The worksheet data should appear in a new document as literal text, separated by tabs.

In addition to using the Open... command to open an entire Excel worksheet as a new document, Word for Windows lets you import Excel charts and worksheet data into existing documents. In fact, you can import either an entire worksheet or a portion of a worksheet.

MICROSOFT EXCEL

There are several forms in which Excel's worksheet data can appear in a Word for Windows document. First, the data you import can be literal text separated by tabs. If you want, however, you can create two types of links between a Word for Windows document and an Excel worksheet: regular links or auto update links. If you create a regular link, Word will update the document's worksheet data only when you tell it. If you create an auto update link, Word will update the document's worksheet data automatically, as soon as a change is made to the source worksheet.

Inserting a chart into a document

To insert a Microsoft Excel chart into a document, first activate Microsoft Excel, then activate the chart you want to copy. Next, choose the Select Chart command from the Chart menu, and choose the Copy command from the Edit menu to copy the chart to the Clipboard. Once you've done this, activate Word for Windows, and place the cursor in the location in which you want to place the chart.

If you want to paste the chart into the document with no link to the worksheet on which the chart is based, simply choose the Paste command from the Edit menu. However, if you want to link the chart in your document to the source worksheet so that it will reflect any changes you make to the worksheet, choose the Paste Link... command from the Edit menu to bring up a dialog box like the one shown in Figure 21-14.

Figure 21-14

The Paste Link dialog box lets you link a chart in your Word for Windows document to an Excel worksheet.

To create a regular link to the source worksheet, make sure that the Auto Update check box is deselected, then choose OK. To create an auto update link to the source worksheet, select the Auto Update check box, then choose OK.

Regardless of which method you use to paste the chart into your document, the chart will initially look just like the one you placed on the Clipboard. However, if you use the Paste Link... command to insert the chart, you can activate the Field Codes setting on the View menu to see that the chart is actually the result of a DDE or DDEAUTO field. For example, if use the Paste Link... command to create a regular link to the source worksheet, Word will insert into your document the field

{dde Excel Chart1 "" * mergeformat}

which will initially return as its result the chart you placed onto the Clipboard. Similarly, if you use Paste Link... to create an auto update link to the source worksheet, Word will insert the field

{ddeauto Excel Chart1 "" * mergeformat}

which will also return the chart you copied. Word will update the DDE field only when you move the cursor to the field code (or to the chart it returns) and press the [Update field] key ([F9]). However, Word will update the DDEAUTO field automatically whenever you change the data in the source worksheet upon which the chart is based.

You can import an Excel chart into a Word for Windows document by manually inserting a DDE or DDEAUTO field. The forms of these fields are

{DDE Excel *chartName* "" * mergeformat}
{DDEAUTO Excel *chartName* "" * mergeformat}

Entering DDE and DDEAUTO fields manually

where *chartName* is the name of the chart you want to insert. If you use the Field... command on the Insert menu to enter one of these fields, Word will update the field for you automatically as soon as it enters the field into your document. If you use the [Insert field] key ([Ctrl][F9]) to enter one of these fields, however, you'll need to update the field manually by pressing the [Update field] key.

You can use any of the techniques we've discussed earlier in this chapter to insert data from an Excel worksheet into a document. If you're running both Excel and Word for Windows under the current Windows session, and you've opened the worksheet containing the data you want to insert, you can use a simple cut-and-paste procedure to move the data from Excel into Word. However, if the data is likely to change in the source worksheet while your document is open, you'll want to use the Paste Link... command, which will use either a DDE or DDEAUTO field to create a regular link or an auto update link, respectively. Finally, if the data is stored in a worksheet file on disk, you'll want to use the File... command on Word's Insert menu, which will insert either literal text separated by tab marks or an INCLUDE field. Fortunately, all of these techniques allow you to specify either a range of data or an entire worksheet. Let's consider each technique.

Inserting worksheet data into a document

To insert data from an open Excel worksheet into a Word for Windows document, you should first decide if you want to copy literal text into the document, or if you want to link the data in the document to the source worksheet.

Inserting data from an open worksheet

**Inserting
unlinked data**

To copy unlinked worksheet data into a document, first activate the appropriate worksheet and highlight the range of cells you want to copy. Next, select the Copy command from Excel's Edit menu to place the cells you highlighted onto the Clipboard. Now, switch to Word for Windows, activate the appropriate document, and place the cursor where you want the Excel data to appear. Finally, choose the Paste command from the Edit menu to insert the data into the document. When you do, the data you selected will appear at the location of the cursor.

Inserting linked data

If you want to create either a regular or auto update link to the data in the source worksheet, you'll need to use a slightly different cut-and-paste procedure. After you copy the Excel data to the Clipboard, activate the Word for Windows document, move the cursor to the desired spot, and choose the Paste Link... command from the Edit menu to bring up a dialog box like the one shown in Figure 21-15. Notice that you can see both the name of the source worksheet and the selected range along the bottom of the Paste Link dialog box.

Figure 21-15

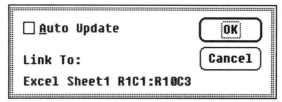

The Paste Link dialog box lets you create a link between a Word for Windows document and an Excel worksheet.

If you want to create a regular link between the document and the worksheet, leave the Auto Update check box deselected and choose OK to complete the Paste Link... command. However, if you want to create an auto update link, select the Auto Update check box before choosing OK. As we mentioned earlier, creating a regular link means that you'll have to manually update the data in the document to reflect changes in the source worksheet. If you create an auto update link, however, Word will automatically update the data in the document as soon as new data becomes available in the source worksheet.

When you choose OK in the Paste Link dialog box, Word will insert either a DDE or DDEAUTO field that returns the data from the source worksheet. The form of these fields are

{DDE Excel *worksheetName range* * mergeformat}
{DDEAUTO Excel *worksheetName range* * mergeformat}

where *worksheetName* is the name of the source worksheet, and *range* is the range of cells you specified. For instance, if you place onto the Clipboard cells A1:B5 of the worksheet BUDGET.XLS, executing the Paste Link… command will insert one of the following fields:

{dde Excel BUDGET.XLS R1C1:R5C2 * mergeformat}
{ddeauto Excel BUDGET.XLS R1C1:R5C2 * mergeformat}

As you probably noticed, the range references from Excel appear in R1C1 form in the DDE and DDEAUTO fields.

The data returned by the DDE and DDEAUTO fields will be in the form of a table. Consequently, you can use any of Word for Windows' table-manipulating features to edit or format the data once you've inserted it into the document.

You can enter DDE and DDEAUTO fields with the Field… command on the Insert menu or with the [Insert field] key ([Ctrl][F9]). If you use the [Insert field] key to enter a DDE or DDEAUTO field, remember to use the [Update field] key ([F9]) to update its result as soon as you enter it.

So far, we've shown you how to import data that is stored in an open Excel worksheet. If you want to insert into a Word for Windows document data from an Excel worksheet you've saved on disk, first place the cursor in the location you want to insert the worksheet. Next, select the File… command from the Insert menu to bring up the dialog box shown in Figure 21-5.

Inserting data from a worksheet on disk

When the Insert File dialog box appears, change the entry in the Insert File Name text box from *.DOC to *.* so you can view all the files saved on your disk. Next, use the Files and Directories list boxes to select the worksheet file you want to include in the document.

If you don't want to link the imported data to the source worksheet file, you should leave the Link check box deselected and choose OK to complete the command. Word will then insert the specified data and display it as literal text.

On the other hand, if you want to link the imported data to the worksheet file so you can update the data later with the [Update field] key, select the Link check box before choosing OK. Word will then insert into the document an INCLUDE field that takes the form

{INCLUDE *worksheetName range*}

where *worksheetName* is the full path name of the source worksheet, and *range* is the range of cells you want to insert. The INCLUDE field returns the worksheet data as literal text, separating columns of data with tab marks.

For example, let's suppose you want to insert cells A1:C10 of the worksheet file FORECAST.XLS (which is stored in the directory C:\EXCEL) into the current document, and that you want to link this data to the worksheet file. To do this, first place the cursor in the appropriate location, then choose the File… command from the Insert menu. When the Insert File dialog box appears, use the Directories list box to choose the C:\EXCEL directory, and change the entry in the Insert File Name text box from *.DOC to *.*. Next, select the file FORECAST.XLS in the Files list box, then enter *A1:C10* into the Range text box. Finally, select the Link check box and choose OK to complete the command. Word will then insert into your document the field

{INCLUDE C:\\EXCEL\\FORECAST.XLS A1:C10}

which will return the data in cells A1:C10 of the source worksheet. Notice that Word doubled the backslash character in the worksheet's full path name to avoid confusing this argument with a switch argument. Also notice that the *range* argument for the INCLUDE field appears in A1 form instead of in R1C1 form. If you want to enter an INCLUDE field into a document with the Field... command on the Insert menu or with the [Insert field] key, make sure that the field you enter takes this same form.

If the data stored in the source worksheet file changes after you use an INCLUDE field to import it into Word for Windows, you can update the field's result by moving the cursor into the field code (or field result), and pressing the [Update field] key ([F9]).

SATISFACTION

The Best

GUARANTEED

Appendices

Appendices

In Appendix 1, we will cover basic Microsoft Windows elements common to all programs—the mouse, menu commands and icons, dialog boxes, and so forth. Appendix 2 provides the names of the icons you'll encounter as you work with Word. In Appendix 3, you'll find a comprehensive list of the keyboard and mouse techniques we've discussed throughout the book. Appendix 4 provides the forms of Word's fields, and Appendix 5 lists the characters in the ANSI and OEM character sets.

In this appendix

Windows Basics *A1*

*I*n this appendix, we'll take a tour of the Microsoft Word for Windows screen (or desktop) and explain some basic concepts and procedures you'll need to know to work in the Microsoft Windows operating environment. If you are new to the Windows environment, or if you want to brush up on your basic Windows skills, you should take time to read this appendix and familiarize yourself with the various concepts and techniques. On the other hand, if you are experienced in another Windows application, we suggest that you skim this appendix just to be sure that you're familiar with our terminology.

SCREEN ELEMENTS

Applications that run under Microsoft Windows are easier to learn and use than standard MS-DOS applications because all Windows applications look essentially the same. In this section, we'll explain the common Windows screen elements that appear in Word for Windows.

Windows

Every program that runs under Microsoft Windows, including Word for Windows, appears inside its own window on the screen. For example, when you begin a new Word for Windows session, you will see a window entitled *Microsoft Word - Document1* like the one shown in Figure A1-1 on the next page.

The Microsoft Word window in Figure A1-1 occupies the entire screen. If you want, you can move and resize this window, and open other program windows without closing this window. We'll show you how to manipulate windows on your screen a little later in this appendix.

In addition to the Microsoft Word window, each document you create appears in its own window. As you'll see later, you can use most of the same techniques to manipulate a document window that you use to manipulate the Microsoft Word window.

Figure A1-1

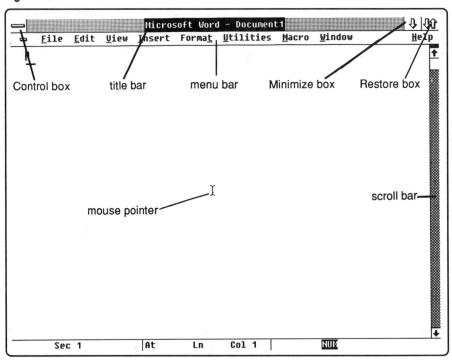

Every application that runs under Microsoft Windows appears in its own window.

Title bar

The top portion of every window contains a title bar. As you can see in Figure A1-1, the title bar of the Microsoft Word window is bound on the left by the Control-menu box (◘) and on the right by the Minimize and Restore boxes (⬇ and 🔲).

A window's title bar serves two purposes: to identify the window's contents and to indicate whether the window is active or inactive. Although you can open several application windows at once, only one window can be active—the window that is ready to accept input or carry out commands. Inactive windows are those that are open on the desktop but aren't being used at the moment.

The title bar of an active window is displayed in a color (or shade of gray) that is different from that of inactive windows. If you haven't changed default colors, the active window's title bar will appear in a dark color, while inactive windows' title bars will appear in a lighter color.

Control menu

The ◘ that appears on the left side of every window's title bar is a Control-menu box. As you'll see later in this appendix, selecting this box brings up the

Microsoft Word window's Control menu, which lets you perform many important procedures, including moving, sizing, and closing the window.

You might have noticed that a smaller box appears at the left edge of the menu bar in Figure A1-1. Choosing this box brings up the document window's Control menu, which performs many of the same functions as the Microsoft Word window's Control menu.

Sizing boxes

The ⬇ and ⬆ on the right side of a window's title bar are the Minimize and Restore boxes, respectively. These boxes let you minimize or restore the size of the Microsoft Word window on your screen. We'll show you how to use these boxes later in this appendix.

Menu bar

Word's menu bar appears right below its title bar. From this menu bar, you can issue instructions to Word. As you can see in Figure A1-1, Word initially offers nine menus: the document's Control menu (the small box on the very left), File, Edit, View, Insert, Format, Utilities, Window, and Help. Later, you'll see an additional menu—Macro. We'll show you how to issue commands from the menu bar in a moment.

Scroll bar

The vertical bar along the right edge of the window is called a scroll bar. Since you cannot usually view the contents of an entire document on just one screen, you'll need to use the scroll bar to view different portions of your document. For more information on scrolling through documents with the scroll bar, refer to Chapter 4.

Mouse pointer

The I-beam shape that appears near the center of the screen in Figure A1-1 is the mouse pointer. You'll see this pointer only if you've installed a mouse on your computer system. As you move the mouse, the pointer will move around on the screen. If you move the pointer to different areas of the Word screen, you'll notice that it can take on a variety of shapes. For a detailed discussion of the pointer, see Chapter 2.

ISSUING COMMANDS

As we explained earlier, you'll use the menu bar to issue commands to Word. When you pull down a menu on the menu bar, Word will display a list of related commands immediately below the menu name. You'll notice that some commands on a menu appear in standard, dark text, while others appear in dimmed text to indicate that they are not currently active. Windows monitors the status of the application you're using and automatically darkens or dims the appropriate commands.

Issuing commands with the mouse

If your computer is equipped with a mouse, you can issue a command by pointing to a menu name and pressing the mouse button. (This procedure is called *clicking on* a menu name.) When you do this, Word will pull down the menu to show a list of available commands. For example, if you click on the word *Format* in the menu bar, Word will pull down the Format menu to reveal the commands shown in Figure A1-2.

Figure A1-2

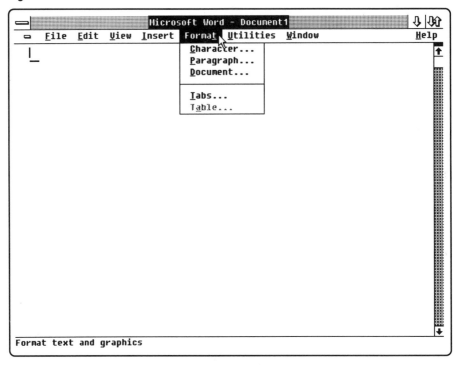

To pull down a menu with the mouse, simply click on the menu name.

If you continue to hold down the mouse button after the pull-down menu appears, you can drag the arrow-shaped mouse pointer through the list of commands. As you drag the pointer, you'll see a brief description of each command on the left side of the status bar at the bottom of your screen. When you highlight the appropriate command, just release the mouse button to issue the command.

After you've pulled down a menu, it stays active until you choose a command, click elsewhere on your screen, or click on the menu name again. For this reason, after you've learned how to use the available commands and don't need the descriptive messages to help guide you, you can speed up the process of issuing a command by clicking on a menu, releasing the mouse button, moving the pointer to the command you want, and clicking again.

Another way to select commands from a menu is by using the keyboard. To access a menu from the keyboard, first press the [Alt] key to activate the menu bar. (The information in the status bar will change to indicate that you've activated the menu bar.) Once you've done this, you can use either of two methods to pull down one of its menus. First, you can press the letter that is underlined in the menu name. For example, to access the Edit menu shown in Figure A1-1, press the [Alt] key to activate the menu bar, then type *E* or *e* (the menus are not case sensitive). At this point, your screen will look like the one shown in Figure A1-3.

Issuing commands with the keyboard

Figure A1-3

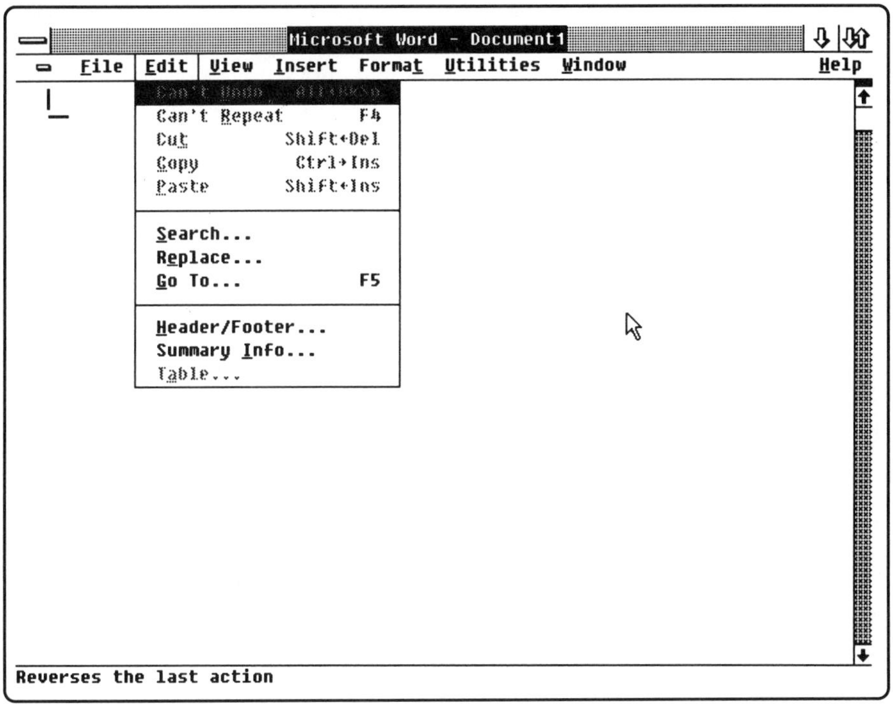

You can access menu commands with either the keyboard or the mouse.

Alternatively, you can access a menu from the keyboard by pressing the [Alt] key to activate the menu bar, using the → and ← keys to highlight the menu you want to use, and then pressing the ↓ key to pull down the menu. For instance, to access the Edit menu, press [Alt] to activate the menu bar, press → once to highlight the name *Edit*, and then press ↓ to pull down the Edit menu. The resulting screen will look like the one shown in Figure A1-3.

You might have noticed that one letter in each of the commands on the Edit menu is underlined. As you'd expect, to select a command using the keyboard, just type the underlined letter. Alternatively, after you pull down a menu, you can use the ↑ and ↓ keys to highlight different commands on the menu. (Using the arrow keys to move the highlight up and down is much like using the mouse to move through the list of commands on the active menu.) As you highlight each command name, you'll see a brief description of the command in the status bar. After you've highlighted the appropriate command in the menu, press [Enter] to issue it.

To access another menu after you've already pulled one down, you can use the [Alt] key technique, or you can use the → and ← keys to move to adjacent menus. If you want to deactivate the menu bar altogether, simply press [Esc].

In many cases, you can bypass the menu bar altogether and use a keyboard shortcut to issue a command. The available keyboard shortcuts are listed on the right side of the menus. For example, as you can see in Figure A1-3, you can issue the Go To... command by pressing [F5]. Similarly, you can issue the Copy command by pressing the [Ctrl] and [Insert] keys simultaneously.

USING DIALOG BOXES

You've probably noticed that some of the command names on the Edit menu in Figure A1-3 are followed by an ellipsis (...). An ellipsis indicates that Word needs additional information to carry out the command. To collect the necessary information, Word will display a special window called a dialog box. For example, when you select the Character... command from the Format menu, you'll see a dialog box like the one shown in Figure A1-4.

As you can see, in several elements can appear in a dialog box, including check boxes, list boxes, option buttons, text boxes, and command buttons. Notice that these elements are organized by category, and that two command buttons, OK and Cancel, appear in the upper-right corner. In this section, we'll discuss the techniques you can use to select options in a dialog box, then we'll examine each type of dialog box element.

Selecting options in a dialog box

If your computer is equipped with a mouse, you can select any option in a dialog box by pointing to the option and pressing the mouse button. This technique is often referred to as *clicking on* an option.

If you're using the keyboard, you must use either of two techniques to make dialog box selections. First, you can make dialog box selections by pressing the [Tab] key repeatedly until you activate the area whose settings you want to change. The dialog box's active area is usually surrounded by a dotted-line highlight. If the active area contains a text box, however, you may not see a dotted-line highlight—instead, you'll see the contents of that text box in inverse type. Once you've activated the appropriate area, use the ↑ and ↓ keys to make your selection.

If you activate a check-box option, you'll need to press the [Spacebar] to select and deselect that check box. We'll discuss these selection techniques as we look at each kind of item you'll encounter in a dialog box.

Figure A1-4

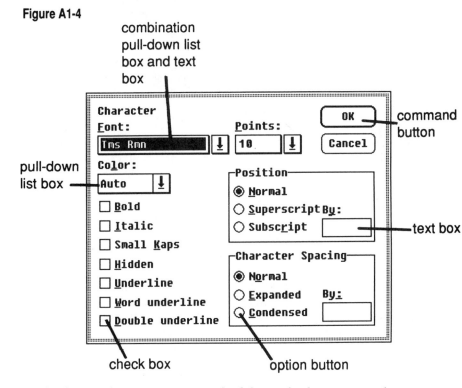

Dialog boxes solicit user input via check boxes, list boxes, option buttons, text boxes, and command buttons.

Alternatively, you can press the [Alt] key in conjunction with the underlined letter in the option you want to choose. (Sometimes, you can just press the underlined letter by itself to make the selection; if you're in a text box when you make a selection, however, you'll need to press the [Alt] key along with the letter.) If the option you select is a list box, you'll then need to use the ↑ and ↓ keys to choose between the options in that list box. We'll discuss list boxes in a moment.

As we've mentioned, dialog boxes can include a combination of check boxes, option buttons, text boxes, list boxes, and command buttons. Let's take a look at these five elements.

Types of dialog box elements

Check boxes

A check box lets you turn a particular dialog box option on or off. To select a check-box option with the mouse, point and click either inside the check box or on the check box's name. An *X* will appear inside the check box to indicate that you've turned that option on. To deselect a check-box option, choose that option a second time. The *X* will then disappear, indicating that you've turned the option off.

To select a check-box option using the keyboard, you can use either of two techniques. First, you can hold down the [Alt] key while you type the underlined letter in the check-box option name. Alternatively, you can first use the [Tab] key to activate the check box (a dotted-line highlight will surround the check-box option to indicate that it is currently activated). Once you've activated the option, you can turn it on or off by pressing the [Spacebar].

Sometimes, a check box will be filled with gray shading. Shading indicates that you've applied that check-box option to some (but not all) of the highlighted areas in the document. If you want to apply the option to all highlighted areas in the document, choose that option. Word will indicate that the option will be applied to the entire highlighted area by placing an *X* in the check box. To remove the option from all highlighted areas in the document, select that option a second time to remove the *X*. Selecting the option a third time will cause shading to reappear in the check box.

Option buttons

Option buttons let you choose a single option from a group of options, much as you'd choose one answer to a question on a multiple-choice exam. For example, the dialog box in Figure A1-4 presents three option buttons in its lower-right corner that let you choose among three types of character spacing: Normal, Expanded, and Condensed. As you can see, the Normal option button—the default selection for this dialog box—is already selected. To select a different option button with the mouse, click on either the button or the button's name. The highlight will then move from the old button to the new one.

To select an option button using the keyboard, you can use either of two techniques. First, you can hold down the [Alt] key while you press the underlined letter in the option button's name. Alternatively, you can first activate the option button area by pressing the [Tab] key until a dotted-line highlight surrounds the option button. Once you've activated the option button area, use the ↑ and ↓ keys to select the option button of your choice.

You may be wondering why some options are depicted by option buttons while others are depicted by check boxes. Here's why: Option buttons are used for groups of options that are mutually exclusive. When you select an option from a group, the previously selected option will become deselected. Check-box options, however, are independent of other options in the dialog box.

Text boxes allow you to answer a dialog box's "fill-in-the-blank" questions. **Text boxes** For instance, to search for a particular phrase in a Word document, you issue the Search… command on the Edit menu and type the phrase you want to locate in the Search For text box.

To make an entry into a text box, first press the [Tab] key repeatedly until you've activated that text box. When you use the keyboard to activate a text box that contains an entry, the text box's entry will appear in inverse type. At this point, you can type a new entry that will replace the existing entry. If, however, you use the keyboard to activate an empty text box, a blinking cursor will appear at the text box's left edge. Any new characters you type will now appear just after the cursor inside the text box.

Activating a text box with the mouse is trickier than activating a text box with the keyboard. When you move the mouse pointer inside the boundaries of the text box, the familiar arrow will change to resemble the shape of an I-beam. If you press the mouse button while the I-beam is inside the text box, a blinking cursor will appear at the I-beam's position. Word will then insert the characters you type just after the cursor inside the text box.

To highlight an existing entry in a text box with the mouse, first position the I-beam at the left edge of the text box. Next, press and hold the mouse button while you drag the I-beam across the characters inside that text box. As you drag across the characters, their appearance will change from normal type to inverse type. After you've highlighted the appropriate characters, any new entry you type will replace the highlighted characters in the text box.

Like option buttons, list boxes let you choose a single option from a group **List boxes** of options. However, Windows uses list boxes instead of option buttons when one of three conditions exist: when you must select one option from a large list of options; when the list of options is dynamic; or when Windows needs to conserve space in the dialog box. You'll encounter two types of list boxes in a dialog box: standard and pull-down.

Consider the dialog box shown in Figure A1-5 on the following page, which appears when you issue Word's Open… command. This dialog box lets you specify the file you want to open by using either the Open File Name text box or the Files and Directories list boxes.

To select an option from a list box with the mouse, simply click on the appropriate option. To make a selection with the keyboard, first press the [Tab] key repeatedly until you've activated the appropriate list box. At this point, a dotted-line highlight will appear around one of the entries in the list. Now, you can use the ↑ and ↓ keys to highlight the appropriate option in the list.

Since list boxes cannot always display the entire list of options at once, you'll sometimes need to use the scroll bars along the right side of the box to find the option you want to choose. There are several ways to scroll through a list box with the scroll bars. If you are using a mouse, you can scroll down the list one line at a time by clicking on the arrows at the top and bottom of the scroll bars. As you move up or down through the list, the white rectangle in the scroll bar (called the scroll box) will move up or down to indicate your relative position in the list. When you reach the bottom of the list, the scroll box will appear at the very bottom of the scroll bar.

Figure A1-5

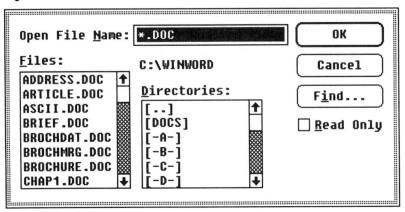

You'll use the list boxes in Word's Open dialog box to specify a file name.

Although scrolling through the list line by line is fine for relatively small lists, you'll find that it is painstakingly slow for large lists. Fortunately, there are two other scrolling methods you can use to move through the list more quickly. First, you can move up or down a boxful at a time by clicking between the scroll box and the top or bottom edge of the scroll bar. Alternatively, you can point to the scroll box, hold down the mouse button, then drag the scroll box to the appropriate location in the scroll bar. When you release the mouse button, the list will immediately scroll to the position that is indicated by the scroll box in the scroll bar.

To scroll through a list box with the keyboard, you can use the ↑ and ↓ keys to move up and down the list one line at a time. Alternatively, you can use the [Page Up] and [Page Down] keys to scroll through the list a boxful at a time. To move to the bottom of the list, press the [End] key. To move to the top of the list, press the [Home] key.

Sometimes, a dialog box will contain a combination list and text box. In these instances, you can change the dialog box's current setting either by making a new entry in the text box or by selecting a new item from the list box. In either case, the entry in the text box will change to reflect the dialog box's new setting.

Pull-down list boxes serve the same purpose as standard list boxes: They let you choose a single option from a large, dynamic list. Unlike standard list boxes, however, a pull-down list box does not appear on the screen at all times. Instead, you'll see only a text box containing the list box's current setting, along with the special pull-down symbol, 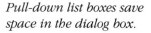. To display the options in a pull-down list box, you must "pull down" the list.

The dialog box shown in Figure A1-4 contains three pull-down list boxes: Font, Points, and Color. You can pull down any of these list boxes with the mouse by pointing and clicking on the appropriate pull-down symbol. For example, if you point and click on the pull-down symbol next to the Font text box in Figure A1-4, the Font list box will drop down, as shown in Figure A1-6.

Pull-down list boxes

Figure A1-6

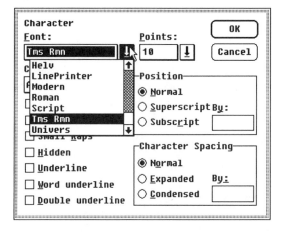

Pull-down list boxes save space in the dialog box.

To pull down a list box using the keyboard, first use the [Tab] key to activate the text box next to the pull-down symbol. Next, hold down the [Alt] key and press the ↓ key. Word will then display the pull-down list box.

Once you've accessed a pull-down list box, you can make selections exactly as you would from a standard list box. When you make a selection from the list, the list box will disappear and your new selection will appear in the box next to the pull-down symbol. If you pull down a pull-down list box by mistake, activate a different area of the dialog box to move out of the list box.

The last dialog box elements we'll discuss are command buttons. The dialog box in Figure A1-5 contains three command buttons: OK, Cancel, and Find…. The OK and Cancel command buttons appear in nearly every dialog box. The OK command button closes the dialog box and carries out the selected command; the Cancel command button closes the dialog box without carrying out the command.

Command buttons

To select the OK command button, either use the mouse to click on it or press the [Enter] key. (The thick outline around the OK button indicates that this is the option that will be selected when you press [Enter]. In other dialog boxes, other buttons may be outlined.) To select the Cancel command button, use the mouse to click on it or press the [Esc] key.

Like the Find... command button in Figure A1-5, some command button names are followed by an ellipsis. Selecting these kinds of buttons opens a new dialog box. In some cases, the button will close the first dialog box before opening the second; in other cases, it will keep the first dialog box open along with the second dialog box. Typically, when you close the second dialog box, you'll return to the first dialog box, where you can continue making selections. As you might expect, you can select a button of this type either by using the mouse to click on the button or by holding down the [Alt] key and typing the underlined letter in the button's name.

Sometimes, a command button will be labeled *Options >>*. When you choose an Options >> button, the dialog box will expand to display additional options.

In our discussions throughout the book, we'll often refer to a command button simply as a button. For instance, we might instruct you to "choose the Options >> button" or "the Cancel button." In addition, we'll typically instruct you to "choose OK" rather than to "choose the OK command button." We think you'll find these conventions make our explanations more readable.

Message boxes

You'll sometimes see another kind of dialog box, called a message box. Figure A1-7 shows the message box that appears when you try to save a document under an invalid file name. Message boxes contain information, warnings, and prompts for further information. They also contain buttons that you use to acknowledge a warning or message, cancel an operation, or issue further instructions. You choose the buttons in message boxes just as you do in dialog boxes.

Figure A1-7

Message boxes are special dialog boxes that contain information, warnings, and prompts for further information.

SIZING AND MOVING WINDOWS

As we mentioned, Microsoft Word for Windows runs in its own window. Additionally, each document appears in its own window. In this section, we'll show you how to size and move these windows with both the keyboard and the mouse.

By default, both the Microsoft Word window and your document window are maximized, which means that Windows expands them to fill a maximum area of the screen. If you're like most Word users, you'll typically want to leave your windows maximized so you can see more of each document on the screen at once. If you want, however, you can restore a maximized or minimized window to the size of a standard, non-maximized window. To restore the Microsoft Word window in Figure A1-1, use the mouse to click on the Restore box (▣) on the right side of the Microsoft Word title bar. Alternatively, you can click twice in succession (called *double-clicking*) anywhere on Word's title bar. When you restore the Microsoft Word window, it will look like Figure A1-8.

Restoring a maximized window

Figure A1-8

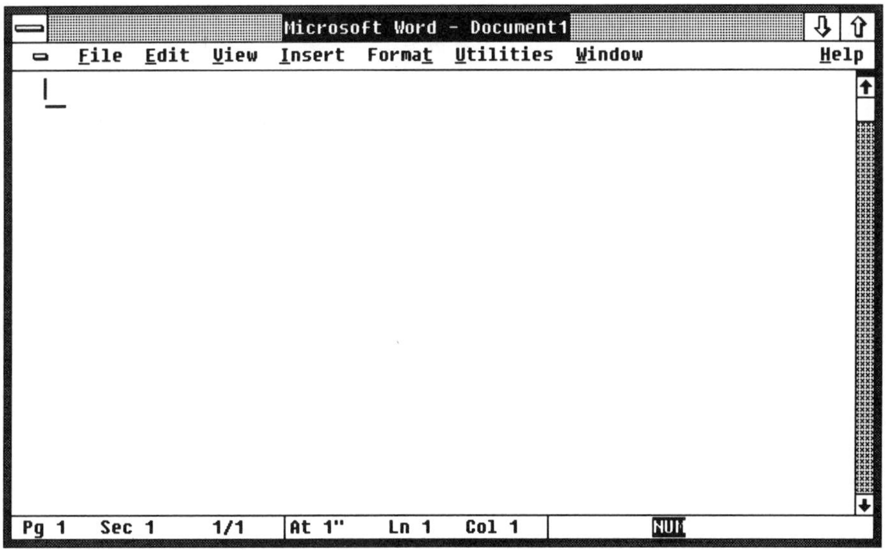

Word will reduce the size of the Microsoft Word window when you click on its Restore box.

To restore the Microsoft Word window using the keyboard, first bring up its Control menu by holding down the [Alt] key and pressing the [Spacebar]. When the Control menu appears, select the Restore command. Alternatively, you can restore the window by pressing [Alt][F5].

Notice that a gray border surrounds the Microsoft Word window in Figure A1-8. This border defines the area of the screen in which Word is running and allows you to use your mouse to resize the window. We'll show you how to do this in a moment.

Now that we've restored the Microsoft Word window, let's restore the Document1 window as well. To do this, you must use the document's Control menu, which is located on the left side of the menu bar. If you're using a mouse, click on the document's Control-menu box to pull down the menu, then select the Restore command. If you're using the keyboard, press the [Alt][hyphen] key combination to pull down the document's Control menu, then choose the Restore command. When you do this, the document window will look like the one shown in Figure A1-9.

Figure A1-9

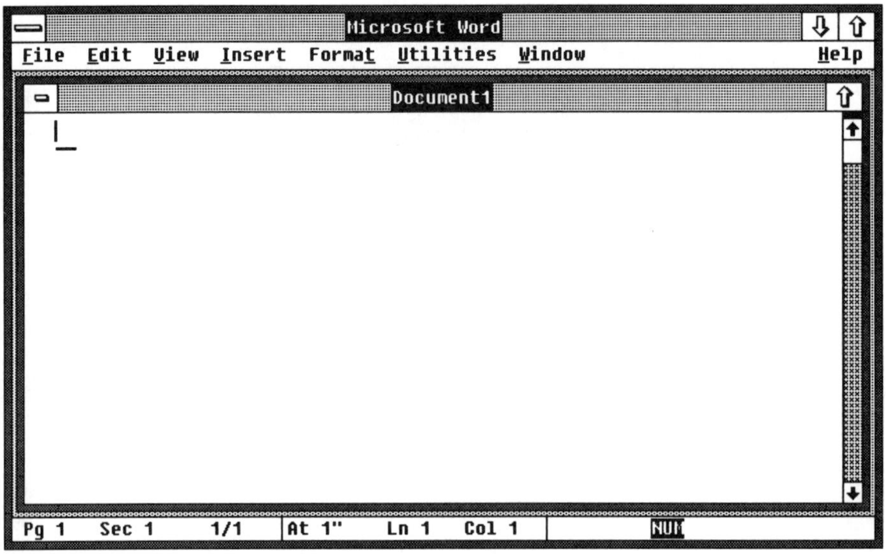

You can manipulate the Microsoft Word window and a document window independently.

Notice that the document now appears within its own window, complete with a title bar, Control-menu box, Maximize box, and window border. In addition, notice that the name of the document, *Document1,* has moved from the Microsoft Word window's title bar to the document's title bar, and that the document's Control-menu box no longer appears on the menu bar.

Maximizing a window

Now that you've seen how to restore a window, let's learn how to maximize it. If you're using a mouse, you can do this either by clicking on the window's Maximize box (the ⬆ symbol on the right side of the title bar) or by double-clicking on the title bar. For instance, if you click on the Maximize box in the document's title bar, your screen will once again look like Figure A1-8.

To maximize a document window with the keyboard, bring up the document's Control menu by pressing [Alt][hyphen], use the ↓ key to highlight the Maximize command, and press [Enter]. (Alternatively, you can use the [Ctrl][F10] key combination, as indicated on the right side of the Control menu.)

When you maximize the document window, the document's Control-menu box will return to the menu bar and the document's name will move to the title bar in the Microsoft Word window.

If you want to maximize the Microsoft Word window using the mouse, point and click on the window's Maximize box or double-click anywhere inside Word's title bar. To do the same with the keyboard, select the Maximize command from the window's Control menu or press the [Alt][F10] key combination. As you would expect, maximizing the Microsoft Word window allows it to fill the entire screen and causes Word to replace the Maximize box with a Restore box.

As we said earlier, you'll typically want to leave both your Microsoft Word and document windows maximized so that you can see more of your document on the screen at once.

Minimizing a program window

To minimize a program window (such as the Microsoft Word window) with the mouse, click on the Minimize box (the ⬇ symbol on the right side of the window's title bar). To do the same with the keyboard, bring up the window's Control menu by pressing [Alt][Spacebar], use the ↓ key to highlight the Minimize command, and press [Enter]. (Alternatively, you can press [Alt][F9], as indicated on the right side of the Control menu.) Figure A1-10 on the next page shows the screen that results when you minimize the Microsoft Word window.

As you can see, minimizing the Microsoft Word window transforms it into a W-shaped icon that lies in the lower-left corner of the screen. This icon includes a label describing the application and the active document, if there is one. If you minimize other applications in addition to Microsoft Word for Windows, those applications will appear in a different shape along the bottom edge of the screen. For instance, if you're using a full-featured version of Windows, a disk-shaped icon representing the MS-DOS Executive window will appear next to the Microsoft Word icon at the bottom of the screen.

Restoring a minimized window

To return the minimized Microsoft Word window in Figure A1-10 to its former size, you can double-click on the Word icon. Alternatively, you can click once on the Word icon to bring up the Control menu, then click on the Restore command. After you restore the Word window, the screen will once again look like the one shown in Figure A1-9.

To restore a minimized window with the keyboard, first bring up Word's Control menu by holding down the [Alt] key and pressing the [Spacebar]. When the Control menu appears, use the ↓ key to highlight the Restore command, and press [Enter]. Alternatively, you can restore the Word window by pressing [Alt][F5].

Figure A1-10

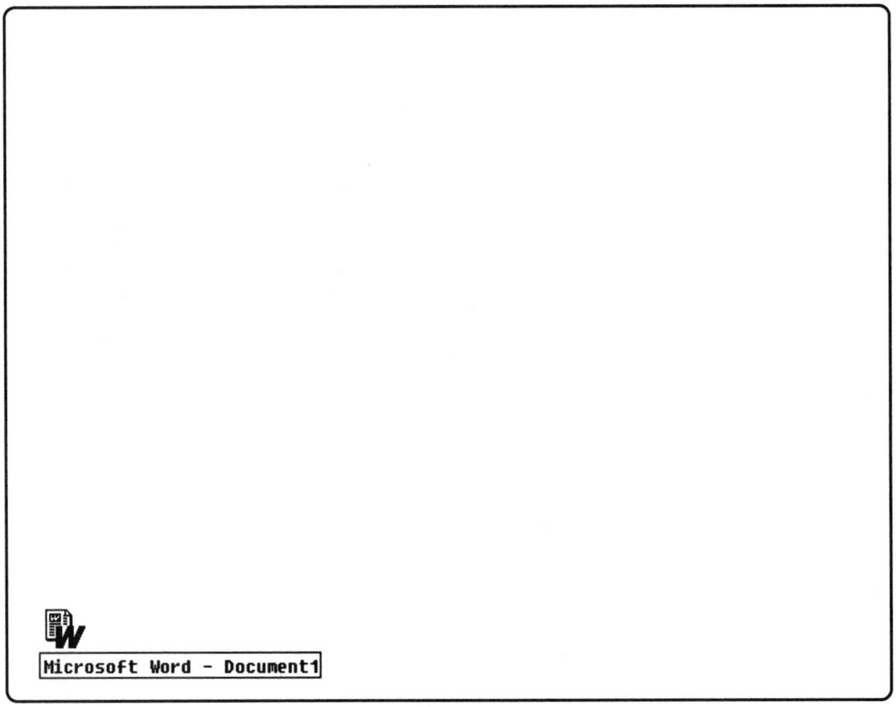

Microsoft Word - Document1

When you minimize the Microsoft Word window, a small Microsoft Word icon will appear in the lower-left corner of the screen.

Manually sizing a window

So far, we've shown you how to completely fill the screen with a window and transform a window into an icon. Now, let's learn how to manually change the height and width of a window.

To resize a window using the mouse, first position the mouse pointer on the border (or corner) you want to move. When you do this, the mouse pointer will change into a double-headed sizing pointer. At this point, hold down the mouse button and drag the border in the direction you want it to go. When you've moved the border to the desired position, release the mouse button.

For example, suppose you want to change the size of the Microsoft Word window in Figure A1-9 so that it occupies only the upper-left corner of the screen. To do this, first position the mouse pointer on the lower-right corner of the window's border. When you do this, the mouse pointer will change into a double-headed sizing pointer. Next, hold down the mouse button and drag the pointer toward the upper-left corner of the screen. When you've reduced the border to the size shown in Figure A1-11, release the mouse button.

Figure A1-11

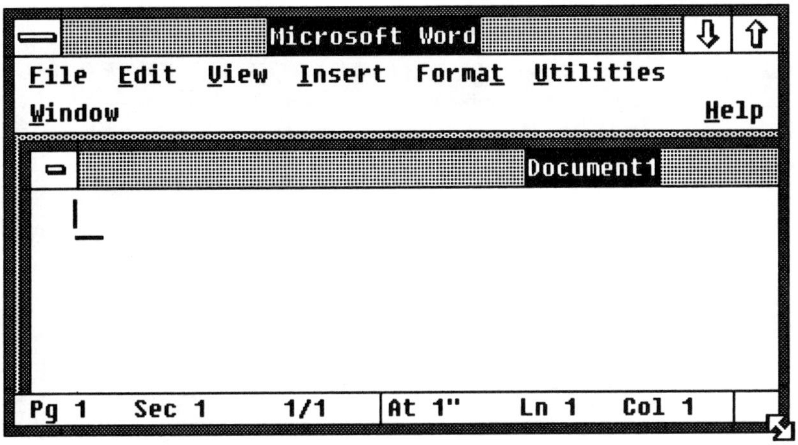

You can manually size a window by dragging the border to the appropriate location on the screen.

To resize a window with the keyboard, first select the Size command from the window's Control menu. A four-headed sizing pointer will then appear in the center of the window, as shown in Figure A1-12 on the next page. Next, press one of the arrow keys to move the sizing pointer to one of the window's four sides. When you do, the four-headed sizing pointer will move to the side you selected and change to a double-headed sizing pointer. If you want to move a corner of the window instead of a single side, press another arrow key after you activate a side to move the double-headed sizing pointer to the desired corner. Once you've activated the appropriate side or corner, use the arrow keys to move the border. To complete the resizing procedure, press [Enter]. If you decide you don't want to resize the window after you've moved the border, just press [Esc].

In addition to moving a window's borders, you can move the entire window. To do this with the mouse, point anywhere on the window's title bar, hold down the mouse button, drag the window to the desired location on the screen, then release the mouse button.

To move a window using the keyboard, first choose the Move command from the window's Control menu. You'll then see a four-headed sizing pointer at the top of the window. At this point, use the arrow keys to move the window around on the screen. When you've repositioned the window, press [Enter] to complete the procedure. If you decide you don't want to reposition the window after you've already moved it, press [Esc].

Moving windows

Figure A1-12

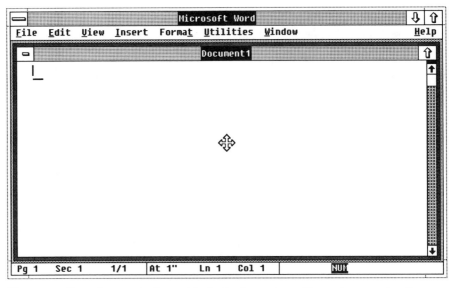

To manually resize a window with the keyboard, you'll need to use the Size command on the window's Control menu.

As an example of how to manually size and move document windows, consider the screen shown in Figure A1-13, which contains two document windows arranged side by side. To create these windows, begin by dragging the right border of the Document2 window to the left until the window fills half the screen vertically. Next, click in the Document3 window and use the same technique to reduce that window to half size. At this point, the two windows will overlap. Finally, click on the title bar of the Document3 window and drag to the right until the two windows appear side by side.

The active document window

Earlier, we mentioned that you can have several program windows open on your screen at once, but that only one program window can be active. As you might guess, the same is true for document windows. The active document window on your screen is the one in which you are currently working. Any commands you issue will apply to the window that is active at the time.

If you've maximized your document windows, the active window is the only document window you can see on the screen. If you haven't maximized your document windows, however, the active document window will appear on top of the "stack" of document windows and will have a unique color in its title bar. For example, notice that Document2 in Figure A1-13 has a white title bar. This is because Document2 is inactive, while Document3 is active.

Figure A1-13

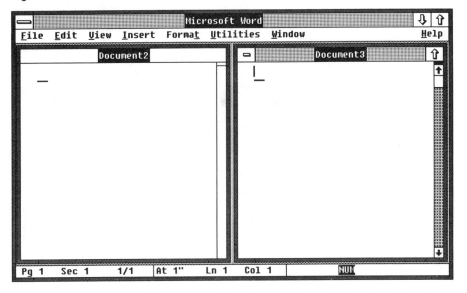

You can create non-overlapping windows by resizing and dragging the windows manually.

In order to edit or make changes to a document, you must first activate its window. To do this, either click on the window with the mouse or select the window name from the Window menu. If you've maximized your document windows, you'll have to use the Window menu, since you won't be able to see the inactive windows.

If you want, you can split a document window into panes to see two portions of your document at the same time. For example, imagine you are writing a sales report and you have presented a table of statistics at the beginning of the document. If you want to refer to these statistics later in the document, you can split your document into two panes rather than scroll back and forth to check the contents of your table. This way, you can keep the table in view as you write the body of your report. You can scroll the two panes independently and even copy data from one pane to the other.

Splitting a window

To split a window into panes, point to the black box (called the split box) that appears above the vertical scroll bar on the right side of the document window. (You'll notice that the pointer changes shape when you place it on the split box.) Now, click and drag the split box downward. When you do, a horizontal line called the split bar will appear in the window and will move up and down with your mouse. When the split bar appears in the desired position, release the mouse button. As you can see in Figure A1-14, Word now gives you two sets of vertical scroll bars to let you move through the two window panes independently. To remove the split bar from your window, just click on it and drag it past either end of the vertical scroll bar.

Figure A1-14

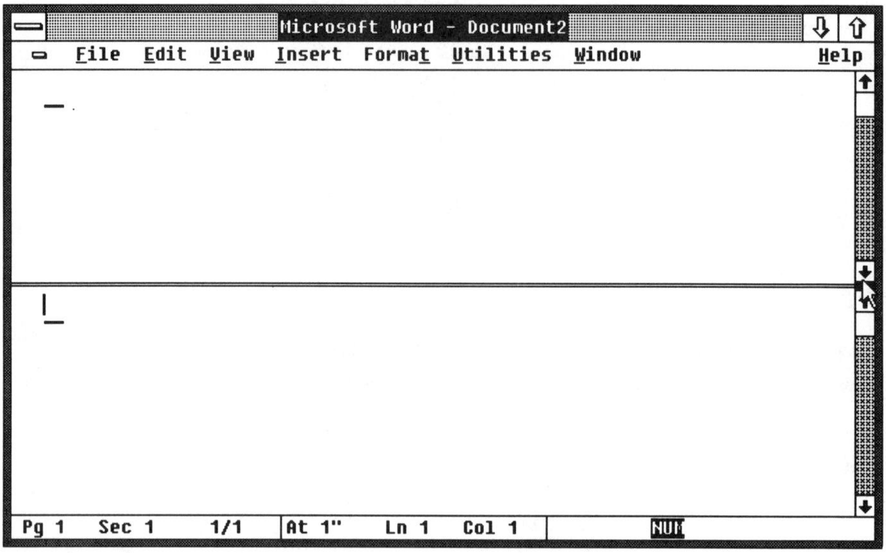

You can use the split bar to split a document window into two panes.

The New Window command

In addition to the split-screen technique, Word offers multiple-windowing capabilities for a single document. By creating multiple windows, you can see different parts of the same document at the same time. This is particularly convenient when you are working with very large documents and you want to see several blocks of text simultaneously.

To create a new document window, just select New Window from the Window menu. For example, if you select New Window while the Document1 window is active, Word will display a new window entitled *Document1:2*. It will also rename your original window *Document1:1*. Subsequent windows will be entitled *Document1:3*, *Document1:4*, and so forth.

Keep in mind that each window is just another porthole through which you can view a single document. Any changes you make in one window will affect the entire document—not just the portion you see in the active window.

The Arrange All command

If you want to view several non-overlapping document windows on your screen, you might be tempted to size and move the windows to make them fit on the screen. Instead of using manual techniques, you can use the Arrange All command on the Window menu to quickly arrange your document windows. When you issue this command, Word will resize and move your document windows to take full advantage of the available space on your screen. Figure A1-15 shows how the Arrange All command will organize your screen if you've opened three document windows.

Figure A1-15

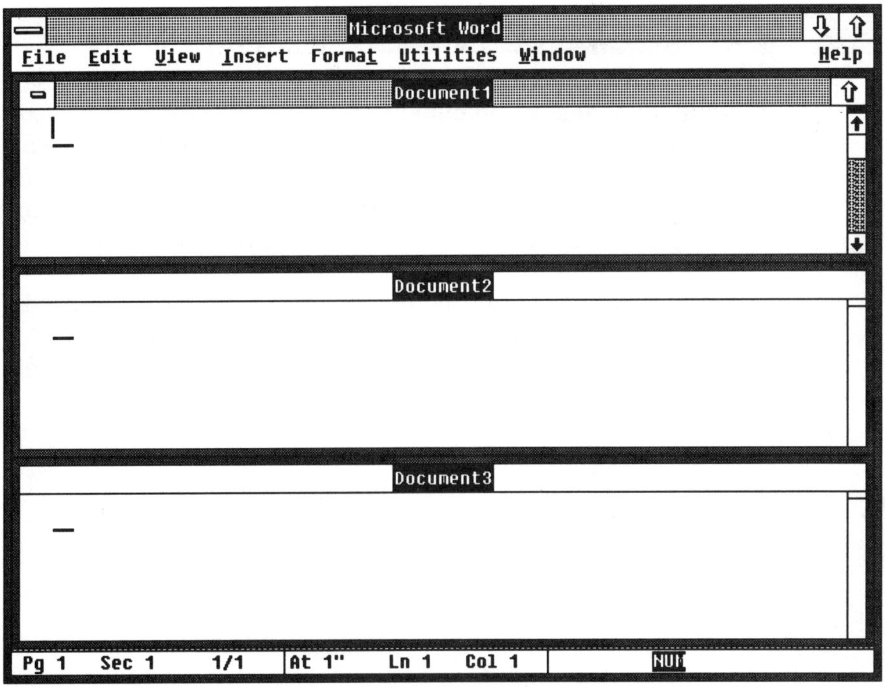

The Arrange All command arranges multiple document windows for you automatically.

Closing windows

After you're finished using a document or an application, you can close its window and remove it from the screen. You'll use the window's Control menu to perform the closing procedure.

To close a window using the mouse, bring up the Control menu by clicking on the window's Control-menu box, then click on the Close command. Alternatively, you can close a window with the mouse by double-clicking on the Control-menu box.

To close a window using the keyboard, bring up the Control menu by pressing either [Alt][Spacebar] (for a program window) or [Alt][hyphen] (for a document window), then choose the Close command.

If you close the only window that is open for a particular document, Word will present a message box like the one shown in Figure A1-16. (You can easily tell if only one window is open for a document since the notation identifying multiple windows will not appear.) We discussed closing and saving document files in Chapter 3.

Figure A1-16

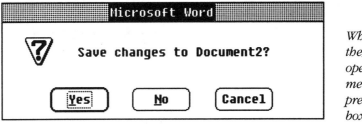

When you close the only window open for a document, Word will present a message box like this.

If you close the Microsoft Word window, you'll see a message box like the one in Figure A1-16 for every document that is currently open. After responding to each message box, the Microsoft Word window will close, ending your current Word for Windows session.

POINTER ICONS

I-beam pointer

Left-arrow pointer

Right-arrow pointer

Hourglass shape

Crosshair pointer

Horizontal split pointer

Vertical split pointer

Downward-pointing arrow

Double-headed sizing pointers

Four-headed sizing pointer

Four-headed outline pointer

Vertical outline pointer

Horizontal outline pointer

"Finger-pointing" hand

Arrow/question mark pointer

**DOCUMENT
WINDOW ICONS**

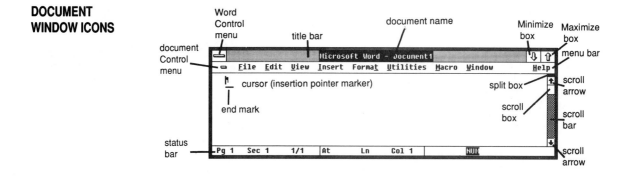

RULER ICONS

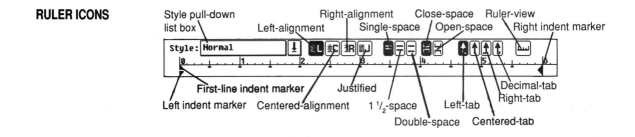

RIBBON ICONS

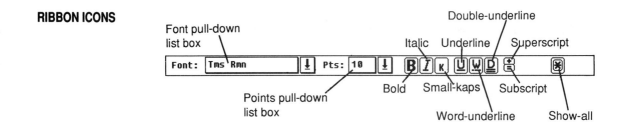

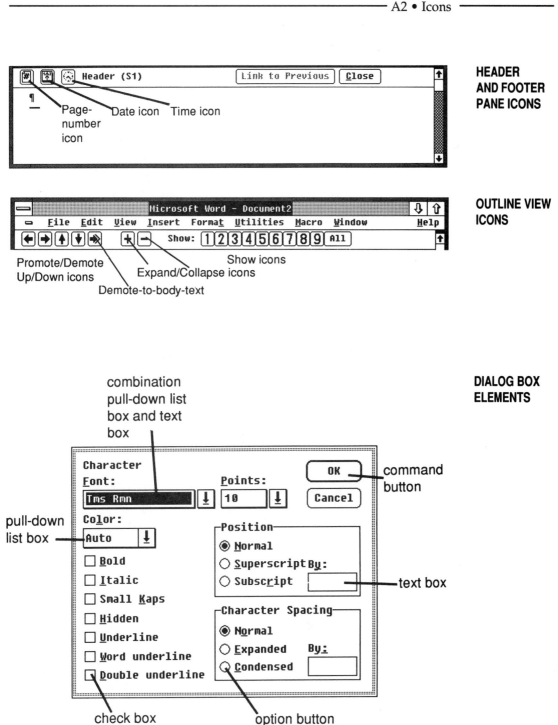

HEADER AND FOOTER PANE ICONS

Page-number icon
Date icon
Time icon

OUTLINE VIEW ICONS

Promote/Demote Up/Down icons
Demote-to-body-text
Expand/Collapse icons
Show icons

DIALOG BOX ELEMENTS

combination pull-down list box and text box

pull-down list box

command button

text box

check box

option button

Keyboard and Mouse Techniques *A3*

*I*n this appendix, we'll provide a comprehensive list of the keyboard and mouse techniques we've mentioned throughout the book. You might want to photocopy these pages and keep them near your computer to help you work more efficiently in Word.

Open a menu	Click on menu name or press [Alt] and menu's key letter	**MENUS**
Open adjacent menu	Press → or ←	
Close a menu	Click outside menu or press [Esc]	
Highlight next or previous command on a menu	Press ↓ or ↑	
Issue a command	Click on command name, open menu and press command's key letter, or open menu, highlight command and press [Enter]	
Activate next element	Press [Tab]	**DIALOG BOXES**
Activate previous element	Press [Shift][Tab]	
Activate particular element	Press [Alt] plus key letter	
Close dialog box with its new settings	Press [Enter] or click on OK	
Close dialog box and cancel command	Press [Esc] or click on Cancel	
Toggle a check box	Click on check box, press [Alt] plus key letter, or activate check box and press [Spacebar]	**Check boxes**

Option buttons	Select an option button	Click on button
	Select next option button	Press ↓ or →
	Select previous option button	Press ↑ or ←
List boxes	Pull down a list box	Click on ↓ or activate list box and press [Alt]↓
	Select an item	Click on item
	Select next item	Press ↓ or →
	Select previous item	Press ↑ or ←
	Select first item	Press [Home]
	Select last item	Press [End]
	Scroll to next windowful	Click below scroll box or press [Page Down]
	Scroll to previous windowful	Click above scroll box or press [Page Up]
	Move to first item beginning with a particular letter	Type the letter
Text boxes	Move cursor into text box	Click on text box or press [Alt] and key letter
Command buttons	Select a button	Click on button or activate button and press [Enter]
	Choose OK button	Press [Enter]
	Choose Cancel button	Press [Esc]
NAVIGATING	Moving the cursor	Click on new cursor position
	Move up or down one line	Press ↑ or ↓
	Move left or right one character	Press ← or →
	Move left or right one word	Press [Ctrl]← or [Ctrl]→
	Move up or down one paragraph	Press [Ctrl]↑ or [Ctrl]↓
	Move to beginning of line	Press [Home]
	Move to end of line	Press [End]
	Move to beginning of screen	Press [Ctrl][Page Up]
	Move to end of screen	Press [Ctrl][Page Down]
	Move to beginning of document	Press [Ctrl][Home]
	Move to end of document	Press [Ctrl][End]
	Move to previous location	Press [Shift][F5]
	Move to next pane	Press [F6]
	Move to previous pane	Press [Shift][F6]
	Move to next field	Press [F11]
	Move to previous field	Press [Shift][F11]

Move to next document window	Press [Ctrl][F6] or [Alt][F6]
Move to previous document window	Press [Ctrl][Shift][F6] or [Alt][Shift][F6]
Move to next text area	Press [Alt]↓
Move to previous text area	Press [Alt]↑
Scroll down one line	Click on down arrow in vertical scroll bar
Scroll up one line	Click on up arrow in vertical scroll bar
Scroll down one windowful	Click below scroll box or press [Page Down]
Scroll up one windowful	Click above scroll box or press [Page Up]

SELECTING TEXT

Select a block of text	Click and drag over text
Select characters or lines	Press [Shift] and cursor-movement keys
Select word	Double-click on word or move cursor to word and press [F8] twice
Select sentence	Press [Ctrl] and click on sentence or move cursor to sentence and press [F8] three times
Select line	Click next to line in selection bar
Select paragraph	Double-click next to paragraph in selection bar or move cursor to paragraph and press [F8] four times
Select column	Click right mouse button next to first character in column and drag to lower-right corner, or press [Ctrl][Shift][F8] and use arrow keys to move to opposite corner
Select document	Press [Ctrl] and click in selection bar, press [Ctrl]5 (use the numeric keypad), or press [F8] five times
Select a large block of text	Click at beginning of block, release mouse button, press [Shift], and click at end of block
Select a picture	Click on picture

EDITING KEYS

Delete selected text	Press [Delete] (or [Backspace] if you've selected Typing Replaces Selection in Customize dialog box)
Delete character to right of cursor	Press [Delete]
Delete character to left of cursor	Press [Backspace]

Delete word to right of cursor	Press [Ctrl][Delete]
Delete word to left of cursor	Press [Ctrl][Backspace]
Cut selected text	Press [Shift][Delete]
Copy selected text	Press [Ctrl][Insert]
Paste text	Press [Shift][Insert]
Copy character format	Highlight text to format, press [Ctrl][Shift], and click on source character
Copy paragraph format	Highlight paragraph to format, press [Ctrl][Shift], and click in selection bar next to source paragraph
Hyphen	Press [hyphen]
Non-breaking hyphen	Press [Ctrl][hyphen]
Optional hyphen	Press [Ctrl][Shift][hyphen]
Non-breaking space	Press [Ctrl][Shift][Spacebar]
Tab	Press [Tab]
New line	Press [Shift][Enter]
New paragraph	Press [Enter]
New page	Press [Ctrl][Enter]
New column	Press [Ctrl][Shift][Enter]

CHARACTER FORMATTING KEYS

Return to character formatting in applied style	Press [Ctrl][Spacebar]
Turn on display of all special marks and field codes	Press [Ctrl]*
Bold	Press [Ctrl]B
Italic	Press [Ctrl]I
Small kaps	Press [Ctrl]K
Change font	Press [Ctrl]F
Change point size	Press [Ctrl]P
Double underline	Press [Ctrl]D
Continuous underline	Press [Ctrl]U
Word underline	Press [Ctrl]W
Superscript	Press [Ctrl]+
Subscript	Press [Ctrl]=
Next largest point size	Press [Ctrl][F2]
Next smallest point size	Press [Ctrl][Shift][F2]
Change case of letters	Press [Shift][F3]
Hide text	Press [Ctrl]H
Strikethrough	Press [Ctrl]Z

PARAGRAPH FORMATTING KEYS

Single-spacing	Press [Ctrl]1
Double-spacing	Press [Ctrl]2
1 $1/2$-spacing	Press [Ctrl]5
Open space before	Press [Ctrl]O
Close space before	Press [Ctrl]E
Return to paragraph formatting of applied style	Press [Ctrl]X

Center paragraph	Press [Ctrl]C
Justify paragraph	Press [Ctrl]J
Left-align paragraph	Press [Ctrl]L
Right-align paragraph	Press [Ctrl]R
Indent paragraph from left	Press [Ctrl]N
Reduce left indent by one tab	Press [Ctrl]M
Create hanging indent	Press [Ctrl]T
Reduce hanging indent by one tab	Press [Ctrl]G
Apply a different style	Press [Ctrl]S
Apply *Normal* style	Press [Alt][Shift]5

Activate and deactivate the ruler	Press [Ctrl][Shift][F10]	**RULER MODE KEYS**
Move the ruler cursor left or right $1/_8$ inch	Press ← or →	
Move the ruler cursor left or right 1 inch	Press [Ctrl]← or [Ctrl]→	
Move the ruler cursor left of the ruler's zero point	Press [Shift]←	
Move the ruler cursor to the ruler's zero point	Press [Home]	
Move the ruler cursor to the right edge of text area	Press [End]	
Set the left indent to the ruler cursor position	Press L	
Set the right indent to the ruler cursor position	Press R	
Set the first-line indent to the ruler cursor position	Press F	
Select left alignment for subsequently set tabs	Press 1	
Select center alignment for subsequently set tabs	Press 2	
Select right alignment for subsequently set tabs	Press 3	
Select decimal alignment for subsequently set tabs	Press 4	
Set a tab at the ruler cursor position	Press [Insert]	
Delete tab at the ruler cursor position	Press [Delete]	
Apply the new ruler settings to the selected paragraphs and deactivate ruler	Press [Enter]	
Cancel the new ruler settings and deactivate ruler	Press [Esc]	

FIELD KEYS

Insert field	Press [Ctrl][F9]
Update field	Press [F9]
Toggle between field code and field result	Press [Shift][F9]
Replace field with its last result	Press [Ctrl][Shift][F9]
Simulate double-clicking a GOTOBUTTON or MACROBUTTON field	Press [Alt][Shift][F9]
Go to next field	Press [F11]
Go to previous field	Press [Shift][F11]
Lock field's result	Press [Ctrl][F11]
Unlock field	Press [Ctrl][Shift][F11]
Insert DATE field	Press [Alt][Shift]D
Insert TIME field	Press [Alt][Shift]T
Insert PAGE field	Press [Alt][Shift]P

TABLE KEYS

Move to next cell and select it	Press [Tab]
Move to previous cell and select it	Press [Shift][Tab]
Move to first cell in row	Press [Alt][Home]
Move to last cell in row	Press [Alt][End]
Move to top cell in column	Press [Alt][Page Up]
Move to bottom cell in column	Press [Alt][Page Down]
Select entire table	Press [Alt]5 (use 5 on the numeric keypad)

OUTLINE VIEW KEYS

Promote selection	Press [Alt][Shift]←
Demote selection	Press [Alt][Shift]→
Demote to body text	Press [Alt][Shift]5 (use 5 on the numeric keypad)
Move selection up	Press [Alt][Shift]↑
Move selection down	Press [Alt][Shift]↓
Show first line in body text paragraphs	Press [Alt][Shift]F
Show heading level 1 entries	Press [Alt][Shift]1
Show heading levels 1 through 2	Press [Alt][Shift]2
Show heading levels 1 through 3	Press [Alt][Shift]3
Show heading levels 1 through 4	Press [Alt][Shift]4
Show heading levels 1 through 5	Press [Alt][Shift]5
Show heading levels 1 through 6	Press [Alt][Shift]6
Show heading levels 1 through 7	Press [Alt][Shift]7

Show heading levels 1 through 8	Press [Alt][Shift]8
Show heading levels 1 through 9	Press [Alt][Shift]9
Collapse text under a heading	Press [Alt][Shift][hyphen] or [hyphen] on the numeric keypad
Display text under a heading	Press [Alt][Shift]= or + on the numeric keypad
Show all text and headings	Press [Alt][Shift]A or * on the numeric keypad

[F1]	Get help on currently selected command, open dialog box, or message box	**FUNCTION KEYS**
[Shift][F1]	Get help on a command, key combination, or region of the screen
[Alt][F1]	Go to next field (same as [F11])
[Alt][Shift][F1]	Go to previous field (same as [Shift][F11])
[F2]	Move selected text to a specified position
[Shift][F2]	Copy selected text to a specified position
[Ctrl][F2]	Increase point size
[Ctrl][Shift][F2]	Decrease point size
[Alt][F2]	Save As... (same as [F12])
[Alt][Shift][F2]	Save (same as [Shift][F12])
[F3]	Expand glossary name
[Ctrl][F3]	Copy to spike
[Shift][F3]	Toggle case of letters
[Ctrl][Shift][F3]	Insert from spike
[F4]	Repeat previous command
[Ctrl][F4]	Close active document window
[Alt][F4]	Close application window
[Shift][F4]	Repeat search or Go to
[F5]	Go to
[Ctrl][F5]	Restore document window
[Alt][F5]	Restore application window
[Shift][F5]	Go to previous position
[F6]	Go to next pane
[Ctrl][F6]	Go to next document window
[Shift][F6]	Go to previous pane
[Ctrl][Shift][F6]	Go to previous document window
[F7]	Check spelling of selected text
[Ctrl][F7]	Move document window
[Alt][F7]	Move application window

[Shift][F7]	Thesaurus
[Ctrl][Shift][F7]	Update source for INCLUDE field
[F8]	Extend selection
[Ctrl][F8]	Resize document window
[Alt][F8]	Resize application window
[Shift][F8]	Shrink selection
[Ctrl][Shift][F8]	Column (block) selection
[F9]	Update field
[Ctrl][F9]	Insert field
[Alt][F9]	Minimize application window
[Shift][F9]	Toggle between field code and field result
[Ctrl][Shift][F9]	Replace field with its last result
[Alt][Shift][F9]	Simulate double-clicking a GOTOBUTTON or MACROBUTTON field
[F10]	Activate menu bar
[Ctrl][F10]	Maximize document window
[Alt][F10]	Maximize application window
[Shift][F10]	Activate icon bar
[Ctrl][Shift][F10]	Activate ruler
[F11]	Go to next field
[Ctrl][F11]	Lock field's result
[Shift][F11]	Go to previous field
[Ctrl][Shift][F11]	Unlock field
[F12]	Save As... command
[Ctrl][F12]	Open... command
[Shift][F12]	Save command
[Ctrl][Shift][F12]	Print... command

Fields *A4*

*A*lthough we introduced fields in Chapter 10, we gave a more detailed discussion of several of Word's fields throughout the latter portion of this book. For your convenience, we'll list the forms of Word's fields in this appendix. (Field arguments enclosed in brackets are optional.)

As you know by now, many fields accept various switch arguments, which change the way the fields work or the way Word formats their results. Refer to Chapter 10 for general information on field switches, and use the index to locate detailed discussions of any of the fields listed below.

{GOTOBUTTON *destination buttonText*}   **ACTION FIELDS**
{MACROBUTTON *macroName buttonText*}
{PRINT *printInstructions*}
{FILLIN *prompt*}
{ASK *bookmarkName prompt*}
{EQ *formulaDescription*}

{= *expression*}   **RESULT FIELDS**
{AUTHOR}
{AUTONUM}
{AUTONUMLGL}
{AUTONUMOUT}
{COMMENTS}
{CREATEDATE}
{DATA *dataDocument*}
{DATE}

{DDE *appName filename [place/reference]*}
{DDEAUTO *appName filename [place/reference]*}
{EDITTIME}
{FILENAME}
{GLOSSARY *glossaryTerm*}
{IF *conditionalTest trueResult falseResult*}
{IMPORT *filename*}
{INCLUDE *filename [place/reference]*}
{INDEX}
{INFO *infoType [newEntry]*}
{KEYWORDS}
{LASTSAVEDBY}
{MERGEREC}
{NEXT}
{NEXTIF *conditionalTest*}
{NUMCHARS}
{NUMPAGES}
{NUMWORDS}
{PAGE}
{PAGEREF *bookmark*}
{PRINTDATE}
{QUOTE *literalText*}
{REF *bookmark*}
{REVNUM}
{SAVEDATE}
{SEQ *identifier*}
{SET *bookmarkName text*}
{SKIPIF *conditionalTest*}
{STYLEREF *styleName*}
{SUBJECT}
{TEMPLATE}
{TIME}
{TITLE}
{TOC}

MARKER FIELDS

{XE *term*}
{TC *text*}
{RD *filename*}

ANSI and OEM Codes **A5**

As we explained in Chapter 16, every letter, number, punctuation mark, and other symbol you can enter into a Word document is defined by a decimal code in either the ANSI or OEM character set. Table A5-1 lists all the characters in these sets, along with their associated decimal codes.

Table A5-1

Code	ANSI	OEM	Code	ANSI	OEM
0 - 31			49	1	1
32	(space)	(space)	50	2	2
33	!	!	51	3	3
34	"	"	52	4	4
35	#	#	53	5	5
36	$	$	54	6	6
37	%	%	55	7	7
38	&	&	56	8	8
39	'	'	57	9	9
40	(	(	58	:	:
41	)	)	59	;	;
42	*	*	60	<	<
43	+	+	61	=	=
44	,	,	62	>	>
45	-	-	63	?	?
46	.	.	64	@	@
47	/	/	65	A	A
48	0	0	66	B	B

Code	ANSI	OEM	Code	ANSI	OEM
67	C	C	107	k	k
68	D	D	108	l	l
69	E	E	109	m	m
70	F	F	110	n	n
71	G	G	111	o	o
72	H	H	112	p	p
73	I	I	113	q	q
74	J	J	114	r	r
75	K	K	115	s	s
76	L	L	116	t	t
77	M	M	117	u	u
78	N	N	118	v	v
79	O	O	119	w	w
80	P	P	120	x	x
81	Q	Q	121	y	y
82	R	R	122	z	z
83	S	S	123	{	{
84	T	T	124	|	|
85	U	U	125	}	}
86	V	V	126	~	~
87	W	W	127		
88	X	X	128		Ç
89	Y	Y	129		ü
90	Z	Z	130		é
91	[	[	131		â
92	\	\	132		ä
93	]	]	133		à
94	^	^	134		å
95	_	_	135		ç
96	`	`	136		ê
97	a	a	137		ë
98	b	b	138		è
99	c	c	139		ï
100	d	d	140		î
101	e	e	141		ì
102	f	f	142		Ä
103	g	g	143		Å
104	h	h	144		É
105	i	i	145	'	æ
106	j	j	146	'	Æ

Code	ANSI	OEM	Code	ANSI	OEM
147	"	ô	187	»	
148	"	ö	188	¼	
149	o	ò	189	½	
150	—	û	190	¾	
151	–	ù	191	¿	
152		ÿ	192	À	
153		Ö	193	Á	
154		Ü	194	Â	
155		¢	195	Ã	
156		£	196	Ä	
157		¥	197	Å	
158		₽	198	Æ	
159		ƒ	199	Ç	
160		á	200	È	
161	¡	í	201	É	
162	¢	ó	202	Ê	
163	£	ú	203	Ë	
164	¤	ñ	204	Ì	
165	¥	Ñ	205	Í	
166	¦	ª	206	Î	
167	§	º	207	Ï	
168	¨	¿	208	Ð	
169	©		209	Ñ	
170	ª	¬	210	Ò	
171	«	½	211	Ó	
172	¬	¼	212	Ô	
173	-	¡	213	Õ	
174	®	«	214	Ö	
175	¯	»	215	×	
176	°		216	Ø	
177	±		217	Ù	
178	²		218	Ú	
179	³	¦	219	Û	
180	´		220	Ü	
181	µ		221	Ý	¦
182	¶		222	Þ	
183	·		223	ß	
184	¸		224	à	
185	¹		225	á	ß
186	º		226	â	

Code	ANSI	OEM		Code	ANSI	OEM
227	ã	¶		242	ò	
228	ä			243	ó	
229	å			244	ô	
230	æ	µ		245	õ	
231	ç			246	ö	
232	è			247	÷	
233	é			248	ø	°
234	ê			249	ù	·
235	ë			250	ú	·
236	ì			251	û	
237	í			252	ü	n
238	î			253	ý	2
239	ï			254	þ	¨
240	ð			255	ÿ	
241	ñ	±				

If you used the Word for Windows Setup program to install either a PCL LaserJet or PostScript printer, you can install the Symbol soft font. Table A5-2 shows you how all the characters in both the ANSI and OEM character sets appear when assigned the Symbol font.

Table A5-2

Code	ANSI	OEM		Code	ANSI	OEM
0 - 32				48	0	0
33	!	!		49	1	1
34	∀	∀		50	2	2
35	#	#		51	3	3
36	∃	∃		52	4	4
37	%	%		53	5	5
38	&	&		54	6	6
39	∋	∋		55	7	7
40	(	(		56	8	8
41	)	)		57	9	9
42	∗	∗		58	:	:
43	+	+		59	;	;
44	,	,		60	<	<
45	−	−		61	=	=
46	.	.		62	>	>
47	/	/		63	?	?

Code	ANSI	OEM	Code	ANSI	OEM
64	≅	≅	103	γ	γ
65	A	A	104	η	η
66	B	B	105	ι	ι
67	X	X	106	φ	φ
68	Δ	Δ	107	κ	κ
69	E	E	108	λ	λ
70	Φ	Φ	109	μ	μ
71	Γ	Γ	110	ν	ν
72	H	H	111	o	o
73	I	I	112	π	π
74	ϑ	ϑ	113	θ	θ
75	K	K	114	ρ	ρ
76	Λ	Λ	115	σ	σ
77	M	M	116	τ	τ
78	N	N	117	υ	υ
79	O	O	118	ϖ	ϖ
80	Π	Π	119	ω	ω
81	Θ	Θ	120	ξ	ξ
82	P	P	121	ψ	ψ
83	Σ	Σ	122	ζ	ζ
84	T	T	123	{	{
85	Y	Y	124	|	|
86	ς	ς	125	}	}
87	Ω	Ω	126	~	~
88	Ξ	Ξ	127		
89	Ψ	Ψ	128		∩
90	Z	Z	129		⌐
91	[	[	130		⌈
92	∴	∴	131		®
93	]	]	132		™
94	⊥	⊥	133		◇
95	_	_	134		Σ
96			135		⎮
97	α	α	136		⎮
98	β	β	137		⎣
99	χ	χ	138		⎩
100	δ	δ	139		⎮
101	ε	ε	140		⎩
102	φ	φ	141		⎧

Code	ANSI	OEM	Code	ANSI	OEM
142		⊗	181	∝	
143		⊕	182	∂	
144		⊃	183	•	
145		⌠	184	÷	
146		∅	185	≠	
147		|	186	≡	
148		⎫	187	≈	
149	o	⌡	188	...	
150	–	⌟	189	|	
151	–	⌝	190	–	
152			191	↵	
153		√	192	ℵ	
154		⇐	193	ℑ	
155		′	194	ℜ	
156		≤	195	℘	
157		∞	196	⊗	
158		π	197	⊕	
159		φ	198	∅	
160		⟨	199	∩	
161	ϒ	⎰	200	∪	
162	′	⌠	201	⊃	
163	≤	|	202	⊇	
164	⁄	⟩	203	⊄	
165	∞	∇	204	⊂	
166	ƒ	♠	205	⊆	
167	♣	≡	206	∈	
168	♦	↵	207	∉	
169	♥	—	208	∠	
170	♠	←	209	∇	
171	↔	|	210	®	
172	←	...	211	©	
173	↑	ϒ	212	™	
174	→	↔	213	∏	
175	↓	≈	214	√	
176	°		215	·	
177	±		216	¬	
178	″		217	∧	
179	≥	ƒ	218	∨	
180	×		219	↔	

Code	ANSI	OEM	Code	ANSI	OEM
220	⇐		238	⎩	
221	⇑	*f*	239	⎪	
222	⇒		240		
223	⇓		241	⟩	±
224	◇		242	⌡	
225	⟨	⇓	243	⌠	
226	®		244	⎮	
227	©	∂	245	⌡	
228	™		246	⎫	
229	Σ		247	⎪	
230	⌠	∝	248	⎭	°
231	⎮		249	⎤	•
232	⎩		250	⎪	•
233	⌈		251	⎦	—
234	⎪		252	⎤	*ν*
235	⌊		253	⎬	″
236	⌈		254	⎦	♦
237	⎨		255		

INDEX

G

N

P

Q

R

T

U

Other Titles From Microsoft Press

WORKING WITH WORD FOR WINDOWS™

Russell Borland

WORKING WITH WORD FOR WINDOWS is the most comprehensive book available on Microsoft Word for Windows for intermediate users. Written by a member of the Word for Windows development team, this example-packed book will be your primary reference to all the exciting document processing, desktop publishing, and WYSIWYG (What You See Is What You Get) features of Microsoft Word for Windows. The book moves from a review of the basics to a full description of Word's most power-packed features. In-depth information, advice, and hands-on examples show you how to: customize the user interface ■ use a variety of fonts and type sizes ■ insert graphics into documents ■ use macros to automate routine editing ■ position text and graphics ■ link text and graphics within documents ■ use on-line help ■ create tables ■ merge print format using styles ■ manipulate text and graphics using fields ■ automate tasks using macros ■ and create templates for standard documents. If you're already familiar with Microsoft Word for Windows, or can pick up the fundamentals quickly, this is the book for you.
656 pages, softcover   7 ³/₈ x 9 ¹/₄ $22.95   Order Code WOWOWI

MICROSOFT® WORDBASIC PRIMER
Building Macros in Microsoft Word for Windows™ and OS/2®

Russell Borland

MICROSOFT WORDBASIC PRIMER is a superb introduction to the basics of macros and WordBasic. Word macros—unlike those that are simply recordings of keystrokes—are stored in WordBasic, a programming language that includes many sophisticated word processing and Windows-manipulating features. With WordBasic, you can customize and enhance Word to an impressive degree. If you are an advanced user of Microsoft Word for Windows and Word for O/2, you will find this book an essential and valuable reference. And you don't have to be a programmer to use WordBasic—it's easy to learn. With the step-by-step tutorials, handy practice exercises, and great examples, included in this book, you'll learn how to create WordBasic macros—from the simple to the advanced. You'll discover how to: add features to Word ■ modify current features ■ automate complex and repetitive editing and formatting tasks ■ debug your macros ■ and more. The result is a more developed and responsive word processing environment.
352 pages, softcover   7³/₈ x 9¹/₄ $22.95   Order Code WOMAPR

MICROSOFT® WORD TECHNICAL REFERENCE
For Windows™ and OS/2®

Microsoft Corporation

Microsoft Word for Windows and Microsoft Word for OS/2 are powerful word-processing applications with many advanced features that give them the flexibility to handle almost any word-processing need. If you're an advanced user of Word and want to delve further into these features to extend and customize the capabilities of Word, this reference is for you. This source of detailed, authoritative information offers clear advice and strategies to utilize Word capabilities with the WordBasic macro language, fields, the Rich Text Format (RTF) specification, and Word's built-in external file converters.
464 pages, softcover   7³/₈ x 9¹/₄ $22.95   Order Code WOTERE

RUNNING WINDOWS,™ 2nd ed.

Craig Stinson and Nancy Andrews

"It can be tough to distingish the truly worthly volumes from the mere rewrites of software manuals. RUNNING WINDOWS is one of the former." **PC Computing**

Build your confidence and enhance your productivity with the Microsoft Windows environment— quickly and easily—using this hands-on introduction. This Microsoft-authorized edition is completely updated and expanded to cover all the exciting features of version 3. You'll find a successful combination of step-by-step tutorials, helpful screen illustrations, and real-world examples that will help you: expertly maneuver through the Windows environment ■ quickly master each Windows built-in desktop accessory ■ tailor the Windows environment to suit your work habits ■ use Windows on a network ■ master the rich features of Windows' built-in word processing, communications, and graphics applications ■ and much, much more. A special section includes techniques and strategies to help you optimize the performance of the Windows environment with extended and expanded memory; swap files; Smartdrive, and RAMdrive. If you're a novice Windows user, this book is the perfect starting point for exploring and understanding Windows. If you're a more experienced Windows user or are familiar with an earlier version, you'll appreciate the in-depth advice, expert tips, and inside information.

544 pages, softcover 7³/₈ x 9¹/₄ $24.95 Order Code RUWI2

WINDOWS™ 3 COMPANION

Lori L. Lorenz and R. Michael O'Mara

"Excellent reference featuring dozens of live examples of how different functions work."
PC Magazine

This up-to-date resource thoroughly covers Windows version 3—everything from installing and starting Windows to using all its built-in applications and desktop accessories. Novices will value the book for its step-by-step tutorials and great examples; more experienced users will turn to it again and again for its expert advice, tips, and information. The authors detail the features and explain the use of Windows' Program Manager, File Manager, and Printer Manager so that you will be able to expertly maneuver through Windows, control the environment, and easily manage files, disks, and printers. Includes a special 8-page section—printed in full color—that highlights Windows' exciting capabilities.

544 pages, softcover 7³/₈ x 9¹/₈ $27.95 Order Code WI3CO

Microsoft Press books are available wherever quality computer books are sold.
*Or call **1-800-MSPRESS** for ordering information or placing credit card orders.**
*Please refer to **BBK** when placing your order.*

---

* In Canada, contact Macmillan of Canada, Attn: Microsoft Press Dept., 164 Commander Blvd., Agincourt, Ontario, Canada M1S 3C7.
In the U.K., contact Microsoft Press, 27 Wrights Lane, London W8 5TZ.

Free Word Tips!

The Cobb Group experts who brought you *Word for Windows Companion* now invite you to examine **3 free issues** of *Inside Word for Windows.*™ This "how-to" journal, also from The Cobb Group, is a gold mine of what's new, what's handy, and what's troublesome with your software. Each 16-page issue brings you easy-to-read articles with step-by-step directions and lots of illustrations to help you save time and learn *the best* ways to use Word for Windows.

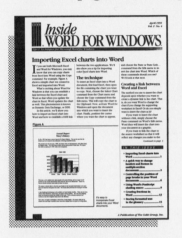

Through *Inside Word for Windows* you'll learn about such topics as:

- using style sheets
- creating side-by-side text
- designing tabular layouts
- integrating graphics into documents
- generating form letters
- printing mailing labels
- using Word's macro capabilities
- customizing your Word menus
- sharing data with other programs

There's more on the back…

You'll work smarter with this free offer!

You'll get answers...

Inside Word for Windows will show you how to work around your word processing problems. You can also share your Word discoveries with other users.

You'll get expert advice about:

- editing
- formatting
- design
- sorting
- printing
- page layout

You'll get the latest news about Word...

When there's information that affects the way you use Word, you can read about it first-hand in *Inside Word for Windows*.

3 Months Free!

You can try *Inside Word for Windows* 3 months <u>absolutely free</u>. All you have to do is mail the card below. There's no obligation, so act now.

Microsoft is a registered trademark of Microsoft Corporation.
Windows is a trademark of Microsoft Corporation.